Wilson Library Bulletin

September 1984

Wilson Library Bulletin

September 1984, Volume 59, Number 1 ISSN 0043-5651

Our cover for September represents a neon sculpture photographed by **Gary San Pietro,** a freelance photographer headquartered in Philadelphia.

Departments

Letter From New York/Editorial 4
Correspondence 6
Upfront/News—*New York Governor Cuomo signs library aid bill; ALA begins search for new executive director; New York Public installs online catalog; Ohio voters approve library levy; Dallas Public gets tough on overdues; San Diego Public receives budget increase; late news.* 8
Library World 70
Marketplace 73
WLB Classifieds 79

Articles

Benevolent Builder: Appraising Andrew Carnegie *Joseph Deitch* 16
U.S. Population Characteristics: Implications for Libraries *Kathleen Falcigno and Polly Guynup* 23
The Only Copyright Law We Need *Daniel Toohey* 27
ALA in Dallas: Moments of Self-Doubt in Times of Great Purpose *The Editors* 31

Features

Dateline—Washington *Dale Nelson* 42
Eye on Publishing *Ann McGrath* 44
Facing the Public *Will Manley* 46
School Library Technology *Patricia Berglund* 48

Reviews

Picture Books for Children *Donnarae MacCann/Olga Richard* 50
The Young Adult Perplex *Patty Campbell* 52
Murder in Print *Kathleen Maio* 54
Front Row Center *Judith Trojan* 56
On Record: Popular Music *Bruce Pollock* 58
Magazines *Gail Pool* 60
Our Profession *Norman Stevens* 62
Current Reference Books *James Rettig* 64

The *Wilson Library Bulletin* is published monthly except in July and August by The H. W. Wilson Company, 950 University Avenue, Bronx, N.Y. 10452. Second-class postage paid at Bronx, N.Y. and additional mailing offices. Copyright © 1984 by The H. W. Wilson Company. The *Wilson Library Bulletin* is indexed in *Education Index, Library Literature,* and *Popular Periodical Index* and abstracted in *Library & Information Science Abstracts, Historical Abstracts,* and *America: History and Life.* Book reviews are indexed in *Book Review Index.* Subscription $30 a year, U.S. and Canada; $35, foreign. Single copies $4, U.S. and Canada; $4.50, foreign (remittance with order, please). Address all correspondence about subscriptions to the publisher. No subscriptions through agents. Telephone: (212) 588-8400

Letter from New York

Editorial

Advertisements for ourselves

At some unmarked and not youthful passage in our lives we come to an appreciation of the confining but nonetheless useful purposes of etiquette—how to employ three forks set to the left of our dinner plate, the conditions under which we can keep the girl ncxt door out all night, how to begin a game of draw poker, when the rules of engagement allow opening fire upon the enemy.

In modern times we have also seen the necessity of exercising a grasp of etiquette in dealing with the federal government. The government of the United States is simple in principle but complex in organization and anyone setting out to influence White House policy, congressional legislation, or Supreme Court decisions is expected, at a minimum, to know how to contact members of the executive branch, when Congress is in recess, what matters are calendared for court attention.

As librarians we have, of course, gone a long way beyond this rudimentary insight. We know something about lobbying, making use of the media, identifying allies in Congress, recording voting habits, undertaking letter-writing campaigns, organizing legislative visits, and generally engaging in self-promotion. We have to understand not only the process of twentieth century American government, but to fathom the rules of persuasion necessary to motivate it.

Like all nonprofit insitutions, however, libraries need the assistance of friends, trustees, regents, school boards, benefactors, commissions, foundations, and local government that, enjoying some neutrality, can intercede for us, arguing our role and significance with a credence we ourselves could not so easily establish. The 1979 White House Conference on Libraries and Information Service marked a recent climax in the effort to seek citizen support and invite lay interpretation of our mission.

The downside of all this activity on our behalf is the danger of losing our voice, of not occupying a central position, not being the first resort in formulating goals. As librarians, citizens, and voters, we also have a right to propound arguments in our behalf.

We were reminded of this compelling option during the inaugural banquet held by the American Library Association at its annual conference in Dallas.

The evening of June 27 did not promise singularity. Situated at our table in the Hyatt Regency ballroom we were witness to the usual introductions, awards, and resolutions. The ritual was not gladdened by a frozen lemon soufflé capable of provoking a food riot at Riker's Island.

The night was permanently altered, however, by the presidential remarks of E.J. Josey—"Forging Coalitions for the Public Good." This was not a ceremonial speech for the record, but a stirring and uncommon defense of libraries coming from an unaccustomed source—ourselves. Not the expected peroration suggesting new ways to provoke government support or attract assistance from organizations sympathetic to our cause, Josey's vision was more ambitiously encompassing—he proposed we align ourselves with the general welfare of the American people:

"The public good, in an even broader sense of the general welfare, is closely related to progress for libraries. So long as the general population is victimized, economic problems will grow, and, as a result, libraries will be inadequately supported. In a time of attack on the basic freedoms and elementary well-being of the most vulnerable sections of the population, professional groups must recognize their stake in the outcome of that attack and their responsibilities to support the freedoms and welfare of the majority of the population. ALA therefore needs to integrate its goals with the goals of greatest importance to the American people, *i.e.*, the preservation of basic democratic liberties, the enlargement of equal opportunity for women and minorities, and the continuance of earlier national planning to raise the level of the educational and economic well-being of greater numbers of the population."

Specifically, Josey recommended working with business and labor to remind the American people of the importance of libraries; creating support for publicly funded institutions; reaffirming our right to federal assistance; continuing strong advocacy in defense of intellectual freedom; maintaining a vigorous national library awareness campaign; and finding ways to use technology on behalf of those with lower incomes. The most important recommendation: "Find specific ways to integrate ALA's priorities with the general, political, and economic welfare of the country."

In its completeness of vision and generosity of concern, it was a remarkable speech—clear, assured, unapologetic.

In spite of all our knowledge of dealing with the federal government and our ability to attract support from a universe of interested parties, there is still merit in occasionally looking to ourselves for answers. As E.J. Josey on this occasion so eloquently verified.

—Milo Nelson

Correspondence

Timely and stimulating

My colleagues and I have enjoyed the new column, "School Library Technology" by Patricia Berglund, very much since its inception in January. The information, ideas and resources covered are timely and stimulating and we are looking forward to its continuation. *WLB* has provided thoughtful, well-researched articles for years and I think that Berglund is contributing significantly to the area of school library media specialists' interests.

Thank you very much for this development in our professional literature.

CATHERINE WILLIAMS
Pomona Senior High School
Arvada, Colorado

Appalling ignorance

I would like to question the usefulness of the "Current Reference Books" section, written by James Rettig, which appears regularly in *Wilson Library Bulletin*. I find that Rettig's reviews of some of the most important reference works published are superficial at their best, and at times reveal an appalling ignorance of the subject matter.

Specifically, in the April issue, Rettig reviewed *Research Guide to Philosophy*, by Terrence Tice and Thomas Slavens. This book is number three in the "sources of information in the humanities series" published by ALA. The review sounds favorable, so I decided to borrow it on interlibrary loan. Instead of the accessible, informative guide I was led to expect, I found the book to be a useless, hodgepodge compilation of meager biographies and misleading, pseudo-technical explanations of philosophies and philosophers. It is neither a book for beginners nor for experts. Moreover, there are a great many books available which will do a better job in explaining, introducing, or expanding the philosophies or philosophers than this book (for a bibliography of these books, consult *Research Guide to Philosophy*).

Rettig concludes his review by stating that "this [book] occupies a niche of its own." Since we are talking about a book about philosophy, I think it is proper to point out to Rettig that nothing can occupy a niche other than its own. He may find several sources in *Research Guide to Philosophy* itself to support the point why some philosophers thought that this was even axiomatic.

An approximate count of the number of pages Rettig had to read for reviewing books in the April 1984 issue is 12,000, and this can be construed as an extenuating circumstance for the superficiality of the reviews. However, what is the point of reading or publishing superficial reviews? If the space and the expertise are not available to *Wilson Library Bulletin*, it would be best to leave the entire column out and let librarians look for more comprehensive, critical, and illuminating reviews of reference books elsewhere.

I think that the American Library Association has done a disservice in publishing *Research Guide to Philosophy*; Rettig—due to lack of space, time, or qualifications—has demonstrated his inability to adequately review this book; and *Wilson Library Buttetin* is not aiding the cause of reference materials selection in publishing a superficial column.

PETER VARI
Asheville-Buncombe Library System
Asheville, North Carolina

Recalculation

Regarding your obituary for Charles W. David ("Month in Review," May 1984). The dates you provide are 1885–1984; however, later in the piece Richard De Gennaro discloses that he died at the age of ninety-one. Not both can be correct.

DENNIS DICKINSON
Beloit College Library
Beloit, Wisconsin

Our mistake. Mr. David died at age ninety-nine.—Ed.

Condescending and patronizing

I find your reviews of the contemporary popular music scene ("On Record: Popular Music") to be completely useless. [The author] is obviously not in tune with the field, in spite of being editor of *Guitar* magazine. As a purchaser of records for today's young listener, I couldn't care less if they do not meet your standards of "substance" and "meaningfulness." Your tone is condescending and patronizing.

What I am looking for in a review is "best of its kind" information, which performer is becoming notable, where the trends are heading. Perhaps your column should be labeled as editorial. I will look elsewhere for purchasing information.

MARGARET HARDING
Crete Public Library
Crete, Nebraska .

Attached to the sixties

While not disputing Bruce Pollock's skills as music critic, I wonder if, with his attachment to the sixties, he is able to objectively review current music. His criticism ("On Record," June 1984) focuses upon the lyric, "at an all-time low," and states few of them deal with "anything but love and/or sexual fulfillment."

Granted, good lyrics can have tremendous impact. They can certainly make a good song great and the guitar solos Pollock dismisses should complement and underscore the emotions expressed in the lyrics. But much of a song's power necessarily derives from the musical underpinning. A song with simplistic lyrics and a good melody can still work as music; the reverse—good lyrics and no tune—does not. Some very powerful music has no lyrics at all. Lest Pollock wax nostalgic for the sixties, let me remind him that out of the same time frame as Bob Dylan came such poetic gems as "Wooly Bully" by Sam the Sham and the Pharoahs, and "Sugar, Sugar" by the Archies. Current music too has its good lyricists in Bruce Springsteen, Billy Joel, and Geddy Lee and Neil Peart (of Rush).

While music can be a platform for meaningful sentiments, the love song has been a large part of every era's pop. Frank Sinatra did not make his millions singing about the federal deficit. Even Dylan broke down and wrote some ("Just like a Woman") and the Lennon-McCartney team wrote a slew.

Instead of reasoned objective discussion of the best in current rock, I feel Pollock's criticisms smacked uncomfortably of "When I was young . . . "

Eleanor Wolven
Yonkers Public Library
Yonkers, New York

Elitist opinions

Bravo Tanya Whitmarsh! Her letter in the May issue voices a gripe I've long nursed in silence: Bruce Pollock's rock column is bad stuff. My reasons for thinking so aren't hers, though.

I don't care for Linda Ronstadt as Whitmarsh does, but in my library system there are plenty of patrons who do. Pollock's column ill serves librarians entrusted with ordering to serve such patrons because he makes no comments on a record's probable appeal for its natural audience. He doesn't answer such questions as "Who is this record for?", "Is it like other popular material by these musicians or other musicians?", "What are the songs about?", and "Is this music played on the radio or MTV?"

In short, Pollock doesn't consider the point of view most useful to a librarian, that of the average rock fan. All he offers are his own elitist opinions. These are nice enough, I suppose, but not as practical advice to librarians. As a former rock reviewer, among the most elitist of the lot, I think I speak with some authority.

Ray Olson
St. Paul Public Library
St. Paul, Minnesota

Pablum on the airwaves

In his article on popular music ("On Record," June 1984), Bruce Pollock comments as to the "absolute lack of substance in today's pop lyrics". Continuing through the article, one finds repeated references to the Top 100, and to various figures from pop music in the 1960s.

Not meaning in the least way to insult, Pollock must realize that we are no longer living in the 1960s—socially, politically, or musically. In the 1960s it was acceptable to speak out against the Establishment, to decry the status quo, to "write music that mattered." Now in the 1980s, with the country experiencing a rapid and vengeful turn to the political right, it is no longer acceptable to be anti-establishment. The rock and roll record industry is a reflection of this new conservatism—by signing only bands that play vapid, meaningless music, full of lyrics that only rehash the traditional girl-meets-boy story, the record companies are effectively acting as an arm of that government, and keeping the bands that sing meaningful lyrics away from mass consumption.

Because social criticism is no longer acceptable, and because radio stations are increasingly regarding their role as advertisers (via programmed play lists, audience surveys, and album-oriented play lists), it is admittedly harder to find music that matters. One must go far beyond the Top 100 lists, if only because those lists represent radio's conservatism. There are many alternatives, and if one looks for them, they are not all that difficult to find. College radio stations are limited to the lower-power left end of one's radio dial. There is an active fanzine industry—magazines that cater to the rabid fans of meaningful rock and roll. Admittedly, some of them may have rather unacceptable names (*Puncture, Savage Pink,* or *Pukin' Blood,* to name just three). However it is in this "underground" medium that anyone can find the social criticism that Pollock longs for. While he may call Laurie Anderson's punk-rock hair "weird," I seem to remember hippies and flower children being called the same thing before they became more acceptable for mass consumption.

Punk rock is music that matters. Unfortunately for Pollock, and for anyone else who relies on the Top 100 lists to form their opinions on popular music, this form of music is not represented by the standard, record industry-sponsored tabulations. Bands such as the Dead Kennedys, MDC, The Dicks, The Big Boys, and umpteen many more are all playing music that matters. If one feels that these bands are too small, inexperienced and raw, and that they do not play to a large enough audience to matter, I wish to remind that the Jim Carroll Band started out as just such a band—playing off nights at a sleazy run-down club in San Francisco to only about twenty paying people. Of course, the Grateful Dead, Jimi Hendrix, and Bob Dylan started out in exactly the same way as today's punk bands.

There are more parallels between today's punk movement and the hippie movement of the 1960s. The social criticism inherent in punk is there for anyone to absorb—should they so desire. As long as one relies, however, on the Top 100 for doses of "music that matters," one will find only pablum on the airwaves, and starve from want of food for thought.

Craig Stockfleth
University of California Library
Berkeley, California

UPFRONT NEWS

Celebrating the July 10 signing of the $15 million New York Library Omnibus Bill are, from left, **Nancy Lian,** *executive director of the New York Library Association;* **Governor Mario Cuomo; E.J. Josey,** *president of the American Library Association;* **Theodore Wenzl,** *trustee, Bethlehem Public Library; and* **Janet Welch,** *executive director, Rochester Regional Research Library Council. The bill increases library aid in the state of New York by $13.3 million. Funding will begin during 1984 and reach the new annual total of $15.3 million during fiscal year 1985, bringing total state aid to libraries to an all-time high of $58.7 million.*

In a ceremony at the Albany Public Library, Governor Cuomo credited leaders of the Assembly and Senate with persistence and cooperation in the negotiations which led to the bill passing unanimously in both houses. The last major increase in library funding was in 1981 when state aid increased from $34.4 to $43.4 million.

The Omnibus Bill directs the commissioner of education to award up to $200,000 per year to support regional bibliographic databases and interlibrary resources sharing; to provide annual grants of $90,000 in support of programs for the preservation of library materials at eleven designated research libraries; and to establish school library systems that will create union catalogs, develop effective delivery systems, promote continuing education for the staff of participating schools, and encourage cooperation with other school library systems in resource sharing.

ALA begins search for new executive director

The Executive Board of the American Library Association held a special meeting in Chicago on July 16 to plan the search process for a new executive director and to appoint a search committee. The present director, Robert Wedgeworth, has announced that he will not renew his contract, which expires August 1985.

The search committee will be chaired by Lillian Bradshaw, past-president of ALA and special assistant to the city manager, City of Dallas. Its members include: J. Dennis Day, director, Salt Lake City Public Library; Marva DeLoach, head, cataloging & records maintenance, Milner Library, Illinois State University; Kathleen Heim, dean, School of Library and Information Science, Louisiana State University; Janis Keene, assistant director, Tulsa City-County Library; F. William Summers, dean, College of Librarianship, University of South Carolina; and Lucille Thomas, assistant director, School Library Services, New York City Board of Education. The committee's staff liaison will be Ernest Martin, associate executive director for administrative services.

The Executive Board instructed the search committee to "conduct a confidential, high level search for an executive director, within the framework established by the board and to present to the board, in non-ranked order, a list of no fewer than three nor more than five names."

Harvard to install video system

A gift from the Digital Equipment Corporation to Harvard University Library will make it possible to provide thirty Interactive Video Information System units, to be located in public areas throughout the university. IVIS units, combining a personal computer and a videodisc player, allow users to interact with instructional material as it is being presented. The first program to be developed for the IVIS system will be a Visual Directory of Harvard Libraries, an interactive videodisc to be produced by Harvard and Digital. The directory will consist of a general tour of Harvard libraries, a description of important collections, scholarly tours, and maps.

UTLAS announces availability of InfoQUEST

The University of Toronto Library Automation Systems has announced the development of InfoQUEST, its new microcomputer-based online public access catalog. InfoQUEST represents a new generation of online catalog, designed especially for the small library. Operating on the IBM Personal Computer or PC-compatible machines, InfoQUEST software is capable of handling file sizes of up to 25,000 records using a hard disk storage device.

One of the system's features is its ability to accept rapid downloading, in batch mode, of records coming directly from a library's file on the UTLAS Catalogue Support System. Unlike other systems, there is no need for costly and time-consuming input of data when locating or updating records.

Richard Sweeney to develop prototype automated library system

Richard Sweeney, executive director of the Public Library of Columbus and Franklin County, Ohio since 1979, has been appointed dean of library and information services at Polytechnic Institute of New York. Polytechnic Institute, embarking on a program to develop a state-of-the-art library system, plans to build a 60,000-square-foot centralized research library at its Brooklyn campus. The multimillion-dollar library and information center will feature the latest information storage and retrieval technology as well as electronic links with Polytechnic's two other campuses at Farmingdale and White Plains. It will quadruple student and faculty study space and tie-in electronically with databases around the world.

"I am very excited about the challenge here at Polytechnic," said Sweeney. "Our goal is to build a prototype library, using the most effective new technologies available."

Sweeney's priorities at Polytechnic Institute will include the new library building program, improving basic library services, and embarking on an automation plan. He will also be involved in designing services for industries locating in MetroTech, the $400 million high technology industrial park being developed by Polytechnic and the City of New York at the Brooklyn campus.

Sweeney pioneered community cable data communications in Franklin County, including remote access to library catalogs and book circulation.

OCLC strengthens online quality control

In June OCLC began improving online quality control of bibliographic records in the Online Union Catalog with introduction of the Enhance capability. Through Enhance, twenty selected OCLC participating libraries are able to edit and replace records in designated formats. The Enhance authorization is similiar to that of CONSER participants, whose quality control efforts are concerned with serials. Enhance is expected to improve the usefulness of records and the quality of cataloging while reducing the number of change requests processed by users and by OCLC staff. OCLC libraries currently catalog 500,000 items per week and add 23,000 records to the database each week.

"Based on estimates supplied by Enhance libraries," according to Richard Greene, Online Data Quality Control Section Manager at OCLC, "more than 50,000 records will be modified annually. As more libraries begin to enhance bibliographic records, quality control will continue to improve. The Enhance capability will complement ongoing quality control efforts whereby approximately 500,000 records are upgraded or replaced annually by OCLC staff, CONSER libraries, medical libraries, and other OCLC users modifying records they input."

OCLC chose the initial group of twenty institutions for Enhance from applications submitted by sixty-six libraries.

New York Public Library installs online catalog

The Research Libraries of the New York Public Library are presently acceptance testing an online public catalog manufactured by Carlyle Systems of Berkeley, California. Designated CATNYP, the initial system includes four terminals connected to a remote processor in New York and, via Telenet, to a host processor in California. Approximately 105,000 records are online. The library has specified thirteen different indexes for searching by keyword, and ten limiting indexes. Silent printers are attached to each terminal and allow the user to print citations in any of four display formats used by the system.

If testing is successful, forty terminals will be installed later this year. Over 1.2 million records will eventually be loaded into CATNYP. Cost of the system is estimated at $300,000.

San Diego Public receives budget increase

The San Diego (California) Public Library received a higher percentage increase in its new budget than any other city department during budget hearings for fiscal year 1984–85. The new budget is $9,313,915 compared to $8,904,500 last year. The City Council of San Diego approved keeping all thirty branch libraries in the system open six days a week, eight hours per day and provided funding for 13.08 new staff positions to make the additional service possible. The council also approved an increase in the book budget, adding $158,000 to the previous year's allocation.

William Welsh honored by Notre Dame

Deputy Librarian of Congress William Welsh received an honorary Doctor of Laws degree in May from the University of Notre Dame. Welsh was invited to accept the honor by the Reverend Theodore Hesburgh, president of the university. The citation read, in part: "Through his expertise the premier library of the land made influential strides in acquisition and cataloging practices. He has been farsighted and creative in recognizing the potential for modern technology in libraries, and his current experimentation in the preservation of library materials has worldwide implications."

Welsh is a 1940 alumnus of the university.

ITT introduces twenty-four-hour news service

ITT Communications Services has introduced a twenty-four-hour news service in the U.S. that provides stock, bond, and commodity prices, market reports, and business news summaries over ordinary telex machines. Called ITT Update, the innovation provides telex service throughout the U.S. and more than 200 other countries.

The on-command system also yields stock quotations, hourly market averages, most-active stocks, dividend reports, market commentaries, world currencies, and current interest rates. The service can be accessed from any of the 200,000 telex terminals in the U.S. and 1.8 million terminals overseas.

To activate the service, the user calls the ITT Update telex number and then enters a three-digit code to specify the desired information category. The cost is approximately twenty cents per minute for access to the database plus the standard domestic telex rate. The several categories include special news summaries from the U.S., Europe, Latin America, Africa, Asia, the Pacific, Far East, and Middle East as well as individual news stories.

LC to translate computer magazine into braille

The Library of Congress National Library Service for the Blind and Physically Handicapped has announced plans to add McGraw-Hill's *Popular Computing* magazine to a group of thirty-six publications that are translated into braille on a regular basis for its 25,000 blind readers nationwide. Frank Kurt Cylke, director of the service, said the library found a growing demand from blind readers and from librarians for more microcomputer information in braille format. "Computers hold great promise for aiding blind and physically handicapped people," observed Cylke. "They call upon logic and use of understandable codes, skills which blind people have in abundance, especially those who know the code of braille. And with special braille terminals, blind computer operators are on a nearly equal footing with sighted individuals."

Molz named acting dean at Columbia

Kathleen Molz, Melvil Dewey Professor of Library Service at Columbia University, has been named acting dean of its School of Library Service. She will serve in the post for the 1984–85 academic year while Richard Darling, dean of the school since 1970, is on sabbatical leave. Darling announced last year that he would retire in June 1985.

Molz joined the Columbia faculty in 1976 as a professor and, in 1980, was named to the Melvil Dewey Professorship, the only endowed chair of librarianship in an American university. She has held library positions at Enoch Pratt Free Library in Baltimore, the Denver Public Library, and the Free Library of Philadelphia. From 1962 to 1968 she edited the *Wilson Library Bulletin.*

Congressional panel foresees end of zip code

Postal automation recommendations recently issued by the Congressional Office of Technology Assessment may spell the end of the zip code, according to *Electronic Mail & Micro Systems,* an industry newsletter. The OTA panel of postal automation experts concluded that the U.S. Postal Service should equip all of its optical character readers with four-line heads, capable of reading all four lines of the address of a typical letter. This would enable the entire address, rather than just the zip code, to be read by the equipment. Online computerized directories would then automatically assign the correct nine-digit zip code, and the corresponding bar-code would be sprayed onto the envelope for later automatic sorting by inexpensive bar-code readers.

The recommended improvement would result in greater address readability since the redundancy in addresses will allow an OCR to misread several characters in the address, yet still correctly recognize it. The current USPS single-line OCR scanners rely only upon the typed zip code: if one digit is missing the letter is missorted. Use of scanners that read all four lines of an address would also mean that the zip code would no longer be needed on envelopes but would be stored in the U.S. Postal Service's computers.

Commerce Department to automate patent applications

The Commerce Department's Patent and Trademark Office has selected Planning Research Corporation and Chemical Abstracts Service to develop and install a multimillion-dollar automated system for processing applications for new patents. Planning Research Corporation will engineer, design, and integrate the system while Chemical Abstracts Service will supply computer software. According to the Commerce Department, the contract could total $300 million over the next twenty years.

The automated system is being developed and installed in three stages. The first of fifteen areas of technology into which the Patent

Shown discussing the scale model of the ***Richard Nixon Presidential Library*** *to be built in San Clemente, California are the former President and Ernest Wilson, Jr., library architect and principal of the firm Landgon Wilson Mumper of Los Angeles. The Spanish-motif styled library will sit on a thirteen-acre bluff overlooking the Pacific Ocean. The Nixon Presidential Archives Foundation plans to reach its targeted goal of $15 million for the construction of the building by the close of 1984. Groundbreaking and construction are scheduled to take place in early 1985.*

Office is organized will be automated by the end of this year. Following evaluation, the remaining fourteen areas will be automated with completion scheduled in 1987. In the final stage the system will be expanded to include the public search room and Patent Depository Libraries.

The U.S. Patent and Trademark Office has twenty-five million documents on file and expects the number to double by the end of the century. It receives 20,000 documents a day and processes more than 100,000 patent applications each year.

ALANET selected to support Illinois network

The Illinois Library and Information Network (ILLINET) has set up its network for interlibrary loans, photocopy requests, and reference questions on ALANET, the electronic mail and information service of the American Library Association. Coordinated by the Illinois State Library and funded through an LSCA grant, the project brings into ALANET eighteen library systems and four reference and resource centers. In July, TWX machines were replaced with the electronic mail/communication network.

One of a number of state library agencies participating in ALANET, Illinois is the first to use the ALANET information service as the basis for its entire statewide interlibrary loan and reference system. Interactive forms for each type of request or referral have been custom-designed for the ILLINET system. The forms can be completed online, with the operator responding to prompts from the system, or can be prepared offline on a microcomputer or word processor and uploaded for savings in cost and time.

Baker & Taylor to provide books to Chinese libraries

Baker & Taylor Company and the People's Republic of China have reached an agreement for supplying scholarly U.S. books to university libraries throughout China. Part of a five-year initiative to rebuild Chinese library collections, the project was made possible by a special loan from the World Bank. Ma Shiyi, director of special purchasing for Beida University in Beijing, and Pedro Mata, president of Baker & Taylor, issued the joint announcement at a news conference at the annual American Library Association conference in Dallas. Title selection will be assisted through the use of Baker & Taylor's *Directions* magazine and approval program database. The database, which will be used retroactively for five years, provides access to over 200,000 scholarly titles. Over 100 university libraries are expected to take part in the project.

Caterpillar Tractor seeks help from library

The Milwaukee facility of the Caterpillar Tractor Company, employing over 600 persons, has asked the Milwaukee Public Library to participate in a series of workshops in connection with the plant's closing in 1985. The workshops are part of the company's program to help their employees find new jobs. A transition team brought in by Caterpillar is offering counseling, resume assistance, and general job search guidelines. The library will provide information on specific resources available for writing resumes, conducting a job search, and locating publications that list position openings.

Bowker purchases software database rights

The R.R. Bowker Company has purchased from PC Telemart, Inc., of Fairfax, Virginia, all rights to its software databases and its present print products. Bruce Gray, president of Bowker, said that the move accelerates Bowker's expansion into reference publishing for the microcomputer industry.

Along with a line of software print products for professional, institutional, and consumer markets, Bowker will begin to publish and market six current PC Telemart directories.

Evans and Hoadley elected to OCLC board

The OCLC Users Council has elected Glyn Evans and Irene Hoadley to six-year terms on the OCLC Board of Trustees, beginning in December 1984. Evans is director, SUNY/OCLC and assistant vice-chancellor for library services, SUNY. Hoadley is director, university library, Texas A&M University, and president of the OCLC Users Council.

The Users Council was established to provide OCLC participating institutions and networks with a formal means of communication with OCLC. The group's sixty delegates meet three times a year to discuss matters concerning OCLC and its users.

The Dougherty County (Georgia) Public Library *recently installed its first online public access terminal (above). The system provides library patrons with author, title, and subject access and indicates if material is on reserve or in circulation. Software for the online operation was developed by library computer programmer R.L. Avery and library director Hal Todd. The software offers an adaptable integrated circulation system to mid-sized public libraries with access to an IBM 38.*

The only known copies of sixteen Dari-language textbooks, urgently needed for the schooling of Afghan refugee children in Pakistan, were recently located in the ***Milbank Memorial Library*** *at Teachers College, Columbia University. Photocopies of the books were rushed to International Rescue Committee headquarters in Peshawar, Pakistan where they will be reproduced for use in camps housing about three million refugees, half of whom are children under age fourteen. The texts present the Dari language, mathematics, and Islamic studies for grades one through six.*

The textbooks were written by Afghan educators who received technical assistance from Teachers College in a textbook project sponsored from 1966 to 1977 by the Agency for International Development. All copies of the textbooks in Afghanistan are believed to have been destroyed after the revolution there, having been replaced by Russian-approved textbooks. The Afghans speak either Dari, a language used only in Afghanistan and Iran, or Pashtu, which is spoken in few other places.

In the photo above, Professor Thurston Atkins of Teachers College and David Ment, head of special collections at Milbank Memorial Library, exhibit the only extant copies of the Afghan textbooks.

WLN to provide original cataloging service

The Washington Library Network has announced that it will provide member libraries with original cataloging and inputting of bibliographic records to the WLN database. Member libraries may send items requiring original cataloging directly to WLN where staff will provide original cataloging, subject analysis, classification, application of content designation, and then input the records into the WLN database. The cataloging service is available for monographs, serials, audiovisual materials, printed music, and sound recordings.

Wisconsin changes library school name

The Library School at the University of Wisconsin at Madison has changed its name to the School of Library and Information Studies. The curriculum of the school has been expanded to include material from the emerging field of information science and the focus of the school has been broadened to include preparation for positions in information-related institutions other than libraries. Such institutions include information analysis centers, data archives, and archives and records management units. The school is also providing instruction that will enable students to become providers of information-related services as freelance professionals.

Some forty-one of the sixty-nine schools accredited by the American Library Association now include the word "information" in their names.

E.J. Josey calls for volunteers

E.J. Josey, president of the American Library Association, has called for 450 volunteers to act as discussion leaders and recorders at the President's Program during the 1985 ALA conference in Chicago. An entire day, July 8, will be devoted to discussions of seven commissioned position papers and speeches by four major public figures on Josey's theme, "Building Coalitions for the Public Good."

The volunteers will be used to stimulate reactions within groups of eight to ten randomly assigned registrants and will record the opinions of the participants. Discussion leaders and reporters must be ALA members and must be able to attend, at their own expense, a training and orientation session during the ALA midwinter meeting in Washington, D.C.

ALA members wishing to volunteer should submit their name, address, and telephone number by November 1 to Carla Stoffle, University of Wisconsin/Parkside, Kenosha, Wisconsin 53141.

Kentucky library benefits from capital funds

A recent influx of capital funds from the city of Louisville, the Jefferson County government, and the Kentucky Department for Libraries and Archives will enable the Louisville Free Public Library to expand library service in the community and renovate existing branch library facilities owned by the library system.

The Jefferson County Fiscal Court unanimously endorsed a capital improvement plan that includes a grant of $950,000 to the Louisville Free Public Library for the construction of four new branch libraries. The library system currently operates twenty branches in addition to the main library located in downtown Louisville. Population shifts over the past decade have created neighborhoods which have been served only by bookmobiles.

Louisville Mayor Harvey Sloane has announced a plan that would give the library approximately $350,000 for repairs and capital improvements to eight of the system's branch libraries built in the early 1900s with Carnegie funds. Improvements will include the replacement of heating and air conditioning systems, lighting repairs, and new plaster and interior painting. The Kentucky Department for Libraries and Archives will contribute an additonal $104,000 to the branch library repair and improvement project.

Dallas Public gets tough on overdues

In a campaign called "Get the Books Back," the Dallas Public Library, which assessed fines of up to fifty dollars per day for overdue library books, retrieved 22,600 books and other library materials with a value of $244,000 in a three-month period. During the same period, fines totalling $119,767 were paid and patrons who had lost or damaged materials paid $27,938. One book, *Mastering Your Nerves,* was discovered in an attic and returned to the library after an absence of forty-five years. Another volume, checked out in 1947, was returned. Its title: *The Irresponsibles.*

The second phase of the "Get the Books Back" campaign consisted of arrest warrants for patrons who did not respond to repeated warnings to return overdue library property.

Geac to automate Bibliotheque Nationale

Geac Computer Corporation of Toronto has signed agreements with Sema, a French systems house, to automate the catalog of the Bibliotheque Nationale. The catalog, to be named the National Bibliotheque Database Management System, will be written by Geac in conjunction with Sema and the Bibliotheque Nationale. When complete, the system will provide online service throughout the institution and, using a packet-switching network, will enable any other library in France to access the database.

In the initial phase of the project Geac will install two Geac System 8000 computers and 105 terminals. The contract, valued at approximately two million Canadian dollars, will require two and one half years to complete.

New York State Library receives translation grant

The New York State Library has received $217,000 from the National Endowment for the Humanities to continue work on translation of the original Dutch archives of New Netherland. The grant covers the period 1984–87 and stipulates that $74,000 be raised from private sources.

The purpose of the project is to translate, edit, and interpret the records of the Dutch in New Netherland and colonial New York. These records, presently in the State Archives, have previously been inaccessible to scholars because of the lack of an authoritative translation. Eleven volumes of translated records published to date have been used by Indian ethnologists, lawyers studying land titles, archeologists studying land sites, and ethnic historians studying European nationalities represented in New Netherland.

ITT introduces volume discounts

ITT Corporation's long distance telephone unit made changes effective September 1 in its ITT Longer Distance service, including the introduction of discounts for high volume callers and the elimination of monthly service charges. In addition, the ITT Longer Distance business and residential services will be consolidated under a common, discounted rate structure and will provide all customers with nationwide calling. Previously, nationwide calling had been limited to ITT's business subscribers. The monthly service charges to be eliminated are a five dollar fee for residential customers and a ten dollar fee for business customers.

"Telephone users can look forward to increased competition among the major long distance carriers," said Stewart Gordon, vice president of ITT Corporation. "ITT is prepared to compete aggressively with AT&T and other carriers such as MCI and Sprint."

Customers selecting ITT as their primary long distance carrier will dial a single digit to reach the ITT network and all long distance calls will automatically be billed to their account. Presently ITT users must dial seven digits to reach the ITT network, and another seven digits to identify their billing code.

Ohio voters approve library levy

Voters in Ohio's Summit County approved an operating levy for the Akron-Summit County Public Library in a recent primary election. Endorsed by fifty-three percent of the voters, it marked the first time in 110 years that the Akron-Summit County system asked voters to approve funds to operate the library.

The library decided to ask area residents for support when it became apparent that the yearly intangibles tax collection, which supports the library, was not keeping up with library costs. In placing the levy on the ballot, the library asked voters to approve operating funds to increase the library materials collection, repair and maintain library buildings, purchase a new bookmobile, and install an automated circulation system. The .89 mill levy will generate $2.5 million a year for the next five years.

Report released on graduate education

The National Commission on Student Financial Assistance recently issued a report on the future of graduate education in America. The subcommittee that prepared the report was chaired by John Brademas, president of New York University. One of the major issues the commission considered was the state of the infrastructure—including libraries—that supports research and training in graduate education. The commission found serious signs of deterioration.

In the report, *Signs of Trouble and Erosion: A Report on Graduate Education in America,* the commission presented several findings that bear on the role of libraries: "Libraries are hard pressed to provide the public and scholars access to their collections and, in the face of an explosion of published knowledge, to maintain current collections. For several reasons, libraries also find it difficult to take advantage of new technologies for bibliographic and indexing improvements and for cooperative arrangements to create networks of knowledge."

The published statement of the commission's findings observes that although expenditures for library materials rose by ninety-one percent in the 1970s, enormous cost increases forced a reduction of twenty percent in growth of new volumes. Expenditures for salaries and wages more than doubled in the same period although staff size increased by only eleven percent. The report also notes that "Far from preserving these collections for future generations, we are permitting them to deteriorate on the shelves. Acids used in paper since about 1850 are literally destroying irreplaceable collections."

A $15,000,000 addition and renovation of the Morris Library at the University of Delaware in Newark is now underway with completion planned for early 1986. In connection with the renovation, the Library Staff Association sponsored a t-shirt contest. The winning design features a book, a computer terminal, and the last three letters of the word "library" hoisted by a power shovel. Some of the library staff (above) recently assembled to display the shirts. ***Susan Tkachick,*** *first row, fourth from left, was the contest design winner.* ***Susan Brynteson,*** *last row, fourth from left, is director of libraries.*

The commission recommends that the federal government increase grants for operating support to all college and university libraries; that the federal government encourage interlibrary cooperation and networking; that the Library of Congress take a leading role in assisting libraries across the country to preserve deteriorating collections; that the Library Career Training program be extended to support advanced study in modern information technology; and that incentives for business and industry to donate equipment to colleges and universities be extended to apply to library materials. Tax incentives to business and industry do not now apply to the donation of library materials.

The commission recommended "dramatic increases in funding" for the College Library Resources program, the Strengthening Research Library Resources program, and the Interlibrary Cooperation Program.

The published statement of the commission also endorses allocating more funds for the Library Career Training program: "New information technologies, networking, and evolving techniques for the preservation of collections all require fresh skills and training. Created in the 1960s, the Library Career Training program supports training for such purposes. Unfortunately, in recent years, less than $1 million has been provided for those efforts, a dramatic reduction from past levels of support. The commission recommends a substantial increase in funds for this program."

Copies of the document are available from the Office of External Affairs, New York University, 25 West Fourth Street, Room 506, New York, NY 10012.

Benevolent Builder: Appraising Andrew Carnegie

by Joseph Deitch

"Dear Saint Andrew," Mark Twain once wrote to Andrew Carnegie, "you seem to be in prosperity. Could you lend me $1.50 to buy a hymnbook with? God will bless you. I feel it. I know it. P.S. Don't send the hymnbook, send the money. I want to make the selection myself."

Ever alert to con artists, no matter how illustrious they might be, Carnegie refused the loan. If Mark Twain did not really have the price of a hymnbook, his local Carnegie library had quite a few he could borrow. Besides, endowing one person with the cost of one book made no more financial sense to the man who enabled millions of people to borrow books than to make a single pound of steel in the Carnegie mills.

Mark Twain was a frequent dinner guest of Carnegie's and the recipient of gifts from Andrew Carnegie, "patron saint of public libraries," that meant more to him than a passel of hymnbooks—gallons of the industrialist's choice Scotch, "the best and smoothest whisky on this planet," according to Twain.

Though Carnegie got no municipal requests for library buildings from Hannibal, Missouri, where Mark Twain spent his boyhood, he provided libraries in twenty-three other Missouri towns.

Huckleberry Finn's creator was not particularly impressed with the Steel King's library benefactions. Putting checks in the mail, nonstop, to pay for libraries was one of Carnegie's "egotistical gambols." Building them all over the United States and other countries made him famous, of course. But "he bought fame and paid cash for it," Mark Twain huffed as he blew smoke rings with his host's Coronas.

Elevating the masses

The Carnegie phenomenon in library history and in the history of philanthropy was the most important movement in mass culture and education since the founding of the public school. In some ways, Carnegie met Horace Mann's ideal for public education better than the American common school did—and does. The Scotsman, a self-made man in the American tradition who quit school at the age of twelve, built libraries across the country "for the elevation of the masses." He wanted the "laboring classes, toilers and wage earners" to have access to books and, through them, to education and betterment.

I discussed the Carnegie era in American public library history with three chief administrators of the Free Library of Philadelphia, where Carnegie built twenty-five branch libraries. He financed fifty-

Joseph Deitch *writes for* The New York Times *and other publications.*

eight in Pennsylvania, including the first four constructed in the United States. Thomas McConkey, chief of administrative services, spoke with obvious affection for the Carnegie branches in his city, eighteen of which are still active units of the library system. All retain the building layouts that James Bertram, Carnegie's Scottish secretary, developed and insisted on before a community's request for a building was approved. "An open-plan Carnegie library has a minimum of partitions, and its shape—parallelogram, square, T-shape or round—makes it possible to provide books and services as part of an integral whole," McConkey said. "You can't beat it for staff accessibility: there they are, out in the open. You go up to them and state your need."

Carnegie and Bertram knew the value of an open plan for security. "Staff could watch patrons to see that they did not steal books or cut them up. This has become even more important in recent years. The open plan was more economical to staff, and it still is. Staffing was cheap in the early years of Carnegie libraries. They employed ladies at low salaries and with little bargaining power. Libraries had larger staffs than they now do. Since we run libraries with fewer staff today, the open plan is absolutely essential," McConkey said. "It was the main recommendation of ALA planners to Carnegie and Bertram and is integral to modern library design, or adaptations of it."

This was a clean break with the tradition of dividing space into small rooms to house special collections, dictated by heating necessities. Rooms were often heated by open fireplaces. Central heating was just coming in when the first Carnegie libraries were built and it made the open plan possible.

Philadelphia employed some of the outstanding architects of the time to design Carnegie branches. The interiors followed four basic plans that Bertram required, with Carnegie's approval. Considerable freedom was allowed for exteriors; hence, the highly ornamental, landmark-type structures seen in many communities.

Towers and stone eagles

The first Carnegie libraries, in the steel towns of Braddock, Homestead, McKeesport and Allegheny, Pennsylvania, were elaborate, Victorian edifices with towers, minarets, stone eagles perched on roofs, and other classical motifs. The Allegheny library has been restored as a centerpiece of the rehabilitated downtown Pittsburgh area. The pioneer Carnegie libraries in Braddock and Homestead are still functioning, but with less support. The four steel cities, personally close to Carnegie, were allowed wide liberties before Bertram stopped departures from the basics.

Bertram would no longer finance ornate buildings with proposed clubrooms, kitchens, dining rooms, boardrooms and reception rooms. One town asked for a community dance hall in the library. Bertram chastised many a community leader for daring to include nonlibrary facilities that waste space and he also criticized local architects for failing to heed his still-useful *Notes on Library Buildings,* sent with applications for libraries. "Economy of space and utility" were the design watchwords. "A schoolboy could do better [in interpreting the *Notes*] than the submitted plans show," he wrote to an architect in Washington State. The almost biblical *Notes* called for adult and children's reading rooms and a combined reference and librarians' room on the first floor, and a lecture room and a staff room in the basement. The basic plans could be interchanged a bit but adding to them could risk the wrath of the curmudgeonly Bertram.

A classic Carnegie library is the Passyunk branch in South Philadelphia. Carnegie gave $1.5 million for the twenty-five library buildings in that city in 1903. The Passyunk branch, which Eileen Boigt, current adult-room librarian, calls the "library of everyone's childhood," has the standard memorial tablet in the foyer. It reads: "This building was given to the City of Philadelphia MCMXIII by Andrew Carnegie, Esq., to be used forever as the Passyunk Branch of the Free Library of Philadelphia." The estate of Stephen Girard, a financier of the American Revolution, provided the land for the library. The building will not only be used forever as a li-

Carnegie and family on an outing

brary; it may last forever, judging from the two-foot-thick foundation walls in the basement that Boigt slapped admiringly during a tour of the building.

Back at her desk, Boigt reveled in the simple logic of the building's layout that Bertram and ALA had devised, with Carnegie's approval, and said she "fell in love with this library the second I saw it." The great skylight has been covered over but the green and yellow walls, incredibly high ceilings, arched windows and beige linoleum floor, with a portrait of a beaming Carnegie on the wall, give the two rooms, in Boigt's words, "a cheerful, bright and sunny look that, we think, makes people want to go to the library and come back. In addition," she said, "this is a very old, middle-class Philadelphia neighborhood, and the library, framed by trees and tall hedges, fits in with what the people like."

One of my old haunts when I was growing up in Philadelphia was the Southwark Branch. That has been converted to a pants factory, so I tried another Carnegie library that I spent pleasant days in, this one on South Broad Street. It was only about eight blocks from my house. The old tan brick building is still a library, and an unusual one. For the past fifteen years, it has been a special children's branch, housing a collection of 16,000 books. Branch head is Diane Sychowski.

"Parents come in, look at the thirty-five-foot ceilings and sixteen-foot windows and say, this is beautiful," Sychowski related. The building is also classic Carnegie—T-shaped, with a big, main reading room leading to a smaller room for story hours and related activities. The walls are a familiar beige, but the oak molding and trim that reminded me of a room in Independence Hall had been painted turquoise or some related pastel horror. Still, the rooms are not overly cheerful and lack the cloying atmosphere that puts reading on the same level with candied medicine.

The kings of industry, politics, and labor. From left, Carnegie, William Jennings Bryan, J.J. Hill, John Mitchell.

Bertram would probably have taken immediate action on Sychowski's complaint that the original rainspouts for the building were put inside the walls, causing an inaccessible leak in one of the pipes to drip pools of water into the basement.

Why have they survived?

All but seven of the Carnegie libraries in this city have survived, including the Wyoming branch, believed the last Carnegie library building to be constructed in the United States. They have survived, physically, because of the quality of the materials, workmanship and design that went into them. In many communities all over the nation, they are still the handsomest buildings in town and have been given landmark status.

Why have they survived? "Library buildings generally have a long life," McConkey said. They become permanent. People identify with churches and municipal buildings like town halls and libraries. They represent respected values. Nostalgia is part of it. "And the people have a degree of control over them. There's no control over, or even interest in, commercial properties slated for demolition. For many, it is unthinkable to tear down a fine old library, and a lot is often done to prevent it."

The second reason for their survival is the foresight shown by Bertram in insisting on four basic building plans. They were all open, dominated by circulation desks. "The open plan became absolutely essential if libraries were to survive. You can run an open-plan library, even today, with a comparatively small staff," McConkey said, "because you can see what's going on from a central location with a few people. The staff is quickly available to the public—it can be spotted immediately, instead of having to wander all over the place for assistance."

That Andrew Carnegie was the "patron saint of public libraries" is easily documented. It all began in 1881 with the gift of a library to his birthplace in Scotland. Carnegie and, later, the Carnegie Corporation of New York which has been equally saintly in its library benefactions, gave $56 million to build 2,509 public libraries in English-speaking nations from 1896 to 1919. Of these, 1,681 were built in the United States—in every state except Delaware and Rhode Island. There has been no comparable philanthropic service throughout library history. Nor has any individual or foundation given money to build institutions, on Carnegie's scale, since his last public library was erected in Philadelphia sixty-five years ago.

The Carnegie family had emigrated to Allegheny, in western Pennsylvania, to seek a better life. Carnegie's formal schooling ended when he was twelve; then it was self-education through libraries. He built public libraries to enable Americans and the working population in many other countries to obtain more education. He used his "surplus of wealth" to pay for the libraries.

Books and buildings to house them were not the only benefit made possible by this man. He pioneered municipal commitment to library upkeep and stimulated funding for other public services, including government-sponsored library construction. The need for competent management of the libraries led to training for professional librarianship. Many towns, physically mundane and often shabby, suddenly found themselves with those Greek temples and Renaissance structures known as Carnegie libraries. Most communities complied with the requirement that they annually report, or document, allocation of money for books, salaries and other upkeep to Bertram. It was more a moral obligation and "was a brilliant and effective way to help guarantee municipal maintenance of the libraries," McConkey said, "and of guaranteeing ongoing support."

A model of its kind

The procedure for obtaining a library was simple and is still a model of its kind. Money would be given if the town or city would donate the site and appropriate at least ten percent of the building cost to maintain a free public library. Many communities gave more than that. The $10,000 or less that Carnegie gave to build about half of his libraries may evoke a gasp when the figure is compared to the cost of building a library today.

In the early years of Carnegie's library giving, the design of the buildings was based on local taste. The main concern of James Bertram, who personally reviewed applications and building plans, was to see that space was not wasted. A lot of space, he found, was being devoted by applicants to what he considered frills. Bertram developed a set of specifications to be followed. With them, he sent applicants sample floor plans drawn up with the help of architects and the ALA.

A "Delivery Desk" and Reading Room

The Carnegie Corporation of New York could not estimate the number of Carnegie libraries still being used as public libraries when I asked for a current figure, but a survey made about fifteen years ago disclosed that, of the 1,681 libraries built, 1,348 were still used as libraries, 1,137 remain as built and 211 had been enlarged. Of Indiana's 164 Carnegie libraries, the largest number in any state, 151 were still in use, 136 stood as built and only five had been demolished. Eighty-six of New York's 142 libraries were still libraries and five had been torn down. Fifty-four of California's 142 libraries were not being used as libraries and thirty-seven had been demolished.

Carnegie regarded Philadelphia as his "second home." He raised from $30,000 to $50,000 the city's estimate for each of its proposed Carnegie branches. McConkey told of two branches that were modernized as part of an effort to attract more people to libraries in the city. The Frankford library, of colonial design with elaborate decorations, has been given a contemporary look by stripping it to the bare walls and starting over again. "Except for a glass wall that replaced a brick wall, Bertram would have recognized the Walnut West branch as a Carnegie library," McConkey said. A key tenet of library promotion in the city is to enable the public to see people using libraries and thus entice more patrons into them. Heavy traffic points, like circulation desks, can be invitingly seen through the big glass walls.

But aside from these two "drastically changed buildings," the other Carnegie branches in Philadelphia are about as they were, except for installation of modern heating, plumbing, lighting and air-conditioning. None have been added to, because the policy is to build another branch in the area if need warrants it. There are now fifty-two branches operating as part of a $22 million budget. McConkey "doubted very much" that the Carnegie branches would have been built by the City of Philadelphia to meet library needs in their neighborhoods. There had been no branches that had not been built by Carnegie when McConkey joined the library system in 1952; prior to that branches were usually set up in rented quarters.

Keith Doms, director of the Free Library of Philadelphia, agreed with McConkey that the twenty-five Carnegies would not have been built by the city. "The city's record for supporting libraries had not, frankly, been outstanding, historically," Doms said. Philadelphia may have been the last city in the country to build a major public library. Its central building was put up long after most eastern cities had built theirs. The reason that Philadelphia was so late in developing public libraries was that it had more private libraries than any other city. "Don't forget that the Boston Public Library went public before we did, and they were not lacking in private libraries," Doms said.

Swimming at the library

When I noted that the construction of the Carnegie libraries coincided almost precisely with mass immigration to this country, from about 1890 to 1920, Doms recalled that these libraries, from his experience in the Pittsburgh area, were also community cultural centers for these people, most of whom worked in the steel mills. Before becoming head of the Philadelphia library system in 1969, Doms was director of the Pittsburgh libraries. The huge Carnegie building in Pittsburgh also had facilities for lyceum-type programs, pipe organs (Carnegie donated 7,000 organs to churches), theatricals, bowling, even swimming. "I recall people saying they were going to the library to swim," Doms said.

Carnegie at work in his private library

Many library users were first-generation immigrants. Carnegie paternalistically combined books and recreation for them. He was, after all, an immigrant himself and these were his people—they needed something more. But the part of the library devoted to books was often more heavily used than the recreation areas. This stemmed from an awareness that advancement in America began with books.

These Pennsylvania cities "were cities of neighborhoods, and they still are," Henry Kapenstein, deputy director of the Philadelphia Free Library, said. "And the Carnegie libraries gave identity to neighborhoods for immigrants and others, much as post offices, banks and other public buildings did. They anchored and linked the community with something it respected." People around the South-side steel mill in Pittsburgh would cluster in the local Carnegie library, particularly on Sundays, Doms noted. With recreation and social activities in the same building, many immigrant steelworkers were reminded of similar facilities in Germany, Hungary, Italy, Poland and other European countries where the library was often part of a complex of related services. "Carnegie may have had that in mind when he built these all-purpose libraries in the steel towns," Doms said. The canny Scot may have also known that the recipients of these benefits would do a better job in his factories. Japanese industrialists now do the same thing.

Doms and his colleagues were asked what it would cost to build replicas of Philadelphia's Carnegie libraries today. Carnegie spent about $50,000 for each of them. "All that stone, marble, steel, bronze, ornamental iron, brick, oak," Kapenstein mused. After some lively debate, the consensus was that they would cost $1.5 million apiece. Doms picked up on a point he had made earlier, that one reason for the survival of Carnegie libraries is the open plan used in all of them. Kapenstein said that this led to the concept of the open shelf—a revolutionary idea compared to the restricted or closed European system. In Carnegie's libraries, patrons "had access to everything they could see," which further endeared them to people. With few telephones and no radio in those early Carnegie-library years, the buildings became communication centers—hives of interaction among the immigrants. "So much so that weddings and even funerals were held in them," Doms said.

High ceilings and labyrinthine halls

The three library administrators were asked to compare the architectural attractiveness of Carnegie libraries with those being built today. They hesitated and grinned. Doms ventured this comment, "Isn't beauty in the eye of the beholder?" Kapenstein said the Carnegies "frequently do not meet today's needs." "Take the central building we're in, opened in 1927," Doms said. "It is monumental in size and expense: it is costly to operate, the building is not as open as it might be to afford easy supervision and reduce staff. The maintenance cost is incredible. The ceiling heights and labyrinthine halls are a waste of space and are impractical, yet some people in the city feel about this building as they do about the Carnegie library in Pittsburgh. It's a landmark."

In some ways, the Carnegie libraries cost more to maintain. But, McConkey said, the roofs of modern libraries have a maximum life of twenty years and air-conditioning systems wear out over the same span, but the roof of a Carnegie library will last one hundred years. It is usually of slate, tile and copper.

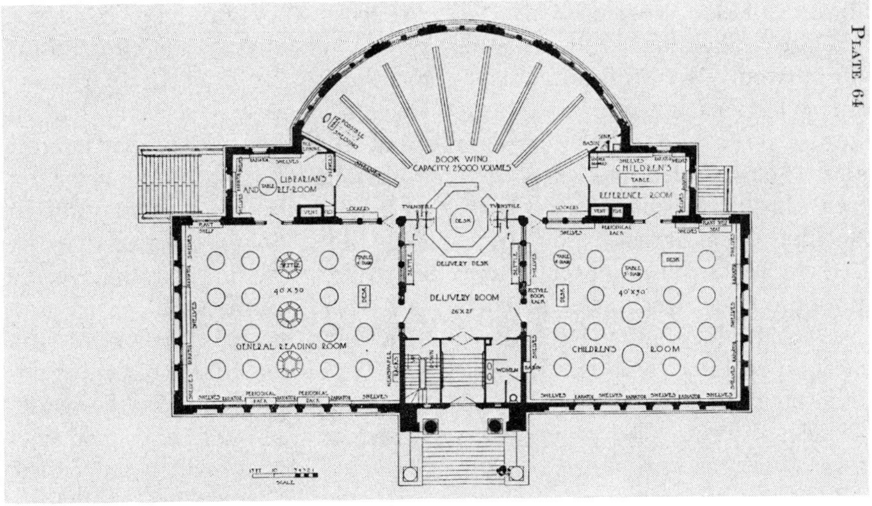

The familiar floor plan of a Carnegie Library

"That is one truism about the Carnegie branches, but there's another one," Doms said. "A 7,500-square-foot Carnegie building is more expensive to maintain than a 7,500-square-foot modern library." The heating, ventilating and electrical systems in most Carnegie libraries have been replaced. McConkey said, "Today's synthetic insulation is more efficient for retaining heat than the Carnegies' thick brick walls. It takes modern insulation to make some Carnegie buildings energy-efficient." A Carnegie library blown away in a tornado in Indiana and another that fell apart in Nebraska were probably victims of shoddy construction and inferior materials.

Skylights, picturesque but with only a few feet of candlepower, have been replaced with fixtures giving fifty to seventy-five feet of candlepower in Carnegie libraries. Arranging passage for the handicapped in the libraries has been difficult, according to Kapenstein. The reason is that the buildings' first, or main, floors are well above ground or basement level, which were given high ceilings as part of design "monumentality" perceived for the libraries, but are hard to ramp. "Like doing the same thing in today's split-level homes," Kapenstein added.

With glass walls and other modern features in the Frankford branch, the plans for the building that Bertram approved eighty-one years ago would be unrecognizable by him today. Would he have approved? Considering that Bertram and his boss were eminently practical men, all felt that he would have at least been positive about the changes. There was also agreement that Philadelphia's Carnegie libraries continue as valuable neighborhood resources and, through their historical architecture, as authentic links with earlier eras in American history.

Another Carnegie?

Does America need, or will it ever get, another Carnegie for libraries? "The tax situation makes that absolutely impossible," Doms said. "We probably do not need another Carnegie. He was the catalyst, remember, that generated the wide spread and implementation of the public library concept. I have always found it interesting that, in Pennsylvania, we had the start of the public library idea—Benjamin Franklin in the eastern part of the state and Carnegie in the West. But Carnegie was the real founding father."

There is no doubt that he stimulated hundreds of other library gifts, buildings and collections, to universities during and after his public library giving period. Doms said the Free Library of Philadelphia is "a library for the people." Carnegie laid the foundation for it with his gift of twenty-five branches. Its special collections include "a fantastic number of Dickens letters, Edgar Allan Poe manuscripts, early children's books, an automotive library that may be superior to the one in Detroit, and a music collection used throughout the world. For seventy-five years, the library has offered vacation-reading clubs for the children of Philadelphia. One of our Carnegie libraries is a children's branch." Doms said.

Holdings at the Central Library, now mainly a reference facility, total five million items—eight million for the entire system. The city's population of 1.7 million includes 500,000 who are functionally illiterate. Many of the latter are migrants from the South and immigrants from poorer nations for whom neighborhood libraries, including Carnegie branches, are vital resources for information, education, and communication.

"The library branch has become a community anchor for many immigrant families, and woe to those who would consolidate, demolish or close it—local politicians are especially aware of this," Doms said. The Carnegie libraries and the branches they brought about are serving the ideal for immigrant masses in the way that Andrew Carnegie and his secretary had in mind when they gave money to erect library buildings in 1,412 towns and cities in America for immigrants in their time. "For meeting this particular need, their libraries have come full circle," Doms said.

Robert Stern, director of the Center for the Study of American Architecture at Columbia University and head of an architectural firm in New York, provided an artistic and visual environmental evaluation of the Carnegie libraries in 1984. "In my travels around the country, I have always been impressed by the dignity, serviceability, and appropriateness of the Carnegie buildings," Stern said. "I am amazed that so little is known about them and that graduate students in art history have given them so little attention."

Exemplifying local traditions

Exemplifying local traditions, Stern said, "they brought significant architecture to small towns in local styles, whether red-brick Georgian in New England or Spanish colonial in the Southwest. The buildings respond to, and exemplify, local traditions. In cities, they reflected the grand architectural style of the day, usually modern French or academic beaux arts. They are still among the most important structures in small towns. They are wonderful monuments in their neighborhoods in New York and are a delight to come upon."

Keith Doms, Free Library of Philadelphia, outside the Passyunk Branch, a Carnegie library still in operation

Contemporary libraries in the United States are no match, architecturally, for the Carnegie buildings. "They are tawdry, many of them. They exemplify what some librarians call the supermarket theory of library service—everything displayed on shelves in clean, well-lighted floor space like so many groceries. And they're boring. You wouldn't catch me dead in an American public library built since 1950," Stern remarked.

Stern did not frequent Carnegie libraries as a boy in Brooklyn, but he did use that borough's Central Library on Grand Army Plaza. "I loved going into that vast hall and feeling about three inches tall and saying to myself, 'Now, at last, I'm someplace.'" Stern deplored the tendency of some library directors and trustees to replace the Carnegie buildings with the strongly advocated supermarket approach. "Keep them. They are small, wonderful buildings, dignified, practical and human that landmark and preservation groups should protect," Stern observed.

Some of New York's branches were designed by such leading architects as Carrere and Hastings, who designed the New York Public Library and Babb, Cook and Willard, who designed the Carnegie mansion on Fifth Avenue. "It was nothing but the best for Mr. Carnegie," Stern said. He added that he was "a creature of libraries, too many of which were designed by cost-cutters and bureaucrats. This is not in the Carnegie spirit. He had a mission—to bring education to large numbers of people through library books, in rooms where people could meet in buildings that would elevate and ennoble the community."

U.S. Population Characteristics: Implications for Libraries

by Kathleen Falcigno and Polly Guynup

Demographic changes in our society create new and changing information needs. Libraries must recognize, understand, and respond to new challenges in order to provide effective service in the years ahead. The *1980 United States Census of Population* suggests several trends of importance to the library community. Specifically, the increases in the number of elderly Americans, citizens living in rural areas, and cultural minority groups have implications for library service. In order to provide more effective and equitable library and information services, and promote a better-informed population, these trends must be carefully examined.

Historically, the chief reason for population growth has been an excess of births over deaths. However, during the 1970s the birth rate dropped to its lowest level in United States history. The final count of the census was 226.5 million, representing an increase of 11.4 percent, the lowest rate of population growth since the depression years of the 1930s. An increase of less than ten percent is expected for the 1980s, and less than ten percent is expected for the 1990s. The differences in growth between regions during the last decade are largely due to the movement patterns of the population. Census data suggest that there has been a shift in the East-to-West and South-to-North migration pattern. During the 1970s, the North-to-South movement became slightly greater than East-to-West. Further, the number of people migrating from southern and western states has declined. Significantly, ninety percent of the net population expansion during the 1970s took place in the southern and western states. These areas experienced an overall growth rate of 21.4 percent. The population in the South grew by 12.5 million during the last decade. This represents an average gain of 3,432 new people a day. The population of the West grew by 8.3 million, or 2,279 new people a day. In the Northeast and Midwest, however, the total population increased by slightly more than two percent (Figs. 1, 2).

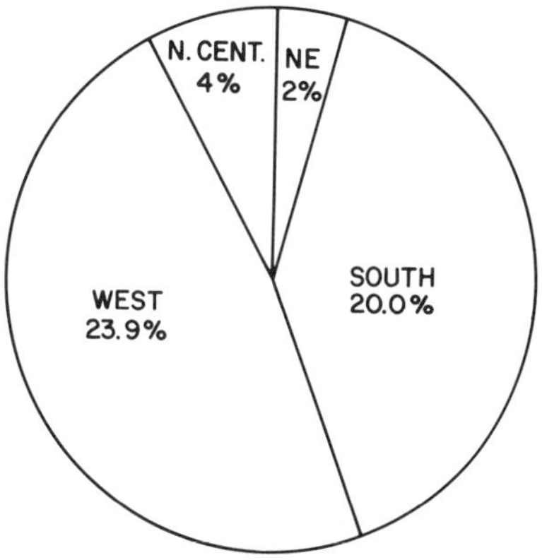

Figure 1

This work was performed in 1983 while the authors were on loan to the National Commission on Libraries and Information Science from the IBM Thomas J. Watson Research Center, Yorktown Heights, New York.

A trend reversed

Most of this migration has been from metropolitan to nonmetropolitan areas. Historically, the metropolitan growth rate outpaced that of nonmetropolitan areas. However, between 1970 and 1980 that trend was reversed (Fig. 3). The population in non-metropolitan areas grew by fifteen percent, while in metropolitan areas, it grew by only ten percent. In contrast, the metropolitan growth rate during the 1960s increased by seventeen percent, while the nonmetropolitan growth rate increased by 3.3 percent.

In the South, metropolitan growth was more rapid than nonmetropolitan growth. In all other areas, however, it was the nonmetropolitan counties which grew the fastest. The most rapidly growing counties in the United States are the nonmetropolitan areas in the West. The growth of small towns

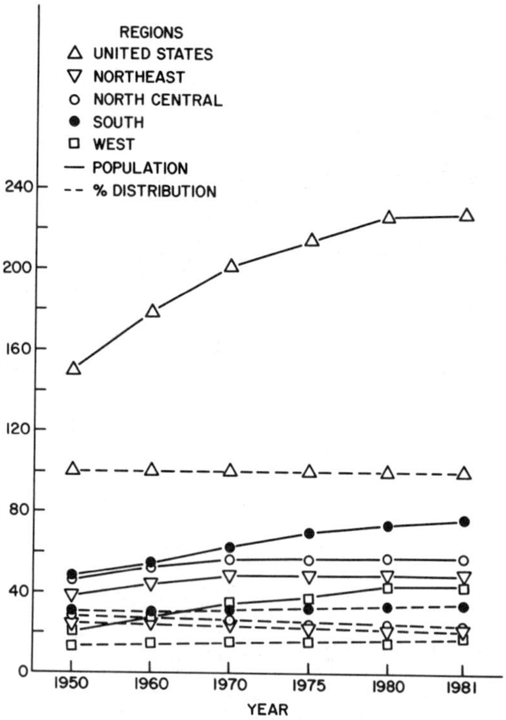

Figure 2 S. Bureau of the Census

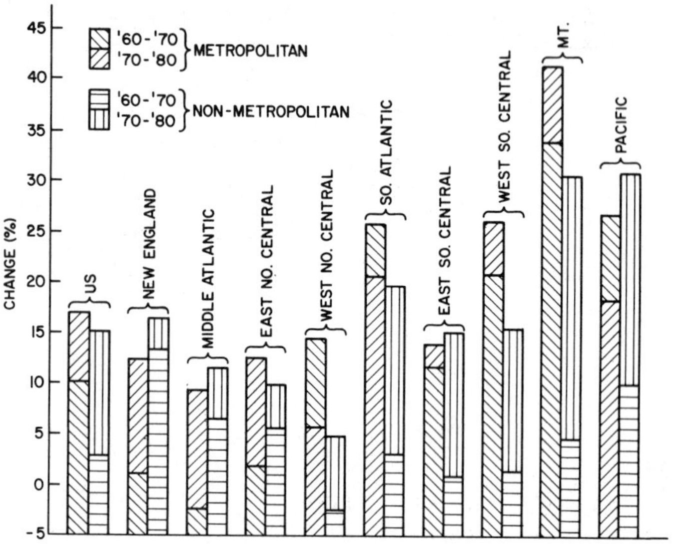

Source: U.S. Bureau of the Census

Figure 3

and rural areas is expected to continue throughout the 1980s with the majority of this growth taking place in the Sun Belt (Fig. 4).

"Library services in rural America," according to Bernard Vavrek, "have existed quietly, and have, at the same time, been overshadowed by American librarianship's preoccupation with the large metro library model." In a national survey conducted by the Center for Rural Librarianship, dealing with public libraries in areas with populations of 25,000 or fewer, it was found that six percent of those libraries responding were without telephones. Considering that communication is one of the cornerstones of library service, these findings point to the need for increased attention to rural library service.

Rural areas are perhaps most often associated with agriculture. However, farm residents number only six million, and are a minority even in the rural population. In the last decade, rural employment was concentrated in four areas: the number of people employed in nonteaching, white collar professional and technical occupations increased by 28. 2 percent; the number of white-collar clerical jobs increased by 28.2 percent; service occupations rose by 26 percent; and the number of blue-collar crafts workers rose by 17.8 percent. These areas provided 82.4 percent of the new nonmetropolitan jobs in the United States. Clearly, people in rural areas have a diverse range of information needs, including small business management, marketing, law, applications of science and technology, and health and nutrition. In addition, since many rural residents formerly lived in metropolitan areas, they have come to expect a wide range of information choices.

Different information needs

Library service policies for rural areas may be influenced by the varying age profiles found in many communities. The overall median age of the rural population is generally the same as the nation as a whole. However, migration has greatly affected the age composition in many areas. In a number of Great Plains and Corn Belt areas affected by a drop in farm employment, the median age has risen to forty as young people have moved away. In these areas, there are more people in their sixties than twenties. In other rural areas, the median age is in the mid-twenties because of job development or high birth rates. Libraries in many rural areas, then, will be dealing with a service area primarily of young or aging adults, with different information needs.

Geographic distribution presents special challenges for libraries in rural areas. High fuel costs and long driving distances can discourage potential users from making the trip to the library. Bookmobiles, a common method of information delivery to rural residents, may not be able to provide the wide range of services required, and in the time frame they are needed. In order to maximize their effectiveness, visits can be scheduled to reach the greatest number of people at a time. Technological developments, such as cable television and videotex, have great potential for providing information to geographically remote areas, and can help link rural and urban communities. Several ventures are underway, but both public and private support are needed to expand them to other areas.

Living longer

According to the census, 11.4 percent of the total United States population is aged 65 or older. In 1970, the total number of individuals over age 65 was 20 million, and in 1981 this number rose to 26.3 million. This constitutes an increase of approximately thirty percent in the last decade. The number of individuals aged 65 or older will rise to 28 million by 1985, and by 1990, over 31 million people in the United States will be aged 65 or older. The older population is expected to grow steadily. The most rapid increase is expected to occur between the years 2010 and 2030, when the "baby boom" generation reaches age 65 (Fig. 5). In addition, Americans are living longer (Fig. 6). The average life expectancy for men is almost seventy, for women it is 77.5. Life expectancy is expected to rise to the mid-eighties by the latter part of this century.

The percentage of elderly Americans reached by library services is relatively small. Perhaps the most comprehensive study of library service to the elderly was conducted by Booz, Allen & Hamilton in 1972. Public libraries serving populations of 25,000 people or more, with a combined service area of 105 million, were surveyed. Approximately fifty-two percent of the total number of elderly Americans lived in the areas surveyed. The total number of elderly citizens reached by library service was 204,541 or less than two percent of the aging in the responding areas. In order to adequately serve this segment of the population, libraries need to assess the information needs of the elderly, provide appropriate materials, and promote an awareness of their programs.

Bringing the elderly together

The information needs of the elderly may be influenced by the psychological and physiological factors of aging. For example, older women outnumber men by a wider margin as age increases. As a consequence, many older women eventually live alone. This may place an emotional and financial burden on many older women, and require them to seek out a wider range of information. By providing information regarding health care, housing, retirement planning, employment, and community services, libraries can help alleviate some of the adjustments facing older citizens. Libraries can bring the elderly together with others their own age or with younger people and, in an informal setting, explore areas of interest or concern to them. Involving the elderly in the planning process is the first step towards assessing their information needs, and in providing library services to this segment of the population.

Working together

Providing access to library services for an increasingly aging population also requires special planning. New electronic information delivery systems which allow information to be transmitted directly into the home can provide an excellent method for ensuring adequate access to information services. Introducing computerized services, however, presents a challenge both in encouraging and educating the elderly to take advantage of them. A recent study sponsored by the National Retired Teachers Association and the American Association of Retired Persons indicates that younger people generally have more positive attitudes towards technology than elderly citizens. More familiar and perhaps at present more easily received methods include home-delivery of materials and transportation services to the library. Almost fifteen percent of the elderly live below poverty level. Considering the cost involved in providing these services, it is clear that libraries, businesses, and government must work together to provide the elderly with the information they need.

The 1980 census reveals that the four major cultural minority groups in the United States are black, Hispanic, Asian and Pacific Islander, and American Indian, Aleut and Eskimo. While the growth rate of the black population has slowed, the Hispanic, and Asian and Pacific Islander population is growing rapid-

Figure 4

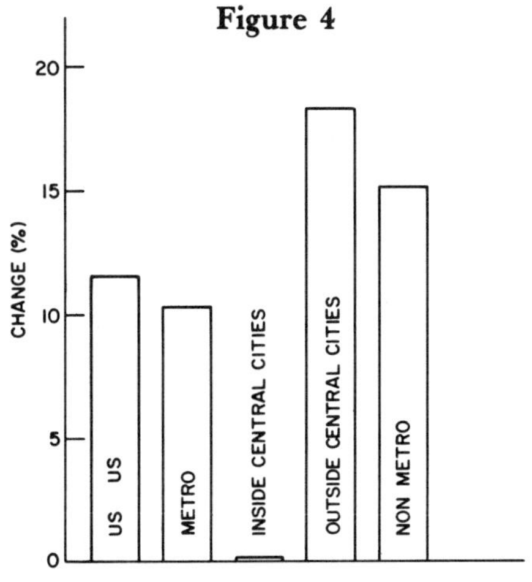

Figure 5

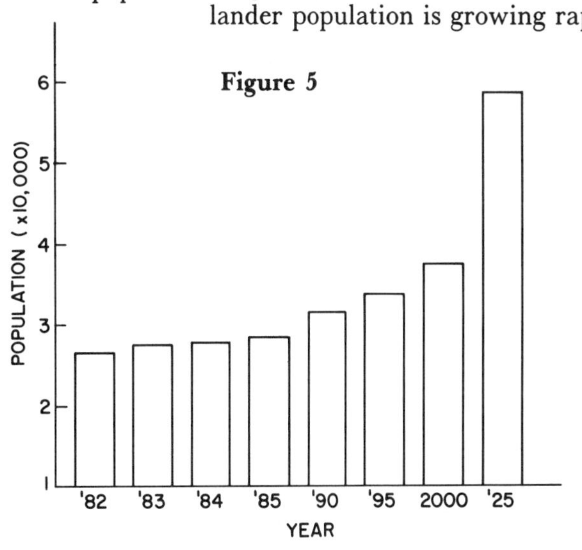

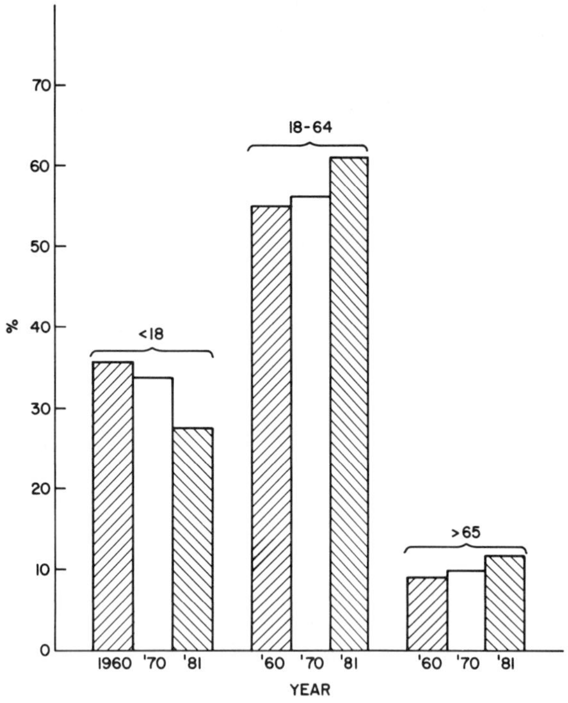

Figure 6

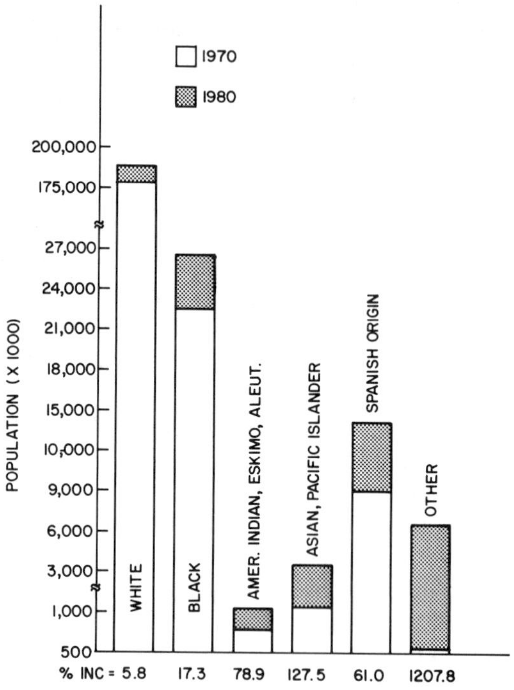

Figure 7

ly. Blacks comprised 11.7 percent of the total population in 1980, an increase from 11.1 percent in 1970. People of Hispanic origin currently comprise 6.4 percent of the national population, experiencing a growth rate of sixty-one percent during the last decade. The number of Asian and Pacific Islanders increased during the 1970s from 1.5 to 3.5 million, an increase of 127.6 percent. American Indians, Aleuts, and Eskimos comprise .6 percent of the population, increasing by 71.8 percent during the 1970s to a total of 1,420,000. During the last decade, the minority population increased from seventeen to twenty percent of the total population (Fig. 7). By the year 2000, almost one-third of the total United States population will be composed of these groups.

Immigration, legal and illegal, has had an impact on the growth rate of many minority groups. *Newsweek* magazine referred to the 1970s as the "Decade of Immigration." There were more individuals admitted to the United States in 1977, 1978, and 1979 than for any year since 1924. There were 4.3 million more immigrants from Europe in the 1970s than there were in the 1960s.

According to a recent Editorial Research Report, "illegal aliens, together with an annual influx of 400,000 legal immigrants, now account for more than fifty percent of the total U.S. population growth." Spanish-speaking Americans have replaced Italians as the largest linguistic minority.

Reexamining policies and services

According to a National Commission on Libraries and Information Science task force report, "while ethnic groups in the country for the last twenty years have been fighting to preserve their heritage, cultural minority groups have had limited access to library and information services. Many studies show that resources of bilingual and bicultural materials in public, school, and academic libraries have been inadequate, and in many cases, nonexistent." If libraries are to attract these groups, they may wish to reexamine their collection policies and services in order to ensure that additonal materials by and about cultural minorities are available. Moreover, in a society increasingly concerned with technological development and computer literacy, language and financial barriers often present special challenges for service to cultural minority groups.

In addition to responding to the changing needs of the population, libraries will be faced with other equally complex challenges. Many urban libraries will be faced with providing services in areas with decreasing tax bases. Libraries in rural areas, on the other hand, will be faced with providing services to an increasing number of people. While technology can be used to provide information services to many people, studies have shown that younger people, as well as those with higher incomes and educational levels are more likely to use and feel comfortable with modern information systems. Moreover, the people generally most concerned about education and libraries are parents. As the population continues to age, and birth rates drop, this area of support may decrease. As a result, libraries may need to reexamine their collections and services, and look for new areas of support in the coming years. ▣

The Only Copyright Law We Need

by Daniel Toohey

Samuel Clemens once said that the only thing God couldn't do was to find any sense in the copyright law. Mr. Clemens lived in fairly active times for copyright laws. When he was born in 1835, this country's second copyright law was four years old. By 1910 when he died, Congress had revised the law twice more, once in 1870 and again in 1909. This writer doesn't know which particular statute prompted the sarcasm, but most people who have any contact with the cumbersome law of copyright leave the experience dissatisfied if not completely undone.

Fewer distant signals

Authors are not the only people who might share Sam Clemens's sentiment. We commoners puzzle over copyright notices posted over photocopiers, we videotape at home while four Supreme Court justices believe that we infringe, we see fewer distant signals on our cable systems because of unexplainable copyright rate increases. Our teachers labor under peculiarly exotic standards for copying classroom materials, standards of "brevity and spontaneity," and "cumulative effect." Librarians display warnings and keep a watchful eye out for "systematic reproduction or distribution" of "related or concerted" copies. We may be fined for "innocent" infringement, and the much relied upon doctrine of "fair use" turns out to be not fair at all, but a pusillanimous doctrine with narrow, grudging application.

Well-intentioned industry groups meet under the sponsorship of Congress to develop "fair use" guidelines that attempt to resolve competing interests informally, and having done so must admit that those who rely upon their conclusions do so perilously.[1]

Nothing in the underlying purposes of copyright prepares one for such a complex, vexatious law. Copyright simply strives to balance two principles: that authors should enjoy a monopoly on their works for a limited time in order to preserve their livelihood in such activities and thereby spur them on to further creation, and that their works should be accessible for people to use them as part of the artistic treasury of the nation.[2]The middle ground between the propositions of monopoly and accessibility is the battlefield where cases are fought in the federal courts and where special interests are lobbied in Congress.

Struggling in vain

The need to balance accessibility with the rights of ownership is increasingly critical as the communications revolution gains speed. Copyright now affects not only large sectors of our economy, but the everyday lives of people, as the librarian on sentry duty at the copying machine well knows. As new technologies enter the marketplace and new economic relationships among users and creators are formed, the traditional administrators of copyright law, Congress and the courts, struggle in vain to keep up. Generally, because of the time it takes for them to act and a backlog of other duties, they fall far behind.

When the United States' first copyright law was enacted in 1790 (called by Congress "An Act for the encouragement of learning"), it protected little more than printing and engraving. A satisfactory protective balance between ownership and use was achieved with periodic legislative review and it occasioned interpretations of the statute by the courts. Technological and economic change occurred more slowly than today and comprehensive revisions to the copyright laws were enacted only every forty years or so until 1909.

Pulled and twisted

When the 1909 statute was superseded in 1976, the old law was exhausted from having been pulled and twisted to fit applications never dreamed of by its authors. Revision was delayed by the impossibility of writing a law specific enough for the problems at hand and general enough to protect new forms of communication as they appeared. The 1976 Copyright Act occupies two and one-half times as many pages as the older law. While the 1909 law defined only two terms, the new law defined more than fifty. These two simple comparisons give only a hint of the statute's complexity. While most statutes lean on legislative intent to assist in interpreting their provisions, the 1976 law actually incorporates sometimes inconsistent documents from House and Senate proceedings. It also incorporates certain FCC

Daniel Toohey *is a member of the law firm of Dow, Lohnes & Albertson, Washington, D.C. He is counsel to several states, colleges, universities, and telecommunications enterprises.*

rules which were in effect at the time but have since been repealed, leaving the law—assuming Sam Clemens was wrong—God knows where.

In spite of Congress' exertions, the 1976 statute lived up to no one's hopes. Only two years after its enactment, various parties were clamoring for major revision. Today the tumult continues. Omnibus legislation is once more in Congress, with little hope of passage. The rapid obsolescence of copyright law is not an indictment of Congress; it demonstrates that the widening scope of property rights under copyright protection cannot be contained in a static federal law. Technology easily outruns Congress's ability to provide adequate protection.

The judiciary, the other principal actor in administering copyright law, fares little better than Congress in maintaining pace with demands for protection. The well-known "Betamax" case is a good example.[3] In January 1984, the U.S. Supreme Court held, by a vote of five to four, that the sale of video recorders is not per se an act of infringement. There are other elements to the decision, but for our purposes, two important aspects of this case stand out.

Stale facts

First, the Supreme Court's opinion rested on fairly stale facts. The case began with the filing of an infringement action in 1976; the Court based its opinion on surveys of video recorder use during a 1978 sample period. As any reasonably alert person will have noticed, video recorder use has expanded dramatically between 1976 and 1984, and "time-shifting" (programs recorded off-the-air for later viewing) was the only issue before the Court, not such practices as private "dubbing" of rented items, black-market rentals and so forth.

Second, the justices repeatedly alluded to a lack of direction from Congress. The majority noted that "one may search the Copyright Act in vain for any sign that [Congress] has made it unlawful to copy a program for later viewing at home" or prohibited selling recorders. Justice Stevens, writing for the majority, said, "It is not our job to apply laws that have not yet been written."[4] The four dissenting justices had words for Congress as well. Besides regarding the majority opinion as a disincentive for Congress to patch the Betamax hole in the law, Justice Blackmun observed in his final paragraph for the minority that, like so many problems created by the interaction of copyright law with a new technology, there can be no really satisfactory solution until Congress acts.[5]

The sound one hears is that of the copyright ball being batted back and forth between two branches of government, with no need yet to awaken the President.

For the judiciary, the responsibility is to determine whether existing law has any currency to the facts at hand. If it does not, courts have two choices. They can apply a statute inadequate to the task, risking an unjust result but one which nonetheless observes the legislature's prerogative to write laws. Alternatively they may despair of Congress ever dealing legislatively with the issue before them and do some judicial lawmaking, behaving as an "activist" court.

In a hailstorm of change

For Congress, the responsibility is to write intelligible, lasting law in a hailstorm of change, with so many other demands upon its time. The author of an omnibus copyright bill wins few votes and is rewarded with few television news interviews. Yet the hapless member who undertakes that assignment must become expert in one of the most tangled, bedeviling areas of law as well as the various sciences and arts it protects, all the while facing some of the nastiest special interests in the halls of Congress. The legislators' reluctance, the long period between statutes, is not surprising. In fact, the present demand for administering copyright is probably beyond Congress's abilities and exceeds the abilities of not a few judges as well.

As a consequence, communications and data processing industries continually produce new forms of copyrightable intellectual property and new methods of exploiting existing works, with no reliable assurance that protection is available under the copyright law[6] or that the process or device is not itself an infringement.[7] The strict penalties imposed by the present law make it very risky to venture into the many "gray areas" of the copyright law, yet technological progress is almost impossible to stop. Usually it will roll right over an outmoded law.

This frustrating state of affairs results from Congress's belief that it must write a painstakingly specific statute. Instead it writes nothing at all and no workable system is at hand to balance, with the force and effect of law, the rights of creators and users of copyrighted materials as those materials become available.

An enormous difficulty

Congress could extricate itself from this enormous difficulty by writing a single law, one which creates a federal administrative agency with all-encompassing jurisdiction over copyright. Unlike the present federal agencies which have jurisdiction limited to a part of the present copyright law, such as the granting and recording of copyrights (the U.S. Copyright Office) or the collecting and dispensing of royalties (the Copyright Royalty Tribunal), the new agency would have broad administrative and adjudicative powers like the Federal Communications Commission (FCC). Fifty years ago Congress passed a law creating the FCC. The Communications Act of 1934 has undergone only moderate revision during the half-century of its regime and yet has survived radical changes in communications and technology. It has enabled the FCC to keep relatively close regulatory pace with many of the same changes in communications technology which have outdistanced the copyright law.

Today federal agencies are more likely to be abolished rather than created in favor of the marketplace as a more effective regulator. But, the marketplace has its limits; its rough and tumble cannot achieve the delicate, shifting balance between protection of ownership and creation on one side and access by legitimate users on the other. An agency, let us call it the Federal Copyright Agency (FCA), could design standards for application of fair copyright principles through regulation and adjudication. The mere act of consolidating the critical government supervision of copyright into a single federal agency would bring immediate practical benefits to the public and to the industries affected by copyright.

"As new technologies enter the marketplace and new economic relationships among users and creators are formed, the traditional administrators of copyright law, Congress and the courts, struggle in vain to keep up."

Problems of narrow scope

The FCA could clarify much of the present confusion about copyright by issuing policy statements and opinions. In the rule-making process, part of which includes public comment, the agency can deal specifically with problems of narrow scope. Through these regulatory devices, the agency could respond more speedily than Congress to strike the important balance between creators and users. By centering rule-making in such an agency, the need for exactingly specific legislation by Congress would be avoided. Congress could do what it is best able to do, set general policy by statute and safeguard implementation through its oversight power, enacting corrective legislation only when necessary.[8]

By means of any federal agency's well-recognized power to waive its own rules, the FCA could recognize special circumstances while promoting uniformity. Occasionally, strict application of a rule produces an inequitable result. In such cases, agencies can waive or suspend the rule without generally repealing it. Congress can achieve a similar result but only in a cumbersome, plodding process involving special legislation.

The FCA might employ compulsory licensing when it is needed to maintain an equitable balance between public use and authors' compensation. More and more, we encounter circumstances where such a system might work well. For example, compulsory licensing might offer a simpler, more easily enforceable method of achieving a balance between the modern library and the authors whose works it stores in so many different formats. Somewhere in the many manifestations of storage, retrieval, book preservation, copying, and format transference there is an opportunity for the compulsory license to simplify in a way which fairly compensates authors and yet allows libraries room to modernize. The ability to apply such compensation schemes to fit unique circumstances, even on a temporary basis, should reduce substantially the need for countless exceptions, provisos, and guidelines in either the agency's rules or its governing statute. But only an administrative agency is equipped to do the constant fine tuning that such a scheme requires.

Promoting consistency

The FCA could be given the power to adjudicate disputes arising under the copyright law, relieving federal courts of the obligation to administer it. Today every litigated controversy under the copyright law is an expensive, federal lawsuit. The fear of such litigation and the inevitable costs and delay undoubtedly chill many legitimate uses of copyrighted works. Through the legal doctrine of primary jurisdiction (which gives the agency first crack over the courts at deciding cases falling within its regulatory ambit) the FCA could promote consistency in the law and avoid the present difficulties flowing from conflicting district court opinions from various jurisdictions. More streamlined administrative proceedings would also permit speedier resolution of claims at less cost to the litigants. Any subsequent judicial review would take place on the basis of a record developed by the agency and doctrines which limit the reviewing court's ability to review the case.

A copyright agency could become expert in the copyright and its subject matter, promoting consistent administration of the law. By consolidating the functions now separately performed by the courts, Congress, the Copyright Office, and the Copyright Royalty Tribunal (CRT), the disharmonies resulting from the independent actions of these entities could end. Thus, for example, the agency could administer the functions performed by the CRT with full authority to interpret and enforce copyright rules and the underlying statutes. Moreover, the agency's continuing participation in these related functions will produce a staff that is thoroughly expert in these matters, reducing the time it now takes government to decide copyright cases.

An agency's ability to develop statistical data on the industries it regulates is also useful, enabling it to anticipate and respond to the demands of new technologies rather than to react to problems already out of control. The need to completely understand the market of copyrightable works and their economic milieu underlies many established doctrines in the field. For example, in administering the doctrine of "fair use," the FCA could monitor developments in affected industries and identify those elements of use that unfairly limit authors' rights or inequitably restrict public benefits. A realistic fairness is the ideal this doctrine has pursued, but it requires attentive experts to make it work.

"Historically, social and economic forces have demanded agency regulation of commerce, communications, trade, and the environment when Congress could no longer keep pace with the level of specificity demanded in order to govern effectively."

A stitch in time

A congressional stitch in time to establish a permanent, effective agency of experts will ultimately save countless hours of futile legislative and judicial work. Congress's present functions force it beyond its proper role which is that of an overseer, a creator of broad policy. Historically, social and economic forces have demanded agency regulation of commerce, communications, trade, and the environment when Congress could no longer keep pace with the level of specificity demanded in order to govern effectively. That same situation exists now in the copyright area and recommends a similar result. The day the idea for the FCA came to me was cloudless, brilliant, with exceptionally low humidity, and a gentle southerly breeze. God likes the idea or He would have made it rain. Besides, it means no more wisecracks from Clemens. ▣

FOOTNOTES

1. For example, Congressman Robert Kastenmaier, Chairman of the House Subcommittee on Courts, Civil Liberties, and Administration of Justice appointed a negotiating committee in March 1979 to establish specific guidelines for off-air recording by educators. The committee met and adopted a set of guidelines, but two of its members dissented, the Motion Picture Association of America and the Association of Media Producers. A member of Congressman Kastenmaier's staff was asked what weight the guidelines would carry. The response made two points: 1) the subcommittee would stand behind the guidelines and make clear that it is Congress's intent that the guidelines represent the appropriate policy behind "fair use," and 2) if educators are sued, and they end up losing, Congress will undoubtedly consider that the courts have not construed the law properly and change it. This information comes from a memorandum sent by the Public Broadcasting Service to all of its managers on January 15, 1982. It is cold comfort indeed to the educator who relies upon these guidelines and is a classic example of the frustration industry groups encounter in their attempts to devise informal standards.

2. Article I, section 8, clause 8 of the U.S. Constitution grants Congress the power to promote the progress of "science and the useful arts" by giving authors and inventors exclusive rights to their writings and discoveries for limited times.

3. Sony Corporation of America *et al.* v. Universal City Studios, Inc. *et al.,* 104 S. Ct. 774 (1984).

4. *Id.* at 796.

5. *Id.* at 819.

6. Until 1980, when the 1976 Copyright Law was amended, much debate centered around the question of whether computer software could be protected by copyright. In Apple Computer, Inc. v. Franklin Computer Corp., 714 F. 2d 1240 (3rd Cir. 1983), decided after the 1980 amendments, the issues included technical questions of whether certain forms of computer programs could be copyrighted.

7. In the Betamax case, *supra* n. 3, the question was whether the sale of Sony's video recorder was itself an infringement because the device did the allegedly illegal recording.

8. When the FCC's comparative hearing process became too protected and cumbersome for deciding among competing applicants for low power television and certain nonbroadcast services, Congress simply authorized the use of a lottery to decide the winner.

ALA in Dallas: Moments of Self-Doubt in Times of Great Purpose

Dallas Times Herald

MONDAY, JUNE 25, 1984

ALA holds national convention in Dallas

The American Library Association (ALA) is the oldest and largest library association in the world. And, this week an estimated 20,000 ALA members and guests gather at the Dallas Convention Center for the association's national convention.

The association's 40,000 members represent all types of libraries — state, public, school and academic; special libraries serving persons in government, commerce, armed services, hospitals, prisons and other institutions.

The association is the chief advocate for the people of the United States to achieve and maintain high-quality library and information services — whether by protecting the right to read, educating librarians, improving library services or making information accessible to everyone.

ALA has influenced the course of America's libraries since its inception in 1876, when such early library luminaries as Melvil Dewey and Justin Winsor issued a call to librarians to form a professional organization. Meeting in Phila-

...jobs. Each year, during National Library Week, the Washington Office sponsors Legislative Day to provide a forum for library representatives across the country to speak to federal legislators.

ALA maintains a vigorous program to defend libraries' rights to shelve and circulate materials presenting all points of view to all people regardless of race, religion, age, national origin or social and political views. A "Library Bill of Rights" was first adopted by ALA in 1939; the present ALA policy statement, dating from 1948, serves as a librarian's interpretation of the First Amendment of the Constitution. The Office for Intellectual Freedom coordinates ALA programs in the area of intellectual freedom and publishes a newsletter monitoring incidents related to first amendment rights.

The Public Information Office of ALA develops national programs of public service advertising and graphics to encourage the use and support of libraries.

BROOKE E. SHELDON has been the president of the ALA.

Sheldon handles presidential term with tremendous success

Brooke E. Sheldon is dean of the School of Library Science at Texas Woman's University in Denton and since June 1983 she has been the president of the estimated 40,000 member American Library Association (ALA).

Her election highlighted about 30 years of public and academic library service. An ALA member since 1967, she has served on its executive board, council and budget assembly. Among many responsibilities for ALA divisions, she has held elective offices in the Public Library Association and the Association for Specialized and Cooperative Library Agencies. She was a delegate to the 1970 White House Conference on Children, and a discussion leader at the 1979 White House Conference on Library and Information Services.

Before her appointment at Texas Woman's University in 1977, Dr. Sheldon taught in the Graduate School of Library and Information Science at the University of Pittsburgh and was director of the Management Institute for State Library Agency Heads, National Commission on Libraries and Information Science. Her profession has taken her throughout the United States, as head of Technical Services and Library Training at Alaska State Library, assistant director for learning at the Leadership Training Insti-

Florida State University, and head of library development for New Mexico State Library. She also has been coordinator of adult services, Santa Fe Public Library; branch librarian, Albuquerque Public Library; and base librarian with the U.S. Air Force in Colorado Springs and with the U.S. Army in Stuttgart, Germany. She began her career in the young adult division of the Detroit Public Library.

Dr. Sheldon holds a B.A. degree in English and economics from Acadia University in Nova Scotia, an M.L.S. from Simmons College in Boston and a Ph.D. in library science from the University of Pittsburgh.

Listed in "Who's Who in America" and "Who's Who of American Women," Dr. Sheldon also is the 1983 recipient of the Simmons College Alumni Achievement Award and is a member of Beta Phi Mu, the library honor organization.

She is the author of numerous publications and serves on the editorial board of "Public Library Quarterly." During recent years, she has been actively involved in training workshops on management, grantsmanship, networking and continuing education, and other topics. She does consulting nationwide for

The temperature in Dallas was in three digits and the distances between hotels, restaurants, meeting rooms, and exhibits great enough to encourage brisk walking habits, induce preoccupation with clocks, and restrict conversation to the manner of a pilot speaking to the control tower. The six-day conference of the American Library Association, its 103rd, passed as swiftly as an elevator falling from the top floor of the Hyatt Regency without benefit of cables.

Although the conference theme, "Paths to Power," was at once too amorphous and ambitious to sit well on the week's events, the yearly meeting was successful for the traditional reasons: there were over 11,000 registrants, the exhibits, embracing more technology than ever before, were historically diverse, there were more job vacancies listed than applicants available, and the opportunities for attending meetings were endless.

The highlight of the conference, however, and one that provided focus for the week, came unexpectedly at the end of the session. The fulcrum was established on Wednesday evening when E.J. Josey, at the inaugural banquet, delivered his presidential address ("Forging Coalitions for the Public Good"). "We need," declared Josey, "to foster the recognition among ALA members that the future of libraries is clearly linked to the welfare of the American people and to reaffirm the inseparable relationship between libraries and the traditional democratic liberties." It was a speech that not only gave meaning to this conference, but promised to cause reverberations in the year ahead. Josey's enumeration of convictions and call to action was the eloquent coda to a week of concern about the free flow of government information, illiteracy, the state of American education, participation in UNESCO, the search for a new executive director, nuclear war, and the validity of the MLS degree.

A budget on target

In presenting his management report at the opening meeting of the Executive Board on Saturday morning, Executive Director Robert Wedgeworth noted that "The most welcome news of the spring was the adoption of the dues increase by the ALA membership." Performance reports, said Wedgeworth, are on target with the budget in balancing revenues with expenditures. He reported that heavy expenditures in May made it necessary to borrow $250,000 to meet the June payroll

but pointed out that ALA still has $375,000 invested in short-term notes.

Wedgeworth related that the Business Council for Effective Literacy has approved a matching grant of $400,000 to the Coalition for Literacy. Benton & Bowles, the advertising agency selected to run the campaign, will concentrate its efforts on informing the public about functional illiteracy, will appeal for volunteers to participate in literacy programs, and will solicit the support of the corporate community at the local level. The campaign begins in October 1984.

In other news, Wedgeworth reported that the W.K. Kellogg Foundation, interested in supporting the development of sites for career assessment for librarians, will not consider the project for funding until the foundation's new fiscal year begins in September.

A quiet revolution

At the annual information update session held by the Legislation Committee, Carol Henderson of the ALA Washington Office reported that Senator Larry Pressler (R–S.D.) has asked Federal Communications Commission chairman Mark Fowler to consider a library private line service. Delivered May 8, Pressler's letter was signed by twenty-seven senators. The letter is reprinted in the June issue of the *Congressional Record.* An excerpt: "In the last fifteen years, a quiet revolution has taken place in libraries as more services and processes have become automated. Caught in the double bind of tighter budgets and increased dependence on telecommunications networks, libraries have adapted data processing and resource sharing through telecommunications to increase their efficiency and provide cost-effective library services to the widest possible population. Thousands of libraries, serving perhaps fifty percent of the nation's population, adapt private, voice-grade multipoint telecommunications circuits to

The Dallas convention center: more exhibits than ever

data transmission. This reduces the labor-intensive nature of library materials processing and enables any library user to gain access to the country's library resources."

Timothy Spray, representing the Office of Management and Budget, told the group that while the free flow of information is a fundamental right and information itself a "societal good," it is not a free good. He cited the necessity of user charges for information and asserted that "government databases should have a healthy fee structure."

Patricia Berger, U.S. National Bureau of Standards, predicted that "gaps in public knowledge may increase" and pointed to the problems of obtaining national security information and timely census data. Referring to "an incipient, international paranoia," Berger said we may return to a period where there is a lack of international scientific information.

OCLC demonstrates the M300 Workstation

Habits of defensiveness

The opening general session was convened on Saturday evening by ALA President Brooke Sheldon and began with the presentation of honorary memberships to Lester Asheim, School of Library Science, University of North Carolina at Chapel Hill, and to Congressman William Ford (D–Mich.). Ford, not present for the occasion, spoke to Sheldon in a pretaped video recording, stressing the need for federal funding for libraries and inviting greater lobbying efforts on the part of librarians.

Frances Fitzgerald, Pulitzer Prize-winning journalist, spoke on the difficulties of politics interfering with education. Fitzgerald, who claimed that textbook interpretations of history change to accomodate the marketplace, stated that "textbooks contain the truths that will sell" and observed that contemporary textbooks "are almost a hum of white noise." She told the audience that "improving education will require a fight" and stated that "now is the time to let go of your habits of defensiveness." "We are," said Fitzgerald, "entering into a new mandarin cycle where we criticize the educators."

Merwine on their mind

The case of Merwine *v.* Mississippi State University, in which the plaintiff sought to prove that "you can be a professional librarian without an ALA-accredited degree," came up as early as Sunday afternoon's joint information meeting of ALA Council and Executive Board. Executive Director Robert Wedgeworth, anticipating criticism of ALA's decision not to file an *amicus curiae* brief in the case, stated that "ALA does not generally become involved at the trial level," citing the expense of such participation, and asserted that "the validity of the ALA MLS is not at issue in the Merwine case." The association is, said Wedgeworth, "committed to a fair and equitable market for services."

Council I got underway with Ella Yates presenting the report from the Freedom to Read Foundation. The report stated that "dominance of the marketplace of ideas is the path to power" and warned that "there is no final victory in the war against censorship."

Dan Lacy, chair of the ALA Commission on Freedom and Equality of Access to Information, reported at length on the work of the group and, in the only substantial business of the afternoon, Council approved a bylaws change recommended by ACRL that would allow each division to specify its representation on the COPES Planning and Budget Assembly. Prior to this action, vice-presidents of divisions provided representation to the Planning and Budget Assembly.

On Monday morning Robert Rohlf, chair of the Committee on Organization, appeared before the Executive Board to ask for a one-year extension for the Independent Librarians Membership Initiative Group. The group, with over one hundred members, has been unsuccessful in finding an ALA unit with which to affiliate. The board agreed to extend the life of the group for an additional year.

In other action the board discussed the merits of creating a new ALA award, the Distinguished Service Recognition Award, to be conferred on individuals who "...in some measurable way, above and beyond the scope of their normal activities, evidenced their support and involvement in librarianship." Persons selected for the award need not be librarians. The board voted to refer the new category of recognition to the ALA Awards Committee.

The system that libraries built

On Monday noon, OCLC departed from tradition by holding its annual report to the library community over a light lunch. In introducing OCLC president Rowland Brown, Russell Shank, chair of the OCLC Board of Trustees, referred to the organization as "the system that libraries built." In his statistic-laden report, Brown noted that there are 10.8 million records in the OCLC system, 5700 dedicated terminals, 1200 dial access terminals, and the utility has recently added three IBM Sigma mainframes. He also announced that OCLC has installed UPS, an Uninterrupted Power System.

Brown stated tht "ultimately the M300 workstation will be the terminal of choice" and asked the audience to "consider replacement" of present terminals with the M300.

In a reversal of policy, Brown said that OCLC intends to cooperate with the Library of Congress, the Washington Library Network, and the Research Libraries Group in developing Linked Systems Programs. Brown pointed out that OCLC will develop internal software program linkage and interfaces with other national networks.

Regarding the network's difficulties with the state of Ohio and exemption from the real estate tax, Brown stated that the exemption clause is very narrowly drafted. In order to qualify, an organization must either be a charitable institution that gives away resources or an organization where teaching takes place on site. OCLC is neither. Observing that the matter has become "a cause célèbre" in Columbus, Brown stated that "our financial strength is held against us." Although OCLC lost its tax case and must now pay real estate taxes to the local school board, Brown reported that the ruling has not changed OCLC's status in Ohio as a nonprofit organization.

Brown said that in the next year there will be "no significant changes in pricing structure," but admitted that there will be "small increases in billable transactions."

Supporter and foe of government secrecy debate

Government secrecy was the subject of a program sponsored by the Intellectual Freedom Committee and the American Association of Publishers on Monday, June 25. Two speakers representing opposing viewpoints discussed how current government policies affect the free dissemination of information.

Richard Schmidt, counsel to the

American Society of Newspaper Editors, reviewed recent incursions on the availability of government information. The Office of Management and Budget has argued that fulfilling the terms of the Freedom of Information Act is costly and an unjustifiable expense. Schmidt said, "The amount of money spent to support FOIA is still less than the Pentagon spends on marching bands." Recent attempts to enforce prepublication review of articles and books written by former government employees drew this criticism from Schmidt: "If an administration can censor the comments of its predecessor, there is potential for mischief—this is really Big Brother sitting up there." Citing additional restrictions on the freedom of the press, Schmidt described the blackout on press coverage of the Grenada invasion as "completely inappropriate in a free society."

Cecile Shure, a consultant and former Department of Defense employee holding "top secret classification clearance at the Pentagon," defended the government's policy of classification and prepublication review of information documents. Shure stated, "The Soviets want our technology for other than peaceful purposes" and cited examples of high-tech theft and industrial spying that led to Soviet development of American-owned technology for military purposes. There has been, said Shure, a "hemorrhage of technology" lost to the USSR, "especially through the academic world."

Shure described how prepublication review and classification is applied, citing the Pentagon's reliance on a "dual use" doctrine designed to identify nonmilitary materials, information, and data that might have military applications. She suggested that even the Apple IIe computer has come under review and reminded the audience that some of the exhibits on display at the Dallas Convention Center might be of great interest to Soviet scientists. "The controls [on the dissemination of information] are not meant to stop the Americans from moving on," said Shure, but rather to protect against misappropriation.

"This administration tends to go after a fly with a howitzer," Schmidt stated in response to Shure's presentation. He warned that we may destroy our basic freedoms in the name of national defense. Shure agreed that "we can't control everything," but she said the administration believes "we're not going to get the cooperation we're asking for" to control leaks of information without mandatory classification and nondisclosure policies. Each speaker encouraged ongoing communication and dialogue to narrow the widening gap between freedom of information and the need for government secrecy.

Reasonable people might disagree

In their morning meeting on June 26 the Executive Board reported the results of actions taken the preceding day in closed session. Jane Anne Hannigan was elected to fill the vacancy in the board created by the election of Beverly Lynch to the office of president-elect; Lillian Bradshaw was elected to a four-year term as an ALA Endowment Trustee; and five names were submitted to the Public Printer for appointment to the Depository Library Council.

A report from the Intellectual Freedom Committee on the circulation of motion pictures and video productions quickly divided the board. The policy statement read, in part, "Just as 'labelling' of books is deemed 'an attempt to prejudice attitudes,' so is the affixing of the Motion Picture Association of America rating codes to motion pictures and video productions." Arthur Curley stated "I have to challenge this as a policy statement by ALA" and remarked that "it is a matter on which ALA should remain silent." At discussion's end the group voted to refer the IFC report to Council without board endorsement. "It is a statement," concluded Curley, "about which reasonable people might disagree."

Judith Farley, chair of the Personnel Committee, noted that COPES plans to recommend an allotment of $164,000 for staff salary adjustments for 1984–85, a six percent increase in salaries already included in the 1984–85 budget. The report noted that a stringent effort must be made to ensure that performance evaluations are not inflated and take account of the "inevitable negative impact on staff morale that such a rigorous readjustment of evaluations has caused." Said Herbert Biblo: "To use staff morale as an argument for fiscal decisions is unwise."

Amendments to amendments

At Council II Joseph Schubert, chair of the ALA Task Force on Excellence in Education, presented the group's statement in response to the publication of *A Nation at Risk*. The report, *Realities: Educational Reform in a Learning Society*, asserts that learning begins before schooling, good schools require good school libraries, people in a learning society need libraries throughout their lives, and public support of libraries is an investment in people and communities. Proposed action: that state aid for public libraries be increased; that state support for re-

WLB conference analysis

Organization: American Library Association, 103rd Annual Conference
Date: June 22–28, 1984
Place: Dallas, Texas
Membership: 38,377 (June 30, 1984)
Attendance: 11,084 (7,952 librarians, 3,132 exhibitors)
Conference quotes: "There has been a gross perversion of the Paperwork Reduction Act."—Caroline Arden; "Now is the time to let go of your habits of defensiveness."—Frances Fitzgerald; "The baby boom generation is not a reading generation."—Ann Branscomb; "Sometimes I get irked when I hear how dirty the OCLC database is."—Rowland Brown; "No government, including ours, loves a free press."—Richard Schmidt; "If things continue as they are there will be 900 million illiterates by the end of the century."—Amadou-Mahtar M'Bow; "UNESCO should be reformed and now is the time."—Leonard Sussman; "We need a universal library card."—Brooke Sheldon.

Significant Council/Membership actions: Referred a motion to enter the Merwine case to Executive Board; Passed a policy statement on circulation of motion picture and video productions; Agreed to appoint a task force to study issues involved in copyrighting bibliographic records; Voted to encourage U.S. membership in UNESCO; Voted to encourage states to pass comparable worth laws; Reaffirmed support for legislative action to guarantee affordable access to telecommunications; Approved joining Citizens Against Nuclear War as a member organization.

source sharing be increased with additional aid provided to school and academic libraries; that federal funds and new initiatives for elementary and secondary school libraries be increased; that federal responsibility for library statistical data be assumed by the National Center for Educational Statistics; and that local, state, and federal agencies developing human services and educational programs include librarians and libraries in their program development.

A resolution from the American Association of School Librarians recommending that ALA designate the month of April as School Library Media Month beginning in 1985 received little support from Council. Dorothy Broderick objected to stressing type of libraries instead of libraries in general and termed the idea "divisive." Brooke Sheldon, presiding over the session, stated "we are more like each other than we are different" and the councilors finally voted to refer the matter to the National Library Week Committee for their recommendation.

A resolution calling for ALA to support the National Decade of Disabled Persons was quickly approved and the body went on to consider the most controversial issue of the session—whether or not ALA should enter the case of Merwine *v.* Mississippi State University as a friend of the court on behalf of Mississippi State University. Wedgeworth noted that Sidley & Austin, ALA legal counsel, estimated the cost of entering the case at between $1,000 and $4,000, a sum that did not strike Council as daunting. Edward Holley, dean of the School of Library Science at the University of North Carolina, Chapel Hill, asserted that "I am not happy in the way the association has addressed this problem" and stated, "We have tried to make the exception the rule." When asked for a legal opinion, Mary Hutchings Reed, representing Sidley & Austin, said "an appeals court is unlikely to make any ruling on the ALA accredited degree."

Council continued to debate, dividing the question, proposing amendments, and taking straw votes to test majority sentiment. One amendment suggested that the association enter the case "... in defense of the ALA accredited MLS should it be determined that that is an issue in this case." Not even language weakened to this extent could win Council approval and at the end of the afternoon's deliberations the assembly voted to refer the resolution to Executive Board recommending that it act in accordance with Council's wishes, inchoate as they were.

Merwine continued

At the membership meeting the following morning, John Berry, editor of *Library Journal,* appeared before a microphone to suggest that the membership set aside the action of Council in referring the resolution on the Merwine suit to the Executive Board, suggesting that Council be given another opportunity for renewed debate on a resolution stripped of confusing amendments. The proposal, which received lengthy debate, was finally defeated.

The members went on to approve a resolution moved by ALA member Vincent Jennings that ALA join the Citizens Against Nuclear War as a member organization. Said Jennings in defense of his motion: "Preventing nuclear war is the ultimate public good." The group also approved a resolution stating that any personal ALA member may attend Council and membership meetings wherever held, even though they may not be registered for a particular midwinter meeting or annual conference. Joan Goddard, sponsor of the resolution, asserted that members registering at conferences do so primarily to attend the programming. William Chait suggested that the resolution be reviewed by COPES, stating that such an innovation would have fiscal implications. Eric

Moon objected, stating that "fiscal implications of an undemocratic association are very great indeed." The resolution passed.

In presenting the treasurer's report, Herbert Biblo reminded the members that ALA's tax-exempt status is being challenged by the state of Illinois and observed that if the case is lost, $350,000 will be due and payable to the state.

Saving the bird books

At the final meeting of Council on June 27, Dennis Day, chair of the Intellectual Freedom Committee, submitted a policy statement on the circulation of motion pictures and video productions for endorsement. The motion was passed only after an amendment was approved deleting the following sentence from the policy statement: "When the manufacturer has affixed the MPAA rating codes to the materials, the MPAA rating codes should not be deleted, excised, altered, or obliterated in any way."

Legislation Committee chair Gary Strong won successive approval of three items, including resolutions that called for support of the concepts embodied in H.R. 5686 extending United States membership in UNESCO; reaffirmed ALA support for legislative action "to guarantee permanent, universal, and affordable access to telecommunications services;" and commended Senator Larry Pressler (R–S.D.) for "his leadership in assuring affordable telecommunications for libraries."

Duane Johnson presented Council Document 46, a resolution asking that the National Audubon Society reconsider their intention to auction off significant holdings in their New York City library. Although some councilors felt this constituted interference with an institution's prerogatives, Arthur Curley emphasized that "we are not censuring the National Audubon Society" and said "I see a positive spirit in the proposal." Council agreed and passed the resolution.

E.J. Josey delivers inaugural, Brooke Sheldon in agreement

In other business of the day, Council approved a motion that state library associations encourage the passage of comparable worth laws in their states; defeated a proposal that ALA urge "the cessation of all military aid and covert intervention in Central America;" approved participation in the Chicago World's Fair of 1992; voted to reaffirm its policy on Abridgment of the Rights of Freedom of Expression of Foreign Nationals; and approved two new awards—the Ralph Shaw Award for Library Literature, sponsored by Knowledge Industry

Councilors-at-large, 1984–1988

Bill Asp; Patricia Berger; Dorothy Blake; J. Dennis Day; Linda Anne Dougherty; Elizabeth Greggs; Dean Halliwell; Charlotta Hensley; Joan Higbee; Monteria Hightower; Phillip Leinbach; Barbara Markuson; Nancy Marshall; Josephine McSweeney; Effie Lee Morris; Roscoe Rouse, Jr.; Gail Schlachter; Elaine Sloan; David Smith; Lotsee Smith; Robert Stueart; Betty Turock; John Tyson; J. Linda Williams; Diana Young

Divisions

The posts are variously designated as vice-pres./pres.-elect or vice-chair/ chair-elect.

AASL—Shirley Aaron
ACRL—Sharon Anne Hogan
ALSC—Linda Silver
ALTA—Herbert Davis
ASCLA—Gail McGovern
LAMA—Ronald Leach
LITA—Lois Kershner
PLA—Patrick O'Brien
RASD—Rebecca Kellogg
RTSD—Marcia Tuttle
YASD—Joan Atkinson

Round tables

Ethnic Material Information Exchange— Susan Freiband

Federal Librarians— Elwynda Chapman

Government Documents— Diane Smith

Intellectual Freedom— John Swan

Junior Members— Anders Dahlgren

Library History— Arthur Young

Library Instruction— Marilyn Berry Segal

Library Research— Maurice Marchant

Map and Geography— Linda Carlson Sharp

Social Responsibilities— Action Council: Kay Cassell; Doris Kirschbaum; Betty-Carol Sellen; Susan Vaughn

Staff Organizations— Steering Committee: Kathleen Prendergast; Barbara Waserman; Janet Woody

Publications and the Carrell Preston Baber Award of $10,000 to encourage innovative research projects to improve library services.

Prior to adjournment Council III voted to approve a resolution asking that ALA appoint a task force "to review the issues involved in the ownership of bibliographic records through copyright, the increasing costs to libraries, the effect of the extended negotiations between OCLC and the networks, and any other barriers to obtaining, using, and sharing machine-readable bibliographic records." The task force is to report its findings at the 1985 Midwinter meeting in Washington, D.C.

For once, more jobs available than job applicants

Prize-winning outreach programs

In order to recognize public libraries that are conducting outreach programs in their communities, the American Library Trustee Association (ALTA) awarded commendations to six exemplary programs from among three hundred reviewed. Representatives of the winning libraries were on hand to receive their citations and explain the programs they conduct.

• Mary Cook Public Library (Warren City, Ohio)—Outreach service to the handicapped elderly by this small library is provided by one librarian who visits nursing homes and boarding houses. He conducts read-aloud book discussion groups and organizes trips and activities for about fifty residents.

• Free Library of Philadelphia—A literacy program for adults supplies tutoring and materials for the library's Reader Development Programs. Library Director Keith Doms estimated the annual cost at $400,000, saying, "We could spend ten times that much and it would be well spent."

• Providence Public Library (Rhode Island)—Child Learning Centers have been developed under Project LIVE (Learning Is Very Enjoyable) to offer workshops, computers, and literacy-building skills to preschool children. Director Annalee Bundy described the project, which costs the library between $75,000 and $115,000 annually, as "a miniature Head Start Program."

• Fresno County Public Library (California)—The Hmong Literacy Program serves the needs of a newly arrived Southeast Asian population in the community. Although the Hmong have no written language, they are offered the opportunity, at library learning centers, to study their own culture and to learn basic survival skills for American living.

• Santa Fe Regional Library (Gainesville, Florida)—Service to homebound patrons is offered by a library-staffed bookmobile that visits between fifty and sixty homebound patrons each week. The face-to-face service offers personalized attention that is welcomed by patrons and their families.

• Santa Fe Regional Library—A branch library established in a local jail schoolroom is staffed by trustee prisoners and the prison teacher. Materials include paperbacks, audiotapes, and law books, and requests from prisoners are filled on a weekly basis.

MLS as minimum qualification draws attention at OLPR program

At a program of the Office for Library Personnel Resources three speakers representing a variety of institutions and opinions examined the role of the MLS degree in professional employment.

Pauline Wilson of the University of Tennessee GSLIS set forth the terms of the discussion by separating the "non-issues" from the real issues. Non-issues, according to Wilson, include the debate over whether librarianship is a profession ("Back in the nineteenth century librarians made a decision to organize as a profession, not a trade, union, or group") and the question of whether ALA should be involved in defending the MLS as a basic requirement for professional employment ("Like unions, one of the purposes of the professional association . . . is to rig the market by setting standards of service, by improving members' knowledge, by lobbving government, and by setting entr) standards").

The real issue, Wilson argued, is how ALA should defend the MLS and whether a legal defense would be appropriate. According to Wilson, "there is definitive evidence that [formal validation of the MLS] may be a will-o-the-wisp." Therefore, before entering specific cases, ALA must determine what general principles it wishes to defend and define its constituency.

Philip Leinbach, librarian at Tulane University, described the practical concerns he faces when hiring library professionals. Arguing that there is not enough proof that the

MLS is a valid selection tool and that legal regulations and other considerations often constrain the selection process, Leinbach said, "My advice is to let the search committee deal with each case as it comes up." But he agreed that "we have some self-interest in protecting the degree we have obtained" and indicated that he prefers to hire in favor of candidates holding the MLS.

Joan Goddard of San Jose (California) Public Library indicated that her library's policy states that "all people are given the opportunity to compete" for library jobs. The selection process depends on a written test, an oral examination and interview, and employment probation. The MLS is not a basic requirement because, as Goddard said, "The person who functions well and has the credentials to be credible in a university library may not function well or be credible to a welfare recipient." According to Goddard, "Each library has a responsibility to analyze its own position."

A lively question-and-answer period followed, highlighted by the remarks of Edward Holley, who has recently testified on behalf of the MLS requirement in a local court case. "My problem," said Holley, "is to make the exception the rule, and the OLPR has been leaning in this direction." Characterizing ALA's reluctance to enter court battles as "short-range thinking," he warned that an "attack on the library profession is an attack on a weak profession." Audience response to these and other criticisms of the uncertain value of the MLS indicated the presence of an issue that continues to concern many in the profession.

Falling in place

The 1984–85 Executive Board met for the first time on Thursday morning, with E.J. Josey presiding. Others in attendance were President-elect Beverly Lynch, past-President Brooke Sheldon, Treasurer Patricia Schuman, Executive Director Robert Wedgeworth, and board members Margaret Chisholm, Arthur Curley, Judith Farley, Elizabeth Futas, Jane Anne Hannigan, Regina Minudri, David Snider, and William Summers.

Janis Keene, chair of COPES, presented the committee's report to the board. Highlights: the year-end general fund operating balance is projected at $108,924 compared with a projected balance of $18,225; revenues are expected to increase by $527,000 over last year but fall short of the budgeted goal by $168,492; expenditures are up over last year by $1,059,000 and are $263,000 less than budget; projected net revenues for the 1983–84 year from revenue-producing units total $661,000, a decline of $121,000 from 1982–83. The recommended general fund budgetary ceiling for 1984–85 was set at $9,548,581. The report states that "while this budget does not provide for new programs, COPES believes that it begins to put the organization on a sounder financial basis and permits restoration of earlier cutbacks in critical areas."

Thomas Galvin appeared before the board to report on the activities of the IFLA Organizing Committee. He noted that Palmer House will be the conference hotel for the 1985 Chicago meeting and reported that more than $100,000 has been raised so far. A second level of fund raising has now begun, observed Galvin, and an appeal is being made to library schools. Although the total cost of the 1985 IFLA conference is estimated at $750,000, Galvin stated that "everything is falling in place."

In other action the board agreed to retain Glenn Tecker to assist in the development of a long-range plan for ALA. Tecker was hired to begin the first phase of a long-range planning process to take place between September 1984 and January 1985. The board also confirmed that the 1988 annual conference will be held from July 9–14 in New Orleans, making use of the city's new convention center.

The board ended their deliberations by commenting on some difficulties associated with the charge given to the Commission on Freedom and Equality of Access to Information chaired by Dan Lacy. Curley remarked that "The commission seems under the impression that it will publish the report to ALA" and stated that, since the board controls the ALA imprint, the nature of authority needs to be studied. The board concurred, stating that whatever the nature of the publication may be, it will not be a report to ALA, but a report by the association. ▣

Future of libraries and the public good

"We need to foster the recognition among ALA members that the future of libraries is clearly linked to the welfare of the American people and to reaffirm the inseparable relationship between libraries and the traditional democratic liberties. Our internal organization problems may be more effectively resolved as we turn to the larger society and join with others in assisting the citizenry to use information services towards the solution of the immediate social problems. There is, in fact, an obvious interconnection of public issues with library issues: the effort to force release of government-controlled information is one part of the fight for intellectual freedom; the reduced availability and increasing cost of government sources of information limit the librarian's ability to provide information. Librarians are in a special position to know of restrictions on government information and to alert the public to act to force a change in policy when needed. The 'right to know' and the 'right to read' cannot be separated in the long run."

—From E.J. Josey's inaugural address, Forging Coalitions for the Public Good.

Only Meckler Publishing offers complete coverage of

SMALL COMPUTERS IN LIBRARIES (SCIL) is a monthly newsletter that offers every librarian the guidance for evaluating microcomputers and associated peripherals. SCIL also keeps librarians informed about reference services for computers, user groups, and materials for more effective microcomputer operations.

Pricing: Available monthly @ $24.00
Editor: Allan Pratt

The M300 and PC REPORT is a monthly newsletter providing information on developments, trends, forecasting, and use of the M300 and IBM PC as a technical processing, library management, and collection access tool. Also, every issue contains practical reports on installations, integration, and effective use. Finally, reports are provided on new programs from library supply agencies written for use on the IBM PC as well as pre-written software available for library applications.

Pricing: Available monthly @ $29.00
Editor: Nancy J. Melin

LIBRARY SOFTWARE REVIEW is the only magazine exclusively designed to provide the library user with information required to make intelligent software evaluation, procurement, integration, and installation decisions. Its coverage is inclusive of both pre-written software as well as software in development for micros, minis, and library oriented mainframe computers. In addition to articles and reviews of software, each issue offers reviews on software books, periodicals, and other materials pertaining to computer software with relevance to libraries.

Pricing: Available bi-monthly @ $69.50
Editor: Nancy J. Melin

Dale Nelson:

Dateline – Washington

Preview of disk technology

In July 1936, families in 150 homes in the New York City area gathered in front of flickering, black-and-white television screens to watch an experimental broadcast of a Felix the Cat cartoon.

By the year 2032, it is very likely that a press demonstration pre sented this summer at the Library of Congress will seem just as quaint and primitive as that first regular American telecast by RCA. Library staff demonstrated the first of six analog videodisks produced during the first phase of an optical disk pilot program begun in late 1982.

"I want to introduce to you a new device that will revolutionize picture research," Elisabeth Betz, picture cataloging specialist in the Prints and Photographs division of the library, told reporters.

Standing beside an eleven-inch video monitor, Betz took viewers on a dizzying, push-button trip through a collection of 539 glass lantern slides gathered by the World Transportation Commission in the 1890s.

Also available on the first disk are five other pictorial collections including more than 23,000 photonegatives, transparencies and photoprints made by the Detroit Publishing Company in the United States, Mexico, Canada, and the Caribbean between 1890 and 1914.

"I just went through the first 12,000 and picked out all of these," Solan Weeks, director of the Detroit Historical Museum, said.

"I had been interested in the collection for years," Weeks said, "but the idea of getting into it was mind-boggling."

Dale Nelson *is a journalist who covers the Washington scene for WLB.*

Using the disk, he said, he was able to go through the collection in about two hours and select the prints that he wanted to see in the original.

Library officials also gave reporters a preview of the second phase of the pilot project—digital optical disks for computerized mass storage, preservation, and retrieval of printed materials.

The disks, except for being silver in color, look very much like long-playing phonograph records. To play them, Integrated Automation of Berkeley, California designed a device that works like, and is called, a jukebox, although it looks more like a big black box than a Wurlitzer.

The jukebox can accommodate one hundred one-sided disks with one million pages of printed material on them. Library officials estimate it will take between fifteen seconds and one minute for users to punch their requests into the jukebox. Each request transfers the material to a magnetic system that holds thousands of pages.

The user sits at a station with a keyboard, a page-shaped video screen and a printer. The system is specially wired so that nothing can be transmitted out of the building.

The first items stored on the digital disks are journal articles and rare documents with pages too brittle to be handled by researchers.

William J. Welsh, deputy Librarian of Congress, says most items are in the public domain, and permission was requested to reproduce copyrighted material.

The library has no plans for outside distribution of disks as part of the pilot project, but an advisory committee is studying the prospect.

"We anticipate there will be a market, and we assume we are going to be talking about some kind of a licensing arrangement with the producers of the materials," Welsh said.

Library officials said they are convinced the optical disk is here to stay, but are equally sure that the equipment they are using will be outmoded before long.

"The salvage value of it will probably be zero, because this is the early stuff," said Joseph W. Price, chief of the science and technology division.

Presidential curbs on hold

Senator Lawton Chiles (D—Fla.), who has been working five years on a bill to curb presidential libraries and other costs of former presidents, received approval from the Senate Governmental Affairs Committee and was hoping for routine approval by the entire body—until he ran into opposition from the White House.

Chiles told the Senate he received a call from Senator Mark Hatfield (R–Ore.), chairman of the Senate Appropriations Committee, saying he had been asked by the White House to put a "hold" on the bill.

Sometimes a hold is put on a bill so that a problem can be straightened out. But Chiles said he feared the White House objection was a "choke hold" that would block consideration during this abbreviated election-year session.

Assistant White House Press Secretary Anson Franklin said one reason for the administration objection is that the bill "changes the rules in the middle of the game"—presumably meaning that President Reagan wouldn't get the same benefits as his predecessors.

Former President Jimmy Carter

Press briefing at Library of Congress to preview disk technology

also opposed the legislation, according to Senator William Roth (R–Del.), chairman of the Governmental Affairs Committee. Senate sources say former President Gerald Ford also asked Senate leaders to put it on the shelf.

Chiles said he would write to the White House and take other steps in an effort to get the bill moving again.

Platforms short on specifics

The Graphic Artists Guild asked the Democratic Platform Committee to go on record against payment of artists on a "work-for-hire" basis. They also asked the committee to favor a change in current tax law that would give artists and writers the same deduction available to others who contribute works of art. A further platform request was for congressional hearings on the impact of technological change on artists and authors.

Despite these and other appeals by scores of groups, most of whom planned to make the same requests of the Republicans, the platform drafters came up with a draft long on general principles and short on such specifics as "work for hire."

Japanese software copyright threatened

A proposal by Japan's Ministry of International Trade and Industry that would strip computer software of copyright protection is causing concern in the American software industry, in the Reagan administration, and in Congress. Since 1964, the United States has treated software as a form of authorship, eligible for full copyright protection. France, the Netherlands, the Federal Republic of Germany, the United Kingdom, South Africa, and Australia have followed the same policy.

Japan's courts also afford software copyright protection. The trade ministry's proposal to undercut this policy did not go to the Japanese parliament at its spring session, but United States trade negotiators believe it still may be submitted.

Presidential trade representative Bill Brock and the Commerce Department went on record against the move and Senator Frank Lautenberg (D–N.J.), former chairman of Automatic Data Processing, unleashed a strong attack at a meeting of the World Computing Service Industry Congress in Tokyo.

Lautenberg, a member of the Senate Commerce Committee, said adoption of the Japanese proposal might encourage similar measures in other nations but would also invite retaliation by steps authorized under the Universal Copyright Convention.

"Nations harmed by such proposals would likely take reciprocal steps to reduce intellectual property right protections," he said. "A nation like Japan, which exports an increasing volume of software, should be wary of such a development. For the markets that it plans to enter would be less than hospitable."

JFK fund-raisers planned

The board of directors of the John F. Kennedy Library Foundation plans a series of dinners around the country and perhaps direct mailings to raise funds toward an $8 million endowment.

John F. Cullinane, foundation chairman, said this summer that $2.4 million had already been raised but much more was needed to update the library's exhibits. He said a five-year fund-raising drive is planned.

"The library has had its light under a bushel," Cullinane said. ◘

Ann McGrath

Eye on Publishing

An electronic OED

Literature lovers may legitimately despair at the awful futuristic idea of taking James Joyce to bed on a computer screen, but few scholars can dispute any longer the vast potential of the database when it comes to reference works. With the information explosion booming on every side, publishers of reference material in all disciplines have to be able to update—and more critically, integrate—their data rapidly and cost-effectively enough to sell a product. Because the database offers a publisher such flexibility, and because it allows a researcher to slice directly through the fat to the meat of his inquiry, the success of future reference works may well be measured more and more frequently in terminal time than in units sold.

The Oxford University Press project to put the *Oxford English Dictionary* online is one current example of how computerization can work even for reference works in the humanities. Ever since the dictionary's self-educated editor, James Murray, put out its first volume one hundred years ago (a 352-page volume entitled *A New English Dictionary on Historical Principles* that covered the language from "A" to "Ant"), its reputation as the authoritative historical dictionary of twelfth-century to modern-day English has remained unsullied. But in its present form—thirteen hardbound volumes of 16,570 pages plus three supplements with a fourth due in 1985—and at its current $1,235 price, the *OED* could only become less and less widely useful.

The New Oxford English Dictionary, as the database version is named, will be prepared over the course of several years at an estimated cost of $10 million. IBM United Kingdom Ltd. is helping—with over $1 million of equipment and expertise. The system on loan from IBM includes a 4341 processor with disk and tape storage units, printers, and terminals. Two of the company's data specialists will collaborate with project lexicographers for two years, aiding with the editing of dictionary entries.

The first phase of the project involves the keyboarding (by hand, since character recognition devices can't handle the range of fonts and symbols used in the dictionary) of the six million words that define and illustrate the work's 500,000 entries. Once that's done sometime this fall, the wealth of historical and linguistic information the dictionary provides can be manipulated in ways impossible before.

For one thing, a fully integrated print edition of the *OED* will be available for the first time—and as the language expands and changes, new words and subtleties of meaning can be easily added. A poet with an interest in all the nuances of a word's meaning through time, for example, will be able to find such a history in one place, and will be able to keep current as new meanings enter the language. For another, since the limitations of space are no longer a consideration, archival material too unwieldy to use before—colorful illustrations of English usage over the past eight hundred years—can be added.

One of the most significant features of the electronic version, according to Jeffrey Seroy of Oxford University Press, will be the subdictionaries it will contain. The extraordinarily complex coding of entries will classify words by category—medicine, for example, or law, sports, or music—so that a specialist can dip into the dictionary precisely where he wants to. If you need to gather all Australian-English words, Seroy says, you should be able to call up a minidictionary containing nothing else.

Exploration of the seemingly endless possibilities for manipulation of the database is still in its early stages; more about the dictionary's potential will be known after the University of Waterloo, Ontario completes its survey of likely users for the new dictionary.

Dickens in all directions

There's good news too from the Modern Language Association, whose MLA *International Bibliography* has been a valuable reference for literary scholars since the first brief version came out in 1921. The bibliography is published annually—giving researchers access to the most recently published books and articles in every significant modern language on literature, folklore, and linguistics—but it has only been available in cumulative form since 1978, when the association drew a deep breath and plunged ahead with computerization. According to Dee Ella Spears, who is assisting with the project, the 1982 edition is now complete and available both in a hardbound version and electronically through Lockheed/ DIALOG. The 1983 edition's 40,000 entries should be added to the database by year's end.

The association's plan to computerize backwards as rapidly as possible is unfolding as scheduled, too—and usage by scholars is increasing dramatically as entries become integrated. When volumes 1970–1975 were added to the database two

(continued on page 79)

Ann McGrath, *a freelance writer based in New York, covers the publishing world for WLB.*

Will Manley:

Facing the Public

Along with the snail darter, the blue whale, the mountain gorilla, and the Ethiopian frankincense tree, you are probably safe in assigning the American children's librarian to the endangered species list.

I figured that along with Rosalyn Carter and the guy who taps the keg at the Baker and Taylor party, I'd be among the most popular people at the ALA conference in Dallas last June. After all, I was there to fill an entry-level children's position. It started at $21,000 a year, which is not much by Reverend Ike's standards, but is certainly enough to make a down payment on a recent model hot tub complete with the latest in floating cocktail tray accessories.

I had always assumed that underemployed children's librarians festooned the land like so many dandelions on a young spring day. It never occurred to me that the world is not overflowing with them. Dedicated, smiling, eternally young, freckled, wearing brightly colored clothes with crayons sticking out of the pockets, and their fingers puppeted, the children's librarians, we assume, are as common in our libraries as clowns in a circus or angels in heaven.

As I saw it, my job would be to somehow find enough time during my three-day conference stay to read all the resumes, screen all the application forms, answer all the interest cards, schedule all the interviews and rate the candidates that undoubtedly would surround me as soon as my 747 touched down upon the hot, humid Texas earth. Not only had I advertised this position widely, I had also boldly put in my advertisement, in capital letters, the alluring bilingual declaration "Children's services are this library's number one (numero uno) priority." No doubt about it. It was time to bite the bullet. Lectures, luncheons, seminars, exhibits, 10 K races, reunions, and poster sessions to say nothing of author brunches, hospitality suites, receptions, cocktail parties, wine and cheese get-togethers around the hot tub, and 5 AM jogs through downtown Dallas were all simply out of the question with the kind of rat race I'd be enduring in my search for the perfect librarian for our children's department.

Why then did I find myself, within seven hours of my Texas arrival, arguing far into the night with an eclectic group of book salesmen, computer vendors, and horror of horrors, academic librarians, over who was the catcher for the Boston Red Sox in the 1967 World Series? To exacerbate things, why did I give this matter such inordinate consideration and reflection that I finally took the time one steamy afternoon to amble over the the Dallas Public Library to consult the *Baseball Encyclopedia* when I should have been concentrating on Newberys, Caldecotts, fingerplays, reading readiness exercises, and, most importantly, children's librarians?

The answer is simple. Children's librarians simply don't exist anymore. After hanging around the Placement Center for just one day, I knew I was in trouble when the only applications I got were from folks whose total experience in working with children had been selling popcorn at Saturday movie matinees or flame-broiling hamburgers at Burger King. To be fair, there were others. There was, for example, the applicant who thought that the Newbery Award had something to do with a certain jazz festival held every year in Rhode Island. But even she was outdone in chutzpah by an unemployed Ph.D. who, with only the need for five words, gave an astounding answer to my question, "A parent is looking for a good book for her seventh-grade son. He is a good reader, but doesn't read very much. What titles or authors would you recommend?" His five words were "*Moby Dick* and *Bleak House*." Score one for elitism. I can see them choking on their Harlequins in Baltimore County.

This bizarre Burger King to *Bleak House* syndrome held form all week to the point where I was sorely tempted to hit the hot tub and cocktail party circuit with a bullhorn in order to urge any and all halfway normal, fully certified librarians to apply for my position. Finally, sans bullhorn, I began to actively recruit librarians who on the surface did not appear to dislike children too actively. However, their response to my "you haven't lived until you've been barfed upon in a two-year-old storyhour" sales pitch was definitely along the lines of "watch this guy, he's the type that might turn the hot tub water up to 350° "

Why don't librarians want to work in children's services anymore? The answer most often given is that it is a road to nowhere. In our world of young, upwardly mobile professional librarians who aspire to fancy titles like administrative systems supervisor (note the acronym), professional services coordinator, and assistant community services director, the simple, direct, and unambiguous title of children's librarian smacks too much of Big Bird, fingerpaints, and Theodor Geisel to be taken serious-

Will Manley *is director of the Tempe (Arizona) Public Library.*

ly in the larger context of career development. "I mean, would you like to start your career", a new M.L.S. was telling me over a bowl of rancid avocado dip recently turned green at a vendor's reception high atop the Hyatt Regency, "as an assistant bibliographic automation analyst or as a children's librarian? Come on, this is 1984," she noted ominously. "But what I want to know," I replied with genuine curiosity, "is why doesn't my $21,000 talk? After all, that academic egghead up in Idaho is only willing to pay you $13,500 for all that uploading and downloading you're going to be expected to do." "But the $13,500 is a springboard to big bucks,"she shot back. "Who do you think the big administrative jobs are going to in the future? That's right, to all of us computer specialists with info to go. As a children's librarian, you have nowhere to go. Nobody takes you seriously. And who wants to work with kids? They're such a mess! Who needs it?"

True, kids are a mess. All you have to do to verify this is to open the newspaper or turn on the television. The media seem to be concentrating on the messy parts. Drug abuse, child porn rings, molestation, child abuse, kidnapping, murder, and rape—you name it and it's a big youth social problem. And our response is becoming all too predictable. Seminars are held on "The Needs of the Latchkey Child", investigations are made into nursery school abuses, and a national commission is appointed to figure out why our public education system is such a big dunce.

We need another Charles Dickens to tell us how badly we're treating our kids. All of the wishy-washy verbiage put out by the consultants has had very little effect. More and more kids are dumped into day-care centers where teachers are barely paid above minimum wage. More and more parents talk hypocritically about how they are stressing quality time with their children as opposed to quantity time. More and more public administrators, in the wake of shrinking tax bases, neo-conservative political philosophies, and burgeoning automation costs, are abandoning their overly costly commitment to youth services. It seems that we are talking more and more about children and doing less and less about them. "Someone else can take care of our children" seems to be the prevalent attitude.

Consider the beleaguered public library director. Beset by inflationary book prices, tighter financial accountability strictures, and the additional pressure of skyrocketing computer systems costs, the temptation is great to relegate children's services to school media centers. Politically, this may be the easy way out. Children are not known to show up at city council meetings, write letters to the editor, fill out written complaint forms or start political movements. And parents, preoccupied with the stresses and challenges of their own occupations, are more concerned about their own library needs than those of their children. As a former school board member, I was always struck by the fact that ninety-nine percent of the parents in the school district never got involved with their children's education until the talk got around to closing schools. Were the parents motivated to get political out of a concern that their kids might have to walk an extra mile or take a bus to get to school? Absolutely not—their biggest fears had to do with the impact a neighborhood school closing would have on their property values.

Parents no longer take responsibility for their children's education. They've handed that job over totally to the professionals, and the professionals have flunked. Consider these statistics: one million school-age children are not enrolled in school, one disabled child out of five is not getting a basic education, up to thirty-three percent of our high school students are chronic truants, and thirteen percent of our seventeen-year-olds are functional illiterates.

We librarians, as part of the public education infrastructure, bear much of the responsibility for this failure. Isn't the decline in reading skills, as represented in the appalling literacy statistics and the disturbing downward trend of S.A.T. scores, a reflection, at least in part, of our inability to motivate children to read? Isn't it also a function of our eroding commitment to the book and our irrational infatuation with computer terminals and audiovisual toys as conveyors of education?

It is easy for us to blame everything that's wrong with kids today on the public schools. But as tax-supported institutions charged with the job of contributing to the public good, our public libraries are also entrusted with the responsibility of serving the educational needs of the entire community, not just people over the age of eighteen. At budget time aren't we always taking credit for this? Don't we mention "education" in the same breath with "information" and "recreation" when proclaiming the holy trinity of public library goals and objectives?

It's particularly fashionable for administrators to talk about the public library as an important source for "lifelong learning". What we can't forget, however, is that there can be no lifelong learning without childhood learning. The great Thomistic maxim that a small mistake in the beginning results in a much larger mistake in the end is never truer than in education. If we don't orient services that are important to the educational needs of young people today, do we really expect them to see us as a source of lifelong learning later on? Educational and humanitarian ideals aside, our future livelihood depends on how seriously we regard children and children's librarians. We can abandon them just like everyone else is doing, or, if we've got any intelligence, we can build our libraries around them and watch a success story blossom that we never dreamed could happen. Next month I'll supply the details. ▣

Patricia Berglund:

School Library Technology

A heartening thing is happening in the educational computing field: school librarians are emerging as leaders.

Ann Lathrop, library coordinator for the San Mateo County (California) schools, thinks she knows why. First, the school library is a better place to put computers than a lab, according to Lathrop. "Some students can't get access to a lab, and some are intimidated by it," she says. "I think students can find a joy in computing in the library that they may never feel in a lab setting. This gives us as librarians a chance to take a real leadership role and become proactive rather than reactive. Also, librarians are uniquely trained in the evaluation of all kinds of media at all grade levels and all subject areas. They are the logical people to get involved in evaluating microcomputer software."

Lathrop is not just a casual observer of the microcomputer scene. She is prominent in educational computing circles, and is nationally known for her pioneering work in software reviewing. She produces reference works about educational software, has organized a prototype public domain educational software library, and is a leader in Computer-Using Educators, the California-based users' group that now numbers over eight thousand members. Lathrop's story offers inspiration to librarians who wonder if there are any contributions they can make to the technological revolution.

After working as an elementary school teacher and as a high school librarian, Lathrop was appointed library coordinator for the San Mateo County Office of Education in 1977. When California's tax-cutting Proposition 13 passed, her job was terminated. Shaken, she returned to school and took some computer programming courses. High tech opportunity did not knock right away. Her classes only proved that "beyond a shadow of a doubt I did not want to be a programmer." Programming is not the only way to enter the computing field, however, and computers were still on Lathrop's mind when her county job was reinstated.

She heard about a group called Computer-Using Educators, and in October 1979 she went to her first CUE meeting. "Truly there are days in one's life that make a difference," she says, "and that day did." A teacher she met at the meeting asked her to go to an upcoming math conference that would have a strong computer component. Although she said "librarians don't go to math conferences," she allowed herself to be convinced.

At that conference, CUE demonstrated computer programs that had been written by teachers. The teachers allowed these programs to remain in the public domain and did not copyright or sell them, so the programs were legally available for duplication. Lathrop and other attendees began talking about how nice it would be if there were a central location where individuals could copy such public domain software.

Lathrop's library instincts took over, and in January 1980 she presented her idea for a public domain educational software library to the CUE board of directors. The San Mateo County Office of Education had agreed to provide space and part-time staff support for this library if CUE members could provide computers and teacher-volunteers to organize and edit the collection.

Fortunately, many of the educators who belonged to CUE knew people in the computer industry, and microcomputers were installed in the San Mateo Educational Resources Center Library in Redwood City. Many teachers volunteered their time during the summer of 1980 to evaluate, edit, revise, and copy donated software. Their program, christened SOFTSWAP, took off. Donated programs continue to flow in from educators and hobbyists. Volunteers examine them, debug them, and transfer them onto dissemination disks for seven computer brands. Boasting more than five hundred programs on eighty disks, SOFTSWAP is now a major source of free software for schools in California. Requests for disks come in from as far away as Buenos Aires and Singapore. The disks are listed in the CUE newsletter and in a catalog available for $1 from SOFTSWAP (333 Main Street, Redwood City, CA 94063). People who visit the center may copy any public domain software they like for the price of a disk. Those who can't visit can order software for a modest fee.

When Lathrop began SOFTSWAP in 1980, there was little educational software in the commercial marketplace. By 1981, more programs were being sold, but the quality was uneven. Lathrop saw the need for product reviews that take into account the realities of software use in schools. She turned to a group of professionals she knew to be skilled reviewers: her fellow librarians. At a statewide school librarians' conference late in 1981, Lathrop organized a software reviewing group and dubbed it the California Library Media Consortium for Classroom Evaluation of Microcomputer Courseware.

Patricia Berglund *is a librarian in the San Francisco Unified School District.*

A new approach

Lathrop and the consortium brought a new approach to software reviewing. They developed an evaluation form and procedures that focus on training the reviewer rather than on producing written reviews. The software is tested in the classroom. "We do not evaluate software primarily to publish reviews," Lathrop says. "We evaluate software to help teachers, librarians, and other educators learn what to look for and to think of what's best for their classsroom. Of course, we do produce some useful written reviews as a by-product of our work." Fifty of these reviews have been published each year since 1982 and the annual reviews are available for $10 a set.

Lathrop's colleague, Barbara Carey, library coordinator for the Butte County schools, developed a sound slide show explaining the consortium's software review form. Copies of the show are loaned to districts throughout the state to help train software reviewers.

The Library Media Consortium's procedure calls for at least two educators to review a piece of software. One review must include information on using the software in the classroom because student reaction to a program is an essential part of the reviewing process. If two evaluators' conclusions differ significantly, the review is not published until more evaluations are received and a consensus is developed. The staff of the SMERC library organizes and edits the reviews and publishes the final product.

In 1982, the California legislature established fifteen Teacher Education and Computer (TEC) centers throughout the state. It also funded a statewide software evaluation project to be developed from Lathrop's software library. The SMERC project became the official TEC Center Software Library and Clearinghouse.

In January 1983 Lathrop organized the first statewide software evaluation forum in Menlo Park, California. There, TEC center staff members were trained to use the consortium software evaluation form. Lathrop also invited representatives from seventeen state, regional, and national organizations to attend the conference forum. The group produced the *1983 Educational Software Preview Guide.*

This year another Educational Software Evaluation Forum was held. The focus for TEC center staff was integrating courseware into daily classroom activities. Twenty-seven other organizations were also represented. The participants started with a list of over 1,700 programs that had been favorably reviewed at one or more of the participating sites. Group members discussed and analyzed their evaluation data and selected 500 titles for their *1984 Educational Software Preview Guide.* This guide, Lathrop is careful to note, "is designed to assist educators in locating software for preview. It is not intended to endorse these products for purchase without examination." The guide costs $10 and is available from Lathrop's office and from many state department of education offices.

Local involvement

Lathrop says, "In California, we have involved teachers and librarians at the local level in our evaluation, rather than expecting the state department of education to do all evaluations at the state level. We have also brought together representatives from evaluation groups all over the country to pool their results instead of having us try to evaluate everything ourselves. I think what's unique about what I have done is that I have worked with so many different groups and helped to build bridges between them."

She sees the annual *Educational Software Preview Guide* as a basis for a national directory of exemplary software. "What we are doing," she says, "is trying to create for the computer software field some of the same reference tools we find so useful in the library field."

On her own, Lathrop works on another reference work, a software equivalent of *Book Review Digest.* It is *The Digest of Software Reviews: Education,* marketed through School & Home CourseWare, Inc. of Fresno. A quarterly publication, it summarizes reviews of computer courseware found in more than seventy journals.

Lathrop is anxious to see software used more effectively in the classroom. In 1983, with coauthor Bobby Goodson, she wrote *Courseware in the Classroom: Selecting, Organizing, and Using Educational Software* (Addison-Wesley, pa $10). One of her current projects is a training package that would help teachers integrate computer programs into the curriculum.

She recommends that librarians keep computers available for use in the library and also on carts "so they can be a normal, everyday, acceptable part of the library and classroom environment. Rotate them through the rooms just like a projector." She further recommends that software circulate from the library media center for classroom use. Despite her interest in educational software, she would not restrict the use of other types of computer programs in the school. "I believe that a wide variety of good software should be a part of the library media center collection. Just as we have our recreational books, I think we need recreational software," she says. "Logic and problem-solving programs, thought-provoking adventure games, word processing programs and other tools are all appropriate for use in the library."

Discussing access to the software, Lathrop says that, if possible, all useful software programs should have both title and subject entries in the card catalog. If the collection is too large, however, she would file diskette titles rather than title cards for every separate program on a diskette.

(continued on page 79)

Donnarae MacCann/Olga Richard:

Picture Books for Children

The four tales reviewed this month are from ancient Judaic and Native American tradition, and from the imagination of a modern Yugoslav writer. **Jonah and the Great Fish** (retold and illustrated by Warwick Hutton) is a simple rendition of the story that Bible authorities say was written about four centuries after the age of Jonah, the prophet. It is generally viewed as an object lesson on the universality of human experience, although children will not realize this unless some of the story's background is filled in for them. Jonah's commission from God was to convert the people of Nineveh—Assyrians who had been among the worst oppressors of Judah. It is not surprising that Jonah objected to his mission; yet God's impartiality was demonstrated when Jonah survived his trial in the fish's belly, and came forth to enjoy an exceptional success in reforming the Ninevites.

To young children, this tale contains a message of reassurance. A "totally Other" guides, corrects, and fulfills the destiny of individuals, as well as the appointed mission of "a great fish."

Warwick Hutton draws the whale, sea, and sky so that all appear tremendously dramatic. They suggest tension and trauma, and yet the artist's technique is not complicated. The power he evokes comes from his careful choice of scale: a small boat against the huge, dark, overpowering elements of nature. There is drama in the contrast between large, freely painted masses of dark colors (for sky and sea) and the frail, pen-and-ink lines used for

From *Buffalo Woman*

the figures and the boat. Placement is important also. Hutton centers the figures while the imposing, diagonal forms flow out of the picture plane on three sides. The effect is original and expressive.

The Native American legend **Buffalo Woman** is also a parable about universality, but it is a love story rather than an adventure tale. Paul Goble's gracefully constructed narrative introduces a reverent hunter who thanks his buffalo prey for offering meat for the people. In a gesture of mutual respect, the Buffalo Nation sends him a wife (a metamorphosed buffalo), and they live happily with their son until the hunter's relatives let their prejudices surface. The wife is "without a family" and "her ways are different." Buffalo Woman and Calf Boy begin a long journey back to the Buffalo Nation. The distraught husband follows and Calf Boy suggests how his father can meet the tests that will jeopardize his life in the Buffalo Nation. The tips, combined with his bravery and devotion, win the hunter the privilege of being transformed into a buffalo. An endless, harmonious relationship, says the narrator, was thus sealed between the People and the Buffalo Nation. "Mitakuye oyasin—We are all related."

Goble's illustrations are facile and talented, yet they are somewhat boring. Most of the pictures are predictable scenes in which flowers and birds are repeated in the same precious way. The design is static in the manner of greeting-card decorations, rather than in the manner of decorators such as Matisse or Braque.

Goble has used his talent and commitment to create an attractive package, a charismatic surface appeal in *Buffalo Woman.* The book is handsomely planned, painstakingly executed, and stylishly colored. But we think he could be creating something more than conventional "squeaky clean" patterns, as the imaginative, schematic drawing on the last page demonstrates.

A second tale from the nations of the Great Plains, **The Story of Jumping Mouse** (retold and illustrated by John Steptoe), features a holy quest and an exemplary mouse. This character bears some resemblance to the "Christ figure" in Christian literary tradition. A divine helper, Magic Frog, gives the mouse powerful new legs to help him in his journey to the "far-off land." It is then Jumping Mouse's turn to be a gift-giver. First a "fat mouse" detains him with notions of the easy life, but the protagonist rouses himself ("I didn't come all this way to settle down under a berry bush") and moves on. He gives a blind buffalo a new name, "Eyes-of-a-Mouse," thereby losing his own eyesight. Next a dying wolf receives a new sense of smell and becomes

From *The Story of Jumping Mouse*

Olga Richard *and* **Donnarae MacCann** *are the authors of* The Child's First Books.

"Nose-of-a-Mouse." These friends now guide the disabled hero to the far-off land, but he can no longer resist crying out in his helplessness. Magic Frog suddenly reappears and summarizes the pilgrimage theme: "Your unselfish spirit has brought you great hardship, but it is that same spirit of hope and compassion that has brought you to the far-off land."

The supernatural frog urges Jumping Mouse to make one more effort: "Jump high." And as the air lifts Jumping Mouse, Magic Frog calls out to him that his new name will be "Eagle," and assures him that he will live in the far-off land forever.

The text is succinct, although Steptoe uses dignified and somewhat elaborate dialogue, as befits the magical setting. The beauties of nature have been evoked intermittently, as when the narrator describes "cool breezes that blew down from the mountain peaks," and "the rhythm of the wolf's padding paws."

As the book's illustrator, Steptoe draws upon a style that he used with great brilliance in *Mother Crocodile* (Delacorte, 1981). Yet he is also moving in an entirely new direction. He creates mixtures of black and white, and is able to animate the surfaces and depict a rich environment with more success than most artists can achieve with a full range of color. He also designs arrangements that are handsome, asymmetrical, and unusual in their intricate weaving of negative and positive spaces.

Steptoe's style calls for a special kind of looking. While his basic drawings are simple and realistic, initially appearing to be almost photographic, he nonetheless produces a unique quality of organic growth in his landscapes. Tonality, space, and surface effects are used for intense, dynamic renderings of nature.

Grozdana Olujic's **Rose of Mother-of-Pearl** shares several plot features with *The Story of Jumping Mouse.* An unusual protagonist (an oyster) longs for another world, but it is the upper world at the surface of the sea, not the mouse's "far-off land." And she meets a coral who, like the self-satisfied "fat mouse," says in effect: "This is the ideal place; know where you belong and stay there." But Rose of Mother-of-Pearl is hopelessly discontented, and only in the end do thoughts of timelessness and peace overshadow her sorrows.

There is no magic helper, however, for Rose of Mother-of-Pearl. Instead a child and a poet know the truth about her feelings, and that is enough. Her longing becomes a "tide of sorrow" that "seemed to fill her being and condense into a solid, gleaming droplet." She no longer thinks of either the upper or lower worlds, because as the longing grows, a pearl grows within her, "glowing like a tiny sun." She has "found a world within herself."

When she is pried loose by a pearl diver, Rose sees, for just a second, a world where "clouds are airier than foam" and "the salt breath of the sea [is] mingled everywhere with the sweet scent of rosemary." Her pearl goes to a fancy shop, but the empty shell is given to a boy who hears a sea sound while "all night long the early moon drifted across the sky."

In a sense the resolution is satisfyingly childlike: a sympathetic character shares the truth about what the oyster has lived through. But on the other hand, it was a "terrible desire of Rose of Mother-of-Pearl," and the author makes it clear that the undersea world was as delightful as the realm of sun and flowers. The protagonist is quite a tragic case, and yet she finds pride and peace in her "shining little sun" within. Existential questions spin off from this blend of magic and psychological realism, but the narrative as a whole remains within a child's range.

This book comes from a connoisseurish small publisher, Toothpaste Press. But one need not be addicted to bibliomania to appreciate the precision and care exercised in *Rose of Mother-of-Pearl.* Little more than a pamphlet in format, the feel of the paper (Ragston) and the look of the typeface (handset Italian Olde Style) are marvelous. Page margins are generous, particularly the outer and tail margins, and this leaves a feeling of space and air that is luxuriously restful. The line drawings are suitable to the book's design: thin, simple, black-line, with minute suggestions of detail—all unassuming, quiet, and in tune with the delicate surface of the slightly off-white Ragston. Kathy Jacobi did the illustrations and pochoir stencils (a stencil process for adding color to a print). The coloring is low-keyed and suited to the minimal intrusion of the line drawings. The typeface makes the visual statement for the book, however, and the block of black and white made by the type has a direct appeal. In contrast, Jacobi's quaint and charming illustrations have a somewhat faded look about them. They are probably more "precious" than they need to be. ▣

This month's books

Goble, Paul. **Buffalo Woman.** Bradbury Press, 1984. $12.95. ISBN 0-02-737720-2 LC 83-15704

Hutton, Warwick. **Jonah and the Great Fish.** Atheneum, 1984. $12.95. ISBN 0-689-50283-4 LC 83-15477

Olujic, Grozdana. **Rose of Mother-of-Pearl.** Translated from Serbo-Croatian by Grozdana Olujic and Jascha Kessler. Illus. by Kathy Jacobi. Hot Chocolate Books (Toothpaste Press, Box 546, West Branch, Iowa 52358), 1983. pa$6. ISBN 0-915124-90-4 LC 83-18254

Steptoe, John. **The Story of Jumping Mouse; a Native American Legend.** Retold and illus. by John Steptoe. Lothrop, Lee & Shepard, 1984. $12.50. ISBN 0-688-01902-1; 0-688-01903-X (lib. bdg.) LC 82-14848

Patty Campbell:

The Young Adult Perplex

"And thick and fast they came at last, and more and more and more," said the Walrus to the Carpenter. He was referring to oysters without feet, but the quote is just as applicable to the recent proliferation of young adult paperback series. Four years ago the first teenage romances burst onto the marketplace with rocketing sales figures. Since then, publishers have been eagerly flinging money and flashy promotion into brand-name series. A generation of YAs trained by television commercials to be knee-jerk consumers gobbled it up, salivating obediently at logos and matched formats.

The chain bookstores stacked the series in eye-catching displays for easy brand-name recognition like so much detergent or breakfast cereal, and the kids, who were hanging around in the shopping mall anyway, marched right in and plunked down their allowances and their McDonald's wages for yet another version of the same book they bought last week. Originality was out. Surprises were out. After all, you want to feel sure that one box of Cheerios will be pretty much like another.

Young adult librarians reacted to this situation with pitiful myopia. We sat around and had the same old debates about literary quality versus popularity and we wrote and read individual reviews of the things, and we worried about the lies they told young people about life. In other words, we treated them like books, when it was plain to everybody else involved, even to the kids themselves, that what we were dealing with here was a commodity, a product. The market had shifted from the library to the bookstore and profit was all that mattered. While we were doing little plot summaries and evaluations of the five titles we were buying for the library in any one month, Waldenbooks or B. Dalton's hauled them in by the truckloads and shoveled them out to the shredder at the end of the week if they didn't sell.

Naturally, we have gotten confused. We thought we invented the game, and now other people have changed the rules and not even given us a scorecard. To be fair, it has to be acknowledged that some publishers (often the same ones who are producing brand-name books out of the other side of their house) are still playing by the old rules. Excellent YA fiction and nonfiction are still being written and published. But somehow it is all beginning to seem alarmingly anachronistic.

Disheartening as the situation may seem to those who care about what goes into young minds, some consolation and a restored perspective can be found in the history of

Patty Campbell *is a freelance writer who teaches young adult literature at UCLA. She is currently at work on a book about YA novelist Robert Cormier.*

young adult literature. At regular intervals during the past century one "trash" series after another has risen on a wave of popularity and canny merchandishing, swept past teachers and librarians who viewed with alarm, and ebbed away in a few years to leave not ruined lives but only a pleasant residue of nostalgia. The Stratemeyer series, Horatio Alger, Tom Swift, the Big-Little Books, Nancy Drew, the Hardy Boys, Sue Barton—all had their day. Some of the modern series seem to be consciously modeled on these older patterns. Diana Winthrop and Donna Rockford are granddaughters of Nancy Drew. The boarding school story has been revived, although that experience is surely remote from the lives of today's teens. New American Library has even dug up the fifty-year-old corpse of Sue Barton, Student Nurse and is reprinting the series intact with only a change of cover design.

So let us dig in and wait it out. In the meantime, here is a scorecard so you can tell the players.▣

Romances

- Sweet Dreams (Bantam)—The grandmama of the whole phenomenon is now into title #72, and includes a nonfiction spinoff.
- Wildfire (Scholastic)—The other matriarch of romance. Also includes nonfiction self-help.
- First Love From Silhouette (Pocket Books)
- Caprice (Berkley)
- Two by Two YA Romances (Warner)—Read the girl's story, then flip it over and get the boy's point of view (or at least what girls would like to think is the boy's point of view).
- Magic Moments (New American Library)—A new series, not to be confused with Sweet Dreams' *Magic Moments* by Debra Spector.

Romances with Reader Participation

The gimmick of providing the reader with a choice of outcomes at crucial points in the plot is perhaps the only original idea to come out of this deluge of schlock.

- Turning Points (New American Library)
- Make Your Dreams Come True Romances (Warner)
- Follow Your Heart Romances (Pocket Books)—For ages ten to twelve.

Speculative Fiction with Reader Participation

See *WLB,* February 1984 for review

- Time Machine (Bantam)
- Be An Interplanetary Spy (Bantam)

Based on Dungeons and Dragons™, the following three series are complex game-stories using dice, maps, and score sheets.

- Fighting Fantasy Gamebooks (Dell)
- Endless Quest Books (Random House)
- Dragontales (New American Library)—two each month, one with a girl as protagonist and one with a boy.

Horror

See *WLB,* May 1983 for review

- Twilight (Dell Laurel Leaf)
- Dark Forces (Bantam)
- Plot-Your-Own-Horror Story (Wanderer Books)

Mysteries

- Diana Winthrop Mystery (Signet Vista)
- Donna Rockford Mystery (Scholastic)
- Windswept: A Mystery Romance (Scholastic)
- Burchardt & Decker Mysteries (Avon Flare)

Theme Series

These follow one set of characters throughout although the protagonist may vary from book to book.

- The Girls of Canby Hall by "Emily Chase" (Scholastic)—A boarding school story. The only racially integrated series.
- Sweet Valley High, "created" by Francine Pascal (Bantam)—Two sisters, one good, one evil.
- The Zodiac Club (Putnam Pacer)—A new series focusing on the astrological signs of the characters.
- Mirrors (Putnam Pacer)—Starts January 1985. Adventures in the world of fashion.
- Seniors (Dell Laurel Leaf)—Four very different girls are high school friends.
- Electric High (Warner)—A breakthrough series about a young rock singer, it dares to take place in 1984 instead of a thinly disguised 1954.
- Sue Barton, Student Nurse (New American Library)
- Perfect Image Books (Putnam Pacer)—Although this series is hardcover, it follows the paperback formula. The first title, *Fantasy Summer* by Susan Beth Pfeffer, is a sentimentalized *Bell Jar* about a group of girls who have won a summer on the staff of a teen fashion magazine.

Reprint Series

Many paperback publishers have made responsible use of the brand-name concept by promoting logo-identified series of reprints of quality YA books. Sometimes the editors disguise these as romance lines by choosing past titles that deal with boy-girl relationships. Most of them also include occasional new nonformula fiction and nonfiction.

- Two Hearts Romances (Putnam Pacer)
- Young Love (Dell Laurel Leaf)
- Flare (Avon)
- Starfire (Bantam)
- Signet Vista (New American Library)
- Laurel Leaf (Dell)
- Fawcett Juniper (Ballantine)

Kathleen Maio:

Murder in Print

There was a time, not so very long ago, when gay and lesbian characters seldom appeared in mysteries. When they did appear, their inversion/perversion was usually only implied by the author through the character's affectations or through the sly hints and disapproval of others. Needless to say, such characters were often murderers. That is, when they weren't victims. They were never protagonists or series sleuths.

The last fifteen years or so have seen a change. One of the key architects of that change has been Joseph Hansen. His new novel, **Nightwork** (Holt, 1984, $12.95), is the seventh in the Dave Brandstetter series begun in 1970. Brandstetter, a death claims investigator for Pinnacle Insurance is a moral, compassionate, middle-aged guy who happens to be gay. *Nightwork* focuses on the death of an independent trucker whose fatal accident turns out to be the result of a carefully placed explosive. The vividly portrayed characters include frightened widows, an elderly reclusive transvestite, and teen-aged boys all too familiar with violence and death.

Hansen's brand of realism does not require him to tie up everything in a bright ribbon at book's end. Brandstetter stumbles upon the murderer's identity, but several equally criminal and tragic subplots are given no easy solution. This slim volume, while not one of Hansen's best, is still a very fine novel of suspense. And Dave Brandstetter remains a quietly heroic and very believable detective.

Nathan Aldyne, who is Dennis Schuetz and Michael McDowell, also has a new book out. **Slate** (Villard, 1984, $12.95) is the third in a series that features gay bartender Daniel Valentine and his straight friend, Clarisse Lovelace. Clarisse is now in law school, and Valentine is the manager of a soon-to-open gay bar called Slate. Clarisse and Valentine move into apartments above the bar, and are welcomed to the neighborhood with a party at Mr. Fred's Tease 'n' Tint salon next door. When Clarisse returns home she finds a body in her bed, and the craziness begins.

Aldyne's characters, both gay and straight, are first-class eccentrics. Clarisse and Val are a late twentieth-century variation on the screwball husband/wife sleuth teams of the thirties and forties. While no one could claim that Aldyne's gay characters are realistic, they are neither stereotyped nor negatively portrayed. In fact, Clarisse remains a shadowy figure compared to Valentine and the other gay men who people these pages.

Some may find *Slate* too farcical, with snappy dialogue that, at times, seems a little too studied. Non-homophobic readers will find Aldyne's latest a very agreeable tale of light suspense.

While gay male detectives are becoming more common and acceptable, lesbian sleuths are rare. In fact, the best example of a lesbian detective I have found is a paperback original from Canada (*A Reason to Kill* by Eve Zaremba) published in 1978. Last year, Naiad (Box 10543, Tallahassee, Fl 32302), a small lesbian press, published the first in a series of mysteries featuring an amateur sleuth named Nyla Wade. The publication of ***Mrs. Porter's Letter*** by Vicki McConnell was a hopeful sign, but a grave disappointment. The narrative and the dialogue were stiff and unnatural. In an even greater outrage, the cover gave away the mystery. By labeling the book "A Lesbian Mystery," the author and publishers were being admirably up-front about the book's content, but they also provided the key to the novel's puzzle.

McConnell's second Wade mystery has just been released. ***The Burnton Widows*** (Naiad, 1984, pa $7.95) doesn't expose its puzzle on the cover, and qualifies as a murder mystery. McConnell's writing is still awkward and, in violation of fair play, she keeps a great many circumstantial clues from the reader.

McConnell has not yet perfected her craft as a writer but she writes mysteries for a constituency that has long been ignored. While many readers will be impatient with the writing (and perhaps offended by the love scenes and Wade's obsession with vulval, vaginal, and breast imagery), interested readers who don't expect too much may appreciate a mystery that not only vali-

---

Kathleen Maio *is a freelance writer based in Somerville, Massachusetts. She has contributed to* Twentieth Century Crime and Mystery Writers, Murderess Ink, *and numerous magazines.*

dates, but celebrates lesbian history and lifestyle. The rest of us must wait for a female counterpart to Dave Brandstetter.

A Naiad non-mystery title may interest mystery readers. ***The Price of Salt*** by Claire Morgan is a 1952 lesbian novel, reprinted this year with a new introduction by the author. "Claire Morgan" is an early pseudonym of crime writer Patricia Highsmith.

There is a new paperback reprint line, the Quill Mysterious Classic series from Morrow. The first four titles have been released, all with excellent cover designs by Irving Freeman and Steve Macanga. They are: ***Bury Me Deep*** by Harold Q. Masur, ***The Asphalt Jungle*** by W. R. Burnett, ***The Bigger They Come*** by A. A. Fair (Erle Stanley Gardner), and Frederic Brown's ***Night of the Jabberwock.*** The price for each is $3.95.

The print is a trifle small, and there are a few more typos than seem acceptable, but the selections are fine ones. I'm delighted to have *Night of the Jabberwock* with Doc Stoeger's wild night of murder and mayhem in hand again. Morrow is planning on reissuing eight titles per year. The first four are an impressive start. Morrow is to be commended for starting with the first books in mystery series like Fair's Bertha Cool and Masur's Scott Jordan case files.

In the paperback original category, we have ***Sick of Shadows*** by Sharyn McCrumb (Avon, 1984, $2.95). A pathetic, unbalanced bride is murdered just before her wedding, in the small Georgia town where her family, the Chandlers, are wealthy landed gentry. The suspects are the rest of her loony clan. The detectives are Sheriff Wesley Rountree, Deputy Taylor, and the victim's cousin, Elizabeth (with a little last minute help from her brother, Bill).

The Chandlers are an interesting, if unsympathetic lot. They are perfect suspects, and entertaining to watch despite the fact that it is easy enough to spot the murderer among the rest of the crazies. Still, this is an unusual and very promising debut.

A promising hardcover debut can be found in Jeremiah Healy's ***Blunt Darts*** (Walker, 1984, $12.95). Here we are introduced to John Francis Cuddy, widower and private eye. It is unfortunate in a way that Healy has set the first of his series in Boston. Cuddy is an independent cuss with a smart mouth and a heart of gold. We know where he eats, what he drives, and what he wears.

It is hard, therefore, to avoid comparisons with Robert Parker's immensely popular Spenser series. Healy ironically acknowledges such a possibility by having Cuddy relax with a Spenser novel. But such comparisons are unfair. Cuddy and Spenser may jog a similar route, but their characters are not alike. Cuddy's case, involving the troubled, missing son of a rich judge, externally seems Spenserian. But Healy's story is tighter than most of Parker's recent efforts, and there is a gut-wrenching twist at the conclusion that will make it easy for readers to remember and admire Healy and his hero.

One wonders whether nun mysteries are experiencing a revival. Two recent mysteries both feature elderly sisters as amateur detectives. ***And Then There was Nun*** (Vanguard, 1984, $10.95) is the third in a series written by Ralph McInerny under the pen name Monica Quill, featuring Sister Mary Teresa (Emptee) Dempsey of the Order of Martha and Mary (the M & M s).

The series characters are derivative of Rex Stout. The fat, irascible Sister Emptee stays home and cogitates while young Sister Kim does the legwork. There are plenty of readers who like this sort of thing. Normally I wouldn't complain. But *And Then There Was Nun* contains the type of howler (one the author or editor should have caught) that can ruin a book for a mystery fan. Through a coded diary (full of clues not fully or fairly provided to the reader) the murder victim refers to the drug that killed her. The code is broken on the last page as angel dust, the addict's term for cocaine. Angel dust is, of course, phencyclidine or PCP, not coke. When a book's characters and story line are strong enough, such a gaffe is often forgiven. It is harder to overlook in a lackluster effort by a mystery veteran.

Another nun, Sister Mary Helen, makes her first appearance in ***A Novena for Murder*** (Scribner, 1984, $12.95). The author brings authenticity to her nun-sleuth. She

is Sister Carol Anne O'Marie, a nun herself for over a quarter of a century.

Sister Mary Helen is a nice, savvy, seventy-five-year-old sister who loves reading mysteries but hates being put out to pasture at a small Catholic girl's college. That is, until the college has its own set of homicides to investigate. Sister Mary Helen joins forces with two Irish-Catholic detectives.

This is an old-fashioned mystery. In nine days, murderous sinners confess, a free-loving female cop sees the error of her ways and gets married, and there are happy endings (in the college chapel, of course) all around after the case is closed–and a novena is completed. ▣

Judith Trojan:

Front Row Center

If Michael Jackson didn't exist, we'd have to invent him. With all the ballyhoo surrounding the Jackson Family "Victory Tour" this past summer and Michael's considerable talents as a solo performer, it's easy to catch the fever and forget the trailblazers who preceded him. He inherited his throne from the crooners of the thirties and forties, the rock and rollers of the fifties, and the rock groups of the sixties and seventies. Frank Sinatra, Elvis Presley, and the Beatles filled a void and spoke to the needs of their particular generations; but they also appealed to a wider, more broadly based audience as well. They made Michael possible.

In light of the current Michael mythology, it's a good time to take a look at two fine short films that chart the rise of rock and roll idols Frankie Lymon and Paul Anka. Although *I Promise to Remember: The Story of Frankie Lymon and the Teenagers* and *Lonely Boy* track careers that peaked a mere five years apart, their different stories make for fascinating viewing and indirectly suggest the barriers that had to be broken before someone like Michael Jackson could make it into the rock and roll pantheon.

After viewing ***I Promise to Remember,*** filmed by Steven Fischler, Jane Praeger, and Joel Sucher for the PBS series *Matters of Life and Death,* it is clear that if the Jacksons had come onto the music scene in the late fifties, they might have easily been lost in the sea of black teenage groups with young lead singers. In 1956–1957, Frankie Lymon and the Teenagers broke the color barrier to become the first sucessful black crossover group; they attracted black, white, and Hispanic audiences in the United States and abroad. Smash-hit concerts in forty-eight states and Europe, TV appearances on *The Ed Sullivan Show* and Alan Freed's *Rock 'n' Roll Party* brought them fame but no fortune. Their songs made it to the top of the charts, but they received only spending money and a limousine for their efforts. At the time, black juvenile acts were often exploited by promoters who pocketed most of the money earned by their clients. Lymon and the Teenagers co-wrote their hit "Why Do Fools Fall in Love," which is recorded to this day by top talents like Diana Ross. They never received a penny in royalties because the song lacked an author credit.

Black-and-white clips highlighting TV performances by the group or Lymon as a solo, interviews with a record producer, disk jockey, Lymon's onetime manager, and two of the Teenagers—Jimmy Merchant and Herman Santiago—confirm the talent and spunk of Lymon and his junior high school buddies who were discovered singing on the streets of Harlem. At age thirteen, Lymon was an electrifying song and dance man, a fifties version of Michael Jackson. Dapper in his preppy "letter sweater" or a suit and tie, he looked like a miniature Nat King Cole who just couldn't stand still.

Merchant and Santiago recall the

From *I Promise to Remember*

Judith Trojan *is editor-in-chief of* Sightlines *magazine, editorial coordinator at the Educational Film Library Association in New York City, and a staff member of the American Film Festival.*

formation of their group and the fifties trend of harmonizing on street corners, a forerunner of today's breakdancing craze. The men also relate, with no bitterness, Lymon's split for a solo act. Neither he nor the Teenagers recovered from that move and their careers went downhill. Lymon, the son of professional gospel singers, turned to drugs. At age seventeen, he was blackballed in the industry. Lymon is shown in a TV clip as an adult lip-syncing a hit record he made when he was thirteen. It's a ludicrous attempt at a comeback, especially since his adult voice was a cross between Frank Sinatra's and Paul Anka's. Frankie Lymon simply wasn't marketable as an adult.

Although the film is only twenty-seven minutes long, *I Promise to Remember: The Story of Frankie Lymon and the Teenagers* sets up an interesting element of suspense regarding Lymon's present-day whereabouts. At the end of the film, one of his brothers acknowledges the heroin overdose that killed him in 1968. Lymon was twenty-six years old. As his fan club president giddily remembers the excitement and adulation generated by Frankie Lymon in his heyday, it's obvious that he had the right stuff to be a teenage idol. But as a young, black performer in the fifties, he was an easy mark for sleazy promoters and drugs. In the seventies and eighties, there have been more options for Michael Jackson and his brothers.

In jolting contrast to Lymon's tragically mismanaged career, Paul Anka's rise was so well orchestrated that by 1962, after five years of hard work and obscurity, his longevity in the business as a major talent and heartthrob was assured. ***Lonely Boy,*** the classic National Film Board of Canada cinema verité study of nineteen-year-old Anka on stage and off, is surprisingly fresh twenty-two years after it was made. The performance sites, Anka's hairline, and the age of his audiences may have undergone some drastic changes since then; but the film's production values and Anka's talent and honesty, even at such a young age, make this film popular among contemporary audiences.

From *Lonely Boy*

While performing at Atlantic City's old Steel Pier, New Jersey's Freedomland Amusement Park, and at the Copacabana, New York City, Anka is polished and charming. Fainting, sobbing teenage groupies are everywhere, but Anka's gentle way with these girls is a lesson in star diplomacy. Off-stage, Anka discusses frankly how he remade himself into sexy star material by working out in a gym, losing lots of weight, and retraining his unruly hair into a fashionable pompadour. His devoted manager mentions Anka's nose job as well.

For its trailblazing, cinema verité camerawork and its backstage look at the making of a teenage idol who also appeals to adult audiences, *Lonely Boy* remains at the top of the music film field and deserves a second look. Although *I Promise to Remember* is no match technically with *Lonely Boy,* the former is an above-average compilation documentary with a special poignancy all its own. Its view of the underbelly of the fifties black music business will surely put Michael Jackson's career into perspective. Both films are suitable for junior high through adult audiences.

For more ambitious programs, try piggybacking these two short films with Taylor (*An Officer and a Gentleman*) Hackford's first dramatic feature, ***The Idolmaker.*** This largely unknown but critically acclaimed film, set in New York City in 1959, traces the evolution of a talented songwriter into an agent who turns unknown boys with "the look" into rock stars to rival Elvis. Reminiscent of Robert De Niro, Ray Sharkey gives a suitably intense performance as the songwriter/agent who becomes "somebody" by pushing others into the spotlight that he covets for himself. The grooming and marketing of late fifties rock and rollers like Fabian and Frankie Avalon is passionately recreated in *The Idolmaker* with top-notch characterization, fine period detail, and original music. ▣

This month's films:

I Promise to Remember: The Story of Frankie Lymon and the Teenagers. 16mm & video. color & b/w. 27 min. 1983. Producers: Steven Fischler, Jane Praeger, & Joel Sucher. Dist: The Cinema Guild, 1697 Broadway, New York, NY 10019. 16mm—$425 (rental $50). Video—$350.

The Idolmaker. 16mm color. 119 min. 1980. Director: Taylor Hackford. Cast: Ray Sharkey & Tovah Feldshuh. Released by MGM/UA. MPAA Rating: PG. Dist: MGM/United Artists Entertainment, 1350 Avenue of the Americas, New York, NY 10019. Rental—$175.

Lonely Boy. 16mm & video. b/w. 26½ min. 1962. Directors: Wolf Koenig & Roman Kroitor. Dist: The National Film Board of Canada, 16th Floor, 1251 Avenue of the Americas, New York, NY 10020. 16mm—$500 (rental $50). Video—$300 (rental $50).

Bruce Pollock:

On Record: Popular Music

In the video age, **Warrior,** by Scandal, featuring Patty Smyth is a veritable TV mini-series of a four-hundred-page romance novel, starring Goldie Hawn as the naive waif and Roman Polansky as the nefarious record biz sharpie, with Louise Lasser as Mary Hartman, Bruce Dern as Bruce Springsteen and the young Warren Beatty as the crusading journalist turned novelist/screenwriter, who exploits the waif and the sharpie by profiting from the telling of the tale.

Profit and exploitation are what this tale is all about. For those who don't follow the rock and roll scoreboard on MTV, let me lay some pipe. It's all about Patty Smyth, lead singer for Scandal. She provides the most glorious burst of musical energy, sass, and pizzazz the entire video age has produced. She hailed from that storybook land of the undiscovered just minutes before her low-rent, three-minute stint astride the rock and roll cameras gave us "Goodbye to You." In one swoop she justified—in fact redeemed—two years of torpid boredom and vacant space on music television. On the wings of Patty's preening, pouting, sly, slick, and wet-lipped rendition of the song, an image, a band, a Top Forty single, and a career were borne. I don't recall the video of the follow-up, "Love's Got a Line on You," but the tune was another instant car-radio smasheroo, evoking all the passion of summer love: knee deep in evanescent, incandescent, up-all-night yearning known only to the eternally teenage and the recently divorced—all the gooey, heartstruck chords that make classic rock and roll so naggingly unforget-

table, like your first botched romance.

And the glory of it, the reverberating thrill of it, besides the magnificent Grace Slickian cool of the girl, and her lordly command of her larynx, was the absolute amateurishness of it. If you watched the video you could swear you saw the band's high school cronies snickering in the wings, Patty's stage mother pacing, her frantic vocal coach beseeching her to 'go for it.' And Patty gamely (gaminly) held back a smile of triumph as she danced and pranced to beat the band, the fans, and the boys in the grandstand. Free-floating and not giving a damn, she achieved a TV perfection unrivaled since Bob Dylan debated Tommy Sands on The Les Crane Show, in 1965.

Fast-forward a year or so if we must. On the strength of Scandal's up-from-nowhere showing, a full-length album is to be done (the two surprise hits emanated from a no-frills Columbia five-song EP). The naive kids in the band travel down Corporate Boulevard in limos for a taste of multinational rock. Innocence meets commerce. Beauty meets the money men. (Fade to a station break, but you already know the ending.)

If you didn't want to wait for the album, the advance video of "The Warrior" was warning enough. There our Patty, naive and nubile yet coyly hip at first, now stepped into a lurid production number in a twenty-first-century makeup job out of 2000 B.C. This is someone's idea of a Pat Benatar or Olivia Newton-John flick, an obvious showcase paving the yellow brick road to Grauman's Chinese Theatre. The song is one of those annoyingly prevalent pop anthem types, all sound and fury, signifying next to nothing. Patty seems lost in all the scenery, like Debbie Harry at the Grammy Awards mouthing platitudes on the podium next to Geroge Burns.

Could the album be anything but downhill from there? Yes and no. Sharp Mike Chapman (of the aforementioned Debbie Harry and Blondie fame) was assigned the production job, and he had done wonders for Suzy Quatro. Zack Smith, the founder of Scandal, discoverer of Patty Smyth (pronounced Smythe, as in 'Can you answer the doorbell, Jeeves old boy?') has since quit the band, along with the original drummer (the bass-player, too, may have been swept out in the purge). They probably weren't cut out for the hectic, dissolute, no-roots, fast-bucks life at the rock pinnacle. Poor Patty seems to be careening toward that life.

She may be in luck, however; this album probably won't be the vehicle that lands her in the living rooms and jukeboxes of our hearts. And maybe by the next album she'll have wrested the reins from whoever is choking back all her glorious once-in-a-teenage-rampage potential.

Cynically, at first, I listened through the album, expecting ten

Bruce Pollock *is editor of* Guitar *magazine and the author of* When the Music Mattered: Rock in the 1960s.

variations on the "Goodbye to You"/"Love's Got a Line on You" formula that had brought Patty and Scandal such a quick joyride to success. Sadly, utterly frustrated, I was not even awarded so much as an echo of that former summer love. Oh, traces maybe, on "Less Than Half" and "All I Want," the album's two best cuts. They contain its most soaring moments, when Patty's early-morning, rolling-out-of-bed, sultry power takes hold in cosmic stretches, causing headlights on the road to wink in unison and countless near-collisions of transported dreamers.

Otherwise, here is the relentlessly slick packaged product: Patty as Pat Benatar, Patty as Suzy Quatro, Patty as Debbie Harry, Patty as no one even remotely familiar. Around meaningless stocking-stuffer songs provided by concerned outside sources when the band's original material proved wanting (or nonexistent), Patty's voice wavers and crashes, all soaring sound and no substance. Occasionally, as on "Beat of a Heart" and "Say What You Will," the sound of her voice is enough. Interestingly, these songs, and the two others mentioned, were written by Patty and her Scandal alumni, perhaps in the days before they were so scandalized. The imported ditties, the title tune, a mock-Journey anthem, a couple of hokey fillers, as airplay-designed as they are, offer only noxious fumes that dull the purified breezes Patty is so capable of producing.

So good luck Zack, in your search for the next Patty Smyth, and good luck Mike Chapman in your future endeavors. Good luck to *The Warrior* as it battles its way up the charts. But not too much. In fact, a whopping stiff might be just the antidote to Scandal's sudden success. Give Patty the chance to turn her head back around to quality songs like the ones that launched her star trip—songs that sing from the blood and settle in the loins like a poignant Windsong perfume commercial. Such songs are waiting to meet a voice like Patty's. And such a marriage would produce such sparks to light the summer night sky, such overnight ratings to make J. R. blush and Grant Tinker proud.

And so Patty, goodbye to you, until next week, same time, same station. ▣

This month's album:

Scandal, featuring Patty Smyth. **Warrior.** Columbia PG 39173

Patty Smyth: A glorius burst of musical energy

Gail Pool:

Magazines

Ethel Heins

Back in 1924, children's literature was not yet a "field," children were not yet a "market," and only a couple of hundred rather than a couple of thousand juvenile titles were published each year. It was an exciting time for children's literature, a field that was just beginning to receive real attention in this country. Children's departments in public libraries and school libraries were springing to life. And Bertha Mahoney Miller, who had established the Bookshop for Boys and Girls in Boston, started the **Horn Book,** a magazine dedicated to children's literature.

The early *Horn Book* was an eccentric publication. One never knew what one would find within its covers, from a short story by Sarah Orne Jewett to a short piece for children—perhaps something by Alice-Heidi, the doll who had "fallen out of Santa's pack as he flew over the Garden and was fortunate enough to land in the Bookshop."

But one always knew that one would find a celebration of books "that offered delight as well as nourishment" to the child. Before long all the staples of the present-day *Horn Book* had appeared: articles by authors about their work, critical essays about the role of children's books, analytical pieces about children's literature or illustration, and lists and short reviews of books selected for their literary quality. The *Horn Book* quickly made itself indispensable to all those involved in children's literature, especially librarians, who were closely involved in the magazine's development.

Today, the *Horn Book* has long since become an institution, the goal of most magazines that has also been the death of a few. A strong editorial identity—the key to a magazine's success—can also form a stranglehold, chaining a magazine to its past. The *Horn Book* is at just such a difficult stage in its life cycle. To move with the times and still adhere to its editorial identity is probably the main challenge confronting the magazine in its sixtieth year of publication.

Constancy has certainly been the keynote of the *Horn Book.* The magazine has maintained its original purpose, comparable standards, and even, to a large degree, a similar format through the tenure of five editors. But the field it serves has undergone enormous change in recent years.

Children's publishing today is big business: sales of juvenile titles amounted to $250 million in 1982. Numerous review media now perform a function the *Horn Book* once performed alone, and they are a part of that big business. Although the *Horn Book* may view itself as a different sort of publication than *School Library Journal* or the *Bulletin of the Center for Children's Books*—it is, after all, a small, independently owned, high-quality literary magazine—these review media offer it stiff competition both for readers and for advertising dollars. Librarians without time for leisurely essays about children's literature may turn for selection help to the most service-oriented review medium; school librarians, involved in selecting all media, may have less interest in a predominantly literary review. Publishers, increasingly selective in their efforts to reach a diminishing library market, may not always view the *Horn Book* as the most visible vehicle for their advertisements. The *Horn Book,* once a necessity in the library, is no longer viewed as indispensable. It has lost

The Horn Book **before (left) and after its cover redesign**

Gail Pool *holds an M.L.S. degree from Simmons College and presently works as a freelance writer based in Cambridge, Massachusetts.*

its once-secure niche.

Faced with declining circulation, the *Horn Book* has looked for ways to find new readers and to make itself more attractive to its old ones. Librarians still form the *Horn Book*'s largest single subscriber group, and the magazine has just changed its publication schedule to accommodate school librarians' needs: it will now appear in alternate months from September, avoiding the awkwardness (for schools) of two summer issues.

An audience that editor Ethel Heins—who retires this year after a decade in the position—has sought to encourage has been academics in the field of children's literature, a discipline the *Horn Book* helped develop by providing a forum for reflective essays. It is for these academics that Heins has continued to emphasize long literary essays which, she realizes, some librarians may find irrelevant and even boring. Though she is wary of the "pseudoscholarly" writing that is readily available in the field, she feels the *Horn Book* must offer something of interest to the academics who form an increasing proportion of its readership.

Yet another effort at audience diversification seems to be taking the *Horn Book* in the opposite direction. The magazine is seeking a more general readership by making itself available in bookstores. The goal is to reach parents, children's literature aficionados, illustrators—all those who want an education in children's literature.

Whether the *Horn Book* can succeed in pleasing librarians, academics, and general-interest readers with the same editorial content remains to be seen. But it is unlikely any magazine can both specialize and generalize at the same time. It seems to me that the *Horn Book* will have to identify its audience more precisely. This is not strictly a marketing problem. The magazine may need to reconsider who they are addressing and what, in contemporary terms, most needs saying. The issue is as much related to editorial as to marketing questions.

Although the *Horn Book* is a magazine with a cause—a magazine that believes in what it is doing more than most magazines do—it lacks vitality. To some degree, the problem is stylistic. The preponderantly positive book reviews—following a longtime editorial policy—are characterized by blandness, lacking punch. The longer essays seem stylistically mechanical: the same writer who comes to life in *Top of the News* moves all too formally and woodenly across the pages of the *Horn Book,* suggesting that a heavy editing process has deleted the writer's personality and left us with a toneless voice.

But the lack of vitality runs deeper: it is as if the magazine were refusing to be engaged. Although the brief editorials address some controversial topics ("Bits and Bytes—and Books?", April 1983, for example) the lengthy essays seem to be avoiding such issues. Many of the subjects, such as "Children: The Inexhaustible Source of Human Energy" or "Chesterton and Children's Reading," are of less than compelling interest, and the articles that do approach more biting issues often lack bite. This is strange in a field that is filled with unsettled and hotly debated issues, from sex in literature to computers in literacy.

The *Horn Book* has not built its reputation as a unique magazine as a selection tool or as a service publication—though it has served as both—but as a critical voice addressing the vital issues in children's literature and publishing. There is still room for that voice, I think, but it isn't being heard. It is safest to deal with the proven and perennial issues of yesterday such as "literary quality." To tackle the unmapped world of the contemporary is to run the risk of being trendy, foolish, or wrong. And yet it is only by taking that risk that the *Horn Book* can adhere to its identity: as an adventurous and pioneering magazine willing to explore new territories. ▣

A welcome effort

Children's Periodicals of the United States (Greenwood Press, 1984. 589p. $49.95) is a first and very welcome effort to bring some order to this field.

Edited by R. Gordon Kelly, the volume offers profiles of 423 titles published during the past two hundred years. The sketches are full and detailed, those for the longer-lived periodicals running to several pages. To avoid the "parochial and moral" judgments that Kelly feels characterize much of the previous work done in this field, the emphasis here is descriptive rather than evaluative. Entries are packed with specific information about the editorial content and publishing history of each magazine.

Since the sketches have been written by about fifty contributors, they vary both in style and in analytical quality. Most are well written; a few seem longwinded or vague. Some offer perceptive insight into "the social meanings mediated by the publications," while others seem a bit naive.

The entries, all of which are signed, are arranged alphabetically, which allows for ready access to titles. A historical introduction and chronological index help compensate for the alphabetical organization.

The guide's real strength lies in the wealth of information it provides. For its full descriptions of the magazines, its bibliographies, publication histories, and location sources (libraries holding complete or nearly complete files), *Children's Periodicals of the United States* is a much needed work.

Norman Stevens:

Our Profession

At the start of the third year of this column, I find library literature alive and well. The short summer break leaves me with a profusion of interesting material to consider. Some is reviewed here; some is set aside for another column; some, regretfully, must be passed over. Several good basic textbooks, a variety of material on library automation, and several of the increasingly popular essays of personal testimony from a range of librarians are among the volumes that have fallen by the wayside. Sometimes, though, personal testimony is so entertaining and informative that it merits review. That is certainly the case with R. C. Benge's **Confessions of a Lapsed Librarian,** the most outrageous work of library literature that I have read in some time. An outspoken radical English librarian, Benge manages to cover everything from dead cats and tramps in English libraries to sex with Nigerian women. Much of what he has to say in this very personal recounting, especially in the chapters on his experiences in World War II and in Africa, tell more about Benge and his view of the world-at-large, than they do about Benge's views of our profession. That is just as well. When he discusses his experiences in British public libraries and in British professional education, his radical view of librarianship comes across loud and clear. Disillusioned by the failures of Communism in Europe, Benge turned to the Third World to make his contributions to librarianship and spent much of his subsequent career in Trinidad, Ghana, and Nigeria. His sense of purpose in making those choices is not always reflected in the initial portions of the text. He concludes with an essay on "The Mystique of Information" and another on "Library Objectives in Africa" which forcefully present his philosophy of librarianship and challenge us to think about all that he has reported about his life and times. One can hardly wait for Benge's colleague Eric Moon, who promoted this book, to recount his library experiences in England and in the colonies.

Just as personal, although tame by comparison, is Sheila Nickerson's **Writers in the Public Library** which recounts her year as a writer-in-residence in Alaska. With support from the Alaska State Library and the Alaska State Council on the Arts, Nickerson spent a year visiting public libraries in fourteen communities scattered across the state. A writer, not a radical, Nickerson's cause is the belief that the "time is overdue for the professional writer to play a larger role in helping librarians to make the library a place where both reading and writing can unlock the human record, awaken a sense of purpose and self-identity." The depth of that belief is reflected as she recounts her experiences in that role. It is also reflected in her fine summary of similar programs in other public libraries in the United States, the consultant in poetry program at the Library of Congress, and related activities and events. The summary, added to the obvious value of Nickerson's Alaskan experiences, make *Writers in the Public Library* a useful guide for librarians seriously interested in doing more to promote reading and writing and to strengthen the bond between librarians and writers.

Although not as directly personal as Benge's and Nickerson's biographical tales, Genevieve Casey's **Library Services for the Aging** carries the same sense of purpose, built around a strong personal conviction. Casey's work makes a direct and concise case for the contemporary American public library to develop and/or strengthen its service for the aging. She neatly balances an examination of such general themes as the demography of aging, the intellectual competence of older adults, education for older adults, and the meaning of aging, against a consideration of such professional themes as trends in public library service to the aging, library service in nursing homes, education for library service to the aging, and planning library service for this important segment of our population. Casey has done a marvelous job of packing her text with an array of detail and statistics that are very much to the point, never confusing or overshadowing the point she is trying to make. She considers the existing data and studies on public library service to the aging and raises some challenging questions about the implications of those studies. She also analyzes some recent data she has helped gather from eight states with large aging populations. Above all, she offers her own conviction about the significance of quality service to the aging, along with many sound suggestions for improving public library service to these citizens.

Evelyn Geller's **Forbidden Books In American Public Libraries, 1876–1939,** like most works derived from doctoral disser-

Norman Stevens *is university librarian at the University of Connecticut and the author of* Communication Throughout Libraries.

"Strange! I've tried all the adult book shops in town and not one has even *heard* of Dostoyevsky."

tations, is anything but personal. Yet her careful analysis of the change in our professional attitudes towards censorship from 1876, when the newly founded American Library Association sought to avoid controversial literature and endorsed the concept of the librarian as a moral censor, to 1939 when ALA adopted its first Library Bill of Rights, provides a view of many librarians that standard biographical sources fail to reveal. After a short prologue on the moral values espoused by the Boston Public Library of 1853, the first major public library in this country, Geller divides her examination of the issue into three periods: the first, from 1876 to 1900, when librarians were concerned with neutrality and avoided controversial literature; the second, from 1900 to 1922, when closed-shelf collections were seen as an effective means of dealing with competing demands; and the third, from 1923 to 1939, which saw the emergence of the ideology of freedom. Geller's review is based on, among other things, a page-by-page analysis of the major library journals over the entire period and is carefully set against the broader background of major social and literary changes in the United States. Although not as lively as Benge's tales, Geller's text makes for good reading because she makes the individuals and the incidents she describes come alive. Throughout the text Geller seeks to determine why and how such a dramatic change in attitude took place and how librarianship chooses its values. Some of Geller's conclusions (e.g., that there is a long-term trend towards greater freedom of expression in sexual matters but towards greater control of political expression) are not a direct result of her study and are open to question. In general, though, all of the points she raises challenge our views on a number of vital questions. That is perhaps most true of her concluding discussion of the elitist-populist, neutrality-advocacy, and censorship-freedom dilemmas which have been, and are, such a significant part of our thoughts about the provision of controversial material to readers.

Contemporary American librarianship is often a blend of the theoretical and the practical. Just as the second half of Nickerson's work complements her personal experiences by speaking to the practical question of how to promote better relationships between librarians and writers, so Linda Schexnaydre and Nancy Burns' **Censorship** complements Geller's historical view of censorship issues. A specific guide to planning a one-day workshop on censorship in libraries designed to educate administrators, board members, librarians, and teachers on dealing effectively with challenges to intellectual freedom, *Censorship* offers much practical material in a compact format. There is virtually no supporting theoretical justification for the authors' clearly held views. Instead the emphasis is entirely on the techniques of conducting an effective workshop that will train participants to handle censorship challenges more successfully. In that respect *Censorship* seems to succeed, and may be the most useful of this month's books; as entertainment, neither *Censorship* nor the other three works can come close to Benge's fascinating sketch of his life. ▣

This month's books:

Benge, R. C. **Confessions of a Lapsed Librarian.** Scarecrow, 1984. 223p. $16. ISBN 0-8108-1676-8 LC 83-20405

Casey, Genevieve. **Library Services for the Aging.** Shoe String Press, 1984. 168p. $21.50, pa $14.50. ISBN 0-208-01946-4; 0-208-01947-2 LC 83-16218

Geller, Evelyn. **Forbidden Books in American Public Libraries, 1876–1939.** Greenwood Press, 1984. 234p. $29.95. ISBN 0-313-23808-1 LC 83-12566

Nickerson, Sheila. **Writers in the Public Library.** Shoe String Press, 1984. 276p. $24.50. ISBN 0-208-01872-7 LC 83-14859

Schexnaydre, Linda and Nancy Burns. **Censorship: A Guide for Successful Workshop Planning.** Oryx Press, 1984. 114p. $18.50. ISBN 0-89774-093-9

James Rettig:

Current Reference Books

Correspondence and review copies for this column should be directed to James Rettig, University Library, Box 8198, University of Illinois at Chicago, Chicago, IL 60680.

The Book of Hierarchies, by Lisbeth Mark. New York: Morrow, 1984. 137p. $13.95, pa$5.95. 0-688-02208-1; 0-688-02646-X 83-63030

Hierarchical lists the compiler "found appealing, amusing, and enlightening" make up *The Book of Hierarchies*. This good idea is treat-

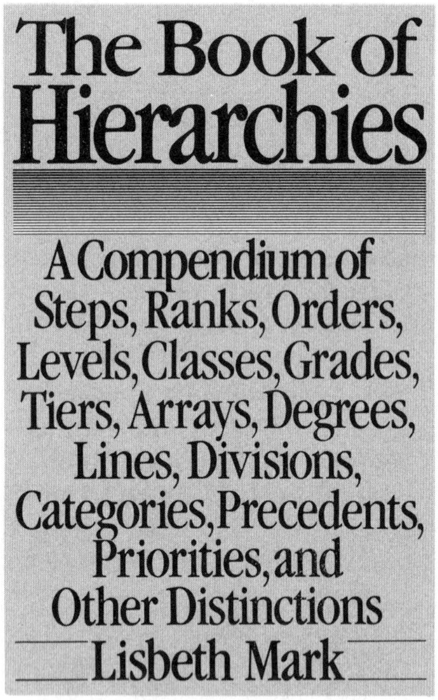

ed glibly, undermining one's confidence in the book's authority. For example, the book opens with the hierarchy of angels and then spoils it with an anecdote about a Jimmy Stewart movie and the supposition that if a guardian angel saves Jimmy Stewart from drowning it moves up a notch in the angelic hierarchy. This supposition contradicts the quotation from Saint Hildegard which states that the angels' hierarchical places are fixed by God. The supposition also contradicts the stated hierarchy, which does not include a rank of guardian angel. Nonetheless, librarians can use this book to find out the relative ranks of orders of British knighthood, grades of beef, champagne bottle sizes, car sizes, judo belts, the Beaufort wind force scale, or Masonic degrees. But they will find these only through luck and fortitude, for the book has no index.

James Rettig *is head reference librarian, University of Illinois at Chicago.*

Callahan's College Guide to Athletics and Academics in America, by Timothy R. Callahan. New York: Harper, 1984. 259p. $17.95, pa $9.95. 0-06-015249-4; 0-06-464081-7 83-48333

First published privately in 1981 and limited to schools in the Northeast, *Callahan's Guide* now covers the athletic offerings of 240 colleges. "Academics" in the title is an afterthought, for each college's one-page entry all but ignores academic programs. Rather, each entry lists the school's men's and women's intercollegiate sports, NCAA or NAIA division, coach's name, conference record, recent won-lost records, national rank, number of athletic grants, and phone number. Criteria for inclusion are not explained, making it impossible to understand the presence of Notre Dame but the absence of the University of Michigan. While *The Blue Book of College Athletics* (Akron: Rohrich Corp.) omits rankings and the number of scholarships, it gives more information about the athletic programs and facilities of many more colleges. Furthermore, college admissions offices can supply information about both athletic and academic programs. At best, *Callahan's* is marginal, far less important to a reference collection than a college's athletic program is to its overall mission.

The Child Care Encyclopedia, by Penelope Leach. New York: Knopf, 1984. 708p. $22.95. 0-394-52532-9 83-48013

The author of the highly regarded *Your Baby and Child* (Knopf, 1978) has heeded readers' requests "for 'something similar which deals with older children as well.'" In A-to-Z order, she explains how to cope with accidents, eating, infection, sleep, toilet training, and the usual gamut of expected and unexpected physical needs of children from birth through the teens. Clear articles, brimming with common sense, explain problems thoroughly and treat not only the child's physical needs, but also social and emotional needs (e.g., divorce and remarriage of parents, adjustment to school) from both the child's and the parents' point of view. Numerous *see* references overcome the lack of an index. The lengthy articles fulfill Leach's intent to "contribute to the kind of thinking and family discussion which will help avoid problems." However her decision to cluster most discussion of sex under "Adolescence" means many parents will find the information when trying to solve a problem they might have prevented. Because this serves both ready-reference and more general needs, it merits consideration for both reference and circulating collections.

The Complete Book of U.S. Presidents, by William A. DeGregorio. New York: Dembner Books, dist. by Norton, 1984. 691p. $22.50. 0-934878-36-6 83-23201
The Presidents, edited by Henry F. Graff. New York: Scribner, 1984. 700p. $65. 0-684-17607-6 83-20225

Although *The Complete Book* will invariably remind users of Joseph Kane's *Facts About the Presidents* (4th ed., New York: H.W. Wilson, 1981), their differences are as great as their similarities. DeGregorio's more discursive approach treats each president in terms of thirty-nine categories, some not touched on by Kane (e.g., capsule biographies of cabinet members, quotes from contemporaries praising or damning the man). Without embellishment or interpretation, DeGregorio reports facts in a telegraphic style. An index, principally of personal names, supplements the arrangement of topics under each president. Neither Kane nor *The Complete Book,* which complement each other in emphasis and arrangement, creates a cohesive picture of a president's life or achievements. For such a view, one must go to *The Presidents* or a similar source.

Edited by Columbia University historian Henry Graff, *The Presidents* consists of biographies of every president except Ronald Reagan. Thirty-five specialists wrote the long biographies (each approximately fifteen large, two-columned pages). It appears that the authors were given considerable editorial freedom, since some emphasize a topical and others a chronological approach. The biographies evaluate and interpret the presidencies and recommend further reading. Librarians may balk at including this in the reference collection since the *Dictionary of American Biography* covers all of the deceased presidents (except Truman, Eisenhower, and Johnson). However *The Presidents* merits recommendation since its biographies are more recent than the *DAB*'s and since it offers a second perspective.

Eerdmans' Book of Famous Prayers, compiled by Veronica Zundel. Grand Rapids: Eerdmans, 1984. 125p. $12.95. 0-8028-3593-7

One would think that in a medium-sized academic library at a Catholic university it would be easy to find a copy of St. Francis of Assisi's prayer for peace or the Gaelic blessing beginning "May the road rise to meet you. . . . " But neither was readily available; indeed, in the latter case the only source available was an Abbey Press catalog in a staff room. A thorough table of contents and indexes by author and theme make it a breeze to find the famous prayers in this anthology. One hundred prayers, all from Christian authors, are organized chronologically. They are accompanied by brief biographical headnotes about their authors. Prayers have been selected from Thomas Aquinas, Martin Luther, John Wesley, Cardinal Newman, Thomas Merton, and many others. Anthologies are problematical additions to reference collections, but this one can be useful.

Emily Post's Etiquette, by Elizabeth L. Post. 14th ed. New York: Harper, 1984. 1,018p. $16.95, thumb-indexed $19.95. 0-06-181683-3; 0-06-181684-1 83-48375

The update of *The New Emily Post's Etiquette* (Funk & Wagnalls, 1975) takes into account recent social changes, especially the fact that women have permanently entered the work force at all levels. Thus it pays much more attention to behavior on the job and in business situations and much less atention to dress. Keeping in step with the times, a new section on unmarried couples who live together and an expanded section on divorce have joined the book's mainstays—explanations of socially proper seating arrangements, forms of address, and the duties of a good host or hostess. Whatever the effects of the women's movement have been, Post avers that "femininity is still more attractive in a woman than masculine capability and in no way denies the fact that her helplessness is a thing of the past." This never interferes with common sense; hence a woman is permitted to give a waiter her own order rather than convey it through her escort. The tone is matter-of-fact and the advice sensible, save for an unconscionable leniency toward smokers. People know, of course, how to comport themselves in their everyday world. However, everyone gets a bit apprehensive approaching new situations and *Emily Post's Etiquette,* updated for the eighties, can help put them at ease.

Fatherhood U.S.A., by Debra G. Klinman and Rhiana Kohl. New York: Garland, 1984. 321p. pa $14.95. 0-8240-9012-8 84-7986

The compilers are staff members of The Fatherhood Project, a nationwide research project launched in 1981 at Bank Street College "to encourage the development of a wide range of options for male involvement in childrearing." They discovered hundreds of resources that share their purpose and have organized the resources by type. Two-thirds of the book consists of directories of organizations that relate to various aspects of fathering, including expectant fathers, school-father cooperation, college courses on the male role, support and discussion groups, divorced fathers' rights groups, and programs for working fathers. This last section is disturbingly small, distressing evidence that although women's roles have expanded greatly, society still looks at men almost exclusively as laborers. The activities of many of the organizations are described in detail. The final section of the book is a selective, briefly annotated bibliography of books treating the same topics as the directories. The information in *Fatherhood U.S.A.* is, the compilers admit, incomplete; hence the perforated "Feedback Form" which readers can use to send them additions. Its incompleteness testifies to the difficulty in locating these organizations and, by extension, the importance of adding this book to library collections.

Football Rankings, compiled by Lowell R. Greunke. Jefferson, N.C.: McFarland, 1984. 196p. $15.95. 0-89950-108-7 83-25595

Bar bets, friendly arguments between Ohio State and University of Michigan alumni, and the curiosity that lists inherently inspire—all can be settled by *Football Rankings.* It reprints every weekly Associated Press ranking of the top twenty college gridiron teams from 1936 through 1983. Lists indicate the number of first-place votes and total number of points received by each team. From 1961 through 1967, when AP ranked only the top ten, the lists include other unranked teams that received votes. An index by school allows a fan to trace a favorite team. Fans place stock in polls, despite the silliness exemplified by the 1971 preseason poll in which Northwestern received one first-place vote and was thus ranked twentieth until the first kickoff. This compilation is a convenient source for some of college football's better known off-field history.

Foundations, edited by Harold M. Keele and Joseph C. Kiger. Westport, Conn.: Greenwood, 1984. 516p. $49.95. 0-313-22556-7 83-10750 ISSN 0271-9509 (The Greenwood encyclopedia of American institutions, no. 8)

The most recent volume in this series maintains the standard of accuracy set by its predecessors. Foundation officials, historians, and others wrote the brief histories of the 234 largest active foundations in the United States, all with 1980–81 assets of $30 million or more. These award fifty-five per cent of all foundation grants annually. The histories recount the founder's purposes in creating the foundation, and describe each foundation's growth, funding activities, and governance. Recommended sources for additional information, typically annual reports and statements filed with the IRS, are also provided. Some of the founders are adulated; one might falsely conclude that philanthropists never have faults or weaknesses. Appendixes list the foundations by value of assets, family connection, location, founding date, and name changes. The index lists personal names, corporate names, and subjects. The subject entries lead to information about the foundations' attitudes towards certain types of beneficiaries. Thus, although a history, this can also be used with other tools in planning grant-seeking strategies.

Funk & Wagnalls Speller. New York: Harper, 1984. 204p. pa $4.95. 0-06-091144-1 83-48465

Only users of microcomputers with spelling correction programs can risk being without one. There should be one on every desk, beside every typewriter, and at every reference desk for those occasions (or is it ocassions?) when the spelling or syllabication of a word is not known. At such times a spelling dictionary comes speedily to the rescue. *Funk & Wagnalls* treats more than 30,000 words without indicating the accented syllables, making it an also-ran when compared to a well-worn personal favorite, *Follett Vest-Pocket Word Divider* (Follett, 1964) with 50,000 words, accents included. Nonetheless, *Funk & Wagnalls* is a serviceable dictionary, destined to replace at least one tattered copy of *Follett.* However, the paperback format of *Funk & Wagnalls* is a drawback in heavy, long-term use.

Her Way, by Mary-Ellen Siegel. 2nd ed. Chicago: American Library Association, 1984. 415p. $35. 0-8389-0396-7 83-22375

Astronaut Sally Ride has replaced Joan of Arc as the portrait on the binding and 125 biographies in the first edition (1976) have been dropped because they have been judged sexist, racist, poorly written, or inaccurate. With the addition of 322 titles, *Her Way* is now a guide to some 1,700 children's biographies of 1,100 women who can serve as positive role models for young girls. New subjects include Rosalyn Carter, Jane Pauley, and Donna Summer. As in the first edition, a capsule biography precedes the brief annotations, which include grade level. A section annotating collective biographies follows the alphabetical section of individual biographies. Indexes by nationality and occupation remain and an author-title index has replaced the name index.

The multiple indexing approaches make this useful in story-hour programming as well as in helping boys and girls select good biographies of famous women past and present.

McGraw-Hill Concise Encyclopedia of Science and Technology, edited by Sybil P. Parker. New York: McGraw-Hill, 1984. 2,065p. $89.50. 0-07-045482-5 83-26794
McGraw-Hill Dictionary of Science and Engineering, edited by Sybil P. Parker. New York: McGraw-Hill, 1984. 942p. $32.50. 0-07-045483-3 83-26768

These offspring from comprehensive works exhibit their parents' best qualities of accuracy and currentness, offer ready-reference convenience to all libraries, and are affordable for branches and other small libraries. The *Encyclopedia* excerpts nearly all of the articles in the fifteen-volume *McGraw-Hill Encyclopedia of Science and Technology* (reviewed in *WLB,* September 1982), depending heavily upon their opening paragraphs. The 7,300 brief articles, many illustrated, range widely over scientific and technical fields. A 30,000-entry index follows a selective bibliography and appendixes of measurement conversion tables, abbreviations, mathematical constants, and other useful data. This is more comprehensive than *Van Nostrand's Scientific Encyclopedia* (5th ed., Van Nostrand Reinhold, 1976) which is not as strong on technology.

The *Dictionary* was distilled from the *McGraw-Hill Dictionary of Science and Technology* (3d ed., 1984) by using a smaller type size and selecting approximately 36,000 of its 98,500 terms, their definitions reproduced verbatim. As in the original, an abbreviation identifies the field to which each meaning applies. Appropriate *see* references have been made. Few libraries owning the parent works need the offspring; others will want them as the next best thing.

The 100 Best Companies to Work For in America, by Robert Levering, Milton Moskowitz, and Michael Katz. Reading, Mass.: Addison-Wesley, 1984. 372p. $17.95. 0-201-15774-8 84-322

Undoubtedly since this book's May publication, the personnel offices of

The 100 Best Companies have been the one hundred busiest. The trio who wrote *Everybody's Business* (Harper, 1980), an anecdotal look at the history of American corporations, interviewed top officers and employees from throughout the organization to select the best, based on the criteria of pay, benefits, job security, opportunity for advancement, and ambience. A header above the company write-up rates it in these five areas on a five-point scale and summarizes in a few words its biggest advantage and disadvantage. Each write-up explains the company's philosophy and describes what it is like to work there, information job seekers crave but can rarely find. Companies range from giants like IBM to veritable cottage industries like Celestial Seasonings, from the very specialized like the Los Angeles Dodgers to the widely diversified like Johnson Wax. In addition to indexes by place and type of business, an appendix lists the top ten companies in each of the five categories. One wishes such information were available on many more companies.

Shakespearean Criticism, vol. 1, edited by Laurie L. Harris and Mark W. Scott. Detroit: Gale, 1984. 683p. $70. 0-8103-6125-6 84-4010
Literature Criticism from 1400 to 1800, vol. 1, edited by Dennis Poupard. Detroit: Gale, 1984. $68. 0-8103-6100-0 83-20504 ISSN 0740-2880

The formula that has worked successfully in *Contemporary Literary Criticism* and *Twentieth Century Literary Criticism* has been applied to Shakespeare's works. The debut volume covers five plays including *Hamlet* and *Henry IV,* parts I and II. The *Hamlet* section spans more than two hundred double-columned pages. Excerpts from critics from Shakespeare's age to the present follow a brief introduction on the play's history and the major critical issues surrounding it. Despite their students' inability to tell the wheat from the chaff of Shakespearean criticism, high school and undergraduate teachers persist in assigning term papers on Shakespeare. If students can be convinced they need more than just the excerpts, *Shakespearean Criticism* can help them sift through the criticism, although the lack of a thematic index all but negates its usefulness for subject access. Nevertheless, it is more manageable than either the subject catalog or a bibliography on Shakespeare. The same formula has been applied to world authors from 1400 through 1799, extending the coverage of Gale's literary criticism series from Chaucer's death to the present. Approximately three hundred authors, mostly European and many of them English, have been selected for treatment in *Literary Criticism.* Among the first volume's sixteen subjects are Aphra Behn, Daniel Defoe, Samuel Richardson, and Ts'ao Hsuĕh-sh'in. The copious selection of critical excerpts, from twelve pages for minor authors up to 112 pages for Swift, implies that many authors will appear in but one volume of *Literary Criticism,* unlike *Twentieth-Century Literary Criticism,* which is often updated. The excerpts come from respected critics and can be useful, painless introductions to secondary sources. The title index is essential. A cumulative author index covers fifteen Gale literary criticism guides. None of these collections of excerpts replaces the originals; they merely serve as helpful introductions.

Television Comedy Series, by Joel Eisner and David Krinsky. 866p. $49.95. Jefferson, N.C.: McFarland, 1984. 0-89950-088-9 83-42901

Television Comedy Series differs from other TV series encyclopedias in scope and purpose by limiting itself to about 150 sitcom series and by excluding those presented live, those introduced after the 1979–80 season, those not in syndication, and those "banned" for offending various ethnic groups. Because of its historical significance, "Amos 'n' Andy" is the one exception to the last two criteria. The compilers claim complete success in listing every episode of these series. Series headnotes list the dates the series originally aired, number of episodes, producer, cast, director, summary of its basic situation, and success in syndication. The titled episodes, arranged by date of production, include names of writers and guest stars and a brief plot summary. Using the extensive personal name index, one can track an actor's sitcom appearances. Browsing through the plot summaries, one realizes how nearly sufficient the introduction's list of seventy-two stock plots is in describing sitcoms. Amidst much dross (e.g., "My Mother the Car") there are bits of gold (e.g., "The Honeymooners"), with both gold and dross treated factually.

The Third Reich, 1933–1939. Santa Barbara: ABC-Clio, 1984. 239p. $28.50. 0-87436-379-9 83-21527
The Third Reich at War. Santa Barbara: ABC-Clio, 1984. 270p. $28.50. 0-87436-393-4 83-27168

These companion bibliographies of articles treat the period spanning Hitler's rise as chancellor and the burning of the Reichstag to the end of the thousand-year Reich just twenty-two years later in the fire and rubble of Berlin. The citations and their annotations have been drawn from the extensive ABC-Clio database. Topical chapters give order to the 932 items in the first and the 1,061 items in the second bibliography. Thorough keyword subject indexes and author indexes enhance the topical approach. Interest in the era will likely increase as the fortieth anniversary of the end of the war approaches.

Third World Resource Directory, edited by Thomas P. Fenton and Mary J. Heffron. Maryknoll, N.Y.: Orbis Books, 1984. 283p. pa $12.95. 0-88344-509-3 83-6783

United States activities in Central America and other regions are likely to be significant issues in this fall's political campaigns. The resources listed in this guide can be used to buttress the arguments of those who charge that the United States does more harm than good in the Third World. Briefly annotated listings for organizations, books, periodicals, pamphlets, audiovisual materials, curriculum guides, and simulation games are organized by world region in the first half of the book and by topic (e.g., food and hunger, human rights, transnational corporations, women) in the second half. Many items were produced by religious and other special interest groups. Some of the annotations mention United States involvement in foreign countries and a few cite Soviet involvement. If one recognizes the compilers' political point of view, this directory can be used effectively to find information sources on a current hot topic.

Torture in the Eighties. Amnesty International (New York: Dodd, Mead, distributor), 1984. 263p. pa $5.95. 0-939994-06-2

From the cover's grim photograph of wrists manacled in steel and stretched by a steel chain high above the victim's head through to the last page, *Torture in the Eighties* chronicles tale after tale of the physical indignities that sixty-six nations have imposed upon their citizens. Whereas the summaries of policies in the *Amnesty International Annual Report* (reviewed in *WLB,* February 1984) outrage one's sense of justice, Torture's accounts of practices savage one's sensibilities. Even though described in a reportorial manner, some countries' routine techniques of dealing with political prisoners are unspeakably horrific. Eight pages of grisly photographs of victims reinforce this. Introductory chapters describe efforts to combat torture, focusing on case studies of Northern Ireland and Brazil. The two Amnesty International reports complement one another and offer authoritative, objective accounts of emotionally charged issues.

Twentieth Century Music, by Richard Burbank. New York: Facts on File, 1984. 485p. $35. 0-87196-464-3 80-25040

In his lively anecdotal introduction surveying the development of twentieth-century Western music, Nicolas Slonimsky, the irrepressible and witty sage of music reference works, commends colleague Burbank's work and expresses his hope "to bring up to date the events tabulated in *Music Since 1900*" (4th ed.

Scribner, 1971), Slonimsky's own chronology, which covered the years 1900 through 1969. Until then, and even after, one must second his endorsement of Burbank with its 1979 cutoff date. Each year's events are grouped into six categories: opera; dance; instrumental and vocal music; births, deaths, and debuts; and related events. Facts are chronicled in a clear and lively style, exemplified by E. Power Biggs's death notice: "He also performed contemporary music, edited music, loved baroque music, and hated electronic organs." The index permits retrieval of thousands of facts, although the lack of topical subdivisions under very active performers or orchestras (e.g., eighty-two dates under Serge Koussevitzky) means many look-ups in some cases. Photographs of composers and performers add to the enjoyment this useful chronology will give music lovers.

Union List of Film Periodicals, edited by Anna Brady, Richard Wall, and Carolynn N. Weiner. Westport, Conn.: Greenwood, 1984. 316p. $35. 0-313-23702-6 83-22585

Although some librarians have predicted that printed union lists of serials have no future in the incipient post-Gutenburg electronic age, the day is yet to arrive. Until it does, printed union lists will continue to play an important role in document delivery, an area of library service that lags far behind libraries' success in identifying documents. This union list of more than a thousand film periodicals in thirty-five American libraries will simplify the work of scholars and librarians in locating and obtaining obscure items. Entries list title, place of publication, ISSN, publication dates, title changes, and library holdings. An asterisk tags incomplete holdings statements. The computer-printout typeface conveys information in a legible albeit offputting way. The titles are indexed by country of publication. This list will give an added dimension to collections where there is particular interest in film.

The Unlisted Market Guide, 1982– . Unlisted Market Service Corporation (30 Glen Head Rd., Glen Head, NY 11545). 2v. looseleaf $195/yr.

Unlisted Market Guide is an investor's guide to corporations whose stock is traded over-the-counter. Most of the companies have paid a $750 fee to be included, a practice similar to the Moody's manuals. Although it now treats only about 350 companies, many of them are not in *Moody's OTC Industrial Manual* which covers more than 1,000. Both services offer a year-end balance sheet, a list of officers, the stock's price range over a year, stock performance data, and address and telephone number. *Market Guide* excels by describing the companies' services or products, their operations, the results of those operations, and recent developments. A fact box preceding each description lists price range, share earnings or loss, price-to-earnings ratio, monthly trading volume, revenue per share, equity per share, and number of shares outstanding. Although the typeface and word-processor spacing are unattractive, it is easier to pick out discrete bits of information than from the densely printed pages of *Moody's*. *Market Guide* reports are updated quarterly and it is rapidly gaining on *Moody's*, adding approximately fifteen new reports in each weekly update. This dynamic guide, a welcome addition to the family of corporate and investment information sources, will get even better as it gets bigger.

Women of the Future, by Betty King. Metuchen, N.J.: Scarecrow, 1984. 273p. $18.50. 0-8108-1664-4 83-20130

A selective guide to science fiction novels, novellas, and English-language anthologies that have women as principal characters, *Women of the Future* approaches the subject by decade. After a preliminary chapter on the history of women in science fiction, six chapters cover the 1930s through the 1980s. Selected books of each decade are described in a standard format listing the main character's name, physical characteristics, and mental/emotional characteristics and summarizing the plot. Less important works are relegated to unannotated bibliographies at the ends of the chapters. Indexes to characteristics, themes, titles, and authors facilitate the book's use as a self-selection, reader's advisory tool. Libraries with a strong interest in either science fiction or women's studies will find this worth acquiring. ▣

Library World

Announcements

The Western Illinois Library System has elected new officers. They are: **Viletta Hillery,** pres.; **Elvira Hulin,** vice-pres.; **Cheryl Culbertson,** secy.; and **Ruth Schillinger,** treas.

Stephen Kochoff has received the 1984 George Virgil Fuller Award from the Columbia Univ. SLS. The award is given to a doctor of library science degree candidate who shows both high achievement on the comprehensive examinations and competence in planning a dissertation designed to make a significant contribution to library literature. Kochoff is presently marketing manager for Turner Subscriptions.

The Council of National Library and Information Associations, Inc., has elected officers for the coming year. They are: **Adele Lerner,** vice-chair/chair-elect; **Jack Ellenberger,** secy./treas.; and **Norma Yueh,** director.

John David Marshall is the 1984 recipient of the Tennessee LA's Frances Neel Cheney Award for outstanding contributions to the world of books and librarianship. He is a professor at Todd Library, Middle Tenn. State Univ., Murfreesboro.

Effie Lee Morris has been given the 1984 Women's National Book Association award. The award is presented biennially to a living American woman who has made an enduring and unique contribution to the world of books and through books to society. She presently teaches at Mills College.

Robert Palmer has been awarded the first Fulbright grant as a librarian to the People's Republic of China for 1984–85 by the Board of Foreign Scholarships and the United States Information Agency. He will be a consultant, teacher, and coordinator of seminars and workshops. Palmer previously served as a Fulbright librarian in Kathmandu, Nepal and Kabul, Afghanistan.

Gail Peck has been chosen as the first Sara Rebecca Reed Memorial Scholar at the Indiana Univ. SLIS. The award will be given annually to an outstanding doctoral student in memory of Sara Rebecca Reed, who was associate dean of the Indiana Univ. GLS from 1971 to 1975. Peck, in her second year of study at Indiana, was formerly project manager and library services manager with the Pittsburgh Regional Library Center.

Nancy Van House has been awarded a National Science Foundation grant for a study of occupational segregation among information professionals. She is a professor at the Univ. of Calif., Berkeley SLIS.

New Posts

John Amrhein, formerly university librarian at Kutztown Univ., Penn., has been appointed library director at Calif. State College, Stanislaus. He had been with Kutztown since 1971 and was previously circulation librarian at Kent State Univ. in Ohio.

Daniel Armstrong has been named director of the Tippecanoe County (Ind.) PL. He was formerly director of the Plymouth (Ind.) PL.

Robert Brooks has been appointed director of the Guggenheim Memorial Library, Monmouth College, N.J. He was formerly acquisitions librarian at Monmouth.

June Iris Brown is now assistant humanities bibliographer for Howard-Tilton Memorial Library, Tulane Univ., New Orleans.

John Callahan has been named head of technical services for the Virginia Beach PL. He was previously librarian at the Great Neck branch of the Virginia Beach PL.

Sara Castro-Klaren is the new chief of the Library of Congress Hispanic Division. She formerly taught Latin American and comparative literature at Dartmouth College, where she also served as chair of the department of Spanish and Portuguese from 1979 to 1982.

Elena Cevallos has been appointed acting assistant dean of public services at Hofstra Univ. (N.Y.) Library.

Emil Ciallella, former library director of the Central Falls (R.I.) Free PL, is now chief librarian of the Richard Salter Storrs Library, Longmeadow, Massachusetts.

Oakley Coburn is the new head librarian at Sandor Teszler Library, Wofford College, Spartanburg, S.C. He had been circulation librarian at Wofford from 1972 to 1976.

Kenneth Cooper has been named chief executive of the British Library. He was formerly director-general of the British National Fed-

John Amrhein

Carol Desch

Richard Dick

Paul Ericsson

Arlene Schwartz

eration of Building Trades Employers. Cooper succeeds **Sir Harry Hookway,** who retired.

Robert Costa, formerly director of the Cambria County (Penn.) library system, has assumed the position of city librarian for the Richmond (Va.) PL. He replaces **Howard Smith,** who retired.

Kathleen Cotter has been appointed professional assistant librarian in the reference/reader's advisor department of the Providence (R.I.) PL. She was formerly assistant to the dean of the University of R.I. GLS, as well as a member of the library's reference staff.

William Davis, public library consultant for the North Texas library system, Ft. Worth, has accepted the position of LSCA coordinator for the State Library of Iowa.

Carol Desch has joined the N.Y. State Library as assistant in library services at the Division of Library Development. She was formerly head of reference and information services at the Bethlehem PL, Delmar, New York.

Patrick Dewey is now administrative librarian for the Maywood (Ill.) PL.

Richard Dick has been appointed director of local systems and microcomputer applications for OCLC. He was most recently executive vice-president of Avatar Systems, Inc., a company which he helped found in 1981 and which was recently acquired by OCLC.

Richard Dougherty, director of the Univ. of Michigan Library, has been named acting dean of the Univ. of Michigan SLS. He succeeds **Russell Bidlack,** who retired.

Paul Drake has been appointed head of the serials/interlibrary loan department at Roger Williams College Library, Bristol, R.I. He was formerly coordinator of the Western Interrelated LS at Warwick (R.I.) PL.

Susan Eilering is now reference/collection development librarian (engineering) at the Columbia Univ. libraries.

Christine Erdmann has been named public services librarian at Beloit College libraries, Beloit, Wisconsin. She was formerly science and special collections librarian at Whittier College, Whittier, California.

Paul Ericsson has been appointed head of technical services at Westport (Conn.) PL.

David Espenscheid has joined the staff of Liberty Baptist College library as cataloger.

Ann Friedman is now Rockville (Md.) regional librarian. She was formerly system planning officer and assistant coordinator of children's services for the Montgomery County (Md.) Department of Public Libraries.

Janice Holladay, formerly acting assistant director for reader services at the Univ. of Rochester (N.Y.), has been named assistant director.

Michael LaCroix has been appointed director of library services for Wingate College, Wingate, N.C. He was previously director of library services at Greensboro College, Greensboro, North Carolina.

Robert Lang has assumed the position of adult services librarian for the Homewood (Ala.) PL. He was formerly reference librarian for the Houston-Love Memorial Library, Dothan, Alabama.

Bruce Langdon has been named director of libraries for Cleveland State Univ. He was formerly director of the Wilson Library at the Univ. of Minnesota.

Kathleen Lohman has been appointed associate director of the library development group at the Illinois State Library. She was previously associated with the Dolton (Ill.) PL as administrative librarian.

Shirley Long is now branch coordinator for the Providence (R.I.) PL. She was formerly head librarian at the Washington Park branch of the Providence PL.

Holly Lovejoy-Nesvold has been promoted to technical services librarian at Beloit College libraries, Beloit, Wisconsin. She was formerly a technical services staff member.

Alexander Moyer is now assistant acquisitions librarian for Howard-Tilton Memorial Library, Tulane Univ., New Orleans.

George Needham has become director of the Fairfield County District Library, Lancaster, Ohio. He was formerly coordinator for adult services at Charleston County (S.C.) library.

Patrick O'Brien has been appointed director of the Dallas PL. He was formerly director of the Cuyahoga County (Ohio) PL, and prior to that was assistant commissioner for the Central Library and Cultural Center in Chicago.

Diane Parker has accepted the position of library director at Western Washington Univ., Bellingham. She was formerly director of the science and engineering library for the State Univ. of N.Y. at Buffalo.

Francisco Pinell, formerly director of services to the blind at the San Francisco PL, is now outreach supervising librarian for the San Diego PL.

Eva Radvan has been appointed international, comparative, and foreign law librarian for the Columbia Univ. libraries.

Leah Ross, formerly community librarian for Little Falls (Md.) Library, is now the Bethesda regional librarian for the Montgomery County (Md.) PL.

Fred Sandner, formerly audio-visual librarian at Asnuntuck Community College, Enfield, Conn., is now head of audio-visual services for Mercy College libraries, Dobbs Ferry, New York.

Arlene Schwartz has been named special assistant to the county librarian at Los Angeles County PL. She was previously manager of the ILLINET bibliographic data base service.

JoAn Segal, formerly executive director of the Bibliographic Center for Research (BCR) in Denver, is the new executive director of the Association of College and Research Libraries (ACRL). She had been at BCR since 1978, first as resource sharing program manager and later as interim executive director. She was named executive director in 1981.

John Sheridan has been named head of Tutt Library at Colorado College. He was formerly head librarian at Transylvania Univ., Lexington, Kentucky.

Paula Smith has been appointed assistant director for consultant, technical and extension services for the Rochester (N.Y.) PL. She was formerly director of the Musser PL, Muscatine, Iowa.

Linda Springer is now branch services administrator for the central library of the Atlanta-Fulton PL. She was formerly with the St. Charles City-County library district in Missouri.

Michael Steinfeld, former director of the Mt. Kisco (N.Y.) PL., is now town librarian and director of the Brookline (Mass.) PL.

Sidney Verba has been appointed director of the Harvard Univ. library. He was formerly Clarence Dillon Professor of International Affairs and associate dean of the faculty of arts and sciences for undergraduate education at Harvard. Verba succeeds **Oscar Handlin,** who retired.

Brenda Wright has been named public information officer for the central branch of the Atlanta-Fulton PL. She was previously acting director of public relations at Southern Technical Institute, Marietta, Georgia.

Mark Baer has retired as manager of the corporate library at Hewlett-Packard Corp. in California. A past-president of the Special Libraries Association (SLA), he was director of libraries at Hewlett-Packard for over seventeen years.

Linda Hillegass has retired. She was assistant library director at Lincoln City (Neb.) libraries since 1979.

Stephen Kees, chief librarian for the Niagara College of Applied Arts and Technology, Welland, Ontario, has retired.

Charlotte Leonard has retired from the Dayton and Montgomery County (Ohio) PL. She had been coordinator of children's services since 1964.

Gil McNamee has retired as director of the business library of the San Francisco PL.

Beverly Toy, associate university librarian for the Univ. of Calif. at Irvine, has retired.

Theresa Carroll, former town librarian of the Brookline (Mass.) PL, has died.

Valmai Kirkham Fenster has died. She was assistant professor of library science at the Univ. of Wisconsin-Madison Library School.

Howard H. Williams, reference librarian at Swarthmore College from 1967 to 1975, has died.

PLACE • MARKETPLACE • MARKETPLACE • MARK
MARKETPLACE • **MARKETPLACE** • MARKETPLACE
PLACE • MARKETPLACE • MARKETPLACE • MARK

Announcements

☐ Robert Fitzgerald, distinguished poet and translator, assumes his duties this fall as Consultant in Poetry at the Library of Congress, succeeding Anthony Hecht. His translation of Homer's *The Odyssey,* published in 1961, won the first Bollingen Award for Translation, and *The Iliad,* published in 1974, the first Landon Translation Award from the Academy of American Poets. He will initiate the fall season of LC literary programs with a reading on October 1.

☐ The National Information Center for Educational Media (NICEM), the world's largest database for instructional technology, is moving its government relations and sales office to the headquarters of the Association for Educational Communications and Technology (AECT), 1126 Sixteenth St., N.W., Washington, DC 20036. The database will move from its original home at the University of Southern California to the offices of Access Innovations, Inc., Box 40130, Albuquerque, NM 87196.

☐ The Public Library Association has established the Leonard Wertheimer Multilingual Award. The award will be granted annually at the ALA annual conference to a person, group, or organization in recognition of the important work they have done in enhancing and promoting multilingual public library services. Nominations with supporting documentation must be made to the award committee by December 15 of the year preceding the award. The National Textbook Company is providing support for the PLA award. Leonard Wertheimer, a retired Canadian librarian, is an international authority on multicultural public library services.

☐ The LAMA Public Relations Section's annual Swap & Shop had an added feature at this June's ALA conference. "Best of Show" materials, selected by a panel of public relations experts, were exhibited. Winners in the thirteen categories were: Bookmarks, DeKalb LS, Decatur, Ga.; Annual Reports, First Regional Library, Hernando, Miss.; Special Programs, Freiberger Library, Case Western Reserve Univ., Cleveland; Friends, Allen County (Ind.) PL, Fort Wayne; Calendars, Onondaga County (N.Y.) PL, Syracuse; Newsletters, Richland County (S.C.) PL, Columbia; Fundraising, Rutgers Univ. Library, New Brunswick, N.J.; Dedications, Broward County (Fla.) Library; National Library Week, Akron-Summit County (Ohio) PL; Summer Reading Programs, Louisville (Ky.) Free PL; Materials Lists, Monroe County (N.Y.) LS, Rochester, and Ferguson Library, Stamford, Conn.; Services, Policies, Orientations, Arlington Heights (Ill.) Memorial Library and Rutgers Univ. Library; Miscellaneous, Onondaga County (N.Y.) PL and Detroit PL. Circulating copies of the winning materials will be available from ALA's P.R. Info Bank.

Children's Specials

☐ Addison-Wesley publishes Kids' Care, a series of single-topic guides for parents. Among recent titles are *How to Cut Kids' Hair, Emergency First Aid for Children,* and *Childproofing Your Home.* Of particular interest to children's librarians is *How to Choose Good Books for Kids* by Kate Hall McMullan. The author provides guidance for parents on how to select books for different age groups and on how to motivate beginning readers. Annotations are provided for over one hundred popular children's books that range from lap books to books for middle graders. The 64p. paperback costs $3.95 and is available from Addison-Wesley General Publishing Group, Reading, MA 01867.

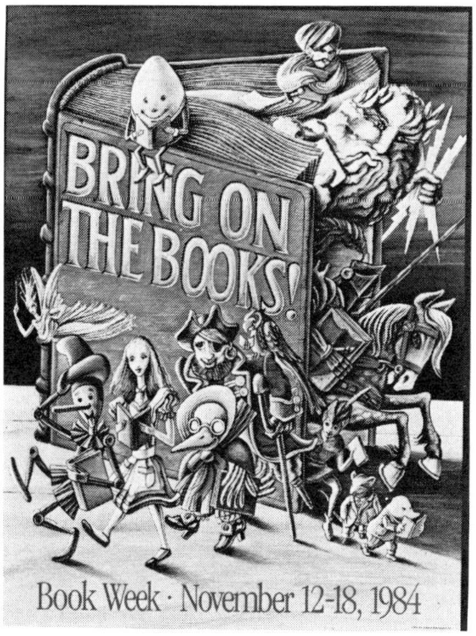

☐ Children's Book Week, November 12–18, 1984, marks the sixty-fifth anniversary of this annual event sponsored by the Children's Book Council, Inc. The 1984 theme is Bring on the Books! To help celebrate, the Council offers a variety of materials including two posters. The full-color 17´´ x 22´´ poster by Gerald McDermott features a cast of familiar storybook characters. It costs $3.50. For preteens and teenagers a familiar environment is shown in Ken Robbins' hand-tinted 17'' x 22'' photographic poster for young adults ($4.95). Children's Book Week materials are available separately or in prepacked kits. An illustrated brochure is available from the Council. Send SASE to The Children's Book Council, Inc., 67 Irving Place, New York, NY 10003.

□ Many librarians will remember Farmington, Connecticut's successful television "Turn Off" program. In response to the interest generated by the program, the Farmington Library Council has compiled an official TV Turnoff Kit. The kit includes a rationale, a planning guide, a publicity plan, sample press releases and bumper stickers, an evaluation card, and a bibliography for children, parents, and professionals. Alternatives to TV viewing and evaluation ideas are also included. Kits cost $7.50 each, with checks payable to the Farmington Library Council. Send orders to: Nancy DeSalvo, Farmington Library, 6 Monteith Dr., Box 407, Farmington, CT 06032.

□ The Vanessa-Ann Collection presents posters from award-winning illustrators of children's books. All posters are reproduced as 18'' x 24'' unframed lithographs on high-quality paper. Among the illustrators represented are Diane Goode, Rachel Isadora, Donald Carrick, Anita Lobel, Tomie dePaola and Tasha Tudor. Unsigned posters range in price from $12 to $20. In signed and numbered limited editions of 500, the posters cost $70. Framed posters are also available. For details write to The Vanessa-Ann Collection, Box 9113, Ogden, UT 84409.

□ The Westchester (N.Y.) Library System has published *Books to Share,* an annotated list of notable children's books of 1983, selected by the children's librarians of the Westchester system. The ten-page list is divided into four sections: Picture Books; For Younger Readers; For Older Readers; and For Parents and Other Professionals. Individual copies cost $1. For orders of ten or more, the cost is 50¢ each; 100 or more, 25¢ per copy. Write to Westchester LS, 8 Westchester Plaza, CWEP, Elmsford, NY 10523.

Continuing Education

□ "Handling Books in General Collections," a ten-minute, slide-tape show designed for staff training in general book collections, has recently been produced by the National Preservation Program Office at the Library of Congress. It covers appropriate shelving for ordinary and oversize books and appropriate techniques for the removal and replacement of books on the shelves. In addition it describes correct methods for the transport, general handling, and photocopying of books. The show consists of eighty-two slides in one 35mm slide carousel and one inaudibly pulsed cassette tape. Three copies of the program have been added to the audiovisual loan program of the preservation office and may be borrowed under the terms of the program. Persons interested in scheduling and shipping information should contact LC, Preservation Office, National Preservation Program Office, Audiovisual Loan Program, Washington, DC 20540. Phone: 202/287-5213.

□ Fort Hays State University is sponsoring its twelfth literature study tour during the summer of 1985, traveling to South America including Brazil, Paraguay, Argentina, Chile, Peru, Ecuador, Colombia and Venezuela. Graduate or audit credit is given for the thirty-two-day program. In each country there will be seminars, visits to libraries, bookstores, and museums, and opportunities to meet colleagues in the host country. For further information about the tour program write to Donna Harsh, Department of Education, Fort Hays State Univ., 600 Park St., Hays, KS 67601-4099.

□ The 1985 program of Management Skills Institutes geared for basic, mid-level, and advanced professional development has been announced by the Office of Management Studies, Association of Research Libraries. Basic institutes will be held in Philadelphia in April and in Denver in October. The fee, including all materials, is $325. Advanced institutes are scheduled for March in Berkeley, California and for November in Boston. The fee is $490. Enrollment for each institute is limited. Interested persons should write to Donna Reilly, OMS, ARL, 1527 New Hampshire Ave., N.W., Washington, DC 20036.

Film and Video

□ Copies of *Rights in Conflict? The Library and the New Patriotism,* a sixty-minute video on the issue of who will decide what materials will be collected and circulated by publicly-supported libraries, are now available from the Northwest Indiana Area Library Services Authority. Selling for $125, the videocassette is featured in either $\frac{3}{4}$'' or $\frac{1}{2}$'' VHS format. Copies may also be rented for $75, and previews can be arranged. For further information, contract Bill Crowley, Administrator, NIALSA, 1919 81st Ave. W., Merrillville, IN 46410.

□ *Lots of Kids Like Us* is a twenty-eight-minute film made especially for young children living in a home where a parental drinking problem exists. It dramatizes healthy ways for children to deal with alcoholism in the family. "You are not alone" and "it's not your fault" are major messages of the film. Also shown are specific problem-solving techniques and additional information on the impact of alcoholism on family members. The 16mm film may be rented for $70. Purchase price is $425 in all formats—16mm, $\frac{3}{4}$'' video, $\frac{1}{2}$''VHS, and $\frac{1}{2}$'' Beta. For further information write Gerald T. Rogers Productions, 5225 Old Orchard Rd., Suite 6, Skokie, IL 60077.

□ Video Outreach circulates educational videocassettes for secondary school and college classes to copy and keep. The videotapes are available to educators, on request, for free duplication in either $\frac{3}{4}$'' or $\frac{1}{2}$'' format. Among titles available are *The Link Between Us . . . Electronics,* and *Electronics . . . Your Bridge to Tomorrow,* from the Electronic Industries Association, and *When All The Citizens Help* and *Thief,* from State Farm Fire and Casualty Company. For more information write to Video Outreach, c/o The JN Company, Box 388, Woodbury, NY 11797.

Finding Aids

□ The sixteenth edition of *University Press Books for Secondary School Libraries* and the sixth edition of *University Press Books for Public Libraries,* both covering titles published during 1983, are now available to librarians at no charge. The annual bibliographies are published for AASL and for PLA by the American University Press Services. Titles in both bibliographies are arranged in Dewey order. Each listing includes author; title; number of pages; illustrations, references, bibliographies or indexes; dimensions; price; month and year of publication; and publisher. Each listing is annotated, with quotes from reviews where possible. If CIP is included, it is noted and LC and ISBN numbers are given. Librarians may obtain copies of the bibliographies at no charge by writing on library letterhead to AUPS, One Park Ave., New York, NY 10016.

□ From Abaco Island in the Bahamas to Goodwill Zwelithini, king of the Zulus, the *National Geographic Index 1947–1983* provides a complete listing of articles that have appeared in the magazine by subject, by author, and by photographer. Books, map supplements, television films, and other materials produced by the Society are entered by medium and by subject. The 606p. hardcover index, which costs $13.95, also includes a list of Society-sponsored research projects and expeditions and an introduction to the magazine by editor Wilbur Garrett. To order, write National Geographic Educational Services, 17th and M Sts., N.W., Washington, DC 20036.

□ The Comsearch series helps grantseekers to explore potential foundation funding sources and to identify foundations which have giving interests similar to their needs. Comsearch are computer printouts of foundation grants of $5,000 or more, classified in ninety-nine subject areas. They are available in four categories. Comprehensive, broad topics cost $30; more specific topics are $16.50; geographic printouts are $25; and special topics cost $16.50. For a brochure that lists the ninety-nine classifications or for further information write to The Foundation Center, 79 Fifth Ave., New York, NY 10003.

From the GPO Presses

The following titles are a sample of recent works available from the Government Printing Office. Specify the stock number, price, and quantity when ordering publications. You may pay by check payable to Superintendent of Documents, or by giving a Visa or Mastercard number with its expiration date. Send to Superintendent of Documents, United States GPO, Washington, DC 20402. Or call the order desk at 202/783-3238.

□ Twelve case studies in a new guide, *How Plain English Works for Business,* describe how business organizations have simplified their warranties, credit contracts, insurance policies, and product information booklets. The 107-page guide, stock number 003-000-00631-0, is available for $4.75 from Department 36-GK.

□ Are our public schools on the crest of the current wave of computer technology? A newly released report, *Instructional Use of Computers in Public Schools,* Spring 1982, provides some answers with a statistical view of our public schools—the availability of computer-based instruction, the extent of computer usage, teachers' computer literacy, needs for courseware and major needs for improving computer-based education. The twenty-seven-page report, stock number 065-000-00197-7 is available for $1. Send prepayment to Department 36-GL.

Idea Exchange

□ The statistics on missing and abducted children are frightening to any parent. In a cooperative pro-

gram between the Chicago Public Library and the Chicago Police Department Bureau of Community Services, thousands of Chicago children came to library branches this summer to be fingerprinted by police officers. Fingerprints are retained by parents or legal guardians for identification purposes, and each child who is fingerprinted receives a library card application. Many parents brought their children to be fingerprinted after watching the television movie, "Adam," about a kidnapped child. According to Elizabeth Huntoon, head of the Chicago Public Library's Children's Services Department, "Our aim is to make this service available to as many school age and pre-school children as possible."

□ To help increase funds for book purchasing, the Marshalltown (Iowa) Public Library compiled a cookbook entitled *Library's Pantry... Restocked.* Recipes were contributed by city council and library board members, Friends of the Library, and staff. Illustrated with teddy bears and calligraphy, the cookbook sells for $5 plus $1 postage and handling. The Friends of the Library are handling distribution and sales, and checks should be made out to that organization. To order a copy of the cookbook or for how-to details write to Marshalltown PL, 36 N. Center St., Marshalltown, IA 50158.

□ A recent issue of *Rural Transportation Reporter* noted the response to library closings in small and rural communities in Finland. The town of Visilahti instituted free taxi routes that take local residents to the regional library twice each month. The government pays the tab—one-tenth of the operating expense of a bookmobile.

□ Credit card companies are quick to point out the special recognition accorded holders of their "gold card." In Allen County, Indiana, the Friends of the Library used the gold card incentive in a direct-mail campaign. The campaign, launched last January, offers a gold plastic library card to new members of the Friends group who donate $25 or more. Video PSA's on local television, billboards, brochures, bumper stickers, and newspaper coverage of the campaign augmented the direct-mail campaign. During its first six months, the appeal has netted the organization more than $30,000 and the membership rolls have grown from 182 to more than 1,500.

□ The Irving (Texas) Public Library System produced library postcards to help celebrate the groundbreaking of their new Central Library. The 85,000 square-foot facility is scheduled for completion in the summer of 1986. Library director Lamar Veatch invites library colleagues to send for a copy of the postcard. Please enclose a SASE and write to City of Irving, Department of Libraries, Box 152288, Irving TX 75015–2288.

□ The Parlin-Ingersoll Library in Canton, Illinois will offer a series of programs and book discussions on the "American Experience" beginning this fall. Five different themes dealing with American life will be featured for two months each. "Small Town Life and Local Heritage" will be the opening theme, and will feature special speakers, displays, a creative writing workshop, and book discussions. Further information on the series may be obtained by contacting Randy Wilson, Parlin-Ingersoll Library, 205 W. Chestnut, Canton, IL 61520.

□ The Minneapolis Public Library is encouraging everyone to "Read. . . . By All Means" through a year-long focus on the importance and pleasure of reading. The campaign began in February 1984 and aims to raise public awareness of literacy concerns, leading into the library's centennial next March. A series of free programs is being held at libraries to promote the reading habit, bolstered by bold graphics bearing the slogan. Programs have ranged from local celebrities reading from their favorite works and talking about the importance of reading in their lives to dramatizations and films based on literary works. The Basic Skills Hotline number is made available at all programs.

Media Center World

□ A source book for both media specialists and classroom teachers, *Ready for Reference: Media Skills for Intermediate Students* provides a research, study, and information skills program that integrates media skills instruction with subject skills instruction. Detailing practical activities for students in grades 3–6, the book incorporates reproducible activity worksheets, pretests and posttests, developmental skills activities, and lesson plans. The 290p. paperback costs $19.50 from Libraries Unlimited, Box 263, Littleton, CO 80160–0263.

□ Georgia-Pacific's Consumer Paper Products Division has announced the Coronet Education Program in which registered schools (k–12), preschools, and libraries will be offered free educational materials in exchange for proofs-of-purchase from Coronet paper products. The program begins this month and will continue through March 23, 1985. More than 100 items, from finger paints to computers, are described in the Coronet Education Program Catalog. Each school or library intending to participate must register by November 15. Requests for registration forms or additional information should be addressed to Coronet Education Program, Box 14636, Baltimore, MD 21268.

☐ The SAT looms as a major hurdle for many college-bound high school students. The *Video SAT Review,* produced by Charlotte Dial and Dial Productions, is a comprehensive package which includes an interactive two-hour videocassette, three study booklets (math, verbal, and anxiety reduction), a sample SAT test, and the do's and dont's for parents. The cassette features Katherine Kendall, founder and director of an educational consulting firm that assists students in all phases of college selection and test-taking. For more information write to Dial Productions, 12077 Wilshire, Suite 614, Los Angeles, CA 90025.

Products and Services

☐ G.K. Hall offers a line of audio books. The unabridged recordings are read by professionals such as Claire Bloom and Ben Cross and are packaged in full-color, book-like plastic cases. The cassettes are recorded in Dolby System stereo, playable on standard cassette players. Among the six-cassette audio books published in June were *Trial Run* by Dick Francis (read by Tony Britton), *A Calf for Venus* by Norah Lofts (read by Roger Rees), and *Monsignor Quixote* by Graham Greene (read by Cyril Cusack). Six-cassette audio books cost $39.95 each. For more information write to G.K. Hall Audio Publishers, 70 Lincoln St., Boston, MA 02111.

☐ The Hollinger Corporation is marking its 35th anniversary of manufacturing archival products with a new 16p. catalog. Starting with the document case known as the Hollinger box, the catalog pictures and describes over forty conservation/preservation products and supplies in many sizes. All products are acid free and manufactured to meet archival standards for permanent, durable storage. Several items have been added including archival box labels, unbuffered tissue, and polypropylene sleeves and pages for long-term storage of photographs, negatives, and film. For a copy of the new Hollinger catalog request one on institutional letterhead from Archival Products, The Hollinger Corp., 3810 S. Four Mile Run Dr., Box 6185, Arlington, VA 22206.

☐ The Danish Library Design Bureau offers modular furniture systems for libraries including box shelving systems and counters that can be varied to flexibly fulfill many functions. The firm also markets library sign systems, exhibit systems, and steel shelving. Their consultants can assist in space analysis and planning of library facilities. For further information write The Danish Library Design Bureau, 1980 Post Oak Blvd., Suite 1710, Houston, TX 77056.

☐ Advanced Handi-Bind is a document binder and paper drill that binds documents .002´´ to 2´´ thick in less than thirty seconds. It can be used for on-site binding of current periodicals, temporary binding of volumes to be filmed later or with missing issues, or binding many flimsy sheets such as office documents and computer printouts. The machine uses plastic-tube heat-compression molding and consumes about 400W of power. For information, write or call Advanced Binding Methods Inc., 85 Channel Dr., Port Washington, NY 11050. Phone: 516/883–6805.

☐ The Book Protectors Company's Book Glove has a fully patented two-envelope design that comes in five adjustible sizes. The tight-fitting design provides extra strength and support and prevents the gaps and sags often found in book covers. Book Gloves are available in four materials: clear, heavyweight vinyl; opaque, heavyweight vinyl; Dupont Tyvek; and lightweight polypropylene. For a brochure write to Book Protectors Company, 4807 Bethesda Ave., Bethesda, MD 20814.

Professional Reading

☐ British novelist Brigid Brophy was one of the original forces in getting the Public Lending Right enacted in Great Britain. In *A Guide to Public Lending Right,* Brophy answers such questions as: Who counts as an author? What happens in the case of multi-author works? How is payment calculated? and Are there nationality requirements? She also shows the effects of PLR on editors, agents and publishers, and tells how writers and illustrators go about applying for PLR registration. The role of libraries is also detailed. The 178p. hardcover book costs $21.50 from Gower Publishing Company, Old Post Road, Brookfield, VT 05036.

☐ *The Library Forms Illustrated Handbook* by Elizabeth Futas includes forms used for technical services, public services, administrative services, audiovisual services, and special collections. It examines the practical function of forms in those categories. The volume details the value of carefully designed forms in preventing duplication, saving time, consolidating information, and standardizing procedures. *The Library Forms Illustrated Handbook,* an 875p. looseleaf publication, costs $75 from Neal-Schuman Publishers, 23 Cornelia St., New York, NY 10014.

☐ *Computers: The Non-Technological (Human) Factors* is a bibliography reflecting the consensus of expert opinion on the most useful literature in computer ergonomics. The book contains a 17-page introduction that defines terms, discusses the historical development of the field, explains the information crisis facing computer designers, and discusses basic computer ergonomics. It includes 61 annotations of books and documents relating to computer ergonomics, including user-friendliness, basic human factors engineering, VDT health hazards, computer graphics, and artificial intelligence. The 96p. softcover bibliography costs $34.95 from The Report Store, 910 Massachusetts St., 5th Floor, Lawrence, KS 66044.

Software

□ In *The Complete Guide to Writing Software Users Manuals,* Brad McGehee shows how to write manuals for the many new computer users who need instructions in clear English, not computerese. He emphasizes how to target the audience for a program and how to plan, organize, and write a manual, whether it is being written along with a program or for a program already in existence. He discusses optional features that can go into a manual such as tutorials, reference sections, and glossaries. For mail order, send $14.95 plus $1.50 postage and handling to Writer's Digest Books, 9933 Alliance Rd., Cincinnati, OH 45242.

□ Think Small Computers has acquired Computer Cat, the Apple-based online library catalog. The firm has served as maintenance contractor for Alpine Software, the program's author, for the past three years. Computer Cat has a number of new features. These include a 13-character field for ISBN and LC numbers; the ability to create in dexes which can be saved on floppy disks; extended editing capabilities; and built-in multiuser capabilities. The enhanced version of Computer Cat, known as Level 4, lays the groundwork for a circulation system that will support either barcodes or keyboard entry, and uses a stand-alone, patron data-entry subsystem. For price information on these products write to Think Small Computers, Inc., 8600 Concord Lane, Westminster, CO 80030.

□ Micro-Systems Software offers a full-feature word processing software package for leading desktop computer systems. M-Script includes automatic word wrap; insert; delete by character, word, line or block; full screen editing; block moves for "cut and paste" editing; headers and footers; special print formatting; and global search and replace. M-Script supports left, right or center justification and provides user-defined printer control codes and tab stops. Online help is available and M-Script comes with a user's manual and reference card. The program retails for $79.95 at software dealers. For more information write to Micro-Systems Software, Inc., 4301-18 Oak Circle, Boca Raton, FL 33431.

□ After a two-year evaluation, IBM has announced the availability of its "Writing to Read" system for teaching children to read and write using the IBM PC/JR computer. Using a computer with natural speech capability, pupils learn 42 phonemes through a series of 30 words. The IBM PC/JR speech attachment uses the computer's sound reproduction capability to pronounce the words while the pictures and phonemes appear on the color display screen. "Writing to Read" will be available this month through IBM National Marketing Division branch offices.

Write for These

□ The Library of Congress has recently published *Oscar Wilde at Oxford,* a lecture delivered by noted biographer Richard Ellmann at the Library on March 1, 1983. Tracing Wilde's life at Oxford University, Ellmann examines the way Wilde "brought himself to full consciousness" during this period. Single copies of the 30p. illustrated lecture are available free upon request from the Library of Congress, Central Services Division, Washington, DC 20540.

□ *Ames Energy: A Consumer's Guide to Energy Conservation* has been published by the Ames (Iowa) Public Library. The bibliography lists energy related books, pamphlets, and videocassettes that are a part of the Ames collection. Individual entries are annotated, and the entire bibliography is approximately fifty pages long. For a copy, send $2 to Ames PL, Information Services, 210 Sixth St., Ames, IA 50010.

□ A collection of capsule evaluations of astronomy books published during 1983 is now available from the Astronomical Society of the Pacific. Organized by subject and level of difficulty, the reviews can help librarians choose among the many available astronomy books. The reviews also include a special box featuring the dozen "books of the year" which the Society's book reviewer chooses each year. The reviews are available to librarians for a one-dollar donation to Astronomical Society of the Pacific, Book Reviews, 1290 24th Ave., San Francisco, CA 94122.

□ A new poster, ready for the 100th anniversary of Eleanor Roosevelt's birth on October 11, is available from TABS. Printed on ivory paper, the red-and-black 11- by 14-inch poster features a smiling, waving Eleanor Roosevelt and two smaller photos of her visiting a coal mine and reading the 1948 United Nations Declaration of Human Rights. The poster, accompanied by a brief biography, costs $2.50 plus $1.50 postage and handling from TABS, 744 Carroll St., Brooklyn, NY 11215.

□ Upstart Library Promotionals has published a new 24p. full-color catalog of library promotion aids. The catalog is full of bright ideas to help librarians and teachers celebrate Children's Book Week and promote reading and library use. The new catalog is free to librarians and teachers. Write to Upstart, Dept. PR, Box 889, Hagerstown, MD 21741. ▣

Eye on Publishing *cont. from page 44)*
years ago, usage jumped nearly seventy percent over the next several months. The 1969 volume should be available in December, at which point the file will contain some 600,000 entries.

Starting with those entries added in the 1981 edition, citations can be accessed by subject, an enormous bonus for scholars interested in interdisciplinary research. Before, says Eileen Mackesy, editor of the bibliography, you could only find Dickens if you knew he was English and lived in the 19th century. With the addition of the subject index, you can approach Dickens from countless directions—how he viewed women, for example, or how he treated religious themes.

School Library Technology *(cont. from p. 49)*
The future for computers and media centers does not look entirely rosy to Lathrop. One of the things that distresses her deeply is that in many schools the money for books is being diverted to buy computer software. "I think that this is a time when we need more money, not less, for books," she says. "Also, I am disturbed by the high expectations that are beginning to grow up around software."

WLB Classifieds

Classified Advertising *is accepted six weeks preceding date of issue. Charges are: minimun 3 lines—$10; each additional line—$2.50. If voucher forms are required, please send them when submitting copy. All advertisements for positions must exclude reference to race, creed, color, age, and sex as conditions for employment. The publisher reserves the right to reject any advertising considered unacceptable as to wording or appearance or for any other reason. Submit classifieds to: Brian Bavolar, Wilson Library Bulletin, 950 University Ave., Bronx, NY 10452.*

Joblines

ATTENTION LIBRARY EMPLOYERS: Need to list a vacancy in a public library or state library agency? Contact the PLA JOBLINE, sponsored by the Public Library Association, division of ALA. Recorded listings run for two weeks, 24 hours a day. $30 for PLA members; $35 for non-PLA members ($10 additional for phone orders). Listngs may also be sent via ALANET to ALA 0105. Job listing forms and more information available from PLA Office, 50 E. Huron St., Chicago, IL 60611. Or call 312/944-6780, ext. 412. Note to job seekers: PLA JOBLINE message is 312/664-JOBS.

Positions Open

ELEMENTARY LIBRARIAN - effective September 1, 1984. Must be NYS certified school librarian. Horseheads Central School District, Horseheads, NY 14845.

Announcements

THE FOOTLOOSE LIBRARIAN newsletter & network. Money-saving travel news + U.S. & overseas librarians offering Bed & Breakfast, housing exchange, more. "Good, practical information" M.S., IN; "An excellent publication" S.R., Tunisia. Free brochure. TFL, Box 972, Minneapolis, MN 55440.

LOOKING FOR an UNABASHED speaker—ask MA & PA about Marvin Scilken, the U*N*A*B*A*S*H*E*D Librarian. Also ask MI, VT, NH, AR, HI, etc. Box 511, Orange, NJ 07051-0511.

MILITARY BOOKS for identification of shoulder patches, medals, insignia ... U.S. and foreign. Military history, etc. Send for free catalog, M.C.N. Press, Box 52033 WLB, Tulsa, OK 74152.

NEWSLETTER FOR YOUR SUMMER, SPRING, CHRISTMAS COURSES in London, Paris, Mexico, Hawaii, etc.! Earn Univ. of Calif. units, tax benefits; visit libraries, theatre productions, galleries. Exciting study/vacation options for librarians, plus work in foreign libraries. Subscription: $25/yr. NEWSLETTER, Box 5513, Santa Monica, CA 90405.

THE ONE-PERSON LIBRARY: A NEWSLETTER FOR LIBRARIANS AND MANAGEMENT. Professional isolation is one of the major problems of working alone. We want to change that. This new newsletter is informal, informative, and, above all, quick and to the point. Charter subscriptions (one year, 12 issues) for $35, a savings of over 20%. Pre-paid orders to OPL RESOURCES, LTD., Box 948, Murray Hill Station, New York, NY 10156.

WANTED: LIBRARY MANUSCRIPTS/AIDS. Publisher seeks outstanding original book manuscripts and unique new products with strong appeal to librarians and reading teachers. Send description of manuscript or product with SASE to: Jeff Glover, Upstart, Dept. A, Box 889, Hagerstown, MD 21740.

For Sale

BRUCE TEGNER judo/karate/aikido/self-defense books price rise in effect now. Current catalog from Thor Pub. Co., Box 1782, Ventura, CA 93002.

CAN-DO CARDS: RESEARCH REPORTING. A proven step-by-step method for teaching students in grades 4-8 how to write research reports. Send for your spiral-bound set of student activity cards to The Curriculum Exchange, Box 985, Marblehead, MA 01945. $6.95 postpaid, Canada $8.95 in US funds.

"...get ideas from every issue."
M.S. High School Media Center, NY
Subscribe (and send *your* nitty gritty ideas) to THE U*N*A*B*A*S*H*E*D Librarian™, the "how I run my library good"℠ letter, Box 2631, New York, NY 10116. Four issues $20 US funds (add $5 Canadian and foreign postage).

HOBBY BOOKWATCH: Military, gun and hobby book review. Approximately 600 new titles each year. Small and large publishers. One year, $2; two years, $3.50; three years, $5. Published six times a year. For free sample write: HB, Box 52033, Tulsa, OK 74152.

HOLIDAY Magazine Oct. '58—Spring '72. Best offer. Box 234, Hannawa Falls, NY 13647 or call (315) 265-3386.

Librarians Love TFL!
"Everyone on our staff is interested in the Travel Exchange, either as a traveller or a host" M.H., San Diego. Free brochure on THE FOOTLOOSE LIBRARIAN newsletter & travel network. TFL, Box 972, Minneapolis, MN 55440.

LIBRARY NEWSLETTERS. Let a librarian prepare camera-ready copy for your newsletter. $1 for samples. Library Newsletter Service, Box 637, Belleville, NJ 07109.

1985 LIBRARIANS PLANNING CALENDAR—a 14-month planning calendar (2′ x 3′). Easy "write on/wipe off" use. Legal holidays, major library events and more are shown. Includes a "Directory of Library Events." Ready Fall - $18. Grenoble Books, 2567 Fisher Bldg., Detroit, MI 48202 313-874-1059.

PERFORMING ARTS TRAVEL GUIDE: A practical guide to best festivals of U.S., Canada, including music, dance, theater, folk. All necessary information for travel planning: dates, places, prices, accommodations. Just published. "Best Festivals of North America." 144 pages, 5 indexes, CIP, ISBN 0-916401-01-4. $4.95 U.S., $5.95 Canada. From your wholesaler or Printwheel Press, 2674 E. Main, #C-124, Ventura, CA 93003.

"Practically the only source of down-to-earth ideas"—West Virginia state library consultant

SPECIAL BACK ISSUE OFFER EXTENDED TO OCTOBER 31, 1984

THE U*N*A*B*A*S*H*E*D Librarian™, the "how I run my library good"℠ letter, is offering back issues, numbers 1 through 37 ONLY, at a special price.

A GOLD MINE OF NIFTY LIBRARY IDEAS, FORMS, PROCEDURES, AND LIBRARY HUMOR

REGULAR BACK ISSUE PRICE—$5

SPECIAL PRICE—Up to 3 issues—$4 each; 4 or more issues—$3 each

Current (paid) U*L subscribers deduct an additional 10%. Check must accompany order. Billing for libraries only for orders totaling over $20. All payments in US funds. Canadian and foreign orders add $1.25 per issue up to 4 issues (25¢ per issue for each additional). Order from: THE U*N*A*B*A*S*H*E*D Librarian™, Dept. BO/WLB, Box 2631, New York, New York 10116. Six to eight weeks delivery.

PRACTICE QUESTIONS for academic quiz shows. For more details write Tim Ballard, Box 502, Bardstown, KY 40004.

PUT SEARS TO WORK. 1,200 "see" and "see also" cards plus Manual/List of Headings with DEWEY numbers. From *Sears* 12th ed., $49.95. Woods Library Publishing Co., 9159 Clifton, Evergreen Park, IL 60642.

SCIENTIFIC AMERICAN, 35mm. Microfilm (Positive). v. 208-247 (1963-1982). Missing v. 234-235 (1976). In very good condition. $150 for 19 reels. Call or write Trinity Western College Library, 7600 Glover Road, Langley, B.C. V3A 4R9. Phone: (604) 888-7511.

SOLID OAK SHELVING

AT COMPETITIVE PRICES! Now acquire hardwood furniture shelving by Direct Purchases from manufacturers: KANECREST—The Kane Company in Tennessee. Quite possibly the most beautiful expandable system in the world today. Call for FREE 'Packet Parcel': Guide, Large Solid Oak Sample, and Prices Delivered on hundreds of combinations, one for every need. Shipped UPS prepaid to help you make your selections and place your order. Costs no more and in some cases less than thin gauge metal or laminated press wood. Perhaps the first major and only really significant engineered wood shelving improvement of this century. Call now 615-588-6113 between 10 and 4 EST giving name, position, institution, and UPS delivery address.

"WOW!" "Do not pass go without collecting this PR gem..." LJ
GO, PEP AND POP! 250 TESTED IDEAS FOR LIVELY LIBRARIES
by Baeckler and Larson
Order from: The U*N*A*B*A*S*H*E*D Librarian™, the "how I run my library good"℠ letter. Dept. GPP/WLB, Box 2631, New York, NY 10116. Send $4.50 check and mailing label with order. Libraries add $1 for billing. Canadian and foreign add $1 in US funds. 6 to 8 weeks delivery. LC 75-20328 CIP.

Credits: p. 15 — C. Frederick Mullison; 16-19 —The Bettmann Archive; 22—Ron Williams; 23-26—U.S. Bureau of the Census; 31-54—Oscar & Associates; 43—Library of Congress; 50—Bradbury Press; 51—Lothrap, Lee & Shepard; 52—Eileen Goudge and Cloverdale Press/Dell; Riverview Books; Byran Preiss Visual Pubs; 56—Cinema Guild; 57—Film Board of Canada; 58—Columbia Records; 59—Buff Herr/Columbia; 63—Ed Arno; 64—Morrow; 65—Scribner; 67—McGraw-Hill; Addison-Wesley; 76—Phil Moloitis.

Wilson Library Bulletin

October 1984

Wilson **Library** *Bulletin*

October 1984, Volume 59, Number 2 *ISSN 0043-5651*

Our cover for October was taken by freelance photographer **Tom Dunham** who was attracted by this arrangement of peppers at a roadside stand. Dunham lives in Hopewell, New Jersey.

Departments

Letter From New York/Editorial 84
Correspondence 85
Upfront/News 87
Calendar 94
Library World 150
Marketplace 152
WLB Classifieds 159

Articles

Newspapers and Electronic Databases: Present Technology *Barbara Newcombe and Harish Trivedi* 95
Treasure in the Library Attic: Von Ranke at Syracuse *Bruce Coville* 99
Serials Cancellations: Taking Advantage of Online Union Lists *Scott Bruntjen and Ruth Carter* 104
Working Less and Enjoying it More: Alternative Work Schedules *Katharine Shanks* 107

Features

Special Report: Winning the Miracle Mill *Ronald Chepsiuk* 109
Dateline—Washington *Dale Nelson* 112
Eye on Publishing *Ann McGrath* 114
Facing the Public *Will Manley* 117
Online Update *Martin Kesselman* 118
Future Libraries *Tom Surprenant* 120
Situation Report: NCLIS *Toni Carbo Bearman* 122
Vantage Point/Opinion *Philip Thompson* 124

Reviews

Picture Books for Children *Donnarae MacCann/Olga Richard* 128
The Young Adult Perplex *Patty Campbell* 130
Murder in Print *Kathleen Maio* 132
Front Row Center *Judith Trojan* 134
On Record: Popular Music *Bruce Pollock* 136
Magazines *Gail Pool* 138
Our Profession *Norman Stevens* 140
Software for Libraries *Patrick Dewey* 142
Current Reference Books *James Rettig* 144

The *Wilson Library Bulletin* is published monthly except in July and August by The H. W. Wilson Company, 950 University Avenue, Bronx, N.Y. 10452. Second-class postage paid at Bronx, N.Y. and additional mailing offices. The *Wilson Library Bulletin* is indexed in *Education Index, Library Literature,* and *Popular Periodical Index* and abstracted in *Library & Information Science Abstracts, Historical Abstracts,* and *America: History and Life.* Book reviews are indexed in *Book Review Index.* Subscription $30 a year, U.S. and Canada; $35, foreign. Single copies $4, U.S. and Canada; $4.50, foreign (remittance with order, please). Address all correspondence about subscriptions to the publisher. No subscriptions through agents. Telephone: (212) 588-8400

Letter from New York

Editorial

A nation of distracted readers

We were bemused to learn that the new twenty-cent commemorative stamp issued by the U.S. Postal Service on October 16 at the Library of Congress was to bear the legend "A Nation of Readers" and to display President Abraham Lincoln reading to his son Thomas—affectionately known to his father as "Tad." A renowned photograph taken by Matthew Brady, there seemed a semblance of fitness in that the portrait is part of the holdings of the Library of Congress and, as a press release from that institution noted, "The image underscores the need for parents, in a Nation of Readers, to stimulate family reading." The news release went on to point out that "It is appropriate that a stamp depicting President Lincoln as a reader be issued in cooperation with the Library of Congress, because Lincoln frequently used the library when he served as both congressman and President."

A measure of aptness, perhaps, but also a degree of misapplication. We are not, after all, prevailingly a nation of readers anymore than we are a nation of astronauts, systems analysts, or break dancers. The languid slogan associated with the stamp was, we imagined, wedded to the portrait of Lincoln to give it strength, to accompany a weak and even untenable idea with an image strong enough in historic repercussions to mask the absence of applicability.

Lincoln was a reader, but certainly not in a modern understanding of this activity. We know of his interest in the Bible, Shakespeare, history, and law, but his reach was neither random or eclectic—he was a most judicious reader. With less than one year of formal education, Lincoln necessarily became his own tutor, reading and rereading a small stock of books. In his breadth of reading it is not easy to accept him as a model for us, a nation of people taught to undertake reading even before entering school. Accustomed to reading at home and at work, we also read in commuter trains, subways, airplanes, waiting rooms, restaurants, hospitals, prisons, in elevators and on beaches. And we have more to read than did our sixteenth President: not only more books, magazines, and newspapers, but more memos, bulletins, statements, contracts, street signs, printouts, and advertisements of all sorts. We are a nation of readers because we have very little choice in the matter, which is one reason we demonstrate concern over our large number of functional illiterates.

This is, after all, the decade of the information explosion, the age of online access to databases, optical disk storage, satellite communications, and earth relay stations. Never having lived in such a milieu of high technology communication, how can Lincoln possibly serve as a meaningful emblem for us?

But here we have Lincoln and Tad gathered together over a book. Lincoln in formal wear, bespectacled, sitting in a Victorian armchair, a book spread upon his knees. Robert Lincoln called this "One of the most characteristic and excellent portraits" of his father. Tad, neatly combed and dressed, with a watch fob on his vest, is intent upon the book opened by his father. It is a warm and comforting photograph, full of dignity and serenity. Or so it seems.

In fact, Lincoln's beloved son William had died shortly before Brady took this likeness, sinking the President into one of his deepest periods of introspection and grief. Lincoln himself would be assassinated within months, Tad to die thereafter, Mrs. Lincoln to struggle against losing her sanity. The Civil War had yet to be resolved and Lincoln was still the subject of withering criticism. Tad and his father were hardly as composed and at peace as the double portrait would suggest.

There is a further anomaly. The volume open upon Lincoln's lap is not a book from which the President is reading, but a portfolio of photographs supplied by Brady as a prop to focus the attention of the sitters. The photograph was not taken at the White House, but at Brady's studio and it has less to do with reading to Tad (somewhat old for this ritual) than with asserting the value of a father and son sharing a moment together. That the staging of the picture would suggest that Tad was being read to from the scriptures was something Lincoln expressed concern about to Brady.

We are not strictly a nation of readers, but a nation of distracted readers—a continent of citizens devoted to so many preoccupations, interests, causes, and events that we don't have time to devote attention exclusively to any single activity. We can only say that we aspire to being a nation of readers and that, to the best of our ability, we are.

So we have Tad and his father together in this portrait for all time. Not, as it turns out, merely reminding us of books and reading, but of companionship and love. Which is the result of reading and finally all that they had time for. It will be true of us as well.

—Milo Nelson

Correspondence

Notably misleading

Contrary to the implications in your June editorial ("A matter of degree,") I am not an advocate of scrutinizing the value and purpose of the MLS degree as a legitimate requirement for truly professional positions. There is absolutely no question in my mind regarding the value and purpose of the MLS, and whether we call it a professional credential, a "selection device," or something else, the degree is valid when properly used. On the other hand, I believe there are exceptional individuals who can demonstrate equivalent professional knowledge, skills and abilities in relevant areas of librarianship who should not be denied a fair opportunity for consideration for professional positions. These exceptions should not become the rule, but neither should they be ignored.

Regarding the quotations attributed to me, your editorial freedom is at once disappointing, even though I must admit to a degree of satisfaction in that the library press is finally responding to the minimum qualifications issue. (Incidentally, your December 1983 editorial is acknowledged in this observation.) The quotation, "the MLS is simply not required in some of our positions," is taken out of context, misquoted and notably misleading. The second quote, "Do not impose the MLS as a degree requirement as an absolute minimum requirement if alternative qualifications might be equally acceptable," is also taken out of context and misquoted.

I urge *WLB* readers to acquire the full text of my presentation to the ALA Council at the last midwinter conference. It is available as Council Document No. 10, "ALA, the MLS and Professional Employment," and may be obtained by sending a No. 10 SASE to OLPR/ALA, 50 East Huron St., Chicago, Illinois 60611. While the statement is important as a means for giving a perspective on the issue, the footnotes and "additional sources" in the appendix will lead your readers to much additional material which will help them understand our circumstances more fully than were represented in your editorial.

KEITH COTTAM
University of Wyoming Library
Laramie

A crucial role

Leave it to the good judgment of Marvin Scilken ("Correspondence," March) to be the person to recognize another one of Will Manley's perceptive and constructive ideas.

Upon reading Manley's "textbook" essay (December 1983) I had intended to write an endorsement of that notion as expressing a conviction about collection development that I have held for many years. Indeed the "contradiction" he mentions always seemed particularly evident to me when I listened to colleagues patiently trying to explain to bemused readers why our library did not buy textbooks. Actually, there never was a rationale given, rather it was a simple, unadorned assertion.

Everyone knows that for subjects like mathematics, the sciences, the technologies, psychology, economics, statistics, management, marketing, and yes of course, computer science, it is the "straightforward and systematic" (Manley) style with questions and problems that make a textbook the appropriate source for learning a subject.

Happily, the library where I work has recently adopted the policy of actively adding this type of material in both the reference and borrowing collections. Since I have been closely involved in this project, I wish to comment on the subject of Manley's observation about the difficulty of locating satisfactory textbook reviews and to recommend the following sources in addition to *Choice* whose coverage is, of course, in the undergraduate to professional range. They include: 1) *Science Books and Films* with coverage at all levels and inclusion of most social and all physical sciences, but very little technology; 2) the book-length compilation based on this quarterly, the AAAS *Science Book List Supplement,* for retrospective buying; 3) one or more of the following very reasonably priced sources: *SciTech Book News, New Technical Books,* and *Technical Book Review Index*—all strong in the technologies; 4) *Curriculum Review* with convenient arrangement by subject area and elementary/secondary level.

Scilken's emphasis on the crucial role that gifts play in textbook collection development is so true. As one who has practiced active solicitation of gift books for years, I can report that excellent results can be achieved in the subject areas of psychology, mathematics, economics, and business, but as this enumeration indicates, gift sources at lower academic levels where students are not usually buying their texts do not yield sufficient quantities.

FRED OSER
Monmouth County Library
Shrewsbury, New Jersey

Speaking up for small communities

Will Manley's column ("Facing the Public") in June 1984 was marvelous. Finally someone spoke for the small communities. Maybe it is about time publishers and corporations started to pay more attention to their small steady accounts rather than in wooing the large accounts. Activity does occur in small places!

HAZEL YLINIEMI
Fargo, North Dakota

Poorly represented

Being a "small librarian," the ninety-eight-pound variety, I thoroughly enjoyed Will Manley's article in the June *Wilson Library Bulletin*. My whole staff (all four of them) liked it, too.

It has always been a sore point with me that most workshops, seminars, and library meetings, as well as programs presented at conventions, seem geared to the 117 communities with libraries that serve huge populations. I always wondered about the other 5,862 of us. I never had the figures to prove it, but I suspected that there were surely more "small" libraries than "large" and felt we were very poorly represented or completely forgotten when these workshops, and seminars were being planned.

Thank you, Will, for at least acknowledging our existence. You're right, I know where New York City is and I doubt that very many "Big City" librarians know where Ironton, Ohio, is.

FLORENCE MILLER
Briggs Lawrence County Public Library
Ironton, Ohio

Confusing friendliness with service

Will Manley ("Facing the Public," June) confuses friendliness in the small public library with service. As director of a "larger" small public library in a town of 25,000 I find that some of the staff, who have lived their entire lives here, do, in fact, know a large percentage of the patrons on a first name basis. And the local newspaper does carry "personal" news as a matter of course. What Manley has overlooked (or, perhaps, has not observed) is the closed nature of the "public" library: racial minorities and poorer white persons get a different view of the library. Also, spending most of the time on the reference desk discussing social events with friends is not the same as helping a patron find the relevant GED study guide. Maybe my spending some time working in the Department of Human Resources in a major urban area (Houston) has helped me become a little better aware of the importance of Information and Referral and its special application in a public library.

Also, discussion of professional training invariably exposes the prejudices of the individual's experiences, whether it be against cataloging rules (obviously Manley's albatross), statistics, or reference. If one has gleaned an overall idea of library service from his or her academic training then I feel it has been of some use. Perhaps having the town librarian get a master's degree in library science isn't such a bad idea—"censorship" doesn't exist in the eyes of the censor. Exposure to different points of view probably wouldn't hurt these small-town librarians.

One major point that Manley overlooks is that in a large city one has a wide variety of options; in a small town there generally aren't any options. These local librarians are in a much more powerful position that their big city counterparts. Shouldn't they be better educated? Shouldn't the librarians in these towns strive to have the best materials (and skills) available to help their patrons fulfill their human potential? And shouldn't he or she strive to make the library "public" and not exclusive?

I'm sorry Manley is so paranoid about big cities and feels that life is so idyllic in the smaller ones. Small collections are not the problems in small city libraries; small minds are.

JOHN SIGWALD
Unger Memorial Library
Plainview, Texas

Liberating children from ignorance

Thank you for the thought-provoking article in the "Young Adult Perplex" column of the June issue. Censorship of young adult materials in high schools is especially distressing because if teens do not find reading materials relevant to their problems in school libraries, not only will they be less prepared to deal with those problems but they are also more likely to give up reading itself.

I was somewhat disappointed by the tactics the censored authors attempted to use to counter the incident in the article. A more positive approach than boycott (and one which would have had much greater effect on the students as well as the censors) would have been for those authors who did speak at the event to have spoken on the censorship issue, explaining why freedom to read is important. Refusal to speak plays into the hands of the censors because the students remain unenlightened on the matter.

I also take issue with the last paragraph of Sonia Levitin's otherwise commendable statement of the case against censorship. We who oppose censorship are not attempting to liberate children from their innocence but from their ignorance. Indeed, we hope to help them retain their innocence (their freedom from evil and guilt) by allowing them to make themselves aware of the reality of evil and the possibility of good.

This etymological quibble aside, I thoroughly agree with Levitin. The two most fundamental points we can emphasize regarding the censorship issue are: (1) no one has the right to deprive others of the freedom to inform themselves, and (2) ignorance is the greatest danger to children; knowledge is their greatest asset.

MIKE BALDWIN
Gladys Harrington Library
Plano, Texas

Remembering the ladies

Having just returned from the ALA conference in Dallas, I read the article on the Dallas Public Library by Pamela Lange and Gerald Saxon (*WLB*, June) with great interest. I have the utmost respect and admiration for Lillian Bradshaw, but the statement on page 706, " . . . and the first woman to be elected president of the American Library Association," made me cringe to think that two staff members of such a large public library had not checked their facts. If they had looked no further than the *ALA Handbook of Organization*, they would find fifteen women preceded

continued on page 158

UPFRONT NEWS

Staff of the Detroit Public Library and representatives of the Citizens' Committee for Library Millage, recently gathered in front of the library to celebrate the passage of Proposition L, increasing the institution's funding from property taxes by one mill. The increase will raise an additional $5 million for the library each year for the next five years and enable DPL to restore hours at the main library and branches, reopen the rare book room, reinstate the film department, and restore funds for the purchase of new books. The millage campaign lasted only six weeks and was approved by a vote of nearly three to one. The library will operate during fiscal year 1984–85 on a total budget of $15,222,339.

Pictured above (in center, microphone aimed at him) is **Paul Scupholm,** *executive director, Friends of the Detroit Public Library, and to his left,* **Jane Hale Morgan,** *DPL library director.*

John Crerar Library receives Kresge grant

The John Crerar Library at the University of Chicago has received a $500,000 challenge grant from the Kresge Foundation. An additional $1.2 million must be raised by February 1985 under the terms of the grant, at which point fundraising will be complete. The $22 million library, to be opened this fall, combines the medical and science collections of the old Crerar Library, formerly located at the Illinois Institute of Technology in

Chicago, and those of the University of Chicago. The merger, one of the largest ever undertaken between two science libraries, will add 350,000 volumes in applied science to the university's holdings. The three-story, 160,000-square-foot library is located in a new "science quadrangle" on the university campus.

The Crerar Library was established in 1894 with a bequest in the will of John Crerar, a Chicago industrialist and philanthropist.

NLM now offering MEDLINE subsets

The National Library of Medicine is now offering subsets of its MEDLINE bibliographic database for use on personal and institutional computers. A subset licensing policy and agreement have been adopted, and the library can provide citations from MEDLINE and its backfiles on magnetic tape for local storage and reuse.

More than four million citations from biomedical journal articles from 1966 to the present are available. Subsets may be defined by subject, time period, language of publication, journal title, and other limiting factors. Requesters may lease a one-time subset or ask to receive monthly or quarterly updates as new citations are added to MEDLINE.

Charges for the service vary with the size of the subset and medium of distribution, whether updates are chosen, and whether or not the subset is intended for use by more than one person. Those leasing subsets are prohibited from republishing, duplicating, or offering the subset for sale to others.

Rutgers acquires crime collection

In an austerity move earlier this year, the National Council on Crime and Delinquency, headquartered in San Francisco, closed its East Coast office and put its collection of criminal justice books and documents up for sale. The collection is considered one of the oldest and most complete libraries on crime in this country. Rutgers University, the successful purchaser, recently moved the $150,000 acquisition into the John Cotton Dana Library on the school's Newark campus, where it is administered as a separate collection.

The new quarters, permitting public access to the material for the first time in two years, houses 8,000 books; 37,000 reports; 175 subscriptions to criminal justice journals, newsletters, and law reviews; 3,000 newspaper clippings; and 6,000 documents on microfiche. James Finckenauer, acting dean of the School of Criminal Justice at Rutgers/Newark, called the purchase "a comprehensive acquisition of the best literature in the field."

Scottsdale PL offers twenty-four hour renewal service

The Scottsdale (Arizona) Public Library has added a new service for the convenience of library users—a twenty-four hour book renewal service that enables patrons to renew books by telephone at any time of the day or night. A person wishing to renew a book dials a special renewal number. A telephone answering/recording device provides the caller with the new due date which the caller is asked to post on the return slip in the book being renewed. Callers then reveal their library card number and book numbers which are recorded for processing by the staff during normal business hours.

The service facilitates the processing of most renewal and circulation transactions, excluding transactions with overdue books which must be handled in person. The twenty-four hour renewal service was created to increase the number of renewals processed while decreasing "in person" staff required for this activity.

Library to computerize bookmobile

The Westminster (Colorado) Public Library has received a grant of over $11,000 to link the library's bookmobile with the city's mainframe computer. Believed to be the first such project in the nation, the library's card catalog will be brought to every location the bookmobile stops. The library plans to install a computer terminal in the bookmobile and use a radiophone link to the mainframe computer, providing over two thousand bookmobile patrons with the opportunity to search for and request any item held in the city's main or branch libraries. The grant was awarded through Title I of the Library Services and Construction Act.

The Orange (New Jersey) Public Library is presently observing its 100th anniversary. Funds raised during the library's celebration will be used for renovation of the eighty-four year old building, a historic landmark. Pictured above (from left) are **Don Wilson,** *library board president,* **Roseanne Monacelli,** *head of the anniversary observance, and* **Marvin Scilken,** *library director.*

Chicago librarian stabbed

Linda Feldman, employed by the Chicago Public Library, was stabbed in the side on August 23 by a man who witnesses said became angry when he could not locate a book on alchemy. The incident, which took place in the business, science, and technology section on the eleventh floor of the main library, has provoked renewed staff demands for stronger security. The library system's security force has been reduced by forty-six percent since 1981.

Feldman was taken to Northwestern Memorial Hospital to undergo surgery to repair liver damage suffered in the attack. The assailant, Harold Peavy, was charged with attempted murder and held pending a court hearing.

Kathleen Prendergast, library union leader, said "you have a real critical situation here with security. This is going to focus attention on our arguments that security guards have to be restored."

Holley to relinquish deanship

Edward Holley, dean of the School of Library Science at the University of North Carolina at Chapel Hill, has asked to be relieved of his responsibilities as dean on June 30, 1985. Holley will return to full-time teaching as a member of the school's faculty. In a letter to Chancellor Christopher Fordham, Holley stated "my decision to leave the deanship is not caused by any disenchantment with the school or the university. I have enjoyed being a dean at the University of North Carolina. However, I have the strong conviction that the school needs new leadership in facing the challenges posed by emerging technologies and other prospective changes in library and information science education during the rest of this decade." Holley has been dean of the School of Library Science since 1972.

NEDCC assists in Andrea Doria project

The Northeast Document Conservation Center, Andover, Massachusetts, participated in the salvage of paper currency removed from the *Andrea Doria* safe and will undertake restoration of the water-soaked bills. Mary Todd Glaser, NEDCC senior conservator, served as consultant to the *Andrea Doria* project and was one of two paper conservators present when the safe was opened August 16 on live television. The contents of the safe comprised small denomination bills, mostly United States and Italian currency. The money was later wrapped and placed in a home freezer.

The material will be freeze-dried and samples sent to NEDCC for treatment. Once the bills are dried, they will be separated, washed for removal of salt, alkalized, and dried again. NEDCC will also experiment with methods to strengthen the paper, either by sizing or polyester film encapsulation.

NEDCC was contacted by Peter Gimbel, organizer of the salvage venture, because of the center's extensive experience in treating paper, especially water-damaged materials. NEDCC specializes in conservation of artifacts and art on paper and provides services for libraries, museums, and historical organizations that do not possess in-house facilities for preservation work.

An exhibit honoring the **Center for Book Arts: The First Decade,** *opened in September at the New York Public Library. Among the 132 contemporary, handcrafted books are a cookbook shaped like a cake and a fabric book that doubles as a necklace. The exhibit, which continues until the end of November, illustrates the modern movement to create art within a book format. "In an unusual reversal," remarked Frank Mattson, curator of the NYPL Rare Books Division, "the text becomes subordinate to the image, provoking a different response to the printed word and the book as a whole."*

The rare and fanciful creations include an **Elvis Presley Scrapbook** *(above) with pop-up pages edged in pink lace, by Joni Mabe, and a handbound edition of* **Moby Dick,** *adorned with a sculpted, removable whale, by Philip Smith.*

Louisiana State offers MLS enhancement

The School of Library and Information Science at Louisiana State University in Baton Rouge has developed a joint degree program in library and information science and systems science with the institution's Department of Computer Science. The joint degree program is intended to prepare information professionals knowledgeable in systems and computer applications in such core topics as control theory, operations research, computer science, information systems analysis, modeling, and simulation. The course of instruction is expected to prepare graduates for careers in library systems development, online bibliographic retrieval research, and administration of information centers. Students enrolling in the joint degree program will earn two master's degrees for a total of fifty-five graduate credits. Earned individually, the two degrees, would require sixty-seven graduate credits.

Tulsa receives its largest single contribution

The Tulsa (Oklahoma) City-County Library System has received $600,000 fron Donna and Roger Hardesty, the largest single contribution ever given to the library. The donation has enabled the library to surpass its goal of raising $2 million to create an endowment fund. The benefactors are owners of the Hardesty Company, a commercial real estate firm headquartered in Tulsa. In presenting the gift Donna Hardesty said "Libraries play a vital part in the growth of our city and our people. They are a reflection of our commitment to our educational system and our future." Pictured above are (from left) Donna and Roger Hardesty and Pat Woodrum, director of the Tulsa City-County Library.

Compact discs given to Library of Congress

The Library of Congress has accepted a collection of 1,000 commercially produced compact discs donated by the Compact Disc Group, and organization comprised of leading equipment manufacturers and independent record companies. Every compact disc from the organization's affiliated companies produced to date will be presented to the library.

The Library of Congress is also engaged in a program to test and evaluate compact discs as a permanent preservation medium for its recorded collections. Laser-read compact discs, renowned for their distortion-free sound, suffer none of the degradation of sound associated with conventional vinyl recordings.

RLIN established new supplier link

The Research Libraries Information Network has modified its acquisitions system to make it possible for users to send their online orders, claims, and cancellations directly to participating suppliers, bypassing the normal printing and mailing routines. Suppliers who have installed RLIN-programmed video terminals use the RLIN acquisitions "local site printing" facility to identify communications awaiting them from libraries. The first supplier to establish an RLIN user account and install the necessary hardware is the Faxon Company of Westwood, Massachusetts.

New Jersey receives supplemental appropriation

New Jersey Governor Thomas Kean recently signed Senate Bill 2000, a supplemental appropriation of $658, 000 to be used for the state's multitype library network. State Librarian Barbara Weaver called the appropriation "a giant step forward for library services." The funds are to be expended during the present fiscal year.

Dallas Public to receive Republican records

The Dallas Public Library has been designated the official repository for the written records pertaining to the Republican National Convention held in Dallas on August 20–23. It is estimated that the material, which will be housed in the Dallas History and Archives Division, will require approximately a year to process. When processing is complete, the material will be available to the public.

SOLINET receives preservation grant

The Southeastern Library Network has been awarded $168,401 by the National Endowment for the Humanities to establish a cooperative preservation program. The funding will enable SOLINET to help libraries and archives develop and coordinate local preservation programs. SOLINET staff will study the feasibility of coordinating existing treatment services, will monitor new technologies such as mass deacidification, and will seek additional funding sources for subsequent phases of the initial two-year project.

Frank Grisham, SOLINET executive director, said "Up to now, most people have thought of SOLINET only as a provider of library automation services. But we realize it is just as important to preserve collections as to catalog them."

Task force to study state of U.S. books abroad

A task force formed at the request of the National Security Council and comprised of experts from the American publishing community, the academic world, and the government has been organized to study and make recommendations on improving the state of U.S. books abroad. The U.S. Books Abroad Task Force, a special subcommittee of the United States Information Agency's Private Sector Book and Library Advisory Committee, convened for the first time on June 13. The task force members, meeting at the Center for the Book at the Library of Congress, devised an outline for a comprehensive study of American books overseas. Among the topics to be covered in the study are copyright law and protection of intellectual property; dissemination of information on the content of American books; extent of private, governmental, and cooperative exhibits at national and international book fairs; export procedures; participation by U.S. publishers in professional meetings and conferences; economic problems of the book export trade; and the USIA book translation program.

The Salt Lake City Public Library, *curious about how much walking their librarians do while on the job, attached a pedometer to be worn by the librarian at a service desk in the fiction department. The findings showed that on the slowest day the librarian walked two miles, on the busiest more than four. The library, which has 135 employees, also calculated that their staff covers approximately 415 miles a week while serving Dallas patrons. In the photo below,* ***Lenore Lewis,*** *head of the fiction department, gives her pedometer a momentary rest.*

A $3 million addition to the ***Finkelstein Memorial Library,*** *Spring Valley, New York (see rendering above) was recently approved by Rockland County voters. Voter turnout on the referendum was markedly higher than in previous years. The three-story addition will provide shelving space for 75,000 books, twice as much seating, a larger children's reading room, expanded audio-visual services, and computerized circulation control.*

The expansion is expected to be completed in two years. At present the library is storing books on the floor, in hallways, and in a storage trailer outside the facility.

Reduced fines force Mississippi library system to reduction of hours

The Monroe County (Mississippi) library system, facing declining revenue from penal fines collected for the violation of state law, has been forced to close all library facilities on Saturdays, including the library's bookmobile operations. Penal fines received in 1983 were $120,000 less than those received in 1981. In addition to closing the library system on Saturdays, the library board agreed to eliminate positions, impose a hiring freeze, and reduce acquisition of films, records, and videocassettes.

The library board will place a request for an additional one-quarter mill tax before the voters in the general election on November 6. The library's present half-mill tax has been in effect since 1972. During that period it is estimated that the county's population has increased 12.2 percent and use of the library has increased by 78.4 percent.

CRL now accepting deposits

The Center for Research Libraries, which for the past several years has been unable to accept deposits of library material because of limited shelf-space, is once again available for deposits. The restriction was lifted following the construction of a second building for the center. Categories of material eligible for deposit from member institutions include serial publications issues in the United States, Canada, and the United Kingdom that did to the holdings of a title already in the center's collections. Serial publications from other countries are acceptable if the run to be deposited is substantially complete and is retrospective at least five years.

The center will also accept the deposit of small quantities of children's book and foreign doctoral dissertations. Copies of the revised policy for making deposits are available from the center. Member libraries wishing to make deposits of material must obtain authorization and shipping instructions from the center prior to dispatching material.

IBM introduces new Personal Computer

IBM has introduced a new top-of-the line Personal Computer with significant performance improvements. The new IBM Personal Computer AT —which uses an advanced, high-speed Intel 80286 microprocessor—can be used as a stand-alone system or as a multi-user system. It offers up to three million characters of user memory and 41.2 million characters of online storage. The Personal Computer AT incorporates a high-capacity diskette drive and expanded fixed-disk drive options. The unit delivers almost five times the user memory and more than twice the information storage capacity previously available on IBM PCs.

The new system is compatible with most existing IBM Personal Computer hardware and software. Prices for the Personal Computer AT start at $3, 995.

ITT to build earth station

ITT World Communications has received approval from the Federal Communications Commission to build a satellite earth station in New York City's financial district. The $2.2 million facility will go into operation in 1985, providing direct digital communication services between the U.S., Europe, and Latin America. The facility will permit high speed transmission of data via digital circuits operating at fifty-six thousand bits per second.

The Lexington (Kentucky) Public Library *recently opened its newest branch library. The Northside Branch (photo above) is situated on ten acres of bluegrass countryside donated by Julia McCullough of Louisville. Money for the $700,000 facility came from a State Library Construction Grant and the Lexington-Fayette Urban County Government.*

The Northside Branch is the first public library in Kentucky to have a computerized circulation system and to offer an online interactive computer catalog.

Rock Island PL receives building funds

The Rock Island (Illinois) Public Library has received $1.8 million in general obligation funds towards a $2.38 million rennovation, restoration, and expansion of its present facility. The funds to improve the eighty-one-year-old building were approved unanimously by the Rock Island City Council. The balance of funds necessary for the renovation will be raised through private contributions.

The 12,000 additional square feet of space provided by the expansion (see architect's rendering above) represents a sixty-four percent increase in space. The library plans to centralize the book collection, double patron seating capacity, and provide enhance security for library material.

Chicago High School students pass in review at the recent rededication ceremonies for the **Hall Branch** *of the* **Chicago Public Library.** *The $1 million renovation fratured the creation of a computer-equiped young adult center, a special storytelling section, increased accessibility for the handicapped, and a new audio-visual department featuring cordless headphones for listening to pre-recorded programming throughout the library.*

Calendar

Announcements should be sent at least 60 days in advance to "Calendar," WLB, *950 University Ave., Bronx, NY 10452.*

OCT. 16—*Preservation and Conservation of Library and Archival Materials,* workshop. Kansas City, Mo. Sponsor: Midwest Cooperative Conservation Program. Inf.: Preservation Workshop, The Center for Research Libraries, 5721 Cottage Grove Ave., Chicago, IL 60637.

OCT. 16–17—*Management of the Online Catalog,* institute. Columbus, Ohio. Cosponsors: Ohio LA and Columbus Area Library and Information Council of Ohio. Inf.: LAMA/ALA, 50 E. Huron St., Chicago, IL 60611.

OCT. 17–19—*Iowa LA,* annual conference. Hotel Fort Des Moines, Des Moines. Inf.: Elaine Estes, Des Moines PL, 100 Locust St., Des Moines, Iowa 50309.

OCT. 17–19—*Southeastern LA/Mississippi LA,* biennial conference. Mississippi Coast Coliseum and Convention Center, Biloxi. Inf.: Kay Miller, SELA Conference Committee, Univ. of Southern Miss., Southern Station, Box 5053, Hattiesburg, MS 39406-5053.

OCT. 18–20—*Ohio Educational Library Media Assoc./Ohio LA,* concurrent conference. Hyatt Regency Hotel and Ohio Center, Columbus. Theme: "Libraries: Learning For Life." Inf.: A Chapman Parsons, OLA, 40 S. Third St., Suite 230, Columbus, OH 43215.

OCT. 19—*New Information Technologies and Libraries,* workshop. Drexel Univ., Philadelphia. Inf.: Janet Goldwater, College of Information Studies, Drexel Univ., Philadelphia, PA 19104.

OCT. 19—*Teaching Library Concepts,* workshop. Drexel Univ., Philadelphia. Inf.: (see above for address.)

OCT. 20—*San Joaquin County Authors' Symposium,* annual conference. Univ. of the Pacific campus, Stockton, Calif. Theme: "Much Ado About Nothing." Inf.: San Joaquin County Authors' Symposium, Inc., Box 4905, Stockton, CA 95204.

OCT. 21–24—*New York* LA, annual conference. Concord Hotel, Kiamesha Lake. Theme: "Partnership Is Power." Inf.: Nancy Lian, NYLA, 15 Park Row, Suite 434, New York, NY 10038.

OCT. 21–24—*Middle Atlantic Regional Library Federation,* conference. Baltimore Convention Center. Inf.: Andrew Lisowski, Gelman Library, George Washington Univ., Washington, DC 20052.

OCT. 26–27—*Oral History for Librarians and Archivists,* workshop. International Graduate School, St. Louis. Inf.: International Graduate School, 55 Maryland Plaza, St. Louis, MO 63108.

OCT. 27—*Books Come Alive! II,* conference. Mankato State Univ., Minn. Inf.: Mary Ann Vande Vusse, Minn. Valley Regional Library, 100 E. Main, Box 3446, Mankato, MN 56001.

OCT. 29–31—*Online '84,* annual conference. San Francisco Hilton and Tower. Sponsor: Online, Inc. Inf.: Online, Inc., 11 Tannery Lane, Weston, CT 06883.

OCT. 31–NOV. 1—*National Association of State Educational Media Professionals (NASTEMP),* annual conference. Atlanta. Inf.: Theresa Fredericka, Ohio Department of Education, 65 South Front St., Columbus, Ohio 43215.

NOV. 2–3—*Harriet Dickson Reynolds: In Celebration of the Child,* symposium. Houston. Sponsor: Houston PL Inf.: Ann Hornak, Houston PL, 500 McKinney, Houston, TX 77002.

NOV. 8—*Connecticut Educational Media Association,* conference. Theme: "Pathways To the Future." Inf.: Diane George, Branford Intermediate HS, 185 Damascus Road, Branford, CT 06405.

NOV. 10—*Festival of Books For Young People.* Iowa Memorial Union, Iowa City. Sponsor: Univ. of Iowa SLIS. Inf.: Ethel Bloesch, SLIS, Univ. of Iowa, 3087 Library, Iowa City, IA 52242.

NOV. 11–14—*Information Industry Association,* annual meeting. Sheraton Palace, San Francisco. Theme: "The Information Nation: New Actors, New Factors." Inf.: Liz Nanni, IIA, 316 Pennsylvania Ave. S.E., Suite 400, Washington, DC 20003.

NOV. 18–20—*Rhode Island LA,* annual conference. Sheraton Islander, Newport. Inf.: Tanya Trinkaus, West Warwick PL, West Warwick, RI 02893.

DEC. 2–4—*Educational Media Association of New Jersey,* annual conference. Hyatt Regency, New Brunswick. Theme: "Today's Libraries: The Road to Excellence in Education." Inf.: Sally Young, 8 Townsend Rd., Mendham, NJ 07945.

DEC. 7—*Appraisal and Conservation of Records,* workshop. American Antiquarian Society, Worcester, Mass. Sponsor: Northeast Document Conservation Center. Inf.: Records Workshop, NEDCC, 24 School St., Andover, MA 01810.

DEC. 13–15—*Arizona State LA/Arizona Educational Media Association,* annual conference. Phoenix Civic Plaza, Phoenix. Theme: "The Future Is Now . . . or Never." Inf.: Jean Murphy, Mesa PL, 64 E. First St., Mesa, AZ 85201.

JAN. 2–4—*Association for Library and Information Science Education,* annual conference. Shoreham Hotel, Washington, D.C. Theme: "Undergraduate Preparation for the Information Profession." Inf.: Jan Phillips, ALISE, 471 Park Lane, State College, PA 16801.

JAN. 18–21—*COMMTEX International.* Anaheim Convention Center, Anaheim, Calif. Inf.: International Communications Industries Association (ICIA), 3150 Spring St., Fairfax, VA 22031.

Newspapers and Electronic Databases:

Present Technology

Barbara Newcombe and Harish Trivedi

Aside from the great moments inscribed in stone, papyrus or parchment, history tends to slip away from us. The mundane record of events that are less than world-shaking may be published in one form or another, but becomes virtually impossible to trace after a few years. Newspapers and magazines, television, radio, and teletext/videotex create records. Preserving, controlling, indexing and retrieving these records, whether partially or in full, has always presented problems. The processes are costly in terms of labor and of space. Retrieval does not happen unless these functions have been successfully implemented.

Libraries maintained for newspaper publishing are incredibly large. All significant articles published in the paper must be analyzed, entered into the storage system, and readied for retrieval. In the case of a large metropolitan daily, this process involves at least one thousand entries for news clips and about one hundred entries for photographs and other graphics. In addition to photographs that were published in the paper, at least twice that many are considered worth keeping for possible future use.

Analyzing the news

There are several ways to record analyses of stories. One is to mark up as many copies of a single story as are needed. For instance, mark one copy for the byline, one for each personal or corporate name prominently mentioned, one for subjects covered, and one for the location of the story. Each copy is then cut and filed—which means a lot of paper is handled and a lot of space is used up. Another way is to underline the items on a single copy of the article. These indicators or headings are typed onto index cards. The single copy of the story is pasted in a scrapbook, filed in a unique place, or microfilmed. The index cards indicate where to find the full text of the article. The indexing may also be stored on a computer. The latter two methods require an extra step before the text can be read. With the older, multi-copy method, the text is in one's hands as soon as the proper file is found. With the other methods, the index must first be consulted and sifted. Next the searcher follows the index pointer to find the story. But oceans of space have been saved at the expense of staff time. Choice depends on whether floor space is more expensive than the local wage scale.

Photographs are far bulkier than clippings. Not too long ago, "cuts" (metal photo-engraving plates) were stored in addition to the actual photo. If negatives were sent to the morgue, that was another format to accommodate.

Although photographs can be identified in almost as many ways as news stories, description is usually kept to a minimum. It is too costly to reproduce the actual photo for multiple filing. An alternative is photocopying the original print. One newspaper makes microfilm copies of photographs for indexing. These 35mm film clips are mounted into aperture cards onto which all relevant information has been printed by a computer. A more common method is to use the good old index card solution. Index cards take up space and, subject headings and humans being what they are, the consistency of the headings will waver.

The Library of Congress is experimenting with optical disc storage. This will enable pictures to be transferred to a disc using a laser beam to record the image. An enormous amount of picture information can be stored in compact form. If successful, fragile, fading photos will be preserved. It may be some time before the cost of optical disc technology is low enough to permit it to be used in newspaper libraries, where it is so badly needed. Old news photographs, especially those on glass plates, are treasures of our society. It is a pity to allow them to fade into a void and it is equally sad watching news clips fall to dust.

Progress in storage/indexing

Not quite in the nick of time, storage/indexing systems based on computers

Barbara Newcombe *is manager of the Editorial Information Center,* Chicago Tribune *and* **Harish Trivedi** *is director of Reference and Research Services, Dayton Newspapers, Inc., Dayton, Ohio.*

have arrived. News librarians, particularly those working with mark-cut-paste-fold-file methods, immediately sensed that here was a solution. It has been slow to unfold—certainly not fast enough to prevent newsprint of a certain age and acid content to self-destruct. Progress is being made, however. During the past ten years, a lot has happened. *The New York Times* became available electronically in abstract form and later in full text. The *Toronto Globe and Mail* became available full-text, followed by Dow Jones News Service including edited versions of the *Wall Street Journal* and *Barrons*. Mead Data Central introduced on its NEXIS system a full-text database consisting of over thirty newspapers, magazines and news services.

As of January 1984 fifteen newspapers could be searched full-text for a fee. During a six-month period the number of entries under "News" in the *Directory of Online Databases* (Cuadra Associates, Santa Monica, CA) increased by twenty-one percent. The directory must issue quarterly updates to stay even remotely current. Wire services—Associated Press, United Press International, Reuters, TT–Nyhetsbanken, PT Newswire, Mediawire—are retrievable full-text via various online services.

Two years ago the authors surveyed newspapers around the world. Dividing the responses into developed and developing countries, we found that of responding newspapers in developing countries, none used a computer in the library and only eight percent of those in developed countries did so. In January 1984 a survey made among daily newspapers belonging to the Inland Daily Press Association found that ten percent used computers to at least some extent for storage and retrieval. This includes online index storage and microform text retrieval as well as fully electronic handling.

There are new faces in the small group of software developers aiming at the newspaper library market, and some of the old faces have faded from the scene. In June 1983 Homer Martin presented a comparison of nine newspaper library systems to the Newspaper Division of the Special Libraries Association. In June 1984 Martin made the same presentation and this time the count was twelve. One on the 1983 list had been dropped and one had survived in somewhat changed form.

Information as a salable commodity

The Inland Daily Press Association survey found that small- to medium-circulation papers were reluctant to consider installing electronic systems because of the cost. Nor could they see that there might be a market for their indexed material. Nevertheless, two-thirds of the respondents said they allowed free public access to their library files. This practice is costly in terms of library staff time. The idea of information as a salable commodity developed slowly. The customer pays to buy his daily newspaper, of course. Beyond that transaction, both producer and customer feel the information should be free—this in spite of the fact that much value has been added. The stories have been read, categorized, processed and stored. As a business product, the information is now much more useful and more expensive.

The marketing potential of newspaper and news magazine databases (current history, social trends and events) is not fully appreciated by many newspaper publishers. One need only look at nearly 2,000 commercial databases in the market and their usage charges. According to a survey conducted by Martha Williams there are more than 2,000 publicly available databases and they are increasing at a rate of twenty to thirty percent each year. In 1982 online connect time usage for the information center/library community amounted to 1.3 million hours and $127 million. The average expenditure per hour was $120.59. The Yankee Group is an international market research and consulting organization specializing in computer systems and telecommunication. In 1982 they estimated the market for data and image storage to be in excess of $175 billion annually and growing at a rate of more than twenty percent per year. A significant share of the storage system market may be diverted to nonmagnetic media such as optical disc storage by 1990. A survey on the use of commercial online databases in newspaper libraries was conducted in 1983 by Lany McDonald of the *Raleigh News and Observer* library. According to the survey, the number of database searches performed each month by newspaper libraries ranged from one to over eight hundred. The median response was thirty. Of these searches, approximately two-thirds were full-text. Costs for these services were charged against the library budgets in thirty-one out of thirty-nine cases, and budgets ranged from $600 to $150,000 per year. The average annual budget was approximately $22,500.

Paving the way to networks

Available technology is not yet fully used for the storage and retrieval of information from news media. Most newspapers that use an electronic composition system purge the data after publication of the newspaper or magazine. Even though installation costs for online full-text systems are relatively high, the increasing labor costs of white-collar workers and the rapidly decreasing costs of electronic storage with enlarged storage capacities should not be overlooked. Standardization of systems and cooperation among newspapers, hardware vendors, and programmers would greatly speed progress in this direction. Standardized procedures and format would also prove to be an attractive feature for future marketing strategies. A possible alternative to standardization would be development of interfaces that would be able to translate between systems—the ability to transfer data and programs between one newspaper and another, between machines of the same generation, and between machines of current and future generations of technology.

Most importantly, recognition by newspaper executives of the need to cooperate would pave the way to the establishment of newspaper information networks. Small- and medium-size newspapers could save considerably on the development of full-text databases if they store only news stories and articles written by their own writers, editors, and commentators. National and international newspaper databases could be relied on for other types of information. This would also result in development of a newspaper database with a strong local slant. Use of Vu/Text Information Services, Data Times/Datatek and NEXIS could provide such an alternative in much the same way that specialized databases now use Dialog or BRS. This would be like a news supermarket. As *The New York Times* and *Washington Post* well know, there is a difference between how reporters use an electronic library of their stories and how the general public (including business corporations) use that same database.

Preparing the news for storage

There are three main ways by which news is prepared for electronic storage today. One is full-text with no added subject analysis. This is typified by NEXIS, the service offered by Mead Data Central. News can be searched by headline, byline, date, place of origin, and name of publication. Any word in the body of the story can be searched. But you cannot search by subject, for instance, U.S. foreign relations. Obviously, not every story dealing with that subject will contain that phrase. Few reporters will ever want to search the phrase. Future historians may very much want to do so.

Another way to prepare the text is by using controlled vocabulary. This is costly on the pre-storage end. It allows conceptual searching because human analysis has been added. The disadvantage is that the intervention was human and there is a lack of consistency. It is interesting to note that the original *New York Times Infobank,* vintage 1974, used this method. Six years later they added the ability to search their story abstracts in full-text. Shortly thereafter they added full-text of the stories. The thesaurus, which had 601 pages in 1982, was shortened to 73 pages when full-text became available.

A third method is to add "enhancement" terms to the text of the story. This is used in the Vu/Text system. Words such as "major story," "opinion," "analysis," "commentary," and "statistics" are added because they help the searcher understand the kind of story that is available. Here, once more, is a problem of inconsistency. Do these terms mean the same thing to all users? The advantage of enhancement is that modern journalistic prose strives to be different. In contrast to the hard sciences, the soft sciences continue to present problems in language control. Looking at how best to handle semantic confusion, news content analysis will have to find the best of two worlds. Free searching of full-text can turn up the needle in the haystack (e.g. when did Reagan say "I've had it up to my keester"?). Controlled vocabulary will give future Ph.D. candidates more than they may want on "political candidates" or "oil production." Enhancement will pull out the stories on "biographies" of political candidates or "statistics" on oil production. Recently one indexer was asked why he added the word "history" to a rather long story on toxic waste when the same word was already in the body of the story. He wisely replied that no good searcher working with a full-text system would ever use "history" as a general search term if all that was needed was a historical summary. Using such a general term would inundate the searcher with unnecessary material. Therefore he chose to add the word to the enhancement field.

Another way to speed searching is to expand on a method the old Infobank offered. If you only want biographies on a person, you type in BIO. If you only want reviews, you type in REV. Numbers or alphanumeric codes can be assigned to a restricted list of common types of news stories—for example, letters to the editor. Such codes are already common in business and financial databases such as Dow Jones and ABI/INFORM.

Information Access Corporation's newspaper and magazine databases do not, at this time, offer major newspapers full-text. The bibliographic citations include in-depth indexing using Library of Congress subject headings plus a special field of "descriptors." This field had to be added because it proved impossible to intelligently analyze daily news using LC headings. The IAC products are available on Dialog and NEXIS. Dialog, a powerful and popular system, offers a wide range of subject-oriented databases that can easily be used to supplement the IAC databases when necessary.

Answering in-house queries

Most queries from reporters and copy editors involve a "quick fact." Spelling, dates, quotes, and names are the most commonly required facts. As newspaper libraries began using the large computerized databases, such as Dialog, BRS, and Orbit, they found eager customers. Reporters never enjoyed plowing through printed indexes. Now a trained library online specialist does the plowing—effortlessly and electronically. Editors and management appreciate that. Less time is expended at a lower salary level. Even though online costs are considerable (ranging from a few dollars per search to hundreds of dollars), it is worth the apparent extra cost for the added benefit of richer research and, theoretically, more interesting news stories.

As the systems available for computerizing newspaper libraries proliferate, as more and more databases are available electronically, it becomes virtually impossible to be proficient in all of them. Competing newspaper chains will find they are trying to sell a product that is written in a different language than other news products. Efforts are underway to eliminate some of the need to memorize another language. This can be done—at considerable human expense—by buying special software that makes the machine automatically perform boring log-on steps. Once logged on, the searcher must still know the unique commands rigidly demanded by each system. No mercy and no results if you happen to use a space instead of a period.

One entrepreneur recently introduced a regional business news database. He chose to imitate the language used by Dialog. Although not identical to Dialog, there is enough similarity to make this new product seem easier to use. One does not hesitate to log on. It is as if when travelling in a foreign country all the telephone systems used exactly the same procedures as those in the United States.

Equipment necessary to reach into this world of data varies also. At first some of the vendors (NEXIS and Dow Jones) tried to restrict use to their brand of terminal. This meant having at least two terminals occupying precious desk space. The keyboards were also slightly different. For many libraries this meant acquiring one terminal for BRS, Orbit, and Dialog and another for NEXIS—which also offered Dialog. Librarians fumed. Online user groups groused via their electronic bulletin boards. Dow Jones never tried to force the issue and offered DJNRS on any compatible terminal. Recently Mead announced NEXIS and LEXIS users could obtain software for PC terminals such as Wang, Apple, IBM and Xerox. The new AT&T personal computer will soon join the club. This is a welcome step.

Questions for news publishers

As more newspaper publishers consider storing and selling their printed product, they must carefully explore questions of copyright, invasion of privacy, inclusion of corrections and retractions, whether or not to store syndicated columns and features. Developers of news-related databases should assess the benefits of a uniform approach to these issues, regardless of the software or hardware they use or the ownership of the databases. Questions are being raised as to whether a syndicated columnist should be paid each time the column is accessed in a database. Or are these rights—similar to those of musicians—relinquished when the articles are published? Certainly all newspapers that are not now copyrighted should take immediate steps to protect their product. Theoretically anyone with financial resources could develop a news database and market it. A uniform approach to these questions should be an important priority by all persons involved in news production and marketing.

There is also a need to improve communications between top management in the publishing industry and information specialists. Failure on this front increases the chances of having managers from the business side of a newspaper's operation take over. It is necessary to reposition the information system's function in the organizational hierarchy. Managing the information resources needs to be intimately related to electronic data processing. Ensuring that each has equal status will free each to devote energy to meeting opportunities for future growth.

Activity abroad

There is also interest and activity outside the United States in this area. According to Patrick V. Drotos of INCA-FIEJ Research Association, West Germany, the current trend in Europe has been the creation of full-text news databases using disc-based systems. This is clearly demonstrated by the installation of the Docu/Master system at Politiken newspapers in Copenhagen, the creation of TT Arkiv AB by the Swedish TT news agency, and the AGORA database in G. CAM by Agence France Presse. A disc-microfiche hybrid system was installed by the ANSA news agency in Rome in 1980. In the ANSA archive, COM fiche has been linked to an online disc-stored index. It is open to remote searching by agency bureaus and client newspapers and businesses. Remote subscribers still need to have a complete collection of microfiche stored on location to recall the full text of stories. A similar system is in use in Zurich, at Ringier Dokumentations Zentrum.

In Drotos's opinion, the Nikkei publishing group (Japan) offers the most significant electronic information service in Asia. It has developed NEEDS-IR. This is made up of a disc-microfiche hybrid archive system started in 1970 and several digital databases known as NEEDS-TS/I, NEEDS-II and QUICK. The service offers industrial, economic, and political information gathered from a global network plus computer economic modelling software.

In India, as in many developing countries, the flow of information is government-controlled in one form or another. Radio, television and telecommunications are under government supervision, while the print media are indirectly controlled by an "import quota on newsprint" allotted to various news publishing groups. The free flow of information is hampered by outmoded equipment and shortsighted government policies. However, the Indian government has encouraged development of databases for the textile and chemical industries. In the print media only *Gujarat Samachar* has done pioneering work in electronic publishing.

Technology is influencing a familiar part of our daily life—the newspaper. Publishers should think in terms of the resale and exploitation of material that has usually been dumped in the morgue. Reporters must learn to use and demand excellent results from a powerful new tool. Librarians must learn how to manipulate the raw material in order to satisfy public and private needs. Researchers need to develop a way to standardize access to the treasure store and simplify and improve their assessment and synthesis. Equipment should be as standard as electric light bulbs and typewriters.

All news media, especially newspapers, are the memory of the community and, as Lou Thomas and Anne Jennings wrote in *Guidelines for Newspaper Libraries,* "the library is the memory of the newspaper." ▣

Treasure in the Library Attic: Von Ranke at Syracuse

Bruce Coville

Twenty years ago, the finest collection of primary source materials ever assembled by one man for the study of western history sat deteriorating on the top floor of Syracuse University's Carnegie Library. Heat was destroying the bindings. Fluctuating humidity was accelerating the decay of low-quality paper. And mold was growing in a first edition of Martin Luther's *Table Talk* (one of three copies known to exist in the United States, currently valued at $100,000).

Even worse, no one really cared,

because the collection, containing some 17,000 books, 4,000 pamphlets and 430 manuscripts, and with a current estimated value of about $3 million had achieved an unjustified reputation of being "worthless."

This collection was the private library of "the father of modern history," a German scholar named Leopold von Ranke. Ranke's name may not be familiar to many persons other than historians. He has been compared with Herodotus and Thucydides, and is considered a national intellectual hero by the people of Germany.

Ironically, one of the reasons Ranke is not as well known here as he should be is his very influence on our historical tradition. In the early part of this century a large percentage of American historians had studied under Ranke, or under professors trained by him. Eventually a reaction to this dominance set in, especially after the First World War, when interest in his work suffered the fate of most things of German origin.

Ranke, with his insistence on using the archives and documents of an era to explain the past "as it really was" (an idea more radical then than it may sound now), pointed historians in the direction they have been moving ever since. The professional discipline was indelibly marked by his philosophy and teaching.

The collection at Syracuse has a double importance. It is a major historical resource, and it is also a vital key to the study of Ranke. Yet for nearly a century this collection, once intended to be a great scholarly resource, has been virtually inaccessible to researchers. The material was not restricted, but the great mass of it had never been properly cataloged.

The problem is summed up in the comments of Walter Peter Fuchs, professor of history at the University of Erlangen and the leading German authority on Ranke, who came to Syracuse in the 1950s to use the collection. Fuchs found he had made a bootless journey. "It was impossible to use," he later stated. "I would have had to organize it first, and that would have taken a lifetime."

Bruce Coville, *editor of* Seniority *magazine, lives in Syracuse, New York*

James Powell *with library specialist* **Liz Williams**

As it turned out the task didn't quite take a lifetime. But it did take many hands, a grant from the National Endowment for the Humanities, and multinational interest. Today, after an effort that has spanned seven years and cost nearly a quarter of a million dollars, the Ranke collection is finally the research tool it was intended to be—not only for scholars at Syracuse University, but also for persons who have access to OCLC terminals.

And thereby hangs a tale. Our story has two heroes: a librarian and a professor, their roles separated by nearly a century.

The librarian was Charles W. Bennett, who joined the Syracuse faculty in 1871, the year of the university's founding. Bennett, who had studied under Ranke at the University of Berlin, was chairman of the university's history department, and, from 1874 to 1884, university librarian. It was Bennett's initiative and persistance that resulted in the university's acquisition of the library.

The professor is James Powell, a historian who came to the university in the early 1960s, when the common wisdom held that the Ranke collection "wasn't worth much."

Powell began to investigate and found otherwise. "They didn't know," he says now, with a trace of wonder. "They had no idea what was in there." Grinning slightly, he describes the situation as "suddenly finding yourself sitting on one of the richer collections in the United States."

How did it get there?

In 1874 the university library consisted of slightly over two thousand books. In Bennett's words, "All felt how meager and totally inadequate was such a collection; chagrin and shame was felt when strange visitors made inquiry respecting the library."

Early in 1875 a wealthy cleric named John Morrison Reid, along with his wife Caroline, spent some time with Bennett's family. Conversations between the two men convinced Reid of the university's need for books. A short time later the Reids provided $5,000 for the purchase of new books, along with expenses for Bennett to travel to Europe to purchase them (certainly a more pleasant, if time-consuming, method than scanning publishers' catalogs). While in Europe Bennett became aware of the Ranke library, and what seemed its incipient availability.

Upon his return Bennett reported to Reid regarding his mission. During this report he said, half in jest, "When Leopold von Ranke dies you must purchase his library for the historical department of Syracuse University. Then let the professors in each of the departments find friends to make like purchases for them, and Syracuse will be the best furnished institution of the land for original scholarly work."

Reid, interested but unable to commit the money required, told Bennett to keep an eye on "the treasure." Bennett and Syracuse University were not the only ones interested in Ranke's library. Several other universities, including Harvard, Yale, and Cornell were intrigued by the possibilities of the collection. But for Bennett it took on the stature of a quest.

However Ranke, whose death had seemed imminent at the time of Bennett's initial book-buying foray, confounded everyone interested in the purchase of his library by living for another eleven years. When he did finally succumb in 1886, at the age of 91, the fate of the library semed a foregone conclusion: it would be purchased by the Prussian government.

Bennett was about to embark for Europe to research a book of his own when he received world of Ranke's passing. Knowing that at least six other universities were after the collection, he decided to sidestep traditional channels and contact Otto von Ranke, the historian's oldest son. The result was not encouraging, as the family was anxious for the collection to stay in Germany. However Ranke, impressed by Bennett's ardor, promised him first refusal of the library if the government should turn it down.

"I had not the remotest thought of the possibility of his success," Ranke was to write later, certain the Prussian government would soon be making their offer.

The family had only two requirements: they wanted a satisfactory financial settlement, and a guarantee that the library would be kept together. To their dismay the Prussian government, absorbed in preparations for what seemed an imminent war, made no satisfactory offer. Their price was too low and they intended to divide the collection among royal and university libraries. Eager as they were to see the collection kept in Germany, the family was even more determined that it should be kept together.

In March 1887, with the Rankes frustrated by months of Prussian foot-dragging, Bennett took a gamble. He sent Otto von Ranke an ultimatum—all of the family's wishes would be met, but only if a decision was made within the next two weeks. Ranke bit, and the collection, all eighty-three crates and nineteen tons of it, belonged to Syracuse. It arrived in March 1888. But now that they had it, what should be done with it? Things got off to a flying start with the dedication, in 1889, of a new building constructed specifically to hold the collection, along with the rest of the university's library. They went steadily downhill for the next eighty years. A large part of the problem was simply that the university had bitten off more than it could chew. This was coupled with a general retrenchment in funding for universities during the next decade.

"It was a perfect example of a mismatch of resources and personnel," says Powell. "They would have done the job if the money had been there to continue development. But there were huge problems involved in making it what it was intended to be. And they weren't just involved with cataloging. They needed to build a history collection to go with it, and a faculty to go with both."

Efforts were made. In 1890 the Chancellor reported "the work of cataloging and arranging the library has gone forward as rapidly as possible . . . the librarian has toiled incessantly all day and far into the night to advance this work."

It was like writing in sand, for in 1895 the librarian's efforts were washed away by the tide of the Dewey decimal system. The cataloging effort had to start all over again.

The university began to regard the collection as an albatross. "They were embarrassed by having it," says Powell. "They started to invent stories that it was worthless as a defense mechanism."

In fact the collection came to be the subject of all manner of rumors. In 1937 the Syracuse library director wrote "the value of the collection now is chiefly sentimental," and complained about maintaining something

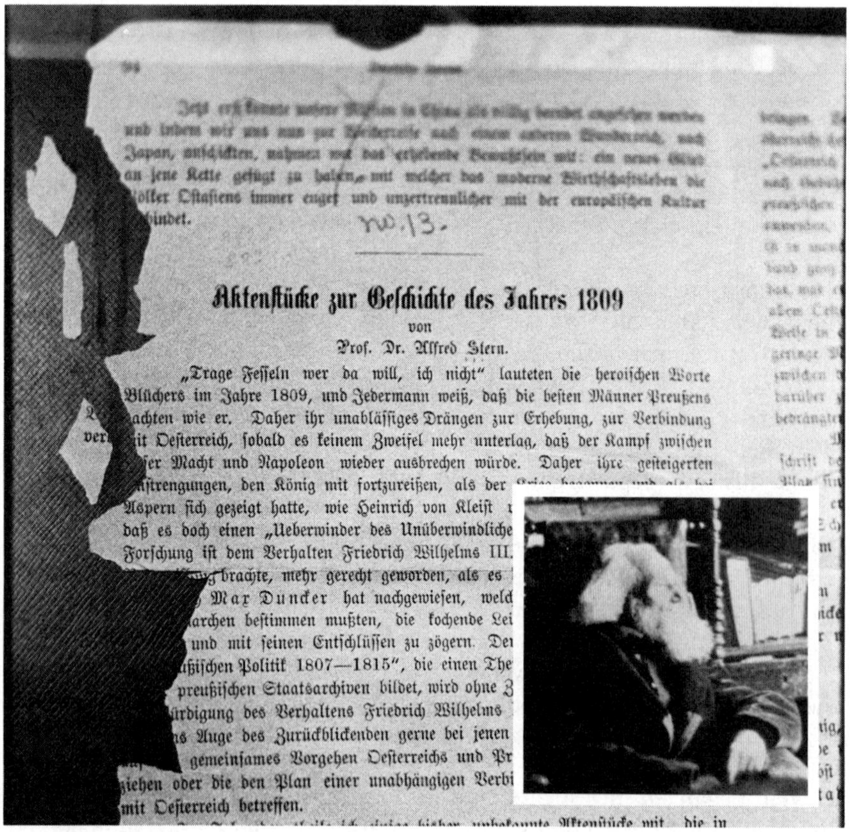

Present and past: *A disintegrating manuscript, Von Ranke in his library*

The **Mercurius,** *an early serial that was, says Powell, "the* ***Newsweek*** *of its time," and a hand-illustrated page from the oldest manuscript (1391) in the collection—the apocalyptic predictions of Telesphorus of Cosenza.*

The Treasures of Ranke

Two people know the Ranke collection intimately—Professor James Powell, whose enthusiasm has carried the project to its current stage, and Professor Edward Muir, who cataloged the manuscript collection. Herewith some of Powell and Muir's favorite items from the collection, notable for rarity, monetary value, or simply because they are unique and surprising:

- The Libellus of Telesphorus of Cosenza: This is the oldest manuscript in the collection (1391), a hand-illustrated set of apocalyptic prophecies in the tradition of the twelfth-century Abbott Joachim, whose views on the history of the world, past and future, were adopted by some "dissident thinkers" in the next century. (See photo)
- *The Autobiography of Benjamin Franklin*: This would hardly seem unusual, except it is a first edition—in French. Few people realize that Franklin's autobiography was published in Paris, shortly after his death, before it ever saw print in English.
- *The Institutes of Christian Religion* by John Calvin: Though the first complete edition appeared in 1559 and this volume is from the late 1560s, Powell has a special fondness for it because of its exquisite binding.
- Several volumes of *The Mercurius:* This was a seventeenth-century journal or serial which Powell likens to "A *Newsweek* of its time." (See photo)
- A Reformation pamphlet by Thomas Muntzer, a radical reformer killed in the Peasant's Revolt of 1525.
- The Ranke family letters: In a neat twist, historian becomes historical source here. Ranke married an Englishwoman (the great aunt of poet Robert Graves); her letters, included in the collection, form an interesting account of nineteenth-century family life, and a picture of what it was like for an Englishwoman to live in Germany at the time.

that was of use only to graduate students who could read German. (In reality the library contained thousands of volumes in English and French.) Even more startling was a 1949 letter from a foundation supporting German-American relations, suggesting that as they had heard the collection was still in boxes (this some sixty years after its purchase) perhaps the foundation would make a good "resting place" for the books.

Jeremy Jackson, an assistant professor of history at Syracuse, summed up the fate of Ranke's library in 1972 when he wrote, "Neglected for understandable reasons, its reputation declined; given no life, it seemed to have none to give."

Enter Professor James Powell, whose interest began in the late 1960s, despite being told over and over that there was nothing of real value in the collection.

"I'm a queer duck," says Powell. "I was always interested in books and libraries, so I couldn't stay away from looking at it. And I started to see that there was important stuff in the collection."

Restoring the collection

Powell tried to get some action on taking care of the library, but nothing was accomplished for several years—largely due to the rumors about the collection's worthlessness, which carried a life of their own. Finally he wrote a proposal for the National Endowment for the Humanities.

The NEH resisted on two points. One, according to Powell "was the traditional gossip among librarians that it was just another collection of old junk." The second was their belief that "no university in its right mind would allow a major collection to be hidden." According to Powell, the situation of the Ranke library can be found echoed in several other major collections gathering dust in universities around the country.

One of Powell's greatest concerns, and a factor creating some urgency, was the physical condition of the library. "It was stored on the top floor of an old building. The heat was destroying the books. It was a mess!"

Ironically, the oldest and most valuable material was the least damaged, largely because of the quality of the paper and the craftsmanship in the binding.

In 1977, ten years after Powell first became interested in the library, the NEH provided a grant of $50,000, with the availability of an additional $50,000 to match privately raised funds. Matching funds were raised, much of them from German sources. Additionally the Deutsche Forschungsgemeinschaft, the official West German Research Foundation, donated over one hundred volumes of the *Monumenta Germania Historia,* an ongoing project reprinting historical source materials relating to Italy and Germany.

With the money in hand, work began on three fronts: restoration, cataloging of the main collection, and cataloging of the original manuscripts.

For the latter project the university hired Edward Muir, who was given the responsibility of identifying the title, author and date of each manuscript, and finding out if there were other copies in existence and if they had been published anywhere. Considering that these were handwritten materials, often several centuries old, and in a variety of languages, the task was a challenging one.

Despite some of the unexpected treasure in the collection, there was no Eureka sensation, says Muir. "You pick up a manuscript and it isn't 'Aha, here's this great unknown thing!' You go through a long research just to find out what it is. It's more a slow accumulation of information."

Initially Muir had expected the project to take two to three years. Indeed, he had finished the "crude cataloging" in that time. But because of the nature of the manuscripts (with titles, authors and quotes from the beginning and ending of each manuscript spanning several languages), typing and proofreading took several more years. In December 1983 the Syracuse University Press published *The Leopold von Ranke Manuscript Collection of Syracuse University: The Complete Catalog.*

For the first time in a century the Ranke manuscripts had become a truly usable historical resource.

The cataloging of the main collection continues. In a spacious room on the top floor of the Ernest Stevenson Bird Library, with huge windows that provide a panoramic view of the campus—a far cry from the overheated "attic" of the old Carnegie Library—two researchers pore through the Ranke collection volume by volume, noting presentation copies and those books with handwritten annotations by Ranke. Ranke took notes in four languages, sometimes all in the same volume; added to the peculiarities of his script, deciphering them is almost a task for a cryptographer.

When the information for each book is complete the material is typed into a computer terminal, entering it in the OCLC catalog and making it immediately available to literally millions of users. About eighty percent of the books have been cataloged; approximately fifty percent of the collection is online. One wonders what Ranke, who refused to organize his books for fear he would not be able to find them, would have made of the process.

Down the hall and around the corner is the George Arents Research Library, where the Ranke collection is now housed. Wandering the stacks, one is first delighted, then awed, and finally overwhelmed by the richness and the variety of the collection. Yet in a way it seems out of place here. The antique volumes, a bibliophile's delight with their leather and vellum bindings, their creamy white paper, and their eccentric sizes, appear strange on the stark metal racks. One feels they ought to be housed in a Victorian mansion somewhere, on soaring chestnut bookshelves, with a fireplace in the background.

Yet here, in their temperature and humidity controlled environment, they will endure. Even more important, they will finally be used. Ranke would be pleased.

Serials Cancellations: Taking Advantage of Online Union Lists

Scott Bruntjen and Ruth Carter

Before the advent of online catalogs, the decisions collections managers made about relying upon resources held in other libraries usually were limited to an inefficient, costly, and often haphazard examination of the collections of a few neighboring libraries. The concept of a regional collection as the sum of the capabilities of all libraries within a region was not well developed and had not replaced the traditional focus on collections of individual libraries.

In virtually all cases that supported the regional collection concept the decision to share resources, substituting access for ownership of material, was limited to the initial decision of whether or not to purchase a specific title.

A definable effect

While there were no easy-to-use, comprehensive sources available to help in the initial purchase decision, there was even less information about the effect that the removal of an item from one library would have on the capabilities of another library. The removal through weeding of a single monograph would have a certain definable effect on another library that had a resource-sharing agreement to provide access to that title. The cancellation of a serial subscription provides a long-term loss of access that is difficult to measure. Unknown quantities of information would have been provided in the future had the serial been continued in the collection.

It is known that online catalogs with enhanced searching capabilities provide better access for the library patron. It is less well-recognized that such catalogs also provide new sources of information to collection managers. An online catalog provides new approaches to current information about the collection and it provides a method to communicate information about that collection to locations outside the library. The mere existence of the online catalog changes the range of possibilities that collection managers can employ for the coordinated sharing of resources. Yet enhanced collection management decision-making information provided by such catalogs, at least theoretically, has not been recognized or used except experimentally.

With the support of the Council on Library Resources, the Pittsburgh Regional Library Center (PRLC) explored what might be done using some of the collection management information provided by a multi-library online catalog: the online union list of serials. The results of the PRLC Serials Cancellation Project provide some insight into the problems and opportunities of multi-institution collection management decision-making using the online catalog as a tool.

In the expanding economy of the 1960s and early 1970s, independent collection building was acceptable since many libraries had adequate financial resources. By the mid-1970s, however, this financial base began to erode. While several studies, such as the 1975 Association of College and Research Libraries' "Standards for Academic Libraries," recognized the fact that a single library's collection should be considered as part of a larger collection resource, there were no widely accepted methods to implement multi-institutional cooperation for collection development and maintenance. Only ad hoc efforts existed.

A few isolated attempts

During this same period libraries began to construct online national union catalogs as a by-product of shared catalog records using the Online Computer Library Center, the Research Libraries Group's RLIN system and other such bibliographic utilities. There were a few isolated attempts to coordinate collection management decisions by examining the holdings of other nearby libraries using the online databases prior to making purchases. These efforts were not universal or coordinated, and, perhaps more significantly, were normally limited to purchase decisions. Less effort was made to cancel a holding and no opportunity was present in the systems to inform other libraries about the consideration of an item for future cancellation.

With the success of shared cataloging, technical services librarians looked to the same national sources to display local holdings for union lists of serials. The Conversion of Serials Project (CONSER), which began in the mid-1970s, provided the necessary catalog base for serials holdings information. Outside funding from a number of sources provided the needed capital to develop union listing capability. Virtually all online activity, however, was concentrated on database building rather than on database maintenance. This focus reflected collection development decisions that

Scott Bruntjen *is executive director, Pittsburgh Regional Library Center, Chatham College, Pittsburgh.* **Ruth Carter** *is head, cataloging department, University of Pittsburgh.*

were less concerned with weeding than with acquisition.

To the credit of the national utilities, procedures were established that required adherence to national standards. This adherence was one of the major factors in assuring the development of data that could be exchanged. For serials holdings, current thought was focused on building a database, not on providing collection development information related to the cancellation of a title.

The standards for recording serials holdings information called for closing the entry only when the last issue actually arrived. Consequently, even for a library that maintained its online union list information, the last entry could not be closed until months, or even years, after the decision had been made to cancel a serial. Thus the database accurately represented serial holdings but there was no provision to include online the intent to terminate or to acquire a subscription at a later date. The standard reflected "holdings," not collection management intentions.

The need to cancel

In most growth environments maintenance is left until later. American libraries building online union catalogs provided no exception to this rule. With the dramatic drop in purchasing power of the United States dollar in foreign markets in 1980 many libraries were faced with the need to cancel expensive serial titles, many of which were held by relatively few institutions. The shared cataloging experience, the development of library standards that reflected the need to coordinate collections, and the resource-sharing interests of a number of regional networks brought librarians to the difficult position of wanting to preserve at least the last copy of an active title in a region while bringing serial budgets into line with the suddenly reduced purchasing power.

Although a number of groups had a management information gold mine in the form of an online union list of serials, standards and procedures that focused on holdings and disallowed information about future intentions worked against using the union list for coordinated deacquisition. Librarians exchanged computer printouts of their journal holdings with handwritten marginal notes about possible cancellation decisions. The printouts, even those that came from an online system, could not represent the current status without those marginal notes, for the standards called for keeping an entry open until that last issue arrived, no matter how long that took.

Although the Pittsburgh area had a long history of cooperative collection development, directors and collection management staff were not using management information systems during a period when massive cancellations were being made. The one lesson that was learned from the 1980 experience was that there must be a way to utilize what had been considered catalog and reference information only, for collection management.

A more effective method

At the same time that the need for rapid communication of cancellation information was recognized, the Pennsylvania Union List of Serials (PaULS) was being built. The Pittsburgh Regional Library Center, having experienced the loosely coordinated cancellation projects and simultaneous development of PaULS, proposed to the Council on Library Resources that PRLC find a more effective method of making future serials cancellation decisions utilizing the PaULS list on OCLC. In 1981 the Council awarded PRLC a grant to develop and test an online, distributed method of communicating serial subscription cancellation decisions to the personnel most interested in minimizing the damage to regional collections.

The PRLC region and the state as a whole were well suited to the test. Included were libraries that participate in OCLC, in RLIN, and libraries that did not have direct online access to either. Two regional networks, PRLC and PALINET, were included. A large union list of serials, PaULS, was available for serial online information. Libraries throughout the region had given strong support to resource sharing.

The organization of the Serials Cancellation Project, as it became known, was superimposed on the structure that had been developing the Pennsylvania Union List of Serials. That project, which had been funded since 1979 by the State Library, included 250 libraries in five states and had produced an online union list of serials on OCLC of more than 60,000 titles and 200,000 holdings.

Outside advice was provided to the project by an advisory committee composed of seven individuals representing libraries, networks, bibliographic utilities, national standards organizations, and other interests. At their first meeting, the advisory committee recommended that librarians who would use the tool become acquainted with its operation through a series of workshops. It also recommended that the American National Standards Institute (ANSI) Subcommittee E, a group that was considering detailed holdings statements for serials, be requested to consider a modification of the serials holdings standard. Specifically, the advisory committee suggested that collection management intentions and decisions be reflected online in addition to actual holdings information. The education of the collection managers and the modification of the ANSI standard were the two most difficult efforts.

Agreeing on a code

As there was no standard code to indicate an acquisition status of "cancellation entered, but currently being received," it was necessary to agree on a code to represent that information. The information would be communicated along with other union list data contained in the local data records of OCLC's Serials Control Subsystem. This topic was brought to the attention of OCLC's Union List Task Force in June 1981.

In the absence of an approved code for the acquisition status described above, OCLC mandated use of a note to convey a decision to cancel a particular serial subscription. The Union List Task Force members agreed upon the following notation:

Cancellation effective with (vol): (no.) (year): (month)

It was understood that the issue and date cited referred to the last issue expected to be received.

Instructions for recording and reporting the information were communicated to participants. The information was included later in the PaULS procedure manual. All reporting libraries were furnished with a revised version of the PRLC union list report form, which created a standard method of reporting information and facilitated processing of the data by project staff. During the project period, cancellation information was centrally entered on the union list, although the procedure was designed to work in a decentralized input mode as well.

The project called for libraries to report a cancellation first when the decision was made and second when the actual holdings were closed. This two-step reporting caused confusion. In part this may be because many librarians prefer not to use limited resources on something that is essentially regional serials collection integrity insurance. Once the last issue is received, the holdings are closed; the intent to cancel is superseded. The value of the intermediate work is only realized if another library looks at the intent during the period when the cancelling library is waiting to receive the last issue and close the holding. This is most likely to happen in the very circumstances which were the genesis of the project: a time when many libraries decide to undertake massive cancellation projects nearly simultaneously.

In the spring of 1982 the project staff conducted six workshops in Pennsylvania and West Virginia. During the workshops it became evident that despite a decade of involvement by libraries in this region in online systems, there was little direct use of OCLC or RLIN by collection managers.

Considering new codes

In addition to providing education for collection development librarians, the serials cancellation project worked to influence the authors of the newly developing ANSI standard for detailed serials holdings. From the advice received from the project's advisory committee, the staff requested that ANSI consider several new "acquisition status codes." In the current ANSI standard for serial holdings at the summary level the library has the opportunity to describe the status of the acquisition in the following ways:

0 information not available
4 currently received
5 not currently received

The serials cancellation project proposed to add four new codes:

2 acquisition under consideration
3 on order but not yet received
7 cancellation under consideration
8 cancelled but last issue not yet received

The rationale was that this technique would provide notice about future collection management intentions as well as current holdings information. With that additional information, the serials statements could influence the actions of collection managers in other libraries.

The ANSI subcommittee reviewed this concept but did not accept it as pertinent to the standard they were writing. That standard was a holdings standard, not one that conveyed other types of information. During this same period, however, development began on the MARC communications format for holdings and locations. The proposed new MARC format was a response to the need to communicate holdings among systems and from systems to vendors in a standardized way. When it is accepted, the format can be expected to influence the design of records in local systems as well as in those of the national bibliographic utilities and commercial systems. Therefore, even though the Serials Cancellation Project did not influence the creation of a new acquisition status code, it did lead to inclusion of a suitable field in the proposed MARC communication format for holdings and locations.

At the project advisory committee's second meeting in the fall of 1982, agreement was reached about the successes and the needs of the effort. In essence, the availability of an online, comprehensive listing of serials information has great potential for regional collection development. While national utilities such as OCLC or RLIN are potential hosts for this data, the current development of linked local library systems has far greater potential usefulness for the distribution of this type of information.

A number of observations

A number of observations can be made about the project results. Negatively, perhaps, it was found that most librarians do not like to spend resources on contingency plans, that database maintenance tends to be neglected, and that even with a decade of use few librarians other than technical services or interlibrary loan staff are acquainted with the potential and the detailed use of online systems. The third condition can be changed but the first two need careful consideration as libraries convert their holdings to online catalogs.

Discussions at the advisory committee meetings and at the workshops included expressions of interest in expanding the scope of collection development records. As an example, there was support for indicating titles that are on order. Some participants wanted to go a step further to include titles being considered either for ordering or for cancelling.

The project demonstrated that within an online environment, libraries can accomplish resource-sharing tasks that have been accepted philosophically but not practically. Rather than a minimal, haphazard approach to regional collection development and resource-sharing, libraries can choose to use the decisions made in the past decade about standards and database building and can provide better knowledge of resources for their communities. ◙

Working Less and Enjoying It More: Alternative Work Schedules

Katherine Shanks

The American way of life is synonomous with the freedom of choice. In our society alternatives and choices are integrated into almost every aspect of daily life. It is inconsistent, therefore, that so little choice is available to the employee in work schedules. Employers should realize that there is no moral or ethical value in the eight-hour day, five-day week, and fifty-two week work pattern. Society has decreed this as the norm, and jobs have been designed to fit into this precedent. Leaders, however, should begin to think in terms of scheduling jobs around the tasks and the people who perform those tasks, rather than an arbitrary schedule. Research has shown that alternative work schedules (flextime, permanent part-time, and job-sharing) will improve job performance and decrease absenteeism.

A more fully integrated life

The term alternative work schedules encompasses all variations of the standard work schedule; that is, an eight-hour work day for five days a week. Chief among such systems are:

- Flextime (Flexible Working Hours). Employees may vary their starting and stopping times within limits, but work the contracted number of hours in a specified time period (day, week, or month).
- Permanent Part-Time Employment. Regular employment (not temporary or casual) carried out during working hours which are distinctly shorter than the normal.
- Job-Sharing. A version of permanent part-time employment in which two (or more) individuals share one job. The workers are part time while the job is full time.

Katherine Shanks *is a part-time librarian for the American Association of Petroleum Geologists, Tulsa, Oklahoma.*

Alternative work schedules allow family, leisure, or education projects to dovetail with employment. Because the employee has greater flexibility for integrating work life and home life, both employee and employer reap benefits. Leaders in the business world are beginning to recognize that alternative work schedules can be very effective. According to the Bureau of Labor Statistics's 1980 figures on full-time nonfarm wage and salary workers, 7.6 million people (11.9 percent) were on flextime and 12.5 million (13.9 percent) were part-time. It is estimated that 15 to 20 percent of private sector employers offer flextime. Comparable figures are not available for job-sharing, but it is believed that there are thousands in the work force.

Although library managers are allowing some alternative work scheduling, there is little support or documentation in library literature. This is an interesting paradox. Alternative work schedules have proven to be most beneficial to working women, and approximately seventy-five persent of library employees are women.

The women's movement and the growing influence of women's organizations on academic, professional, and community institutions have played a tremendous role in social change. These organizations have taught women that it is acceptable to pursue careers, and no justification is needed. Alternative scheduling for the working woman is the next step in the process of advancement for women.

Human capital investment is an economic theory that considers education and training as an investment in the individual, contributing to that person's worth in terms of potential productivity. From this point of view, women who have degrees in librarianship and do not work are wasting valuable resources and assets. This is a loss not only to themselves, but to society as well. Alternative work scheduling can reclaim some of these individuals for America's work force.

Coordinating career and family

Alternative work schedules make it possible to efficiently coordinate career and domestic domains. Working mothers (particularly those with children at home) are often asked, "Why do you want to work since you don't have to?" Work is basic to the conduct of individual lives. Apart from the tangible rewards of work—finishing a job or collecting a paycheck—very often the process of work is itself most satisfying. Work is essential to a person's existence and satisfaction; it challenges a person's capacity to think and act and is a major source of human enrichment.

The standard eight-hour day and forty-hour work week were established in the 1930s. Union strength and legislation were instrumental in cutting the extended hours characteristic of the early 1900s. This pattern lasted until the labor shortage created by World War II. Work schedules were then established that focused on production; shift work was common and men and women equally shared the work until the end of the war. After the war, schedules and patterns again reverted to the standard pattern. It is time once again to consider alternative work schedules.

Rhythms and stages

Psychologists recognize that work behavior varies from one individual to another, and it varies over time for the same individual. Two important sources of these individual difference are circadian rhythms and life cycle stages. Recognition of the existence and implications of these cycles is important in order to help employees maintain effectiveness.

Biologists state that circadian rhythms are individual cycles of temperature, heart rate, metabolic rate, and urine constitution. These personal rhythms vary greatly, and have been shown to be correlated with work performance. If an individual's circadian rhythm is out of synchronization with the required work schedule, then it is unlikely that she will reach her productive potential. When one considers the inflexible work hours of most organizations, it is clear that some human factors, such as circadian rhythms, have not been considered. If one is allowed to coordinate peaks in his biological cycle with work demands, then overall improvement may occur. For example, an employee who is constantly tardy may have a work schedule that is incompatible with his circadian rhythm. With a minor adjustment, frustration would decrease and productivity would increase.

As individuals pass through various stages of life, personal attitudes and values will change—these are recognized as life cycles. However, most organizations assume no differences among life stages. Employees deserve the right to choose between financial advancement and individual values and the quality of life.

Flextime is a work schedule that allows employees to choose schedules for work and nonwork activities. The organization treats the individual as a whole person, with a life outside, as well as within, the organization. Flextime is limited by the number of hours that must be worked for the employer during a reporting period. These reporting periods are commonly a day, a week, or a month. In the United States, hours are usually contracted by the week.

New freedom of choice

The fundamental feature of flextime is that it gives the worker a new freedom of choice and autonomy. This flexibility enhances the quality and dignity of a working life by offering the employee more control. Job satisfaction is greatly increased because flextime treats employees as responsible adults. Persons are free to pursue educational goals, follow leisure interests, do necessary shopping, run errands, and arrange for child care. In short, there is an opportunity for individuals to make appropriate tradeoffs between work and non-work concerns.

Not only are there benefits to the individual, but there are social benefits as well. The greatest societal benefit is that it provides employment opportunities for many often-overlooked groups, particularly women.

There are some disadvantages to the company or organization that allows a flextime schedule. Communication lines may break down and it may be harder to find times to hold meetings that require everyone's presence. For this reason, more consideration must be given to planning meetings and communications.

Another disadvantage is that some kind of record-keeping system for workers' hours may be necessary. When all hours are fixed, there is no need to establish a system that records working hours, but with flextime, the employer must develop a system for accruing hours.

Supervisors who follow the classical management style may feel threatened and insecure when flextime is initiated. Those who have never trusted employees enough to let them work without supervision may, especially at first, feel uncomfortable with flextime.

A wide range of workers can benefit from a flextime schedule. Some of them are:

- Working mothers who have the opportunity to stay home to see the children off to school in the morning, or to be at home to greet them as they return in the afternoon.
- Single adults who enjoy an active night life are given the chance to sleep late; hence, they are more productive while at work.
- Executives or managers who prefer to work longer hours on some days to complete projects can take off on others.
- Older employees who are nearing retirement may adjust schedules so that they are more involved in hobbies or activities that will carry them into retirement.
- Single parents are given the chance to adapt to the necessary distractions of parenting without guilt.

It has been shown that flextime raises morale, reduces tardiness and absenteeism, controls employee turnover, and makes recruiting easier. All of these benefits are available at very little cost to the employer.

Part-time work has always existed, but the concept of permanent part-time is relatively new. Permanent part-time positions are available indefinitely, regardless of the jobholder. Permanent part-time work also connotes some career-relatedness, with potential for upward mobility.

There are a variety of ways that permanent part-time work can be inaugurated. Employees can agree to work a minimum number of hours per week, and be on call for more. Or, they can work a fixed number of hours at mutually convenient times. In either case, the organization or library will have the benefit of adjusting schedules to match peak demands, and the individual can balance work with nonwork activities. Many permanent part-time workers are individuals who would otherwise not be able to work, or would give less than full commitment to work that demanded longer hours.

Attracting talented people

There are several advantages of having permanent part-time workers in the organization. Part-time scheduling can lead to reductions in overtime payments, turnover, absenteeism, and time lost for work breaks. Another organizational advantage is that permanent part-time work often attracts talented people who might not otherwise be available to work. Valuable employees who want to quit full-time but do not want to stop working can be retained on a part-time basis.

In the American economy, there are often shortages in particular job categories and in particular locations. Permanent part-time work creates a large applicant pool of people willing to assume routine, entry-level jobs who perform with greater than average productivity. Employers have found that those who begin work with routine part-time jobs often stay to work full-time for the organization. Such jobs allow persons to gain experience in the world of work. Another advantage for the organization is that minority quotas can be partially met for the affirmative action goals of the Equal Employment Opportunity Commission. The government makes no distinction between part-time and full-time workers in estimating percentages of women and minorities at work.

The company that uses part-time employees can plan to meet actual demands, and avoid paying overtime. Part-time workers can be scheduled to meet emergencies and special projects, and to provide public service when demand is at its peak. Hence, there will be better service to customers or patrons, a decrease in backlogs, and an elimination of work logjams.

The greatest advantage to the employer is that the productivity of part-time workers equals and often exceeds that of full-time workers. It is believed that a half-time worker (one who works four hours a day) produces approximately three-fourths the amount of work as a full-time worker. They do not become fatigued with tedious jobs because they are required to produce for a shorter period of time.

Some women's organizations have been at the forefront in advocating permanent part-time scheduling. It allows women to raise a family and not lose touch with career interests and training. Women who drop out of the labor market fall behind those who continue; this is a major rationale behind permanent part-time work. The most significant statistic, however, is that researchers have determined that permanent part-time work is particularly good for both women and children's psychological health—it even has shown to have a positive effect on marital satisfaction. While women make up the majority of part-time employees, some young couples are experimenting with each partner working part-time so that both may share in child-rearing.

There are some disadvantages for organizations that have a poorly designed program for part-time workers. Scheduling is more complex, and there can be additional costs for administration and training of part-time workers. Some companies have complained that part-time employees do not show the same commitment to the organization that full-time workers do.

For the employees there are, likewise, some disadvantages to part-time work. Certainly those who work part-time will advance much more slowly than full-time workers. Also, there are few (if any) benefits allowed. In addition, a person working part-time is likely to have higher commuting expenses.

Job-sharing, work-sharing

Job-sharers are two individuals who hold a single position. It is a rather new concept in the work world, and provides a new work method. Job-sharing seeks not only to increase the number of part-time opportunities, but also the quality of positions available (managerial and administrative positions). Job-sharing differs from part-time employment in that there must be collaboration between the two part-time workers who share the job.

Most job-sharers are women who value responsiblity and enjoy working fewer hours. Entitlement to fringe benefits is on important aspect of job-sharing as opposed to part-time work. Most job-sharers receive fringe benefits, either on the same basis as full-time employees or on a specially arranged, prorated basis.

Organizations benefit from job-sharing because there is better coverage with two individuals working on the same projects. If necessary, job-sharers can cover for each other during vacations and emergencies.

During downturns in the economy, the customary way for companies to cope is to lay off employees who are not needed, and rehire them when economics improve. This strategy has disadvantages in that some of the recalled, trained workers do not return. Also, when layoffs occur, there is usually a disproportionate loss of blacks and women, because these groups usually lack seniority. As an alternative to layoffs, some employers are implementing work-sharing, a form of job-sharing. A group of workers choose to reduce their hours of work and accept less pay. The trade-off, of course, is between less work/less pay for more people versus more work/more pay for fewer people. The main problems with work-sharing are that workers cannot qualify for unemployment compensation; fringe benefits for the employees are very expensive for employers; and senior employees may resent the loss of the ordinarily more favored position. Perhaps the greatest benefit of work-sharing is that net unemployment costs do not increase and society as a whole is less disrupted.

New sources of talent

There are disadvantages for individuals who share jobs. Many workers feel that even though they are often more effective than their full-time counterparts, they are not treated equally in terms of promotion and job tenure. There is slower progress on the salary scale, and a slower rate of seniority. By far, the greatest problem encountered by job-sharers and part-time workers is that they are often resented by their coworkers. Other em-

continued on page 158

Special Report:

Ron Chepesiuk

Winning the Miracle Mill: Greenville County Library Is Back on Its Feet

Tony Messineo

"It's never over 'til it's over." So said baseball great Yogi Berra in what has become one of his most famous "Yogiisms." It could very well have been the slogan, or perhaps more accurately, the battle cry of the Greenville County Library from 1979 through much of 1981. During that period, the library was involved in a pressured up-and-down struggle against the court claims of a local business. The odds were long that the case would be resolved in the library's favor. But Greenville County hung in there, and gave truth to Berra's words.

Ron Chepesiuk *is head of special collections, Dacus Library, Winthrop College, Rock Hill, South Carolina*

In recent years, South Carolina, like many other states, had encouraged economic growth by granting tax exemptions to new industries or to existing ones that expanded their operations. The exception was school taxes, which all industries had to pay immediately. The law favored the Greenville County Library in June 1979, when the South Carolina General Assembly enacted legislation stating that all taxes levied for the library were for "educational purposes." There were absolutely no exemptions. Overnight, the Greenville County Library became the best financially supported public library in the state—a library whose resources were used by the county as a drawing card to attract new industry.

The library enjoyed its status until 1979 when Hollingsworth on Wheels, a local construction company, challenged the statute. Its lawyers argued that the Greenville County Library was not eligible for the special taxes and asked for a refund of the taxes Hollingsworth had paid during the 1978–79 fiscal year. In August 1979 the local Master-In-Equity ruled in favor of the firm. In February 1980 the case was brought before the 13th Judicial Circuit, where the decision was reversed.

The lawsuit was shaping up to be a major court case bringing into question the basic educational function of the library. In the meantime, however, the library was forced to tighten its belt. On July 1, it was notified that, pending the outcome of the lawsuit, $170,000 for the 1981 fiscal year would be withheld. With a court docket backlog of nearly two years, no one expected the Supreme Court to decide the case quickly. Time dragged on as each side filed briefs. Amicus briefs were filed by the powerful State Chamber of Commerce and the South Carolina Textile Manufacturers Association in favor of the Hollingsworth Company.

When the State Supreme Court finally filed its opinion on May 18, 1981, it was a sad day for the Greenville County Library. In its decision, the court concluded that "the taxes for the library and museum are not taxes for a school purpose nor are school taxes. The library and museum satisfy recreational and social needs as well as educational needs. However, they are not schools and they do not serve a school purpose." The Supreme Court decreed that a library is not a school in the formal sense; that is, it doesn't have a classroom. Therefore, under South Carolina law, it is not eligible for the special taxes.

Greenville County Library director, Anthony Messineo, remembers the time as one of anxiety and uncertainty. With one legal sweep, the library's income had been decreased by twenty percent. He had been the library's director for only six months, and now he was faced with a situation in which essential programs would be jeopardized and the book collection adversely affected. "We really didn't know what our losses would be," he recalled. "There were all kinds of rumors floating around. It seemed as if everyone had a different guess."

The largest estimate was put at $87,000, far short of what the actual loss turned out to be. The courts ordered the library to pay back $557,405 to fifteen Greenville County businesses. This included tax revenues for the years 1977 through 1980. The largest sum, totaling approximately $224,000, went to the giant Michelin Corporation.The Hollingsworth on Wheels share of the tax refund bonanza amounted to just over $33,000. The situation could have been much worse. "Many companies didn't know that they could file claims," says Messineo, "and we weren't about to shout it from the rooftops."

Where could the library turn for relief? There was no choice. The library went to the Greenville County Council and asked for a special appropriation in the form of a millage increase for the library. However, like other parts of the country, it was the worst of times. The council was feverishly planning sharp budget cuts for fiscal year 1981–82. Another discouraging sign was that there had not been a tax increase in the county in five years.

The situation looked bleak indeed. In January 1981, the *Wilson Library Bulletin* reported B. O. Thomason, Jr., legal counsel for the Greenville County Library, as saying that a mill increase to compensate for the decreased level of support would almost certainly not be approved. But feeling that they had nothing to lose, the library decided to request a mill increase from $7\frac{1}{4}$ to $8\frac{1}{4}$, or about $236, 000 in additional money—not enough to make up for the lost income, but enough to stave off disaster.

There were no delusions about the initial chance for success. "I don't think any of us thought that the council would say yes right off the bat," says Messineo. On May 26, just eight days after the court decision, the library made its pitch to the council. The answer it received: No, by a convincing vote of nine to four.

The library's back was now against the wall. In three weeks, the council would make its final decision on the 1981–82 budget. How could the library get the council to change its mind? It was no easy task considering a simple majority was not enough. Nine out of the twelve councilmen had to vote yes.

The library administration knew that the only chance it had was to appeal to its constituency—the public—those who would suffer if the millage increase were not granted. "This is and has always been a good library," explains Messineo. "We thought that because it was a good library, we should be able to get strong community support. If we didn't get support, maybe the library was not doing its job."

Ironically, Messineo thought that the lack of time actually might be an advantage for the library. The opposition couldn't muster its defense. He explains, "It takes time to find out what's happening. Then you have to think about it before organizing and finally, once you organize, you have to have some method of fighting."

A peaceful world restored—the interior of Greenville County Library

Messineo says that the strategy the library mapped out was simple. "We didn't want to embarrass anybody publicly. We planned to treat them like the responsible adults that they were and just go for the mill. Let them know the consequences of not getting the appropriation and try to get the word out as quickly as possible and to as much of the public as we could."

Before beginning the public relations campaign, Messineo realized that the library's own house must first be in order. Rumors were rampant about possible layoffs, and he didn't want the staff to panic. He says, "I didn't want the staff to feel uncomfortable with the developments that were breaking day by day." Regular staff meetings were held and frequent internal memos provided facts and figures for the staff so that patrons could have a better understanding of the situation, advised the staff on how to get the message across, and instructed them to encourage library supporters to attend the council meetings.

Not all of the staff were enthusiastic about the library's chances of success. Verena Bryson, then the library's assistant director for community services, remembers one day when a large group of library volunteers were stuffing envelopes with campaign literature. A key staff member went up to the volunteers and told them that they were wasting their time. The library was going to lose the mill, so it would be better for the staff to implement the cutbacks than to send out the mailers.

"I couldn't believe it," Bryson recalls with anger, "I could have literally killed the person." He later apologized publicly in the library's house organ, saying that he was wrong.

With little time to lose, Messineo and his administrative staff concentrated on a media blitz. Advertising was out of the question because it cost money. Instead, the library turned to television and radio. Since he had been in Greenville for only six months and didn't know many people in the community, Messineo depended heavily upon the judgment of Bryson, a native of Greenville County who had twenty-two years experience working for the library. Messineo says, "I told Verena that anytime you see a microphone or camera, get me in front of it. When I came to work in the morning, Verena would grab me and point me in the right direction." By the end of the first week, Messineo was making as many as three television interviews a day.

In the beginning, the library wasn't getting much coverage from the newspapers. Messineo felt, however, that it was more important than television coverage. He explains, "People can clip articles, save them and refer to them. I believed that if newspapers printed the story, more people would know about our dilemma."

So he went down to talk to the editors of the local newspapers and told them that he was disappointed in the publicity the library was getting. The campaign for the mill increase was very important, and there would be an adverse effect upon the community if the library was not successful. "The newspapers reacted very reasonably," says Messineo. "They asked how we can help and began to publish our material verbatim."

The sympathetic press turned out to be a big factor in the campaign. The newspapers published several letters to the editor which appeared with bold headlines—"Library Must Be Saved," "Library, a Local Responsibility," "Budget Cuts Are Shameful"—and were effective in getting the library's message across. In one letter, the writer pointed out the irony of a situation in which manufacturing concerns, scouting areas to locate, always check the cultural facilities. "A library is a major asset, and our library is very creditable," he wrote. "It seems logical that all manufacturers should feel obligated to help in its support."

Editorials appeared often. The editor of the *Greenville News* wrote that unless the mill increase was restored, "a vital community resource will be diminished and the community as a whole . . . will suffer, as information, which a growth area needs, becomes less accessible." Bryson recalls, "We were getting so many editorials that Tony began to worry that the opposition was going to panic and mobilize. But that didn't happen."

In each of the stories relating to the campaign, one point was hammered home—the effect on the community. In a story which described the effect on a branch library in Greer if the county council did not approve the mill increase, Messineo was quoted as saying, "No local funds are available for purchasing books and only money provided by state and federal grants will be used for this purpose. This will not only affect books and magazines, but also business services such as Dun and Bradstreet."

The library's media campaign quickly proved successful, as it began to receive unsolicited contributions from citizens who wanted to help. Bryson says that the publicity had a snowball effect. "Once you start getting publicity, the people from the media keep coming back for more."

Under the pressure of growing public support for the library, the opposition within the council began to weaken. A few days before the council was to meet and decide on the mill, Messineo got a call from a library supporter. The chairman of the county council had given a speech to the Lions Club, and its members were criticizing the council for not supporting the library. Under pressure, the chairman said he would support the millage increase. "Once we had that," says Messineo, "I knew that we had turned the corner. If we could not get the whole council to vote yes, we would certainly get at least enough to win."

On June 16, the county council met. Nine out of the twelve voted in favor of the library request. In a stunning reversal from the first vote of just three weeks before, the library had squeaked by, getting the needed two-thirds majority to win. County council members were the first to admit that they had not anticipated the public outcry. Councilman Butler Hines, one of the four councilmen to support the initial library request, told one reporter after the meeting that "the public clamor made it hard for many of my colleagues to oppose the library."

The council had voted for the extra mill, but the increase was to last for only one year. In addition to the back payments to the companies, the library lost $232,000 when the mill was reduced in value. To hold down costs for the 1981–82 fiscal year, the library implemented a number of budget cuts, which included a reduction in bookmobile service, closing branch libraries on weekends, raising photocopy fees, and increasing fees.

In April 1982, the library made an appeal to the council that the millage increase be made permanent. The library administration argued that it "acted in good faith," trying to keep down costs and discouraging the efforts of library supporters who wanted to establish a lobbying group that would come to the council and insist that more than one mill be given to the library to offset losses. The council agreed.

Although it has been over three years since the run for the "miracle mill," Messineo says that the library is just starting to get back on its feet and shake off the debilitating effect of three years of retrenchment. "The future looks bright," he says, "We just got a foundation grant of over $200,000 that will allow us to install an automated circulation system."

As for the lessons for other systems, Greenville County Library officials believe that it really depends upon the circumstances and the library. Verena Bryson says, "Each public library would have to approach a similar situation differently. It depends a lot on your county council—the people you have in government." She adds, "If you provide what the people want, they will stand up for you. We assumed that our library was a good one. Obviously, the support that we got shows that the people shared that opinion." ▣

Dale Nelson:

Dateline–Washington

Unanimous consent for NARS and LSCA

To judge by the *Congressional Record,* you would think the Senate had a lively debate the night it passed the National Archives and Records Administration Act and the Library Services and Construction Act.

The first item for consideration when the Senate took up the archives act, setting up the National Archives as an independent agency instead of a part of the General Services Administration, was an amendment by Senator Charles Mathias (R–Md.).

Mathias's amendment was an essentially new bill, making a number of changes but preserving the general purpose of returning Archives to independent status with the archivist appointed for a ten-year term by the president.

The Senate then turned to an amendment by Senator Robert Dole (R–Kan.) designed to prevent disclosure of income tax records under a portion of the bill requiring federal agencies to turn over to the archivist "any information or data which the archivist finds necessary to carry out his duties."

Dole said the bill "might be misconstrued as indicating changed congressional intent regarding the confidentiality of tax records."

Mathias replied that he thought this concern was without basis, but he was willing to accept the amendment to pave the way for the bill, which was needed to correct "governmental inefficiency, confused lines of responsibility and authority, duplication of efforts, and prolonged decisionmaking."

Senator Daniel Patrick Moynihan (D–N.Y.) also joined the debate, saying the General Services Administration had been "the only voice of dissent" to making Archives an independent agency.

The Senate then turned to the library act and took up an amendment by Senator Robert Stafford (R–Vt.) authorizing assistance to a number of specific libraries.

Stafford spoke for his amendment and called the bill "an example of successful federal, state and local partnership."

Senator Lowell Weicker (R–Conn.) also supported the Stafford amendment and said that "federal encouragement of library sciences is necessary and must be continued."

Senators Dole and Mack Mattingly (R–Ga.) also expressed strong support for the bill, which was then passed unanimously.

At least that's what the *Record* says.

In fact, hardly any of these worthies were anywhere near the Senate. President Reagan was playing host at a fish fry at the White House, with practically the whole Senate in attendance.

The bills were passed by the sort of legislative legerdemain that keeps the Senate functioning when most of its members are attending committee meetings or are otherwise engaged.

Majority Leader Howard Baker (R–Tenn.) arrived on the nearly empty Senate floor bearing what he described as "an incredible amount of stuff here that has been handed to me."

A few moments later, he amended this to the more decorous phrase "a great many items that appear to be cleared for action by unanimous consent."

He then went through the list, offering amendments on behalf of absent senators, asking unanimous consent that their statements be inserted in the record as read, and asking unanimous consent that the bills be considered passed.

Minority Leader Robert Byrd (D–W. Va.) was on hand to protect the interests of Democratic senators. But since the senators had been put on notice that the bills would be considered in this way, and none had objected, the bills were passed.

Other items in Baker's "incredible amount of stuff" included authorizations for space research and natural gas safety programs and an addition to the Bon Secour National Wildlife Refuge.

Presidential libraries and the private sector

Although the White House opposes a Senate bill that would place restrictions on presidential libraries, it is supporting a measure passed by the House to stimulate private support of the institutions.

The House bill requires that twenty percent of the money raised for libraries of future presidents be put in an endowment fund to help defray operating expenses. For the libraries of President Reagan and his predecessors, it calls for the establishment of endowments within the National Archives Trust Fund.

At present, the libraries are built by private subscription but maintained by the federal government.

The bill also requires the establishment of minimum standards designed to assure that the buildings and equipment of future presidential libraries are suitable for archival purposes.

The Senate bill would limit a former president to one library of 60,000 square feet for a one-termer

Dale Nelson *is a journalist who covers the Washington scene for WLB.*

and 70,000 for a president who serves two terms. It also restricts Secret Service and office expenses.

The bill was held up in the Senate at White House request, and M.B. Oglesby, Jr., an assistant to President Reagan, wrote Lawton Chiles (D–Fla.) that his bill "unwisely and unnecessarily restricts the privileges and prerogatives of former presidents."

Oglesby added that the administration "does support efforts to encourage the participation of the private sector in the development and operation of the libraries of former presidents."

He said the House bill "would, if enacted, provide us with a useful tool to encourage greater public participation in the construction and operation of presidential libraries and to help defray day-to-day operating costs."

"This would help some," Chiles agreed, "but there would still be no restraint on the size and number of libraries. The bigger and fancier they are, the more they cost to keep going, and that means keep going forever."

Representative Jack Brooks (D–Tex.), speaking for his own bill in the House, said, "Nobody wants to shortchange history by putting undue restrictions on our presidential libraries, but, at the same time, it is clear that we must get the costs of those libraries under control."

Restoring Jefferson and Adams

Just before it recessed for the Republican National Convention and the Labor Day holiday, Congress appropriated $81 million for the Library of Congress to restore and renovate its two original buildings.

The money will be spent on the Thomas Jefferson Building, which dates to the nineteenth century, and the 1930s beaux-arts style John Adams Building.

But the lawmakers took precautions to avoid the kind of delays and cost overruns that dogged the library's James Madison Building, which fell years behind schedule and turned out to be the most costly public building ever erected in America.

The library asked for $111.5 million for the project, but the House, wary of previous cost overruns, voted to provide no funds, at least for the present.

Senate-House conferees and the full House agreed to the compromise offered by the Senate.

The Senate formula limits expenditure for the buildings to the $81 million appropriation and requires George White, Architect of the Capitol, to submit a construction schedule within ninety days. The schedule is to spell out milestones and estimate how much it will cost to reach each one.

If the cost of any milestone turns out to exceed the estimate, the architect will have to come up with recommendations for cutting future costs to keep the overall cost within the estimate. ▣

Ann McGrath:

Eye on Publishing

Cambridge looks back on four centuries

Cambridge University Press may enjoy only a meager twenty-five-year operating history in the United States, but over at the home office 1984 marks the beginning of a fifth century of continuous publication. For four hundred years—ever since the Press's first printer Thomas Thomas brought out that 1584 Cambridge title—the publisher's influence as an academic press dedicated to the dissemination of scholarship has been deepening and spreading. Today CUP, billing itself the oldest press in the world, employs close to a thousand people and brings out some nine hundred titles a year. In commemoration of the quadricentennial, the American branch is publishing M. H. Black's *The Cambridge University Press: 1584–1984, A Short History.*

During its four-hundred-year history, Cambridge has published the works of some of the world's greatest thinkers: Isaac Newton, John Milton, and John Donne, to name but a few. Gradually, the Press has developed a strong three-pronged publishing mix. Probably best known of its works are the CUP histories, led by *The Cambridge Modern History* in twelve volumes, which was completed in 1912. Subsequent histories chronicle the development of India, Poland and the British Empire, as well as of ancient and medieval civilizations. The success of these ambitious histories has led the Press to concentrate on single-volume reference works as well, such as those on China, Russia, and Africa. The first installment of Joseph Needham's work-in-progress, *Science and Civilisation in China,* appeared in 1954; the project figures among CUP's most formidable.

Cambridge came out with its first "Geneva version" Bible in 1591; since then—and particularly since printer John Baskerville's exquisite 1763 Bible appeared—Bibles have represented a second significant CUP focus. And, in spite of the fact that libraries have tightened their belts radically over the past few years, Cambridge continues to fare well with its sixty-plus scholarly journals. As another boon to the scholar, CUP maintains an unusually sizeable backlist; most of its substantial works are still in print.

And sister university presses?

In addition to its venerable tradition and unshakable foundations, Cambridge University Press enjoys an advantage most American university presses must envy: a healthy confidence in its ability to remain financially and editorially independent. Still, with the economy showing no immediate signs of faltering, the recent convention of the Association of American University Presses finished on an upbeat note. The association's new president, Leslie Phillabaum, is optimistic about university presses' ability to continue providing access to those truly important pieces of scholarship that "by definition, are not commercial, or profitable," and that the trade press can just not afford to handle.

Hopefully, since libraries and university presses are so closely bound, library coffers will be better able to fund book purchases as the economy improves. "College and research libraries are our biggest single market," explains Phillabaum. "And the problem is compounded by the fact that when acquisitions fall off, we have to raise our unit prices. I don't know what the answer is, except to try to encourage state and local support for libraries and education in general."

What else are university presses doing to, as Phillabaum puts it, "keep the doors open"? For one thing, the presses are using the production efficiency of computer typesetting when possible to offset the costs of producing quality books on acid-free paper that are sturdy enough to withstand library usage. For another, they are stretching editorial specializations to create room for general interest trade-type titles related to those specialties. LSU Press, for example, publishes both scholaly, extensively documented studies of the Civil War and histories of the period appropriate for the average reader. As a result, new markets can open up. The History Book Club, for instance, can offer the university press much broadened exposure. LSU has even made successful forays into chancy fiction and poetry publishing—about ten titles of the Press's sixty come out in both fields each year. *A Confederacy of Dunces* is the Press's most well-known recent success.

In addition, Phillabaum and the association's new executive director, Frances Gendlin, are seeking ways to make university presses more visible. They are looking into the creation of a university press book club, for example. They are exploring the means to crack the international market in a bigger way, and they hope to put in place more formalized lines of communication with library and other professional organizations. "We need a way to have a constant dialogue with libraries," Phillabaum says. "We need to be able together to explore our mutual situation, because it seems to me that what helps one will help the other."

Ann McGrath, *a freelance writer based in New York, covers the publishing world for WLB.*

Quality trade publishing—the Knopf legacy

Generally speaking, the terms "university press" and "quality publisher" are synonomous. Not always so with the average trade press. Alfred A. Knopf, of course, has historically been an exception. With Alfred Knopf's death in August, the publishing world lost one of its most dedicated patrons and certainly one of its greatest achievers. The imprint Knopf left—figuratively, with his relentless pursuit of the best in literature, literally, with that "Alfred A. Knopf" tradition of elegant book design—is a deep and lasting one.

Perhaps Knopf's most significant contribution was his insistence on providing plenty of space in American letters for a broad range of foreign talent—artists and philosophers whose ideas might not have reached the American mass market so readily without his championship. The Knopf author roster reads like a literary Who's Who; it boasts sixteen Nobel Prize winners and twenty-six who won Pulitzers. Among them are Thomas Mann, T. S. Eliot, Wallace Stevens, John Cheever, John Updike, and Gabriel García Márquez. To make money was important, but it was never everything. A book's subject matter always defended it more eloquently to Knopf than did its potential for immediate commercial success.

The philosophy worked, and remains a model for young independents today. Knopf's first bestseller, his edition of W. H. Hudson's *Green Mansions,* was published when the house was only one year old, and it has been followed by a steady stream of successes both before and after Alfred A. Knopf became part of Random House in 1966. Mann's *Death in Venice* was one, as was John Hersey's *Hiroshima* and Willa Cather's *Death Comes for the Archbishop.*

The works' inherent beauty and worth have always spoken for themselves. Knopf's borzoi—his colophon—continues to attest to the tremendous pride and care he took in their presentation.

"Congratulations! It's a book!"

A sense of humor, too

Knopf may figure among the more intellectual of the trade publishing houses, but it is by no means stuffy. Its recent publication in this country of Kit Williams's new untitled masterpiece suggests a certain streak of mischief.

An untitled book? Williams, remember, is the innovative British artist whose blockbuster puzzler *Masquerade* (Jonathan Cape/Schocken) led thousands of readers a few years ago on a treasure hunt through the English countryside. This time, the search is for the book's title itself, on one lone copy sealed inside an exquisitely decorated mahogany box. Deduce the title correctly—and express it most creatively in some artistic form other than the written word—and you win the titled copy, the box, and the pure gold bee that adorns it.

Knopf is not alone this year in recognizing the puzzler's huge appeal to even non-readers. Since *Masquerade* (which has sold over a million copies) and Thomas Chastain's more recent *Who Killed the Robins Family?* (William Morrow) proved their salability, several publishers have entered the market with puzzle books of their own that offer the reader with the best answers a concrete reward. The Englishman who solved the *Masquerade* riddle dug up a $35,000 gold hare. The readers who solved the Robins family mystery split $10,000.

Pocket Books has three such books coming out this year that promise $15,000 to the reader with the most appropriate solution—*Prize Meets Murder, The Medical Center Murders,* and *This Prize Is Dangerous.* Three more are planned. Morrow is bringing out a Robins family sequel, *Revenge of the Robins Family,* and will give $10,001 to whomever can track the culprits. Most ambitious of all is Intra Vision/Warner's *Treasure,* to be published this fall. *Treasure* takes its readers on a search of the continental United States for a buried gold horse containing the key to a safety deposit box—and $500,000.

Conclusion? Not only does reading pay—it pays.

Will Manley:

Facing the Public

"No, Jack and the Beanstalk does not have any chase scenes!"

When people start getting idealistic about children, I know that their contact with them must be minimal. When I hear someone using adjectives such as "lovely," "adorable," and most especially "wonderful" to describe little boys, I know that person hasn't been any closer to children than the latest "Leave It to Beaver" rerun. When I overhear two elderly people in a grocery store line talking about preschoolers with such words as "bright," "precocious," "advanced," and especially "precious," I know they are referring to grandchildren who are no closer to them than the other side of the continent.

Did you ever wonder why Mr. Rogers can do a children's television show day after day after day with the same kind, loving, gentle, understanding, and perfectly rational demeanor? Has it ever struck you as slightly odd that he can relate warmly and patiently to children with nary a whine or a whimper to say nothing of a scream? One day recently I finally discovered it's because he rarely has a child on his show. All his children are located conveniently thousands of miles away from him on the other side of the television screen.

Years of watching Mr. Rogers have made me a very guilty person because as a father I chronically fail to live up to his role model as the rational, gentle, imperturbable, sensitive, all-knowing, and all-loving parent. I think of Mr. Rogers whenever one of my kids lets the gerbils run loose in the crawlspace under the family room, clogs up the toilet with Play-Doh, knocks over a pyramid of pickle jars in the grocery store, or starts screeching in the middle of a crowded reading room just after I have lectured a group of parents about the need to take more responsibility for their children in the library. At times like that a little vein just along my temple begins to pulsate irregularly and then I generally lose my temper, raise my voice, throw something, and often threaten capital punishment. But within three minutes a terrible guilt trip sets in as I begin to reflect on how gently but effectively Fred Rogers would have handled the situation. And the terrible thing is that Mr. Rogers is always on in my house. My kids love him, which makes me feel even guiltier. They even tape him on the VCR. Morning, noon and night, rerun after rerun, and videotape after videotape there is the ubiquitous Mr. R. in my living room singing and smiling, taking off his coat, putting on his sweater, slipping off his shoes, lacing up his sneakers, feeding his fish, and taking us to the land of make-believe.

But that's precisely the point. The idealistic world of Mr. Rogers, where justice is always done, feelings are always understood, and children are universally loved and appreciated is soporific fantasy—and pefect fodder for a passive, hypnotizing medium like television. Eventually, however, it rings hollow. Just once we'd like to see Fred throw his shoe or raise his voice a mere decibel or two. Or better yet, we'd like to see a little boy or girl really get on his case, maybe by dumping some hot tomato soup on his freshly cleaned three-piece suit. I suspect the surprisingly deep-seated hos-

---

Will Manley *is director of the Tempe (Arizona) Public Library.*

tility I feel for Mr. Rogers is shared by other parents and teachers who live in the midst of the chaos of children and experience daily the maddening frustrations of sibling rivalries, chipped teeth, broken bones, and prolonged psychological warfare. I would love to see Mr. Rogers ride from Omaha to Denver in a snowstorm during the middle of the night, in a car that has engine knock, with a constipated two-year-old yelling for a nonexistent piece of bubble gum.

I stress the dangers of idealizing children because last month in this column I strongly suggested that public libraries should begin to consider not only beefing up their sagging juvenile programs, but acutally making them the number one service priority. By strongly advocating that children's services should be re-emphasized, therefore, I do not want to give the misleading vision that all that is involved is a Disney-like amble down a yellow brick road of children's librarianship which is filled with nothing but fun, fantasy and fulfillment.

Part of our ambiguity toward children is that from "Leave It to Beaver" to "Mr. Rogers Neighborhood" we've been bombarded on television with idyllic family situation comedies that look like absolutely nothing that we're familiar with in our own lives. Exasperated, we tend to throw up our hands and conclude that we're just not capable of dealing effectively with children. So we relegate our responsibilities to people or agencies that we mistakenly assume have some professional expertise in that area. In that vein more and more public libraries, boxed in by tight budgets, are shrugging off their responsibility for children to the public schools, specifically to the school media centers.

Therefore, in advocating that public library services for children should be strengthened, not phased out, it is important to arrive at a neo-realistic attitude toward children. They are not the cute, kind, innocent, and naturally loving creatures portrayed on television. They are loud, uncompromising, cantankerous, obstreperous, selfish, and very difficult to communicate with. Young children also have a number of redeeming features—curiosity, spontaneity, and an enthusiasm for learning.

Making a commitment to children's services beyond the usual token weekly story hour, therefore, is asking for hassles and unpredictable problems as well as a busier library. The important first step is to make the commitment, but this will not be easy. It involves putting more money and more staff into the children's department, and any administrator knows full well that changing budgetary priorities always meets traumatic resistance. That's why so few administrators have the courage to effect change. But when the change involves building up children's services at the expense of adult services resistance can be even stronger.

W.C. Fields's observation that "anyone who hates kids and dogs can't be all bad" wouldn't be a cliché today if it didn't meet with such universal approval. My home state of Arizona is filled with retirement communities and complexes where a rowdy band of Salvadoran rebels would be welcomed with greater enthusiasm than a demure group of children. And if you want to induce mass hysteria in Sun City you don't need to turn off the pacemakers and hearing aids, just take a field trip of second graders to the annual Wayne Newton concert. As a library administrator, I've never encountered anything close to the amount of criticism directed at me when I became director of the Tempe Public Library and quickly began to shift money, resources, and personnel into children's services and away from adult services. Several library board members, a hard-line bloc of professional staffers, and a goodly number of library patrons resented bitterly the fact that the library was being turned into a "nursery school" (less kind critics used the term "zoo") and was being "overrun by screeching young savages." I was accused of everything from ageism to looking after my own self-interests (I have three young children).

Although now, two and one-half years later, the criticism has somewhat abated, there are still many patrons who are simply not comfortable being around children and are not reluctant to make their opinions known. This residual pocket of resistance aside, the decision to emphasize children's services has had a tremendously positive impact on the adult use of our library. In two and one-half years, registration for adult borrowing cards has doubled and the circulation of adult books has almost tripled.

The lesson here is simple. If you are understandably reluctant to embrace the idealism of inculcating a love for books in the hearts of children because they do not fit neatly into our happy stereotype of the ideal library patron who is neat, purposeful, potty-trained, quiet, and studious, then give serious consideration to embracing the very practical potential children have in acting as the catalyst for bringing many adult users into the library for the first time.

Although one would think that parents should bear the responsibility for getting their sons and daughters involved in the library, it doesn't work that way anymore. The growing phenomenon of the one-parent family on the one hand and the two paycheck family on the other has radically changed family dynamics. Preoccupied with the dual burdens of pursuing a paycheck and running a household, parents unfortunately have less time and attention to devote to their kids. What has resulted is a generation of children who have had to become far more independent and street-wise than their predecessors. If we take the time to analyze this sociological transformation we will quickly realize that the only way to get whole families involved in a weekly library habit is to appeal directly to the children, not to their parents. Having been won over to the library, the child will prevail upon the parent to also get involved. This public relations process works more effectively than you can imagine. Next month we'll show you how to put the nuts and bolts into place. But be warned: children are not library-trained. ▣

Martin Kesselman:

Online Update

In keeping with the update theme for this column, I attended Dialog Update '84, Dialog's annual users conference, in Washington, D.C. on July 12 and 13.

Update '84 began with a refresher session the first morning and then for the rest of the two days, provided attendees with a choice of two Dialog applications sessions, two database update and reviews and two what's new on Dialog sessions. In addition, there were two luncheons and a Database Bazaar. A proceedings volume given to attendees at registration included database information, applications, and search examples provided by database producers and Dialog staff. Some sessions included separate handouts which, like the proceedings, were clear and easy to follow and a good source for later review.

The refresher I attended, led by Anne Caputo, was well-organized and included a review of database construction and how it can affect retrieval, when and how to use Boolean commands and proximity operators, the use of the expand command, including, in some files, expanding into a database's thesaurus online, limiting capabilities, sorting and printing options, and cost and exit commands.

Cost-effective searching was stressed throughout the session. For example, proximity operators [(w), (f), (s) and (c)] as a rule use less computing time than Boolean commands (and, or, not) and limiting is always cheaper than selecting the equivalent online field (such as limiting to accession numbers versus selecting publication years). The use of limit can provide even greater cost savings: if you know in advance that you want to limit a search, such as to English, use the limit all command at the start of your search rather than at the end.

The refresher also included a review of using Dialindex to determine which files have information on a topic and which should be searched first. Dialindex is a collection of file indexes for Dialog databases and provides the number of hits for a given search statement in those files specified by the searcher individually or by subject category. The refresher concluded with a review of Dialorder for ordering documents online.

The Dialog applications sessions, presented by Dialog staff, focused on subject-specific search strategies, database selection, cost-effective search techniques and database specifics. Representatives of database producers were also present to comment on the applications dealing with their files. I attended the sessions dealing with biomedical research and the use of Dialog for ready reference.

The biomedical research applications session concentrated on cross-file searching with a review of database coverage of medical specialty areas, depth of indexing by various databases in these areas, and the document types they include. Sample questions were reviewed as an exercise in choosing appropriate biomedical files.

The session on ready reference included examples and tips on the use of Dialog to locate answers quickly, at low cost and with few citations retrieved. Examples reviewed included verifying a title on LC MARC, searching for information on individuals in a directory file such as *Marquis Who's Who,* locating unusual companies through the *Electronic Yellow Pages,* and researching "hot topics" in *Magazine Index.*

Other applications sessions included one on chemical research, highlighting the use of chemical substance files; two on business, covering company, financial and statistical data, and management, marketing and advertising information; one on legal research, with techniques for tracking federal legislation and regulations and searching for patent and trademark information; and one on computers and software which advised attendees on searching the computer science and popular microcomputer literature and on locating computer hardware and software reviews.

In contrast to the Dialog applications sessions, the database update and review sessions were presented by the database producers themselves. Sessions were offered on files in business; science and technology; biomedicine, chemistry and patents; social sciences and humanities; legal and government; and reference, multidisciplinary, and news. Many of these sessions featured reviews of new databases on Dialog such as PsycAlert in the social science and humanities session and the DIF (Drug Information Full-Text) file in the session on biomedicine, chemistry and patents.

The Dialog update not only reviewed existing databases and features, but provided attendees, through the What's New on Dialog sessions, a look at the newest Dialog capabilities and a preview of exciting forthcoming developments. Of the four What's New sessions offered, including ones on business information services and chemical information, I attended those dealing with full-text databases and new value-added services from Dialog.

The What's New session on full-text databases reviewed effective search techniques on these files including the importance of searching by specific fields such as title and the use of proximity operators. In full-text databases the entire document is online and every word (excluding stopwords) of the original author is searchable, providing access to specific names of products, places, and people and to terminology that may not appear in titles or indexes, as well as

Martin Kesselman *is life sciences librarian at Bobst Library, New York University.*

access to footnotes, references and tables. Some new and forthcoming full-text databases on Dialog include the *Academic American Encyclopedia, Everyman's Encyclopedia* from Great Britain, *Facts on File,* which should have much appeal for ready reference information, *Moody's Corporate News,* and Standard and Poor's *Corporate Descriptions.* Dialog has a new format for printing the entire full-text document online or offline at a cost of seven dollars per record.

The What's New session on value-added services was a miscellany of new Dialog capabilities and features. Major equipment developments include three mainframe computers working in tandem and the establishment of Dialog's own telecommunications network. When signing on through Telenet, Tymnet or Uninet, you will be connected to one of the three computers, depending on the telecommunications system you use. The same telecommunications service must be used if you have to sign on again after being dropped from the system. Starting with the West Coast, Dialog's new telecommunications network, Dialnet, was made available this past summer. Unlike the other networks, Dialnet operates on all three computers (you'll be signed on to the least loaded CPU), providing maximum reliability and economy. In addition, Dialnet's back-up links insure circuit protection to help eliminate drops from the system. During fall and winter 1984 several East Coast locations will be added; other states will be phased in during 1985 and 1986. Priced at six dollars per hour, Dialnet is now the lowest cost telecommunications network. Both 300- and 1200-baud access are provided as well as a leased-line option for high-volume users, with which 9600-baud access is possible.

A new file available in August, through an agreement with the U.S. Bureau of the Census, is CENDATA. This file provides up-to-the-minute access to census data, as it is updated throughout the day and includes the latest press releases. Besides searching CENDATA through regular Dialog commands, users can choose, through a different logon procedure, an option to search the file via a menu-driven interface.

A new special feature available on selected Dialog business files such as *Disclosure, Electronic Yellow Pages* and *Million Dollar Directory,* is REPORT. With REPORT, searchers can print selected fields from retrieved items in a tabular format. The use of REPORT requires a different logon procedure.

Available this fall is a new print format specifically for downloading ("printing" search results onto a microcomputer's disc) that will facilitate post-processing for searchers using microcomputers and appropriate software. In addition, Dialog's New Technology Applications division is developing its own software to assist searchers with manipulating downloaded records. Dialog notes, however, that these downloaded records are still under copyright restrictions.

Beginning in October, Dialog will institute two new payment plans: a prepayment option with a minimum of $1000 for a discount of from $5 to $15 per hour and a non-prepayment commitment contract, with a minimum of $5000 committed, for a discount of from $5 to $10 per hour. At present, institutional accounts for Knowledge Index, Dialog's low-cost after hours online service, are still not allowed (payment is by credit card). Dialog did mention however, that the New Technology Applications division, headed by Charles Meadows, is looking into developing a service that will help meet the special needs of academic and public libraries.

Future Dialog developments were also presented during Roger Summit's speech, "Dialog Directions," at Friday's luncheon. Summit, Dialog's president, besides noting his enthusiasm for Dialnet, provided attendees with a preview of Dialmail, Dialog's electronic mail service coming this winter. Dialmail will make possible several applications such as swapping reference questions, transmitting interlibrary loan requests, arranging meetings, two-way communications with Dialorder suppliers, and announcements or training schedules from database producers. A very welcome feature will be the overnight delivery of offline prints and SDIs to a searcher's electronic mailbox. This service, although more expensive than typical offline printing costs, will be cheaper than online printing.

As to some new directions, Summit noted that a research and development group, the New Technology Applications division, has recently been established within Dialog. This group is working on projects such as front-ends to the Dialog system, beginning with an easy-to-use menu-driven interface Dialog is testing with the new CENDATA database. Other projects include computer assisted instruction software for training in the use of the Dialog system and a demo software package to use with personal computers. This division is also heavily involved with Dialog II, a rewrite of Dialog's search software. Dialog II, which incorporates many of the suggestions of searchers over the years, will be phased in over the next few years and will be backwardly compatible with the present Dialog system. Dialog II features include options for tailored print formats, a new proximity operator, (n), which allows for term adjacency in either direction, and multifile searching, the ability to search several Dialog files at once (this last feature should be available sometime in 1986). Summit sees as another direction for Dialog an increased marketing effort aimed at end-users and an introduction of online services earlier in the academic system, such as in high school. Dialog would also like to see increased use of online services in public libraries.

Whereas the national online conferences, such as Online '83, and the National Online Meeting deal with a wide range of topics and developing trends in the online field and are geared more towards the "online scholar," Dialog Update provides experienced searchers a very practical hands-on approach to learning efficient and cost-effective search techniques for the Dialog system. ▣

Tom Surprenant:

Future Libraries

Libraries interested in the application of electronic technologies to help resolve information problems have been taking a keen interest in the various optical disk projects initiated by the Library of Congress. These pilot projects will have a profound effect on the use of this valuable technology in libraries throughout the world. At the same time that the Library of Congress is showing how we might use the disk, the business segment of our culture is busily developing products that will eventually allow us all to apply what LC will be doing on a grand scale.

If we are to believe the market predictions of the past few months, our culture is on the verge of yet another revolution in information handling: an entire new family of optical digital disks and associated equipment. This is the result of over twenty years of research and development aimed at creating a viable commercial use for the laser in information technology. Over five years ago the read-only or play-only video disk was introduced. Now, the addition of digital capabilities for that disk creates two new types based on the laser, which have great potential for library use. They are the write-once/read, and read/write/erasable optical disks.

The key to the use of the disks is the ability to digitize the information that will be used. This is a fairly expensive operation and, while it only needs to be done once, the cost will inhibit rapid acceptance of the technological innovations. However, libraries that have computerized circulation systems and online catalogs have created the type of database that can be easily moved to the optical disk format. New laser devices can read print directly into digitized form, without manual keying. One can foresee the time when price, ease of use, and reliability will become less critical, setting the stage for a comparatively easy transition into digitizing information. Each of the three types of disk has a number of uses in the information environment.

The capacities and capabilities of optical digital disks are staggering. While compatibility will be a problem, there are already formats emerging that can give us some idea of its potential.

So far, the read-only optical disk has been used primarily for home entertainment and industrial training. With the potential for adding more types of information in digitized form, the read-only disk takes on a new dimension in the technological mix. Read-only technology could be applied to home computers so that many software programs can be stored on a single disk. This will replace the many magnetic disks now used to hold equivalent material. The prospect of using the read-only optical disk as an alternative or supplement to print will be very enticing to publishers because the medium lends itself nicely to both book and periodical production. We may also see various large archival files available for sale to local libraries.

The expanded use of the optical disk for interactive purposes, such as encyclopedias and other bibliographic tools, has the potential to enhance both library use and the teaching role of the institution. We may also see less reliance on telecommunication access to bibliographic utilities. Retrospective databases, available on disk, could be updated at regular intervals. The in-house disk database search would be supplemented by online access for the most up-to-date information. Another alternative is for the utilities to produce full-text databases to be sent to libraries on optical digital disks on a subscription basis. Searching would be reserved for online use. Creative use of the disk for both retrospective and current information searching may change the entire nature of bibliographic utilities.

The write-once/read optical disk has direct application for in-house production of local access tools. The card catalog stands out as a leasing prospect for this type of conversion. It will be fairly easy to use the technology to create a digitized card catalog which will provide a tamper-proof configuration for public use. Used in combination with the computer, which would store the most recent holdings and coordinate them with disk data, this technology could assist librarians in maintaining a major access tool. Other possible uses of the write-once disk are for archival information, internal records, local databases of all types, and some subscription databases.

The read/write/erasable optical disk will have many uses in the library. Because of its tremendous storage capacity this format could easily replace the hard disk drive and the floppy disk. This makes the optical disk a candidate for use as a primary and/or backup device for computer

Tom Surprenant *is director, Graduate School of Library & Information Studies, Queens College, City University of New York.*

New demands for access and use: *Reference Technology Inc., Boulder, Colorado, has developed an information delivery system incorporating laser optic technology. Shown above, a laser optical disc capable of containing up to two gigabytes (two billion bytes) of information. The company's* CLASIX *Dataplate*tm *can accommodate digital data, video still-frames, full-motion video, analog or digitized audio, and digitized high-resolution images.*

circulation systems. In fact, it could be used for any application where information changes rapidly, such as statistical records, specialized current bibliographies, and all forms of word processing.

The capacities and capabilities of optical digital disks are staggering. While compatibility will be a problem, there are already formats emerging that can give us some idea of its potential. A single 4.72-inch optical disk can store 550 megabytes of information. That is equivalent to the contents of approximately 700 novels or 275,000 pages. Hard figures are difficult to obtain but it has been projected that a 100-megabyte disk will cost around $60. The equipment needed to play the disk will probably cost about $1,000. The ability to handle all three types of disk formats may add to the equipment cost but the additional cost will not be great, because the laser is used to both read and write. When you compare this with the current hard disk drives, costing $3,300 for a 40 megabyte disk, it is easy to see that the optical digital disk is going to be a major competitor. It also retains its competitive position when other comparisons are made. The hard magnetic disk drive is highly susceptible to dust, heat, fingerprints, and smoke. The optical disk, on the other hand, is not prone to such problems and needs much less care and attention.

This technology carries implications for librarianship. It has been predicted that the optical digital disk will be introduced into the American market late this year or early next year. It is estimated that, by 1990, there will be 553 million disks in use. The pressure on librarianship will come from patron demands for access and use. We will have to meet the needs of our clientele, especially if databases and other types of bibliographic tools are available on disk. The problems of copyright and the use of material will become apparent as we store and use more information on disk. For instance, will we allow a researcher to bring in a write-once disk and copy an archive for use somewhere else? It seems certain that the entire nature of the library will change if the move into electronic publishing utilizes this technology. Finally, the growth of the interactive database will be enhanced by the optical digital disk, which will decentralize information and increase the potential for personal databases, accessible through the personal computer, and tailored exactly to the needs of the user.

The impending introduction of yet another technological innovation will have far-reaching effects on how we handle information and will create many of the same problems that we now experience with the computer. We need to take a long look at this technology in an attempt to place it in proper perspective. We have only just begun to consider the potential of the digital disk. It will be up to librarians to supply the creativity necessary to assign a proper place for the optical digital disk in the world of information.

Toni Carbo Bearman:

Situation Report: NCLIS

In nearly four years of talking with librarians and information professionals about NCLIS, I have listened to a wide range of perceptions about what the National Commission on Libraries and Information Science is, what it has achieved, and what it ought to be doing for libraries and information services in the nation. From these conversations I have gained a wealth of good ideas, as well as the realization that NCLIS needs to be better known and better understood throughout the library/information community. Over the next few months I hope to share with you relevant news about the current activities of NCLIS, with particular emphasis on how it is grappling with the major trends and events affecting library professionals. My comments reflect my own views and not necessarily those of the commission or of the United States government.

NCLIS is a permanent, independent executive branch agency—minuscule by federal standards—that resulted from a recommendation of the National Advisory Commission on Libraries established in 1966 by President Johnson. NCLIS was created by PL 91–345 in 1970 to advise the President and Congress on national policies for America's library and information needs. The commission was set up to be an impartial and objective advisor to both branches of the federal government. The commission meets four times a year; its meetings are announced in advance in the Federal Register, and visitors are welcome. Between meetings, the commissioners and staff carry out NCLIS programs and activities in accordance with the priorities established by the full commission.

The commission is composed of the Librarian of Congress and fourteen other members appointed for staggered five-year terms by the President, by and with the advice and consent of the Senate. By law, five members are professional librarians or information specialists and "the remainder shall be persons having special competence or interests in the needs of our society for library and information services, at least one of whom shall be knowledgeable with respect to the technological aspects of library and information services and sciences, and at least one other of whom shall be knowledgeable with respect to the library and information . . . needs of the elderly."

Currently NCLIS counts among its members a university president, a bank president, three heads of information-related businesses, a junior high school librarian, a special librarian, an attorney, and an octogenarian who has made stellar contributions to the cause of libraries and education throughout her life. NCLIS has eight full-time and two part-time staff members, and an annual budget of approximately $700,000. Our small staff is augmented by a senior program officer on loan from the National Agricultural Library and by cooperative projects with other agencies and the private sector.

NCLIS accomplishments

The commission can be credited with a number of significant contributions to the development of library and information services in the United States since 1970. In its early years, the commission performed several comprehensive assessments of the library and information needs of the American people, and published a document outlining a National Program for Library and Information Services that was endorsed in principle by all the major United States library and information service organizations. Just a few of the commission's other activities over the years are: initiation of the Continuing Library Education Network and Exchange (CLENE); planning and coordination of the first White House Conference on Library and Information Services (a massive undertaking that involved the time and energy of 100,000 citizens); extensive technical assistance to Congress on the reauthorization of LSCA and other library-related legislation; and task force studies on computer-to-computer protocols, school library media programs, the role of special libraries in nationwide networks, library and information services to cultural monorities, community information and referral services, and public/private sector interaction in the provision of information. A complete record of the commission's activities is contained in its *Annual Report* for 1980–81, subtitled "A Decade of Accomplishment." Single copies can be obtained free from NCLIS.

Toni Carbo Bearman *is executive director, National Commission on Libraries and Information Science.*

Current activities

Future columns will detail NCLIS programs. To set the stage, however, I'd like to provide a brief overview of some of our objectives and activities during the current fiscal year.

NCLIS is in the process of disseminating the results of three recently completed task force reports and encouraging the implementation of their recommendations. They are all on topics of immediate interest and concern to the profession: library and information services to cultural minorities; community information and referral services in libraries; and the role of special libraries in nationwide networks and cooperative programs. NCLIS is working with all appropriate organizations and agencies to help implement the recommendations.

One of the commission's priorities is improving library and information services to meet the changing needs of the American people. In the September issue of *WLB,* we published the results of a study of current United States population characteristics and their implications for library and information services. During 1983 NCLIS laid the groundwork for an important new progam on the information needs of the aging. The commission is already working with other groups and agencies to learn more about the library and information needs of elderly Americans and the current state of library and information services to this significant population group. Our next goal is to establish a blue-ribbon panel to make a report with specific recommendations for improving library and information services for the nation's elderly. Hopefully the panel will come up with strategies for more effective use of public libraries by the elderly and ways of furthering cooperation between state and local agencies and the public library in this increasingly important area of service.

Another NCLIS program that strives to improve library and information services to meet changing needs is our National Rural Library and Information Services Development Program. Working closely with the library/information community, the United States Department of Agriculture, cooperative extension services, and the nation's state universities and land-grant colleges, NCLIS is helping to provide America's rural communities with the broad range of information services and products they need to meet the diverse and changing information needs of their citizens. Under the program, the rural library will be strengthened even more as an essential community institution, taking on the role of a comprehensive community learning/information center that utilizes computer and telecommunications technologies.

This year NCLIS approved the establishment of a national advisory board to help guide the rural program, and planning is underway to determined the need, concept, and objectives, for the board.

An issue that has concerned all of us this year is the role of libraries in restoring excellence in American education. At its January 1984 meeting, the commission passed a resolution noting the total absence in the "Nation at Risk" report of recommendations on the role of library and information resources in elementary and secondary schools, and the omission of references both to the importance of library and information resources to underpin all of learning and to the essential skills and proficiencies involved in finding and using information effectively. The resolution also urges the establishment and support of strong school libraries throughout the country. Commissioners and staff later participated in the series of seminars on "Libraries and the Learning Society" sponsored by the Department of Education.

The impact of fees for library and information services on access to information is a controversial issue facing our profession. Many librarians are totally opposed to charging fees for any services. Others have been charging fees for some services, such as computer searches, for years. In order to provide information on current practices and to answer such questions as, "How many public libraries are charging fees for any kind of service?" NCLIS is researching the current status of library fees and plans to undertake a study that will provide an overview of current library practices.

Another area of current concern is the impact of new information technologies on access to information for all components of our population. Later this year we will publish a study, completed with the assistance of two IBM librarians on loan to the commission, of the most significant new information technologies for 1985 and beyond.

NCLIS is participating actively in the collaborative effort to help the nation's estimated twenty-six million adults who are functionally illiterate, and we are also working with the Department of Defense in a pioneering project to help adult illiterates through community volunteer literacy programs based in local public libraries. The NCLIS/United States Army Reading Project is designed to transfer technology developed to increase reading skills in the military to library-based literacy programs. Two public library demonstration sites—Baltimore, Maryland, and Weirton, West Virginia—are testing the computer-assisted instruction program. The project is generating great interest and has the strong support and cooperation of everyone involved.

Satellites and international policy

In the important area of national information policy, NCLIS was asked last year by the Department of Commerce to assist with the development of information policy guidelines for the archiving of data from the Nation's weather- and land-sensing satellites. The commission assembled a distinguished blue-ribbon panel of experts to consider the interests of all users of satellite data and to develp guidelines and recommendations. A primary consideration here was the importance of protecting the needs of the public and insuring continued access to satellite data. The panel's report to the commission will be published this fall.

As the secretariat for the United States National Committee for UNESCO's General Information Program (PGI), NCLIS represents the interests of the American library/information community with regard to the PGI and serves as an official advisor to the State Department on related matters. This year the commission was asked by the State Department to insure full participation in the PGI for the remainder of the year, to monitor any changes in the program during the year, and to coordinate the development of a proposal for alternatives to UNESCO library- and information-related

continued on page 158

Vantage Point/Opinion

Philip R. Thompson

American Education, Entrepreneurship, and the Public Library

About one year ago, the National Commission on Excellence in Education warned that "the educational foundations of our society" are "being eroded by a rising tide of educational mediocrity that threatens our very future as a nation and a people."[1] Fearful of seeing their own children float as aimlessly as flotsam and jetsam on this tide, parents are withholding an estimated 30,000 to 100,000 children from the public schools and educating them at home, violating state truancy laws in the process but also winning their cases in court with great regularity (ninety-five percent by some estimates).[2]

Compulsory school attendance has an old but only recently successful history in the United States. In the nineteenth century, self-education was the prevailing theory and was responsible for the creation of the vast public library system in America. It argued that once children had been taught to read in the public schools, they would further their education through the free and voluntary public libraries. The hope that making books free and available to all citizens would lead to an educational uplift of the masses proved overly optimistic. So did the alternative theory that compulsory school attendance would lead to a well-educated citizenry.

Beginning with studies undertaken in the 1960s by the U.S. Department of Education, it was clear that half or more of the nation's gifted children (those with IQs over 130) were dropping out of high school or receiving grades so low that their entrance into college was doubtful.[3] For the five percent of the nation's children defined as gifted, segregation into special classes or home education achieved better results than compulsory education. After all, Abraham Lincoln and Andrew Carnegie educated themselves; had they been compelled to attend public schools they might never have entered the history books.

Little by little, the legal barriers to self-education are being overturned. Standardized testing as a measure of educational ability and attainment is already widely accepted and gains converts steadily. Indeed, many states prefer standardized tests to high school diplomas as a measure of literacy. Public schools are openly called a disgrace in urgent need of reform. Critics even describe our public schools as "the twelve year sentence" and "the national child aging vats."[4]

There has been a national exodus from the public schools into self-education or other alternative education, concentrated among the five percent of the nation's children classified as gifted. Some states have attempted to tap this new educational trend with new educational policies. For example, North Carolina has a secondary school of science and mathematics that recruits gifted children from across the state and that boasts a faculty consisting entirely of Ph.Ds. Private business, too, has attempted to capitalize on this trend. The Educational Testing Service in Princeton, New Jersey, has expanded its list of standardized knowledge tests used to award college course credits to measure high school equivalency education. No state or city has taken full advantage of the options available to swell or even ride this tide.

As the world moves toward high technology, the better paying jobs require higher levels of education in science, mathematics, and English. These skills can be taught in formal classrooms, but inventive and entrepreneurial abilities are far harder to instill. The closest approximation to nurturing the innovative mind and entrepreneurial daring was the public library movement in the late nineteenth century, which enlisted the support of such philanthropists as Andrew Carnegie, Enoch Pratt, and Samuel Tilden.

Libraries held an attraction for Carnegie and others that went beyond educational uplift for the common man (Carnegie declined most entreaties to support university libraries) and this was the idea that libraries are centers of learning whose boundaries are those of knowledge itself, capable of continual expansion. To a self-educated entrepreneur like Carnegie, there are also no boundaries to what may be invented or accomplished, which is why he used so much of his accumulated wealth to further the spread of free libraries.

Another attraction that free li-

Philip Thompson *is a research librarian at the College of Urban Affairs, Cleveland State University.*

braries must have held for Carnegie arises through his association with Social Darwinism, a nineteenth century philosophy which, after being rejected and ridiculed throughout most of the twentieth century, is now making a surprising comeback. Thus, in the widely read *In Search of Excellence*, Thomas Peters and Robert Waterman state that, "The truly adaptive organization evolves in a very Darwinian way."[5]

> Libraries held an attraction for Carnegie that went beyond educational uplift for the common man

Darwinian evolution assumes three processes: a process that continually creates new variants, a process whereby all variants—new and old—can be copied, and a process of selective retention whereby some variants are retained and others eliminated. The modern synthesis of evolutionary biology describes the process of new variation as mutation, the process of copying as DNA replication, and the process of selective retention as differential reproduction or natural selection (which is called natural to contrast it with the selection of plant and animal breeders).

It is the argument of Peters and Waterman that the large, successful American corporations can act like populations of organisms. They tolerate within them the continual birth of new ideas, they put into place mechanisms whereby these variants can be copied and spread, and they then select from among the available variants those which seem best able to solve corporate problems. What Peters and Waterman argue works well in the late twentieth century, Andrew Carnegie advocated in the late nineteenth century.

According to Carnegie, a philanthropist had an obligation to see that all citizens of his state could learn to read in free and nearby public schools. They could then continue their education in free and nearby public libraries. Neither the state nor the philanthropist had, according to Carnegie, any obligations beyond that point. These were Carnegie's own words: "In bestowing charity, the main consideration should be to help those who will help themselves; to provide part of the means by which those who desire to improve may do so; to give those who desire to rise the aids by which they may rise; to assist, but rarely or never to do all."[6]

In an age where inequality of resullts (even when based on inequality of merit) tends to have a bad name, invoking the philosophies of Andrew Carnegie may provoke more heat than light, yet one can argue that recent educational history has shown that Carnegie had a far keener appreciation for developing a system to encourage entrepreneurship and innovation than the educational bureaucracy that followed him.

Among the characteristics of gifted children are an ability to teach oneself to read, a capacity for divergent thinking, and persistence in problem solving, all of which can lead to conflict in formal classroom instruction. For example, gifted children will often give answers to questions or solutions to a problem which, when given careful consideration from another point of view are supportable, but which differ from the correct answers given in the textbook or those formulated in the mind of the teacher. Their answers may be seen as incorrect and graded as such. Similarly, gifted children may wrestle with a problem until they feel they have mastered it to their own high standards of perfection while the teacher feels that the problem or subject has been adequately covered and that the class as a unit should move on. These characteristics frequently cause gifted students to be labeled troublemakers and rebels by teachers. As late as 1970, over half the schools sampled in a survey of gifted children reported that they had no gifted children. Since five percent of the school age population is classified as gifted, this result underscores the conclusion that most teachers do not care to discover who the gifted children are in their classrooms.

When one adds that gifted children are, by virtue of their very giftedness, unusual as children, they stand to be similarly ridiculed and rejected by their peers. The resulting frustration and social isolation frequently lead gifted children to become withdrawn, conceal their intellect, or drop out of school. Of course, not all gifted children follow this pattern so one could say that this is merely an affordable social cost of compulsory school attendance. And yet one of the arguments used by advocates of truancy laws is that schooling is a socializing experience. When one is the class scapegoat one is more likely to find it a socially alienating experience.

Ironically, the very characteristics that make gifted children unsuited to formal classroom instruction—the ability to learn to read by oneself, the tendency to persist at a problem until it is solved to self-imposed standards of perfection, and the tendency to seek novel answers to questions and original solutions to problems—make self-education through libraries the ideal learning environment for them. No one is compelled to attend a library, there are no right or wrong answers in a library, and one is free to try to read every book in the collection.

> No one is compelled to attend a library, there are no right or wrong answers in a library

If parents are willing to pay the costs of going to court to win the right to educate their children at home and then pay the costs of educating the children of others through taxes, then imagine how eager these parents would be to simply move to a state that not only allowed them to do this legally but also subsidized them by allowing self-education through public libraries coupled with a program of monitoring using standardized knowledge tests. Imagine how many more parents there must be who have hesitated to challenge state truancy laws but would willingly move to a state that gave them the education they wanted for their children. Therefore, an innovative public education system is an incentive to the in-migration of the highly-educated family with gifted children.

In addition to the above benefit, gifted children are those most likely to become inventors and entrepreneurs as adults. Imagine the deferred benefits such a state would reap in the next generation, with its harvest of such innovative and entrepreneurial adults, drawn from the school-age children across all other parts of the country. Indeed, there is so much to be gained—both immediately and in the long run—through improving the quality of public education and so little to be sacrificed or paid-out that it is clear that only strong, conservative forces interested in the perpetuation of educational mediocrity could prevent widespread reform of this kind.

American education *has* changed since the time of Andrew Carnegie. Nevertheless, there is no reason not to suppose that the best qualities of Social Darwinism could be combined with the best qualities of mass public schooling. Compulsory school attendence laws ensure that everyone has, as nearly as possible, the same education regardless of individual differences, a fact which may account for much of their political support.

Rather than work to create a uniform, national educational system, perhaps we should instead consider letting the fifty states become educationally competitive. For example, perhaps the high capital investment required to start an automobile or steel company has led to a climate of business conventionality in Detroit and Pittsburgh while the low capital investment required in publishing, fashion design, computer software, and country music have kept New York City, San Jose, and Nashville entrepreneurial and innovative. If so, it would then be appropriate policy for Detroit or Pittsburgh to become more economically competitive with other metropolitan areas through creating new, innovative educational systems, experiments in social planning that would lure highly-educated parents of gifted children into their local economies and also create more entrepreneurs within the ranks of their next generation of workers.

Th Apple computer corporation—now worth $1.2 billion—was begun in a garage by Steven Jobs and Stephen Wozniak; former high school and college drop-outs. Jobs, who in the seventh grade refused to go to school at all, now owns stock worth $210 million and Apple is still the principal competitor for IBM in the personal computer market, even though IBM is one of the "best run" American corporations studied by Peters and Waterman. Although Jobs eventually earned his high school diploma, so that he could matriculate at Reed College, he also soon dropped out there.

Steven Spielberg, whose credits include the movies *Jaws, E.T.,* and *Raiders of the Lost Ark,* and who will soon have the distinction of having made three films with combined gross earnings of over one billion dollars, received grades so low in high school that he could not enter a major film school, his first choice, and instead had to accept earning a B.A. in English from California State College at Long Beach. Billy Joel, the pop recording artist who has had records selling over one million copies each or making over one million dollars each, never did graduate from high school.

Joseph Wambaugh, who has written four novels about police work selling over fifteen million copies in all, and who has produced and directed the movie version of one of his novels, *The Onion Field,* described himself as a "terrible" high school student. Wambaugh enlisted in the Marines after graduating from high school, though he did eventually earn an M.A. in English. Neil Simon, who makes over one million dollars annually as a writer and is the author of *The Odd Couple* and *Barefoot in the Park,* graduated from high school at sixteen, though academically undistinguished, to assume an Air Force engineering scholarship at New York University. At eighteen he entered the service to leave it when his enlistment was up, then a corporal. Robert Redford, whose first major break was acting the male lead in the Broadway play *Barefoot in the Park,* described his high school as "a cultural mud sea" and entered college on a baseball scholarship, which he soon forfeited through his failure to regularly attend practice and his classes. Just think where these people would be today had they graduated from high school with honors.

The power of the state to compel its citizens to attend a public school for a fixed number of years is based on its necessity to ensure an educated citizenry. But there are now many, better alternativcs to the formal classroom for achieving and demonstrating the education necessary for a democratic and economically thriving nation. The public library has always been free and voluntary; the public school may soon become so.

Footnotes:

1. National Commission on Excellence in Education, *A Nation at Risk,* full text of the report published in *The Chronicle of Higher Education,* May 4, 1983.

2. "Little Redwood Schoolhouse," *Newsweek,* December 5, 1983.

3. Christopher Johnson, "Smart Kids Have Problems Too," *Today's Education,* February/March 1981.

4. William F. Rickenbacker, editor, *The Twelve Year Sentence* (La Salle, IL: Open Court, 1974).

5. Thomas J. Peters & Robert H. Waterman, *In Search of Excellence* (New York: Warner Books, 1982).

6. Andrew Carnegie, *The Gospel of Wealth and Other Essays* (Garden City, NY: Doubleday, Doran & Co., 1933).

Donnarae MacCann/Olga Richard:

Picture Books for Children

The "naughty child" character is part of a longstanding tradition. This wrong-doer has been used to spoof adult manners, as in Thomas Bailey Aldrich's 1869 novel, *The Story of a Bad Boy,* or to poke fun at childhood manners, as in Heinrich Hoffmann's book of nonsense rhymes, *Struwwelpeter.* The theme of living with a little malcontent has had many variations both as entertainment and as a gleeful tension reliever.

The *New Yorker* cartoonist, James Stevenson, has created several books about a particular grandfather's boyhood exploits. The latest, **Worse Than Willy,** focuses on Grandpa and his hellion of a brother. Both characters have the witty hallmark that Stevenson introduced at the beginning of the series: the same heavy mustaches are worn in babyhood as in the grandfathering years. In the recent sequel, Grandpa is blown out to sea, captured by pirates, and rescued by his sibling rival, Wainey. Mary Ann and Louie know their Great-uncle Wainright as a sedate gentleman, hardly the sort to have braved a storm, propelled himself onto a pirate vessel with a pair of suspenders, outwitted an octopus as well as the pirates, and carried his big brother to safety.

Wainey's story is used by Grandpa as an object lesson for the children concerning the trauma of coping with a new baby. But the reader may also find the villainy of the infant somewhat cathartic. At least the youngest member of a household can hammer, smash, rip, scream, and come through it all with no fracture in family solidarity.

Stevenson uses felt tip pens with great ease and energy. His line work is so bold that we suspect he had his sketches well planned in advance. Then he picked up a pen, shifted into higher gear, and ended up with the super-charged, frenetic cartoons about Grandpa. The design is perfectly controlled and readable visually.

He places color washes here and there, often merely to suggest space, to complete the composition, or to delineate foliage and background objects. At times however, the color use is richer than that, and adds to the sense of what is being described. For example, in the illustration reproduced on this page, Stevenson builds a dynamic sense of the storm by using shades of color in little bits and fragments. The result is a "howling gale" created by using color shades like scattered collage pieces.

From *Worse Than Willy!*

In Mordicai Gerstein's **Prince Sparrow,** it first appears that tantrums are an occupational hazard in the world of royalty. When the royal heir has a fit of temper, "no one would spank or even scold her. She was a Princess." The temperament seems to go with the territory. But as the tale develops into a parable about privilege—about a lonely life in a gilded cage—a remedy emerges in the form of mutual respect. A sparrow flies into the room as the Princess listens to a story about an enchanted bird/prince. She makes the childlike, but mistaken, connection that this bird is a bewitched prince, and supplies him with an elegant cage. The analogy between sparrow and Princess is clear when the bird indicates how he will surely tear himself to bits if he has to live behind bars (even the fanciest bars).

Gerstein makes use of turn-of-the-century manners in art, but the drawing technique has a contemporary, sketchy aspect as well. The Princess has a burdensome weight of flowing hair (as in one of Dante Gabriel Rossetti's portraits), the narrow window casements are elaborately framed, and interiors are furnished with ornate tubs, plumed pens, etc. The brattiness of the Princess is suggested as the illustrator caricatures her features and body language, but then the bird's beneficial influence is reflected in drawings that are more passive. Focus shifts from mannerism to situation. As the Princess addresses the sparrow ("I think you are an enchanted prince"), the reader sees an interesting arrangement of light areas (moonlight) coming through the window and contrasting with solid shapes of floor, bed, canopy. A tall chair is nicely placed in the light areas, but does not detract from the moonlight effect because Gerstein draws the chair with a delicate, thin line. With such visual control, the author/illustrator keeps the sentimental Victorian features in the narrative from seeming overly prosaic.

It is a pleasant surprise to see humans rather than dressed-up beasts as protagonists in the Gerstein and Stevenson books. In Thacher Hurd's

---

Olga Richard *and* **Donnarae MacCann** *are the authors of* The Child's First Books.

From *Prince Sparrow*

Mama Don't Allow, we return to the widespread anthropomorphic treatment of human experience. A young possum/person—residing in Swampville—practices on his new saxophone and forms a band with a trumpet-playing rat and several birds. But their loud, squawky music causes the townsfolk to grumble, rebel, and finally insist that "Swamp bands play in the swamp!!" The "sharp-toothed, long-tailed, yellow-eyed alligators" have nothing but praise for this combo and hire the entertainers for the upcoming alligator ball. Since Possum and friends are also billed as "Swamp band soup," it is fortunate that they have a soporific number in their repertoire. The alligators are soon dozing, and even the possum mother can now exclaim to her musical son, "Oh, how nice."

Hurd uses bright, bold color with no concern for tradition. For example, instead of depicting background objects as grayer and paler to suggest distance, the artist makes hills and sky as brightly colored as the clothing in foreground figures. This impetuosity is in keeping with the drama in the storyline. Hurd knows the rules, but is simply being discriminating in their use. Diminishing sizes are used to indicate distance, while raw hues of reds, greens, blues, violets, and yellows are distributed loosely throughout the compositions. On the opening page of text, the reds and blue-purples in a mountain range on the left side of the doublespread come forward with a big swoop into the interior of the possum home on the right side. This sweep of color supports and accents the hero's "Wow" as he sets eyes on his birthday saxophone. Throughout the book, themes and colors are compatible in underscoring the noisiness and impudence of youth.

Rotten Island is like the world before the Flood: "From cursing and blaming, scratching and shoving, they took to serious fighting, and all their deepest demons of hate tore loose. . . . It was every rotten one for his own rotten self against every rotten one else." In visual terms this is a nonthreatening world. The childish tantrums are similar to the tantrums of the Princess in *Prince Sparrow.* Like Steig, children enjoy devising creatures that are amazingly creative in their design. No matter that the jagged teeth suggest a hideous persona. A gorgeous geometric surface treatment, as in Steig's goggle-eyed insect with chopping mandibles, turns a monster into an object of fun. And the incongruities and strings of adjectives set the same tone in the text: "They loved their rotten life. They loved hating and hissing at one another, taking revenge, tearing and breaking things, screaming, roaring, caterwauling, venting their hideous feelings."

From *Mama Don't Allow*

The structure of the allegory is so simple that teachers could use the book as an antiwar, antipollution, anticommunism, anticapitalism, antiracism fable. The island's first inhabitants are initially described in terms of their violence, aggressiveness, and ugliness. They are then shown to have fits at the sight of something unlike themselves (they see a flower), they destroy each other in their fury, and the flowers are left to multiply and attract a beneficent population of birds.

From *Rotten Island*

As in Steig's *New Yorker* drawings, there is a commentary here in relation to our times, but Steig lets the viewer sort out the implications. An alien world is paradoxically fascinating and incredible. To a child the closest analogy may be an elementary school playground at recess time: at the peak of a competitive game, children sometimes shove, shriek, and glare almost as senselessly as Steig's seriocomic monsters. Then they take pens in hand (like Steig and their other artist friends) and create rich, harmonious, other-wordly designs. ▣

This month's books:

Gerstein, Mordicai. ***Prince Sparrow.*** Four Winds Press, 1984. $10.95. 0–590–07907–7 83–11558

Hurd, Thacher. ***Mama Don't Allow.*** Harper, 1984. $11.95 0–06–022689–7 83–47703

Steig, William. ***Rotten Island.*** David R. Godine, 1984. $12.95. 0–87923–526–8 84–40755

Stevenson, James. ***Worse Than Willy!*** Greenwillow, 1984. $10.50 0–688–02596–X 83–14201

Patty Campbell:

The Young Adult Perplex

Bonn, West Germany—An official government agency for censoring books for youth! Shades of *Fahrenheit 451*! Last year in Munich when I first heard of the existence of the Bundesprüfstelle für jugendgefahrende Schriften I was intrigued. How could such a bureau function in a democracy that is ostensibly committed to free speech? Our itinerary led south, and my curiosity was never satisfied. Now this year we are back in Northern Europe, and I have fumbled my way through the bureaucracy to make an appointment with the Bundesprüfstelle. The bureau head, Rudolf Stefen, is away on holiday, but the second-in-command, Elke Monssen-Engbeding, will be glad to talk to me.

On the doorstep of the agency, upstairs in a very pleasant and unbureaucratic-looking shopping mall, I decide to concentrate my questions on matters of function and let the ethics of censorship fall where they may. After all, we know that free access for youth is the only right position, I think smugly as I go up the steps. In less then five minutes my convictions are to be badly shaken.

In their modern, book-lined offices I am welcomed cordially by Monssen-Engbeding and two of her colleagues, jurists Waltraud Diop and Christine Bolchenberg. They have decided to pool their knowledge of English for the interview, and they giggle a bit about it. Far from the dour repressive types I had expected, these young women are cheerful and matter-of-fact. As I entered the office they clicked off a TV monitor. "Much of our work right now is with videos," they explained. By this, they meant videotapes made for home viewing. Television broadcasting in Germany is government-originated and has its own set of standards.

Coffee is served, and we begin by putting our heads together—with the help of a dictionary—to work out an acceptable translation of the name of the bureau. They are part of the Ministry of Health and Youth, and Bundesprüfstelle für jugendgefahrende Schriften translates into English as Federal Authority for Evaluating Books (or Writings) Dangerous to Youth. They are insistent on the term "dangerous". "'Problem books'—no, that is too soft. Here, we show you." And they turn on the monitor. "This video is called 'Eaten Alive'." We settle back to watch.

From the first frame the screen is filled with images ghastly beyond lunacy. A pile of gnawed blood-clotted human limbs in the grass, crowned with a staring severed head. A few feet further on, a wild-eyed woman tearing with bloody mouth at a handful of dangling intestines. A group of people standing over a naked young woman spread-eagled on the ground. A man raises a long knife to the sky, then bends over and seizes her breast; the knife descends; the camera moves in for a close-up.... "Stop!" I implore, cringing. "Turn it off, please!" They smile a bit at my reaction and put on another tape. "This one was made in America. It's called 'Mother's Day.'" Again not one second is wasted: a man slams a machete through the closed window of a car to decapitate the driver; the head falls forward and blood spurts up from the veins. He drags a girl from the other seat, slams her onto the hood of the car, unzips his fly to rape her while a second man batters her with his fists. Screams, blood, smashed teeth.... An older woman appears and commands them to stop. "That is Mother," Diop explains. "They are her sons and they must bring young women to Mother because she loves to kill." The bloody victim begs for mercy and so do I. "Please, that's enough. I'm sorry, but I can't watch this. How can you look at it all day long?"

They shrug. "So you see why we say this is dangerous to youth."

"Dangerous to youth! I'd say these things are dangerous to everybody!" I hear myself say.

"Yes, but in Germany it is forbidden to control media, the press," they admonish. "Adults must be able to decide for themselves if they want to look at this."

Thus chastened, I listen sympathetically as they explain the workings of their organization. The BPS has jurisdiction only over the reading and viewing of young Germans under the age of eighteen. They do not have power to judge all published materials, but only those books, magazines, newspapers, and videos referred to them for examination by local Youth Welfare Agencies: the Bundesprüfstelle itself cannot initiate a hearing. The actual evaluation is done by a board of twelve people meeting once a month in Bonn. The shifting membership of this board is drawn from a pool of seventy-two experts from eight different areas: art, literature, booksellers, publishers, youth organizations, youth welfare boards, teachers, and the clergy. In addition the pool includes twenty-seven representatives from the "Lände," or local states. The experts are appointed for a three-year term by their own organizations, such as the Teachers' Guild, and they are paid only their travel expenses. But where are li-

Patty Campbell *teaches young adult literature at UCLA and is a library consultant and freelance writer. She is currently researching a book in Europe.*

braries represented here? The term for booksellers also includes librarians, they explain, and in addition a number of the representatives from the Lände are heads of libraries.

When a hearing is held, the publisher first presents a defense. Then he leaves the room, and the board reaches their decision. Eight votes are required for a judgment. In about twenty percent of the cases they decide the video or book is not dangerous. Publishers may appeal to the courts on grounds of faulty procedures, but not for the decision itself. Once a book or video is forbidden, or "indexed" ("'Forbidden' is not the right word," my hosts said. "Because for adults, you see, it is not forbidden"), it is listed in an official publication called the *BPS Report*. Video shops, bookstores, and libraries may subscribe at a small charge, although subscriptions are not obligatory.

How is the law enforced? In the case of videos, an indexed tape may not be sold to anyone under eighteen, nor displayed where they might see it. Advertising, too, is restricted to rooms for adults only. The same rule applies to books in libraries and bookshops: the indexed titles cannot be displayed, sold, or loaned to young people. Enforcement is up to local police; they make unannounced inspections from time to time to make sure that indexed items are not on display. ("It is the duty of the police to control the shops because there is a law.") If they find a violation, the matter goes to court, and the penalty is a fine (or prison) based on the daily income of the defendant.

The image of a policeman strolling in to check the shelves and then hauling the head of the department off to court is a particularly chilling one for American librarians. How does this affect library collection policies? A local constable would probably only point out the shelving error if he found an indexed book in the open stacks, admitted the three jurists. They had never heard of a case in which a library was fined. However, indexing has a chilling effect on purchase. The jobber informs libraries when a book on order is indexed, and then "they send it back to the publisher," fearing that owning a forbidden book might cause them to inadvertently break the law if it wandered onto the wrong shelf.

For the same reasons serious bookstores are reluctant to purchase indexed material. This exerts financial pressure on publishers of indexed books, although the effect on videos is not so clear. The BPS can bring additional pressure to bear in the case of books in series or magazines. If three individual issues in a year are indexed, then the BPS has the option of indexing the entire magazine or series for one year unless the publisher agrees to clean up its content. As an example, the jurists show a copy of "Exquisit Bücher," a pornography series by a large Munich publisher. I also notice in the *BPS Report* that *Hustler* magazine has been proscribed until January 1985. *Bravo,* the most popular teen magazine in Europe, has several times been under fire for articles endorsing drug use.

The criteria for judging materials are laid down quite specifically in the law. Violations fall into seven categories. "Gewalttätigkeit" or excessive violence, is the most common offense of videos, as I had seen. "Pornographie" was also no surprise. "Drogenkonsum" refers to the promotion of drug abuse. "Frauendiskriminierung" is the depiction of women as "things to buy." Most interesting politically are the remaining three categories: "Rassenhass," "NS-Ideologie," and "Kriegsverherrlichung"—racial hatred, Nazi ideology, and the glorification of war. Such books are available in Germany, but only outside the regular commercial bookselling channels, the jurists clarified, from "special" publishers who sell only by mail order.

Certain considerations override the seven deadly sins listed above. The most obvious, of course, is literary quality. Is it art or pornography? is the question most frequently debated by the board. *Fanny Hill,* for example, is available to young people, as are the works of Henry Miller and the Marquis de Sade. Historical importance, too, can justify a work: *Mein Kampf* is not indexed. If a book is out of print and only available in a limited number of copies the board might not bother indexing it. And they cannot consider political books, with the exception of the three categories of racial hatred, Nazism, and glorification of war. Judgments in these areas can be complex. For instance, a collection of pages from *Der Adler,* a Nazi magazine originally disseminated during World War II, was subject to indexing because the collection was published in 1977, although copies of the magazine itself are not restricted.

Do they attempt to differentiate between what is appropriate for young children and what is appropriate for teens? No, that would be too confusing, they answer. Do they ever judge children's or young adult books? No again, they are only protecting young people from harmful books written for adults.

What was the most controversial BPS case? "Oh, Harold Robbins," they remember, chuckling. "A book called *Goodbye, Janette.* Many loud people objected." But the judgment stood nevertheless. Later, glancing through the *BPS Report* for other familiar names, I see that 513 videos and 298 books have been indexed. ("The work of four years," they said.) Most are plainly hard-core pornography. There are a number of comics, particularly the works of Georges Pichard, U-Comix, and the American In-and-Out Comics. The venerable *Marijuana Grower's Guide* from And/Or Press in Berkeley is listed along with other drug titles, and *The Story of O* in a number of editions. There are some books of Nazi propaganda. Among the videos, Bruce Lee is the most frequent offender, and cannibalism seems to be a popular theme.

As I am leaving, the jurists ask a parting question. "How are these things handled in America?" I am at a loss to sum it up in a few sentences. "Well, with us," I falter, "it is not so clear. It can be very confusing. Not all in order as it is with you."

Kathleen Maio:

Murder in Print

For many of us, the detective novel is one of the great comforts of life. In the classic mystery, we comfort ourselves with the myth that violence and death can be conquered through

brave resolve and calm reasoning. The comedy-mystery is an even more soothing invention. It is both comforting and defiant as it allows us to laugh at death and bloodshed.

While the comedy-mystery never entirely disappeared, it seems to do best during troubled times. The late depression and World War Two years saw a proliferation of the comedy-mystery, especially the screwball variety, which seems to recognize the lunacy of life without marring the fantasy with harsh reality.

In the fifties and sixties there was a move toward greater realism, but in recent years I have noticed a resurgence in the comedy-mystery. It is not for me to theorize whether this phenomenon bodes ill for the nation's economic and military outlook. I do, however, feel confident in crediting Charlotte MacLeod as one of the leaders and most gifted practitioners of the late-twentieth-century screwball mystery.

Kathleen Maio *is a freelance writer based in Somerville, Massachusetts. She has contributed to* Twentieth Century Crime Writers, Murderess Ink, *and numerous magazines.*

MacLeod's latest, **The Convivial Codfish** (Doubleday/Crime Club, 1984, $11.95) is a perfect example. The fifth in her series featuring Sarah Kelling of Beacon Hill and her extensive and thoroughly zany clan, we now find Sarah married to art detective Max Bittersohn. With the Christmas rush and their new-found wedded bliss, Max and Sarah are at first slow in their response to the obstreperous cries of distress from Sarah's Uncle Jeremy. It seems that while overseeing the annual Scrooge Day blow-out, Exhalted Chowderhead Kelling was somehow stripped of The Great Chain of the Comrades of the Convivial Codfish.

It is a crime of the most vicious nature to old Jem. Less so to Max until the theft is followed by an attack on Jem, the murder of one of his elderly comrades, and the poisoning of passengers on a train carrying innocent revellers.

MacLeod is in great form. The detection is carried on at a feverish pace by Max, with a little help from Sarah, as they track a disappearing sommelier. The comedy, heavy on the farce, and laced with holiday cheer and malice, is hilarious. Most of MacLeod's characters are outlandish souls, but the author handles normalcy (evidenced in cameos like a trio of hard-working caterers, or an overworked nurse) just as nicely.

Fans of MacLeod's several series, under her own name and the pseudonym of Alisa Craig, need no encouragement to read *The Convivial Codfish*. Those who haven't yet sampled her brand of comic detection could well start with this title.

As proof that the comedy-mystery never has a completely fallow period, I should note the paperback reprinting of the first two of three mysteries starring Dr. William Blow and close friend, fellow scholar, and neighbor, Professor Gideon Manciple.

She Died Because . . . (Harper/Perennial, 1984, $2.95) by Kenneth Hopkins was originally published in 1957 and introduced the dottiest, most doddering detectives you would ever want to meet. Blow gives new meaning to the term "absent-minded professor." He and Manciple seem to back into all the vital clues and plot developments long before the long-suffering police.

Fans of Charlotte MacLeod and related authors might well enjoy the escapades of the two learned gentlemen in *She Died Because . . .* and its sequel, **Dead Against My Principles,** also reprinted by Harper. Devotees of hard-hitting realism should avoid MacLeod and Hopkins.

Fans of realistic mysteries will probably enjoy Rick Boyer's second mystery, **The Penny Ferry** (Houghton Mifflin, 1984, $13.95). Boyer won a well-deserved Edgar Award for best first mystery with *Billingsgate Shoal* (1980), his first novel about oral surgeon Charles (Doc) Adams. It

was a nicely complex novel, part detective story, part political thriller, that contained a sensitive portrait of its hero, an affluent and successful fellow with a bad case of mid-life crisis.

The Penny Ferry continues in the tradition of the first novel, with fewer melodramatic excesses. Doc still has a tendency to get into big trouble when he gets bored. This time, he investigates when a trusted messenger fails to deliver an expensive piece of dental work to his office. Eventually, the messenger turns up dead. And thus starts a trail of murder and violence that is possibly linked to organized crime, and seems fantastically yet undeniably linked to the infamous trial and execution of Sacco and Vanzetti.

Some, especially those who read the first Adams adventure, may wonder why Doc doesn't wise up and butt out when he sees the amount of violence leveled against himself and his family. In fact, the sadistic elements of Boyer's story are not for the faint of heart. There is no denying the skill of Boyer's bloody story, however. His prose is tight and tense, with an occasional wonderful bit of imagery. But it is the way he weaves history and present day crime, so that both are intensely suspenseful, that is the real attraction. And it will be a strong attraction for many mystery readers.

Death Turns a Trick was one of my favorite first mysteries of 1982. Now, Julie Smith and her "Jewish feminist lawyer" sleuth, Rebecca Schwartz return with **The Sourdough Wars** (Walker, 1984, $12.95). Set in San Francisco, Schwartz's current case involves the proposed auction of a "starter" to one of the Bay City's most revered sourdough breads. When the owner, the lover of Rebecca's law partner, is found murdered, Schwartz and her reporter boyfriend Rob Burns start detecting.

Smith's plot is a good puzzler full of the facts and lore of sourdough baking. There's a lot of wise-cracking dialogue, as Rebecca and Rob seem to find a body at every turn. Beneath the backchat and the crime-a-minute pace, though, there is an underlying believablity that makes Smith's novel of the unusual challenges facing "Today's Action Woman" especially satisfying.

Rex Burns's police protagonist, Gabe Wager, returns in **Strip Search** (Viking, 1984, $13.95). This time Wager is investigating the seemingly random and meaningless murders of two exotic dancers. When things don't move on the case, Wager starts a private investigation on his own, using large amounts of his own cash. When one of his snitches is also murdered, Gabe intensifies his inquiry, which includes an unauthorized undercover masquerade as a drug dealer.

There is plenty of well-constructed suspense here, but it's too hard to figure the motivation (prior to the informant's death) for Wager's obsessive investigation. Why turn vigilante, and threaten his career and possibly his life, for a stripper he never met? And although Burns captures the isolation of the modern cop, his expressions of the existential are often too heavy-handed.

The Thin Woman by Dorothy Cannell (St. Martin's, 1984, $13.95) doesn't have to worry about being heavy on the existentialism. It is a frothy fantasy of a mystery. It chronicles the story of Giselle Simons, an obese interior designer with a compulsion for food and self-hatred. After making a command appearance, with a paid escort in tow, at the castle homestead of her rich Uncle Merlin, her uncles dies, leaving her his estate—but only if she drops sixty-three pounds and finds a hidden treasure.

Cannell's first novel is a crazy concoction. It is also great fun to read. Despite her light tone, Cannell expresses the pain of being fat in a thin world. But if you think Ellie learns to love herself as is, think again. This is a thoroughly retrograde fantasy

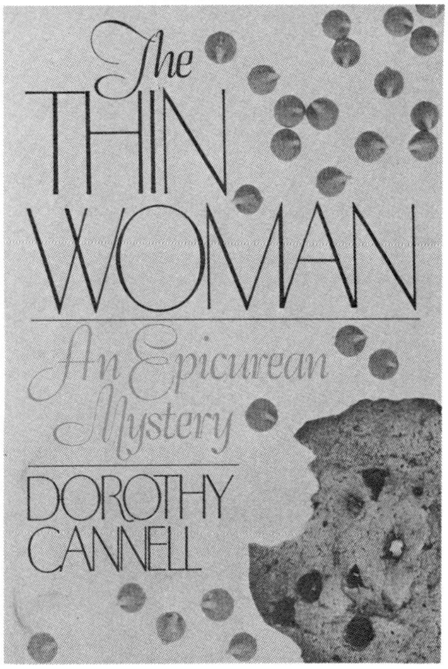

wherein a woman is transformed by love, wealth, adventure, and weight loss—not neccessarily in that order.

Libraries with collections of popular culture and Sherlockiana will want to purchase **The Baker Street Reader: Cornerstone Writings About Sherlock Holmes** edited by Philip A. Shreffler (Greenwood, 1984, $27.50). Shreffler brings out the big guns, like T.S. Eliot, Edmund Wilson, and of course, Vincent Starrett. Yet there is little duplication of pieces that libraries would already have in other collections. This is a well-balanced anthology that will provide the interested reader with a serious but lively introduction to Sherlockian studies.

Judith Trojan:

Front Row Center

Judith Trojan *is senior editor of* Sightlines *magazine, editorial coordinator at the Educational Film Library Association in New York City, and a staff member of the American Film Festival.*

Courage is a common theme in nonfiction cinema. In this column I have reviewed numerous documentaries that focus on courageous individuals fighting the physical and emotional ravages of war, toxic chemical contamination, terminal illness, and debilitating handicaps among other things. But no matter how broad-based its definition, a show of courage always embodies strong personal conviction and commitment. It is appropriate that one of the newest and most touching film profiles of courage is titled **The Good Fight.** The feature-length documentary by Noel Buckner, Mary Dore, and Sam Sills examines the personal, humanitarian, and political reasons why 3,200 Americans defied United States government censure to fight the spread of fascism in Spain during the Spanish Civil War (1936–1939). As members of the Abraham Lincoln Brigade, these Americans joined with volunteers from fifty-one other countries to prevent Franco's takeover of Spain's legally elected democratic government.

Eleven survivors of the brigade form the heart and soul of *The Good Fight.* Prior to their commitment to the war effort, several of these veterans were champions of socialist causes as members of the early American Communist Party. Some were American immigrants or members of minority groups who felt a kinship with the oppressed Spanish peasants about to lose their hard-won democracy. Others were frightened by reports of Hitler's support of Franco; and all were appalled by Franco's slaughter of innocent men, women, and children. Representing diverse vocations and mixed political and ethnic persuasians, the eleven brigade veterans seem to have been motivated by a common concern for global human rights. As they recall their reasons for supporting the loyalist effort in Spain, the hardships faced in fighting on alien turf, the futility of using hand-me-down, World War I weapons against sophisticated German and Italian weaponry, and the tragic consequences of noninterventionist blockades, the veterans still evince great pride in having made this early attempt to stop Hitler.

A fine historical documentary, *The Good Fight* illustrates the reminiscences with striking old photographs featuring the veterans, terrifying archival war and newsreel footage, and hard-hitting narration read by Studs Terkel. Also fascinating is a clip from *Blockade* (1938), a lesser Hollywood film of the period that starred Henry Fonda as an impassioned Spanish peasant fighting for his homeland. To their credit, the filmmakers refrain from the heavy-handed approach evident in *Blockade* and several other films on the subject. They play down Communist politics and sentimental testimony from their witnesses, minimalize period music, and keep the war footage of carnage at a bearable level.

Although the story is coolly told, few will be unmoved by the stars of this film. Of the 3,200 Americans who fought as members of the Abraham Lincoln Brigade, half were killed. Their courage, stemming from youthful idealism and from strong political and humanitarian conviction, would seem to be the stuff of American heroism of the first order. Long forgotten, these veterans have given us a second chance to remember and honor them in *The Good Fight*.

The Good Fight is appropriate for senior high school through senior citizen audiences. United States and world history classes and programs covering the pre-World War II political climate in Europe should find much clarified by *The Good Fight*.

Serious programs on the Spanish Civil War would be incomplete without a screening of Joris Ivens's 1937 classic, **The Spanish Earth.** With commentary written and read by Ernest Hemingway, *The Spanish Earth* is both a poetic and propagandistic view of the loyalist cause against Franco. Hemingway's narrative, Virgil Thomson's and Marc Blitzstein's lush music, and Ivens's beautiful cinematography raise the plight and character of Spanish peasant farmers to super-heroic proportions.

Two other films, now out of general distribution except in large public library collections, also cover the period. Abe Osheroff, one of the eleven Abraham Lincoln Brigade veterans featured in *The Good Fight*, produced his own film on the subject ten years ago. His hour-long **Dreams and Nightmares** opens effectively with a history of the Spanish Civil War and a personal account of his involvement. Unfortunately, the film deteriorates into a leftist political whine about the continuing repression he senses in Spain in the early seventies. Finally, for lighter programs, try the Hollywood version of Hemingway's **For Whom the Bell Tolls,** starring Gary Cooper and Ingrid Bergman, if you can find an old 16mm print floating around. ◙

This month's films:

The Good Fight. 16mm & video. color/b&w. 98 min. 1983. Producer/directors: Noel Buckner, Mary Dore, & Sam Sills. Dist: First Run Features, 153 Waverly Place, New York, NY 10014. 16mm lease—$1,295 (rental $175). Video lease—$700.

The Spanish Earth. 16mm. b&w. 53 min. 1937. Scenario & direction: Joris Ivens. Commentary written & spoken by Ernest Hemingway. Music: Virgil Thomson & Marc Blitzstein. Dist: The Museum of Modern Art, Circulating Film Library, 11 West 53 Street, New York, NY 10019. Rental: $50.

Dreams and Nightmares. 16mm. color/b&w. 60 min. 1974. Producer/writer: Abe Osheroff. Director/editor: Larry Klingman. Dist: Currently not in distribution. Try large public library film collections for loan.

For Whom the Bell Tolls. 16mm. color. 170 min. 1943. Director: Sam Wood. Cast: Gary Cooper, Ingrid Bergman, Akim Tamiroff, & Katina Paxinou. Dist: Currently not in distribution.

Bruce Pollock:

On Record: Popular Music

It is by no mere whim or abject commercial ploy that Billy Squier's fourth album under his own name, sixth overall, is entitled **Signs of Life.** Like everything this most canny rocker has done in his nearly exemplary career, the title reverberates with unconscious symbolism, and veritably reeks of unintentional autobiography.

On the surface a prototypical faceless eighties rocker, certifiably gold, but hardly a synonym for Michael Jackson, Squier offers his share of white noise but leavens it with a massive, naked, roughly poetic ongoing lifestory in song that is no less affecting for its apparent accidental nature. If you read between the lines enough—not unlike the works of Dylan in the acid-soaked sixties—you will find the man, unadorned, breathing, human. Which is saying something in this techno-age.

Signs of Life, then, is an allusive title that nonetheless speaks with uncommon poignancy to the Squierologist. Apart from his well-publicized collapse near the end of the final mixes for his previous album, 1982's *Emotions in Motion,* Side Two of that album seemed to mark a precipitous musical if not personal deterioration, lending credence to rumors that Squier had retired from the rock and roll game to join his father in the sneaker business. The last few songs on *Emotions* sound tired, exhausted actually. And is it again just an accident that the very last song is entitled "Listen to the Heartbeat"? For two years Squier's legions did just that, ig-

Bruce Pollock *is editor of* Guitar *magazine and the author of* When the Music Mattered: Rock in the 1960s.

Billy Squier

noring the dire rumors and casting about for the odd glimpse of "The Stroke," his signature hit, in its MTV incarnation.

Thus, it is either the height of calculation—exhibiting a knowledge of his audience far beyond the ken of mortal rock stars—or the essence of instinctive creative genius, or some deft and/or lucky combination of the two, that has Squier begin this new work with what sounds like modern-day medical apparatus designed to revive the failing heart attack victim!

"All Night Long" is a frantic rocker that not only justifies its existence with a winning hook and danceable rhythm, but comes with an even higher purpose. It is there leading off the new album (and Squier is as devious and driven as a grandmaster in positioning the songs on each of his albums) to reassure his fans that indeed there is life in the old (34) boy yet. He can go, if necessary, all night, and did, if you caught the show that toured America this past summer. Beyond that message is a lyric that is sensitive and revealing. It pictures Squier as the ultimate rock and roll survivor, realizing it perhaps not for the first time, but with a power and directness arising from a year away from the boards and the studio that has made him appreciate it more fully than ever before.

Abounding with refreshed vibes and an array of energetic sounds, most of Side One features the positive, aggressive rock that Squier has made his trademark. The man knows how to make a record, utilizing the studio, his producer (in this case Jim Steinman), and all the available gadgets, sounds, and technologies. You can get lost in the density and the texture. But if you do you'll miss the lyrical odes and warnings to himself that are as much Squier's stock-in-trade as his sheer blinding technique. While "Rock Me Tonight" may reside with a multitude of similarly one-track anthems, as Paul McCartney might reply, "What's wrong with that?" Lust is as basic to rock lore as doleful dirges sung to underage lovers left abandoned on the railroad tracks.

From *The Good Fight*

And if the video of that song seems to imply that Squier himself is the object of his own lust, a few listenings to the audio version should reaffirm the tune's inherent male-female equation.

Since he achieved mega-success only an album ago, Squier's penchant for paranoia may be new to most listeners. But his preoccupation with the subject is easily on a par with his obsession with stardom. Here's a guy who no sooner achieves his life's ambition of a million-selling album—after years and years of abject and bitter and even humiliating failure—than he opens his next album (*Emotions in Motion*) with the sarcastic ode "Everybody Wants You," a rebuke to the very forces that granted his dream. It was as if he were saying, "I finally made it, but who needs it?" Yet that initial bitterness gives way by the third song on the album to the stunning, indeed redeeming honesty of "Learn How to Live," a humble ballad of self-discovery made even more meaningful by the whopping success that came before he wrote it.

Squier will do that, disarm you with his vulnerability even as he tries to intimidate you with his insouciance. In *Signs of Life* songs three and four, "Eye on You" and "Take a Look Behind Ya," are shifty odes to celebrity and chancy fame, exhibiting his thanks-but-no-thanks attitude in a format fans of Queen and Led Zeppelin have come to expect from Squier. But with "Reach for the Sky," he ends Side One on a note of vulnerability, in effect offering as nifty a credo for the modern rock star as you're apt to find. And to find it on what is ostensibly the album of a yanker and cranker is a bonus unexpected only by the uninitiated. For the rest, the bonuses are what make Squier one of the most consistently surprising musicians at work today in the rock sphere.

As are most album flip-sides in the business today, Side Two of *Signs of Life* is a safe haven where fans will most likely outnumber foes in appreciating its casual merits. Yet even here among throwaway rockers like "Fall for Love," "Can't Get Next to You" and "Hand-Me-Downs" is the occasional revealing lyric, the inevitable cry of pain and love that is the essence of rock and roll purity, buried in layers of artifice, multitracked voice-on-voice, and relentless wall of sound. To top off an album called *Signs of Life* there's "Sweet Release," a song about dying, another Robert Plantian plaint into the void. Could this song be a veiled tribute to his late grandmother, or is it perhaps a soap opera flourish designed to lure listeners back to the coffers for album number seven?

Surely Squier must realize he doesn't need such a flourish by now—unless each album is a life and death struggle for him, with the muse, the fates, the forces of commerce. If there's any other rocker extant (singer-songwriter types excluded) to whom the foregoing might apply with greater relevance than Billy Squier, let him or her step forward now, or deliver to me an album to prove it.

Until then Billy Squier's catalog should suffice. ▣

This month's album:

Billy Squier. ***Signs of Life.***
Capitol SJ-12361

Other Billy Squier albums:
The Tale of the Tape.
Capitol ST-12062.
Don't Say No.
Capitol ST-12146.
Emotions in Motion.
Capitol ST-12217.

Gail Pool:

Magazines

The media change their shape these days as readily as Proteus on the beach. While some of the hybrid forms seem hardly worth trying to hold on to, others are very successful, providing the impetus for new combinations. After all, if people enjoy watching records to the tune of millions of dollars—as they do on cable's MTV—might they not want to take a videotape tour of a photography exhibit? Or log into classified advertisements?

The American Arts Project hopes to find an audience that wants to listen to a magazine. The magazine concept has been floating around electronic circles for some years now, and magazines in various guises have linked up with cable, with television, and with videotape. But *The American Arts Project,* which bills itself as a "monthly magasette," seems to be the first United States effort to bring the magazine format to audiotape.

The initial idea for creating a magazine on cassette belongs to Jake Holmes, a singer and commercial writer responsible for such advertising copy as the recent Burger King campaign and such well-known jingles as "Be All That You Can Be" (for the Army) and "The Spirit of Massachusetts Is the Spirit of America." Holmes and Daniel Roth, cofounder and publisher, narrowed down the magazine's subject matter to the arts in America—hardly too narrow, since their concept ranges from poetry to art appraisal to Broadway musicals—and launched the series in 1983.

The first *American Arts Project* tape includes an interview with composer Philip Glass and a panel discussion on American theater with *New Yorker* critic Brendan Gill. Later tapes feature readings by William Burroughs and Nikki Giovanni, interviews with Virgil Thomson and Louise Nevelson, and a symposium called "Back in the World: Writing After Vietnam," with veterans reading from their work. Future projects include an interview with John Huston and one with composer Jule Styne.

At the marketing level, Holmes and Roth obviously hope to tap plugged-in America—the joggers, exercisers, and commuters hooked to their Walkmen and tape decks who have created a giant maw for cassette programming. At the more creative and ambitious level, they have viewed the cassette as a distinct medium and tried to create an original type of programming suitable to the form.

"There are things you can do with the cassette medium you can't do with print, video, or radio," says Roth, an unabashed (and not unbiased) fan of the medium. "It's closest to a record, but records aren't topical. Here, you have the sound qualities of a recording, the electricity of a live performance, the recency of a magazine, and the intimacy of the oral word."

One characteristic of the series is its independence of the written word. No text accompanies the tape. Though liner notes on a hardbound card, a permanent printed part of the cassette, will tell who the performers are and why they're there, this is as far as the publisher wants to go in accommodating print-oriented souls. Still more important perhaps, the tapes aren't really based on a text. Interviews and panel discussions, though edited, are not translations of the printed word, as books on tape—even dramatizations—must in some sense be.

A second characteristic is the series' emphasis on live as opposed to studio performances. "There is an electricity, an energy in the air at a live performance that is missing from a studio reading," says Roth who believes the live element renders the tapes "kinetic" and enables them to avoid the static quality which he feels characterizes books on cassette.

As a prime example of what *The American Arts Project* hopes to do, Roth cites the Vietnam tapes, featured in volume one, numbers four, and five, in which veterans read from their work. The event, held at the West Side YMCA in New York City, was organized by *The American Arts Project.* Roth and Michael Stephens, an *American Arts Project* panelist who served as moderator of the symposium, invited the veterans, sold tickets (to an SRO crowd), and recorded and edited the final product. The creation and recording of not only the tape but the event itself represents the kind of original programming *The American Arts Project* is striving to achieve.

Original programming, of course, is expensive, and *The American Arts Project* is still feeling its way toward profitability. Advertising plays no part in revenues—there are no ads on the tapes—so the entire income depends on circulation. To encourage sales, *The American Arts Project* has already reduced its original $96 subscription price to a more feasible $79 for twelve issues. The publishers have changed a subscription-only policy to include single copy sales as well, and they will market the magazine through museum bookstores and Waldenbooks. In addition, to increase revenues, they have plans for spinoffs and special issues, such as the Vietnam tapes, which will be reissued as

Gail Pool *holds an M.L.S. degree from Simmons College and presently works as a freelance writer based in Cambridge, Massachusetts.*

two one-hour tapes and marketed separately.

The decision to pursue single copy sales seems to be a wise one because it's hard to know how large an audience of individual subscribers *The American Arts Project,* as it now stands, could find. A problem with the series is that the tapes include not only a diversity of content—which is all to the good—but a diversity of sophistication that make it unlikely one person would find all the tapes of interest. *The American Arts Project* may have to tighten its focus more clearly on one audience. On the other hand, the diversity presents no problem for libraries, which serve a variety of patrons who can check out only those tapes they find of interest. Roth is hoping *The American Arts Project* will find a "solid, loyal following" among libraries. His interest in the library market is clear from his attendance at ALA and his responsiveness to librarians' queries about ISSN (there is now a number), packaging (the tapes will be blister packed), and cataloging problems (magazine or cassette), which he is trying to resolve with the assistance of a librarian at New York Public Library.

Roth's belief that *The American Arts Project* is the sort of thing that "should be in libraries" is not without foundation. This is a high quality series, a serious effort. It may be particularly appealing and useful to young adults as an introduction to artists and issues. There is good treatment of a diversity of artists, including women, too often ignored in the arts.

The cassette format has it limitations along with its strengths: outstanding in its presentation of musical features, it is obviously weak in its capacity to treat the visual arts. One wonders whether some visual material (pictures, not text) might accompany the features on the visual arts. An interview with Louise Nevelson, for example, would be enhanced by some illustrations of her work, especially for those unfamiliar with the sculptor's unique style. Affordability may be at war here with the ideal—it usually is—but the relevant question may be whether *The American Arts Projct* can really develop the cassette as a distinct new medium.

The American Arts Project, like most new and innovative ventures, has a struggle ahead of it. Certainly as the tape field grows, other endeavors will give this project a run for its money. At the moment the magazine format—the inclusion of several different features on each tape—gives it a distinct place. But as books on cassette continue to expand conceptually to include interviews and panel discussions as well as live readings—features of *The American Arts Project*—the magazine will have to fight to maintain its share of the competitive market, a share it deserves for the quality and origniality of its effort. ▣

Not for left-handed computers users

Those who, like myself, have pined for an American humor magazine will be happy to learn that such an animal now exists. It is called *Mole,* and it is published in Washington, D.C., a suitable home for political satire.

Editor and publisher Gary Wasserman, a former political science professor at Columbia University, launched his pilot issue in the summer of 1983, and it tested sufficiently well on a national basis for him to begin bimonthly publication this past spring.

Mole is nonpartisan in its attacks and social as well as political in its satire, and parts of it are very funny. Some of the short features are successful as one liners: its fake ads (Asbest-O-s cereal, loaded with minerals) or its "Editorial Declaration of Principles," comprised of a blank page noting "This space available for advertising." "Kennedy World: The Ultimate Kennedy Magazine," a spoof of the sensationalist press treatment of the clan ("Ted and Jackie Beg JKF: 'Bless Our Love Child'") was very good. But some of the humor is forced, some is adolescent, and some—like the regular feature "Sandra's Day: Diary of a Mad Supreme"—strikes me as just not funny. I hope *Mole* moves in the direction of sophistication and wit à la *Punch* and away from the adolescent *Lampoon*-type humor that has characterized too much of the American comic style.

Wasserman is hoping to build circulation sufficiently to generate some advertising. But he is aware of the trouble humor magazines have acquiring ads in the American magazine world geared to specialized publications and targeted audiences. "Now if you had a magazine for left-handed computer users . . . " he quips.

The amount of press *Mole* has received so far is a fair indication that many people have been awaiting a satirical magazine and are eager to like this publication. There are enough good things in this bold magazine to make it well worth watching.

Subscriptions: $12/6 issues from *Mole,* Box 43403, Washington, D.C. 20010. A free sample is available on request.

Norman Stevens:

Our Profession

As librarians we work in different settings and with different kinds of materials. To be effective we must be able to adapt readily to the circumstances in which we find ourselves and to deal effectively with information in any format. This month's books reflect the diverse situations that we may encounter and suggest helpful ways of dealing with them.

The use of a library degree in an alternative, but related, career has received considerable attention in recent years as librarians, like others, find that their immediate job market may be limited or may not best suit their abilities. Betty-Carol Sellen and Dimity Berkner's **New Options for Librarians: Finding a Job in a Related Field** is the most helpful tool yet available for those seriously interested in such matters. The first part of the text, which deals with changing career directions, starts with a report on a survey of five hundred persons with library school credentials who are employed outside libraries. That survey, which gives a broad picture of what some people are doing and the options that exist, is followed by six essays that deal with everything from how to make a change to running your own information business. The second part of the text consists of twelve essays that explore possibilities for work in such environments as contract service companies, information brokers, research firms, information management, networks, sales and marketing, library publishing and journalism, book and serial vendors, abstracting and indexing, associations, public relations, and communications and media. These essays, which were written by different authors based on personal experience, are largely descriptive of the kind of positions that are available and the kind of work that is involved. In one sense *New Options for Librarians* offers little that is new or earthshaking but it does a solid job of presenting a range of information that should be of substantial help to those considering an alternative career.

For many persons in developing countries librarianship itself may be an alternative career. Faced with a shortage of trained information professionals, many developing countries have had to turn to others to run their libraries, and to provide them with training. Clairc Guinchat and Michel Menou's **General Introduction to the Techniques of Information and Documentation Work** is an outgrowth of training programs that UNESCO has sought to provide. It is a manual for those in developing countries who are beginning a career in an information unit with a secondary-level degree but without any basic training in library and information science. Guinchat and Menou have developed a work that is detailed and straightforward without being simple or condescending. This manual, which has been published in both an English and a French edition, should serve for many years as an extremely valuable handbook for its intended audience. It is substantially better than most available American manuals designed for the training of library technical assistants and is recommended wholeheartedly for such purposes. Guinchat and Menou cover all aspects of our work in a challenging fashion that deals with the concepts and philosophy of librarianship and not simply the technical details.

Much to Herbert White's dismay, since he does not want to encourage the notion that those with no library background can run a special library, Guinchat and Menou's work could also serve admirably as a self-teaching manual for those untrained persons in this country who have special librarianship thrust upon them as an alternative career. In **Managing the Special Library** White takes the view that effective special librarianship requires skilled professionals. His text, subtitled *Strategies for Success Within the Larger Organization,* is aimed at such professionals. It concentrates not on basic library routines as practiced in special libraries but on the unique elements of special libraries, especially in the context of relationships with the parent organization. White, in his typically iconoclastic fashion, does not hesitate to forcefully express his opinions as he deals with the myriad problems that face the special librarian trying to provide quality service in an organization where library service may not be highly valued. As he ranges over topics from standards, professionalism and salaries to management communication, White speaks his mind as he describes ways for negotiating a successful library program. The flavor of his views can be found in his notion that "the greatest problem with management is not opposition but indifference" and that the special librarian must develop a "conscious plan to win over a group of people who are probably not instinctive or experienced library users." Since almost all librarians work in a larger institutional setting, White's words of wisdom may have value for all of us.

By comparison Elizabeth Ferguson and Emily Mobley's more conventional treatise **Special Libraries at Work** seems tame. It is a much more straightforward text covering all aspects of special librarianship. It will serve as a manual for students and new special librarians and perhaps as a refresher and handbook for the experienced special librarian. It is far more descriptive, and far less prescriptive, than White's work and makes a fine contrast to it. With Guinchat and Menou's text it might

---

Norman Stevens *is university librarian at the University of Connecticut and the author of* Communication Throughout Libraries.

well serve as a self-teaching manual for the neophyte coming into a special library. The experienced special librarian may find little of value in Ferguson and Mobley but will find much in White that requires careful consideration. The newcomer, or student, will find much of value in Ferguson and Mobley but may find some aspects of White's provocative statements beyond his or her immediate comprehension.

For special librarians, as for many of the rest of us, access to information from the government is increasingly important. The sheer mass of government publications presents a variety of challenges to our ingenuity. Peter Hernon and Charles McClure, who are recognized as experts in this field, have put together in a single volume a comprehensive treatment that covers every conceivable aspect of dealing with this vital body of material. **Public Access to Government Publications: Issues, Trends, and Strategies** does not approach the subject, as it usually is treated, from the perspective of a form of material that requires special handling by libraries (although it deals more than adequately with all of the issues involved in handling government publications). It approaches the issues from the perspective of the importance of providing increased public access to information produced and published by the government. Hernon and McClure emphasize the need to critically assess current practices and traditional assumptions, suggesting ways in which government publications and information services can be made more effective, and stressing the need for a research base from which issues can be examined. By looking at how information is produced and distributed by the government, how libraries process and use it, and the role of networks and other cooperative activities, Hernon and McClure place the issues in a broad perspective.

A recitation of the chapter headings indicates the comprehensive treatment. They cover public access to depository collections, federal information policies and public access, government publications as an information source, bibliographic control of United States government publications, developing collections of United States government publications, technology, reference and referral services, microforms, technical reports, administrative considerations, integrating government information resources into library services, physical facilities and space management, processing depository publications, planning and evaluating services, cooperation and resource sharing, restructuring the GPO depository system, local and state information resources, the publications of international organizations, education of the documents professional, and mainstreaming government publications. Everything is neatly placed in the context of the the policies and practices of contemporary librarianship. This is by far the most comprehensive and useful treatise on government publications yet published. It will rank with the first edition of Osborn's classic work on serials as a landmark publication. It will assist, just as that work did for serials, in giving government publications the recognition and status they deserve in library collections. ▣

This month's books:

Ferguson, Elizabeth and Emily R. Mobley. **Special Libraries at Work.** Shoe String Press, 1984. 206p. $21.50, pa $14.50. ISBN 0-208-01938-3

Guinchat, Claire and Michel Menou. **General Introduction to the Techniques of Information and Documentation Work.** UNESCO, 1983. 340p. pa $10.50

Hernon, Peter and Charles R. McClure. **Public Access to Government Publications.** Ablex, 1984. 457p. $49.50, pa $25.00. ISBN 0-89391-100-3

Sellen, Betty-Carol and Dimity S. Berkner. **New Options for Librarians.** Neal-Schuman, 1984. 300p. pa $19.95. ISBN 0-918212-73-1

White, Herbert S. **Managing the Special Library.** Knowledge Industry Publications, 1984. 151p. $36.50, pa $27.50. ISBN 0-86729-088-9; 0-86729-087-0

Patrick Dewey:

Software for Libraries

Buying the microcomputer has turned out to be the easy part; finding all the right software is a never-ending battle. When selecting software, one key to success is to keep all of the end-users in mind—kids, students, senior citizens, librarians—just as we do when we select books.

There are groups, however, for whom it is difficult, but not impossible, to find proper software. For instance, finding software for a three-year-old in a public library microcomputer center has usually been more difficult than for other patrons. This situation seems to be rapidly ending as new products surface. One delightful package just released is **Dinosaurs** by Julie Harris (Advanced Ideas, 1984), created for kids two and one-half to five years of age. Everyone is fascinated by the large skeletal remains of long extinct animals. Five separate games are based upon the dinosaur theme: match the dinosaur; distinguish the meat eaters from the plant eaters; guess which dinosaur goes with which name; guess where the dinosaur belongs (water, land, or sky); and match and count dinosaurs. Each game is easy to play. Just depress one of two keys to make a choice. The animals are different colors and shapes. While it improves the program, a color screen is not mandatory. When guessed correctly, the Pteranodon will flap its little wings and fly across the screen. Completion of each unit is rewarded by a parade of six dinosaurs marching across the screen. This provides positive reinforcement for color recognition, shape differentiation, and elementary counting—just the sort of skills that preschoolers should be mastering. To lessen the moderate noise level, the sound may be switched off. For use with: Apple II+, IIe. Cost: $39.95.

Patrick Dewey *is administrative librarian, Mayfield (Illinois) Public Library and author of* Public Access Microcomputers: A Handbook for Librarians.

Challenging adult patrons

A real challenge is to see how many adult, and, especially, retired or elderly patrons, can be tempted into trying out the microcomputer. Just what can we buy to get them interested? Sometimes, we may look to classics. **Sargon III,** a chess program by Dan and Kathe Spracklen (Hayden, 1983, 1984), inherits a long-respected name. Its predecessor, *Sargon II,* could play at seven different skill levels, but when operating at an advanced level, it often deliberated over a single move for six hours. The new version operates with lightning speed—eight of its nine levels take only ten minutes or less to complete a turn. This is an important development for public access centers. Patrons can now play high-level chess in real time. To achieve all this, *Sargon III* has not sacrificed ease of play; virtually anyone who knows how to play chess can sit down at the keyboard and begin, without reference to the excellent manual. Unlike *Sargon II,* chess notation (e.g., A1) now appears on the screen to aid those who don't know the difference between square A1 and A2. The screen can be "flip-flopped" back and forth between a high-resolution graphic representation of the chessboard and pieces and a list of moves that have taken place during the game. With the aid of the Apple Macintosh's mouse, a button control device, chess notation may be bypassed altogether. The Macintosh version does not require flipping back and forth between screens since the chessboard and pieces, and the list of moves, are always visible. Adding a completely new dimension to *Sargon III* is a second disk which contains a library of chess problems (opening, tactical, endgame, checkmate). That, and 107 master tournament games from 1951 to 1980, can be pressed into action. For use with Apple II+, IIc, IIe, Macintosh, Commodore, IBM PC & jr., and, later this year, Atari. Cost: $49.95.

Patrons will eat it up

Many libraries promote better health by featuring lectures, films, and fliers on the subject. **The Eating Machine** (Muse Software, 1983), by Barbara S. Thorne, could be promoted concurrently with such activities, and is a great way to get health buffs into the library. The graphics could pass for those often associated with educational packages for the younger grades, but the program itself—a specialized database which lists the nutritional content of some five hundred foods—will definitely appeal to adults of all ages. Diets may be analyzed according to the minimum daily requirement of iron, calcium, vitamins A and C, and protein. Bar graphs show just how close to the desired intake a planned diet comes. Any excess of sodium is reported, and a breakdown of calories is given by fat, carbohydrates, protein, and alcohol. Portions may be adjusted up or down. Any good book on nutrition will divulge the calories and vitamins contained in many foods. This program, however, saves all of the calculations associated with figuring out what the banana split sitting on the counter is worth in calories. This makes it very much a kind of "What if?" spreadsheet for nutrition. ("What if I eat two candy bars instead of one?") As foods are added to each meal of the day (breakfast, lunch, dinner, and snack are possible), the program maintains a running total. The database may be modified by including information taken directly from labels or recipes for a total of up to 732 foods. Nine different age categories, plus gender, are taken into account when default values are calculated for recommended daily allowances of vitamins and calories, but these may be modified up or down, depending upon any special requirements of the user. While it seems unlikely that this will provide a precise count of daily calorie or vitamin intake, it should give many users serious pause to reflect on their eating habits. The software uses a program and a data disk. The entire database may be printed out if desired. Two drives are convenient but not required. Five nutrition experts are listed as consultants in the sixty-five-page, easy-to-use manual. For use with: Apple II+, IIe. Cost: $49.95.

A Basic introduction

For those wishing to delve into the internal workings of the microcomputer, and learn to tell it what to do, **Basic for Beginners** (Society for Visual Education, 1983) is a highly interactive package for use with the fourth through sixth grades, and seventh and eighth grade remediation. If a public library has a cooperative or referral microcomputer program with a local school, this would be a good software choice. For that matter, it would be a good introduction for anyone curious about Basic computer programming, including adults. Learning is effected through a series of multiple-choice questions, and program-building exercises (for example, "What would be the output of this program if you typed it in and ran it?"); the learner is forced to think about what is happening and why one thing works and not another. A wrong answer will loop back for a review of the missed material. On the reverse side of both diskettes are

"Write a program" exercises. Here the learner is given the result of a program (e.g., a rectangle), and then asked to write a program that will produce it. Errors return helpful counsel from the computer. Disk #1 includes such elementary concepts as: defining a computer program as a set of instructions; flowcharting, PRINT, REM, INPUT, and IF . . . THEN commands; and the text commands TAB, HTAB, VTAB, FLASH, NORMAL, and INVERSE. Disk #2 covers more advanced topics: GOSUB . . . RETURN, GOTO, and FOR . . . NEXT commands; nested loops; subroutines; the graphics commands of PLOT, COLOR, HLIN . . . AT, VLIN . . . AT; and simple animation. The teacher's manual contains careful objectives, and reproducible worksheets to be used with the diskettes. A classroom management system allows retention of progress for up to thirty students, but it may be bypassed altogether. The student guide contains a chart of the Apple keyboard, an example of how to make a flowchart, and a glossary. One pretest is supplied, as well as a separate posttest for each diskette. For use with: Apple II+, IIe Cost: $99 includes backups; $79 without backups.

Inhouse bibliographer

Entering items in a bibliography can be tricky and time-consuming when done manually. For those lucky enough to have a microcomputer for internal library use, **Personal Bibliographic System**, (Personal Bibliographic Software, 1983), by Victor Rosenberg, will be useful. A separate, newly released and enhanced version, the **Professional Bibliographic System** (1984), is available for the IBM-PC. With PBS the user need not know anything at all about order or punctuation. When entering data, a prompt is given for each field, and, depending upon the material, the author, title, and other information are entered. Notes as well as abstracts can be appended, and an index line is available. The program itself is quite easy to understand and use, rarely requiring reference to the manual. In addition, word-processing capability permits the user to rearrange and edit entries as needed. The *Personal Bibliographic System* will accommodate twenty-two different document types, and it uses the formats compiled by the American National Standard for Bibliographic References. Appended to documentation are a sample bibliography and a list of references about bibliography. Index. Separate versions of the program are available for Apple II+, IIe, Terak Computer, Victor 9000, and IBM-PC. Cost: $250. The updated version, the *Professional Bibliographic System,* for the IBM-PC: $395. Requires: 2 disk drives, 80 columns, and 64K. ▣

Publisher addresses for this month's software:

Advanced Ideas, 2550 Ninth Street, Suite 104, Berkeley, CA 94710.

Hayden Software Company, 600 Suffolk Street, Lowell, MA 01853.

Muse Software, 347 N. Charles St., Baltimore, MD 21201.

Society for Visual Education, Inc., 1347 W. Diversey, Chicago, IL 60614.

Personal Bibliographic Software, Inc., Box 4250, Ann Arbor, MI 48106.

James Rettig:

Current Reference Books

Correspondence and review copies for this column should be directed to James Rettig, University Library, Box 8198, University of Illinois at Chicago, Chicago, IL 60680.

Advertising Slogans of America, compiled by Harold S. Sharp. Metuchen, NJ: Scarecrow, 1984. 543p. $35. 0-8108-1681-4 83-20431

Bereft of the illustrations, music, or rhythm which originally gave them vitality and context, advertising slogans easily sound pompous ("World's greatest newspaper"—Chicago *Tribune*); inane ("Coke is it!"—Coca-Cola); ironic ("The vanishing breed"—DeLorean autos); laboriously literal ("For your eyes"—Murine eye drops); or overly obvious ("For use by one user"—Scot Tissue). A few retain their wit, ("The support of a nation"—Paris Garters). *Advertising Slogans* lists approximately 15, 000 slogans used by 6,000 American businesses. Slogans appear twice in the alphabetical list, once by company name and once by first word. Since the slogans were gathered from television, radio, films, books of past advertisements, newspapers, magazines, and other sources, each one could have been assigned, if not a precise year, at least an approximate date. This would have facilitated study of the evolution of the language of advertising. As it stands, the book serves its limited purpose well and can add a bit of the din of the marketplace to popular culture collections.

James Rettig *is head reference librarian, University of Illinois at Chicago.*

The Almanac of Investments, edited by Alan Crittenden. Crittenden Books (Box 1150, Novato, CA 94948), 1984. 514p. $24.95. 83-051608

Brokerage offices in Sears stores have sprung up to help people choose among the incredible variety of investment opportunities available today. This printed guide will help bewildered novice investors sort out their options for increasing their money by putting it into baseball cards, gold, real estate, insurance, bonds, wine, stocks, horses, or beer cans. Twenty-five chapters review each of these and other investments, telling their history, pointing out their pros and cons, comparing their rates of return, explaining how to invest in them, citing tax benefits, and including brief bibliographies of books and current periodicals. Numerous anecdotal sidebar stories give credence to the publisher's claim that the book "is part *People's Almanac* and *Everybody's Business*." The lucid articles take investments seriously but discuss them in a light, conversational tone. Caveats about investing in books do not apply the *Almanac* itself, for it can help interested readers select ways to increase their interest.

American Drama Criticism, Supplement I to the Second Edition, compiled by Floyd Eugene Eddleman. Hamden, CT: Shoe String, 1984. 255p. $29.50. 0-208-01978-2 83-25410 (Drama explication series)
Twentieth-Century Short Story Explication, Supplement II to the Third Edition, by Warren S. Walker. Hamden, CT: Shoe String, 1984. 348p. $35. 0-208-02005-3 80-16175

These supplements extend the usefulness of standard reference works. The supplement to *Drama Criticism* lists interpretations of 1,300 North American plays published between 1978 and 1982. The second edition's format, listing playwrights alphabetically by name with citations to criticism of their plays arranged by the plays' titles, has been enhanced by the addition of a general section for some playwrights.

The supplement to *Short Story Explication* covers explications published in books and periodicals from 1979 through 1981. It increases the number of authors by 246, bringing the third edition's total to 1,298. Both of these bibliographies are often found in ready-reference desk collections for their convenience and ease of use. Students will find them especially helpful.

Business Forms on File, edited by Richard P. Zeldin. New York: Facts on File, 1984. looseleaf $75. 0-87196-881-9 84-5950

Personal Forms on File, edited by Richard P. Zeldin. New York: Facts on File, 1984. looseleaf $75. 0-87196-880-0 84-5956

A librarian's decision on whether or not to add either of these to a reference collection is, in effect, a declaration of his or her position on the long-standing controversy of whether librarians should provide instruction or information. Using the heavy opaque stock and looseleaf format of *Maps on File* (reviewed in *WLB,* January 1982), *Personal Forms* arranges forms into eight categories (e.g., accounting, government procurement, legal, taxes). The thorough table of contents is more convenient than the index. Personal forms include a Naval Academy application, auto maintenance schedule, safe deposit box inventory, certificate of citizenship, terms of agreement for an unmarried couple living together, selective service registration, daily record for tips, and a genealogy checklist. Conspicuous by its absence is the popular IRS 1040EZ. Business forms include a balance sheet, government bid bond, claims compensation for occupational disease, corporation estimated tax, an insurance checklist, and a postage meter application. Even though the publisher offers an annual updating service, many of the forms are subject to revision. Most are available free for the asking from government agencies or other organizations. Librarians who favor instruction will give patrons a phone number or address from which appropriate forms can be requested; those who favor "information" will buy these volumes and put the forms in patrons' hands for photocopying.

China, compiled by Peter Cheng. Santa Barbara: Clio Press, 1983. 390p. $55. 0-903450-81-X (World bibliographical series, no. 35)

Poland, compiled by Richard C. Lewanski. Santa Barbara: Clio Press, 1984. 266p. $40. 0-903450-58-5 (World bibliographical series, no. 32)

The *World Bibliographical Series,* an ambitious project which eventually will cover every country in the world, deserves to be well-known and well-used. The annotated bibliographies of books in English, plus a few foreign-language exceptions of unique character or indisputable import, cover geography, tourism and travel, flora and fauna, prehistory, history, politics, foreign relations, language, arts, and other topics relevant to each country. The books feature integrated author, title, and subject indexes. Because they are compiled by experts on the individual countries, the bibliographies complement the United States Defense Department's *Area Handbook* series (SuDocs D101.22:). Librarians can serve their patrons by promoting the use of both series.

Computer Books and Serials in Print 1984. New York: Bowker, 1984. 551p. $49.50. 0-8352-1814-7 ISSN 0000-0779

In common with every other guide to books on computers, this was surely incomplete and out-of-date the day it was published. Since it does not evaluate computer books, it is one guide that can truly be called useful and which will remain useful. It presents the usual *BIP* information on more than 12,000 domestic and foreign books and pamphlets and 1,500 serials relating to every phase of the computer world. The extensive subject index, employing more than six hundred LC subject headings, offers far more extensive coverage and more precise retrieval than does the *Subject Guide* to *BIP.* In addition to LC headings, proper names (e.g., Atari 800, VAX-11) enrich the subject index. Complete bibliographic information appears in every entry in the subject, author, and title indexes. Serials are treated in separate subject and title indexes. Not to be mistaken as a simple spin-off from *BIP, Computer Books and Serials* is a useful bibliographic tool in its own right.

Dictionary of Medieval Civilization, by Joseph Dahmus. New York: Macmillan, 1984. 700p. $60. 0-02-907870-9 83-25583

The short, objective articles on people, places, events, books, religious rites, institutions, religious orders, weapons, and other bits and pieces of life in the Western world between the fourth and sixteenth centuries complement the longer articles in the multivolume, encyclopedic *Dictionary of the Middle Ages* (reviewed in *WLB,* February 1983 and November 1983). The book touches on every aspect of medieval life, including articles on popes, kings, colleges, legal practices, battles, architecture, and legends. Needed *see* references have been made, but *see also* references ought to be more numerous. For example, the Premonstratensians figure prominently in the article on the Dominicans, but no cross-reference has been made to the article on the Premonstratensians. The addition of illustrations would have added clarity to some articles. Overall, however, this one-volume dictionary is an excellent source of brief, accurate information on things medieval.

Dun's Latin America's Top 25,000. Dun's Marketing Services (Three Century Drive, Parsippany, NJ 07054), 1984. 1,274p. $250. ISSN 0733-1592

To be updated annually, *Dun's Latin America's Top 25,000* borrows the successful format of *Principal International Businesses* (Dun & Bradstreet International) and applies it to corporations in Latin America. For the book's purposes, Latin America includes Mexico, Central America, South America, and the Caribbean. The criteria for selecting the 25,000 companies are size, number of employees, and location. The introduction does not specify cut-off points for size (presumably measured by annual sales) and number of employees. The directory, organized by country, lists company name, address, sales in local currency, SIC numbers, number of employees, type of business, and president or equivalent officer. This lists more companies for most countries than does *Principal International Businesses*. Both the index by SIC numbers and the index by company name include the address. *Principal International Businesses* will serve most libraries' needs; *Latin America's Top 25,000* offers the depth needed in very specialized international business collections.

The Encyclopedia of Drug Abuse, by Robert O'Brien and Sidney Cohen. New York: Facts on File, 1984. 454p. $40. 0-87196-690-5 82-5034
Drug Abuse and the Elderly, by Douglas H. Ruben. Metuchen, NJ: Scarecrow, 1984. 247p. $20. 0-8108-1677-6 83-20463

O'Brien and Cohen's A-to-Z collection of articles on drugs and their misuse recognizes that drug abuse is far more pervasive than indicated by the popular images of street junkies shooting heroin or Hollywood stars snorting cocaine. In addition to the well-publicized drugs from outside the medicinal pharmacopoeia, the encyclopedia describes prescription drugs, substances such as glue which are misused, diseases, body organs, ethnic groups, technical terms, drug administration techniques, and organizations. Broad topics such as pregnancy, gastrointestinal tract, and withdrawal are treated in articles of one to two pages. The encyclopedia approaches its multifaceted subject objectively. Extensive appendixes present street language for drugs, statistical tables, organizations involved in research or treatment, and a bibliography. This will be useful to young and old in public, college, high school, and hospital patient libraries.

The *Encyclopedia* cites several reasons why the elderly can easily lapse into drug abuse. Although older Americans comprise only ten percent of the population, they consume one fourth of all prescription drugs. As the population ages, consciousness and concern about the elderly and

drug abuse will increase. Thus Ruben's 787-item annotated bibliography of books, articles, conference papers, and research reports comes at an opportune time. Its eight topical chapters cover alcohol, illegal and legal drugs, medication, epidemiology of drug abuse, education and prevention, and institutionalization. Items are arranged by main entry. The lists of descriptors following the annotations facilitate browsing. The descriptors also appear in the subject index. The thorough annotations clarify the descriptors' meanings, some of which are very broad. The bibliography identifies and organizes a great number of recent items on a topic of growing interest. Researchers, geriatric and other health care professionals, and social workers specializing in serving the elderly will be able to find many helpful publications by using this bibliography.

Everyday Phrases, by Neil Ewart. Blandford (distributed by Sterling), 1983. 162p. $9.95. 0-7137-1354-2

"You pays your money and takes your choice" and some four hundred other popular expressions are explained in *Everyday Phrases*. Anecdotal articles tell how "Best foot forward," "Peeping Tom," "Ready when you are" and similar phrases came into being and how their meanings have remained stable or changed. Instead of cross-references within the alphabetical sequence, an index leads the user to the entry on "Black sheep" under "S" and so on. The articles are chattier than those in *Brewer's Dictionary of Phrase and Fable* and are more likely to veer off into entertaining asides. The businesslike Brewer's almost always gives fuller citations for expressions with literary origins. The plausible explanations in *Everyday Phrases* sometimes offer alternatives to *Brewer's* and, of of course, it explains some phrases (e.g., "Catch-22") not in *Brewer's*. However, li-

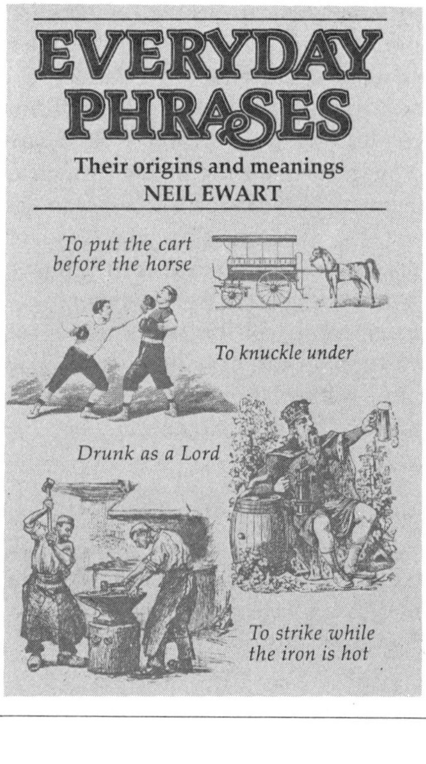

brarians who pay their money and take their choice will continue to choose *Brewer's* as a first source for origins and meanings of colloquial phrases.

The Facts on File Dictionary of Religions, edited by John R. Hinnells. New York: Facts on File, 1984. 550p. $24.95. 0-87196-862-2 83-20834

A surprising amount of information about the world's living and ancient religions is packed into this compact dictionary with its 1,150 wide-ranging entries. Articles of eighty to several hundred words, written by twenty-nine scholars from around the world, present clear definitions of religious concepts, groups, practices, and sacred texts. Roman numerals following entry words identify the article's author and the appropriate section of the sixty-four-page bibliography in which to find the references made within the articles. Just as numerous as the bibliographic references are the cross-references to other articles. There is so much in this dictionary that it requires both a synoptic index and an alphabetical index. The latter greatly expands the book's utility by identifying discussions of particular persons and common English names for foreign technical terms used as entry words. The method of citing bibliographic references is too subtle for many users, but the clarity and range of definitions should serve them well. The more selective, but also more current *Facts on File Dictionary* complements S. G. F. Brandon's *A Dictionary of Comparative Religion.*

Information on Music, Vol. III, Europe, by Guy A. Marco. Littleton, CO: Libraries Unlimited, 1984. 519p. $55. 0-87287-401-X 74-32132

And the beat goes on—if one may apply a phrase from a pop song to the three volumes of Marco's annotated guide to reference sources on serious music. The first volume (1975) covered universal sources, the second covered sources on the Americas, and the present volume covers sources on Europe. Because "Europe" includes all of the Soviet republics, much of Asia is also covered here. The 2,300 entries are organized into chapters on individual countries, each of these organized by type of tool and topic. The sources in English and other European languages include books, journal articles, and articles in such standard encyclopedias as the *New Grove.* Because of its focus on Europe, the volume duplicates only 167 items listed in Sheehy's *Guide to Reference Books* and 198 listed in Vincent Duckles's *Music Reference and Research Materials* (3rd ed., Macmillan, 1974). Indexing is by author, title, and subject. Marco's newest volume enriches music bibliography.

International Historic Statistics: The Americas and Australasia, by B. R. Mitchell. Detroit: Gale, 1983. 949p. $95. 0-8103-0520-8 82-23410

Economists, historians, and others in the United States may have one quibble with this companion to *International Historical Statistics: Africa and Asia* (New York University Press, 1982) and *European Historical Statistics* (2nd ed., Facts on File, 1981). Distances, temperatures, and other physical measures are expressed in metric units. The introduction offers practical caveats to users of any historical statistics. The eighty-plus tables are arranged into eleven groups such as climate, population, agriculture, industry, communications, prices, and education. Most of the statistics date from the nineteenth century, although some are as old as 1738 and others as recent as 1975. Footnotes qualify the data in the tables and cite their diverse sources. The table of contents adequately substitutes for an index. Users of historical statistics always face difficulties. This book eliminates the greatest difficulty: locating the numbers to be interpreted.

Knowledge Encyclopedia, edited by John Paton. New York: Arco, 1984. 415p. $16.95. 0-668-06137-5 83-73345

Although not stated, *Knowledge Encyclopedia* was first published under the same title in Britain (Leicester: Windward, 1979). Only a few of its 2,500 brief entries belie this British background (e.g., "motor car" rather that "automobile," an article on "parliament" but none on "Congress"). Other signs are more subtle, for example, a preference for British scenes in the six hundred color illustrations or British variations in spelling. By avoiding the most notoriously transient topics, the encyclopedia has not dated much. Geographic entries, except those for major countries, do not exceed other entries' one-paragraph length, nor are they disproportionate in number. Numerous articles on scientific and technical terms are clear, but range towards the higher end of the elementary-to-high school reading level continuum. Picture captions and marginal sidebar notes add detail to the brief articles. Internal *see also* references and an index supplement the alphabetical arrangement. These articles tell in dictionary-like fashion what things are; most fail to tell about them.

Major Modern Dramatists, Vol. 1, compiled and edited by Rita Stein and Friedhelm Rickert. New York: Ungar, 1984. 570p. $65. 0-8044-3267-8 78-4310 (A library of literary criticism)

The first volume in the *Library of Literary Criticism* series to focus on a genre rather than a nation, *Major Modern Dramatists* reprints excerpts of criticism on thirty-five American, British, Irish, German, Austrian, and Swiss playwrights of the post-Ibsen era. They were selected for their international reputation, frequency of translation and performance of their plays outside their native countries, and the existence of extensive criticism of their work. The dramatists are grouped by country and the excerpts from reviews, articles, and books are arranged in chronological order by date of publication. The list of "Plays mentioned" arranges them by author and gives the year of first performance. The list does not tell on which page(s) a play is discussed; references may be scattered over twenty or more pages. In contrast, the "Index to Critics" gives precise page references. An undergraduate can use this for an overview of the critical legacy of Albee, Wilder, Yeats, Brecht, or Wedekind, but other tools offer better access to criticism of individual plays.

Modern Business Language and Usage in Dictionary Form, by J. Harold Janis. Garden City, NY: Doubleday, 1984. 506p. $19.95. 0-385-14489-X 80-1656

The title needs to specify "in Dictionary Form" since one can lose sight of that organizational principle when

opening the book and landing in a long section on general usage, such as the nine-page treatment of forms of address or the eight pages on capital letters. To these articles on style, usage, punctuation, grammar, sentence structure, and model letters, the dictionary weds articles on words used in the business world. This makes for a curious whole. Slang terms (e.g., guesstimate, golden handcuffs) and more conventional terms (e.g., front office, over-the-counter) are briefly defined and usage is often illustrated by a quote. Definitions sometimes suggest preferable alternatives. The attempt to serve, in one volume, the purposes of both the *Secretary's Handbook* (9th ed., Macmillan, 1969) and Jerry Rosenberg's *Dictionary of Business and Management* (reviewed in *WLB*, October 1983) fails. This marriage cannot be saved simply by putting all its pieces into one alphabetical order.

The Oxford Companion to Children's Literature, by Humphrey Carpenter and Mari Prichard. New York: Oxford, 1984. 586p. $35. 0–19–211582–0 83–15130

Children's Periodicals of the United States, edited by R. Gordon Kelly. Westport, CT: Greenwood, 1984. 591p. $49.95. 0–313–22117–0 83–8574 (Historical guides to the world's periodicals and newspapers)

Originally proposed to the Oxford University Press in 1958 by Peter and Iona Opie, the *Oxford Companion* treats children's literature from Mother Goose and Beatrix Potter to Judy Blume and Robert Cormier. Emphasizing the nineteenth and twentieth centuries and the United Kingdom and the United States, its 2, 000 articles summarize plots, identify characters, offer capsule biographies of authors and illustrators, describe genres, and characterize the children's literature of various countries. The 136 illustrations convey the flavor of famous illustrators' work. The critical articles include numerous *see also* references. Despite the authors' apologies for their imagined failure to produce the book the late Peter Opie would have written, the newest *Oxford Companion* has set a standard any future single-volume encyclopedia of children's literature will be hard pressed to meet much less exceed.

Similar self-effacement surfaces in the preface to *Children's Periodicals* which asserts that "Ten years from now, it would be a different, doubtless better book." Yet it recognizes itself as sui generis and as a foundation upon which others will build to complete the history of American children's magazines. Frank Luther Mott's monumental *History of American Magazines* (Harvard University Press, 1930–1968) does not treat these adequately. *Children's Periodicals* begins to fill that void by telling the stories of magazines from *The Children's Magazine* (1789) to *Seventeen*. The articles by nearly fifty experts describe each magazine's purpose, history, and editorial policy shifts; list footnotes; include a brief bibliography; name repositories holding large runs; and summarize publication history, including changes in title and editors. A bibliography lists 423 titles whose histories await telling. Other appendixes list the titles by state and city of publication and by year of birth. This trailblazing work belongs in every collection supporting the serious study of children's literature.

The Private Lives of English Words, by Louis G. Heller, Alexander Humez, and Malcah Dror. Detroit: Gale, 1984. 334p. $44. 0–8103–1012–0 84–8095

Words About Words, by David Grambs. New York: McGraw-Hill, 1984. 409p. $17.95. 0–07–024048–5 83–22254

Treating them as if they were people with pasts entertaining enough for gossip, *Private Lives* explains the etymology and development of four hundred English words. The forward and introduction explain the processes of linguistic change which account for the transformations the four hundred words have undergone. It is not clear how words were selected for inclusion. The articles, some as long as a page, avoid technical terms for the processes of change. Two appendixes link words and processes, one appendix listing the words and then the processes each has undergone, the other appendix reversing this, listing the forty-plus processes and then the words illustrating each one. The index cites headwords, variant forms, and meanings. The articles are much longer and much more readable than those in standard etymological dictionaries. They would be suitable for syndication as a newspaper feature that would entertain readers as much as it would educate them.

Words About Words defines and illustrates through quotations approximately 2,000 words related to "the craft of prose writing." Words for the linguistic processes, which *Private Lives* takes pains to illustrate (e.g., back-formation, functional shift, pejoration), are defined along with hundreds of others, many of them journalistic slang. The selection complements traditional dictionaries of literary terms which emphasize the vocabularies of poetics and rhetoric. The illustrative quotations come from a variety of sources, most contemporary, including the day's cognoscenti of language, John Simon, William Morris, and William Safire. Twenty "Special Entries" list related words and their definitions (e.g., propaganda devices, footnote abbreviations, rhetoric terms) or short articles on topics relevant to careful writers (e.g., the "Fog Index" of clarity, the elements necessary to prove libel). With its clear definitions and well-chosen illustrations, *Words About Words* is a wonderful word-hoard for writers.

Psychiatric Glossary, by the American Psychiatric Association. Washington: American Psychiatric Press, 1984. 142p. pa $7.95. 0-88048-027-0 84-473

Essentially a reprint of the fifth edition of the APA's *A Psychiatric Glossary* (Little, Brown, 1980), extensive comparison of the two shows that only the list of references has been revised. It has doubled in size by the addition of two books published by the APA. Librarians not already acquainted with the glossary should know that it is very selective and defines terms in simple language the lay reader can comprehend. In addition to enjoying the authority of the APA, it conforms to APA's *DSM III,* or *Diagnostic and Statistical Manual of Mental Disorders* (3rd ed., APA, 1980). Robert Goldenson's *Longman Dictionary of Psychology and Psychiatry* (Longman, 1984), much broader in scope and covering a greater number of technical terms, also conforms to *DSM III.* Both the *Glossary* and the *Longman Dictionary* are useful and authoritative guides to the vocabulary of psychiatry.

U.S. Government Directories, 1970–1981, compiled by Constance S. Gray. Littleton, CO: Libraries Unlimited, 1984. 260p. $35. 0-87287-414-1 83-26801

Donna Larson's *Guide to U.S. Government Directories, 1970–1980* (reviewed in *WLB,* April 1982) and Gray's *U.S. Government Directories, 1970–1981* share the purpose of listing and annotating directories published by the United States government over nearly identical periods. They differ in both content and arrangement. Larson's 842 directories are arranged by SuDocs number and are indexed by subject; Gray's 575 directories are grouped into twelve topical chapters and indexed by title and subject. Although smaller, Gray includes somes titles not in Larson. Both give title, author, issuing agency, date, length, and SuDocs number: however Larson also lists GPO stock numbers and depository item numbers. Since Gray limits her book to depository publications, inclusion of item numbers would have been prudent. Their absence, the broad topical arrangement, and the fuller annotations imply that Gray's book is meant for library users rather than librarians. Larson's more inclusive book will be most librarians' first choice.

Who's Who in Frontier Science and Technology. Chicago: Marquis Who's Who, 1984. 846p. $84.50. 0-8379-5701—X 82-82015

Researchers on the outside of "the invisible college" can peek inside thanks to the work done by the compilers of *Frontier Science and Technology.* It presents brief biographies of more than 16,500 scientists working at the cutting edge of research and applications in approximately 350 specialties. The biographies present the typical who's who data plus identification of one or two specialty areas and a brief description of current work. The subject index groups the 350 specialties into twenty-four broad areas, enabling users to identity leading researchers in high energy astrophysics, solid state chemistry, or gas cleaning systems. Among the few who made additional comments is Don Swanson of the University of Chicago's Graduate Library School who says one of the problems he would like to solve is "how to find information in a library." This can be used much as any other who's who is used and can also help to identity prospective speakers or potential employees for highly specialized positions.

Word Processors and the Writing Process, compiled by Paula R. Nancarrow, Donald Ross, and Lillian Bridwell. Westport, CT: Greenwood, 1984. 146p. $29.95. 0-313-23995-9 83-22749

Three English professors compiled this bibliography of articles, ERIC documents, book chapters, and unpublished papers to bring together available publications on this question: "What information might help those who are interested in the way computers can help writers, especially university students, with the art and craft of writing?" Needless to say, most entries date from the past five years, although some go back as far as fifteen years ago. Most entries include rich descriptive and evaluative annotations. Their clarity shows that using a computer to create the camera-ready copy had no detrimental effect on the compilers' writing. A computer-generated index provides subject access to the entries, which are arranged by author. The compilers are to be complimented on their perspicacity in creating this bibliography at this time—before the body of relevant items becomes unwieldy but at a time when it needs to be organized so the field can continue to advance. It will attract attention at universities and colleges where computer centers support widespread word-processing and text-editing for students and faculty.

Library World

News of announcements, new posts, retirements, and deaths should be sent to "Library World," WLB, *950 University Ave., Bronx, NY 10452.*

ANNOUNCEMENTS

Eunice Lovejoy has been given the 1984 Exceptional Service Award of the Association of Specialized and Cooperative Library Agencies (ASCLA) for contributions to the field of library service for disabled and elderly people. She is currently a research scientist for Information Science and Library Systems at the Battelle Columbus Laboratories Library, Columbus, Ohio.

Charles Rusiewski received the 1984 Honor Award from the Illinois Association for Media in Education. The award is presented to a member of the association who has made an outstanding contribution to school library media programs in the state of Illinois and who has held a leadership role in the organization. He is editor of the association's professional newsletter and has been media director at Nashville (Ill.) Community HS since 1958.

NEW POSTS

Jaia Barrett has been appointed program officer with ARL. She is the recipient of the 1984 CIS/GODORT "Documents to the People" Award and is currently head of the public documents department at Duke Univ.

David Brunnell has been named executive director of the Bibliographical Center for Research, Denver. He was formerly assistant network coordinator for the Federal Library and Information network (FEDLINK) of the Library of Congress and previously worked at BCR as systems specialist from 1977 to 1979.

Michael Buckland has been appointed assistant vice-president, library plans and policies for the Univ. of California at Berkeley. He was formerly acting assistant vice-president as well as dean of the UC Berkeley SLIS.

Jane Byers has been named director of the Waukesha PL, Waukesha, Wisc. She was formerly assistant director of the Fond du Lac (Wisc.) PL and the Mid-Wisconsin Federated Library System.

Timothy Connor is now head of public services at Harvard-Yenching Library, Harvard Univ. Libraries.

Beth Ferg, formerly public information offiicer of the Tuscon (Ariz.) PL , has joined the staff of the Scottsdale (Ariz.) PL as administrative services manager.

Katherine Gates has been appointed children's librarian at the Rochambeau branch of the Providence (R.I.) PL. She was formerly library assistant at the Johnstown (N.Y.) PL.

Jane Byers

Renee Gold has been named director of information services for the Special Libraries Association. Formerly associate editor of *Wilson Library Bulletin,* she is now in charge of SLA 's publishing program, the information resources center, and public relations.

Jo Griffith is now information services librarian at the Richland County PL, Columbia, S.C.

Patricia Harris has been named assistant director for library development with the Virginia State Library. She was formerly regional library consultant for the Ohio State Library, and previously headed a branch of the Greene County (Ohio) PL.

Jeffrey Heynen has been appointed program officer with ARL. He is currently president of the Information Interchange Corp.

Susan Jurow has accepted the position of training program specialist with the ARL Office of Management Studies. She was formerly assistant to the director of the Northern Regional

Renee Gold

David Remington

Charles Rusiewski

Karen Simmons

Library facility at the Univ. of California-Richmond.

Manuel Lopez is now head of the reference department for the Lockwood Library at the State Univ. of N.Y. at Buffalo.

Bruce Manzer has assumed the position of chief of the science and technology research center for the New York PL. He was formerly head librarian at the Univ. College of Bahrain.

Beata Panagopoulos has been named serials cataloger for the Harvard College Library, Harvard Univ. libraries.

Neel Parikh has been appointed coordinator of children's services with the San Francisco PL. She was formerly supervising librarian with the Alameda County (Calif.) library system.

Barbara Preschel is the new executive director of the Public Affairs Information Service (PAIS). She was formerly a faculty member with the GSLIS at Queens College, City Univ. of N.Y.

Joseph Pukl is now head of the order department at Thomas Cooper Library at the Univ. of South Carolina. He was assistant order librarian with the USC library since 1979.

David Remington, formerly head of the Cataloging Distribution Service, Library of Congress, has been appointed director of the Pend Oreille County Library, Newport, Wash.

Karen Simmons has been named director of library services for the American Institute of Certified Public Accountants (AICPA). She had been chief librarian of AICPA since 1975.

Paula Smith has assumed the position of assistant director for consultant, technical and extension services for the Monroe County (N.Y.) library system. She was formerly director of the Musser PL, Muscatine, Iowa.

David Turkalo has been appointed reference librarian in the business industry science department of the Providence (R.I.) PL. He was formerly a library assistant with the Taunton (Mass.) PL.

Tom Walker has been named systems coordinator for the Charleston County (S.C.) library. He was formerly deputy director of the Brampton (Ontario) library.

Paula Warnken is now director of libraries at Xavier Univ., Cincinnati. She was formerly acting director and head of reader services at Xavier.

Duane Webster, director of the ARL Office of Management Studies, has been appointed deputy executive director of ARL.

RETIREMENTS

Susan Haskin, deputy state librarian of the Library of Michigan, retired in September.

Catherine McCarthy has retired. She was formerly head of the reference and professional library for the Massachusetts Board of Library Commisssioners.

Dorothy Naughton, director of the Waukesha (Wisc.) PL since 1975, has retired.

DEATHS

Helen Scribner has died. She had been head of cataloging at the Virginia State Library from 1943 to 1977.

David Waite, president of the Copyright Clearance Center, died in August. Prior to his position at CCC, he founded and was president of Information Dynamics Corporation.

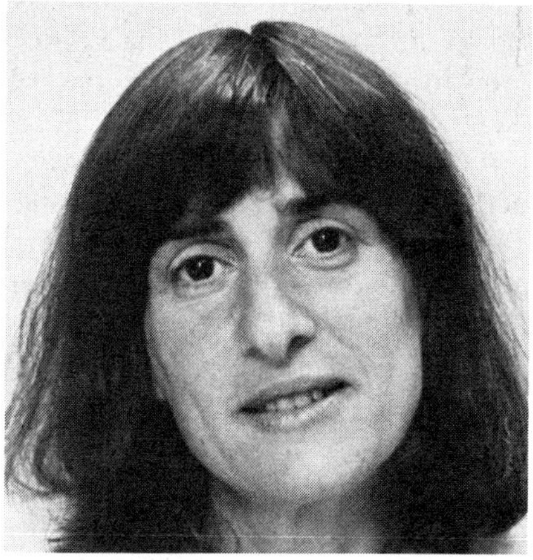

Paula Warnken

The Storymakers

Announcements

☐ In conjunction with the 1985 National Library Week, with the theme "A Nation of Readers," a national photography contest is being sponsored by the American Library Association in cooperation with the Library of Congress. The entrants for the national contest will be winners of competitions held by local libraries during National Library Week (April 14–20). Cash awards and a visit to the Library of Congress are among the prizes. For guidelines for local library contests, contact "A Nation of Readers" Photo Contest, Public Information Office, ALA, 50 E. Huron St., Chicago, IL 60611 or call 312/944–6780.

☐ Several children's book award winners have recently been announced. The 28th Annual Dorothy Canfield Fisher Children's Book Award was won by Pat Rhoads Mauser for *A Bundle of Sticks* (Atheneum, 1982). Jan Hudson, author of *Sweetgrass* (Tree Frog Press), is the recipient of the 1984 Canadian Library Association Book of the Year for Children Award. Ken Nutt, illustrator of *Zoom at Sea,* written by Tim Wynne-Jones and published by Groundwood Books, received CLA's Amelia Frances Howard-Gibbon Illustrator's Award. Kentucky children in grades three through eight voted Martha Alexander's *Move Over Twerp* (Dial Books, 1981) as their choice for the second annual Kentucky Bluegrass Award. *A Light in the Attic* by Shel Silverstein (Harper, 1981) was named the winner of the 1984 William Allen White Children's Book Award. It is the first book of poetry to win the award in the program's thirty-two year history.

☐ A new joint degree program has been established at the University of Maryland by the College of Library and Information Services and the Geography Department. Leading to the simultaneous award of the MA in geography and the MLS, the program requires fifty-six graduate hours of credit. The curriculum provides offerings in computer-based spatial analysis and information management. For information contact Anne MacLeod, College of Library and Information Services, 4105 Hornbake Library Bldg., Univ. of Maryland, College Park, MD 20742, 301/454–3590.

☐ A network-wide bulletin board is now featured on ALANET, ALA's electronic mail service. The bulletin board allows participants to post announcements and exchange ideas in a variety of categories such as Fund Raising, Microcomputers, Solutions Wanted, and Youth Ideas. The bulletin board joins ALANET's present services, including electronic newsletters, electronic mail and interactive forms, and databases such as ABI/INFORM. Contact Joel M. Lee, ALANET System Manager, ALA Headquarters Library, 50 E. Huron St., Chicago, IL 60611, 312/944–6780.

Children's Specials

☐ The theme for the 1984 Children's Book Festival in Canada is "The Storymakers." Sponsored by the Children's Book Center, the week-long celebration runs from November 17 to 24. During the week seventeen Canadian children's authors will be visiting schools and libraries throughout the country. Festival kits (including a poster, catalog of the best Canadian children's books of the past four years, and bookmarks), banners, filmstrips on authors, and posters can be ordered from a brochure available from the Children's Book Centre, 229 College St., 5th Floor, Toronto, Ont. M5T 1R4.

☐ A study conducted by the Dallas PL and North Texas State University concluded that story hours help children acquire listening skills. Preschool children were presented with live story hours and videotapes and films of story hours. A control group saw no story hours. The children seeing live story hours scored higher in the acquisition of listening skills than those in other groups. "Storyhours *Do* Make a Difference," a fifteen-minute slide/tape program based on the study, consisting of eighty-three color slides, an audiocassette tape, and a script of the tape can be borrowed for up to three weeks for a charge of $8. The study itself, *What Research Tells Us About Storyhours and Receptive Language,* can be purchased for $4.20. Order from Frances Smardo, Early Childhood Librarian, Dallas PL, 1515 Young, Dallas, TX 75201.

☐ Lancaster Horvath Productions is a new company offering recordings of traditional children's songs with accompanying songbooks. Their first release is "A Keepsake of Nursery Songs and Lullabies," with twenty-five selections. The cassette is $9.95; cassette and songbook together are $12.95. Releases scheduled for 1985 will be suitable for older children. For a catalog write Lancaster Horvath Productions, 111 Monte Ave., Piedmont, CA 94611.

☐ New full-color posters from noted children's books are available from The Peaceable Kingdom. Posters, $7.95 each, are from Clement Hurd's *Goodnight Moon* and *The Runaway Bunny,* Maurice Sendak's *Where the Wild Things Are,* Chris Van Allsburg's *The Wreck of the Zephyr* and William Steig's *The Amazing Bone.* Order from The Peaceable Kingdom, 2954 Hillegass Ave., Berkeley, CA 94705.

Continuing Education

☐ ALA is offering two new opportunities for fund-raising training. A kit of library organizations that want to sponsor fund-raising workshops is available from ALA's Public Information Office. The kit includes a ninety-minute videotape of Brooke Sheldon's 1984 President's Program, "Raising Funds for Libraries: Paths to the Public Sector"; an instruction manual for trainers; fifty copies of five brochures; fifty copies of a general bibliography on fund-raising; and fifty copies of a fund-raising list from the Library Administration and Management Association. The package is available for $200 from Public Information Office, ALA, 50 E. Huron St, Chicago, IL 60611.

☐ Organizations that do not want to create their own workshops may be interested in cosponsoring the institute "Fund Raising for Libraries" from ALA's Library Administration and Management Association Fund Raising and Financial Development Section. The one-and-one-half-day institute is designed to increase the awareness of librarians, trustees and friends from libraries of all types and sizes of the benefits and techniques of private sector fund-raising. Other LAMA regional institutes are "Management of the Online Catalog" and "Getting on the Air." For more information contact Roger H. Parent, Executive Director, LAMA, ALA, 50 E. Huron St., Chicago, IL 60611, 313/944-6780, ext. 298.

Film and Video

☐ Winner of the Environmental Health Award at the Fifth Biennial John Muir Medical Film Festival is *Water: A Clear and Present Danger,* a twenty-six-minute film produced by ABC 20/20 on the health hazards of groundwater contamination. An Honorable Mention at the festival was given to *Toward Immortality,* a twenty-seven-minute film produced by the Gannett Documentary Unit. Medical experts discuss theories on how people can prolong their life span and possibly control the aging process. Both films are distributed by Coronet/ MTI, whose catalog can be obtained by writing them at 3710 Commercial Ave., Northbrook, IL 60062 or calling 800/323-5343.

☐ The Consumer Interest Research Institute, a nonprofit organization that focuses on public policy alternatives, recently released a video program entitled *Taking the Long View: Social Security and Medicare.* The production includes a thirty-five-minute videotape and study guide. It is designed to encourage retirement organizations, unions, businesses, and community groups to learn about Social Security and Medicare issues and the ways that consumers can affect public policy. The video can be stopped at three points to hold discussion after the major sections: payments, benefits, and funding; issues of women's equity; and the future development of Medicare for all Americans. A guide for discussion leaders accompanies the tape. Nonprofit organizations can purchase the videotape and guide for $50. For further information write to: CIRI, 1825 K St., N.W., Suite 503, Washington, DC 20006.

☐ The arena is an ice hockey rink, but the message of *First Goal,* a twelve-minute, free-loan, color film is universal: "A game should be fun!" Hockey star Bobby Orr, teaching youngsters the fine ponts of hockey, also listens to their complaints and frustrations. Special concerns among the young participants are overzealous parents and coaches. The film reminds us that the role of organized amateur sports is to provide a framework for learning the game, playing as part of a team, and having fun. Produced by Nabisco Brands, *First Goal* won a silver medal at the International Film and TV festival. It may be ordered on free-loan from Core Communications. Specify preferred format—16mm film or ¾'' videocassette—along with preferred and alternate show date. Write to Core Communications, Inc., Distribution Operations, 117 Sharpe Ave., Staten Island, NY 10302.

☐ Centre Productions Inc. is now distributing five films by producer/ director Robert Godfrey, three of them new. *Free Climb* is a shortened educational version of the award-winning film narrated by Robert Redford, and *Chance of a Lifetime* is a documentary on the Outward Bound program. The new films are *Sherpa,* twenty-eight minutes, on the impact of Western culture on the Tibetan mountain guides of Nepal; *Territory in Conflict,* twenty-eight minutes, on the environmental and human issues raised by a proposed mining operation in a small Colorado town; and *From the Heart,* twenty-eight minutes, on concert pianist Larry Graham. All are available for purchase or rental in 16mm and all video formats. Previews are for prospective purchasers only. Contact Centre Productions, 1800 30th St., Suite 207, Boulder, CO 80301, 800/824-1166.

Finding Aids

☐ The second edition of *Alternative*

America provides addresses of over 13,000 "alternative, progressive, innovative, experimental" groups and organizations such as bookstores, communes, ecology groups, radio stations, small presses and alternative technology organizations. Arrangement is geographical with title and keyword indexes. Priced at $19.95, *Alternative America* can be ordered from Resources, Box 134, Cambridge, MA 02238.

☐ Another publication providing access to information that is often hard to find is the *Native American Directory*. Covering both the United States and Canada, it lists dates of celebrations, and addresses of organizations, schools and colleges, libraries, museums, crafts guilds, urban centers, and Native American media, such as television and radio stations and periodicals. The directory is available for $18.95 plus $3 shipping charge from the National Native American Co-op, Box 5000, San Carlos, AZ 85550-03001.

☐ *Brick, A Journal of Reviews* is published three times per year, providing thoughtful review essays of Canadian books. A recent issue included reviews of Ken Dryden's *The Game,* Guy Vanderhaeghe's *Man Descending,* and Allison Mitcham's study of northern Canadian literature, *The Northern Imagination*. Individual issues cost $2 and subscriptions cost $5.50 per year. For further information write to Brick Books, 219 Ilderton, Ontario, N0M 2A0 Canada.

☐ For the would-be entrepreneur, franchises are available in areas as diverse as accounting, lawn spraying and transmission repair. As well as listing over 2,500 of these opportunities, the *1984 Franchise Annual* provides advice on investigating franchises, sample contract clauses, and a summary of state laws in this area. The directory section includes address, number of units in operation, royalties, and approximate investment required. It can be ordered for $22.95 from Info Press, Inc., 728 Center St., Box 550, Lewiston, NY 14092.

From the GPO Presses

The following titles are a sample of recent publications available from the Government Printing Office. Specify the stock number, price and quantity when ordering. Payment is by check payable to Superintendent of Documents or by Visa or Mastercard (give card number and expiration date). Send to Superintendent of Documents, United States GPO, Washington, DC 20402. Or call the order desk at 202/783-3238.

☐ Five "how-to" booklets produced by the National Center for Appropriate Technology describe home energy-saving projects. *Solar Greenhouses and Sunspaces: Lessons Learned* (S/N 061-000-00622-2, $2.25) examines greenhouse components including framing, glazing, storage, ventilation and control mechanisms. *Using the Earth to Heat and Cool Homes* (S/N 061-000-00620-6, $1.75) provides a guide to using the earth directly or in conjunction with heat pumps to heat and cool, with a focus on installation, economics, reliability and performance. *Moisture and Home Energy Conservation* (S/N 061-000-00615-0, $4.75) shows how to detect and correct moisture problems in the home. *Window Insulation: How to Sort Through the Options* (S/N 061-000-00632-0, $2.50) includes sections on choosing the right design for the window, how to choose an installation method, and how to size up insulation needs. *Major Energy Conservation Retrofits* (S/N 061-000-00635-4, $3.25) contains advice for builders, architects, and skilled homeowners in selecting the most cost-effective procedure for insulating existing residential structures. When ordering, send prepayment to Department 36-HG.

☐ The Environmental Protection Agency has published three reports on the impacts of the greenhouse effect. *Can We Delay a Greenhouse Warming?* (S/N 055-000-00235-5, $6) analyzes the options to slow the build-up of carbon dioxide in the atmosphere and the resulting rise in global temperatures. *Projecting Future Sea Level Rise: Methodology, Estimates to the Year 2100, and Research Needs* (S/N 055-000-00236-3, $5) estimates a sea level rise of four to seven feet by 2100, and discusses the impacts of such a rise and the possibility of reducing economic and environmental losses by planning for them. *Potential Climatic Impacts of Increasing Atmospheric CO2 with Emphasis on Water Availability and Hydrology in the United States* (S/N 055-000-00241-0, $4.50) focuses on possible changes in precipitation, evaporation, soil moisture, run-off, and other water-related conditions that could accompany a doubling of atmospheric carbon dioxide. When ordering, send prepayment to Department 36-HM.

☐ Another important environmental issue, acid rain, is the subject of a report prepared by the Congressional Research Service, *Acid Rain: A Survey of Data and Current Analyses.* Major points covered include emissions sources, atmospheric processes, impacts of acid rain on terrestrial and aquatic ecosystems, strategies to mitigate acid deposition, and benefits and costs of controlling acid rain. *Acid Rain,* stock number 052-070-05930-3, is available for $14. Send prepayment to Department 36-HN.

Idea Exchange

☐ Not even in the Nieman-Marcus catalog can you find a children's pup-

pet show (priced at $40) or a new wing for a regional library (for $400, 000), but these and many more products and services are displayed in the catalog "Tell Sacramento You Care with a Gift to Your Public Library," sponsored by the Friends of the Sacramento PL. The catch is that when a patron, business or organization places an "order," the library is the one who receives it. Complete with enticing descriptions, prices and order numbers, a copy of the glossy catalog can be obtained from Lann Jurgens, Sacramento PL, 7000 Franklin Blvd., Suite 540, Sacramento, CA 95823.

☐ An LSCA grant has enabled the Rockford (Ill.) PL and the Rockford Public Schools to establish Assignment Alert, a communications program designed to help students and teachers. By filling out a one-page form, teachers can alert their school library and the Rockford PL to upcoming assignments that will require library resources. Materials can then be organized and if necessary, put on reserve. For further information contact Judith Long, Head of Extension Services, Rockford PL, Rockford, IL 61101, 815/965-6731.

☐ County extension agencies as well as libraries receive many calls on home and garden questions. A program to provide information on these popular topics has been developed by the Columbus and Franklin County (Ohio) PL and the Franklin County Cooperative Extension Service. Over 125 tape-recorded messages on subjects ranging from freezer failure to slug control, created by the Extension Service, are available to callers to the Main Library. Pamphlets have been distributed listing the tapes, but callers may request them by topic as well as specific name. Contact Pat Groseck, Columbus and Franklin County PL, 28 So. Hamilton Rd., Columbus, OH 43213, 614/864-8050.

☐ Libraries can sponsor a weekly column in their local newspaper, "Answers from the Library." The column, which has appeared in the *Monroe* (Mich.) *Evening News* for the past eight years, uses a question-and-answer format to cover reference questions on a variety of topics. Several subscription options are available for libraries who wish to sponsor the column, starting at $26 a year. For a brochure with subscription information, write Marie Chulski, Monroe County LS, 3700 So. Custer Rd., Monroe, MI 48161.

Magazine Notes

☐ *Japan and America: A Journal of Cultural Studies* recently began publication. The journal's purpose is to provide in-depth coverage of Japanese culture. Each issue has a theme.

The inaugural issue had Space as its theme, with articles about theatrical space, the Noh theatre, architecture, and human space and culture. A comparative approach is used, and both scholarly and creative material (i.e., poems, koans, and artwork) are included. Book reviews and translation studies will also be featured. *Japan and America* is published three times per year and an annual subscription costs $22.50. For information write to Japan and America, Box 774, Pleasant Grove, UT 84062.

☐ A quarterly publication devoted exclusively to exploring creativity will debut in November. *Creative Person* will focus on easing the sense of isolation experienced by persons who draw extensively from themselves to create. Artists, writers, musicians, scientists, designers, and choreographers are among the persons who will share their observations about nurturing a talent, of being "different." The magazine will feature interviews with successful people, articles relating to creativity, professional advice, and occasional round-table discussions, essays, poems, and short fiction. Sample issues are $3. The quarterly costs $12 per year. For information write Creative Person, 1000 Byus Dr., Charleston, WV 25311.

☐ Millions of Americans generate sideline or full-time income from a variety of homebased craft, publishing, consultant, and computer businesses. Barbara Brabec, a marketing consultant to homebased workers, edits *National Home Business Report*, a 24p. newsletter published bimonthly. The introductory issue featured articles on business checking accounts, on teaching workshops, and on making money from art. Hints from homebased workers are a regular feature. Subscriptions cost $18 per year, with an additional $1 charge if invoicing is required. Write to Barbara Brabec, Box 10423, Springfield, MO 65808.

Media Center World

☐ Ideas on library skills instruction,

games and contests, reading encouragement, computers, special events, library management and public relations are found in *What's Right with Library Media Centers in San Diego County,* a 74p. paperback. K–12 library media specialists from throughout the county describe their programs, with addresses and phone numbers given. It is available for $5 from Superintendent of Schools, San Diego County Office of Education, 6401 Linda Vista Rd., San Diego, CA 92111–7399, Attention: Kay Niemeyer.

☐ Two years ago, at San Jose State University, a taped program entitled *Learning to Speak English* was developed. There are now nine languages available: Korean, Vietnamese, Mandarin, Cantonese, Tagalog, Ilocano, Spanish, Cambodian, and Laotian. The classroom edition of the program has four two-sided tapes in each language along with worksheets, flashcards, tests and teaching suggestions. Library editions include the same tapes and a read-along booklet containing complete text of the English portion of the tapes and instructions. For further information write to California Language Laboratories, Box 176, Cupertino, CA 95014.

☐ The Young Adult Services Division of the American Library Association is looking for artists aged thirteen to eighteen to design a cover for the ALA-YASD booklist "Best Books for Young Adults," an annual annotated list of outstanding books. The design should be 9-by-3¾ inches in black ink on white paper and must include the words "Best Books for Young Adults 1984." The artist's name, school, age and addresss must be on the back. The winner will receive $50. YASD encourages librarians to hold cover design contests to generate entries. Send designs by December 1 to Betty Carter, 2310 Lexford Lane, Houston, TX 77080.

☐ Media specialists considering making software available for circulation may be concerned about how to order and process this new medium. The second edition of *Processing Computer Software for the School Media Collection,* by David L. Bullers and Linda L. Waddle, has been revised to reflect changes in cataloging guidelines and to include a flowchart of tasks associated with ordering, receiving, cataloging and processing. Samples of catalog cards, storage containers, checkout cards, card pockets, and package labels are shown. It can be obtained for $6 from David L. Bullers, 3333 Viking Rd., RR #1, Waterloo, IA 50701.

Products and Services

☐ Baker & Taylor has reduced the price of cataloging and processing from 99¢ to 89¢ per book. Each book is provided with an attached book pocket, spine label, Mylar jacket, book card inserted into the pocket, and a set of catalog cards. Improvements in productivity were cited as the source of the savings. Information can be obtained from Baker & Taylor's four regional sales departments: eastern, 201/722–8000; midwestern, 815/472–2444; southern, 404/335–5000; western, 702/786–6700.

☐ The Simplex Camera 16 is a compact microfilmer from Alos Micrographics Corp. that weighs only thirty-eight pounds. The 16mm rotary camera is operated much like a photocopier, with documents fed in and automatically recorded on film. Formats are accepted up to eleven-by-seventeen inches. Features include an interchangeable film head, a removable glass bank and guide for cleaning and lamp change. Contact Alos Micrographics Corp., 239 E. Plains Rd., Box 407, Walden, NY 12586, 914/778–7511.

☐ Computerized custom searches of information from most of Gale Research Co.'s directories are now available. Requests for information on organizations can be limited by geographic location, subject, publications, size or other criteria. The amount of information can also be specified, from just name and address up to the full information as contained in the published directories. The client will be provided with a cost estimate. For more information, or to request a search, call John Schmittroth, 800/521–0707 or 800/223–GALE.

☐ A new catalog from Knox Manufacturing features an assortment of audiovisual products plus a guide to selecting projection screens. The guide includes charts to determine the right screen based on room size and seating capacity, type of projection equipment, and lighting conditions. There is also a guide to screen fabric selection. In addition to screens, the catalog features slide viewers, storage

units, stands, projector carts and other accessories. For a copy of the catalog write Knox Manufacturing, 111

Spruce St., Wood Dale, IL 60191.

☐ Telex Computer Products, Inc. is introducing a new family of displays for IBM 3270 users. The first displays available are a twelve-inch monochrome model, the Telex 078, and a twelve-inch color model, the Telex 079. The models are plug-compatible with IBM's 3178 and 3179, respectively. The screens can be tilted and swiveled and have coiled-cable adjustable keyboard. Both display 1,920 characters, and attach directly to either an IBM 3274/3276 controller or a Telex 174/274C/276 control unit. The 078 is priced at $1,550 and the 079 at $2,195. For more information contract Telex Computer Products, 6422 E. 41st St., Tulsa, OK 74135, 918/627–1111.

Professional Reading

☐ The second edition of the Association of Canadian Map Libraries' *Guide for a Small Map Collection,* by Barbara Farrell and Aileen Desbarats, is directed to those without formal map librarianship training who are in charge of or are setting up a map collection. Following a brief description of maps and how to use them are chapters on such subjects as acquisitions, storage, access, and reference service. Sources for further reading are given. Copies are available from the Association, c/o National Map Collection, Public Archives of Canada, 395 Wellington St., Ottawa, Ont. K1A 0N3.

☐ Institutions considering disaster planning and cooperative strategies for coping with emergencies will be interested in a disaster manual produced by the Special Collections Interest Group of the San Antonio Council of Research and Academic Libraries (CORAL). The publication contains sections on emergency procedures for controlling disasters and for salvage of water-damaged materials. It includes lists of recommended emergency supplies to keep on hand and sources of other supplies and assistance that can be obtained in the San Antonio area. Also included are reading materials and sample forms. When the forms are completed, the manual can serve as an institution's disaster plan. Copies of the *Disaster Manual for San Antonio-Area Libraries and Other Collections-Holding Institutions* can be ordered for $8 from Robert A. Houze, CORAL Executive Director, 9831 Greentree, San Antonio, TX 78230.

☐ The University of Toronto publication *Preservation of Library Materials: A Report of the Collection Preservation Committee,* is now available to other libraries at a cost of $5 to cover handling and postage. The report outlines the problems of collection conservation and preservation and describes the methodology used in the survey of the collections undertaken by a computer-generated random sampling scheme. Proposals for restoration and maintenance, and a summary of recommendations and estimated cost are included. Requests for the report should be sent with prepayment to M. Davison, Chief Librarian's Office, Univ. of Toronto Library, 130 St. George St., Toronto Ontario M5S 1A5 Canada.

☐ To aid catalogers, two sources have published enhancements to the Library of Congress *Cataloging Service Bulletin.* Oberlin College Library's *Library of Congress Rule Interpretations for AACR 2: A Cumulation from Cataloging Service Bulletin Numbers 11–24,* compiled by Lois Lindberg, Alan Boyd and Elaine Druesedow supersedes their previous cumulation for numbers 11–16. It is available for $20 (including quarterly updates through no. 28), with additional copies at $17 each, from Alan Boyd, Oberlin College Library, Oberlin, OH 44074. The *Cataloging Service Bulletin Index* for numbers 1–24, Summer 1978–Spring 1984, prepared by Nancy Olson, a professor at Mankato State University, can be ordered for $7 from Soldier Creek Press. Standing orders can be also placed for this annual cumulative index, and the index to the earlier bulletin, *Index to the Library of Congress Cataloging Service Bulletin, No. 1–125, June 1945–Spring 1978,* is still available for $7.50. Order from Soldier Creek Press, Box 863, Lake Crystal, MN 56055.

Software

☐ The use of microcomputers can have special benefits for handicapped students, and educators are faced with the need to find software these students can use. *The SpecialWare Directory,* a 98p. book distributed by Oryx Press, lists companies that produce over 200 programs and software or courseware products suitable for special education. Arrangement is by company, with ordering information and a description of products, giving curriculum areas, grade levels, hardware requirements, format, handicapping condition for which it is appropriate, and instructional design or approach. Priced at $16.95, the directory can be ordered from Oryx Press, 2214 North Central at Encanto, Phoenix, AZ 85004-1483, 800/457–ORYX.

☐ Designed to handle overdue books in junior and senior high school libraries, OVERDUES software, part of the LIBRARY HELPER software program from Southern MicroSystems (SMS), is able to print overdue notices as well as the entire overdue list, delete overdue records when books are returned, and sort by record number, homeroom code, date due, student's name, title of book, author of book, and Dewey number. OVERDUES, priced at $69, includes a manual and a program diskette and is available for the Apple II, II+, IIe and IIc. Contact SMS, Box 2097, Burlington, NC 27512–2097, 919/226–7610 or 800/334–5521.

☐ Three corporate libraries who are users of Sydney Dataproducts, Inc.'s Easy Data Integrated Library System are working with Sydney on a serials enhancement to the current system. The new software package will extend the system (which handles such functions as cataloging, ordering, and circulation for collections of up to 150,000 titles) to monitor incoming periodicals, claim missing issues, order and renew subscriptions, and route issues within the organization. It is scheduled for availability in early 1985. A microcomputer version of the Easy Data System, for collections with fewer than 10,000 titles, to run on IBM PC and PC-compatible machines, will be available in the late fall. Contact Sydney Dataproducts, 11075 Santa Monica Blvd., Suite 100, Los Angeles, CA 90025, 213/479-4621.

Write for These

☐ The magazine *50 Plus* has published two new booklets on retirement. *65 Mistakes to Avoid in Retirement,* priced at $2.50, covers activities in retirement, financial matters, health, and personal relations, drawing on retirees' personal experience. The latest edition of *Your Social Security Benefits,* updated annually, is also available. The 48p. booklet costs $2. Both can be ordered from 50 Plus Booklets, Dept. WLB, 850 Third Ave., New York, NY 10022.

☐ The need for technical standards is displayed in a poster from the Library and Information Technology Association. Captioned "Without Technical Standards, Systems Cannot Grow," the poster depicts the golden spike ceremony of 1869, when the tracks of the Union Pacific and the Central Pacific Railroads were joined at Promontory, Utah. The poster can be obtained for $5 prepaid from LITA, ALA, 50 E. Huron St., Chicago, IL 60611.

☐ While the percentage of women in the general labor force rose dramatically from 1970 to 1980, the percentage of disabled women in the labor force declined. These and other data from Census Bureau records are examined in *Disabled Women in America,* a statistical report recently published by the President's Committee on Employment of the Handicapped. Single copies of the report are available free from the Committee, Washington, DC 20210.

☐ Recent additions to the Bibliography and Reference Circular Series published by the Reference Section of the National Library Service for the Blind and Physically Handicapped include *Mobility and Mobility Aids for Visually Handicapped Individuals,* a 40p. bibliography that lists and annotates selected books, articles and reports published since 1972, and *Guide to Spoken-Word Recordings: General Nonfiction,* a 42p. directory of distributors, which includes a subject index. Guides to literature, general nonfiction and foreign language recordings have also been published. Copies of any of these publications are available free on request from the Reference Section, National Library Service for the Blind and Physically Handicapped, Library of Congress, Washington, DC 20542.

Situation Report *(cont. from p. 123)*

programs, should the United States withdraw from UNESCO at the end of the year. NCLIS also cosponsored the first international meeting on "Information and Productivity—Implications for Education and Training," held in the United Kingdom in July, in cooperation with the British Library's Research and Development Department and the Library and Information Services Council (U.K.).

From this brief overview you can get a sense of the breadth and diversity of NCLIS's 1984 program menu. We have many exciting future plans, which I'll discuss in forthcoming columns.

Shanks *(cont. from p. 108)*

ployees perceive those who work fewer hours as being less serious about their profession.

Employers fail when they treat job-sharers as casual or intermittent help rather than seeing them as valuable employees. Organizations that recognize and hire college graduates for whom full-time work is not attractive will find new sources of talent and a lower turnover rate among valuable employees.

When one considers these three alternative work schedules, they all offer certain common advantages. They cost little or nothing to institute, they require no changes in technology to implement, there is no need for organizational restructuring, and they help improve productivity. Eventually most American employees will be working under some form of alternative employment schedule. Libraries should be at the forefront of this movement.

Correspondence *(cont. from p. 86)*

Mrs. Bradshaw.

And of course we have had some fine women presidents since that time. Mrs. Bradshaw was the first woman president in my own attendance of ALA and she will always be a "standout" for me, but these other ladies did their bit and should be at least remembered.

MARY LOUISE RHEAY
Cobb County Public Library
Marietta, Georgia

Looking for Jane Austen

I would appreciate hearing from anyone who knows the location and/or owner of original Jane Austen letters, letter fragments and autograph signatures other than those listed in R. W. Chapman's Oxford edition of *Jane Austen's Letters* as I hope to publish a facsimile edition of all manuscript letters.

JO MODERT
15 Northbrook Drive
Mt. Vernon, Illinois 62864

Credits:
p. 90—Bob McCormack; 99—Paul Pearce; 115—Ed Arno; 116—Chuck Vadun; 128—James Stevenson/Greenwillow; 129—Mordicai Gerstein/Four Winds; 129—Thacher Hurd/Harper; 129—William Steig/David Godine; 132—Harper & Row; 133—St. Martin's Press; 133—Viking Press; 134-35—Robert Capra; 143—Hayden Software; 144—Crittendon Books; 145— Macmillan; 146—Facts on File; 146—Blandford; 148—Doubleday.

WLB Classifieds

Classified Advertising is accepted six weeks preceding date of issue. Charges are: minimum 3 lines—$10; each additional line—$2.50. If voucher forms are required, please send them when submitting copy. All advertisements for positions must exclude reference to race, creed, color, age, and sex as conditions for employment. The publisher reserves the right to reject any advertising considered unacceptable as to wording or appearance or for any other reason. Submit classifieds to: Brian Bavolar, Wilson Library Bulletin, 950 University Ave., Bronx, NY 10452.

Positions Open

THE AMERICAN LIBRARY ASSOCIATION, the oldest and largest national library association in the world, seeks an Executive Director who will provide leadership in a 39,000-member organization charged with promoting and improving library and information services, the advancement of the profession, and the free flow of information worldwide. As chief operating officer of the Association, reporting to its Executive Board, the Executive Director is responsible for administering a staff of approximately 220 persons and a budget of $12 million. Candidates should have demonstrated management experience; broad knowledge and understanding of libraries, information services and related fields; and the ability to work with and relate to people in a wide variety of organizational and cultural environments. Minimum qualifications include a masters degree from an ALA-accredited program. Salary range: $70,000–$90,000 per year. Position available August 1, 1985. Letter of application with resume should be sent by December 1, 1984 to: Executive Director Search Committee, American Library Association, 50 E. Huron Street, Chicago, IL 60611. All replies will be held in strict confidence. Affirmative Action—EOE.

ASSISTANT LIBRARIAN. Must have Masters Degree in Library Science. Duties include organizing and performing original cataloging of growing historical collection, along with some reference work. Also involves supervising activities associated with cataloging and periodicals for the main collection. Apply to Lujuanna Clayton, Isothermal Community College, Hwy. 74 Bypass, Spindale, NC 28160. Equal Opportunity Employer.

THE UCLA GRADUATE SCHOOL OF LIBRARY AND INFORMATION SCIENCE is seeking to make a one-year visiting appointment in the area of cataloging and subject analysis. This appointment could lead to a permanent position. Applications are desired from candidates with a doctorate, or from persons about to receive one, with demonstrated experience or strong potential in teaching, with interest and competence in theoretical and empirical research, and with knowledge of professional practice. Rank and salary will depend upon record of experience and competence with the following established ranges: Assistant Professor ($25,500 to $29,000), Associate Professor ($30,600 to $34,300), Professor ($37,100 to $49,600), all on a nine month academic year basis. The appointment will be as of Fall Quarter, 1985 or earlier. Inquire and send resume with a list of references to: Robert M. Hayes, Dean, Graduate School of Library and Information Science, University of California, Los Angeles, California 90024. Applications close November 30, 1984.

Announcements

THE FOOTLOOSE LIBRARIAN newsletter & network. Money-saving travel news + U.S. & overseas librarians offering Bed & Breakfast, housing exchange, more. "Good, practical information" M.S., IN; "An excellent publication" S.R., Tunisia. Free brochure. TFL, Box 972, Minneapolis, MN 55440.

MILITARY BOOKS for identification of shoulder patches, medals, insignia . . . U.S. and foreign. Military history, etc. Send for free catalog, M.C.N. Press, Box 52033 WLB, Tulsa, OK 74152.

NEWSLETTER FOR YOUR SUMMER, SPRING, CHRISTMAS COURSES in London, Paris, Mexico, Hawaii, etc.! Earn Univ. of Calif. units, tax benefits; visit libraries, theatre productions, galleries. Exciting study/vacation options for librarians, plus work in foreign libraries. Subscription: $25/yr. NEWSLETTER, Box 5513, Santa Monica, CA 90405.

1-800's PLUS FOR LIBRARIANS—1985. The Directory of Toll-Free and Collect-Call Accepted Telephone Numbers provides numbers needed and most used by librarians. December 1984—$22. Grenoble Books, 2567 Fisher Bldg., Detroit, MI 48202 or call (313) 874–1059.

THE ONE-PERSON LIBRARY: A NEWSLETTER FOR LIBRARIANS AND MANAGEMENT. Professional isolation is one of the major problems of working alone. We want to change that. This new newsletter is informal, informative, and, above all, quick and to the point. Charter subscriptions (one year, 12 issues) for $35, a savings of over 20%. Pre-paid orders to OPL RESOURCES, LTD., Box 948, Murray Hill Station, New York, NY 10156.

REFERENCE REPORT—Your monthly guide to the publishing activities of reference book publishers. Send for sample issue. Grenoble Books, 2567 Fisher Bldg., Detroit, MI 48202 or call collect (313) 874–1059.

For Sale

BRUCE TEGNER'S COMPLETE BOOK OF SELF-DEFENSE again available in hardcover edition Oct. 1 '84; 0–87407–510–6, $10.95. Other Bruce Tegner titles in hardcover and trade paper from your jobber or the publisher: Thor Pub. Co., Box 1782, Ventura, CA 93002.

BRUCE TEGNER judo/karate/aikido/self-defense books price rise in effect now. Current catalog from Thor Pub. Co., Box 1782, Ventura, CA 93002.

"... get ideas from every issue."
M.S. High School Media Center, NY
Subscribe (and send *your* nitty gritty

Schmittroth
Encyclopedia of Information Systems and Services
International
1985
Sixth Edition
GALE
Schmittroth
Encyclopedia of Information Systems and Services
United States
1985
Sixth Edition
GALE
1985
Encyclopedia of Information Systems and Services
Sixth Edition
Edited by John Schmittroth, Jr.

Wilson Library Bulletin

November 1984

Wilson **Library** *Bulletin*

November 1984, Volume 59, Number 3 *ISSN 0043-5651*

Our cover for November is a detail of an illustration from **B. Kliban**'s 1985 *CatCalendar* published by Penguin Books. This year the Kliban cats, available in bookstores, are in full color.

Departments

Letter From New York/Editorial 164
Correspondence 165
Upfront/News—*CBN University dedicates $13.2 million library; Boston College dedicates $28 million library; OCLC to spend $2.6 million on telecommunications; CCC signs license agreement with General Electric; California funds state literacy program; FBI recovers stolen library stamps; late news.* 166
Calendar 172
Library World 230
Marketplace 232
WLB Classifieds 239

Articles

Retrospective Conversion: Investing in the Future *Richard Boss* 173
Public Libraries and Literacy: A New Role to Play *Gary Strong* 179
Keeping a Dream Alive: Cooper Union Library *Irene Iwan* 183
IFLA in the Third World: The Nairobi Meeting *Esther Dyer* 187

Features

Special Report: Doing Business with Philadelphia *Art Milner* 191
Dateline—Washington *Dale Nelson* 194
Eye on Publishing *Ann McGrath* 196
Facing the Public *Will Manley* 198
School Library Technology *Patricia Berglund* 202
Library to Library *Rod Henshaw* 204
Portrait: Marvin Scilken *Joseph Deitch* 205

Reviews

Picture Books for Children *Donnarae MacCann/Olga Richard* 208
The Young Adult Perplex *Patty Campbell* 210
Murder in Print *Kathleen Maio* 212
Front Row Center *Judith Trojan* 214
On Record: Popular Music *Bruce Pollock* 216
Magazines *Gail Pool* 218
Our Profession *Norman Stevens* 220
Software for Libraries *Patrick Dewey* 222
Current Reference Books *James Rettig* 224

The *Wilson Library Bulletin* is published monthly except in July and August by The H. W. Wilson Company, 950 University Avenue, Bronx, N.Y. 10452. Second-class postage paid at Bronx, N.Y. and additional mailing offices. The *Wilson Library Bulletin* is indexed in *Education Index, Library Literature,* and *Popular Periodical Index* and abstracted in *Library & Information Science Abstracts, Historical Abstracts,* and *America: History and Life*. Book reviews are indexed in *Book Review Index*. Subscription $30 a year, U.S. and Canada; $35, foreign. Single copies $4, U.S. and Canada; $4.50, foreign (remittance with order, please). Address all correspondence about subscriptions to the publisher. No subscriptions through agents. Telephone: (212) 588-8400

Letter from New York

Editorial

The sorrows of being streetwise

In most urban areas of American there is a branch of learning that has to do with one's ability to understand what is happening in the street. Because this knowledge is largely intuitive we have—in books, films, and television presentations—tended to romanticize people who are "streetwise." They are, we are told, savy individuals who know how to identify unsafe areas, how to cope with danger, recognize the differences between an Electrolux salesman and a drug dealer, are able to distinguish a prostitute from a visiting aunt, can discern when a pocket is bulging with a revolver rather than a bagel, and are able to speak the language of the street in such a way as to be immediately understood and respected.

On any given day there are thousands of such people on the streets in the nation's major cities, exhibiting their own lifestyle, language, and values. Over the years we have titillated ourselves by incorporating some of their argot into our vocabularies and credited the streetwise with a sort of legitimate intelligence necessary for a career in the local neighborhood.

It is only in the past several years, when we became aware of the presence of so many illiterate adults across the land, that we have had second thoughts about gilding life on our city streets and so uncritically endorsing the easy and superficial lessons acquired there.

"What's coming down?" Nothing very good. The U.S. Department of Education estimates that twenty-seven million American adults are functionally illiterate, meaning that they possess only marginal skill in reading, writing, and speaking. For them, composing a letter, writing a check, or filling out a job application is a major event. An additional forty-five million adults are thought to be only partially literate, with the pool growing by about 2.3 million persons each year, including high school dropouts, immigrants, and refugees.

Adult illiterates are found in every region of the country, with the highest rates of illiteracy in our central cities. The high number of illiterate people, so difficult to comprehend, is attributable not only to traditional reasons—substandard teaching and curtailed schooling—but to the fact that accelerating technological advances have changed the requirements for literacy in the United States. The standards for minimum acceptable literacy are higher today than at any time in our past.

A report from the Business Council for Effective Literacy notes that families at or below the poverty level are five times more likely to be functionally illiterate than families with an income of $15,000 or above, that fifteen percent of our workforce is functionally illiterate, and that an estimated three-fourths of those currently unemployed are illiterate. Even among managerial and professional workers the deprivation is present, with eleven percent of the people in this group thought to be illiterate.

The cost of welfare and unemployment compensation due to illiteracy is estimated at $6 million annually. AT&T alone, it is reported, spends $6 million a year to provide basic reading, writing and math skills to 14,000 employees. The cost of crime due to illiteracy is also set in the billions of dollars.

There are now a number of organizations, including libraries, that have taken up the cause of reducing illiteracy statistics. Among them are the National Adult Literacy Project, the Coalition for Literacy, Laubach Literacy Action, and the Literacy Volunteers of America.

Libraries, sometimes guilty of embracing social causes only tenuously connected with their main purposes, here have a concern of obvious and apparent relevance. As Gary Strong, California State Librarian, points out in this issue (*Public Libraries and Literacy: A New Role to Play*), there is a compelling need for libraries to become involved in statewide literacy initiatives. Future issues of *WLB* will report on other statewide campaigns in which libraries have assumed a leading role.

The campaign against illiteracy has now captured the attention of government, foundations, private business, and non-profit associations. It is inevitable that all this activity will arrest the spread of illiteracy and reduce the proportions of the problem. It is a crusade that libraries should willingly join.

There is no joy in being streetwise. A full and purposeful education, which presupposes a high degree of literacy, is the only deliverance from that confining experience.

—Milo Nelson

Correspondence

No news from the bottom

I wish to applaud heartily Will Manley's observations concerning the "small library" and the lack of library media coverage ("Facing the Public," *WLB,* June).

I must take exception with just one of his observations, however. In discussing why the content of such journals as *LJ Hotline* is "monopolized by news from these metropolises," you state: "Certainly when we talk about advancing the bibliographic applications of computer technology, building highly sophisticated and comprehensive book collections, and devising innovative programming, we're talking about the big libraries."

This observation has little merit in reality, particularly as concerns innovative programming. We small library people are often in the vanguard of innovative programming and are usually eager and willing to share our successes with the larger library community. The library press chooses simply to ignore us.

For example, fourteen months ago our library sent a detailed press release outlining our Public Access Microcomputer program. We were one of the first and we offer our community of 14,000 four Apple IIes, over seventy software packages, and extensive courses in computer literacy, basic programming, and word processing. The library press uniformly ignored news of our project, soliciting stories instead from Long Island, Seattle, Cleveland, and so forth.

My public services librarian recently composed another article for the news media concerning refinements in our program. No one has seized the opportunity to publish these innovative activities of a quite small library. Instead, we are informed of the belated efforts of Minneapolis Public Library and other large libraries who follow in the wake of "small" library successes. Wow! You mean they're finally purchasing computer software there?

There is just no room for news from the bottom when there is so much more important news from the top: cherry pit spits at Mesa, noon Fonda workouts at Houston, and any silly program or funding increase reported by large libraries with full-time PR staffs.

And every once in a great while the press needs to squeeze in a cute story about a quaint small town library with a precious collection of romance paperbacks.

No, Mr. Manley, the reason for the lack of small library exposure in the library press does not lie with a lack of pioneering or creative programs nor with a lack of librarian interest in public relations. The reasons are much more obvious. After all, how much money does the average small library have to spend with Wilson and Bowker? How many influential committees in ALA do small librarians sit on?

RANDY WILSON
PARLIN-INGERSOLL LIBRARY
CANTON, ILLINOIS

Safe bridges

I read the editorial in the June 1984 issue of *WLB* ("A matter of degree"). I thought the observations and points made should be heeded. I believe that a person needs to obtain the necessary skills required for performance on the job in all fields. Certain criteria must be met. Different jobs require different abilities. There should be different levels of attainment. If requirements are not necessary, structures will be broken down. If we proceed down the path of eliminating requirements for jobs, eventually the schools and universities would no longer need to provide educational training or direction. We could close the doors.

I underlined the following key statement from the editorial: "a profession where penalties for misjudgment and error are relatively inconsequential." This reminded me of an article I read about a supposedly qualified engineer who admitted he could not read blueprints and had not passed required tests. In this case a bridge collapsed and lives were lost. The error was of great consequence.

Would our society prefer people with the necessary skills and qualifications to build a safe bridge or would our society prefer that people without the necessary skills build the bridge? There *is* a difference.

KAREN TOMPKINS
BATTLE CREEK, MICHIGAN

WLB welcomes letters from its readers. Correspondence should be sent to Wilson Library Bulletin, 950 University Avenue, Bronx, N.Y. 10452.

UPFRONT NEWS

A new $13.2 million library (top photo) was dedicated October 13 at **CBN University,** *Virginia Beach, Virginia. The 152,000 square-foot Georgian-designed library will support graduate education at* CBN *University, an institution that shares a 685-acre campus with its sponsoring organization, the Christian Broadcasting Network. The library, with an auditorium, classroom, chapel, and faculty offices, is capable of holding 600,000 volumes and one million microforms.*

The library will be linked to its neighboring $27 million International Communications Center (lower photo) to launch national and global mass education programs through satellite communications. One of the first programs to be telecast over the CBN *Cable Network, which goes into 25.1 million U.S. households, will be "Sing, Spell, Read & Write," a series to teach children and illiterate adults how to read. Daniel Hedges, director of continuing education, said "The potential for influencing the world is extremely significant."*

Illinois dedicates library addition

The University of Illinois Library at Urbana-Champaign recently dedicated an eight-story library addition capable of accommodating two million books on fifty-five miles of moveable shelves. The moveable shelving, manufactured by Spacesaver Corporation of Fort Atkinson, Wisconsin, consists of forty-five-foot units, weighing up to 16,235 pounds, that move aside on hidden wheels to form an aisle. Hugh Atkinson, university librarian, said, "By eliminating most aisle space we have reduced construction cost from about $9 a volume to $4.25. At this cost, it is cheaper to build instead of rent storage space, and we can afford sprinklers, air conditioning, and humidity control. If we had built the stacks in the traditional way, we could have gotten in about 950,000 volumes on ten decks. For the same appropriation, we have seven decks for two million books."

The addition was constructed at a cost of $3.55 million for the building and $3.3 million for the shelves. It is estimated that the new space will accommodate acquisitions until the 1990s. The library adds about 180,000 volumes and 98,000 periodicals a year.

OCLC to spend $2.6 million on telecommunications

OCLC has announced that it intends to spend $2.6 million on computer equipment and software to modernize its telecommunication network. OCLC President Rowland Brown said "In less than a year the OCLC telecommunication system will be state-of-the-art. The new system will vastly expand our telecommunications options, both technologically and economically." The decision represents an acceleration of OCLC's planned expenditures for redesign of the telecommunication network. "OCLC," said Brown, "has had to readjust its capital budget to take advantage of the opportunities presented by the new telecommunication implementation schedule."

Among the features of the telecommunication network, to be in place by the summer of 1985, will be an OCLC-controlled packet-switched network; off-the-shelf hardware; custom software for the OCLC polling protocol; telecommunication service alternatives to multidrop leased lines; and dial-up use of the OCLC network rather than through value-added networks.

The OCLC telecommunication network is an interstate, multipoint, synchronous polled network using private lines leased from AT&T. It is a star configuration consisting of over 180,000 miles of leased telephone lines on 218 circuits with an average of twenty-one terminals per circuit, with a total of 3,470 modems. These circuits are linked to OCLC's telecommunications center in Dublin, Ohio, which comprises twenty-six D-116 minicomputers, a distributed communications processor, and modems. There are also Tymnet and Telenet minicomputers for the 1,200 dial-access authorizations for the OCLC system.

The OCLC network will use a distributed architecture with central control available from any Advanced Communication Processor node. The ACPs are specially designed computer digital switching equipment that will replace OCLC's D-116 minicomputers, in use since 1974. The ACPs will enable OCLC to use wire, satellite or microwave transmission.

CCC signs license agreement with General Electric

The Copyright Clearance Center has signed a photocopy license agreement with the General Electric Company granting GE the right to legally copy articles from thousands of copyrighted publications. Effective for one year, and renewable for a second, the license covers copies made by GE employees for internal use at all its sites throughout the United States. GE purchased the authorizations to copy from books and journals issued by publishers represented by the CCC. Copying fees were established independently by each publisher. The cost of the license for GE was established through the use of statistical sampling and modeling techniques developed by consulting econometricians from the Massachusetts Institute of Technology.

Harry Manbeck, General Patent Counsel for GE, said "We believe the agreement with CCC provides a workable way for General Electric to observe publishers' rights, while maintaining completely unrestricted access to the scientific, technical, and business information we need via photocopy." David Ladd, U.S. Register of Copyrights, has also approved the CCC licensing system, calling it "A successful voluntary solution which could further affect other difficult copyright-technological issues such as those now posed by electronic libraries and optical disks. It would maintain the principle of copyright while meeting the needs of users, and it would employ a voluntary mechanism rather than direct government intervention."

The Copyright Clearance Center was established in 1977 by photocopy users, authors, and publishers in response to the desire of Congress that a service be created to facilitate implementation of the U.S. copyright law that took effect January 1, 1978. The CCC is located in Salem, Massachusetts.

California funds state literacy program

California Governor George Deukmejian has approved the use of $2,635,000 in state funds for a 1984–1985 California Literacy Campaign. Gary Strong, state librarian, said, "This is a significant step for the state to take on behalf of the millions of adults in California who need help learning to read and write in English."

The California State Library launched the campaign in January 1984 with federal Library Services and Construction Act funds to twenty-seven public libraries to coordinate literacy programs in over one hundred communities. The libraries work in partnership with groups and agencies at the local level to design their own services. "All of us involved with the campaign," said Strong, "are proud that even in the early months of this demonstration, the legislature and the Governor perceived that these services are addressing the urgent needs of many Californians who are not able to use existing education and volunteer programs."

Rutgers receives grant from Getty Trust

The J. Paul Getty Trust, through its Center for the History of Art and the Humanities, has given $50,000 to Rutgers University Library in support of the *Lexicon Iconographicum Mythologiae Classicae,* a pictorial dictionary of classical mythology. The *Lexicon* is an international project of thirty-seven countries and will constitute the only complete reference to all ancient representations of classical mythology from the period 800 B.C. to A.D. 400.

Rutgers University Library is the center for the project in the Western hemisphere and is responsible for all American material in the *Lexicon.* The grant from the Getty Trust will release federal matching funds from the National Endowment for the Humanities.

FBI recovers stolen library stamps

The FBI has announced the recovery of eighty-two postage stamps valued at $500,000 that were stolen from the New York Public Library in 1977. The stamps were among 153 that were removed from panels stored in oak cabinets located near the information desk at the main library facility at Fifth Avenue and 42nd Street. The theft occurred on a weekend when the library was closed. Among the stamps stolen was a rare twenty-four-cent airmail stamp known as an "inverted Jenny." Issued in 1918, the stamp bears a picture of a Curtiss-Wright JN-4 "Jenny" biplane that was printed upside down. The stamp is valued at $150,000.

The stamps, identified in sale catalogs, were recovered from stamp dealers and auction houses. Although the FBI has identified suspects in the library burglary, the statute of limitations has expired.

Boston College dedicates $28 million library

Boston College, Chestnut Hill, Massachusetts, recently dedicated a new $28 million central research facility, the Thomas O'Neill, Jr. Library. Named after the Speaker of the U.S. House of Representatives, a 1936 alumnus of the college, the five-story structure replaces Bapst Library as the institution's main library. Bapst Library, which has served students since 1928, will be renovated and reopened in 1986, housing the university's special collections.

The O'Neill Library, capable of holding 1.25 million volumes, also houses the university computer center, a 140-station public computer terminal area, nine classrooms, research office space, and the university's telecommunications center.

The Boston College Library Information System incorporates all available Geac functions, including automated circulation, acquisitions, an online catalog, and the MARC Record Management System.

The O'Neill Library forms a quadrangle with three of the university's original neo-Gothic buildings. The cornice line of the new building was kept low and a gray-pink granite was selected to harmonize with the old Roxbury puddingstone facades.

Minudri and Sager to run for ALA president

Regina Minudri, director of the Berkeley (California) Public Library and Donald Sager, city librarian, Milwaukee (Wisconsin) Public Library, have been selected by the nominating committee of the American Library Association to run as candidates for president in the 1985 elections. The term of office is for 1986–1987. Alphonse Trezza, associate professor, School of Library and Information Studies, Florida State University, Tallahassee, has announced that he will enter the presidential race as a petition candidate.

Library collection of magic material to be sold at auction

The Hampden-Booth Theatre Libary in New York City has decided to dispose of its collection of more than 10,000 items on magic at an auction to be conducted by Swann Galleries, the country's largest antiquarian book auction house. The collection, amassed by John Mulholland (1898–1970), a world-renowned professional magician, consists of rare books, props, theatrical posters, broadsides, playbills, and Houdini memorabilia. The collection was acquired by the Walter Hampden-Edwin Booth Theatre Library after Mulholland's death fourteen years ago. Valued at $600,000, the collection, housed at The Players Club, is being sold because it is too large to be maintained within the limited confines of the Hampden-Booth Theatre Library and the library, as a separate arm of a nonprofit institution, lacks staff and funds to give the collection the care warranted by its importance. A spokesman for the library said, "It pains us to have to part with it piecemeal, but for the past eighteen months we have offered this collection intact to an institution or single buyer with the provision that it be readily available to scholars and researchers—to no avail."

John Lowry, president of Swann Galleries, attempted to find a buyer for the entire collection. "We must have approached just about every logical party here, in Europe, and the Far East." Among the parties contacted was the University of Texas, which already has a major magic collection. "They had indicated an interest in acquiring the Mulholland when it wasn't for sale. Now, what with the drastic curtailment in federal library funding, they were no longer interested."

The magic collection will be auctioned off in three separate sales: on December 6 and on dates to be set in June and December 1985. The sale is expected to raise in excess of half a million dollars for the Hampden-Booth Theatre Library.

Delaware acquires Brinnin papers

The University of Delaware, Newark, has acquired the papers of John Malcolm Brinnin, poet, biographer, and critic. Brinnin was director of the Poetry Center in New York City from 1949–1956 and was responsible for organizing Dylan Thomas' reading tours in this country. Besides his volumes of poetry, Brinnin is the author of *The Third Rose: Gertrude Stein and Her World* and *Dylan Thomas in America*.

Brinnin's papers include over 7,500 pages of primary source material for the study of modern American poetry, including correspondence with such writers as Truman Capote, Richard Eberhart, T.S. Eliot, Denise Levertov, Robert Lowell, Katherine Anne Porter, and Alan Tate, among hundreds of other contemporary authors. The collection also includes manuscripts of all of Brinnin's own work.

Residency fellowships available at Wayne State

The Rockefeller Foundation Residency Program in the Humanities has given $150,000 to the Walter Reuther Library of Labor and Urban Affairs, Wayne State University, to create two full-time residency fellowships for the 1985–1986 academic year. Scholars will be selected based on the quality and significance of their research proposal and its relationship to the holdings of the Reuther Library. The library holds the world's largest collection of labor union records, more than ninety-five million items.

Deadline for applications is December 1. Persons wishing to apply for the fellowships should write to Director, Reuther Library of Labor and Urban Affairs, Wayne State University, 5401 Cass, Detroit, MI 48202.

The Huntsville-Madison County Public Library *in Huntsville, Alabama recently established a new dimension of library service with the opening of a branch library in the city's new super-mall. The Madison Square Branch was custom-built by a local contractor and occupies only 261 square feet of space. In addition to regular shelving there are paperback carousels and sloped shelving commonly used in bookstores. The branch is stocked with paperbacks, bestsellers, and popular titles, but patrons may request books from the main library.*

The library reports that reaction from the public has been favorable, with many people surprised they do not have to purchase the books. The new branch is open the same hours the mall is in operation.

EBSCO to distribute CHECKMATE serials system

EBSCO Industries, Inc. has signed an agreement with the Cooperative Library Agency for Systems and Services, enabling it to market and distribute CHECKMATE, the microcomputer-based serials control system developed by CLASS.

CHECKMATE is a serials system for the IBM PC/XT which provides small and medium-sized libraries with searching, check-in, claiming, routing, and management report capability. As an authorized distributor of CHECKMATE software, EBSCO will demonstrate and install the serials control system. Software maintenance will be provided by CLASS.

Cleveland Public upgrades positions

The Cleveland Public Library has upgraded 240 clerical positions following a job classification study intended to eliminate pay inequities associated with positions traditionally filled by women. The study, made with the assistance of Yarger and Associates, also addressed the issue of comparable worth. The consultants found that while professional-level salaries were properly competitive, wages paid to clerical workers were not. The library's board of trustees unanimously adopted the recommendations of Yarger and Associates. Judge George Trumbo, president of the board of trustees, said "The Cleveland Public Library is now a model of enlightened personnel practices. Other units of government might study us, with profit."

Kellogg awards grant to Michigan cooperative

The W.K. Kellogg Foundation has awarded a grant of $836,200 to the Upper Peninsula Region of Library Cooperation to help fund a centralized database of library material. Headquartered in Marquette, Michigan, the cooperative represents school, public, academic, and special libraries. An automated library system has been planned whereby records of all library resources will be entered into a centralized database accessible through any local library. Membership in the cooperative is open to any of the 163 libraries in Michigan's Upper Peninsula.

Ground was recently broken for a new $5.1 million facility for the **Cumberland County Public Library** *in Fayetteville, North Carolina. The ceremony climaxed a two-year, community-wide effort to secure a new central library. The campaign was assisted by a private fund-raising drive which brought in $1.2 million. Unexpectedly low bids will make it possible to fund items previously left out of the plan, including landscaping, moving expenses, a sprinkler system, and additional furniture. The library, scheduled for completion in 1986, will incorporate a $500,000 computer system.*

Pictured in the photo above are (from left) Sara Hodgins, State Department of Cultural Resources; J.L. Dawkins, city council; Dorothy Brower, library board of trustees; Charles Speegle, county commissioner; Jerry Thrasher, library director; and Robert Ray, chair of the library building fund.

CAS resumes service to Poland

Chemical Abstracts Service is resuming delivery of its *CA Search* tapes to the Technical University of Warsaw after a two-year interruption of service. Shipment of the tapes to Poland stopped in 1982 when the U.S. Department of Commerce declined to renew CAS's validated export license for the tapes, holding that the tapes themselves, not the information they contained, represented technology that could not be exported to Poland or the U.S.S.R. As a result of CAS's appeal of that decision, the Commerce Department has determined that the tapes may be shipped to Poland under a general export license.

The *CA Search* computer-readable file contains bibliographic information and index entries paralleling much of the content of CAS's *Chemical Abstracts* publication.

Delaware establishes affirmative action internship

The University of Delaware, Newark, has begun an Affirmative Action Intern Program designed to provide full-time professional work experience in a large academic library to minority graduates of ALA-accredited library schools. The program recognizes that the existing library job market makes it difficult for newly graduated librarians to compete successfully for positions in large research libraries.

During the course of the internship, the librarian is provided with an orientation to the library, selects a home department, is given specialized training, attends workshops, serves on committees, and is provided with travel support for two national meetings of ALA. The intern is offered a one-year, noncontinuing contract.

The first incumbent of the program is Rosemary Oyoko, who received her MSLS from Case Western Reserve University in August 1984.

ALANET adds library supplier menu

The Library Supplier's Service Center is the latest menu to be added to ALANET, the electronic mail and information service of the American Library Association. The menu offers three promotional services: interactive forms for purchase orders and claims; special categories in ALANET's systemwide bulletin board; and electronic newsletters for announcing new products and services.

Order and claim forms are available to ALANET customers of Turner Subscriptions, Ebsco Subscriptions, Ambassador Book Service, Faxon Company, and ALA Publishing Services. Other vendors participating in ALANET include Quality Books, Blackwell North America, Texas Instruments, and MicroStuf, Inc.

A recent ground-breaking took place for a new central library for the **Irving (Texas) Public Library System.** *The $7.2 million facility (see artist's conception above) will be completed in the summer of 1986 and is expected to serve the library needs of the community "well into the next century."*

SUNY/ Stony Brook permanent home for Yeats

The William Butler Yeats Archive at the State University of New York at Stony Brook, the most complete collection of Yeats material outside Ireland, has been made a part of the permanent collections of the university library.

The archive, formerly located in the university's Center for Contemporary Arts and Letters, has been moved to the library's Special Collections Department to permit its permanent maintenance and availability to scholars under professional archival conditions. The archive consists of about 80,000 frames of microfilm. The original materials are in the possession of the Yeats family and the National Library of Ireland in Dublin.

OCLC to acquire LSP computer equipment

The OCLC board of trustees has authorized acquisition of hardware for OCLC's computer link in the name-authorities phase of the Linked Systems Project. LSP involves computer-to-computer links between the Library of Congress, the Research Library Information Network, the Washington Library Network, and OCLC.

In the name-authorities portion of LSP, OCLC-affiliated NACO (Name-Authority Cooperative) libraries will have online input via the OCLC system into the LC Name-Authority file. Present plans call for transmission of additions and corrections from the Library of Congress to each of the bibliographic networks on a daily basis.

While the first phase of LSP development is limited to the transfer of authority information, it is part of a broader program underway at OCLC. According to OCLC President Rowland Brown, "OCLC will be linking with many networks and local systems, both in the U.S. and abroad. LSP is only one type of linkage, and as such is very important but only one part of the planning activity OCLC is undertaking for its open system architecture."

LSP has been funded primarily by the Council on Library Resources. OCLC will seek third-party funding to help defray the cost of software development on the Data General 16-bit Eclipse S/280 minicomputer, which will serve as an interim system until the implementation of OCLC's overall system redesign.

MIDLNET assets transfered to CRL and ALA

The dissolution of the Midwest Region Library Network has resulted in the transfer of its remaining assets to the Center for Research Libraries and the Washington office of the American Library Association. The transfer of funds was the final action of the MIDLNET board, chaired by John McGowan, university librarian at Northwestern University.

The Center's portion of the award is $88,637 and it will be used for the immediate acquisition of material approved for purchase in fiscal year 1984 but not acquired because of lack of funds.

MIDLNET was founded in 1975 under the auspices of the Committee for Institutional Cooperation. The organization provided a number of services to its members, most specifically the brokering of OCLC. With the growth and expansion of state and national networks, many MIDLNET projects were no longer competitive. The organization was therefore dissolved and the MIDLNET board of trustees was assigned the task of determining which organizations would receive its remaining assets.

Calendar

NOV. 18–20—*Rhode Island LA,* annual conference. Sheraton Islander, Newport. Inf.: Tanya Trinkaus, West Warwick PL, West Warwick, RI 02893.

NOV. 29–DEC. 1—*Western School Conference.* Banff, Alberta, Canada. Theme: "Lead? Who? Where? Leadership and School Libraries in Western Canada." Inf.: Warren Grabinsky, 2110–24 Avenue, Vernon, British Columbia V1T 1K9 Canada.

DEC. 1–5—*California LA,* annual conference. Westin Bonaventure Hotel, Los Angeles. Theme: "Faster, Firmer, Further." Inf.: CLA Headquarters Office, 717 K Street, Suite 300, Sacramento, CA 95814–3477.

DEC. 2–4—*Educational Media Association of New Jersey,* annual conference. Hyatt Regency, New Brunswick. Theme: "Today's Libraries: The Road to Excellence in Education." Inf.: Sally Young, 8 Townsend Rd., Mendham, NJ 07945.

DEC. 4–6—*Online Information Meeting.* Novotel, London. Inf.: Jean Mulligan, Learned Information (Europe) Ltd., Basselsleigh Road, Abingdon, Oxford OX13 6LG England.

DEC. 6—*Effective Reference Service: An Introduction For Support Personnel,* seminar. Boston. Inf.: AJ Seminars, 11205 Farmland Drive, Rockville, MD 20852.

DEC. 7—*Appraisal and Conservation of Records,* workshop. American Antiquarian Society, Worcester, Mass. Sponsor: Northeast Document Conservation Center. Inf.: Records Workshop, NEDCC, 24 School St., Andover, MA 01810.

DEC. 13–15—*Arizona State LA/ Arizona Educational Media Association,* annual conference. Phoenix Civic Plaza, Phoenix. Theme: "The Future Is Now . . . Or Never." Inf.: Jean Murphy, Mesa PL, 64 E. First St., Mesa, AZ 85201.

DEC. 13—*Information Sources In Business and Economics,* seminar. Barbizon Plaza Hotel, New York. Inf.: (see Dec. 6 for address.)

DEC. 13—*Thesaurus Construction,* seminar. George Washington Univ., Washington, D.C. Inf.: (see Dec. 6 for address.)

JAN. 2–4—*Association for Library and Information Science Education,* annual conference. Shoreham Hotel, Washington, D.C. Theme: "Undergraduate Preparation for the Information Profession." Inf.: Jan Phillips, ALISE, 471 Park Lane, State College, PA 16801.

JAN. 16–19—*Medical Library Association,* winter institute. Belleview Biltmore, Belleaire, Fla. Inf.: MLA Education Dept., 919 North Michigan Ave., Suite 3208, Chicago, IL 60611.

JAN. 17—*Massachusetts LA,* midwinter conference. Framingham State College. Theme: "The Library As An Educational Institution." Inf.: Milles Cavanaugh, South Hadley LS, South Hadley, MA 01075.

JAN. 18–21—*COMMTEX International.* Anaheim Convention Center, Anaheim, Calif. Inf.: International Communications Industries Association (ICIA), 3150 Spring St., Fairfax, VA 22031.

FEB. 8—*The World of Rare Books,* workshop. Drexel Univ., Philadelphia. Inf.: Janet Goldwater, Office of Continuing Professional Education, Drexel Univ., Philadelphia, PA 19104.

FEB. 8–14—*Art Libraries Society of North America,* annual conference. Hyatt Regency, Los Angeles. Theme: "L.A.: Metaphor For the Future." Inf.: Pamela Jeffcott Parry, Executive Director, ARLIS/NA, 3775 Bear Creek Circle, Tuscon, AZ 85749.

FEB. 15—*On-Line Literature Searching,* workshop. Drexel Univ., Philadelphia. Inf.: (see Feb. 8 for address.)

FEB. 18—*1985 Congress For Librarians.* St. John's Univ., New York. Theme: "Downloading/ Uploading Online Databases and Catalogs." Sponsor: Division of Library and Information Science, St. John's Univ. Inf.: Dr. James Benson, St. John's Univ. DLIS, Jamaica, NY 11439.

FEB. 21–23—*Triple I '85,* conference. Hyatt Regency O'Hare, Rosemont, Ill. Theme: "Bridges To Excellence." Sponsors: Illinois Association for Media in Education, Illinois Association for Educational Communication and Technology, and the Illinois Association for Supervision and Curriculum Development. Inf.: Triple I '85, 225 Edgewood Drive, East Peoria, IL 61611.

FEB. 22—*Library Automation: A Seminar On the State-of-the-Art,* workshop. Drexel Univ., Philadelphia. Inf.: (see Feb. 8 for address.)

MAR. 3–8—*Audio-Visual Institute for Effective Communications.* Univ. of Indiana, Bloomington. Sponsor: International Communications Industries Association. Inf.: ICIA Training Department, 3150 Spring St., Fairfax, VA 22031.

Major Meetings

American Library Association
Mid-winter meeting
January 5–10. Washington
Annual meeting
July 6–11. Chicago

Canadian Library Association
Annual conference
June 13–18. Calgary (Alberta)

Medical Library Association
Annual conference
May 24–30. New York

Public Library Association
National conference
April 2–5. St. Louis

Special Libraries Association
Winter meeting
January 30–February 1. Philadelphia
Annual conference
June 8–13. Winnipeg (Manitoba)

Retrospective Conversion: Investing in the Future

Richard Boss

Why do libraries undertake retrospective conversion of their manual files to machine-readable form? The seemingly obvious answer is that they do it because they are going to install an automated system, and this requires a machine-readable database. However, the library administrator has to look beyond the immediate need and consider how the database will be used over time.

In the past, a number of libraries have seen the creation of the database as a relatively short-term requirement: a library was going to automate circulation and so it was decided to input the last name of the author, a truncated title, a call number and a label number into the database. Other libraries look further ahead and consider ways in which they might want to use a record—originally created for a circulation control system—in the future. Administrators in these libraries consider their current needs and attempt to project five or so years ahead to their future needs, and use the results of both examinations to determine the required characteristics of the database.

Accommodating full records

In the past, a number of libraries were constrained in their decisions about the nature of the database by costs or by technical limitations. Today most supermicro, mini, and mainframe-based systems can accommodate full bibliographic records. The cost of storing a full record is slightly greater than for a brief record, but not much more because the unit cost for storage drops as the size of the database increases. The risk in choosing to create brief records is that the record might have to be modified or upgraded in the future, an undertaking that will result in a higher investment than would have been the case if a full record had been provided in the first place.

Even if planning begins with the assumption that full records are to be created—and let's assume these are full MARC bibliographic records—it is still important to be clear as to why the retrospective conversion is being undertaken. For instance, if the immediate aim is to create a database to support circulation, with a long-term objective of using the same database to support a patron access catalog within four or five years, the most useful circulation database would focus on the most active parts of the collection—these would be converted first. On the other hand, if the file is to be a patron access catalog database, it might make more sense to convert everything from a certain date. Then users can be told, "If it was published before x date, look in the card catalog; after that date, look in the online catalog." A library might also plan to use the retrospective conversion to provide access to records that are difficult to locate in the present environment—the materials that have only been partially cataloged, for instance. This would be appropriate if the partial cataloging was the result not of a judgement about the usefulness of the material but because appropriate support was not yet available. This was often the case in processing microforms. It was difficult to get sets of catalog cards for microform collections, but today it is possible to obtain machine-readable records from bibliographic utilities for a number of microform series, enabling this material to be recorded in a database at relatively modest cost.

Conforming to standards

Decisions have to be made with regard to the standards of the database. A database is a long-term investment, a resource with the same kind of life as a card catalog. Under these circumstances, it makes sense to conform to the AACR-2 and MARC II standards for cataloging. If these standards are adhered to rigidly, the database is likely to outlast several different generations of computer hardware and software. In the same way that catalog cards are periodically refiled into new cabinetry, a database can be moved from a library's first computer system into a second computer system, and into a third. Computer systems are likely to be replaced at faster intervals than card-catalog cabinetry. It is estimated that the average life expectancy of an automated library system is just beyond seven years. Compare this to the twenty to twenty-five year retention schedule for card-catalog cabinets. Because of the likelihood that the database will be moved, the transportability of the file is an important consideration. Much as the details of the MARC format have been criticized, it is the only standard available, and adherence to that standard is essential if transportability is to be achieved.

A standard should be multi-institutional, spanning many organi-

Richard Boss *is senior consultant, Information Systems Consultants, Bethesda, Maryland.*

zations. With bibliographic utilities, bibliographic services, computer system vendors, computer output microform vendors, and libraries all conforming to the same standard, an individual library can obtain a record from an external source, load it, process it, output it, and send it to a COM vendor without incurring a reformatting charge to utilize that record. The record can be handled by a variety of computer programs because it conforms to the industry standard.

Unfortunately, the only standards currently available relate to bibliographic records. A library's database is going to contain records other than bibliographic records. At a minimum, these other records will include copy-specific information and patron information, and there may be other types of records also. Copy-specific information consists of descriptive elements that pertain to a particular physical entity, to a particular copy or manifestation of a bibliographic record. As more libraries share computer systems, it is becoming increasingly common to regard the call number as copy-specific information since different libraries using the same system often wish to attach a different call number to a single bibliographic record. Locations within the library system are copy-specific information, as are the specific label numbers on individual books. Descriptions of the condition of an item are also usually encompassed in the copy-specific record.

There are problems relating to standards for copy-specific information, particularly in the serials area. For example, libraries follow different practices in binding their volumes—some bind more issues together than do others. Varying practices for the recording of issues means that it is difficult to automatically derive summarized holdings statements for inclusion in products such as union lists. Standards are only now being developed for representation of holdings in machine-readable form. The ANSI Z39 Committee has prepared draft standards, but these may be under discussion for some time to come.

This means that in some areas libraries have to create their records without the benefit of standards, and must anticipate what the standards might be. In this situation, the best advice is to follow the standards/practices that are prevalent in the industry, particularly those prevalent among the major turnkey vendors. This course provides a format and a consistency that may be less expensive for the library to change when a standard is developed and it is time to convert the records to that format. When this happens a vendor is able to spread the costs of preparing conversion programs over a number of clients. A library that has "gone it alone" may also have to bear all of these costs alone.

There are no standards for patron records and almost everyone will create patron records differently. The advice to follow here is to create records with as much detail as possible and to use a different field, and a different field tag, for each data element. Then if a computer program must be written to convert the data into a standard format, the data will be formatted so that every required element can be automatically identified by the computer and translated into the appropriate field in the new record without requiring human intervention. The essential considerations are consistency and the maximum separation and identification of data elements. Do not include multiple elements of data in a single field even though it is anticipated that they will be used together virtually all of the time.

There has been a dramatic transformation in the attitudes toward standards on the part of librarians involved in automation. The change has been partly due to personal experience and partly due to the literature. Whereas two or three years ago there was considerable reluctance to adhere to standards such as MARC as a format for loading records and for retaining records in an automated system, there now seems to be a very strong positive bias in favor of maintaining and following standards.

Creating bibliographic records

There has been a similarly dramatic change in relation to record length. In the early days of turnkey automated library systems, many libraries created only brief bibliographic records; today, more and more libraries create full records even if they initially intend only to use them to support circulation control. One of the reasons for this change is the way in which disk storage capacity is sold. The larger the disk drive, the lower the cost per thousand or million characters stored. That is, a sixty million character device does not cost one-fifth of a 300 million character device, or—if you want to use the jargon of the industry—a 60 MB drive does not cost one-fifth of the price of a 300 MB device. It costs up to seventy-two percent of the price of the larger device. When a library selects a larger storage device it realizes considerable economies in terms of the unit cost of storage and for that reason more and more libraries have overcome their concern about creating full-length bibliographic records.

Librarians, particularly those in institutions other than academic libraries, often ask why they should consider loading full MARC bibliographic records when they have no intention of displaying all of that information on the screen and confronting users with a screen filled with bibliographic information. Even if only a one-line or brief display is envisaged, there may still be a desire to provide the ability to qualify or refine a search. For example, a user may want to qualify a search by language, limiting the retrieved items to those in English, Dutch or German. Alternative requirements may be limitation by date of publication, by the presence of a bibliography, or by publisher. Although the results of the search may be displayed in a brief one- or two-line format, many elements are needed to provide the searching precision required in these examples.

There are a number of sources of

support for the retrospective conversion of bibliographic records. First, there are the bibliographic utilities. The major advantages of a bibliographic utility include the size of their bibliographic databases which are much larger than any other available sources files. This means a higher hit rate. On OCLC, for example, there are more than ten million bibliographic records. These records include materials other than monographs. More than 475,000 of the OCLC records are for recordings and scores, for instance. The UTLAS database contains almost as many monograph records as OCLC —eight million plus—but only about two-thirds the records for recordings and scores. The RLIN database, while it is more difficult to size, apparently contains about two-thirds the number of monograph records on OCLC and forty percent the number of records for recordings and scores. The WLN database is about forty percent the size of OCLC in terms of bibliographic records for monographs, and apparently about thirty percent the size in terms of scores and musical recordings. Nevertheless, any one of these utilities is at least twice as large as ninety percent of the other resource database options that are available.

The second advantage in using a bibliographic utility to support retrospective conversion is that all of them are basically online systems, although some off-line options are now available. This means that an operator can search for a record, display it, adapt it, download it, and send it for inclusion on an archival tape all as part of one session.

But the bibliographic utilities have disadvantages in that they are a very expensive way of maintaining an online database. A library using these systems for retrospective conversion pays a share of the costs of the associated hardware and software. In the case of OCLC there is $20 million worth of computer hardware located in Dublin, Ohio. In contrast, a stand-alone system such a MiniMARC uses only $25,000 worth of micro hardware and floppy disk storage in order to accomplish retrospective conversion or, for that matter, current cataloging. And the utility approach carries extensive telecommunications costs. With the restructuring of the telephone company, the cost of telecommunications as a percentage of the total OCLC budget is expected to rise from fifteen percent to twenty-five percent. Of course, OCLC charges are going to go up, as will the charges of the other bibliographic utilities.

There are so many unknowns in the current telecommunications picture that it is impossible to predict the outcome. There are some reasons to believe that so-called private networks—networks of leased lines crisscrossing the country—will become more and more expensive and that dial-up access will actually go down slightly in cost. In this scenario, in two or three years libraries may find that dialing up into OCLC or another bibliographic utility will be more cost-effective than using leased lines of the type that are now being used. Telecommunications costs are in inherent characteristic of the bibliographic utility approach, and this poses potential problems.

A saleable service

OCLC was the first bibliographic utility to recognize that retrospective conversion was not only a saleable service that might bring in income, but also that it could enhance the utility's database. Thus, when OCLC first began to offer retrospective conversion there was no charge for it. If a library had a terminal and was paying the set telecommunications charge for that terminal, no extra charges were incurred for using the OCLC system to support retrospective conversion. At that time so much of the retrospective conversion effort was keying records for which the file contained no matching records, that the operation enhanced the database, adding new records that could then be resold to other libraries. The database is now so large that many of the records required in a retrospective conversion are already in the database and there is less enhancement of the file through the addition of new records during a conversion.

The percentage of computer resources being used for retrospective conversion had been rising, to the extent that some eighteen months ago over fifty percent of OCLC's computer resources were being used to support online retrospective conversion. At that time, the rates for retrospective conversion began to rise and they are now at a rate of twenty-two cents for off-hours retrospective conversion. If the conversion is done during prime time the charge is now ninety cents per record. Charges from regional networks usually are higher than OCLC prices.

RLIN introduced a retrospective conversion rate recently. Their rate is still substantially higher—about three times—than that of OCLC. And so far, RLIN has been little utilized for retrospective conversion, although that may change now that it offers a separate retrospective conversion rate. Previously, most RLIN members have chosen to use the REMARC approach to retrospective conversion.

The bibliographic utility approach to conversion may change in the future. Witness, for example, OCLC's introduction of the Model 300 terminal. This will allow a less communication-intensive approach to conversion. A library could input its search keys —ISBN, ISSN, LCCN—transmit the search online, have the results transmitted after the search was performed and download those records. Online editing could be done locally and the results batched before being transmitted back to OCLC. This would considerably reduce the telecommunications charges currently entailed in doing online conversion through the utilities.

A second source of retrospective conversion support is the stand-alone system. At present, there is only one: MiniMARC. MiniMARC utilizes a small microcomputer, a printer, a series of floppy disk drives, a screen with keyboard, and a microform index. The microform index is searched by Library of Congress card number, by author, or by title to retrieve a reference that will indicate the location of the machine-readable record on one of the 1,300 floppy disks in the system. This information is used to retrieve the record which can then be edited online and transferred to a second diskette that contains the library's developing database. If the library has a local automated system provided by CLSI, Data Phase or Geac, the record can be transferred directly to the system via a cable interface. The system, including floppy disk and microform index updates, costs about $55,000. If used efficiently, with batched searches of the indices, the average cost per record—for ongoing cataloging or retrospective conversion—will be about eighty-eight cents per item, exclusive of labor costs. If the system is used more intensively—by working a double shift of operators, for instance—the workload can be increased and the unit cost lowered to around fifty cents per item.

Obviously the hit rate will not be as high as on OCLC or another bibliographic utility. Public libraries have achieved a relatively high hit rate on MiniMARC as have academic and special libraries with collections of recent, primarily English-language titles. In a large-scale, double shift operation, fifty cents per item plus labor costs is relatively competitive.

MiniMARC will undergo a major change later this year. The database will no longer be stored on floppy disks but on digitally encoded videodisk. The disk will contain not only the records but also the indices, eliminating the need for a separate microform search. It is anticipated that the new hardware configuration will not cost any more than the old system, because the company actually will realize substantial economies in not having to work with the floppy disks and microform. The labor costs of working with the sytem should decrease, possibly to the point where this approach to cataloging support will be fully competitive with the lowest cost retrospective conversion option.

The commercial bibliographic services provide the third option for retrospective conversion support. Services are provided by companies such as Auto-Graphics, Blackwell North America, Brodart, Sciences Press, the Computer Company, and General Research Corporation. There are about a dozen companies offering such services. Historically, these organizations have subscribed to the MARC tapes, mounted them on their computer systems, and searched libraries' holdings against these files to extract matching MARC records. Search requests can be submitted in one of several ways: brief search keys can be submitted on magnetic tape; cards or other forms of records can be sent to the service, which keys search statements onto tape, or libraries can submit the search keys typed with an optical character recognition ball on a typewriter, and the service uses an electronic scanner to convert these to machine-readable form. If the search keys are ISBNs, LCCNs or some other control number, the systems can produce a fairly high reliability in the match. But if these numbers are not readily available in a library's existing records, it will have to develop a search key from elements of the author/title name or an author/title/publisher/date key. The more points in such a key, the more reliable the match is going to be, but the more it is going to cost to prepare the search key. On a number of occasions multiple matches will be retrieved. These and all single records thought to be exact matches would be printed out on edit sheets. The printouts have to be reviewed manually, corrections marked and keyed, and resubmitted to the service for reprocessing. After reprocessing, the whole manual checking and editing process has to be performed again.

Compared with the process of online matching and editing supported by the utilities and, to a certain extent, MiniMARC, there is a much greater labor cost, and much greater potential for error in the bibliographic service approach. Even though the average bibliographic service charges between twelve and twenty cents to match and extract a record from the MARC database, labor costs and error rates are substantially higher.

Use of personal microcomputers

Recognizing that there were some real problems, a number of bibliographic services have started to go a different route. They now provide libraries with a personal microcomputer on which to enter the search keys. Libraries send the diskettes to the vendor, who reformats them onto magnetic tape, performs the matching and extraction operation, outputs the results on tape, and reformats the tape onto diskettes, which are sent back to the library for online editing and correction. This ability adds to the cost of vendor services. A library may only be paying between twelve and twenty cents for the actual extraction of the record, but it also must pay for the microcomputer, for the computer programs, for reformatting the diskettes to magnetic tape, the magnetic tapes to diskettes, etc. By the time all of those charges are added, including labor costs, the result may not be a reduction in the overall cost of the retrospective conversion. What may have been achieved is a shift in the allocation of these costs, with the personnel component being reduced, and the operations and expenses category increased. Comparisons have to be conducted very carefully because it is impossible to say that one process is less expensive than another if all that is assessed is the bill received from the vendor or the amount of labor expended by library staff.

The strengths of the bibliographic services have been in terms of the total amount that a library has to pay to an outside organization, and that bill tends to be low. The main disadvantages of the bibliographic service approach to retrospective conversion is the prospect that internal labor costs will be higher and the hit rate will probably be lower because most of the vendors only mount the LC MARC tapes.

Some vendors have enhanced their databases with contributed records from their other customers—all but one of the companies offering these services realize significant income from producing COM catalogs, which give them a potential source of records other than the MARC tapes. However, these supplementary records are often of uneven quality and may not be MARC records. Thus, when a service offers a resource file, it is important to examine the composition of the file in relation to factors other than its size.

The largest database available through such a service is one that offers not only LC MARC tapes, but the REMARC tapes. The REMARC file contains machine-readable records for some three to four million items cataloged by the Library of Congress before it began producing its cataloging in machine-readable form. Carrollton Press, the developer of the file, has negotiated access rights with several vendors. The cost for using a REMARC record is fifty cents as compared with twelve to twenty cents for a MARC record.

A fourth approach to retrospective conversion is to obtain a machine-readable database developed by a library with a similar collection. It might be possible to negotiate favorable terms to use the database and load it into the converting library's local automated system. The first library to try this on a large scale was Tacoma Public Library in Washington and it is therefore often called the "Tacoma Method."

There is, however, a potential problem. The local system is usually configured on the basis of the expected size of the local database and the projected activity levels against that file. Mounting a large external database of bibliographic records, undertaking the extraction and editing of these records, and transferring them to the local database can, for the period of the conversion, severely overload the local sytem. Response time on the system can be downgraded so that it requires several minutes to display the results of a simple search. A library intending to use the Tacoma method for conversion should ensure that the system has the required interim capacity in terms of both data storage and processing power. Once the conversion is complete, the extra capacity should be justified in terms of some required future application.

Most retrospective conversion in academic and special libraries has been done using bibliographic utilities. Public libraries generally have used the commercial bibliographic services. This pattern has only begun to change in the past year or so as a number of academic libraries, especially research libraries, have started doing retrospective conversion using the REMARC file, either directly with Carrollton Press or through another vendor that has a contractual relationship with them.

Converting patron records

In an academic environment a library can often obtain a dump of machine-readable student and faculty records. A special computer program usually has to strip off confidential information and format the records so that they can be loaded into the library system. Once the records are mounted, patrons can be asked to verify the data and the library's records can be amended to reflect any changes. The objective is to reduce the amount of necessary keying. A number of libraries with very large potential users have found it more efficient to register patrons "from scratch" and key the information. This is because the percentage of potential users who actually use the library is too small for the efficient conversion of all available records.

There really is no way to obtain copy-specific information from an external source. This data has to be newly entered in each library. One may, however, add copy-specific information into the bibliographic utility database at the time of cataloging or retrospective conversion.

What are the costs of conversion? First of all there are equipment costs. These will vary according to the conversion approach used, but might include the costs of one or more of the following: an electric typewriter with an OCR ball, a computer terminal with or without a modem, a microcomputer, etc. If a vendor provides the personal computer or some other piece of equipment as part of a retrospective conversion contract, the library is still paying for the equipment, it's just a question of how that cost is being recovered by the vendor. This may be by selling the library the piece of equipment, or by recovering two or three cents every time a record is processed. A library might want to investigate buying the equipment outright. Then, when the conversion is over, the library has equity in the equipment.

Typically, a fully configured dumb terminal or a dedicated terminal costs some $5,000 by the time it is up and running. For a micro that is fully configured with software, another $2,000 should be allowed in order to make it operational. If substantial retrospective conversion is to be undertaken, one unit may not be enough. On the other hand, if the library already has bibliographic utility terminals and these are not utilized all the time, the conversion project may be fitted in without requiring an investment in additional terminals.

Vendor charges are the area where the greatest variations occur. Different vendors have varying ways of dealing with cost, negotiating different rates for different sized conversions. Most often, dramatically different prices mean that the costs have been moved around in some way. Per record charges might be disguised by the imposition of a set-up charge or a database maintenance charge, or various other kinds of charges. To determine the actual vendor charge per record, all of the costs must be added. Generally the commercial bibliographic services that use the off-line approach will have seemingly lower charges than the bibliographic utilities.

The telecommunications changes for accessing a bibliographic utility are approximately fifty cents per hour for OCLC dedicated terminals (figured on the division of the monthly per terminal charge of around $170 and system availability of some 325 hours a month) and up to thirty dollars per hour for dial-up access over regular telephone lines. The difference is due to the fact that OCLC has a large telecommunications network and realizes low costs by putting many terminals on a single line. OCLC telecommunications costs are expected to rise to over one dollar per hour in the foreseeable future. Tymnet and Telenet, which might be used for dial access, cost five to seven dollars per hour so the bibliographic utilities offer a real telecommunications bargain, even if it is assumed that prices will rise. Tymnet and Telenet are value-added services which not only provide telecommunications but also convert computer protocols so that any one of several different kinds of terminals may be used to access other services such as Dialog, BRS and SDC. A library using such a telecommunications service is provided with, and paying for, additional services.

Dial access charges vary substantially depending upon location and time of day. Access to a remote system can cost as little as fourteen cents for a minute, or as much as fifty-one cents for a minute. This is an area in which an active user can quickly lose money. Right now the rule is that if the total number of transactions—acquisitions, cataloging, interlibrary loans, and serial transactions—performed with utility support is under 2,500, dial access is most advantageous. If the figure is over 4,000 transactions, the bibliographic utility's telecommunications system is the most cost-effective. In the 2,500 to 4,000 range, a library must analyze its local situation to determine the best approach.

Elusive labor costs

Labor costs are an area in which it is very difficult to obtain hard data, despite the fact that labor represents a very significant part of the cost of retrospective conversion. The state university system of Florida undertook the conversion of one million bibliographic records for its nineteen campuses. Carefully maintained cost records revealed that, in 1980, the average cost of labor for an online retrospective conversion on OCLC was sixty-seven cents. If that cost is added to the cost per record of using OCLC for off-hour conversion, the total cost is eighty-nine cents to do an online retrospective conversion during non-prime hours. And terminal, membership, and telecommunications charges have to be added to that figure. That is the lowest cost retrospective conversion that anyone has ever documented.

It is possible that someone will develop a lower cost approach to online conversion, but even if a lower cost can be achieved, this may not be sufficient reason for it to be universally adopted. Consider a library with 250,000 records, access to four OCLC terminals, and plans to achieve the conversion by using operators before 9:00 a.m. and after 5:00 p.m. On this workplan, it would take 4.7 years to complete the conversion!

There are all sorts of arguments about how much it costs to do an off-line retrospective conversion, but the most reliable information seems to suggest that it costs at least eighty-eight cents per record when the search keys are created on a personal computer, diskettes are dispatched to the vendor, and diskettes are returned and mounted on the personal computer for editing. To this cost must be added twelve cents or more for extraction and the charges for reformatting the floppy disks to and from tape several times. These charges may well add up to eight cents per record, bringing the total cost up to at least $1.08.

In an off-line conversion with the vendor doing the data entry and library staff handling printouts of matched records, the library's labor costs very quickly rise to $1.25 per bibliographic record. Add the twelve cents or more extraction fee, the charge for entering the search keys and the cost of the printouts, and the vendor charge per record very quickly goes up by about thirty cents, for a total of $1.55 per record. It is very difficult for the commercial services to beat the cost of a retrospective conversion done online using a bibliographic utility during off-hours, but the project can usually be completed more quickly.

The bibliographic utility picture immediately changes when it is used during prime time. On the one hand the bibliographic utilities (at least OCLC) anchor the low end of the retrospective conversion cost continuum when used in off-hours, but used during prime time they represent the top end in costs.

There is one more expensive approach that has not been mentioned, and that is to use EKI or Saztec to key and code the entire shelflist at two to six dollars per record depending upon the kinds of services performed. Only libraries with very unique databases should consider this approach.

Because so many libraries are frustrated by their inability to take advantage of the off-peak retrospective conversion charges, OCLC has set up a retrospective conversion service. It employs 150 operators using terminals directly wired to the system, thus not incurring any telecommunications charges. Because of the low impact of such activity on the system, prime time rates are not charged, so for about one dollar per record—including both the system charges and the labor charges—the service can key from the shelflist creating a machine-readable record that the library can load into its local system for online editing.

The database has been created, and the rule-of-thumb suggests that this database has cost approximately one dollar per bibliographic record. If the library has created a full MARC bibliographic record that conforms to the standard, virtually any vendor of an automated system should be able to load that database without charging a reformatting or tape loading charge. That's one of the advantages of adhering strictly to the standards.

Most local library systems can retain records in the MARC format. And most can output the MARC record with the tags. If the system cannot output the record with the tags, it is not worth considering as it does not

continued on page 238

Public Libraries and Literacy: A New Role to Play

Gary Strong

California is estimated to have at least 2.5 million adults over the age of sixteen who cannot read and write English well enough to handle the minimal demands of daily living. They cannot read traffic signs, product labels, or job advertisements. They cannot write checks, fill out application forms, vote, or read their children's report cards. These Californians, both native and foreign-born, are unable to participate fully in the social and economic life of the state.

The magnitude of illiteracy in the United States is overwhelming. It is believed that at least twenty-three million persons, or one fifth of the adult population of the United States, are unable to read. The adverse impact of illiteracy on communities can be inferred from the following national estimates:

- Forty percent of adults with incomes under $5,000 are functionally illiterate.
- Over one third of mothers receiving Aid for Dependent Children are illiterate.
- $6 billion is spent annually on welfare and unemployment compensation due to illiteracy.
- $6.6 billion is spent per year on 700,000 illiterate prison inmates.
- One million students drop out of high school in the United States each year.
- Forty percent of all minority youth may be functionally illiterate.[1]

Public libraries offer a unique opportunity for attacking the alarming problem of illiteracy in America. While many public libraries have a marvelous tradition of advising adult readers and a few have maintained literacy programs for many years, no major statewide effort involving libraries has been mounted to eradicate adult illiteracy in the United States. The recently issued *Alliance for Excellence* calls on "libraries to become active in adult literacy education programs at local, state, and national levels."[2]

California's information economy continues to expand and diversify, demanding new talent and offering new opportunity. At the same time, a growing number of adults are unable to take advantage of these new horizons. The problem of adult illiteracy increases at alarming rates. The high school drop-out rate, likewise, remains high—over thirty per cent this year statewide. As California moves toward an information-based economy, assembly-line employment is rapidly declining. Many adults with limited literacy skills are finding it increasingly difficult to cope under these conditions. The ability of many adults to retrain and move into new careers is curtailed.

Believing that public libraries could become significant partners in enhancing the "Learning Society,"[3] the California State Library set a program in motion to assist public libraries in meeting their long-term goal as learning centers. California law states that "it is in the interests of the people and of the state that there be a general diffusion of knowledge and intelligence through the establishment and operation of public libraries. Such diffusion is a matter of general concern inasmuch as it is the duty of the state to provide encouragement to the voluntary lifelong learning of the people of the state." The law further states, "the public library is a supplement to the formal system of free public education, and a source of information and inspiration to persons of all ages, and a resource for continuing education and reeducation beyond the years of formal education."[4]

Since 1911, when the County Library law was enacted, California public libraries have been established to provide this basic level of learning support to the people. Today, the one hundred and sixty-nine public library jurisdictions offer a network of services in over eight hundred communities. California public libraries have always taken a leadership role in innovative service delivery. It is quite natural that public libraries once again move forward to support the major concern of reaching out to the millions of citizens who cannot read and write English well enough to meet their living requirements.

The California Literacy Campaign

The California Literacy Campaign has a single purpose. It is to lay the groundwork for a statewide, long-term structure that will reach and help adults in California attain an English-language ability they want and need. The campaign will be successful to the degree that public policy, as established by state and local officials, fully acknowledges the damage caused by illiteracy and endorses the need to eradicate it.

This statewide commitment was

Gary Strong *is Librarian, State Library of California, Sacramento.*

evidenced by a proclamation issued by Governor George Deukmejian recognizing the California Literacy Campaign and urging "citizens and leaders of our state to join [him] in supporting this important program."[5]

A further step in this commitment came in the form of money. The California State Librarian set aside $2.5 million in Library Services and Construction Act funds during 1983–1984 to fund adult illiteracy programs in public libraries. These projects were intended to complement the efforts of formal education agencies and the volunteer sector who have worked for many years on this problem. A number of libraries were already participating with community groups to combat illiteracy. It was believed that libraries have a vested interest in reading and an informed public and would want a larger role. The intent of the campaign is to draw statewide interest in public library involvement and to enable public libraries to mobilize their communities to take action on behalf of adult learners.

The State Library is committed to provide specialized suppport to local projects. The management staff made the California Literacy Campaign a top priority for the State Library. Carmela Ruby serves as the principal consultant to the LSCA-funded projects and works to forge ongoing relationships within state government and with national literacy groups. Gail McGovern carries the responsibility for developing public relations and publicity programs that support the projects and raise statewide awareness. All geographic consultants provide ongoing support as a part of their responsibility in long-term library development activities. Staff of the State Library Services Bureau are called upon to compile statistics, conduct literature searches, and acquire and catalog specialized resources.

In addition, the library has added specialized expertise. At present two staff members support the effort. The literacy specialist is Al Bennett. He has an extensive background in adult literacy work and provides ongoing consulting support to the projects statewide. His role is to make sure that local project staff have the necessary skills to succeed. He advises on methods and activities and conducts training and skill-building workshops.

The other area of specialized expertise is in community organizing. Edna Mayhand brings extensive background in community organizing to the project staff. She works with project sites to insure that they develop the necessary coalitions to build a support base.

Specialist assistance from the California Department of Education and its adult education program, the California Youth Authority, the state universities and colleges, B. Dalton Booksellers, Laubach, Literacy Volunteers of America and many others has been available to assist in drawing together a common focus on literacy. Inspiration came from the many individuals who have been striving for years to put literacy on the national agenda. Among them is Jonathan Kozol who spoke movingly to Californians of the frightful deprivation illiteracy causes. He helped people realize they could do something about it.

The first priority of the California Literacy Campaign is to insure that the services offered by public libraries are offered in concert with and in addition to those available from other providers in each community. The Adult Basic Education programs, the training programs offered by colleges, and the many programs supported by volunteer organizations across the state are some of the opportunities that were already available. These existing efforts allow public library programs to provide services that will offer new opportunities for the illiterate adult.

The local projects

In inviting local project applications, the State Library sought libraries that would provide a basic commitment to general criteria. The projects needed to concentrate on placing a maximum priority on helping more adults learn to read and to write English. Believing that adult illiteracy is a problem that a specific community must address through its local officials, agencies, and interested groups, libraries were required to identify these potential partners. Above all, projects needed to address how the personal energies and commitment of concerned individuals might be tapped.

Many public libraries needed to refocus their thinking. Applicants were required to concentrate on coordinating and providing adult illiteracy services at the community level. Libraries accustomed to working on jurisdiction-wide or multi-jurisdiction programs needed to shift their focus to the individual community where local policy is developed and decisions are made on a day-by-day basis. It is at that level that coalition-building for literacy becomes effective; that tutors can be recruited; and most important, that the hard-to-reach adult illiterate can be identified, encouraged, and taught to read.

The county libraries typically serve many communities, both cities and communities in unincorporated areas. Larger city libraries serve several communities as well. A smaller city library's service area may be just one community, coextensive with the city, or it may serve two or more communities.

For the purposes of the various projects, it was suggested that a community be identified by having several, although not necessarily all, of the following characteristics:

- Community-specific service clubs, e.g. Soroptimists; Lions.
- A community public library (possibly a branch of a larger city or county system).
- A community college campus.
- A community-specific high school.
- A post office with the community name.
- A community-specific branch of a service agency, e.g. DMV, EDD, Social Security.
- A Chamber of Commerce.
- A realtor's association.
- A separate governing body, or if within a larger jurisdiction, a sepa-

rate supervisorial or council district.

• A planning council and/or neighborhood organization.

• A community-specific newspaper.

• Many residents who identify with the community.

• Several cultures and/or neighborhoods.

In completing their applications, libraries were asked to identify, target, and involve each of the communities the program would serve; describe why each of the communities chosen meets the needs of illiterate adults that have been identified; and describe the process by which each community will design its own service program to meet local needs.

Applicants were also asked to describe each coalition or partnership that would support the local program and implement its activities. The application included a plan for forming a local coalition to begin work by February 1, 1984; a description of tasks, in terms of how each coalition representative would specifically contribute to solving the community problem of adult illiteracy; an array of public and private agencies, including, but not limited to, current providers of literacy services; and a description of how such a coalition or partnership would mobilize local government and private commitment and support.

Students identified in the programs must be at least sixteen years old and must not be enrolled in another educational program or literacy program. The program goal was set so that as a minimum for every $10,000 granted, fifty adult learners would be identified and service/tutoring to them would have begun by October 1, 1984.

While the State Library did not specify methods to be followed by the various public libraries in support of individual projects, applicants were required to identify either innovative or proven methods that would be used for teaching adults to read and write English and specify why they are appropriate. No method was funded that depended exclusively upon self-teaching.

What constitutes a literate adult could be defined by the local program or could be defined by each student. Elaborate testing methods were considered less important in these projects than a focus on the student's assessment of competencies that he or she acquired in order to function better. It is hoped that the adults tutored under the public library effort will achieve the confidence to move on to other programs such as those offered by Adult Basic Education or in the community colleges or be able to enter job-training programs otherwise denied them. Evaluation by all concerned in the projects must, however, address the individual student's goals as defined by the students themselves, and show how the community program has allowed the students to progress toward their goals.

Each library project applicant was to determine the materials that would be required for the literacy program. These included literacy materials to be used by the students, tutoring resources, and the professional literature on the topic of literacy for use by tutors, trainers, library staff, community agencies, and individuals. Long-term utility to the community was considered so that the community could respond to new needs and approaches as they were discovered.

Because the emphasis of the campaign is on an active role for the public library in delivering literacy services, funds were not granted for upgrading library collections, including materials in languages other than English; materials which address multi-cultural needs; materials for skills-building, consumer topics, high-low interest, and the like for the reader, including the new reader. These resources are already the basis of good public library service.

It was specifically not the purpose of the California Literacy Campaign to establish large new organizational structures. However, time and energy are required for integrating the library and community roles in the literacy program, mobilizing the community, coordinating community groups, managing tutors, providing public relations and publicity, and coordinating activities of various literacy providers. Grant funds support coordinators for community-level programs. No funds were granted for vans, bookmobiles, or microcomputer hardware under this grant program.

The range of applications that were funded is indeed exciting. Highlights of several projects demonstrate their variety.

The Modoc County Adult Tutorial Program is administered by a coordinator and paid tutor-administrators in three locations in this remote rural county. Both the Laubach and Lindamood methods are being used, and an experimental approach to language experience has been introduced to the Northern Paiute Indian Community.

The Tri-City Literacy Coalition is a cooperative program among the Carlsbad and Oceanside public libraries and the Vista branch of the San Diego County Library. In addition to the local community, Literacy Volunteers of America and Laubach Literacy Council are closely involved.

Project Pasadena Reads has intensively assessed the community's needs, with the result that two approaches to tutoring are being developed: that of Laubach, and an innovative approach suited to the learners' levels, for which the materials, format, and tutor training are being developed by a community Materials Committee. The Ventura County project also has developed its own methodology.

The Fresno and Merced projects have unique teaching challenges. They serve an English-as-a-second-language population, with a heavy influx of Hmong and Lao refugees. The San Bernardino County project will provide literacy training for adults through the Cino, Yucaipa, Barstow, and Twenty-nine Palms branch libraries. The training of tutors draws on the LVA and Laubach methods as well as those developed by The Literacy Council of Alaska, a former Right-to-Read and Adult Basic Skills Academy.

The Placentia District Library has been involved with Literacy Volunteers of America for four years and will help four more public libraries in Orange County become LVA affiliates who can then serve other nearby public libraries.

The Los Angeles Public and Los Angeles County Libraries will establish "reading centers" in twenty-one branches that will reach out to neighborhoods through community coalitions.[6]

Many programs will provide "enabling funds" to students and volunteer tutors who cannot afford transportation, child care, materials and other expenses of tutoring or being tutored. Each program is expected to involve "adult learners" in the planning and development of the programs.

The State Library further provided initial statewide training and publicity. At the preapplication stage, workshops were held to acquaint potential applicant libraries with background information on the California Literacy Campaign and the emphasis that it would take. Once projects were funded, basic literacy awareness and public relations awareness workshops were completed. The State Library also provided a standards manual for publicity and promotion.[7]

Community-based literacy programs

The California Literacy Campaign encourages community-based literacy programs using the criteria defined in a 1983 study funded by B. Dalton Booksellers.

- The program has a local base and focus. It serves a definable constituency within a given locality, using indigenous staff.
- The program is independent, that is, it is autonomous and locally managed and operating outside the formal public education system. Decisions regarding program content and methods are made at the local level.
- The program serves learners traditional programs do not reach. It serves the "hard to reach" populations such as the poor and those at the second-grade reading level.
- The program has objectives of economic and social self-sufficiency which seek empowerment of the individual and development of the community and it seeks to end dependence.
- The program incorporates the learner's own objectives into the program design. It seeks to meet learner's expressed needs rather than develop a prescribed set of skills.
- The program emphasizes participation, with teachers or tutors playing a facilitative rather than a didactic role.[8]

The State Library has established guidelines to assist public libraries in developing permanent support structures to teach nonreaders. To attain this goal, public libraries participating in the campaign were required to form coalitions of adult nonreaders and other community organizations. Community coalitions of adult nonreaders, local governmental entities, community leaders from both the nonprofit and profit sectors, churches, welfare departments, labor, police departments, the criminal justice system and other organizations are formed to broaden the understanding of the importance of eradicating illiteracy. Public libraries were asked not only to identify existing partners such as Friends of the Library and literacy organizations, but also to establish working relations with other organizations in the community such as churches and community centers, in order to take the learning programs to the nonreaders. Community coalitions enable libraries to seek out and recruit adult nonreaders as well as tutors.

The future for the California Literacy Campaign

In May 1984, Assemblyman Tom Bates contacted the California STate Library and asked if he could help keep the California Literacy Campaign alive. With less than a month left in the state budget process, he submitted a budget augmentation of $3,500,000 to support the campaign from state general funds under the provisions of the California Library Services Act. Working very closely with the California Library Association, and library supporters statewide, the California State Library successfully supported the augmentation through the legislative process with a compromise budget of $2,635,000 for 1984–1985. The Governor approved the budget augmentation, calling for a Program Effectiveness Review before including the program in his 1985–1986 budget. In August, the California Library Services Board adopted preliminary program objectives to transform the California Literacy Campaign into a state-supported program base. The California State Library and the library community in California face incredible challenges over the next few months to insure that the campaign receives continuing state support. Given citizen support to date, there is no doubt. California Public Libraries can lead their communities in their continuing role as the "people's university." ▣

References

1. California State Library. Data Sheet. *Adult Illiteracy: Selected Statistics.* 1984.
2. U.S. Department of Education. *Alliance for Excellence: Librarians Respond to A Nation at Risk.* 1984.
3. National Commission on Excellence in Education. *A Nation at Risk: The Imperative for Educational Reform.* 1983.
4. California. Education Code. Section 19300.
5. California. A proclamation by the Governor. November 8, 1983.
6. California State Library. *Profiles of the 1984 Public Library Adult Literacy Programs in the California Literacy Campaign.* July 1984.
7. California State Library. *Standards Manual: California Literacy Campaign.* All Write Enterprises, Inc. (1983).
8. Association for Community-Based Education. *Adult Literacy: Study of Community Based Literacy Programs.* 1983.

Keeping a Dream Alive: Cooper Union Library

Irene Iwan

New York's first public library, now a private academic library specializing in architecture, art and engineering, celebrates its 125th anniversary this fall. The Cooper Union Library opened in November 1859 as part of the unique Cooper Union for the Advancement of Science and Art, the first tuition-free college in the United States, founded by industrialist and philanthropist Peter Cooper "open, free of charge, to boys, girls and adults from all levels of society . . . who can bring a sertificate [sic] of good morrel [sic] character from parent guardian or employer." The college, still tuition-free, today admits students on the basis of competitive exams to professional schools of architecture, art and engineering. The library that supports the institution's academic programs is currently a member of the Research Association of South Manhattan, a consortium that includes New York University, the New School, and Parsons School of Design. As a consortium member, it is part of the pilot project for the Geac integrated automated library system, utilizing the Geac circulation system and online catalog and RLIN cataloging.

The Cooper Union, 1984

Peter Cooper

Discussion of the Cooper Union and its library would be incomplete without a biographical sketch of the man whose vision it was. Peter Cooper, whose ancestors were among the earliest settlers in New York State, was

Irene Iwan *is Senior Assistant Librarian at the Cooper Union for the Advancement of Science and Art in New York City.*

born in New York City on February 12, 1791. The Cooper family moved frequently during Peter's childhood, leaving him no opportunity to attend school, a fact he always regretted, and which later severely handicapped him as an inventor. Having neither the training or knowledge to implement his technical ideas, he often wasted time and money on impractical devices. He was driven to succeed, and spent his free time working on inventions and reading all the books he could get his hands on. It was at this time he conceived of his lifelong dream: an evening school for the working classes, a public forum for the exchange of ideas, and a free reading room and research library.

At the end of his apprenticeship to a coachmaker, he went to work as a mechanic at a Hempstead, Long Island manufacturing firm, and managed to save enough of his wages to begin his own business a year later. Shortly after his marriage to Sarah Bedell, Cooper returned to New York City and opened a grocery store in the area where the Cooper Union now stands, then known as Bowery Village, a summer resort for New Yorkers. The Coopers bought much of the real estate in the area. Still restless, he sold the grocery in 1821 and purchased a glue factory. He learned all there was to know about glue manufacture, improved the process, and made his fortune selling Cooper's Glue, used by manufacturers of everything from pianos to books, and Cooper's Gelatin, the first gelatin sold in America. In 1837 he founded the Trenton Iron Works, which produced the world's first rolled iron beams for structural use, the basis for skyscraper architecture.

In addition to being an extremely successful and honest businessman and investor and a dedicated husband and father, Cooper remained a prolific inventor and active citizen. Among the many patents he held were those for a musical cradle (1815); an endless-chain device for towing boats, used on the Erie Canal (1820); the first rotary steam engine (1820); improvements in the methods for making salt (1824) and glue (1830); shutter fasteners (1877); and an endless-chain device for the propulsion of railway cars (1879). His most famous invention was the first steam engine for railroads—the Tom Thumb.

Politically active, Peter Cooper served as alderman for New York City's Sixteenth Ward, when he proposed and supervised the construction of the city's Croton water system (completed in 1842) and proposed the establishment of free schools and paid police and fire departments. In 1875, he was the Greenback presidential candidate.

As successful and varied as his life was, Peter Cooper always regretted the lack of a formal education. It remained his dream, while amassing a fortune, to build and endow a tuition-free, independent college, free from tax support and political contol. Over the years he continued to acquire land in the Bowery Village area, until he owned the entire block between 7th Street and Astor Place and between Third and Fourth Avenues, on which to build his vision—"a union of science and art."

The Cooper Union

Construction of the original Cooper Union building, now a city and national historic landmark, began in 1853 and represented major architectural as well as ideological foresight. Cooper worked on every detail of the six-story sandstone, brick and iron building, a forerunner of the modern skyscraper. It was the first large building to use wrought iron beams, made in Cooper's ironworks, then the largest in the nation. Although elevators were yet to be invented, he constructed a cylindrical shaft for the round elevator he envisioned. The elevator is still in operation today. A huge lecture hall was built in the basement so that, in the event of a fire, people would run up rather than down the stairs, lessening the chance of trampling. Most famous among the many historic public debates that took place in the Great Hall was Abraham Lincoln's 1860 "Right Is Might" campaign speech.

The Cooper Union opened on November 2, 1859. The charter and deed of trust conveyed to the Board of Trustees "all that piece and parcel . . . to be forever devoted to the advancement of science and art" and held them personally liable for any debt in excess of $5,000 at the end of any year. Today, the college continues to operate free of debt, largely from its endowment, alumni contributions, and rent received for the land on which the Chrysler Building stands. The charter further stipulated "The Cooper Union shall be devoted . . . to regular courses of instruction . . . free to all who shall attend . . . on the application of science to the useful occupations of life and on social and political science . . . to the support and maintenance of a free reading-room, of galleries of art, and of scientific collections . . . and to a school for instuction in the arts of design."

There was some public objection to education for the masses and the association of all social classes. Cooper's motives were greeted with suspicion. However, all courses were filled during the first night of registration, and Cooper's dreams were realized.

Over the years the curriculum has undergone many changes. Today, the institute offers a five-year program leading to a Bachelor of Architecture degree; a four-year program leading to the Bachelor of Fine Arts degree, with specialization in graphic design, painting, drawing, photography, film, video, printmaking and sculpture; and Bachelor and Master of Engineering degree programs in chemical, civil, electrical and mechanical engineering.

The original plans for the Cooper Union included a museum to house "examples of natural wonders . . . which would demonstrate the true philosophy of life." This was yet another of Cooper's progressive visions; at the time there were no museums in New York except the New York Historical Society and P.T. Barnum's "emporium of hoaxes, gadgets, uplift, exotica, and nature's dirty tricks." The Museum for the Arts of Decoration was not opened until 1897. In 1963 it was closed, largely for financial reasons. The trustees ruled that this "afterthought . . . does not contribute substantially to Cooper Union's broad education program in engineering, science, art and architecture." In 1967, the museum's holdings, including its reference library, were transferred to the Smithsonian Institution to create the Cooper-Hewitt Museum, also known as the Smithsonian Institution's National Museum of Design. It was stipulated that the collection be retained intact in New York City and supported by private funds. The museum is housed in the mansion of a former friend and financial protégé of Cooper's, Andrew Carnegie.

The Cooper Union Library

The charter of the Cooper Union provided for "the support and maintenance of a free reading-room . . . to improve and instruct those classes of the inhabitants of the City of New York whose occupations are such as to be calculated, in the opinion of the said board of trustees, to deprive them of proper recreation and instruction." The bylaws gave power to the Committee of the Reading-Room and Cabinets to "establish, furnish and maintain a comprehensive free reading-room for the working classes . . . for both sexes, with the books, plans, maps, pamphlets, publications and papers of the day, and all other conveniences, which they deem fit and proper to fulfill the aim and objects of the founding of the Cooper Union."

The new library, with a collection of almost 4,000 books and 400 periodicals, was the first public reading-room in New York. Open from 8 A.M. to 10 P.M. it aimed to draw workers from "less desirable places of resort." From the first day it was wildly successful: during the first year over 160,000 people visited the library, an average of 3,000 per week. By 1894, over 700,000 visitors were counted each year. While the tremendous popularity of the library confirmed Cooper's belief in its need, it placed an enormous physical strain on the collection and catalog. Almost half the books had to be rebound or replaced each year, and an average of 30,000 catalog cards had to be rewritten. The French and German catalogs, in almost constant use by the large immigrant population, were rewritten annually. Compounding the problem was a fixed classification system that required cards to be corrected each time books were shifted. This problem was alleviated when the library converted to the Dewey Decimal classification system in 1901, a project which took five years to complete.

Thieves stole many of the books and mutilated others to sell the illustrations. The library also suffered from overcrowding due to the many loiterers who sought refuge there. In 1881, upon the trustees' recommendation, a ticketing system was introduced to limit attendance. A day ticket was given to anyone not unclean, intoxicated or disorderly; a season ticket to those who registered their names. This system greatly cut down the incidence of book theft, as passes had to be returned to a guard who inspected exiting patrons. Yet, a May 1883 article in *Library Journal* reported "the reading room of the Cooper Union is a popular resort for eccentric people . . . most of the harmless lunatics at large in the city at one time or another have found their way there." Growth of the library collection depended on private donations, which did not materialize as anticipated. The trustees appealed for public support for "free books for the use of the great masses . . . to be read at home in the midst of their families . . . the true antidote to low drinking shops, to intemperance, vice and crime." With contributions few and far between, Peter Cooper ultimately came to the aid of the library with a $150,000 donation.

As the curriculum of the school evolved, more library support was required, causing philosophical tension between the library's public service and educational responsibilities. In 1910, the librarian of the Pratt Institute was invited to prepare a study of the Cooper Union Library. Pratt had responded to the same situation by transferring its public service unit to the new Brooklyn Public Library system. The report issued as a result of the study suggested that the New

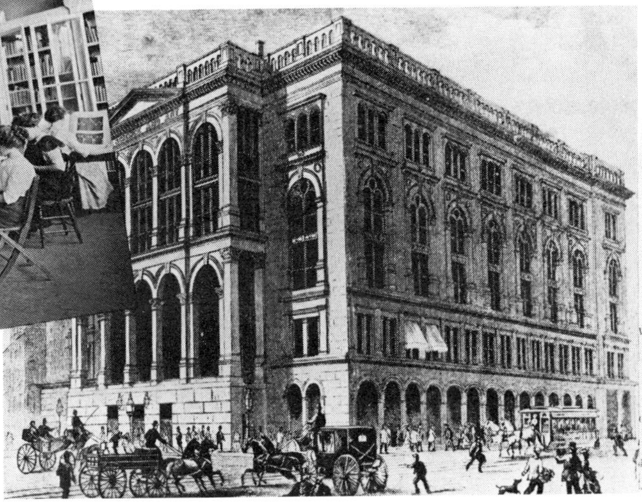

REGULATIONS

I Open daily, Except Sundays, from 8 A.M. to 10 P.M.

II Free to all Except Children unaccompanied By Parents or Guardian.

III CONVERSATION not Allowed.

IV Gentlemen Will Not wear their Hats.

V Books, Magazines, Papers, To be Handled With great care and Left in the Places where found.

VI Cleanliness in Person and Habits Required.

VII Smoking strictly Prohibited.

Gentlemen are Expected to TAKE care of their OATs And Hats, as They Are Liable To BE ken away Through Mistake OR by DESIGN.

York Public Library system, conceived and developed long after the Cooper Union, could now meet the library needs of the public. It recommended that the Cooper Union concentrate on improving the collection and services needed to support the institute's curriculum. A forcible reply was issued by Cooper's granddaughters, quoting his stated intent to always maintain a public library, and rejecting any suggestion that the Cooper Union Library abandon public service. As a result, the only suggestion of the Pratt report that was adopted was the establishment of a separate student's reference library in 1912, mostly comprised of science and engineering texts.

In 1938, administration of the combined Architecture and Art School library was transferred to the Main Library and technical services were centralized. The stated book selection policy by this time was the support of the educational programs of the Cooper Union. While the public was still welcome, attendance steadily declined. Most patrons came only to use the extensive national newspaper collection.

The library came into possession of over 50,000 original manuscripts, letters, pamphlets and ledgers of Peter Cooper and his son-in-law, Abram S. Hewitt, who had been Mayor of New York from 1886 to 1888, from the estate of Hewitt's son in 1940. Included in the collection were many documents relating to the history of New York City such as the laying of the Atlantic cable; the construction of the Brooklyn Bridge; the development of the public water supply system; planning for the rapid transit system; construction of the first skyscraper; testing the Bessemer steel process; expansion of western railroads; and correspondence detailing the controversial Tilden-Hayes presidential campaign. These documents constitute an important part of the Cooper Collection, the Cooper Union archive.

As the institute's academic programs continued to mature, the library eventually phased out public service altogether. By 1972, when plans were being made to merge the Art and Main Library collections to form one central college library, the public was admitted only to consult items held in the selective government documents depository collection, or with a continuing education registration card. All departments were moved to temporary quarters and the entire Foundation Building was gutted and renovated, according to the plans of Cooper graduate John Hejduk, dean of the School of Architecture. The exterior of the building was left intact, but a totally new structure was built within. The new library, located on the main floor to facilitate use by all departments, opened in 1974. It provides study space for 125 readers and has shelf space for 100,000 volumes and a separate slide/picture collection.

In 1975, the presidents of New York University, Cooper Union, and the New School for Social Research (including Parsons School of Design), commissioned a study of the library services of the four institutions to determine possible cooperative efforts that would reduce costs and improve services and resources. As a result of the study, a $250,000 grant was received from the Mellon Foundation in 1977 to develop a computer software program to establish a combined COM catalog and centralized acquisitions system and the official plan for the Research Library Association of South Manhattan was announced. Under the original contract, general management of the consortium was vested in the president of NYU. Reciprocal borrowing privileges were arranged for the undergraduate students and faculty of the four schools, and the Bobst Library at NYU began to process acquisitions and provide OCLC cataloging for all the libraries. CLSI circulation terminals were installed in each of the libraries and, as a byproduct of the circulation system, a consortium catalog was begun. In an effort to standardize records, Cooper Union once again changed its classification system, and began conversion to the Library of Congress system.

Under the new arrangement, the Bobst Library maintains a core humanities and general research collection for the consortium. Cooper Union transferred its holdings in these areas to NYU and now acquires and maintains a working collection in the areas of art, architecture, engineering and humanities. Concern over the effects of the consortium on the resources, services, and identity of the Cooper Union Library was initially expressed by much of the Cooper community. Widespread use of the consortium facilities by Cooper Union students and faculty, and return of administrative and acquisitions functions to the Cooper Union (the most controversial aspects of the original contract) have since alleviated these fears. In 1981, NYU joined the Research Libraries Group (RLG), greatly expanding the resources available to the consortium and adopted RLIN cataloging. An RLIN terminal at Bobst's main reference desk provides immediate access to bibliographic citations and location information of the holdings of major research libraries across the United States. NYU also installed a Geac computer for the consortium's integrated acquisitions, cataloging, and circulation. In September 1983 the Geac catalog, known as BOBCAT, came online—New York City's first computerized public access library catalog. The database contains over 350,000 records for books, magazines, music scores, sound recordings, and films and other media, representing twenty-five percent of the holdings of the consortium. It is searchable by author, title, a combination of author and title, subject, call number, ISBN, ISSN, and author, title or subject keyword. Terminals have recently been installed at the Cooper Union library.

Technology, cultural movements and economic conditions have greatly changed the world around the Cooper Union for the Advancement of Science and Art during the past 125 years, yet, in all its efforts to keep pace, one question still seems to guide the institute and its library—Is this what Peter Cooper would have wanted? ▣

IFLA in the Third World: The Nairobi Meeting

Esther Dyer

Pictured above in Nairobi are (from left) **Mr. Mussisci,** *chair of the Kenyan Organizing Committee;* **Vice President Mwai Kibaki** *shaking hands with* **Amando Brisso,** *UNESCO;* **Hans Peter Geh,** *IFLA Vice President;* **Margaret Wijnstroom,** *IFLA Secretary General; and* **Mr. Soisan,** *IFLA Executive Committee.*

The fiftieth general conference of the International Federation of Library Associations and Institutions (IFLA) met in Nairobi, Kenya at the Kenyatta Conference Center on August 17–24. Nearly seven hundred delegates from more than seventy countries joined more than two hundred Kenyan librarians at the IFLA General Conference to celebrate the organization's fiftieth anniversary. The theme of the congress was "The Basis of Library and Information Services for National Development," chosen to underscore the indispensability of library and information services in national development and in specific areas such as the promotion of the reading habit and adult education, manpower for library and information services, and library and information systems and services.

When it was proposed that IFLA hold its Golden Jubilee congress in Kenya, many members were skeptical about the venue. Yet IFLA, committed to the development of librarianship in Third World countries, had never held a conference in Africa. Remembering the needless qualms over the 1980 conference in the Philippines, there was less trepidation and more enthusiasm for a safari to Africa. Indeed most European and American delegates combined business with pleasure and took time to visit the game reserves and to sample the scenic beauty of Kenya.

The Kenyatta International Conference Center (KICC) in downtown Nairobi is an impressive and flexible facility accommodating the needs of all sizes of conference groups. Composed of a large plenary sessions hall, tower, and amphitheater with a conical African style roof, the KICC occupies a total of 500,000 square feet. Finding meeting rooms, however, proved to be a major obstacle since the identification plates to many rooms were missing and had been hurriedly written in black marker on teak

Esther Dyer *manages the archives and library reference center of Blue Cross Blue Shield of Greater New York. She is chair of IFLA's statistics section.*

wood, visible only at certain angles. We were informed that costs were prohibitive and prevented the duplication of maps to the elegant but confusing conference center, so perseverance proved the key to finding meeting rooms.

Registration was no easy matter, complicated by currency restrictions. The national bank that received registration fees did not forward to the Kenyan organizing committee a list of sources of funds. Dollars had to be matched with registration forms and some were hopelessly lost. Registration often took more than an hour, despite the determined efforts of Peter Weche, Kenyan organizer, and the volunteer staff responsible for this herculean task. East and West German participants were listed as coming from a single nation. My own registration did not appear among the USA delegates. In perusing all registration forms, I finally found myself listed under Barbados. Invitations to events and badges were not ready on schedule, causing further confusion.

Registration and the perennial hunt for meeting rooms were borne with the good grace of the seasoned conference-goer. Unfortunately, the major government and private funding—necessary for IFLA to succeed—did not meet expectations, and the organizing committee had to cut corners in several areas. The primary problem was the lack of copying facilities and the time it took to have anything typed or copied. A limited number of papers were available for distribution and even fewer papers were available in translation. In theory, all papers should be translated into the offical IFLA languages—English, French, German and Russian—and ready for delegates at all meetings. In practice, due to problems in securing speakers for Nairobi (some perennial IFLA attendees presented two, three or more papers as did several Kenyan representatives), many papers were hand-carried by speakers or sent with friends who read them. Participants had to make do. Nor was it easy for committee members to get access to typewriters and other office machines, normally required during the week to adequately conduct the business of IFLA. The headquarters staff spent the better part of one day testing some two hundred typewriters in the KICC to find five that worked. Committee members did what had to be done in the only way possible, and handed in material in longhand. Quite an irony for a conference that flies the banner of high technology.

The magic

The magic of an international meeting was apparent despite the minor irritants. The fiftieth IFLA conference attracted a number of participants from African countries who shared experiences and enabled regular IFLA attendees to gain insight into some of the problems facing countries in development. Discussions of the rapid transition from the oral tradition to the written record and the introduction of technology proved to be both fascinating and inspiring. African nations are compressing such changes into the span of a few years while they evolved more slowly in other societies. From this perspective the meeting of IFLA, the international organization committed to library development worldwide, was inspiring for those in attendance and a landmark event in the development of libraries in Africa.

The importance of libraries and of the IFLA congress in Kenya was eloquently described by His Excellency, the Vice President of the Republic of Kenya, Honorable Mwai Kibaki, in his provocative speech during the opening ceremonies. He stressed the importance of libraries in the social and economic development of all countries and especially in developing countries that stand at the crossroads of primitive and technological society. In Kenya, as in other African nations, several obstacles must be overcome before the nation can fully enter the information age. These obstacles include: the prohibitive costs of publishing reading materials; the difficulty in establishing an appropriate infrastructure for the publishing industry; and the environmental conditions to be overcome in rural areas to provide adequate access to reading materials and to promote literacy. The oral tradition is dying and with that cataclysmic change comes an even greater need for published materials to carry on the history and to become the vehicle for the transfer of knowledge. Today the nation is attempting to store the available information by developing and using the university library system and incorporating modern technology. According to Vice President Kibaki, Kenya must move speedily from oral history to today's computer so that the oral historical records are not lost to posterity.

In Kenya today, even when a library is built, it is often impossible for the people to use it properly. Users are not allowed to borrow books, prohibiting many from having access to knowledge. Even if borrowing were allowed, most homes are without electricity and the conditions are such that books would be destroyed. Barriers such as time and distance from the library combine to make the reading population outside the schools quite small. Vice President Kibaki spoke with conviction, and no one could doubt the sincerity of his and the government's concern with libraries and literacy, and their genuine interest in developing appropriate information infrastructures.

The Minister for Cultural and Social Services, Kenneth Matiba, in his closing remarks to the congress, echoed the theme of Vice President Kabaki. He stressed the urgent need for more primary schools and recreational centers with library facilities, thus creating awareness in the community of the importance of reading for both pleasure and educational advancement. The Minister pledged continued government support for these events.

"School libraries need facilities," "Conference was a 'great success'," "Emphasis on reading and low readership explained" were headlines on the closing day of the IFLA conference in the *Daily Nation,* one of two national dailies in Nairobi. In commenting on press coverage, IFLA President

Elsa Granheim said, "I cannot remember seeing so many newspaper columns ever during any IFLA conference. I hope the media will continue taking an interest in library services." Indeed, at all levels of government and in the media the recognition of the role of libraries in national development was apparent.

The gift

Some members of IFLA also tried to leave a lasting and practical monument to librarianship in Kenya. The final stage of preparation for the conference began two years ago with a preliminary visit of IFLA dignitaries to Nairobi, where they met with ministry and other government officials. During these meetings the Kenyan officials asked IFLA if the organization could help in developing school libraries, as part of Kenya's national fight against illiteracy begun in 1978. IFLA contacted the Dutch Public Library Service with good results. The support of Dutch librarians and of IFLA exhibitors (Swets and Zaitlinger, Springer Verlag, K.G. Saurs, and Elsevier) was generous enough to provide books, typewriters, television sets, tape recorders, and other materials to equip two model school libraries. Bomefa, a library equipment supplier, designed an exhibit for the conference that was to have fully equipped the two libraries with shelving, desks, and other furnishings. The proposed donation totaled more than $60,000 including a check for $6,500 to cover costs of establishing the two model school libraries.

While this gift responded to the government's plea for help, Kenyan internal politics proved an insurmountable obstacle. Although the Minister of Culture cleared all bills of lading and welcomed the gift, the ministry that deals with import/export held the materials at the docks in Mombasa and requested duty for the gift in excess of $20,000. IFLA officers and the publishers met with government officials but in the end too little was done too late. The almost tribal rivalry among the different ministries proved fatal to the project.

Publishers were forced to use creative tactics and plain bribery to free their goods. Even then most had to be content with displaying printed brochures and a few other items. Undaunted, the intrepid exhibitors located themselves in the central meeting place, where they carried on the business of meeting clients and greeting potential customers. Exhibitors rescued their goods by shipping them back home or on to Zimbabwe for an international book fair. At the closing ceremonies, the cash gift was given to the Ministry of Culture to help in the development of school libraries, but the major portion of the gift—equipment and some books—went to Gambia, where the materials were accepted without restriction.

The conference was an exercise in futility for the exhibitors who had come with the best of intentions and who left with little to show for their efforts. As disappointing as this was, however, the tragedy of Kenyan politics is such that Customs also refuses to clear cargo containers of food donated by charitable organizations to alleviate the severe drought and famine conditions in much of the country. Local representatives of the charities are faced with the same dilemma as the publishers and library providers—they are asked for a tax on a donation that could ultimately help Kenya. Clearly, Kenya is experiencing growing pains. Red tape and rivalry are combining to impede progress in many areas.

Despite this disappointment, when I asked Margreet Wijnstroom, Secretary General of IFLA, whether the first IFLA conference in Africa had been a success, she replied affirmatively, citing the burgeoning interest of African librarians in the organization and the level of participation of Kenyan librarians. She felt that, in retrospect, the Golden Jubilee conference of IFLA would reaffirm the organization's commitment to librarianship in the Third World and would provide tangible evidence of the organization's efforts in this direction. An editorial in *Mwalimu,* a Kenyan educational journal, reinforced the importance of holding IFLA in Kenya. "The first mark will be left on Kenyans who have not known much about libraries and what they stand for." Further, the international congress has "created an international fraternity that facilitates the sharing of international wealth of knowledge contained in world libraries." And lastly, the interaction among often competing library factions in Kenya will be channeled into constructive cooperation to assure the success of the congress.

The social programs

The IFLA conference program was a bit compressed. Traditionally, IFLA is held from Saturday to Saturday, with committee meetings conducted on the first day. Thursday is generally tour day. However, the Nairobi conference began on Sunday for committee members and Thursday morning became the time for the second required committee meetings. Accompanying persons and some participants were able to take advantage of the full-day tours offered to the tea plantations, the Earth Satellite Station, the Mayers farm, and the Akamba Carving Center at Wamunyu. For those of us embroiled in IFLA committee work, the visit to the National Game Park in the afternoon was a delight. Photographing zebras, elephants, lions and other wildlife was a welcome change of pace.

The Minister for Culture and Social Services, the Honorable Kenneth Matiba, entertained IFLA delegates at a cocktail party in the garden of the Parliament Building on Monday evening. The event provided the group with an opportunity to mingle with old friends and strike up new acquaintances. While many who made the pilgrimage to Kenya were expecting stereotypical hot and muggy weather, the climate was surprisingly mild. During the day, the temperature hovered between sixty and seventy degrees, and at night fell as low as forty.

A highlight of the social program was the visit to the Bomas (homes) and the large conical-shaped amphitheater provided an appropriate background for a special presentation of traditional tribal dances for all the IFLA participants.

Most participants availed themselves of the opportunity to see the sights of Kenya and some of the surrounding countries. Conversation focused on after-conference plans and the potential excitement of a safari. I went on safari with fourteen other Americans and although I'm not an outdoorsman, the beauty of the scenery and the wonder of the animals in their native habitat were enough to prompt me to take the sunrise game tours and to thoroughly enjoy myself.

Pre- and postconferences

A preconference seminar on Education for Librarianship at the Grassroots Level addressed a host of issues including: national planning for education; availability of materials and the problems of import duties; school libraries as a foundation for a literate society; and curriculum content for education and training programs for information workers. Unlike many seminars, the focus was on practical and attainable measures that could be used in the immediate future to advance the profession in Africa. The recommendations of the seminar ranged from developing a module to teach core skills to librarians, to establishing model job descriptions and organizational structures based on a representative survey of library systems in different countries.

The postconference on Statistics for English-speaking African Countries was sponsored by the Section on Statistics. As chair of the section, I had a close view of the problems inherent in organizing such a seminar. Securing speakers—IFLA pays no honorarium nor does it reimburse expenses for speakers—was difficult, and identifying appropriate participants from the African nations was even more challenging. Karl Neubauer, ISBN international director, managed to secure some funds from IFLA and UNESCO to partially underwrite the travel expenses of participants. It remained for us to complete negotiations with hotels for rooms and receptions. The local organizer, Peter Weche, was most helpful but haggling over hotel charges was akin to buying in the markets or bazaar. There was ample opportunity to practice negotiating skills. Communications are not easy between Africa and Europe or the United States, and it was not until the opening reception that we were sure of who would attend. In all, nearly thirty participants from ten African nations, plus nine speakers participated in the two days of deliberation addressing the themes of management use of statistics; UNESCO statistics; national planning; and standards for statistical analysis. As with most IFLA meetings, the program was only a part of the attraction of the seminar—the interactions with colleagues and the exchange of ideas and information were paramount.

Program highlights

Some two hundred programs were offered at the Nairobi conference addressing the special concerns of a variety of libraries. Due to problems in interpretation and availability of papers in translation, many of the sessions had spotty attendance and failed to hold the attention of participants. There were some notable exceptions, however. For example, the International ISBN Agency premiered its new film "ISBN and Its Uses" which explains the international numbering system for books, the structure of the ISBN and the administration of the system. The film shows potential applications for publishers and the book trade, and for libraries. It is available from the International ISBN Agency in Berlin.

A sampler of program titles illustrates the richness of the schedule: "Library and Information Services for Cultural Minorities" by E.J. Josey, President American Library Association; "The Dissemination of Patent Information by Libraries," Eckhard Derday (Germany); "Problems Concerning the Function of Librarians in Management Positions" by R. Bruyne (Netherlands); "Library Service for the Blind in Kenya" by J. Ng'anga'a (Kenya); "The Basis of Library and Information Services for National Development", by J. Dosunmu (Nigeria); "Serials for the Poor" by T. Mlaki (Tanzania), and "Library and Continuing Education With Implications for Developing Countries" by David Bender, Special Libraries Association.

The association plans ahead

The committees and divisions were kept busy by putting the final touches on their new medium-term programs, due to go into effect in 1986. The timetable for future conferences is so tight that committees are asked to determine next year's program session by the end of October. Committees were also concerned with securing representatives from many member countries on their committees. IFLA is composed of over 1,100 associations and institutions representing 120 countries. As such, it provides a forum for intellectual discussion, exchange of ideas and new approaches to old questions, and the cultivation of the kinds of new questions that sprout in international soil. IFLA is an expensive professional item for most American librarians. Few members are subsidized by their institutions, and most of them depend on the tax deduction for attending a professional meeting to help them finance their participation. Some colleagues from other countries are fully reimbursed but as the world economy tightens, these institutions are becoming less and less eager to send representatives. External financing and funding for participation from developed as well as developing countries may prove to be a major challenge for IFLA in the years ahead. The fifty-first general conference will be held next year in Chicago, Illinois, August 18–25, and will provide an opportunity for American librarians to attend what promises to be one of the largest IFLA congresses ever. Planning ahead, IFLA is scheduled to be in Toyko, Japan (1986); Brighton, England (1987); Australia (1988); and, tentatively, France (1989). ▣

SPECIAL REPORT:

Art Milner

Doing Business With Philadelphia

An advertising agency with a new account, a wine distributor, recently needed information quickly in order to form its advertising and public relations campaign for the client. A call to the Free Library of Philadelphia's Computer Based Information Center yielded immediate results. Using the PTS Prompt database, the high speed printer rolled out nine abstracts from trade and other publications.

The agency learned that the average American annually drinks a total of 182 gallons of all kinds of beverages—beer, milk, soft drinks, wine, coffee and water. The South, with only thirty-two percent of the population, accounts for forty-eight percent of the nation's tea consumption. And the Northeast, with twenty-two percent of the population, drinks thirty percent of the wine. Eighty-five percent of all wine in the United States is imbibed by only fifteen percent of the population.

The abstracts also revealed that we probably will drink our wine from boxes and cans in the future. Fifty percent of all wine in Australia is now packaged in boxes. Projections for 1995 show that the same will happen in the United States, with boxes and cans prevailing in the industry.

Art Milner *is the public information officer for the Free Library of Philadelphia.*

Pat Kelker, *librarian in the Computer Based Information Center, helps a patron select from the more than 130 available databases.*

While the wine saga may make great trivia talk for the uninvolved, for the advertising agency it was vital. With the information supplied by Free Library resources, the agency was able to recommend a marketing and advertising campaign, pinpointing markets by regions, demographics, drinking habits and a host of other criteria.

An attorney is handling a negligence case on behalf of the parents of a six-year-old girl who was killed in an auto accident. He dials the government publications department at The Free Library of Philadelphia. Objective: to compute the potential earnings of the child had she lived an average lifetime in order to determine the amount of damages to be sought in a suit against the insurance company of the defendant.

"Were the parents professional people?" the librarians asked. "The parents are both physicians," was the reply. Once the age of the child and the occupation of the parents were disclosed, several different sources were consulted. The staff was then able to come up with the solution. In a few minutes, the attorney had the figure he needed.

The question and response were part of a routine day for librarians in the Government Publications Department. Last year the department answered more than 13,000 telephone queries and 12,000 in-person requests for information.

The services of the department, like all units of the Free Library, are free and callers remain anonymous unless they choose not to be. "Our job is to give information. Who you are and for what purpose you want the information is your own business," says William Felker, head of the Government Publications Department. "We simply want to furnish information if we can."

Many callers, however, mention their occupations and the reasons for their call. Felker, therefore estimates that about forty percent of those seeking information in the department are attorneys, searching for information by phone or in person.

While the Government Publications Department is heavily used by attorneys, a reccent survey conducted by the Free Library's Office of Planning and Development disclosed that corporate and business-related clients view the entire library as an information resource.

During the weeklong survey of corporate use conducted in the Central Library, regional libraries, and the Free Library's Mercantile Library, 438 business or business-related clients were interviewed. Almost every department was consulted by members of the business community.

Advertising agencies, financial and insurance institutions, marketing offices, attorneys, manufacturers, and radio and television news departments were among major categories, as were architectural and engineering consultants and a variety of other organizations, representing the entire spectrum of business activity.

Of those surveyed, attorneys were among the heaviest users, often working on behalf of their corporate or business clients.

What kinds of information are lawyers after? The Equal Opportunity Employment Act, the much-amended Security and Exchange Act of 1934, and questions on municipal and federal finance and tax reform bills head the popularity list.

The review of expenditures in *The Census of Governments* which contains the budgets of most large cities was in demand during the 1976 financial crises in New York and Philadelphia.

The Government Publications Department can almost count on several calls a day on the Social Security Act of 1934. A change in the bill has been made almost every year since its enactment so attorneys are continually calling to find the latest versions.

Intent of the law is a frequent objective of attorneys who call the department. Lawyers review the paperwork that accumulates during a bill's trip through Congress. Supporting such a search are the *Digest of Public General Bills* and *The House Calendar*. Also used frequently are transcripts of congressional debates, and *Congressional Record* and its predecessors. *Congressional Committee Prints* are ideal for the layman or the expert who is in a hurry.

Included also in the holdings of the department are a full run of *The Federal Register;* all editions and revisions of most titles of *The Code of Federal Regulations* since the first edition was published in June, 1938; *Statutes at Large; Revised Statutes;* reports of presidential commissions; census materials and statistics; decisions of regulatory agencies; and annual reports.

Often attorneys' questions relate to everyday litigation. Recently, a department librarian received a question about safety belts. Objective: to find specifications for the manufacture of safety belts in order to decide if a suit against a seat-belt firm should be instituted following an automobile accident. The specifications were found in the *Code of Federal Regulations.*

With the aid of microfilm printers, such as the one operated by **Sheri Reinhart,** *library assistant in the Microforms and Newspapers Department, businesses can copy magazine and newspaper articles available only on microfilm.*

"Because of the resources of the Government Publications Department," says Kelker, "we are a natural resource for the business community." For example, *The American Statistics Index* and *Statistical Reference Index* can be used to find sources of income and demographic information including educational level or the number of skilled workers in a given area. The service is used frequently by those planning new plants or service organizations. *The Survey of Current Business, Employment and Earnings, The Area Wage Survey* and the *Consumer Price Index* are used constantly while the *Patent Gazette* provides abstracts of patents.

For those who wish to do business with government, two volumes are indispensable—*Department of Commerce Standards* and *The General Service Administration Standards.* "For example," says Felker, "if you want to sell sheets to the Veterans Administration hospitals you need to know such details as the size and quality. The Defense Department has its own volume of specifications."

For business, and the advertising and public relations agencies and the consultants who work on their behalf, the resources of the library can often mean the difference between failure and success. At the Free Library, users now have the choice of using the Computer Based Information Center with more than 130 databases with charges ranging from forty-two cents to two dollars per minute or using conventional print or microfiche sources. Often, computer-based information saves enormous amounts of time and is able to accomplish objectives impossible without them. Some case histories tell the story:

- A toy manufacturer needs studies done on memory with regard to sex differences; articles written on marketing of toys; recent surveys of advertising recall; the names and addresses of all toy corporations in the U.S. broken down by share of market, number of employees, also alphabetized and listed according to zip code.
- The marketing manager of a small textile firm needs information on: organic dyes and the pigment industry since 1976; references to government-funded inventions for deriving polymetric compositions from flour; a list of manufacturers of children's, women's, and men's clothing in the U.S. broken down by region and share of market.
- A public relations firm with a variety of clients and working under a deadline needs to have: a list of items published about Michael Jackson in the last few months; articles on the possible impact of energy on lifestyles; the effect of voice on the mechanical performance of rats; and articles about bras for joggers.

These were all problems that were

solved in hours, often in minutes, by the Free Library's computerized information services—a battery of about 150 specialized data banks covering some one hundred million citations on almost every conceivable subject.

John Reiff, president of JRA Associates, a Philadelphia-based marketing communications agency, is a frequent user of the computerized information services.

"For a client who specialized in temporary office and storage space and trailer rental," says Reiff, "we needed statistics on short-term trailer use. We found it by using the Computer Based Information Center.

"The Japan Market Research Institute needed information on toys," continues Reiff. "Using the computer capabilities of the Free Library we came up with share of market, trends-in-toys articles and other information. It helped us to construct a successful campaign." For another client, an oil transport firm, Reiff says he was able to come up with valuable information on transport of oil by tankers and barges.

There is no charge for the use of three of the Free Library's databases: Viewtext, the full-text printout of the *Philadelphia Inquirer* and the *Philadelphia Daily News;* the Vocational Information through Computer Systems (VICS); and the IAC Search Helper.

Vilma Lieberman, who heads the Free Library's Computer Based Information Center, says she first determines the objective of those who need information before agreeing to do a computer search. "I do it to save the user money." Often the same objective can be accomplished by using the conventional print or microfiche sources, for which there is no charge. "For example," she says, "the PTS database has a price tag of two dollars per minute with a charge of forty-eight cents per citation. That could be more than the traffic will bear for a business just starting up." Recently, she suggested the relatively inexpensive *Electronic Yellow Pages* rather than a complex computer search for a young man starting a business. He had no need to begin with a national search. The *Yellow Pages* yielded a list of potential customers to fill his immediate needs.

In other library department, Blue Cross of Pennsylvania researchers were able to determine the number of doctors in the state per 100,000 population and, using the Newspaper Department, were able to confirm the date of an editorial in the *Philadelphia Inquirer*. "We were able to find the farewell address of Dwight D. Eisenhower when he left office in 1961. We needed it for a speech to be given by one of our executives. The text was found in *Vital Speeches* and saved the day."

The Free Library staff learned a long time ago that the corporate information needs of business mirror those of their eclectic nonbusiness counterparts.

"Recently," says a librarian for a large insurnce firm, "I called the Literature Department to find the title of two public relations publications." She continued, "A few weeks ago one of our members of the board knew the subtitle of a needed book, *Everything Insurance Companies Don't Want You to Know*. But the title eluded him. The library gave me the title and also found the book. We also found the full text of a newspaper article through Viewtext, the database of the *Philadelphia Inquirer* and the *Philadelphia Daily News*."

The Free Library's computerized information services print out facts to whet the appetite of any marketing or advertising person. For example, stored in the data banks is information on 117,000 plants operated by 67,000 companies accounting for more than ninety percent of the total United States industrial activity. In addition, there are more than five million abstracts and articles covering business and economics.

"A printout from a keyboard terminal," says Jim Woy, who heads the Free Library's Mercantile Library, "can contain a precise rundown on certain plants including the number of workers, production figures, market share of a particular product, and even current growth figures—and the information is usually updated quarterly.

"When an abstract is received," he says, "it contains the name of the publication in which the information appeared, its author and date. Then you just head for the library shelf." By using the computerized information services at Mercantile, continues Woy, one can obtain current forecasts for industry and projections for products, keep up-to-date on the competition, or get information on mergers and acquisitions.

One service that Woy is particularly proud of is the computer's ability to come up with lists of corporations in almost any order and classification.

At the Mercantile Library marketing managers eager to promote national or regional sales receive information in minutes that marketing dreams are made of. For example, the top one hundred United States manufacturing companies may be printed out in descending order, or according to share of market, number of employees, or other valuable categories.

There is, of course no way to pinpoint which clients are using the library for business purposes. Pursuing their corporate objectives, they may easily be mistaken for Shakespearean experts in the Literature Department, or a historian in Social Science and History. Take the case of Cece Hinds, a public relations account executive at Lewis and Gilman, one of Philadelphia's larger advertising agencies. "Dixie Marathon, a former client," Hinds says, "was about to hold its first national sales meeting in a decade. Regional meetings for the client had been the rule before. Therefore we needed a dramatic opener. The solution was to link significant events in the operations of Dixie Marathon during the past decade to those of the world and the nation. Events and graphics describing them would then be presented as a slide film titled 'Reflections' and projected on a large screen."

During a two-hour visit to the li-

continued on page 238

Dale Nelson:

Dateline Washington

Deacidification at LC

Congress has approved the Library of Congress's plans for book deacidification, but not without warning library officials that using volatile gas to prolong the life of books could be dangerous to people.

In the weeks before their pre-election adjournment, both the House and Senate authorized the appropriation of $11.5 million to build a plant at the Army's Fort Detrick (Md.), about fifty miles from Washington, to deacidify books with the aid of diethyl zinc (DEZ).

The library estimates that each year more than 77,000 books, out of its collection of about eighty million items, deteriorate so badly that they can no longer be used. Library officials told Congress that pumping DEZ into the books would prolong their life expectancy, estimated at thirty to forty years, by two to five times.

The officials also acknowledged, in House hearings, that the gas is highly flammable when brought into contact with air or water. But they said they had worked out precautions during tests and "there will be absolutely no safety risks to personnel or books with the Library of Congress process."

The House Public Works Committee, however, in approving the authorization, expressed the hope "that the Library of Congress would not become complacent with the safety achievements they have achieved to date and would continue their research to develop additional innovative methods to eliminate the hazardous risks associated with the use of DEZ."

The facility is expected to be able to handle 500,000 books per year at first and 1.5 million per year eventually. The cost is estimated at $3.50 per volume initially, dropping to $1.80, which compares to a cost of about $30 per volume for putting the books on microform.

The proposed facility will consist of twin vacuum chambers rectangular

Dale Nelson *is a journalist who covers the Washington scene for WLB.*

in shape to accommodate pallets loaded with books. The building will include staging areas for book loading and unloading, a series of rehumidification rooms, and a test chamber to be used for further development work. The Army Corps of Engineers will construct the facility in consultation with an engineering and architectural firm. The cost of the building is estimated at $3.5 million. The remaining $8 million of the appropriation will go for laboratory facilities, equipment and other expenses. The expenses are authorized over a period of five years.

The process involves loading books and other library materials into a chamber which is then sealed and into which gaseous diethyl zinc is injected. The gas reacts with the paper, neutralizing the acid and leaving a thin residue of zinc oxide to prevent further deterioration.

"The cost of constructing this facility is a small price to pay in order to preserve the very embodiment of knowledge—the hand-held book," Representative James Howard (D–N.J.), chairman of the Public Works Committee, told the House.

Nonprofit record lending

Congress also revisited what Representative Hamilton Fish, Jr. (D–N.Y.) called "the difficult problem of the adaptation of our copyright law to new technologies."

Both houses approved legislation prohibiting the rental, lease or lending of phonorecords without the authority of the copyright owners.

The bill was aimed at commercial record rental establishments that rent phonorecords for periods of twenty-four to seventy-two hours, for fees ranging from ninety-nine cents to $2.50 per disc. The House Judiciary Committee was told that many of the establishments also sell blank cassettes and one of them advertised, "Never, ever, buy another record."

The House added to the Senate-passed bill a provision exempting nonprofit libraries and educational institutions. In recommending the change, the Judiciary Committee said it intended "that the legislation not interfere with the usual lending activities of nonprofit libraries or the educational programs of nonprofit educational institutions when the rental, lease, or lending of phonorecords is part of their customary activities and not in the nature of a commercial enterprise.

"These activities must be directly related to the ordinary lending activities of the nonprofit library or the educational mission of the nonprofit educational institution," the committee said. "By requiring the lending activity to be 'for nonprofit purposes,' the committee does not intend to bar a small fee to cover administrative costs of the lending program, if that is customary. However, this provision is not intended to allow nonprofit libraries and nonprofit educational institutions to engage in record rentals for the purpose of raising funds to support other activities."

Nixon files to be opened

Not only the Watergate tapes but White House files on outer space, education, peace, American Indians, and recreation policy are expected to be in the first batch of materials from the Nixon presidency made available by the National Archives.

The timetable for release of the material is uncertain as the General Services Administration and Justice Department are trying to draw up new rules governing use of the collection. Former Nixon aides successfully challenged the original rules last fall.

The tapes and papers are being prepared in a brick warehouse on a dead-end street in Alexandria, Virginia, in a project that has cost the government an estimated $5 million.

The collection includes forty million pages of documents, three million feet of movie film and videotape and 350,000 official White House photographs.

"When the papers are finally opened, the heavy demand for materials from the speical Watergate files is expected to be so great that most of the staff will have to work on research requests," James Hastings, project director, recently told *The Washington Post.*

Gang Busters given to LC

Hitler addressing the Reichstag, the last train ride on the Sixth Avenue El, and Beverly Sills singing a Rinso White commercial are part of an archive of the early days of radio that has been presented to the Library of Congress.

RKO General, Inc., presented the library with a collection of news, music and drama discs, as well as scripts, musical arrangements and information about the operation of WOR-AM in New York.

The collection covers sixty years beginning on February 22, 1922, when WOR went on the air from Bamberger's Department Store. The station became a subsidiary of RKO in 1955.

Radio historians have expressed particular interest in a group of materials relating to the radio work of Phillips H. Lord, a producer and writer whose name is familiar to those who remember "Gang Busters." Scholars will be able to hear transcriptions of "Gang Busters" programs, examine drafts of scripts for the program, and view copies of FBI documents that formed the basis for episodes of the program.

The collection is split among the Motion Picture, Broadcasting and Recorded Sound Division, the Manuscript Division, and the Music Division of the library.

Reading stamp

President Lincoln reads to his son, Tad, on a twenty-cent commemorative stamp honoring "A Nation of Readers."

The stamp was designed by Bradbury Thompson of Riverside, Connecticut, who also designed the Library of Congress commemorative stamp of 1982.

Librarian of Congress Daniel Boorstin and Postmaster General William Bolger were featured speakers for an October 16 first-day-of-issue ceremony at the Library of Congress.

Ann McGrath:

Eye on Publishing

"Now will you believe me when I say there are too many books being published?"

Some three years ago, the Association of American Publishers surveyed its membership about experience with foreign book piracy. Just how serious was the problem? the Association wondered. Certainly British publishers, who typically had exported more than half their books, seemed to think there was cause for concern. But except for those houses with significant export trade or foreign operations—publishers like John Wiley, McGraw-Hill, Prentice-Hall, Addison-Wesley and Harper & Row—American firms hadn't made much noise. Most were happily preoccupied with domestic business, the lion's share of their trade.

The evidence turned up by that questionnaire, as well as the Association's longstanding concern about copyright issues, lit a fire under the AAP. "We found a total of sixty-eight countries where piracy had occurred," says Carol Risher, the group's director of copyright and new technology. Since then, a lot has happened. Working as one of six members of the Alliance for Intellectual Property Protection (with the Recording Industry Association of America, the Motion Picture Association of America, the International Anti-Counterfeit Coalition, the National Music Publishers Association, and the Computer and Business Equipment Manufacturers Association) the AAP has prodded Congress into action and can proudly report that progress has indeed been made.

How large a problem are we talking about? Alexander Burke, an executive vice-president with McGraw-Hill Book Co. and former president of McGraw-Hill International, has estimated that if you consider all types of intellectual property theft—of films, software, computers, sound recordings and even blue jeans as well as books—piracy worldwide has reached outrageous proportions. More than $10 billion in counterfeit merchandise hits the market each year, he thinks. Books, says Risher, are particularly vulnerable to counterfeiting. "All you have to do is take a U.S. book and create a photo offset plate," she explains. "There is no design work or creative effort involved at all."

Of that $10 billion annual total, probably $1 billion represents losses to publishers of English-language books. And it's likely, Risher says, that seventy percent of those are pirated from U.S. publishers. The underground nature of piracy—and the historically lackadaisical attitude on the part of many governments in culprit nations about cracking down—means the estimates can only be estimates, but they are enough to make businessmen and politicians interested in both intellectual property rights and trade sit up and take notice.

In his presentation this past September to the Senate Judiciary Committee's Subcommittee on Patents, Copyrights, and Trademarks and to the House Foreign Affairs Committee's Subcommittee on Western Hemisphere Affairs, Register of Copyrights David Ladd noted three fundamental conditions that have sustained book piracy historically—in the United States as well as abroad—and that continue to do so. One, he said, is the failure of certain countries "to acknowledge a property interest of an author, publisher, or both to control the circulation of intellectual works." Second is "the allure of profits to be made, with a minimum of investment and risk." Third is a demand for works that cannot be met at locally acceptable prices.

Since there is no such thing as an international copyright—no automatic protection in any country for the works of foreign authors—Ladd underlined the need for efforts among concerned states to define, strengthen, and standardize their requirements

Ann McGrath, *a freelance writer based in New York, covers the publishing world for WLB.*

for eligibility under existing copyright law. The need for protection is growing, he believes, because the "information age" is upon us. "Informational works and technologies have drawn the world, and its markets, closer together—indeed, created true world markets," he reported. "They have affected the content of national and regional cultures and how they define themselves. The stakes in revenues, employment, and trade balances are huge and growing, absolutely and relatively."

The intellectual property rights coalition members have worked hard to educate Congress, and have met with the Secretary of State, the Secretary of Commerce, Trade Ambassador William Brock, and the Commissioner of Customs. In August 1983, when President Reagan's Caribbean Basin Economic Recovery Act became law, a publisher-pushed amendment defending the integrity of intellectual property passed into law with it. Any of the twenty-seven countries eligible for American aid under the program, declared the amendment, would be required to beef up their laws protecting United States copyrights, patents, and trademarks. The Dominican Republic, consequently, is currently working with help from the coalition on an acceptable protective law.

Without a doubt, says Risher, government trade policy can be publishers' most potent weapon in the piracy war. Most recently, the coalition has focused its efforts on getting Congress to attach similar caveats to the "generalized system of preference" program, which helps developing countries get their exports duty-free entry into the United States market. The legislation that had been introduced—which was passed by the 98th Congress just prior to the session's close—"links the trade benefits a country can expect, to whether it has put in place adequate and effective protection for intellectual property," Risher explains.

In addition, representatives from this country, including Burke of McGraw-Hill and Leo Albert, chairman of Prentice-Hall International, travelled to offenders Taiwan, Singapore, and Korea last spring and summer to convince the governments of those countries to cooperate. Taiwan is now working on its copyright law, Risher says; Korea and Singapore, which both have laws on the books, need to expand protection to cover books not originally published within their borders. "South Korea is probably responsible for about $100 million of book piracy annually," Risher estimates. "The whole Pacific Basin? For $250 million." Burke and Albert estimate that, for all intents and purposes, the book marketplace in South Korea exists entirely because of pirated works.

An educational videotape about book piracy in Arabic, Chinese, Spanish, and English—featuring Brock, Burke, Albert, Register of Copyrights Ladd, author Bette Bao Lord, and *Time* magazine writer Richard Schickel—has been produced by the United States Information Agency for distribution to cultural institutions overseas.

All kinds of books are susceptible—best-sellers, paperbacks, hardcover works, textbooks. Textbooks and professional books are particularly popular ripoff targets because they are generally so expensive; their reproduction on inferior grade paper, often with poorly copied illustrations, can be exceedingly cheap to accomplish, and the books can be priced just slightly below the authorized edition—at a level that affords the pirate a substantial profit, yet offers poverty-stricken students a powerful incentive to buy. Often these books are even exported to third markets, where piracy is a crime, but where they are frequently indistinguishable from the original work.

"But imagine a medical textbook with black-and-white pictures," Risher says. "How can you tell the veins from the arteries?"

Worse yet, even a book's contents are not sacred. Bette Bao Lord, author of *Spring Moon,* describes in the USIA videotape her horror at examining an unauthorized Taiwanese "edition" of her bestseller: "They had taken the second half of the book and completely chopped it up, added words, added whole pages, changed about I would say one third of the book, but pirated it and sold it as if it were my work.... I worked six years on this book—each word was put in for a special purpose.... And having to see pages, sections, chapters mutilated—it's incredible to an author!"

In Lord's case, at least, the affront had more to do with the integrity of her art and her reputation than it had to do with royalties. Do principles more elevated than the bottom line also motivate publishers? Yes, in the sense that they're determined to create and safeguard an environment within which all phases of publishing—writing, publishing, bookselling, and librarianship—can flourish. They undoubtedly have the immediate well-being of their companies at heart; $1 billion in annual losses is not to be sneezed at. But AAP lobbyists recognize that long-range individual survival is closely dependent on the health of the entire publishing ecosystem. And certainly on the affirmation by the local population of the value of original effort.

"We come in and we establish our own subsidiary," Burke has said. "We help provide jobs to that country, and we help develop a publishing industry, a whole publishing community." The ultimate capacity of books to flourish in any country, he believes, relies on the strength and commitment of such a community—not just on the numbers of foreigners publishing there.

Copyright protection is also essential, Risher points out, if native writers are to entertain any hope of publishing their works at home. Speaking purely in economic terms, she says, a beginning writer's work has virtually no chance of getting published in his own country if he's competing against pirated works—already written, designed, illustrated, edited. The result is cultural, artistic, and literary aridity. The incentive to create is destroyed. And the best books are cheapened, distorted, or cannot even be found. ▣

Will Manley:

Facing the Public

It's reassuring to know in this day and age of fiber optics, videotape cassettes, and the "total" library computerized system that the substantive issues that confront serious librarians who have made the daily, on-going process of "facing the public" their first priority are the same issues that faced librarians at the turn of the century.

Consider the following dialogue that took place sixty years ago between Carol Kennicott, a new arrival to the village of Gopher Prairie, and Miss Ethel Villets, the deathless head of the Gopher Prarie Public Library, in *Main Street,* Sinclair Lewis's classic portrayal of small town America.

Mrs. Kennicott opens the conversation by saying, "I'm sure you will agree with me in one thing: The chief task of a librarian is to get people to read."

Miss Villets replies, "You feel so? My feeling, Mrs. Kennicott, and I am merely quoting the librarian of a very large college, is that the first duty of the conscientious librarian is to preserve the books. It may be all very well in cities where they have unlimited funds, to let nasty children ruin books and just deliberately tear them up, and fresh young men take more books out than they are entitled to by the regulations, but I'm never going to permit it in this library."

"What if some children are destructive?" Mrs. Kennicott questions, "They learn to read. Books are cheaper than minds."

But Miss Villets is ready with a quick rejoinder, "Nothing is cheaper than the minds of some of these children that come in and bother me simply because their mothers don't keep them home where they belong. Some librarians may choose to be so wishy-washy and turn their libraries into nursing homes and kindergartens, but as long as I'm in charge, the Gopher Prairie library is going to be quiet and decent, and the books well kept."

Such a discussion takes place at least fifteen times a day in my library between patrons, between patrons and librarians, and between librarians. Computer down-time, budget cuts, censorship squabbles, perverts, peepers, and delinquent borrowers are the problems that serve as fodder for many library literature articles. Some of these are legitimate concerns that working librarians have to confront on a daily basis. But none of these noteworthy issues has hit me personally with anywhere near the impact of the "children's issue" in our Tempe library.

The problem has arisen because over two years ago we decided that children, even very young children, are people. That's an assumption that, we came to learn very quickly, is not shared by most people over the age of twenty-one. They may give it some lip service, but what they're really thinking is: "Keep those kids out of sight—abort them, dump them in

Will Manley *is director of the Tempe (Arizona) Public Library.*

day care centers, and lock them up in schools." We are seeing more and more segregation and discrimination in this country on the basis of age, and this reflects an attitude of fear.

And no wonder! There's nothing more terrifying than two-year-old children. They're unpredictable, spontaneous, loud, obstreperous, curious, and still young enough to resist all attempts at being drugged and brainwashed by television. They make demands on our time. Providing them library services is one of the most labor intensive processes that we can engage in. That's because, as any parent knows full well, we can't stick a two-year-old in front of a television monitor, film screen, or a computer terminal and expect to keep his or her attention for longer than you can say "Jack Robinson."

Serving the two-year-old patron epitomizes the fact that even in this day of high technology, librarianship, the art of bringing people and books together, is still a highly personal, human relations oriented profession. Any library practitioner who is directly involved with the end process of serving the public knows full well that libraries are bewildering in their complexity not only to chidren, but also to about 95.9 percent of the adults who use them.

The chronic attempts that public librarians make to educate the general public in the use of the library are noble, but impractical. While such programs reach and teach a few interested patrons, the vast majority of our users can't or won't take the time to learn the intricacies of deciphering the card catalog or interpreting the idiosyncrasies of useful reference materials.

Given this fact of life, the most important message to get across to the public is that librarians are friendly, accessible, helpful, knowledgeable and communicative people. And you would think that if there was an area in which librarians could be expected to excel it would be communication. You would think that the organizers and providers of thousands of books would know a little about the process of transferring thoughts and emotions from one person to another.

But let's face it. Librarians have not usually been very good communicators, a conclusion drawn directly from the perceptions of libraries and librarians held by the general public. A terrifyingly telling comment made at the first White House Conference on Library and Information Services by a youth delegate was: "Librarians don't like to talk to people." As attractive, likeable and outgoing as we all hope we are, we have to admit that the old stereotypes not only linger in people's minds, but from the evidence of the above quotation, are apparently surfacing anew in the perceptions of young people. The dingy, brown, dusty stacks, the restrictive quiet, the trauma of fines—a Freudian analyst would have a field day poking around in that corner of the collective psyche that harbors library neuroses.

Granted, many folks, young and old, have had their consciousness raised. Many now see the public library as a little more colorful and dynamic than the above picture but the stereotypes still pop up in a commercial here, a novel or movie there. The reason that many people have a negative image of libraries and librarians and that embarrassing stereotypes persist in people's minds and in the popular media is that too many people do not use the public library and therefore neither understand it nor ascribe any value to it. Librarians are apt to assume, unfortunately, that there will always be a great number of people who do not want to and never will use the public library. By doing so we are devaluing ourselves and our institutions in the eyes of the public. Thus the challenge of insuring the longevity of our libraries relates to one fundamental issue—serving the entire community and not just a select few. If most of the people in this country began to use their public libraries on a regular basis and profited from the experience the old stereotypes would vanish quickly, and there would be much less anxiety about our survival.

That's where the two-year-old child comes in. The leaders of every significant social, political, or religious movement or institution, from the Roman Catholic Church to the Soviet Communist Party, know that the key to their long-term success lies in the indoctrination of young people to the institution's goals, objectives, and ideals. The younger the better. There is much talk about the uncertain future of the public library. We get concerned, brainstorm, and come up with short-term fixes (ambitious new user fees, private sector fundraising, circulation of video games, etc.) to long-term problems. But we talk very little about long-range strategic planning—about the need to put ourselves into a position where, twenty years from now, we'll not only still be around, but we'll be stronger than we are now.

The most effective form of long-term planning is to concentrate on serving that two-year-old child right now. Until recently, most librarians wouldn't even consider including such an uncivilized, uncontrollable creature in their service program, but today circumstances are changing. Two seems to be the last year that many children are still at home all day with a parent; they usually are not sentenced to the daily routine of institutional regimentation until the age of three. So at two, we can, through quality story-hour programming, take advantage of the opportunity to work jointly with parent and child to instill in both of them a strong feeling for the value of books and libraries.

Once this initial enthusiasm is established, the follow-up is crucial. Not only must we make developing juvenile book collections a priority, we must also provide comprehensive book-oriented programming for children of all ages in which the talents of enthusiastic children's librarians are highlighted and encouraged. Systematic efforts must be made through the schools to introduce young people to the public library and to insure that they are all card-carrying registered borrowers.

We may not realize it, but our futures are in the hands of our children's librarians. ▣

We make it easy for you to use WILSONLINE

The Wilson Company provides several user aids that clearly explain WILSONLINE benefits and search procedures.

- *Online help command*—a menu of common situations faced by searchers using WILSONLINE with detailed explanations of their solutions.
- *Online explain messages*—users can request detailed explanations for each system command, message, and feature.
- *Quick Reference Guide*—a one-place look-up summarizing system commands and features.
- *WILSONLINE Guide & Documentation*—a complete user's manual describing search procedures and databases in detail.
- *A WILSONLINE training program* offered at regional sessions throughout the U.S.
- *A toll-free phone number*—a professional searcher will be available to answer your questions if you need help while searching.
- *Accessibility*—WILSONLINE is available Monday, 7:00 A.M. through Sunday 7:00 A.M., except 3:00 A.M. to 5:00 A.M. each morning. (Eastern Standard Time).

WILSONLINE Databases

The records in the WILSONLINE databases contain the same information as the Wilson Company's printed indexes, as well as additional features which enhance retrieval. Articles are indexed by professional librarians and specialists in the subject areas covered by each database. Each database provides at least one year of indexing coverage.

Available now
The following Wilson databases are available now for online searching:

Applied Science & Technology Index
Biological & Agricultural Index
Book Review Digest
Business Periodicals Index
Cumulative Book Index
Education Index
Index to Legal Periodicals
Readers' Guide to Periodical Literature
Journal Directory
Publishers Directory
Name Authority File
LC MARC File

Available in 1985
Other Wilson indexes, listed below, will become available for online searching in 1985.

Humanities Index (February 1985)
Social Sciences Index (February 1985)
General Science Index (May 1985)
Biography Index (July 1985)
Art Index (October 1985)
Library Literature (October 1985)
Bibliographic Index (November 1985)

How to open your WILSONLINE account

To receive a Rate Schedule and Order Form with complete information on WILSONLINE subscription rates, rates for non-subscribers, and prices for training sessions, offline printing, telecommunication access, and *WILSONLINE Guide & Documentation*, and a brochure describing WILSONLINE service in depth, please call the Wilson Customer Service Department, toll free, 1-800-367-6770 (In New York State, call 1-800-462-6060).

THE H.W. WILSON COMPANY
950 University Avenue, Bronx, New York 10452

Publishers of Quality Reference Works Since 1898

Patricia Berglund:

School Library Technology

Are you terrified of typewriters? Do your palms sweat when you have to dial a telephone? Are you afraid of computers?

For most people, the answers are no, no and yes. According to the computer magazine *InfoWorld,* ninety percent of us are so afraid of computers that we will go out of our way to do a task the old way rather than adapt to using the new technology. If you are among that ninety percent majority, you may feel nervous and guilty. The following thoughts may help you relax.

I know a retired librarian who went to her local library to look up an article on computers. She really didn't give a fig about computers; she just wanted to read the article because an old friend had written it. While she waited for the page to bring the magazine, she remarked to the librarian, "I'll die without ever understanding computers." With a perfectly straight face, he replied, "Many people have."

Think about it. His statement puts a lot of things into perspective. The world has gone on a long time without computers and people's lives have been satisfactory. If you really and truly don't want to use a computer, don't use it.

That said, let me add that you should think calmly and clearly about the subject before rejecting computers for life. Most working librarians will find that using a computer will save them time or produce a better, more accurate end-product.

If you use a typewriter very much, the computer is a godsend. All corrections are made electronically—no more erasers or correction fluid. The printed page is perfect every time. Type size and page placement can be changed in a second. Extra touches like automatic centering, page numbering and footnote placement are available at the touch of a button.

Patricia Berglund *is a librarian in the San Francisco Unified School District.*

"I get a cave's worth of drawings on one disk."

Once you learn how to use the computer for writing—whether for letters, reports, catalog cards or overdue notices—you will never go back to a typewriter.

If you keep card files or lists of any length, you should think about using the computer to save and sort those facts or numbers. If you prepare budgets or manage statistics, the computer is an excellent assistant. Computers let you compose music, draw pictures, or practice biofeedback relaxation techniques. The possibilities are endless.

Maybe you agree that a computer is a helpful tool, but you're just plain afraid to use one. They seem so hard to understand, so expensive and fragile. You think you'll make mistakes and look foolish. You're afraid you'll break it. If you feel that way, don't be too hard on yourself. Barbara Varenhorst, a California school psychologist, says, "No generation has had to cope with such monumental changes in one lifetime." Richard Byrne, a lecturer on computer use at the University of Southern California gets a big laugh along with knowing nods from students when he quotes Paul Valéry: "The problem with our times is that the future is not what it used to be." We feel a natural uneasiness as we try to adapt to all the new things that are rushing into our lives.

One solution is to replace fears with facts. That's not always easy to do because teachers and computer professionals sometimes make computing seem harder than it is. Teachers who entered the field early were mostly hobbyists who enjoyed the technical details of computer construction. They are interested in electronics and assume, wrongly, that their students are too. They natter on about RAM, ROM, chips, and motherboards without ever letting you touch the machine. This approach makes as much sense as teaching driving by reciting the history of transmissions and drawing diagrams of clutches. It confuses people, makes them feel stupid and contributes nothing to the goal of learning to use the machine.

The only thing you need to know about electronics is how to work the on/off switch. Useful learning takes place with your hands on the keyboard. Avoid teachers who focus on the inside of the computer or on paper and pencil exercises. Avoid, also, teachers who tell you that you need to learn computer programming if you want to use a computer. Programming is difficult for many people, and a waste of time for almost everyone. Richard C. Carlson of the Stanford Research Institute says, "The last computer skill really necessary for the great majority of the population . . . is programming. The systems are so easy to use that you do not need to know how to program."

When you choose a class or talk to a computer salesman, you encounter another unsettling aspect of computer use: the language. Computer professionals seem to want to make themselves appear brilliant by making their speciality seem esoteric. "Won't boot" proclaims the computer pro with a problem. If he'd only say "won't start" (which means the same thing), anyone over three could understand him. When he uses jargon, he feels special, and you feel intimidated. To hold your own, mentally translate his words into plain English. Documentation—which sounds like something you need for an IRS audit—becomes instructions. Word processing is typing. Database management is filing. If you can't guess the meaning of a term, insist on a clear explanation. If the expert can't provide one, it reflects on his intelligence, not yours.

A common fear among potential computer users is that they will look foolish if they make mistakes. Rational thought and realistic expectations will help you dispel this myth. When you take typing, you do not expect to be a touch typist after one lesson. When you study piano, you know that you'll fumble for weeks or months before you produce any real music. Errors are normal occurrences and not reflections on your intelligence or dexterity.

Try to keep the same realistic viewpoint when you begin to use a computer. You will be controlling the machine by touching keys on the keyboard. The skills you learn are not difficult ones, but proficiency takes time. At first, every movement will be studied. Often you'll forget what to do next or hit the wrong key. You might have to start over. If you feel inept, take a deep breath and remember that trial and error is the only way to learn computer use. Everyone goes through the same process of practicing, making mistakes, practicing some more, and gradually improving. In time you will memorize the combination of keystrokes that produce desired results, and your movements will become automatic. The average adult will take about twenty hours to reach this point. You can also cheer yourself up during the learning period by reminding yourself that your eventual gain in productivity will more than offset the time it took you to learn the skills.

Your learning will be impeded if you are worried about damaging the computer, but many new users are frightened of that very thing. This fear usually springs from lack of information. Personal computers are neither particularly fragile nor particularly expensive, but they are unknown. You drive off in a new $10,000 car without a second thought yet freeze up when you think about touching a $1000 computer. Your fears are not proportional to the actual potential for damage posed by each activity. Keep things in perspective and remember that there's almost nothing you can do to damage a computer unless you pull something out of it while it's running or start playing around inside it. Three-year-olds use computers everyday, and their prodding and pounding doesn't hurt the machines. You won't hurt it either.

Adam Osborne reminds us that computers are powerful tools, but just tools nonetheless. "The computer is to the mind what the spade is to the arm," he says. Computers are not alive. They are not smarter than you are. If you can work a record player, if you can take pictures, you can use a computer. Try it. ▣

Rod Henshaw:

Library to Library

With this issue, WLB begins offering an occasional column on a traditional, but rapidly changing library activity—interlibrary loan. Future columns will look at new developments in networking, electronic mail, loan policies, the British Lending Library, and national planning for resource-sharing.

Rod Henshaw presently serves on both the RASD/ILL Committee and the OCLC Interlibrary Loan Advisory Committee.

Interlibrary loan is an activity common to libraries of all sizes and types. What was once a peripheral, has now become a prominent and vital service. Few responsible librarians would argue against the imperatives for resource-sharing; even under the best budgetary and collection management situations, local self-sufficiency is elusive if not illusionary.

Yet, the library literature continues to abound with attacks on the merits of interlibrary loan. The detractors maintain that interlibrary loan is too slow, too costly, and is used by too few patrons, overlooking the fact that the same arguments could be used against any library service when viewed in an isolated context. The proposed alternatives, perhaps fueled by the past decade which saw many stagnant or declining library budgets, seem to reside in a future grounded in the "no growth" society expounded by some economists. More importantly, the opponents of interlibrary loan overlook the historical antecedents and developments on which this service is based.

Resource-sharing, via a system of interlibrary loan, was an important element even in the earliest days of professional librarianship in America. As early as 1853, librarians began to recognize the need for cooperative relationships, and in 1876, in the very first issue of *Library Journal*, Samuel Sweet Green suggested that "...an agreement should be made to lend books to each other for short periods of time." By 1919 the American Library Association had adopted the first national interlibrary loan code. This initial code, which has since undergone numerous revisions, clearly articulated the purpose of interlibrary loan: "To aid research" and "to augment the supply of the average book to the average reader." Shortly thereafter, a standard interlibrary loan form was adopted, as well as a set of abbreviations for citing verification sources.

The leadership for these early accomplishments was provided by librarians from the oldest and largest of the public and university libraries of that era. As a group, they represented libraries that had built enormous collections through the efforts of a generation of diligent scholar-librarians. Long before the information explosion had detonated, they had the foresight to recognize that it was not enough to merely acquire, label, and shelve books. They saw that if librarianship was to be a profession, it would have to commit itself to creating ways and means of providing access to information.

This commitment to access provided the framework for a long list of developments, focusing to a large degree on bibliographic control through classification systems and cataloging standards. For resource-sharing, it bore fruit in such projects as *The National Union Catalog* and *The Union List of Serials*. By the 1940s teletype technology had become an accepted and widespread device for the exchange of interlibrary loan requests. With the introduction of the photocopier, libraries had the ability to reproduce journal literature which was in itself a further incentive for expanding union list and interlibrary loan activity.

The impetus for resource-sharing became even stronger immediately following World War II. Higher education, faced with tremendous increases in enrollment and research, spent vast sums of money in building large library collections. Public libraries, inheriting a legacy of free access and confronted with a society that was increasingly information-dependent, expanded their services and collections. But as budgets spiraled upward, the demands for services heightened. In one avenue of response, the library community fought for and achieved, through the Library Services and Construction Act, federal funding for resource-sharing. This facilitated the creation of numerous state and regional interlibrary loan networks which, by the 1970s, began to use the online union catalogs of such systems as RLIN and OCLC.

Computer and telecommunications technologies have brought the threshold of automation within the grasp of even the smallest of libraries. This may allow more and smaller libraries to satisfy many of their interlibrary loan needs without resorting to larger public and academic libraries. There is also a growing number of commercial suppliers who provide documents with consistent speed and cost. Blending these new realities into an efficient and coherent system of document retrieval and delivery is a complex challenge for network planners. Librarianship is demonstrating a professional maturity in its managerial and research methodologies which, when combined with a heritage of access, should allow for the continuance and growth of responsible resource-sharing. ▣

Rod Henshaw *is head, interlibrary loan, Iowa State University Library, Ames.*

Joseph Deitch:

Portrait: Marvin Scilken

The unabashed librarian at work—Marvin Scilken

Marvin Scilken's pungent and iconoclastic views of library operations and policies and his support of practices not taught in library schools generally delight, sometimes irritate but always provoke and challenge readers of his quarterly called, quite logically, *The U*N*A*B*A*S*H*E*D Librarian.*

Scilken's literary cousin is certainly H. L. Mencken, whose favorite American institution was the Enoch Pratt Free Library in Baltimore. While Scilken has never characterized librarians as part of "boobus Americanus," as Mencken labeled most professors, politicians and professional pedagogues, he is not afraid to upset applecarts if it means making librarians more efficient. What the Sage of Baltimore, a grammarian's grammarian, would have thought of *The U*N*A*B*A*S*H*E*D Librarian*'s secondary title, *How I run my library good,* is open to speculation.

Perhaps the nearest geographical approach to a Menckenian view of Scilken, as librarian, editor and publisher of unabashed opinions and of better ways to do things in libraries, came in an interview with Anna Curry, director of the Enoch Pratt Free Library. "For him, there are no sacred cows," she said. "Everything is subject to challenge. There is no other professional reading like *The U*N*A*B*A*S*H*E*D Librarian.* You may not agree with his ideas or with the practices he reports, but he gets you to think. And your analogy to Mencken is correct. Both upset applecarts and are provocative. Marvin is contributing to the improvement of the profession."

Scilken got into the library field through *The New York Times,* which he reads cover-to-cover every day, a feat unmatched since Samuel Johnson, in his prime, tossed off four books a day, according to Boswell. Nothing escapes Scilken's eye, including the small-type public notices on the weather page. In 1960, he spotted a New York State notice that offered to train people to become librarians at state expense, and to wire collect. Scilken did, and got a wire back telling him to report to the Donnell Branch of the New York Public Library to take a competitive examination for a scholarship.

Scilken passed the test but "hemmed and hawed" about making libraries his career. He finally "took himself up" to the library school at Columbia, only to be told that he was too late for that term. Were there other schools in town? There was Pratt. He zipped down to Brooklyn, and was promptly admitted.

Scilken is director of the Orange (N. J.) Public Library, which is celebrating its 100th anniversary this year. The library building, designed by Stanford White of McKim Mead and White, is surely one of the finest examples of Greek revival architecture in the United States. The natural setting for its white exterior, with Ionic columns spread across the facade and under the pediment, is a hillside overlooking the wine-dark Aegean Sea, with carts pulled by donkeys and oxen in front of it, not whizzing cars and trucks.

The building's pure, classical motifs are continued on the inside, where the main floor is divided by gray marble columns. It is in this copy of an ancient Greek temple that Scilken makes discoveries for improving library service and writes about them in *The U*N*A*B*A*S*H*E*D Librarian.* His office, lined with old and rare books that once routinely filled the library's open shelves, is a scholar's den. Around the corner is the circulation desk surrounded by tiers and carts packed with books, mostly current or recent, for every taste and need.

Scilken, a portly New Yorker who works in shirtsleeves with a gentle, almost self-effacing approach, talked about the life cycle of best-sellers at his library.

"An issue was, What to do with old best-sellers," he recalled. "A trustee suggested distributing them to doctors' and dentists' offices, supermarkets and banks for people to take. We like to meet people's needs in a reasonable time, so we buy many copies of books in demand or that are likely to be. The throwaways were mainly former best-sellers with instant appeal. Even discards need appeal—if it's a dog in the library," Scilken cautions, "it will be a dog out of it," a bit of critical pithiness that may not get quoted in *New York Times Book Review* ads but will help librarians get out from under mountains of former best-sellers in their buildings.

Joseph Deitch *writes for* The New York Times *and other publications.*

Scilken's impulse to spread the word about exemplary library practices and start his one-man crusade began when he got a rejection slip from a library journal that refused the first you-can-do-it-too article he had written, on disposing of retired best-sellers gathering dust on overcrowded shelves. "Make room for younger best-sellers," is a Scilken watchword.

Visualizing more rejections, Scilken decided to collect useful library practices from around the country and to publish them himself. Thus, in 1971, was born *The U*N*A*B*A*S*H*E*D Librarian,* the quarterly compendium of ways to improve the operation of libraries as reported by librarians themselves.

"They're solid ideas—stuff they never told us about in library school as perhaps too practical or simple but are, nevertheless, affecting a lot of libraries for the better," a librarian at a busy reference desk in Bergen County, New Jersey, commented. In what ways? "In saving money, time, labor, space and personnel."

The founding idea for *The U*N*A*B*A*S*H*E*D Librarian* was to report and correct Library of Congress cataloging errors and similar gaffes found elsewhere. The Library of Congress? "Nobody's perfect," Scilken said. "Not only errors but differences in philosophies and approaches affecting administration. The Orange Public Library stocks 100,000 books, LC sixteen million. What's good for LC may not be good for all of us smaller libraries. For example, the Dewey classification fits us better than the LC system."

A "terrible thing that has happened to the library profession is the constant changing of the Dewey decimal system," Scilken said, and he urged, that "old numbers be used for old subjects and new numbers for new subjects," thus insuring that all books on a given subject will be in one place. The Dewey decimal expert at the Library of Congress thinks that libraries should reclassify, that they will actually change the numbers on books. But most libraries do not reclassify. Newer libraries that buy their cataloging shelve books as they come in from central processing.

"There should be a coherent philosophy," Scilken said. "Most people take books by browsing. Therefore, all books, new and old, on a subject should be in the same number category."

Dewey numbers are always changing. The Orange Public Library is on the sixteenth of nineteen Dewey editions. If Scilken knew then what he knows now, he said he would still be on Dewey 14, the last of the older classifications.

The circulation of *The U*N*A*B*A*S*H*E*D Librarian,* which, editorially, has noted that progress is often best achieved by using old or standard methods, is about 1,200, with subscribers all over the world, except in China. It meets a clearinghouse need for practical ideas submitted by library personnel who describe methods and procedures—tips, shortcuts, hints—with zeal, conviction and humor. All contributors say, in effect, "This works in my library, maybe it will in yours." The publication is edited by Scilken and his wife, Mary, a nursing professor at Pace University.

Not only is there no other professional reading like *The U*N*A*B*A*S*H*E*D Librarian,* but it is the only idea clearinghouse for and by library personnel who want to help each other without having to prepare long dissertations for possible publication. Contributors sum up "how they run their libraries good," in a few paragraphs to a couple of pages. No one knows how many of the thousands of successful practices published in UL's thirteen-year history have been adopted by libraries. But they have all met the editor's criteria for soundness and feasibility. Scilken will reject articles that are theoretical, speculative, or "too scholarly."

"Something you'll never learn in library school may be the most important task of all: keeping the library clean," is a point made in a "survival book list" that Scilken published in one UL issue. "I'd like a nickel," the contributor added, "for every time a librarian with sleeves rolled up has emerged from a library washroom, mop in hand, muttering, 'They never told me about this in library school.'"

Copyable practices from the field are often followed by editor's notes reporting that he does the opposite of what is proposed. A reprinted editorial that condemned defacing books—from discreet pencil checks to yellow underlining and inked marginal notes—prompted Scilken to declare that the Orange Public Library encourages readers to write on the back inside book covers where a rubber-stamp message declares "Tell the world this book was (followed by three columns, "good," "bad," "so-so")

A good many of Scilken's own contributions to UL are based on his professional experiences and daily challenges. He studies his library users, benevolently tries out ideas on them and meets needs as they arise. These efforts, naturally, also increase circulation. Like a good store manager, he "merchandises" and strategically displays his product.

"We want to make our books hard to resist by putting new ones near the entrance, so they'll be seen and be taken out, and we do this as soon as they are received," he said.

Unlike some library directors, Scilken buys what the people of Orange want to read, not what he thinks they should read or what he likes to read. His library is far from handsomely supported, but Scilken's merchandising nets more circulation per borrower than libraries with bigger budgets. "And we get books to people quickly—nobody waits more than a month for titles in demand," he said.

Some public libraries are automatically supported because of community demographics. Their trustees and directors do not have to compete for funds with other municipal services. Many have to assert themselves with city council members and other politicians. Scilken became aware of these budget facts of life a long time ago and advocates continued interaction with local decision makers. That is why, for example, he produced posters reading, "Libraries are where the voters are."

"And they are—a survey showed that fifty-four percent of voters are library users and people who said they voted in a lot of elections were heavy library users," Scilken said. "So these posters tell politicians that great numbers of their constituents are library users who expect libraries to be at least adequately supported." Some six thousand of Orange's population are library households with one or more active voters apt to support candidates who include the library among their main municipal interests.

As Scilken and I talked, the wife of the Mayor of Orange swept into the director's office and picked up two shopping bags full of printed matter on the library's 100th anniversary. She is directing the six-month celebration program, and is living proof that political and governmental interaction with libraries can be a two-way process. Much of this part of the director's approach to library communications has been stated dozens of times by him and others in *The U*N*A*B*A*S*H*E*D Librarian*.

Leafing through the periodical, I asked why there are stars between letters in U*N*A*B*A*S*H*E*D. The idea was his brother-in-law's, a designer for Harper & Row. He may have been inspired by Leo Rosten's 1937 novel, *The Education of H*Y*M*A*N K*A*P*L*A*N*, about an unabashed New Yorker learning grammar and pronunciation in night school ("O Kaplan, my Kaplan, our fearful trip is done. . . . ").

"It's a terrific gimmick because it lifts the title right off the cover," Scilken said. "The stars in the name came after K*A*P*L*A*N but they predate M*A*S*H."

Scilken leaned back and thought a moment when I asked what libraries should be today. "They should be responsible to their clienteles as the people see their own needs. There appears to be a flight from the book. Libraries think they're in the information business, or so they have been led to believe. They should not be, not in the sense that I perceive that they think they are. Libraries will not be successful sitting people down in front of computers. That isn't in the cards. We are in the book business. What we should do is give people all the books they want as quickly as we can with as hassle-free service as possible."

Scilken has achieved a reputation as a budget watchdog. His own library receives less than average support, a factor in his policy of vigilance in protecting libraries from being cheated. He became incensed when he learned that many trade publishers were giving libraries smaller discounts than bookstores for the same books. When he placed an order with a publisher, he was told that he would have to pay the full list price, plus shipping, because, unlike booksellers, he was "taking no risk." He was, in fact, taking a larger risk than bookstores. His risk was that no one may read the book, which could not be returned, he argued in a publishers' trade journal. This is how, in part, publishers, are subsidized, he said, and he concluded:

"Instead of libraries subsidizing publishers, perhaps publishers should subsidize libraries for the services they perform in maintaining and enlarging America's book-reading public." This statement rubbed a university librarian the wrong way. Proposing the same discount for libraries and booksellers "flies in the face of logic," he said. What the library profession needs is "increased knowledge about publishing and the distribution of books." The rebuttal to Scilken and to a resolution that was later passed at an ALA conference appeared in a journal on the practice and theory of library acquisitions. For Scilken, the rebuttal belongs more to theory than practice for those counting dollars on the purchasing firing line.

Children's library service should be funded by publishers, Scilken said. Only by developing readers at a young age will there be book readers and buyers. Moreover, the only people who buy novels and general trade books are those who read for pleasure, and the only institution that encourages people to read for pleasure is the public library.

"I have this funny theory that, to be a good reader, a child needs exposure to lots of books when learning to read," Scilken said. "And, unless you have friends and relatives with books who are willing to lend them, the only place to get books is the library. We are, then, the basis or source for readers that publishers need to survive."

The original unabashed librarian said that libraries should not be too concerned about people who do not use the library. "Most libraries have all the members they are ever going to get," he said. Attempts at change, to bring in more people, won't work. Given "the same director, buying policies, budget and hours, no public relations in the world will attract more members." Community adult programs in libraries "are foolishness." They are fine if a library wants to present or house them. "But it should not think that people who go to these events are going to join the library after the lecture on buying government securities; they may, but probably won't."

Card-holders in a town's library are those who are "willing to play your game, to put up with you—bring books back on time and generally do what you want them to do. Cajoling people to join can backfire: all people say they love the local library whether they use it or not. So you get people to join, they take out books and don't return them and you enmesh them in the overdue system. From moderate library supporters, they can become active dislikers. They have overdue books in the house they don't want and owe you money and are afraid to go into the library.

"So what have you gained? You've lost books and a friend. Library use should be voluntary. Let there be no lures." Scilken walked to the circulation area and got affectionate looks from the staff. He gestured at shelves and carts full of books, many new, including a cartful of pulp romances.

"Give the people what they want," he said. "It's their library."

Donnarae MacCann/Olga Richard:

Picture Books for Children

Books from small presses have been reviewed with great infrequency in this column. Small press books are often less accessible and there is a temptation to appreciate and respond to the steady flow of mainstream books. To make some amends, we will focus this month and next on books from two small, specialized presses: Third World Press and Coffee House Press (formerly Toothpaste Press).

We begin with a cultural publishing house that emphasizes books by and about Africans and black Americans: Third World Press. Three black poets in Chicago, Carolyn Rogers, Johari Amini, and Haki R. Madhubuti (Don L. Lee) decided in 1967 to "provide in-depth reflections of ourselves by ourselves." The company has published works by major black scholars, editors, essayists, poets, and writers of fiction. Its children's line includes books by such major literary figures as Gwendolyn Brooks, Sonia Sanchez, and Mari Evans.

Singing Black by Mari Evans has been described as an alternative nursery rhyme collection for the very young—alternative in the sense that no mainstream nursery rhyme collections, as far as we know, include African and Afro-American names, specific references to African values, and verses about black self-esteem. In the latter category are verses like the following:

Sing a song of brothers
Whistle all day long
Black and proud and beautiful
  And Strong
  Strong
  Strong!

Olga Richard *and* **Donnarae MacCann** *are the authors of* The Child's First Books.

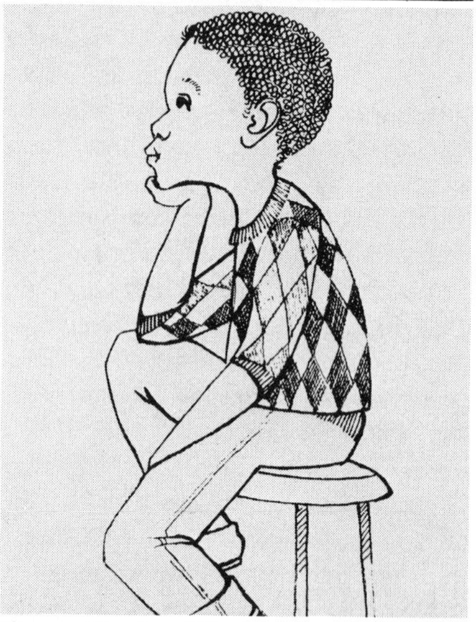

From *Singing Black*

Verses about "umoja" and "kuumba" are explained in footnotes, "kuumba" being the Swahili word for "creativity" and "umoja" meaning "unity."

Umoja! umoja!
Means we work together
  In sunshine
  And rain-time
And all kinds
  Of weather!

Some rhymes have a specific tie-in with the customs of Afro-American culture:

Chicken, rice and gravy
  Sweet potato pie
Daddy says my stomach's
  Bigger than my eye!

There are poems about childhood that refer to Afro-American experience only through the illustrations. For example, this verse about bedtime:

"Go to bed, go to bed"
That's what they say
  So my pj's and I
    walk
      slowly
        away

As soon as I'm big
  And they are just three
I'll say "go to bed, go to bed"
  Like they do me

And I'll stay up all night
  When I'm big
  and they're
    three!

Throughout the book there are many examples of Ramon Price's superb drawing skill and rhythmic design sense. The style is minimal in its treatment of line, the portraiture includes much differentiation, and the form of each youngster is well understood. The reproduction on this page is a simple, direct drawing with a lovely line and a subtle suggestion of depth produced by line thickness and overlapping legs and arms. Price suggests more than he shows, and he arranges all the images in a loosely structured, but graceful page design.

In 1981, Third World Press published a picture book for a slightly older age group, **The Day They Stole the Letter J** by Jabari Mahiri (illustrated by Dorothy Carter). It chronicles the fantastic events in the day of two small boys in a black community. Jelani and Jerome pay a visit to the friendly barber shop of JoJo—a wood-carver and storyteller as well as the neighborhood barber. JoJo's voodoo sets the plot in motion as the boys carry off one of his carved letters: a large "J." Everything with a "j" as its initial letter disappears if the carving is misused. JoJo follows the children to the place where they have foolishly buried the letter, and by correcting their mistake, he causes jumbo jets to return to Jersey City, jam to return to the peanut butter and jelly sandwiches, a jug of juice to return to the refrigerator, and so on.

All this remarkable magic might appear somewhat abrupt in the context of everyday inner city life. But Jelani's story opens with a bit of alliterative word play as he wonders about words, letters, and his own identity as "Jelani" or "J" for short.

The initial lightness of tone prepares the way for suspension of disbelief later.

Voodoo is one of a number of African and Afro-American references in the narrative. JoJo's own use of "the powers" is preceded by an account of trial by fire—the capacity to walk on burning coals that was practiced at some indefinite time in Haiti. Voodoo is used as one means of underscoring the idea of wholeness and self-appreciation. For example, the magical, carved "J" (a symbol of Jelani's identity) is said to come from sacred wood; thus "it can never be buried and have its beauty hidden without some strange things happening." But in an entirely different kind of scene, the idea of wholeness is presented again: Jelani has misspelled a word by omitting a letter, and his sister reminds him, "You've got to have *all* the letters or you can't make the word." While Jelani's mother is portrayed as a nonbeliever of JoJo's stories of "powers," the narrative hints that strong self-concepts are supported by both ancient and modern traditions.

From *The Day They Stole the Letter J*

This juxtaposition of the seen and unseen worlds is expressed visually by blending the textural and architectural features of the city with some boldly nonobjective designs. Dorothy Carter demonstrates a particular talent and a great courage for large visual ideas. She is adept at breaking up areas into ingenious shapes, as can be seen in the example reproduced here. The abstract planes and curves in this drawing do not detract from a straightforward understanding of the scene. In a very subtle way, they add a sensitive sculptural quality to the portraits. Carter creates a range of textural features throughout the book—from rug-like textures to the simulation of sheer window curtains.

Unfortunately, a heavy gray monotone overlays many of the illustrations and tends to make the work look dated. The publisher explained that this problem resulted from working with a new printer, lacking the necessary resources to allow for corrections. For some small presses, a high degree of perfection in the printing process is a luxury that must be subordinated to other goals.

Another Third World Press book is a photographic picture book that shows no sign of technical problems. **I Want to Be...** by Dexter and Patricia Oliver with photographs by Dexter Oliver, is an alphabet book about careers. An occupation has been chosen to represent each letter (architect for "A", botanist for "B", etc.), and children have been posed to illustrate the workers at their jobs. The props and characters have been well planned in each photo. For example, the architect has a large, partially rolled drawing on his work table and several floor plans pinned to the wall in the background. The geometric quality in the props are echoed in the garment worn by the young architect. On the zoologist's page, a young person is seen among her test tubes, scissors, tweezers, and microscope. Her white jacket, notebook, and trays accent the composition.

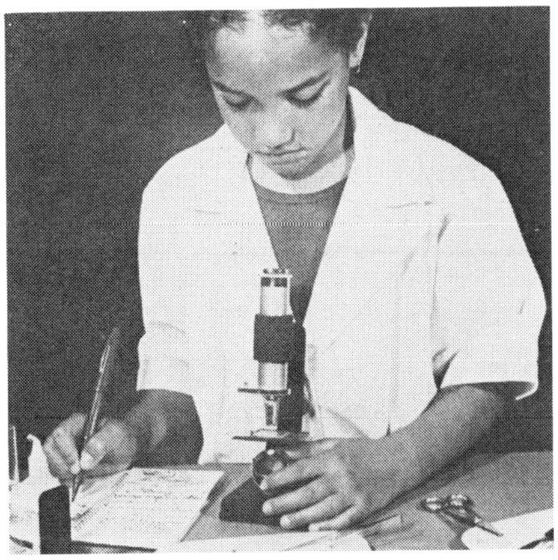

From *I Want To Be...*

No feeling of patronization is produced by the use of the children. On the contrary, the treatment is sincere and we hardly notice that the leading characters are children. The result is a highly motivating presentation of career choices.

I Want to Be... represents one of the stated goals of Third World Press: to "assist students and teachers in learning and teaching specific nonreligious academic subjects." *Singing Black* and *The Day They Stole the Letter J* are examples of another goal: "to portray aspects of Afro-American and African experience." A third objective involves changing "political, social, and cultural attitudes of Afro-Americans by advancing specific Black ideologies." However, the ideological content in the children's books is broadly inclusive. The word "possibilities" expresses their general thrust. As Haki Madhubuti stated in an interview, when speaking of the very young child: "I think that literature—if it's working—talks about the possibilities, about what you can become, what is beautiful in the world....We have to think about what is best for the child, and we can do that in ways that do not compromise the intelligence or development of the child. I'm pretty sure that can be done." ▣

This months books:

Evans, Mari. *Singing Black.* Illus. by Ramon Price. Third World Press (7524 S. Cottage Grove Ave., Chicago, IL 60619), 1978. $2.50

Mahiri, Jabari. *The Day They Stole the Letter J.* Illus. by Dorothy Carter. Third World Press, 1981. $8.95, pa$3.95

Oliver, Dexter and Patricia Oliver. *I Want to Be....* Illus. with photographs by Dexter Oliver. Third World Press, 1974. $5.95, pa$2.95

Patty Campbell:

The Young Adult Perplex

Near Thessaloniki—There is something about being in Greece that makes a person feel like sitting on a rock and looking out to sea while pondering the nature of civilization. I have been doing a lot of this lately, trying to digest the strange and wonderful experiences of the past few days. Why do some cultures rise and fall and others endure? How can a society search for new and better ways without destroying that which is valuable from the past? How can the culture-bearers—that's us, fellow librarians—transmit values so that the young accept them rather than reject all that went before as an automatic part of growing up? Can a society in transition agree on which values should be passed on? We have just come from the remote southern corner of Yugoslavia where we have found some insight into these questions. Now I am rock-sitting and trying to sort it all out.

"When you come down into Macedonia from Titograd," said *Let's Go,* our usually trustworthy guidebook, "the change is abrupt. The air is stagnant, dust lies thick on the trees, and horse-drawn carts rumble along Europe's most antique roads. Blood feuds are still common in small villages, newborn babies still kiss the muzzle of a gun, and fighting ability is the test of a man. A word of caution—this part of Yugoslavia is quite primitive." We enter the ancient land of Macedonia with some apprehension. What if we run out of gas or have engine trouble and are stranded here among these fierce people?

Patty Campbell *is a freelance writer who teaches young adult literature at UCLA.*

Within twenty miles we begin to doubt the perceptions of the Harvard students who wrote *Let's Go.* Every "fierce" Macedonian child greets us with a welcoming wave and a sweet smile. Some of the younger women wave, too, particularly when there are no men around. Their husbands and fathers give us stern, straight, but not unfriendly looks from behind tremendous mustaches. It is evidently beneath male dignity to wave. The teenage boys without exception stick out their thumbs for a ride. Evidently contact with foreign tourists is part of the bravado of coming-of-age—what do they learn on these rides? We are kept busy returning greetings as the road winds steeply up into the mountains.

I have long been fascinated by this land from which came Alexander the Great to conquer the known world, a culture that in modern times endured many centuries of harsh Turkish rule and yet kept a passionate sense of identity and allegiance to its own ways. The strange wild harmonies and mystical circling dances of Macedonia are the oldest in Europe, and on our car radio it is this eerie archaic music that accompanies our ascent of the sheer valleys. The road is a tiny level ribbon in a vast vertical landscape. Occasionally we see a village perched beside it or impossibly high above on the green slopes. As the late afternoon wanes, there are walkers beside the highway, young boys driving flocks of sheep or goats with the help of a dog and a long stick, women

in groups of two or three coming home from visiting or from market. The women wear traditional ankle-bloused harem trousers of patterned cotton, cut wide and full between the legs, and the younger ones walk proudly with a small graceful flip of the heel and hip to cope with the clumsiness of the extra fabric. Men, too, sometimes wear traditional garments—a pillbox cap, or even a turban, an embroidered jacket flung dashingly over one shoulder. Few tourists come this way—this is not a show for visitors, but ordinary people wearing their everyday clothes.

There are horses and wagons on the road, but not the plodding nags we have seen on the coast. These teams prance along with flying manes, and jaunty red pom-poms decorate their bridles. I catch a startling glimpse of a woman sitting under a tree spinning thread from a hand-held spindle. Is it possible that in this land where Volkswagens and modern tractors are parked in the yard a woman should produce cloth by a method older than the Industrial Revolution, older even than the spinning wheel? Then we see two more spinners, and know that it is.

The next day we come down into Ohrid, the exquisite lakeside town that was the center of Slavic culture for centuries, and here we have the enormous good fortune to be guests of a Macedonian family. Our genial host is Ilija Djoreski. We meet him by chance in the exchange office, where he helps us cope with the complexities of buying gasoline coupons. He has worked for fifteen years in Germany, he explains, but on holiday he comes straight back to beautiful Ohrid to renew ties with family and friends. He speaks a little English and is anxious to practice it with us. After we go to the bustling market—a scene right out of the Middle Ages, with villagers in exquisitely corded and embroidered costumes, heaps of tomatoes and peppers, donkeys grazing by the gates—we invite him to lunch. "No," he insists, "you must come home with me to eat. You are a guest in Macedonia."

In the next few days we are to hear those last words many times. The family welcomes us warmly. The center of social life is the big dining room table in the apartment of Ilija's brother Dimitri, and there—when we are not sightseeing or swimming in the lake with our host—we are plied with glasses of slivovitz, the fiery plum brandy that sustains the courage of Yugoslavia. There we are fed lavishly by Dasha, Dimitri's pretty wife, who produces an amazing variety of traditional dishes from limited ingredients: tomatoes, peppers, onions, cheese, eggs. Neighbors and friends drop in during the day and stay to drink a glass and discuss politics and business. We are introduced casually as Americanska visitors. Ilija translates only sporadically, but smiles and handshakes are international. We swim happily in a sea of Macedonian dialect, trying to pick up a few words to augment our meager grasp of Serbo-Croatian.

The extended family lives in a large modern house which Ilija and Dimitri own together. They built it themselves, which is usual in Yugoslavia, and the gleaming kitchens would do justice to any house in California. The family had owned another house by the lake, but after World War II the government allowed them to retain only one property. They chose this one because it had more land, which they have since sold. "It is not too good to seem to own too much in Yugoslavia," Ilija tells us without rancor. On each floor is a separate apartment: Ilija has bachelor quarters at the top, then Dimitri and Dasha and their four-year-old son Slavco on the second level. A third brother, Stefan, is severely retarded, but is accepted warmly without condescension into the daily life of the household. He lives on the first floor—with their mother, we are told, but we are never introduced to her. Once from the balcony I glimpse a mysterious bent figure in black tending the chickens and little Slavco cries happily, "Baba! Babinitza!" And while we are looking at a photo album Dasha warns me that Baba never has her picture taken.

In many other ways the sixteenth and the twentieth century live in harmony here. The music on the radio or on Ilija's expensive German tape player is sometimes modern pop and sometimes ancient dance songs. We drink tea from herbs gathered on the mountain while we watch aerobics on television. Ilija teaches us to understand the pride Yugoslavia has in their ongoing independent social "experiment" with its unique combination of communism and free enterprise, and he also gives us a sense of the history of his people. The phrase "in the village" comes often into the conversation: "We do it this way now, but of course in the village . . . "

And then one day when we go to visit a tenth-century Byzantine church we see how respect for the old customs is handed on. Ilija is a bit embarrassed not to be able to interpret the "Bible pictures" in the frescoes for us. He had no religious education in school, he explains. The communist state has no sympathy with the church, and Ilija is a sophisticated cosmopolitan, an agnostic. Yet he lights a candle for each member of his family and insists that we do the same. And then he takes Slavco's small unwilling hand and teaches him the sign of the cross.

Eventually, over the protests of our hosts, we must leave. We exchange gifts, take photos, have a last glass of slivovitz, wave fond goodbyes. We cross the tension-filled border into Greece and in a few hours we stand amidst the ruins of Alexander's birthplace at Pella. Here he walked with his tutor Aristotle, that greatest of culture-bearers, who, it is written, taught him a love of reading so strong that he slept always with a copy of Homer's *Iliad* under his pillow. The empire Alexander created is gone, reduced to this heap of rubble. But the *Iliad*? And the identity of the Macedonian people?

Life is too short to spend the whole day sitting on a rock by the sea, as Democritus observed. It's time to go for a swim. ▣

Kathleen Maio:

Murder in Print

There have been many mysteries written by English authors about Spain. Memories of old national rivalries aside, Spain attracts many British to her shore as retirees, expatriates, and holiday trippers. Occasionally these folks write suspense novels featuring España, but the plots and characters remain very English. The novels of John and Emery Bonett are a good example. Their Inspector Borges mysteries take place on the Costa Brava (where the couple moved in the early sixties). Yet, except for Borges and an infrequent walk-on by a Spanish servant, their characters are English through and through. And Borges himself seems more Cantabrigian than Castilian. So much so that when he finally solves a mystery in London (*The Sound of Murder*, 1970), he seems like a native.

David Serafin is also a British writer. But the major attraction of his work is that he writes so well of Spain. **Madrid Undergrouund** (St. Martin's, 1984, $11.95) is the third in his series of mysteries featuring Superintendent Luis Bernal of Madrid's Brigada Criminal.

Bernal and his investigators are faced with the job of tracking a psychopath who stashes the bodies of his victims on Madrid's extensive subway system. The novel is written in a dry, reportorial style. But this classic police procedural, while staying closely focused on a set of crimes and their detection, still manages to convey the social tensions facing Spain before the first free election after the death of Franco. Here and there, Serafin's British voice comes through (for example, a Spanish general has all the bluff and bluster of Colonel Mustard in an Agatha Christie story), but his portrait of Spain still rings true and adds great interest to this suspenseful police story.

R. D. Rosen uses a slightly less exotic locale in his first mystery, **Strike Three You're Dead** (Walker, 1984, $12.95). Rosen sets his mystery in Providence, Rhode Island, a locale he claims looks "like a place you ended up when they kicked you out of everywhere else." Proud citizens of the Ocean State may resent Rosen's repeated jabs at their capital, but baseball buffs will especially enjoy this tale of murder in the clubhouse of the newest team in the American League East, the Providence Jewels.

Rosen's central character and amateur detective is center fielder Harvey Blissberg, who feels obliged to investigate when his friend and roadroommate, pitcher Rudy Furth, is slugged to death in the team whirlpool. The investigation gives him insights of friend Furth, and numerous opportunities for a little wiseacre humor. Rosen handles comedy, suspense, and even Blissberg's romance with a local sportscaster with the skill of a seasoned pro. *Strike Three You're Dead* is a winning rookie effort.

Slightly less satisfying is Susan Dunlap's **An Equal Opportunity Death** (St. Martin's, 1984, $12.95). Dunlap's heroine, Vejay Haskell, is a gas meter reader, a second career she acquired after dropping out of the success-obsessive world of San Francisco, and moving to a cabin community on the banks of the Russian River. When the local bartender is murdered and Vejay is the last person to see the fellow she becomes a major suspect. She responds by breaking into the scene of the crime, concealing evidence from the police, and otherwise doing more harm than good.

Vejay has her good points, as do the rest of the characters in Dunlap's novel. There are plenty of hustles and

Kathleen Maio *is a freelance writer based in Somerville, Massachusetts. She has contributed to* Twentieth Century Crime and Mystery Writers, Murderess Ink, *and numerous magazines.*

shady deals in this backwater. But the backwater literally steals the show. The natural raging violence of the Russian River is used as a foil to intensify the impact of the human violence, but it ends up adding too melodramatic a touch to the novel's suspense. Not a memorable mystery, but one that promises better things to come.

On the small press scene, we have a country mystery that completely misses the mark. **Green Mountain Murder** (Landgrove Press, 1984, $3.95) is the second novel by B. Comfort to feature a had-I-but-knownish heroine named Liz Bell. Those who read the first novel will be confused. Although the protagonist has the same name and a similar history to the heroine in Comfort's first novel, she has a different hometown, life, lover, and pets.

Those who haven't met Liz before will likely find her dizzy dame routine sorely trying as she bumbles into danger and is battered for her trouble. The story likewise bumps along in a choppy fashion, the author never developing a scene fully before going on to the next. All this is a shame, because Comfort has some nice pithy comments to make about the development of Vermont. But her commentary cannot sustain an entire novel.

Asia Rip by George Foy (Viking, 1984, $16.95) is one of the most impressive first mysteries of the year. The evocative title is taken from one of the shoals off Cape Cod. The novel focuses on the men who fish those waters, specifically Lars Larsen, who investigates the disappearance of a friend's boat and thus plunges himself into a bloody nightmare.

Foy's knowledge of the North Atlantic fishing industry is extensive and there is a harsh realism to his narrative—whether on the icy waters of the ocean or the filthy streets surrounding the Fulton Fish Market in New York. His story powerfully links organized crime to the men who go down to the sea in ships. Of those men, Lars Larsen is a compelling hero.

Now I am the type of reader who tends to scoff when a man with a wounded (and infected) shoulder is shown climbing a superstructure, or forging a raging river without a boat, but Foy's storytelling is so strong and true that I was able to suspend my disbelief. And there is enough tension to this story to keep the most skeptical reader hooked.

While George Foy creates his brand of excellent suspense with nonstop action and violence, others take a much different approach. Dorothy Salisbury Davis brings back her series character Julie Hayes in **Lullaby of Murder** (Scribner's, 1984, $12.95).

Davis's talent is for quiet, "psychological" suspense. I am fascinated by her ability to show those small, daily acts of spiritual violence people commit. And I don't know of anyone better at showing, through dialogue, controlled conflict and the countless ways people fail to communicate with one another. Her characters snipe at one another with words, not weapons.

This time out, Julie investigates the murder of her boss, gossip columnist Tony Alexander, a man hated and feared by many—and deservedly so. Davis has created a fascinating cast of characters. Not the least of them is Julie, who grows with each novel in her painful progression towards full, independent womanhood. The mystery is good, too.

So much of the history of the mystery genre remains untapped. It is with great anticipation that each new volume of historical analysis is published. One such volume is **Victorian Masters of the Mystery: From Wilkie Collins to Conan Doyle** (Ungar, 1984, $11.95, pa$6.95) by Audrey Peterson. The title indicates the major problem with Peterson's book. She writes almost exclusively of Collins, Dickens, LeFanu, and Sir Arthur, all of whom have been studied extensively elsewhere. Peterson touches on several writers whom she refers to as "minor voices," but even these are familiar names, except for James Payne, whose contribution to the mystery appears minor indeed.

Peterson has little new insight on the history of suspense fiction, but the study is a readable introduction to several leading figures in nineteenth century mystery literature.

Regarding historical figures of twentieth century mystery fiction, Shadow fans will appreciate the hardback reprint of two notable adventures for Lamont Cranston in **The Shadow and the Golden Master** (Mysterious Press, 1984, $15.95). Fu Manchu fans may question how well Shiwan Khan stacks up as a yellow menace, but those who remember The Shadow will greatly enjoy this facsimile edition, replete with ads for the Shadow pencil "lite" and disguise kit. ▣

Judith Trojan:

Front Row Center

Christopher Reeve and Madeleine Potter—A dark view of feminism

During his lifetime, Henry James conquered all literary avenues except one. A successful novelist, critic, short story writer, and travel writer, James set no precedents as a playwright. Adept at weaving penetrating psychological character studies that defied visualization on the nineteeth century stage, James lived too soon to tap the potential of sound cinema. Such Jamesian gems as *Washington Square, The Europeans, The Turn of the Screw, Daisy Miller, The Golden Bowl, The Spoils of Poynton* and, now, *The Bostonians* have all reached the screen and done quite well by the translation.

On paper, Henry James dealt an ironic hand. His brand of action-adventure took place in the minds of his characters. Through them, James was able to embody the political and moral disorder endemic to the late nineteenth and early twentieth centuries. By focusing on young innocents who were tugged this way and that by the changing social order, James mirrored the forces of social and moral upheaval at work in middle and upper class American and European society as a whole.

This theme was nowhere more evident than in *The Bostonians*, published in 1886. The novel, with its dark view of the early feminist movement, is perhaps more relevant today than it was nearly one hundred years ago. Aware of its timeliness, James Ivory and his partner, Ismail Merchant, have produced an exquisite film version of the novel. Specializing in literary adaptations that feature small groups of exotic misfits, producer Merchant and director Ivory tackled James's *The Europeans* in 1979. They are right for Henry James; they take him seriously. *The Bostonians* also boasts a core group of Merchant-Ivory collaborators including screenwriter Ruth Prawer Jhabvala, cinematographer Walter Lassally, and composer Richard Robbins. With this production team, *The Bostonians* was bound to be a top-notch effort.

Like the Anglo-Indian settings of many of Merchant-Ivory's original films, *The Bostonians* is set in striking locales—the drawing rooms and boudoirs of upper class Bostonians and New Yorkers circa 1875. Ostensibly

Judith Trojan *is editor-in-chief of* Sightlines *magazine, editorial coordinator at the Educational Film Library Association in New York City, and a staff member of the American Film Festival.*

an unfriendly look at the apostles of women's suffrage, *The Bostonians* uses the movement to tell a more universal love story. While James refrained from including overt sex in the novel, Ivory's usual coolness is tempered by both implicit and explicit sexuality in the film.

The music, gorgeous period interiors and costumes are the first thing you'll notice. The rich, dark Victorian city interiors lighted softly by gaslight, the spare rustic Martha's Vineyard beach house and seascape, the beautifully detailed city and country dresses set the time, place, and mood in which this story of good cause, passion, and jealousy unfolds.

Verena Tarrant, a rosebud of a child-woman, personifies the Jamesian innocent who is pulled between the demands of the feminist cause and the natural demands of her hormones. With a talent for public speaking, she studies to become an orator for women's suffrage under the tutelage of pinched, wealthy spinster Olive Chancellor. Chancellor, played in a masterfully repressed manner by Vanessa Redgrave, uses the movement's high aims to veil her very real hatred for men and her sexual desires for her protegé. It's a thin veil, however; and by film's midpoint, everyone takes Olive's true feelings for Verena for granted. Ironically, Olive does not have emancipation in mind for Verena; she wants to possess the girl and extracts from her a short-lived vow of celibacy.

Olive's chief rival for Verena's affections is Basil Ransom, Olive's distant cousin, played by Christopher Reeve. A Confederate veteran, Ransom is up from the South to practice law in New York. A chivalrous chauvinist, Ransom would like nothing more than to outfox Olive and win Verena as his wife, thereby disengaging her from public life and the movement. Although they are political and sexual opponents, Olive and Ransom have much in common.

Scenes between Ransom and Verena are often tumultuous, limited by Olive's stopwatch and Verena's guilt for displeasing Olive. Scenes between Olive and Verena, on the other hand, begin placidly enough, but tenderness soon gives way to mistrust and recrimination. When it becomes apparent that Verena will not be able to abide by her promise of celibacy, Olive's possessive demands push the girl even closer to a union with Ransom. Olive's slow, subtle dissolution is completely drawn by Vanessa Redgrave. Although older than the Olive of Henry James's creation, Redgrave ably projects the movement's contradictions and the high-minded rationalizations that sexual repression can take. Christopher Reeve looks every bit the part of Basil Ransom—tall, dark, and handsome with a continual glint in his eye. Unfortunately, Reeve reads his lines with a lackluster Southern drawl that lessens Ransom's appeal. Newcomer Madeleine Potter is lovely as Verena. Her gentle voice and uncloying sweetness, her wild red hair and and slightly chubby looks enable her to play a convincing teenager on the verge of womanhood. Although Verena has intelligence and a mind of her own, she is just a bit too young and unworldly to know when and who not to trust.

Vanessa Redgrave and Madeleine Potter—A more universal love story

Despite its deliberate pace, the film continually fascinates on various levels. Aside from its topical focus on feminism, its fine production values, and strong lead performances, there's also something to be said for the film's incredible ensemble of character performers. Jessica Tandy is the doddering old abolitionist Miss Birdseye, who makes an ironic go-between for former slaveowner Basil Ransom and Verena. Linda Hunt is the practical Dr. Prance, Ransom's asexual soulmate. Wallace Shawn is the pudgy, pushy newspaper reporter out to make a buck off Verena, the suffrage media star. Wesley Addy plays Verena's loony father, a mesmeric healer who also uses Verena for profit. And, finally, there's Nancy Marchand as Mrs. Burrage, the witty and wise New York society matron who courts Verena as a bride for her son, Henry.

Unpopular in its day as a novel, *The Bostonians* on film has much to recommend it to a contemporary audience. A fine complement to school and library programs covering the work of Henry James, the film is also a perfect program choice for women's studies groups and audiences interested in Victoriana. Film students concerned with successful translations of novels into film will find *The Bostonians* to be a gold mine. Henry James would be pleased as well. ▣

This month's film:

The Bostonians. 35mm. Color. 120 min. 1984. Director: James Ivory. Producer: Ismail Merchant. Screenplay: Ruth Prawer Jhabvala, based on the novel by Henry James. Cast: Christopher Reeve, Vanessa Redgrave, Madeleine Potter, Jessica Tandy, Nancy Marchand, Wesley Addy, Linda Hunt, and Wallace Shawn. Released by Almi Pictures, Inc. No Rating. For future availability on 16mm, contact: Almi Cinema 5, 1585 Broadway, New York, NY 10036.

Bruce Pollock:

On Record: Popular Music

The Bangles—the new Beatles?

I have had in my life, since my extended adolescence ended and the real world of post-rock-and-roll experience (house, car, kids, debts) began, at least two of what I would call "radio epiphanies." Consisting of an aural encounter, usually on a car radio while driving to some godforsaken outpost, with not less than three but sometimes as many as six absolutely stunning, classic, tasteful, exhilarating songs in a row, such epiphanies give rise to outrageous, exotic thoughts of total freedom, bliss, contentment, of the power rock music once had to transform and unite, solve problems, offer advice, hope, and solace, do the shopping, and walk the cat named Dog. After my first I remember thinking: If I could have just an hour of this a day, I could probably withstand anything life could toss at me: washing dishes, changing diapers, working for a living. After the second I suddenly understood what it meant to be young and alive on a Saturday night in the heart of America in the heart of rock and roll, eternally sixteen and aching with unsatisfied lust and unknown destinies and unfulfilled potential—and I was only on my way to the Chinese restaurant to pick up some egg rolls to go!

Bruce Pollock *is editor of* Guitar *magazine and the author of* When the Music Mattered: Rock in the 1960s.

Now radio is radio and rock is rock and some people may reach an emotional peak every time they hear Boy George segue into Cyndi Lauper out of Prince by way of Huey Lewis via Michael Jackson through Billy Joel. And one man's epiphany is undoubtedly another's apoplexy—just ask a Van Halen fan. So I won't bother mentioning the specific components of that first long-vanished radio set that sent me rhapsodizing. But the second, more recent encounter is still whirling in my brain, along with the possibilities of a new musical renaissance around the bend, of bands with songs that miraculously speak to me at the same time they speak to girls and guys young enough to be my babysitters and their late dates: an almost mythical coming together of the generations once again around music.

Two cuts into the Bangles' first full-length LP, **All Over the Place,** somewhere in the middle of "Live," sung by Debbi Peterson, the thought hits: if there were to be a Beatles in the eighties it would have to be four women. Four women whose light and soaring harmonies evoke a pristine, bygone musical age, whose individual and collective personas could cause a generation of young and impressionable women to grow their hair long and drop out of society, whose lyrics and melodies could so awaken in the hearts and loins of young Americans a buried sense of joy and possibility that they might inspire a legion of followers and thereby alter the course of history. Creativity would flourish and common sense go out the window. It would be a little like the moment in *Solid Gold Cadillac* when the picture turns from black-and-white to color. What I mean is, Bam! A new consciousness would take hold, sweep the country, really shake things up for a while.

Now admittedly that's a lot to ask of a band with but one EP to its credit, but the Bangles seem geared for the task, up for it, asking for it even, from their slightly English accents to their modern but melodic sensibility, neither a creation of men's music nor a sisterhood-solidarity cliché of women's music. Aside from the Beatlesque intimations, the message of the Bangles is clear and strong: girls may want to have fun (re: Cyndi Lauper), but they also have to "Live." They are becoming more aware in their relationships, getting ready to stop accepting second best. While these don't sound like revolutionary sentiments right off the bat, neither did "I Wanna Hold Your Hand" in 1964. And beyond any proselytizing, this is an album of delights no matter where your epiphanies lie.

Close on the closing chords of "Live," by the Bangles, "Long Gone Dead," the title tune of Rank and File's LP, immediately flashed me back to 1965. There was the distant sound of an autoharp, evoking the Lovin' Spoonful, the straining harmonies of the Byrds, the folk/rock sentiments of Dylan. Gunning in on that Chinese restaurant I envisioned flower children once again lining the promenade, accosting me for spare change—the Summer of Love II in my very backyard. I didn't know whether to laugh or cry or leave town. Because as much as the song triggered free association of familiar scenarios, it also struck me as being incredibly naive, even lame, laughable. What do these dewdrop college kids know about streetlife, domestic tragedies, domestic wines, life and death or even life only? They probably weren't even born when Dylan prowled the blood-scarred land and every other week someone was assassinated. Like a true reactionary I put them through by far a sterner test than I'd subject on your average loud rock band, the ones with amplifiers like Sherman tanks coming to occupy your city. In fact, just the notion of a new wave of effete folk bands offering a glistening vision of right and wrong to the sneering populace (myself among them) seemed at once a preposterous and pompous proposition. I resented their optimism (and when I saw their video felt ashamed of their unsuave amateurishness). Then, on hearing the entire album, resented their inability to bring it all off convincingly. They wouldn't be Dylan at all, or even the Byrds—they were more like Aztec Two-Step!

But if Rank and File were Aztec Two-Step (a pair of innocuous but pleasant harmonizers from the seventies), Aztec Camera is the second coming of someone like Donovan (who is making a comeback of his own, or perhaps has already come and gone). Led by a teenage Scottish folksinger named Roddy Frame, the band's first album, *High Land, Hard Rain* (Sire 1–23899), gained high critical marks, though I found it impossible to get through. "Oblivious," however, is remixed on this four-cut maxisingle (45 RPM) and the other cuts are oddities no Roddy Frame connoisseur would want to neglect. Something of a South American flavored sambaesque refrain, "Oblivious," in the context of the songs preceding it, suggests an open-ended expanse of musical possibility—man does not live by folk/rock alone. There are other shores, the accumulated wisdom of the seventies, for instance; the wizardry and vigor of the eighties. I was perfectly willing to accept those into my life—I might even buy a pair of straight-legged pants. Which is not to recommend Aztec Camera to anyone—just to place it in the context of a Saturday night eating take-out Chinese again.

The cool jazz-blues inflections of "That's the Way It Is," by The President, widened that expanse further. I thought of the dear departed Colwell-Winfield Band, the long gone dead strains of Keef Hartley. Wonderful. But the rest of the album was as lame as Little River Band meets Air Supply. One for the home-cassette and then the dumpster. Too bad.

Still, I'm asking myself, what is this radio station I've tuned into, this amazing show of nothing but songs I'd never heard before by groups almost all new to me? Obviously there is an audience of red hot teenagers out there cruising to this music even as I'm cruising for dinner through the lights of Saturday night. "Eve of Destruction," by Red Rockers, sewed it up, the mood, the time frame. As ludicrous as it seemed when it hit the top of the charts in 1965, sung by Barry McGuire, its updating nearly twenty years later by a group of teenagers does not immediately seem an utter camp concoction on the order of Weird Al Yankovic. Whether a true tribute, or by imitation or accident, the Red Rocker version sounds serious. And the album surrounding it is dark and foreboding, with brooding songs and a sinister air—as if there might just be something happening out there on the glaring weekend road; something I know next to nothing about.

Do you, Mr. Jones? ▣

Rank and File—A flashback to 1965

This month's records:

The Bangles. *All Over the Place*. Columbia BFC 39220.
Rank and File. *Lone Gone Dead*. Slash 1–25087.
Aztec Camera. *Oblivious*. Sire 20219–0 A.
The President. *By Appointment of the President*. Columbia FC 39360.
Red Rockers. *Schizophrenic Circus*. Columbia BFC 39281.

Gail Pool:

Magazines

The United States has a reputation for provincialism. We are famous for our neglect of foreign languages. Our schools give world history short shrift. We tend to group items together in such categories as "foreign films"—and even "foreigners"—as if they all came from a single country, a tendency oddly reminiscent of some so-called primitive cultures that divide the universe into "we," often synonymous with "human beings," and "they," i.e., everyone else.

Such provincialism seems inappropriate today. That a world increasingly interdependent politically, economically, and culturally calls for a more global viewpoint has long since been recognized by *World Press Review, Worldview,* and *World Literature Today,* three publications which, though very different, share an international perspective.

World Press Review's objective is to provide Americans with access to world news. As its title implies, the magazine surveys the world's leading publications, reprinting those articles and items judged most significant.

"Comfortable and self-absorbed on our vast continent, Americans may be unaware that forty of the world's fifty top newspapers . . . are published outside the United States," says *World Press Review* editor Alfred Balk in the magazine's tenth anniversary issue (May 1984). *World Press Review* tries to make available top quality material most Americans would not otherwise see, and perspectives we would not find in our own excellent but very American press.

Each issue of *World Press Review* includes long articles (sometimes grouped around a theme, such as the UNESCO controversy) and a rundown of events as reported in different parts of the world ("Moscow Beat," "Africa Beat"). Regular departments include "Looking at the U.S.," a compilation of quotations about the United States from various papers, and "The World in Cartoons," which reprints as many as thirty cartoons per issue. A small quantity of original material features a series of dialogues between the editor and leading figures in the world press.

World Press Review is successor to *Atlas,* a more scholarly version of the world news digest, which was founded in 1961 by Quincy Howe and which ceased publication in 1972, when it ran out of funds. In 1974 Balk, formerly with *Saturday Review* and *Columbia Journalism Review,* revived the magazine, now a nonprofit publication sponsored by The Stanley Foundation.

"Like all public affairs magazines, *World Press Review* loses money," notes Balk. He stresses that he won't compromise the magazine's quality for advertising or circulation. Nevertheless, he seems determined to succeed commercially. He hopes to increase advertising revenues; to find outlets for *World Press Review* material in cable television, book publishing, and newspaper syndication; and to market the magazine abroad. Most important, he has tried to enhance the magazine's viability by making it more "journalistic." Shorter and more timely articles, a greater diversity of subjects, glossy covers, and improvements in graphics have helped boost the magazine's circulation to 150,000.

World Press Review has probably gone about as far as it can toward popularization without sacrificing its quality and usefulness. Brevity, as Balk remarks, is the trend in publishing, but it can be taken too far. How useful are one-line quotations taken out of context, such as those found in several sections of *World Press Review*? The short paragraphs in the various "beats" tend to lack the background information needed for useful comprehension. With the recent addition of "Travel Briefs," "Business Briefs," and "The World Economy" (also "briefs"), an increasing proportion of the magazine seems to be divided into paragraph-length items.

World Press Review provides a unique service, at its best bringing home both the insight and the foresight of the foreign press. We need to know how other countries view world events and how they view the United States. The publication's strength clearly lies in its longer articles, and it is doubtful it can do justice to its ambitions by packaging the magazine as a "quick read."

For an examination of the context and implications of world events, it would be hard to find a better source than **Worldview,** a plain and plain-spoken publication that deserves more attention than it has received.

Worldview was founded in 1958 to provide a forum for the exchange of views in the areas of ethics and foreign affairs. Initially an eight-page

Gail Pool *holds an M.L.S. degree from Simmons College and presently works as a freelance writer based in Cambridge, Massachusetts.*

publication, *Worldview* today runs to thirty-two pages, comprised of editorials, articles, and book reviews. Editorials are outspoken. Articles are long, but no longer than they need to be for thoroughness. And the book section is unusual in that it reviews books *not* reviewed everywhere else, and its reviewers tend to be concise, lively, and literate.

Two characteristics make *Worldview* especially unusual. The first is its ethical stance. "We look at the long-term implications of events and decision-making processes," says editor John Tessitore. "We ask, 'Is this good for people? Is it bad for people? Is it correct or incorrect for a government to be doing this?'" *Worldview*'s ethical stance derives from its relationship with the Council on Religion and International Affairs, its founding and sponsoring organization. But Tessitore stresses that the magazine is published as an independent entity, a claim to which the publication's diversity of views lends credence.

Which brings us to *Worldview*'s second characteristic: its function as a forum. The liberal Henry Steele Commager may appear in the same issue as neoconservative Peter Berger. Tessitore suggests that magazines that are identified with the left or the right end up preaching to the converted, reinforcing readers' beliefs and providing them with comfort, while *Worldview*, by offering a variety of views, may cause readers some discomfort.

Worldview has gone through changes in its twenty-seven years—at one point it was a glossy sixty-page publication. Today it is on a course set in 1980, when its new editor came aboard along with Robert Myers, president of the Council on Religion and International Affairs. Editorially the course seems excellent. But like many magazines that emphasize editorial quality, *Worldview* appears to have neglected business. It is not available on newsstands—apparently because *Worldview* does not think its circulation of 25,000 warrants such distribution. But with a small budget

for promotion and advertising, one wonders how *Worldview* is to gain visibility. Because it is subsidized, survival may not be at issue. But just as overcommercialization poses dangers, a lack of commercial sense entails risks of its own. Economic complacency can isolate a magazine from readers' needs and eventually sap it of vitality. Apparently, Myers believes in "the test of the marketplace." He has extensive magazine experience and was founder of *The Washingtonian*. Perhaps under his direction *Worldview* will become more actively competitive.

International crises force us to look at events in other countries; but we are able to comfortably ignore world literature, which doesn't, after all, start wars. True, there are trends, and from time to time countries, even whole continents, are "in"—witness the boom in Latin American literature in the United States. But generally we focus on American writing, and when someone from another country wins the Nobel Prize for literature, we are often unfamiliar with the author's name, let alone his or her work.

Since 1927 **World Literature Today** has been quietly but consistently examining international writing. Started as *Books Abroad* by Roy Temple House, the magazine is sponsored by the University of Oklahoma. Initially a small publication aimed simply at obtaining and noting foreign books, it has grown to be a substantial quarterly. Issues run to a couple of hundred pages, with one section devoted to essays about writers and issues, and a second section comprised of approximately three hundred reviews of books in all languages from Estonian to Japanese, and not excluding English.

World Literature Today's review section presents information one simply doesn't find elsewhere, as well as a fascinating overview of the world's creative output. Articles in the first section are generally interesting. A recent issue included "Reviews of Latin American Literature in U.S. Magazines: Aid or Impediment to Understanding?", an examination of review media undertaken all too infrequently in the general press.

There is a tendency to relegate university and literary magazines to the category "academic," and assume they will interest only a tiny audience. In the case of *World Literature Today,* this attitude seems especially formulaic. Given its unique subject matter, the publication is a resource that should have wider availability than its present circulation of 2,000 permits.

World Press Review, Worldview, and *World Literature Today* offer an international perspective rarely found in our newspapers or magazines. The cliché has it that the globe is shrinking; but reality suggests that the chasms between countries may be deepening. These three publications help provide the bridges we need. ▣

This month's magazines:

World Literature Today. Quarterly. Individuals: $23/yr.; Institutions: $35/yr. Subscriptions: 630 Parrington Oval, Room 110, Norman, OK 73019.

World Press Review. Monthly. $17.95/yr. Subscriptions: Box 915, Farmingdale, NY 11737.

Worldview. Monthly. $19.95/yr. Subscriptions: Box 1935, Marion, OH 43305.

Norman Stevens:

Our Profession

Too often the motivation to produce a particular work is not clear and the work then suffers. Interest in, and sometimes even a passion for, the subject are often what makes a person's work stand out. A high level of personal intensity certainly characterizes, in one way or another, each of this month's books.

Eugene Garfield's work, as revealed in his **Essays of an Information Scientist,** shows intense personal involvement that clearly sets his work apart from that of most information scientists. This volume is the sixth in a series that compiles the multitude of essays Garfield has written under the title "Current Comments" for *Current Contents,* a publication he founded and edits. The range of topics covered in these fifty-two essays, and another twenty-three of his pieces from other sources published between 1954 and 1983, is truly astonishing. Sometimes, as when he deals with automobile horns or graffiti, he is exercising his editorial right to confront pet peeves that have little to do with information science. Sometimes, as when he deals with snoring or cleft lip and palate research, he is commenting on how information science assists science, or how scientific research has advanced our understanding of a particular issue. Those topics may be of limited interest to most librarians even though they are presented in Garfield's usual articulate manner.

But he also touches issues that are of real significance to librarians. In this volume his four essays on research and science in the Third World, as well as his two essays on the use of citation analysis for faculty evaluation, are outstanding contributions that truly challenge our conventional wisdom. Garfield does not simply dash off a weekly essay; each often involves not only considerable thought but considerable research. It is refreshing to note the extent to which he credits his staff for their assistance in his work. Garfield also recognizes and pays tribute, in both personal essays and in essays based on citation analysis, to a number of important individuals. All of these personal elements help set Garfield's work apart from much of our literature.

As a shy person, I have some difficulty in accepting, let alone trying the kinds of suggestions made by Janette Caputo in **The Assertive Librarian.** Nevertheless I can appreciate the intense personal interest which she has in her subject, and I can commend her work, even over Powdermilk Biscuits, to other librarians who may no longer wish to be a shy person. Building on her experience in offering assertiveness-training workshops for librarians, Caputo provides a practical professional manual. She builds on the best and the most solid literature, not on the popular and the trivial, and has done an outstanding job of putting the findings of that literature into library settings.

Especially fascinating is her summary of assertive rights for librarians, library users, and governing boards. That includes the cherished right of librarians to dislike a patron as well as the right of patrons to dislike libraries (but not, I note, librarians). Like most self-help books this one should be read thoroughly and understood if it is to be used; it should not just be skimmed for a few casual ideas. Above all it should not be taken as the only approach to survival in our profession.

Since 1971 Bill Katz has memorialized the best of the current professional literature, much of which reflects a high level of personal interest. Katz may have overlooked the contributions of alternative librarianship, which are often intensely personal. In any case we now have the first of a series of biennial anthologies from that other world of librarianship. Sanford Berman and James Danky, probably the two most passionate advocates of an alternative view, have identified, with no help from an established jury, what they regard as the best contributions on out-of-the-mainstream librarianship. Their anthology covers such diverse topics as alternatives, AV, censorship, just for fun, kids, nukes/peace, people, service/advocacy, women, and work. Their selection of some sixty-seven articles, including four by Berman, contribute to our understanding of issues not always fully appreciated. Like Caputo's assertiveness, all of the issues of alternative librarianship are not for me, and may not be for others; but it always helps to know what those not in the mainstream are thinking and saying. Their choice of library humor, however, is particulary unsatisfying. The three pieces specified as such are all distinctly sophomoric.

No issue of concern to librarians can raise more intense personal feelings than censorship. The four articles on censorship in Berman and Danky all advocate the presentation of alternative views. They come out strongly against censorship but raise interesting questions on such issues as self-censorship, whether words and images affect human behavior, and feminist concerns over pornography and violence. More traditional, but far more effective, are the more than fifty essays in **The First Freedom Today.** Compiled by two respected librarians who have a strong personal regard for the First Amendment, these essays all speak eloquently, and often with personal intensity, on a broad range of contemporary censorship issues.

An almost complete recasting of

Norman Stevens *is university librarian at the University of Connecticut and the author of* Communication Throughout Libraries.

the first edition (1960), *The First Freedom Today* begins with two excellent sections that provide historical background and some new views on the First Amendment. It then deals with such important issues as creationism, fair trials, freedom of information, libel and privacy, obscenity and pornography, radio and television, school censorship cases, secular humanism, and textbooks. All of the material, much of it by nonlibrarians, strikes a positive note. Robert Downs and Ralph McCoy have done an outstanding job of identifying and selecting material. Their collection is the best single available source book for educating ourselves and others on the issues of censorship so that we can act in an assertive fashion.

Unfortunately *A Nation at Risk*, the 1983 report of The National Commission on Excellence in Education, failed to refer directly to the role of libraries in educational reform. Fortunately librarians have been assertive enough to insert library concerns into the debate engendered by that report, and a body of articulate librarians, with an intense personal interest in the role of the library in the educational process, came forward to speak on the issues. **Libraries and the Learning Society** contains six papers by such librarians on how academic, public, and school libraries, and library education fit into society's concerns about quality education. These papers were prepared for a series of seminars sponsored by the Department of Education's Center for Libraries and Education Improvement in 1983 as part of its Libraries and the Learning Society project. They served as the basis for discussion at seminars that will be summarized in a report from the project. There is not much here that is new to librarians but it is all well presented. The material should be of substantial benefit in reawakening our consciousness and in teaching us how to present our views to others in a forthright fashion. ▣

This month's books:

Berman, Sanford and James P. Danky. **Alternative Library Literature, 1982/1983.** Oryx Press, 1984. 338p. $29.95. ISBN 0-89774-132-3.

Caputo, Janette S. **The Assertive Librarian.** Oryx Press, 1984. 242p. $19.50 ISBN 0-89774-085-8. LC 83-4252.

Downs, Robert B. and Ralph E. McCoy, editors. **The First Freedom Today.** ALA, 1984. 341p. $40. ISBN 0-8389-0412-2. LC 84-461.

Garfield, Eugene. **Essays of an Information Scientist. Vol. 6, 1983.** ISI Press, 1984. 673p. $25. ISBN 0-89495-032-0 LC 77-602

Libraries and the Learning Society. ALA, 1984. 145p. $9. ISBN 0-8389-3313-0 LC 84-11163.

Patrick Dewey:

Software for Libraries

Patrick Dewey *is administrative librarian, Maywood (Illinois) Public Library and author of* Public Access Microcomputers: A Handbook for Librarians.

An excellent educational game for ages eight and up teaches the names, abbreviations, and capitals of the fifty states. The program disk for **Game of the States** (Milton Bradley, 1984) is self-documenting, and includes five separate games: name the state; name the capital city; abbreviation; name the neighbors; and major cities. Four of the five games have two skill levels. The graphics and color are pleasing, and the action can be timed at a pace set by the learner, or untimed. The use of only three keys to play any of the games at level one makes it ideal for the youngest elementary school students. Level two sometimes requires spelling out state names or capitals. Instructions, once learned, can be bypassed. Games may be short or long, depending upon how many states one wishes to play. The game may be played either solo or with a friend. An accompanying brochure contains instructions and a list of the fifty states, capitals, and abbreviations. For use with 48K Apple II, or IIe. Cost: $39.95.

Customized requests

Fiction Finder (Calico, Inc., 1983), by William M. Fabian and Varon Fugman, provides librarians with an efficient method for producing customized lists of books for individual patron fiction requests. *Fiction Finder* is a specialized database that holds up to one thousand book titles, each of which may be coded in a number of ways. Up to twenty-seven title categories (e.g., science fiction, westerns, romances, best-sellers, etc.), may be entered. Each title may in turn be coded in up to eight different user-definable ways (e.g., long, short, part of a series, college level, easy reading, etc.). Results can be displayed on the screen or printed for the patron. As with most databases that require custom entry, this one may take awhile to get started—entering one thousand titles, even from a list, takes time. But one can start out small and work up to any number of titles. Many classic or perennial titles remain in the database for good, others may be added or deleted as best-sellers come and go. School librarians may be able to bypass some of the work by drawing upon predetermined reading lists, or by seeking the help of teachers. Calico software is designed and tested by librarians. The program is unlocked, and users are urged to make a backup. For use with the Apple II. Cost: $39.95.

Removing the tedium

Readability Calculations (Micro Power & Light Co., 1984), by Michael Schuyler, will calculate the relative difficulty of text according to nine readability formulas. The use of such formulas has been a tedious process, involving counting syllables and calculating sentence length. This automated system removes the tedium and provides graphs and charts as well. The user types in samples of text, and the formulas are then calculated automatically and results given. Besides being a practical program, it can also be fun. For instance, I took a romance novel and compared it with software reviews found in a library magazine.

The romance had a fourth-grade reading level or less using one formula (fourth grade is the bottom line for the Dale-Chall). The software reviews received a college-level reading score. It can also be a bit humbling to type in one of your own manuscripts, so be warned. Analysis of material reveals a number of other facts, including the Flesch reading ease score, the number of syllables per hundred words, the number of words in the text containing more than three syllables, the number of sentences per hundred words, and the reading level according to several readability formulas. An explanation of what all this means, and how to interpret the graphs and charts, is outlined in the printed documentation and is also part of the program. For further study of readability calculations, a bibliography is provided.

Many librarians will find this program useful, especially when they desire a general understanding of the relative difficulty of books being recommended to patrons. School or academic librarians should be able to recommend it to teachers. It is also a fine tool for writers at work on documentation, training manuals, or any material aimed at a specific age group. In short, this is an extremely impressive, powerful, and useful program. Some of the problems noted by reviewers of the earlier Apple II version have been remedied. Perhaps the most exciting change in the new IBM version is the ability to analyze files created with a word processor, which will allow routine sounding of an author's entire output. Formulas used in analysis: Dale-Chall, Fry, Flesch, Flesch-Kincaid, Fog, ARI, Coleman, Powers, and Holmquist. For use with the IBM-PC, PC-XT, and PCjr. Requires 64K with DOS 1.0, or 128K with DOS 2.0. A tutorial and instructions for the easy production of a backup copy are contained in the manual. Cost: $49. 95. Apple II version: $44.95.

A magic typewriter

The Writing Workshop: The Milliken Word Processor (Milliken, 1984), by Irene and Owen Thomas is one of the most exciting programs to be seen so far this year. It is also perhaps the easiest word processor in the world to learn. Written with the student in mind, it should not take anyone more than thirty minutes to be able to command this simple "magic typewriter." This is not meant to be a full-fledged word processor, nor is it meant as a system for the whole family. It has a specific task: to help and encourage elementary school writers to write. The program is divided into three parts: writing tools, the typewriter, and the file cabinet. It uses some icons—graphics representing the file cabinet, the typewriter, and so forth. By far, the best graphic is the file cabinet, a representation of a cluster of file folders. Each is labelled as files are stored. Most of the other icons are little more than window decoration, since the commands—nearly all mnemonic—each consist of one letter. Editing commands allow the user to move blocks of text, find text, and clear the page. The student may push the cursor to the beginning of the text, or to the end. The program does not allow for normal scrolling.

The IIe version is somewhat easier for students to use, since no control characters are required. Instead, it uses the IIe's four directional keys for cursor control, and the cap shift for upper/lower case. The II+ version requires the user to learn several control commands. The entire program loads into memory during the boot process (it uses Diversi-DOS, a special high-speed disk operating system that improves execution time). The program disk may then be removed and put away until the next session. The "file cabinet" disk—an ordinary preformatted disk which is included and ready for use—is then inserted, and the student is off and running. The list of obvious shortcomings, which prohibit the use of the Milliken Word Proccessor as a tool for serious writing, includes an inability to justify text and limited formatting options. Surprisingly, the program allows for the chaining of files. The documentation, though excellent, will rarely be needed, since most important instructions are online in the form of a superb help file. A special student activities section provides twenty exercises for students to begin and continue their writing, including brainstorming, revising, and writing letters. Suggestions for the teacher are also included. This program is an excellent first stop for the teacher or parent. The disk may be used on any of the Apple II family of micros. Cost: $69.95, with backup disk, and preformatted file disk.

SAT Math I (MicroLab, 1983) is a module to assist students preparing for the SAT. MicroLab came out with its first SAT module for English preparation several years ago. This new module provides interactive testing, tutoring, and familiarity with the SAT format. The two-sided disk program covers algebra, geometry, probabilities, exponents, square root, fractions, ratios, quantitative comparisons, and more. A pretest allows the student to see where he or she stands, with selective tutoring on missed topics. A posttest permits a student to gauge progress. Special commands include quitting at any time, skipping ahead to bypass certain questions, and returning to the introductory page of any unit to make another selection. This will be an excellent addition any library where patrons request SAT material. For use with Apple II, IIc, IIe. Cost: $35.

Publisher addresses for this month's software:
Calico, Inc., Box 15916, St. Louis, MO 63114.
Micro Power & Light Co., 12820 Hillcrest Rd., Dallas, TX 75230.
MicroLab, Inc., 2699 Skokie Valley Rd., Highland Park, IL 60035.
Milliken Publishing Company, 1100 Research Blvd., Box 21579, St. Louis, MO 63132.
Milton Bradley Company, Microcomputer Software Department, 443 Shaker Rd., E. Longmeadow, MA 01028.

James Rettig:

Current Reference Books

Correspondence and review copies for this column should be directed to James Rettig, University Library, Box 8198, University of Illinois at Chicago, Chicago, IL 60680.

Actor's Encyclopedia of Dialects, by Donald H. Molin. New York: Sterling, 1984. 256p. $19.95, pa $12.95. 0-8069-7044-8; 0-8069-7628-4

Actor, director, producer, and dialect coach at various times during a career played out in several countries, Molin has created this book for actors who wish to acquire rather than merely imitate dialects. To that end he has developed his own phonetic notation, keyed in three ways for English speakers in the United States, the United Kingdom and Canada, and Australia and New Zealand. Twenty-three chapters explain how to speak 136 regional dialects from twenty-six countries. American dialects have been excluded. Each chapter describes vowel and consonant changes and the the language's rhythm and pace. Detailed tables present changes for the language as a whole and for its dialects. A tape cassette (price not stated) can be ordered separately. It will greatly facilitate using the book to fullest advantage. To be realistic, however, most aspiring or accomplished actors will prefer to consult their ear rather than this book.

Business Publications Index and Abstracts, 1983 Cumulation, prepared by Management Contents. Detroit: Gale, 1984. **Abstracts.** 2v. $250. **Subject/Author Citations.** 2v. $250. 0-8103-1519-X ISSN 0739-618X

James Rettig *is head reference librarian, University of Illinois at Chicago.*

Keeping track of the hard-copy indexes that have expanded into online access is nearly as futile as bailing a boat with a sieve. *Business Publications* merits note because it reverses the trend. Until recently it was only accessible online as the *Management Contents* database. Now available in hard copy both monthly and annually, two of the cumulated volumes contain the year's abstracts and citations in abstract-number order while the other two contain subject and author citations without the abstracts. Print, of course, offers less flexibility than computer searching. Heavy users of the online version might save money by printing only accession numbers, referring users to the hard copy for citations and abstracts. However, this could lead to sloppy searching. One can appreciate the incentive to diversify formats since the database producer earns a much higher profit on hard copy sales. Charges for online searches must be shared with a telecommunications system and the host system. Libraries must weigh carefully the cost of this cumulation, adding the costs of the 1980–1982 retrospective cumulation and separate subscriptions to future monthly and annual issues.

Critical Survey of Poetry: Foreign Language Series, edited by Frank N. Magill. Englewood Cliffs, NJ: Salem Press, 1984. 5v. $250. 0-89356-350-1 84-5365

Matthew Arnold's assertion in 1865 that "Poetry is simply the most beautiful, impressive and wisely effective mode of saying things, and hence its importance," sounds utterly anachronistic 120 years later. Yet libraries retain poetry collections and schools maintain poetry curriculums because poetry *is* important. If high school and college students need secondary sources such as Magill's *Critical Survey of Poetry: English Language Series* (reviewed in *WLB,* March 1983) to discern the importance of poetry in their own language, how much more they need the *Foreign Language Series*! Like its English counterpart, this series, treating approximately 200 poets from all ages and lands, lists each poet's principal poems and collections, mentions major works in other genres, assesses cumulative achievement, offers a brief biography, analyzes major themes, and lists selected secondary works. Both the essays on twenty-five national literatures (e.g., Catalan poetry, Italian poetry since 1800, Third World poetry) and those on individual poets (e.g., Catullus, Nikos Kazantzakis, Michelangelo, Omar Khayyam, Tu Fu) treat the reader as someone willing to learn the importance of poetry and capable of understanding why, twenty-seven centuries after capturing in words the image of the "wine-dark sea," Homer remains relevant.

Current Issues 1985. Close Up Foundation (1235 Jefferson Davis Highway, Arlington, VA 22202), 1984. 213p. pa$5. ISSN 0743-0388 78-643561

Each year since the late 1970s, the Close Up Foundation, "a nonprofit, multipartisan organization dedicated to encouraging citizen involvement in government," has published *Current Issues* as background information for high school students and teachers participating in week-long seminars sponsored by the foundation in Washington. Each year it surveys ten foreign policy and ten domestic policy issues facing the country. These include defense, international trade, Central America, the Middle East, the domestic economy, environment, education, civil rights, agriculture, and immigration. The unbiased, consistently objective expositions of these topics identify key questions, offer historical background, describe current issues, and juxtapose pro and con arguments likely to be heard during the coming year. The succinct discussions so assiduously avoid drawing conclusions or favoring any viewpoint that the book's usefulness, especially as a starting point for high school debaters, will remain intact whatever the results of this month's elections.

Currier & Ives. Detroit: Gale, 1984. 1,029p. in 2 v. $250. 0-8103-1638-2 83-20844

Valued today as collector's items and depictions of nineteenth-century American life and manners, lithographic prints produced by Nathaniel Currier, James Merritt Ives, and Charles Currier have been cataloged before, but never as thoroughly as they have been here. This catalog's 7,500 numbered entries, alphabetized by print title, include stock number, size, coloration, description, artist's and lithographer's names, publisher, date, notes on variants, and symbols for institutions holding originals. Title variations have been noted through careful cross-references. Approximately 1,000 reproductions, indexed by title, display the Currier & Ives style, sometimes realistic, more often stylized. Indexes provide access by site depicted, date, subject, and artist/lithographer. A concordance translates entry numbers. The compilers acknowledge that this catalog will be subject to revision and addition; nonetheless, for now it is the best treatment of the Currier & Ives oeuvre.

Dictionary of American Temperance Biography, by Mark E. Lender. Westport, CT: Greenwood, 1984. 572p. $45. 0-313-22335-1 83-12589

Today when even Evanston, Illinois, home of the Woman's Christian Temperance Union, has repealed its prohibitions against the sale of liquor, it is easy to forget the power that temperance issues once held in American society. This biographical dictionary of 373 temperance leaders demonstrates the strength of the movement from the 1670s, when Increase Mather published his *Wo to Drunkards,* to its culmination in 1919 when the Eighteenth Amendment was ratified. Even after repeal, the movement continued, but the dictionary emphasizes individuals involved in research and treatment during the post-1933 period. A header lists each subject's birth and death dates, educational background, and career history in who's-who fashion while the profile, one or two pages long, focuses on his or her anti-drink activities and concludes with a brief bibliography. Appendices list biographees by birthplace and religion, and there is an index. The subject is not everyone's cup of tea, but the dictionary will serve well in libraries where there is a call for such information.

Drug Use and Abuse, by Gregory A. Austin and Michael L. Prendergast. Santa Barbara: ABC-Clio, 1984. 2 v. $110. 0-87436-414-0 84-3015

Its selectivity and its presentation distinguish *Drug Use and Abuse* among drug abuse bibliographies. The compilers selected 238 federally funded drug research projects conducted between 1970 and 1980. The 125 studies reported in the first volume were conducted on adults, the 113 in the second volume on adolescents. The studies have been organized by purpose (e.g., characteristics of opiate use, drug use among women, studies on marijuana). The lengthy entries of two to three pages consist of a bibliographic citation, a summary table identifying the characteristics of the population studied and the methodology and instruments used, an explanation of the study's purpose, a list of findings, and a statement of conclusions. Each volume has ten indexes: author, topic, drug, sample type, sex, age, ethnicity, location, methodology, and instrument. Oddly, the index to the second volume is cumulative. The detailed abstracts and the exhaustive index allow a user to determine the sort of studies that have been attempted and what they have revealed. It will be invaluable to drug abuse researchers and helpful to casual, term-paper writers.

Eighteenth-Century English Literary Studies, by Waldo S. Glock. Metuchen, NJ: Scarecrow, 1984. 847p. $52.50. 0-8108-1658-X 83-20057

The annual bibliography on eighteenth-century British literature published from 1926 through 1975 in *Philological Quarterly* lives on today in the multidisciplinary, international annual, *The Eighteenth Century: A Current Bibliography* (New York: AMS Press). For his bibliography, Glock has selected the most significant articles and books, excluding most biographical and bibliographical items, on twenty-five British authors. Descriptive annotations written by Glock enrich the 3,500 entries for books and articles published from the early 1920s through 1980. There is a generous list of scholarly treatment of each author (312 entries for Fielding, 571 for Swift) arranged by the works they treat. The list of nearly two hundred basic books and background articles on the period is not annotated. The annotations for individual authors reveal that some of the articles may be too specialized for undergraduates. Yet they, along with graduate students, will appreciate the bibliography's convenience and its helpful annotations.

Encyclopedia of Psychology, edited by Raymond J. Corsini. New York: Wiley-Interscience, 1984. 4v. $199.95. 0-471-86594-X 83-16814

Of the three English-language psychology encyclopedias, this newest one will most likely receive the heaviest use. To students and other lay readers, its 1,500 signed topical articles will be more satisfying and offer coverage of more topics than the briefer articles in H.J. Eysenck's *Encyclopedia of Psychology* (London: Search Press, 1972) or the rather daunting disquisitions in Benjamin Wolman's *International Encyclopedia of Psychiatry, Psychology, Psychoanalysis, and Neurology* (New York: Van Nostrand Reinhold, 1977). Between these it confidently occupies that middle ground on which most readers feel comfortable. Its 650 biographical entries are a unique strength. Many of the articles conclude with cross-references to related articles. In general the intelligent lay reader can understand the articles, although social science jargon obfuscates the meaning of a few. In the pragmatic style increasingly popular in the social sciences, bibliographical references within the text are extremely brief, just sufficient to refer to the full entries in the extensive bibliography in the concluding volume. Name and subject indexes are separate. A must purchase for academic libraries, this authoritative, encyclopedic exposition of psychologists, theories, tests, and applications of psychology will also find favor in public libraries.

The Encyclopedia of Second Careers, by Gene R. Hawes. New York: Facts on File, 1984. 444p. $49.95 0-87196-692-1 82-5195

If imitation is the sincerest form of flattery, the United States Bureau of Labor Statistics should feel sincerely flattered by *The Encyclopedia of Second Careers,* for 273 of its 444 pages are principally rewritten versions of the occupational profiles published in the *Occupational Outlook Handbook*. The originals, enlivened as they are by photographs, give a fuller picture of what a job requires and involves. *Second Careers* embellishes this core section with lists of careers by type, income level, ease of entry, and educational requirements. Most of the pairings in the list of occupations indicating what sort of second career they can lead to are self-evident, for example, computer programmer leading to computer system analyst. Other trimmings include profiles of the job prospects in fifteen current boom cities; a rudimentary eight-page explanation of how to find and land a job; a directory of community colleges, technical institutes, trade schools, and correspondence schools; a short survey of career change information sources; and an index. The book's mostly cosmetic appeal to career changers cannot substitute for the *Occupational Outlook Handbook* or for professional career counseling.

The Great Song Thesaurus, by Roger Lax and Frederick Smith. New York: Oxford, 1984. 665p. $75. 0-19-503222-5 83-24927

Popular Song Index, Second Supplement, by Patricia P. Havelice. Metuchen, NJ: Scarecrow, 1984. 530p. $32.50. 0-8108-1642-3 83-7692

The Great Song Thesaurus could have been subtitled "A Chronology of Popular Taste," for its main section lists the songs popular in the English-speaking world from Elizabethan times through the 1970s. From the seventeenth century onward, "English-speaking world" is largely equated with the United States. A separate section lists songs popular only in Britain. Annual lists open with a few facts of political or entertainment history. The lists themselves, divided into the categories of Top Hits, Adaptations, Revivals, and Notables, indicate the popularity of hits as measured by sheet music sales, record sales, or air play. To learn the composer, writer, or performer of most songs, the user must turn to the alphabetical title section. Other sections list British and American award winners; lyricists and composers and their works; songs made popular through theater, film, radio, and television; and a subject/keyword index. The *Thesaurus* tells very little about the songs other than that each was popular at a particular time. It also proves the saying that there is no accounting for taste; in 1966 the top seller was "The Ballad of the Green Berets." There is nothing else like the *Thesaurus*; one questions the need for it.

Libraries that buy the *Thesaurus* should also have song indexes on hand, for users of the *Thesaurus* will likely want to find the words to some fondly but hazily remembered songs. Since 1975, Havelice's *Popular Song Index* has been a standard in this field. The second supplement increases its utility by indexing 156 collections published between 1974 and 1981. As before, entries in the title and first-line index and the composer or lyricist index are keyed to a bibliography of collections. Overlap with the 203 collections indexed in *Find That Tune* (reviewed in *WLB,* June 1984) is slight since Havelice continues to emphasize the traditional over the contemporary. *Popular Song Index* will continue to identify sources of old standards.

A Guide to Reference Books for Small and Medium-sized Libraries, 1970–1982, by G. Kim Dority. Littleton, CO: Libraries Unlimited, 1984. 410p. $28.50. 0-87287-403-6 84-7849

Reference Sources for Small and Medium-sized Libraries, edited by Jovian P. Lang and Deborah C. Masters. 4th ed. Chicago: American Library Association, 1984. 252p. pa$20. 0-8389-3293-2 84-6513

Mary Barton and Marion Bell's venerable *Reference Books: A Brief Guide* (7th ed., Baltimore: Enoch Pratt Free Library, 1970) long ago lapsed as small libraries' "Winchell." These libraries now have two candidates to be their "Sheehy." Dority's guide follows the organization of *American Reference Books Annual*: Forty-three topical sections are subdivided by reference genre. The 1,179 entries' mostly descriptive annotations conclude with citations of reviews in standard reference review media, including *ARBA*. The 1970–1982 period signifies the book's emphasis, not its limits; significant older works have been included. The index, a critical feature in any guide to reference works, meets the standard Eugene Sheehy has set for access by author, title, and subject/type of work. It is a commendable guide, but Lang and Masters outshine it.

Several changes differentiate the Lang and Masters product from its predecessors, *Reference Books for Small and Medium-sized Libraries* (1969, 1973, and 1979). None of these editions was worthy to be small libraries' "Sheehy" since they excluded out-of-print titles and virtually ignored reference tools for children and young adults. No longer. The new edition includes these and also notes online availability. The twenty-two chapters, each prepared by a member of the ALA/RASD committee responsible for the book, are divided by narrower disciplines or type of resource. The breadth of the 1,788 entries, the succinctness of the descriptive annotations, the tagging of works appropriate for juvenile and young adult collections, and an index equal to the task make this the "Sheehy" small libraries need.

An Index to Microform Collections, edited by Ann Niles. Westport, CT: Meckler, 1984. 891p. $95. 0-930466-75-6 84-4452 (Meckler Publishing series in library micrographics management, no. 11)

The practicality of microform publishing to preserve and distribute scarce monographs has long been accepted despite most people's strong aversion to reading microfilm for extended periods. It is mystifying, therefore, that microform has been resisted as a medium for reference tools, a use requiring only seconds rather than hours of reading. This weighty volume testifies to the strength of that resistance. An index to an eclectic collection of twenty-six widely held microform collections of monographs from nine micropublishers, its twenty-six chapters list the contents of each set alphabetically by author. Entries for the 9,000 plus works include author, title, date, and reel or fiche number when available. Author and title indexes indicate where an item appears. Because the quality of the guides to the twenty-six collections varies and because few have yet been cataloged title-by-title in OCLC, this volume will be helpful in verifying interlibrary loan requests.

The International Dictionary of Films and Filmmakers, edited by Christopher Lyon and Susan Doll. Chicago: St. James Press, 1984. **Volume I: Films.** 536p. $50. 0-912289-04-X **Volume II: Directors and Filmmakers.** 611p. $50. 0-912289-05-8 83-24616

At a cursory glance, these two volumes seem very similar to *Halliwell's Film Guide* (reviewed in *WLB,* September 1982) and *Halliwell's Filmgoer's Companion* (7th ed., New York: Scribner's, 1980). But the differences are significant. *Films* covers works most often studied as art; *Halliwell's Film Guide* covers popular films. Thus *Films* boasts a smaller but more international selection of films. Both works list cast and other credits, but *Films* goes further, citing reviews and criticism and including a critical essay of several hundred words by a film specialist. *Films,* then, neither replaces nor competes with *Halliwell's.* It makes its own strong contribution to film studies reference.

Filmgoer's Companion offers capsule biographies of actors, directors, producers, writers, and others in the business. The third and fourth volumes of the *International Dictionary* will cover actors and writers and production artists. The overlap between its second volume and *Filmgoer's Companion* is minimal. *Directors/Filmmakers* gives each director's biographical facts, lists films, cites publications by and about the director, and assesses his or her work in a critical essay. Truly international in scope, it covers Woody Allen, Jean Cocteau, Susumi Hani, Leni Riefenstahl, Steven Spielberg, and approximately five hundred others. Students of film will eagerly await the other two volumes of this analytical set.

Library Research Guide to Psychology, by Nancy E. Douglas and Nathan Baum. Ann Arbor: Pierian Press, 1984. 65p. $17.95, pa $9.95. 0-087650-156-0; 0-87650-175-7 84-60640 (Library research guide series, no. 7)

Similar in purpose and audience, *Library Research Guide* and *Library Use: A Handbook for Psychology* (reviewed in *WLB,* December 1983) offer unexpected contrasts. Both explain the use of fundamental reference tools such as *Psychological Abstracts* in the context of the library search strategy. The *Research Guide,* more elementary and selective than *Library Use,* covers the *Social Sciences Index* (which *Library Use* does not mention) but not the Buros books or numerous other specialized tools covered by *Library Use.* The *Research Guide* treats fewer titles in greater detail. It makes a useful companion to bibliographic instruction sessions. After mastering the how-to provided by the *Research Guide,* students will be prepared to expand their knowledge using the additional resources introduced by *Library Use.*

The Marshall Cavendish Illustrated Encyclopedia of World War I, edited by Peter Young. New York: Marshall Cavendish, 1984. 12v. $399.95. 0-86307-181-3 83-20879

Some 540 articles, most between 3,000 and 5,000 words in length, capture the scope and the spirit of the "war to end war." Arranged in the chronological order of the events they treat, the articles address both broad topics (e.g., trench warfare, the Italian forces, revolution in Russia) and narrow ones (e.g., the death of Kitchener, the *Lusitania,* the first flame attack). The table of contents reveals the war's scope; articles discuss campaigns and political situations in western Africa, the Falklands, China, and Singapore as well as along the bloody, entrenched western front in France. The battles receive their due, of course, but the temper of the times really comes through in articles about generals, kings, government ministers, the home front, slang, technological innovations, political movements, and strategy controversies on both sides. All articles conclude with brief bibliographies of additional readings. The length of the articles, the level of the writing, and the copious color maps and illustrations are similar to *American Heritage* magazine. The authors, most of them British, maintain their objectivity except for a few who wrap themselves in the Union Jack but stop short of calling the Germans Huns. An occasional editorial slip, such as the presence of an introductory phrase saying "In this week's article," gives credence to the impression that many of the articles were previously published in a popular British history magazine. Although they follow the progress of the war from the Archduke Ferdinand's assassination to international combat, they do not fit together as an organic whole. Instead, like a row of books supported by bookends, they are held together by introductory sections on one end and the concluding sections and index on the other. Introductory materials include a brief summary history of the war and a chronology. Concluding sections include another chronology and A. J. P. Taylor's summation of the significance of 1914–1918 from the perspective of "fifty years after." The set gives a vivid, if not systematic picture of the war and its effects; it is appropriate but not essential for public and academic libraries.

Musicals! by Richard C. Lynch. Chicago: American Library Association, 1984. 197p. $19.50. 0-8389-0404-1 84-468

Managers of amateur theater groups and summer stock companies and coaches of high school drama troupes trying to decide which musical to produce as their annual show will sing for joy as they clutch a copy of *Musicals!* It will simplify their task, for it identifies and describes, alphabetically by title, nearly four hundred musicals currently available for production. Entries list the years of New York productions and the book from which the musical was derived as well as its composer, lyricist, published libretto, condensed version, inclusion in anthologies, publisher of score or vocal selections, licensing agent, label numbers of recordings, and cast size divided by age and sex. Descriptive annotations characterize the musicals, note famed productions, warn about special needs such as a dog, and identify top songs. This last feature brings entry after entry to life, even in the minds of readers who can't carry a tune in a portable radio. The book includes the time-tested favorites (e.g., *South Pacific, Camelot*)) as well as the mostly forgotten (*By Hex, Sunny*) and the unexpected (*Rocky Horror Show*). Directories of licensing agents and music publishers and an index by composer, lyricist, and librettist are the book's curtain closers.

The Olympics, by Bill Mallon. New York: Garland, 1984. 258p. $25. 0-8240-8926-X 84-4072 (Garland reference library of social science, v. 246)

The timing of this unannotated bibliography is perplexing since, had it been delayed a year or two, it would have been published at low tide of the quadrennial ebb and flow of Olympics publishing. Then it could have become a reservoir for the inevitable flood of books about the 1984 Olympic games. Whatever the reasons for publishing it now, it is limited to books dealing principally with the modern Olympics. The first section includes publications of official Olympic organizations, organized according to type of group. The second section lists books published in more than twenty languages, arranging them according to language. There is no index. Even large research libraries will own only a small fraction of these books and official reports. Standardization of some organizations' names into French may have introduced complications, which will become evident only when a library attempts to negotiate an interlibrary loan request. Since the popular English-language secondary books already on hand in most libraries will satisfy most patron interest in the games, few will want this, regardless of its merits.

The Presidential-Congressional Political Dictionary, by Jeffrey M. Elliot and Sheikh R. Ali. Santa Barbara: ABC-Clio, 1984. 365p. $28. 0-87436-357-8 84-6316 (Clio dictionaries in political science, vol. 9)

Elliot and Ali's dictionary must run against the incumbent, Plano and Greenberg's *American Political Dictionary* (6th ed., New York: Holt, Rinehart, 1982). Plano and Greenberg justify substituting fourteen topical chapters for the alphabetical order expected in a dictionary by saying their order dovetails "with the chapters or groups of chapters found in most textbooks on American government." Elliot and Ali offer no such explanation for their twelve chapters. This distracting scheme is made workable only by a good index. The two-part entries first define, then explain the significance of hundreds of terms relating to the presidency and the Congress. Cross-references knit together terms whose relatedness defies the chapter categorizations. When an entry is common to both books, Elliot and Ali's treatment is longer but not always more enlightening. The chapter evaluating each presidency is inferior to other books, which do the job more thoroughly (e.g., DeGregorio's *The Complete Book of U.S. Presidents* reviewed in *WLB,* September 1984). Since it also covers terms from state and local politics, most libraries will vote for the Plano and Greenberg book, due to publish a seventh edition next year.

Theological and Religious Reference Materials, by G.E. Gorman and Lyn Gorman. Westport, CT: Greenwood, 1984. 526p. $49.50. 0-313-20924-3 83-22759 ISSN 0742-6836 (Bibliographies and indexes in religious studies, no. 1)

The first of four volumes identifying and annotating reference materials for the study of religion, this volume covers general and biblical sources. The sixty-four page section of 154 general reference sources, organized by main entry, could have been omitted despite the author's defense that these are useful; Sheehy does the job better and organizes the sources more sensibly. Chapters on various types of general theological sources (bibliographies, dictionaries, biographical directories, handbooks) and sources for Bible study are also arranged by main entry. The generously long annotations explain how similar works relate to one another. The Gormans have stretched the definition of a reference source to include textbooks and "major topical surveys." The scope includes non-Judeo-Christian religions, although this is not evident in the first volume, which emphasizes biblical resources. Author, title, and subject indexes are separate. The Gormans' planned work greatly exceeds the scope of either Robert Kepple's *Reference Works for Theological Research* (2nd ed., Washington: University Press of America, 1981) or James McCabe's *Critical Guide to Catholic Reference Books* (2nd ed., Littleton, CO: Libraries Unlimited, 1980). When complete, it appears that the Gormans' work will be as definitive as any bibliography can be, but less convenient to use than Kepple and McCabe.

The Twentieth Century: An Almanac, edited by Robert H. Ferrell and John S. Bowman. New York: World Almanac, 1984. 512p. $24.95. 0-345-31708-4 83-051725

Not an almanac, but a chronology of world history, *The Twentieth Century* raises the curtain on a scene that includes the Boers at war against Britain, the "Boxers" in China attacking foreigners, Russia asserting control over Finland, the Irish demonstating against British rule, and Carrie Nation smashing saloons. It closes in 1983 on a scene of a guerrilla car-bombing in South Africa, a Russian fighter destroying a Korean airliner, the United States' invasion of Grenada, a terrorist attack on United States and French barracks in Beirut, and the televising of *The Day After.* Two World Wars, many smaller wars, two atomic bombs, thousands of smaller bombs, assassinations, and incredible advances in transportation, communication, and health care fill the interim. Achievements, atrocities, political changes, significant births and deaths—all mingle on the pages in the haphazard ways of history while developments in the arts, science, technology, and the social sciences are summarized at the end of each year's chronology. The index refers to page numbers rather than specific dates. Photographs and capsule biographies make the book as engaging as its arrangement and index make it all accessible.

Twentieth-Century Author Biographies Master Index, edited by Barbara McNeil. Detroit: Gale, 1984. 519p. $60, pa $25. 0-8103-2095-9; 0-8103-2096-7 84-10349 (Gale biographical index series, no. 8)

Since the second edition of Gale's *Author Biographies Master Index* citing sources of biographical information on authors of all centuries was published just last fall, what need, one may ask is there for this new work covering only authors of this century? The introduction answers that it "aims in particular to make the most useful information on twentieth-century authors affordable for small libraries which may not require the extensive coverage" of the larger set. Some 30,000 of its 170,000 citations are unique to *Twentieth-Century,* having been gathered since *ABMI* was put to bed. The format, immediately recognized by users of other Gale biographical master indexes, registers names exactly as they are entered in the fifty-nine standard, widely held source works indexed. As the introduction accurately states, this offers affordability to libraries that do not have adequate funds to buy *ABMI* or *Biographical and Genealogy Master Index* (reviewed in *WLB,* September 1981).

Worldmark Encyclopedia of the Nations, edited by Moshe Y. Sachs. 6th ed. New York: Wiley, 1984. 5v. $199.95. 0-471-88622-X 83-26013

Since for all practical purposes, the *Worldmark Encyclopedia of the Nations* has reached the quarter-century mark—the first edition was published in 1960—it deserves reassessment. An Achilles among reference works treating world governments, it alternately enjoys a long, uneventful life between editions and a glorious but fleeting fame with each new edition. Of late it has led the former life, neglected on reference shelves because the fifth edition was published in 1976, a time when the Shah ruled Iran, Gerald Ford was President, and Leonid Brezhnev enjoyed good health. Now it reasserts itself until events once again sideline it. For at least several years it will shine, for no other survey of nations and government makes as much information as economically accessible. The first volume is devoted to the United Nations and its agencies, explaining their purposes, origins, organization, and activities. The other volumes profile 172 countries, systematically describing nations in terms of fifty points dealing with their physical attributes, form of government, history, education, foreign relations, economy, military, communications, population, and culture. *Worldmark*'s Achilles' heel, of course is that it is updated at best once every four years. Unlike the Achilles of legend, this does not kill it but rather progressively lames it as time passes. The set has always held and justifiably continues to hold great appeal to small libraries since it economically and single-handedly delivers as much information as a phalanx of competing, overlapping annuals. Buy it and use it.

Library World

ANNOUNCEMENTS

Marie Bruce, director of the Huntington Memorial Library, Oneonta, N.Y., has received the 1984 Robert B. Downs Award. Sponsored by the Univ. of Illinois GSLIS, the award is given for outstanding contributions to the cause of intellectual freedom in libraries.

NEW POSTS

Phyllis Andrews has been appointed head of the Rush Rhees Library reference department at the Univ. of Rochester, N.Y. She was formerly reference librarian and bibliographer for English and American literature at the Univ. of Rochester libraries.

John Aubry has been named reference librarian/bibliographer for the rare book and manuscript library as well as curator for the Herbert H. Lehman Suite of the Columbia Univ. libraries, New York.

Robert Audretsch has accepted the position of director of the Summit County Library, Frisco, Co. He had been director of the Three Rivers Regional Library Service System, New Castle, Co. since 1978.

Susan Barnes has assumed the position of head of reference for the health sciences library of the Columbia Univ. libraries, New York.

Linda Beaupre has been promoted to associate director of general libraries at the Univ. of Texas, Austin. She had been associate director for public services since 1980.

Daniel Davila, formerly chief librarian and dean of learning resources and cultural affairs at Passaic County (N.J.) Community College, has been named chief librarian at Queensborough Community College of the City Univ. of New York.

Susan Davis has been appointed assistant librarian in the university libraries at the State Univ. of New York, Buffalo. She was previously head of serials at the Kemper Library of the Illinois Institute of Technology.

GraceAnne DeCandido has been named editor of serial publications for SLA. She will be responsible for editing and production of SLA's quarterly journal, *Special Libraries,* and the monthly newsletter, *SpeciaList*. DeCandido was formerly coordinator for the Archon retrospective conversion/conservation project at New York Univ.

James Deffenbaugh is now collection development/acquisitions librarian at the Earl Gregg Swem Library of the College of William and Mary. He was formerly bibliographer for philosophy and theology at the Univ. of Notre Dame libraries.

L. David Devine has been appointed manager of the library division of Sydney Dataproducts, Inc. in Vancouver. He was previously marketing manager for the Library Product Group.

Jane Dorn, formerly librarian with the Nuclear Waste Policy Library of the South Carolina governor's office, is now children's librarian for the Richland County (S.C.) PL.

Susan Dow has been named head of the documents department in the law library at the State Univ. of N.Y. at Buffalo. She was formerly public services librarian for the Urban Institute Library, Washington, D.C.

Daniel Eckert has assumed the position of assistant reference librarian at St. Michael's College, Winooski, Vt. He had been reference librarian at Phillips Memorial Library, Providence College since 1980.

Walter Fraser has been appointed director of library services for Advanced Library Concepts of Sacramento, Calif. He was formerly library technical services consultant with Advanced Library Concepts and had been head of the systems and automation department with the Univ. of Calif. at Davis.

John Fuchs, formerly interim director of the learning resources center at Pikes Peak Community College, is now director of the Berkshire Athenaeum, Pittsfield, Mass.

William Fulton is now assistant head of technical services for Mercy College libraries, New York.

Dorothea Hiebing has been named director of the office of library development for the state library of Iowa. She was formerly public library consultant to the Wisconsin Division for Library Services.

Thomas Hinders has been appointed technical services librarian at the McDonald Memorial Library, Xavier Univ., Cincinnati.

Bernita Ingle has been appointed coordinator of the community information and referral service of the Muncie (Ind.) PL.

Virginia Kane is now with the Irving (Texas) PL system as technical services coordinator. She was formerly manager of the technical services division for the Calcasieu Parish PL System, Lake Charles, La.

Stephen Kershner has accepted the position of joint director of the Baldwin PL and Bloomfield Township PL in Michigan. He was previously director of the Geauga County PL.

Bettina Manzo, formerly reference librarian at the Univ. of Wyoming, is now reference librarian at the Earl Gregg Swem Library of the College of William and Mary.

Linda Mark is the new assistant editor for the *Wilson Library Bulletin*. She had been head of the serials division at Pierian Press and was previously an editor at Pierian from 1975 to 1983.

Mark McAteer has been named head of the circulation department at St. Michael's College Library, Winooski, Vt. He was formerly young adult librarian at Stoughton (Mass.) PL.

Colin McKirdy has been appointed associate university librarian for systems at Tufts Univ., Mass. He was formerly information systems manager at the Univ. of Lowell, Mass.

Miriam Meier, formerly mobile services librarian at the Albany (N.Y.) PL, has been promoted to branch librarian at the New Scotland Branch of the Albany PL.

Ray Olson has been appointed to the *Booklist* staff as assistant editor for adult books. He was previously a member of the reference staff of the art and music department at the St. Paul (Minn.) PL.

Deborah Ottsen has joined the staff of the Oklahoma State Univ. library as assistant cataloger. She was formerly serials librarian at Karrmann Library, Univ. of Wisconsin, Platteville.

Russell Pease has joined the staff of the university libraries at the State Univ. of N.Y. at Buffalo as assistant director for public services at Lockwood Memorial Library.

Patricia Peterson has been named assistant library director of the Lincoln City libraries, Lincoln, Neb. She had been coordinator of branch extension services with the Lincoln City Libraries since 1976.

Glenis Ratcliffe has been promoted from branch librarian to adult services librarian at the Albany (N.Y.) PL.

Beth Rile has been appointed assistant librarian at Wabash College, Crawfordsville, Ind. She was formerly catalog librarian at Wichita State Univ., Kansas.

Gail Sacco is now branch librarian at the Delaware branch of the Albany (N.Y.) PL.

Alan Schaplowsky has been appointed head of serials acquisitions at Columbia Univ. libraries, New York.

Thomas Surprenant has been named director of the Queens College GSLIS, City Univ. of N.Y. He was previously associate professor with the Univ. of Rhode Island GLS and will serve in the same capacity at Queens College in additon to his duties as director.

Donna Thomas is now assistant documents librarian in the Oklahoma State Univ. library. She was formerly manager of the Valencia branch of the Tuscon (Ariz.) PL.

Alice Tiffeault has joined the staff of the Mercy College (N.Y.) libraries as reference and library instruction librarian.

DEATHS

Bradford Chambers, director of the Council on Interracial Books for Children, has died. He had been director of the council for the past eighteen years and was previously children's book editor at *Parents* magazine.

Linda Beaupre

Daniel Davila

Walter Fraser

Dorothea Hiebing

PLACE • MARKETPLACE • MARKETPLACE • MARK
MARKETPLACE • MARKETPLACE • MARKETPLACE
PLACE • MARKETPLACE • MARKETPLACE • MARK

Announcements

☐ A scholarship for students in library automation has been established by the Library and Information Technology Association and C.L. Systems, Inc. The $1,500 scholarship will be granted to a student entering a master's degree program, with an emphasis on library automation, at an ALA-accredited school. It will be awarded on the basis of academic excellence, evidence of commitment to a career in library automation, and prior experience. Applicants should not have completed more than twelve hours toward an MLS prior to June 1, 1985. Completed applications must be postmarked no later than December 15, 1984. For an application and reference form, write LITA/CLSI Scholarship, c/o LITA, ALA, 50 E. Huron St., Chicago, IL 60611.

☐ The National Geographic Society's staff library has reopened its reference reading room to the public. The facility had been closed to the public since July 1983 due to construction. The library's refurbished quarters now include a second reading room where visitors may use the resources of the Society's map library, not previously available to the public. The library houses 78,000 books, 100,000 maps, 800 atlases, 750 periodical titles, and a vertical file of more than 1.5 million clippings. There is a particularly extensive collection of materials relating to polar exploration. For more information contact Susan Fifer Canby, National Geograhic Society Library, 1600 M. St., N.W., Washington, DC 20036, 202/857-7787.

☐ The Technologies Committee of the Public Library Association's Community Information Section is collecting information for a directory on the use of new technologies in providing community information services. "Community information" is meant to encompass not only general information and referral but also such services as community bulletin boards, car-pool databases and lists of adult education courses. "New technologies" includes cable TV, computers, electronic mail, and computerized typesetting. To provide information on your library's services, send for a questionnaire from Jane Light, Redwood City PL, 881 Jefferson Ave., Redwood City, CA 94063.

☐ Richard Scarry, author and illustrator of over 200 children's books, has deposited the original artwork for twenty-seven of his books with the Babbidge Library at the University of Connecticut in Storrs. He also provided funds for the purchase of equipment for its storage, and Random House, Scarry's publisher, has donated copies of the published books. Scarry decided to make the gift after his agent read about the deposit in the Babbidge Library of 5,000 illustrated books by children's book collector Billie Levy. The drawings are housed in the Babbidge Library's Special Collections Department.

Children's Specials

☐ In response to a survey recommendation that children's services in Ohio public libraries should become more involved in the decision making process in the library, the Ohio LA has published *A Guideline to Planning Public Library Service to Children in Ohio*. The 32p. booklet is designed to aid trustees, directors, and children's librarians in the planning process by evaluating the library's present service to children and formulating goals for developing the highest level of library service to children. The *Guideline* is available for $3.25 prepaid from OLA Publications, 40 S. Third St., #230, Columbus, OH 43215.

☐ Children at the Gardiner (Me.) PL can view videotapes of such classics as *Strega Nona* and *Where the Wild Things Are* at a moment's notice. Thanks to the proceeds of a book sale, the library has set up a twenty-five-inch color television and a VCR in the children's room. Tapes are shown on demand, often to a single viewer. Due to the ease of operation of the equipment, children can play the tapes themselves. The tapes are also available for one-day check out.

☐ The video generation children, like the ones at the Gardiner PL, now have their own book: *The Kid's Guide to Home Video* by Daniel and Susan Cohen. Following a brief history of TV are discussions of cable, VCRs, video disc, two-way TV, and tips on making your own videos. MTV gets its own chapter, but other programs for children are covered as well. The economics (but not the legalities) of buying, renting, borrowing, and swapping tapes are presented. It is even suggested that libraries are a good source! Published by Pocket Books, the 120p. paperback costs $2.25.

Continuing Education

☐ Designed to meet the needs of mid-career librarians, Career Connections provides guidance in establishing career goals, improving skills, identifying continuing education options, and enhancing career network support. Individual and small group sessions are held at Career Connections in Santa Fe, New Mexico, and programs for groups of up to twelve can be scheduled for other locales. A follow-up consulting service is available for one year after attending the workshop. For more information contact Barbara Conroy, Career Connections, Box 9331, Santa Fe, NM 87504, 505/983-9217.

☐ A fifteen-credit program leading to the Certificate in Community Information Management is being offered jointly by the University of Pittsburgh School of Library and Information Science, Graduate School of Public and International Affairs, and School of Social Work, beginning in the fall of 1984. The program is designed to provide both skills and a credential for community planners, resource specialists, entrepreneurs, and outreach librarians. Further information is available from the admissions office of the school in which the applicant wishes to enroll.

☐ A seminar entitled "English Libraries and Librarianship" will be held May 19–June 7, 1985 at Oxford University, England, conducted by the University of Oklahoma in cooperation with Oxford's Bodleian Library. The session is designed for librarians with an interest in cross-national comparisons of the social role and present practices of libraries and the relationship of individual libraries to a national library system. For more information contact CLS, Library, 1700 Asp Ave., Suite 226, Norman, OK 73037, 405/325-1061.

Film and Video

☐ The Labor Institute of Public Affairs of the AFL-CIO has produced a videotape on pay equity for women. It profiles a library clerical worker at the University of Maryland who is also president of a local union. The twenty-three-minute tape includes information on the current position and history of women in the workforce and depicts the lobbying efforts of the library worker for a comparable worth study of the state employee system. *Pay Equity,* available in ¾-inch and ½-inch VHS or Beta, can be rented for $5 or purchased for $40 from the Department of Education, AFL-CIO, 815 16th St., N.W., Washington, DC 20006.

☐ A series of nine pamphlets on AV techniques—three tip sheets and seven bibliographies—has been produced by NAVA, the International Communications Industries Association. The tip sheets on slides, overhead transparencies, and video offer hints for producing materials, effectively using the media, setting up the meeting room, and other points. The bibliographies cover general AV communications, motion pictures, TV and video, still images for projection, operation and maintenance of AV equipment, designing AV facilities, and AV periodicals. A sample copy of each can be obtained by sending a self-addressed, business-size envelope with three-ounce postage to ICIA, 3150 Spring St., Fairfax, VA 22031, 703/273-7200. Pamphlets can also be purchased in quantity.

☐ Recent events have reminded many in the United States that Central America is a region they know far too little about. Icarus Films has compiled a catalog of their offerings on Central America, including new releases on Nicaragua, Honduras, and El Salvador. Films are available for rental or sale in 16mm or for sale only in ½-inch video. For the Central American Film Library or the complete Icarus catalog, write Icarus Films, 200 Park Ave. S., Suite 1319, New York, NY 10003.

Finding Aids

☐ Eager stage parents can find help in *Getting Your Baby into Modeling and TV Commercials.* As well as providing a directory of over 250 talent agents and personal managers for baby and child models, the guide covers such topics as getting started, finding an agent, auditions, legal requirements, and opportunities after babyhood. The booklet is available for $3.50 from Pilot Books, 103 Cooper St., Babylon, NY 11702.

☐ Self-publishers, whether individuals or organizations, can locate printers that do small press runs in the second edition of *Directory of Short-Run Book Printers,* by John Kremer. Over 190 printers are listed, about half of them with detailed information on minimum, maximum and optimum print runs, sizes and bindings, standard terms, and other features. Advice is also given on dealing with printers. The 160p. book is available for $11 from Ad-Lib Publications, Box 1102, Fairfield, IA 52556.

☐ Innovation in technology is considered by some to be the key to economic growth in the future. To aid smaller firms in this endeavor, the *Guide to Innovation Resources and Planning for the Smaller Business* has been produced by the Department of Commerce and the National Technical Information Service. Federal, state, local and private agencies that offer assistance in such areas as financing, information-gathering, and management are listed with address, description of services, who is eligible, and how to apply. The guide can be ordered for $13.50 from NTIS, Springfield, VA 22161.

From the GPO Presses

The following titles are a sample of re-

cent publications available from the Government Printing Office. Specify the stock number, price and quantity when ordering. You may pay by check payable to Superintendent of Documents or by Visa or Mastercard (give card number and expiration date). Send to Superintendent of Documents, United States GPO, Washington, DC 20402. Or call the order desk at 202/783–3238.

☐ Access to the publications of the Bureau of the Census—print, computer tape, fiche and maps—is provided by the *Bureau of the Census Catalog 1984*. Arranged by broad areas with a subject index, the descriptions give subject content, frequency, geographic areas covered, and price. Ordering information is included and a resource section provides addresses and phone numbers for state and local data agencies. The 268p. catalog, stock number 003–024–05668–2, is priced at $7. Send prepayment to Dept. 36–JP.

☐ Illustrated with photographs, historical drawings, schematics, and maps, *Volcanoes* is a nontechnical digest of information about volcanic types, how they explode, where they are found, and the scientific monitoring going on today. The 45p. booklet, stock number 024–001–03472–7, is available for $2. Send prepayment to Dept. 36–HY.

☐ A new booklet from the Department of Labor, *A Working Woman's Guide to Her Job Rights,* shows women how to get a job, how to protect themselves on the job, and how to secure benefits after retirement. In each section laws and services that are available to assist workers and to protect them from discrimination on the basis of sex, race, color, religion, national origin, age or handicap are cited. The 56p. publication, stock number 029–002–00069–0, is available for $2.25. Send prepayment to Dept. 36–JD.

☐ Published by the Patent and Trademark Office, *General Information Concerning Trademarks* provides information about trademarks and how to apply for them. It answers questions concerning examination procedures, time periods for renewals, and fees. Copies of the necessary forms are included along with a review of the drawing requirements. Explanations of the different types of trademarks and a list of goods and services for which trademarks can be applied for are also provided. The booklet, stock number 003–004–00605–6, is available for $1.75. Send prepayment to Dept. 36–HV.

Idea Exchange

☐ Child-Care Resource and Referral is a new service being offered through the cooperative efforts of the Houston PL's Community Information Service and the Houston Committee for Private Sector Initiatives. The purpose of the service is to assist working parents in finding and selecting child care and to aid community efforts to develop child care services. Persons who call the referral service receive child care options, names of child care providers, and selection guidance. In addition to serving parents, the program gives child care providers information about licensing requirements, staff training, and parent education. For more information contact Carolyn Rinyu or Charles Masling, Community Information Service, 500 McKinney, Houston, TX 77002, 713/229–9177.

☐ In observance of National Library Week in April, the Atlantic County (N.J.) Library compiled a booklet based on Patricia and Gordon Sabine's *Books That Made a Difference.* Local readers, children and adults, submitted brief descriptions of how books, from Beverly Cleary's *Ramona and Her Mother* to Dante's *Divine Comedy,* have affected their lives. A clip-and-save page lists all the books mentioned. For more information contact Kathy Anderson, Atlantic County Library, 2 S. Farragut Ave., Mays Landing, NJ 08330, 609/625–2776.

☐ Filled within ten minutes of the opening of registration, a certified American Red Cross babysitting course was offered at the Mesa (Ariz.) PL this past summer. Restricted to young adults aged eleven to fifteen, the weeklong sessions taught first aid, accident prevention, child development, child and infant care, and babysitting business practices. The YA department sponsored the classes, with funding from the Friends of the Library. A list of certified graduates of the course is kept at the library for interested parents.

Magazine Notes

☐ A newsletter that might be of interest to those outside its geographical area, *The Great Lakes Storyteller's Gazette* provides short articles (how to write a storyteller's resume, pros and cons of scary stories for kids) and news of events in the region. The bimonthly is available for $6 from Great Lakes Storyteller's Gazette, 715 Washington, Grand Haven, MI 49417.

☐ *The Smith Kettlewell Technical File,* published quarterly, is a technical journal for blind and visually impaired electronics hobbyists. It includes information on electronics and radio theory, data on integrated circuits, and instructions for building electronic aids and other devices, as well as hints on soldering, using power tools, and tape editing and storage. The magazine also periodically contains bibliographies. It is available in braille or large print for $15 per year or on talking book disc for $8 per year from Smith Kettlewell Eye Research

Foundation, 2232 Webster St., San Francisco, CA 94115.

☐ Every month *Connections, the Businesswoman's Travel Newsletter* features a city with basic travel information (map, climate, public transportation) plus special tips for women, such as areas to avoid at night and hotels that offer amenities for women. A separate section provides a selection of more general tips. Both sections are three-hole-punched to fit in a binder. A year's subscription is currently $24 and will go up to $36 January 1, 1985. Contact *Connections,* Box 6117, New York, NY 10150, 212/832-2052.

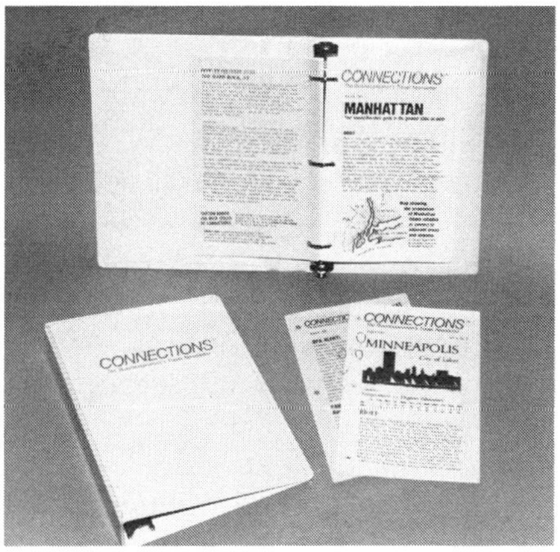

☐ A new publication devoted to the use of the IBM PC family of microcomputers, including the OCLC M3000 workstation, in libraries, *M3000 and PC Report* includes articles on applications in individual libraries, news from OCLC, IBM, and networks that use the hardware, and reviews of books, periodicals, and software. The newsletter, appearing eleven times yearly, is available for $29 for institutions, $20 for individuals from Meckler Publishing, 11 Ferry Lane West, Westport, CT 06880.

Media Center World

☐ The activities of media specialists throughout the country aiding classroom teachers in reaching their lesson objectives are profiled in *Supporting Classroom Instruction Through the School Media Center: A Collection of Case Studies.* Selected from the responses to a survey as examples of the best programs, the descriptions are arranged by subject area and grade (K–12), with name and school of media specialist given. The collection, edited by George K. Sheppard of Idaho State University, is available for $5.95 prepaid, $6.95 billed, from Contemporary Issues Clearinghouse, Dept. A, 1410 South 2nd St., Pocatello, ID 83201.

☐ Cliffs Notes, whose ubiquitous black and yellow covers are familiar to generations of students, has entered the media age. *Cliffs Cassettes—Companions to the Classics* are audio tapes on works of literature consisting of narration interwoven with selected dramatized passages presented by actors and accompanied by music typical of the period. Each thirty- to fifty-minute cassette presents the listener with the themes and historical background of the work and information on the life of the author. Titles available include *Canterbury Tales, Great Expectations, Huckleberry Finn,* the *Odyssey, The Scarlet Letter* and several Shakespeare plays. The cassettes are priced at $7.95.

☐ Since the publication of the first edition of *Instruction in School Library Media Center Use, K–12,* by Thomas L. Hart, in 1978, the number of items developed for library instruction has doubled. The recently published second edition, by the same author, lists activities, games, tests, software, AV materials, and other resources. The table of contents permits identification of materials by subject and grade level. The book is available for $12.50 from Publishing Services, ALA, 50 E. Huron St., Chicago, IL 60611.

Products and Services

☐ Tandberg of America, Inc. has introduced a direct selling program, replacing its representative network, for its audiovisual product line. Customers will now be able to purchase Tandberg products directly from the company in Armonk, N.Y. The new program also features price reductions on most products, product warranties extended from ninety days to one year, and, except for their computer interactive cassette, a thirty-day trial period. An information kit with product descriptions and price lists can be obtained from Tandberg of America, Inc., Box 54, Armonk, NY 10504, 800/431-2430.

☐ Sidney Kramer Books, Inc., a retailer of books on economics, political and military affairs, business management, area studies, and computers, is developing an online database for libraries. The service will permit access to the Stanley Kramer database of over 35,000 in-print and on-order titles to make inquiries on a book or to place an order. Testing with a pilot group of approximately ten libraries will begin January 1, 1985. Libraries interested in joining this group should contact William Kramer, President, Sidney Kramer Books, 1722 H St., N.W., Washington, DC 20006, 800/423-BOOK.

☐ Designed for text storage, heavy office typing and printing, the TW-3000 TECwriter from TEC America has recently been enhanced. Compatible with most microcomputers and small business computers, the TECwriter now has the capability of interfacing with a modem to provide an electronic mail system. The 13,000-character memory, which is optionally expandable up to 29,000 characters, allows up to 255 frequently used phrases or sentences to be stored and recalled, an improvement over the previous model's 3,000-character lim-

it. The TECwriter uses a 100-character daisy wheel and can accommodate proportional spacing. The suggested price is $1,245. Contact TEC America, 19250 Van Ness Ave., Torrance, CA 90501, 213/320–8900.

TECwriter TW-3000

Professional Reading

☐ "Women in Librarianship Bibliography 1983" is a six-page listing of publications issued during 1983 that relate to the status of women in librarianship. Compiled by Katharine Phenix for the ALA Committee on the Status of Women in Librarianship, the citations include articles and books that address pay equity, the Equal Rights Amendment, salary and position levels of women librarians, and association activities related to women's issues. Copies can be obtained for fifty cents prepaid from the ALA Committee on the Status of Women in Librarianship, 50 E. Huron St., Chicago, IL 60611.

☐ The Washington Library Network is publishing a series of booklets designed to assist libraries using microcomputers. The first in the series, *Printers . . . Printers . . . Printers . . .* , is a guide to selecting printers compatible with the IBM PC. It covers over thirty-five data categories on more than twenty-five printers and features such information as durability, noise rating, graphics capability, and capacity to handle card stock. Manufacturers' addresses are given. The booklet is available for $8 prepaid from Washington Library Network, Washington State Library AJ–11, Olympia, WA 98504, Attn: Microcomputer Consulting Service.

☐ The Council on Library Resources has been assessing the extent of current retrospective conversion activities and exploring options for a national conversion policy. *Issues in Retrospective Conversion,* the report of a study conducted for CLR by Jutta Reed-Scott, considers available methods of conversion, the economics involved, and proposals for eliminating duplicate efforts. The study concludes with a recommendation for a national strategy and a method for implementation. Priced at $3 prepaid, the report can be obtained from Council on Library Resources, Inc., 1785 Massachusetts Ave., N.W., Washington, DC 20036.

Software

☐ Output measures such as circulation per capita, reference success rate, and percent of population with library cards are automatically calculated for up to 250 libraries by OUTPUTM, a microcomputer program that can run on the IBM PC, PC–XT, and the Columbia microcomputer. It can store up to ten years' worth of data in twenty categories including annual circulation, annual reference transactions, holdings, and population. Documentation is included with the disc. The cost is $99 with checks payable to the CUP Foundation. Send orders to Center for the Study of Rural Librarianship, College of Library Science, Clarion University of Pennsylvania, Clarion, PA 16214.

☐ A revised edition of A-C-C-E-S-S microcomputer network system software has been developed and the price has been reduced. A-C-C-E-S-S is a telecommunications program for the Apple II series of microcomputers (except IIc) which can be used as a bulletin board system or as a network system for messages and orders. The new package includes menu-driven capability for all functions and permits the selection of a number of popular modems. Two disc drives and a clock card are required. The price is now $250. Contact Information Intelligence Inc., Box 31098, Phoenix, AZ 85046, 602/996-2283.

☐ There are now four editions of Elsevier's *Software Catalog:* catalogs covering science and engineering, and business have been created from material taken from the microcomputer and minicomputer catalogs. A brief description of the software, type of warranty, hardware needed, date of release and other features are given in each catalog. Addresses are provided for distributors and there are subject, systems, language, and microprocessor indexes. The 1984 edition of *Software Catalog: Microcomputers* costs $75, *Minicomputers,* $115, *Business Software,* $35, and *Science and Engineering,* $29.

Write for These

☐ Demonstrating that there's a world of library stamps beyond "Does Not Circulate," the new Kidstamps catalog, produced by two librarians, of stamps created from the work of over forty noted children's illustrators includes for the first time designs of Leo and Diane Dillon, Paul Goble, Rosemary Wells, and Charles Mikolaycak. Stamps depict favorite book characters, two complete alphabets, book plates, and the theme of books and reading. Custom designed stamps can also be ordered. To obtain the catalog free (normally $1.50), request on school or library letterhead from Kidstamps, 1585 Maple Rd., Cleveland Heights, OH 44121.

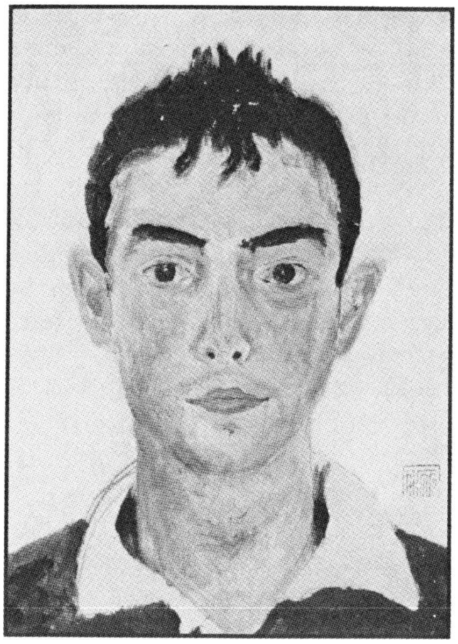

Self-portrait by William Carlos Williams

☐ A table-top display with a selection of pamphlets on public library service to the unemployed, sponsored by the AFL–CIO/ALA (RASD) Joint Committee on Library Service to Labor Groups, was shown at the ALA conference in Dallas. This display and the free pamphlets are now available for loan to state library association conferences. In addition to the brochures on their job and career information services from fourteen public libraries, the material includes publications from the AFL–CIO and the Joint Labor Committee. The shipping cost is approximately $10. The display can be borrowed through Arthur S. Meyers, Muncie PL, 301 E. Jackson, Muncie, IN 47305.

☐ "The Happy Genius of the Household," a lecture on the writings of William Carlos Williams, presented by Reed Whittemore, professor of English at the University of Maryland and Interim Consultant in Poetry at the Library of Congress, has been published by LC. The 32p. illustrated booklet contains the complete lecture as delivered at the library on November 1, 1983, and includes introductory remarks by then Consultant in Poetry Anthony Hecht. The publication is available free from Central Services Division, LC, Washington, DC 20540. ◙

Milner *(cont. from p. 193)*

brary, says Hinds, she was able to develop the facts with the help of librarians who provided her with reference works including *Facts on File* plus other volumes. She learned when: mini-skirts became popular (1969), hot pants emerged and retreated (1971); Billie Jean King defeated Bobby Riggs (1972); the United States put the first man on the moon (1969); the gross national product reached one trillion dollars (1970); Tom Dempsey kicked a record sixty-three yard field goal for the New Orleans Saints (1970); the Viet Nam War ended (1975); and double digit inflation was reached (1978).

Despite the results of the week-long survey confirming substantial use of Free Library business services, there is no doubt that there are thousands of businesses unaware of the library as a powerful tool in achieving success. The perception is that sophisticated business people use the library frequently while the small entrepreneur, or those getting started in business are not familiar with library services.

For libraries the message is clear. As a service to the community and as enlightened self-interest in building a potentially powerful constitutency, a promotion directed to the business community is imperative. The use of direct mail and trade publications are methods that come to mind immediately. Seminars for business led by marketing executives, attorneys and others offer other excellent opportunities. Informal interviews with users who consent to be quoted yield excellent case histories for appropriate use in media. As a result, business leaders, and government officials will view the library rightly as a necessary and vital service to the community.

Boss *(cont. from p. 178)*

provide a method for transporting that database to the library's next system. The only way around this would be to maintain an archival tape for transfer. This is a complex procedure, since all changes made in the records on the local system would have to be duplicated on the archival tape in the MARC format. This does not fully cover the situation, because only bibliographic records are represented. Copy-specific information has usually been added to the records on the local system.

Consider the addition of this copy-specific information. The usual approach is to bring each book to a terminal or bring each shelflist card to a terminal, call up the associated bibliographic record and attach to that record all of the copy-specific information about the physical item associated with that bibliographic record. At the same time the book is going to have to be handled again to have machine-readable labels attached. Counting the cost of the labels, this process will cost around thirty cents per item for the copy-specific conversion and labelling. In a public library, where the ratio of items to records can be ten to one, this can represent a very high total cost.

Libraries are now seeking to create the copy-specific information at the same time that the bibliographic record is created. This can be done by entering the copy-specific information into appropriate fields. Location symbols, accession numbers, copy number information and label numbers can be input in this way.

The availability of label numbers introduced a chicken-and-egg situation because a library does not know what label format its proposed automated system will use until it has selected its system vendor. More and more libraries have decided that they want to undertake conversion and record copy-specific information produced by their current cataloging activities before knowing which label format will be used in their automated system. These libraries are willing to gamble that they will be able to select a system that uses their chosen format, or to persuade the system vendor to support the format they have chosen.

A database to outlast both hardware and software

Such an approach is possible because there are only two basic formats supported by the turnkey system vendors. One is Codabar—a barcode technology—and the other is OCR-A, an optical character recognition technology. The first uses bars, the second uses letters that are shaped so that they can be scanned optically by a special wand. However, each vendor has developed its own format for using the chosen symbology. And here is the gamble. Of the turnkey vendors, CLSI has the most widely installed base. CLSI has not only prepared labels for hundreds of libraries, but other major vendors have inherited CLSI customers. Those vendors have had to support the CLSI labels so that the libraries would not have to replace them. This means that all of these vendors have written computer programs to recognize a CLSI-formatted barcode label.

It is a gamble, because at any time the vendors could say, "if it isn't our label we won't support it." But a number of libraries are realizing that if they can label a book at the time it is cataloged or convert and scan that label to enter the label number in the 049 field, then when they take their records and load them into the local system, the computer program will separate out this information and hang it neatly at the bottom of the appropriate bibliographic record. This will cut down the amount of work to be undertaken when the system is installed.

What must be kept in mind is that a library is building a database that will outlast any piece of computer hardware or software. Without a database, a computer system is useless.

WLB

Classifieds

***Classified Advertising** is accepted six weeks preceding date of issue. Charges are: minimun 3 lines—$10; each additional line—$2.50. If voucher forms are required, please send them when submitting copy. All advertisements for positions must exclude reference to race, creed, color, age, and sex as conditions for employment. The publisher reserves the right to reject any advertising considered unacceptable as to wording or appearance or for any other reason. Submit classifieds to: Brian Bavolar, Wilson Library Bulletin, 950 University Ave., Bronx, NY 10452.*

Positions Open

DIRECTOR, Sullivan County Public Library. Salary negotiable. Position available after mid-October. Send letter of application and vita to: Harold Medsker, President of the Board, Sullivan County Public Library, 100 S. Crowder, Sullivan, IN 47882.

LIBRARIAN/ARCHIVIST. The Monmouth County Historical Association is seeking an energetic and creative individual to manage and promote an important local New Jersey history research collection and library under the supervision of the Director. Responsibilities include day-to-day management of the library, development and preservation of collections, development and promotion of library programs, supervision of volunteers and interns, grants preparation and publication development. Qualifications include an MLS or equivalent experience, knowledge of management and archival management, strong writing skills, familiarity with history and genealogy research and ability to work effectively with Board of Trustees, volunteers and diverse public. Salary range is $14,000 to $18,000, depending upon qualifications. Send cover letter, resume and three letters of recommendation to Director, Monmouth County Historical Association, 70 Court Street, Freehold, New Jersey 07728.

THE UCLA GRADUATE SCHOOL OF LIBRARY AND INFORMATION SCIENCE is seeking to make a one-year visiting appointment in the area of cataloging and subject analysis. This appointment could lead to a permanent position. Applications are desired from candidates with a doctorate, or from persons about to receive one, with demonstrated experience or strong potential in teaching, with interest and competence in theoretical and empirical research, and with knowledge of professional practice. Rank and salary will depend upon record of experience and competence with the following established ranges: Assistant Professor ($25,500 to $29,000), Associate Professor ($30,600 to $34,300), Professor ($37,100 to $49,600), all on a nine month academic year basis. The appointment will be as of Fall Quarter, 1985 or earlier. Inquire and send resume with a list of references to: Robert M. Hayes, Dean, Graduate School of Library and Information Science, University of California, Los Angeles, California 90024. Applications close November 30, 1984.

Announcements

THE FOOTLOOSE LIBRARIAN newsletter & network. Money-saving travel news + U.S. & overseas librarians offering Bed & Breakfast, housing exchange, more. “Good, practical information” M.S., IN; “An excellent publication” S.R., Tunisia. Free brochure. TFL, Box 972, Minneapolis, MN 55440.

LIBRARY/MUSEUM STUDY TOUR in Honolulu/Maui. Holiday leisure and learning 12/27 to 1/4. Tour only from $300; include air and hotel from $850. Teacher's Travel, Box 5513, Santa Monica, CA 90405.

MEDIA NOTES NEWSLETTER. Although the issues have been reduced to two a year, the $10 subscription still secures six issues over a three-year period. A former president of the American Association of School Librarians once commented, “In every issue of MEDIA NOTES there has always been at least one key idea that has benefited me as an educator and media professional.” Subscribe to MEDIA NOTES, the newsletter that takes a lighthearted look at the school media field. MEDIA NOTES, Box E, Avon, CT 06001.

MILITARY BOOKS for identification of shoulder patches, medals, insignia . . . U.S. and foreign. Military history, etc. Send for free catalog, M.C.N. Press, Box 52033 WLB, Tulsa, OK 74152.

NEWSLETTER FOR YOUR SUMMER, SPRING, CHRISTMAS COURSES in London, Paris, Mexico, Hawaii, etc.! Visit libraries, theatre productions, galleries. Exciting study/vacation options for librarians, plus work in foreign libraries. Subscription: $25/yr. NEWSLETTER, Box 5513, Santa Monica, CA 90405.

THE ONE-PERSON LIBRARY: A NEWSLETTER FOR LIBRARIANS AND MANAGEMENT. Professional isolation is one of the major problems of working alone. We want to change that. This new newsletter is informal, informative, and, above all, quick and to the point. Charter subscriptions (one year, 12 issues) for $35, a savings of over 20%. Pre-paid orders to OPL RESOURCES, LTD., Box 948, Murray Hill Station, New York, NY 10156.

For Sale

BRUCE TEGNER'S COMPLETE BOOK OF SELF-DEFENSE hardcover edition is again in stock. ISBN 0-87407-510-6 $10.95. Thor Publishing Co., Box 1782, Ventura, CA 93002.

BRUCE TEGNER judo/karate/aikido/self-defense books price rise in effect now. Current catalog from Thor Pub. Co., Box 1782, Ventura, CA 93002.

CHRISTMAS STORY PROGRAMS by Carolyn Sue Peterson and Ann D. Fenton. A collection of finger plays, poems, songs, and stories with full size traceable patterns for flannel board and puppets. Order from MOONLIGHT PRESS, 3407 Crystal Lake Drive, Orlando, FL 32806. Send $7 plus $1 shipping and handling.

“. . . get ideas from every is[...]ssue.”
M.S. High School Medi[...]a Center, NY
Subscribe (and sen[...]d your nitty gritty
ideas) to The U[...]*N*A*B*A*S*H*E*D

Librarian™, the "how I run my library good"℠ letter, Box 2631, New York, NY 10116. Four issues $20 US funds (add $5 Canadian and foreign postage).

HOBBY BOOKWATCH: Military, gun and hobby book review. Approximately 600 new titles each year. Small and large publishers. One year, $2; two years, $3.50; three years, $5. Published six times a year. For free sample write: HB, Box 52033, Tulsa, OK 74152.

Librarians Love TFL!

"Everyone on our staff is interested in the Travel Exchange, either as a traveller or a host" M.H., San Diego. Free brochure on THE FOOTLOOSE LIBRARIAN newsletter & travel network. TFL, Box 972, Minneapolis, MN 55440.

LIBRARY MUST SELL entire collection of 152 16 & 8mm sound films. Old-time classics & documentaries. $13,000 or best offer. For non-commercial use only. Library catalog: (503) 440-4310. Douglas County Library System, Rosenburg, Oregon. Offers accepted until 12/1/84. Library reserves right to refuse all offers.

LIBRARY NEWSLETTERS. Let a librarian prepare camera-ready copy for your newsletter. $1 for samples. Library Newsletter Service, Box 637, Belleville, NJ 07109.

The MILITARY BOOKMAN—Military, Naval, and Aviation History. Out-of-print and rare books, 3 catalogs per year. 29 East 93rd St., New York, NY 10128 or call (212) 348-1280, Tues.-Sat. 10:30-5:30.

PRACTICE QUESTIONS for academic quiz shows. For more details write Tim Ballard, Box 502, Bardstown, KY 40004.

PUT SEARS TO WORK. 1,200 "see" and "see also" cards plus Manual/List of Headings with DEWEY numbers. From Sears 12th ed., $49.95. Woods Library Publishing Co., 9159 Clifton, Evergreen Park, IL 60642

SOLID OAK SHELVING

SUPERB[LY] ENGINEERED, this solid oak fur[niture bolts together into] sound unibuilt s[helving! Known as] Kanecrest Solid Oak [Demountable-] Remountable Systems with [hundreds of] combinations! Call 615-588-611[3 today] between 10 and 4 EST for FREE 'Packet Parcel', shipped prepaid via UPS. Includes Guide, Large Oak Sample, and Prices Delivered. By all means, compare all prices and costs before ordering thin gauge metal or laminated press wood. SAVE with Direct Purchasing from manufacturer in Tennessee: KANECREST, the Kane Company for this genuine furniture shelving in beautiful solid oak. Call now. Give name, position, institution, and UPS delivery address for your free 'PACKET PARCEL'!

TEACH RESEARCH REPORTING with Can-Do Cards, a proven step-by-step approach recommended for students in grades 4-8. $6.95 postpaid to The Curriculum Exchange, 71 Longview Drive, Marblehead, MA 01945.

"WOW!" "Do not pass go without collecting this PR gem . . . " LJ

GO, PEP AND POP! 250 TESTED IDEAS FOR LIVELY LIBRARIES by Baeckler and Larson. Order from: The U*N*A*B*A*S*H*E*D Librarian™, the "how I run my library good"℠ letter. Dept. GPP/WLB, Box 2631, New York, NY 10116. Send $4.50 check and mailing label with order. Libraries add $1 for billing. Canadian and foreign add $1 in US funds. 6 to 8 weeks delivery. LC 75-20328 CIP.

INDEX TO ADVERTISERS

Gale Research Company .... 4th cover

Holt, Rinehart & Winston 221, 236

Social Issues Resources Series . 161

H. W. Wilson Company
2nd cover, 162, centerfold, 3rd cover

Credits:

p. 168—Lee Pellegrini; 191-92—Ron Williams; 194—The White House; 196—Joseph Farris; 198—Joe Warner; 202—David Jacobson; 205—Don Cohen;; 212—St Martin's Press; 213—Viking; Scribner's; 229—World Almanac. /EBX

STATEMENT OF OWNERSHIP, MANAGEMENT AND CIRCULATION *(Required by 39 U.S.C. 3685)*

1. TITLE OF PUBLICATION Wilson Library Bulletin

2. DATE OF FILING Oct. 9, 1984

3. FREQUENCY OF ISSUE Monthly except July & August

3A. NO. OF ISSUES PUBLISHED ANNUALLY 10

3B. ANNUAL SUBSCRIPTION PRICE $30.00

4. COMPLETE MAILING ADDRESS OF KNOWN OFFICE OF PUBLICATION 950 University Avenue, Bronx, New York 10452

5. COMPLETE MAILING ADDRESS OF THE HEADQUARTERS OF GENERAL BUSINESS OFFICES OF THE PUBLISHER 950 University Avenue, Bronx, New York 10452

6. FULL NAMES AND COMPLETE MAILING ADDRESS OF PUBLISHER, EDITOR, AND MANAGING EDITOR
PUBLISHER The H. W. Wilson Company, 950 University Avenue, Bronx, New York 10452
EDITOR Milo Nelson, 950 University Avenue, Bronx, New York 10452
MANAGING EDITOR None
OWNER *(If owned by a corporation, its name and address must be stated and also immediately thereunder the names and addresses of stockholders owning or holding 1 percent or more of total amount of stock. If not owned by a corporation, the names and addresses of the individual owners must be given. If owned by a partnership or other unincorporated firm, its name and address, as well as that of each individual must be given. If the publication is published by a nonprofit organization, its name and address must be stated.)*
The H.W. Wilson Company, 950 University Ave., Bronx, N.Y. 10452; Florence A. Arnold, 950 University Ave., Bronx, N.Y. 10452; Angelina & Vincent DiGiorgio, 100 Edgewater Drive, Coral Gables, Fla. 33133; Howard Haycraft, 950 University Ave., Bronx, N.Y. 10452; Molly Costain Haycraft, 950 University Ave., Bronx, N.Y. 10452; John Jamieson, 950 University Ave., Bronx, N.Y. 10452; Edward S. Kelley, 28 Kent Shore Drive, Carmel, N.Y. 10512; Arthur & Hannah F. Johnson, 43 Shore Drive, West Barrington, R.I. 02890; Karl Koether, 7 Timbers Trail, Suffern, New York 10901; George I. Lewicky, 950 University Ave., Bronx, N.Y. 10452; Ida E. Rigg, 34-48 81st Street, Jackson Heights, N.Y. 11372; L. M. Weins, 950 University Ave., Bronx, N.Y. 10452; The H. W. Wilson Foundation, Inc., 950 University Ave., Bronx, N.Y. 10452

8. KNOWN BONDHOLDERS, MORTGAGEES, AND OTHER SECURITY HOLDERS OWNING OR HOLDING 1 PERCENT OR MORE OF TOTAL AMOUNT OF BONDS, MORTGAGES OR OTHER SECURITIES None

9. FOR COMPLETION BY NONPROFIT ORGANIZATIONS AUTHORIZED TO MAIL AT SPECIAL RATES *(Section 433.12 DMM only)*
The purpose, function, and nonprofit status of this organization and the exempt status for Federal income tax purposes
☐ (1) Has not changed during preceding 12 months
☐ (2) Has changed during preceding 12 months

(If changed, publisher must submit explanation of change with this statement)

10. EXTENT AND NATURE OF CIRCULATION

		Average No. Copies Each Issue During Preceding 12 Months	Actual No. Copies of Single Issue Published Nearest to Filing Date
A.	TOTAL NO. COPIES *(Net Press Run)*	18,910	19,500
B.	PAID AND/OR REQUESTED CIRCULATION		
	1. SALES THROUGH DEALERS AND CARRIERS, STREET VENDORS AND COUNTER SALES	None	None
	2. MAIL SUBSCRIPTION	15,165	14,569
C.	TOTAL PAID AND/OR REQUESTED CIRCULATION *(Sum of 10B1 and 10B2)*	15,165	14,569
D.	FREE DISTRIBUTION BY MAIL, CARRIER OR OTHER MEANS, SAMPLES, COMPLIMENTARY, AND OTHER FREE COPIES	1,315	2,400
E.	TOTAL DISTRIBUTION *(Sum of C and D)*	16,480	16,969
F.	COPIES NOT DISTRIBUTED		
	1. OFFICE USE, LEFT OVER, UNACCOUNTED, SPOILED AFTER PRINTING	2,430	2,531
	2. RETURN FROM NEWS AGENTS	None	None
G.	TOTAL *(Sum of E, F1 and 2—should equal net press run shown in A)*	18,910	19,500

11. I certify that the statements made by me above are correct and complete.

Frank W. Miller, Vice President

PS Form 3526, July 1984

Wilson Library Bulletin

December 1984

Wilson Library Bulletin

December 1984, Volume 59, Number 4 ISSN 0043-5651

Our holiday cover for December was taken by **George Obremski,** a freelance photographer based in New York City.

Departments

Letter From New York/Editorial 244
Correspondence 245
Upfront/News—*President Reagan signs LSCA reauthorization; Buffalo (New York) Public Library under threat of closure; ALA Executive Board confronts AASL list of proposals; Virginia libraries receive record grant; Roger Parent appointed deputy executive director of ALA; U.S. Secretary of Education resigns; AAP begins campaign to halt copyright abuses in schools; late news.* 246
Calendar 253
Library World 294
Marketplace 296
WLB Classifieds 303

Articles

User Friendly: Washington's Martin Luther King Library *Carolyn Crowley* 254
Sharing Resources in Illinois: Statewide Library Computer System *Bernard Sloan* 259
Access to Materials in Pennsylvania: Interlibrary Delivery *Dwight Huseman* 262

Features

Special Report: "Old Jeff" *Fred Chamberlain* 264
Dateline—Washington *Dale Nelson* 267
Eye on Publishing *Ann McGrath* 268
Facing the Public *Will Manley* 270
Online Update *Martin Kesselman* 272

Reviews

Picture Books for Children *Donnarae MacCann/Olga Richard* 274
The Young Adult Perplex *Patty Campbell* 276
Murder in Print *Kathleen Maio* 278
On Record: Popular Music *Bruce Pollock* 280
Magazines *Gail Pool* 282
Our Profession *Norman Stevens* 284
Software for Libraries *Patrick Dewey* 286
Current Reference Books *James Rettig* 289

The *Wilson Library Bulletin* is published monthly except in July and August by The H. W. Wilson Company, 950 University Avenue, Bronx, N.Y. 10452. Second-class postage paid at Bronx, N.Y. and additional mailing offices. The *Wilson Library Bulletin* is indexed in *Education Index, Library Literature,* and *Popular Periodical Index* and abstracted in *Library & Information Science Abstracts, Historical Abstracts,* and *America: History and Life.* Book reviews are indexed in *Book Review Index.* Subscription $30 a year, U.S. and Canada; $35, foreign. Single copies $4, U.S. and Canada; $4.50, foreign (remittance with order, please). Address all correspondence about subscriptions to the publisher. No subscriptions through agents. Telephone: (212) 588-8400

Letter from New York / Editorial

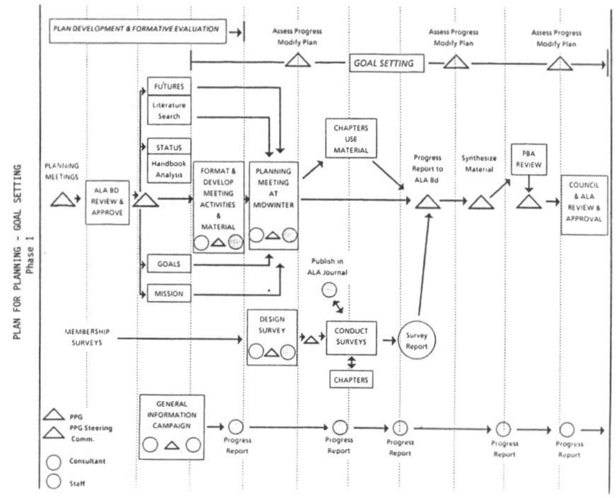

The long-range strategic planning bomb

Since the time that frontiersmen mounted trees in eighteenth-century America to gain a keener appreciation of the geography ahead, it has been a singularly American habit to attempt to see beyond the present. From the private explorations of Daniel Boone, to the organized expeditions of Lewis and Clark, to the institutionalized voyages of modern astronauts, we have proved to be not only a nation of discoverers, but a people who wish to anticipate what is discovered. Curiosity about what might befall us is a national trait. It is not for nothing that we developed the Gallup Poll and the Ballistic Missile Early Warning System. Our interest in the future is as unbounded as our concern with the past is limited, which is one reason we spend millions of dollars on space exploration and are simultaneously content to watch ill-funded archeologists chip away at remote excavations for years on end. We are interested in receiving predictions on virtually everything, including tomorrow's weather, pork belly futures, and the likelihood of getting out of bed the morning after a nuclear attack.

Planning for the future, such a tedious concept when we were young, is seen as the very stamp and hallmark of maturity. Life insurance, reserved cemetery plots, perpetual calendars, umbrellas, smoke detectors—these are the symbols of a life lived with prudence and forethought. We were not schooled to believe there could be such a thing as excessive planning any more than it was possible to be excessive in amount of socks owned, number of foreign languages spoken. All this innocence, however, was recently lost as the result of a trip to Chicago.

The occasion was the autumn meeting of the ALA Executive Board during which time the group heard a report from a committee that had met to do something most people would consider eminently sensible—develop long-range objectives. The title of the committee's printed statement, "Report of the ALA Plan for Planning Group," threatened a certain impreciseness that was borne out by further reading of the paper (Executive Board Document #22). The committee had gathered, we are told to "assess the ALA planning environment" and to "select major steps in ALA Strategic Long-Range Planning."

Although one commendable sentence in the report declares that "Planning activities and the strategic plan itself should be simple, clear, and free of planning jargon," the document then plunges into a plan for action that is only occasionally explicable. The committee, managing to turn a simple assignment into an obscure declaration that is breathtakingly unintelligible, is overcome with randomly applied terms such as "process technique," "working parameters," "agreed upon values," "status assessment," "outcomes," "futures research," "mission review," and enough "time-frames" and "target dates" (see inset) to intimidate Cronos himself.

Even when the committee frankly set out to explain what they did, it is difficult to understand precisely what was accomplished: "The unique characteristics of ALA's planning environment were addressed using small group/large group analysis and consensus decision-making techniques to develop a set of 'Primary Characteristics for the Planning Process'."

The ALA Strategic Long-Range Planning Process will, in the words of the report, ask such questions as "Why do we exist?," "Where are we now?," "What do we want in general?," and "What's out there that may affect us that we should know about?" Who knows. The Loch Ness Monster? Satellite weapons?

That the long-range study will require an outside consultant, need a team of fifteen staff members, take three phases, demand $80,000, and extend to the summer of 1986 seems less of a problem than solving the basic riddle of why such a plan is necessary, what difficulties exist that the effort is expected to correct.

The final goal of this ambitious soul-searching is, apparently, to give "The management tools needed by the association offices and staff to ensure that collaborative planning occurs and achieves its purposes." If one could penetrate this thought, there might be hope of understanding the committee's work.

Mice and men not only make plans that oftentimes go astray, they often go astray in the making of plans. In the absence of a compelling need for a long-range plan, the best plan might be not to undertake a plan.

—Milo Nelson

Correspondence

A proposal to seriously consider

It seemed to me that the recommendations made by Daniel Toohey in "The Only Copyright Law We Need" (*WLB,* September) made such good sense and conformed to the principle of Occam's razor so well that I took the liberty of sending an unauthorized photocopy to Congressman Robert Kastenmeier (D-Wis.) with the suggestion that the House Judiciary Committee seriously consider the proposal.

We here in western New York have had our problems with the copyright law—*Encyclopedia Brittannica* v. *B.O.C.E.S.* It seems to me that Judge Curtin has ruled that the "fair use" guidelines have no standing in his court.

HERBERT SULLIVAN
Grand Island Central School District
Grand Island, New York

Underpaid, undervalued, overworked

I was greatly interested in Will Manley's September column about children's librarians, and want to share with you my opinions.

For too long, educators, librarians, day care workers, and all those who work with children have been considered second-class citizens. They have been put in this position for several reasons. First, they are usually women, whose value in the work force has traditionally been undervalued. Second, working with children has long been considered less important than "serious, adult" work.

Women, today more than ever before, have an opportunity to achieve financial and social success in the workplace. What young woman would willingly choose to be underpaid, undervalued, and overworked when she can be praised, emulated, and make enough money to support her children?

I agree that work with children is valuable, and critical for the future of our world. In fact, I think it is the most important work to be done today. However, I don't blame anyone who chooses something that promises more benefits.

Directors, city commissioners, legislators and parents must demand that librarians be compensated for being the multi-faceted people they are—early childhood specialists, children's literature experts, actors, storytellers, musicians, singers, babysitters, and accountants. We will go back to the field when you offer us:

- A living wage. Mr. Manley, you are the exception in offering $21,000 to an entry-level children's librarian. I've scanned the jobs in *LJ Hotline* for a long time, and most list something around $15,000. Many women today are single heads of households who wind up living close to poverty level trying to support a family on that minimal wage. Library directors are in a position to get more money for their staff. Either do it, or don't be surprised when we go to law school.
- A chance for promotion. Create opportunities for us to grow and achieve status. Who wants to devote fifteen years to a profession and still be a Librarian I because there are no II, III, or IV positions, and you topped out in your salary classification in 1975? We want to feel like we're going somewhere.
- Respect. People think working with children is "fun" and not really work. Well, it is enjoyable, as any job should be, but it is also highly specialized, demanding work, and anyone who denigrates it knows nothing about it. Specifically, library directors must give children's librarians equal status with reference, cataloging, and other professional librarian positions. Reference librarians, without training and experience, could not do what children's librarians do. Let us know we're valuable to you.

My own experience is a good example of someone forced to leave children's work. In the Santa Fe Regional Library in Gainesville, Florida, there are no professional positions in the children's department, (except for the supervisor). I am therefore now in reference, making the maximum salary of $19,500, and every day missing the kids. There are no opportunities for promotion—I already hold the highest nonsupervisory position. There are no opportunities for a raise—I am at the top of the pay scale. The only way I can return to the children's field is to leave a city I love, and many dear friends. My husband would also be forced to leave his job to come with me, or we'd have to work out a commuter relationship. My eight years of experience have been very valuable, and I'd like to be a supervisor, but who hires someone for a supervisory position who does not already have supervisory experience? Even if I could just pick up and go, most positions only offer a substantial cut in pay. My personal dilemma aside, I feel the problems I am facing are illustrative of the problems in the profession as a whole.

I would make a damn good children's librarian. I once was.

FRANCES DOWNEY
Santa Fe Regional Library
Gainesville, Florida

WLB welcomes letters from its readers. Correspondence should be sent to Wilson Library Bulletin, 950 University Avenue, Bronx, N.Y. 10452.

UPFRONT NEWS

Some of the leaders in American librarianship were on hand at the Chicago Public Library for a recent meeting of the U.S. Organizing Committee for the fifty-first General Conference of IFLA, *the International Federation of Library Associations. The conference is to be held in Chicago, August 18–24, 1985. The theme for the 1985 conference is* Libraries and the Universal Availability of Information.

Pictured above are (clockwise from far end of table) **Robert Wedgeworth,** *Executive Director,* ALA; **Amanda Rudd,** *Commissioner, Chicago Public Library;* **William Walker,** *Art Libraries Society of North America;* **Irvin Pizer,** *Medical Library Association;* **Shirley Echelman,** *Association of Research Libraries;* **Vartan Gregorian,** *President, New York Public Library;* **Kathleen Molz,** *School of Library Service, Columbia University;* **Thomas Galvin,** *Graduate School of Library and Information Science, University of Pittsburgh;* **William Welsh,** *Library of Congress;* **Toni Carbo Bearman,** NCLIS; **Pat Moholt,** *Special Libraries Association; and* **Robert Doyle,** ALA *coordinator for* IFLA.

President signs LSCA reauthorization

President Reagan signed HR 2878, Library Services and Construction Act amendments, on October 17. The five-year extension provides for the existing Title I—Public Library Services, Title II—Public Library Construction, and Title III—Interlibrary Cooperation and Resource Sharing. The measure also provides for three new titles: Title IV—Library Services for Indian Tribes, Title V—Foreign Language Materials Acquisition, and Title VI—Library Literacy Programs.

The LSCA reauthorization was among more than 150 bills passed during the final days of the 98th Congress.

Buffalo and Erie County Library under threat of closure

The Buffalo and Erie County (New York) Public Library has been confronted with a county directive ordering the closing of all public libraries in Erie County, including the central library, as of January 1, 1985. County Executive Edward Rutkowski ordered department heads to eliminate nonmandated county services (which includes library services) because of a projected revenue shortfall in the 1985 budget. Rutkowski was quoted in the *Buffalo News* as saying "he had instructed department heads to make such plans because the county legislature has so far shown no inclination to repeal a law limiting property tax increases."

The Buffalo and Erie County Public Library, representing fifty-two city and suburban libraries with 400,000 registered borrowers, has issued an appeal to both the executive and legislative branches of county government, outlining the impact such a decision would have.

Donald Cloudsley, director of the library, told *WLB* that the county has been $75 million in debt for the past two years because of cost overruns at the county medical center, problems associated with a $62 million domed stadium that was never built (and over which the city lost a lawsuit), and "some bad decisions" generally.

Rutkowski has stated that only $16 million will be available in 1985 for optional services like libraries which, by that time, will require $52.9 million. Cloudsley said, "We have lots of friends in the legislature but where they will come up with this sort of money I don't know." Cloudsley, meanwhile, as a cost-saving procedure, has directed that circulation at all libraries in the system be halted, an unpopular move that made headlines after it was announced. Citizens groups are protesting the scheduled closing.

ALA Executive Board confronts AASL list of proposals

A controversial list of proposals and recommendations formulated by the American Association of School Librarians was responsible for the most lengthy discussion and spirited debate at the fall meeting of the ALA Executive Board in Chicago. Those present at the October 24–25 meeting included President E.J. Josey, President-elect Beverly Lynch, past-President Brooke Sheldon, Treasurer Patricia Schuman, Executive Director Robert Wedgeworth, and board members Margaret Chisholm, Arthur Curley, Judith Farley, Elizabeth Futas, Jane Anne Hannigan, Regina Minudri, David Snider, and William Summers.

Presenting his management report, Wedgeworth reported that the State of Illinois has granted ALA's request for a real estate tax exemption on its property, thereby removing a potential tax liability. He stated that the General Fund ended the 1984–85 fiscal year "on target." Total revenues were $8,692,810 and total expenditures $8,668,898, leaving an excess of $23,912. While personal memberships in ALA have increased, there has been a slight decline in organizational memberships and in enrollment in divisions.

Wedgeworth took account of three recent promotions at ALA headquarters: Roger Parent, Deputy Executive Director, Deborah Robertson, Public Information Officer, and Barbara Macikas, Assistant Conference Manager.

Reporting on the September meeting on accreditation sponsored by the Association for Library and Information Science Education, Wedgeworth said the group agreed to explore expanding the scope of the accreditation program to include professional degrees beyond the Master's, broadening the governance of the accreditation program, and expanding the financial base of the program to include participation from other organizations and outside funding. He noted that ALA has obtained a $46,195 grant from the U.S. Department of Education to study participation of other associations in the accreditation of programs in library and information science.

Wedgeworth told the board that ALANET subscribers now number 124, with over 600 mailboxes on the system.

Regina Minudri provided "a walk-through" of a written report on the meeting of an Executive Board subcommittee with a subcommittee of the AASL Board of Directors, both groups formed to attempt to reconcile areas of disagreement. The document summarizes seven AASL positions: AASL wishes to act as the "singular voice" for school librarians; supports a differentiated dues structure allowing school librarians to join AASL without requiring them to join ALA; wants to have responsibility for investing unexpended balances in any of their accounts; wishes to engage in revenue-generating activities including the right to determine when and where to hold conferences; desires to contract with ALA for certain services and not others; favors determining its own employment policies for the executive staff officer and staff; and asks for the right to affiliate with other national and educational associations of its choice. AASL had also requested that it be allowed to publish and hold copyright, but later relinquished this proposal.

"What you have here," said Schuman, "is a division saying it doesn't want to be a division," adding "We would be chipping away at the definition of a division by approving these specific recommendations." Other board members agreed. This is, said Lynch, "a good example of a division usurping the overall context of ALA." Stating that "AASL is challenging the policies of this association," Curley remarked that "elements of the 'operating agreement' are present here." Although Wedgeworth observed that "they want to be the single voice of their constituency," there was no agreement that this was desirable. Said Lynch: "When does a division speak for the association as a whole?"

The board, reacting to the challenge of the proposals put forward by AASL, also reacted to the absence of any representatives of the division at a meeting that had been rescheduled to allow for their presence. "It is an insult to ALA," reproved Lynch, "that no one came to represent AASL. It is an outrage. I will say it publicly."

At discussion's end a statement by Curley summarized the mood of the board: "Come on you guys, if you want to be a part of ALA, be a part of ALA." The board voted unanimously to present the AASL recommendations as an information item to Council at the ALA midwinter meeting in Washington, together with the board's reaffirmation of its belief in the present bylaws governing the association's divisions.

Barbara Markuson, chair of the Committee on Program Evaluation and Support, presented her report on the second day of the session. Markuson stated that ALA could "take pride in the results of restraint, economy, and continued creative actions in revenue generation." Expenditures were under budget by $107,429 with revenues only one-tenth of one percent below target. The board approved a $9,545,667 budgetary ceiling.

Markuson stated that a request was submitted to COPES for two additional staff positions but that the permanent positions had already been filled and asked for a clarification on the practice of creating positions prior to budget approval. Curley commented that having fixed levels of staffing is "a rather archaic management practice" and said while budget ceilings are desirable, staffing ceilings are not. Snider disagreed, saying, "A call for a ceiling is not restrictive." He pointed out that with present practice there is "an element of saying we really don't know what we are doing so we need this flexibility." The board voted to refer the matter to the Finance and Audit Committee.

William Jackson, representing the Endowment Trustees, reported to the board. He stated that the transfer of endowment funds from the First National Bank of Chicago to the Northern Trust Company had only recently taken place, the negotiation taking longer than planned. As a result, there was "a gap in time when no one was looking at our investment account" and a meeting with bank officers revealed that there were virtually no earnings for the past year. Admitting that there might have been a loss of as much as $100,000 in funds at market prices during the transition period, Jackson asserted that "this is merely a loss on paper, with no change in actual, real assets."

The board was briefed by Sheldon on a "Strategic Long-Range Plan." The scheme calls for retaining Glenn Tecker Associates as consultants to guide ALA through the process and will involve $80,000 in contractual costs. Concerned about the cost of the study, the board was also wary of the purposes of the project. Complained Lynch: "There is no clear understanding of the objectives." The board agreed to present the proposal to Council, along with some brief documentation, but the vote was not unanimous: seven for, three against, one abstention.

Eileen Cooke, ALA Washington Office, informed the board that President Reagan had signed a five-year extension of the LSCA into law. She also related that Senator Claiborne Pell (D–R.I.) intends to introduce legislation calling for a second White House Conference on Libraries and Information Service. Said Cooke: "Many people groan and then, in the next breath say, maybe it's not a bad idea." *—M.N.*

ICIA seeks lower postal rate for software

NAVA, the International Communications Industries Association, has urged the U.S. Postal Rate Commission to amend the *Domestic Mail Manual* to allow computer software to be mailed under the special fourth-class rate and the library rate. The U.S. Postal Service has filed a request with the commission to change the postal regulations to allow for the mailing of software under the fourth-class rate. The commission is also being asked to reduce the rates for computer software. The rule change will eliminate what ICIA calls "unfair discrimination" against software. Under present regulations, 16mm films and other audio-visual products are eligible for the special fourth-class rate, but software is excluded.

In a letter to the commission, Kenton Pattie, representing ICIA, said "The authors of the original regulation could not have anticipated the rapid growth of the computer software industry and the widespread applications for these products to libraries, educational institutions, and other non-profit organizations."

ICIA, the trade organization of the communications industry, is located in Fairfax, Virginia.

Virginia libraries receive record grant

The Fauquier County and Fairfax (Virginia) County public libraries have jointly been awarded a $195,806 grant from the National Endowment for the Humanities, the largest NEH grant ever given directly to individual public library systems. The gift will fund presentation of literature discussion programs in forty public libraries in Virginia, with the theme "Literary Reflections of the New South." Humanities scholars from Virginia colleges and universities will deliver lectures and lead discussions. Edwin Clay III, director of the Fairfax County Public Library, said the suc-

Lehigh University, *Bethlehem, Pennsylvania, has received $181,600 from General Motors Corporation to support construction of the university's $10.8 million library and computer center. The building is now in its final stages of construction.*

cess of previous discussion series "confirms our belief that adult programming based upon books, lectures, and discussions is desired by our patrons."

National Library of Wales computerizes

The National Library of Wales in Aberystwyth is being equipped with the most advanced integrated computer system in a single library in the United Kingdom. The library has placed a multi-million dollar order with Microdata Corporation's subsidiary in England to provide computer hardware and software for automating the institution's operations. Installation of the system, based on the company's M9000 32-bit supermini computer with nineteen online VDU terminals and the new URICA library software, is underway by Microdata Information Systems, Hertfordshire, England.

URICA is a new software package that is compatible with libraries of all sizes. The system is designed to take advantage of the relational database of Microdata's M4700 minicomputers and M9000 superminis. URICA has five integrated modules covering information retrieval, acquisitions, serials control, circulation, and cataloging.

The National Library of Wales will be the first in the United Kingdom to offer direct access to a locally held computerized catalog offering comprehensive search and inquiry facilities. Users will be able to choose whether to input and receive information in Welsh or in English.

Brian Evans, project leader of the library's automation team, said "The final system should enable us to unlock the treasure of great richness that we have in our library in a manner never possible before." Within five years the database is expected to hold over a million records.

Microdata, a subsidiary of McDonnell Douglas Corporation, is headquartered in Newport Beach, California.

UMI to upgrade delivery service

University Microfilms International, Ann Arbor, Michigan, plans to make popular periodicals on microfiche available on a quarterly delivery schedule. It had been UMI's policy to deliver its microfiche periodicals on an annual and semi-annual schedule. The frequency change is in response to requests from librarians, who indicated a desire to receive select periodicals on a more timely basis.

The delivery frequency of select periodicals on microfiche will now be a customer option. The customer may elect delivery either annually or quarterly—thirty to forty-five days after the end of each three-month period. Approximately 400 popular periodicals will now be available from UMI under the accelerated delivery option, with new titles available later if market interest warrants.

New Jersey library barters for legal services

The Atlantic County Library, Mays Landing, New Jersey, has adopted a barter system for legal services with the county's legal department. Library director Joseph Green came up with the barter agreement after finding that collection agencies have only limited success in taking action against severely delinquent borrowers.

With the present procedure the library attempts to retrieve delinquent materials by overdue notices, invoices, and phone calls. If these efforts fail and the materials are of $50 value or more, the case is sent to the county counsel's office which issues a letter warning of an impending suit. If the letter is unsuccessful, the county counsel's office files suit in Superior Court, seeking the cost of the book, fines, court costs, and attorney fees. In exchange for their work, the county counsel's office is entitled to equivalent time on the library's WESTLAW database. According to Susan Lothian, assistant county counsel, "Access to WESTLAW is very useful to us, since research sources are limited locally."

Council on Library Resources gives grant to CRL

The Council on Library Resources has awarded a $8,800 grant to the Center for Research Libraries to study and evaluate its current membership, governance, and fee structures. Warren Haas, president of the CRL, said, "We are hopeful that this study will go beyond a survey and analysis effort. We see this as an opportunity to think broadly and creatively about the future character of the center."

The evaluation is prompted by changes in the expectations of the member research libraries and the resulting impact on the center's collections and services. Information Systems Consultants of Bethesda, Maryland has been given the contract to conduct the study. The consultant team will be headed by Richard Boss.

Center for Rural Librarianship offers electronic mail service

The Center for the Study of Rural Librarianship at Clarion University of Pennsylvania has established an electronic mail service to provide rapid transmission of messages via microcomputer terminals. This new service, Ruraline, is part of TYMNET's OnTyme-II network which now has more than 500 member libraries.

The OnTyme-II message system will allow users to send a message simultaneously to any number of recipients. Network members and online user groups can exchange messages and local libraries may refer reference questions to regional centers or to the Center for the Study of Rural Librarianship via Ruraline. The mail system will store announcements of conferences, news items, and cooperative activites in an online file.

The OnTyme-II electronic bulletin board service originates from the Bibliographical Center for Research in Denver.

Chicago Public approves Data Phase installation

The Chicago Public Library board of trustees has formally accepted a Tandem computer system and Data Phase ALIS software. Both hardware and software have met required contract specifications. The online library automation installation at the Chicago Public Library is one of the largest such projects ever undertaken in the United States. Data Phase also plans to develop a telecommunications network that will provide the library with long-range technological capabilities.

Data Phase, located in Shawnee Mission, Kansas, specializes in designing software for library use. The ALIS system is presently in use in over 800 libraries nationwide.

Gale Research offers database license service

The Gale Research Company is now making information from its publications available on computer tape and diskette. Through the company's new Database License Service, clients may obtain copies of Gale's directories and other publications for internal use on their own computer facilities. The tapes can be ordered to contain all of the information for a publication, or be limited by subject category or geographic location. The thirteen titles presently available include *Business Organizations and Agencies Directory, Encyclopedia of Associations,* and the *Research Centers Directory.*

The basic price for the service ranges from $2,000 to $5,000 per year or edition, depending on the publication.

OCLC begins microcomputer exchange

OCLC has inaugurated an exchange program for IBM PC and M300 workstation microcomputer programs. The OCLC Microcomputer Program Exchange (OMPX) will collect and distribute public domain programs relating to library operations. The OMPX collection will contain three types of material: contributed programs from IBM PC and M300 workstation users written in BASIC and other languages; command files and templates for use with commercially available programs such as DB Master, VisiCalc, Supercalc, Lotus 1-2-3, dBase II, and similar products; and data files, such as names and addresses of library schools and professional literature.

OMPX is the successor to the LIS/PX (Library and Information Services Program Exchange) begun last year by Allan Pratt at the University of

The Orbis Imago, *Gerardus Mercator's cordiform map of the world, 1538, the earliest dated map to apply the name "America" to both the North and South American continents, is part of* Treasures of the New York Public Library, *a major exhibit that will run from February 15 through May 24, 1985 at the Central Research Library in New York City. The exhibition, embracing ten centuries and scores of cultures, will showcase 250 of the library's most significant holdings, including a letter Christopher Columbus wrote to his patron Luis de Santangel in 1492 reporting his discovery of the "New World."*

The Mercator map shown below is the Flemish cartographer's first published world map. Drawn when he was twenty-six, it depicts a double cordiform (heart) projection, breaking the world sphere into halves. It is one of two known impressions.

Items in the exhibit were selected for their historic impact, aesthetic beauty, and bibliographic rarity. An illustrated catalog is available from the library for $12.

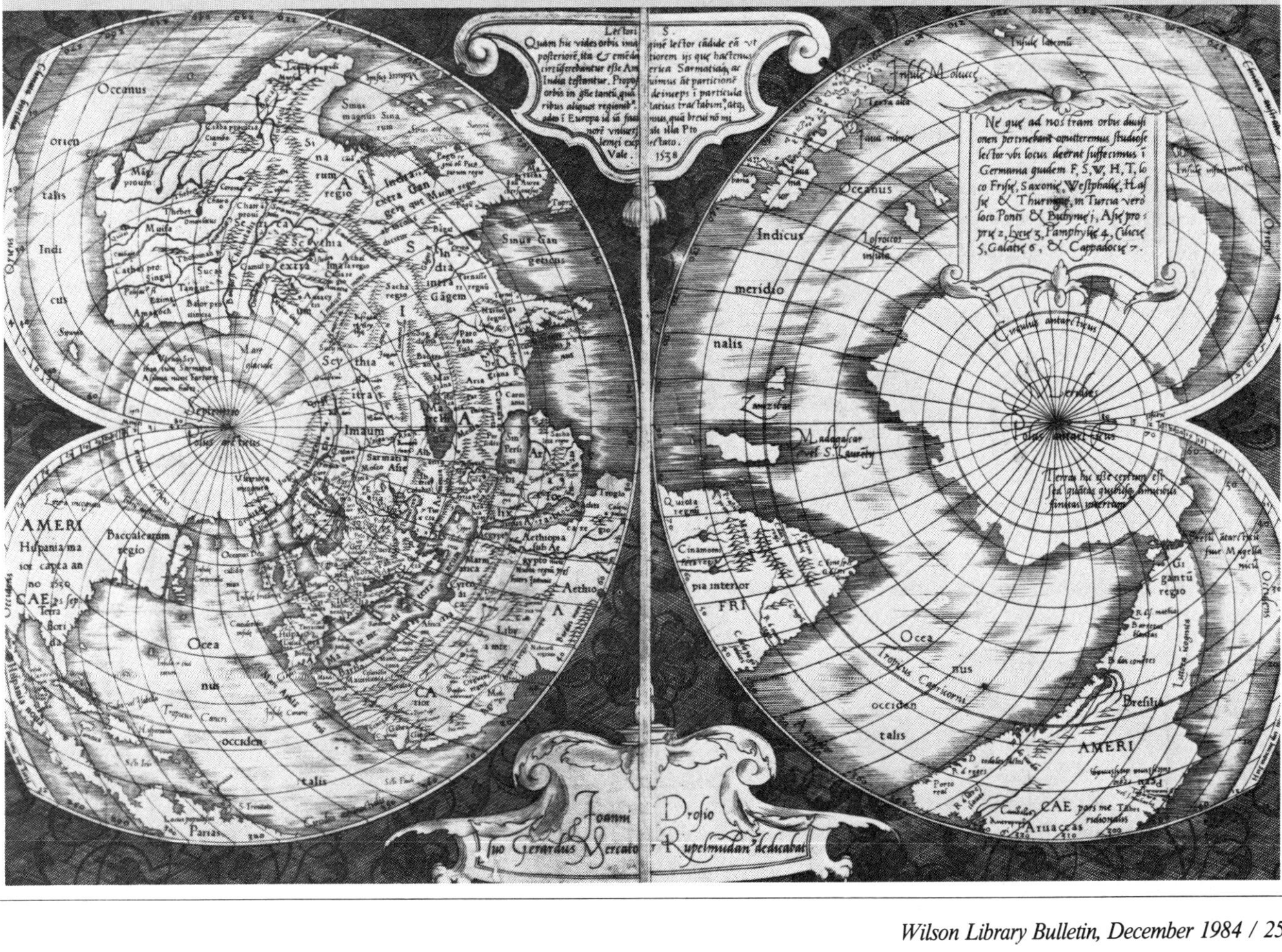

Arizona Graduate Library School. The disks which were formerly available from LIS/PX are now part of the OMPX collection.

Dallas Public receives literacy grant from Dalton

The Dallas Public Library has received a grant of $6,000 from the B. Dalton Bookseller National Literacy Initiative. After the library raises $12,000 the bookseller will contribute an additional $6,000 to the campaign. Lee Shuey, coordinator of the library's new literacy program, said "The grant will help support our volunteer tutoring program, which is targeted to begin in January. Our intent is to teach area adults who want to learn to read, write, and compute."

Houston voters approve bond issue

Voters in Houston, Texas have approved $15.25 million in bonds for the development of the Houston Public Library system. Proposition 8, which was part of the city's nine-part capital improvement package, passed by sixty-two percent of the vote. The library bonds will fund the construction of three new branches over the next five years. The capital improvement plan also calls for the purchase of sites for three new branches in unannexed sectors of the city.

Library director David Henington said, "Houston voters have once again shown their commitment to quality library service. We are grateful for their support."

Bell resigns as Secretary of Education

Education Secretary Terrel Bell has announced his resignation, the first member of the Cabinet to make the decision not to remain for President Reagan's second term. Citing "personal reasons" for his decision to leave, Bell will become a professor of school administration at the University of Utah. He denied that differences with the Office of Management and Budget over levels of federal spending for education had been responsible for his decision to leave government service.

Bell called *A Nation at Risk,* a report that criticized the quality of elementary and secondary public education, one of his major achievements. Bell said he was leaving the department during "a real renaissance in education. It's been a joy to have been a part of that."

AAP attempts to halt copyright abuses in schools

The American Association of Publishers recently announced that they have reached an agreement with the public schools of Anne Arundel County, Maryland that stipulates when teachers may reproduce copyrighted material. The agreement is the first of its kind with a public school system in an effort to curtail the misuse of copyrighted materials, according to Carol Risher, director of copyright for the AAP. "In schools around the country," said Risher, "teachers who are very eager to expand the resources that they bring to their classrooms, and who face a tightening economy, run off materials they pick up at conferences, such as a sample workbook. Frequently, they don't know they're breaking the law, and sometimes they know but don't care because they think it is for a noble purpose."

William Patry, a lawyer for the AAP, said the agreement allows a teacher to seize "the teachable moment" and copy something like a news clipping or magazine article. But it prohibits a teacher from reproducing a literary work and passing it out to classes year after year. The guidelines also limit how much material may be reproduced, limit how much may be reproduced from a single source, prohibit copying for the purpose of creating an anthology, and require that photoreproduction of a work must be at the inspiration of an instructor rather than a system-wide decision.

Roger Parent *has been appointed deputy executive director of the American Library Association. Since 1979, Parent has been executive director of the Library Administration and Management Association. Prior to that he served as development librarian at Princeton University, as director of the Mercantile Library Association in New York City, and as a business reference librarian at Bernard Baruch College, City University of New York. Parent holds a B.A. in liberal arts from the University of Massachusetts and an MLS from Simmons College.*

Data Research upgrades turnkey systems

Data Research, St. Louis, Missouri, has upgraded the performance of its turnkey systems by incorporation of Digital Equipment Corporation's VAX 8600 mainframe computer. The availability of the new hardware will increase the number of terminals that may be configured on a Data Research system. DEC will support up to 512 terminals per VAX 8600 processor, and due to their compatibility with DEC's VAXCluster multiprocessor computer interconnect and hardware interfacing, up to fourteen processors may be locally interconnected to form a single high-performance automation site.

The VAX 8600 has a performance level up to five times that of the previous mainstay of the DEC VAX product line, the VAX-11/780. The machine is rated at approximately 4.2 million instructions-per-second. All software currently supplied by Data Research will operate on the VAX 8600 without modification.

The major market for the new library system is expected to be university libraries and large public libraries.

Calendar

Announcements should be sent at least 60 days in advance to "Calendar," WLB, *950 University Ave., Bronx, NY 10452.*

JAN. 2–4—*Association for Library and Information Science Education,* annual conference. Shoreham Hotel, Washington, D.C. Theme: "Undergraduate Preparation for the Information Profession." Inf.: Jan Phillips, ALISE, 471 Park Lane, State College, PA 16801.

JAN. 16–19—*Medical Library Association,* winter institute. Belleview Biltmore, Belleaire, Fla. Inf.: MLA Education Dept., 919 North Michigan Ave., Suite 3208, Chicago, IL 60611.

JAN. 17—*Massachusetts LA,* midwinter conference. Framingham State College. Theme: "The Library As An Educational Institution." Inf.: Milles Cavanaugh, South Hadley LS, South Hadley, MA 01075.

JAN. 18–21—*COMMTEX International.* Anaheim Convention Center, Anaheim, Calif. Inf.: International Communications Industries Association (ICIA), 3150 Spring St., Fairfax, VA 22031.

JAN. 22—*Marketing Techniques For Librarians,* seminar. George Washington Univ., Washington, D.C. Inf.: AJ Seminars, 11205 Farmland Drive, Rockville, MD 20852.

JAN. 22—*Information Sources in Business and Economics,* seminar. Norris Medical Library, Los Angeles. Inf.: (see Jan. 22 for address.)

JAN. 29—*Abstracting and Indexing,* seminar. Hotel Bellevue, San Francisco. Inf.: (see Jan. 22 for address.)

FEB. 1–3—*Winter Education Conference '85.* Franklin Plaza Hotel, Philadelphia. Inf.: Ellen Gerber, SLA , 235 Park Ave. S., New York, NY 10003.

FEB. 1–3—*Marketing and Public Relations,* institute. Philadelphia. Inf.: (see Feb. 1 for address.)

FEB. 8—*The World of Rare Books,* workshop. Drexel Univ., Philadelphia. Inf.: Janet Goldwater, Office of Continuing Professional Education, Drexel Univ., Philadelphia, PA 19104.

FEB. 8–14—*Art Libraries Society of North America,* annual conference. Hyatt Regency, Los Angeles. Theme: "L.A.: Metaphor For the Future." Inf.: Pamela Jeffcott Parry, Executive Director, ARLIS/NA, 3775 Bear Creek Circle, Tuscon, AZ 85749.

FEB. 15—*On-Line Literature Searching,* workshop. Drexel Univ., Philadelphia. Inf.: (see Feb. 8 for address.)

FEB. 18—*1985 Congress For Librarians.* St. John's Univ., New York. Theme: "Downloading/Uploading Online Databases and Catalogs." Sponsor: Division of Library and Information Science, St. John's Univ. Inf.: James Benson, St. John's Univ. DLIS, Jamaica, NY 11439.

FEB. 21—*U.S. Government Publications and Services,* seminar. Hotel Bellevue, San Francisco. Inf.: (see Jan. 22 for address.)

FEB. 22—*Library Automation: A Seminar On the State-of-the-Art,* workshop. Drexel Univ., Philadelphia. Inf.: (see Feb. 8 for address).

FEB. 26—*Introduction To Basic Cataloging,* seminar. Norris Medical Library, Los Angeles. Inf.: (see Jan. 22 for address.)

FEB. 27—*Information Sources in Science and Technology,* seminar. George Washington Univ., Washington, D.C. Inf.: (see Jan. 22 for address.)

MAR. 4–5—*Univ. of North Carolina Librarians' Association,* spring conference. Univ. of North Carolina, Chapel Hill. Theme: "Preservation in the '80's." Inf.: Libby Chenault, Rare Book Collection, Wilson Library 024–A, Univ. of North Carolina, Chapel Hill, NC 27514.

MAR. 4–6—*Management Skills,* institute. San Francisco. Inf.: (see Feb. 1 for address.)

MAR. 4–6—*National Federation of Abstracting and Information Services,* annual conference. Crystal Gateway Marriott Hotel, Arlington, Va. Theme: "New Developments in Electronic Publishing and Information Services." Inf: NFAIS, 112 South Sixteenth Street, Suite 1207, Philadelphia, PA 19102.

MAR. 6–8—*Libraries, Books and Culture,* seminar. Univ. of North Carolina, Chapel Hill. Co-sponsors: Univ. of Texas GSLIS and Univ. of North Carolina SLS. Inf.: Univ. of Texas at Austin GSLIS, Education Building 564, Austin, TX 78712–1276.

MAR. 8—*Midstream Career Changes For Librarians and Other Information Professionals,* workshop. Drexel Univ., Philadelphia. Inf.: (see Feb. 8 for address.)

American Library Association
Midwinter meeting
January 5–10. Washington
Annual meeting
July 6–11. Chicago

Canadian Library Association
Annual conference
June 13–18. Calgary (Alberta)

Medical Library Association
Annual conference
May 24–30. New York

Public Library Association
National conference
April 2–5. St. Louis

Special Libraries Association
Winter meeting
January 30–February 1. Philadelphia
Annual conference
June 8–13. Winnipeg (Manitoba)

User Friendly: Washington's

Carolyn Crowley

Austerely modern—Martin Luther King Library

Martin Luther King Library

Washington, D.C.'s Martin Luther King Library functions as an exciting, unusual community center. It is the central facility of a twenty-six branch public library system established in 1896. The eleven-year-old building is austerely modern. Designed by the late Mies van der Rohe, the 420,000-square-foot library is constructed of concrete, grey glass, and black steel. The Martin Luther King Library is located at 9th and G Streets, N.W., between two subway stops in central Washington—near the major department stores and two blocks from the new convention center. It has become a refuge for young and old alike.

At The Other Place

Each week, about 2,500 students visit the Young Adult Services Division, known as The Other Place. "We need rollerskates here after school," laughed Desiré Grogan, chief of the Young Adult Division. Along with a variety of paperbacks, hardcover books, and magazines for teenaged patrons, the collection includes records, educational and recreational filmstrips, and videotapes. There are also four Commodore PET Series 2001 professional computers with instructions, recreational tapes, and programs for skills development in math, vocabulary building, and reading comprehension. The staff offers term paper clinics, SAT preparation workshops, financial aid seminars, college and career workshops, and a computerized tutoring service. There is a rap corner, furnished with comfortable bean-bag chairs.

Charles Foster, a seventeen-year-old high school senior, likes to spend time after school at The Other Place. "I like to come here with my friends to talk with them and have some fun. There's a controlled atmosphere here. It keeps me out of trouble but I'm a nice person anyway. I come here almost every day."

He was there recently reading *Return of the Native*. He admitted he had waited until the last minute to begin reading Thomas Hardy's work for his three-page book report due that week. "We do one every month. I don't like doing book reports but I like to read. I could be doing better in school but I don't try hard enough." He's doing well enough, though, to look forward to attending college.

Donna Fleming, a fourteen-year-old ninth grader, also goes to The Other Place almost every day. "It's quieter here than at home. There are three kids at my house. My mother picks me up at 6:30. Until then I experiment on the computers, read, do homework—every night I have two hours—and listen to music."

Celebrating curiosity

The collection at the Martin Luther King Library—some 429,000 books and 1,321 magazine titles—is a monument to the love of knowledge and to human curiosity. Nowhere is this more apparent than in the Telephone Reference Division. There, surrounded by a five-tier wheel holding over six hundred reference volumes, a vertical file of 10,000 newspaper and magazine clippings, and additional books that line the walls, sit two reference librarians. They receive six hundred to eight hundred calls each week.

"We try to answer questions in three minutes. Ninety-five percent of the time we succeed," said reference librarian Bill Stephenson. "The more intellectual the questions are, the easier it is to find the answer. It's hard to find the answers to questions we think are silly."

He cheerfully spends his days answering telephone inquiries on the distance between cities, where to find birth and marriage certificates in the United States, and the meanings of slang terms.

"People sometimes call asking the date," Stephenson said. "We get long-distance calls from bill collectors wanting to verify people's addresses and addresses of their neighbors in the District. We don't give out names of those living nearby. Someone once wanted to know if cockroaches have

---

Carolyn Crowley *is a freelance writer based in Washington, D.C.*

Answering questions in three minutes—the telephone reference section

teeth." (They do, according to Stephenson.)

The books he consults the most are a thesaurus, *The Encyclopedia of Associations, Who's Who in America, Webster's Third Unabridged Dictionary, Editor and Publisher Yearbook, Books in Print,* the *World Book Encyclopedia* and the *World Almanac.*

"Ninety percent of the calls are from adults. Up to 5:30 it's government employees," Stephenson said. School children call too. "Children are cheating when they call about their homework," he laughed. "But they're always prepared and listen attentively. Seldom do we have to repeat answers for them."

Stephenson enjoys his work. "This is a challenging job. The gratification you receive from the patrons is overwhelming. I'm never bored. Each call is different. You must have a sense of adventure for this job because each question is an adventure."

District history

The seventy-eight-year-old Washingtoniana Division includes materials that chronicle events in the nation's capital as far back as the early nineteenth century. The division houses 14,000 books that contain the social, cultural, economic and, of course, political history of the District of Columbia. In August 1982 the library acquired the working morgue and photo library of the *Washington Star.* The acquisition was a gift from the *Washington Post,* the buyer of the *Star*'s building. The collection includes thirteen million news articles filed by name and by subject and one million photographs.

"There was competition for that collection. We had the widest access and the largest space for it. That's why it came here. We moved six divisions to make room for it. All the media in D.C. have used us," said assistant head librarian Kathyrn Ray. In January 1984 about 4,300 people did research in the *Star* collection and 969 people called for assistance. "That's our average, not our busiest though. February and March are the busiest," Ray said.

Among the most popular of the Washingtoniana collections are the real estate references. They include plans from 1887, property assessments from 1873, and a complete set of city directories, first issued in 1822. Residents and out-of-towners who are thinking of buying and selling property frequently call or visit this division to check on assessments and taxes or to compare sale prices of nearby properties.

Service for the blind and handicapped

The American Foundation for the Blind has identified some 9,000 blind readers in the District of Columbia. "If we reached 5,000, that would be our optimum. We serve fewer than 3,000. About 2,500 don't know we exist. A number of them have never been readers," according to Grace Lyons, chief of the system's Library for the Blind and Physically Handicapped.

Martin Luther King Library is one of the country's fifty-six regional libraries to receive material from the National Library Service (NLS) of the Library of Congress. The national book collection contains 38,000 titles and the service offers seventy magazines on disc and in braille. The District of Columbia library sends out or delivers reading materials to borrowers who return them by postage-free mail. Anyone who is unable to read or use standard printed materials because of temporary or permanent visual or physical limitations may receive service.

Visually-impaired patrons may choose to use the library's Visualtek, a machine that enlarges words up to sixty times their printed size. The library also owns a Kurzweil Reading Machine, which electronically converts printed and taped texts to lifelike speech. Another library service valued by visually-impaired patrons is a monthly in-person reading service for personal correspondence, bank statements or bills.

"There's no way national programs such as the National Library Service of the Library of Congress and Recordings for the Blind in Princeton, New Jersey can meet every need of our visually or physically handicapped. We have highly skilled disabled people in Washington," said Lyons. Some of those gaps are filled by volunteer readers, who record publications for the blind at the Martin Luther King Library.

Lucille Holmes, an eighty-one-year-old volunteer, averages twelve hours a week reading for the Washington Volunteer Readers for the Blind. A retired Voice of America broadcaster, she is one of 200 volunteers who tape publications for the blind for nationwide distribution. In 1983 they taped 38,118 pages and 681 requested items for individuals and agencies. Holmes is also recording *Access to the World,* a publication that provides information about air, bus, train and ship travel and lists hotels accessible to the handicapped.

Up-to-the minute news—wire service in the lobby

Literacy, music and black studies

The library does not have adequate funds to run literacy classes. It has for many years, however, offered information on tutoring programs. The Sociology Division has a collection of books for adults with literacy problems and for those who want to teach an adult to read. "There are a lot of adults who've gone to school in this country who are illiterate," said Ann Ross, director of the division. "In the 1960s libraries started being concerned and gathered collections but the materials were few and mostly children's and easy young adults' books. Libraries scrounged for materials. We started our collection in 1976.

"Librarians must be sensitive in knowing when someone needs materials like this. Some people come in saying 'I can't read'. But that's unusual." Ross added, "More people are willing, however, to admit they can't read today than ten years ago because of the attention illiteracy has received and because they know they aren't the only ones in the world who can't read."

No other library in the Washington metropolitan area has such a large collection of printed music scores, free to the public. Some of these are miniature scores that can be carried to concerts. The Music Division owns 26,000 scores—from song books, to musical comedies, to chamber music. It also has 700 orchestral sets for loan.

The Black Studies Division houses almost 15,000 contemporary and historical volumes in all subject areas by and about Afro-Americans and people of African descent throughout the world. Also there are more than thirty Afro-American-owned newspapers.

This large first-floor room has a wide range of clientele. One man who visits about four times a week is a freelance writer who is researching the Dred Scott case for an article in a scholarly journal.

Some of the other clientele are "regulars who get out of the damp, cold and rain here," the chief of the program, Alice Robinson, said. "We have scholarly researchers, transients, lots of students and bag people. They read a lot. Some have Ph.D.'s and have just flipped out. They couldn't take the pressures."

Another popular feature at the library is the AP news wire service teletype machine which types out up-to-the-minute news dispatches in the lobby. At times of national and international crisis large crowds gather to follow the latest news developments.

Dial-A-Story

Children and adults alike enjoy the library's Dial-A-Story. The Children's Services Division is the only one in the metropolitan area producing weekly recorded folk tales. Since the service began in 1976 almost three million callers have listened to the three-and-one-half minute recorded folk tales from around the world.

"The dominant European cultures have given us the best known folk tales," commented Maria Salvadore, coordinator of children's services.

"African folk tales are popular too. We try to introduce a number of cultures. The stories are for five to five-hundred-year-olds," Salvadore said. "Folk literature is for everyone. The appeal of folk tales is their predictability, especially for a child. It's comforting to know what's going to happen next. Our purpose is to interpret literature for children, encourage reading, and encourage use of the local library." Every week there is a different tale. The recording operates twenty-four hours daily, a boon to both junior-sized and adult insomniacs.

The Martin Luther King Library also provides meeting rooms for community groups, free sign language classes, a weekly authors lunchtime speakers program, free assistance in filling out District income tax forms, films, and concerts. It has become an important place in the accelerating revival of the downtown area as well as a focal point for city celebrations and special events.

Funding and the future

The popular programs at Martin Luther King Library have faced funding problems like most library systems. Hardy Franklin, director of the District of Columbia Public Library since 1974, noted that the fiscal cutbacks a couple of years ago were difficult for the system. The Martin Luther King Library was "really screaming and hurting. Now financing has drastically improved." In fiscal 1985 there is a $1.4 million increase from the mayor's office, a $125,000 increase from City Council, and a $100,000 increase in the book budget from Congress's House Subcommittee on D.C. Appropriations.

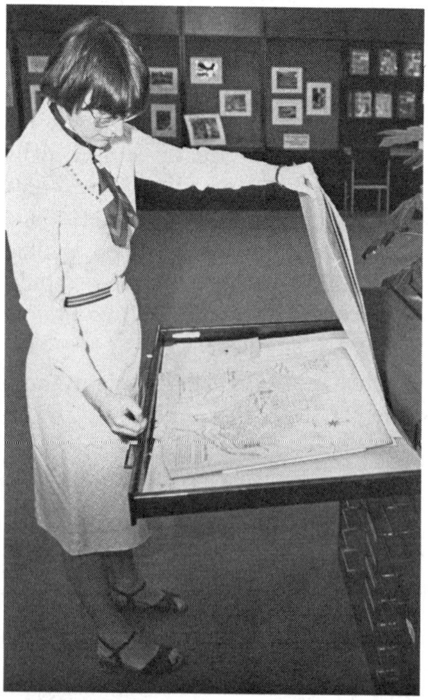

Kathryn Ray with Ellicott's plan of the City of Washington

"This year and in 1985 we've gotten increases all along the line," Franklin emphasized. Ninety-six percent of the library's funds come from the District government. "It's a misnomer we're supported by the federal government," Franklin said.

In a pilot cooperative project begun this fall under Title III of the Library Services Construction Act, the District of Columbia Public Library provides public access terminals to the University of the District of Columbia, two District high schools and to the Martin Luther King Library. Students have access to the library's community database, which provides listings of District government services and the services offered by 1,000 community groups. The database listings include contact person, cost, location and telephone number. Students will also have access to the library's bibliographic database.

"They will see what materials we own," Franklin said. In the next fiscal year he hopes this project can be expanded to all thirty District high schools. Funding requirements for next year's project are not yet determined.

A 1979 borrowing agreement with all public libraries in surrounding areas enables the District's 600,000 residents to borrow from all greater-Washington metropolitan libraries. Since 1896 they had been denied this privilege. "We're lending more than we're borrowing," Franklin reported.

Last June, the library began renting videocassettes of popular movies for $2 a day. It offers a selection of 400 titles. "We have the best buy and variety in town. Rentals are picking up steam," Franklin commented. The library rented 542 tapes during the first sixteen days of the program.

In July, a cable company proposed a library studio for the District of Columbia Public Library. Programming for the library studio would include book discussions, job bank information, adult education classes, children's programs, preschool storytelling programs, and bibliographic instruction.

The Martin Luther King Library is "not difficult to maintain or supervise," Franklin said. "It will meet our needs for the next twenty years. We're in good shape for a central library facility."

Sharing Resources in Illinois: Statewide Library Computer System

Bernard Sloan

On June 1, 1984 the Sheean Library at Illinois Wesleyan University in Bloomington, Illinois, and the A.C. Buehler Library at Elmhurst College in Elmhurst, Illinois, became the twenty-fourth and twenty-fifth academic libraries in Illinois to join the Statewide Library Computer System (LCS). The addition of these libraries to the system boosted LCS holdings to 8.1 million titles and 13.2 million volumes, and pushed the number of terminals supported by the system past the six hundred mark.

LCS, now maintained by the University of Illinois Office of Administrative Information Systems and Services, provides member libraries with local and interlibrary known-item searching and circulation capabilities. The system has achieved a number of milestones during the fiscal year ending June 30, 1984:

• At the end of fiscal 1983, participating libraries converted 11,930,278 holdings to machine-readable form. By the end of fiscal 1984 LCS holdings had passed the thirteen million mark, with a tally of 13,205,430 volumes. Thus LCS participants saw a 10.6 percent increase in resources available through the system over the course of the fiscal year.

• Interlibrary circulation activity, both local and remote, was at record levels during fiscal 1984. 30,544 interlibrary circulation transactions were initiated during March, a record for a single month's activity. Interlibrary circulation activity for the fiscal year totalled approximately 275,000 transactions, an increase of more than thirty-five percent over thc previous fiscal year. During October, LCS saw the 500,000th interlibrary circulation transaction initiated since the system went statewide in 1980.

• With the addition of the system to the Booth Library at Eastern Illinois University, in February 1984, LCS is now in place at every state-supported university library in Illinois.

• On December 11, 1983, LCS marked its fifth anniversary as an operational system in the state of Illinois. The University Library, University of Illinois at Urbana-Champaign, began using LCS on December 11, 1978. On July 7, 1984, Statewide LCS was four years old.

• During the course of the fiscal year, the number of LCS terminals increased by forty percent. At the end of fiscal 1983, the system supported 421 terminals. By the end of June 1984, LCS boasted a network of nearly 600 active terminals, spread across a distance of 340 miles, from the Rockford branch of the University of Illinois Health Science Center to Southern Illinois University at Carbondale.

• Total system activity increased by more than twenty percent during fiscal 1984. More than 31 million transactions were initiated by system users during the year. By way of comparison, LCS processed 'only' 16.4 million transactions during the first year of statewide operation. Despite this dramatic increase in system activity, records kept by the University Library at the University of Illinois at Urbana-Champaign show response time to be less than two seconds per transaction.

Once labelled a 'project' or an 'experiment', the Illinois version of LCS ended fiscal 1984 as an established system. Having maintained a relatively low profile for a number of years, LCS is now a library automation 'giant.' In several respects, LCS could be called the largest single circulation system in the United States. Hank Epstein, president of Information Transform, Inc., has estimated that LCS supports three times as many terminals as the next largest circulation system, with five times the holdings of the next largest circulation system. He also estimates that LCS interlibrary circulation activity, at 300,000 annual transactions, is at least ten times greater than that of most other large circulation systems. With LCS, the citizens of Illinois have the largest resource-sharing pool of currently held library materials of any state.

LCS was developed in the late 1960s (as the Library Circulation System) by IBM for the Ohio State University. The system became fully operational at OSU in December 1970, and it is still operating at OSU today. LCS began modestly enough in Illinois as the circulation system of the University of Illinois. In 1977, the University of Illinois received funding from the Illinois Board of Higher Education (IBHE) to automate library circulation at its campuses in Urbana-Champaign and Chicago. The LCS software installation and modification were handled by the Urbana campus office of Administrative Information Systems and Services and the system operated through an IBM 360/75 computer located in the Urbana campus academic computing center. In addition to the programming workload, the University Library in Urbana-Champaign underwent a massive data conversion project to convert manual collection records to machine-readable form. The system became operational on the Urbana-Champaign campus in December 1978.

Bernard Sloan *is management analyst for the Statewide Library Computer System, University of Illinois at Urbana-Champaign.*

A statewide pilot project

At about the same time LCS was implemented at the University of Illinois, action on another front laid the groundwork for what would eventually become Statewide LCS. Representatives of the Illinois Board of Higher Education and the Illinois Association of College and Research Libraries were investigating the possibility of developing a computer-based library network to facilitate resource-sharing among libraries in Illinois. They chose LCS for a pilot project designed to link fourteen academic libraries with each other, and with the University of Illinois. Work on this project began in the summer of 1979. The fourteen libraries selected to participate in the project received funds from the IBHE through the Higher Education Cooperation Act to help defray the costs of joining the system. These funds were to be used for the purchase of equipment and for retrospective conversion of bibliographic data into machine-readable form. Individual institutional grants ranged from a few thousand dollars to slightly more than $100,000. Significant changes to the software were made to accommodate the multiple-institution structure of the network pilot project. The Learning Resources Center of Triton College in River Grove, Illinois, became the first of the fourteen in the pilot project to go online on January 16, 1980. Twelve more libraries in the pilot group were added to the system by November of that year. The data processing group also finished work on the University of Illinois Chicago campus libraries in 1980. LCS is now operational in twenty-five academic libraries across the state of Illinois, including the libraries of every state supported university.

The University of Illinois at Urbana-Champaign (UIUC) has placed nineteen LCS terminals in regional library headquarters and in the Illinois State Library in Springfield as part of the University Library's role as a Research and Reference Center in the Illinois Library and Information Network (ILLINET). While the library systems did not enter their holdings into the LCS files, they used the terminals to locate and charge materials from the UIUC Library. During the past fiscal year a project has been underway in which the library systems use the terminals to locate and charge materials owned by other LCS libraries.

Resource-sharing with LCS

One of the primary reasons for expanding LCS beyond the University of Illinois was to facilitate resource-sharing among participants. The design of the statewide system makes resource-sharing less time and labor intensive than with the more traditional interlibrary loan methods. Anyone with access to an LCS terminal may search the files of any participating library, using the same command structures and syntax as are used at the user's library. Points of access include author, title, author/title, and call number. While subject searching capabilities are not available, anyone with a knowledge of classification systems within a given subject area may 'browse' the shelflists of each library using the shelflist position search. The LCS record contains location, circulation, and availability data which help to increase the efficiency of the remote borrowing process. Not only does one know that another library owns a particular title, but one may also determine if there is a circulating copy, and whether that copy is available for use.

If a preliminary search fails to locate the item locally, or if the item is locally owned but unavailable for circulation, the searcher proceeds to check the files of other LCS libraries. Once an available copy is located, the searcher may enter a 'charge' transaction to request the item. A page slip is printed on a terminal located within the holding library, where library personnel use the information to retrieve the book from the shelves and determine its destination. The item is then shipped to the requesting library via the Intersystems Library Delivery Service and regional library system delivery services. In some instances, the only paperwork required of library staff is the delivery form.

LCS first went statewide on July 7, 1980. Prior to that there were two LCS's. The first LCS, used by the University of Illinois libraries, ran on an IBM 360/75 in the UIUC Computing Services Office in Urbana. The other LCS, used by participants in the resource-sharing pilot project, was on an IBM 370/168 in the University's Administrative Computing Center in Chicago. The systems merged into one LCS on the 370/168 IBM in July 1980. Since then, more than 600,000 interlibrary circulation transactions have been initiated. And resource-sharing activity continues to grow. During March 1984, a record 30,533 interlibrary circulation transactions were initiated. Slightly more than 83,000 interlibrary circulation transactions were recorded during the first quarter of calendar 1984. This figure is only 4,800 transactions fewer than the total recorded for all of fiscal 1981.

A review of interlibrary circulation statistics shows several interesting aspects of resource-sharing activity. For example, not all resource-sharing involves 'haves' lending to 'have nots'. The six smallest LCS libraries, each having less than 60,000 titles in their LCS files, lent 7,339 items to other libraries via LCS during fiscal 1983. This same group of libraries loaned 1,530 items in a single month (March 1984). During March, four of the five smallest libraries were not lenders. The highest ratio of lending to borrowing (16.62:1) was at the fourth smallest library. The second highest lending-to-borrowing ratio (7.15:1) was at the second largest library. Interlibrary circulation activity accounted for 7.7 percent of all applicable circulation activity for March.

Interlibrary cooperation, as measured by LCS, does not stop with the twenty-five participating academic libraries. A review of terminal activity data for a recent month reveals that the eighteen regional library systems and the Illinois State Library accounted for 4.2 percent of a total system activity of some 3.3 million transactions. The same data reveals that these terminals initiated 9,500 charge transactions for the month. Such activity, when taken with the levels of interlibrary circulation among the participating academic libraries, represents a substantial contribution to library resource-sharing at the statewide level.

Public access to LCS

Public access to computer-based library systems has been a 'hot topic' in library literature. But public access to LCS has been going on for years. Triton College, the first library added to the system in the statewide pilot project, has allowed public access to LCS for four and one-half years. The University of Illinois at Urbana-Champaign provided such capabilities even earlier. The significance placed on public access by participating libraries has increased so that fully one-third of all LCS terminals are public access terminals. In a recent survey, LCS library personnel identified 222 out of 564 active terminals as being public access terminals. This represents thirty-nine percent of all LCS terminals.

Public access is not limited to onsite use of library terminals. Remote public access to the system may be gained in a number of ways. Currently, most remote patron access is achieved by dialing directly into the system using a home or office computer. Five LCS libraries have dedicated a total of eleven computer 'ports' to direct-dial remote patron access. Patrons using these dial access 'ports' initiated nearly 27,000 transactions during March 1984. A second method for gaining remote access to LCS involves the placement of LCS terminals in public areas of academic departmental offices. The University of Illinois at Urbana-Champaign has placed five of its terminals in areas such as the psychology department. These five terminals initiated more than 5,000 transactions during March 1984. A third method of remote patron access is only in its infancy, but the concept shows promise. Three participating institutions, the University of Illinois at Urbana-Champaign, the University of Illinois at Chicago, and Lake Forest College, have made arrangements whereby users of their respective academic computing networks may gain access to LCS through these networks. Eight LCS computer 'ports' have been dedicated to access by these academic computing networks. Although this approach to remote access to LCS has been operational for a relatively short time, users of these academic networks initiated nearly 8,500 LCS transactions during March. One indication of the potential popularity of such an approach may be found in an advertisement in the *Daily Illini,* the student newspaper at the University of Illinois at Urbana-Champaign. A private residence hall in Champaign arranged to be connected to the Computing Service Office academic computing network. In one advertisement touting the benefits of living in the residence hall, access to LCS received top billing.

LCS use from public access terminals is quite extensive. During March 1984, patrons using the 221 public access terminals initiated 1.3 million transactions, nearly thirty-eight percent of the system workload for that month. And public access is not restricted to bibliographic searching. During one recent month users of one of the busier public access terminals initiated 281 charge transactions, 156 renewals, and 94 saves. Giving circulation capabilities to public access terminals means that, in many cases, library personnel at the patron's library may not be involved in the interlibrary circulation process until the requested item actually reaches the patron's library.

Today, LCS is a unique and successful large scale computer-based library system. No one can argue with the system's significant contributions to resource-sharing and librarianship in Illinois. But without the hard work and cooperation among diverse groups of people and the institutions they represent, Statewide LCS may not have amounted to much more than an admirable idea that failed.

Participation in LCS

LCS is now operational in twenty-five academic libraries across the state of Illinois, including the libraries of every state-supported university. The following libraries used the system as of the end of fiscal 1984. State-supported university libraries are indicated by an asterisk.

Catholic Theological Union, Chicago
*Chicago State University, Chicago
DePaul University, Chicago
*Eastern Illinois University, Charleston
Elmhurst College, Elmhurst
*Governors State University, Park Forest South
Illinois Institute of Technology, Chicago
*Illinois State University, Normal-Bloomington
Illinois Wesleyan University, Bloomington
Judson College, Elgin
Kankakee Community College, Kankakee
Lake Forest College, Lake Forest
Millikin University, Decatur
*Northeastern Illinois University, Chicago
*Northern Illinois University, DeKalb
St. Xavier College, Chicago
*Sangamon State University, Springfield
*Southern Illinois University at Carbondale
*Southern Illinois University at Edwardsville
*Southern Illinois University School of Medicine, Springfield
Triton College, River Grove
*University of Illinois at Chicago
*University of Illinois at Chicago, Health Sciences Center
*University of Illinois at Urbana-Campaign
*Western Illinois University, Macomb

Access to Materials in Pennsylvania: Interlibrary Delivery

Dwight Huseman

The electronic age has created nearly unbelievable accessibility to library materials. Accessing an item through the OCLC Interlibrary Loan Subsystem and determining a lending institution is the first part of the process. There must also be a way for the lending library to send requested materials. Telefacsimile is one way to do it, but that can be a costly process. The United States Postal Service and UPS are other ways. More than 120 academic, public, school and special libraries in Pennsylvania have found still another alternative that they consider to be cost-effective, efficient, convenient, and even congenial. That alternative is the Interlibrary Delivery Service of Pennsylvania (IDS). It has been endorsed by the Pittsburgh Regional Library Center (PRLC) and the Philadelphia Area Libraries in Network (PALINET) as an "effective means for delivery of library materials."

IDS is a cooperative association that has delivered more than two million library items since it was organized in 1969. In addition to its more than 120 members, the cooperative currently has an agreement with Solid State (a New York State library delivery service) that enlarges the service area to include more than 160 libraries in New York State.

IDS was begun by a group of fourteen academic libraries and one public library in Pennsylvania, as the Area College Library Cooperative Program (ACLCP) Delivery Service. It has since been renamed the Associated College Libraries of Central Pennsylvania. It applied for and received an LSCA grant from the State Library in the amount of $10,500 for the delivery of library materials among fourteen ACLCP libraries, three regional resource centers, seven district centers and eleven Philadelphia-area college and university libraries. The pilot project began in October 1969 and continued through 1971. Delivery of library materials was scheduled twice a week.

During its first three months the new delivery service delivered nearly five thousand items to participating libraries. By December 1971 the delivery of 35,000 items was reported and membership had increased to thirty-seven. A six-member management committee was appointed, half of whom were appointed to a one-year term, the other half to a two-year term. The delivery service was successful. A new grant was requested from the state. This new grant would place LSCA funds and participating library funds on a fifty-fifty basis, down from the previous formula, which placed federal funds at sixty-six percent and participating library funds at thirty-three and one-third percent.

The ACLCP Library Delivery Serice increased in size and service. Between April 1971 and April 1972 the membership in the cooperative had increased to sixty-three libraries and the volume of deliveries increased by 150 percent. From February to April 1971 it delivered 10,612 items. From February to April 1972 it delivered 26,174 library items. The management committee, now called the Advisory Committee reported that the unit cost of delivery per item in 1971 had decreased from forty-three cents per item to thirty-six cents per item in 1972, despite the fact that two trucks were now being used and deliveries had increased from twice a week to three times a week. By December 1972 another change was observed. The name ACLCP Library Delivery Service was confusing and misleading to many of the members. The service was renamed the Interlibrary Delivery Service of Pennsylvania (IDS).

Membership grew modestly during the next two years, increasing to seventy-five members in 1973 and remaining constant in 1974. A grant of $130,000 from LSCA provided the impetus for statewide expansion. New members were accepted on the basis of a two-year commitment. They were assessed $200 for the first year, and $400 for the second year. Membership expanded statewide with the addition of seventy-seven members, bringing the total to 152 members in 1975. Before the end of 1976 IDS members numbered 156.

The new statewide system consisted of three interconnected routes, one operating from the Harrisburg area, a second from the Philadelphia area, and the third from the Pittsburg area. Designated libraries managed the routes and provided the drivers for delivery trucks. They were reimbursed for their services by IDS. About this time IDS also incorporated as a nonprofit organization, elected a twelve-member board of directors, and adopted a constitution and bylaws. IDS currently has a thirteen-member Board of Directors, one of whom is elected as a member-at-large because of his or her special expertise in finances or transportation. The two-year statewide expansion of IDS was a success. While there was a membership decline when some trial members were confronted with paying the full cost of the service, IDS continued to serve libraries throughout the state, even after some new members had withdrawn.

A 1979 crisis period nearly spelled the demise of IDS. A number of factors

Dwight Huseman *is serials and systems librarian for Gettysburg College, Gettysburg, Pennsylvania.*

contributed to this crisis. Batelle, Columbus Laboratories had been contracted by the State Library of Pennsylvania to make a general study of interlibrary delivery services throughout the state. Their 1979 report attributed the relative decline of IDS to several factors. Its inability to carry letter mail was one problem cited. Its loss of membership after the trial period, and a change in headquarters location were other factors listed as contributing to its decline. IDS had changed its headquarters from the Lancaster Public Library to the Dauphin County Library at about the same time as the membership decline was occurring. Other, weightier factors included the sudden rise in gasoline prices; high repair costs for the rented vans; uncontrolled driver wages paid by local libraries at local pay scales; and wage increases made without IDS consultation. High insurance rates and an inability to find a new headquarters and coordinator for IDS also contributed to the membership decline. IDS headquarters had been centered in Lancaster Public Library for seven years, but Dauphin County Library was only able to manage the service for a few years. The need to change the location of its headquarters twice within three years came upon IDS at a particularly difficult time.

During the crisis period of 1979 there were motions proposed to the Board to suspend service or reduce services in order to gain better control of the deficit. Ultimately the crisis served IDS well. In June 1979 the executive committee of the Board of Directors invited a transportation consultant to attend the July Board meeting. David Paden, chief executive officer of D.L. Paden and Associates in Philadelphia, reviewed the realities of a cash-flow problem, an abysmal safety record, and the technical skill required to operate a truck service. He recommended that the librarians suspend truck service in favor of a professional delivery firm. He also recommended that member charges be based upon the extent to which each library used the service rather than having each member pay the same amount for vastly different levels of service.

At its August meeting, the IDS Board of Directors met with a representative of Purolator who indicated that the use of the Purolator delivery service could be cost-effective for IDS. At this meeting Paden reminded the Board that if a service such as Purolator took over the delivery service no overhead management structure, such as that required for route management, would be needed. Vans would no longer be required.

Further contacts with Purolator and with the Pittsburgh Regional Library Center and its director, Scott Bruntjen, led to a crucial meeting of the Board on October 2, 1979 at which the group acted to establish a new pattern of service for IDS. The Board's actions included closing down the truck system, establishing Purolator as its delivery service, establishing a graduated fee schedule and contracting with the Pittsburgh Regional Library Center to serve as its administrative headquarters. Library cooperation in delivery service was entering a new, more effective era for IDS. Purolator began deliveries to libraries on behalf of IDS on November 12, 1979.

The Interlibrary Delivery Service of Pennsylvania has experienced change and development in its more than fifteen years of service. From its beginnings with thirty-four members and a single truck to its becoming a management cooperative which contracts for its administrative headquarters service and its delivery service, IDS has remained constant in its service goals. The *Users' Manual* of IDS declares "The Interlibrary Delivery Service of Pennsylvania is a nonprofit delivery service designed to facilitate the transmittal of interlibrary loans and other educational items among its members." IDS was organized to insure speedy, safe, cost-effective delivery of library materials and it continues to meet this goal.

In a 1982 unpublished study made at Lehigh University, items shipped from Lehigh University across the state to Carnegie Mellon, and items shipped to Penn State and Drexel University all reached their destinations the next delivery day. IDS remains on a three day per week delivery schedule. Items shipped through Purolator on April 26th reached their receiving libraries on April 28th, demonstrating a consistent pattern of safe, speedy delivery.

IDS has continued to provide cost-effective service. In 1972, costs were noted at thirty-six cents per item. Considering the impact of inflation since the early 1970s, IDS members are probably paying little more than that today. A comparative cost study made in 1981 at Lehigh University suggested that the same item sent through IDS at $1.09 would have cost $3.73 through the United States mail and $8.24 through UPS.

IDS has been an effective means of resource-sharing among school, academic, public, special, and research libraries of varied sizes. Libraries pay on a graduated scale only for what they send, and are not limited in any way to the number of items that they may receive. Does IDS accomplish its goal of safe, cost-effective service to the satisfaction of its members? Surveys of the membership taken in 1981 and 1983 indicate a high level of satisfaction among members.

In 1981 more than ninety-six percent of those responding observed that pick-up and delivery schedules were being met. More than ninety-five percent noted that billing procedures were satisfactory. More than ninety-eight percent of those responding noted that the statistical gathering methods were adequate. IDS headquarters provided effective service most of the time to more than ninety-five percent of the respondents. The question of items lost in shipment was irrelevant to nearly all respondents.

IDS stands as an example of what library cooperation and resouce-sharing can do. It provides a service that helps libraries achieve their purpose—to place the right resources into the hands of a patron at the right time. ▣

Fred Chamberlain

Special Report: "Old Jeff"

The Jefferson Market Courthouse Branch Library

The Jefferson Market Courthouse Branch of the New York Public Library, affectionately known as "Old Jeff," is located in Greenwich Village, Manhattan, at the intersections of Sixth Avenue, Greenwich Avenue and West 10th Street. The building is something of a phoenix. The beginning of "Old Jeff" goes back to the year 1832. At that time, certain lots in New York City were set aside for public use, and each of these lots included a market, a municipal court and a volunteer fire station with a watchtower and alarm bell. These structures were made of wood. In 1870, the Commissioner of Public Works declared the old Jefferson Market "an obstruction to the streets, a nuisance to the neighborhood and detrimental to public health." Wreckers demolished the original wood Jefferson Market complex.

The second stage of "Old Jeff's" life was orchestrated by two very talented architects: Frederick Clarke Withers (1828–1901) and Calvert Vaux (1824–1895). Withers was a prominent designer of churches and Vaux had already teamed up with Frederick Law Olmsted to fashion the layout for Central Park. Both architects worked in a style that the Municipal Art Society called "Italian Gothic-Eclectic." By the general public it was called the "Lean Bacon Style" because of variations in the brick and granite.

An article in the *American Architect and Building News* (June 15, 1878) had this to say about the new Jefferson Market complex: "The buildings are of brick, those of the court house and bell tower being faced with Philadelphia brick, and those of the prison with Croton fronts. The stone used is from Berlin, Ohio, and its color contrasts well with the red brick. The carving, which forms an important element of design, was done under the direction of Mr. William Simon. The interior walls of the main halls and the staircase are lined with stone, with ornamental arches over the doorways, windows, etc., and enriched with a large amount of carved foliage. The interior of the court rooms and offices are trimmed with black walnut and cherry wood wainscotting, doors, etc., and floors of the vestibules and halls laid with ornamental tiles." The cost of the building, without the architects' fees, was $360,000. Imagine how much a building like this would cost in today's dollars! Today much of Simon's stonework remains exactly as it always has been.

The construction of the Jefferson Market Courthouse was started in 1874 and completed in 1877. By that time "Old Jeff" was being widely acclaimed as one of the most beautiful buildings in America. In 1885, a poll of architects voted the Jefferson Market Courthouse among the ten most beautiful buildings in America. From this peak the structure slowly began its slip into the shadows of decay and

Fred Chamberlain *is a freelance photographer based in New York City.*

Main reading room with catwalk crossing

vacancy. It wasn't until 1906 that "Old Jeff" was back in the news. The trial of Harry K. Thaw focused national attention on the courthouse. Thaw had been held at the prison adjoining the courthouse for the murder of Stanford White.

In September 1929 a demolition notice was served and approved for the three buildings that comprised the jail, and the Jefferson Market building.

In 1930, the Hogarthian Women's House of Detention (perhaps the only Art Deco prison in the world) was built on the site of Vaux and Withers's prison. From this point on it was downhill for "Old Jeff." By 1945, it had ceased functioning as a courthouse and took on various tenants, including the Public Works Department, several Civil Defense groups, the Bureau of Census, a health insurance program, and the Police Academy.

By 1958, the Jefferson Market Courthouse was on the city's auction block, and was considered an eyesore. An article in the *New York Times* called it "one of New York's gaudiest and most controversial landmarks . . . widely regarded by the public as a monster," and claimed that "by 1960 the structure had become what might be called a sooty red elephant." Not very nice words for a landmark building. However, New York seemed dedicated to tearing down its past to make way for the future.

When a bank considered purchasing the Jefferson Market Courthouse, Greenwich Village citizens decided to compete with the bank for the building. The bank wanted the land for apartments, which would have meant tearing down "Old Jeff." The citizens, on the other hand, wanted to save the building. Margot Gayle and Judge Harold Birns, then the City Commissioner for Housing and Buildings, decided that they were not going to stand by and let the wreckers get "Old Jeff." After targeting the clock on the watchtower as their goal, they formed the "Committee to Get the Clock on Jefferson Market Courthouse Started." The first attempt at saving the courthouse came on Christmas Eve when the Committee telephoned Mayor Robert Wagner, asking to rehabilitate the structure and present it as a gift to Greenwich Village. To repair the clock and meet their goal would cost $3,400. By September of 1961 the clock was fully electrified and working.

Around that same time, the New York Public Library was looking for a new branch location in Greenwich Village, and the community group saw a golden opportunity. Margot Gayle formed a new group, the "Committee for a Library in the Jefferson Market Courthouse." This time Margot Gayle was joined by lawyer Philip Wittenberg as cochair-

Old Jeff's basement reference room

person. Members of the committee included Maurice Evans, Lewis Mumford and e.e. cummings. This time objections to the committee's proposal came from representatives of the New York Public Library who were seeking a new building constructed specifically to their needs. However, the committee drafted the support of Mayor Wagner, James Felt (chairman of the City Planning Commission) and Edward Dudley (Borough President of Manhattan). The committee felt almost certain that with these people backing them, their goal of making a library out of "Old Jeff" was much closer than before.

The Department of Public Works approached the committee and asked a committee member, architect Giorgio Cavaglieri, to estimate costs for renovating the building for library use. In 1962, having consulted with representatives of NYPL and the Department of Public Works, Cavaglieri gave his estimate of $950,000. The budget for a branch library at this time was only $400,000. Although the renovation of the Jefferson Market Courthouse would cost twice that of a new branch library, the plans and the working drawings of the committee were approved in October 1964. "Old Jeff" was back in business.

The Jefferson Market Courthouse was about one-hundred years old. The craftsmanship of that period was much different than it is today, and painstaking attention to detail was given to the repair work. Elderly craftsmen were sought to restore badly deteriorated features. To keep an old building like this in its original state and to comply with today's building codes was nearly impossible. To make "Old Jeff" accessible to the modern public, some regulations were waived.

Reconstruction presented a number of problems. During the time of neglect, a leaky roof damaged the structural ironwork with heavy rust. The main gable was out of plumb by about five inches. The old slate roof was replaced with terne metal, the interior stonework was repaired, and nearly all the existing ceilings were reconstructed. New elevators, doors, and window sashes were installed throughout. The stained glass and the existing woodwork were repaired and the exterior of the building was "freshened-up."

Giorgio Cavaglieri's modernization of the facility does not attempt to hide or disguise anything. The new doesn't clash or distract from the old. New glass and metal doors lead one into old, "spruced-up" interiors. While the plasterwork is pure white, most of the other modern details and fixtures are black. There is a wonderfully comfortable balance of the new invading the old throughout the library. One of the most striking examples is the elevated catwalk on the second floor.

On November 27, 1967 the Committee for a Library in the Jefferson Market Courthouse ceased to exist. On that day, the new library branch was officially opened. It was stocked with an initial collection of 40,000 books from the old Jackson Branch Library. And Giorgio Cavaglieri was not to be outdone by Frederick Withers or Calvert Vaux. Another award was bestowed on the property in 1968—an honor award from the American Institute of Architects.

Sculptural detail from the facade

Dale Nelson:

Dateline Washington

Last acts of the 98th

There was champagne for the archivists, money for Indian libraries, and action on international copyright protection, book preservation and a library of terrorism as the 98th Congress came to a close.

The champagne, provided by the National Association of State Archives and Record Administrators, was broken out by top federal archives officials when Congress passed legislation giving them an independent agency.

The new National Archives and Records Administration replaces the National Archives and Records Service, previously part of the General Services Administration. GSA officials recommended that President Reagan sign the bill, saying the final version had satisfied their earlier objection that too much records-management authority was being assigned to the Archives. The new agency was given a fiscal 1985 budget of $95 million and a staff of about 2,400.

Funds for library services for Indian tribes are contained in a five-year reauthorization of the Library Services and Construction Act. Funds are also authorized to set up literacy projects at libraries to help meet the needs of some 25 million illiterate Americans.

Overall, the bill provides authorization levels of $145 million in fiscal year 1985, $155 million in 1986, $165 million in 1987 and $175 million in each of the following two years. It requires each state to develop a long-range plan on how best to meet networking and resource-sharing goals.

Copyright and other intellectual property rights came in for consideration in connection with a five-year extension of the Generalized System of Preferences, which accords duty-free treatment to products from developing countries. The Senate adopted an amendment by Senator Frank Lautenberg (D–N.J.) requiring the President to consider intellectual property rights protection as a factor in designating beneficiary countries under the system.

Tucked away in the $173 million authorized for improving embassy security in the aftermath of the Beirut bombing in September was $134,000 for an interagency terrorist computer library.

The State Department told Congresss there was an urgent need for its Office of Counter Terrorism and Emergency Planning to become part of the system, known as DESIST. Officials said the office would contribute information on host governments' terrorism policies and responses and would gather terrorism information provided by other agencies. The request included $108,000 for equipment and construction, $21,000 in salaries and benefits for a computer analyst, and $5,000 for staff support.

Finally, the Library of Congress received authorization for its $11.5 million book deacidification facility, to extend the lives of books produced after the age of rag paper.

As retiring Republican Majority Leader Howard Baker Jr. told the Senate:

"As I understand it, the Library of Congress has built and is planning to put in operation very large autoclaves, that is pressure chambers, in which these books can be put and they can leach the acid from the paper and preserve them for hundreds of years into the future.

"I have thought about that many times, and I wish I could designate some of the pages that would not be deacidified so they would disappear very quickly."

First funds for Reagan library

Meanwhile John Buckley, a spokesman for President Reagan's campaign for renomination, said a million dollars in leftover campaign funds might be put in a trust fund for the Reagan presidential library. He said the money also might be given to Citizens for the Republic, the political action committee that Reagan started after losing the Republican nomination in 1976.

Carter library vs. the National Trust

Federal highway and environmental agencies have smoothed the way for the highway that former President Jimmy Carter says is essential to his presidential library, but the National Trust for Historic Preservation is carrying on the fight against it.

The Federal Highway Administration approved the 2.4-mile route, linking downtown Atlanta to the proposed library site by way of some of the city's most historic neighborhoods. Carter has said that the parkway is essential if the library is to be built at the site in Atlanta's eastern suburbs.

The Advisory Council on Historic Preservation contended that the parkway would hurt several historic communities, and asked the Council on Environmental Quality to intervene. On September 25, the council declined, declaring that "the issue is not one of national importance."

The commission added, however, that any parkway development beyond the 2.4 miles "would have a serious impact and should be opposed." The advisory council had argued that construction of the parkway would "inevitably create pressure" to build other highway links in the area.

Caution Inc., an Atlanta citizens' group, filed suit, charging that the decision to proceed would cause significant problems in preserving the historic character of the communities.

The Trust for Historic Preservation then filed for an injunction in U.S. District Court in Atlanta, saying that thirty historic sites, ranging from the Sweet Auburn National Historic Landmark to the Jackson Hill Baptist Church, would be destroyed, rendered useless or severely degraded.

Dale Nelson *is a journalist who covers the Washington scene for WLB.*

Anne McGrath

Eye on Publishing

Stratemeyer finds new home at Simon & Schuster

Ron Buehl has spent most of his career watching and influencing children's and young adult publishing. He reminisces about a time when the demand for children's books depended almost exclusively on the health of library budgets—a period during the early 1960s, for example, when Dell transacted some eighty percent of its juvenile business with institutions. Then the economy faltered and library funding began to dry up. Suddenly, the secret to survival appeared to be to court the bookstore market in a major way. "When I left Dell in 1977," Buehl recalls, "we were doing seventy percent of our business with bookstores and only thirty percent with libraries."

Buehl is now at Simon & Schuster, as vice-president and publisher of its juvenile division, where he is making impressively giant strides toward bringing the company's juvenile business back to life. "Simon & Schuster reacted to the economy during the 1970s and dropped out of juvenile work," Buehl says. "Five and a half years ago we came back."

Much of the division's subsequent success, of course, has been due to its gaining rights in 1979 to publish the Stratemeyer Syndicate's popular series books (Nancy Drew, the Hardy Boys, Tom Swift, the Bobbsey Twins) in paperback, under the Wanderer imprint. Interestingly, however, plans for future development include not only continued and even more aggressive marketing of the Stratemeyer works but a concentrated effort to give the division's Messner library imprint a real shot in the arm.

There is no question that Stratemeyer represents the practically unshakeable foundation upon which less certain ventures can be built. "It's a tremendous acquisition for us," Buehl says. "It offers great opportunity to develop even further characters such as Nancy Drew and the Hardy Boys, who are already household words. We'll publish the Stratemeyer books with renewed energy, and use some aggressive marketing and merchandising techniques to realize wide new audiences." The Nancy Drew, Hardy Boys, and Bobbsey Twins books together have sold some 250 million copies worldwide in seventeen languages. Simon & Schuster, since taking the series on in 1979, has put out six million copies of seventy-seven titles.

Edward Stratemeyer launched his company in 1906, editing stories for Horatio Alger. Shortly thereafter he began publishing his own books—the Rover Boys series made its debut in 1910. An avalanche of popular books for young readers followed, either written or conceived by Stratemeyer. When he died in 1930, he had published some 800 works in nearly 150 juvenile series under sixty-five pseudonyms.

Stratemeyer's daughter, Harriet Adams (perhaps better known by the pen name Carolyn Keene, shared with a number of Nancy Drew series authors), carried on at the helm for another fifty years. She died at age eighty-nine in 1982.

The transition period has been an exciting one for Buehl, who is fascinated both by the history—the relics—of the Syndicate arriving on his

Anne McGrath, *a freelance writer based in New York, covers the publishing world for WLB.*

doorstep by the boxloads ("We've discovered everything from toilet paper to early manuscripts," he says) and by the possibilities for rejuvenation of the series. "We have to breathe new life into them," he says. "The characters are showing signs of age and need updating. Nancy, for example, doesn't reflect the reality of 1980s girlhood."

What does this mean? First, it means sorting throught the hundreds of cards that trace each character's activity throughout his or her series life in order to understand the personalities. Then, ideally without introducing any inconsistencies with past behavior, modern conflicts and preoccupations can be explored in new episodes. "We want Nancy's readers to identify with her as well as follow her through another adventure," Buehl explains. "Maybe her relationship with her boyfriend can be more concrete. Or maybe we could do more with world problems. We'll need to repackage the books, too. The covers are looking dated."

Simon & Schuster will continue to publish the series in paperback and in a limited number of library hardcover copies. Grosset & Dunlap, publishers of the familiar yellow-spined hardcover editions, will also carry on.

The other main thrust of Buehl's game plan to buttress his juvenile division is to collect all of Simon & Schuster's imprints directed at young readers under a single management. Archway, for instance, the racksize paperback line of reprints and originals for the twelve-and-older group, has been brought into the juvenile division where it can be profitably teamed up with the Wanderer line. Plans for Archway include development of its own series like the Moonstone mystery romances scheduled to come out early next year.

Plans are also on the drawing board to fully develop Simon & Schuster's Messner juvenile library imprint, which Buehl describes as a "stepchild" of the division that has suffered from inadequate distribution. "Messner was wasting away as part of the trade division," he says, "because library publishing was not seen as a profit center. But now money is coming back into the library world. The great thing about Messner is that it should allow us to acquire quality books for hardcover and then perhaps put them out in paperback under the Wanderer or Archway imprints. At the moment Messner is contemporary nonfiction, but I think we can develop quality fiction also. It's aimed at libraries, but wherever possible we'll cross over to the trade market, too." Acquiring the right works for institutions, he thinks, will almost certainly mean reviewable fiction and nonfiction that can go into paperback.

Juvenile publishing, it appears, holds substantial promise at Simon & Schuster. Although Buehl chooses not to discuss the current contribution of his division to the house's total output, he hopes that in about five years books for young readers will represent twenty percent of the firm's business.

Times Books acquired by Random House

Random House and the New York Times Company have announced an agreement in principle to transfer ownership of the Times' book publishing operation, Times Books, to Random House. Books compiled from *New York Times* material, which have represented the backbone of Times Books' business, will now be published by Random House.

Times Books has been working for the past several years at strengthening its trade list. The association with Random House, with its well-developed sales and marketing operations, is expected to further the imprint's progress toward this goal.

In other Gulf & Western news...

Gulf & Western Industries, Simon & Schuster's parent, has been busy these past few months. In what appears to be a determined effort to expand its publishing business, the conglomerate made clear its intention to acquire Prentice-Hall. Prentice-Hall initially rejected a bid of $70 per share, and prepared to consider possible better offers. A $71-a-share, $705-million deal was closed as we went to press, making Gulf & Western a significant presence in just about every area of publishing. Simon & Schuster, already one of the giants in hardcover trade and mass-market paperback publishing, is joined by the giant among college textbook publishers.

Gulf & Western actually entered educational publishing last winter, when it bought the publisher Esquire and made it part of Simon & Schuster. Esquire (no relation to the magazine) publishes elementary and secondary school texts through its Allyn & Bacon, Modern Curriculum Press, Cambridge Company, and Globe Book Company. Many publishing industry observers consider Prentice-Hall's preeminence in the school and college markets to be the perfect foil for Simon & Schuster's trade strength.

Prentice-Hall was founded in 1913 by two college professors who wanted to publish textbooks on finance. Its first title, *Materials of Corporate Finance,* led a stream of college and professional books that now flows at a rate of some one thousand titles a year. The Englewood, New Jersey house, which ranks first as a publisher of college texts ahead of McGraw-Hill, has approximately 13,000 titles in print. Other segments of its business include loose-leaf information services about tax and regulatory issues, college preparatory books and civil service examination books, atlases, travel guides, and home-improvement guides. It also operates the largest publisher of data processing industry training material and is moving strongly toward book and computer-disk packages.

Simon & Schuster, by contrast, is known for its hot sellers. Recent titles include *Wired,* the John Belushi story, and *The Kennedys.*

Gulf & Western intends to keep the Prentice-Hall management in place and to let the publisher maintain its identity. ▣

Will Manley:

Facing the Public

"A BOOK? HOW DOES IT WORK?"

Somebody, perhaps the Surgeon General, or better yet, the Librarian of Congress, ought to declare that reading too much "library literature" can be hazardous to your health.

From the looks of things, the very term "library literature" is approaching an elevated oxymoron status generally reserved for such inanities as "moral majority" or "military intelligence." Look over your recent ALA yearbooks, scan the new lists from library publishing houses, flip through a year's worth of *Library Journal,* or if you really want to get depressed, study the advertising trends in *Publishers Weekly.*

What you are confronted with is technology—hardware and software of all sizes and shapes quickly becoming obsolete so that it can be superseded by hardware and software of new sizes and shapes. The hazard in all of this is that if the average librarian who got into the profession because he "likes people" takes his library literature too seriously he will begin to think of his job more in terms of technology and less in terms of people.

"We're here to serve the computer, not those folks who just want a good book to read" is an attitude that is more widespread than we care to admit.

And why shouldn't it be? Technology is what gets the emphasis in our profession, whether in conference programming, vendor exhibits, library literature, or the rarified air of library school ivory towers. Just check out your basic library school (oops, I mean library and information science school) curriculum. Most likely they've got a list of courses on audiovisual technology, online searching, and computerized cataloging that will keep you busy until the final days of Armageddon, but if it's something in the area of library public relations you want, they've probably got an obscure footnote that directs you to a wimpy, generic public relations course in the business school where a gray-haired proponent of the "trickle down" theory will try to teach you how to hoodwink an unsuspecting public into buying something so obviously inferior as an American-made automobile or missile system.

I don't know how many bright, liberal arts types in our profession I've bumped into in the past five or six years who will actually admit after a martini or two that their only career regret is that they "didn't have the opportunity to work in the forties, fifties or early sixties before libraries became so technically oriented." There's a great inferiority complex that goes along with having the ability to talk intelligently about the role of monarchy in Shakespearean tragedy and yet not being able to give a working definition of the terms ROM and RAM. How weary are the uses of the world when you can readily decline an array of irregular Latin nouns and yet not be able to complete a simple program in BASIC? What does it profit a librarian to master the whole world of twentieth century naturalistic literature and lose one's soul in the inability to do a simple online literature search?

The humanistically oriented librarians are either not getting ahead in the library profession or getting out of the profession altogether. It's the technocrats, the professional managers with MBAs, MPAs, or computer degrees who are now unfortunately moving up the ladder, calling the local shots, and populating library director meetings and regional conferences. Listening to them talk is like sitting in the high school cafeteria listening to teen-aged boys talk about automobile engine mechanics. They're experts at getting where they want to go fast. The problem is they have no place to go. So it is with the library technocrats. They know all about processes and systems of delivering information and providing access, but they have absolutely no vision about the information they should be delivering or the books to which they are providing access.

Just once I'd love to open the librarian want-ads and find one asking for a librarian with a degree in philosophy, fine arts, or heaven forbid, literature. But the changing face of librarianship is representative of the changing face of other "cultural-educational" professionals. For instance, publishing houses are being run by bottom line accountants and

---

Will Manley *is director of the Tempe (Arizona) Public Library.*

colleges and universities are beginning to be dominated by business and engineering specialists. The liberal arts major, a person who was never greatly admired by practical people, is more out of favor today then ever before.

In a way this is a little bit hard to understand, especially in libraries and especially with the full scale arrival of computer technology. After all, everyone, including myself, agrees that automation has been a great benefit to libraries. Increasing access to collections, enhancing resource-sharing, and recording, tabulating, and processing all our circulation transactions, automation has freed us from time-consuming busywork and has given us the potential to concentrate renewed attention to our primary and humanistic responsbility of facing and serving the public in our daily function of bringing people and books together.

But unfortunately this renaissance of humanism has not taken place. Technology has derived a life of its own. Although the bibliographic applications of computerization are simply a means to the ultimate end of serving library users, we are devoting an inordinate amount of attention to systems analysis as opposed to public relations. In other words, an impressionistic perusal of the substance of our professional literature, our professional conferences, and our spending trends would indicate that we regard machines more highly than people.

This is unfortunate because there is no direct correlation between how good your library is and how sophisticated your automated systems are. Effective library services do not turn on how complex your computerized circulation system is. There is a very direct correlation, however, between how well you treat library users and how good your library is. That is why some of the best libraries in this country are among the smallest, with nary a microchip on the premises. It is in this context that libraries can give excellent, personalized service. In fact, when library users are confronted with an array of new technology with which they are relatively unfamiliar and uncomfortable, the dynamic, personable public services librarian takes on an even more significant role.

It's ironic that as a country we are so schizophrenic about technology. On the one hand we're enamored of our technological prowess and proud of our national leadership in this area. We believe that for every serious problem we get ourselves into there is a technological "fix." For instance, we irrationally assume that "Star Wars" defense systems will render nuclear weapons harmless and that clean, cheap, and limitless solar energy will make a mockery of oil shortages. It's the new American mythology that if we can put a man on the moon we can solve any problem here on earth with enough technological research and development.

On the other hand we fear and mistrust technology almost as much as we revere it. Virtually our entire national literary tradition from James Fenimore Cooper to John Cheever deals with the tensions between the American glorification of nature and the rise of technology, a conflict best expressed by literary critic Leo Marx as the "machine in the garden" phenomenon. In other words, we tend to mistrust technology and its applications as we observe it poisoning our air, contaminating our water, despoiling our landscape, disturbing our peace, and threatening our lives. That is the side of us that opposes nuclear energy, abhors hazardous waste dumps, is repulsed by strip mining, and is sickened by oil spills. It is also the part of us that defiantly bends, folds, and mutilates computer cards, punches out vending machines, rips telephones out of the wall, and swears at automatic bank tellers.

Henry David Threau wrote as intelligently about technology as any American. In our day and age of razors that flex their heads, dolls that go to the bathroom, pens that tell time, ovens that clean themselves, typewriters that remember, golf clubs that talk, missiles that seek and destroy, and tanks that drive themselves, we find it somewhat quaint and curious that Thoreau felt it necessary to get away from the technological distractions and diversions of his day and "go to the woods to live deliberately, to front only the essential facts of life." After all, we think of Thoreau's time—the middle of the 1800s—as the heyday of the Jeffersonian agrarian ideal and the flourishing family farm.

Thoreau, however, was a poet with the vision of a prophet. He realized that very slowly and imperceptively technology was beginning to change the face of America. In his sojourn in the woods surrounding Walden Pond he concluded that "there is an illusion" about all the modern improvements in American life. He postulated that there is not always a positive advance with them and that many of the new inventions were simply "pretty toys, which distract attention from serious concerns." He wrote, "They are but improved means to an unimproved end. We are in a great haste to construct a magnetic telegraph from Maine to Texas but we have nothing important to communicate."

Thoreau's assessment of technology as an improved means to an unimproved end has never been truer. Video technology has never been more finely tuned but television programming has never been more mediocre; military hardware has never been deadlier while prospects for global peace have rarely been gloomier.

The challenge, therefore, for librarians is to insure that technological advances in libraries go hand-in-hand with a renewed commitment to serving people, that the commitment to online searching be matched by a commitment to reader's advisory services, that the dollars invested in systems research and development be matched by the dollars invested in staff development, and that the attention devoted to evaluating the effectiveness and response time of our computers be matched by the attention we devote to communicating with the people who pay the taxes to support our libraries. ▣

Martin Kesselman:

Online Update

Probably the biggest development right now in online searching is the use of microcomputers as "smart terminals" along with the use of front-end software and gateway services. Front-ends and gateways make the online search process easier and more cost-effective for novice end-users and experienced online searchers alike. A front-end is basically an interface between the user and the online system that translates many of the online system's search commands and search processes into a format that is easier to use. Front-ends can be located on the search service itself as with BRS *After Dark,* on separate software on a user's microcomputer as with *In Search,* or on an intermediate host computer as with the *Easynet* gateway service. The BRS *After Dark* front-end software, a user-friendly menu-driven system to search selected BRS databases evenings and weekends, has previously been discussed (see Online Update, *WLB,* May 1984). This column will explore front-end software packages used with a microcomputer, and the next generation of front-ends, gateways.

Front-ends

Just as with many communications software packages, front-end software can store phone numbers and passwords, automatically log on, prepare a search strategy offline and transmit (upload) it to the online search service at high speed and transmit (download) search results to disk on a microcomputer. Additional features provided by front-ends include assistance with database selection, with setting up a search strategy, and with saving search strategies and results. A wide range of front-end packages are available, some geared for use by end-users with no online experience and others with features that require online searching experience. Some packages can only be used for particular databases or with one particular online system whereas others can be used with several online systems.

Search Helper provides access via Dialog to Information Access Corporation's databases—*Newsearch, Magazine Index, National Newspaper Index, Trade and Industry Index* and *Legal Resources Index* as well as *Management Contents. Search Helper* is menu-driven; it first asks what database to search, then whether the user is interested in a person or subject, whether additional terms to narrow the search are needed, and after reviewing the search strategy created by the software, if the user would like to make modifications. For multiword phrases or author's names, the software automatically adds adjacency operators. The software then logs on to Dialog, uploads the search strategy and downloads up to twenty citations. The next twenty citations can be requested, but this counts as a second search. A typical search costs approximately $2.50 with an annual *Search Helper* license that costs $200 plus $1750 for 700 prepaid searches. A drawback to *Search Helper* is that users can only "and" terms together, not "or" or "not" terms as is possible by searching on Dialog directly. Still, because *Search Helper* is simple to use and can provide short searches on current topics at low cost, it can be very suitable for public libraries and for undergraduates in academic libraries, and an appropriate vehicle for setting up a daytime end-user search service. IAC is even making a coin-operated system available as an option. *Search Helper* runs on the IBM PC, Eagle and Apple microcomputers. A demo diskette is available.

With flashy color graphics, Menlo's **In Search** facilitates searching on Dialog and assists with database selection. After the user chooses from four main subject categories such as Biology and Medicine and from thirty to forty subject or document-type terms within each category, càtalog cards for appropriate databases are displayed with descriptions. For developing and running an online search, *In Search* provides several options and help screens through a command box at the bottom of the screen. Dialog's blue sheets are part of the software and can be accessed at anytime during the search session. *In Search* highlights the search terms in the retrieved references and simplifies revising search strategies by automatically re-searching any part of a strategy that is affected by revisions. Successful search strategies can be saved to be reloaded and used later. Effective use of the software and experience with Boolean operators can be gained by using the tutorial disks and manual. *In Search* costs $399 and is available for the IBM PC and compatibles as well as the Texas Instruments Professional Computer. A demo diskette is also available.

ISI's **Sci-Mate** is comprised of two integrated software packages, the *Universal Online Searcher* and the *Personal Data Manager.* With the *Universal Online Searcher,* users have the option of searching BRS, Dialog, NLM and SDC through menu-driven prompts or through their native command languages. The *Universal Online Searcher* includes functions such as browse, which expands into a database's online index; search, which has numerous help screens; display/offload, which displays and downloads all, none or selected records; and save strategy, which retains the entire search strategy or any portion. If the *Personal Data Manager* is also used, records can then be downloaded into this database management package directly according to a chosen format (template). Additional records can be added by the user, and all records searched, tagged, and annotated. *Sci-Mate* has an extensive manual, a

Martin Kesselman *is life sciences librarian at Bobst Library, New York University.*

telephone hotline and a bimonthly newsletter—*Sci-Mate Matters.* The *Universal Online Searcher* sells for $440, the *Personal Data Manager* for $540, and both for $880. *Sci-Mate* can be used on the IBM, Vector, Apple, and TRS-80 microcomputers and those with the CP/M operating system.

SDC's **Search Master** is comprised of two program modules: pre-search and run-search. Menu-driven pre-search allows you to enter your search offline, and once a strategy has been prepared, run-search automatically logs you on to the chosen online system and database and runs the search. A unique feature of pre-search is that it allows users to create their own preformatted search strategies or scripts which can be filled in when doing a specific search. An online library of these scripts, designed by database producers and other specialists, will be available as a file through the SDC Orbit online system. *Search Master,* which runs on the IBM PC, sells for $299 and can be used for searching SDC, Dialog, NLM and BRS.

Informatics' **PC Net/Link** simplifies access to twelve online services including BRS, Dialog, SDC, NLM, Mead Data, Dow Jones, Questel, OCLC and RLIN. The database selection process is menu-driven beginning with a choice of twenty-six primary headings each of which is further divided into as many as twenty-six subheadings. A user selects one main heading and up to two subheadings and descriptions of the relevant databases are displayed. Searches can be prepared offline to be uploaded. The user needs to know each online service's command language, but the software can display summaries of each system's basic commands. *PC Net/Link* runs on the IBM PC and sells for $550.

Gateways

Unlike front-end software packages, gateways connect you to an intermediary computer which in turn provides a connection to several online services. These gateway services, because they are based on mainframes and minicomputers, can provide a great deal more transparency to the casual end-user who is not familiar with online information sources. One exception is *Superscout,* which is a gateway service for the experienced searcher. Gateways are the wave of the future and have just become available.

Users of **Superscout** are provided a free diskette from the Business Computer Network (BCN), which allows access to the BCN host computer by calling a toll-free number. The BCN computer provides a gateway to several online systems including Dialog, BRS, Newsnet, CompuServe and Billboard. It will also include the low-cost after hours services of BRS *After Dark* and *Knowledge Index.* The user is signed on to the selected system but then is on his own. The advantage of this service is that the user need not have passwords and receives one bill that includes searches on all services used the previous month. There is a flat access fee of $5 per month for up to twenty searches, with additional searches at twenty-five cents each. Online charges of each database and online service are additional. BCN offers a free user guide with search examples, a newsletter and twenty-four-hour customer service.

Information Transfer (IT) from Data-Ease, available now as a front-end software package for the IBM PC and compatibles with hard disks and for several brands of minicomputers, will be available as a gateway service in early 1985. The user types in information requests in natural language and appropriate databases are displayed in a ranked order with descriptions and costs. The software then sets up a search strategy and provides options for the user to remove any unwanted lines, combine two lines to search them as a phrase, edit mistakes, add synonyms or limit the search further by adding additional terms. Keying in a question mark will elicit a help screen. The search is then run with the choice of printing, displaying or downloading results. The initial release of the software sells for approximately $550 for the micro version and provides access to databases on BRS and Dialog. Early in 1985, as a gateway service with dial-up access, *Information Transfer* will be available at per search charges.

Telenet's **Easynet** provides access currently to approximately sixty databases on Dialog, BRS and SDC produced by members of the National Federation of Abstracting and Indexing Services (NFAIS), which has agreed to cosponsor this service. Databases produced by NFAIS members on Newsnet as well as several other online systems will be added shortly. Access to *Easynet* is through a toll-free phone number. After giving a credit card number, the user is presented with menus to choose a topic, and is asked whether the topic deals with a person, place, subject, or organization. Further menus help refine the search. There is a $5 access charge plus a $5 vendor/database charge for ten records, $5 for each additional ten records, $2 for abstracts and $8.50 for *(continued on page 302)*

Addresses:

Business Computer Network, 2533 South Highway 101, Suite 210, Cardiff by the Sea, CA 92007, 800/541-0199.

Data-Ease, Inc., 3130 Mayfield Rd., Cleveland Heights, OH 44118, 216/371-5640.

Informatics General Corp., 6011 Executive Blvd., Rockville, MD 20852, 800/638-6595.

Information Access Corp., 11 Davis Dr., Belmont CA, 94002 800/277-8431.

Institute for Scientific Information, 3501 Market St., Philadelphia, PA 19104, 800/523-4092.

Menlo Corp., 4633 Old Ironsides, Suite 400, Santa Clara, CA 95050, 408/986-0200.

SDC, 2500 Colorado Ave., Santa Monica, CA 90406, 800/352-6689.

Telebase Systems, Inc., 134 North Narbeth Ave., Suite 6, Narbeth, PA 19072, 215/664-6168.

Donnarae MacCann/Olga Richard:

Picture Books for Children

From *A Visit from St. Alphabet*

This fall, Allan Kornblum, Cinda Kornblum, and David Duer turned Toothpaste Press—a small press notable for fine printing—into Coffee House Press. The children's books known as the Hot Chocolate Fairy Tale Series will be available as part of the Coffee House list. We reviewed the first "Hot Chocolate" fairy tale, *Rose of Mother-of-Pearl,* in our September column. This month we will cover two titles by poet Dave Morice that we overlooked in 1982 and a 1980 Morice title, *A Visit from St. Alphabet,* that was one of "Toothpaste's" best-sellers.

In making a general evaluation of the work of Dave Morice, *A Visit from St. Alphabet* has the cleverest text, and *The Happy Birthday Handbook* has the most artistically consistent illustrations. *Dot Town* is a blend of several graphic styles, but the book design overcomes any visual inconsistency. The text is an appealing collection of verses that have narrative continuity and rhythmic diversity.

A Visit from St. Alphabet is superlative word play for a wide-ranging audience. A quotation is perhaps the best way to introduce it:

> 'Twas the night before X, when all through the Y
> Not a letter was stirring, not even an I;
> The S's were hung by the T's with care
> In the hopes that St. Alphabet soon would be there;
> The Z's were nestled all snug in their beds,
> While visions of W's danced in their heads;
> And U in your kerchief, and I in my cap,
> Had just settled our words for a long writer's nap. . . .

The nonsensical parody continues in this vein and concludes with this couplet: "But I read in the sky, ere he wrote out of sight,/'Happy Alphabet to all, and to all a good writer!'"

With such fanciful versifying, it is surprising that Morice did not move in a similar direction in the illustrations. His Santa is a tired image carried over from the nineteenth century, and some scenes are so mercilessly hatched and cross-hatched that it is an effort to sort out the overload of technique and imagery. Morice seems to have sensed the need to break out of the conventional mold, but he finds a more innovative approach only spasmodically, as in his depictions of the reindeer and sleigh.

But like all the Coffee House books, *A Visit from St. Alphabet* is a pleasure to examine in terms of its layouts, paper quality, and beautiful typeface. These features create a unity that the illustrations lack.

In *The Happy Birthday Handbook,* the viewer receives a strong sense of the artist, as well as an awareness of meticulous book design. The protagonist is conceived in the form of a hand—a child/hand in a realm of hand-shaped folks. Homer Hand is lonely on his birthday because all his friends seem to be someplace else, and the ice cream he buys for himself doesn't cheer him up. The isolation of this hapless Hand is underscored by the simplicity of the por-

From *The Happy Birthday Handbook*

Olga Richard *and* **Donnarae MacCann** *are the authors of* The Child's First Books.

trait and the few disparate objects placed in each scene (an umbrella, a tree, etc.). But the composition changes as Homer's surprise birthday party is foreshadowed. There is first a cozy composition of fence posts and a curving line of clouds—a design that encloses Homer within a more fully visualized context. Then the friends appear in a supportive cluster, and the compactness of the whole design expresses the coming together of different elements: the narrative climax, the psychological shift in characters, the change of mood. The cleverness that Morice brings to this rather familiar sounding plot is evident in his simple treatment of line and in his uncluttered, straightforward technique, which is so minimal that it soon strikes the reader as comical. The hand/person, "handbook," and super-sparse image are all part of a singularly whimsical vision.

In a third Morice book, *Dot Town*, individual illustrations have many special qualities, but these traits are not carried over to the next picture. The minimal, uncontrived approach that is handled so well in *The Happy Birthday Handbook* is predominant on some pages, and then Morice switches to the tight, complex type of renderings that characterize *A Visit from St. Alphabet*. There is, however, a farcical mood throughout, and the pictures extend the range of the plot action suggested in the verses.

The Dots of Dot Town are not as infinitesimal as the "Who" in Dr. Seuss's Whoville (see *Horton Hears a Who* published in 1954) and unlike the plot in the Dr. Seuss story, the Dots are not caught in a moral dilemma. But the busy, bourgeois activities are similar in Dot Town and Whoville, and the size contrasts are similarly intriguing. The disparity in scale between the human and Dot worlds is presented in the first verse:

A tiny Dot can stand
At the edge of a person's hand,
On a fingertip or a thumbtip,
And shout, "The view is grand!"

The second verse requires the presence of the illustration to produce the comical effect. In conjunction with the following verse there is a series of portraits of Barbie Dot, Donald Dot, Trixie Dot and so on.

From *Dot Town*

How do you make a dot?
It's easy, is it not?
Two arms, two legs, a head,
And a name you like a lot!

Other verses capitalize on the child's fascination with birthdays, circuses, inventions.

We hope the Dave Morice books will not be neglected by libraries because of their miniature size and soft covers. But librarians might be interested to know that the new goals of Coffee House Press are described as the creation of "fiction, children's books and poetry titles of interest to a wide audience," and that some will "combine offset technology and film-laminated covers with the beautiful margins and choice of type that have distinguished Toothpaste Press books." Furthermore, Smyth sewing and glued wrappers with flaps will enable the books to "hold up in any bookstore or library."

Finally a word about where Coffee House Press came from and how it grew. Given the enormous capitalization of some commercial publishing companies, the creation and prosperity of a company such as Coffee House Press can seem somewhat mysterious. But there is really nothing imponderable about commitment and vision. Under the name Toothpaste Press, the enterprise started in 1970 with a mimeographed magazine that sold for a dollar and was sold by local shopkeepers in a small college town. "After learning the letterpress ropes with a few pamphlets and broadsides," says the author of the 1978 Toothpaste catalog, "we are now committed to publishing what's new in poetry using what's old in printing: handset type, letterpress printing, needle-and-thread binding."

Keeping pace with social progress, a 1983 advertisement announced a new goal—the "desire to uncover contemporary and nonsexist examples of one of the oldest and best-loved literary forms . . . : the fairy tale." If Coffee House Press can fulfill this purpose and bring gender inclusiveness to a problematic genre, then the press will serve children as a positive agent of change, as well as an artistic standard-bearer. ▣

This month's books:

Morice, Dave, **Dot Town**. Coffee House Press, 1982. $8.50.
Morice, Dave. **The Happy Birthday Handbook.** Coffee House Press, 1982. $7.50.
Morice, Dave. **A Visit From St. Alphabet.** Coffee House Press, 1980. $5.
Note: Coffee House books are distributed by Bookslinger, 213 E. Fourth St., St. Paul, MN 55101.

Patty Campbell:

The Young Adult Perplex

This month's column is an excerpt from Patty Campbell's forthcoming book, Robert Cormier, *to be published in August 1985 by Twayne Publishers. Used with permission of Twayne Publishers.*

You are riding the bicycle and you are on Route 2 thirty miles west of Boston on your way to Leominster, Massachusetts, and you're pedaling furiously because this is an old-fashioned bike, no speeds, no fenders, only the warped tires and the brakes that don't always work and the handlebars with cracked rubber grips to steer with. A plain bike—the kind Bob Cormier rode as a kid years ago. It's cold as you pedal along, the wind like a snake slithering up your sleeves and into your jacket and your pants legs, too. But you keep pedaling, you keep pedaling.

It's crazy to be riding a bicycle here on the snowy highway in the midst of winter. But this is a pilgrimage, a journey to Cormier country, and riding a bike—an *old* bike—is the only right way to do it. This is the kind of bicycle Adam Farmer rode on his perpetual haunted journey to find his dead father, and Cormier's words from the beginning of *I Am the Cheese* echo again in your head as you struggle uphill against the bitter wind. "I am riding the bicycle and I am on Route 31 in Monument, Massachusetts, on my way to Rutterburg, Vermont, and I'm pedaling furiously because this is an old-fashioned bike. . . . "

You look back over your shoulder but there's no one following.

The low hills are covered with patches of snow, and the naked trees are rows of black pen-scratches slashed between the white ground and the white sky. You labor on, careful to stay in the tracks of clear pavement left by the snow tires of cars. Near the brow of the hill is a sign: "Leominster. The Pioneer Plastic City. Population 38,000." As you come over the crest you see the town straggling across the little valleys below, a jumble of clapboard and dull red brick from the turn of the century. An ugly New England mill town, but with a comfortable air of homeyness and endurance.

Leominster and the neighboring town of Fitchburg are where Robert Cormier has lived all of his life. As Monument, Massachusetts, they are the setting for his stories, the theater where his characters struggle against the ominous powers of malice and tyranny that gather like the dark snowclouds behind these hills of Leominster. The people in his novels are creatures of his own mind, but the stage sets for their grim dramas are the street and schools and houses of these two tiny towns where Robert Cormier's own life has been acted out. It is to visit these places that you have made this cold, slippery journey—to see these real places in "Monument" where Jerry Renault and Adam Farmer and Amy Hertz and Miro Shantas walked and worried and dreamed, and to see what kind of man could be the creator of these brave and tormented people.

You follow the directional signs off the highway to a smaller road. At the top of the hill you pause to rest, breathing heavily, and to settle the newspaper-wrapped package more securely in your bike basket. It is soggy now from the damp cold air and some of the Scotch tape has begun to pull free. You turn up your jacket collar around your ears, push off, and sail in one long swoop down Main Street through the town and on to the town square, the Common on the north of the center of the business district where Main Street widens out to form a triangle. This is where Jerry Renault waited for the bus, leaning wearily against a telephone pole after a grueling football practice. On the Common by the Civil War cannon and the flagpole the grass has long

Patty Campbell *teaches young adult literature at* UCLA *and is a library consultant and freelance writer.*

About Twayne's Young Adult Authors Series

In 1985, Twayne Publishers will offer a new series of critical studies of young adult authors. Each hardcover volume, approximately one hundred pages long, will examine the life and work of one contemporary YA author. The first volumes Twayne will publish are on Robert Cormier (by Patricia J. Campbell), M.E. Kerr (by Alleen Pace Nilsen), and Judy Blume (by Audrey B. Eaglen). Also under contract are books on Paul Zindel (by Jack Forman) and Rosa Guy (by Jerrie Norris). Contributions are sought for volumes on S.E. Hinton, Norma Klein, Isabelle Holland, and Norma Fox Mazer.

—Ron Brown, series editor

been covered with snow, and no hippies lounge about or cross the street to challenge Jerry to start his own war, his Chocolate War. A bus pulls up with a hiss and a stench of exhaust.

You cross the square, wheeling the bike through the crosswalks, and look up at the third floor of the rooming house from *Take Me Where the Good Times Are*. Behind these windows Jean Baptiste in his lonely insanity clung to the secret companionship of his family of dolls. Even from where you stand on the sidewalk you can smell the lonesome smell of fried things cooked on a hotplate.

Careful of the traffic now, you pedal slowly down Pleasant Street to Mechanic Street and turn left. A few blocks farther on, you come to the heart of Cormier country, the district called French Hill. This is the neighborhood of Cormier's childhood. Here he grew up in a warm, close community of family and friends, all French Canadian immigrants who had come to New England in the early part of the century to provide manpower for the newly built factories. The narrow clapboard houses stand sturdy and square, three stories with white-trimmed shutters and balconies. Each is apart on its own bare little plot of land, but no fences separate neighbors and friends. "Tenements" they are called hereabouts, but these decent working-people's homes are nothing like the disreputable tenements of New York City.

You wheel along the quiet streets and stop for a moment in tribute in front of the pale green house where Alph LeBlanc in *Now and at the Hour* fought his silent losing battle with cancer—and where Cormier's own father died in his son's arms. Above the bare branches of the elm trees you can see the spire of St. Cecelia's Church—or St. Jude's Church in Monument. Around the corner of Sixth Street you pass number 121, where Cormier lived as a little child and where the Midnight Raiders from *Eight Plus One* plotted their vegetable raids. Down the block is the bar called the Happy Times in *A Little Raw on Monday Mornings,* where lonely middle-aged Gracie had her one night of fun, and where Cormier father and son came to watch baseball games together on television. Through the widely spaced houses and tree trunks you can see downhill across Mechanic Street to the factories where Cormier's relatives and his characters Alph and Gracie and Tommie worked all their lives on the comb machines.

You turn back to town now and, trying to avoid the traffic in the square, you turn left into a narrow alley. A mistake, you soon realize—it goes nowhere. But a voice in your head says, "Lose something, honey?" and you look up to discover Fat Arthur's fire escape. The iron railings and banisters and rungs are cagelike and you remember that he sat there in the pages of *I Am the Cheese* like a prisoner in his weight and bulk. Hurriedly you back out of the dank alley and steer determinedly up Mechanic Street and then north toward Fitchburg.

Your legs churn with rhythm, tempo, and as you fly along the road you think about the meanings of the word "monument": A structure erected as a memorial for valiant deeds. A place preserved as having special historical importance. An inscribed stone in remembrance of the dead. An exceptional example of something. From the Latin for "to remind, to warn." One by one you measure them for appropriateness as you bicycle through Monument, Massachusetts.

It's a long way to Fitchburg, and long before you get there your hands are rigid claws around the handlebars. At last you reach the outskirts, and, a minute later, the center of Fitchburg. Although this town is almost the same size as Leominster, Main Street seems more "downtown." You wobble through the stream of cars and trucks and pull up in front of the neo-Grecian facade of the public library. Should you go in for a minute? It would feel good to get warm, but time is short and you have miles to go before the dark comes. You put one foot out to balance yourself, and step deep into a snowbank. The icy prickles down your boot make up your mind for you. You go under the gray stone arch of the old Carnegie part of the building, and push open the door where Amy and Adam first met. She was coming in and he was going out, you remember, and they collided, spilling books everywhere; before they finished picking them up he was madly in love.

But you're just cold. In the sudden welcome warmth and light you stroll up and down the aisles, rubbing the feeling back into your cold fingers. In the fiction section you find Cormier's three early adult books—*Now and at the Hour, A Little Raw on Monday Mornings,* and *Take Me Where the Good Times Are*. Where is *Eight Plus One,* you wonder? In the short-story section? Or probably upstairs in the Young Adult room, along with *The Chocolate War, I Am the Cheese,* and *After the First Death*. The librarian smiles pleasantly at you, and you are tempted to stay to talk with her about your pilgrimage. You have heard that Robert Cormier serves on the board of trustees for this library. But you glance out the window and see that the late afternoon light is starting to fade.

Hurrying now, you pedal along Main Street a little farther, past the spot where the *Fitchburg Sentinel* offices used to be. A new building stands there now, but you imagine Cormier standing at the window of the office where he worked for so many years as associate editor. At another window Amy's father gazes out, taking a moment's break from his work as editor of the *Monument Times*.

At the intersection of Main and Mechanic Street (a *different* Mechanic Street) you pause at the curb and peer up the street to your right, where the hospital looms on a rise. Adam thinks his father is there sometimes, and Barney could have been there, too, waiting out his short life in The Complex, yearning for the Bumblebee to fly anyway. You think you glimpse a high fence, too, that could

(*continued on page 302*)

Kathleen Maio:

Murder in Print

Dorothy L. Sayers angers many people. Some are offended by the elitism of her aristocratic sleuth, Lord Peter Wimsey, pampered by devoted "servants" like Bunter and Miss Climpson. Others are offended by Sayers' snobbish writing style—the way she'll toss off an unattributed quotation from John Donne or untranslated quotation from Aristotle. But for those of us who love her mysteries, erudition and all, her biggest offense is that she turned away from detective fiction during the stirrings of World War II never to return to it again. She left us with but a dozen novels and a handful of short stories.

There are few sights more pathetic than that of a mystery fan who has just devoured the last novel by a favorite author. We comfort ourselves by reading their "straight" novels, their newspaper and journal appearances, or, in the case of Sayers, anything from religious philosophy to translations of *The Divine Comedy.* The publication of the Avon anthology *Lord Peter* in 1972 was a blessing to Sayers fanatics for its inclusion of the theretofore unpublished story, "Talboys." This embarrassing yet fascinating story saw Lord Peter and wife Harriet Vane with three sons. The newest comfort for Sayers devotees is the publication of **Love All and Busman's Honeymoon** (Kent State University Press, 1984, $19.95), edited by Alzina Stone Dale.

The volume contains Sayers' first professionally produced plays. *Busman's Honeymoon* was written with Sayers' lifelong friend, Muriel St. Clare Byrne. It is the original form of the story for which Sayers' novel of the same name is "but the limbs and outward flourishes." Those who agree with Sayers that there is "an intolerable deal of saccharine" in the novel may feel more kindly towards the play. Although not without the love element, it is a lean, businesslike piece of work concerned primarily with providing a fair-play mystery for the play-going public.

Love All, never before published, is a play I had the good fortune of reading in manuscript form as "Cat's Cradle" at the Marion E. Wade Collection at Wheaton College. It is a sophisticated sex comedy of the type identified with Noel Coward. But since the author is Sayers, the play is feminist as well as witty. It argues, with humor, that a woman requires meaningful work of her own, beyond that of helpmate and mother.

Alzina Stone Dale's introduction does a good job of placing the two plays within the context of the rest of Sayers' work. By researching and discussing the form of the Sayers/Byrne collaboration, she tells us how the author worked. Sayers scholars and fans will find this volume fascinating, entertaining, and a comfort against the void.

One author who hasn't stopped writing but who can hardly keep up with demand for his work is Frank Parrish. His latest, **Death in the Rain** (Dodd Mead, 1984, $12.95), continues the adventures of West Country rogue, Dan Mallett. Dan's proclivities for poaching and pinching the valuables of the local nobs make him a key suspect when an old woman is murdered during a robbery.

This time out, he loses his spot as number one suspect in favor of a young woman, to whom he is very

much attracted. If Dan isn't absolutely certain of his new lady's innocence, neither is Natasha sure that Dan isn't the murderer and thief. Still, the two investigate side by side. They elude the police, but not the meddling of Dan's aged and crippled mother.

This is not Parrish's strongest mystery. But the tale of Dan and Natasha's courtship (guided by Mrs. Mallett, who views a Surbiton accountant's daughter as the quickest way to force her son back to the straight and narrow) is filled with warmth and humor. For most readers, Parrish's characters, the occasional glimpses of the flora and fauna of rural England, and the naked chase scene in *Death in the Rain* will guarantee full satisfaction.

Marcia Muller's new Sharon McCone novel is **Leave a Message for Willie** (St. Martin's, 1984, $11.95). This time out, Sharon is hired to protect a likeable fence named Willie from a mysterious fellow wearing a

Kathleen Maio *is a freelance writer based in Somerville, Massachusetts. She has contributed to* Twentieth Century Crime Writers, Murderess Ink, *and numerous magazines.*

yarmulke who keeps tailing him. Sharon finds Willie's shadow murdered, and the mystery expands to include more murder and some very dangerous adult games.

We also get intriguing glimpses into the private life of Muller's sleuth as she contemplates further commitment to her latest lover. The author is smart enough to avoid spending too much time on Sharon's domestic scene and never loses sight of the story line. She makes it clear that Sharon may dribble snowcone on her chin, but she still knows how to take care of business.

Three first mysteries are all very different and quite good. T.J. Binyon, who has reviewed crime fiction for the London *Times*, has produced his first

suspense novel in **Swan Song** (Dial Press, 1984, $14.95). Binyon has traded on his experience as a student and teacher of Russian literature and culture to produce a satisfying novel set in Moscow and the rural Vologda oblast.

Vanya Morozov finds himself in a no-win situation when he is forced by an old acquaintance now with the KGB to track and spy on a woman, significant to both their pasts, who is now a central figure in a religious cult. Vanya is an academic, unused to espionage and mountain hikes. There are no easy answers or actions for him as he tries to do the right thing by his friends and conscience, while insuring his own survival.

The plot, which concerns more than a small band of religious dissidents, is a complicated one. Still, Binyon's realistic and sympathetic hero, and his effective use of locale and culture, keep everything hanging together. Despite the international spies and drug-induced orgies, *Swan Song* remains a story of love and jealousy and the yearning for spiritual fulfillment.

Alison Smith makes her debut in **Someone Else's Grave** (St. Martin's, 1984, $11.95). Here is a classic village mystery set in a small New England town called Coolidge Corners. The action begins when an elderly spinster sets out to decorate the graves in the town's old cemetery and finds an extra body inadequately buried in a recently opened grave.

Chief Judd Springfield must end an outbreak of violence that escalates to include the murders of three women and an attack on another. Smith shows real skill in setting up a large number of suspects and even more in her portrayal of small-town life and a homey, caring detective.

The latest entry into the hard-boiled field is William J. Reynolds with **The Nebraska Quotient** (St. Martin's, 1984, $13.95). Reynolds

sets his story in Omaha and names his hero Nebraska. Nebraska has retired from the detective business to support himself as a freelance journalist while he works on "The Book." When his crooked ex-partner collapses into his apartment with a mortal bullet wound (and with a set of incriminating pictures stuffed in his undershorts), Nebraska is back in the game.

The plot is standard material with political corruption, sexual treachery, and heartland Mafia, against which our hero stands tall. It doesn't matter that you know exactly where a plot like this is going so long as you enjoy getting there. And Nebraska, a member in good standing of the wise-ass school of private eyes, makes it a pleasant journey. Some of the dialogue and Nebraska's interior asides alone are worth the trip.

Not a first novel, but a first to the Doubleday list, is **Striving with Gods** by Jo Bannister (Doubleday/Crime Club, 1984, $11.95). Like William Reynolds's Nebraska, Bannister's protagonist, Clio Rees, has turned from her original profession, in this case physician, to become a writer of mysteries. The mystery develops when Clio is informed that her dearest friend, a gay man named Luke, has died with a young boy in an apparent suicide pact. She doesn't believe the police scenario, and uncovers evidence of a double murder and cover-up. It soon becomes clear to Clio, and the reader, that this is a case of medical conspiracy as well as homicide.

Bannister's book is more thriller than mystery. And Clio is more avenging fury than detective. We know early on who the prime conspirator/murderer is. The major question is whether Clio will survive long enough to build a case. A murder attempt and chase scene go on a bit too long but Bannister keeps her thriller tight with good characterization and the no-nonsense voice of her heroine. Clio's wry narration shows strength, but contains an edge of self-criticism along with self-awareness. It is a voice that tells a suspense story exceedingly well. ▣

Bruce Pollock:

On Record: Popular Music

An old record business axiom so hoary it's hard to believe has just been proven to me once again: It all comes down to the song. Think of the timeless simplicity, the bedrock inevitability: you either like a song or you don't. And while radio—and now TV—can numb you into submission, seduce you into humming something you can barely tolerate, personal classics are almost instantly recognizable, taking place in the form of radio epiphanies, moments when the art form of popular music can make everything suddenly glowing and right, if only for three minutes and twenty-two seconds.

The song it came down to for me a few days ago was not an instant classic, but it certainly sports all the earmarks of compelling balladry that go into the making of an evergreen. I heard it the first time from the lips of an absolutely mediocre aspiring Borscht Belt chanteuse. I recognized it as the same type of adult-sensibility tune as last year's "Always on My Mind." When the song turned up again, as the emotional finale for an upcoming Sheena Easton special, I knew my original instincts had been right. Not two days later, perusing a day-old newspaper discovered on a train, I noted that the same song, "The Wind Beneath My Wings," had been given a country music songwriting award. Obviously, it had been a country hit (as was "Always on My Mind") and minimal research could turn up the original artist, album and label.

But that song, worthy as it may be, is not the point. The point is—as it's always been—It all comes down to the song. So I have compiled a list of songs that to me are classics, obscure gems in many cases, that deserve further recognition, and that elevate the albums on which they are found into the ranks of the sought-after. It is hoped that the aspiring song buff (not always the same thing as a record buff) will be moved to seek out these sometimes hard-to-find albums and perhaps discover his or her own epiphanies as well.

Bruce Pollock *is editor of* Guitar *magazine and the author of* When the Music Mattered: Rock in the 1960s.

• "God's Song," by Tracy Nelson, on *Homemade Songs.* Flying Fish FF052 (1978)

Under-appreciated, misused and nearly always mumbling through inappropriate material, the wailing blues power of Tracy Nelson's voice comes through loud, clear and unadorned on one of Randy Newman's most withering lyrics.

• "Sunday Bloody Sunday," by U2, on *Under a Blood Red Sky.* Island 7-90127-1-B (1983)

This is a message song that serves to disprove the odious notion—rampant in some quarters—that today's rock has no substance. Its statement is as powerful and compelling as war itself.

• "Power," by the Doobie Brothers, with John Hall and James Taylor, on *No Nukes.* Asylum ML801 (1979)

Since the demise of Phil Ochs, I generally shy away from overtly political songs. But this is a song that transcends its ominous message with some thrilling and soulful harmonies.

• "Still in Saigon," by the Charlie Daniels Band, on *A Decade of Hits.* Epic FE 38795 (1983)

If you're looking for the best song about Vietnam, forget Springsteen, forget Billy Joel—this Dan Daley gem is it. As convincingly portrayed by the Charlie Daniels Band, this tale of a frazzled returning vet was my choice for 1981's song of the year—the Grammy committee didn't even see fit to nominate it.

• "Stoney," by Jerry Jeff Walker, on *Bein Free.* Atco SD 33-336 (1970)

A perfect evocation of that particular wanderlust that gripped many in the late sixties; the scenes and characters one encountered on the road, on the lam, as sung by the ultimate urban cowboy.

• "(Talk to Me of) Mendocino," by Kate and Anna McGarrigle, on *Kate and Anna McGarrigle.* Warner Bros. BS 2862 (1975)

Girls, of course, get wanderlust too, and the McGarrigle sisters, being no exceptions, are exceptional, in this poignant and sweet tale of a bi-coastal coming of age.

• "New Orleans Ladies," by Louisiana's Le Roux, on *Louisiana's Le Roux.* Capitol SW 11734 (1978)

My particular street of dreams was in the French Quarter in New Orleans, where I once rented an apartment for a single day with a girl from Rhode Island, a fiasco that will live in infamy between the lines of this melancholy song by an otherwise hard-boogying southern band.

• "Boulder to Birmingham," by Emmylou Harris, on *Pieces of the Sky*. Warner Bros. MSK 2284 (1975)

In a career of admirable interpretations, Emmylou has written a song that stands as one of her finest moments, a brilliant, blazing portrait of a love gone to flames—where country music crosses into bluegrass, and bluegrass into eternity.

• "The Moon's a Harsh Mistress," by Linda Ronstadt, on *Get Closer*. Asylum 60185-1 (1982)

Despite some snide and possibly unwarranted comments lately made about Ronstadt in certain quarters, she hits some high notes on this stark and unyielding Jim Webb ballad that prove her worthy, beyond a doubt, of whatever fame and riches fate has rewarded her.

• "P.F. Sloan," by Jim Webb, on *El Mirage*. Atlantic SD 18218 (1977)

Though there's something to be said for the songwriter as the only true interpreter of his/her own work, there's also something to be said for leaving well enough alone—or to the pipes of Ronstadt, Nelson, et al. In the case of Jim Webb the latter statement stands in most cases. The exception is this haunting song about a missing person.

• "The Road," by Danny O' Keefe, on *The O'Keefe File*. Warner Bros. PRO A-760 (1979)

The most (and perhaps only) believable song about everyday rock on the circuit, by a sweet-voiced, star-crossed singer-songwriter. Luckily for O'Keefe, the song was covered by Jackson Browne on a best-selling album. His own album was never released commercially. The original allbum that contains this song, *O'Keefe,* on Signpost Records, is most likely out of print.

• "Romeo and Juliet," by Dire Straits, on *Making Movies*. Phonogram BSK3480 (1980)

Beyond the brilliant guitar work by Mark Knopfler is an equally brilliant and biting love song to a coy and shallow contemporary Juliet.

• "Romeo Is Bleeding," by Tom Waits, on *Blue Valentine*. Asylum 6E-162 (1978)

Here's a song that could be an entire episode of "Hill Street Blues": the street as seen in vivid drab, deftly painted by a master sidewalk portrait (and con) artist.

• "Livin' It Up," by Rickie Lee Jones, on *Pirates*. Warner Bros. BSK 3432 (1981)

A desultory yet plucky saga of some local losers, set to a bebop score. But the title chant is eerie and sad.

• "Old Friend," by Gretchen Cryer and Nancy Ford, on *I'm Getting My Act Together & Taking It on the Road*

Taking in many of the imponderables of life, love, and relationships, this is perhaps the most adult of all the adult-sensibility pop songs in vogue these days—and easily the most sensitive. From the cult theatrical piece, it is performed by its writers, who starred in the play. It makes Carly Simon's "That's the Way I've Always Heard It Should Be" sound as naive as "When You Wish Upon a Star."

• "Waiting for the Moving Van," by David Ackles, on *American Gothic*. Elektra 75032 (1972)

A man returns to the house that he lived in with his wife for ten years, and reminisces about their married life, cut short by divorce, as he waits for the movers to cart the memories away. Sure it's sentimental—but who says only the French can write sentimental songs?

• "Once in a Lifetime," by Talking Heads, on *Remain in Light*. Sire SRK 6095 (1980)

Contemporary anomie, urban angst, suburban ennui—with a good beat, so you can dance to it. This song has recently been revived (if that's the right word) in the recent documentary on the Talking Heads, *Stop Making Sense*.

• "Take This Longing," by Leonard Cohen, on *New Skin for the Old Ceremony*. Columbia KC 33167 (1974)

Notorious for his dour sentiments, bleak outlook, and melancholy songs (my favorite type), Cohen outdoes himself in this abject plea for acceptance. There is a slightly more palatable Judy Collins version of this somewhere, but Cohen's loneliness rings truer.

• "Turned Up Too Late," by Graham Parker, on *Heat Treatment*. Mercury SRM-1-1117 (1976)

The flip side of melancholy is rage, and on this, one of the few pure rockers in the set, Graham Parker is outrageously enraged and engaging as the spurned lover turning into the spurner—a theme as old as Buddy Holly's "Maybe Baby."

• "American Dreamer," by Laura Nyro, on *Nested*. Columbia JC 35449 (1978)

Laura Nyro has fallen upon some hard times and critical impassiveness of late, but this song redeems her years of struggle. Sly, wry, perceptive (which she is rarely accused of being in public), along with charming, warm, seductive, and (amazingly) self-aware, it's the quintessential post-comeback Nyro song. ▣

Gail Pool:

Magazines

It's hard to say whether Americans are more obsessed with eating or with losing weight, but in magazines, food intake seems to have the edge. We find recipes in *Natural History,* restaurant reviews in *Fortune.*

Yet despite our devotion to the table, we have few magazines dedicated entirely to food and cooking. In an era of specialization, where even the most obscure activity can boast its own publication, the popular field of cooking has only four major magazines: *Bon Appetit: America's Food and Entertaining Magazine, The Cook's Magazine: The Magazine of Cooking in America, Food & Wine: The Guide to Good Taste,* and *Gourmet: The Magazine of Good Living.* All four cater to the "epicurean" market, leaving Middle American cooking to the women's magazines which, with their substantial food sections and mass circulations, garner most of the food industry's advertising and probably inhibit new entries into this field.

There is certainly no confusing the epicurean magazines' approach to food with that of *Woman's Day* or *Good Housekeeping.* The fancy books are for people genuinely interested in cooking, not those who simply have to get a nightly meal together. They are also for those who have the time and money to cook just what they want, whether venison or zabaglione, not those who have to stretch one pound of ground beef eight ways in one-half hour after work.

Although these magazines differ in personality and editorial thrust, they share some characteristics. All are handsome publications. *The Cook's Magazine* runs subdued watercolor designs on its covers. *Gourmet* has long been known for its art work. *Food & Wine* zooms in on its colorful food. Although *Bon Appetit* has a tendency toward clutter—the price it pays for its advertising success—all four magazines aim for an attractive design consistent with their aesthetic approach to food.

A second and less fortunate characteristic of all four is their lack of humor, a lack especially peculiar in view of their subject. Not that food isn't a serious issue. But these magazines aren't dealing with famine in India or ecological problems of the twenty-first century. They focus on eating and living well.

How appealing humor can be in this type of magazine was apparent in *Cuisine,* a cooking publication which CBS Inc. acquired in 1982 and decided to fold in October 1984. *Cuisine,* which could poke fun at the cocktail party or at gourmet hedonism, had a lightness and a perspective sorely needed by these others which, because they are too serious for their subject, seem to take themselves too seriously, skirting the sandpit of pomposity and, when it comes to critiques of wine, often falling in.

Whatever their similarities, however, the differences among the four magazines are greater and point up the variety of avenues to the subject of food. Of the four, the least well-known is the most interesting: **The Cook's Magazine.** This bimonthly focuses considerably more than the others on the specific and fascinating properties of food itself, and considerably less on entertainment and travel. In addition to recipes and cooking techniques, *The Cook's Magazine* offers in-depth articles about food—salt, for example, or maple sugar—which provide a colorful and detailed background most of us lack about our culinary culture.

The Cook's Magazine puts its emphasis on American food, from the fiddlehead fern to the New York egg cream, and each issue includes a section on regional cooking in America. Also in each issue is a consumer section, with a thorough rating of a cookware product (such as kitchen timers or skillets), assessed in *Consumer Reports*-style, complete with chart and supplementary discussion.

Like its fellows in the epicurean field, *The Cook's Magazine* is undoubtedly read by an upscale audience, but—perhaps because it pays so little attention to the entertainment circuit or the gourmet tour—it does not seem to cater to the interests of the rich. Moreover, as is clear from its honest consumer section and its rejection of cigarette advertising, it doesn't cater to advertisers either. This is an independent and unusual magazine, making its own editorial way.

In contrast with *The Cook's*

Gail Pool *holds an M.L.S. degree from Simmons College and presently works as a freelance writer based in Cambridge, Massachusetts.*

Magazine's broadly informative focus, **Food & Wine** is more of a service publication, a rich person's guide to the cuisine and restaurants of the world. There is a "how-to" and a "where-to" quality to the editorial material, both in articles ("What Makes a Superb Wine List") and in restaurant reviews.

Food & Wine's emphasis is international and somewhat travel-oriented, as is fitting, perhaps, in a magazine owned by American Express. A wide variety of foreign dishes appear in its pages and these recipes, which are accessible but challenging, are *Food & Wine*'s main strength. Despite the magazine's upscale mode, ingredients do not seem all that expensive, or so exotic it would take a week to locate them. These are dishes an average interested cook might like to try.

But apart from its recipes, *Food & Wine* seems somewhat flat. Perhaps its service orientation accounts for the merely serviceable prose of its articles and reviews. The best culinary writing can engage the interest of those who may never eat a particular dish, or visit the restaurant or even the country in which the dish is prepared. Such imaginative writing is not the strong point of *Food & Wine,* a magazine for real and not vicarious travelers.

Gourmet's prose, on the other hand, can satisfy both. The oldest of the four publications (founded in 1941) and the classiest, *Gourmet* is also the best written, with the richest use of language, and even a touch of wit.

Gourmet's approach to food is that it is only part of a "lifestyle," and, in its case, a very rich lifestyle. In their current advertising campaign, Conde Nast—the company that now publishes *Gourmet*—emphasizes that the magazine is not simply a food publication but, as implied by its subtitle, a magazine of "good living." Whether or not *Gourmet* can persuade upscale nonfood advertisers that its audience is the one to reach, and *Gourmet* the best way to reach it, its articles do cover travel, museums, and such topics as "Golfing in Gerona"—a world of opulent living above and beyond food.

Nevertheless, *Gourmet* does devote a high percentage of its editorial to fancy food and cooking, which brings it into close competition with **Bon Appetit,** the largest and richest magazine in the group, and the one which is probably the best positioned for the young upwardly mobile professionals advertisers love. Of the two, *Gourmet* is the more handsome, literate, and aristocratic magazine. *Bon Appetit,* a Knapp publication, is too bustling, too socially aggressive, too Yuppie to really have class. But when it comes to recipes, and for many readers it does come down to recipes, *Bon Appetit* seems to me the winner.

Bon Appetit, like *Gourmet,* is for serious cooks. The recipes in both magazines are complex, the techniques often demanding. But *Bon Appetit* has adapted some of its recipes toward the average person's reality in such departments as "Too Busy to Cook?" While *Bon Appetit*'s version of simplicity is hardly at the "boil and broil" level, its efforts to make some of its recipes more do-able have undoubtedly won it readers. A second, and somewhat less tangible, factor in the success of *Bon Appetit*'s recipes is that they seem more appealing than those in *Gourmet*; less exotic, a bit more conventional, perhaps, but more sumptuous, the ones you'd like to eat.

Gourmet these days is struggling to escape its pre-Conde Nast reputation as a magazine that presented food as objets d'art, dishes to be admired but not actually prepared and eaten. The magazine has begun to simplify some of its recipes and now has a "quick" department, "In Short Order." It also seems to be moving toward the inclusion of more conventional dishes (October's issue had a section on brownies). But in developing a more mainstream selection of recipes to challenge those that have made *Bon Appetit* indispensable for many cooks, *Gourmet* risks losing some of the qualities that have made it distinctively *Gourmet.* The magazine's challenge, as it shifts its identity, will be to hold the readers who enjoyed the exotic character of its editorial matter, while attracting the broader market it wants and needs.

In the magazine world, the epicurean field has blossomed only recently, and just how stable it is remains to be seen. Most of the magazines are young and the past five years have seen a lot of activity: Conde Nast's acquisition of *Gourmet, The New Yorker*'s partial acquisition of *The Cook's Magazine,* the folding of *Cuisine.* These magazines have shaped themselves around the upscale market, whose size and depth is not yet clear, and they're competing fiercely for an elite group of readers and a relatively small group of advertisers.

Most important to their survival, obviously, is the popularity of epicurean cooking, which could turn out to be a passing fad. Just as Americans are torn between feasting and fasting, we are torn between culinary pleasure and convenience. It has been said we want to eat well but cook fast. The more popular of the gourmet magazines, perhaps already sensing the turning tide, have begun to tell us it can be done. After all, it's their business to survive. But not even a gourmet magazine can tell you how to have your cake and eat it too.

This month's magazines:

Bon Appetit: America's Food and Entertaining Magazine. Monthly. $15/yr. Subscriptions: Box 2424, Boulder, CO 80302.

The Cook's Magazine: The Magazine of Cooking in America. Bimonthly. $18/yr. Subscriptions: Box 2998, Boulder, CO 80322.

Food & Wine: The Guide to Good Taste. Monthly. $16/yr. Subscriptions: Box 3004, Harlan, IA 51537.

Gourmet: The Magazine of Good Living. Monthly. $18/yr. Subscriptions: Box 2980, Boulder, CO 80302.

Norman Stevens:

Our Profession

Published somewhat later than usual this year, Katz's standard **Library Lit. 14—The Best of 1983** makes a fine companion to Sanford Berman and James Danky's alternative version, reviewed last month. The larger size, greater white space, cartoons, and other trappings of *Alternative Library Literature* make it appear more lively but in terms of content it is a standoff between the two. It is surprising to note, for example, that Katz's volume concludes with Celeste West's interview with "sex positive" publisher Joani Blank which would have seemed a natural for the alternative volume. While, in fact, this edition of the old best is slightly more staid than the new best, there is little distinction between the real press and the alternative press, or between these two selections. The difference is in the taste of the selectors. With the steady increase in professional library journals, and some signs of increased attention to library issues in other journals, there is ample room for more than one judgement as to what represents the best of library literature.

Katz groups his material in three sections: "Libraries and Librarians" (nine articles), "Communication and Education" (fourteen articles), and "The Social Prerogative" (seven articles). Many of the articles are the usual examinations of such issues as the purchase of poetry by public libraries, bibliographic control of library and information science literature, or the present state of libraries and information services in China. Informative but dull. But there are several notable exceptions which, because they challenge our basic assumptions, make for more lively reading. Those include: one Luddite's ramblings about technology, a troublemaker's unwarranted attack on library education, a disrespectful consideration of the best of current management theory as misapplied in libraries, an envious look at the economics and management of the New York Times Information Bank, and that outrageous interview with a "sex positive" publisher.

There is a need for Bruce Shuman's **River Bend Revisited** which gives sound assistance in thinking about how to deal with the troubled patron. Using the case study approach, which is usually dull and unimaginative, Shuman has put together a lively assortment of forty situations that public librarians, and sometimes academic and school librarians, face in today's troubled world. Divided equally between cases defined as emergencies and hazards and those described as mere nuisances (although the dividing line is not readily apparent), Shuman forces us to consider such problems as potential child abuse, accidents, bomb threats, arson, extortion, belligerence, graffiti, alcoholism, exhibitionism and other sexual activities, smoking, creationism, religion, fortune telling, and garlic. Quite an assortment! All are the kinds of cases we are unprepared to deal with because the topic has been ignored in library education and seldom covered in our journals (even in the literature of how-I-run-my-library-good school). More attention has been paid in recent years to the question of the problem patron and Shuman's casebook is an excellent summary of the field. Caputo's *The Assertive Librarian* (reviewed in last month's column) will need all of her skills in tackling these cases.

With those problem patrons, why any library should want to market its services is beyond me. Various studies, especially those conducted by Chen, which demonstrate how few people think of the library as an information resource have led to a strong interest in marketing our services. If libraries are going to use marketing techniques, librarians will need a body of literature translating marketing concepts to the library as a non-profit organization. Gary Ford, chairman of a unversity marketing department, offers in **Marketing and the Library** (a special issue of the *Journal of Library Administration* volume 4, number 4) one of the first, but undoubtedly not the last, texts on the subject. In his view libraries do

---

Norman Stevens *is university librarian at the University of Connecticut and the author of* Communication Throughout Libraries.

not need modern marketing techniques to survive but they do need them to prosper. He laments the lack of articles on empirical marketing research in a library setting and suggests the need for such studies conducted by marketing academics or professionals. Reports of such studies will undoubtedly appear soon.

The volume begins with Barbara Conroy taking yet another look at *Megatrends* and how marketing and strategic planning can help libraries respond to the impacts that Naisbitt identified. Bored as I am with the overemphasis that has been placed on John Naisbitt's work, Conroy did not hold my attention. The remaining articles are more intriguing and warrant examination. Anne Matthews looks at how libraries might segment their markets as an effective means of developing programs and marketing techniques to appeal to those homogeneous segments. Andrea Dragon and Tony Leisner consider some of the basics of implementing a marketing program. Darlene Weingand looks at distribution strategies and how changes in the way in which we make our services available can improve our standing. Finally Ford reprints Theodore Levitt's classic article "Marketing Myopia" from the *Harvard Business Review* of 1960. He suggests the need for an organization to think about doing the things that will make people want to do business with it. Eighty pages is not much for your money but, given the present state of our knowledge about marketing and libraries, it represents a fair start.

Neil Radford's careful historical narrative, **The Carnegie Corporation and the Development of American College Libraries, 1928–1941** is, in part, a tale of primitive marketing. After having supported library buildings, including 108 at colleges and universities, at a total cost of just over $4 million the Carnegie Corporation terminated such grants in 1917. In 1928 William Warner Bishop, Sarah Bogle, and Carl H. Milam met to draft a set of proposals to persuade philanthropic foundations to support college and university libraries. Their marketing of the proposals led to a Carnegie Corporation program that resulted in grants totalling $1,636,800 to 248 academic libraries to purchase basic books, as well as Shaw's *A List of Books for College Libraries* (1931); Mohrhardt's *A List of Books for Junior College Libraries* (1937); a program run through the University of Michigan to purchase books for libraries from those grants; various studies of college libraries, including a number by William M. Randall which in turn led to the publication of *The College Library* (1932) and later to his and Francis L. D. Goodrich's *Principles of College Library Administration* (1936). Over that period the Carnegie Corporation contributed more than $3 million to the development of college libraries.

Radford tells the story of those activities in a style that is fluid and easy to read. He does an especially careful job of evaluating the impact of the program. He concludes that library service in the recipient colleges was improved, but probably only temporarily, that college administrators were stimulated to think about the importance of good library service, that nonrecipients were not significantly encouraged to improve their level of library service on their own, and, on the whole, that the program was worth the money and the effort expended. To us an average grant of $6,600 over a thirteen-year period seems insignificant in comparison to the large gifts now being requested to fund automation. It will be interesting for future historians to attempt to assess the impact of such greater largess. One suspects that the earlier work of the Carnegie Corporation will seem more significant than Radford's cautious assessment suggests.

The best of this month's books is clearly Lowell A. Martin's **Organizational Structure of Libraries.** Using his long professional experience to good advantage, Martin has produced a text that is an excellent blend of theory and practice and should serve as the standard guide for many years to come. In Martin's terms "organization is taken to mean the formal and informal structure through which decisions are reached and individuals perform job tasks that contribute to the goals of the enterprise." Within that broad definition he deals with the theory of organization, contemporary concepts of organization, the organization of library services, the librarian's view of organization, the external and internal organization of libraries, specialization by level, direction and decision-making, coordination, and library workers and the organization. Martin does not seek to identify and recommend the "perfect" library organization; nor does he seek to force theoretical concepts into practical situations; instead he stresses the need for adaptability and flexibility as he considers how libraries can best be structured to accomplish their mission. His presentation of a series of organization charts, including a slightly irreverent one of heaven, is typical of the concise way that he addresses the issues. This is a book that is easy to read yet contains a wealth of sound advice. Martin's book is not to be missed. ▣

This month's books:

Ford, Gary T. *Marketing and the Library.* Haworth Press, 1984. 80p. $19.95. ISBN 0-86656-307-5 LC 84-668

Katz, Bill. *Library Lit. 14—The Best of 1983.* Scarecrow Press, 1984. 372p. $20. ISBN 0-8108-1717-9 LC 78-154842

Martin, Lowell. *Organizational Structure of Libraries.* Scarecrow Press, 1984. 294p. $14.50. ISBN 0-8108-1696-2 LC 84-4859

Radford, Neil A. *The Carnegie Corporation and the Development of American College Libraries, 1928–1941.* American Library Association, 1984. 257p. pa $29.95. ISBN 0-8389-3295-9 LC 83-25710

Shuman, Bruce. *River Bend Revisited: The Problem Patron in the Library.* Oryx Press, 1984. 186p. pa $22.50. ISBN 0-89774-125-0 LC 81-4372

Patrick Dewey:

Software for Libraries

Easy as PIE

Many Apple owners who do a lot of writing consider **PIE Writer** by Thomas Crosley (Hayden Software, 1983), formerly *Apple PIE,* to be the most full-featured, non-CP/M word processing program available. It is one of the oldest micro word processors around. *Apple PIE* was originally produced by Programma. When that company folded, the program was acquired and improved by Hayden Software. *PIE* is a program with a great deal of power and can cope with a book, thesis, technical document, or other complicated project. *PIE* is really two programs in one: a text editor, and a formatter. The editor is used to create a document or to edit an already existing one; the formatter is used to print documents either on the screen (softcopy) or on paper (hardcopy). *PIE* offers just about every trick in the book, including a wide range of auxiliary commands. These can provide word or line count, offer global search and replace, wraparound, scrolling forward or backward, saving tab settings to disk, and many other features. It is also possible to use abbreviated forms of all of the regular Apple commands from the command processor (e.g., C = Catalog; %D = Delete, etc.). It also supports boldface printer options, various types of underlining, loading or saving a range of lines, and chaining files. *PIE* is relatively easy to use, not nearly as difficult as many other word processors. Most people can conquer the basic routines in just a few hours. Many of the format commands (they determine just how the finished document will look) are simple (e.g., .pp = paragraph; .ul = underline; .11 = line length, etc.). Approximately 3,000 words can be stored in the buffer at one time, depending upon the hardware. One big jump is that the new *PIE* supports telecommunications and Mail Merge. The software comes with an excellent tutorial as well as a help screen. An eighty-column card, a Ramcard, and a lower case adapter increase the utility of the Apple version, but are not essential. *PIE* is a highly recommended and extremely valuable program, appropriate for both patrons and for library staff. For use with the Apple II, II+ or IIe. Cost: $149.95. Compaq+ and Portable, or IBM PC, PC jr. Cost: $199.95. The version used for this review was the Apple II+.

Patrick Dewey *is administrative librarian, Maywood (Illinois) Public Library and author of* Public Access Microcomputers: A Handbook for Librarians.

Fewer misteaks

The Sensible Speller IV (Sensible Software, 1983) is one of the more versatile spelling checker programs around, designed to work with a variety of Apple word processors, including most DOS programs (e.g., *Pie Writer, Applewriter,* etc.), CP/M (e.g., *WordStar, Magic Wand,* etc.), *Word Handler,* and *PFS: Write.* A *Pascal* version is available separately. The program checks the spelling of a document against 80,000 words from the *Concise Random House Dictionary* contained on the dictionary disk. Up to 10,000 user-selected words can be added. The program operates in a user-friendly, straightforward manner. Set-up and operation can be carried out in minutes, and a document may be read and corrected just as quickly. Other writing problems can, of course, be missed, including missing words, misused homonyms, and punctuation. While *The Sensible Speller* can help one appear to be a better speller, the program cannot substitute for careful proofreading. Complete with backup disk for the Apple II, II+, IIe. Cost: $125.

A heavy-duty copy program

Anyone dealing with diskettes knows just how easy it is to destroy the data contained on them. Backup copies are often needed. While some manufacturers supply two original diskettes for users, most do not. Many manufacturers now also explain on the package that it is perfectly legal to make an archival copy, but they copy-protect their product, making normal copy procedures difficult. That's when a good "heavy-duty" copy program, such as the recently updated **Essential Data Duplicator III,** by Donald Anthony Schnapp (Utilico Microware, 1984), is needed. Most copy programs do about the same thing. If the programs requiring duplication are not too tricky, they all work about the same way: stick in the disk and in three to ten minutes you have a copy. For some though, it's not that simple, and parameters—changes in the copy program—are required. *EDD* provides a list of such parameters for many commonly purchased programs, and promises that a new list of parameters will be sent to all registered owners of *EDD* at least four to six times each year. They also provide some telephone backup. This can be a goldmine for the person de-

termined to backup everything. If the required parameters are listed, copying is a rather uncomplicated affair. The documentation also has a discussion of how users can work out the parameters on their own. Doing so is rather technical, even with *EDD*'s help. Details are also given on how various copy-protection schemes work and how to circumvent them. There is even a section on "tricks of the trade." For use with the Apple II, II+, IIe. Cost: $79.95.

Searching for a college

Peterson's **College Selection Service** (Peterson's Guides, 1984) is a specialized database for patrons seeking college information. The package comes with two two-sided diskettes, two copies of the documentation (Counselor/Student Manual), a reproducible student work sheet, and a copy of Peterson's *Guide to Four-Year Colleges*. The program is self-documenting, but a look at the manual will save time. Data is included on approximately 1,700 accredited four-year colleges in the United States and Canada. Users can search through eighteen different categories, including location, majors, campus life, costs, sports, admission requirements, housing, public/private, etc. Searching may be refined by the use of AND or OR commands. A list of the search results may be displayed at any time, providing that the number has been reduced to fewer than forty. It is also possible to review choices and change any of the variables if the search has not produced the desired information. A summary may also be printed out. All colleges in the final list are cross-referenced to Peterson's *Guide to Four-Year Colleges,* where students will find more complete data. This is an excellent package that will help students get past the tedium of searching the 2,000 pages of the complete Peterson's *Guide.* It is a good supplement to the college catalog collection and other library reference tools. While an eighty-column display is not required, the use of this program is greatly impaired without it. With only forty columns, users must "flip-flop" back and forth between the right and left sides of the output. Available for the Apple (64K) II, II+, IIe, IBM PC (80K), and TRS-80 Models III, IV. Cost: $145. The Apple version was used for this review.

Trolls and dark passages

The **Zork** (Infocom, 1981, 1982, 1983) series of adventures (*Zork I, II,* and *III* have emerged from the "great underground empire") have long set the standard for excellence in computer games. The format is simple, the games give the sense of being part of a Tolkien adventure of trolls and dark passages, or a *Dungeons & Dragons* role-playing game. These games are all text—no graphics—so be prepared to do a lot of reading. Play begins on a forest path, and from there events unfold according to a player's cleverness in avoiding traps, skill in fighting fiends, and luck in unravelling puzzles in a world of fantasy. The puzzles are not difficult, but they do require mental alertness (if not gymnastics), and judgement. As a librarian, I am delighted to find that players must make logical sentences, as well as spell correctly in order to play. The adventures can take weeks to complete, but the program is forgiving. If you get knocked off by some nasty critter, just start over. Games may also be saved so it's easy to backtrack several moves. Some criticism can be levelled at the violence in the programs. It's certainly true that a troll or two may be stabbed or otherwise dispatched, but trolls aren't particularly nice creatures anyhow. I eagerly await *Zork IV.* Available for: Apple II, IIe, Atari, TRS-80, and DEC Rainbow. Cost: $39.95. Also available on eight-inch CP/M disks. Cost: $49.95.

Publisher addresses for this month's software:

Hayden Software, 600 Suffolk Street, Lowell, MA 01853.

Infocom, 55 Wheeler St., Cambridge, MA 02138.

Peterson's Guides, Dept. 4204, 166 Bunn Drive, Box 2123, Princeton, NJ 08540.

Sensible Software, 210 S. Woodward, Suite 229, Birmingham, MI 48011.

Utilico Microware, 3377 Solano Ave., Suite #352, Napa, CA 94558.

James Rettig:

Current Reference Books

Correspondence and review copies for this column should be directed to James Rettig, University Library, Box 8198, University of Illinois at Chicago, Chicago, IL 60680.

American Newspaper Journalists, 1926–1950, edited by Perry J. Ashley. Detroit: Gale, 1984. 410p. $82. 0-8103-1707-9 84-8182 (Dictionary of literary biography, v. 29)

Many of the fifty-four journalists profiled here are big names in American journalistic history—individuals like Heywood Broun, Robert McCormick, H. L. Mencken, Ernie Pyle, and Grantland Rice. Yet this volume lacks the exuberance of earlier volumes of this series. The fault lies not in the reportorial biographies, but in their subjects. Journalism between 1926 and 1950 had not yet become the province of J-school graduates, but it was becoming increasingly professional, especially after the founding of the American Newspaper Guild in the 1930s. The period's journalists were by no means a dour lot, but few were as colorful as their predecessors in the era typified by Ben Hecht and Charlie MacArthur. That does not, of course, in any way diminish the usefulness of the present volume as a trustworthy source of evaluative biographies of major journalists of the century's second quarter. It is exactly that.

Arthurian Legend and Literature, by Edmund Reiss, Louise H. Reiss, and Beverly Taylor. New York: Garland, 1984. 467p. $48. 0-8240-9123-X 83-47612 (Garland reference library of the humanities, v.415)

This international bibliography of some four hundred medieval treatments of the Arthurian legend differs from earlier bibliographies by adopting a broad subject arrangement. Most of the subjects are characters from the tales; other subjects include reference works, history, and literary contexts. The arrangement, complemented by an author/title index, calls attention to the connection between works from different countries and different centuries. A subject index offers more refined approaches to the works. Several thousand selected secondary items from the past century and a half have been annotated descriptively. An index to critics provides author access. A second volume will cover post-medieval treatment of the Arthurian legend. This first volume will help scholars trace critical trends and develop new insights.

James Rettig *is head reference librarian, University of Illinois at Chicago.*

Atlas of European Architecture, by Brian Sachar. New York: Van Nostrand Reinhold, 1984. 369p. $33.50. 0-442-28149-8 83-1171

Both too wide and too hefty to be a pocket vade mecum, the *Atlas*'s tall, narrow trim size nonetheless suggests just such a use. Its organization reinforces the suggestion. Twelve chapters on countries of western Europe are organized internally by city, each city's list of significant buildings arranged chronologically. Norway, Ireland, Portugal, and Luxembourg are omitted. Each of the 3,489 entries includes name of the structure, date of construction, address, name of the architect, a sentence noting special features, and coordinates for the structure's location on either the national map or a more detailed city map. Black-and-white photographs, not much larger than a postage stamp, illustrate selected entries. Two indexes, one by architect and artist, the other by city and town, permit ready-reference access. The brevity of the entries makes this unsuitable as a reference tool and the heftiness of the volume makes it unsuitable as a guidebook. The *Atlas* is a book in search of a purpose.

American Women: Three Decades of Change, by Suzanne M. Bianchi and Daphne Spain. Washington: GPO, 1984. 39p. pa$3.50. S/N 003-024-05743-3 (U.S. Bureau of the Census, Special Demographic Analyses, CDS-80-8) SuDocs C3.261:80–8

Newspaper and magazine stories frequently mention that women are marrying later, are becoming better educated, and are earning only fifty-nine percent of what men earn. Sometimes patrons ask for proof of statistics that are blandly cited as having come from "a government report." With so little to go on, the search for the anonymous report often fails. Librarians will want to acquire this and to acquaint themselves with its contents. The report charts changes in American women's lifestyles from 1950 through 1980, focusing on marriage, childbearing, family living arrangements, educational attainment, earnings, and poverty. Graphs and tables neatly summarize the text, which frequently cites sources in its extensive bibliography. The report treats important issues; no public or academic library can make an adequate excuse for not having it.

Bed and Breakfast North America, by Norma S. Buzan. 3rd ed. Betsy Ross Publications (3057 Betsy Ross Dr., Bloomfield Hills, MI 48013), 1984. 342p. pa$10.95. 0-943232-03-1 82-138156

As in the first edition (reviewed in *WLB,* June 1982), listings of bed and breakfast agencies in the greatly expanded third edition cluster along the Atlantic and Pacific seaboards. However the increased number of entries for the vast region between the coasts indicates that, like many trends originating in New York or California, the bed and breakfast alternative is catching on. The directory not only describes the services of B&B booking agencies, but also describes typical lodgings. The second half of the book, organized by state, showcases small inns throughout North America. Since luxury accommodations as well as reasonably priced ones are described, one must regret the omission of San Francisco's Nob Hill Inn, a hostelry whose exterior appearance and interior appointments recall an earlier, more elegant age and readily inspire romantic fantasies. Even without the alluring pictures found in the *Country Inns of America* series (Holt, Rinehart), the descriptions of both inns and B&B establishments evoke far more charm than any Rodeway or Best Western room ever could. *B&B North America* has matured and will give travel collections an extra dimension.

Books and Real Life, by Nancy Polette. Jefferson, NC: McFarland, 1984. 117p. pa$15.95. 0-89950-119-2 84-42607

Subtitled "A Guide for Gifted Students and Teachers," *Books and Real Life* is an item for the professional collection in school and public libraries. It identifies picture books and junior novels that can help gifted children bridge the gap that so often exists between their intellectual ability and their emotional maturity. Most of the books deal with "the losses of life which all humans will face at one time or another." It differs from *Books to Help Children Cope with Separation and Loss* (reviewed in *WLB,* October 1983) in that instead of annotating the books, it suggests exercises and discussion topics teachers can use to help children interpret the books. Questions for the eighty-three books in the first section are geared to younger children. Questions for the forty-five junior novels in the second section emphasize problem-solving and decision-making. A subject index identifies the books by type of situation, among them death, fear, friendship, rejection, and sibling rivalry. Even though the absence of Robert Cormier and Judy Blume from the book is inexplicable, teachers will appreciate the helpful approaches to helping young readers appreciate the books.

British Foreign Policy, 1918–1945, compiled by Sidney Aster. Wilmington, DE: Scholarly Resources, 1984. 324p. $20. 0-8420-2176-0 84-5339

One of a series of five volumes on the diplomatic history of the major European powers between the wars, *British Foreign Policy* lives up to its subtitle's billing as "a guide to research and research materials." The guide to research materials comes first, a twenty-five-page survey of British research libraries and archives, their holdings, finding guides, and publications. The guide to research follows, an annotated bibliography of books and articles organized topically into eight chapters, all subdivided by topic or type of work. The brief descriptive annotations frequently cite related works, sometimes making comparative evaluations. Items in foreign languages have been included selectively. The annotations show that scholars do not fully agree in their interpretations of the conduct of the belligerent countries between the wars. This wide-ranging guide will help scholars continue their disputations and devise new interpretations.

College 101, by Ronald T. Farrar. Princeton: Peterson's Guides, 1984. 177p. pa$6.95. 0-87866-269-3 84-9534

Compared to *The College Catalog* (reviewed in *WLB,* October 1983), a C+ effort if viewed generously, *College 101* rates an A+. Written by a journalism professor in question-and-answer format, *College 101* delivers practical information and common-sense advice to the college-bound not only on how to cope, but also on how to thrive in college. Its chapters deal with dormitory living, study habits, getting along with professors, social life, financing, counseling, and planning for after graduation. Librarians will second Farrar's strong endorsement of the need to develop library skills and will take heart from his characterization of librarians as "good-humored, genuinely caring individuals who are glad to help." Since Farrar answers the questions asked by students preparing for college, high school and public libraries should make his answers available to them.

The Complete Guide to Citing Government Documents, by Diane L. Garner and Diane H. Smith. Bethesda, MD: Congressional Information Service, 1984. 142p. pa$12.95. 0-88692-023-X 84-11357

The "Bible" of style manuals, *The Chicago Manual of Style* (reviewed in *WLB,* November 1982) offers a scant thirteen pages of general rules for citing public documents. The *MLA Style Sheet* (2nd ed., New York: Modern Language Association, 1970) incorrectly advised including the SuDocs classification number for United States Government publications to "facilitate ordering from the GPO." Even for editors of style manuals, the citation format to government publications is largely terra incognita. Many, therefore, will warmly welcome the thorough guidance the *Complete Guide* promises in its title and delivers in its text. With rules based on principles of clarity and consistency and numerous examples illustrating those rules, it explains how to cite publications of governments and international organizations. The bibliographic vagaries of government publishing necessitate numerous short discussions of the how and why for citing specific documents (e.g., the U.S. Constitution or budget) or types of documents (e.g., ERIC documents, international court reports). The rules permit options when options do not diminish clarity. The fine index speeds specific rule retrieval. Editors of future general style manuals would do well to condense their chapters on citing public documents into a single citation—to the *Complete Guide.*

Computer Publishers and Publications. Communication Trends (distributed by Gale), 1984. 379p. $90. 0-8103-0540-2 ISSN 0740-4805

Half *Literary Market Place,* half *Directory of Publishing Opportunities,* this new annual complements *Computer Books and Serials in Print* (reviewed in *WLB,* October 1984) by giving additional information about 275 publishers and 600 periodicals. Introductory essays similar to those found in the *Bowker Annual* review the computer publishing scene in 1983, discuss computer book selection, and recommend titles for core collections in public and academic libraries. The publishers directory lists address, ISBN prefix, chief officers, type of audience for its books, number of titles published in recent years, representative titles, and bestselling titles. An index sorts the publishers by type of audience (consumer, educational, or professional) and by specific computer brands. The periodicals directory, organized by title, lists publisher, type of audience, format, frequency, circulation, price, advertising policy and rates, and parent company. Each description also tells whether the periodical buys articles and whether it focuses on a particular machine or manufacturer. Periodicals are indexed by publisher, type of audience, specific computers treated, place of publication, and frequency. Among the many new books in this volatile field, this and *Computer Books in Print* stand out as useful and well-edited.

The Consumer Health Information Source Book, by Alan M. Rees and Jodith Janes. 2nd ed. New York: Bowker, 1984. 530p. $35. 0-8352-1877-5 84-14213

Librarians, especially in public libraries, must grapple with the ethical issues surrounding answers to medical questions. They may find pragmatic solutions in the *Consumer Health Information Source Book.* A complete revision of the first edition (1980), it describes and evaluates 935 books and articles on health published for general readers since 1979. They are arranged in nineteen topical chapters. In addition to such perennially important topics as pregnancy, human sexuality, cancer, heart disease, and mental health, the new edition includes subjects such as AIDS, herpes, and job burnout, which have received considerable publicity only recently. The lively annotations characterize the books fully and evaluate them boldly, rating them on a scale ranging from "Exceptional. Highly recommended" down to "Prosaic writing that results in dull reading. Mediocre." Since the scope of the items on a page is often broader than a heading in the index, the subject index references to page numbers are somewhat ambiguous. Use of entry numbers for the items and in the index would have been more precise. Nonetheless, the *Source Book* offers trustworthy advice about current information sources on topics that sometimes engender life-or-death interest.

Contemporary Authors Autobiography Series, vol. 1, edited by Dedria Bryfonski. Detroit: Gale, 1984. 431p. $70. 0-8103-0004-1 ISSN 0748-0636
J. D. Salinger, by Jack R. Sublette. New York: Garland, 1984. 257p. $42. 0-8240-9077-2 83-48268 (Garland reference library of the humanities, v.436)

No critic, whatever the acuity of his judgment, can offer the perspective an author brings to his or her own work and life. Therefore this newest member of the *Contemporary Authors* series is especially welcome. Twenty-three authors, including Daniel Berrigan, Erskine Caldwell, James Purdy, and Irving Wallace, accepted the editor's invitation to write an autobiography in the 10,000- to 15,000-word range. They also supplied photographs from their own collections. Most of these spirited autobiographies begin with descriptions of their parents and progress to the present, charting personal and literary development along the way. The authors' frank insights about themselves will work like the Sirens' song on anyone interested in contemporary writers, seducing them into extended browsing. Future volumes will present more literary lives; however it will be very surprising if J. D. Salinger is among them.

Readers of Salinger's small corpus—only one novel and thirty-five stories—who want to know more about this reclusive writer must turn to the 153 items in the biography section of Sublette's annotated bibliography. Covering items from 1938 through 1981, it organizes its 1,462 items into primary and secondary works, each group subdivided by type, and indexes them by author and by title of works treated. The casual term paper writer will be able to use this, but it really serves the needs of the Salinger scholar, for it identifies unpublished primary materials, letters, dissertations, reviews, and foreign items. Only through study of such works can Salinger's readers learn more about him.

Do-It-Yourself Medical Testing, by Cathey Pinckney and Edward R. Pinckney. New York: Facts on File, 1984. 266p. $14.95, pa$7.95. 0-87196-705-7; 0-87196-972-6 82-12069

As a matter of policy, many libraries will not consider this book; they do not collect medical self-diagnosis books lest they be misused. Despite the disclaimer that it "is not to be considered a substitute for the professional judgement of a physician," the "M.D." following Edward Pinckney's name could induce some to place false confidence in their evaluations of do-it-yourself tests. The 160 tests, grouped by type (e.g., urine, heart, eye, ear, etc.), vary in complexity. Some require special equipment ranging in cost from a few dollars up to two hundred. Descriptions state normal conditions, list needed materials, explain the test procedures, and explain what various outcomes mean. If used prudently, the tests can advise a person whether or not he should consult his physician. That, of course, is a big "if."

Macmillan Dictionary for Students, edited by William D. Halsey. New York: Macmillan, 1984. 1,190p. $16.95. 0-02-761560-X 84-3880

Earlier editions of this fine dictionary

were published in 1979 as the *Macmillan Contemporary Dictionary* and in 1981 as the *Macmillan Dictionary*. Its 90,000 entries, 120,000 definitions, and 19,000 brief etymologies include proper names of famous persons, places, and organizations. Numerous idiomatic expressions are explained under their keywords. The word stock was selected from "the language of everyday speech and conversation" and from subjects studied in school. Illustrations, many in two colors, clarify definitions but are used sparingly. Precision, clarity, and conciseness characterize the definitions. Appendixes include a simple style manual, a brief chronology of United States history, and a glossary of computer terms. The dictionary will satisfy junior high school students' need for pronunciations, meanings, and spellings of familiar and unfamiliar words.

Macmillan Illustrated Almanac for Kids, by Ann Elwood and Carol Orsag. New York: Macmillan, 1984, c1981. 429p. pa$7.95. 0-02-043040-X 83-26296

School and children's librarians who somehow missed the *Almanac for Kids* when it was published in hardcover in 1981, should not let that happen again. The first chapter, "What Kids Think," surveys 310 kids on their opinions about twenty-five questions important to kids (e.g., relationship to parents, worries, ideal age for various activities). It seemed appropriate to solicit the opinion of my household's resident fourth grader. She pronounced it "interesting, helpful, fun, never boring, ... and written in words that are easy to understand." She liked the mix of topics—brief biographies of famous kids and adults, animal stories, sports, the law and kids, health and emotional problems of youth, science, the arts, and odd facts—all treated from a kid's point of view. Many of the brief articles suggest organizations or books that can supply additional information. The appealing photographs and drawings coordinate well with the text. The *Almanac* speaks engagingly to the concerns of children. More than one copy will become well-worn by fourth graders and others who turn to it to satisfy curiosity or to find entertainment.

Memorable Film Characters, compiled by Susan Lieberman and Frances Cable. Westport, CT: Greenwood, 1984. 291p. $29.95. 0-313-23977-0 84-10844 ISSN 0742-6933 (Bibliographies and indexes in the performing arts, no.1)

Several flawed assumptions run through this book like cracks in a piece of polished marble; they simply cannot be ignored. The book lists film characters by name, identifies each in a sentence or two, and names the film and the actor or actress who played the character. The first flawed assumption is that people remember characters by name only and not by film as well. Since film characters have no existence apart from their films, people generally speak of them in terms such as "Who played God in *Oh God*?" Many sources organized by film title identify characters and their actors. These render this book with its film title index largely superfluous. And *Who Was Who on Screen* (3rd ed., New York: Bowker, 1983) renders the actor index redundant. Another flaw is the lack of sufficient *see* references from last names when only a first name is used for entry. For example, a user who remembers the Jarrett family in *Ordinary People* but not their first names (Calvin, Beth, and Conrad) must look in the film title index rather than under Jarrett in the character list because there is no *see* reference from Jarrett to the first names. *Memorable Film Characters* is forgettable.

Microcomputer Software Buyer's Guide, by Tony Webster and Richard Champion. New York: McGraw-Hill, 1984. 422p. pa$19.95. 0-07-068967-9

Computer professionals have long been acquainted with the comprehensive (and expensive) Datapro Guides to computer equipment and software. Now the thousands of microcomputer owners relatively new to the computer scene, whether they operate their machines for business or personal use, can benefit from a comparable guide priced for their needs. These readers will learn little from the ninety-five-page overview of microcomputing, but they will value the guide to popular spreadsheet, word processing, database management, integrated packages, and product families of software. These describe the programs' hardware requirements, features, operations, and documentation and make an overall evaluation of each program. Facsimiles of start-up screens and help screens and tabular summaries permit easy comparisons. Since some programs cost several hundred dollars, this economical guide can quickly pay for itself in libraries that are shopping for quality microcomputer software.

The Morrow Book of Quotations in American History, by Joseph R. Conlin. New York: Morrow, 1984. 352p. $17.95. 0-688-02068-2 84-60613

Clearly Conlin, a history professor at California State University at Chico, disagrees with Henry Ford's assessment of history as "more or less bunk." Yet he includes Ford's injudicious remark along with Khrushchev's "We will bury you" and Sitting Bull's characterization of Americans as "all liars" because all of these "address the meaning of the United States." That meaning, of course, derives from statements contradicting one another which, as a whole, weave the varied fabric that is the United States past and present. The founding fathers are well represented, but politicians and pundits of the past forty years have been favored. Thus the natterings of Spiro Agnew occupy nearly as much space as Alexander Hamilton's exhortations. A subject index citing page numbers rather than specific quotations offers alternative, albeit awkward, access to the quotations, arranged alphabetically by speaker. The quotations illustrate the ineffable American psyche.

Because of its subject matter's broad appeal, this will be more useful than many other specialized quotation books.

Presidential Also-Rans and Running Mates, 1788–1980, by Leslie H. Southwick. Jefferson, NC: McFarland, 1984. 722p. $49.95. 0-80050-109-5 83-25577

Joe Lane, John McLean, and John Bell are not household names, yet all once commanded the political spotlight as the presidential candidate of a major political party. Needless to say, all lost. DeGregorio's *Complete Book of U.S. Presidents* (reviewed in *WLB,* September 1984) and other books provide abundant information about the winners and Paul Boller's *Presidential Campaigns* (New York: Oxford University Press, 1984) tells how they vanquished their foes. But since hard luck stories about losers possess an ineluctable fascination—witness the loyalty of Chicago Cubs fans—one cannot dismiss this book as an also-ran to DeGregorio. It profiles the eighty-eight men who failed to attain the presidency or vice-presidency in the elections of 1788 through 1980, listing standard biographical data and describing their characters, their careers, and their losing campaigns. The analysis of how well each man would have performed if elected is as dubious and as much fun as any other "what-if" speculation. This supplements DeGregorio, but lack of demand for biographies of these losers may send the volume to the circulating collection.

The Professional Secretary's Handbook. Boston: Houghton Mifflin, 1984. 583p. $10.95. 0-395-35604-0 84-3756

Index entries such as "radiation and VDTs," "FORTRAN," and "LCD display on electronic typewriters" testify to the changes in offices and in secretarial jobs in recent years. Explanations of the capabilities and use of electronic typewriters, word processors, microcomputers, and electronic mail glitter besides the traditional topics in secretarial handbooks. The authors take a practical approach to the new and the old aspects of the secretary's job (e.g., English usage, formatting documents, mail handling, telephone skills, recordkeeping, and scheduling). Secretaries, of course, need a copy handy for daily reference. Public libraries need it for the occasional writer of business letters or memos who seeks the standards for such communications.

TV Trivia Teasers, by W. Wilson Casey. Ann Arbor: Pierian Press, 1984. 245p. pa$9.50. 0-87650-164-1 84-81219

TV Trivia Teasers borrows its title from the author's syndicated column, "TV Teasers," and its significance, such as it is, from a national craze. Racks at grocery store checkout counters burgeon with paperbacks offering "strategies" for winning Trivial Pursuit and the *Atlantic* has published an article complaining about the game's errors and ambiguities. Librarians should not be surprised, therefore, if this is but the first wave of an invasion of specialized trivia books aimed at the same audience. The popular board game has created a new publishing market. So, complete with answer key and index, questions are arranged here in four sections for comedy, mystery and adventure, films, and a general catch-all section. Scattered throughout are eighty-six "photo teasers," uncaptioned portraits of stars who must be identified. Librarians should be aware of this trivial phenomenon, but they need not buy into it.

Winning Money for College, by Alan Deutschman. Princeton, NJ: Peterson's Guides, 1984. 209p. pa $7.95. 0-87866-261-8 83-22151

Nearly every college and university offers little-known scholarships available only to those who have a certain ethnic background, whose parents work in as certain industry, or who belong to a certain civic group. Just as unknown are national scholarship contests, some with no entry restrictions, others with qualifications similar to those cited above. Many of the fifty programs described were established to advance high school students possessing outstanding talents (e.g., piano, welding, engineering) promoted by the sponsoring organizations. Descriptions list eligibility requirements, rules, procedures, helpful hints, deadlines, and the name of a contact person. In the cases of essay competitions, a recent winning entry is reproduced and in the cases of tests, sample questions are printed. The author has personally demonstrated the book's potential. A Princeton University student, Deutschman has won thousands of dollars for his education through speaking, writing, and scholarship competitions. If more students knew about such opportunities, more would vie for a share of the bounty.

Women Novelists, 1891–1920, by Doris Robinson. New York: Garland, 1984. 458p. $38. 0-8240-8977-4 83-49334

Since Norma Ireland's *Index to Women* (Westwood, MA: Faxon, 1970) indexes 945 collective biographies, this index to biographies of women novelists might strike some as superfluous. But close examination reveals that the two differ considerably. Since many of the 290 works indexed by *Women Novelists* focus on its thirty-year period or on novelists, few of them are also in Ireland. Furthermore, *Women Novelists* cites obituaries in periodicals and selected monographic biographies and autobiographies of its 1,565 authors. The women included were writing novels at the turn of the century or their works were first translated into English during that period. In the index by country, British and North American novelists outnumber all others. Like all-purpose and other specialized indexes to collective biography, *Women Novelists* greatly simplifies the search process for biographical information on minor figures. ▣

Library World

News of announcements, new posts, retirements, and deaths should be sent to "Library World," WLB, *950 University Ave., Bronx, NY 10452.*

ANNOUNCEMENTS

Margaret Kimmel has assumed the office of president of the United States Board on Books for Young People, the U.S. section of the International Board on Books for Young People.

The School Library Media Specialists section of the New York Library Association has announced its officers for the coming year. They are: **Frances Selip**, pres.; **Yvonne Hudson,** vice-pres./pres.-elect; **Hazel Podraza,** second vice-pres.; **Jean Williams,** secy.; and **Ethel Keefer,** treas.

Officers of the South Carolina LA for 1984–1985 are: **Carl Stone,** pres.; **Susan Roberts,** vice-pres./pres.-elect; **Thomas Raines,** second vice-pres.; **Helen Callison,** secy.; and **David Cohen,** treas.

Richard Talbot has taken office as president of the Association of Research Libraries, succeeding **Eldred Smith.** He is director of libraries at the Univ. of Massachusetts.

Newly elected officers of the Guam LA are: **Harry Uyehara,** pres.; **Joan Nichols,** first vice-pres.; **Cheryl King,** second vice-pres.; **Alice Hadley,** secy.; and **Beth McClure,** treas.

NEW POSTS

Elizabeth Aversa has been named assistant professor at the college of information studies of Drexel Univ., Philadelphia. She was previously assistant professor at the Florida State Univ. SLIS.

Cheryll Bixby has been appointed assistant librarian in the university libraries of the State Univ. of N.Y. at Buffalo.

Dale Brown is now director of libraries and instructional resources for the public schools of Alexandria, Va. Brown formerly served with the Alexandria school system as supervisor of libraries, media, and textbooks.

Doris Brown, formerly associate director for technical services at DePaul Univ., Chicago, has been promoted to director of libraries at DePaul.

Jim Brown has assumed the position of branch manager of the Kathryn M. Linnemann Library, St. Peters, Mo. He was formerly data processing librarian at Olin Library, Washington Univ., St. Louis.

Daniel Cleary has been appointed assistant librarian for reference/government documents at the Stephen B. Luce Library, SUNY Maritime College, Bronx, N.Y.

Carol Cook has joined the staff of the Providence (R.I.) Athenaeum as bibliographer/librarian.

Marilyn Crouch, previously central library manager for the Anaheim (Calif.) PL, is now assistant director of the Roseville (Calif.) PL.

Helen Dagley has been named audio-visual librarian for the state library of Iowa. She was formerly head of audiovisual services for the Quincy (Ill.) PL.

John Montag

Susan Miller

Jonathan Lauer

Linda Wallace

Sherman Hayes

Linda Elliott has been appointed assistant head librarian for the Oak Lawn (Ill.) PL. She was formerly city librarian for the main library of the San Luis Obispo City/County Library System.

Fred Fernow is now business services librarian for the St. Charles City-County Library District, St. Peters, Mo. He was previously public services librarian at the Reistertown branch of the Baltimore County PL.

Vee Friesner, formerly director of the library development division of the Kansas State Library, has become the program officer of the Public Library Association.

Edward Gaynor has joined the staff of the Auburn Univ. libraries as catalog librarian.

Sherman Hayes has been named director of the Solomon R. Baker Library at Bentley College, Waltham, Mass. He was formerly assistant to the director of the Univ. of North Dakota libraries.

Philip Jones is now general reference librarian for the Howard-Tilton Memorial Library, Tulane Univ., New Orleans.

Gail Junion has joined the staff of the Univ. of Rochester's River Campus library, Rochester, N.Y. She was previously associate professor and coordinator of cataloging at Bowling Green State Univ., Ohio.

Deborah Ann Kegel, formerly reference assistant at the main library, Indiana Univ., Bloomington, is now science and technology reference librarian at Auburn Univ.

Michael Kinney has been appointed librarian-in-charge of the Llewellyn Library, a branch of the Milwaukee PL. He was formerly head of a branch library with the Palm Beach (Fla.) County Library System.

Barbara LaGodna, previously director of the Horshoe Bend Regional Library, Dadeville, Ala. is now catalog librarian at Auburn Univ.

Jonathan Lauer, formerly head of public services at Wheaton College (Ill.), is now library director at Aurora College (Ill.).

Sandra Lockett has been named librarian-in-charge of the Center Street Library, a branch of the Milwaukee PL. She was formerly head of the government documents department at the Univ. of Iowa law library.

Jacqueline Mancall has been promoted to associate professor at the College of Information Studies, Drexel Univ., Philadelphia. She has been a number of the Drexel faculty since 1979.

Susan Miller has been appointed director of the East Shore Area branch library of the Dauphin County (Pa.) Library System. She was previously director of the Lebanon (Pa.) Community Library.

John Montag has been named director of the office of information services with the state library of Iowa. Montag was previously assistant professor of libraries at the Univ. of Nebraska at Lincoln.

Lizabeth Nicol has joined the staff of Auburn Univ. libraries as automation manager.

Arlene Noble has been appointed assistant to the head of original monograph cataloging at Columbia Univ. libraries, New York.

Thomas Pearson, formerly director of the Vermillion (S.D.) PL, is now supervisor of the Divoll branch of the St. Louis PL.

Robert Roehr has been promoted to manager of the St. Louis PL main library. He had been manager of branches and community services for the library since 1980.

Ellen Scaruffi has been appointed curator for the Bakhmeteff Archive of the rare book and manuscript library with the Columbia Univ. libraries, New York.

Stephanie Sigala has joined the staff of Auburn Univ. libraries as head of the architecture library.

Bob Smith, previously automated circulation coordinator of the Cuyahoga County (Ohio) PL, has been named chief librarian of the Livonia (Mich.) PL.

Sarah Spurgin has assumed the position of the reference librarian for the humanities and history division of the Columbia Univ. libraries, New York.

Carla Stoffle has been appointed associate director for public services at the Univ. of Michigan library, Ann Arbor. She had been assistant chancellor for educational services at the Univ. of Wisconsin at Parkside since 1978.

Robert J. Veenstra, formerly science reference librarian at the Univ. of Missouri in Kansas City, is now head of the veterinary medical library at the Auburn Univ. libraries.

Linda Wallace has been named director of the public information office of ALA. She had been community relations coordinator for the Mideastern Michigan Library Cooperative since 1976.

Sandra Wenner has joined the staff of the Auburn Univ. libraries, as bibliographic instruction and humanities reference librarian.

Diana Zinnato has been appointed catalog librarian at the Swarthmore College library. She was formerly assistant librarian for technical services at the College of Physicians of Philadelphia.

MARKETPLACE

Announcements

☐ Clifton Daniel, journalist and author of *Lords, Ladies and Gentlemen: A Memoir,* will be the speaker at the centennial banquet of the New York Library Club on January 24, 1985. This will be the first event in a year-long schedule of activities commemorating the founding of the club in 1885 by Melvil Dewey. The club offers lectures, programs, special events and field trips to those interested in books and libraries. For more information on the centennial events, contact The New York Library Club Centennial, Rockefeller Center Station, Box 1052, New York, NY 10185.

☐ Using the Family Registry Index, a list of genealogists maintained by the L.D.S. Genealogical Library in Salt Lake City, researchers can locate others working on the same topic to share information and coordinate work. Microfiche copies of the index are available at the library in Salt Lake City and at branch libraries in the United States and Canada. Listing and using the service is free of charge. Registration forms can be obtained from any of the libraries or by writing Genealogical Dept.—Family Registry, 4th Floor, West Wing, 50 E. North Temple St., Salt Lake City, UT 84150.

☐ The International Reading Association (IRA) annually presents Broadcast Media Awards for outstanding television and radio programming relating to reading and literacy. Entries for the 1985 award must have been broadcast during 1984, must be directed toward the general public, and must be informational rather than instructional. Required for entry are three ¾-inch videocassette tapes (for TV) or three cassette tapes (for radio) and three transcripts. The deadline is February 20, 1985. For information and entry forms, write Public Information Office, IRA, 800 Barksdale Rd., Box 8139, Newark, DE 19714.

☐ A Title II–C grant of $70,000 from the Department of Education will be used to develop online access to the videotape archives of the children's television program "Mr. Rogers' Neighborhood." The archives are located in the Nesbitt Room of the library of the University of Pittsburgh School of Library and Information Science. The program originated at Pittsburgh public broadcasting station WQED and has been produced there throughout its thirty-year history. Tapes of the programs, as well as puppet images and production sets, are being placed in the collection by Fred Rogers.

Children's Specials

☐ The students in grades four though eight in Florida have chosen the winners of the first annual Sunshine State Young Reader's Award: James and Deborah Howe for *Bunnicula.* The first and second runners-up were, respectively, *Ramona Quimby, Age 8,* by Beverly Cleary, and *The Great Gilly Hopkins,* by Katherine Patterson. The program is cosponsored by the Florida Association for Media in Education and the School Library Media Service of the Florida Department of Education. The twenty nominees for the award are chosen by the award selection committee from books recommended by students, teachers, and media specialists throughout the state.

☐ The Association for Library Service to Children has recently published *Coordinators of Children's Services and of Young Adult Services in Public Libary Systems Serving at Least 100,000 People.* A revision of the 1981 compilation, the directory includes 544 public library systems and lists 395 coordinators for children's services and 173 coordinators for young adult services. It also includes the fifty state library agencies and lists twenty-four consultants in children's or young adult services at the state level. To order send checks for $7.50 payable to ALA to ALSC/ALA, 50 E. Huron St., Chicago, IL 60611.

☐ A poster created by Vera B. Williams is the first in a planned series of commissioned works celebrating the Boston Globe-Horn Book Award for illustration. Williams won the award in 1983 for the picture book *A Chair for My Mother.* Although subsequent posters will be available for sale only, the first one is being sent to *Horn Book* subscribers in honor of the magazine's sixtieth anniversary. Copies of both the poster and the anniversary edition of the *Horn Book* are available to nonsubscribers for $5 each prepaid from The Horn Book, Inc., 31 St. James Ave., Boston, MA 02116.

Continuing Education

☐ The Citizen Exchange Council is offering two library-related tours to the Soviet Union next spring. "Children's Literature in the USSR," April 4–17, 1985, will travel to Moscow, Leningrad and Tallinn, Estonia, with visits to schools, publishing houses, and libraries, and will provide opportunities to talk with educators, authors, illustrators and publishers. The cost, including airfare from and to New York, is $1799. "The Book and Libraries of the Soviet Union and Eastern Europe: Collections, Computers and Cooperation," May 29–

June 16, 1985, will visit libraries and book dealers in Leningrad, Kiev, Moscow, Warsaw and Prague. The cost is $2299. For more information contact Citizen Exchange Council, 18 E. 41st St., New York, NY 10017, 212/889-7960.

☐ The University of Wisconsin-Madison School of Library and Information Studies, in cooperation with the Robert M. LaFollette Institute of Public Affairs, offers a program that combines study in the areas of public administration, economics, political science, business, urban and regional planning, law, and sociology with library and information studies. The specialist's sixth year certificate is a twenty-four hour program for those with the MLS and some professional experience. Students entering with a BA can combine the MA degree with the certificate in a fifty-four hour program. Contact the SLIS, University of Wisconsin-Madison, 600 North Park St., Madison, WI 53706, 608/263-2900.

☐ The topic for next year's Congress for Librarians at St. John's University is uploading and downloading online databases and catalogs. The February 18 program will address such aspects as reference work, production of a bibliographic database, copyright law, and the policies of RLIN and OCLC. Registration is $35. Contact the Division of Library and Information Science, St. John's University, Grand Central and Utopia Parkways, Jamaica, NY 11439, 718/990-6161.

Film and Video

☐ The spring 1984 special theme issue of *Top of the News,* "Films, Young People, and Libraries," is available as a reprint from ALA'S Young Adult Services Division. Eleven articles discuss such topics as visual literacy, trends, young adult filmmakers, and film programming. The reprint also includes a movie book bibliography and two annotated lists, one on films for young adults and one on notable children's films, filmstrips, and recordings. *Films, Young People, and Libraries* can be ordered for $6.50 from YASD, ALA, 50 E. Huron St., Chicago, IL 60611.

☐ "Children in Action," a five-part series of videotapes that focus on the social, emotional, physical, and cognitive aspects of the preschooler's development, has been produced by the Library Video Network. Each tape is accompanied by a program guide, reproducible discussion guides and related activities for handouts, a list of resources, and a bibliography of references and books for children. In the tapes, libraries are stressed as important sources of materials and information. About 15 minutes long, the tapes can be viewed separately or as a series, and are available in VHS, Beta and ¾-inch format. For information about rental or purchase contact Library Video Network, 1811 Woodlawn Dr., Baltimore, MD 21207, 301/265-6983.

☐ "Visions of Paradise" is a series of five half-hour color 16mm films or videotapes (all formats) produced and directed by Allie Light and Irving Saraf. Each film features an American naive artist. The subjects of the films, while varying in ethnic background and artistic medium, are all self-taught and began pursuing their art late in life. For a copy of the catalog, or information on rental or purchase, contact Light-Saraf Films, 131 Concord St., San Francisco, CA 94112, 415/469-0139.

Finding Aids

☐ Old house restorers, American history buffs, and those who simply believe they don't make things the way they used to will find plenty to fulfill both their fantasies and their practical needs in *The American Historical Supply Catalogue: A Nineteenth-Century Sourcebook,* by Alan Wellikoff. Sources of tin ceilings, Victorian hardware, clothing, pot-bellied stoves, old-fashioned toys, and, yes, even Levi's button-fly denim pants are list-

From "Visions of Paradise"

ed in this illustrated catalog. The 256p. paperback is available for $16.95 from Schocken Books, 200 Madison Ave., New York, NY 10016.

☐ *Kachinas, a Selected Bibliography,* by Marcia Muth, lists over 100 sources on the Pueblo Indian mythological beings, which are often represented by dancers and by dolls. Illustrated with drawings of several of the figures, the bibliography is arranged by main entry and lists books, articles and reports. The 32p. pamphlet is priced at $4.95 and is published by Sunstone Press, Box 2321, Santa Fe, NM 87504.

Kwikwilyaga kachina

☐ Updated for the first time in five years, *Directory of Foundations of the Greater Washington Area 1984* covers 400 grant-making organizations with financial and grant data, a list of the five largest grants awarded by each, and names of trustees, managers, and directors. There is also guidance on the grant-seeking process. The 90p. directory is available for $10 plus $1.50 for postage and handling from Jamie Kopp, Community Foundation of Greater Washington, 3221 M St., NW, Washington, DC 20007.

From the GPO Presses

The following titles are a sample of recent publications available from the Government Printing Office. Specify the stock number, price and quantity when ordering. Payment is by check payable to Superintendent of Documents or by Visa or Mastercard (give card number and expiration date). Send to Superintendent of Documents, United States GPO, Washington, DC 20402. Or call the order desk at 202/783-3238.

☐ Results of the first national study on the selection of school principals have been published by the Department of Education in *Selecting American School Principals: A Sourcebook for Educators.* Part I focuses on common practices in selecting principals, and the roles of superintendents and school boards in the selection process are described. Part II discusses alternative approaches being used in some districts, and provides ideas on developing better principal selection procedures. The report, stock number 065-000-00195-1, is priced at $2.50. Send prepayment to Dept. 36-JJ.

☐ *The Energy-Wise Homebuyer* from the Department of Housing and Urban Development discusses the factors that should be considered in examining a new or used house. The guide provides a checklist of energy-efficient features to look for, with diagrams and illustrations. It also shows how to obtain and analyze information on past energy usage and what energy-saving techniques can be applied in a used house. The 60p. publication, stock number 023-000-00518-2, is available for $5.50. Send prepayment to Dept. 360-JT.

☐ A new periodical from the Department of Agriculture will cover ideas, trends, and research in rural development. To be issued three times a year, *Rural Development Perspectives* will present the results of new research in rural development and explain what they mean to rural policymakers, community and regional planners, officials of local government, and social science researchers. Each issue will include, besides articles, a digest of research from various sources and reviews of books. An annual subscription to *Rural Development Perspectives,* List ID RDP, costs $10. Send prepayment to Dept. 36-JQ.

Idea Exchange

☐ It may not have the cachet of Cannes, but the amateur film festival at the Milford (Connecticut) PL, now in its fifth year, has been a rousing success. Scheduled for late June (so that newly completed student films can be entered), the festival offers cash and other prizes. All films are shown without prescreening, which provides an element of surprise even to the organizers. Arthur Bargar, Media Librarian, is willing to share his expertise. He can be contacted at the Milford PL, 57 New Haven Ave., Milford, CT 06460, 202/783-3290.

☐ Patrons of the member libraries of the Corn Belt (Illinois) LS can keep track of the due dates of their books on the Illinois Literary Heritage Calendar. Produced by the system and funded by the People's Bank of Bloomington (which also distributes copies), the calendar features a theme

From the Illinois Literary Heritage Calendar

every month with reading lists and information on library services. Authors' names are also listed on their birthdays, with information on their connection to Illinois. The calendar is illustrated with original drawings and photographs.

☐ In conjunction with the showing of a film on the images of women in advertising, a "Bad Ad" contest was held last fall at the Billerica (Massachusetts) PL. Patrons were asked to contribute offensive or stereotypical ads to a bulletin board. To provide balance, "good ads," those portraying people in realistic situations, were also sought. After six months, letters were sent to the producers of the ten worst and ten best ads. The advertisers' side of the question was presented in a talk at the library by a Boston advertising executive.

Magazine Notes

☐ Written for both serious amateurs and professionals, *Culinary Arts News* provides information on cooking and wine schools and classes in the United States and abroad. Arranged geographically, the entries give a detailed description of the curriculum, teachers, and facilities, and an evaluation. Each issue also features general articles and restaurant reviews. Subscriptions to the quarterly newsletter are $30 per year from *Culinary Arts News,* Box 153, West Springs, IL 60558.

☐ The Bio-Integral Resource Center, an organization that promotes least toxic pest control through integrated pest management (IPM), publishes two periodicals. *The IPM Practitioner* is a technical monthly newsletter that includes articles, journal abstracts, research notes, and book reviews. The November issue carries an article "Least Toxic Pest Control for Libraries." The subscription price is $25 for individuals and $50 for institutions, and single issues are $2.50. *The Common Sense Pest Control Quarterly* is intended for nontechnical readers and provides practical advice on using least toxic pest control methods. It is available for $30 for individuals and $50 for institutions. Send orders to BIRC, 1307 Acton St., Berkeley, CA 94706.

Library pests from *The IPM Practitioner*

☐ *Adventure Years Digest* is a new monthly newsletter that condenses articles of interest to child care professionals from over 150 publications. Child development, preschool instruction, programming, and management are among the principal topics covered. A subscription is $24.95 and sample issues can be obtained from Discovery House, Ltd., 29-24 40th Ave., Long Island City, NY 11101.

Media Center World

☐ *LiveWire,* a new periodical from the National Council of Teachers of English, to be published five times during the school year, is designed to meet the need of teachers in grades K-7 for classroom activities in the language arts. Librarians will be particularly interested in the feature "Choosing and Using Children's Books," which examines ways of approaching a specific book or author. Subscriptions are $15 from NCTE, 1111 Kenyon Rd., Urbana, IL 61801.

☐ Eight new classroom video series are included in the Agency for Instructional Television's 1985 catalog of educational materials. Among the new series are "Child Sexual Abuse," with programs for three different age groups and for parents, "16 Tales," folktales from American ethnic groups, and "Old Enough to Care," six programs on growing up and aging. To obtain the catalog, contact AIT, Box A, Bloomington, IN 47402, 800/457-4509.

☐ Follett Library Book Company is offering two new catalogs of interest to media specialists. For the first time they are issuing a secondary school catalog of books, arranged by subject and broken down by grade. In the software area, Follett is now distributing only Apple material, and has five curriculum-oriented software catalogs: administrative, language arts, mathematics, science, and social science/art. The catalogs can be obtained from Follett, 4506 Northwest Highway, Crystal Lake, IL 60014, 800/435-6170.

Professional Reading

☐ Prepared by the Preservation Committee of the New York University Libraries, the *Disaster Plan Workbook* is an outline of a model disaster plan for libraries, published in a looseleaf binder. Individual libraries can fill in portions of the pages or add their own pages as indicated. The sections cover emergency procedures (fire, flood, bomb threat, natural disaster, etc.), computer systems, safety equipment, resources, personnel (who to contact), branch library plans, insurance coverage, and appendixes include floor plans and a reading list. Copies are available for $10, with checks payable to New York University. Order from Collection Management Office, Elmer Holmes Bobst Library, New York University, 70

Washington Sq. S., New York, NY 10012.

☐ The *Kentucky Library Association Intellectual Freedom Manual* was published as the summer issue of *Kentucky Libraries*. The 40p. booklet contains information on handling censorship issues, lists resources for reference and advice, and includes a bibliography on intellectual freedom. The manual can be obtained for $3, with checks payable to KLA, from Executive Director, KLA, Paducah PL, 555 Washington St., Paducah, KY 42001.

☐ The Virginia Library Association has published the *Virginia Library Automation Directory,* based on a survey of Virginia libraries conducted last fall. It includes entries for over 100 libraries in Virginia that use automation, with name of contact person, activities automated, and vendors used. There is a vendor/system index and a directory of all vendors mentioned. The 39p. directory costs $6 prepaid, $7 billed from the VLA Publications Office, 80 South Early St., Alexandria, VA 22304.

Products and Services

☐ Useful for presentations to small groups or for editing slide shows without setting up a screen, the Kodak Cinemasound III sound slide projector is equipped with a built-in screen, along with a sixteen-watt amplifier and a six-inch speaker. It can also project onto a large screen. Weighing nineteen pounds, the projector, based on the Kodak Ektagraphic III ES projector, has a two-year warranty on parts and labor.

☐ Visually impaired readers with a taste for glamor and romance can thank Thorndike Press for making available in large print for the first time both Judith Krantz and Harlequin romances. The Krantz novels to be published are *Mistral's Daughter, Princess Daisy* and *Scruples*. In the Harlequin agreement, thirty-six of those titles will bc published each year. Contact Thorndike Press, Box 157, Thorndike, ME 04986, 800/223-6121.

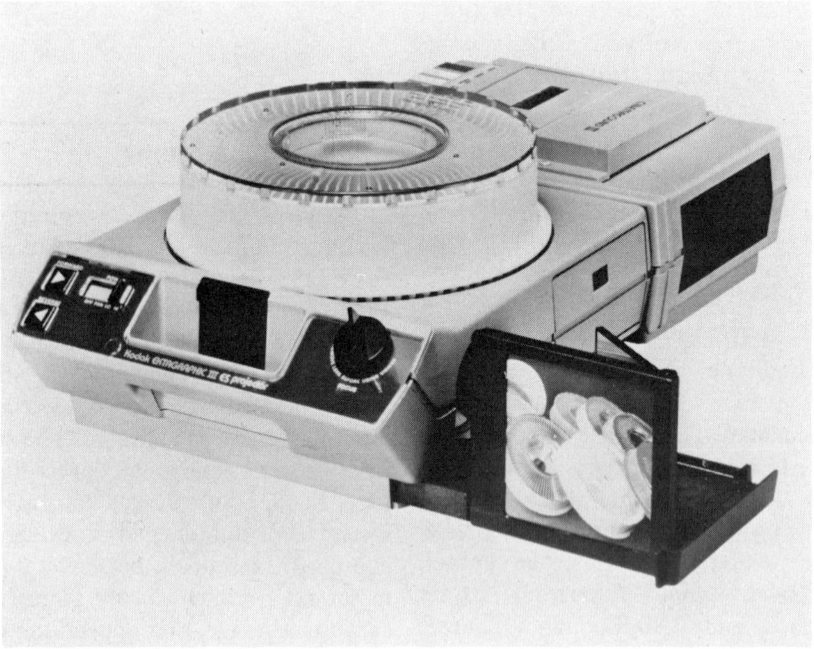

Kodak's Cinemasound III

☐ A book return from Highsmith is designed to withstand extreme environmental conditions. The All-Weather Book Return is made of

Highsmith's All-Weather Book Return

polyethylene with stainless steel hardware, and comes with a book truck made of one-piece construction with integral handles and two swivel and two rigid casters. Small openings located in the bottom of the book truck and the deposit door slide prevent damage to materials if liquids are forced into the return. It is available in curbside or sidewalk access styles, both designed with raised side panels to accommodate optional letterboards for mounting signs. Contact Highsmith, Box 800L, Highway 106 East, Fort Atkinson, WI 53538, 800/558-2110.

Software

☐ Spell-A-Vision from Cross Educational Software is designed to help the older child and adult poor speller by reinforcing the visual memory of correctly spelled words. Each of the eight disks, including one on sound-alikes and one on "spelling demons," covers 1,000 words, each presented in the context of a sentence that shows or defines its meaning. New spelling lists can be added by the user. There are Spell-A-Vision versions for the Apple II, Commodore 64 and IBM PC, at $19.95 per disk, or $150 for the entire series. Write for a free catalog

from Cross Educational Software, Box 1536, Ruston, LA 71270, 318/255-8921.

☐ The National Council of Teachers of English Committee on Instructional Technology has compiled *Guidelines for Review and Evaluation of English Language Arts Software.* The 4p. booklet advises on software evaluation on the basis of such features as teacher management, instructional strategy, content, and ease of operation. Single copies are free to members who send an SASE to NCTE, 1111 Kenyon Rd., Urbana, IL 61801.

☐ SoftStyle's Printworks provides simplified control over more than thirty models of dot matrix printers on IBM PC and compatible systems. It allows menu selection of printing modes and characteristics, and has such features as special fonts, a custom font editor and lengthwise-rotated printing, eliminating the need to learn printer control codes and providing the functions of several printer utilities that must otherwise be purchased separately. Printworks is available for $69.95 from SoftStyle, Inc., 7192 Kalanianaole Highway, Suite 205, Honolulu, HI 96825, 808/396-6368.

Write for These

☐ The nuclear arms issue and the response of religious groups is a topic of much interest. A guide to the Catholic position is a 14p. bibliography compiled by Catherine Pilley on the National Conference of Catholic Bishops' statement "The Challenge of Peace—God's Promise and Our Response." The books and articles cited are from volume 22, issues 1–9 (January 1983–June 1984) of *The Catholic Periodical and Literature Index* (Abridged Edition). A single copy of the bibliography is 50c. Order from the Catholic Library Association, 461 W. Lancaster Ave., Haverford, PA 19041.

☐ A list of over 1,900 statistical publications issued by nearly 1,000 associations, commercial publishers, research organizations, universities, and state governments is available free from Congressional Information Service. The 44p. booklet, excerpted from CIS's *Statistical Reference Index,* indicates whether the publication is included in the Statistical Reference Index Microfiche Library. Write Statistics Sources, Congressional Information Service, 4520 East-West Highway, Suite 800, Bethesda, MD 20814 or call 800/638-8380.

☐ Basic information about more than 170 periodicals that carry materials about reading can be found in *Contributor's Guide to Periodicals in Reading,* from the International Reading Association. Information includes audience, type of material published, editorial process, a brief statement of purpose, and address, frequency and circulation. Single copies of the 28p. booklet are available free by sending an SASE with two-ounce first class postage to IRA, Box 8139, Newark, DE 19714, Attn: Contributor's Guide to Periodicals in Reading.

Online Update *(cont'd. from p. 273)*

the actual article. *Easynet* is also developing a gateway service for experienced searchers.

Even BRS, SDC and Dialog are getting into the front-end/gateway act. As already mentioned, BRS's *After Dark* software provides a front-end to the BRS system for various end-user services and SDC has developed *Search Master* as a disk-based software package. Dialog is currently experimenting with front-ends by offering the option to search their new database, CENDATA, the database of the U.S. Bureau of the Census, through a menu-driven format. Dialog is also providing a gateway to search the *Official Airline Guide* electronic edition. Other offerings of front-end and gateway services by database producers, vendors, and others are sure to follow, opening up the world of online information to many new users as well as increasing the accessibility of numerous online systems for the experienced online searcher. ▣

Young Adult Perplex *(cont. from p. 277)*

hide an automobile graveyard.

After a minute you make a U-turn and start back south toward Leominster. Several miles off to the west you know is the sinister presence of Fort Devens—or Fort Delta. There too are the culvert and the high railroad bridge where the terrorists held Kate and the children prisoner in the school bus. Two separate places, actually, although Cormier put *this* bridge across *that* culvert in his mind and in his book to make the set for *After the First Death*. You would like to visit these places, but they are miles away, and besides, they wouldn't let you into Fort Delta, you tell yourself.

One more stop left, now, an important one, and then on to the final destination. At the thought of what lies at the end of your journey a shiver of anticipation—or is it dread?—travels through your stomach. You pedal faster and try to block out your thoughts by concentrating on the pain in your calves. Tempo, rhythm.... Your feet rise and fall, around and around. Overhead the street lights begin to wink on.

Breathing hard, you pass Notre Dame Preparatory School where Cormier's son Peter, with his father's approval, refused to sell chocolates. This is Trinity School, where Jerry Renault dared disturb the universe, and up ahead is your last stop, the athletic field. You take a small side road that brings you around and above. You lean your bike against a tree and pick your way through the little wood until you can see down the slope to where a few players are finishing a late football practice under stadium lights. The paint on the shabby bleachers on the far side of the field is sickly green under the illumination. The ground has been cleared of snow, but the muddy puddles near the goal posts are frozen slick. The cries and thuds of the practice are like the brutal fight sounds that Brother Leon heard as he stood hidden and gloating here among these trees. Now the tired players are leaving the field with their helmets under their arms. Suddenly the lights are switched off and the dark falls over your head like a blanket. Your ears ring with an animal roar from the empty grandstand. The night has come on while you have been standing here.

In the darkness: You blunder back through the trees, stumbling over rocks, and grab your bike with stiff hands. Your ears sing with pain from the bitter cold as your legs churn urgently toward the final destination. Not too far, now, not too far. But what will you find at the end? Because the object of your pilgrimage is, of course, Robert Cormier himself. What kind of man could have written these books that show so clearly the face of evil? What kind of man can look so deeply into the heart of darkness?

The houses are far back from the road now as you sail past, and a line from *Take Me Where the Good Times Are* sneaks into your mind: "There's a dark and lonesome spot in every town where the bright, shining stores come to an end and the buildings rise out of the darkness, the pale street lights flickering in the tree branches like candles for the dead." Almost there, almost there, you tell yourself. Then you hear a faint rhythmic clinking of a bicycle chain making a duet with your own. Close behind a swishing of tires. Someone else crazy enough to ride a bike in this terrible dark cold? You hesitate in surprise to listen, and he sweeps past, bent over his handlebars, doggedly pedaling on and on, through his fantasies and through his fears—Adam in his father's old jacket with his knit cap pulled down over his ears. Up ahead he fades into the blackness and somewhere you hear a dog barking a bark with a snarl in it.

Your front wheel swoops wildly. You fight for control and narrowly miss falling into the snow that gleams dully from the side of the road. But there it is, two doors farther on, the Cormier house, tucked under tall black pines like the witch's cottage in the woods. What will you find when you knock on the door? It doesn't matter; you are desperate for light and warmth.

You wheel your tired old bike up the driveway and lay it against the front porch. You take your package out of the basket, the package that holds your well-thumbed copies of *Chocolate War* and *I Am the Cheese*. Was it childish to have brought them for Cormier to autograph, you wonder fleetingly?

But then you are at the door knocking, and it opens immediately. A slight man with wispy gray hair and a crooked smile like sunshine holds out his hand. Behind him you see a handsome motherly woman and a pretty dark-haired girl. "Come in, come in," he cries in a voice full of welcome and concern. "We've been worried about you! You must be just frozen! Connie's made some hot chocolate for you—come in!" And you step out of the dark into a house full of comfort and warmth. ▣

WLB Classifieds

__Classified Advertising__ is accepted six weeks preceding date of issue. Charges are: minimum 3 lines—$10; each additional line—$2.50. If voucher forms are required, please send them when submitting copy. All advertisements for positions must exclude reference to race, creed, color, age, and sex as conditions for employment. The publisher reserves the right to reject any advertising considered unacceptable as to wording or appearance or for any other reason. Submit classifieds to: Brian Bavolar, Wilson Library Bulletin, 950 University Ave., Bronx, NY 10452.

Announcements

THE BERMUDA LIBRARY announces the launching of the *Bermuda National Bibliography,* a quarterly publication with annual cumulations. The first annual issue (1983) is free of charge. The annual subscription for 1984 is BDA or US $6 including postage, cheques and drafts payable to the Accountant General. Please address enquiries and orders to: Head Librarian, The Bermuda Library, Par-la-Ville, Hamilton 5-31 Bermuda.

THE FOOTLOOSE LIBRARIAN newsletter & network. Money-saving travel news + U.S. & overseas librarians offering Bed & Breakfast, housing exchange, more. "Good, practical information" M.S., IN; "An excellent publication" S.R., Tunisia. Free brochure. TFL, Box 972, Minneapolis, MN 55440.

MILITARY BOOKS for identification of shoulder patches, medals, insignia . . . U.S. and foreign. Military history, etc. Send for free catalog, M.C.N. Press, Box 52033 WLB, Tulsa, OK 74152.

NEWSLETTER FOR YOUR SUMMER, SPRING, CHRISTMAS COURSES in London, Paris, Mexico, Hawaii, etc.! Visit libraries, theatre productions, galleries. Exciting study/vacation options for librarians, plus work in foreign libraries. Subscription: $25/yr. NEWSLETTER, Box 5513, Santa Monica, CA 90405.

THE ONE-PERSON LIBRARY: A NEWSLETTER FOR LIBRARIANS AND MANAGEMENT. Professional isolation is one of the major problems of working alone. We want to change that. This new newsletter is informal, informative, and, above all, quick and to the point. Charter subscriptions (one year, 12 issues) for $35, a savings of over 20%. Pre-paid orders to OPL RESOURCES, LTD., Box 948, Murray Hill Station, New York, NY 10156.

For Sale

BRUCE TEGNER'S COMPLETE BOOK OF SELF-DEFENSE hardcover edition is again in stock. ISBN 0-87407-510-6 $10.95. Thor Publishing Co., Box 1782, Ventura, CA 93002.

CAN-DO CARDS: RESEARCH REPORTING—A proven method for teaching students in grades 4–8 how to write research reports. $6.95. The Curriculum Exchange, 71 Longview Dr., Marblehead, MA 01945.

FOR SALE: Charming 27-page brochure (SECRET PLACE), includes illustrations that enhance the listing of books for the preschool and kindergarten child. Bibliography includes books for parents, picture books, stressful situations (*I'm Sick, I'm Scared, I'm Sleepy*), jealousy, death. An attractive and enticing list. Send orders with check for $1.75 to Wessie Connell, Roddenbery Memorial Library, Cairo, Georgia 31728.

". . . get ideas from every issue."
M.S. High School Media Center, NY
Subscribe (and send *your* nitty gritty ideas) to The U*N*A*B*A*S*H*E*D Librarian™, the "how I run my library good"℠ letter, Box 2631, New York, NY 10116. Four issues $20 US funds (add $5 Canadian and foreign postage).

HOBBY BOOKWATCH: Military, gun and hobby book review. Approximately 600 new titles each year. Small and large publishers. One year, $2; two years, $3.50; three years, $5. Published six times a year. For free sample write: HB, Box 52033, Tulsa, OK 74152.

LEARN *CALDECOTT* AND *NEWBERY* TITLES the easy way—two fun, Bingo-type games for an entire class. Offered to you by two practicing librarians. Painless approach to recognition of these award-winning titles for only $15 each. Contact H.M. Mudpies, Inc., Box 37151, Raleigh, NC 27637-3151.

Librarians Love TFL!
"Everyone on our staff is interested in the Travel Exchange, either as a traveller or a host" M.H., San Diego. Free brochure on THE FOOTLOOSE LIBRARIAN newsletter & travel network. TFL, Box 972, Minneapolis, MN 55440.

LIBRARY NEWSLETTERS. Let a librarian prepare camera-ready copy for your newsletter. $1 for samples. Library Newsletter Service, Box 637, Belleville, NJ 07109.

THE MILITARY BOOKMAN—Military, Naval, and Aviation History. Out-of-print and rare books, 3 catalogs per year. 29 East 93rd St., New York, NY 10128 or call (212) 348-1280, Tues.-Sat. 10:30-5:30.

PRACTICE QUESTIONS for academic quiz shows. For more details write Tim Ballard, Box 502, Bardstown, KY 40004.

PUT *SEARS* TO WORK. 1,200 "see" and "see also" cards plus Manual/List of Headings with DEWEY numbers. From *Sears* 12th ed., $49.95. Woods Library Publishing Co., 9159 Clifton, Evergreen Park, IL 60642.

SOLID OAK SHELVING

ACCEPTING ORDERS NOW for Spring deliveries in all continental states. SAVE with direct institutional purchases from manufacturer in Tennessee for genuine furniture shelving in beautiful solid oak: Kanecrest Solid Oak Demountable-Remountable Systems. Call now 615-588-6113 between 10 and 4 EST for FREE 'Packet Parcel', including Packet Guide, Large Solid Oak Sample, and Prices Delivered. Make your selections from hundreds of combinations. Place your order direct for Spring delivery. Give name, position, institution, and address for UPS Prepaid Delivery of your 'Packet Parcel'! Every major library should have one! The Kane Company, Box 10505, Knoxville, TN 37939-0505.

"WOW!" "Do not pass go without collecting this PR gem . . . " LJ
GO, PEP AND POP! 250 TESTED IDEAS FOR LIVELY LIBRARIES by Baeckler and Larson. Order from: The U*N*A*B*A*S*H*E*D Librarian™, the "how I run my library good"℠ letter. Dept. GPP/WLB, Box 2631, New York, NY 10116. Send $4.50 check and mailing label with order. Libraries add $1 for billing. Canadian and foreign add $1 in US funds. 6 to 8 weeks delivery. LC 75-20328 CIP.

Credits:
p. 264–66—Fred Chamberlain; 268, 284—Catharine O'Neill; 270—Artemas Cole; 274, 275—Coffee House Press; 278—Dodd, Mead; 279—Dial Press, St. Martin's Press; 280—Island Records; 281—Elektra/Asylum Records; 287—Peterson's Guides.

INDEX TO ADVERTISERS

Facts on File 288
Gale Research Company .... 4th cover
OCLC 241
United Nations Publications 242
H. W. Wilson Company .... 2nd cover, 3rd cover

Wilson Library Bulletin

Start the new year right…

950 University Avenue, Bronx, New York 10452

☐ Please enter my subscription to 10 monthly issues of *WLB for one year* @ $30 in the U.S. and Canada, $35 in other countries.

Name ______________________

Address ______________________

City ______________ State ________ Zip ________

Publishers Directory 1984-85

. . . A Guide to More Than 9,000 New and Established, Commercial and Nonprofit, Private and Alternative, Corporate and Association, Government and Institution Publishing Programs and Their Distributors; Includes Producers of Books, Classroom Materials, Reports, and Databases.

Fifth Edition. Edited by Linda S. Hubbard. (Formerly published as *Book Publishers Directory.*) 1,729 pages in 2 vols. Publishers, Subject, and Geographic Indexes. Published by Gale Research Co., 1984. ISSN 0742-0501. L.C. No. 82-640252. ISBN 0-8103-0412-0. $200.00/set.

Dealing with a distinctive and growing area of publishing that is of increasing importance to librarians, researchers, booksellers, and others, Gale's *Publishers Directory* (formerly *Book Publishers Directory*) has gained rapid acceptance. The revised and expanded fifth edition provides authoritative information on some 9,300 presses in the United States and Canada that are not listed in *Literary Market Place*, an increase of 2,000 over the previous edition.

The publishing organizations described in the directory represent a broad spectrum, including: Small presses in the literary sense . . . Groups promoting special interests . . . Museums and societies in the arts and sciences . . . Divisions within universities that issue special publications . . . Religious institutions . . . Corporations that produce important publications in their areas of specialization . . . Government agencies . . . and more. Also covered in the new edition are producers of books, classroom materials, reports, and databases. A separate section is devoted to small press distribution. Typical entries in this new section provide complete contact information, year founded, principal officers, regional offices, a brief description, subject specialties, terms to publishers, special services, discount and returns policies, and more.

All information in Gale's *Publishers Directory* is obtained by mailing questionnaires to the publishers. Entries provide the most recent address, telephone number, date founded, ISBN prefix, and CIP (Cataloging in Publication) information in easy-to-read headnotes. The body of a typical entry includes the publishing house's principal personnel, a description of the aims of the organization, subjects covered in the firm's publications, discount and returns policy, and a list of representative titles.

Three indexes aid in retrieving specific information from any of the entries. The Publishers Index puts into one alphabetic sequence the names of the presses, both first and last names, and includes references to all publishers listed in *Literary Market Place.* The Subject Index gives the full names of presses under the 275 subjects that have been indicated by the publishers, or which were apparent from the titles of their publications. Finally, the Geographic Index serves as a source of addresses for area mailings and for locating publishers of local interest.

Publishers Directory is available at Gale's 5% Standing Order discount.
All books published and distributed by Gale are sent on 60-day approval.
Deduct 5% if you send check with order. Add 10% outside the U.S. and Canada.

GALE Research Co. • Book Tower • Detroit, MI 48226

To order by phone: **800-223-GALE tollfree.** In Canada, Michigan, Alaska, and Hawaii: 313-961-2242.

Wilson Library Bulletin

January 1985

Wilson **Library** *Bulletin*

January 1985, Volume 59, Number 5 *ISSN 0043-5651*

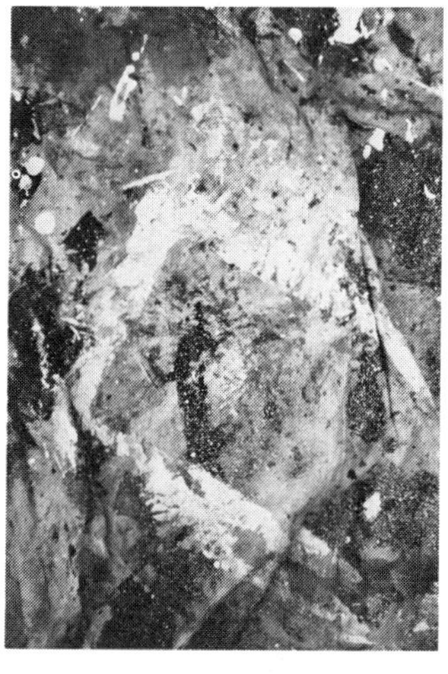

Our abstract cover for January is a detail of a painter's dropcloth taken by **Gary San Pietro**. San Pietro, a fine arts photographer who lives in Philadelphia, is a frequent contributor to *WLB*.

Departments

Letter From New York/Editorial 308
Correspondence 309
Upfront/News—*Columbia University dedicates rare book library; Los Angeles Public Library receives major funding for renovation; Pennsylvania adopts comprehensive plan for library development; Cuadra Associates to market database directory; Xerox awards $12.5 million to universities; late news.* 310
Calendar 314
Library World 361
Marketplace 362
WLB Classifieds 367

Articles

Enlarging Micros: The Mainframe Connection *Nancy Melin* 315
Managing Research Libraries: An Interview with David Weber *Russell Fischer* 319
Ladies of the Club: An Arkansas Story *David Taylor* 324
Mission Possible: AASL in Atlanta *Karen Lawrence* 328

Features

Dateline—Washington *Dale Nelson* 330
Eye on Publishing *Anne McGrath* 332
Facing the Public *Will Manley* 334
School Library Technology *Patricia Berglund* 336

Reviews

Picture Books for Children *Donnarae MacCann/Olga Richard* 338
The Young Adult Perplex *Patty Campbell* 340
Murder in Print *Kathleen Maio* 341
Front Row Center *Judith Trojan* 342
On Record: Popular Music *Bruce Pollock* 346
Magazines *Gail Pool* 348
Our Profession *Norman Stevens* 350
Software for Libraries *Patrick Dewey* 352
Current Reference Books *James Rettig* 354

The *Wilson Library Bulletin* is published monthly except in July and August by The H. W. Wilson Company, 950 University Avenue, Bronx, N.Y. 10452. Second-class postage paid at Bronx, N.Y. and additional mailing offices. Copyright © 1985 by The H. W. Wilson Company. The *Wilson Library Bulletin* is indexed in *Education Index, Library Literature,* and *Popular Periodical Index* and abstracted in *Library & Information Science Abstracts, Historical Abstracts,* and *America: History and Life*. Book reviews are indexed in *Book Review Index*. Subscription $30 a year, U.S. and Canada; $35, foreign. Single copies $4, U.S. and Canada; $4.50, foreign (remittance with order, please). Address all correspondence about subscriptions to the publisher. No subscriptions through agents. Telephone: (212) 588-8400

Letter from New York

Editorial

Another unnecessary rescue

We know nothing of the daily activities of the Center for the Book in the Library of Congress, aware only that it was established by the federal government in 1977 to promote books, reading, and study of the written word. The essential purpose of the agency has always seemed to us grandly redundant, like a Center for Crime in a New York City subway tunnel, a Center for Chocolate at Hershey corporate headquarters, or a Center for a Needle in a Haystack located in a haystack.

But, if holding a mirror up to the Library of Congress seemed a superfluous labor, there is no denying that the Center has sponsored and given its name to a number of useful meetings, forums, symposia, exhibits, and promotions. The Center would be of use, we supposed, to the extent that it refused to become as narcissistic as its name suggested. That has seemed to be the history of this office, up until the publication last month of *Books in Our Future,* the fruits of a study undertaken by the Center for the Book.

A report to our national legislature from the Librarian of Congress, the document is the result of a study proposed by the Joint Committee on the Library and approved as Senate Congressional Resolution 59. The measure, agreed to in late 1983, suggested that "A timely study of the changing role of the book in the future is highly desirable."

The Library of Congress, the Center for the Book, and an advisory body of twenty-five individuals thus joined that growing band of committees that set out in search of "the book"—the presumed motive being to ascertain if the device is still valuable, influential, and of utility. But the ultimate goal was to stage an argument to determine whether or not books will be rendered obsolescent by high technology.

As librarians we have learned how to acquire, describe, catalog, shelve, list, retrieve, lend, borrow, bind, preserve, withdraw, sell, and discard books. We could also, should it be necessary, become expert in eliminating books and mastering a replacement technology. Persistently teased with this possibility, we hoped that *Books in Our Future* would challenge and startle us with futuristic likelihoods. Instead we are confronted with a predictable and tiresome tract that, incapable even of living up to its title, rushes to reassure us of an "American Renaissance of the Culture of the Book."

"We Americans," the document opens, "have a habit of writing premature obituaries." Having announced its position in advance, the paper then labors on to argue that books are here to stay, that "Our civilization is a product of the Culture of the Book," that the Library of Congress possesses some eighteen million books, that books are "everyday fixtures of our lives," and "measures of our civilization." Proclaims the statement, "We find books everywhere."

We are delivered from several pages of this committee prose to a long passage of statistics assembled to show that the book publishing industry is flourishing, the amount of money spent on buying books increasing ("Books have become visible in drugstores, supermarkets, and airports") and the number of book publishers in the U.S. growing.

Television comes in for the usual conventional analysis and is found to promote "new forms of passivity" while "Readers of books are likely to be alert citizens."

Absent of any logical progression, the report then takes up the "twin menaces" of illiteracy and aliteracy (a person who can but stubbornly refuses to read) and discovers new ways in which to defend the use of books. Generous in what it is willing to worry about, the document is despondent because senior citizens are not reading enough books, depressed because sixty percent of the nation's prisoners are illiterate.

Books in Our Future then stumbles into a consideration of coexistence of the book with emerging technology, the argument it had been waiting to pose. It is apologetic. "The traditional book, of course, lacks the novelty, the commercial hype, and futuristic romance which have surrounded more recent technologies of communication." No matter. "The Culture of the Book will continue to be enriched by new technologies." The committee, declaring that the book is "user-friendly," also asserts that "we must aim to make all Americans book-friendly." Smiling weakly on computer technology, the authors of the report can't resist a sour aside: "We must do our fallible best to suggest the extent and the limits of the roles of the new computer technology."

The final portion of the report ("A Manifold Program for a Massive Problem") returns to the challenge of illiteracy, comfortable that the book has an unassailable role to play in its solution. *Books in Our Future* is willing to endorse anything, from establishng a family library for the vice-president's house to preferred postal rates, from encouraging Chicago Mayor Harold Washington to present official visitors with books to making use of technology developed by the Department of Defense. It applauds the fact that children in Butte, Montana can ride free on city buses by displaying their library cards and encourages the U. S. Information Agency to continue developing a plan for strengthening U.S. books abroad.

The authors of this report, a year in the making, set out on an errand that wasn't necessary. The book as an instrument for the diffusion of learning is not imperiled and does not require rescue. It is not the instituion of the book we need worry about, but the habits of its readers.

—Milo Nelson

Correspondence

Jobs going begging

Children's librarians do exist. I know; I'm about to be one. Manley is correct ("Facing the Public," September) that there aren't many of us, but I place the blame on the library schools, not on the students.

Public service courses are a thing of the past at the University of Arizona Graduate Library School, and this school is no exception. Reference is the only subject left where we get some training in how to deal with the public in libraries. All the other courses deal with technical, administrative, bibliographic, or computer services.

I arrived at the University of Arizona a year-and-a-half ago with a desire to be a children's librarian. Several courses in children's services were listed in the catalog, but the professor who taught these courses had resigned and was replaced by a computer expert. I am typing this letter on one of the school's eight new computers—a great boon to all students, but hardly a substitute for courses in human services.

The image of children's librarians does need to be upgraded, and systems like the Tucson Public Library are doing this by appointing children's librarians to positions of higher responsibility. Library schools do not intentionally perpetuate a negative image of children's services, but by ignoring this essential aspect of librarianship the schools are saying that it is no longer relevant or important.

The University of Arizona Graduate Library School is about to be investigated for reaccreditation; it will be interesting to note if the ALA committee remarks the lack in children's service courses.

I hear that Will Manley has filled his vacancy. There are other children's jobs going begging now. Until the library schools turn back to emphasizing the people in libraries, a large portion of whom are children, these jobs will continue to be vacant.

George Pilling
Tucson, Arizona

Treasure abuse

Conceive of a university library which was pioneering in computerization in the dark ages of the late 1960s and early 1970s. Add this to an aged and decrepit Carnegie building with roof leaks, unusable space, and half the book collection stored ten blocks away in a warehouse, and a new university library building in the planning stages, too small before ground was broken to hold accumulated collections. On the second floor of the warehouse an accumulation of more than a thousand manuscript collections was being gathered, ranging from a few pieces to something over 700 cartons, all awaiting processing. Put several ambitious and aggressive persons in the field to add to the collections on a constant basis. Stir in a generous dash of competition between the university's chief and deputy chief administrators, each vying to bring in the most material without regard for the future commitment in processing time. Even with one of the largest, if not the largest, special collections staff in the country at the time (twenty-two trained and competent persons) working full-time, could a dent be made in this backlog?

Yes, the Von Ranke collection is a treasure, but it is just the tip of the iceberg at Syracuse University. How do I know all this? I was there, trying to deal with manuscript and rare book cataloging on a day-to-day basis. While child abuse is the current social condition being dealt with, someone someday will come up with treasure abuse. The subject is wide open and really something an up-and-coming young librarian can get his or her teeth into.

Glenn Skillin
Philadelphia, Pennsylvania

Our most important resource

Consider this an overdue letter, delayed by a busy schedule, a direct reflection of concerns raised by Will Manley in his excellent series of columns in your September and October issues.

I write not only to express my pleasure in his essays, but to be sure you, as editor, know that we remain out here and reading, and welcome the attention of professional journals such as yours to the concerns that Manley raises.

The single best reason to support services to children, not only library, but similar services, is that children are the nation's most important resource. Whatever may be in second place does not even come close. It may sound like a cliché to say it, but the point is we rarely act as though we understand, much less believe it. It seems a shame to me that newly established governments, whether totalitarian or free, usually understand perfectly and act upon this truism while established, free societies, are so quick to overlook it, or pay lip service only to it. The point about books and libraries is that even in today's computer-conscious world, the government requires them for its continuing existence. Thinking is hardly possible without information in areas of history, economics, philosophy, government, science and literature as is primarily available through books, and therefore through public libraries. If children are not educated, taught to read and value books, eventually there will be no point in libraries as we know them.

I hope future issues of the *Bulletin* will expand upon the topic of services to children, and ways to encourage libraries to specialize in providing them, from a broad spectrum of views.

Barbara Porte
Nassau Library System
Uniondale, New York

UPFRONT NEWS

On December 6, Columbia University dedicated its new $3 million-dollar Rare Book and Manuscript Library (left) built atop Butler Library on the institution's Morningside Heights campus. The glass-walled, crystal pavilion houses 500,000 rare books, 22 million manuscripts, and thousands of art works.

The two-story structure, designed by the New York architectural firm of Cain, Farrell & Bell, is built on the sixth floor setback on the south side of Butler Library. Extensive use of glass walls and partitions, and a skylight running the entire length of the 230-foot library, give a sense of openness to a structure deliberately windowless except for two high circular windows. Panes of laminated solar-gray glass, designed to block ultraviolet rays, are used in the skylight.

The rare book collection, begun with the founding of the university, was formally organized as a separate unit of the libraries in 1930. Last year library users consulted more than 15,000 rare books and two million manuscripts, producing scores of biographies, critical studies, and dissertations.

An inaugural exhibit, "Treasures from the Collections," displays the range of the library's holdings, from a 4,000-year-old Mesopotamian cylinder seal to a hand-corrected typescript of Howl *by poet and alumnus Allen Ginsberg.*

"Legions of scholars, authors, and appreciative lovers of books will be here for generations to come," said Columbia President Michael Sovern at the library's decication, "enjoying the feeling of openness, the exquisite use of glass and wood, the striking design that brings light and access to the treasures of the written word."

Los Angeles Public Library receives major funding for expansion and renovation

The Los Angeles Public Library has received a financial commitment from the Community Redevelopment Agency of $110.4 million for the expansion and renovation of the central library facility. Two major office towers—Library Tower, designed by I. M. Pei and Partners, and Grant Place Tower, designed by Johnson-Burgee—will be constructed near the library site by Maguire/Thomas Partners. In return for the rights to build, Maguire/Thomas will provide most of the private funding to be contributed to the library. Their total contribution exceeds $62 million, approximately $49 million in direct cash payments, and payments of costs in excess of $13 million for library parking, construction of a new street, and relocation of utilities.

A second element in the financing program is a sale-leaseback arrangement with Blythe, Eastman, Dillion, allowed under federal law, which provides an additional $27 million from the sale of tax benefits. The library will be repurchased at a later time using CRA tax allocation bond proceeds.

The 75,000 square-foot western portion of the central library site now used as a surface parking lot will be sold to Maguire/Thomas Partners for the construction of a subterranean parking garage for 600 cars. The grade level will be landscaped as a public open space reminiscent of the original park on this site. The main entrance to the library building will front on Flower Street. Located within this open space will be a maximum of 10,000 square feet of retail shops and restaurant space to be built and owned by Maguire/Thomas Partners.

In addition to the open space on the west lawn of the library, Maguire/Thomas will develop and give to the city a new public space across Fifth Street, Bunker Hill Steps. Located between the new Library Tower and the Wells Fargo Building, the Steps will be an integral part of the Library Tower project. Designed by landscape architect Lawrence Halprin, the Steps will include waterfalls, gardens, and terraced landings.

"This is a precedent-shattering program for Los Angeles," said Mayor Tom Bradley. "First, it allows the library building to be preserved and upgraded to a top quality stature, without placing an undue financial burden on the city of Los Angeles. Second, it represents an outstanding merging of public and private interest for the public good—preserving the central library."

As pressure mounted to tear down the library and sell the land to developers to generate funds for a new library facility, Robert Maguire III undertook a study seeking a feasible alternative to save the library and update its facilities, to maintain its open space, and to devise a financing plan that could provide the funds.

"We were able to accomplish some enormously important city planning issues with this study," Maguire said. "The plan surpassed our expectations, not only recommending how to save the library and enhance it to international stature, but establishing the library block as the true center of downtown, and creating some exciting new public space in the library garden and across the street with the Bunker Hill Steps."

Under the proposed package, the existing central library building will be restored and improved producing 160,000 square-feet of space. The children's wing east of the main building will be replaced by a 200,000 square-foot expansion, providing a total of 360,000-square feet. Design of the renovation is being performed by the New York City architectural firm of Hardy Holzman Pfeiffer Associates, renowned for their expertise in refurbishing historic landmarks.

CRL receives money from Atlantic Richfield

The Center for Research Libraries has received $25,000 from the Atlantic Richfield Foundation in support of the center's building campaign. The first part of the four-phase building program includes the construction of the center's new facility at 6050 South Kenwood Avenue in Chicago and the renovation of its original site on South Cottage Grove Avenue.

The center's building program began in 1980. The Kenwood facility was completed in 1982 and contains most of the institution's service operations, staff, and its more frequently consulted collections. The Cottage Grove building is used for retrospective conversion projects of bibliographic records, preservation projects, and the housing of most of the center's monographs.

In addition to the gift by the Atlantic Richfield Foundation, the center's building campaign has been supported by the Carnegie Corporation and by the Ford and Rockefeller foundations.

Nevada voters approve library bond

Nevada voters, by a margin of fifty-seven percent, have approved a statewide $10 million bond issue for the expansion and construction of public libraries. Major support came from two counties with urban centers, in the face of opposition from Nevada's remaining fifteen counties.

Asking voters to take "The first step . . . it's long overdue," communities that wish to expand or construct a new facility must now seek matching funds through local bond issues or other funding sources.

Money for the campaign was raised from private sources and special fund-raising events.

Search committee established for Register of Copyrights

The Library of Congress has formed a search committee for a new Register of Copyrights to replace David Ladd who resigned the position effective January 2, 1985. Members of the committee are Dan Lacy, special consultant to McGraw-Hill, Stanley Gortikov, president, Recording Industry Association of America, and Robert Wedgeworth, executive director, American Library Association.

The Register of Copyrights, who is appointed by the Librarian of Congress, is responsible for carrying out the provsions of copyright law. The Copyright Office, a part of the Library of Congress for nearly 115 years, oversees the deposit of works for copyright as part of the registration process. The Copyright Office employs nearly 600 persons.

The Register also has the responsibility of serving as principal technical adviser to the United States government on national and international copyright matters and advises Congress on copyright legislation.

Des Moines voters approve bond issue

By a sixty-four percent margin, voters in Des Moines, Iowa have approved a bond issue for automation of the Des Moines Public Library. The integrated automation system will include an online catalog, computerized circulation system, and a security system. Automation of the facility is expected to take two years. Upon completion, library users will have access to the 800,000 volumes in the main library and its five branch libraries.

The **St. Louis (Missouri) Public Library** *recently staged a Printmarket to raise money in support of the institution's NEH Challenge Grant for restoration of the main library. The benefit, which featured old and rare books and prints, raised $3,000.*

Pennsylvania adopts comprehensive plan for library development

Pennsylvania Governor Richard Thornburgh has announced a comprehensive proposal to "open the doors of information to all Pennsylvanians at every publicly-supported library in the Commonwealth." Called "Access Pennsylvania," the proposal calls for initiation of a statewide library card system; a plan of state reimbursement for resource-sharing to encourage interlibrary lending; revision of the formula used to aid public libraries to allow greater aid to economically distressed communities; and development of a course that teaches school children to use library computer catalogs to search for information.

Thornburgh's announcement of the "Access Pennsylvania" program coincided with the annual meeting of Pennsylvania Citizens for Better Libraries (PCBL) in Harrisburg. "Access Pennsylvania" was developed from the recommendations of a ninety-five-member planning council organized in 1982. The council convened at Thornburgh's request when he received the PCBL "Citizen of the Year Award" in 1981.

The proposal calls for a budget of $3 million in additional state funds and $1.5 million in federal funds which will be included in the governor's budget request for 1985–1986.

"Our complex society has created an increasing need for information on the part of every citizen," said Thornburgh. "This proposal will help make necessary knowledge easier for Pennsylvanians to obtain as they seek to meet the challenges and opportunities of the information age."

Cleveland Public to acquire new DEC hardware

The Cleveland Public Library recently announced that it has become the first Data Research customer to integrate new Digital Equipment Corporation VAX 8600 hardware into its library automation system. The DEC hardware will allow for a substantial increase in the number of terminals able to be configured on a single Data Research ATLAS turnkey system. The hardware will support up to 512 terminals per VAX 8600 processor, with up to fourteen processors able to be interconnected on a VAXCluster multiprocessor.

In addition to its main library, the Cleveland Public Library presently has thirty-one branches and several subcontracted libraries on its automated system, running more than 180 online terminals. The VAX 8600 will initially be used to supplement three VAX 11/780s in the Data Research ATLAS system in place at the library.

Cuadra Associates to market database directory

Cuadra Associates, Santa Monica, California, plans to license its *Directory of Online Databases* to online service vendors so that they can offer it online. Cuadra Associates also plans to sell *Directory* data on floppy disks for use in both large and personal computers. According to Carlos Cuadra, president of the organization, the growth in online databases and in vendors of online services has intensified the need for tools to help users identify the most appropriate databases for research efforts. Cuadra, who has published the *Directory* since 1979, said "Our first issue identified 400 online databases of all kinds, offered on fifty-nine online services. Today, a total of 2,435 online databases developed by 1,189 database producers are being offered on 362 online services." The firm estimates that the number of online databases available to the public has grown more than five hundred percent in the past five years, with three new databases introduced every business day.

AMIGOS and SOLINET boards explore cooperation

The AMIGOS board of trustees and the SOLINET board of directors met recently in New Orleans to explore possible cooperative programs and to discuss issues surrounding contract negotiations with OCLC and OCLC copyright claims.

The group discussed ways of making selected services reciprocally available, including the AMIGOS collection analysis service and SOLINET programs in preservation, microcomputer-based service to small libraries, and the regional serials project with thirteen southeastern ARL libraries.

In reviewing the OCLC claim of database ownership, the two boards agreed that "appropriate uses of the database be governed by a cooperatively developed and approved code of responsible use" and agreed upon "continued opposition to any exculsive claim by OCLC of ownership of the database."

Xerox awards $12.5 million to universities

The Xerox Corporation has awarded computer system grants worth $12.5 million to thirteen universities in the United States and England. The grants provide each school with the Xerox Development Environment, an advanced software and hardware development system used at Xerox since 1978. The system uses Xerox network service products and runs on the 8010 Star high-performance workstation. Each grant includes a system of workstations, laser printers, and computers for filing and communicating information. Individual systems are configured into two or more Ethernet networks based on the Xerox network system architecture. The architecture consists of communication protocols to enable products to work together in a local area network.

Computer scientists and others will use the equipment for research and teaching in the areas of distributed computing applications, programming languages, network architectures, and software development tools. Other groups will use the equipment for research in management, artificial intelligence, and office automation.

The schools selected are Brown University, California Polytechnic State University at San Luis Obispo, University of California at Berkeley, Cornell University, University of Maryland, Massachusetts Institute of Technology, New York University, Princeton University, University of Rochester, Stanford University, University of Texas at Austin, University of Wisconsin at Madison, and Cambridge University, Cambridge, England.

Ziff-Davis sells off twenty-four publications

On November 21, Rupert Murdoch announced his purchase of twelve trade publications of the Ziff-Davis Publishing Company for $350 million. The announcement came one day after CBS, Inc. said it would acquire twelve consumer magazines from Ziff-Davis for $362.5 million, thought to be the highest price ever paid for a group of magazines. The total price realized by Ziff-Davis exceeded estimates made when the twenty-four publications were put up for sale.

In 1983 Murdoch paid $100 million for the *Chicago Sun-Times.* His other American holdings include the *New York Post, Boston Herald, San Antonio Express,* and *Village Voice* newspapers, and *New York, New Woman,* and *Star* magazines.

The group of publications Murdoch acquired from Ziff-Davis includes eight magazines, one newspaper, and three newsletters, most of them dealing with the travel and aviation industries.

Oklahoma users given free search time

The Library Commission of the Metropolitan Library System in Oklahoma County, Oklahoma City, Oklahoma, has agreed to give county residents up to $20 worth of computer search time per month at no charge. It is estimated that the dollar allowance will more than cover searches required by average library users. The library system presently subscribes to four information networks. The most heavily used is *Datatimes,* a service that indexes news from the *Daily Oklahoman* as well as legislative and business information.

The new policy, which will be reviewed after a year, will allow residents, property owners, and students in Oklahoma County with full borrowing privileges to be given up to $20 worth of free online searches per month. Costs in excess of that amount must be paid by the user.

Brian Aveney

Aveney to edit electronic journal

Brian Aveney has been appointed editor of *Information Publishing,* a new electronic journal to be published by Information Access Company and available on Dialog beginning in January. Aveney edited *Information Technology and Libraries* for the American Library Association from 1981 to 1983 and until recently was director for research and development for Blackwell North America.

He was recently appointed to the ALA Task Force on Bibliographic Databases which is examining the question of copyright of library cataloging records.

Calendar

Announcements should be sent at least 60 days in advance to "Calendar," WLB, *950 University Ave., Bronx, NY 10452.*

JAN. 29—*Abstracting and Indexing,* seminar. Hotel Bellevue, San Francisco. Inf.: AJ Seminars, 11205 Farmland Drive, Rockville, MD 20852.

FEB. 1–3—*Winter Education Conference '85.* Franklin Plaza Hotel, Philadelphia. Inf.: Ellen Gerber, SLA, 235 Park Ave. S., New York, NY 10003.

FEB. 1–3—*Marketing and Public Relations,* institute. Philadelphia. Inf.: (see above for address.)

FEB. 8—*Effective Communication: Meetings and Group Dynamics,* workshop. Univ. of Michigan, Ann Arbor. Cosponsors: Univ. of Michigan SLS, Michigan LA Academic and Research Libraries Division. Inf.: Univ. of Michigan SLS, 580 Union Drive, Ann Arbor, MI 48109-1346.

FEB. 8—*The World of Rare Books,* workshop. Drexel Univ., Philadelphia. Inf.: Janet Goldwater, Office of Continuing Professional Education, Drexel Univ., Philadelphia, PA 19104.

FEB. 8–14—*Art Libraries Society of North America,* annual conference. Hyatt Regency, Los Angeles. Theme: "L.A.: Metaphor For the Future." Inf.: Pamela Jeffcott Parry, ARLIS/NA 3775 Bear Creek Circle, Tuscon, AZ 85749.

FEB. 15—*On-Line Literature Searching,* workshop. Drexel Univ., Philadelphia. Inf.: (see Feb. 8 for address.)

FEB. 18—*1985 Congress For Librarians.* St. John's Univ., New York. Theme: "Downloading/Uploading Online Databases and Catalogs." Sponsor: Division of Library and Information Science, St. John's Univ. Inf.: James Benson, St. John's Univ. DLIS, Jamaica, NY 11439.

FEB. 21—*U.S. Government Publications and Services,* seminar. Hotel Bellevue, San Francisco. Inf.: (see Jan. 29 for address.)

FEB. 22—*Library Automation: A Seminar On the State-of-the-Art,* workshop. Drexel Univ., Philadelphia. Inf.: (see Feb. 8 for address).

FEB. 26—*Introduction To Basic Cataloging,* seminar. Norris Medical Library, Los Angeles. Inf.: (see Jan. 29 for address.)

FEB. 27—*Information Sources in Science and Technology,* seminar. George Washington Univ., Washington, D.C. Inf.: (see Jan. 29 for address.)

FEB. 28–MAR. 1—*Management of the Online Catalog,* institute. California State Library, Sacramento. Inf.: Roger Parent, American Library Association, 50 E. Huron St., Chicago, IL 60611.

MAR. 4–5—*Univ. of North Carolina Librarians' Association,* spring conference. Univ. of North Carolina, Chapel Hill. Theme: "Preservation in the '80s." Inf.: Libby Chenault, Rare Book Collection, Wilson Library 024–A, Univ. of North Carolina, Chapel Hill, NC 27514.

MAR. 4–6—*Management Skills,* institute. San Francisco. Inf.: (see Feb. 1 for address.)

MAR. 4–6—*National Federation of Abstracting and Information Services,* annual conference. Crystal Gateway Marriott Hotel, Arlington, Va. Theme: "New Developments in Electronic Publishing and Information Services." Inf: NFAIS, 112 South Sixteenth Street, Suite 1207, Philadelphia, PA 19102.

MAR. 5–9—*Music LA,* annual conference. Seelbach Hotel, Louisville, Ky. Inf.: Marion Korda, Dwight Anderson Music Library, School of Music, Univ. of Louisville, 2301 South Third St., Louisville, KY 40292.

MAR. 6–8—*Libraries, Books and Culture,* seminar. Univ. of North Carolina, Chapel Hill. Cosponsors: Univ. of Texas GSLIS and Univ. of North Carolina SLS. Inf.: Dr. Davis, GSLIS, Univ. of Texas at Austin, Education Building 564, Austin, TX 78712–1276.

MAR. 8—*Midstream Career Changes For Librarians and Other Information Professionals,* workshop. Drexel Univ., Philadelphia. Inf.: (see Feb. 8 for address.)

MAR. 8–10—*Materials and Machines,* institute. San Francisco. Inf.: (see Feb. 1 for address.)

MAR. 10–13—*Alaska LA,* state conference. Centennial Hall, Juneau. Theme: "Libraries: the Link That Strengthens the Community." Inf.: Barbara Pavitt, Alaska State Library, Pouch G, Juneau, AK 99811.

MAR. 15–16—*Hawaii LA,* spring conference. Honolulu. Inf.: Kimberly Nakano, Univ. of Hawaii at Manoa, Hamilton Library, Room 104B, 2550 The Mall, Honolulu, HI 96822. ▣

American Library Association Annual conference
July 6–11. Chicago

Canadian Library Association Annual conference
June 13–18. Calgary (Alberta)

Medical Library Association Annual conference
May 24–30. New York

Public Library Association National conference
April 2–5, 1986. St. Louis

Special Libraries Association Annual conference
June 8–13. Winnipeg (Manitoba)

Enlarging Micros: The Mainframe Connection

Nancy Melin

Librarians have become quite accustomed to routine online access to mainframe databases, even those that may be thousands of miles away. For the past fifteen years they have worked at inhouse terminals, connected via modems or dedicated telephone lines, with access to the bibliographic databases of OCLC, RLIN, Dialog, BRS, or local computer facilities.

Nancy Melin *is editor of* Library Software Review, Small Computers in Libraries, *and* M300 and PC REPORT.

The advent of the microcomputer offers many new possibilites for connecting libraries to mainframe databases that can significantly simplify and enhance a variety of library activities.

Mainframe computers, both inhouse and offsite, offer many well-known advantages. One is, of course, a database of unlimited size capable of accommodating millions of records including data that may be needed in the future. Mainframe processing power—especially for number crunching and for calculating highly complicated spreadsheets—is another advantage. It has still not yet achieved its greatest potential. And the use of the mainframe to process electronic mail, including inhouse applications as well as the ability to transmit documents and information across the oceans, is becoming commonplace through such methods as EDUCOM's MailNet. It connects the University of Southern California to the University of Stockholm via a computer at MIT.

Power and size are not everything, however. The microcomputer offers certain benefits and meets certain needs that mainframes and minicomputers can't even approach. Unlike the larger machines, microcomputers may be kept on a desktop and require little environmental accommodation. And they are relatively inexpensive. Capability, in terms of speed and added function, is very extensive even in a stand-alone situation. Micros are especially suited to perform a number of repetitive and frequently boring tasks—recording and analyzing statistics, for example—and can thus free workers for other project-planning activities. Finally, unlike larger hardware, even the biggest micros may be considered portable. They can be regularly and frequently moved to any location needed.

To date, most librarians have had less experience with microcomputers than they have had with mainframes. The decision by OCLC, WLN, UTLAS, and others, to provide microcomputers as database terminals or workstations will result in their integration in all aspects of library activity both for staff and for patron use. Why have these agencies selected microcomputers instead of dumb terminals? How can their use benefit librarians?

Over the past few years, especially with the popularization of Apple and IBM computers for home and office use, the availability of software has mushroomed. This is especially true for such "business" activities as word processing and spreadsheet analysis. In fact, there is so much available now—much of it even more sophisticated than the microcomputers on which it is programmed to run—that software selection tools have become a separate selection problem themselves.

The use of a microcomputer to serve as both a library processing tool as well as a terminal for remote access to databases offers special advantages. These benefits range from the mundane to the sophisticated. For instance, the use of a single device to serve two different purposes saves space. It follows that purchase of a single device rather than two separate ones is cost-effective. A microcomputer that is used as a 'terminal' is also cost-effective because only a single set of cables and other associated hardware—such as a printer—need be purchased.

Microcomputers make it possible to selectively download information stored on a mainframe computer and to reformat it as needed. With the availability of new online search software, complex user interfaces can be simplified and extensive offline preparation of database searches is possible. Both offer substantial savings in terms of telecommunications and training costs. Microcomputers are also operationally efficient. A single terminal, capable of performing several different activities, may be used continuously instead of sitting idle when a particular activity is complete as happens with a dedicated dumb terminal. The use of a microcomputer for data processing also promotes information security. Information may be retained on floppy or hard disks with selective access.

In spite of the recital of advantages of both the micro and the mainframe, the advantages of each are again their weaknesses. The mainframe is expensive and complicated. It requires tight security and an air-conditioned environment. MIS professionals must be employed to keep it running. The microcomputer offers only a small database and requires substantial time for data entry. In combination with one another, through a micro-to-mainframe link, librarians may have the best of both worlds.

Technical considerations for the link

Technically speaking, what is the micro-to-mainframe link? Currently, microcomputer-to-mainframe connections consist of simple terminal emulation. This means that the microcomputer adopts the characteristics of a specified terminal so that it can execute mainframe computer programs. To accomplish this, special hardware, software, and system requirements must be met. Products necessary for this work range in price and complexity from the simple and inexpensive to the sophisticated and costly.

One of the simplest may be IBM's asynchronous communications package. With it, the micro "pretends" that it is a dumb (nonprogrammable) generic mainframe terminal. The software costs less than $100. But, as with most everything, you get what you pay for in the form of less sophistication for this type of communications link. The micro is limited to very basic operations. Users are able to do little more than type simple single letter commands.

An example of second-level communications effort is the emulation circuit board. Digital Communications Associates' Irma board is one standard product. An emulation board allows the micro to send data, in the form of statistics or text, to the mainframe and to receive processed information back. Communication is accomplished through a network of coaxial cables. Therefore its use is limited to environments where the micro-to-mainframe link is on site. Circuit cards of this type cost between one and two thousand dollars. The additional cost of stringing cable may bring costs up several times more. Another example of a communications link that can be accomplished via a terminal emulation approach involves the use of telephone lines to transmit and receive data. In this configuration, using a modem along with a software communications package, the microcomputer can also be made to act like the mainframe.

A third possible linkage option involves the use of specially written software both for the microcomputer and for the mainframe. This is desirable when the micro is required to perform such tasks as error-checking for unwanted data and remote or automatic uploading and downloading of information, as is accomplished through the OCLC *Micro Enhancer* software programs.

The categories of micro-to-mainframe links available today may be characterized in four ways:

- *Terminal connections in which the PC emulates a dumb terminal*

Modems and communications boards are required. Many vendors supply these and refer to their equipment as PC-to-mainframe links. Advantages are that the PC can make a physical connection to the mainframe and data can be viewed. The limitations are that the PC is essentially a "dumb" terminal; that the PC can only view the data with no possibility for downloading or uploading; PC capabilities are not available during emulation.

- *Simple data transfer in which mainframe files are transferred in bulk to the PC.*

The advantage is that data from the mainframe computer is available for PC users. There are four limitations: customized programming is required for the mainframe; customized programming is required for the PC; there is no data selectivity because entire files must be transferred; and processing is often slow and inefficient.

- *Selective data access category.*

Data is extracted from files, transferred to the PC and reformatted to popular PC software. The advantages are several: only the needed information is downloaded; information is made usable by existing PC software; PC data may be uploaded to the mainframe; and no programming is required. The limitations are that there is no communication with other PCs; access is typically limited to only one file at a time; and processing is often slow and inefficient.

- *Nongeneric links.*

Primary access is to vendor's programs and data files. The signal advantage is that the PC has access to information from specific applications or databases. The disadvantages are that in most instances the vendor's application programs must be purchased and that it is often dificult to access other applications and databases.

How librarians can use the link

Typically micro-to-mainframe users are organizations with installations in several different locations. For librarians installations may be understood to mean remote databases for either searching or processing activities—Dialog or OCLC, for example. Several library specialist suppliers have developed new commmunications products for this market.

Data Phase has announced its new ALIS networking program for use in linking incompatible library systems for resource-sharing. Phase I involves such breakthroughs as the availability of Data General and Tandem computers to interface. More important to us here, however, is the promised integration of microcomputers into their system. Now micros may be used to access Data General and Tandem systems and will be part of a new Data Share Network provided via UNINET. The system is intended to access library information directly into businesses, homes, and educational institutions.

Faxon's LINX NETWORK services are also available for access via microcomputers including OCLC's M300 Workstation. Since the M300s are hardwired via dedicated telephone lines, potential microcomputer users of the LINX network will need to purchase a modem as well as communications software. WILSONLINE, the H. W. Wilson Company's database system, can also be accessed via micro-to-mainframe connection. With these possibilities and with add-on equipment, there are several economic and operational advantages to microcomputer-to-mainframe links. If the M300 is not connected to OCLC for library cataloging, interlibrary loan, acquisitions, or serials work, or to WILSONLINE for periodical or book indexes, it may be accessing Faxon's LINX Network for serials information. Or it may simply be employed in word-processing, statisics-processing, or spreadsheet analysis in its role as a microcomputer.

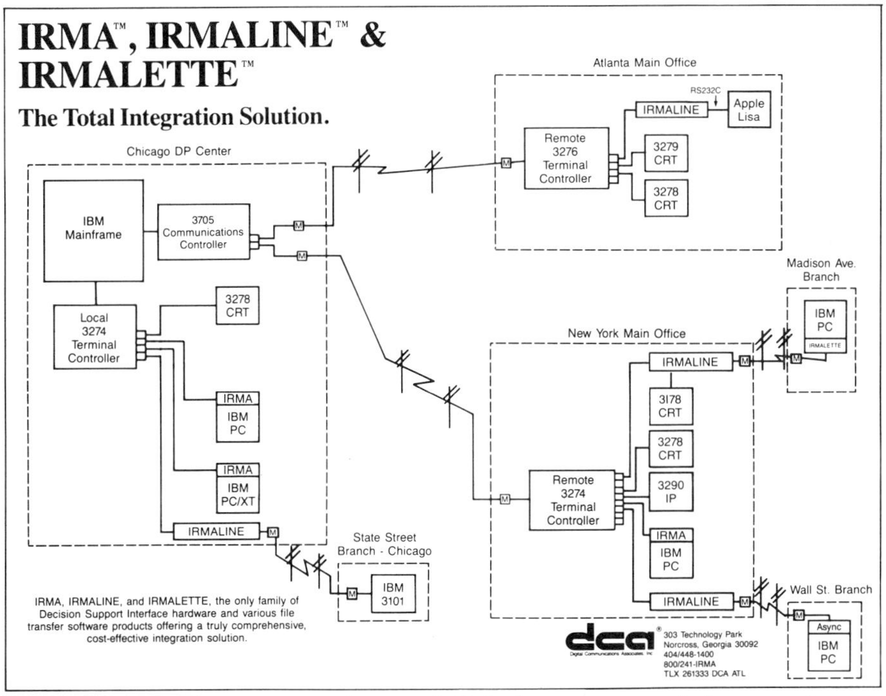

This schematic shows connections and links between a mainframe and microcomputers using IRMA products from DCA. Connections may be made within buildings or across the country.

Availability of software

Software designed to assist in the micro-to-mainframe connection is becoming easily available. Such software employs the processing power of the PC to mediate between researcher and the mainframe database. It offers a simpler user interface for novices and a more powerful searching tool for experts. Such software is available in two types. The first is composed of programs that are "loosely coupled" to a specific mainframe database. These programs are an extension of intelligent communications software programs and generally permit automatic log-on, query, and downloading from a host mainframe computer. The second category includes software that has been "tightly coupled" to one or more particular databases. By tailoring programs for interaction with a host computer, software designers are able to create user interfaces that require little user knowledge of either micro-to-mainframe communications or the formal database query process.

Earlier this year Informatics General Corporation announced its PC/Net-Link. Specially designed microcomputer software provides a subject catalog of online databases from all retrieval services and automatically logs on to any one for which a password is available. Menlo Corporation's InSearch is a similar service. This type of software has two significant advantages. It increases communication speed by tightening up the connection between the micro and the mainframe. It also allows for post-processing work. SciMate from ISI, for example, offers automatic log-on and query and includes a local database manager to store downloaded information and to manipulate it.

Another kind of software for use in the micro-to-mainframe link allows downloading from a mainframe into a specific microcomputer program. This will be especially valuable for local micro-to-mainframe access where information stored on the mainframe—statistics, financial data, and text, for example—is to be used at the desktop level.

Informatics recently announced a combination of new products which make it possible to both download and upload Lotus 1-2-3 and dBASE II files between micros and mainframes. The program names are Lotus/Answer and Visi/Answer on the PC and Answer/DBM on the mainframe. Even more timely is Cullinet's new Information Database package for its GOLDENGATE software, to be used in micro-to-mainframe links. It includes a relation database manager, a spreadsheet, a graphics system, a word processor, and a communications tool. It is hailed as the "missing link" for true communications between a micro and a corporate mainframe.

At Reed College, software has been developed which enables a Macintosh computer to link with a mainframe to offer a complete graphics/text package. Acting as dumb terminal, the Macintosh is logged on to a mainframe and instructed to display a computer graphic designed by the mainframe program. Then, using the graphics capability of the Macintosh, the figure may be redrawn, enhanced, and inserted into a text file.

PC-PLOT-III allows the IBM PC to emulate eight different terminal configurations. This means that a user can work on a mainframe graphics program and then switch over to a full-screen editing software on the mainframe. PC-PLOT can be used on a small system, and costs $95. It requires only 96K RAM and a single disk drive and runs either via a modem or in a hardwired configuration.

The future is a bright one for micro-to-mainframe connections. Industry specialists and computer users agree that future communications will offer much greater capabilities with easier use. They predict that mainframe manufacturers will include the PC in mainframe architecture and simplify many current communication problems. ▣

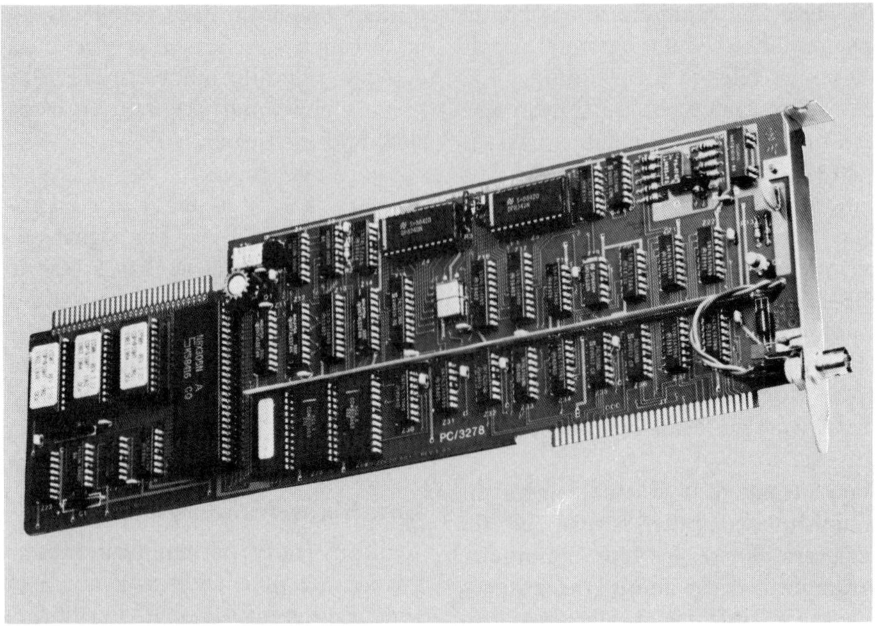

IRMA from Digital Communications Associates is a representative circuit board that fits into any available slot in an IBM PC. It comes with a software package containing a 3278 terminal emulator and two file transfer facilities.

Planning for the micro-to-mainframe connection

As librarians undertake micro-to-mainframe links, they must engage in systematic planning. The planning team should be representative of all users as well as administrative staff. Some questions that must be answered include:

- What mainframes must be accessed to include current and future applications?
- Will any of the user's microcomputer applications need to be uploaded to the mainframe?
- Will modems and cables need to be purchased?
- Will the micro-to-mainframe connection help eliminate terminals?
- Will more microcomputers have to be purchased?
- Will additional space be needed?
- Will a centralized microcomputer center be developed?
- Are the current information processing facilities large enough to handle current and anticipated hardware needs?

Managing Research Libraries: An Interview with David Weber

Russell Fischer

David Weber's library career stretches over thirty-five years and includes positions at two of America's most prestigious universities, Harvard and Stanford. Before embarking on a library career, Weber earned a bachelor's degree in history from Colby College in 1947, and a year later he received a library degree from Columbia University. He also holds a master's degree in history, which he earned at Harvard in 1953.

Weber began his library career in 1948 as a cataloger at Harvard University. In 1950, he became assistant to Harvard library director Keyes Metcalf, and a few years later Weber assumed the position of assistant director of university libraries at Harvard. Moving to Stanford University libraries in 1961 as an assistant director, Weber rose to the position of associate director, and then in 1969, he was appointed director of university libraries.

At Stanford, Weber oversees a library system with an operating budget of nearly $14 million, collections of over 2.7 million volumes, and a staff of 379 people. Under Weber's direction, Stanford University libraries have built and refurbished several library buildings on campus, shown a marked growth in the size and quality of the collections, become leaders in library automation, and assumed an important role in both local and national library networks.

Russell Fischer *is director of library services, San Jose City College, California.*

The following interview took place in Weber's Stanford office last May.

What do you regard as the director's main function in a large research library?

Guiding the organization as a whole in terms of its long-range goals and establishing standards for achievement, those are what one might put under the heading of nurturing an organization. I think those are key. The facilitating of the goals and objectives that are set out by individual departments or by my colleagues as directors, that is also very important. In addition, assisting with public relations or university relations, relations with faculty, with students, with university administrators where the library director can play a minor role. And finally, although not last I'm sure, is fund raising and assistance with donor relations and the development of friends and supporters for a university research library.

Ideas and the new areas to be pursued can come from anyone—from faculty members, university officers, and library staff at all levels. But a director can, by finding ways in which those ideas can be supported and encouraged, fit them into a coherent program that assists with the pursuit of long-term goals and objectives of the library organization, objectives that the faculty and university administration will support. That is a way of facilitating the organization toward achieving those goals and that can be very satisfying. You have not a personal pride in having achieved anything, but it's a vicarious pleasure in helping your colleagues and seeing the organization rise to greater achievement over time.

One may be frustrated in what one can achieve in one or two years because you never can do half of what you set out to do. You need to recognize that over time, if you look over five years or ten years, a tremendous amount can be achieved, and the distance that any academic institution can come is quite significant. The Stanford library, over my time here, is very fortunate to have had dramatic change in its collection, the staff, in becoming one of the leaders, I believe, among research libraries of the country. I don't believe that any of the people who were here in 1961, when I first came to Stanford, would have claimed that for Stanford then.

What are the principal problems in managing a large research library?

Maintaining an effective closeness to faculty and university officers is, if not a principal problem , a principal need. One must be able to understand and respond to faculty expectations, to understand enough of what the provost, the vice-presidents, and deans need and what they're trying to do. If the university officers are moving toward a somewhat greater degree of centralization or decentralization, or more emphasis on academic computing, or stronger efforts at being good neighbors with other institutions, then the library must be aware of those goals.

The library plays a support role for the faculty and for the university, and therefore must be in tune with what university officers believe. The library contributes to the university and can share in achieving some of its accomplishments.

Also, nurturing staff, developing staff sharing in a modest way in hiring the academic staff of the library—nothing can be more important. I think there is also a problem in juggling all of the issues that exist on one's desk day after day—the financial aspects, balancing personal and institutional needs, and determining what is in the best interests both of the individuals and of the institution. Maybe one would do well to go into circus work when one retires!

How do you succeed in balancing all of those issues and challenges?

With difficulty. [Laughs.]

Well, historically I would say that my mother and father's perspective on education and my upbringing have contributed; so that I'm keenly interested in scholarship, in education, in students, in publishing, and in the book arts. If one has interests from one's childhood of that range, one's hardly narrow. Secondly, I think the challenge of Stanford and the lively faculty members and the very bright students and the remarkably fine administrators to work with, encourage one to perform at a high level. There's a good deal of emphasis here on teamwork. The other point I would make is that if you have a fine and talented staff, that also can help to cope with all of the issues.

One of the significant changes in libraries during my thirty-five-year career has been the growth in business complexity. I'm reminded that when I became director of libraries in 1969, we had none of the offices that I will mention, which shows the change, but it also shows the kind of specialists that I can turn to to help with the management of a large research library: a financial officer with an MBA, a building projects manager with an architecture degree, a personnel officer and a sizeable personnel office, a fund-raising officer or a "development" officer as we call it, a community relations officer or team if you will, a systems office, a publications office, a graphics office, and a security office.

Furthermore, to get to the academic side, we had no subject curators until about 1963. Now there are over thirty curators or bibliographers who handle almost all the collection development work.

So I don't have to do much around here. [Laughs.] I can turn to people with expertise in many different areas. With a remarkable group of people of this sort, you're more like an orchestra leader where you may say, "Well what piece shall we play today?" As long as they're all playing in harmony everything goes well, and the audience—the faculty and students—is very pleased.

There are currently a lot of changes and new developments occurring in education and in the library world. What do you read to keep up with current issues and new developments?

A very few journals in higher education but certainly the *Chronicle of Higher Education* would be among them. There's a new journal called *California Higher Education*, and I've found occasional interesting articles there, particularly as it covers publicly supported higher education. It's important to us all that the state of California provides stronger support for community colleges, the state university system, and the University of California, because if there are weaknesses in one segment of higher education other segments suffer too. We benefit by having strengths in all segments and a healthy competition.

In the past fifteen years, I probably have read more heavily about higher education, in general, than many librarians do. To my mind that is very stimulating because that is the milieu in which we work; and we are enriched as a profession, and we succeed as a profession only as we understand that larger dimension.

Are there any books that you have read and reread throughout your career or any things that you continually go back to?

I very seldom read anything twice and that isn't because I have a good memory. It's because I hope to distill out of it some thoughts that will stimulate and contribute to putting one and one together and getting three, something new, something to be pursued. But there are so many stimulating things to read that one can go on in several lifetimes and not get all of the pleasure or all of the new ideas that would benefit.

I find considerable satisfaction delving back from time to time in history and reading the 1876 survey of libraries entitled *Public Libraries in the United States* done by the federal government with chapters written by thirty or forty librarians, from different types of libraries, who were leaders at the time. It's interesting how the same problems that we may face today have their antecedents—personnel, buildings, collections, cooperation. There's a lot one can learn from reading some of our forebears in library work from fifty, eighty, one hundred years ago. They were very wise with what resources they had.

How well do you think library schools are preparing librarians for careers in large academic libraries?

They must be doing a fair job because we continue to employ bright and talented librarians who received their graduate degrees two, four, six years ago. So it certainly is not going steadily downhill. But at the same time, just as there was considerable criticism of the library school curriculum and faculty in 1947–1948 when I went to school, and I attended what was then regarded as one of the best library schools, there is widespread belief today that the schools are doing an inadequate job in preparing people for academic libraries and particularly for research libraries.

There's good reason for that. The number of people who go into the profession is relatively small; and, given that there are over fifty accredited library schools in the country, it is impossible to have a large enough faculty to cover, in depth, all of the qualities that one would like to have in those coming out into the field. So given the market that exists, there are real problems in having strong faculties for research libraries where we're talking about the smallest part of the market. Public libraries, school libraries, governmental libraries, must be much larger aspects of the library market than the kind of research university that I share some responsibility for. So it is incumbent upon us to seek from anywhere in the country, and indeed abroad, men and women who have the mental ability to be creative and to grow. It's imperative they have good undergraduate preparation, and hopefully, they have pretty good preparation in librarianship.

Stanford is not one of the institutions that requires a graduate library degree for appointment to our academic staff. We list positions requiring "the MLS or equivalent," and some of our very able librarians have the equivalent. If an individual has a real strength in a subject field and has a certain basic knowledge of bibliography and what libraries are and how they serve institutions, and if an individual is stronger than those with a graduate library degree, we will choose the one that has the strength and not merely the degree. I realize that we're in a minority on that, but I think that we may have a stronger staff holding to those high standards.

Fortunately, the Association of Research Libraries and the Council on Library Resources are giving a good deal of effort to urging improved curricula for research librarianship. And there are programs at places like Michigan, UCLA, Chicago, and North Carolina that hold some promise of providing entry-level improved training and mid-career advanced training for research libraries. This kind of extra effort is to be encouraged and I think will hold out some good promise for maintaining the flow of highly qualified people into the field.

David Weber

What are library schools not doing that they should be doing to prepare librarians for careers in research libraries?

The areas where we at Stanford feel a particular need (and areas where I understand we are not alone, on the basis of what other ARL libraries have said about graduate library education) would lead me to cite several matters. New librarians need a broader understanding of the academic environment and of the teaching and research that go on in a research university. It is incumbent upon those who go through library school and go into research librarianship to have that grounding.

Another area would be managerial skills even recognizing that different libraries will vary. There needs to be a good sense of managerial methodologies and options, techniques that can be applied. I think that within the latter group, I would single out interpersonal skills and supervisory skills as being a particular need. We all too often, I think, obtain people who of necessity are expert in the bibliography of a certain language or field or who are technically skilled in computer science or whatever. But at the time they have supervisory responsibilities added, their backgrounds are frequently inadequate. I think that was so with myself and with a great many individuals throughout the profession.

The demands of a large and complex library and the need to work with staff in setting goals, setting common objectives to be pursued, and to understand how all of the parts fit together requires a major team effort. Furthermore, to help individuals with their careers puts a major burden on those with supervisory responsibilities to guide, to counsel, and to help those they supervise. So it's important that librarians have good interpersonal skills.

I know there are some in the field who would add to my list particular knowledge such as operations research or financial analysis, but to my mind they're not as critical as those skills I have singled out. In a very large university library, one can hire people who possess special skills. I'm not at all sure that the majority of librarians need those special skills at the time they are coming out of graduate school.

In a recent issue of American Libraries *[January 1983], Patricia Battin wrote that many librarians do not have a strong intellectual commitment to librarianship and that many young librarians cannot articulate their professional career goals. Would you agree with those observations?*

I have high admiration for Pat Battin, who I believe is a very distinguished librarian. But I don't think that my own conversations with people in the profession, and specifically those here at Stanford, would support her observations. Speaking of my colleagues and acquaintances who are librarians, I would say that there is an enthusiasm for librarianship on the part of the vast majority; and there is an intellectual commitment, if by that is meant that they read in the field, enjoy contributing to the profession, and are enthusiastic practitioners in their work.

If a strong intellectual commitment means pursuing an extremely earnest, thoughtful, and academic approach to librarianship, and striving to find a philosophy of it, indeed, there probably are a small number who are so committed or who are groping at the outer reaches of their own capacities. There are certainly at Stanford, among those librarians that I work with, a good number—I think it would be at least half—who are very active in their profession outside of their work. That's one measure of strong intellectual commitment. I believe that one third of our academic staff play some part in professional associations. There are a smaller number who publish, but that seems to be growing, and they've made good contributions to the profession.

In terms of encountering young librarians who cannot articulate their personal career goals, I've not had that experience. Although they may not know, anymore than I did when I started, what their ultimate goals are (I did know that I was interested in academic libraries, in scholarly publications, and in the bibliographic organization of materials), I think today one would find at least that much articulation among young librarians. They're very dedicated, highly motivated, professional people, and I'm sure they can articulate at least their near-term goals. Obviously, if one tries to look ahead five, ten, or twenty years, it becomes highly speculative. It doesn't surprise me at all that people can't say what they'd like to be doing in twenty years.

A couple of political and social changes during your career have been affirmative action and the emergence of the women's liberation movement. What has been their impact on the library profession?

Certainly, affirmative action and equal employment opportunities have been important federal policies which, in the past twelve to fourteen years, have urged improved personnel practices in higher education. In turn, not only the universities but the libraries have responded to that change; and a major consequence, because of federal requirements, has been the establishment of the library personnel office which did not exist in the 1960s. It was about 1972 that we created the library personnel office at Stanford, and that has grown to be an extremely important and valuable part of our organization. We're not alone in that. Yale, Columbia, Harvard, Michigan, UCLA, Berkeley,—I suppose all of the larger libraries have one or more people who perform that function within the library, not merely relying upon a university personnel office.

You also mentioned women's liberation; I guess I don't see that as having any specific impact. Libraries have always benefited by having women librarians, women managers, and certainly during my time at Stanford there's been as much diversity of ethnic background as there was when I came here. We currently have two department chiefs who are outstanding black women librarians, and one of my four associate directors of libraries is an extremely able woman librarian.

Perhaps the most striking change however in this area of personnel has been the improved codification of policy and practice. Even there, Stanford libraries in 1961 had a good operating personnel manual for library staff. It had a manual before any other part of the university did. We now have a whole section in our policy and procedure manual that covers a wide variety of personnel matters, and in fact, many of our departmental policies and procedures also deal with personnel matters. All of these supplement the university's policies on personnel management. That codification, of course, was encouraged by affirmative action.

During the past ten years, many academic institutions and libraries have experienced diminishing financial support. In terms of collection development and new buildings, Stanford appears to have avoided that situation. Would you explain why?

If there is a simple answer, it probably is that the majority of faculty and the principal academic officers have felt that the library must be maintained even in relatively austere times. Some of the faculty who were here back as far as the fifties and even the early sixties would be aware of the large gaps in the collection and how far the library has come, with faculty help, in trying to fill those gaps. The faculty and academic officers were aware that one couldn't turn the spigot on and off in a library because when it's turned off someday you're going to have to pay for those materials; and you may pay much more dearly than you otherwise would.

To maintain a good, strong, steady collection development program, without it hurting other parts of the university, has certainly been a very deliberate intent, at Stanford, over the years. There has been between the library and the provost an understanding which dates back fifteen years that we would maintain our collection development effort and not increase it or decrease it. If you can picture all of the world's publications as being in a pie and the portion that we get being six or seven percent of the new publications, we want to maintain a budget that will enable us to maintain the same size slice of the pie each year; and I think we've done so.

In terms of buildings for housing the collections, with only a couple of exceptions, every one of the libraries has been rehoused in the past twenty years. The Cubberly Education Library and the Lane Medical Library are the only two that have not been rehoused, but even there improvements and changes have been made. That kind of library building really is very difficult financially for any university or college. Our hope is that there will be much less building of new facilities in the remainder of the century. We plan to use some kind of auxiliary storage for growth over the next twenty years; so that we won't have to add to every library when it grows out of space.

There have been studies of collection use that indicate many books and periodicals in large academic libraries are rarely or never used. Have these studies had any impact on the collection development practices at Stanford?

To answer your question in a word, I would say no. They have not affected our collection development. Paul Mosher, my colleague, has spent much more time than I thinking about and discussing the Pittsburgh study and Trueswell's studies. To my mind, there is a degree of validity in those studies. Obviously there is a statistical base for them. But it is not the be-all and end-all. Although they can be a guide and provide input into decisions that can be made—whether one is collecting enough in a field, whether one has enough copies of an item, whether one can withdraw items from the collection and put them in an auxiliary or storage facility—it is only part of the input.

The study by Simon and Fussler at Chicago showed that there may be four or five times as much use of the collections as recorded circulation shows, and in some fields there will not be a perfect correspondence with those recorded circulations. Those items that are used briefly in-house obviously will not have the circulation record that items like reserve books will have.

Fortunately, our faculty, even though there is a heavy quantitative basis to much of their studies, rely on us for sound judgement as to what should be in the collection, and we in turn are very fortunate in having three things that make up the ingredients of a good collection development program. One is an adequate book budget, so that we're not always falling short of what faculty need. Second is an outstanding group of subject specialists. And third is an understanding university administration and an understanding faculty. Those elements feed back to each other. If you have one and two, you may have three as well. And we're fortunate at Stanford in having all three; so that the environment in which the collections are built does not force us into some of the hard statistical decisions that may, in fact, be appropriate at other institutions. I'm just glad that I don't work under those circumstances.

In your opinion, what are the most significant issues now facing research libraries?

Recruiting our future leaders is number one, and that means assisting with recruitment into library schools and helping young people get their beginning jobs. That is very dificult given the tight job market now. If we don't have good quality education in graduate library schools, and if we do not help people in their early years as librarians, we will have extreme difficulties in the future.

Second would be financing research libraries, and there certainly is need for more initiative on the part of librarians in finding diverse sources of income. Not just reliance on tuition and endowment, but also developing gifts and finding foundation or other university sources that will provide more financial support.

A third significant issue is of course further development of automation or information technology. I believe we're only halfway now to the whole growth in the application of computers in benefit of academic libraries. So there's a long way yet to go in that area.

A fourth would be the formidable task of conserving or preserving our research collections—not all of them, but those collections that must be retained for future students and scholars. That is an extremely large task, technically difficult, and it's very formidable in cost.

A final issue I would mention is to find the right areas in which we can rely on collaborative efforts or partnerships or networks, partnerships like the Research Libraries Group which I believe to be essential in the support of research libraries.

I think that further development in support of shared programs and the costs of them is a major need of research institutions.

What would your advice be to someone who aspires to become the director of a large research library?

The important recommendation, I believe, is to enjoy your work—to find a position that is rewarding and stimulating. Don't worry about where you'll end up. One spends so many hours of one's life working that you really ought to relish it. If your job excites you, you will develop in the profession because your excitement will carry you into studying, knowing the people, and contributing back to the profession. And in turn, you will have responsibility or committee work thrust upon you, whether you want it or not.

If you have extra capacity, then the man or woman you work for will ask you to undertake an extra project, to write up a proposal, to help with something. And in turn, the chances to advance will come. It may be wrong for a person to set a goal of being this or that. It isn't surprising that the possibility of advancement may go through one's mind. But I've not been one to set my goals and say that I shall strive to attain a particular rank or position, but merely to strive to be the best librarian I can, to be the best colleague, to enjoy the work, to have some fun of it. It's a lot of work, and one ought to enjoy it.

One ought to be able to go home and share with one's husband or wife some of the pleasures of the day. Sure you're going to share some of the frustrations, some of the errors you made, some of the situations you wish could have worked out better. However, day in and day out, year in and year out, there ought to be a lot of pleasure in your work. To my mind, the constant change, the constant challenge, the constant developments make librarianship the most exciting career that I can think of. ▣

Ladies of the Club: An Arkansas Story

David Taylor

A river boat town's cultural anchor. The oldest library building in Arkansas, for many years it was painted a vibrant pink that, along with the mansard roof, was an attempt to lend a touch of the Mediterranean to the sleepy Delta town of Helena, Arkansas.

They may be backwoods cousins to the mighty stone edifices in Dallas or New York, and online is still a country mile down the road. But the Center for the Study of Rural Librarianship estimates that rural libraries account for eighty-two percent of all the libraries in America, and their stories speak a nation's history.

Born after the upheaval of the Civil War, nurtured by the optimism at the turn of the century, the town library in Helena, Arkansas, has been steadily shaped by the progressive legislation that bestowed free education and libraries upon America. It was added to the National Register of Historic Places in 1975, and now amid budget restrictions this small library like its country cousins tries hard to maintain basic services to a people spread far from city lights.

But the story of the library in Helena is really about southern ladies, not coy belles cooing over their beaux, but resourceful and determined women who moved here from the North and East after the Civil War and replanted the culture of literacy they brought with them. The ladies succeeded splendidly in this rural town of 11,000, founding what is now the oldest library association in Arkansas and constructing the first town library building in the state.

David Taylor *is assistant professor of English, Moravian College, Bethlehem, Pennsylvania.*

Helena on the Mississippi

First settled in the early 1800s, the Mississippi delta is that flat, leaf-shaped plain of dark alluvial soil that stretches from Memphis two hundred miles south to Vicksburg, Mississippi. In its heart sits Helena, the state's only seaport on the Mississippi River. As a key outlet for the delta's rich harvest of cotton, soybeans, and rice, Helena came of age during the heyday of the steamboat, when from behind the river levee could be heard the musical bells and whistles of the *Lovin' Kate* or *Jim Lee,* big wheelers that plied Mississippi waters from St. Louis to New Orleans.

It was as the quintessential riverboat town that Helena earned her reputation. Travelling thorugh Arkansas, British geologist G. W. Featherstonhaugh was warned of "a place on the Mississippi called Helena where 'counterfeiters, horsestealers, murders, and sich like' took shelter 'agin the law.'"

Another Arkansas traveller, Bernard DeVoto, wrote of "Helena and Natchez and all the waterside slums, the shanty boats with their drifting loafers; the boats of medicine shows, daguerreotypes, minstrel troupes, doctors, thugs, prophets, saloon keepers, whoremasters. . . . It was a cosmos."

Although obviously outnumbered, ladies and gentlemen were also part of these southern communities. Members of the frontier aristocracy, they lived the good life of an agrarian ideal based on chattel slavery and infused with a code of gentlemanly conduct, hospitality, and fierce allegiance to family and place. This was a time when true ladies said "cow frogs" because the word "bull" was too vulgar. The Civil War, far from destroying the essence of this unhurried and genteel life, intensified it. Even today the New South and Yankee industrialization are found only at the edges of Helena, a place where long ago is not so far away.

A burning desire

During the 1870s a group of the town's volunteer firemen, the Rescue Hook and Ladder Company, maintained in their game room a small subscription library of newspapers, magazines, and some of the "best books being published," according to their estimation. The library's growing popularity forced the men to move their collection, now numbering 533 well-circulated volumes, to a small frame building and to incorporate as the Helena Library Association in 1878. Their desire was modest: "To promote literature and encourage art and science with succession for 100 years." Unfortunately the library lasted only a few more years before interest burned out, but the splendid century dream of the Hook and Ladder Company was rescued by some clubwomen.

In 1888 the women of a literary group named the Pacaha Club, the Indian word for Helena, began working toward a permanent library. At a public meeting on February 29, the forty ladies in attendance chose their name, the Women's Library Association, and adopted a charter modelled after the Ladies' Library Association of Kalamazoo, Michigan. From then until this day the Pacaha Club has provided all but two of the library board's presidents and museum directors.

The Association's first president was Sally Alexander Sanders, a schoolteacher arrested during the Civil War for trying to smuggle boots to Confederate soldiers amassed on the outskirts of town for the Battle of Helena. Along with Gettysburg and Vicksburg the battle was one of three key losses for the South on July 4, 1863. Other member were the wives of the town's mayor, judge, and leading businessmen. "They had the time, money, and ambition," observed Mrs. Dale Kirkman, current president of the Helena Library Association and granddaughter of the WLA's second president. "For a library to stay in a place like Helena we had to have women like that."

The ladies wasted no time. They quickly put together a collection of 821 books—including those of the Hook and Ladder Company—secured one room in the Grand Opera House and on April 24, less than a month after their first meeting, opened for business above the vaudeville stage as a subscription library and free reading room. Within one month they had acquired a plot of land for a library building and bought forty shares of building and loan stock, paid in part by several husbands. A local architect began drawing plans.

Their premiere was an unqualified success. In her first annual report to the association the club secretary offered congratulations: "The women of Helena have certainly every reason for being proud of the first year's work of the Library Association. It was originated by women, has been controlled and directed by women, and has flourished wonderfully." She concluded, "Our efforts have provided the gentlemen with an occasion to help."

A misfortune that befell the men provided the capital needed to begin construction. When the fraternal lodges of the city were forced to give up their meeting rooms at the local school, the women made them an offer. The lodges could be the first renters of the proposed two-story library building if the men would back a town bond issue. They did, and by September of 1891 Arkansas's first town library building was completed at a cost of $6,000. Its French mansard roof and paired gable dormers stood out amidst the Greek revival and Victorian structures of the town's financial district, providing advertisement for a building owned by women and meant for the enrichment of the mind, not the pockets.

Now came the hard part. At first the actual library was relegated to a small room downstairs, with the second and third floor of the building rented in order to pay off the mortgage. It was only in 1914 that the main floor of the building was used for library purposes. During that twenty-three year period "Library Hall" became famous for the dances of the Young Men's Cotillion Club, bazaars, benefit concerts, and plays, even once serving as a skating rink—all put on by the WLA to raise money. By the turn of the century the library was functioning as Helena's country club, city club, and civic center all in one, a home for religious services, school classes, an art studio and all manner of social groups.

Something important had happened. Until now Helena's pride was mired in the past and her role in the

Dale Kirkman, museum director and president of the Helena library board, works in the Arkansas Room. The staircase in the background was the renters' private entrance when the upper stories were let to raise funds.

Civil War, its memories lingering like smoke after a cannon's shot. But the new library and the galvanizing spirit of the WLA sparked a new, progressive civic pride. The activity at the library became almost daily news in the paper and rivaled the weather as a topic for conversation, giving a focus to the efforts to give the town a cultural anchor. More than just a new building, this library was a turning point in the life of a notorious riverboat town.

Main room of the Phillips County Museum, one of the most important local museums in the state. Ensconced upon its walls are the portraits of the seven Confederate generals from Phillips County.

Margaret Ready: A future perfect for the past

Beginning in 1888 with the donation of a letter written by Revolutionary War hero Lafayette, many museum items were given to the library group. Meeting the growing need for a building to display them became the goal of the WLA's president in 1916, Margaret Ready, who led thirteen years of almost daily fund-raising similar to that used to finance the library. In 1929 the $21,000 museum wing was finished, helped greatly by matching funds donated by Ready, perhaps Helena Library's most important figure.

A charter member of the WLA, she served twenty-seven years as its president and carried the library into the twentieth century of modern librarianship. Under her stewardship it was the first in Arkansas to receive tax funding under a 1911 state law that allowed one-half mill of a tax levy for the support of libraries. With its share of Helena's general tax, the WLA could declare the library a free one in 1919 and itself the Helena Public Library Association. Margaret Ready and the "new" tax-supported library were tested during the Depression years, depending upon the slot machines in town to provide the library's share of the city's revenue.

In 1939, after years of hauling collections of books to the county's many rural schools without libraries, Margaret Ready and other library directors acquired the first funding for a Phillips County Library Board, headquartered in the Helena Library. Even today the trust fund she set up for the library figures prominently in its $104,000 budget, ten percent of which is gifts and bequests. And interest earned by the Ready trust was used in 1962 to build the Margaret R. Ready addition that houses the offices and stacks of the tri-county regional library, also located in the Helena Library building.

Ready's contributions were recognized shortly before her death with the dedication of a museum courtyard and sundial to this clubwoman who lighted the way for over a quarter of a century. In accepting she said, "I have had so much joy in library and museum work throughout the greater portion of my life that the time given to these two are like the hours this dial records—only the sunny ones."

Perhaps the museum was the greatest accomplishment for this tall, austere woman remembered as always wearing black. Dedicated as "a memorial without being so named to those who have lived and wrought in our midst," the Phillips County Museum is the first in the state devoted exclusively to local projects and the first added as an annex to a library. It tells the story of Helena through collections of Indian artifacts, Civil War relics, personal effects of the town's citizens, period costumes, and a wealth of archival material.

Nearing completion is one of museum director Dale Kirkman's current projects, a collection of 2,000 photographs of Helena that provide a montage of history sweeping over one small delta town blessed with women of vision and drive who preserved that record. As the century-old epigraph over the Confederate money display reads: "Representing nothing on God's earth now/And naught in waters beneath it/As a pledge of a nation that's dead and gone/Keep it dear friend, and show it."

Bread upon the waters

After several years of intense lobbying by the Helena Library Association and the town's newspapers, one mill of the Phillips County general tax was granted to the library in 1948, making possible a four-branch county library system of which Helena is the hub. The county library board provides staffing, books, and other library resources to the branches if the towns in which they are located provide a home.

In 1950 the first branch added was in the town of Marvell, which agreed to support a library built in 1924 by the Mother's Club, a literary group inspired by the Pacaha Club. The free but private library run for twenty-six years by the club sits on the elementary school playground and, in a unique symbiosis, serves as library for both the town and the school.

The next branch, added in neighboring West Helena, is also a woman's story. When Mrs. E. G. Nelson moved in 1916 from Illinois with her husband, the local manager of Chicago Paper and Mill, she was struck by the lack of a library in her new hometown. The one-room structure she persuaded her husband to donate served for sixty-three years as the town's library, replaced in 1979 by a brick structure next door.

But there is still life in Mrs. Nelson's library. "We just couldn't bear to tear it down," said Carolyn Cunningham, librarian here for twenty-three years. "Everybody in town grew up in that little place." So the quaint structure is now being restored as the West Helena Museum, modelled after the one in Helena.

A last branch was added in the small town of Elaine in 1974 when another group of women banded together as the Elaine Library Board and launched a community effort to renovate an abandoned cafe on the town's main street. The library that resulted was completely a product of volunteer labor and donated furniture, even the gaily painted mailbox that serves as a book drop.

In 1961 the library received an LSCA demonstration grant to form the Phillips and Lee County Regional Library, with neighboring Monroe County added under a similar grant in 1969. The major benefit of the system is bookmobile service to the tri-county area, a necessity in intensely rural southeastern Arkansas. With a collection of 24,000 volumes and a circulation of 16,000 in Phillips County alone, operation of the bookmobile garaged at Helena demands all of the annual $65,000 in state aid that has replaced the original grants.

"Its is money well spent," Betty Reynolds, bookmobile librarian for nineteen years, firmly believes. "This service means a great deal to the people around here. For many it's simply their only means of having books. Not everybody in this part of the country can come in to a library, you know." So she goes to them—the elderly for whom she selects books and delivers to their doors, the young children for whom the bookmobile is the school library in nearly forty locations.

In 1980 the library building underwent a $57,520 restoration made possible by the Arkansas Historic Preservation Program, matching funds from the Department of the Interior, and contributions by the people of Helena and Phillips County. Much-needed repairs were completed on the library's regal but leaky mansard roof and gutter system, the exterior was repainted from a vibrant pink to a more sedate rose, and the Arkansas Room, a repository for regional and state historical documents and a local center for genealogical studies, was remodeled.

The house that served for sixty-three years as West Helena's town library.

A century's troubled dream

Today, the first ladies of the club would be impressed by the new microcomputer with its modem for an OCLC link, and the plans to become part of the AMIGOS network of libraries that promises electronic mail and cataloging services. They would be encouraged by last year's increase in circulation from 35,000 to 46,000 and the LSCA grant spent on the adult nonfiction collection.

But there are financial problems that have forced the Helena Library to cut one staff position and have cut branch operation by one day each week. The success of a petition to the county court for an increase in the tax levy to support the library may determine whether services are cut back even more.

"We just cannot continue to operate on the budget we've been getting," says Laura Dietz, chairman of the Board of Trustes of the Phillips County Library System and of the Phillips-Lee-Monroe County Regional Library. "For the past eight years we have gradually eaten into the library's $100,000 reserve fund, which is now down to $20,000, just to meet basic operating expenses. And we haven't added any new programs. We've had to use reserves just to carry on, to do the things we have been doing for years."

The problem is one of budget stagnation rather than reduction. The library has received no increase in funding since the one mill county tax allotment in 1948. Arkansas's attorney general ruled that to have the millage increased, the issue must be placed before each county's voters. The library in Phillips County will be one of the first in the state to do so, and county library boards across Arkansas will be watching.

"We believe that the tax referendum has an excellent chance of being passed. We're counting on it," Dietz continued. "The city councils of town branches want the library to maintain what it has and to grow, which means increasing the book collection, expanding hours—especially in the evenings—and upgrading our reference collection."

When asked about options if the tax initiative did not pass, she concluded, "The Board of Trustees will just have to sit down and assess where we'll go. One thing's for sure—we can't continue with the kind of budget we've been getting."

Perhaps it's not to worry. After all, the Pacaha Club has met in the library on the first Tuesday of May every year since 1891. One doubts that that granddaughters and nieces of the original ladies of the club will let anything untoward happen. Tradition has a way of hanging on down here.

A postscript

Tradition barely hung on. The referendum to increase funding for the library by raising property taxes in Phillips County passed by only 136 votes in last November's balloting. The six-tenths of a mill increase will mean an additional $40,000 to $60,000 per year. That should keep the wolf from the ladies' door.

Mission Possible: AASL in Atlanta

Karen Lawrence

"Your mission, should you choose to accept it, is to coordinate a successful national conference—well-attended, with a variety of continuing education opportunities for school media specialists, with challenging keynote sessions, and with ample opportunity to view the latest products available from a broad range of publishers, suppliers, and library vendors." That charge, to Theresa Fredericka and her conference committee, did not "self-destruct" as it would in the popular TV series. The mission was not only possible, but was accomplished during "Challenge '84: Mission Possible," the third national conference of the American Association of School Librarians, held from Octobcr 31 to November 4 in Atlanta. With registration topping 3,200, the conference shattered attendance records. Attendees were challenged with a wider mission: to work toward the provision of excellence in education for all children in our country.

The conference opened with a series of educational tours of Atlanta-area media center facilities. Educational seminars and program sessions filled the four-day program, affording attendees the opportunity to learn about everything from running a successful puppet program to running computer programs. Sessions included a number of programs that emphasized personal development including interpersonal communication, self-image and professional image, accountability, management skills, career planning, and executive dress.

Lobbying and educational excellence

Thomas Hart, professor at Florida State University, presided at a spirited session that challenged school library professionals to become legislative activists. The Florida Association for Media in Education maintains an ongoing legislative program. They have established rapport with state legislators, who let the organization know about the major emphases of each new year's legislation. The organization has a network of fifteen regional representatives who can mobilize school librarians in their regions in support of important state legislation.

Mary Cunningham: *"Become more savvy . . . more adept at recognizing corporate games in which you are being used as a pawn."*

Hart introduced Mary Margaret Rogers, FAME association executive and lobbyist-activist. She underscored the importance of legislative programs in state media organizations, including an organized statewide network. "Support of key legislation is important," Rogers noted. Librarians should "take advantage of the leadership system and lobby appropriate leaders especially hard." She stressed that library activism also involves defensive issues—killing bad bills and keeping good legislation from repeal.

In a program about the recently released *Alliance for Excellence: Librarians Respond to "A Nation at Risk"*, a panel of educators and librarians responded to the recommendations and suggested means for their implementation. Paula Short, of Texas Women's University, applauded the recommendation that the curriculum be strengthened by teaching the use of library resources. The return-to-basics movement "implies passive learning, while this recommendation fosters independent, active learning." She implored librarians to exert their professional expertise in dialogue with other educators and administrators, and to strive to be curriculum-supportive.

Kenneth Neal of the Utah Office of Education stressed the need to be imaginative and creative with the report, noting that there is "nothing staggeringly new." He remarked that dissemination of the report is crucial. "We can talk to ourselves just so much. We must get the report to those involved in the decision-making process." Gainesville (Georgia) City School Superintendent Ed Cook was upbeat about *Alliance for Excellence,* but stressed the dual needs for wide dissemination and for standards of implementation.

Theme sessions

Two theme sessions were held during the Atlanta conference. Mary Cunningham, president and chief executive officer of Semper Venture Capital and author of *Powerplay: What Really Happened at Bendix,* spoke to a filled auditorium. In her opening remarks she stated that "information is power and those who control access to information are powerful." She noted that one of her early role models was an elementary school librarian who was powerful yet approachable, and remarked that "unless approachable, believable persons

---

Karen Lawrence *is assistant editor of the* Wilson Library Bulletin.

The AASL Idea Festival provided table exhibits that shared successful programming ideas.

such as yourselves are present in school libraries, the underprivileged would be shut out."

Cunningham discussed some of the impediments to realizing personal and professional potential, using examples from her experience at Bendix and subsequent personal doubt and conflict. She remarked that prejudice in the business and professional world have become more subtle. The laws are in effect and behavior is beginning to change, but attitudes have a long way to go regarding women and other minorities. She urged her listeners to sustain savvy, a combination of maturity and sensitivity, in order to build a constituency, and she emphasized that professionals should avoid slipping into a defensive posture.

Dorothy Blake, an AASL past-president, introduced her boss, Alonzo Crim, as keynote speaker at the second theme session. Crim, superintendent of Atlanta's public schools since 1973, focused his remarks on the creation of a community of believers surrounding young people. The most current and pressing concern is the provision of quality education for all children. "In our roles we don't have to create the good ideas but we should be able to identify them and to bring together those who can bring ideas to fruition." The schools need to show evidence of people who believe in young people, who invite them to express themselves, and who confront them and challenge them.

Foot-weary conferees relaxed in the Exhibit Hospitality Area.

Challenging AASL

Although the national conference was a program meeting rather than an association business session, members of the AASL Board of Directors were available at a challenge forum to hear member concerns and answer questions about the association. There was considerable discussion of last March's *Future Structure Report* and of subsequent action on that issue. Judith Davie read a unanimous decision by the North Carolina affiliate of AASL. The document urged that school libraries should improve their ability to work within ALA and encouraged that steps be taken to improve AASL communication within the present structure of ALA. David Rose reminded the board that the AASL Affiliate Assembly had requested a timetable for action on the issue and that his state (California) had requested significant change or federation within one year. Several members were concerned about the language used in the priorities that were presented to the ALA Executive Board Subcommittee. Specifically, members were dissatisfied with references to AASL as the "singular" voice for school librarians. Many members remarked that they felt ill-informed regarding action subsequent to last March's report and wished to know how the priorities were established. Committee members elaborated on the process and the chronology. Jean Lowrie remarked that she had seen discussion of an independent AASL come and go over the years and "each time the decision has been made that strength is with the association as a whole."

Among other concerns addressed to the board: more outreach is needed to reach current members of AASL; the organization should work to involve young members and building-level media specialists who are often unable to attend conferences such as the Atlanta meeting; AASL could increase its membership by focusing on the larger issues that affect the profession as a whole; AASL members should be endorsed and promoted as ALA council candidates; new standards for media centers need to be written and published.

Mission proceeding

The emphasis of the Atlanta meeting was on programming rather than organizational politics. The school media specialists who attended the Atlanta conference brought with them their ideas and goals for excellence in educational media programs. They returned home with shared knowledge, expertise and innovative programming ideas in addition to the enthusiasm and mutual support so necessary for implementing true alliances for excellence. That mission is still being accomplished. ▣

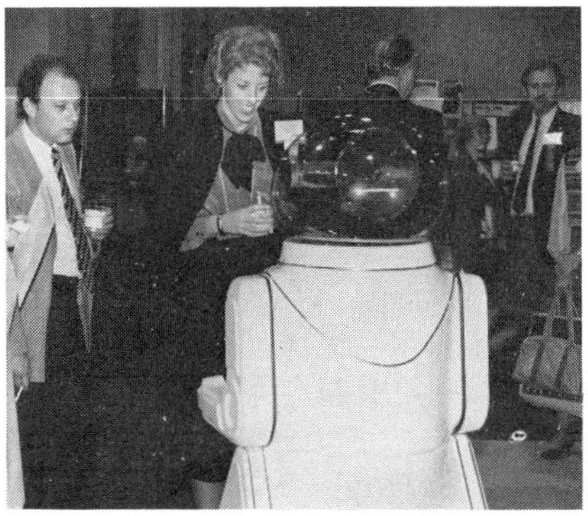

At the exhibitors reception: making a robotic friend.

AASL awards

AASL/SIRS Intellectual Freedom Award: Vicki Hardesty, Findlay (Ohio) High School

AASL Distinguished Library Service Award for School Administrators: Marilyn Scott, Anchorage (Alaska) School District

AASL President's Award: Rheta Clark, South Glastonbury, Connecticut

Dale Nelson: Dateline Washington

Copyright vs. First Amendment

Victor Navasky, editor of *The Nation,* thought he had hot news on his hands when someone gave him a copy of former President Gerald Ford's unpublished memoirs. Navasky was wrong, but the manuscript is turning out to be news in a way he did not anticipate: it could lead to a landmark Supreme Court ruling on the balance between copyright law and the First Amendment.

The court heard arguments on Election Day on an appeal by Ford's publishers, Harper & Row, of a federal appeals court decision that ruled *The Nation*'s publication of an article based on the memoirs was a legitimate part of the "harvest of knowledge so necessary to a democratic state."

The Association of American Publishers sided with Harper & Row, arguing in a friend-of-the-court brief that "if the First Amendment is the moral force of publishing, copyright is its commercial foundation" and urging the court to "keep both copyright and the First Amendment in vital balance."

The justices are expected to decide the case before July.

The Ford memoirs, *A Time to Heal,* were published by Harper & Row in the spring of 1979. Harper & Row sold to *Time* magazine, for $25,000, the right to serialize excerpts from the book before its publication. Before the *Time* excerpts were published, however, a copy of the entire 200,000-word manuscript was provided to Navasky. He has never said who gave it to him.

Navasky testified that he believed at the time that the book's account of a conversation between Ford and then White House chief of staff Alexander Haig about the possibility of pardoning former President Richard Nixon for Watergate offenses was "hot news." He later found out that Ford had testified about it before a congressional committee. *The Nation* still contends that the article, containing Ford's views on Watergate-related matters, was newsworthy.

At any rate, the magazine rushed the piece into print and had it on the newsstands on April 3. *Time*'s first installment was to appear on April 16 and the book on May 1. After the article in *The Nation* appeared, *Time* canceled its plans to publish excerpts and refused to pay Harper & Row the $12,500 balance of the $25,000 it had agreed to.

Harper & Row sued for copyright infringement. *The Nation* argued that its quotations and paraphrases of the memoirs were "fair use" because the material was news. U.S. District Judge Richard Owen agreed with the book publishing firm, saying, "*The Nation* took what was essentially the heart of the book."

The 2nd U.S. Circuit Court of Appeals reversed Judge Owen's decision, saying, "*The Nation* article drew only upon scattered parts (of the book) and not the total entity with its unique and protected mosaic."

Harper & Row, in its appeal to the nation's highest court, said the circuit court's "artificial definition of expression will deny an author protection for important elements of authorship."

The Nation argued, "To allow anyone to copyright facts, information, or news would contravene the very purpose of the copyright clause of the United States Constitution" which the Constitution states is "to promote the progress of science and the useful arts."

The Association of American Publishers brief argues that the circuit court failed to consider the intention of Congress, in its 1976 rewrite of the federal copyright law, "to limit fair use of unpublished works to exceptional cases."

During oral argument, Justice Sandra Day O'Connor asked Edward A. Miller of New York, representing Harper & Row, whether the article would have amounted to copyright violation if it had appeared in *The Nation* after Ford's book was published. "I can't answer yes or no," Miller said. "It would depend on the economic harm."

Floyd Abrams, representing *The Nation,* said the article involved only 300 words of direct quotation from the Ford book.

Is "lust" a four-letter word?

In another First Amendment case, the high court is being asked to determine whether the Washington State Legislature exceeded constitutional bounds in declaring that works appealing to

Dale Nelson *is a journalist who covers the Washington scene for WLB.*

"lasciviousness or lust" are obscene.

Among those challenging the 1982 Washington law are the Washington Library Association, Washington Library Media Association, Community College Librarian and Media Specialists Association of Washington, Madrona Publishers of Seattle, and the American Civil Liberties Union of Washington.

Under a rule laid down by the Supreme Court in 1973, one of the tests for obscenity is whether the average person, applying contemporary community standards, would find that the work, when considered as a whole, appeals to the prurient interest. The Washington legislature followed this, but defined prurient as "that which incites lasciviousness or lust."

The 9th U.S. Circuit Court of Appeals struck the law down, saying "lust" does not fit within the Supreme Court's definition of "prurient" as "a shameful or morbid interest in nudity, sex or excretion."

"Indeed, the word has acquired such acceptable connotations that, prior to his election in 1976, presidential candidate Jimmy Carter confessed in a popular national publication that he had "looked on a lot of women with lust (and)... committed adultery in my heart many times," the circuit court said.

"We do not think that President Carter was describing a shameful or morbid interest; rather, he was obviously expressing a healthy, wholesome, human reaction common to millions of well-adjusted persons in our society," the jurists said.

Spokane County Prosecuting Attorney Donald Brockett, in his appeal to the Supreme Court, asked "whether a state legislature should be compelled to research present existing contemporary meanings of isolated words in the obscenity test before enacting obscenity statutes." The lawmakers, Brockett argued, should not be "constrained by a state's best guess of the acceptable meaning of words in contemporary usage."

The court will hear arguments on the case early this year.

Security in presidential libraries

Concern about security at presidential libraries is expressed in a report by the inspector general of the General Services Administration.

The report to the National Archives and Record Service said there had been no security survey at the Eisenhower Library in Abilene, Kansas, since November, 1981, at the Truman Library in Independence, Missouri, since June, 1980, and at the Hoover Library in West Branch, Iowa, since the summer of 1979.

The report also said these surveys did not appear to have been very thorough. The one at the Eisenhower Library, for instance, was largely limited to a review of security alarm systems and security staffing. Reports on the 1979 survey at the Hoover Library dealt almost exclusively with the museum display area.

In the meantime, security staffing at the libraries has decreased significantly for budgetary reasons. Since the 1980 survey at the Truman Library, for instance, the security staff there has been cut from twelve persons to six.

Library officials told the inspector general there had been no serious security incidents at the libraries in recent years but the report nonetheless recommended evaluation of security requirements to see that the buildings, grounds and holdings of the libraries are adequately protected.

Archivist Robert Warner said National Archives had made arrangements with GSA's Office of Oversight to conduct security reviews at the three libraries.

Library friend in the Senate

A lawmaker with a reputation as a friend of libraries will be moving up to the Senate when Representative Paul Simon (D–Ill.) takes over the seat of Republican Senator Charles Percy in January.

Simon, House sponsor of the Library Services and Construction Act, defeated Percy in one of the most closely contested Senate races of the November election. Simon has been chairman of the House Subcommittee on Postsecondary Education for four years.

Simon is one of Congress's most prolific authors, having written nine books. His wife, Jeanne, served on a presidential library commission during the Carter administration.

Gershwin Room at LC

The Library of Congress has announced plans for a George and Ira Gershwin Room, to be opened after the restoration of its 1897 Thomas Jefferson Building is completed. The restoration is expected to begin next summer.

The Gershwin Room will be furnished with George Gershwin's piano and Ira Gershwin's library, as well as desks, paintings and posters that belonged to the two brothers. The items on display were donated by Mrs. Ira Gershwin. ▣

Anne McGrath:

Eye on Publishing

American Book Awards given to three writers

The American Book Awards, sponsored by the Association of American Publishers, recognized authors in only three categories in 1984—a marked drop from the twenty-seven categories in which writers and book designers were honored a year ago. Harriet Doerr's *Stones for Ibarra* (Viking Press) won the prize for outstanding first novel; Ellen Gilchrist's *Victory Over Japan* (Little, Brown) received the general fiction award; and Robert V. Remini's *Andrew Jackson and the Course of American Democracy, 1833–1845, Volume III* won the nonfiction award.

The decision to accept nominations in only three genres came after spirited discussion among the AAP membership, led by a number of dissenting paperback publishers—whose books took nearly half of the prizes in 1983—and a determined group who argued that the awards should more closely resemble the prestigious Booker McConnell prize given in Britain to one outstanding novel. This group reasoned that knocking out all but the most fundamental literary categories would substantially increase the importance of those awards given. As a result, no prizes were given this time in the previous categories of graphics or children's books, and paperback books—while accepted as nominees—were no longer considered as a separate category.

Harriet Doerr's novel follows Californians Richard and Sara Everton to Ibarra, Mexico, where they intend to work a copper mine that has been in Richard's family. The story deals with Richard's discovery shortly after their arrival that he is dying, and with Sara's inability to face the truth. *Stones for Ibarra* was selected from a group of three first novels; the other two nominees were *Tapping the Source,* by Kem Nunn (Delacorte Press) and *Edisto,* by Padgett Powell (Farrar, Straus, & Giroux). Doerr, who was born in 1910, lives in California and received her bachelor's degree from Stanford University in 1977.

Ellen Gilchrist's *Victory Over Japan* is a collection of fourteen short stories about Southern women that span the years from World War II to the present. Her book was also chosen over two other nominees: *Foreign Affairs,* by Alison Lurie (Random House) and *The Anatomy Lesson,* by Philip Roth (Farrar, Straus & Giroux).

The nonfiction judges found themselves faced with perhaps the most difficult decision of all. Their five nonfiction nominees included Eudora Welty's *One Writer's Beginnings* (Harvard University Press), a work which, had the rules allowed, would have shared the 1984 prize. Only one winner could be named, however, and the final volume in Robert Remini's exhaustive study of Andrew Jackson's presidency gained the edge. Remini is a history professor and Distinguished Professor of the Humanities at the University of Illinois. The other three entries were Ernst Pawel's *The Nightmare of Reason: A Life of Franz Kafka* (Farrar, Straus & Giroux), Howard Feinstein's *Becoming William James* (Cornell University Press), and Richard Marius's *Thomas More* (Alfred A. Knopf).

Each of the three American Book Award winners receives $10,000. Simon & Schuster contributed $1,000 in prize money for each of the eight runners-up.

The Holy Book wars

All is not peace and tranquillity in Holy Book publishing these days. For the past several months, in fact, competition for bigger and bigger chunks of the $110 million Bible market has really been heating up. Nelson, Tyndale, Zondervan, and Oxford University Press have all outdone themselves with efforts to popularize editions of the Bible and market them to the masses.

Thomas Nelson Publishers reasoned that, if it's true that the majority of Americans don't already read the Bible, the logical approach would be to carve a whole new readership out of those stubborn masses: to lure the secular-minded into the fold with answers—biblical answers—to decidedly laic questions about such things as stress and sexual preferences. The result? *The Bible,* a $5.95 paperback published last summer, that appended forty such questions and their biblically inspired answers to Nelson's New King James Version translation. The publisher launched a determined effort this past fall to promote its Bible in the pages of *USA Today* and on the radio.

Tyndale House Publishers has reached essentially the same conclusion about the thrust its marketing strategies should take. Ever since Kenneth Taylor founded the firm in 1962 to make the Scriptures as contemporary as possible—in *The Living Letters, Living Prophecies, Living Gospels, Living Psalms and Proverbs,* and, in 1971, *The Living Bible*—the firm's efforts to spread the teachings of God among the uninitiated have been leading toward publication of the new $9.95 paperback *The Book.* This new Bible has the same simplified, readable text as *The Living Bible,* but boasts a new, non-biblical blue cover more palatable to those who like to read in public. Tyndale added a preface to its new version that—like Nelson's addition—directs troubled readers to possible sources of guidance in handling their worldly problems. Where will *The Book* be sold? In all the traditional outlets, of course, and, appropriately enough, in the supermarket.

Two other competitors for Bible dollars this year will be Oxford Uni-

Anne McGrath, *a freelance writer based in New York, covers the publishing world for WLB.*

versity Press, with its updated *Oxford New International Version Scofield Study Bible,* and Zondervan, with the *New International Version Reference Bible.* The Scofield was originally published seventy-five years ago; this new edition is available unindexed for $24.95, or indexed for $29.95. The Zondervan book, designed with a center column reference system for the more serious reader and selling for around $20, is to be featured in national magazine advertisements as one important element of a healthful breakfast. "Start your day with something nourishing," the message goes.

Even as all these new and improved Bibles are joining the lineup on the bookstore shelves, the battle continues to rage in other quarters over whether what we really need is a "unisex" Bible that rejects to as great a degree as possible the concept of God as a male figure. If you've started to notice subtle changes in the readings at your church services recently, it may be because those readings have been rewritten as part of a National Council of Churches experiment in which passages free of masculine references were introduced to many congregations starting in December.

The National Council of Churches is attempting to make such substitutions as "Sovereign" for the words "Lord" or "King" and to replace male pronouns used in reference to God with "God." "Follow me," says one suggested rewording, "and I will make you fishers of men and women." The commandment "You shall not covet your neighbor's wife" becomes "You shall not covet your neighbor's wife or husband."

Many religious leaders—notably of the Jewish and Roman Catholic faiths—are strenuously objecting to meddling with the Scriptures, preferring instead to concentrate on reworking hymns and prayers. Still, at least one Catholic translation of the New Testament is in the works that will drop many male pronouns. Other gender-free versions are sure to follow.

Catholics baffled by the Vatican decision nine months ago to deny church approval to the popular introduction to their faith, *Christ Among Us,* will be glad to know that—approved or not—it will be available through Harper & Row. The book, published until last winter by the Paulist Press (a Catholic publisher run by the Paulist Fathers in Ramsey, N.J.), has been widely used since it first came out in 1968 as a textbook in high school and adult religious education classes. In February, apparently in response to a conservative Catholic organization's concerns about the book's "deviations" from traditional church doctrine, the head of the Vatican's Sacred Congregation for the Doctrine of the Faith told Archbishop Peter Gerety of Newark to remove his imprimatur—his official recognition of the work's validity—from the book.

Shortly afterward, the Paulist Press stopped publishing and distributing the book. Harper & Row, convinced of the book's reliability and readability and encouraged both by the fact that nearly two million copies have been sold during its sixteen-year history and that Catholic educators are not automatically dropping it from their curricula, took up negotiations with author Anthony Wilhelm to publish it again.

Small Press Center open

Librarians, collectors, and anyone else intrigued by the work of small independent book publishers can now keep current with the growing small press movement and its achievements in printing and design by visiting the new Small Press Center in New York City. The permanent exhibition facility is operated by the Library Committee of the General Society of Mechanics and Tradesmen of the City of New York and is located in the society's building at 20 West 44th St. Independent publishers who have published at least four titles and have "demonstrated a serious commitment to books of literary, artistic, or social value" are eligible to submit books for display.

"You've been occupying that spot for six months! I'll have to ask you to publish or get the Hell out!"

Will Manley:
Facing the Public

Toward the end of the second presidential debate in October, Ronald Reagan somewhat incoherently began stumbling through his all-important final statement. Inexplicably filled with nostalgia at this tense and crucial moment, he seemed to be harking back fondly to the happy days when he was governor of California. At that time in the sixties he had been asked to put something in a time capsule to be opened in eighty years. Reagan, who was supposed to be debating foreign policy and explaining the nuances of negotiating arms control treaties with the Soviets, instead decided to take us on a guided tour up the coast of California. With the top down in his convertible, the redwood trees waving in the ocean breeze, the coastal mountains sparkling in the radiance of the California sun, and thoughts about what to put in that time capsule dancing in his head, our incoherent President seemed headed straight for a political San Andreas Fault. You could see Mondale smiling in the background waiting for Reagan to steer himself into a major gaffe. But then suddenly and unceremoniously the debate moderator, Edwin Newman, under the pretense that the President's allotted time had run out, mercifully stopped Reagan from committing any further nonsense.

Whether or not Reagan's time had indeed run out or whether Newman, a noted grammarian and advocate of good linguistic taste, simply could no longer listen to the President's fractured English is interesting to ponder. Nevertheless, due to the interruption, we never did find out what Reagan decided was representative enough of America to put into the California time capsule. Personally, my bets are on videotapes of television commercials. What could be more appropriate for someone so mediacentric and unabashedly capitalistic as Reagan? I can see the "great communicator" donating such American classics as the early Alka Seltzer ads or the later editions of the Marlboro Man for posterity. What, after all, is a more characteristic form of American communication than TV commercials?

And I'd be the last person to complain about making a gift of them to future generations, for I appreciate the value of a well conceived commercial. For instance, I'm sure glad that when I drink a frosty can of Lite Beer from Miller in a crowded bar I can enjoy the taste, avoid the inconvenience of getting filled up, rest easy that it has a third less calories than regular beer, and, most importantly, not have to worry about being perceived as a wimp (provided of course that I crush the empty can in my hand).

I'm just as relieved that when I eat my bowl of Frosted Flakes in the morning I don't have to sneak it behind my wife's back or hide it from the children. I'm so happy to know—from the commercial that shows a corporate vice-president in a three-piece suit eating a bowl of Frosted Flakes—that I'm a normal adult, and that there are thousands of other adults who feel the same way I do about Frosted Flakes. It is such a relief to know that I'm not alone.

What bugs me are the elitists who look down upon television commercials. These are the people who watch public television not because they really like opera, Alistair Cooke, Big Bird, or the Boston Pops, but because they don't like commercials. Probably one of the most regrettable creations of technology is the infamous videocassette recorder. With it you can now tape your favorite TV shows, play them back, and with the press of a button bypass all the commercials.

What I like about commercials is that they are so unpretentious and so unabashedly, well, commercial. Personally, I can't imagine why anyone would want to avoid commercials. I've often thought many of them are far superior to the actual programs that they support. Think of all the good things that commercials do for you. They make you feel good about yourself. After watching a day's

Will Manley *is director of the Tempe (Arizona) Public Library.*

"It's fantasy! It's folklore! It's a whole lot more! It's your new public library. Come visit us now and we'll give you every first edition ever published. That's right! Every first edition ever published. It's an offer so incredible, I can't believe I'm saying it. But I am."

worth of television you realize that everyone else suffers from loose dentures, halitosis, hemorrhoids, constipation, bathtub rings, and the heartbreak of psoriasis. Commercials also help you make decisions about life's big questions—do you want a dishwasher detergent that leaves spots on your dishes, or do you want one that transforms dinner plates into mirrors?

Furthermore, television advertising makes you aware of the subtle things in life that you should avoid at all costs, such as ring around the collar, yellow wax build-up, and dirty carburetors. But most advantageously, commercials allow you to enjoy those things in life, such as cigarettes, beer, cookies, coffee, soft drinks, and sugary breakfast cereals, that everyone else makes you feel guilty about consuming.

Despite all the VCRs and all the highbrows who publicly express disdain for commercials, they have gone from being the vast cultural wasteland of the sixties and seventies to becoming the status symbol of the eighties. Everyone has to have one. Traditionally staid professionals such as lawyers, family doctors, accountants, and ophthalmologists, who previously barely condescended to allow their names to appear in the yellow pages of the phone book, now shamelessly hawk their wares on television right alongside Hartz Mountain Flea and Tick Collars and the Goodyear Blimp. And talk about starchy—have you noticed that such venerable institutions as hospitals, medical clinics, and universities have all learned the joys of selling, television-style? Add public libraries to that list and it's obvious that the producers of television commercials have come full circle from the unpretentious, unapologetic, money-grubbing, profiteering entrepreneur to the public, tax-supported, "for the common good" institution.

What has happened is that we in the public sector who have always legitimately been concerned with developing some sort of public relations program have begun to confuse public relations with advertising, promoting, publicizing, and marketing. The upshot of this is that the few big libraries that actually have public relations budgets often squander their money at regrettable attempts to produce low-budget television advertising. If Miles Laboratories can make Alka Seltzer tablets seem like so much fun to swallow that we all want to go out and get an upset stomach, librarians apparently think that they can make public libraries as appealing as indigestion.

To paraphase one of the more tautological rallying calls of the 1984 presidential campaign, "Let Reagan be Reagan," I say we should "Let commercials be commercial." The basic fallacy behind the commercialization of public sector services is the underlying misconception that government has failed because it has not adopted the "superior" modus operandus of the world of private enterprise. Implicit in this misconception is the neoconservative attitude that the so-called "non-essential" services should get off the public dole and start paying their own way as enterprise operations on the order of a municipal golf course.

Consistent with this view is the idea that the free public library is too old hat and in today's world we have to get out and sell. What happens when we sell, however, is that we try to appeal to popular tastes and desires even if those tastes and desires have nothing to do with reality. Just look at the commercials. Pepsi is for those who think young but look old. Budweiser is for men who think that they're rough, tough, and macho—even though most of the people who drink it appear to be overweight, middle-aged wimps. And last but not least, public libraries are for people who are enamored with art prints, phonograph records, videocassettes, and power drills even though most of the people who use libraries are there for books.

To illustrate my point, let me recall a television commercial put out by the Milwaukee Public Library a few years ago. It was a commercial whose only virtue was that it seemed to be shown only at odd times like early Sunday morning or very late during the week. It was definitely not ready for prime time. In fact, I think that its only good purpose is that it served as a fitting introduction to the post-late show test pattern. The commercial was set on an ominously dark city street, where a suspicious-looking man in a trench coat was hurrying away with an armful of records, tapes, art prints, and all the other nonprint trinkets that libraries have succumbed to circulating. In fact, he had everything but a Waring blender and a book. Suddenly a Sergeant Friday policeman-type showed up out of the dark to arrest the man for presumably knocking over a department store. The man's defense, of course, was that he had only been to his local library.

What is objectionable here is not just the message of the commercial, it's the fact that the commercial was produced at all. Commercials are made to sell. Public libraries should not be selling. They are public, tax-supported institutions that exist for the common good. If the services that public libraries provide were saleable and profitable, they would be provided by the private sector.

Public libraries, therefore, should not be wasting money on advertising. Advertising is not only inappropriate for public libraries, it also ironically generates very bad public relations for them. Nothing gets me angrier as a taxpayer than seeing public sector services wasting money on advertising. Those dollars should be spent on the services themselves. Whenever I see a public sector agency advertising on television I automatically assume that that is an agency whose budget has some fat in it.

Public librarians should, therefore, orient their public relations away from the manipulative techniques of private business and begin to develop a program that will spend more time listening to people than talking at them. After all, relationships are a two-way street. Next month we'll discuss some "two-way" techniques that won't cost you a penny. ▣

Patricia Berglund:

School Library Technology

"I love it, I LOVE the program, I love it." Jeanne Harsin, a school librarian, thus declares her undying affection for *Computer Cat,* the computerized card catalog program that she uses at Skyview Elementary School in Windsor, Colorado.

Computer Cat is an old war-horse in the micro market. Introduced in 1981, it was the first online catalog available to small schools using Apple computers. Frequent updates and personalized user support have helped maintain its popularity. The sale of *Computer Cat* to the Winnebago Software Company of Calendonia, Minnesota has put it in the spotlight once again.

Harsin first encountered *Computer Cat* three years ago when she saw it demonstrated at a convention. She was planning the library for a new school at the time, and thought it might make more sense to install a computerized card catalog than a drawer catalog. She told her principal and superintendent about *Computer Cat*: they looked at it, liked it, and purchased it.

"We started from zero," she says. "No one here had any computer background." For Harsin, that ignorance was bliss. "I didn't know all the bad things that could have happened. A computer technician just brought the manual and showed me how to run the computer. My aide and I entered about 2,000 titles that first summer. We put in both books and library media. It went really well."

When school opened, Harsin continued to breeze along. "The students used it, and they loved it," she says. "The teachers immediately used it a lot." There were no problems with crowds at the computer or students who couldn't work the program. "You think one terminal won't work, but it does," she insists. "Not all the children come to the computer every time. You may have five or ten children waiting, and each gets about a minute on the computer. Everyone gets a turn, and it works out."

Harsin reports that first graders use the program as soon as they begin to spell and that second graders are pros. "If they don't know how to spell the whole word, they can call up subjects even with the first letter," she explains. Only two-to-four letters are needed for a sort. Using the computer motivates children to master library skills much more than an old style card catalog, she says. "The kids really get to know the difference between subject and title—they have to know. They also learn better where everything is located because they want to use the computer."

Harsin praises the things the librarian can do with *Computer Cat.* One of her recent projects was to print out all the primary and elementary subject headings so students could refer to that list. Reports, indexes and bibliographies are easy to produce. She also prints her shelflist on paper instead of keeping a shelflist card file. It's much easier to make notes on a paper shelflist, she says. Any inconsistencies in cataloging show up in the printed lists. "Before I had a computer, I had so many mistakes in my card catalog, but I never really knew it. With cards, it's so hard to find the mistakes and get them all changed. Changes are quick on the computer," she notes.

Harsin's trouble-free beginnings were followed by a period in which she gradually became aware of the problems that can arise with computerized card catalogs. *Computer Cat,* like all microcomputer card catalogs, uses a hard disk drive to store records. Power fluctuations, failure to close files—even static—can erase data. There is a checking mechanism that tells the librarian something is wrong, but one must have accurate, accessible back-up copies of all information in order to repair the damage.

Computer Cat gave Harsin the option of using videotape or floppy disks to store her back-up data. She chose videotape, but her school's new videotape machine proved to be incompatible with the Corvus hard-disk system. She has to borrow an old VCR from another school to make her back-ups.

Once Harsin thought she had some database damage, so she set out to rebuild the file from her master record. The computer runs for about six hours to accomplish this task. After five and one-half hours, she bumped the computer with a chair. The program stopped, and she had to start all over. On other occasions, the computer would stop operating every time she called up a certain title. She never did find the reason for the delay.

None of this has dampened her enthusiasm for the program. She wants to see her whole district using computerized card catalogs and computerized circulation systems. Cost, she says, should not hold people back. "The Corvus hard-disk drive costs the same as a wrestling mat. Districts don't hesitate to buy the things they need for sports. They have to change their way of thinking about libraries. Even though schools have card catalogs, they are going to have to do away with those eventually. A lot of people say, 'Oh, this is just a passing fad.' Well, it isn't."

Betty Costa, the school librarian who designed *Computer Cat* with her husband Larry and programmer Stan Crane, is delighted with Harsin's positive experiences, but she doesn't recommend that others plunge into a computerized card catalog project without computer knowledge. She encourages librarians to get a word-

Patricia Berglund *is a librarian in the San Francisco Unified School District.*

Jeanne Harsin *using* Computer Cat *with two students:* Sarina Campbell, *second grade, and her brother* Ed, *fourth grade.*

Betty Costa, *left, discusses* Computer Cat *with a colleague.*

processing program, a database management system, and a spreadsheet. "Get to know what's involved in manipulating small files. Work with small bibliographies or your nonprint collection. Use an inexpensive overdue program. Do it yourself and see what you get," she says.

According to Costa, people should make a written list that describes what they want a library management system to do. Do they want circulation? Do they want a full bibliographic record? Do they want annotations?

Available systems must be studied carefully. For example, some circulation systems claim to have a bibliographic record. To a librarian, that probably means a shelflist-style entry, or a full MARC record, but the person who wrote the advertisement may mean an author, title and call number.

Joann Jones *in the Thompson School District Media Center.*

Jeb Griffith *of Winnebago Software Company.*

When the librarian has narrowed down the list of suitable programs, she should contact the vendor for the names of users. If she is thinking of investing a lot of money in a program, she should not only talk to a librarian who is using it but should visit the site as well, according to Costa.

Site users can discover ways to use programs that even the designers and programmers did not foresee.

Computer Cat was designed primarily for students using a print collection. In Loveland, Colorado, district media coordinator Joann Jones has teachers using *Computer Cat* to access the nonprint collection in the Thompson School District's central office.

Jones's computerization project dates back to 1982 when her district decided to change the organization of its growing collection of nonprint items from accession number to Dewey decimal number. This decision meant setting up a card catalog. Jones found that she could buy the hardware necessary to computerize the collection for about the same price as card catalog furniture. Clerical time, she felt, would be less with the computerized system because an entry is typed once on the computer instead of the five or six times necessary for a card file.

Jones attended a demonstration of six electronic card catalog programs and decided on *Computer Cat.* She and her staff read the manual and realized that modifications of the program would be necessary to adapt it to their collection. They entered 200 titles on the computer and experimented with them to see what changes would be necessary. A place to designate media type was already built into the program, but Jones soon realized that a way to separate material by grade level would be needed. She decided to enter the grade level into the location field and also to append an "E" (elementary) or "S" (secondary) to the title entry. The author field was transformed into a series section, and one subject heading field became a curriculum designation.

According to Jones, entering the material was not difficult, and teachers have no problems looking things up. "This was developed by a librarian, a working librarian," she says. "That has really helped. I sometimes telephone Betty Costa or her husband Larry and they're right there with the answer. I would not have wanted to go to a physical card catalog when a system like this was available."

How will the sale of *Computer Cat* affect the effective personal support system that has been its mainstay? According to the Costas, one of the factors in the sale of their system to Winnebago was Winnebago's willingness to continue the high level of customer support they established. Both Larry and Betty Costa will continue to work personally with *Computer Cat* users until October, 1985. *Computer Cat* software is currently priced at $995.

Donnarae MacCann/Olga Richard:

Picture Books for Children

Picture books do an excellent job in depicting a basic enigma: how to be independent yet connected with others. At least a partial answer is worked out with the aid of the community, family, and extended family in Felicia Bond's **Poinsettia and the Firefighters.** Poinsettia, a pig-child, undergoes a change that will expand her sense of autonomy and self-

From *Poinsettia and the Firefighters*

confidence. She is provided a room of her own in her family's old-fashioned residence. Poinsettia loves her new room until she hears the "lights out" order. Then she faces a long, cold night of unfamiliar sounds and such complete darkness that she can't even see her "hoof in front of [her] face." But the ensuing insomnia holds the key to her rescue. A new plot twist—Poinsettia spotting a fire on the telephone lines—enables the author to show how someone can find a sense of connection at the very moment it is needed.

A firefighter explains to the piglet that the fire alarm did not wake him: "'I'm a night watchman. I stay awake all night.'" And Poinsettia replies, "'I'm a night watcher too.'" In the last scenes she still keeps her night vigil at the window rather than going calmly to bed like the rest of the pigs, but she sees a glimmer of light from the firehouse and thinks of the friendly person who is standing by as a professional night watcher. Of course drowsiness overtakes her anxiety before daybreak.

Olga Richard *and* **Donnarae MacCann** *are the authors of The Child's First Books.*

The text is handled succinctly and credibly, only calling attention to itself at that moment when the protagonist refers to her "hoof in front of [her] face." This line is a playful surprise because everything in the narrative and illustrations point to the fact that this pig population is standing in for the human race. It has an amusing effect because only rarely in anthropomorphic children's books do the animals seem to have a consciousness of themselves as animals.

Felicia Bond demonstrates expanding skills as an illustrator, as well as competence as a storyteller. At first glance, the pages appear to be vintage Bond characterized by small, unobtrusive, patterned shapes. But she experiments with a strong sense of depth in the picture reproduced on this page (where the stairs "creaked v-e-r-y slowly"). She experiments with dark shades produced with interesting layers of color, with radical changes in perspective, and with unusual edges for a composition rather than a standard framing technique (e.g., she dramatizes the exit of the fire truck by surrounding it with bursting, irregular shapes). Bond utilizes the kind of distortions that are frequently achieved in wide-angle-lens photography. She mimics the camera's vertical distortion with gently curving verticals (as in a door, window casing, or bedpost). Then she dramatizes the climactic point in Poinsettia's fantasies by creating a double-page array of these tilted and wobbling objects combined with dark, cavernous spaces. Within the framework of Bond's cozy style—an approach that blends with her narrative interests—she incorporates some strong, courageous innovations.

In **The Biggest Pumpkin Ever,** Steven Kroll uses an ingenious plot to demonstrate separateness and togetherness. Without encountering one another until the climax, a village mouse and a country mouse select the very same pumpkin to care for and use for their divergent goals: to win a pumpkin contest in the village, and to design a jack-o-lantern to amuse the country folk. The parallels between the two protagonists are handled whimsically. The first mouse discovers and tends the pumpkin by day, the second by night. Sugarwater is suggested by a parent of the first mouse to enhance the pumpkin's growth. The same suggestion is made by a big brother of the second mouse. On a cold night both mice children turn up with a pile of blankets to keep out the frost.

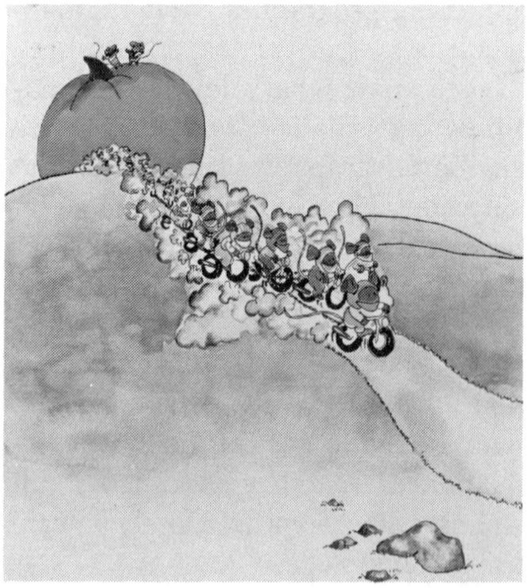

From *The Biggest Pumpkin Ever*

While each episode seems to be building toward a showdown, the unexpected midnight meeting of the mice produces instant friendship. They devise a means of sharing the now hilariously oversized pumpkin: first as a nominee for the prize; second as a jack-o-lantern that lights up the countryside.

The illustrator, Jeni Bassett, uses two visual styles. Her characterization of mice-folk (for example, one hundred field mice on motorcycles) illustrates a style that is spontaneous, humorous, and convincing in its treatment of gesture. But she also seems to strive laboriously for a rendering of plants that is typical of art school exercises. The overworked pumpkin stem on the last double-page is an example of a style that needs to be loosened up. Bassett's droll sense of character is her strong point, and she uses this talent to good advantage in defining Kroll's wise and genial "children."

Coco Can't Wait! by Japanese writer/illustrator Taro Gomi, revolves around a single idea: affection between child and grandparent. It takes only a few parallel lines of text (e.g., "One day Coco wanted to see Grandma very much. And Grandma wanted to see Coco very much.") to convey this message. But the book is full of frantic movement because Grandma lives on the opposite side of town from Coco. Several times we see this devoted pair ride in trains, taxis, or trucks that pass one another on the road, until finally Coco (on her scooter) and Grandma (on her motorcycle) meet at the midpoint and enjoy the present in Grandma's basket: some nice juicy apples.

From *Coco Can't Wait*

If this plot line sounds somewhat bland in its simplicity, it has nonetheless aroused feelings of great pleasure in our three-year-old listeners. The art work is both exquisite and accessible. Gomi uses a stunning range of grays, blacks, and browns, combined with accents in purple, magenta, and orange. Uneven paint textures and changing values against a white background make the pages glow with luminosity, and there are many ingenious scale changes and three-dimensional illusions. The first illustration is a panorama of the countryside with crisscrossing roads and rail lines, foreshadowing the travel motif and the aura of speed that Gomi sustains from page to page.

A grandparent/child relationship is also a central feature in Denys Cazet's **Big Shoe, Little Shoe.** But status and reciprocity are themes that add some complexity. First Louie, the grandchild/bunny, beats Grandpa at checkers; then Grandpa is "one-up" because he has the privilege of going to work; then little Louie is "one-up" by hiding Grandpa's shoes. Eventually a playful equilibrium is reached when Louie puts on the big shoes and climbs into Grandpa's laundry truck as the "worker," and Grandpa shuffles along in his grandchild's shoes as the worker's helper. Child listeners are enthralled by the final jumbling of roles: "'Don't worry, Grandma. Since Little Shoe [grandfather] lost the checker game, I'm going to let him drive the truck.'"

While all this foolery is a rather elaborate way to convey the stresses of youth and age, Cazet has such an exceptional talent for visual characterization that preschoolers can follow the nuances in the relationship with perfect ease. The author/illustrator's drawing skills enable him to complicate a composition with many overlapping objects and never lose a strong sense of clarity, consistency, and humor. He uses a quivery black line that breaks off at times to suggest texture and colors produce an atmosphere of warmth and familiarity. This ambiguity in the color quality is repeated in frames that effectively organize different scenes within a single page. Interiors with lumpy furniture suggest the 1930s, and the lumpy rabbit/people are also cast in that era. ▣

From *Big Shoe, Little Shoe*

This month's books:

Bond, Felicia. *Poinsettia and the Firefighters.* Crowell, 1984. $10.50, lib. bdg. $9.89. 0-690-04400-3; 0-690-04401-1 83-46169

Cazet, Denys. *Big Shoe, Little Shoe.* Bradbury, 1984. $12.95. 0-02-717820-X 83-21362

Gomi, Taro. *Coco Can't Wait!* Morrow, 1984. $10.50. 0-688-02789-X 83-17295

Kroll, Steven. *The Biggest Pumpkin Ever.* Illus. by Jeni Bassett. Holiday House, 1984. $12.95. 0-8234-0505-2

Patty Campbell:

The Young Adult Perplex

Los Angeles—The French have a word for it: réentrée. It appears everywhere on advertising posters in the Paris métro during the time of year that American merchants label "Back to School." But the concept is applicable year-round to any situation of return from a long refreshing sojourn in real or imaginary faraway places. Réentrée is the process of initiating the chain of small ritual acts that reestablish the rhythms and comforts of home after an absence—picking up the mail from the neighbors, phoning your mother, watering the dried-out houseplants. Réentrée is also an attitude of brave new strength, resolve, and perspective. With luck, it may last long enough to scale the slopes of the mountain of work that has accumulated. For this reviewer that mountain is made up of books.

What went on in YA publishing while I was far away enjoying the view from Mount Olympus? The first thing I notice is that there has been a whole lot of it. If output is any indication, the young adult book game is alive and well. Novels predominate. There are a couple of short story collections, but no poetry. Nonfiction (excepting the ever-dependable and timely books of Franklin Watts) has shrunk to a few dozen titles, most of them focusing on beauty and grooming and the problems of dating. Among the fiction there are a few pleasures and surprises and much that is predictable: pallid British junior fantasies, adult memoirs of long-ago adolescence, and a plethora of forgettable growing-up stories that confuse "realistic" with "ordinary." Again predictably, the paperback series ("continuity books," as they are now being called in the trade) have continued to mushroom, and now come close to outnumbering the hardcovers. A number of titles are worth comment. We'll discuss as many as space allows this month, and finish the job next time.

Patty Campbell *teaches young adult literature at UCLA and is a library consultant and freelance writer. She is currently at work on a book about YA novelist Robert Cormier.*

Head and shoulders above anything published this season or last is Terry Davis's stunning new novel, **Mysterious Ways**. This is not a book for younger readers. Its explicit sexual scenes and—more important—its complex and devastating metaphor make it more appropriate for mature, thoughtful, and strong-minded teens. Davis's first novel, *Vision Quest* (Viking, 1979), developed a cult following, and a second novel has been eagerly awaited. In the first scenes of *Mysterious Ways,* Karl Russell, whose journal we are reading, seems like an older version of the young wrestler from the earlier book. He has the same puppy-like eagerness to learn about life, the same antic sense of humor and gangly need for love, the same heartbreaking honesty in his struggles to make sense of it all. But Karl has something more to struggle with—one year ago, his family was killed in a car crash. Now, as a freshman in a small northwestern college in 1968, the painful question of God's ways toward man is never very far from Karl's mind, even when he is studying, running, or horsing around with his girlfriend, Jen. (Davis writes about the horseplay of young lovers better than anybody.) Just when the story has begun to seem predictable, there is a sudden shift in locale, mood, and tone. Karl goes to visit a former roommate in Brazil. On his arrival, Karl learns that his friend has been killed back in America. Alone in a strange and hostile place, Karl is stricken with a shocking Job-like transformation so appalling that all his spiritual struggle seems meaningless. Worst of all is his realization that he has known all along that this hideous thing would happen to him—the signs have been plain to see. In a violent, disturbing, but oddly optimistic conclusion, Davis shapes a metaphor (and perhaps a justification) for God's inhumanity to man.

Coming back down to earth, let's look at some new works by old hands. Paul Zindel's recent books have grown increasingly grotesque. His new novel moves into the realm of the truly preposterous. **Harry & Hortense at Hormone High** are electrified by their first encounter with teenage schizophrenic Jason Rohr. He finds them instantly attractive, and enlists them to help in his grand plan—something vaguely involving heroes, social responsibility, and saving the world. He reveals to them that he is Icarus, son of Daedalus, and that they are reincarnations of Euripides and the Delphic oracle. Suspicious, Harry and Hortense sneak a peek at the school records and learn that Jason's father killed his wife and himself when their son was six, and Jason's behavior has been a little strange ever since. It soon gets even stranger. Jason takes control of the school's public address system to broadcast his message, blows up the records office with dynamite, and escapes through the roof on a homemade feathered flying machine, pausing only long enough to grab a letter from Hortense in which she and Harry urge him to get psychiatric help. Crashing into a bridge, Icarus falls appropriately to his death, and the two friends blame themselves (déjà vu *The Pigman*) until they decide to carry on Jason's cause (whatever that may be). *Harry & Hortense* is a peculiar book that lacks enough of Zindel's redeeming wit.

What becomes of the children of political activists who must go into hiding? Robert Cormier explored this theme in the shadowy, sinister world of *I Am the Cheese*. In **Downtown**, Norma Fox Mazer, one of the finest YA novelists, has turned her hand to the subject with sunnier results. Peter Greenwood (whose peace activist parents Laura and Hal named him Pax

Martin Gandhi) has lived with his Uncle Gene in the only house downtown ever since his mother and father threw a bomb into a war research laboratory, killing two people. Now they are in hiding, and Peter lives for their return, although he feels abandoned and struggles with ambivalent feelings of pride and guilt for their actions. In this he is unlike his girlfriend Cary who is bitter about the drug-addict parents who left her to foster care. Norma Fox Mazer has developed the situation with intelligence and skill and has avoided simplistic judgments. Character has always been her strong point. Pete's mother, the passionate red-headed Laura, cares so deeply for her son that she must act in behalf of all the world's children. She is one of Norma Fox Mazer's most interesting creations.

Sixteen, edited by Donald R. Gallo, is a collection of original short stories by leading YA authors. It is a very good idea, but unfortunately the project falls as flat as a bathmat. The trouble is that most of these pieces simply don't work as short stories. Many seem to be mood studies, character exercises, studies for a book in progress, or unpublished episodes retrieved from the bottom desk drawer to fill Gallo's request for original material. Even the stories by the three authors who have published their own short story collections—Norma Fox Mazer, Joan Aiken, and Robert Cormier—lack the punch and focus we have come to expect from these writers. Two pieces, however, salvage the collection: Diane Duane's "Midnight Snack," with its haunting image of unicorns emerging shyly from the New York subway to feed daintily on moldy cheese Danish from the trash, and Richard Peck's delicious anecdote "Priscilla and the Wimps," in which every word builds with exquisite skill to an explosively comical conclusion.

The Delacorte Press Prize for an outstanding first young adult novel continues to bring wonderful new talent to light. **The Question Box** by Roberta Hughey, an honorable mention in this year's contest, is a delightful first offering by a writer who shows promise of becoming a major voice in YA literature. A former junior and senior high school teacher, she writes classroom scenes of hilarious authenticity. Her insights into the pain of adolescence are tender and wise, and she has the essential knack of weaving serious matters into the plot but keeping a light hand about it. *The Question Box* is primarily a story about loyalty between friends, but Hughey manages to touch on weightier problems—a father with unacknowledged incestuous tendencies, a best friend whose mother lives with a lesbian lover—without swamping the basic plot line or allowing the tone to become lugubrious. According to the jacket flap, Hughey is at work on a mystery for young adults. We look forward to it.

Devil's Race by Avi could have been an interesting psychological study, but in the Lippincott Page-Turner format it has been held within the limitations of the simple horror story. John Proud's ancestor of the same name was hanged as a demon in 1854, he is told by his Uncle Dave. As research for a school project on family trees, John is led by his uncle and his pretty cousin Ann into a wilderness area of the Appalachians to find the grave. There he is confronted by the evil spirit of the dead John Proud, his double. The demon begins a battle to return to life by taking over John's mind and body, and only with Ann's help is he eventually able to save his identity and to destroy the evil manifestation. Although several plot turns are clumsily transparent, the story moves quickly and smoothly and is several notches above the paperback horror stories that have become so popular with teens.

A new series carries the fantasy reader-participation concept several steps further than the excellent Fighting Fantasy Gamesbooks. In **The Shamutanti Hills**, leading British gamesman Steve Jackson (who co-authored the Fighting Fantasy series) has added magic spells to be used at appropriate times in the action. The spells are listed in a separate book, and the reader must memorize at least some of them before play begins. The level of skill depends on the number of spells available in the player's memory. Otherwise, the game is similar to the Fighting Fantasy Gamesbooks—skill, stamina, and equipment scores, battles determined by a code of dice throws, etc. A boon to libraries and to bus-riding readers is the ingenious device of printing dice casts at the bottom of each page, to be chosen by arbitrary page-ruffling rather than rattle and roll. The multiple adventures are exciting and colorful and the many black-and-white drawings add to the fun. ▣

This month's books:

Avi. *Devil's Race.* Lippincott, 1984. 152p. $10.50. ISBN 0-397-32095-7 LC 84-47636

Davis, Terry. *Mysterious Ways.* Viking, 1984. 274p. $15.95. ISBN 0-670-50224-3 LC 83-40227

Gallo, Donald R., ed. *Sixteen: Short Stories by Outstanding Writers for Young Adults.* Delacorte, 1984. 179p. $15.95. ISBN 0-385-29346-1 LC 84-3250

Hughey, Roberta. *The Question Box.* Delacorte, 1984. 187p. $14.95. ISBN 0-385-29358-5 LC 84-7022

Jackson, Steve. *The Shamutanti Hills.* (Steve Jackson's Sorcery!1) Penguin, 1984. 456p. $3.95. ISBN 0-1400-6794-9 LC 84-60574

Jackson, Steve. *The Sorcery Spell Book.* Penguin, 1984. 107p. $2.95. ISBN 0-1400-6793-0 LC 84-60575

Mazer, Norma Fox. *Downtown.* Morrow, 1984. 216p. $10. ISBN 0-688-03859-X Avon Flare, 1984. 208p. $2.50. ISBN 0-380-88534-4 LC 84-91105

Zindel, Paul. *Harry & Hortense at Hormone High.* Harper & Row, 1984. 160p. $11.50. ISBN 0-06-026864-6 LC 82-47697

Kathleen Maio:

Murder in Print

Almost a year ago I noted a small press volume celebrating novelist Jim Thompson (*Jim Thompson: The Killers Inside Him,* Fedora Press, 1983). Thompson's paperback originals of the 50s and 60s represent some of the finest "roman noir" crime fiction this country has ever produced. At the time, I observed that "this new tribute will likely speed along the rediscovery of Thompson's work by a wider audience." Seldom have my prophecies been so accurate. Two publishers have recently released paperback reprints of several of Thompson's most impressive novels.

Morrow's "Quill Mysterious Classic" series has republished **The Killer Inside Me** (1984, $3.50). The publishers claim that it is Thompson's masterpiece, and they may well be right. Seldom has anyone written such a compelling portrait of a sociopath. The author does not, as tradition would dictate, take the part of the honest, compassionate cop/detective desperately hunting a vicious criminal. Instead he takes us inside the killer, who is himself a deputy sheriff.

From the Black Lizard imprint of Creative Arts Book Company (833 Bancroft Way, Berkeley, CA 94710) come three Thompson titles—**The Getaway, Pop. 1280,** and **A Hell of a Woman** (1984, ea $3.95). Each book has a suitably garish cover rather clumsily illustrated and very evocative of its paperback forebears. Each also contains an essay about Thompson. Afterwords geared towards each individual title would have been preferable, but the general essay found in all three volumes will definitely snag many readers who are attracted by the books' campy covers.

The Black Lizard reprints are just as unusual and unsettling as *The Killer Inside Me. Pop. 1280* manages to be both humorous and peculiar. And the conclusion to *A Hell of a Woman* is certainly not your average fictional finis. The focus is on criminals, killers, the evil, the warped, and the weak. Not the type of folks everyone wishes to read about, perhaps. But fans of the hard-boiled school, or of Cornell Woolrich or James M. Cain, will definitely want to sample these paperback reprints of novels that are neither hard-boiled, Woolrichian, or Cain-like. They are unmistakably the work of Jim Thompson, an American original.

It is frustrating to find a mystery that doesn't jell as a final product, despite an intriguing concept and a readable prose style. Such a frustration is **The House That Jack Built** by Eileen Dewhurst (Crime Club, 1984, $11.95).

Here is the story of a sixteen-year-old named Sue Halliday, who has grown up playing the sweet and dutiful daughter on a British soap opera called "The House That Jack Built." The intriguing concept is the unique adolescent difficulties faced by Sue, who has played another character in a make-believe family since she was two weeks old. Sue feels closer to her screen mom than she does to her cool, professional, birth mother.

When Sue's diary (largely devoted to details of a heavy-duty crush on a fellow cast member) is stolen, she is blackmailed into performing certain seemingly innocent errands that implicate her in a larger criminal plot. This mystery plot doesn't work completely. The suspense doesn't move quickly enough and the evil doings don't begin until halfway through the book. In addition, some readers may have a hard time believing that a girl would go so far to avoid having her secret diary exposed.

Young Sue and her two mothers are a fascinating triangle and much of Dewhurst's latest is satisfying. But *The House That Jack Built* is damaged by the implausibilities of a mystery plot that is developed too slowly.

A more unqualified success is **Double** by Bill Pronzini and Marcia Muller (St. Martin's, 1984, $13.95). Pronzini, creator of the "Nameless" detective and no stranger to collaboration, teams up for the first time with Muller, author of the Sharon McCone series. It is a blessed union on all sides.

Private investigator Sharon McCone has for some time been acquainted with Nameless—or "Wolf" as she has nicknamed him—but it is not until they attend a convention of private investigators that things really start popping. A mysterious death and the disappearance of a small boy are the hooks. The two detectives take

Kathleen Maio *is a freelance writer based in Somerville, Massachusetts. She has contributed to* Twentieth Century Crime Writers, Murderess Ink, *and numerous magazines.*

parallel paths, in alternate chapters, towards the solution of a very complex plot. We also get new glimpses into the characters and lives of the two series sleuths. Readers will especially enjoy meeting McCone's eccentric yet completely believable family.

Double could very well be the most entertaining book in either series. Nameless and Sharon McCone work very well together. And so do their authors.

Those who enjoy mystery pastiche may want to pick up L.A. Morse's new book, **An Old-Fashioned Mystery** by "Runa Fairleigh" (Avon, 1984, $2.95). May is the operative word here, for I found Fairleigh's novel neither witty nor puzzling.

The plot involves a handful of extremely unpleasant people brought together for a dinner party on a desolate island. With communication and escape to the outside world cut off, the guests start dying off, in a fairly gruesome manner, one by one. If this is beginning to sound suspiciously like Christie's *And Then There Were None,* there is good reason. Many elements are borrowed from Dame Agatha's tour de force. Unfortunately, tight plotting, a truly suspenseful atmosphere, and an (almost) believable solution, are not among them. It is hoped that Morse will abandon further excursions into the classic puzzle, pastiche or otherwise, and will return to the hard-boiled formula (*The Old Dick, The Big Enchilada*) for which he displays more talent.

On the small press front this month is a first mystery by Barbara Wilson, **Murder in the Collective** (Seal Press, 312 S. Washington, Seattle, WA 98104, 1984, $7.95). The title is a dead giveaway that the book has something to do with the taking of a radical/alternative life.

Pam Nilsen, member of the Best Printing collective, usually worries about politics—among the staff as well as in the world beyond—and about how to sustain the printing business she inherited from her parents. When the sole lesbian member of the collective proposes that Best Printing merge with a typesetting firm called B. Violet, tensions escalate to vandalism and murder. Pam turns from print shop troubleshooter to amateur detective.

There is no doubt that Wilson has a political axe to grind. Through one character she manages to say much about the political turmoil of the Philippines, through the rest she raises issues of feminism, sexual politics, and radicalism in the 80s. Unlike most authors of political mysteries, Wilson wields her axe in a very cunning manner. Her characterization and mystery plot never suffer from polemical overkill. She has produced a very entertaining mystery that may well appeal to the most unpolitical reader.

A political mystery of an entirely different variety is **Priestly Murders** by Joe Gash (Holt, Rinehart and Winston, 1984, $11.95). It is a jaundiced police procedural taking potshots at Chicago city government and at a liberal phony of a priest. Speculation as to whether Gash is lampooning a well-known priest, novelist, and social critic may pique the interest of some readers.

Gash's story is passable enough. A priest is shot down during Mass in a dark and crumbling ghetto church. The most shocking aspect of this crime is that the assailant was dressed in full police uniform, including a masking bubble helmet. Police assigned to the case must verify not only the identity of the killer cop, but also the identity of the intended victim. Was the killer out to get any priest, the murdered priest, or the priest for whom he was substituting?

The police break the case through luck and blind belief in the old adage about the scene of the crime. With less than 165 pages to tell his story, Gash has little time for character development or subtlety. His politicians and priests are evil and power hungry. Police officers aren't much better—hard, racist cowboys of the city. It may be, as Gash contends, that his novel "reflects certain realities about the criminal-justice system" of Chicago. If this is so, the Windy City must be a nasty place to visit, and one wouldn't want to live there either.

From the mean streets to the mean refund and gift-wrap counter, Diane Mayo has just published her second cartoon suspense story in *Murder at the Big Store* (St. Martin's, 1984, $5.95). Her first book, *Murder at Bean & Beluga,* poked fun at her former employer, the New York gourmet shop Dean & Deluca. There will be even less doubt what famous New York department store is now receiving the tart side of Mayo's pen. Those looking for a real mystery puzzle need not apply. Mayo's book will appeal most to conspicuous consumers (and their detractors), and to persons for whom the horrors of holiday shopping and subsequent returns are still fresh wounds. ▣

Front Row Center *Judith Trojan:*

Frieda Lee Mock and Terry Sanders, producer-directors of *Screenwriter/ Word into Image,* an award-winning filmmaking teak based in southern California, talk with Robert Towne.

If you've ever contemplated a screenwriting career as an easy ticket to fame and fortune, think again. Or better yet, watch *Word into Image: Writers on Screenwriting,* a six-part video series produced and directed for PBS by writers Freida Lee Mock and Terry Sanders. These half-hour interviews introduce viewers to six noted screenwriters who admit that their craft can be agonizingly hard work with no guarantees of box office success.

The tapes capture William Goldman, Neil Simon, Paul Mazursky, Eleanor Perry, Carl Foreman, and Robert Towne relaxing at home or at their typewriters, talking about what they do best—writing original or adapted screenplays and, in some cases, novels and plays as well. As they recall their early years in the business, their first screenplays, and their philosophies of plot and character development, clips from their most notable films are intercut to clarify points made in the narrative. Essentially monologues, the six portraits provide a quick view of the world and work of screenwriters, those oft-forgotten artists who unfairly take a backseat to actors and directors in the minds of most filmgoers.

Charlie Chaplin was Neil Simon's first role model. In the program focusing on Simon, the playwright and screenwriter recalls how, as a child, he laughed so hard and long at Chaplin's films that it hurt. Simon aims to recreate this sense of joyful pain for audiences in his plays for the theatre and cinema. Aside from the kick of seeing his audiences doubled over in laughter, Simon shares something quite personal with his audiences. An autobiographical writer, Simon uses his family and friends as models for his characters. The compulsive Felix Unger of *The Odd Couple* was modeled after Simon's fastidious brother, Danny. Simon's courtship of actress Marsha Mason was the subject of *Chapter Two.*

Simon claims to enjoy the process of writing "more and more," and the staging and filming of it "less and less." "Life" is Simon's villain, and confict arises when characters in his works try to deal with that villain. Dotted with riotous clips from *The Odd Couple, Chapter Two, The Sunshine Boys, Plaza Suite,* and *The Goodbye Girl,* Neil Simon's video portrait in *Word into Image* provides a way for viewers to become acquainted with America's most prolific comedy writer.

Neil Simon and Eleanor Perry have little in common except their vocation. While Simon is the contented fat cat of comedy screenwriters, the late Eleanor Perry had limited markets for her work. A serious female writer, she struggled to gain a toehold in the male-dominated film industry. Even with some respected films to her credit, she continually scrambled for work.

In Perry's interview, taped in New York in 1981, she recollects the beginning of her screenwriting career. A fan of French New Wave cinema, Perry had an MA in psychiatric casework and a desire to work outside her home and family. Quite by accident, she discovered the fictionalized psychiatric case history on which she based *David and Lisa.* Clips from the latter and from *Last Summer* underscore her skill in writing about children and adolescents.

Also known for her feminist viewpoint and her ability to craft believable psychological portraits, Perry adapted the groundbreaking *Diary of a Mad Housewife.* Years later she begged for a chance to adapt Harold Robbins's *Lonely Lady* to the screen. She needed the job and laughingly recalls how she promised the film's producers "no integrity" if they let her write the script. They turned her down.

Eleanor Perry's strong-minded desire to write quality scripts on humanist themes may have limited her marketability in an industry known for its crass commercialism, but Perry's small body of work for film and television stands as a testament to her independent spirit. Despite her untimely death, she remains a role model for young women entering the profession today.

While Perry found few outlets for her special talent, Carl Foreman had no takers at all for his work during the infamous McCarthy era. Subpoenaed by the House Un-American Activities Committee, Foreman took "the diminished Fifth Amendment" and his career as a screenwriter in the United States was finished—just as his most notable achievement, *High Noon,* was opening in neighborhood theatres. He remembers that it was "no fun" being blacklisted in a company town, and being condemned by the likes of John Wayne. After watching his similarly blacklisted friends lose their jobs, wives, health, and often their lives, he left the United States for England, where, over a period of twenty years, he reestablished himself as a writer and producer.

Judith Trojan *is editor-in-chief of* Sightlines *magazine, editorial coordinator at the Educational Film Library Association, and a staff member of the American Film Festival.*

Foreman's is the most well-rounded biographical portrait in the series because it flashes back to his childhood in Chicago, his involvement with early labor politics, and his youthful dream to become a Hollywood screenwriter. Perhaps the most political screenwriter of the six, Foreman's scripts (*The Men, The Victors*) often deal with social and thinly disguised political issues. Foreman typically writes about the fight against injustice and about struggles with morally corrupt authority. Seemingly a traditional, thinking-man's western, *High Noon* was, in fact, a "deliberate" metaphor for the mob rule and fear overtaking America during the McCarthy era. Carl Foreman's motto, "Be true to yourself, no matter what the pressures," is obviously the key to his survival.

More than most screenwriters, Paul Mazursky has his finger on the pulse of modern mores. Concerned with the sexual revolution and its effect on white, middle-class Americans, Mazursky is a writer/director who has written successful scripts about open marriage (*Bob and Carol and Ted and Alice*), aging (*Harry and Tonto*), and the plight of newly separated women (*An Unmarried Woman*). His serio-comic dramas speak to the changes people face, yet Mazursky never forgets the importance of an entertaining script.

Mazursky considers the painful process of screenwriting "the black hole," and he lightheartedly reminisces about his early, prolonged inability to sell anything (short stories, scripts, etc.) to anybody. His evolution from serious writer to performer to TV comedy writer and to screenwriter/director is recalled as film clips recap the high points of his career.

Like Paul Mazursky, Robert Towne finds screenwriting a painstaking craft. Admittedly a slow writer, Towne tackles each project as if it were a detective story. Often tapping obscure events in his private life for clues to characterization, Towne began his screenwriting career as one of Roger Corman's protégés. The master of schlock horror and car chase films, Corman gave many fine, young filmmakers their start in Hollywood. But the cerebral Towne, unable to crank 'em out fast and dirty, became a Corman drop-out.

A mellow, if somewhat vague Californian, Towne imparts some not altogether clear screenwriting tips. But it's fun to hear about the *Chinatown* love scene initiated by his heroine's black-spotted eye, and *Shampoo*'s classy origins in Wycherly's *Country Wife*. Robert Towne's anecdotes should give budding screenwriters the courage to go to unorthodox sources for their material.

William Goldman is as energized and cynical as Towne is low key and sincere. A New Yorker, Goldman began his writing career as a novelist with no intention of breaking into screenwriting. Goldman's first script assignment was to adapt the book, *Flowers for Algernon*, for Cliff Robertson. Goldman remembers rushing to an all-night Times Square bookstore to buy a book on screenwriting. He failed dismally with the project. Robertson fired him and, with a rewritten script in hand, went on to produce and star in *Charly* and win an Academy Award for his efforts, no thanks to Goldman. Goldman still had a lot to learn about screenwriting.

With his born-to-win personality, Goldman's inevitable blockbusters have more often than not fallen into the adventure, espionage, and psychological thriller genres. His *Butch Cassidy, All the President's Men, Marathon Man,* and *The Stepford Wives* became instant classics. On the average, he claims, it takes three years to write, sell, produce, and market a commercial feature. It is impossible for writers to predict public taste from such an early vantage point. To Goldman, screenwriters are an unhappy lot because their work is altered to fit the whims of directors, actors, and producers. William Goldman's cold-blooded appraisal of the business and tips on how to prepare a saleable script should give novices a head start in their uphill marketing battle.

Although *Word into Image* profiles a small, very specialized group of artists, the series is never boring, and should appeal to a wide audience. By personalizing the much misunderstood craft of screenwriting, the tapes will provide discussion material for students of film and creative writing, and transcripts of each half-hour program are available to supplement the tapes for classroom use. The inclusion of writers who adapt scripts from other sources and writers who create original screenplays makes for a valuable, educational balance as well.

Liberally dotted with film clips, the series will, at the very least, entertain film buffs and general audiences from senior high through senior citizens. For more expansive library programs, try piggybacking any *Word into Image* profile with a feature film—for example, show *Harry and Tonto* immediately following the Paul Mazursky tape. Such programs will enhance an audience's viewing pleasure by broadening their perspective and appreciation of the cinema. ▣

This month's programs:

Word into Image: Writers on Screenwriting is a series of six videotapes produced and directed by Freida Lee Mock and Terry Sanders for PBS. Individual titles are: *William Goldman, Neil Simon, Paul Mazursky, Eleanor Perry, Carl Foreman,* and *Robert Towne*. video. color/b&w. 30 min. each. prod. 1981. rel. 1984. Dist: American Film Foundation, Box 2000, Santa Monica, CA 90406. ½" Beta VHS—$500 series (rental $210 series); $250 any three titles (rental $105 any three); $100 each (rental $35 each). ¾" —$1,200 series (rental $330 series); $625 any three titles (rental $165 any three); $225 each (rental $55 each). A bound copy of the six transcripts from the series is available for $27.50 or free if the entire series of tapes is purchased.

Bruce Pollock:

On Record: Popular Music

Something of an alien world, the rock and roll sector has provided its adherents their fair share of thrills this year, along with the usual disappointments, comets flaring into sudden view, warhorse planets flaming out into endless space. Here's a close-up look at that sector, with a glance at some of the comets and planets that whirled and burned in the night.

Bruce Pollock *is the editor of* Guitar *magazine and the author of* Popular Music: An Annotated Index of American Popular Songs, Volumes 7 and 8.

Guitar heroes

• *Starfleet Project.* Brian May (Cap MLP 15014)

Queen's Brian May teamed with all-world rock guitarist Eddie Van Halen on these largely aimless blues jams. Queen's own later album fizzled.

• *Built to Destroy.* The Michael Schenker Group (Chrysalis FV 41441)

The legendary German guitarist has inspired countless Metalists, but on his own has proven lacking as a songwriter. This album proved to be no exception.

• *Couldn't Stand the Wearther.* Stevie Ray Vaughan (Epic FE 39304)

With his second album, he continues his one-man electric blues renaissance. A Hendrix disciple without peer.

• *Midnight Madness.* Night Ranger (MCA 5456)

A couple of new axes on the block, Brad Gillis and Jeff Watson, drive this band with a hard-edged and note-filled pop sound. You might remember "Sister Christian."

• *1984.* Van Halen (Warner Bros. 23985-1)

Long a cult favorite among preteen males, this year Eddie's revolutionary fingerboard technique brought him wider plaudits. Perhaps it was his incendiary solo on Michael Jackson's "Beat It" that finally did the trick. He celebrated 1984 with the number one "Jump."

• *Victims of the Future.* Gary Moore (Mirage 90145-1)

Perhaps the best known unknown guitarist around, Moore is second only to Schenker when it comes to gaining the respect of the metal guitar breed. He plays with fire and passion; unfortunately, when he toured America recently, he played to half-empty houses.

• *Orion the Hunter.* Orion the Hunter (Portrait BFR 39239)

Led by Barry Goudreau, the guitar sound behind Boston, this work capitalized on the rock world's hunger for a new Boston album (now years overdue). Laden with signature sounds, it helped to temporarily fill the need.

• *Grace Under Pressure.* Rush (Mercury 818 476-1 M1)

High-tech rock that loses none of its fury, as played by Alex Lifeson, Canada's rock and roll answer to

Wayne Gretzky. Except that Rush has been playing almost as long as Gretzky's been skating.

• *Through the Fire.* Hagar, Schon, Aaronson, Shrieve (Geffen GHS 4023)

On leave from Journey, rock guitar prodigy Neal Schon teamed up with singer Sammy Hagar to produce an album in a couple of weeks. The product sounds it, except for the flashy remake of "A Whiter Shade of Pale."

New music

• *Rebel Yell.* Billy Idol (Chrysalis FV 41450)

A post-punk throwback to Jim Morrison, Idol loves to live the decadent life he sings about. This is as fine a document as can be found of what's left of the rock experience (as opposed to the corporate experience) in the eighties.

• *More Fun in the New World.* X (Elektra 60283-1)

Frenetic rockabilly courtesy of Billy Zoom, married to the backwoods poetry of John Doe, as mordantly sung by Xenene. A critic's band with something for true rock believers.

• *The Crossing.* Big Country (Mercury 812 870-1 M1)

The big sound of folk/rock returned with Scottish echoes and a modern sensibility; cogent lyrics when you can make them out beneath the stirring din.

The classics

• *Undercover.* The Rolling Stones (Rolling Stones Records 90120-1)

Nothing much new here, or terribly inspired. But the band did produce some snappy videos.

• *90125.* Yes (Atco 90125-1)

A slightly refurbished lineup paved the way toward a wholly satisfying reunion by this monument to seventies progressive rock. Trevor Rabin stepped forward to put himself in the rock guitar sweepstakes.

• *Camouflage.* Rod Stewart (Warner Bros. 25095-1)

Rod continued his long decline as a significant rocker, with another polished set of snoozers.

• *The Pros and Cons of Hitchhiking.* Roger Waters (Col FC 39290)

In the absense of Pink Floyd, one of its prime movers, Roger Waters, took up the chalice of psychedelia and waved it briefly before a new generation. Also this year, Dave Gilmour gave us the bluesy (but not terribly newsy) *About Face* (Col 39296).

• *Penetrator.* Ted Nugent (Atlantic 80125-1)

Though his Tarzan act is wearing thin, Ted should be commended for sticking to his macho, hard-rock roots in a difficult, quiche-eating time. Can't take those commendations to the bank, however.

• *Keep Your Hands Off My Power Supply.* Slade (CBS Assoc. FZ 39336)

Another warhorse band found rolling its merry way through England and resurrected on the wings of a smash remake of their "Cum on Feel the Noize." To their credit, Slade wrote rock and roll anthems all the while. "My Oh My" and "Run, Runaway" were a couple of the creamier moments on 45 this year.

Heavy metal

• *Bark at the Moon.* Ozzy Osbourne (CBS Assoc. QZ 38987)

Scourge of harmless bats and chickens, Osbourne has nevertheless brought to the world some of rockdom's finest guitarists, perhaps the best being the late Randy Rhoads. On this LP hear Randy's able successor, Jake E. Lee.

• *Condition Critical.* Quiet Riot (Pasha QZ 39516)

To the consternation of elders everywhere, heavy metal music reigned briefly this year, chiefly due to the efforts of Quiet Riot's screaming lead singer Kevin DuBrow. But after striking it rich with their debut album, they virtually committed harakiri with this collection of bombs.

• *Animalize.* Kiss (Polygram 422-822-495-1)

After practically inventing the genre, and then falling into disrepute as aging dinosaurs, Kiss was forced into stripping off their makeup in an attempt to revitalize the image. When that didn't work, they threw themselves upon the mercy of the music, and in *Animalize* produced a minor miracle of redemption.

• *Flick of the Switch.* AC/DC (Atlantic 80100-1)

• *Defenders of the Faith.* Judas Priest (Columbia FC 39219)

A couple of the staunchest of the heavy breed, these two bands moved, in 1984, closer to the brink of extinction. Their sound has been updated, their comic-book lust and mayhem adapted to a newer, slicker cat. Sure they have their cults, but rock fans are notoriously fickle.

• *Love at First Sting.* Scorpions (Mercury 814 981-1 M1)

Brother of Michael Schenker, Rudolph, created one good smash in the heavy style, "Rock You Like a Hurricane," and rode the storm through a fairly successful American tour. Prospects for long-term stardom seem slight, as slight as the album's other cuts.

• *Shout at the Devil.* Motley Crue (Elektra 60289-1)

• *Stay Hungry.* Twisted Sister (Atlantic 7-80156-1)

• *Out of the Cellar.* Ratt (Atlantic 80143)

Fueled by the apparent heavy metal takeover, these three bands rose in 1984 to fill the need for loud, arrogant, guitar-filled (some call it) music. Dominated by a fashion consciousness that is at the other side of the world from Duran Duran (but nearly touching Boy George), the bedraggled, made-up faces of Twisted Sister perhaps defined the genre: outrageousness for its own sake, attached to pseudo-anthems like "I Wanna Rock." Will any of these bands be around to welcome 1986? Will any of their songs survive puberty? Highly doubtful. Less doubtful, however, is the fact that three new bands will arise from the mire to take their place in the rock pantheon. If you're into such things, you might want to think about Dio, Queensryche, Loudness, Metallica, Fastway, Girlschool and Krokus, and call me in a year. ▣

Gail Pool:

Magazines

Not long ago, a librarian remarked to me that most library magazine collections reflect a female bias and that public libraries, weakest in reaching blue-collar men, might offer more suitable titles to attract them. "What about *Playboy*?" he suggested. "Or *Soldier of Fortune*?"

Both the observation and the suggested titles call up some provocative issues related to magazines and gender. Most obvious, and intriguing, is the editorial gulf between the majority of magazines designated "men's" and those designated "women's." Put simply: it's a long, long way from the suburbs of *Good Housekeeping* to the steamy environs of *Penthouse,* and longer still from the daycare centers of *Working Mother* to the bloody battlegrounds of *Soldier of Fortune.* The dichotomy raises some unsettling questions about media concepts of male and female, and moves us from the issue of a balanced magazine collection to the issue of a balanced culture.

Historically, men's and women's magazines—those publications which address readers specifically in their male and female roles—have developed along separate editorial and business lines.

For the past century, women's magazines have been the success story of magazine publishing: long-lived, lucrative, and large. Today, ten of the top thirty revenue-producing magazines in the United States are women's magazines; eight of these have circulations that top three million, and six top five million.

Numerous historical reasons account for this success. Women, traditionally assigned specific areas of interest (home, fashion, family, food), formed a coherent audience, at once specialized and large—an ideal combination for a magazine. Relatively neglected in newspapers ("lifestyle" pages are new), women welcomed "their own" publications, focused on issues relevant to their daily lives and filled with information (including advertising) useful to homemakers. Most important, since women were attributed with making most consumer purchases, they comprised an audience advertisers were eager to reach. Food, fashion, beauty, child, and home product advertising have handsomely supported the large number of titles in the field.

Editorially, the success of women's magazines reflects a culture absorbed with defining and channeling femininity. The magazines have held readers with a formula of practicality and promise. They have addressed women in their most traditional roles and because women's traditional roles were their work roles, they have focused on work: cooking, housekeeping, or working at life itself, either struggling to save one's marriage or one's figure.

One and all, women's magazines have stressed self-improvement. Traditional home magazines tell readers how to improve family life and the physical home; fashion books show how to improve appearances. Newer types of women's magazines have carried on the self-improvement tradition: *Working Woman* in the field of corporate life; *Self,* in the area of physical fitness; *Cosmo,* in the realm of sexuality. "Women are very optimistic," says Arthur Hettich, editor-in-chief of *Family Circle.* Women's magazines have skillfully mined readers' optimism.

Men's magazines contrast with the women's scenario in almost every way. Although most men in the United States are husbands and workers, the largest male magazines have addressed them as neither: they have left work roles to be catered to by business and trade publications, and conjugal roles to be neglected entirely, while they themselves have focused on entertainment, escape and escapade. Where women's magazines have emphasized self-improvement, men's have explored self-realization—living to the fullest—and they fall into two main types: sophisticated living with a sexual orientation (the original *Esquire* or *Playboy*), at times reduced merely to the sexual orientation; and adventure (*True* or *Soldier of Fortune*). Thus traditional male magazines have addressed men as pleasure seekers, adventurers, even predators—on the mountainside, on the battlefield, in the bedroom—roles central perhaps to masculine fantasy, but peripheral to most daily lives.

On the business side of the fence, the contrast between the two genres is equally striking. Throughout the century, there have been few major men's titles, and few of these have attained large circulations. Even today, only *Playboy* and *Penthouse* have circulations that top three million.

Unlike women's magazines, men's publications have had to struggle for advertising and have garnered most of their revenues from newsstand sales. A diversity of media to reach men, a dearth of personal products traditionally purchased by men, and the blue-collar audiences of adventure magazines have contributed to the advertising problem. In addition, advertisers shun the skin books. Only *Playboy* has broken the advertising barrier. In 1983, even *Playboy* had only half *Good Housekeeping*'s ad revenues. Apart from the element of sleaziness, with which high class advertisers do not want to be associated, advertisers may well consider that a man is more likely to think about buying a car while perusing a newsweekly than while perusing the voluptuous figure of Miss January.

In view of the editorial differences between men's and women's magazines, it is hardly surprising that they

Gail Pool *holds an M.L.S. degree from Simmons College and presently works as a freelance writer based in Cambridge, Massachusetts.*

have met with different fates in the library. Librarians, like advertisers, have found traditional men's magazines troublesome.

Of the skin magazines, only *Playboy* has the editorial quality to justify an average public library's purchase, and even *Playboy* poses problems. At the practical level, readers mangle it, tearing out the centerfold. Some libraries keep it under lock and key, others resort to microfilm; neither solution allows for convenient access or browsing. On an editorial level, many people find the magazine's sexual content offensive, while others find its sexism offensive. Librarians face the question of whether the magazine's editorial content justifies the extra care required to protect the magazine physically and to defend it intellectually.

Soldier of Fortune poses a different set of problems. The publication is virtually a celebration of war. In-depth, well-written, and overtly rightist articles highlight "hot spots" around the globe—Central America is currently a favorite. The magazine depicts war—and war here is not an abstract, political activity, but actual, graphically described killing—as adventurous, manly, and moral.

Weaponry is a main focus of *SOF* in columns, reviews, and almost all the ads. In a sense, *SOF* is much like a hunting magazine, except the prey are not deer but human beings. In a review of battle blades (December 1984), for example, the author criticizes a knife's performance because, "The point is too high, and you would have to push a large part of the arc of the front of the blade through resisting flesh and around bone on a stabbing stroke." Ads for everything from military grenades to submachine guns are eye-opening to those unacquainted with the variety and accessibility of weapons in the United States.

Should a public library acquire *SOF,* parents would undoubtedly request that the magazine, with its "merc" heroes and easily ordered weapons, be kept away from youngsters. Again, the librarian must weigh the publication's editorial value

against potential difficulties.

Thus men's magazines pose "problems," while women's magazines—however cloying, consumerist, and condescending—are popular and safe. Understandably libraries tend to have numerous women's titles and but a few men's—*Esquire,* usually, and, increasingly, *GQ,* both nowadays "service" magazines and as cloying, consumerist, condescending (and safe) as their feminine counterparts.

Yet despite the preponderance of women's titles, I suggest the average collection will not really reflect a female bias and, because of a different and hidden gender gap in magazine reading, may even tend the other way.

While general interest magazines such as *The New Yorker* are read equally by men and women, specific genres, though not necessarily designated men's or women's interest, are in fact read predominantly by one sex or the other. A few categories, mainly those associated with traditional women's subjects such as health, are read mostly by women. But a great diversity of categories, such as business, sports, automotive and home mechanics, science, and political magazines—our main genres, all well represented in libraries—are read mainly by men. Indeed, the readership breakdown of many of our major magazines (*Business Week,* 98% male; *Sports Illustrated,* 79% male; *Scientific American,* 73% male) suggests that they are in a sense men's magazines. Thus a library's collection of women's titles is likely to be more than compensated for by a broad and interesting selection of magazines read mainly by men.

Since men and women play different roles in our society, it is not surprising that we read by gender. But what we read by gender is disconcerting. Most striking in the magazines read by men is their diversity. While *Penthouse* addresses men in their explicitly sexual role, *Business Week, Field and Stream,* and *Popular Mechanics* address men in other masculine roles. Nowhere in the women's field do we find such a contrast as that between *Penthouse* and *Business Week.* Indeed, most magazines for women are remarkably similar in content and approach to life, showing women tied to a narrow range of interests and images.

Of course, the asymmetry in men's and women's magazines only mirrors the asymmetry of the sexes in our culture and economy. Recently, some of our largest men's and women's publications have encountered economic problems, perhaps in response to changes in our demographic, consumer, and sex-role patterns. Whether real change in these magazines occurs will depend upon publishers, advertisers, and readers themselves. In the meantime, the librarian may balance the collection by subject, by political bent, by intellectual style, in any number of ways—but not really by gender. No acquisitions can impart balance to a collection that must reflect the imbalance in the world that creates it. ▣

Norman Stevens:

Our Profession

While not as glamorous as automation and technology, and in fact now dependent on those marvels, the fundamental technical services operations are essential to sound library management. Equally essential is the ability to analyze problems and to carry out effective research, especially in the application of technology to technical services. The four books reviewed this month are not exciting to read, or full of new ideas, but they are solid presentations of basic information about technical services and research techniques. They are recommended for content and not for style or readability.

Stephen Ford's *The Acquisition of Library Materials* (1973) has served as a standard guide to acquisitions matters for over ten years but ten years is now a long time in librarianship and his work was very much in need of replacement. Rose Mary Magrill and Doralyn Hickey's **Acquisitions Management and Collection Development,** which builds on Ford's work, is a fresh approach to the subject. The inclusion in the title of "management" and "collection development" indicates the extent to which, in ten short years, we have moved away from a focus simply on the acquisition of materials to also take into account the examination of acquisitions patterns in an organized fashion and the direction of the acquisitions process. Some of Ford's material has been retained but, in general, Magrill and Hickey offer a new approach and new information on the essentials of acquisitions.

After two brief but highly effective background chapters on collection development issues, the authors deal in detail with the organization of collection development, the organization of acquisitions work, bibliographic searching, purchasing individual items, vendor-controlled order plans, purchasing special types of book materials, purchasing nonbook materials, the acquisition of serials, gifts and exchanges, and evaluation. Throughout there is a wealth of detail, an excellent selection of pertinent bibliographic citations, and good suggestions on how policies and procedures should be established. Without being overly prescriptive or too specific, Magrill and Hickey provide sensible thoughts on this basic component of our work. Designed as an overview of the field, this text serves that purpose well. It will be especially useful to students and beginning professionals.

Written by two authors, but with considerable assistance from others, Magrill and Hickey's book offers a unity of style and thought that is not found in Irene Godden's **Library Technical Services.** The focus on all aspects of technical services work

Norman Stevens *is university librarian at the University of Connecticut and the author of* Communication Throughout Libraries.

The Best of 1984

- Peter Hernon and Charles R. McClure. *Public Access to Government Information* (Ablex)
- Lowell A. Martin. *Organizational Structure of Libraries* (Scarecrow)
- Gary R. Purcell with Gail Ann Schlachter. *Reference Sources in Library and Information Services* (ABC-Clio)

During 1984 many good professional library publications were issued and in this column I have reviewed a number which I found to deserve attention. Three stand out as meriting special note as we start a new year. Hernon and McClure's work on government information forcefully calls our attention to the importance of those publications in library collections and of providing access to them. It should become a classic serving documents librarians and library administrators for many years to come. Martin's treatment of library organization is a model of what a text in library administration should be. It will help train the next generation of librarians in understanding and thinking about this essential component of our work. Purcell and Schlacter provide those engaged in the research and study of library issues with the first comprehensive reference book of librarianship. Each of these publications will endure. Each of these authors deserves our thanks.

makes it more effective here to use specialist authors to cover different segments of the field; but, as always, that approach sacrifices something in style, uniformity, and content.

Godden has made sound choices in her selection of content and authors. Her general introduction, which sets the tone of the work, is followed by chapters on technical services administration (Leslie Manning), the context and the potential of automation (Karen Horny), acquisitions (Marion Reid), bibliographic control (Betty Bengston), preservation and materials processing (A. Dean Larsen), and circulation functions (Leslie Manning). Each chapter is brief, detailed, and descriptive. Reid compresses, for example, in forty-three pages what Magrill and Hickey cover in 229 pages. Inevitably, as in the other chapters, something gets lost—the nuances of many of the issues, and the broader sense of what the area is about. This more abbreviated overview of the entire field of technical services works best in Godden's introductory chapter and Manning's especially sensible chapter on technical services administration. Together those two chapters furnish a sound idea of the purpose of the technical functions that support all of our work. Designed as a text, like Magrill and Hickey, it too will be especially useful to students and beginning professionals.

The unity of theme found in Godden is lacking in the latest volume of **Advances in Librarianship,** a collection of eight bibliographic essays on topics of current interest. It is remarkable, therefore, how successful this volume is. There is a certain degree of unity provided by the essays on collection management (Marcia Pankake), collection evaluation (Paul Mosher), and the identification of important science literature (C. D. Hurt), all of which deal with the same acquisition theme as Magrill and Hickey and much of Godden. Here, however, the emphasis is on a detailed analysis of the literature relating to a specific aspect of the acquisitions process. Intended for the experienced practitioner rather than the student or the beginning professional, these three essays offer a solid summary of the recent literature along with some challenging ideas based on an analysis of that literature.

Two of the other essays, one on IFLA (Robert Vosper) and the other on library automation in Latin America (Marietta Daniels Shephard), continue the attention that the series has paid to international and foreign librarianship. *Advances in Librarianship* is one of the few sources of useful information on library work outside the United States regularly available to us, and these two essays are welcome for that reason.

The remaining essays are on separate themes. Joan Durrance's examination of community information systems and Nancy Williamson's review of subject access in online systems are fairly standard treatments of their subject. Durrance's plea for the need for evaluation of community information services, and Williamson's suggestion that the development of subject access systems through online public access catalogs built from the top down may be less successful than the techniques used in videotex systems that are being built from the bottom up, warrant careful consideration. Charles McClure's essay deals with management information systems (MIS), information resources management (IRM) systems, and decision support systems (DSS) and their potential role in library management. McClure does a reasonable job of presenting the literature, much of it from other fields, and explaining the techniques and concepts of these exotic systems. He concludes that few libraries currently operate anything approaching these systems, that model building is far ahead of actual implementation, and that research on management information systems for libraries is sparse. His thoughts about the research that needs to be done, and on other future considerations, are well taken; but whether or not his conclusion that it is "intuitively satisfying" to assume that MIS and DSS for libraries is a "good thing" is open to question.

McClure has become one of the outstanding professional experts on the application of research techniques from other fields to librarianship. In that role he is providing an important service by raising questions about the potential use of techniques such as MIS and DSS that are not now being used. In **Research for Decision Making,** he and Robert Swisher offer a basic text on the importance of research to the examination of problems in librarianship and on the components of research including research design, data gathering, sampling, methods of data description, covariation, and statistical decision making. Using relevant examples throughout the book, Swisher and McClure describe some complex techniques in a relatively straightforward manner. While useful to the practicing librarian undertaking a research study, this text is likely to be more useful as a library school text in courses that deal with research methods. Along with such works as *Research Methods in Librarianship* by Busha and Harter, and *Scientific Management of Library Operations* by Dougherty, Heinritz, and Kaske, it gives library and information science a group of texts that should support more satisfactory teaching of a range of research techniques. ▣

This month's books:

Godden, Irene P. *Library Technical Services.* Academic Press, 1984. 272p. $32. ISBN 0-12-287040-9.

Magrill, Rose Mary and Doralyn J. Hickey. *Acquisitions Management and Collection Development in Libraries.* ALA, 1984. 229p. $20. ISBN 0-8389-0408-4. LC 84-9288.

Simonton, Wesley. *Advances in Librarianship. Volume 13.* Academic Press, 1984. 264p. $32. ISBN 0-12-024672-4.

Swisher, Robert and Charles R. McClure. *Research for Decision Making.* ALA, 1984. 209p. $25. ISBN 0-8389-0398-3.

Patrick Dewey:

Software for Libraries

If you've seen long, computer-produced banners lately, they were probably generated by **The Print Shop** (Broderbund, 1984). Written by David Balsam and Martin Kahn, *The Print Shop* is a versatile program for generating banners, letterheads, signs, greeting cards, and kaleidoscope designs. It is also extremely user-friendly through every step of the selection process. To produce a greeting card, simply select from a prepared format or make a custom card. Eight predesigned cards are included, including notepaper and an invitation. Customs cards may be made by selecting borders and illustrations. Size and placement of the illustrations are chosen by the user and there are eight different fonts. The program includes two kaleidoscope displays which may be "frozen" and used as background for any of the creations. This should prove a useful program for numerous library chores, and for public access. Any of the functions can be performed in minutes. Once the design has been printed out, the print shop across the street can do the rest. Greeting cards are printed on a single sheet of paper which folds into a regular card. You can even put your own motto, message or initials on the back of the card where the publisher's name usually goes. Once you've "experimented" with the product, a more convenient shorthand method of use is available by just typing in numbers which represent the various designs and choices. Only one warning to librarians—some of the features (especially the banners) use ribbons at an incredible rate, so some rationing or caution for public access is advised. *The Print Shop* will work with many dot matrix printers, including Scribe, Imagewriter, Epson, Okidata Microline, Prowriter, and others. Make certain that your printer—make and model—will work with *Print Shop*. For use with Apple II+, IIe, IIc,; Commodore 64. Dot matrix printer with graphics capability required. Cost: $49.95.

Patrick Dewey *is administrative librarian, Maywood (Illinois) Public Library and author of* Public Access Microcomputers: A Handbook for Librarians.

Restoring lost data

Lifesaver, by John Worthington and Donald Lee, (Micro Lab, Inc., 1983) is a utility program for use on so-called "blown" diskettes. Diskettes may lose data or have data scrambled for various reasons, one of the most prevalent being the magnetic field. A disk may be inadvertently written over with other data, or reinitialized. In both cases, there may be permanent data loss. Nothing will retrieve it. There are less drastic problems—for example, when a file is simply deleted. *Lifesaver* will easily restore such a file so long as it has not yet been written over. Similarly, restoring DOS is also a simple matter. Very often, a small data loss makes an entire file inaccessible. *Lifesaver* will analyze each track on the disk and attempt to retrieve all existing data. Files that are retrieved will have various degrees of damage, and each file is labelled according to how much data were recovered. In some cases, there may be complete files, in others there may be very little data left. The primary function of such a utility program would seem to be for word processing, database management, or other user-created files—especially for users who consistently forgot to "back it up." There is even a section on how to split open a mud-stained diskette, wash it off, and pack it back into a new, clean jacket! *Lifesaver* can be used with Apple-based DOS, Pascal, CP/M, Pilot, Fortran, or Apple III. Cost: $25.

An electronic coloring book

Two new programs are available in the Creative Paths series from Springboard Software. **Rainbow Writer** is appropriate for ages four and up and **Mask Parade** is appropriate for ages four to twelve. *Rainbow Writer* is an excellent graphics system that can be learned in fifteen to twenty minutes. Essentially an elaborate electronic coloring book, the user selects from nine icons or small pictures located along the bottom of the screen. For instance, the "paint can" provides ten different palettes of colors. Each palette is a range of ten colors and designs (solids, stripes, brick walls, etc.), and samples displayed along the left side of the screen. Most of the screen is taken up by the picture being colored or drawn. Eight different sets of pictures include animals, the seasons, space, fairy tales, flowers, and birds. Each set has from three to four pictures. They are similar to the pictures found in paper coloring books—blank until the user chooses "crayons" that allow him or her to draw in different ways, including single, small, large dots, groups of dots, etc. There is also a "hat of tricks" icon, which permits the user to draw different size lines, circles, and boxes. Just for variety, a "mirror" choice allows free-style drawing but duplicates whatever is input (e.g., a line drawn on the top of the screen is drawn at the same time on the bottom of the screen). Free hand drawing on a blank page is also allowed. Each picture set can be colored in predetermined ways, or by the use of a "fill" command that allows quick, first-time success at drawing pleasing and colorful creations in just minutes. Finished products may be saved to disk. This is a spectacular, user-friendly system. For use with: Apple II+, IIe, IIc, Commodore 64, IBM PC jr. Cost: $34.95. Another recommended product in this series is *Mask Maker* which is similar to the familiar *Facemaker,* by Spinnaker Software, but goes a step farther. Children will have lots of fun combining silly faces, spectacles, feet, neckties, and jewelery. The finished products are printed out and may then be cut out and worn! For use with: Apple II+, IIe, IIc, Commodore 64, IBM PCjr. Cost: $39.95.

Managing the small library

Library Management Programs (Random House, 1984, first published by The Library Software Co., 1983) are a group of packages for the small library, particularly school libraries that do not have access to an automated circulation system. Included are *The Overdue Writer, The Overdue Collector, The Bibliography Writer* and *The A-V Catalog Writer.* All are simple and easy to use. They are not for everybody and they do not do everything. But having said that, they will fill the needs of many librarians in small school libraries. **The Bibliography Writer,** will produce professional-looking bibliographies, but the program is limited to books and periodicals. Cost: $49.95. **The Overdue Writer** and **The Overdue Collector** work together, and are actually a small circulation system. The promotional materials for the programs note that users need only have access to a micro for up to twenty minutes per day, since book information may be input at the end of the day's activity. *The Overdue Writer* tracks checkouts, allows searches, and prints lists, overdue notices, and bills. At the end of four or five weeks, records for books not yet returned are kept in a printed file, and the disk may be reused for a new circulation period. With the aid of *The Overdue Collector,* records of delinquent borrowers can be kept in an active computer file for as long as is necessary, and additional bills can be printed. Cost: *The Overdue Writer,* $149.95; *The Overdue Collector,* $49.95. **The A-V Catalog Writer** will catalog up to one thousand audiovisual items on a single data disk, including up to three subject headings. Each item is input using media type, shelf-list number, title, producer, contents, copyright date. Each item is given a discrete number. The list may be printed out in its entirety, or in part (just one subject, for instance). Cost: $69.95. All programs are for use with Apple II, IIe, or TRS-80 Model III, IV. Requires 80-column printer.

New utility for Terrapin

Terrapin Logo (Terrapin, Inc., 1982, 1983) has been available for several years now, with a new version (3.0) due early this year. To enhance this popular language, a new utility package, **Utilities II,** has been created. Designed for children, Logo is a teaching language but it will learn the basics of programming, with loops, graphics, and designs. Few things could be as simple, and the language will progress to advanced topics. In the center of the screen sits a tiny "turtle," which draws a line according to the user's instructions. Programs are called "procedures" and are built from "primitives" or the elementary commands (forward, backward, etc.). The documentation is massive (375 pages), but excellent. Cost: $99.95. *Utilities II* comes with a small booklet that explains what it does and how it should be used with Logo. It also provides examples of graphics, and several educational games (e.g., Hangman, Argue). For use with Apple II+ (64K). ▣

Publisher addresses for this month's software:

Broderbund Software, 17 Paul Drive, San Rafael, CA 94903.

MicroLab, Inc., 2699 Skokie Valley Road, Highland Park, IL 60035.

Random House, Inc., 400 Hahn Road, Westminister, MD 21157.

Springboard Software, Inc., 7808 Creekridge Circle, Minneapolis, MN 55436.

Terrapin Inc., 222 Third St., Cambridge, MA 02142.

Current Reference Books

Correspondence and review copies for this column should be directed to James Rettig, University Library, Box 8198, University of Illinois at Chicago, Chicago, IL 60680.

American Peace Directory 1984, edited by Melinda Fine and Peter M. Steven. Cambridge: Ballinger, 1984. 225p. pa$12.95. ISSN 0740-9885

Although admittedly incomplete, this first effort to identify organizations in the United States "which support the establishment of a stable peace with a minimum level of military force" is a qualified success. The compilers are on the staff of the Institute for Defense and Disarmament Studies in Brookline, Massachusetts. The five alphabetical directory sections list addresses, phone numbers, contact persons, and program emphases of 181 national groups, 3 educators' groups, 69 educational programs, 408 local peace groups, and 767 local chapters of national groups. Indexes list the groups by state and zip code, program focus, and name. A superfluous list of members of the House of Representatives by state and district is mirrored by an alphabetical list by name. The introduction carefully explains the distinctions among the groups' constituencies, purposes, and structures. It resembles a 1960s undergraduate discussion of the nuances among political philosophies espoused by protest groups of that period. However, this should not detract from the directory's success in fulfilling its purpose—facilitating communication among peace groups. Libraries can use this to refer patrons to local and national groups that focus on issues such as disarmament and the nuclear freeze movement.

The Atomic Papers, by Grant Burns. Metuchen, N.J.: Scarecrow, 1984. 309p. $22.50. 0-8108-1692-X 84-1390

Every reference work is at least implicitly a political document. Even a literary bibliography, by its inclusions and exclusions, declares its compiler's membership in a particular critical camp. *The Atomic Papers,* an annotated 1,100-item bibliography on atomic power, with a particular focus on nuclear weapons, lists books published since 1945 and articles published since 1980 that discuss the pros and cons of the issue. The decidedly anti-bomb annotations make this an overtly political reference work. One representative annotation speaks of "the Reagan administration's reckless nuclear positions . . . and the whole whimsical entertainment of the 'winable' nuclear war option." Even the selection of sources has been politicized; mainstream magazines indexed by *Readers' Guide* have been avoided in favor of alternative press journals. Subject and author indexes supplement the chapters' topical arrangement. Since nuclear weaponry and related issues are popular topics with high school and college debaters and term paper writers, students will be attracted to this bibliography for its convenience; however they should be cautioned about its strong bias.

Biography and Genealogy Master Index, 1984 Supplement, edited by Barbara McNeil. Detroit: Gale, 1984. 914p. $170. 0-8103-1508-4 82-15700

It appears that rather than issue a cumulative third edition of this ambitious, comprehensive, and expensive cumulative index to other reference works, Gale has decided to issue annual supplements. In the absence of an explicit statement about the future of *BGMI* (reviewed in *WLB,* September, 1981; January, 1983; January 1984), one can only speculate. The new supplement indexes 370,000 entries in some eighty-five editions and volumes of approximately fifty titles. Since some titles are serials that index themselves (*Current Biography, Contemporary Authors*), libraries may decide the cost outweighs the convenience. Many of the indexed works are new editions of standard annuals (e.g., *Who's Who, The Annual Obituary*). The remainder are monographic works. Some, like *British Writers,* are well known and frequently consulted, while others, such as *Who's Who in Real Estate* are more esoteric and consulted mostly by specialists. The convenience of *BGMI* cannot be disputed; each library must judge whether the supplement's added convenience is worth its cost, especially since *BGMI* and its supplements are available on Dialog.

James Rettig *is head reference librarian, University of Illinois at Chicago.*

Black-Jewish Relations in the United States, 1752–1984, compiled by Lenwood G. Davis. Westport, CT: Greenwood, 1984. 130p. $29.95. 0-313-2332-2 84-4685 (Bibliographies and indexes in Afro-American and African studies, no. 1)

Black-Jewish relations commanded the national spotlight last year when Jessie Jackson called New York "Hymietown" and Louis Farrakhan inflamed the controversy by threatening the life of Milton Coleman, the *Washington Post* writer who reported Jackson's remarks. Despite the time span cited in the title, this 1,200-item bibliography does not include articles about the Jackson-Farrakhan incident. The bibliography is divided into three sections according to type of publication (books, dissertations and theses, and periodical and newspaper articles). Each section is organized topically. Most of the dissertations treat conditions in particular cities. Many of the chapters in the book and article sections deal with the opinions of individual black leaders regarding Jews. Others deal with slavery, abolition, affirmative action, desegregation, the PLO and Arabs, and anti-Semitism. Within each chapter, items are arranged by author. Book entries have been annotated. The articles were culled from a variety of sources, including black newspapers. The topical chapters are defined narrowly so that the personal name index offers the only additional access needed. Davis's bibliography offers an excellent starting point for historians, sociologists, and political scientists.

The Book of Fees, by Lois Cunniff. New York: Morrow, 1984. $12.95. 264p. 0-688-03275-3 84-9042

Librarians are conspicuously absent from the forty professions whose fees are explained in *The Book of Fees.* Whether or not the public yet realizes that "fee" increasingly supplants "free" library service, they do know it costs to have a will drafted or a tooth drilled or a piano moved. Not only does the book explain what accountants, appliance repairers, brokers,

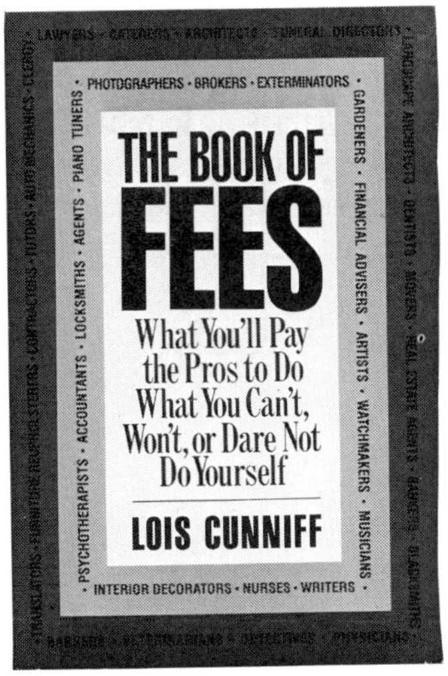

contractors, detectives, funeral directors, gardeners, locksmiths, photographers, translators, veterinarians, and others charge for their professional services, but also how those fees are calculated, often quoting the professionals themselves. It tells how to negotiate a lawyer's fee; how health insurers arrive at "usual, customary, and reasonable" payment schedules, and how much to tip personnel in upscale beauty salons. Fees charged in various major cities and parts of the country are compared and are displayed in chart form when a profession has many specialties or performs a variety of procedures. This book removes the mystery surrounding the costs of infrequently used services such as architects and furniture restorers. Consumers will feel more comfortable and better prepared if they consult *The Book of Fees* before hiring one of these professionals.

Children's Literature from A to Z, by Jon C. Stott. New York: McGraw-Hill, 1984. 318p. pa$12.95. 0-07-61791-0 84-4425

A poor man's (or poor library's) version of *Something About the Author* (Detroit: Gale, 1971-), *Children's Literature* offers short critical biographies of approximately 150 authors and illustrators of children's books. Biographies of subjects both living and deceased include summaries of significant works and overall career assessments. Articles on genre (e.g., biography, folktales, picture books); the Caldecott and Newbery awards; and famous tales (e.g., Cinderella, Hansel and Gretel, Snow White) are integrated into the alphabetical sequence of authors. Because the book is intended as a guide for parents and teachers, each article concludes with short tips for stimulating discussion with children. Many of these tips will be obvious to all but very ingenuous adult readers of the children's books. Where *Something About the Author* often runs autobiographical commentary on its thousands of writers, *Children's Literature* consistently offers chronological biographies. The former format involves greater risk but can yield greater excitement; the latter, while predictable, is dependable. Since *Something About the Author* and its short-lived two-volume companion, *Yesterday's Authors of Books for Children,* cover all the authors in *Children's Literature,* libraries owning those will gain little from *Children's Literature.* Other libraries obviously need it.

Dictionary of Animals, edited by Michael Chinery. New York: Arco, 1984. 379p. $17.95. 0-668-06155-3 84-716

The only traces of a British accent in his attractive import are metric measurements, occasional variant spellings, and a few popular names used in England but not in the United States. Organized in dictionary form by popular names, articles of no more than several hundred words describe each animal's physical features, habitat, food, and behavior. The articles, written in a simple style, conclude with the animal's scientific name. Bountiful color illustrations of the sort *National Geographic* would proudly publish assure the book's appeal to children in the upper grades. Occasional thematic articles (e.g., carnivores, marsupials, parasites, rodents) discuss characteristics of groups of species. The index includes both popular and scientific names. The dictionary will be popular and useful in school and public libraries.

A Dictionary of Classical Reference in English Poetry, by Eric Smith. Totowa, N.J.: Barnes & Noble, 1984. 308p. $39.50. 0-389-20430-7 83-12273

As knowledge of Graeco-Roman literature and history becomes a greater rarity, people capable of truly understanding English poetry become equally rare, for the Graeco-Roman heritage informs much of that poetry. The need for works such as this dictionary of references will continue to increase. For eighty-five frequently studied British poets, it identifies hundreds of mythological characters, antique historical figures, and ancient authors alluded to or named in their major poems. A fact-packed paragraph identifies the classical figure, followed by citations to allusions, that list poets, poems, and line numbers. Thus one can trace the treatment of a particular mythological figure from Chaucer down through the centuries. The index by English poet permits one to reverse the procedure, seeing which classical figures captured the imagination of each poet. This dictionary touches but a small part of our literary heritage. But preservation and remedial efforts must begin somewhere and must abide by realistic ambitions. This is a good beginning.

A Directory of Public Vocational-Technical Schools and Institutes in the U.S.A., edited by Marliss Johnston, 2nd ed. Mankato, MN: Minnesota Scholarly Press, 1984. 333p. $65. 0-933474-37-7

Although it is much more current, this directory does not fully supplant *Lovejoy's Career and Vocational School Guide* (5th ed., New York: Simon & Schuster, 1978). *Lovejoy's* lists some schools (particularly proprietary schools) and indexes some curricula that are not included in the *Directory*. This is not to say *Lovejoy's* is superior. The newer *Directory* lists by state more than 1,400 publicly supported vocational schools, including, address, phone number, name of contact person, and programs. In many cases the duration of programs is stated in terms of weeks, semesters, or years. An extensive program index cites states and entry numbers. High school and public libraries should have the *Directory* to help students learn what programs are available and where they are offered.

European Writers: The Age of Reason and the Enlightenment, edited by George Stade. New York: Scribner's, 1984. 2v. $130. 0-684-17914-8 83-16333

In unwelcome tribute, many libraries' sets of *American Writers* (New York: Scribner's, 1974–81) and *British Writers* (reviewed in *WLB,* December, 1981) have been marred by readers' underlining or mutilated by razor-toting vandals posing as patrons. These transgressors can be commended for their taste even as they are condemned for their deeds. Like *The Middle Ages and the Renaissance* (reviewed in *WLB,* February 1984), *The Age of Reason* excludes British authors. The well-written, in-depth articles survey each author's life, analyze major themes and significant works, and offer selective bibliographies of primary and secondary works. Among the thirty authors treated are Descartes, Pascal, Vico, Voltaire, Diderot, Lessing, and the Marquis de Sade. When complete, the series will collectively offer an impressive overview of Western civilization's development as reflected in its best literary and philosophical works. Librarians can expect the pages of *The Age of Reason* to suffer the same sorts of unwelcome flattery experienced by other volumes in the series.

The Facts On File Dictionary of First Names, by Leslie Dunkling and William Gosling. New York: Facts On File, 1984. 305p. $17.95. 0-87196-274-8 84-4175

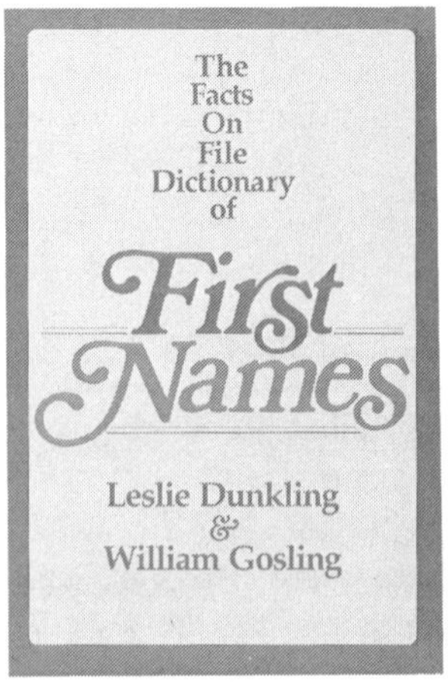

First published by J. M. Dent in England in 1983 as *Everyman's Dictionary of First Names,* this is a far livelier treatment of names than E. G.

Withycombe offers in *The Oxford Dictionary of English Christian Names* (3rd ed., New York: Oxford, 1977). With 4,500 names and more than 5,000 variants and nicknames, *Facts On File* is also more comprehensive and more cosmopolitan, noting popularity trends and variants of names not only in Britain, but throughout the English-speaking world. *Oxford* explains etymologies in scholarly fashion and tends to account for surges of popularity of names by relating them to literary characters. *FOF* does this too, but it also links popularity to the prominence of like-named entertainers and other public figures. An appendix lists the top fifty first names for boys and girls in Britain and the United States from 1925 through 1982. Produced by two specialists on names, the *FOF Dictionary of First Names* is first-rate.

Indexing and Abstracting, 1977–1981, by Hans H. Wellisch. Santa Barbara: ABC-Clio, 1984. 276p. $45. 0-87436-398-5 84-3064

In the last century, England's Lord Chief Justice John Nolan proposed that Parliament pass a bill "to deprive an author who publishes a book without an index of the privilege of copyright, and moreover, to subject him for his offence to a pecuniary penalty." Had the MPs enacted the bill, indexing would have matured sooner and no doubt something comparable to Wellisch's international bibliography and it predecessor, *Indexing and Abstracting* (Santa Barbara: ABC-Clio, 1980) would have been compiled long ago. Recently, however, a force stronger than law has affected indexing. That force, the computer, did not appear in the index to Wellisch's 1980 volume; the new volume has many entries for online systems and databases. The 4,000 books, articles, dissertations, and conference papers in twenty-six languages treat indexing techniques, indexing languages, indexing of specific formats, types of indexes, professional issues, history, and even humor in indexing. It covers a similar array of topics in abstracting. The three indexes (author, title, subject) are, as one would expect in such a work, carefully crafted. Its appeal will be greatest in library schools, but it can be helpful to anyone curious about how verbal systems can be used to make stored information retrievable.

Lisa Birnbach's College Book, by Lisa Birnbach. New York: Ballantine, 1984. 515p. pa$9.95. 0-345-30918-9 84-90910

A thorough reading of Birnbach's introduction leads one to conclude that since she threatens to perpetrate "future updated editions," her book is meant to be taken seriously. Nearly every page brims with evidence that preppy maven Birnbach, who made one-day visits to all 186 colleges she describes, needs to return to school before she attempts to write another reference book. Birnbach's profiles, punctuated by quotes from students, focus on campus social life, listing best dorm, best pizza parlor, favorite drink, favorite drug, parking situation, popular hang-outs, status of Greek life, and the like. Her narratives swell with exaggeration and caricature. All of this overshadows the few bits of information about academic programs, things like most and least popular majors, best professors, and best study spots—items open to dispute. But Birnbach says these aren't important in her book. Nor, it turns out, is truth. If she returns to campus, Birnbach should attend journalism classes to learn how to find and report facts. One can open to almost any school and find one or more errors. For example, she erroneously reports that this reviewer's college dormitory of some fifteen years ago, a circular building featuring cramped pie-slice rooms, was a Holiday Inn five years ago. Errors are so abundant that *The Chronicle of Higher Education* (September 19, 1984) ran a long article in which numerous college officials found fault after fault with Birnbach's book. One hopes it will be perceived as a one-shot put-on; it certainly isn't a reference book.

Literary Criticism Index, by Alan R. Weiner and Spencer Means. Metuchen, N.J.: Scarecrow, 1984. 685p. $49.50. 0-8108-1694-6 84-1371

We have bibliographies of bibliographies. Here we have an index to bibliographies. Surely, a bibliography of indexes to collective reference tools must be in the works. It all sounds confusing, but most of these tools dispel confusion. Indeed, this index addresses a very real problem. Students with a shallow sense of their cultural history are baffled by literary bibliographies that presume a knowledge of the author's nationality and period or a work's genre. This index requires only that a user know the author's name. Under each author, the user will find references to bibliographies, indicating which ones include citations to general criticism and criticism on particular works. References include page number, eliminating any problems caused by the bibliographies' diverse forms of organization. Most of the eighty-six bibliographies concentrate on British and American authors. The index covers a good range of monographic bibliographies, but would be more useful if it also indexed Lewis Leary's *Articles on American Literature, 1968–1975* (Durham, N.C.: Duke University Press, 1979), a very heavily used bibliography. This is more a tool for librarians to use to set patrons on the right path than for patrons to use without considerable explanation or assistance. Yet the net effect will be time saved for both parties and a more satisfied patron.

McGraw-Hill Dictionary of Chemistry, edited by Sybil P. Parker. New York: McGraw-Hill, 1984. 665p. $32.50. 0-07-045420-5 84-12205

McGraw-Hill Dictionary of Electronics and Computer Technology, edited by Sybil P. Parker. New York: McGraw-Hill, 1984. 582p. $32.50. 0-07-045416-7 84-12211

McGraw-Hill Dictionary of Engineering, edited by Sybil P. Parker. New York: McGraw-Hill, 1984. 659p. $32.50. 0-07-045412-4 84-12206

Just as the *McGraw-Hill Encyclopedia of Science and Technology* (reviewed in *WLB,* September 1982) has spawned specialized subject encyclopedias such as the *McGraw-Hill Encyclopedia of Astronomy* (reviewed in *WLB,* June 1983), the *McGraw-Hill Dictionary of Scientific and Technical Terms* (3rd ed., New York: McGraw-Hill, 1984) has spawned these specialized subject dictionaries. *Chemistry* defines 9,000 terms, *Electronics* 10,000, and *Engineering* 16,000, reprinted verbatim from the parent work's 98,500 entries. Entries in *Chemistry* and *Engineering* include tags identifying each term's narrow discipline (e.g., analytical chemistry, crystallography, design engineering, mining engineering). These dictionaries offer convenience and economy to small libraries and branch libraries that need narrow subject coverage. But libraries should not buy these dictionaries if they are to be shelved in the same collection. It would be more economical to buy the parent work for $70.

Movie Guide for Puzzled Parents, by Lynn Minton. New York: Delacorte, 1984. 368p. $19.95, pa$12.95. 0-385-29284-8; 0-385-29336-4 83-23971

In *Halliwell's Film Guide* (3d ed., New York: Scribner's, 1982) and similar sources, most libraries have all of the brief film plot synopses they need. However public libraries that circulate videocassettes of feature films may want to tether a copy of *Movie Guide for Puzzled Parents* to the cassette catalog or cabinet because, unlike other film guides, it specificially evaluates each film's suitability for children and adolescents. The 1,500 reviews selected from Minton's movie review column, published in *McCall's* since 1973, manage to pack a lot of information into their hundred or so words. The reviews summarize, pick out highlights, point out weaknesses, and evaluate. Minton's sentences tend to be too ambitiously long and become confusing. However she clearly describes each film's treatment of sex, violence, and language and predicts their effect on young viewers. Reviews generally conclude with a recommended minimum age for viewing. These are the things parents want to know before taking a film home for the family. They will especially appreciate the checklists of movies for various age groups and on various themes. Librarians can expect that copies of this book will become well-worn by parents trying to find films suitable for their children and, one suspects, by young people in search of forbidden fruits.

Our Mutual Friend, by Joel J. Brattin and Bert G. Hornback. New York: Garland, 1984. 197p. $37. 0-8240-8986-3 83-49325 (The Garland Dickens bibliographies, vol. 1)

The first of a series of bibliographies devoted to single Dickens novels, the annotations of criticism of Dickens's last complete novel show the variety of interest the novel has generated. A number of articles in *Notes & Queries* debated the accuracy of Dickens's use of railroad signals; other articles and dissertations have considered the novel's social theme, symbols, and significance. Some few annotations manage to evoke the spirit of the novel, giving rise to images of Gaffer Hexam's Thames, Boffin's dustheap, and the Veneerings' dinner party. Following the opening section on the text and early editions, secondary works are organized into sections of criticism published during various periods through 1983; special studies such as notes, sources, and historical background; biography; and bibliography. The subject entries interspersed within the index's numerous author entries are not as helpful as they could be, because some are followed by as many as fifty undifferentiated entry numbers. Although indisputably a reference work by virtue of its organization, its specialized nature dictates placing this helpful bibliography in the circulating collection in academic libraries.

Parents as Sexuality Educators, edited by Susan U. Snyder and Sol Gordon. Phoenix: Oryx, 1984. 212p. $55. 0-89774-087-4 83-42840

Every mother and father hears the question sooner or later: "Where do babies come from?" Unless they intend to stonewall their children until those children make them grandparents, parents need answers appropriate for the context created by the child's age and their own beliefs about sex. This bibliography describes print and audiovisual resources parents and professionals can use to answer perennial questions. Resources are arranged by age group and by special topics such as homosexuality, teen pregnancy, single parents, sexual abuse, and the disabled. Many of the annotations explain the item's ethical perspective, a real aid in selection. But other annotations are throwaways such as "Provides essential information in the area of sexuality." The scope ranges far afield from the title, citing among its 2,500 items works on sex and aging, divorce, public policy questions, changing male-female relationships, and stepparenting. Parents, if they turn to the library, will benefit from the bibliography's guidance, but it will be most useful to professionals working with children and teenagers.

The Random House Thesaurus, edited by Jess Stein and Stuart B. Flexner. College ed. 812p. $14.95. 0-394-52949-9 84-4914

Thesauri often confer mixed blessings on their users. On the one hand, the user finds a more vivid word than the one that first came to mind; on the other hand, that word is often inappropriate, especially when compared to the tried-and-true word whose rejection occasioned consulting the thesaurus. Two features in the *Random House* should discourage farfetched substitutions. First, each of the 11,000 entry words is illustrated in a complete sentence, permitting the user to plug synonyms in and test their fit. Second, highly specialized and very broad synonyms are labeled as such, warning the user to check a dictionary to learn their connotations. It shares this feature as well as lists of antonyms, indicators of parts of speech, and usage labels with another thessaurus in dictionary rather than traditional form, *Webster's Collegiate Thesaurus* (Springfield, MA: Merriam, 1976). *Webster's* is organized to indicate degree of similarity by separating words into lists of synonyms and related words, an approach suitable for some users. But others will prefer *Random House*'s appeal to intuition through examples and will rely on that power for guidance in choosing words. Both approaches are valid, acceptable, suitable, proper, fitting, applicable, effective. . . .

Scribner Desk Dictionary of American History. New York: Scribner's, 1984. 631p. $24.95. 0-684-18154-1 84-14019

The Concise Dictionary of American History (New York: Scribner's, 1983) condenses every article in the eight-volume *Dictionary of American History* (rev. ed., New York: Scribner's, 1976). The shorter *Desk Dictionary* distills selected articles down to essentials, translating the fluid prose of the originals into dictionary-definition prose, functional and to the point. A handful of the 6,000 entries describe events since 1976; 1980 census figures are used throughout. The *Desk Dictionary* is fine for office use by historians who can place the brief articles into context, but most libraries should, at the very least, have *The Concise Dictionary* and ideally, have the complete encyclopedic eight-volume dictionary.

Slogans, edited by Laurence Urdang and Ceila D. Robbins. Detroit: Gale, 1984. 556p. $65. 0-8103-1549-1 84-10197

With approximately 6,000 slogans, *Slogans* is more selective than the 15,000-item *Advertising Slogans of America* (reviewed in *WLB,* October 1984). Although more selective, *Slogans* has a slightly broader scope, encompassing political slogans and some British advertising slogans. The arrangement by type of product, with slogans indexed by first word and by company or product name, is more versatile than *Advertising Slogans'* arrangement by slogan and company. Unfortunately neither source gives dates of slogans. Browsing through the slogans can be tedious and leaves one with the impression that "you had to be there to get it." Advertising executive S. Heagan Bayles strengthens that impression in his anecdotal introduction telling how he helped increase sales of Pall Mall cigarettes with the slogan, "Filters the smoke on the way to your throat—filters the smoke and makes it mild." Apparently you had to be there—in the days before health warnings on cigarette packs—to get it. Slogans merit preservation since they mirror the values of their times. So, until a slogans dictionary founded on historical principles comes along, *Slogans* and *Advertising Slogans* will do. And both are welcome to use that line as a slogan.

Tests, Supplement, edited by Richard S. Sweetland and Daniel J. Keyser. Kansas City: Test Corporation of America, dist. by Gale, 1984. 426p. $65. 0-9611286-4-X 84-8773

The supplement to *Tests* (reviewed in *WLB,* November 1983) increases its usefulneses by describing more than five hundred new psychological, educational, and personnel tests. Most of the descriptions are longer and more informative than the 3,000 in the base volume. The same easy-to-read format tells each test's title, author, age level, scoring procedure, cost, and publisher. The supplement includes one-and two-page facsimile samples from seventy tests published since 1980. The samples note the page numbers of the tests' descriptions but, curiously, the descriptions of these tests fail to refer users to the samples. This missing link would have been very helpful. Few supplements have the convenient feature of a cumulative index. This one boasts three cumulative indexes: publisher, title, and author. It also has cumulative directories of scoring services and of tests that can be used with the visually impaired. *Tests,* now in its third printing, has demonstrated its usefulness and popularity. Yet librarians will understandably bristle at having to pay $65 for the 426-page supplement barely a year after paying just $69.95 for the 900-page base volume. The difference seems to be a result of the supplement's distribution by a second publisher; the base volume was marketed directly by the Test Corporation of America.

Ward's Directory of 51,000 Largest U.S. Corporations, edited by Bald-win H. Ward. Baldwin H. Ward Publications (929 Petaluma Blvd. N., Petaluma, CA 94952), 1984. 1,523p. pa$195, hardback $10 extra. 0-913482-00-5

Because Ward's business directories rank and sort companies in numerous useful ways, one wishes that they were published promptly as announced and updated at specified regular intervals. Like *Ward's Directory of 55,000 Largest U.S. Corporations* (reviewed in *WLB,* June 1982), *51,000* ranks 8,500 publicly held and 42,500 private companies by sales within three-digit SIC categories and lists them in state and zip code order and alphabetically. The ranking of public corporations includes thirty bits of financial data (including selected ratios) gathered from 10-K reports, annual reports, and questionnaires. Unfortunately the year in the "This Year" column is not specified. An innovation in this edition is the linking of divisions and subsidiaries with their parent companies in the geographic and alphabetical sections. Special features include lists of the top 1,000 companies ranked by profitability, growth rate, number of employees, highest current ratio, and several other factors. *Ward's* many rankings distinguish it and give it utility no other directory has. One must, nevertheless, exercise caution with it. For example, *Ward's* ranks the defunct Goldblatt Bros. department stores of Chicago as the 971st largest employer and includes some religious orders and nonprofit organizations which, although legally corporations, are conspicuous misfits in a business directory. In libraries this popular directory, sold out-right rather than leased, will receive such heavy use that the flimsy hardcover binding will not survive. It will be more economical to buy the paperback and send it out for a binding that will protect it until the appearance of its successor.

Webster's II New Riverside University Dictionary. Boston: Houghton Mifflin, 1984. 1,536p. $14.95, pa$3.95. 0-395-33957-X; 0-395-36341-1 83-3799

Although it is a serviceable desk dictionary for home, dormitory, or office, *New Riverside* lacks some of the desirable features that mark *Webster's Ninth New Collegiate Dictionary* (reviewed in *WLB*, September 1983) as the best in its class. Drawing on the Merriam-Webster Company's database of thirteen million words, *Webster's Ninth* dates the first appearance of words and consistently gives pronunciation of all forms derived from a root. The absence of these from the *New Riverside* becomes apparent only when the two dictionaries are compared side-by-side, an exercise that makes one want these features. The two define approximately the same number of words, but definitions in *Webster's Ninth* tend to be pithier. *New Riverside* includes more than three hundred engaging word histories emphasizing the evolution of meaning as much as of form. Usage notes, similar to those in *Webster's Ninth*, explain current conventions. More than nine hundred entries include lists of synonyms. In its coverage of new words (e.g., freebase, lunar excursion module) *New Riverside* distinguishes itself. Like many other generic "Webster's" desk dictionaries, *New Riverside* proves that Noah Webster laid a firm foundation for dictionaries providing correct spellings, meanings, pronunciation, and brief etymologies. Nevertheless, without detracting from *New Riverside*'s merits, *Webster's Ninth* has built more on that foundation than any other dictionary.

What Can I Do with a Major In . . . ? by Lawrence R. and Anita Malnig. Rev. ed. Abbott Press (Box 433, Ridgefield, NJ 07657), 1984. 240p. $24.95, pa$17.95. 0-912678-1-X; 0-912678-0-1 83-73269

A reference book editor once told this reviewer that a good reference book's purpose and organization should be so self-evident that a dog can understand it. Some reference works, for example the *Mental Measurements Yearbook,* fall short of this whimsical ideal but are nonetheless good and useful. Add to this category *What Can I Do. . . .* It helps students recognize the wide range of occupations they can choose, whatever their college major and however narrowly vocational their curriculum. It approaches the question asked in its title from two directions. First it lists majors, their job possibilities, types of hiring institutions, and the jobs graduates in each major have landed between 1960 and 1980. Just how the sample of graduates was selected is not explained. The absence of engineering from the majors is a minor flaw. The second approach lists occupations and tells how many workers each major supplied over that twenty-year period. Identifying numbers borrowed from the *Dictionary of Occupational Titles* have been expanded in this edition from three digits to six to indicate the relative degrees of contact with data, people, and things in a job. Completely new to this edition are three-letter codes assigned to the jobs to indicate which three of six possible principal personality traits characterize people holding each job. Once one has read the front matter explaining the codes, they can be used to match personality as well as interests to the demands of a job. *What Can I Do . . .* can alert students to career possibilities they might otherwise overlook.

Women in Western European History: The Nineteenth and Twentieth Centuries, compiled by Linda Frey, Marsha Frey, and Joanne Schneider. Westport, CT: Greenwood, 1984. 1,024p. $55. 0-313-22859-0 81-20300

This bibliography's companion volume, published in 1982, covered the period from antiquity through the French Revolution. This successor includes four major sections: a general one for both the nineteenth and twentieth centuries, followed by sections for the period before World War I, the period between the world wars, and the post-World War II era. Each section's geographic subsections are richly divided by subjects dealing with politics, economics, religion, society, literature, culture, and significant figures both male and female. The bibliography sweeps far wider than the traditional concerns of marriage and family. Most of the 10,487 entries, indexed by subject, personal name, and author, are for books, the great majority in English. The bibliography can be a helpful starting point to researchers working on nearly any topic about Western women and women's history. ▣

Library World

News of announcements, new posts, retirements, and deaths should be sent to "Library World," WLB, *950 University Ave., Bronx, NY 10452.*

Doris Brown

Linda Elliott

NEW POSTS

Camila Alire has accepted the position of director of the learning resources center at Pikes Peak Community College, Colorado Springs. She was formerly assistant to the dean at the Univ. of Denver GSLIM.

Larry Black has been appointed executive director of the Columbus and Franklin County PL system, Ohio. He has been with the library system since 1977 and was appointed assistant executive director in 1983.

Michael Borries has been appointed serials cataloger at the Columbia Univ. libraries, New York.

Doris Brown, formerly associate director for technical services at DePaul University, Chicago, has been promoted to director of libraries.

Christine Cairo has been named coordinator of children's services of the Indianapolis-Marion County (Ind.) PL. She was formerly head of the children's and young adult departments at the Kokomo PL.

Clara DiFelice has been named audiovisual/outreach coordinator for the Palm Springs (Calif.) PL. She was previously an assistant professor at Washington and Lee Univ., Lexington, Virginia.

David Donaldson has been appointed administration librarian of the Air Force Base Library, Altus, Oklahoma. He was formerly director of library/audiovisual services at Purdue University.

Marion Donaldson is now director of the Lawton (Ok.) PL system. She was previously director of the Hobart PL, Merrillville, Indiana.

Linda Elliott has been appointed assistant head librarian for the Oak Lawn (Ill.) PL. She was formerly city librarian for the main library of the San Luis Obispo City/County Library System.

Barbara Grether has joined the staff of the Danville Community College's Learning Resources Center as public services librarian.

Martha Gould has been promoted to director of the Washoe County library system, Reno, Nev. She was formerly assistant director of the system.

Patricia Harris has been named assistant director for library development with the Virginia State Library, Richmond. She was previously public library consultant for the Louisiana State Library, Baton Rouge.

Donald Hartman has joined the staff of the university libraries of the State Univ. of New York at Buffalo as assistant librarian.

Martha Johnson, formerly coordinator of instructional media services at Kalamazoo College's Upjohn Library, Kalamazoo, Mich., is now the director of the learning resources center, Danville Community College, Danville, Va.

Douglas Lehman has been appointed director of library technical services at Miami-Dade Community College, Miami, Fla. He had been reference librarian at the north campus library of Miami-Dade Community College since 1981.

Catherine O'Connell, formerly assistant director of the Washington County Free Library, Hagerstown, Md., is now director of the Saginaw, Mich. PL system.

Charles Manley has been named assistant director of the Washoe County library system, Reno, Nevada. He had been head of reference for Reno Central Library since 1975.

Irene Stoller has assumed the position of director of the Paramus (N.J.) PL. She was formerly director of the Madison (Wisc.) PL.

Josephine Williamson, formerly catalog librarian for Wofford College, Spartanburg, S.C., is now collection development librarian at the Daniel Library, The Citadel Military College of South Carolina, Charleston.

Announcements

☐ The Enoch Pratt Free Library (Baltimore) and the Mary Weir Library (Weirton, West Virginia) have been selected as sites for testing the adaptability for civilian use of adult learning programs developed by the Armed Forces in a joint project of the National Commission on Libraries and Information Science and the United States Army Human Engineering Laboratory under the Army's Technology Transfer program. A Navy-developed computer-assisted instructional program for improving adult literacy was singled out for its adaptability to public library use. The two test libraries were chosen because both had active volunteer literacy programs, access to knowledgeable computer personnel, and a strong commitment to combatting adult illiteracy. If the tests are successful, the program will be expanded.

☐ Author/illustrator Arnold Lobel has been selected as the 1985 recipient of the University of Southern Mississippi's Silver Medallion for his contributions to children's literature. Winner of many other awards, including the Newbery Award for *Frog and Toad Together,* Lobel will receive the Silver Medallion during the eighteenth annual Children's Book Festival, March 7–8, 1985, at the university. The festival will feature many writers and illustrators of children's literature and include book sales, autograph parties, exhibits, and banquets. For more information contact Jeannine Laughlin, Southern Station Box 5146, Hattiesburg, MS 34906, 601/266–4231.

☐ The African Studies Program of Indiana University, Bloomington, is offering an assistantship, dependent upon funding, to a student in the School of Library and Information Science at the university. The assistantship involves working fifteen to twenty hours a week under the supervision of the African Studies Area Specialist in the University Libraries and provides a stipend of $4,000 for the 1985–1986 academic year and a fee remission for the fall, spring, and summer semesters at the SLIS. Candidates must be admitted to the SLIS. Deadline for applications is February 15, 1985. For more information write to Nancy Schmidt, African Studies Area Specialist, E660 Main Library, Indiana University, Bloomington, IN 47405.

☐ The Library Public Relations Council is seeking entries for its Share the Wealth Packet, a cross section of the newest and best in library publicity. Libraries are asked to submit flyers, newsletters, annual reports, booklists, stationery, posters, book bags and other materials produced during 1984. Entries will be judged for originality, visual impact, effectiveness, and clarity of message. The deadline for entries is March 15, 1985. Five copies of each item should be submitted and 300 copies held in reserve in the event the item is selected. Mail entries to P. Charles Livermore, Packets Chair, Jersey City PL, 472 Jersey Ave., Jersey City, NJ 07302.

Puppets from Nancy Renfro Studios

Children's Specials

☐ Using an adaptation of Hansel and Gretel as an example, Nancy Renfro guides the neophyte puppeteer through an entire production, from first concept to publicity, in *Puppet Shows Made Easy!* Inexpensive ideas are given for making puppets, costumes, sets, and stages. The 80p. paperback costs $9.95; a kit consisting of the book, a forty-minute filmstrip and cassette on creating a puppet show, a forty-minute filmstrip and cassette of the Hansel and Gretel puppet play, and a script costs $69.95. To order or to request a catalog of other books, puppets, and kits write Nancy Renfro Studios, 1117 W. 9th St., Austin, TX 78703.

☐ The Task Force on Standards for Youth Services in Public Libraries of New York State of the New York LA has prepared *Standards for Youth Services in Public Libraries of New York State,* intended to help librarians and administrators assess their youth services and make plans to reach desired goals. Materials, services, and facilities standards are outlined for children's and YA services, and staffing and management are discussed. The 28p. booklet costs $5 plus $1 for postage from the NYLA, 15 Park Row, Suite 434, New York, NY 10038.

☐ The Child Study Children's Book Committee has published *Books to Read Aloud with Children Through Age 8,* an annotated list of 350 titles. The booklist costs $4. Other publications of the committee are *Children's Books of the Year 1984* ($3.50) and *Paperback Books for Children* ($3); all three can be obtained for $9.50 from the Child Study Children's Books Committee at Bank Street College of Education, 610 W. 112th St., New York, NY 10025.

☐ Cap'n O.G. Readmore, the alley cat developed by ABC Entertainment in cooperation with LC's Center for the Book, has been expanding his media exposure. He stars in three new thirty-second reading messages for TV and is now hosting the ABC Weekend Specials. During the coming year, ALA will develop a poster encouraging children to take a trip with a book and the Cap'n. He was featured on a first-day cover of the new Nation of Readers stamp, and finally, the ubiquitous Cap'n is the hero of *The Adventures of Cap'n O.G. Readmore* by Fran Manushkin, a 32p. book for children published by Scholastic, Inc. for $3.95. Can an appearance on the "Tonight Show" be far behind?

Continuing Education

☐ The ALA Office for Library Personnel Resources and the Standing Committee on Library Education have compiled the second annual edition of "ALA Is Continuing Education," a brochure describing ALA's continuing education activities and resources. Some of the workshops listed are available for cosponsorship by groups such as library schools, state or regional library associations, state library agencies or library systems. Also covered are publications such as training packages and course syllabi, and sources of continuing education grants. To obtain a single copy, send a self-addressed, stamped #10 envelope to ALA/OLPR, 50 E. Huron St., Chicago, IL 60611.

☐ The Canadian School Library Association sponsors two-day workshops for superintendents, principals, teachers and teacher-librarians on resource-based learning and the integration of the library resource center with the school's curriculum. The program stresses cooperative planning and teaching through role-playing and problem-solving sessions. School jurisdictions or school library associations interested in having this workshop brought to their area should contact Gene Burdenuk, Faculty of Education, University of Western Ontario, 1137 Western Rd., London, Ont. N6G 1G7, 519/679-2757.

☐ The Office of Management Studies of the Association of Research Libraries has announced its 1985 Basic Library Management Skills Institutes. The sessions focus on first-line supervision and middle management skills such as problem-solving, staff motivation, decision-making, performance appraisal, conflict management, and communication. They will be held April 14–17 in Philadelphia and October 27–30 in Denver; on-site institutes may be scheduled by libraries wishing to cosponsor a session. The registration fee is $325; travel and housing are extra. To obtain a registration form write Office of Management Studies, ARL, 1527 New Hampshire Ave., NW, Washington, DC 20036.

Film and Video

☐ A red, white and blue poster urging patrons to "Use Your Film Library" is available free from Centre Productions. To obtain a copy, write Poster, Centre Productions Inc., 1800 30th St., Suite 207, Boulder, CO 80301 or call 800/824-1166.

☐ Maryland Public Television has released several new programs on the arts. They include documentaries on the Rowe String Quartet, Louis Comfort Tiffany, and four twentieth century British writers, and performances of ballet, opera, jazz, and gospel music. Fifteen-minute previews can be obtained at no charge; full program previews are $10 per order. Programs are available for rental or purchase in all video formats. For more information write Maryland Public Television, Owings Mills, MD 21117.

☐ The 1985 Southern Africa Media Center catalog features three new films. *Woza Albert!* (fifty minutes, 16mm and ¾-inch video, $75 rental) is a BBC film of the play, *Namibia: Africa's Last Colony* (fifty-five minutes, ¾-inch video only, $65 rental) is another BBC production, and *Allan Boesak: Choosing for Justice* (twenty-eight minutes, 16mm and ¾-inch video, $55 rental) is on the Coloured (mixed race) minister elected head of the World Alliance of Reformed Churches. For the catalog contact Southern Africa Media Center, California Newsreel, 630 Natoma St., San Francisco, CA 94103, 415/621-6196.

From Southern Africa Media Center catalog

Finding Aids

☐ Access to oral history collections in Alaska is available through the *Alaska Oral History Index,* prepared by the Program for the Preservation of Oral History and Traditions of the University of Alaska Rasmuson Library. Comprised of thirty-one microfiche, the index lists over 5,500 audio and video tapes. To obtain the index, priced at $12, write Ron Inouye, Oral History and Traditions, Alaska and Polar Regions Dept., Rasmuson Library, University of Alaska, Fairbanks, AK 99701.

☐ Printed simultaneously in print and electronic formats, the *Data Base Directory,* published by the American Society for Information Science and Knowledge Industry Publications, lists almost 1800 numeric, full-text, and bibliographic databases. The online directory is updated continuously and *Data Base Alert,* a newsletter, updates the printed directory every month. For each database, information is given on subject, price, producer, time coverage, file size, vendor, search aids, etc. The 608p. print directory costs $120 ($96 for ASIS members) from Knowledge Industry Publications, Inc., 701 Westchester Ave., White Plains, NY 10604.

☐ Another new publication in the database field is Marquis Who's Who *Directory of Online Professionals.* Over 6,000 individuals are listed including searchers, educators, information brokers, researchers, consultants, and vendors. Entries include information on current position, area of specialization, education, career history, and address. There are indexes by type of job, database subject expertise, and geography. The directory can be obtained for $85 plus $3.50 for shipping from Marquis Who's Who, Inc., 200 E. Ohio St., Chicago, IL 60611.

☐ Prospective nursing students and nurses interested in further education can find over 500 institutions offering baccalaureate, master's, and doctoral degrees in nursing in the *Directory of Degree Programs in Nursing* by Marcia Anderson and Barbara Schmidt. Information is given on head of nursing program, degrees offered, accreditation, admissions requirements, and curriculum for each degree program. The 280p. book is available for $29.95 from Arco Publishing, Inc., 215 Park Ave. S., New York, NY 10003.

Idea Exchange

☐ Contributions of $100 ($200 for businesses) will literally be helping to "Pave the Way" to the front entrance of the new Reynolds Corner Branch Library of the Toledo-Lucas County (Ohio) PL. Sponsored by the branch's friends chapter, the campaign will sell 100 signature blocks of granite to be used as a walkway; funds raised by the sale will then enable the friends to commission a bronze sculpture for the courtyard of the new building. The statue will be dedicated in the spring of 1985.

☐ Several area libraries have joined forces to develop library services at Winchester House, a Libertyville, Illinois nursing home with over 350 patients. An LSCA grant has enabled the group to hire a librarian for an onsite facility with books, periodicals, audiovisual materials, and microcomputers. Cook Memorial PL is administering the project, Condell Memorial Hospital will provide health and nutrition information and staff for programs, Waukegan PL will contribute programming and make videotapes available, and the College of Lake County will offer telecourses and other services.

☐ Local newspapers (like library publications) receive many more press releases than they can publish. The Kirkland (New York) Town Library collects a week's worth of unused press releases from the *Courier* and makes them available in binders in the magazine rack. Patrons can request to keep a press release or picture; otherwise they are discarded after four weeks.

Winner of Omaha PL logo contest

☐ Both a new logo and increased public interest in the library were the result of a logo contest held by the Omaha PL last fall. Media publicity plus a mailing to high schools, colleges and art schools in the Omaha area and to artists on the Nebraska Arts Council list generated over 280 entries. The panel of judges was from the library, the community and the arts. Winner Janeen Macrino, a supervisor of graphics for the Union Pacific Railroad, was awarded $500 by the Friends of the Library.

Magazine Notes

☐ Now in its second year, *Fiction Monthly: The Bay Area's Fiction Magazine,* a 12-to-16p. tabloid, publishes original short fiction, interviews (Anne Rice, Gilbert Sorrentino), and book reviews. There is a useful list of manuscripts wanted by little magazines and small presses, writing contests, conferences, and assorted literary notes from all over the country. An interesting feature is "The Browser's Guide," reviews of Bay area bookstores. Subscriptions are $13 for ten issues from *Fiction Monthly,* 545 Haight St., San Francisco, CA 94117.

☐ Another lively literary tabloid is *The Bloomsbury Review,* which publishes book reviews and interviews (mythologist Joseph Campbell, poet Robert Creeley). A unique feature is the extended overviews of current publishing in a specific area; recent issues have covered gardening, biography, cookbooks, and children's books. Subscriptions to the monthly magazine are $12 from *The Bloomsbury Review,* Box 8928, Denver, CO 80201.

☐ A new non-tabloid, and even non-print journal will be made available in January 1985. Edited by Brian Aveney, *Information Publishing: An Electronic Journal* is published on IAC's *Trade & Industry ASAP* full-text database and indexed in the *Newsearch* and *Trade & Industry Index* databases. The journal is soliciting articles on online information databases, library online services, electronic publishing, and such components of information technology as microcomputers, videodiscs, and satellites. For more information contact Information Access Company, 11 Davis Dr., Belmont, CA 94002.

Media Center World

☐ "Junior High Contemporary Classics," a bibliography that appeared in the December 15, 1984 *Booklist,* is available as a reprint. The list of fifty high-appeal works of fiction for grades 7–9 was compiled by the magazine's children's and young adult editorial staff. To obtain a single copy send a self-addressed #10 envelope with 37¢ postage to Booklist/Junior High Classics, ALA, 50 E. Huron St., Chicago, IL 60611.

From *Van Gogh in Arles*

☐ Public and school librarians have contributed their ideas on joint programs in *The School/Public Library Workout Book: A Guide to Cooperating with Public/School Libraries,* published by the Virginia State Library and the Virginia Department of Education. The ideas are relatively easy and inexpensive to implement. The booklet stresses the importance of strong commitment and good communication to successful cooperation. To receive a copy send a self-addressed 9½-by-6½-inch envelope with 35¢ postage to Christina Dunn, Library Development Branch, Virginia State Library, 11th St. at Capitol Square, Richmond, VA 23219.

☐ In conjunction with the exhibit held at the Metropolitan Museum of Art last fall, the museum has produced *Van Gogh in Arles,* a sound/slide program with forty slides and a thirty-minute cassette. The works in the exhibit were painted during a fifteen-month period, Van Gogh's most productive, when he lived in Arles. Order for $19.95 plus $2.95 shipping from The Metropolitan Museum of Art, Museum Special Service Office, Middle Village, NY 11381.

Products and Services

☐ The new Series 3000 workstation from CL Systems functions both as a stand-alone microcomputer and as a system terminal. In the CLSI LIBS 100 system the workstation operates as a terminal, but as a separate computer it has word processing, spreadsheet, and database management capability. The Series 3000 can be configured with a floppy disk or a floppy disk plus Winchester disk drive. The system has an LSI-11/23 processor with 16-bit data and 22-bit addressing capability. For more information contact CL Systems, Inc., 1220 Washington St., West Newton, MA 02165, 617/965-6310.

☐ Micro Design has introduced a

CLSI Series 3000 workstation

new line of microfiche readers designed to take up less vertical space. The Model 425 has an 11–by–11–inch screen, the Model 475 an 11–by–8½–inch screen, and the Model 495 a 14–by–11–inch screen. All three readers are available with a selection of drop-in lenses and a dual-lens option. For more information contact Micro Design, 857 W. State St., Hartford, WI 53027.

☐ Chemical Abstracts Service is introducing two new Chemical Abstracts Service Source Index (CASSI) services. CASSI 1907–1984 Cumulative (which supercedes the 1907–1979 cumulation) is a bibliography with library holdings information for approximately 60,000 scientific and technical publications cited in *Chemical Abstracts*. The new CASSI KWOC index, on microfiche, provides key-word access to titles in the cumulative. For more information contact CAS, 2540 Olentangy River Rd., Box 3012, Columbus, OH 43210, 614/421-3600.

Professional Reading

☐ A project of the California Spanish Language Data Base, *Bilindex* offers standardized Spanish equivalents to over 13,000 current Library of Congress subject headings. The main list in arranged like the LC subject headings volumes, with main headings, see also, see from and see also from references, and scope notes, all in Spanish. An English index is included. The 501p. book is available from California Spanish Language Data Base, 604 William St., Oakland, CA 94612.

☐ Profiles of more than thirty integrated online library systems are featured in *Integrated Online Library Systems: Principles, Planning and Implementation* by David Genaway. Specific functions, subsystems available and planned, equipment needed, price ranges, and locations of installed systems are noted. There are also guidelines for planning, evaluation, and implementation, a vendor survey form which can be reproduced, and a directory of vendors. Available for $36.50 in hardcover and $28.50 in paper, the 151p. book is published by Knowledge Industry Publications, Inc., 701 Westchester Ave., White Plains, NY 10604.

☐ International ILL will benefit from the third edition of IFLA's *A Brief Guide to Centers of International Lending and Photocopying,* covering policies in ninety countries. For each country the system of international lending is explained, and where no central authority exists, addresses of major libraries that can satisfy requests are provided. Method of mailing, type of request form preferred, charge, method of payment, loan periods, etc. are given. This edition includes for the first time information on photocopying centers. Copies are available for £10 or four British Library Lending Division International Coupons from IFLA Office for International Lending, British Library Lending Division, Boston Spa, Wetherby, West Yorkshire, U.K. LS23 7BQ.

Software

☐ Online search results can be edited with *Search Companion* from Aaron/Smith Associates. Available for IBM PC and PC–compatible computers with a minimum of 128K memory, the software allows the user to eliminate codes and unwanted information from the downloaded search and reformat as desired. *Search Companion* costs $295 from Aaron/Smith Associates, Inc., 1422 W. Peachtree St., NW, Suite 518, Atlanta, GA 30309.

☐ Over 500 educational programs on twenty-eight disk sides for the Apple II family of computers are available for less than 40¢ a program on Educational Computing Network's Delta collection. Subject areas include business, computer languages, computer programming, foreign languages, games, home economics, teacher utility, telecommunications, and the Bible. The collection is priced at $179 from Educational Computing Network, 12680 Hollyglen Circle, Riverside, CA 92503.

☐ Avant-Garde has produced one math program for young children and three for high school through college. With *The Magic Cash Register* (Apple II, 64K, one disk drive) children become cashiers in their own make-believe stores. They choose what to sell, what to charge, and how to give out change. An accompanying coloring book includes play money to cut out. *Introductory Algebra* and *Intermediate Algebra* (Apple II, 48K, one disk drive) have hundreds of exercises with three levels of difficulty. *Logic Workout* (Apple II, 48K, one disk drive or Commodore 64, 64K, one disk drive) introduces classical logic and syllogisms with a short tutorial on theory followed by problem solving. Each program is $34.95 from Avant-Garde Publishing Corp., Box 30160, 1907 Garden Ave., Eugene, OR 94703.

Write for These

☐ To aid in charting a career course, *The Dewar's Guide to Career Development* gives advice on goal-setting and planning alternate routes, a survey of changing occupational fields, a self-awareness questionnaire, and a bibliography. The 40p. booklet can be obtained for $1 from the Dewar's Center for Career Development, 110 E. 59th St., Suite 1100, New York, NY 10022.

☐ For career guidance in the teaching field, *A Career in Independent School Teaching* describes the difference between public and private school teaching, how to apply for a private school position, and salary and benefits. The 19p. pamphlet is free from the National Association of Independent Schools, 18 Tremont St., Boston, MA 02108.

☐ Kids of all ages who received model trains for Christmas may need some help to keep the hobby going. *Introduction to Scale Model Railroading* offers information on costs, sizes, where to put it, and how to lay track. The 31p. booklet is free from Kalmbach Publishing Co., 1027 N. 7th St., Milwaukee, WI 53233.

WLB Classifieds

Classified Advertising is accepted six weeks preceding date of issue. Charges are: minimum 3 lines—$10; each additional line—$2.50. If voucher forms are required, please send them when submitting copy. All advertisements for positions must exclude reference to race, creed, color, age, and sex as conditions for employment. The publisher reserves the right to reject any advertising considered unacceptable as to wording or appearance or for any other reason. Submit classifieds to: Brian Bavolar, Wilson Library Bulletin, 950 University Ave., Bronx, NY 10452.

Positions Open

LIBRARIAN/EDITOR

WILSON LIBRARY BULLETIN has immediate opening for an assistant editor. Duties include writing, editing, proofreading, and reporting on professional meetings. MLS from an ALA-accredited library school and demonstrated writing and editing ability. Competitive salary and benefits. Send resume and salary history to Director of Personnel, H. W. Wilson Company, Bronx, New York 10452.

Announcements

EARN UNIVERSITY CREDIT for your personal travels/vacation anywhere in the world. Write Univ. of Calif. Travel/Study, Box 16501, Irvine, CA 92714.

THE FOOTLOOSE LIBRARIAN newsletter & network. Money-saving travel news + U.S. & overseas librarians offering Bed & Breakfast, housing exchange, more. "Good, practical information" M.S., IN; "An excellent publication" S.R., Tunisia. Free brochure. TFL, Box 972, Minneapolis, MN 55440.

GET OUT OF THE WAREHOUSE BUSINESS! Stop stacking and storing books! Get in the library business! Invite, attract, lure more patrons, students into your library with proven Kanecrest 'Classic' Solid Oak Display Shelving Systems! Book shelving counselors serving Eastern Half of U.S. No obligation. Call 10–4 EST 615-588-6113 for free Packet Guide featuring solid oak sample, free estimating, delivering, and installing services!

MILITARY BOOKS for identification of shoulder patches, medals, insignia . . . U.S. and foreign. Military history, etc. Send for free catalog, M. C.N. Press, Box 52033 WLB, Tulsa, OK 74152.

NEWSLETTER FOR YOUR SUMMER, SPRING, CHRISTMAS COURSES in London, Paris, Mexico, Hawaii, etc.! Visit libraries, theatre productions, galleries. Exciting study/vacation options for librarians, plus work in foreign libraries. Subscription: $25/yr. NEWSLETTER, Box 5513, Santa Monica, CA 90405.

THE ONE-PERSON LIBRARY: A NEWSLETTER FOR LIBRARIANS AND MANAGEMENT. Professional isolation is one of the major problems of working alone. We want to change that. This new newsletter is informal, informative, and, above all, quick and to the point. Charter subscriptions (one year, 12 issues) for $35, a savings of over 20%. Pre-paid orders to OPL RESOURCES, LTD., Box 948, Murray Hill Station, New York, NY 10156.

For Sale

BOSC DIRECTORY - FACILITIES FOR LEARNING-DISABLED PEOPLE. A guide to over 400 facilities from 42 states. More detailed, more comprehensive, more helpful. Includes day and residential centers and schools, clinics, group homes, independent living centers, special college offerings and others. Ten significant articles by experts to help parents and professionals with facility selection and other problems. 8½'' by 11'' —200 pp., indexed, ISBN 0-9613860-0-2. $28 plus $2 for postage & handling. BOSC, Dept. W, Box 305, Congers, NY 10920.

BRUCE TEGNER'S COMPLETE BOOK OF SELF-DEFENSE hardcover edition is again in stock. ISBN 0-87407-510-6 $10.95. Thor Publishing Co., Box 1782, Ventura, CA 93002.

CAN-DO CARDS: RESEARCH REPORTING—A proven method for teaching students in grades 4–8 how to write research reports. $6.95. The Curriculum Exchange, 71 Longview Dr., Marblehead, MA 01945.

ENTERTAINMENT INDUSTRY BOOKS
$10.00 Each/Prepaid

1) The Record Industry Book

2) The Music Industry Book

6) The Managers' Entertainers' & Agents Book

7) Film/TV Law

9) Music/Record Business & Law

10) Motion Picture Distribution

11) How To Be A Music Publisher

13) How To Start A Record Or Independent Production Co.

14) How To Register A Trademark

15) © Copyright; Your Introduction

16) Copyright Registration Forms PA & SR

18) How To Sell Your Song

22) Delson's Dictionary of Radio & Record Industry Terms

23) The Movie Industry Book; Pt. II

$25.00 Each/Prepaid

3) The Publisher's Office Manual

4) The ULSL Master Producer's & British Music Scene Book

$150.00 Each/Prepaid

8) Film Superlist: (1894–1939)

17) Film Superlist: (1940–1949)

AUTHOR: Walter E. Hurst, Attorney
Seven Arts Press, Inc. Dept. W/L/B
Box 649, Hollywood, CA 90078.

". . . get ideas from every issue."
M.S. High School Media Center, NY
Subscribe (and send *your* nitty gritty ideas) to The U*N*A*B*A*S*H*E*D Librarian™, the "how I run my library good"℠ letter, Box 2631, New York, NY 10116. Four issues $20 US funds

(add $5 Canadian and foreign postage).

PHOTOGRAPHS OF FAMOUS and interesting people. Darwin, Geronimo, Longfellow, Hitler, Queen Victoria, circus freaks, and many more. Free list. Glimpse of Time, Rte. 1, Box 428, Bandon, OR 97411.

HOBBY BOOKWATCH: Military, gun and hobby book review. Approximately 600 new titles each year. Small and large publishers. One year, $2; two years, $3.50; three years, $5. Published six times a year. For free sample write: HB, Box 52033, Tulsa, OK 74152.

Librarians Love TFL!
"Everyone on our staff is interested in the Travel Exchange, either as a traveller or a host" M.H., San Diego. Free brochure on THE FOOTLOOSE LIBRARIAN newsletter & travel network. TFL, Box 972, Minneapolis, MN 55440.

LIBRARY NEWSLETTERS. Let a librarian prepare camera-ready copy for your newsletter. $1 for samples. Library Newsletter Service, Box 637, Belleville, NJ 07109.

THE MILITARY BOOKMAN— Military, Naval, and Aviation History. Out-of-print and rare books, 3 catalogs per year. 29 East 93rd St., New York, NY 10128 or call (212) 348–1280, Tues.-Sat. 10:30–5:30.

PUT *SEARS* TO WORK. 1,200 "see" and "see also" cards plus Manual/List of Headings with DEWEY numbers. From *Sears* 12th ed., $49.95. Woods Library Publishing Co., 9159 Clifton, Evergreen Park, IL 60642.

SOLID OAK SHELVING

ACCEPTING ORDERS NOW for Spring deliveries in all continental states. SAVE with direct institutional purchases from manufacturer in Tennessee for genuine furniture shelving in beautiful solid oak: Kanecrest Solid Oak Demountable-Remountable Systems. Call now 615-588-6113 between 10 and 4 EST for FREE 'Packet Parcel', including Packet Guide, Large Solid Oak Sample, and Prices Delivered. Make your selections from hundreds of combinations. Place your order direct for Spring delivery. Give name, position, institution, and address for UPS Prepaid Delivery of your 'Packet Parcel'! Every major library should have one! The Kane Company, Box 10505, Knoxville, TN 37939–0505.

"WOW!" "Do not pass go without collecting this PR gem . . . " LJ
GO, PEP AND POP! 250 TESTED

THE THREE BEARS

Goldilocks and the 3 bears are paper bag puppets; chairs, beds, bowls go on the flannel board. All are printed on stiff colored paper ready to cut out and use.

To order send $3.50 plus $1.00 shipping to MOONLIGHT PRESS, 3407 Crystal Lake Dr., Orlando, FL 32806.

IDEAS FOR LIVELY LIBRARIES by Baeckler and Larson. Order from: The U*N*A*B*A*S*H*E*D Librarian™, the "how I run my library good"℠ letter. Dept. GPP/WLB, Box 2631, New York, NY 10116. Send $4.50 check and mailing label with order. Libraries add $1 for billing. Canadian and foreign add $1 in US funds. 6 to 8 weeks delivery. LC 75-20328 CIP.

INDEX TO ADVERTISERS

American Psychological Association 306
California Spanish Language Database......... 331
Gale Research Company .... 4th cover
OCLC 305
H. W. Wilson Company .... 2nd cover, 3rd cover

Credits:
p. 310—Joe Pineiro, Columbia Univ; 321—Stanford Univ. News; 324-27—David Taylor; 333—Ed Arno; 335—Morrow, Arco; 336—D. S. Brewer, Facts on File; 337—Patricia Berglund; 338—Crowell, Holiday House; 339—Morrow, Bradbury; 342—Doubleday/ Crime Club; 343—St. Martin's Press, Holt Rinehart; 358—McGraw-Hill.

Wilson **Library** *Bulletin*

Spend the year with us. . .

Customer Services
H.W. Wilson Company
950 University Avenue, Bronx, New York 10452

☐ Please enter my subscription to 10 monthly issues of *WLB* for one year @ $30 in the U.S. and Canada, $35 in other countries.

Name ____________________

Address ____________________

City ____________________ State __________ Zip __________

Wils[illegible] Library Bulletin

February 1985

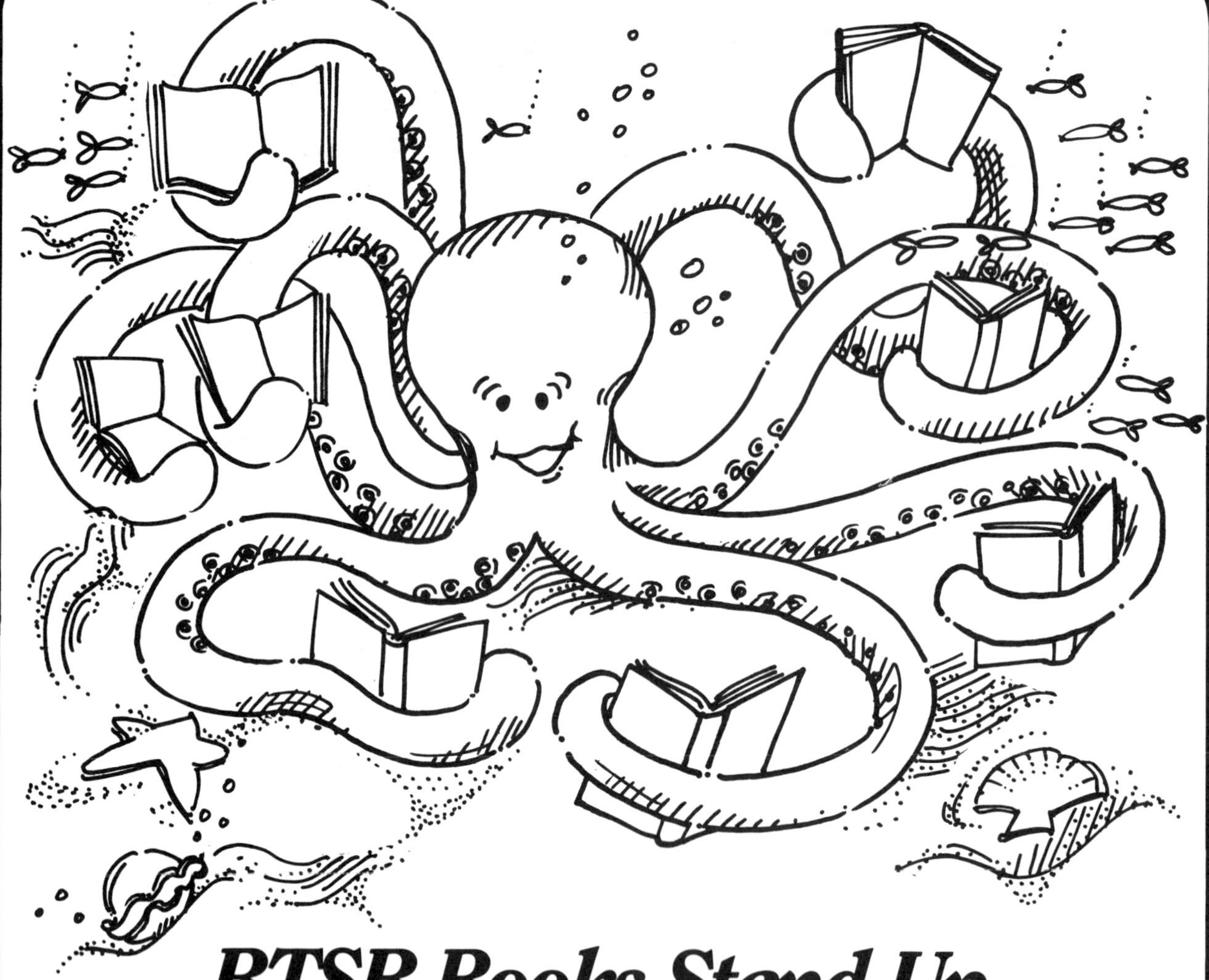

Wilson **Library** *Bulletin*

February 1985, Volume 59, Number 6 *ISSN 0043-5651*

Our winter scene for February was taken by **Robert Monroe,** a freelance photographer who lives in Cuddebackville, New York.

Departments

Letter From New York/Editorial 372
Correspondence 373
Upfront/News—*New York Public Library closes catalog room; Crerar completes merger with University of Chicago; RLG signs agreement with British Library; UTLAS acquired by International Thomson; Enoch Pratt Library awarded $1 million grant; University of Texas at El Paso opens $22.8 million library; OCLC introduces SC 350; Postal rates increase; late news.* 375
Calendar 380
Library World 426
Marketplace 427
WLB Classifieds 432

Articles

Expanding Service: Public Access Microcomputers *Don Julien* 381
Preservation Using Pesticides: Some Words of Caution *Mary Davis* 386
Consumer Health Information: A Prognosis *Ellen Fecher* 389

Features

Special Report: A CHOICE Assignment *Virginia Clark* 392
Dateline—Washington *Dale Nelson* 394
Eye on Publishing *Anne McGrath* 396
Facing the Public *Will Manley* 398
Portrait: Eileen Cooke *Joseph Deitch* 400
Library to Library *Rod Henshaw* 403

Reviews

Picture Books for Children *Donnarae MacCann/Olga Richard* 404
The Young Adult Perplex *Patty Campbell* 406
Murder in Print *Kathleen Maio* 408
Front Row Center *Judith Trojan* 410
On Record: Popular Music *Bruce Pollock* 412
Magazines *Gail Pool* 414
Our Profession *Norman Stevens* 416
Software for Libraries *Patrick Dewey* 418
Current Reference Books *James Rettig* 420

The *Wilson Library Bulletin* is published monthly except in July and August by The H. W. Wilson Company, 950 University Avenue, Bronx, N.Y. 10452. Second-class postage paid at Bronx, N.Y. and additional mailing offices. Copyright © 1985 by The H. W. Wilson Company. The *Wilson Library Bulletin* is indexed in *Education Index, Library Literature,* and *Popular Periodical Index* and abstracted in *Library & Information Science Abstracts, Historical Abstracts,* and *America: History and Life*. Book reviews are indexed in *Book Review Index*. Subscription $30 a year, U.S. and Canada; $35, foreign. Single copies $4, U.S. and Canada; $4.50, foreign (remittance with order, please). Address all correspondence about subscriptions to the publisher. No subscriptions through agents. Telephone: (212) 588-8400

Letter from New York

Editorial

Putting a price on our head

The price of living in modern America is to some extent the burden of being aware of the cost of everything, not just the expense of food, clothing, and shelter, but the price of health, education, government, energy, travel, recreation, and even death. We are continually encouraged to think about simple arithmetic—doing the numbers, costing-out, the bottom line. In buying a hamburger we want to be sure we are getting the most beef for our money, in constructing a high tech weapon we insist upon the most bang for our buck.

There is comfort in understanding the specific value of things, which is why there is so little joy on used car lots, so much discomfort upon entering a museum where a "suggested fee" is in effect.

Accustomed as we are to stateable values place upon goods and services, it is no surprise that for the past several years librarians have been interested in placing an assessment upon a library school education. The feasibility of setting a salary standard for librarians has been debated now for over fifteen years.

The question arose again at the Midwinter Meeting of the American Library Association in Washington, D.C. The issue before the ALA Council was whether or not to endorse a resolution calling for formulation of a minimum annual salary for entry-level librarians possessing the MLS degree because, the resolution declared, "It is important to take a beginning step in upgrading salary standards." The proposal stipulated that job openings listed in ALA publications carry the statement "The American Library Association has established a minimum recommended salary of $17,500 for a full-time beginning librarian in 1985."

There were objections to the proposal. Members of Council pointed out that a recommended minimum salary would be impracticable because of geographical salary variations, differences in size and type of libraries, and disparities in individuals. It was predicted that a minimum salary guideline would work against graduates seeking higher positions and salaries and that organizations now offering comparatively high entry-level wages might readjust them downward, such as the federal government and private and corporate libraries.

Speakers opposing the resolution noted that a non-binding guideline would be incapable of enforcement and that setting a minimum salary might violate provisions against price-fixing embodied in the Sherman Anti-Trust Act. Numerous Councilors rose to object to the figure of $17,500, finding the sum inappropriately low. None of these arguments were new.

At the end of debate it was agreed that the resolution be referred to the Office for Library Personnel Resources, asking for an opinion and requiring that it be provided to Council at the annual conference of ALA in Chicago this July.

We favor the proposal. None of the arguments against adopting the resolution are without merit, it is just that they all collapse so completely in the face of the higher need to take a stand on this issue, declare our value, and take steps to attain the higher salaries we deserve and that have historically eluded us. It is, after all, only a guideline and local employers can adjust the agreed upon standard because of geography, type of institution, and the talents and promise of an individual applicant. It is unlikely that organizations now offering salaries above a recommended minimum would scale them down and suffer the corresponding loss of prestige, improbable that highly gifted and motivated library school graduates will be strictly held to the suggested minimum, implausible that such a subtle action as a salary guideline would violate federal statutes against price-fixing.

As things stand now there is no adequate guideline for establishing the salary of an entry-level librarian, many institutions depending on the annual salary survey in *Library Journal* to devise a wage. The survey, which reflects salaries paid to recent graduates of accredited library schools, is only a guide to what has taken place, not to what should take place.

State library associations in Connecticut, Massachusetts, Minnesota, and Rhode Island have all implemented guidelines for entry-level librarians and found them workable. This year the New Jersey legislature is expected to approve a minimum starting salary for public school teachers of at least $18,500. The measure, which would create the highest statewide minimum pay for teachers in the nation, has already been approved by the state assembly and endorsed by Governor Thomas Kean.

We are all familiar with the occasional reminiscing done with colleagues about starting salaries in librarianship, always astonished to learn about friends who began careers as recently as ten years ago at $10, 000, $6,000, or even less. We know what it took to get from that position to the present one—years of experience, promotions, advancement to other library systems, relocation, retraining, added degrees, and publications. It is not so difficult to evaluate our present worth based on what has transpired since our professional training in library school. But it is not too much to expect that a price be put on our general skills at the outset.

Over the years no one has been very successful in assessing what we believe to be our minimum worth—not school boards, superintendents, boards of trustees, local governments, city councils, boards of regents, university presidents, corporations, or the federal government. It would be a valuable innovation if we took the initiative, this year, by ourselves putting a price on our heads.

—*Milo Nelson*

Correspondence

WLB welcomes letters from its readers. Correspondence should be sent to Wilson Library Bulletin, 950 University Avenue, Bronx, N.Y. 10452.

Very special people

A big hurrah for Will Manley's support for children's librarians (*WLB*, October 1984). For those of us who truly love children's work there is no place to go, nor is there much prestige associated with the position.

Young readers grow into adult readers who attend city council meetings. We need more good children's librarians and more aggressive children's programs. There should be story times every week in every community. And most of all, there needs to be support from the library profession. We need to cultivate those who choose to work with children, for they are very special people.

STEPHANIE BAUERSFELD
West Valley Regional Branch Library
Reseda, California

Life outside the workplace

I read with interest Katherine Shanks's article, "Working Less and Enjoying It More: Alternative Work Schedules" in the October 1984 issue of your magazine. The Campbell County Public Library serves a county of approximately 25,000. We employ forty-seven people, twenty of whom are permanent part-time employees.

We also have three job-sharing positions. It started with the business manager's position more than two years ago and worked so well that we now have job-sharing at both the circulation and reference desks as well as in the business office.

As Public Information Officer it is necessary for me to be available for special programs and events as well as making myself available to the media at their convenience. Because this doesn't always fit in with my part-time schedule, I work on a flextime basis which gives me the freedom to do my job as it should be done without restricting me to traditional working hours.

All permanent part-time employees receive paid holidays and vacations as well as having insurance benefits available as do our full-time employees. I understand that regrettably this is the exception rather than the rule for part-time workers in most businesses.

Although the part-time positions are scheduled to facilitate the smooth functioning of the library, the fact that we do offer a variety of work schedules keeps our employee application file full of eager hopefuls. This obviously allows us to pick and choose our employees carefully so that we maintain a first-rate staff.

For those of us employed by the Campbell County Public Library our jobs provide us with stimulating and challenging positions while allowing us the freedom of a life outside the workplace. All of which makes for happier, more productive employees and that, of course, certainly reflects in the quality of service we provide our patrons.

KAREN HILL
Campbell County Public Library
Gillette, Wyoming

A waste of time and money

Patty Campbell ends her November 1984 column with the line "Life is too short to spend the whole day sitting on a rock by the sea. . . ." May I add that a busy school librarian's life is much too short to spend reading Campbell's travelogue.

Opening the pages of the November issue to Campbell's column, one expects to find an article devoted to a critique of, or a discussion of some aspect of young adult literature. Instead one finds that one has been invited to a slide-show presentation of Campbell's latest vacation. Articles of this type in a periodical such as *Wilson Library Bulletin* are a waste of my time and my school system's money.

DIANE BOOTH
Holyoke High School Library
Holyoke, Massachusetts

Library service built on success

I would like to present a few differing views from those of Rod Henshaw ("Library to Library," *WLB*, November 1984) on interlibrary loan.

Resource-sharing has become the sacred cow of the library profession in the eighties in the way that outreach was in the late sixties and early seventies, and one expresses a dissenting opinion at considerable risk of being labelled a reactionary or worse.

While conceding that resource-sharing has some value and that no library can be totally self-sufficient, I submit that interlibrary loan deserves all the criticism it gets and more.

It is too slow. Most library users are not willing or able to wait the one to six weeks it takes to receive an interlibrary loan. Most customers won't wait even one day to negotiate an interbranch loan in an urban library system. To depend upon interlibrary loan in more than the most minimal way is to deny customers the level of service they want and expect.

Interlibrary loan is too often used as a substitute for adequate local collection development. One barely hits the produce key on the OCLC terminal these days before the ILL requests begin to accumulate for titles that have just been published. In a study I did of interlibrary loan activity in Iowa public libraries in 1982, seventy-three percent of all public library interlibrary loan requests were for in-print items and forty-four percent were for items published within the last five years.

Interlibrary loan is too expensive. The average list price of items requested in the Iowa study was $12.07, yet the estimated cost of a completed interlibrary loan transaction was between $25 and $30.

Focus on resource-sharing at the state agency level diverts much needed attention from areas of far greater potential value to library users. If the energy and dollars devoted to building networks, union catalogs, and regional systems, were devoted to developing adequate local support, implementing standards for local library service, and teaching librarians the skills of measuring their markets and building collections tailored to those markets, there would be less need for interlibrary loan.

Every interlibrary loan request for an in-print item that is not totally outside of the scope of the collection of the requesting library should be viewed as a failure on the part of that library.

I'd rather see library service built on success.

MICHAEL PHIPPS
Omaha Public Library
Omaha, Nebraska

Measuring up

Re: "Facing the Public," November 1984. Any library practitioner who is directly involved in the end process of serving very young children knows that providing a child-sized toilet and a changing table should be a number one priority. Human dignity requires human consideration for any age or handicap. Does the Tempe Public Library measure up?

VICTOIRE GRASSL
Everett Public Library
Everett, Washington

Love letter

This is an overdue love letter to Will Manley for his recent, eloquent columns in support of children's services. If more administrators held his views and made them public, not only would children be better served, but youth-serving librarians might be able to shrug off some of the paranoia engendered by the contempt of their child-loathing colleagues.

I would like to add to his plea for more attention and resources devoted to kids in public libraries, especially for the "invisible" clientele—adolescents. It is well known that the few young users we manage to cultivate are often lost as adolescents because of pervasive and hostile neglect by public librarians, and as the "generalist" concept becomes pervasive, the problem is certainly being exacerbated. Of course, few administrators want to talk about that, but perhaps he will turn his excellent "crap detector" onto the subject.

It is obvious that our thought processes about public librarianship are enriched by his column.

MARY CHELTON
Voice of Youth Advocates
University, Alabama

Which is cart, which is horse

In your editorial in *WLB,* November 1984 you state: "The high number of illiterate people ... is attributable not only to traditional reasons ... but to the fact that accelerating technological advances have changed the requirements for literacy in the United States. The standards for minimum acceptable literacy are higher today than at any time in our past."

I am curious to know upon what information you base this assertion. Would you please let me know the source of this conclusion. If it is your own observation, could you amplify your statement and explain how you came to believe this.

There is more to my request than simple curiosity. I believe that increasing technology, rather than requiring literacy of a higher order, is actually a contributing factor to illiteracy, or at least to a decline in the level of what we consider literacy. Thus, we appear to have different views of which is cart and which is horse. If I am right, the condition will worsen and the rift between verbal literacy (reading/writing at a fairly high level of skill) and minimal literacy will widen, and those on the minimal side will have increasingly less reason to improve their skills. Additionally, I think that technology will increasingly reduce the deprivations caused by illiteracy and provide compensations which will enable the minimally literate to move through life in reasonable comfort. What they will *not* be able to do is discriminate, express, or appreciate anything above this basic level which is not a handicap so much as a danger.

My conclusion is based on my observations of the literacy level of college students, particularly those in education, the education and work on a daily basis of school teachers and librarians and the expectations they have of their students, the level of language in widely circulating print media, the circulation statistics of libraries, and various reading score levels over the years. The applications to which computers are being put in schools, the kinds of equipment commonly used in businesses, and other technological "advances" prompt me to *my* view. What is yours based upon?

ANN DONOVAN
Central Washington University
Ellensburg, Washington

We were only playing a hunch, based upon personal observation that elementary school children confront higher mininum literacy standards than were faced by our generation. We would bet that high technology will raise such standards generally, but we would also put a little money on your position.—Ed.

UPFRONT NEWS

On January 18 the **New York Public Library** *closed the Public Catalog Room of its Central Research Library at Fifth Avenue and 42nd Street for the first time since the building opened in 1911. The closing will launch a year-long project which entails major restoration of the Public Catalog Room ("315") and its conversion from a card catalog system to a computerized bibliographic system. The "315" project will launch the second phase of the library's $45 million restoration program. The renovation was begun with major grants in the amount of $800,000 each from the Kresge Foundation and the Pew Memorial Trust.*

The 8,000-drawer card catalog will be replaced by the 800-volume Dictionary Catalog of the Research Libraries of The New York Public Library, 1911–1971, *which includes bibliographic information on material cataloged before 1972. The book catalog was recently completed after more than ten years of work. Approximately fifty computer terminals will be installed to serve as the library's catalog for material accessioned after 1971. The library's online public access catalog is known as* CATNYP *(Catalog of The New York Public Library) and was developed by Carlyle Systems, Inc. of Berkeley, California.*

Rodney Phillips, chief of the General Research Division, said "Using the computer system will enable us to serve better the one million researchers who use Room 315 each year. CATNYP *is very easy to use, fast, and sophisticated. It is also more current than the present system of printed catalogs which we are now using; a search that would have taken ten minutes in the printed catalogs will now take thirty seconds."*

MIDLNET assets dispersed

The Midwest Regional Library Network has been dissolved as a corporation and all remaining assets dispersed between the Center for Research Libraries in Chicago and the Washington Office of the American Library Association.

Since its creation in 1975 under the auspices of the Committee for Institutional Cooperation, MIDLNET enlarged its membership and provided a variety of services to its members, the brokering of OCLC being its principle activity. With the growth and expansion of state and national networks, many of MIDLNET's projects were no longer competitive or attractive to its membership.

RLG signs agreement with British Library

Sir Frederick Dainton, chairman of the British Library board, and Richard McCoy, president of the Research Libraries Group, have signed a memorandum of understanding to begin a program of cooperative activity between the two organizations. A dedicated telecommunications line between RLG and the British Library is to be installed later this year. The first traffic on the line will extend work on the *Eighteenth-century Short Title Catalogue*. The separate versions of the ESTC in Great Britain and the United States will be unified in work done on the RLIN network. The agreement will also initiate a series of cooperative programs to benefit scholarship on both sides of the Atlantic. The organizations intend to coordinate preservation activities, exchange records and files between their databases, and explore the value of direct electronic communication for interlibrary lending.

Record budget increase for Pennsylvania library

The Dauphin County Library System, Harrisburg, Pennsylvania, has received a forty-five percent increase in its 1985 budget, the largest budget increase in the history of the system, according to library director Sarah Long. The increase, from $1,081,733 in 1984 to $1,566,084 in the present year, is being funded by a two-mill special library tax imposed by the Dauphin county commissioners.

Although the law has provided the mechanism for municipal offficals to support libraries in Pennsylvania in this way for some time, Long says this is the first instance in Pennsylvania of county officials levying a library tax. DCLS will retain its private, non-profit status.

Making use of an LSCA Title I grant from the Pennsylvania State Library, the Dauphin County Library System paid for a $19,000 survey of attitudes toward the special tax. Conducted by the Harrisburg firm of Cromer and Young, the survey revealed that sixty-three percent of county residents would pay up to 2 1/4 mills in support of the library and that only ten percent would react adversely to the special tax. No adverse publicity followed the announcement of the tax levy.

UTLAS acquired by International Thomson

The University of Toronto, UTLAS, Inc., and International Thomson Organization have signed a letter of intent under which International Thomson Limited will acquire UTLAS from the University of Toronto and will make "a significant capital contribution" to the information utility. A long-term association between the University of Toronto and UTLAS is anticipated to develop under which the university will continue to be served by UTLAS.

International Thomson is a Canadian-based multinational firm with an interest in library information services. In the past few years the company has placed emphasis on the electronic distribution of information and the formation of databases.

UTLAS has been supplying online database services to Canadian libraries since 1973. In recent years it has also added a number of U.S. and Japanese libraries to its user network. Over 2,000 libraries of all types and sizes receive products and services from the bibliographic system.

Enoch Pratt awarded $1 million grant

The Enoch Pratt Free Library, Baltimore, Maryland, has been awarded a $1 million challenge grant by the National Endowment for the Humanities. "The news of the award has very nearly sent us into orbit," said Anna Curry, director of the library. "This is precisely the stimulus needed to launch the major fundraising campaign on which our trustees have been working so hard."

The NEH grant requires a three-to-one match by the private sector and allows the institution three years in which to raise these funds. The Enoch Pratt Library, which will celebrate its centenary in 1986, is presently engaged in its first major capital improvement campaign, with a provisional target of $10 million.

If the projected fundraising goal is met, $2 million will be used to complete renovation of the central library, $2 million will be designated for restoration of branch libraries, and $6 million will be used to augment the library's endowment fund.

"At the completion of a successful fundraising campaign," said Curry, "we will find ourselves once again secure in the position we have held for so many decades as one of America's leading public libraries. A first-rate library is what Baltimoreans deserve, and it is what they are going to get."

Chicago PL to install communications network

The Chicago Public Library has selected Doelz Networks, Inc. of Irvine, California to install a data communications network to help solve the communications problems of its $2 million computerized library circulation system designed by Data Phase Corporation. The new $600,000 data communications network from Doelz will enable the library system to connect terminals in its eighty-seven library facilities with multiple Tandem computers in the central library. The communications network consists of sixteen links formed with seventy-nine Doelz Elite One multipoint concentrator switches, all of these terminating at the central building. The network is expected to provide all branches with access to identical information. Each library in the system has a network node that can be connected to several terminals. This will eliminate telephone company involvement when the library wishes to add or delete terminals from the network.

The network, now installed and operating, was reviewed during installation for the Chicago Public Library by the consulting firm of Arthur Anderson and Company.

AMIGOS and SOLINET to integrate records with OCLC

OCLC has entered into agreements with AMIGOS and SOLINET so that bibliographic records converted to machine-readable form by the retrospective conversion services of the regional networks will be tapeloaded into the OCLC Online Union Catalog. Tapeloading will consist of records previously converted by AMIGOS and SOLINET as well as those from ongoing projects. An estimated minimum of 250,000 holdings will be added by tape in the next year.

AMIGOS began its retrospective conversion service in 1978 and has developed its SHARES database especially for conversion of non-current cataloging to machine-readable form. The SOLINET retrospective conversion service has converted over 1.1 million records since its establishment in 1983.

The bibliographic records on tape provided to OCLC by the two regional networks will have OCLC control numbers that will be matched with records in the OCLC database. When a match occurs, the holding symbol of the library will be attached to the bibliographic record in the OCLC database.

The University of Texas at El Paso recently held a celebration to mark the opening of its $22.8 million central library. The new six-floor facility contains an auditorium, twenty-nine meeting areas, and over seventy study rooms for faculty. The current collection is 710,336 volumes, with a capacity for 1.2 million items. Construction of the new library was the first priority of Haskell Monroe when he became president of the university in 1981.

Crerar completes merger with Chicago

The John Crerar Library recently completed its merger with the University of Chicago and a new library has opened for service on the university campus at 5730 South Ellis Avenue in Chicago. The $22 million project includes a building that houses the combined science collections of the two institutions, known as the John Crerar Library of the University of Chicago. The merger is thought to be one of the largest in American library history and is unprecedented in that it represents the first merger of two ARL libraries.

The facility will serve the needs of scholars, researchers, and the general public in the fields of biologial and physical sciences, medicine, and technology. The library opened with 900,000 volumes and current subscriptions to more than 6,000 serial titles. Among special features of the collections are 27,000 rare books which are housed nearby in the Special Collections Department of the Joseph Regenstein Library.

Grants from the Mellon Foundation and the U.S. Department of Education made it possible to create machine-readable records for several thousand titles and to convert them from the Dewey Decimal Classification to the Library of Congress Classification prior to the opening of the library. All future materials added to the collections will have LC Classification and will be processed through the University of Chicago's Library Data Management System.

The new library is part of a two-acre landscaped science quadrangle on the University of Chicago campus which links several buildings devoted to the physical and biological sciences. An underground passageway connects the library to the university's medical center.

The Crerar Library's original benefactor was John Crerar (1827-1889), a New Yorker born of Scottish immigrants. He moved to Chicago in 1862 to establish a railway supply company. When Crerar died in 1889 his will stipulated that a large part of his estate be used "for the erection, creation, maintenance, and endowment of a free public library."

The Los Angeles County Public Library has designated $50,000 from the 1984 California Public Library Fund to automate its multilingual information and referral service. The County Library's CALL—Community Access Library Line—has been serving residents of southern California since 1979, using a manual retrieval system for over 5,000 agencies.

CALL, which originated with a LSCA grant to provide information via a toll-free telephone line to underserved minority communities in the Los Angeles area, collected original data to service the information needs of the Hispanic, Black, Asian, American Indian, and hearing impaired communities. Today, as an adjunct to the library's referral service, CALL continues to provide information and referrals in English, Spanish, Chinese, and Japanese.

Since late 1984, CALL librarians have been locating information about local organizations and events in STAR, a turnkey database system designed by Cuadra Associates in Santa Monica. STAR provides multi-user capability allowing staff members to do Boolean searches, database definition, data entry, or printing from terminals at their workstations.

Pictured in the photo above (from left) **Linda Crismond,** County Librarian, **Marilee Marrero,** CALL coordinator, and **Carlos Cuadra,** president, Cuadra Associates.

Paulson appointed to Forest Press

Peter Paulson, director of the New York State Library, has been appointed executive director of Forest Press, publisher of the Dewey Decimal Classification. Paulson will succeed John Humphry who is retiring from the position. The appointment is effective May 1, 1985.

Paulson has been director of the New York State Library since 1972 and a member of the library staff since 1952. He has served as president of the New York Library Association and chair of the ALA Committee on Legislation.

Forest Press, a division of the Lake Placid Education Foundation, is located in Albany, New York.

Kennickell appointed Public Printer

President Reagan has named Ralph Kennickell, Jr. as Public Printer. As the twenty-first Public Printer, Kennickell will head the U.S. Government Printing Office, one of the largest printing and information disseminating organizations in the world. With more than 5,500 employees, the GPO is the largest industrial employer in the District of Columbia.

Before his appointment as Public Printer, Kennickell served the Reagan administration at both the Treasury Department and the Small Business Administration. A native of Savannah, Georgia, Kennickell went to work in 1971 for the Kennickell Printing Company, a family-owned firm since 1892. Kennickell is thirty-nine years old.

WLN acting director appointed

Washington State Librarian Roderick Swartz has announced the appointment of Norris Stussy as acting executive director of the Washington Library Network. Stussy most recently served as assistant director, operations and enforcement division, Washington State Lottery.

Zipkowitz elected to NEDCC

Fay Zipkowitz, director, Rhode Island Department of State Library Services, has been elected chair of the board of directors of the Northeast Document Conservation Center, Andover, Massachusetts.

NEDCC is governed by the directors of state library agencies in its eight-state region, including New York, New Jersey, Maine, New Hampshire, Massachusetts, Connecticut, Rhode Island, and Vermont.

Maurice Freedman *(right) director of the Westchester (New York) Library System and* **Benedict Leerburger,** *president of the WLS board of trustees, toast the twenty-fifth anniversary of the Westchester Library System at their annual meeting at system headquarters in Elmsford, New York.*

The main feature of the program was a speech by Henry Goldstein, president of the Oram Group, one of the nation's oldest fundraising firms. Goldstein spoke on fundraising for public sector institutions. The Oram Group has been engaged by WLS to determine the feasibility of soliciting funds to automate the county's public libraries.

Postal rates increase in February

A postal rate increase affecting all classes of mail took effect February 17. A first class stamp has gone up ten percent to twenty-two cents with additional ounces remaining at the previous seventeen cents. The second class rate for classroom materials has increased thirty percent, the third class nonprofit bulk rate fourteen percent, and the fourth class book rate eight percent.

The impact on the fourth class library rate is an average 15.2 percent increase. Postage for a two-pound package now costs fifty-four cents. The USPS calculates the eventual average increase for the library rate at twenty-one percent. The library rate is now in Step 14 of a sixteen-step phased rate schedule leading up to a rate which will reflect the full attributable costs of library rate mail.

OCLC introduces SC 350

In January OCLC introduced Serials Control 350, a microcomputer-based system that provides librarians with local serials control as well as access to the OCLC Online Union Catalog containing over 600,000 serials bibliographic records.

Serials Control 350 (SC 350) was developed for use with the OCLC M300 Workstation, a modified IBM Personal Computer. It supports a full range of technical service needs, including bibliographic record selection and transfer, automatic check-in and claiming, routing, binding, financial control, report generation, and public searching capability.

LS/2000, OCLC's Local Library System, will provide an interactive link with SC 350. The link will allow libraries to transfer summary and detailed holdings information into the LS/2000 Online Catalog and Circulation System in order to maintain an integrated local library system.

SC 350 users can access local serials records twenty-four hours a day, seven days a week from their M300s.

Any OCLC member library is eligible to use SC 350. Equipment needs include the M300 workstation, a hard disk storage device, and the software needed to support the service.

Information Access Company's new InfoTrac^tm computer-assisted videodisc referenced system allows up to four users to simultaneously access almost 500,000 citations drawn from more than 1,000 magazines with coverage from 1982 to the present. Menu-driven software assists the user in defining a search and offers alternative subjects and subheadings to refine the search strategy. Citations selected are printed on a silent printer. The InfoTrac^tm database is contained on a single twelve-inch videodisc. Subscribers receive an updated cumulated disc each month.

Calendar

FEB. 28–MAR. 1—*Management of the Online Catalog,* institute. California State Library, Sacramento. Inf.: Roger Parent, American Library Association, 50 E. Huron St., Chicago, IL 60611.

MAR. 3–4—*Music OCLC Users Group,* annual meeting. Seelbach Hotel, Louisville. Inf.: Don Hixon, University Library, Univ. of California, Box 19557, Irvine, CA 92713.

MAR. 4–5—*Univ. of North Carolina Librarians' Association,* spring conference. Univ. of North Carolina, Chapel Hill. Theme: "Preservation in the '80's." Inf.: Libby Chenault, Rare Book Collection, Wilson Library 024-A, Univ. of North Carolina, Chapel Hill, NC 27514.

MAR. 4–6—*Management Skills,* institute. San Francisco. Inf.: Ellen Gerber, SLA, 235 Park Ave. S., New York, NY 10003.

MAR. 4–6—*National Federation of Abstracting and Information Services,* annual conference. Crystal Gateway Marriott Hotel, Arlington, Va. Theme: "New Developments in Electronic Publishing and Information Services." Inf.: NFAIS, 112 South Sixteenth Street, Suite 1207, Philadelphia, PA 19102.

MAR. 5–9—*Music LA,* annual conference. Seelbach Hotel, Louisville, Ky. Inf.: Marion Korda, Dwight Anderson Music Library, School of Music, Univ. of Louisville, 2301 South Third St., Louisville, KY 40292.

MAR. 6–8—*Libraries, Books and Culture,* seminar. Univ. of North Carolina, Chapel Hill. Cosponsors: Univ. of Texas GSLIS and Univ. of North Carolina SLS. Inf.: Dr. Davis, GSLIS, Univ. of Texas at Austin, Education Building 564, Austin, TX 78712-1276.

MAR. 8—*Job Training: Developing Training Plans For Your Staff,* seminar. Thompson Conference Center, Univ. of Texas at Austin. Inf.: Mel Boggins, GSLIS, EDB 564, Univ. of Texas at Austin, Austin, TX 78712-1276.

MAR. 8—*Midstream Career Changes For Librarians and Other Information Professionals,* workshop. Drexel Univ., Philadelphia. Inf.: Janet Goldwater, Office of Continuing Professional Education, Drexel Univ., Philadelphia, PA 19104.

MAR. 8–10—*Materials and Machines,* institute. San Francisco. Inf.: (see Mar. 4-6 for address.)

MAR. 10–13—*Alaska LA,* state conference. Centennial Hall, Juneau. Theme: "Libraries: the Link That Strengthens the Community." Inf.: Barbara Pavitt, Alaska State Library, Pouch G, Juneau, AK 99811.

MAR. 15–16—*Hawaii LA,* spring conference. Honolulu. Inf.: Kimberly Nakano, Univ. of Hawaii at Manoa, Hamilton Library, Room 104B, 2550 The Mall, Honolulu, HI 96822.

MAR. 18—*Children's Literature Workshop.* Creese Student Center, Drexel Univ., Philadelphia. Cosponsors: Drexel Univ. College of Information Studies and the Free Library of Philadelphia. Inf.: Anne B. Tanner, College of Information Studies, Drexel Univ., Philadelphia, PA 19104.

MAR. 23—*Office Automation and Library Productivity,* workshop. Madison Building, Library of Congress, First St. and Independence Ave., S.E., Washington, DC 20540.

MAR. 24–26—*Nonfiction, Independent Study and the Gifted Child,* conference. Sheraton Westport Inn, St. Louis County, Mo. Cosponsors: Lindenwood College and Book Lures, Inc. Inf.: Nancy Polette, Education Dept., Lindenwood College, St. Charles, MO 63301.

MAR. 27–29—*North Carolina Community College Learning Resources Association,* annual conference. Greensboro Sheraton, Greensboro, N.C. Theme: "The Past a Foundation; the Future a Challenge." Inf.: Lynette Finch, Nash Technical College, Box 7488, Rocky Mount, NC 27804.

MAR. 27–30—*Kansas LA, Kansas ASL, Kansas Association for Education, Communications and Technology,* annual triconference. Broadview Hotel, Wichita. Inf.: Kay Mounkes, Hillcrest JHS, 9300 Nieman, Shawnee Mission, KS 66214.

MAR. 29—*Archives and the Law: Keeping It Straight,* seminar. Education Bldg., Univ. of Texas at Austin. Inf.: (see Mar. 8 for address.)

MAR. 29–30—*Subject Analysis,* symposium. North Carolina Central Univ., Durham. Inf.: D. McAllister-Harper, North Carolina Central Univ. SLS, Durham, NC 27707.

MAR. 31–APR. 3—*Softcon,* international conference and trade fair. Georgia World Congress Center, Atlanta. Inf.: Softcon, c/o Northeast Expositions, 822 Boylston St., Chestnut Hill, MA 02167.

APR. 8–11—*Catholic LA,* annual convention. Marriot Pavilion Hotel, St. Louis. Theme: "The Library: Gateway To Global Understanding." Inf.: John T. Corrigan, CLA, 461 W. Lancaster Ave., Haverford, PA 19041.

American Library Association
Annual meeting
July 6–11. Chicago

Canadian Library Association
Annual conference
June 13–18. Calgary (Alberta)

Medical Library Association
Annual conference
May 24–30. New York

National Library Week
April 14–20

Public Library Association
National conference
April 2–5, 1986. St. Louis

Special Libraries Association
Annual conference
June 8–13. Winnipeg (Manitoba)

Expanding Service: Public Access Microcomputers

Don Julien

Purchasing a microcomputer for library public service can be likened to buying an airplane. A computer shuffles data quickly; the applications are what vary. Similarly, an airplane does one thing—it moves someone or something from one location to another, varying only in its application or use. One can purchase the airplane for personal use, making deliveries or taking business trips as the need occurs (staff use). One can set up an air service, providing pilot and attendants for regularly scheduled flights (database searching, in which the client expects to be able to come in at a specific time and receive prompt service). One can provide the aircraft on long-term lease (circulating computers). One can reserve the airplane for flight instruction (computer literacy). One can rent the airplane by the hour (public access computers). What would be readily apparent is that all of these services cannot be supplied at the same time by the same airplane. Some uses will automatically exclude others; several may be compatible through careful scheduling (e.g., flight instruction in the morning, rentals in the afternoon). The second point that should come clear is that no one airplane is suitable for all types of services. A scheduled flight service would require a larger and more complicated airplane than a flight instruction model. The final point in the comparison, particularly if you are wondering why we are talking about airplanes, is to reconsider and repeat the question: "Why are we talking about airplanes?" If other flight services exist, perhaps you should be providing travel agent services (rather than offering database searches, instruct users in database selection and search strategies). If flight instruction is readily available, perhaps a ground school might be more appropriate (perhaps you should enhance your computer book and magazine collection before considering a hands-on computer literacy program). If most of the clients who need airplanes have already purchased them, perhaps the need is for maps, and airport directories (circulating or review software).

Bailing out of the example, we can move on to a model for identifying needs and target audiences and for selecting appropriate services, equipment, and locations. Fritz Zwicky in his *Discovery, Invention, Research Through the Morphological Process,* Don Koberg and Jim Bagnall in their *Universal Traveler,* and J. Adams in *Conceptual Blockbusting* outline a method of clarifying options through morphological forced connections. The attributes of the subject under study are listed. After each attribute, list as many alternatives for that attribute as you can. Then go through the attributes, selecting one alternative from each list, combining them into new forms.

This approach can be applied to public service microcomputer projects. The elements of a project can be listed: Needs, Clientele or Population, Skill Level, Type of Service, Type of Equipment, and Site or Location. Under each heading, a number of options can be identified, as in Figure 1. Items can be selected from each column, forcing relationships and analysis of each combination. You need not be restricted to only one item from each list, but the more items you select, the more conflicts you will encounter as you select from other columns. Theoretically, you would work from left to right, but more than one library has found itself working from right to left. In one case, a college library was the surprise recipient of two Apple computers, courtesy of the dean, who stipulated that they be made available for student use. In this case, an outside force dictated the location, the equipment, the type of service, and the target population. The library was left with the task of deciding what need would fit those restrictions. The easy solution, and probably the one the dean expected, would be to merely make the equipment available as a homework tool, much like an electric typewriter. The librarian had loftier ideas, but will probably face an uphill battle working back across the columns to get software, and staff and system enhancement support. Most projects that start with

Don Julien *is director, Lake Hills Library, Bellevue, Washington.*

the equipment and location and work to the left usually end up working back to the right again when the needs that are finally identified dictate a change in the structure of the project.

Needs

The most common and most inaccurately cited need for a public service microcomputer is to increase computer literacy in the 'community', whether that community is a student body, a business, or a town. Computer literacy is rarely defined, although it is usually expected to mean that everyone is going to become excited about having a computer in the library. It seems to include vague notions of understanding the inner workings of the computer, how to program it, and how to use available programs. The debate continues in the general popular computer magazines as to what computer literacy really is, especially when defining the role of the schools. One author noted that as computers become easier to use and microprocessors find more uses in everyday tools such as kitchen appliances, heating controls, and automobiles, the only skill necessary would be the one that has powered modern civilization: the willingness to use things without worrying about how they work. He continued to say that for children, the computer is as exciting as flash cards; the value of a computer in the family is not as an educational tool, but as a shared adventure of discovery. Many computer programs are rather dull until a parent and child sit down together and explore.

A narrower definition of computer literacy might call for awareness of the potential of computers, a grasp of what a computer does well and what it cannot do, and a rough understanding of major applications. In a computer literacy program, the worst place to start is with the equipment. Books, general magazine articles, videotapes, and films effectively describe 'what a computer can do'. Unfortunately, the person who wants to become computer literate generally just wants hands-on experience with the computer. The expectation is much like that of television: turn it on, watch for awhile, and if you get bored, turn the channel. People who want to 'see what it does' have not made the connection that the computer takes something from the human mind, speeds it up, juggles it around, and returns it in a form that should make sense. Unfortunately, this requires, first, that there be something to be juggled, and, second, that a user tells the computer what to do with it. Any computer literacy project should start with a self-exploration process that discloses the tasks an individual wishes to relegate to a mechanical process.

What is usually touted as computer literacy is really a combination of several needs. The chart separates these because each will probably require a different approach. The most common needs that can be separated out are learning how to program the computer, gaining experience on several different brands of computers, and becoming aware of major computer applications. Other goals include: using the computer as an educational tool, with drill and self-learning programs; extending or manipulating data from print resources; using the computer as a homework tool, much like a public typewriter; programming, either by staff or by the public; previewing software; using the computer for in-house applications, such as booklists, local databases, indices and files, reports and statistics and other enhancements of the library's public services; extending library service beyond library walls, through such services as database searches, networks, bulletin board communications, and at-home access to library files (catalog, local databases); using the computer for games (Flesh Public Library in Piqua, Ohio, saw justification for games in the library, providing a separate Atari game console in addition to the public access microcomputer).

Population

Targeted population can be broken down in many ways. The most popular breakdowns have been by age and by socioeconomic status. Each category has special needs and interests. Preschoolers, for example, require simpler programs with less emphasis on reading skills and they usually need more adult help and guidance. College students may require access to several computer languages; business professionals may require a microcomputer with sufficient memory to handle or demonstrate major software for business applications. Socioeconomic factors may indicate whether members of the community have personal computers and need support and training, or whether a vocational training program is needed. It is tempting to ignore this column or to choose several items from it, but many of them conflict. Many adults feel ill at ease when confronting an unfamiliar piece of equipment. Often equipment suited for business applications is not suited for game use unless options are added. Special keyboards designed for children or the elderly may be distracting or uncomfortable for touch-typists. A circulating computer purchased with parents in mind will be different from one purchased for college students or for professionals.

Skill level

Similar to population considerations is the skill level of the target population. The user's familiarity or lack of familiarity with computer applications and programming will influence hardware and software selections. Both the Apple Macintosh and the Epson QX-10 emphasize ease of use for people with little computer experience. On the other end of the spectrum are the complex spreadsheet/database management/word processing programs such as Lotus's 1-2-3 and Symphony and Ashton-Tate's Dbase II and Framework. Devotees of these programs proclaim ease of use—after one has devoted hours to learning how to use them. If the user population is sophisticated and adventurous, programming capabilities in Pascal, Fortran, C, small-c LISP, FORTH, or APL may be required.

If the hardware and software are beyond staff or patron skills, a great deal of staff time might be used in explanations of features, instruction and problem-solving. Equipment and software below the skill levels of the users might not be used.

Type of service

The variety of public services involving computers seems endless. Figure 1 lists some of the more popular services libraries provide. New technological breakthroughs will expand the options.

The number of public access microcomputers in libraries has exploded within the last few years. Only a fraction of that number have been reported in the literature. In Washington State alone I have identified twenty projects. Many of these are in smaller libraries. When national surveys are conducted concerning public access microcomputers, large libraries and systems are the ones contacted; there may be far more public access microcomputers than the surveys indicate.

Many libraries offer only one public access microcomputer, some offer several. A few libraries have closely identified the purpose of their microcomputers and offer dedicated public access—for example, restricting the use to searching job information databases or for vocational training. Baltimore's YMCA initiated an adult functional literacy lab using micros, and the University of Utah's Marriott Library set up a word-processing center. Circulating computers range from inexpensive Sinclairs and VIC–20's to bulky Apples and notebook computers. Many libraries provide formal instruction ranging from workshops to multi-session courses taught by volunteers or paid instructors. Cornell University's library trains students and faculty to perform their own database searches. In areas where home computers are more prevalant, libraries circulate software, some restricting themselves to public domain materials, others circulating commercial programs. A few libraries have established preview centers where their patrons evaluate commercial and public domain software. Not to be ignored as a public service computer is the one dedicated to staff use for in-house and online database searching. And of course, libraries are jumping into the CB of the 80s: the electronic bulletin board service.

Several projects are underway to collect information on microcomputer use in libraries. Patrick Dewey is seeking information on electronic bulletin boards. The Public Library Association's Use of Microcomputers in Public Libraries Task Force is compiling a national database of libraries using micros. The University of British Columbia's School of Librarianship, with the support of the British Columbia Library Association, is compiling a database of applications in British Columbia. The Technologies Committee of the Public Library Association's Community Information section is seeking data on the use of new technology to operate community information programs.

Equipment

Consideration of equipment shows

Figure 1

Needs	Population	Skill Level	Service	Equipment	Location
Computer literacy	Children	No experience	Free public access (one machine)	Videogame console	Public library
Learning how to program	Preschool age	Acquaintance	Free public access (several)	Dedicated learning tools	• Children's department
Multiple machine experience	Young adults	Beginner	Fee public access	Inexpensive micros	College library
Computer applications	Parents	Competent	Dedicated public access	Notebook micros	College computer center
Educational applications	Adults	Advance	Circulating computers	Multipurpose home computers	School library
Extension of print resources	College students		Classes/workshops	Business system	Special library
Homework tool	Professionals		Circulating software	Network-controlled system	Rent-a-computer store
Computer programming	Seniors		Software Center	Peripherals	Museums/Science centers
Software preview	Breakdown by socio-economic factors:		Dedicated staff access	• printer	Student Union buildings
In-house applications (e.g., indexing)	• Income		Bulletin board service	• modem	Pizza parlors
Library service extensions	• Employment			• graphics tablet	Amusement parks
Gameplaying	• Urban/Rural			• game controls	YMCA
					Summer camps
					Senior centers
					Siteless services (computer clubs)

that certain types of microcomputers are suited to specific functions and populations. Videogame consoles are extremely easy to use and well-suited to relatively unsophisticated games, appealing to the early elementary ages. Dedicated learning tools, such as *Little Professor* and *Speak 'n' Spell* are an inexpensive alternative to educational software, especially for the early elementary ages. The inexpensive microcomputers, such as the VIC-20, the TI-99/4A, the Timex/Sinclair and the Radio Shack Model 10 are rapidly disappearing from the market, but are well-suited as circulating computers aimed at families and adults who want a short trial run with a computer or want to learn simple programming.

The notebook computers are good for circulating computer projects where more involved applications are expected. This equipment would be useful for college students working on term papers, programming, and data manipulation, or for business executives who take work with them on trips. Notebook computers range from the relatively unsophisticated and inexpensive Apple IIc, to the sophisticated HP-110 and Data General One with bundled software and IBM compatability, to briefcase systems including modems and printers.

Multipurpose home computers have been the most popular selection for libraries. They are bulky, like stereo component systems, making them unsuitable as circulating computers. They are versatile, lending themselves well to undirected public access and they are expandable, if use patterns dictate a change in services. They tend to be a little more difficult to use, unless someone spends a significant amount of time rewriting programs to simplify procedures. Some, such as the Apple and the Atari, are especially attractive to sophisticated game players. Others, such as the PCjr, which does not have many games written for it, or the Radio Shack models, for which the games are not as attractive, might be more suitable where computer games are discouraged. Business-oriented systems such as the Morrow Decision and the IBM PC are particularly well-suited to programs aimed at business or professionals and for in-house uses that might require more memory or storage capacity. In settings where a central computer is available and applications are limited, a network-controlled system may be more appropriate. Such systems are common in large businesses and in colleges; the library could be linked with the network or the main computer to provide patron access.

Peripherals and enhancements for microcomputers abound. Printers and modems are the most familiar ones. Other peripherals include graphics tables, game controllers such as paddles, trackballs, and joysticks, speech synthesizers, memory expansion boards, language cards, graphics drivers for the printers, mouse, extra disk drives (or hard disk), CPM or Apple card. Purchasers need to know what they want to do before they can make intelligent choices.

Location

This last item is one that is usually assumed. Of course, the library is the best place to have a microcomputer. Or is it? If you gave gotten this far in evaluating and planning a public service computer, you may have to admit that another location could be more suitable. Perhaps fee-based games belong in pizza parlors, or a college student computer lab belongs in the student union building. The list in Figure 1 samples a few of the places that have hosted computer projects. Some have proven especially successful in different locations. Summer camps are suitable for short series of intensive classes aimed at mid-elementary school through teenaged users. If the library lacks the space or staff for a multiple-machine learning lab, let someone else do it or try something else. The Tacoma (Washington) Public Library's COMPULIT lab was a strain on library staff because users expected an expert to be on hand whenever the library was open. The Pacific Science Center in Seattle was able to limit computer lab hours because the public expectation did not demand that it be open the same hours as the Center.

Using the model

A few examples will illustrate how librarians can use the model in planning a service. Let's assume the library is interested in showing adults how to program. There are several choices that will approach the goal. The library can provide a public access computer for the self-directed adult; the library can offer classes in programming; the library can provide circulating computers that the adult can work on at his or her leisure. The public access computer has some drawbacks; if only one is available, a user may have difficulty getting to use the machine and may be limited in the amount of time he or she can spend on it. Also, working on a public access microcomputer is like being in a fish bowl; the self-directed user would have to be able to ignore distraction. Some of these problems could be relieved by having several microcomputers available, perhaps in a separate room. Classes involve paid or volunteer instructors, will usually tie up a room at least twice a week, and may pull a microcomputer away from other functions during the class period. Circulating computers give the learner the time and privacy to work at his or her own speed but there is no human feedback, help or support. Another consideration is the number of people who will be served by the program; an eight-week course might reach twenty people and the computer can be used in the library when class is not in session; a public access computer might serve two hundred patrons during the same period; a computer circulating on two-week loan will reach only four patrons during the eight-week period. However, assuming the availability of a number of low-cost computers, one hundred circulating packages (at about $50 each) can be put together for the same cost as a public access microcomputer. The type of service chosen will determine the necessary equipment: for a class, one might consider a business system that can also be used for library applications outside of class; for a public access computer one might choose a low-cost general-purpose home computer such as the Commodore 64; for circulating computers one could select inexpensive closeout models (buy extras—they self-destruct). Now you can decide whether you should really be doing this. Is the local community college already offering continuing education courses in programming? Are they full? Does most of the target population already own computers? Can they readily afford them? If you had chosen another another age group, such as senior citizens or children, would other locations be more appropriate or convenient? Do you need a site or equipment at all?

Let's try another example: extending library service beyond the library to adults and young adults with computers of their own. The purpose is to provide information on new computer software, books, and magazines that are available in the library, to announce upcoming programs, and to respond to inquiries. There are several ways this can be done. A newsletter is one of the more traditional ways, although newsletters tend to become sporadic, are often out-of-date by the time they are mailed, and are poor vehicles for responding to inquiries. Another method would be to use local cable access and place messages on the character generator on the government, educational or public access channels; the information might be more timely, but there are severe restrictions on length of messages, and there is no effective means to respond to inquiries. One computer-based approach would be to use a commercial electronic mail service such as the Source, but the library and particular users would first have to subscribe to the Source, and might be restricted by the hours of operation. An alternative might be to use someone else's bulletin board service to leave and retrieve messages, eliminating the cost problem but probably enduring severe time limitations. Another computer-based approach would be to offer a library bulletin board service, either afterhours or twenty-four-hours (an unusual approach that requires a dedicated computer but would be easily promotable among local computer owners). A bulletin board service (especially twenty-four-hours) would require at least a multipurpose home computer with expanded memory, a modem, an out-of-the-way site, and a telephone line.

A final example: a software preview service for professionals. This could be done by circulating the software or by establishing a software center. Software circulation can be done without special equipment if the library is not concerned with checking for damage. Many libraries own equipment to check problems or to inspect returned software. Without such equipment a library can expect more problems with missing or damaged software. Needed computer hardware would probably have to be a business system with enhancements necessary to run business graphics, although large memory may not be necessary in a strictly preview setting. A software center gives the library more control over the software, although public access equipment is needed for the user. A major concern of software centers has been monitoring copying, especially of software that has been loaned or deposited by the manufacturer; this requires a trained staff, or a controlled population. A particularly interesting setting would be a software preview center, including not only programs but templates designed for regularly used programs, in a special library for use by employees.

The tough decision

The strongest pressures for public service microcomputers in libraries are often not from the staff, but from library board members, deans, Friends of the Library or interested patrons. In most cases, they are in the machine-fever stage, but the excitement can be contagious. The toughest decision is to say, "No!" True, every community probably has some computing/telecommunications need that the library can address, but any proposed service demands careful consideration. Patron and board interest should be encouraged. Use that enthusiasm to lead plans for a service that works for the library and the community. ▣

Preservation Using Pesticides: Some Words of Caution

Mary Davis

Last March, the National Research Council issued a report stating that only ten percent of the pesticides now in use have been tested sufficiently to fully assess their health risks, and that there is only minimal data on toxicity for another thirty-six percent. This study, and a similar 1982 staff report from the House Agriculture Subcommittee, sound a warning to librarians.

As a general rule, library directors leave the problem of pests to professional exterminators. Robert McComb of the Library of Congress's Research and Testing Office reflected the prevailing view in a letter to me last January, in which he stated that regular visits by exterminators are the usual means of controlling insects. Unfortunately, most professional exterminators rely heavily on chemical pesticides. McComb, taking this for granted, noted that the Library of Congress recommends the application of Sevin, Ficam, or Baygon. Such chemicals, we are now learning, are dangerous. They are also unnecessary. Librarians can protect their health without allowing collections to suffer, if they ask questions about pesticides and seek safe alternatives.

Two classes of synthetic organic insecticides frequently applied in libraries, organophosphates and carbamates, can damage the mind. Both insecticides inhibit the production of cholinesterase, a substance that controls the body's level of acetylcholine. Acetylcholine transmits nerve impulses. In excess it severely irritates nerve endings. The first organophosphates were developed for use as nerve gases during World War II. Cholinesterase activity returns to normal faster after exposure to carbamates than after exposure to organophosphates. However, both substances can cause long-term behavioral changes.

Researchers at Harvard Medical School discovered that repeated low-level doses of the organophosphate sarin altered the electroencephalograms and increased the REM sleep of workers for at least one year following exposure.[1] In an animal experiment, scientists found that exposure to two carbamates at subacute doses caused "mild, but permanent and increasing functional deviations of the nervous system."[2] A publication from the Consumer Affairs Department of the State of California sums up the available evidence: "Chronic exposure to organophosphates observed in workers indicate neurological effects (e.g. memory effects, delayed reaction time)"; with carbamates "secondary effects such as decreased learning ability appears to be long lasting."[3] Organophosphates commonly used in buildings today include diazinon, chlorpyrifos (Dursban), and dichlorvos (Vapona strips). Among the carbamates are carbamic acid (Sevin and carbaryl), propoxur (Baygon), and bendiocarb (Ficam).

Approval by the Environmental Protection Agency (EPA) does not guarantee a product's safety. The pesticides noted above have been registered for use, even though their drawbacks are not limited to their effects on the nervous system. Diazinon and carbaryl, for instance, damage animal fetuses. Diazinon is suspected of being a mutagen and carbaryl of being a carcinogen. Until 1972 Congress did not require testing of pesticides for any quality other than acute toxicity. The compounds were simply fed to animals, and the level necessary to cause the death of half of the animals was noted as the LD-50. Pesticides are still ranked in this fashion. Based on LD-50s, Ficam is the most toxic of the carbamates recommended by the Library of Congress, Sevin the least, and Baygon of intermediate strength. Such rankings say nothing about the ability to cause genetic mutations or cancer.

Now, the EPA must obtain data for the long-term effects of old and new compounds. However, reregistration of pesticides sanctioned before 1972 is proceeding slowly. Many of the tests have been found invalid, but no registrations have been cancelled for this reason. Industrial Bio-Test Laboratories (IBT), the largest independent testing laboratory in the nation, has been prosecuted and three officials sentenced to prison for submitting falsified data to the EPA. Yet carbaryl, registered on the basis of IBT tests, is still widely used.

Pesticide labels reflect the tendencies in testing. They teach avoidance of immediate acute effects but usually neglect to discuss the possibility of low-level cumulative damage. The EPA is aware of the limited meaning of registration. Any claim on a label that a pesticide is "safe when used as directed" violates the Code of Federal Regulations 162.10.

Library directors usually close their institutions during spraying, but this step, though helpful, is not sufficient to protect librarians and patrons. Many pesticides remain lethal to insects for weeks after the products are applied. During this period, peo-

Mary Davis, *who received her MLS degree from Simmons College, is a frequent contributor to magazines concerned with environmental issues. She lives in Georgetown, Kentucky.*

ple can be harmed by pesticide residues and byproducts, sometimes more toxic than the substances themselves. Diazinon, for instance, stays active for up to twelve weeks out of doors. Inside, due to the lack of direct sunlight, rain, and wind, it breaks down even more slowly. Diazinon evaporation allows it to be inhaled; other pesticides may sublimate or enter the air as solid particles. Library staff in a building that is periodically treated are subject to chronic low-level exposure. Library patrons receive smaller doses, but even slight contact with a toxic substance can cause significant harm to some individuals, including children and the elderly, who are particularly sensitive to pesticides. Researchers are unable to identify in advance individuals in the general population who are likely to become ill from such exposures, nor do they know what percentage of the population is hypersensitive.

Fumigation of books in closed chambers protects library patrons, if the chambers are properly vented and the books are thoroughly aired afterwards. This does not automatically solve the problem for librarians. Permissible levels of ethylene oxide, commonly used in the seventies against insects and fungi, have been lowered because the substance has been linked to illnesses such as leukemia and chemical pneumonia. Thymol and o-phenyl-phenol are frequently substituted. These are less dangerous than ethylene oxide, but both can damage the eyes and upper respiratory system. Thymol can also affect the liver, kidneys, central nervous system, and circulatory system. Unfortunately, thymol, a solvent, is not as kind to books as is o-phenyl-phenol. Fumigation by professionals in visiting vans or in conservation centers is safer than using chambers in individual libraries.

If people become ill from insecticide exposure in a library, there may be legal repercussions. Patrons or volunteers not covered by workers' compensation can sue the institution. The victim is not likely to recover damages unless the effects of the insecticide are immediate and obvious. The courts consider chemicals to be innocent until the plaintiff proves them guilty, not an easy task. Therefore, the library will probably suffer nothing more serious than embarrassment.

An employee cannot sue if the pesticide was applied by the employer. Compensation in this event can only be gained through the Federal Employees Compensation Act or the state workers' compensation system, which limits the amount of any award—an unreasonably small sum in some states. If the employer refuses to admit that the employee was harmed on the job, he or she can appeal the decision to a workers' compensation board. However, until a decision is reached, which can take a year or two, the employer may refuse to consider the employee for disability on the grounds that acknowledgment of injury could prejudice the case.

Librarians can do much to avoid creating such situations by following sound general principles of library maintenance that make buildings inhospitable to insects and render the use of pesticides unnecessary. Several of the factors that prevent insects from flourishing also slow the deterioration of paper and inhibit the growth of fungi. The one exception is light—good for insect control, bad for library materials. On this matter librarians may need to compromise. The ultraviolet rays in sunlight and fluorescent lights are damaging to paper. Library staff may therefore decide to light the storage area but to keep books out of direct sunlight and to place ultraviolet-blocking material over windows and fluorescent tubes.

Other factors are less controversial. The temperature should be maintained at 68°F or below, the lower the better and the relative humidity should be kept at fifty percent. With this level of humidity, insects will not find enough moisture in the materials they eat to enable them to survive, according to Richard Smith, president of Wei T'o Associates. Air circulation should be good, and the building should be cleaned regularly. Food should not be allowed, except possibly in a staff room or lounge located away from the stacks. To inhibit the movement of cockroaches and rodents, cracks in floor and walls should be filled and any spaces between entering pipes and walls sealed.

While maintaining these conditions, the staff will need to watch for signs of insects in incoming books and in the building. Traps baited with synthetic pheromones are a good means of monitoring particular species. Once staff members find insects, they should identify them and develop a plan for treating the specific situation, if necessary, with the assistance of an entomologist. The book *Urban Entomology* by W. Ebeling (Richmond, California: Agricultural Sciences Publications, University of California, 1975) is helpful for identifying insects.

Freezing is a promising technique for treating book infestations. At a 1983 conservation meeting, Mary-Lou Florian stated that "we don't have enough information to recommend" freezing. "Eggs and the pupae may be quite resistant."[4] However, the staff at Yale's Beinecke Rare Book and Manuscript Library is enthusiastic about the method. In the late 1970s they gradually froze their entire collection—over thirty thousand volumes—to combat an infestation of a Mediterranean species of death watch beetle, imported in foreign books. The program was developed by conservator Jane Greenfield, working with Charles Remington of Yale's Peabody Museum of Natural History. According to Gisela Noack, current head of conservation, the books were frozen in a blast freezer at -20°F for seventy-two hours. Each volume was wrapped in a polyethylene bag to prevent damage from condensation during thawing. It took a year to run the books through the freezer. Afterwards they were left in their sealed bags for an additional year so that if any eggs hatched, the insects would be contained. "We could not find any recurrence," Noack states. Now the Beinecke staff freezes all incoming materials as a precautionary measure; but they wrap entire boxes rather than individual items in polyethylene.

A number of European institutions have used freezing successfully. Richard Smith is attempting to spread the practice in this country. Wei T'o Associates markets a library Book-Dryer/Insect Exterminator. Although Remington found that a temperature of -10°F for twenty-four hours was sufficient to kill library insects, the Wei T'o freezer holds volumes at -20°F for twenty-four hours as part of a three-day freezing cycle. The cycle kills adult insects, eggs, larvae, and fungi but not spores.

Establishing a low oxygen atmosphere is another technique suggested by Smith. This can be implemented in a vacuum table, from which air is withdrawn and to which nitrogen or carbon dioxide may be added. Another possibility is substituting carbon dioxide for ethylene oxide in fumigation chambers. When using carbon dioxide, all air need not be removed. An increase in the proportion of carbon dioxide kills insects by forcing them to hyperventilate. Similar techniques are already used by the food industry. In the Northwest apples are regularly preserved in atmospheres from which most of the oxygen has been burned away, and in the South grain is stored with carbon dioxide in silos.

Other possibilities for treating books are microwaves and radiation, although microwaves have proven unsatisfactory in museums. There is evidence that gamma radiation, which breaks chemical bonds, may shorten the life of paper. Such radiation is currently being tested at the medical archives of Johns Hopkins University School of Medicine under a grant from the National Endowment for the Humanities.

Control of cockroaches can center in the use of boric acid, a substance to which roaches have not become resistant as they have to many synthetic chemicals. Although boric acid does not give off fumes, it is toxic if swallowed, so should not be used where children can reach it. As a heavy powder, it can be placed in cracks and crevices which form natural traps. Unless deposits become damp, they remain effective indefinitely. Boric acid can also be distibuted in tablet form, either homemade or purchased as Harris' Famous Roach Tablets. The Navy uses Harris' tablets "in massive amounts, on shipboard," according to Shirley Briggs of the Rachel Carson Foundation. She reports that silica aerogel (Dri-Die) and diatomaceous earth are substitutes for boric acid in cracks and crevices. Silica aerogel, which kills silverfish, beetles, ants, and crickets as well as cockroaches, is a fine powder. Although it is chemically inert, the fine particles can irritate the lungs. A professional-quality respirator should be worn when applying any dust, cautions Helga Olkowski of the Bio-Integral Resource Center. The pheromone traps which serve as monitors for cockroaches are helpful in eliminating the insects, but are more expensive than boric acid and tablets.

For termite control, professional assistance will be needed, but libraries should find an exterminator who will treat only the infested areas. Damaged sections should be cut out and replaced; nests should be destroyed, Olkowski says.

Libraries that emphasize non-chemical pest control may use a variety of natural techniques but they must employ chemicals occasionally as a last resort. They are practicing integrated pest management (IPM), best known in agricultural circles. An example of successful urban IPM is furnished by several California facilities for animal research. To combat cockroaches the staff sealed floors and walls, improved sanitation procedures, and applied Harris' tablets, loose boric acid, and baited traps. Between 1973, when the program began, and 1979, they cut their use of liquid and aerosol pesticides by ninety-nine percent.[5]

If a library turns to chemicals, the director should make certain that those chosen are the least dangerous available and are applied with care. Books and articles discussing specific chemicals go out of date quickly. A pamphlet published by the Library of Congress in 1975 recommends placing paradichlorobenzene in "open containers on shelves or in bookcases."[6] Paradichlorobenzene, it is now recognized, should be used only in closed containers; people working near the exposed chemical need to wear full-face respirators. For current information on the hazards of specific insecticides and on alternatives, librarians can consult the Rachel Carson Council (8940 Jones Mill Rd., Chevy Chase, MD 20815) The Center for Occupational Hazards (5 Beekman St., New York, NY 10038) distributes a data sheet and answers questions on fumigation. In return for a consulting fee, the Bio-Integral Resource Center in Berkeley, California will analyze specific pest problems and develop integrated pest management strategies to meet them.

The director of a library that resorts to toxic chemicals needs to be certain that the library is complying with all relevant state and federal laws and regulations. Certain pesticides, for instance, can only be handled by certified applicators. *Pest Control in Museums: A Status Report*, edited by Stephen Edwards, Bruce Bell, and Mary Elizabeth King (Lawrence, KS: Assoc. of Systematic Collections, 1980) furnishes valuable guidance on the regulatory system but does not cover right-to-know legislation recently put into effect in several states. Right-to-know laws mandate that employers furnish employees with information on toxic substances to which they are exposed, including generic and trade names, acute and chronic effects of exposure at hazardous levels, and appropriate emergency treatment.

Whether or not right-to-know legislation is in effect, such facts should be given to staff members before application of chemicals. Librarians need to be able to respond quickly to questions from patrons and they also need to be able to protect themselves. Few physicians are trained to link symptoms like headaches, weakness, and muscle tremors, to pesticides; and

(continued on page 431)

Consumer Health Information: A Prognosis

Ellen Fecher

People have always been concerned with their health. However, in recent years individuals are becoming more actively involved in health matters. Many trends have led to this increased interest in health: the consumer movement, women's rights, and informed consent among others. There is a growing mistrust of doctors. Doctors also have limited time and differing attitudes toward telling their patients about health conditions and treatments.

Today's consumers realize that they need facts in order to make intelligent decisions about their health and to evaluate health care choices. As a result, librarians are faced with a growing number of health-related inquiries from the public.

What type of information is the public seeking? A community survey conducted by Overlook Hospital in Summit, New Jersey found that people were interested in the topics of nutrition, exercise, parenting, sex and venereal diseases. In recent years there has been a transition in disease patterns from infectious to long-term illnesses such as cancer, heart disease and diabetes. In order to cope with these diseases patients and their families must be informed. Healthy people need information in order to prevent the development of these illnesses.

Where are people getting health data? The problem is not that health information is scarce but that it is plentiful and can be obtained from a variety of sources. "The present picture of consumer health information delivery is characterized by fragmentation rather than cooperation."[1]

A Harris Poll found that almost one-third of the United States population obtains most of its health facts from television. Another survey revealed that seventy percent of what the consumer sees on television with regard to health is false or misleading. The Overlook Hospital survey revealed that over fifty-five percent of those polled said that a physician was their first choice in seeking health particulars. The public library was the first choice for eighteen percent of the respondents. This certainly points to a need for community health science collections.

Consumer health information is available and can be obtained from a wide variety of sources. The Overlook survey found that while most people need health data, thirty-eight percent were unable to find medical information. Public library users were particularly dissatisfied. Since the consumer is having difficulties it is apparent that librarians must reexamine their own roles, review problems and look for new and innovative ways to serve the public.

The librarian's role

The general consensus today is that the librarian's role is providing health information, not health education. With education something is learned, and as a result a behavior is modified, an action is carried out or a decision is made. "Information dissemination, on the other hand, may be considered a less aggressive role. The individual is directed to or provided with information without interpretation, without opinion or counseling, and with no attempt to influence the actions or decision making of the individual. Information dissemination facilitates self-education; learning is left to the individual."[2] It is in this area of providing medical information that librarians can and do play a role.

The ultimate responsibility for the procurement of health information rests on the individual interested in a particular topic or concern. Some people are unable to find what they need unaided. These individuals, however, have a right to information. Librarians must be able to provide medical information that is organized and should coordinate that information for the remainder of the health field using skills basic to librarianship.

Some believe that the librarian's role should be more aggressive. According to Dr. Paul Kay, "In assisting and encouraging patrons to think about, to search out, and to evaluate on their own the information they request, librarians, as educational or developmental catalysts, might also be silently intensifying their patrons' abilities to take active and efficient charge of their health and lives at the same time."[3] Dr. Kay urges librarians to try to understand the patron's motivation; for example if the librarian encounters a person too timid to question his or her doctor, the librarian could suggest material which might help the patron work out this problem. This is indeed a change in role bordering on health education, for here in a sense, the librarian is offering an opinion and trying to change the behavior of the patron.

The clarification of his or her role is just one problem that the health science librarian must deal with. There is a scarcity of authoritative material written for the lay person. The quality of existing literature is inconsistent

Ellen Fecher *is former school librarian at Saint John's Preparatory School, Astoria, New York.*

and there is no thorough reviewing process by which this quality can be assessed. Another dilemma is the absence of unified bibliographic control. The National Library of Medicine is being urged to take a leadership role in this area and to provide for the centralized control of consumer materials. However, the mission of the National Library of Medicine is to collect in-depth only for health professionals. It is probable that some other organization will fill this role if the National Library of Medicine does not do so. "Regardless of what agency or organization undertakes the responsibility, there is a need for a national database of consumer health information materials accessible to the public through existing libraries and library networks. There is much to be done to develop standards for quality, to produce union lists and online databases for selection and information retrieval and to establish centers for distribution."[4]

Librarians must be concerned with the possible legal entanglements in providing health information. Essentially if librarians provide information, and if they forgo personal views, remedies, and diagnosis, they should not be charged with practicing medicine or of going beyond the area of librarianship. "According to physician-lawyer Norman Charney, there are possible legal implications in two other areas. One involves the accusation of fraud and misrepresentation, and is theoretically possible if information is misunderstood by an individual and that individual is injured as a result. The second, and perhaps the more likely, accusation of defamation might result from a librarian voicing an opinion about a particular physician or other health care professional."[5] Of course librarians must keep in mind that to deny requested information might be interpreted as an infringement upon an individual's lawful right to know. Medical librarians have discussed these legal issues.

The reference interview poses special problems when dealing with consumer health information. It is generally agreed that patrons seldom ask for what they really want and, therefore, reference questions must be negotiated. In discussing personal medical problems, however, many librarians feel ill at ease. It is particularly important in these situations for the reference librarian to be helpful, frank and reliable and to let the patron know that an interview is needed in order for the librarian to provide good service. As in all reference transactions the librarian should seek feedback, as material given to the patron may be insufficient or too difficult to understand. Providing information about fatal illnesses can be particularly stressful. Librarians should always respect the right of the patron to know. According to Norman Charney, "a librarian should not prejudge a person's reaction to learning about a disease he or she has. The challenge for information providers is to balance an objective, professional approach with a sensitivity to the requester."[6]

Academic health science libraries

Traditionally academic health science librarians are dedicated to serving the needs of faculty members, researchers, health science students and local doctors. The collection usually includes technical biomedical literature that is too advanced for the average consumer. Although few academic health science libraries forbid access to the public, priority of service is given to the library's principal users.

"If the academic health sciences library is to function as a link in a network providing public access to health information, then it must reassess its services."[7] One approach would be to establish a collection of health materials suitable for the general public and to organize a program of service for this segment of the population. Resulting difficulties would include the defense of an expanded budget and identification and loan procedures for the general public.

A second approach would be to offer service only to patients and their families recommended to the library by a health professional who uses the institution. This would cut down on the number of public users and would narrow the scope of information needs—most transactions would deal with specific health problems. This approach, while beneficial, would be very restrictive and would ignore the needs of most of the community.

A third possibility would be to function as a back-up for public libraries. Here academic health science libraries could do much: instruct public librarians in medical terms, health resources, and current medical happenings; supply health information that is not available at the public library; suggest health materials that the average person can understand and that can be of use to librarians serving the general public.

Whatever approach is taken, the academic health science librarian can strive to make physicians, other health professionals, and students aware of consumer needs for health information, and let them know libraries can play an important part in the provision of this information.

Hospital libraries

Traditionally the focus of hospital library service has been the health professional. The degree to which the hospital library serves patients depends largely on how much the staff and management stress patient education. No matter what the emphasis on patient education, however, most hospital libraries will assist in-patients and out-patients, their families, and, to a lesser extent the public.

Librarians have much to offer, especially if they combine efforts with a patient education or teaching department. Librarians can support programs by obtaining requested print and nonprint materials. Programs can be expanded by collecting information and critiques of other items, by ordering literature on specific issues, and by coordinating materials to meet specific needs. Other examples of possible programs are book cart services to in-patients and materials (books, pamphlets, etc.) placed in clinic waiting areas, chronic care units and other locations.

Many communities in the United

States and Canada do not have the benefit of an academic health science library; in these instances the hospital library can support the local public library by providing reference and instructional services. Many such programs already exist. Hospital libraries have been quicker than academic health science libraries to enter into such partnerships.

Public libraries

For many, the public library is the most popular source of consumer health information. In comparison to the aforementioned types of libraries, public libraries are new to the area of health information and yet it is logical that they should assume an important role. Problems faced by public librarians are different from those encountered by librarians in health institutions, for they must supply information for a very broad range of cultural and educational experiences. The public library faces a big challenge in trying to satisfy everyone's needs for health information. One possible solution to this is for public libraries and health sciences libraries to participate in joint collection development.

Public libraries regularly receive requests for health information. However, these requests make up only a small percentage of the entire demand for information made on the library. If the public library is to provide health information it must be dedicated to that role. Librarians must learn more about health resources. "This is essential, not only in order to enable public libraries to build sound collections and to guide the public in their use, but to assess individual needs and to be able to refer people successfully and appropriately to a health sciences library, an agency, or a health care professional."[8]

Online services at public libraries increase consumer access to health information. In a recent article, Tina Roose states that many questions could not be answered at the public library were it not for the online search and that online searches on health topics are extremely popular. At the North Suburban Library System in Chicago, Medline searches have been the most popular searches yearly since 1979. Most of these searches are done for average people who need details on health topics. They need information on treatments, on the courses and outcomes of diseases, and supplementary information to what their physicians have told them.[9]

Cooperation and coordination among libraries is perhaps the most effective way to increase public access to health information. Links between public and hospital libraries have already been formed.

The Metropolitan Cooperative Library System in Pasadena found that the delivery of medical information to the public was a problem. It teamed up with the Veterans Administration's Wadsworth Hospital in West Los Angeles to exchange services.

The Los Angeles County Carson Regional Public Library and the Los Angeles County Harbor General Hospital Regional Medical Library are also involved in a cooperative project—the Consumer Health Information Program and Services/ Salud y Bienestar (CHIPS). Salud y Bienestar translates as health and well-being. This project was funded for three years (1976–1979) by a Library Services and Construction Title I grant. When the grant ended funding was maintained by the two libraries.

The goal of CHIPS—the formation of a health information network—is brought about by working together to initiate activities and in the evaluation of results. Several objectives were established in order to meet the goal. One of the project's objectives is to improve levels of service and increase public and patient satisfaction in the area of consumer health information. Since a good portion of the residents in the area speak Spanish, many tapes in this language have been purchased.

The future of health information

If public librarians are to play an important role in the dissemination of consumer health information, library schools must provide for these new responsibilities. The problems of providing medical information to the public must be covered in general reference courses. Students interested in becoming health science librarians as well as those interested in public libraries must be introduced to the legal and ethical problems in providing consumer health information.

Even hospital librarians are often not recognized as important partners in the provision of health information and health education. Librarians must strive, therefore, to make themselves known to others active in the provision of health information. Cooperation among libraries is important but it is not enough. Librarians, because of their special knowledge of health literature and their familiarity with the public and the kinds of questions they ask, can offer a great deal to physicians. "Librarians must become partners with health professionals, with health organizations, with government agencies, with educators. In order to become effective, we must be recognized; in order to be recognized, we must be effective."[10]

Footnotes:

1. Dottie Eakin, Sara Jean Jackson, and Gale C. Hannigan, "Consumer Health Information: Libraries as Partners," *Bulletin of the Medical Library Association,* 63 (1980), 221.
2. Eakin, p. 223.
3. Paul Kay, "Public Access to Health Information: A Psychoanalyst's View," *RQ,* 22(1983), p. 405.
4. Eakin, p. 224.
5. Eakin, p. 223.
6. Howard A. Epstein, "Patient/ Consumer Information," in *Basic Library Management for Health Science Librarians,* ed. by Patricia Jones Wakely, and Ruby S. May, 2nd ed. (Midwest Health Science Library Network, 1982), p. J-9.
7. Eakin, p. 224.
8. Eakin, p. 227
9. Tina Roose, "Who Are the Consumers? What Are the Questions?" *Library Journal,* 109 (1984), 155.
10. Eakin, p. 228.

SPECIAL REPORT:

Virginia Clark

A CHOICE Assignment

Patricia Sabosik, ***Choice's*** **new editor**

The view from *Choice* magazine's Riverview Center offices is indeed of a river. The broad Connecticut is edged with highway on the Middletown side, but the ten large windows along *Choice*'s editorial row frame views of wooded banks opposite and of a hill topped with appropriately collegiate-looking buildings. This is not the famous brownstone skyline of Wesleyan University, however. That campus, in whose Olin Library *Choice* had its first offices, is a few minutes walk uphill from the river.

Inside the offices, a river of books—joined recently by a tributary stream of film containers and other packages of information—flows from publishers and producers. About 25,000 items arrive each year. Of these, more than 7,000 titles selected as appropriate for undergraduate libraries flow out again, each carefully matched to the reviewer whose subject interests and expertise best fit it. A *Choice* reviewer writing in the April Fool section of the April 1975 *Wilson Library Bulletin* paid admiring if teasing tribute to the sometimes esoteric levels of academic specialization required of reviewers. In mythic autobiography he "submitted his name to *Choice* as an expert in the fields of peanut butter and goat cheese sandwiches, snakes, and all aspects of library science. Taking his last statement as gospel, the book review editor sent him in 1971 a report on ANACONDA for comment. Our man naturally assumed this to be a volume on herpetology, and reviewed it as such. The results were not printed and he was not again asked to review." It seems a pity to dispel such a haunting legend and to let that reviewer continue to struggle in the self-inflicted coils of serpentine ALA acronyms. Reader, he lives! He reads the books *Choice* sends, and he still writes reviews. Reviews bear sometimes staggering evidence of the most attentive reading of formidable material. Some include not-for-publication attachments of detailed supporting evidence and text the brief printed reviews—about six hundred per issue—cannot encompass.

Reviewers—mostly college faculty members with some librarian reviewers—form a pool of about 3,000 persons representing campuses across the United States and Canada. Completed reviews make up another incoming stream at the *Choice* office, a flow of almost tidal regularity despite the sometimes contrary currents of the academic calendar. Reviewers are chosen as subject specialists who can compare and evaluate new works against existing ones, where appropriate.

Choice enters its twenty-first calendar year, its twenty-second volume, still a relative youngster beside such stalwarts of the library review press as *Library Journal* (1876), *Booklist* (1905), or the *Wilson Library Bulletin* (1917). *Choice*'s first editor, Richard Gardner, traced "Reminiscences of Early Years" in a special article in the April 1984 anniversary issue. He paid special tribute to the man whose brainchild *Choice* was, Verner Clapp, president of the Council on Library Resources. Clapp asked the American Library Association to propose a review journal project so that the Council could then offer to fund it—not the usual approach of grant-giving agencies. Clapp's idea proved itself when *Choice* became self-sustaining almost immediately. The journal was named after a contest that turned up four submissions suggesting the title, one of them from the late Eli Oboler. A staff of five assembled in the summer

---

Virginia Clark *is a subject section editor at* Choice *magazine and a member of the original staff.*

Inside *Choice*—**A river of books**

of 1963; the first issue appeared in March 1964, with 209 reviews of 210 titles by reviewers representing just over 100 United States colleges and one Canadian college. *Choice* had planned to review at most 3,000 titles a year but soon raised that figure. Since 1969 staff has numbered about twenty. There are approximately 3,000 reviewers and about 6,600 reviews published annually.

The aim was to supply faculty-written reviews of scholarly titles to librarians who could not wait months or years for scholarly reviews in subject quarterlies. At first the subjects of books selected for review matched the traditional liberal arts curricula typical of most small four-year colleges during the mid-1960s. Since libraries serving other sorts of institutions found *Choice* useful, and since many liberal arts colleges broadened their scope, they expected *Choice* to meet their new demands, and the magazine has tried to do so. A periodicals column and separate business, health sciences, information science, photography, and nonprint sections, including computer software reviews, attest to such response. *Choice* detailed its selection policies within each subject field in its Septemer 1983 issue. Bibliographic essays on special topics, long a standard feature of each issue (except May, which carries an annual "Outstanding..." list) are useful in larger institutions building in-depth collections, sometimes as a result of sudden growth from college to university status.

Reviewers, their interests in peanut butter and goat cheese sandwiches notwithstanding, are a widely varied lot. Special articles in the September and October 1982 issues of *Choice* profiled the reviewer group, described their recruitment, and gave evidence of their scholarly productivity outside the pages of *Choice* by listing one year's output of books they had written or edited. Reviewers are recommended by campus librarians and by their colleagues. Some volunteer their services, still others are recruited to fill particular subject vacancies. All reviewers provide curriculum vitae, which are carefully screened and filed by subject. The five assistant editors of *Choice,* who are in charge of matching book and reviewer in particular clusters of subject fields, are nearly all librarians. They find their contacts with reviewers akin to phone or mail-order reader service. They delight in "perfect" matches of reviewer and book, even on the occasions when a hasty search of their files turns up only the author of the book to be reviewed, signalling that it is time to add another expert on that topic. Bright, occasionally contentious, sometimes classically absent-minded—whatever their other characteristics—reviewers are definitely peripatetic. Tracking their job changes keeps editors and support staff busy. Once in a while reviewers seem to indulge in verbal pranks and it enlivens an editor's day to decide when to allow readers a smile in the midst of otherwise dense and sober prose and when it might seem too much to allow a reviewer to accuse the author of a book on women's history of "skirting the issues."

In September 1980, *Choice*'s familiar brown-and-terracotta cover design gave way to an ongoing series of color cover photographs of undergraduate libraries. In the September 1984 issue, reviewers' names appeared for the first time at the ends of individual reviews instead of in a list of "Consultants for this Issue." These two visible changes suggest many less visible ones in the production process. There have been many, and there are more to come. From the beginning, the techniques used to transform reviewers' words into type were at the frontiers of available printing technology, thanks to Science Press, *Choice*'s first printer. Their stroboscopic Photon presses were a forerunner of today's CRT-driven computer typesetting. Technology has also enabled *Choice* to make its reviews available on cards since 1968; and electronic publishing may make an online database of *Choice* reviews possible. In-house word processing and computer equipment now helps staff in the advertising and subscription departments as well as for editorial record keeping.

Editorial changes will continue as *Choice* watches trends in collection development. The growing internationalization of scholarship and the overseas growth of "American Studies" programs will help *Choice* build its already international circulation.

Choice is officially a publication of the Association of College and Research Libraries division of the American Library Association. It has an advisory editorial board representing various constituencies. Board members' names, especially in the early years, read like a who's who of college librarianship. Both the river outside the office windows and the activities and personnel within are constantly changing, as are the publishing and academic library worlds *Choice* links. The aim remains constant: to serve libraries with more of the best possible reviews of scholarly materials than are offered by any other journal. ▣

Dale Nelson:

Dateline Washington

Books in Our Future

The Library of Congress study, *Books in Our Future,* a year in the making, didn't come up with much in the way of new ideas, but more may spill out when the views of project advisers and consultants are published this year.

As submitted to the congressional Joint Committee on the Library on December 7, the study outlined no new government initiatives to achieve its goal of wiping out illiteracy over the next four years.

The report, commissioned by Congress in November 1983, said that both illiteracy—the inability to read—and "aliteracy"—the lack of will to read by those who are able—are widespread and growing. It called for greater support and visibility of existing government literacy programs.

The letter of transmittal to the committee noted that the conclusions were those of the Librarian of Congress, Daniel Boorstin. A related volume offering the views of project advisers and consultants will be published by the library in 1985 under the auspices of its Center for the Book.

As presented to the congressional panel, the study deplored the declining state of school libraries, saying that the average school is spending less per pupil on its library than it costs to replace a single hardcover book.

As for public libraries, it said, "In the very neighborhoods where people most need constructive leisure and self-improvement activities, libraries often cease to be accessible, though they could serve as avenues to upward mobility, as antidotes to juvenile delinquency and as the most open of universities."

Dale Nelson *is a journalist who covers the Washington scene for WLB.*

Senator Charles Mathias Jr. (R–Md.), chairman of the joint committee, said he hopes public hearings will be held on the issues.

The study predicted that computers will enhance, not diminish, the value of the book, arguing that new technology poses no threat to the book's future.

It attacked the "hasty assumption . . . that time given to new forms of leisure activity is necessarily subtracted from that given to older forms," saying previous studies have shown that the growth of television has not diminished reading.

As though to illustrate the point, ABC telecast a two-part adaptation of Ernest Hemingway's first and best serious novel, *The Sun Also Rises,* December 9 and 10.

Noting that although Hemingway purists would doubtless object to the liberties taken with the author's work, the program's backers argued that, even if it did poorly in the ratings, it would be seen by many millions of people, some of whom would be likely to be drawn to the book.

As a matter of fact, Part I of *The Sun Also Rises* finished forty-eighth in number of viewers as measured by the A. C. Nielsen Company. Part II also fared badly, with a 12.8 rating, just a shade more than half of the viewers for the same network's *Dynasty.*

The television production was the second try at filming the Hemingway classic. The first, a black-and-white movie with Tyrone Power and Ava Gardner, was no smash hit either.

As reviewer Tom Shales noted in *The Washington Post,* "Perhaps the book will remain the definitive version of the book. It has been known to happen."

Archives need permission

Now that the National Archives is an independent agency, a number of lawmakers have indicated they will hold hearings on strengthening its authority to inspect records of government agencies.

The House version of the bill separating Archives from the General Services Administration would have required agencies to furnish information about their records to the archivist. The final compromise, however, retained the previous requirement that the archivist get permission of agency heads before examining their files.

Copying in public schools

For the first time since photocopying guidelines were written in 1976, a public school system has agreed to restrain its teachers from copying material at will and passing it out to their students.

The Association of American Publishers announced in November that the public schools of Anne Arundel County, Maryland, have agreed to abide by the guidelines as to when a teacher may and may not reproduce copyrighted materials.

The guidelines were drawn up by publishers, authors and educators after the latest revision of the nation's copyright laws, but until the Anne Arundel agreement no formal attempt had been made to implement them on a school-by-school basis.

The agreement allows a teacher to copy something such as a news clipping or an article from a magazine to take advantage of what William Patry, a lawyer for the publishers, called "the teachable moment." But it prohibits the teacher from reproducing a poem, semester after semester, and handing it out to pupils.

The agreement is similar to one reached in 1983 in an out-of-court settlement of a lawsuit by nine book publishers against New York University.

Carol Risher of the AAP said she hopes the agreement will serve as a model for other school systems.

Card catalog as icon

Debate blossomed in the letters-to-the-editor column of *The Washington Post* after the newspaper ran an article on the computerization of the Library of Congress card catalog. Library officials say the catalog has been obsolete for nearly two decades and its replacement was long overdue.

Some readers, however, saw it differently.

William Peterson of Greenbelt, Maryland, who said he has been "messing about in libraries on both sides of the Atlantic for more than two decades," wrote:

"Of course we all sympathize with the poor librarians trying to cope with the glut of books, but it is less than candid of them to pretend that computerization is aimed at making the lives of readers easier. From a reader's perspective, it is simply another obstacle to scholarship."

Ferdinand Stibi of McLean, Virginia, said the library was "fast becoming a book cemetery," as researchers abandoned its reading rooms because of their objections to the computer system.

On the other hand, Julia Stam of Silver Spring, Maryland, who said she earns her living with her home computer, wrote:

"The computerized system is to the card catalogue what the car is to the horse and buggy. Few people would deny the romance and pleasure of a beautiful horse and a classy brougham; few people would deny the advantages of a car once one learns how to drive it."

Despited Stibi's report of mass desertion by scholars, library officials said only a recalcitrant minority were arguing for retention of the card index.

"To some people, it's an icon," Bob Zich, the library's director of planning and development, told a *Post* reporter. "It's like a religion."

The real Herbert Hoover

President Herbert Hoover was often seen as a cold and humorless man, but archivists at the Hoover presidential library say the newly disclosed papers of his wife, Lou, show a more warm, compassionate side of his nature.

Hoover, who died October 20, 1964, more than thirty years after leaving office at the height of the Great Depression, left instructions that his wife's files be kept from public scrutiny for twenty years. They were opened at the West Branch, Iowa, library on October 23.

Dale Mayer of the library staff said the material presented such a different picture of Hoover that it was "sort of like being the first person to stumble into King Tut's tomb." ▣

Anne McGrath:

Eye on Publishing

"... years of hunting dangerous, big game had honed my senses to a buffalo skinner's knife edge, and every goosebump on my neck now shouted 'danger!'..."

Scribner-Rizzoli marriage

The Scribner Book Store on Fifth Ave. and 48th St. is a New York City landmark—as handsome and welcoming a place to browse in as any book lover could ask for. It was designed in 1913 by architect Ernst Flagg for Charles Scribner 2nd, and has been a favorite haunt of the city's literati ever since. Fortunately, as a result of an agreement negotiated at the end of last year by Charles Scribner 3rd with Rizzoli International Bookstores, the famous old shop will stay open, with business as usual, right where it is.

Rizzoli International Bookstores is a New York City-headquartered company, part of a bookselling-publishing group owned by a consortium of Swiss and Italian business interests, that has acquired the two Scribner stores (one in Williamsburg, Virginia as well as the one in New York) and the right to add to them to a limited degree. (The Rizzoli bookstore, itself a fine Fifth Avenue shop until last month, has expanded into a new six-floor space on West 57th St.) The intention of both businesses is to cultivate their differences. Scribner will carry on as a bookseller of general hardcover and paperback fiction and nonfiction; Rizzoli, as a highly respected specialist in art, photography, and foreign editions.

Scribner Book Stores' history actually dates significantly farther back than 1913; the business has been run by the family for some 135 years. Last year Macmillan Inc. bought the Scribner Book Companies (Charles Scribner's Sons, Atheneum, and Rawson Associates), and the two bookstores have been operating under a license from the Scribner publishing arm. Rizzoli has outlets in Dallas, Costa Mesa, California, and in Chicago and plans to expand in the near future into the Boston and San Francisco markets.

The New York Review of Books sold

The book review journal that for the past twenty-two years has given *The New York Times Book Review* a run for its money has been sold for $5 million to a forty-year-old former Jackson, Mississippi newspaper editor. Rea Hederman, the *Review*'s new owner, has assured the paper's founders that he is not interested in making editorial changes, and that Robert Silvers, editor since the beginning, will remain in charge.

The *Review* dates back to the 1963 New York newspaper strike, when the absence of the *Times*' Sunday review section was sorely felt. Two of its founders, Jason Epstein, a Random House executive, and Barbara Epstein, a freelance book editor, produced the debut issue in their apartment. Barbara became co-editor, with Silvers. Book critic Elizabeth Hardwick, also a founder, became, and will continue as, "advisory editor."

The politics of the journal have sharpened and mellowed with the times, and its impressive list of con-

Anne McGrath, *a freelance writer based in New York, covers the publishing world for WLB.*

tributors reflects those changes; always, though, it has maintained its reputation as a place where important, scholarly books—however obscure—can be discussed. During the Vietnam War era, the journal looked to the intellectual left for input. Writers Murray Kempton, Noam Chomsky, I. F. Stone, Tom Hayden, and Andrew Kopkind expressed their views in no uncertain terms. Joan Didion's bestseller *Salvador* grew out of her work for the *Review*. Investment banker Felix Rohatyn has published a number of his economic essays there.

Bestselling books of 1984

A *New York Times* survey that tracked the popularity of last year's hardcover and paperback fiction and nonfiction puts *Iacocca,* Lee Iacocca's autobiography written with William Novak and published by Bantam, at the top of the hardcover list. The survey results were arrived at by gathering sales figures from 2,000 bookstores around the country and extrapolating total national sales from them. Many of these most popular books were published prior to 1984, but the rankings are intended to show only how well they sold last year.

The top sellers, in addition to *Iacocca,* were *The Aquitaine Progression,* by Robert Ludlum (hardcover fiction; Random House), *Eat to Win,* by Robert Haas (hardcover advice and miscellaneous; Rawson), *Seeds of Yesterday,* by V. C. Andrews (paperback fiction; Pocket Books), *Megatrends,* by John Naisbitt (paperback nonfiction; Warner), and *The One Minute Manager,* by Kenneth Blanchard and Spencer Johnson (Berkley).

Thoreau in paperback

Thoreau scholars worn out by the unwieldiness of the multi-volume *Journal* will be delighted by the news that Peregrine Smith Books has published the first paperback edition of the work. The new fifteen-volume pocket-size edition adds a botanical index to plant names used by Thoreau to the fourteen volumes in Houghton Mifflin's 1906 edition and includes in the first volume the material referred to as the "lost volume." Peregrine is selling its *Journal*—reproduced from a fine first edition, printed on acid-free paper and slipcased in a marbleized paper box—for $145.

Walter Harding, Thoreau scholar and professor at the State University of New York's Geneseo campus, increases the value of the *Journal* with his volume-by-volume analysis of the progress and pattern of a quarter century of Thoreau's thoughts, painstakingly recorded on a daily basis from late 1837 until the end of 1861. Harding served from the mid-1960s until 1975 as the editor of an authoritative text of Thoreau's work that is being published by Princeton University Press.

Thoreau's *Journal* was published by Houghton Mifflin only after a young editor interested in ornithology persuaded the publisher of its worth and did the editing himself. It came out in two editions—a limited edition that featured a manuscript page in each first volume, and a regular edition printed from the same plates—and was published along with six additional volumes of Thoreau's work. Both editions proved to be immensely popular.

New Hemingway award established

Authors and publishers of English language literature have recently been given new encouragement for their pursuit of literary excellence. The Ritz Paris Hemingway Award—a $50,000 annual prize to be given to the novelist of any nationality whose work comes closest to achieving Hemingway's standards of quality—will be given for the first time in 1985. The idea for the award grew out of conversations between Pierre Salinger, Mohammed al-Fayed (an owner of the Hotel Ritz in Paris), and Sir Hassanal Bolkiah, the Sultan of Brunei, who will underwrite the award. A board of directors that includes al-Fayed and Hemingway's sons Jack and Patrick will administer it.

Candidates for the 1985 prize, nominated by an international group of critics and authors, are under consideration by a distinguished jury: Salinger, William Styron, Mario Vargas Llosa, and James Dickey. Three finalists are to be selected this month, and the winner will be anouced in Paris at the end of March. The institution judged to have contributed most significantly each year to the study of Hemingway's work and his life will also be awarded $100,000.

Hemingway's connection to the Ritz dates back to the day in August of 1944 when he arived in Paris with the Allied troops and proceeded to set up shop in one of the hotel's rooms.

Prize-winning children's books

Winners of two of the most highly regarded awards in children's literature—the John Newbery Medal and the Randolph Caldecott Medal—have been named by the Association for Library Service to Children. Robin McKinley and Trina Schart Hyman will receive their awards at the association's annual conference in July.

McKinley wins the Newbery Medal, given yearly since 1922 to the most outstanding work of children's literature, for *The Hero and the Crown* (Greenwillow Books). Hyman receives the Caldecott Medal, awarded since 1938 to the best picture book, for her illustrations in *Saint George and the Dragon,* retold by Margaret Hodges (Little, Brown).

Three works named Newbery Honor Books are *Like Jake and Me,* by Mavis Jukes (Alfred A. Knopf), *The Moves Make the Man,* by Bruce Brooks (Harper & Row), and *One-Eyed Cat,* by Paula Fox (Bradbury Press).

Those honored as Caldecott runners-up are *Hansel and Gretel,* retold by Rika Lesser and illustrated by Paul O. Zelinsky (Dodd, Mead), *Have You Seen My Duckling?,* written and illustrated by Nancy Tafuri (Greenwillow Books), and *The Story of Jumping Mouse,* written and illustrated by John Steptoe (Lothrop, Lee & Shepard).

Will Manley:

Facing the Public

When you hear administrators talking about the need to get in touch with the people, when you hear politicians talking about "reaching out to the heartland," and when you hear educators talking about "developing a dialogue" with their students, you're usually dealing with people who expect to get a pat on the back.

It's a fact of life that no one, absolutely no one, not the Pope, not Gandhi, not Ronald Reagan, not Michael Jackson, not Joan Rivers, and certainly not Richard Nixon enjoys being criticized. Actually it's not even a case of not enjoying being criticized, it's a case of hating being criticized.

Early in life we learn that if you want to endear yourself to someone you obviously don't greet them with, "Good morning, I think your mother is something that rhymes with 'rich,' I think you're disgusting, and I think your dog is simply insufferable." Even such trendy salutations as "I'm okay; you're fat" will not get you on the world's most popular list.

So in general, most people don't go around insulting each other as a matter of policy. Certainly in the heat of argument insults are somewhat more socially acceptable than they are when you chance upon someone you know at the barber shop and blurt out, "You mean that hair of yours is real? I thought it was a polyester rug!" It is in the midst of argument that one can unleash one's entire arsenal of invective, ridicule, vituperation, scurrility, and abuse and not feel too guilty or gauche about doing it. The risk you take, of course, is that you can fully expect your invective, ridicule, vituperation, scurrility, and abuse to be returned in kind. Generally such arguments, which take place over insignificant occurrences like tubes of toothpaste being squeezed improperly (that is why the new "pump" should significantly decrease the divorce rate), tend to get rather cosmic. Like Vietnam, they get started over something silly, escalate into something serious, and often end inconclusively with one side saying, "all those things I said about you being a wimp, well they're not true." But, of course, they are true, she really did mean to say them, and the truth about you which has abruptly been revealed hurts—you are indeed a wimp.

The moral, I suppose, is don't put yourself in a position to be criticized if you want to avoid the unpleasantnes of being criticized. It's a matter of not casting the first stone. Then why are there so many masochistic-sounding managers, educators, and politicians who say that they want to learn what is on the minds of the people? Why are they asking for trouble? Why are they putting themselves on the firing line? I've got to believe that they think the people love them. They've been sitting isolated in their offices for so long being told what they want to hear from their staff lackeys that they really don't realize that the "people" just might have something negative on their minds.

If librarians really want to take the phrase "facing the public" to its logical conclusion, we must consider doing more than just delivering services that we have envisioned and shaped according to our own professional priorities. We must also "face up" to how our users evaluate those priorities and the quality of those services. Call it a "reality check" if you will.

The irony is the universally known truth that we librarians think two things about ourselves: 1) we're doing a superlative job and 2) we are underpaid. It has never occurred to most of us that those who use our libraries are not deep down fundamentally grateful for our professional competence and helpfulness. Oh, there might be a problem with an overdue or two, but most people, we assume, have a deeply seated respect for the wonderful, unselfish, altruistic work that we do for the common good. Therefore, many of us express no qualms about undergoing a reality check from time to time.

The problem is that a "reality check" for most library administrators involves nothing more than popping one's head out of the office door, walking around the library, seeing students hard at work, observing children smiling at story hour, and maybe even reviewing the usage statistics of the past six months. Sensing that he or she has taken the pulse of the community and that there is satisfaction all around, our library administrator then heads back to the friendly confines of the office with a renewed sense of smugness that should hold sway for at least six more months or until such time that he or she becomes so frustrated from such an important management decision as what should be the main dish at the annual trustees' luncheon that another ego trip around the library is launched. All's well that looks well.

Will Manley *is director of the Tempe (Arizona) Public Library.*

If we're really in need of more concrete affirmations of our goodness than just a few smiling faces, then we might get a little more creative. A very good, inexpensive, quick, and dirty method of "getting in touch with the people" is the "comment bulletin board." The big drawback of the comment bulletin board is that its effectiveness is limited to the people who actually come into the library. Its big advantage is that is gives library users of all types an opportunity to speak their minds in an immediate and personal way. It gives them the outlet to anonymously register comments, questions, and suggestions concerning library services with the full anticipation that their comments will be answered and posted by the library administration.

The best way to get started is to reserve a rather large bulletin board located in a central position in your building for nothing but patron comments. By doing this you will be providing something that everyone will want to consult on a regular basis without your having to go through the hassle of cutting and pasting, painting and illustrating, and tacking and stapling. No longer will you have to worry about having the artistic skills thc high art form of designing a bulletin board requires. Your patrons will do all the work for you. Therefore the comment bulletin board will not only provide an important communication vehicle, but it will also save you the time and agony of doing bulletin board designs.

One thing that you will have to provide is a pile of forms that have ample room for the patron's comments and enough space for your own reply. It adds some interest to the process if you give your forms a catchy heading like "Say It," "Speak Your Piece!," or "In My Opinion." One library I'm familiar with had the dubious taste to label their comment forms as "Bitch Tickets." Predictably, one of the first comments turned in accused the library administration of being sexist and obscene!

Once set up, the bulletin board should be divided into two sections: new comments and answers. A simple set of instructions should be included on the form directing the patron to tack the suggestion to that part of the bulletin board labeled "New Comments," making it clear that people need not provide their names, phone numbers, or addresses. You should personally check the board each day in order to write a prompt response for each new comment and move the entire form to the other half of the board.

So far so good. Now all you have to do is sit back and wait for the bouquets to come your way. I know that's the way I felt when I put up a comment board in the Tempe Public Library several months ago. I fully expected to be told what a great place the library is, what an effective administrator I am, and how grateful the community is to have such a public services oriented library program.

As for responding to such comments, I had some ready answers handy. First of all, I anticipated that the comments I would get over and over again were "How are you able to accomplish so much with only two percent of the municipal budget?," and "The library does so much with so little. What is your secret?"

"The secret," I had already intoned in my head, "is cost-effective management, a realistic sense of priorities, a searching for excellence, an understanding of human needs, and a thorough knowledge of the community. Next question, please!" In my imagination the comment bulletin board would give me the perfect forum to expound authoritatively upon the art of librarianship, the science of modern management, and the future of the contemporary novel. From there I figured I would work in some unsolicited remarks on the budget deficit, arms control, tax reform, and worldwide hunger.

And then reality set in. The first few comment forms were filled out and dropped into the box. To quote Joseph Conrad, my initial reaction to these insignificant tidbits was "the horror, the horror." The first one was from a guy who had a complaint, something that I obviously wasn't very prepared for. But the worst part about it was that it didn't involve something high-minded like a challenge for greater intellectual freedom or an idealistic request to buy thirty-five new copies of *Moby Dick*. Rather, the comment went like this: "I have used this library for many years. I have never been treated as badly as I was last night when I returned a copy of the book, *How to Build a Fireplace,* to that predatory book drop on the north side of your building. The spring attached on the little door of the depository is so tight that when the door slipped from my hand, it slammed against my fingers, which continue to ache quite badly. We're now talking damages—something in six figures without the decimal point. My attorney will be in touch."

"Okay, okay," I told myself, "he'll never be able to prove it was our bookdrop. He probably got his fingers caught in the car door. The next comment will praise us for our great selection of books."

But the next one was a plea for more bicycle racks. The one after that complained about a scarcity of parking spaces. The one after that said that the library was too noisy. The one after that said it was too quiet. And so it went. We didn't have enough romances; we had too many romances. The beeping from the computer check-out was driving people crazy. All the children in the library were driving the adults up a tree.

Finally after a week of this uninterrupted abuse, I called a special meeting of our librarians and asked, "If we're so terrible why are we circulating so many books?"

After several moments of silence, one of the children's librarians bravely asked, "Why did you put that comment board up in the first place? You said you wanted to hear from the public."

"Yes," I answered, "I guess I thought they were going to tell us how great we are."

Let that be a lesson to you. Facing the public is not looking at yourself in the mirror. ▣

Joseph Deitch:

Portrait: Eileen Cooke

Eileen Cooke in the Senate Reception Room

A glance at President Reagan's 1983, 1984 and 1985 budget requests for libraries shows a series of zeros. As the President's older brother once explained, "Ronald never did care much for books." Zero appropriations for the Library Services and Construction Act do not surprise Eileen D. Cooke, director of the American Library Association's Washington office. How, I asked in an interview with her, did she feel when she saw zero for libraries in the President's 1985 budget? "There he goes again," she recalled thinking. Then Cooke, whose leadership has aided in obtaining billions of federal dollars for libraries over the past twenty years, went into action.

The result was a change from zero to $118 million for fiscal 1985, the largest appropriation of its kind for libraries. "The President proposes—in this case, nothing—but Congress disposes, to the tune of $118 million," Cooke said, adding, "It was a classic team effort." On the very day that *The Washington Post* said that the President might veto the LSCA funding bill, which came out of local initiative and pressure, Reagan signed HR 2878 and extended the library-aid law for another five years.

"Intense grassroots efforts by the library community apparently convinced the President of the bill's merits," Cooke said in the *ALA Washington Newsletter*. He may have also been convinced that a veto would have imperiled votes in thousands of library-supporting towns and cities. Gracious in victory, ALA's Washington voice asked library folk to "thank all Senators and Representatives who urged the President to approve the measure, as well as the President himself."

What Cooke called "an unprecedented crash course in practical politics" for librarians and a chance for real-life experience in influencing the legislative process came during ALA's 1973 Midwinter Meeting in Washington. The librarians arrived in the nick of time. President Nixon, an admitted lifelong book-reader and with a much lower deficit to contend with, proposed the termination of federally aided library programs.

The librarians' invasion was "the talk of the town and the envy of the Committee for Full Funding for weeks to come." They had "stolen a march on eveyone [seeking funds] in the education community." Librarians, professional in assembling up-to-date information when needed—"isn't that what libraries are all about?"—did it this time for their profession: to get zeros changed to dollars next to such familiar library programs in the budget as ESEA, LSCA and HEA II.

Strategist Cooke points out that timing is crucial for affecting the legislative process. Regular meetings are cumulatively useful for "nurturing national legislation." But at any level, accurate and timely information is essential if targeted individual or group is to take effective action. Another Cooke truism, proven by good results, is that lawmakers and other budget-influencers are more responsive to public opinion if they are aware that the public knows they are considering funding legislation.

"The fast follow-up and continuing work by members throughout the spring months, coupled with the comprehensive public-relations effort directed by ALA headquarters in Chicago—'Dimming the Lights on the Public's Right to Know'—combined greatly to increase general

---

Joseph Deitch *writes for* The New York Times *and other publications.*

public awareness and eventually it yielded unprecedented media coverage about the plight of libraries and succeeded in convincing Congress to reject the zero budget proposal and appropriate $151.2 million for library programs threatened with extinction."

Why is there an ALA office in Washington? Because the association and its members are concerned with the legislative process and with laws affecting the creation, funding and management of libraries. Every day, Cooke's office provides the executive, legislative and judicial branches of the federal government with authoritative, nonpartisan information about library services and resources, plans, needs, construction, and personnel.

In turn, the office has a feedback role for ALA members and state chapters with news of legislative and administrative developments about libraries and librarianship. Ask Cooke what's happening in Washington of importance to libraries and you get the factual rundown, with commentary, that has established her as one of the most dependable and believable operatives in a city teeming with lobbyists promoting everything from Alaska lands to zero growth. Her office provides library liaison with educational, scientific, business, labor and cultural organizations represented in the capital.

Cooke herself plays the role of advocate in support of library legislation and funding on Capitol Hill, as when, in April of last year, she told the Senate Subcommittee on Labor, Health and Human Services and Education Appropriations that "the gist of my testimony to you today is this: libraries make a major contribution to excellence in education."

Her two-thousand-word statement, documenting the need for strong libraries, was based on her experienced belief that zero dollars next to federal library programs need not mean failure if an effective approach is made, person-to-person, to the right legislators. One of her decisive points to the Subcommittee was the following:

"Despite the contribution of libraries to the development of skills for critical thinking by children, despite the contribution of libraries to an educated citizenry, despite the contribution of libraries to literacy and self-improvement, despite their contribution to scholarship, research and development that keep the U. S. competitive in the world economy—despite all this, the Administration has recommended, for the third straight year, the elimination of Federal library grant programs."

These words—and respect for Cooke—helped get a bill passed, just as she has been getting library-related bills into the hopper and into funding law for many years.

Of special concern, Cooke reminded the Senate Subcommittee, was ALA's Coalition for Literacy, a campaign to help libraries educate the estimated twenty-three million illiterate adults in the country. "Adult illiteracy," she said, "costs over $224 billion every year in welfare payments, crime, incompetence on the job, lost tax revenues and in remedial education." If federal library grant programs "made even a modest contribution to reducing that number of illiterates, which they certainly do, they would pay for themselves many times over. Yet the budget request for these excellent programs continues to be zero."

Six days after Cooke addressed the Senators, the Senate Labor and Human Resources Committee passed S. 2496, extending the Adult Education Act for five years, with amendments and emphasis on adult literacy. Her legislative report for the first six months of 1984 sums up other library and education-related legislation with which she and her office were involved.

In 1981, on the twenty-fifth anniversary of their initial passage, Cooke's office compiled a list of benefits made possible by the Library Services Act and the Library Services and Construction Act. The accomplishments included the building or remodeling of 2,000 public library buildings, better library service for 100 million people, the purchase of 171 million books with combined LSCA, state, and local funds, 17 million persons benefiting from public library services for the first time, and library services for 30 million disadvantaged people. The Washington office helped enact the legislation to make all this possible.

Cooke noted that the ALA and library programs have enjoyed "very good bipartisan support over the years." She recalled that Senator Jacob Javits of New York was one of the strongest supporters of libraries. Senator Javits always said that he helped educate himself through his use of the New York Public Library, and that he had no doubt that his rise to long-time Senate membership was because of the early role of public libraries in his life. "The country is beginning to lose some of that tradition because people often do not come from a reading background," Cooke said.

Cooke thought a moment, then said, "One role we try to play is to remind our members that if we sit back when the President marks it zero for libraries and we say, 'Too bad, libraries go down the drain again,' they forget the potential role of Congress. It has the power of the purse and it is not going to be convinced unless they hear from back home. So we try to get the word out to library constituents as soon as possible. Members have to justify library funding programs because when the budget is tough, the competition is keen. You can just say, 'Libraries are nice, you ought to help support them.' Why should tax dollars come from the federal level if people in the community aren't willing to keep the library going as it should be?"

So the $118 million in federal aid for 1985 came about through action by the people?

"It certainly did. It was the result of good letters, conversations with Congressmen in Washington and on recess back home, and testifying at hearings." Cooke described the task of her office as "a steady role in influencing Congress. What makes it work is if we get the grassroots response. That's often hard to do. People think

'Well, we have a Washington office, so we don't have to worry.' It doesn't work that way."

For example, when Reagan first came into office, Cooke related, the Republicans took over the leadership in the Senate for the first time in thirty years. "They really had to learn to be leaders. The outgoing minority staff in Congress said it would be tough, because when you are in the minority, you can play around with legislation you like and put your foot out and trip the opposition. But when you've got the leadership, you have the responsibility to get programs through."

Cooke recalls having the impression that the newly-elected conservatives believed that anyone working in Washington "was to be avoided at all costs." They were a bunch of "flaming liberals." She therefore made "absolutely no effort whatever to contact Republicans in the Senate. They were going to have a biased view—we [in the library and book world] were pariahs." But she did send a message to ALA members, who were also constituents, about what was happening with the budget and what they must do about it.

The message was that if they had new Senators from their states, they should write to them to explain library programs in everyday, human terms—in terms of service to people who need libraries. "There is a particular role that lay people—trustees, 'friends with a capital F' and others without a vested interest in libraries—can play in influencing legislators, who know that librarians themselves have paychecks to look out for and who are going to say that libraries are great. Or so Congress would say it if was looking for ways to cut back.

"Those in the Friends category helped convince Congress, especially Republicans more supportive of the President's [antilibrary views] than the Democrats, to understand that libraries are for everybody and are not frills in the community, that they need stability and cannot be funded in erratic ways. And that libraries suffered from double-digit inflation way ahead of the rest of the country."

What will the second Reagan term mean for public libraries?

The fact that the President signed an extension of the Library Services and Construction Act for another five years is "very hopeful," Cooke said, "though I am an eternal optimist. You can't be negative and work in Washington very long," she explained.

His signing the extension "is intriguing in itself. If he were consistent with his zero budgeting, he would have vetoed the bill. The second important factor in the second Reagan term works in the opposite direction, and that is that David Stockman is still head of the Office of Management and Budget. Just based on past experience, he will want to cut everything in sight that can be cut, till everybody screams, 'Well, we didn't mean this or that program.' And so they get to their Congressmen, who will say, 'This can't be cut anymore, it's cut to the bone.' It could be Social Security, Medicare or student aid. It's always a matter of whose ox is being gored. When Congress says that it has cut all that it can, there will be a tax increase. Senator Dole, chairman of the Senate Finance Committee, and all reasonable people—Wall Street brokers, economists, everybody, is saying there's no way to avoid a tax increase."

Cooke has examined how the federal dollar is spent and has found that only seventeen cents of every dollar is "controllable." The rest is locked up in entitlement money—defense, student aid and the like. The seventeen cents breaks out to nine cents for the cost of running government operations and eight cents for domestic-aid programs like LSCA and programs under the Office of Educational Loans.

"So it really winds up as pennies, literally, for education and related needs, in contrast to all those billions for defense."

What do libraries get?

About one-tenth of one percent of the budget. "And even that may be a generous estimate," Cooke said. Will one-tenth of one percent enable libraries to meet the challenge reported in *A Nation at Risk*? Libraries would be used as never before as people become part of a learning society. Can libraries do their part with a federal allotment of a tenth of one percent of the budget?

"Absolutely not," Cooke said. "Look, for example, at the deterioration that sets in the finest buildings, as it did across the street in the Supreme Court building and the Capitol steps, where a lot of marble was replaced. Even solid buildings need shoring up. Libraries, to accommodate all that new and heavier use that the government sees for them in a learning society, need to be rewired, made accessible to the handicapped and generally strengthened to meet their new national responsibilities as learning centers."

Libraries will need up-to-date materials, whether for direct education or for family decision-making—can we afford a mortage, can we send our children to college? "I am sure that Caspar Weinberger does not use year-old magazines or newspapers or handbooks and databases for subjects involving his decisions. Technology, though, isn't everything. I agree with Dan Boorstin that the book isn't going to go away, and books cost money. A book costing $8 in 1973 costs $30 today."

Will there be federal funding to help libraries do what they are expected to do in the Alliance for Excellence? "Judging from his budgets, the President is saying there really isn't a federal role in library support. Libraries are a state and local responsiblity. You will recall that he even tried to do away with the Department of Education."

What might be funding priorities to allow libraries to contribute to better education?

"It's almost a chicken-and-egg question, but you certainly need materials, highly trained staff and sound buildings. The three are co-equal." Should libraries continue to leap up, all bushy-tailed, and say they are ready to do the government's or some

(continued on page 431)

Rod Henshaw:

Library to Library

The goal of an interlibrary loan transaction is to obtain a document in a reasonable length of time and at minimal cost to the requesting patron. Each transaction is composed of numerous tasks ranging from the patron interview to verification. Of all the steps involved in the processing of an interlibrary loan, perhaps none is more crucial than the selection of the library from which to borrow. Failure to identify an appropriate lender can mean the difference between a document delivery time of three days or one of three weeks, even using the electronic interlibrary loan systems.

Many interlibrary loan librarians consider the process of selecting a supplying library as one of the most professional aspects of their job, with a long apprenticeship needed to acquire a sound knowledge not only of which libraries give the best service, but also of a complicated system of networks, loan policies, and fees.

However, in most operational settings processing interlibrary loan requests is handled by clerical and paraprofessional staff. The choice of a borrowing source is usually a routine procedure based on protocol conventions. Protocol may be defined, in the interlibrary loan context, as a prescribed sequence in which requests are referred within a delineated group of libraries. Most local and state interlibrary loan networks have a structured protocol to which member libraries must adhere. Many protocols are hierarchical, but some are predicated on borrowing from like-type libraries, and some are based on contractual agreements with designated resource libraries.

Rod Henshaw *is head, interlibrary loan, Iowa State University Library, Ames.*

A protocol can perform two very important functions: it can assist in standardizing workflow in the processing of requests, and more importantly, it can help bring balance to borrowing and lending patterns. This latter concept is endorsed in both the ALA national and model regional interlibrary loan codes. The language of these two documents clearly encourages local initiative for resource-sharing and interlibrary protocols. The intent of both codes is to protect large public and academic libraries from being inundated by requests that have not been channeled through a local or regional protocol. This is very important today, particularly with an interlibrary loan system such as OCLC, which currently has 2,400 designated supplier libraries, but has no formalized system of protocol other than that suggested in the ALA codes.

When a library has exhausted its local borrowing options, the process of identifying a supplier becomes more difficult. Union lists, online and otherwise, can provide a plethora of potential suppliers, but which one is going to provide the best service in terms of delivery and cost? Who will and will not loan?

In addition to reliance on the skills of an interlibrary loan librarian, there are some published guides. The ALA National Interlibrary Loan Code recommends that all libraries engage in lending materials provide on demand a "statement of interlibrary loan policy and charges." As a result, interlibrary loan offices have systematically exchanged these statements for many decades. Also, OCLC's Name Address Directory has a provision for online access to member library policies.

For libraries not utilizing OCLC, and for libraries desiring a convenient ready-reference source, ALA has recently published a second edition of the *Interlibrary Loan Policy Directory*.

Congratulations are in order for the compilers, Leslie R. Morris and Patsy Fowler Brautigam, for their persistent efforts in seeing this project through to publication. In all respects this edition is clearly superior to the previous edition of 1973. Not only is it better organized, but it also includes policies for twice as many libraries. Entries are arranged by state and then in alphabetical order by library within each state. Although a key term index is included, the work would be even more useful with the addition of both an ALA and OCLC code index.

The data presented in the directory is also extremely interesting. For instance, of the 832 libraries listed, 100 presently charge a loan fee. All but a handful levy a fee for photocopy services. Another intriguing entry in light of our discussion of protocol is the number of special arrangements many libraries employ. Many of these arrangements waive all fees.

This seems to confirm the findings of a study recently conducted and published by the Association of Research Libraries (SPEC #92, March 1983). Of the libraries sampled in the study, all participated in a median of four interlibrary loan arrangements, with some institutions participating in as many as ten. Clearly, many libraries are not averse to establishing a multitude of special protocols to achieve favorable, if not reciprocal, loan conditions. As the ARL study suggests, the infrastructure of consortia and reciprocal agreements is both widespread and complex. The structure is a proverbial labyrinth that, rather than facilitating resource-

(continued on page 431)

Donnarae MacCann/Olga Richard:

Picture Books for Children

From Rotten Ralph's Rotten Christmas

Little Goody Two-Shoes would have been amazed by twentieth-century ambivalence about what makes a rascal or a saint. In Judy Blume's **The Pain and the Great One,** the good/bad spectrum is all a matter of perspective and ego. From a little brother's point of view, the "Great One" (his sister) is a pompous, overbearing threat. From a big sister's point of view, the "Pain" (her brother) is a sneaky manipulator of their gullible parents and a constant annoyance. Blume has divided the text into two separate, self-contained sections in which each child testifies on his and her own behalf.

Another narrative about behavior (also involving a pair of rivals under the same roof) reveals the "meany" as one who expresses chronic immaturity. In Jack Gantos's **Rotten Ralph's Rotten Christmas,** the cat-protagonist revels in tricks that represent playtime for him, but anguish for someone else (e.g., he unravels a sweater as it is being knitted). He demands attention (prancing along the piano keys as his friend, Sarah, tries to play), and he has a fit of vengeful jealousy when another cat pays a visit. But nothing this obnoxious "Garfield"-type does can move Sarah to a stronger reprimand than "Stop that." Rotten Ralph may be satirizing the arrested development of the spoiled child, but the characterization of Sarah serves as a wry comment upon overindulgent parents.

The Supermarket Mice by Margaret Gordon is a spoof about how to make your opponent work for you. As the illustration on this page suggests, Bounce is the proverbial mouse persecutor. But a supermarket's resident mouse family studies his principal character flaw—gluttony. They place Bounce in a position where he can "play both sides of the street." He is fed by the management for supposedly eradicating mice, and he is also fed by the mice as he helps them clean up after themselves each night and thus avoid detection. Virtue now has a pragmatic component. The supermarket staffers remark: "Thank goodness we got that cat," while the mice have a cozy, secure evening in front of their TV set, exclaiming, "Thank GOODNESS we've got that cat." Big folks are conned by a united front of little folks—a common motif in the folktale.

Goody Two-Shoes and other eighteenth-century cherubs would have been more comfortable with the distribution of rewards and punishments in David Neuhaus's **His Finest Hour.** Although visually this is the most contemporary of the four books in terms of mood and graphic style, the theme is handled with less ambiguity. Ralph in this story is like Rotten Ralph—an unmitigated stinker—and yet he has managed to be the friend of the exemplary Dudley since babyhood. Dudley is clearly a paragon, but a very passive one. He lets Ralph set up a rigged bicycle race, but perhaps knows by this time that Ralph is his own worst enemy. Ralph's trickery defeats him, while the honorable Dudley is given the coveted place on the local racing team.

The use of language in all four books is credible and expertly sparse. And in each case, the "nice" versus "not-so-nice" character models are handled with humor. The chief stylistic distinctions among the books rest with illustrations.

The loose, bold, sly cartooning by Irene Trivas is well-suited to Judy Blume's narrative. Trivas lets us see the consequences of petty, sibling rivalry (disgust, scorn, envy, anger) by simple gestures that are simply drawn. She tilts heads and suggests

From Supermarket Mice

Olga Richard *and* **Donnarae MacCann** *are the authors of* The Child's First Books.

From His Finest Hour

annoyance and suspicion by skyward and sidelong glances. She draws mouths expressively (although too often the children are pouting), and she portrays body language with understanding and skill.

Line drawing is the basic technique, although the illustrator occasionally enhances texture with a delicate use of color (as in the Great One's skirt as she sits at the piano). Page design is occasionally a problem when Trivas's skillful sketches are carelessly arranged—when drawings on opposing pages underscore an already over-crowded quality in the composition. An example of this flaw is the scene in which the Great One complains about the Pain's game as a garbage collector.

We would like to see Trivas focus on some of the painterly techniques that are merely tucked away in corners of the Blume book. For example, the cat who appears on nearly every page is subtly formed and painted, a vignette depicting the living room is embellished with a lovely bit of flower painting, and there is an exceptionally well-conceived and well-executed portrait of the Great One as she stands in a background doorway.

In the latest "Rotten Ralph" book, as in earlier ones, Nicole Rubel plays a fascinating visual game. Her style includes the use of a multitude of background patterns that have the same valence as the central figures. All objects are brought forward with a two-dimensional emphasis as Rubel flattens the patterns with opaque color and heavy outlines. The illustration reproduced here is an example. Cat designs on the wallpaper are as important visually as the hapless victim tied to the railroad tracks, and the rug beneath Sarah's feet is as prominent as Sarah herself. Our eyes are invited to play the game: "Look here. No, look over here."

Individual figures and patterns seem guileless, almost awkward, but the sum is complex, elaborate, and droll. The mood is "cheeky," and Rot-

From The Pain and the Great One

ten Ralph's clownishness is accentuated by his garish, fiery-red coat. To make sophisticated humor out of slapstick narration is a remarkable gift. It is probably alive in few places outside modern picture books.

Margaret Gordon's *Supermarket Mice* is a strange combination of techniques. The mice and their home interiors are rendered with 1890s cross-hatching, mannerism, and decor. The supermarket they raid every night is staffed by modern comic-book types who seem bold, cold, and oversimplified. The bright, raw colors used for both groups unify the pages. The busy, cozy, mouse world most appealed to our young child informants. Older children might catch some of the humor in the time warp: the juxtaposition of a modern, alienated, commercial milieu with the orderly, nineteenth-century world.

His Finest Hour combines contemporary image-making with a traditional plot about good sportsmanship. David Neuhaus's art is in the minimalist mode, and represents a manner of working that is often called "childlike." His figures and settings are handled with a deliberate and generalized disregard for the conventions of drawing. They are fresh and comical. These qualities are not lost on the perceptive viewer because the very sparseness of the compositions challenges us to make a full examination of everything the artist has done. But appreciation of minimalist art has a lot to do with visual predispositions. The Neuhaus book will probably be laid aside by children who find the very sparseness of the images difficult to process visually. Others will see the ingenuity and cleverness as a special treat. ▣

This month's books:

Blume, Judy. *The Pain and the Great One.* Illus. by Irene Trivas. Bradbury Press, 1984. $10.95. 0-02-711100-8

Gantos, Jack. *Rotten Ralph's Rotten Christmas.* Illus. by Nicole Rubel. Houghton Mifflin, 1984. $12.95. 0-395-35380-7

Gordon, Margaret. *The Supermarket Mice.* E. P. Dutton, 1984. $10.95. 0-525-44145-X

Neuhaus, David. *His Finest Hour.* Viking Kestrel, 1984. $10.95. 0-670-37260-9

Patty Campbell:

The Young Adult Perplex

Good Old Mom is a stock character in young adult fiction. A crashingly obvious statement, because Good Old Mom is a stock character in young adult lives. The adolescent dependency conflict focuses on her, and except for rare tender moments the average teenager regards her as alternately an annoyance and a convenience.

YA authors have treated her in pretty much the same way. In the junior novel she has to be there, or her absence has to be explained. Sometimes she is only a voice offstage, like the balloons from the next room that occasionally nag Charlie Brown. Sometimes she is only a presence against which the young protagonist reacts. In the early junior novels of the fifties, she often served as deus ex machina, delivering a wise little sermonette just when the teen needed to resolve a conflict. When she is fleshed out and appears as a character the result is often a grotesque. Such Moms are memorable: the man-hating dragon-nurse in *Confessions of a Teenage Baboon* by Paul Zindel, the sadistic monster-mom of *The Boy Who Could Make Himself Disappear* by Kin Platt, the cookie-baking, fire-eating, "good Catholic mother" in *The Revolution of Mary Leary* by Susan Shreve, the vicious marshmallow in the first chapters of *To Take a Dare* by Crescent Dragonwagon, the self-absorbed social crusader of *Dinky Hocker Shoots Smack!* by M. E. Kerr, the doggie sportswoman in *Carnival in My Mind* by Barbara Wersba. It is much harder (and much less interesting) to recall the sympathetic mothers in YA fiction. They blend into the woodwork, because after all, Moms are supposed to be nice.

Paradoxically enough, in the greatest YA fiction Mom is usually missing (or so distant from the action as to be virtually missing). Think of *The Outsiders, Catcher in the Rye, The Chocolate War, Lord of the Flies, Center Line.* The motherlessness is a powerful element in the pathos of these classics.

It is rare that Moms are presented as people in their own right with problems and pleasures that have nothing to do with their adolescent offspring. And when they do move through the pages of YA fiction living their own lives, the plot usually revolves around the protagonist's rage or insensitivity toward that state of affairs. This season at least five novels have turned on this theme, with varying degrees of skill and insight.

Beginning at the bottom, **The President's Daughter** by Ellen Emerson White depicts a Mom who is doing the most unmomlike thing possible: running for President of the United States. And winning. Naturally her teenage daughter is, as the kids say, "good and pissed." It embarrasses her at school (who knows if the boys are asking her out because of Mom?), it annoys her when her mother isn't home, and when Mom wins the election, the ultimate teenage disaster befalls her: she has to move and change schools. True, she is reluctantly proud when her mother debates on television, but not so much for the quality of her rhetoric as for the quality of her silk dress and designer coiffure. The book dwells on appearance to a terrifying degree; there are a myriad detailed descriptions of what everybody wore and how their hair looked. "You look nice," is the basic mother-daughter dialogue. We are vaguely aware that Madame President is a liberal, but other than that there is an almost total lack of politics in a novel about politics. Even more disconcerting, there is little mention of the difficulties inherent in being a female presidential candidacy. *The President's Daughter* is a clever, but shallow and superficial book, whose topical relevance ended on November 7.

Torey Hayden's **The Sunflower Forest** shows a mother who has been shut in at home, away from the world, by her loving family—ostensibly to protect her from herself. In this fine novel, blonde Hungarian Mama, with her plain-speaking exuberance for life, her restless intelligence, her inexplicable fits of violent depression, is an unforgettable character. To her daughters, seventeen-year-old Lesley and nine-year-old Megan, Mama's "spells" and eccentricities are just a normal part of life. They and their father join forces in arranging their lives around Mama's need for protection. Gradually Lesley learns that as a young girl Mama had been kept by the Nazis in a "lebensborn" where she was raped nightly by SS officers and made to bear two children. The first child, Klaus, was abruptly taken from her. In retaliation, she smothered the second child to death. In the light of her past suffering, Mama's paranoia seems almost justified, until she becomes obsessed with the idea that a scruffy neighbor child is her long-lost son. Appalled, Lesley tries to dissuade her,

---

Patty Campbell *is a freelance writer who teaches young adult literature at UCLA.*

although she is distracted by her own first romance. The delusion grows, and one day Mama takes a rifle and goes to free "Klaus" from the parents she imagines are his Nazi captors. Tragedy ensues, in a shocking climax. Lesley, stunned and grieving, flees to Wales to a cottage called "Forest of Flowers," where her parents had lived in contentment during the first years of their marriage. She does not find happiness there, but she summons the courage to go back and live outside the conspiracy of protection that has shaped all her former life. Torey Hayden writes with subtle control and extraordinary vividness, and mature YAs are sure to find *The Sunflower Forest* a moving experience.

Binding Ties by C. S. Adler features a teenager who is being surrounded with "protection." In this companion volume to *Footsteps on the Stairs,* shy, quiet Anne lives in a household that is dominated by a triumvirate of mother-figures: wasp-tongued Gram, tough career-oriented Aunt Renee, and her gentle mother, who is recovering from a mastectomy. In some passages that will have less meek teens gnashing their teeth, Anne knuckles under to their meddling with her life, until she falls violently in love with handsome, rebellious Kyle. The situation is complicated when Anne's stepsister, plump extroverted Dodie, comes for a long visit.

C. S. Adler again proves her skill at weaving a convincing story line and creating amusing and interesting characters in a slight but workmanlike novel that will appeal to junior high girls.

What would be the absolutely worst thing that Good Old Mom could do, in the eyes of her teenaged daughter? Get pregnant, of course. And, as sixteen-year-old Cassie in Eve Bunting's **Surrogate Sister** discovers, if Mom is getting paid by strangers to be a surrogate parent, it's a thousand times worse. Mom, a beautiful Rubenesque redhead, has her own reasons. She has lost a child and a husband in a car accident, she loves being pregnant, and she feels she is doing a great service for the childless couple who have chosen her to bear their baby. The whole thing strikes Cassie as bizarre, even gross, especially when word gets out at school and she is subjected to unmerciful teasing. And what will her new boyfriend Sam think? When she finally tracks down the adopted parents of her surrogate brother, her resentment begins to change to understanding. Bunting has taken this subject, which in less skilled hands could be tasteless, and developed it with compassion into an absorbing story.

Norma Klein can always be depended upon for deft, clean plot lines, witty dialogue, and something worth saying. **Angel Face,** although disfigured by a jacket illustration of spectacular unattractiveness, is a worthy addition to her long list of fine YA novels. Good Old Mom here is being divorced—and trying to be a wisecracking good sport about it, when she's not hollering with outrage, because, as everybody reminds her, she and her husband have never gotten along. Caught in the middle is angel-faced youngest son Jason and his brother and sisters. Actually, Jason is more interested in making it with his new girlfriend Vicki; his sisters are away at school, and older brother Ty spends most of his nights sleeping over at his beloved Juliet's house. No one pays much attention to Mom, as she struggles to find an identity in

fruitless job interviews and disastrous dates. Against a foreground of Jason's romance, we see Mom gradually falling apart until, on the way home from taking him to the airport to spend the summer with his father, she crashes into an embankment and is killed—or kills herself. Witty fast-talking keeps the book from being as somber as it sounds in synopsis, and while this is not absolutely top-notch Norma Klein, it certainly is light-years above most of what passes for young adult fiction between paper covers these days. ▣

This month's books:

Adler, C. S. *Binding Ties.* Delacorte, 1985. 192p. $14.95. ISBN 0-385-29293-7

Bunting, Eve. *Surrogate Sister.* Lippincott, 1984. 215p. $12.50, lib. bdg. $11.89. ISBN 0-397-32098-1; 0-397-32099-X LC 83-49483

Hayden, Torey. *The Sunflower Forest.* Putnam, 1984. $15.95. 344p. ISBN 0-399-12946-4 LC 83-27043

Klein, Norma. *Angel Face.* Viking, 1984. 208p. $13.95. ISBN 0-670-12517-2 LC 83-21657

White, Ellen Emerson. *The President's Daughter.* Avon Flare, 1984. 247p. $3.50. ISBN 0-380-88740-1

Kathleen Maio:

Murder in Print

Last year marked the fifteenth Bouchercon, an annual convention named in memory of Anthony Boucher, mystery fan, author, and critic extraordinaire. It is a gathering of mystery folk, both professional and amateur, during which a good time is truly had by all. That includes the most recent convention, "Second City Skulduggery," which took place in Chicago's Americana Congress Hotel.

As far as I know there was no violence at the latest convention. Well, there *might* have been a little bloodless backstabbing, or a possible swindle or two in the book dealers' room, but nothing to mar the enjoyment of the weekend. Nothing even close to the violent and murderous doings in Max Allan Collins's new novel.

Kill Your Darlings (Walker, 1984, $12.95) is set in Chicago, at a Bouchercon taking place at the Americana Congress Hotel. It is, the author claims, just a coincidence—an amazing one to be sure. At Collins's Bouchercon a tough-guy author of '50s and '60s paperback bestsellers, on the verge of a comeback, drowns in his bath. Roscoe Kane was drinking heavily the night of his drowning and his death is termed accidental. But series sleuth Mallory suspects that Kane was murdered.

There are plenty of suspects: a wife, an ex-wife, a gay son, and a few colleagues from the mystery world. Character walk-ons by the score will either entertain or infuriate the reader. The major game in *Kill Your Darlings* is not identifying the murderer, but identifying all the real-life mystery figures parading through Collins's plot.

Some members of the mystery community appear under their real names. Others don't. Still, it doesn't take a genius to recognize R. Edward Porter as Edward D. Hoch (a.k.a. R.E. Porter when he writes for *Ellery Queen's Mystery Magazine*). Collins claims that several of his least sympathetic characters are "composites." Maybe. But who could blame a reader for assuming that an arrogant and successful mystery author whose series character is named Keats ("a private eye named after a poet! Gimme a break!") is based extensively on a real-life mystery star?

Collins said recently, in a letter published in the fanzine *Mystery and Detective Monthly,* that "if this book were any more inside, it'd be inside out." That is its charm. It is also the major problem with *Kill Your Darlings.* Collins's mystery plot is nothing special. Mallory does little detecting. His technique consists of a lot of bluffing and confrontation that ends up paying off. It's the wicked little character sketches of mystery figures and all those little in-jokes on the world of crime publishing that make the third Mallory novel such fun to read.

I fear that readers unfamiliar with mystery fandom may find *Kill Your Darlings* quite slow and dull. But perhaps it should be viewed as a primer on Bouchercons (unrealistic though it most certainly is) for those who wish to join in the fun this fall in Berkeley.

In the first novel category, we have **The Other David** by Carolyn Coker (Dodd, Mead, 1984, $13.95). Andrea Perkins is a talented art authority and restorer. She is also assistant curator of a Florence museum. One foggy day she is given a grimy old painting by an elderly priest. Upon cleaning the panel she makes the astonishing discovery that the painting is a lost Michelangelo, or a reasonable forgery thereof. As she seeks to authenicate the painting she precipitates a criminal plot that includes murder and just about every other major crime.

Andrea is spunky enough. She defends herself well in several dangerous situations. But her role remains largely that of beauteous damsel in distress. I liked the police captain in charge of the case, an Italian-American raised in New Orleans but now one of Florence's finest. I didn't like the other male lead, a megalomaniacal millionaire from Texas who came off as a poor imitation of J. R. Ewing.

Coker doesn't bother to sustain the whodunit part of her novel very long, but she does sustain interest and suspense. *The Other David* is a propitious debut and a good art-world thriller even if Coker is not yet in the same league as Oliver Banks.

Michael Z. Lewin's private eye, Albert Samson, returns in **Out of Season** (Morrow, 1984, $12.95). Albert is once again asked to rattle around in one family's closet and see

Kathleen Maio *is a freelance writer based in Somerville, Massachusetts. She has contributed to* Twentieth Century Crime and Mystery Writers, Murderess Ink, *and numerous magazines.*

what pops out. In this case a well-to-do, middle-aged woman is denied a passport when her birth certificate is judged a forgery. Her banker husband hires Samson to find her real birth record.

The plot is very complicated, but agreeably so. And Samson's deadpan but dedicated approach to detecting, letting other people do as much of the work as possible, is oddly endearing. But I wonder if Samson isn't sometimes too easy-going. A trap is set for a murderer but it backfires with rather tragic consequences. Yet Samson seems little concerned with his culpability. If Samson is sometimes short on guilt reflexes, he is also short on the brassier brand of machismo. *Out of Season* is a pleasing private investigator novel.

On the other side of the pond, Martha Grimes's Inspector Richard Jury returns in **Jerusalem Inn** (Little, Brown, $15.95). The prolific Grimes has settled into her own formula. From her sleuth's frustrated passions to the appearance of feisty, adorable waifs in supporting roles, many elements of Grimes's new novel are reminiscent of earlier work. But this doesn't keep *Jerusalem Inn* from seeming fresh and being completely enjoyable.

Jury is spending a miserable Christmas with a downtrodden cousin in Newcastle when he meets a haunted and haunting beauty in a graveyard. He is intrigued and possibly smitten by her. But before their second meeting she is murdered. Jury horns in on the case which eventually leads to an isolated country house wherein Melrose Plant, his coadjutor, is one of the holiday houseguests.

Despite the fact that Jury's final reasoning and proof would never stand up in a court of law, this is a skilled story in the classic tradition. Repeated episodes of snooker-playing may pall a bit, but perhaps they should be put down to a desire for British local color. Grimes's characters are never dull, from major suspects to cameos. The veneer of melancholoy on Jury makes him a most sympathetic sleuth and the most interesting character of all.

It matters little whether Grimes has settled into her own formula. It is a very fine formula. *Jerusalem Inn* is further proof that Martha Grimes is one of the most gifted disciples of the latter-day British mystery.

New from Jon Breen is a reference volume, **Novel Verdicts: A Guide to Courtroom Fiction** (Scarecrow, 1984, $18.50). This well-organized and entertainingly annotated bibliography tells you everything you ever wanted to know about novels with trials in them—and more.

I must admit that I shudder to think of anyone voluntarily reading the entire oeuvre of Erle Stanley Gardner. Jon Breen has evidently done so. He nobly reports back to us on most of Gardner's massive output in the Perry Mason series and others. Breen may be a Gardner defender, but he is certainly not unaware of that gentleman's hackish ways and occasional blunders. Breen's judgement calls are fair and honest with Gardner and with the many other authors and novels he covers.

For those interested in novels (mostly mysteries) featuring trial scenes and legal trappings, this source will be indispensable. Even those who find courtroom scenes severe trials to their reading pleasure will likely find reference value in Breen's book verdicts.

I found Margaret Maron's novel **Death of a Butterfly** (Crime Club/Doubleday, 1984, $11.95) fascinating. Not for the mystery, which is standard fare about a beautiful but wicked woman who gets her head bashed in. The story starts out slow and is awkward at times, but it works its way out well enough.

No, I was fascinated by the romance given Maron's policewoman sleuth, Sigrid Harald. It is amazingly like Harriet Vane and Peter Wimsey—if Harriet were the detective. Our heroine plays the prickly female with the sophisticated jet-setting suitor who has a comfortable knowledge of ribald French and a penchant for reckless driving. When Sigrid starts quoting "licence my roving hands" while staring at her man-friends's mitts, I began to think I was in a time warp flashing back to chapter seventeen of Sayers's *Busman's Honeymoon*.

Maron may suffer in comparison with Sayers, but she's produced a pleasant quasi police procedural effectively combined with a traditional puzzle mystery.

A police story of an entirely different sort is James Melville's **Death of a Daimyo** (St. Martin's, 1985, $10.95). This is the fourth of a series featuring Superintendent Otani of the Hyogo Prefectural Police. The Superintendent goes to England to visit his married daughter and grandchild just in time for the murder of a Japanese national within the dignified walls of Cambridge University. The murder is linked to the death of a daimyo (mob boss) back home, where his second-in-command must lead an investigation into the power struggles of the new would-be kingpins.

One only wished that Melville had done more with the situations he created. The author spends little time contrasting the cultures of England and Japan except in such superficial matters as how one boards or disembarks from trains and subways. More could also have been made of the milieu of organized crime in Asia. In one hundred and forty-six pages, however, there is little room for such niceties. ▣

Judith Trojan:

Front Row Center

Childhood should be an enchanted time when hugs and kisses come from loving caregivers and not from sexual perverts. As more and more horrifying stories flood the media about neighborhood child molesters and sexual abuse in day care centers, it's time to alert children, their parents, and other primary caregivers about the nature of the crime, how and when to say "no" to sexual advances, and what to do if "no" doesn't work.

Programs featuring films about individual sex abusers and their victims is one way to awaken audiences to the severity of the problem. Since eighty percent of all sexual abuse is perpetrated by family members or friends, it's not necessary to look very far to find likely culprits.

Last November, CBS-TV's *60 Minutes* aired *Cheryl,* a provocative story about a tiny victim of sexual abuse. Now five, Cheryl Henderson's nightmare began at age two, when she was forced to endure court-designated weekend visits with her father. (Her parents had been divorced when she was sixteen months old.) Cheryl returned home from these visits exhibiting emotional and physical signs of molestation. Her mother took immediate action against her ex-husband, but no one believed her accusations. She recalls that prior to their divorce, her husband made no secret of his sexual attraction to young girls. He even admitted that he would have sex with his own daughter.

Although Mrs. Henderson told her divorce lawyers about his threats, her former husband was still granted weekend custody. When she forbid him to take Cheryl, she was held in contempt of court, and threatened with jail and loss of custody. Doctors, police, and social service workers turned a deaf ear to the mother's pleas for help. She was told, in one instance, that "all women" going through a divorce make such accusations against their husbands. A judge called her "a vicious, malicious woman" who needed "to see a psychiatrist." To make matters worse, her ex-husband accused her of molesting their child. Cheryl became mute.

Finally, Mrs. Henderson found a good lawyer and some doctors who were expert in the care and investigation of child sex abuse cases. Dr. Carey English, a specialist who treats a staggering 400 to 500 child sexual abuse victims a year at Martin Luther King Hospital in Los Angeles, confirms the undeniable physical fact of Cheryl's molestation. In addition, court appointed psychiatrist, Dr. Gloria Powell, discusses how she tested Cheryl with anatomical dolls, which proved without a doubt that the father was the molester. Powell claims that most preschoolers are incapable of making up stories about such sophisticated activity.

Late in the program, Powell's testimony indicting Cheryl's father is strikingly intercut with Mr. Henderson's jarring denial of any wrongdoing. Contradicting correspondent Harry Reasoner, Henderson claims that, despite evidence to the contrary, he never sexually abused his daughter. He also states that he plans to regain visitation or custodial privileges.

Cheryl's lawyer is initiating a landmark suit against the system—the legal, medical, and social service personnel who failed to protect Cheryl from her father—but the case may never come to trial. To date, Henderson has not been criminally investigated, nor has a criminal complaint been filed. Cheryl's lawyer states that Henderson will probably gain "custody of Cheryl between now and her eighteenth birthday."

As shocking as this may seem, it's also frightening to consider the sexist double standard at work here. Oddly enough, *60 Minutes* never addresses the question of why Henderson has been treated as innocent, while his former wife has been dismissed as a name-calling maniac. Despite the fact that children are urged to confide in the nearest caring adult if molestation

Judith Trojan *is editor-in-chief of* Sightlines *magazine, editorial coordinator at the Educational Film Library Association in New York City, and a staff member of the American Film Festival.*

From No More Secrets

occurs or is threatened, this program clearly shows that for a child's confidence to be effective, the adult confidant must be believed as well, or the child will be open to further victimization. In Cheryl's case, her mother was also a victim of the system. Cheryl will have to pay the long-term consequences.

Short and slickly edited, *Cheryl* can be effectively used to enlighten senior high through adult general audiences, in addition to medical, therapeutic, and social service professionals and students. Some words of caution should be noted for younger audiences due to the graphic subject matter.

Although Cheryl Henderson's protection seems to be stymied by a web of incompetent bureaucrats, other potential victims of sex abuse could be luckier, especially if they make use of *No More Secrets,* one of the most comprehensive preventive media packages available. Produced by Oralee Wachter, who also penned an outstanding children's book based on the film, *No More Secrets* gently dramatizes—with live-action and animated vignettes—three ways of dealing with common forms of sexual abuse.

A fun outing in the park turns serious for four ten-year-olds when they begin to share confidences about family members who make them feel uncomfortable. Jeannie's brother barges into the bathroom when she's undressing for a bath; he likes to watch. Jeannie's three friends encourage her to speak up and tell her brother to respect her privacy. Sam doesn't want his favorite uncle to call him a poor sport, so the boy obliges his uncle's fondness for wrestling. Sam feels tricked: "I think he teaches me to wrestle just so he can touch me." The other kids tell Sam that he won't be a poor sport if he refuses to wrestle with his uncle. Maureen's father likes to touch her under the covers when he tucks her into bed each night. Her father has sworn her to secrecy about his "game," but her pals advise Maureen to tell an adult friend immediately.

In nonthreatening fashion, simple animated drawings by Jane Aaron illustrate the abusive behavior described by Jeannie, Sam, and Maureen. The animation provides a catharsis of sorts by also depicting each child's newly assertive follow-up behavior. As Jeannie's story triggers Sam and Maureen to recall "icky" incidents in their own lives, *No More Secrets* should encourage young viewers to verbalize and share similar difficulties. Peer disclosure is a positive first step in the prevention process for the potential victim of sexual abuse.

The film comes with a high-quality instructional guide that will enable parents and teachers to use the film with children from ages six to twelve. The guide shows adults how to introduce the topic prior to screening the film, including sample dialogue about touching and private body parts. Post-screening discussion suggestions highlight sample questions and ways to allow children to connect incidents in the film with those in real life. A training film to be used with *No More Secrets* is currently in post-production.

Oralee Wachter's book, *No More Secrets for Me* (Little, Brown, 1983), also comes with a handy pamphlet to educate parents about sexual abuse. The book, for ages three and up, is divided into four stories of increasing complexity. "Talking Helps" is geared for the youngest readers. Darryl is uncomfortable when his teenage babysitter dries and dresses him after his bath. The focus here is on the child's right to privacy, even with a good-intentioned caregiver who has no ulterior motive. "Just in Case" focuses on Nickie, who gets nervous when an elderly neighbor makes advances that are too friendly. Nickie learns to say no and to develop good judgment in dealing with people, especially with innocent-seeming neighbors who come on too strong. In "What If," Greg's camp counselor tries to coerce him into stripping off his bathing suit and playing "a game." Like Nickie, Greg feels tricked and trapped, but he refuses to "play" and tells another camp counselor about the incident.

Based on Maureen's story in the film, "Promise Not to Tell" presents the most sophisticated concept and the hardest adult behavior to deal with. Maureen feels tricked when her father pretends to tuck her in bed. He really wants to touch her under her nightgown. She feels obligated to keep "their" secret until a girlfriend tells her that the secret is "his", not hers. Maureen is encouraged to tell a trusted adult friend.

Simple cartoon-like line and crayon drawings, executed by animator Jane Aaron, illustrate this extraordinarily sensitive book, which should be required reading in classrooms and in households with young children.

Whether you use the film, *No More Secrets,* the book, *No More Secrets for Me,* or both, they will enable your children to be one step ahead of potential abusers. When children learn that they have options—to say "no" and to tell others—they are no longer the passive, naive individuals who are prey to sexually disturbed adults. ▣

This month's programs:

Cheryl. Video. color. 15 min. 1984. Producer: Jim Jackson for CBS News. Dist: Dolores Sura, CBS Broadcast International, 51 West 52nd Street, New York, NY 10019. $350.

No More Secrets. 16mm & video. color. 13 min. 1981. Director: Peter Barton. Producer: Oralee Wachter. Dist: O.D.N. Productions, Inc., 74 Varick Street, Rm. 304, New York, NY 10013. 16mm—$348 (rental $68). Video—$308 (rental $68). Includes 12-page *Instructional Guide.*

This month's books:

Wachter, Oralee. *No More Secrets for Me.* Little, Brown, 1983. 48p. pa $4.95. 0–316–91491–6.

Wachter, Oralee. *Parents' Guide.* Little, Brown, 1984. 8p. pa $1. 0–316–91137–2.

Bruce Pollock:

On Record: Popular Music

Even for an unregenerate sixties adherent (are there really any left at this late date?), 1984 was a remarkably musical year. There was a preponderance of snappy sounds, from hip hop (Hall & Oates) to psychedelic white soul in drag (Boy George). There was a genuine folk/rock resurgence on campus (R.E.M.) and a new champion of the electric blues guitar (Stevie Ray Vaughan). Rhythm and blues got a shot in the arm from the pop antics of Huey Lewis & the News, the soul crooning of Lionel Richie, the mad strutting of Prince, the sexy rejuvenation of Tina Turner. Yes came back, Cyndi Lauper arrived and Duran Duran refused to go away. Michael Jackson's album finally stopped selling (after everyone in the world had bought a copy), just as Billy Idol's new piece of wax began its ascent. All this and Weird Al Yankovic, too? Be still my heart.

As can be expected, my own top ten has relatively little to do with any of the above. And yet, with the absence of a strong underground scene (aside from college radio and the subterranean self-produced independent label movement), it probably has more to do with it than I'd normally like. Regardless, here are the records and songs I found myself playing most this year, along with some explanatory comments.

The countdown

10. *Warrior.* Scandal, featuring Patty Smyth. Columbia PG 39173

Though I was admittedly skeptical about Patty Smyth's meteoric rise to pop power at the expense of her entire band—and even though this band has a long way to go in concert, there's no getting around that voice. When it's attached to the right song, anything can happen. And that's what rock and roll is all about. As I said in my earlier review about "Less Than Half" and "All I Want," the album's two best cuts: "They contain its most soaring moments, when Patty's early-morning, rolling-out-of-bed, sultry power takes hold in cosmic stretches, causing headlights on the road to wink in unison and countless near-collisions of transported dreamers."

Don Henley

9. *Building the Perfect Beast.* Don Henley. Geffen GHS 24026

Sapped of the cynicism of his earlier Eagles youth, Don Henley is almost sympathetic in this rather sad collection of postadolescent songs and stories. The opening cut, "The Boys of Summer," is one of the most moving lyrics of lost love to be heard, and all the way to "Land of the Living," the album makes a statement about surviving as an adult once life in the fast lane hits an unexpected roadblock.

8. *The Magazine.* Rickie Lee Jones. Warner Brothers 25117-1

From the girl who gave us "Chuck E's in Love," this beautiful work is somewhat unexpected. Though "The Real End" is a fine song, it's just about the only one on the disc—the rest are more like a series of set pieces, an extended jazz/rock opera. At turns fiercely poetic and autobiographical, haunting, sad and strange, the Rickie Lee that emerges is someone unknown to the pop business, one part Joni Mitchell, another part Carson McCullers. Sink into it and dream.

7. *Reckless.* Bryan Adams. A&M SP 5013

From Canada, Adams is one of the most soulful and passionate of white singers to emerge in the eighties. On the surface just another rough boy, he is without peer in the realm of the rock ballad. And while "Run to You," the album's hit, is exemplary of the genre, the movie song "Heaven" is one of the decade's best. What's most amazing is the way Adams can make even an ostensibly happy song (like "Heaven") sound unbearably melancholy and foreboding. Maybe the couple in question is happy . . . for now. Surely they deserve this happiness, after years of struggle—and surely, too, such perfect bliss can never last. I hope Bryan Adams enjoys

Bruce Pollock *is editor of* Guitar *magazine and the author of* Popular Music: An Annotated Index of American Popular Songs, Volumes 7 and 8.

his (admittedly fleeting) run at the top.

6. *Mister Heartbreak.* Laurie Anderson. Warner Brothers 25077-1

"*Mister Heartbreak* is the rarest of creatures: a work of poetry that works as music, a work of music that works as poetry. Each poem is placed in a musical setting as exotic and appropriate and hypnotic as the language and the reading/singing of it."

Repeated listenings have not dimmed my opinion of the album, only heightened it, offering glimpses into infinity whenever I can muster up the concentration to revel in its magic for awhile.

5. *Heartbeat City.* The Cars. Elektra 60296

One of the best pure rock records around, the Cars' disc captures a band at their peak, establishing their sound and probing its every variation with delight. Operating on a premise of simplicity, the Cars can get satisfyingly complex even as they convince you that their only aim is moving and grooving. Here's one album (probably the only one) that's actually enhanced by a viewing of the group's videos. "You Might Think" won MTV's award for best of the year. Consistently, the band's eye is as telling and witty as their ear.

4. *Learning to Crawl.* The Pretenders. Sire 23980-1

On an album of blistering intensity and rock solid musicianship, "2000 Miles" is, a year later, still on my turntable. As for the rest: "There are ten great tracks . . . that take Chrissie Hynde from cradle to grave, from emotionally repressed to positively loose, from adopted England back home to Ohio and back again, from the shambles of a band decimated by tragedy to the semblance of a new life. . . . There are moments of incredible poignance, feelings you don't hear much about in rock and roll." On top of that, Chrissie got married this year. Here's to her.

Bruce Springsteen

3. *Born in the U.S.A.* Bruce Springsteen. Columbia QC 38653

After a three-year absence, and maybe a six-year blue period, Springsteen has produced a veritably ebullient album (for him) full of positive virtues and magical soul shouting. Enhanced, of course, by the spectacle of seeing him perform, these songs soar as high as anything he's ever done, while at the same time plunging to the heart of his own and his audience's prime concerns: growing up, getting down, getting out, getting on with it. Me? I'm singing "No Surrender." You can take your choice.

2. *Steeltown.* Big Country. Mercury 822831-1

This is a Scottish rock band with inbred folk influences, bagpipes in their genes, rockets in their pockets. From the opening bars of "Steeltown," they create a dense musical mix of myriad modern and traditional elements, tied to smokey, intense lyrics and jangling melodic jigs. While their message may indeed be worthy, after many listenings I'm still swimming in the tide of the music—a new experience for me. Maybe it's my car stereo's fault. Maybe there should be a lyric sheet along with the cassette. Or maybe one of Big Country's messages is that the sound of the guitar is a message in itself.

1. *All over the Place.* The Bangles. Columbia BFC 39220

Adopting the high harmonies of the Beatles, this group of four women have tied them to lyrics that speak to a generation and melodies that speak to everyone. The album is a seamless succession of insidiously memorable tunes, strong voices, strong sentiments. As I said about my favorite cut, "Live": "If there were to be a Beatles in the eighties it would have to be four women . . . whose lyrics and melodies could so awaken in the hearts and loins of young Americans a buried sense of joy and possibility that they might inspire a legion of followers and thereby alter the course of history." I see no reason to take that back.

Gail Pool:

Magazines

"So the air is full of crud and the water tastes funny and the nine-to-five is a drag. You're tired of the subway, dog crap in the streets, bumper-to-bumper traffic and plastic TV dinners. Maybe the communes—with all that fresh air, sunshine, love and home-baked bread—are really into something."

Thus began an article published in the first issue of **The Mother Earth News,** a thin newsprint magazine that sprang to life in January 1970. From today's perspective, communes seem a footnote to the sixties, and the back-to-the-land movement never took off. But *The Mother Earth News* has probably exceeded its founders' wildest expectations: in 1983, the thick, glossy *Mother Earth* took in approximately $4.5 million in advertising revenues and reached close to one million subscribers.

The Mother Earth News is one of a loosely linked group of magazines usually referred to as "alternatives." The term "alternative," with its connotations of "alternative lifestyle," has for most of us, I expect, a distinctly sixties ring. Our mass media, from *The Big Chill* to news analyses of the presidential election, would have us believe that the eighties put an end to alternatives and that everyone is now mainstream. Certainly, you would never deduce from our popular, yuppie-oriented magazines that a sizeable number of people "want to escape from and stay the heck out of the corporate/consumer rat race"—as *Mother Earth*'s associate editor David Petersen has written. But mainstream media, after all, represent and reinforce mainstream values—one reason that alternative media are so important.

Under the "alternative" rubric falls a disparate group of publications: some depict nonntraditional lifestyles, some are in themselves unconventional types of magazines, and some offer nonestablishment sources of information. Characteristic of most is an underlying philosophy, a cause, a reason for being aside from making money (which most, *Mother Earth* notwithstanding, don't do very well).

Mother Earth is the most successful of the alternatives focusing on nontraditional lifestyles. Underpinning the magazine is a philosophy of self-sufficiency, with an emphasis on getting back to, and living harmoniously with, nature. Today's *Mother Earth* is not a socially or politically radical magazine (it no longer has much to say about communes); and it has probably maximized its audience with its accessible and useful how-to orientation. Articles instruct how to build and repair homes, raise assorted animals, grow vegetables, keep healthy, set up one's own business. *Mother Earth*'s audience appears to be comprised of homesteaders, future homesteaders, those who want to incorporate elements of self-sufficiency into urban or suburban lives—and those who just want to read about it all.

Mother Earth has plugged into an American dream: the powerful lure of self-sufficiency. The unity and strength of its back-to-the-natural message has served the magazine well, distinguishing it from mainstream magazines with similar editorial features—such as *Better Homes & Gardens,* with its home-repair focus, or *Country Journal,* devoted to upscale rural living.

Mother Earth's philosophy has also served to draw together readers, making them feel they are part of a conceptual community—an important aspect of the alternative magazine's role. Although an alternative publication is, by definition, an alternative to something else, it can't succeed by defining itself by what it isn't. *New Age Journal* in its current incarnation brings this point home.

New Age, another alternative lifestyle magazine, was founded in 1974. Recently acquired by Rising Star Associates, *New Age* is in the process of finding a new identity and is still foundering in the misty waters of "personal growth" and "the struggle to be human." *New Age* may want to reach those individuals who feel they don't fit into the mainstream. But these individuals do not form a monolithic group: their reasons for "not fitting" undoubtedly vary. *New Age* will have to decide which reasons it wants to address, whom it is speaking to, if it is to shed its editorial vagueness and develop thc personality it needs.

Both *Mother Earth* and *New Age,* although they depict nontraditional lifestyles, are in themselves traditional types of magazines, with conventional how-to and lifestyle features. A different type of alternative magazine is one that plays with the magazine format itself. Many of these efforts result in magazines that manage to be both flaky and dull. But one magazine that has pulled it off is the **CoEvolution Quarterly,** an eclectic and highly personalized publication.

Founded in 1974 by Stewart Brand, creator of *The Whole Earth Catalog, CoEvolution Quarterly* was initially a supplement to the catalog. Committed to self-sufficiency and survival, early issues had articles on putting food by and home medical remedies. In more recent issues, essays have flourished, with enjoyably unpredictable subjects. "Becoming Part of Gaia" appears alongside a poignant, more conventional piece on Alzheimer's disease. Not all *CQ*'s essays have been winners, but the magazine on the whole has been consistently provocative, informative,

Gail Pool *holds an M.L.S. degree from Simmons College and presently works as a freelance writer based in Cambridge, Massachusetts.*

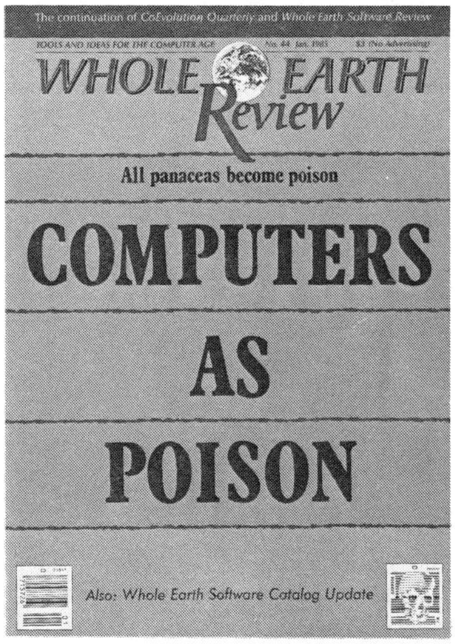

and entertaining.

But *CQ*'s most interesting contribution as an alternative magazine has been in its departure from typical magazine format. Brand takes reader involvement pretty far: book reviews are often letters written by readers; the only advertisements accepted are classifieds from subscribers. While reading *CQ*, one has an awareness of other readers—indeed, one almost has the feeling, encouraged by the magazine's homemade look, that it is written by readers.

CQ avoids conventional information slots. Magazines tend to be tightly formatted; we are used to fitting information into departments. *CQ* breaks down those divisions and proves that a magazine can take some imaginative leaps and still hold the interest of 22,000 readers.

In a sense I should be speaking of *CQ* in the past tense, since its fall issue was technically its last. Brand is merging *CQ* with his ailing *Whole Earth Software Review* to form the *Whole Earth Review*. But I expect, since *CQ* is so much Brand's own, that its character will not be lost in this merger and that the new magazine will bear the same stamp.

While *The Mother Earth News* addresses the issues of nontraditional living, and *CQ* addresses unconventional ways of thinking, a third type of alternative magazine provides "other"—i.e., nonmainstream—sources of information. Usually this type of magazine is specialized—in fields such as health care or political affairs for example. Usually it is written from a distinct political or social point of view. In a sense, these alternatives are based on the premise that all information has a bias. At their best they help us read the bias in the mainstream information we receive—whether from the American Medical Association, the White House, or *The New York Times*—and help us make intelligent, informed choices.

Science for the People, in the field of science and technology, is an example of an excellent "other" source of information. Founded in the seventies and published by the non-profit Science Resource Center Inc., *Science for the People* addresses a range of issues from what the magazine itself calls a "progressive" point of view. Topics such as the dangers of nuclear power or occupational hazards in the workplace are treated in full complexity, but the writing is clear and jargon-free.

Science for the People examines the motivations behind the messages we receive. "Sociobiology and Rape" (January/February 1984), for example, analyzes (and decimates) the "scientific" theories that suggest that rape is "natural" because even birds and bees (and plants!) do it. Other examples of informed insight can be found throughout *Science for the People,* including the special July/August issue devoted to how the media shape our image of science and such articles as "The Politics of AIDS" (September/October 1984).

Recent months have seen increasing concentration of ownership in the publishing industry. One needn't be paranoid to feel uneasy at the prospect of a diminishing number of independent voices in our powerful mainstream press. Such magazines as *The Mother Earth News,* the *CoEvolution Quarterly,* and *Science for the People* do more than add color to our publishing spectrum. In their approach to issues, in their definition of those issues, they offer needed, independent points of view. To make intelligent decisions, one has to be aware of the alternatives. ▣

This month's magazines:

The Mother Earth News. Bimonthly. $18/yr. Subscriptions: Box 70, Hendersonville, NC 28791.

Science for the People. Bimonthly. Individuals: $15/yr.; Institutions: $24/yr. Subscriptions: 897 Main St., Cambridge, MA 02139.

Whole Earth Review, formerly *CoEvolution Quarterly.* Bimonthly. $18/yr. Subscriptions: Box 27956, San Diego, CA 92128.

Note: *American Arts Project,* reviewed in *WLB,* October 1984, is available for $79/ 12 issues. Subscriptions: American Arts Project, 485 5th Ave., New York, NY 10017.

Norman Stevens:

Our Profession

At last there is an opportunity to discuss a handful of books about those items which are the foundation of librarianship. For over five hundred years books have been a fundamental element in human experience. The aspirations of people to acquire knowledge and learning through books, even under the most adverse conditions, have been remarkable. In recent years "the future of the book" has been questioned. We should, perhaps, stop using that phrase for it is clear that the book is alive and well and likely to survive for at least another five hundred years. But what about the future of technology?

Three small books have recently been published, even though one carries a 1981 imprint date, that deal with the subject of the availability of books for and the reading of books by American soldiers in three major wars. These fascinating historical studies are strong testimony to the lasting strength of books and their use in situations where technological substitutes would be impractical. As David Kaser suggests "military personnel in future millenia [will] use their reading skills to while away at least some of the myriad hours of idleness that even then will hang heavy over them." His **Books and Libraries in Camp and Battle** is an impressionistic view of how Civil War soldiers on both sides used books and libraries. Kaser scanned a mass of books, journal articles, and manuscripts looking for reference to books and reading and recorded a representative sample. While not, as he admits, a definitive study, this book is undoubtedly an accurate representation of the role of reading in the life of the Civil War soldier. Kaser has done a fine job of selecting and arranging the material.

His straightforward presentation begins with a description of what is known about the reading habits of American men in 1860, proceeds to identify what Civil War soldiers read, recounts the conditions under which they read, describes the sources of reading matter, and concludes by discussing the aftermath of those reading experiences. By 1860 the literacy rate was high and there was ample reading material available. However, the lack of leisure time limited reading by men and much of their reading was purposeful. Wartime service provided more leisure time and soldiers read purposefully but also for escape. In a well-organized narrative fashion, generously using the soldiers' own words, Kaser cites what they read in camp and battle, libraries and reading rooms, hospitals, and prison camps. The military, private individuals, commercial concerns, and religious and charitable organizations were among the varied means by which material was acquired. Here Kaser's selections provide an intriguing account of the lengths to which individual soldiers went to acquire reading material.

The soldiers' discovery of the pleasures of reading had a lasting impact. Kaser concludes that the reading experiences of Civil War servicemen contributed both to the growth of publishing and to the rapid growth of tax-supported public libraries. Those wartime experiences introduced men to the concept of reading for pleasure which led to a major change in the kinds of material published and acquired by public libraries. The efforts that were made to provide organized access to reading materials during the Civil War also had a marked impact on the future of military library service.

Kaser briefly summarizes subsequent library service to soldiers but Arthur Young, in **Books for Sammies,** takes up the story in more detail. He offers a descriptive history of the role of the American Library Association, and the War Service Committee it established in June 1917 to oversee the Library War Service in providing books to American soldiers in this country and overseas during World War I. ALA raised over $5 million in public donations, secured funds from the Carnegie Corporation to build thirty-six camp libraries, distributed about 10 million books and magazines, and provided, through just over 1,100 library workers, library collections to nearly 5,000 locations. That massive effort, undertaken by a relatively small organization and core of librarians, succeeded through bureaucratization, standardization, cooperation, and publicity. Originally written as a dissertation, Young's treatise is a more organized and less impressionistic view of soldiers' access to books and reading than Kaser's. It offers more information about the mechanics of the process and less sense of the end result. Still Young's text is lively and readable and offers a good picture of how books reached soldiers. He discusses the impact of that program on the growth of librarianship as a profession and concludes that its legacy was the new horizons of professionalism and service that characterized American library service in the postwar period.

John Cole's **Books in Action** is yet another piece of the same story. His focus is the 123 million copies of the 1,322-title Armed Services Editions, which introduced the pleasures of reading to thousands of American servicemen overseas during World War II. Although initiated in the U.S. Army Library Section, the project was planned and carried out by the

Norman Stevens *is university librarian at the University of Connecticut and the author of* Communication Throughout Libraries.

Council on Books in Wartime, a group of trade book publishers, librarians, and booksellers. Cole's succinct nine-page introduction provides a good history of the project. It is followed by an essay by Michael Hackenberg on the Armed Services Editions as an aspect of publishing history, a delightful essay by Matthew J. Bruccoli on his experiences as a collector of the books, a bibliography of writings on those editions, a note on ASE collections in libraries, and a list of the ASE titles. While by no means the entire picture of access to books and reading by servicemen during World War II, *Books in Action* tells an important piece of the story. It complements Kaser and Young; together these three short volumes reaffirm the importance of books and reading to servicemen during wartime. Perhaps before long others will add to this story with work on the subject during the Korean War and Vietnam.

As Kaser points out, more than four million copies of Beadle dime novels were sold during the Civil War. That marked the start of what is now called popular culture. The materials of popular culture, although until recently often outside the interest and scope of libraries in the United States, have had a pervasive influence in our society. Frank Hoffmann, in **Popular Culture and Libraries,** has put together a unique book which addresses, for the first time in any detail, the relationship between this mass of popular materials and libraries. He deals first with the integration of popular culture into library services. His good introductory chapter on the application of popular culture to library services is supplemented by one by William Schurk on the nature and scope of a popular culture collection and one by Haynes McMullen and Jay Daly on teaching the use of those materials in library school. The first part of this book is an excellent introduction to what is a relatively new and still neglected field and warrants careful attention. The second part is a series of eleven chapters on popular literature, popular music, the Hollywood film, comic books and comic strips, pop art, radio, television, the paperback book, the underground press, collectors and collectibles, and fads. Those chapters, each of which includes something about the history and the nature of the materials and a number of bibliographic citations, are a fair starting point but they are uneven and lack sufficient detail to be of lasting value. They serve as a reasonable introduction to a wide range of materials and topics but provide too little information about the ways in which some libraries collect and preserve those materials, or about the role that libraries might play in collecting and preserving them. On the whole this unusual treatment of a significant body of materials calls to our attention the widespread influence of the book, along with some of its technological counterparts, and the problems those materials present to libraries.

Unfortunately Hoffmann pays almost no attention to the contribution that the Library of Congress makes as the major repository of popular culture in the United States. Under the leadership of Daniel Boorstin, with assistance from others including John Y. Cole, executive director of the Center for the Book, the Library of Congress plays a major role in highlighting all aspects of the importance of books in our society including their contribution to popular culture.

In 1983 Boorstin secured a concurrent resolution from Congress authorizing a study of the changing role of the book in the future. The Advisory Committee on the Book in the Future, composed of educators, librarians, publishers, scientists, and others, gathered information from interviews with a broad range of people and discussed the issues. Fortunately Boorstin had the good sense to prepare the first report, **Books in Our Future,** himself. His letter of transmittal is careful to point out that some of the advisers do not agree with some of the conclusions and notes that a supplementary volume with the views of project advisers and consultants will be published in 1985. That can wait. For now Boorstin offers, in the twenty-two brief pages of the first part of his report, an eloquent and stirring picture of the importance of the book to society and of the continuing role that the book will play in our future. He manages to touch on every issue of importance and, in particular, interrelates the book with the new technologies. He affords both their proper roles as he suggests the need for combining technologies in "the adaptable book." Above all Boorstin is troubled by the menaces of illiteracy and aliteracy. He issues a challenge to "use all of our technologies to make the most of our inheritance, to move toward an American Renaissance of the Culture of the Book."

Setting as a potential goal the abolition of illiteracy in the United States by 1989, the bicentennial of the Constitution, Boorstin then proceeds, in the second half of his report, to present a manifold program for a massive problem. He begins with a lengthy catalog listing briefly hundreds of imaginative programs that citizens are doing and can do. The report concludes with a series of broad recommendations, stated succinctly and

(continued on page 431)

This month's books

Cole, John Y. *Books in Action.* Library of Congress, 1984. 78p. $4.95 plus $2 shipping and handling (Library of Congress Information Office)

Hoffman, Frank W. *Popular Culture and Libraries.* Shoe String Press, 1984. 328p. $29.50, pa $18.50. ISBN 0-208-01981-2; 0-208-01983-9

Kaser, David. *Books and Libraries in Camp and Battle.* Greenwood Press, 1984. 141p. $27.95. ISBN 0-313-24483-9

Library of Congress. *Books in Our Future.* GPO, 1984.. 49p. $2.50

Young, Arthur P. *Books for Sammies.* Beta Phi Mu, 1981. 149p. $12.50. ISBN 0-910230-15-3. LC 81-17085

Patrick Dewey:

Software for Libraries

A welcome addition to the growing amount of software available for young and preschool children has been published by Scott, Foresman. **Animals and Insects** (Scott, Foresman & Co., 1983) is a simple matching game wherein children, aged four and up, are presented with easily distinguishable drawings of various animals and insects (e.g., cat, horse, spider) with the name of one spelled out at the bottom of the screen. A moving arrow alternately points from one drawing to the next. To make a selection, the child simply presses the space bar when the arrow is pointing at the correct picture. For variety, the game can be played in the opposite direction: i.e., the child picks the correct word from among three choices to identify the picture. The program is also good for use with people with learning disabilities and with people learning English as a second language. It comes with four sets of flash cards, including the animals used in the software, a "Basic Book" of animal illustrations, and an "Instructor's Guide." For use with Apple II+, IIe, IIc. Cost: $69.95.

Simple library applications

Catalogit!!! and **Overdue Books** (Right On Programs, 1984) are two good programs that are specifically intended for inhouse library use. Both are extremely easy to master. If you harbor some fear of computers but still want to take advantage of the new technology, these programs will give you a good chance of overcoming one while enjoying the other. *Catalogit!!!,* for example, has only three commands on the main menu: enter data, print cards, or quit. It is one of the most straightforward library programs around, requiring no special knowledge and only moments for startup. Included are five hundred continuous-feed catalog cards. *Overdue Books* will support a list of over four hundred student and teacher entries. The program will print the list by date or by teacher, and also provides overdue notices. These programs, while good, are limited in sophistication and lack the ability to handle large numbers of users. They are best suited for small libraries, such as those in elementary schools. For use with Apple II+, IIe, IIc, Commodore 64, Commodore PET (32K). Cost: *Catalogit!!!,* $70; *Overdue Books,* $50.

Patrick Dewey *is administrative librarian, Maywood (Illinois) Public Library and author of* **Public Access Microcomputers: A Handbook for Librarians.**

Educational adventures

The Elysian Fields and Other Greek Myths, by Mark Novembrino, and **Kukulcan,** by Michael D. Giltzow, are two new adventure games (American Eagle Software, Inc., 1984). Both are different from the many ordinary adventures available in that they were apparently written as educational programs using the adventure format. High resolution graphics provide colorful and well-made drawings of people and places in two historical contexts. *Elysian Fields* provides us with a look at ancient Greek mythology, including a glimpse of gods, goddesses, and geography. *Kukulcan* gives a brief but excellent look at ancient Aztec culture. Historical notes in the accompanying guide give an overview of social structure, government, and architecture. Historical notes are also available online throughout the game. A good bibliography suggesting additional reading is included in the *Kukulcan* booklet. Neither of these educational adventures is difficult, and though they could be recommended for use with precocious grade school students, they are more suitable for high school. A hint sheet, with clues, may be obtained by writing the vendor. Game positions may be saved to disk for both adventures. For use with Apple Computers, and Commodore 64. Cost: $39.95 each.

A graphic best buy

The Graphic Solution (Accent Software, Inc., 1982) is an exciting animation kit that permits users to craft shapes and drawings and then capture them in "frames" for animated sequences later. It is a graphics package with a great deal of power. Libraries with public access computers may soon find a graphics or animation club built around this single software package. In some ways, the user can begin immediately. Drawing circles and other forms to make rather elegant and intricate patterns can be done in minutes. Text may be added to graphics, as well as fast or slow motion. Advancing to the creation of "frames" for an animated sequence can take quite a few sittings in front of the monitor, but to help, *TGS* provides 170 pages of documentation, including a nine-lesson tutorial, and a good help menu is available whenever needed. The system also supports screen dumps for computers with a graphics card, and saving work to disk. A remarkable tool, *TGS* is well worth the investment in time for patrons or librarians interested in graphics. Though several years old, this is still the best animation package available for microcomputers. Persons who master this package will have a tool equal in capability and importance to a spreadsheet, a good word processor, or a database management system. A running demo is included on the backsides of disks. $149.95, with backup. Available for the Apple (64K) II, II+, IIe, IBM PC (80K), and TRS–80 Models III, IV. Cost: $145. The Apple version was used for this review.

A premium value

Microzine (Dan Klassen, producer and editor) is very much an electronic magazine. Published by Scholastic six times each year, *Microzine* provides a variety of programs in each issue, and it is highly educational. Learners get practice in following directions, using the computer, puzzle-solving, and reading, as well as being entertained. Each issue comes with a small but excellent manual with easy-to-follow directions. The issue received in December 1984 contained a letter from the editor explaining what was in the issue, and "Zazoo Come Home." "Zazoo" is a highly interactive mystery to be solved (Who stole the short story you wrote for class and left a trail of bubble gum wrappers?). Children are able to alter the path of the story at a number of crucial points as it is told. For instance, after a conversation with Long John Silver and Sherlock Holmes, they are asked which character they would prefer to have along to assist them. Their own name is used as the main character. Stories are primarily text and generally require a lot of reading, but there are numerous colorful and well-done illustrations. The issue reviewed here also contained "Secret Journal," which encourages creative writing through the use of a very simple word-processing system (entries may be saved to disk and protected with a "password"), and an elementary "drawing board," which permits the drawing of circles, lines, fill, and other modes of drawing. To round out its credibility as a magazine, *Microzine* also has letters to the editor, cartoons, and "What's coming" in the next issue. Topics covered in other issues have included writing and taking quizzes, budgeting money, and adventure stories of all sorts. Though *Microzine* has been around for several years now, it is still a premium software value for the elementary grades. It supports keyboard, joystick, or Koala Pad. Cost: $39.95 per issue. Six issues per year. For use with the Apple II+, IIe, and IIc.

Finding money for college

Peterson's Financial Aid Service (Peterson's Guides Incorporated, 1984) is another excellent software package, similar in concept and design to Peterson's service for college placement (reviewed in this column, December 1984). The program is intended to be used with Peterson's 1985 *College Money Handbook* (included), and covers the 1985 to 1986 academic school year. The program generally requires only one of two responses to questions, a "Y" or "N." In this manner, the user slowly sifts through hundreds of possible financial aid packages, depending upon personal financial and social factors. Users are also aided in estimating how much of their own money they will be expected to contribute for college, as well as how much they are likely to need from a scholarship or grant. In helping to find suitable grants and scholarships, the software takes into account handicaps, class ranking, religious affiliation, career area, civic and extracurricular memberships, hobbies, talents, and work experience. There is also a section that calculates the average costs of college by region or type, and individual colleges may be investigated by simply typing in their number. Both private and public sources are covered. If a printer is not available, only convenience is lost, since a reproducible "Manual Student Report Form" is included. In order to reduce the amount of computer time needed, a worksheet is provided to help prepare users. This program is very useful, extremely user-friendly, and a delight to work with. It is very much like having a personal financial counselor. Required hardware is a 64K Apple II+, IIc, IIc with 80 column card, printer optional. The program is "bomb-proof," since a backup copy is permitted (instructions are included). There should be no problem worrying about patrons making illegal copies, since this isn't the sort of program kids (of any size) typically "swap." Includes a counselor/student manual. Cost: $156.

Publisher addresses for this month's software:

Accent Software, 4546 El Camino Real, Suite S, Los Altos, CA 94022.

American Eagle Software, Inc., Box 46080, Lincolnwood, IL 60646.

Peterson's Guides Incorporated, Box 2123, Princeton, NJ 08540.

Right On Programs, 140 E. Main St., Huntington, NY 11743.

Scholastic, Inc., 730 Broadway, New York, NY 10003.

Scott, Foresman & Co., 1900 E. Lake Ave., Glenview, IL 60025.

James Rettig:

Current Reference Books

Correspondence and review copies for this column should be directed to James Rettig, University Library, Box 8198, University of Illinois at Chicago, Chicago, IL 60680.

Abbreviations, by C. Edward Wall. Ann Arbor: Pierian Press, 1984. 2v. $98. 0-87650-179-X 84-60677

Since the 70,000-item *Abbreviations* excludes acronyms and initialisms, it is impossible to compare it closely with the well established 300,000-item *Acronyms, Initialisms & Abbreviations Dictionary* and *Reverse Acronyms, Initialisms & Abbreviations Dictionary* (9th ed., Detroit: Gale, 1984). The two are similar in structure: Wall's first volume lists abbreviations and their meanings and the second volume reverses the list. The problem (or perhaps the virtue) of Wall's book is that most of the abbreviations are not standard but appear to have been culled from an untold variety of sources. They stand bereft of their original context, many appearing as the consonant skeletons of words whose fleshly vowels have been eaten away. A user can learn that "rstr" might mean resistor or restart or restore or restrict or restricted or roaster, depending upon context. This dictionary would serve a higher purpose if the source and context of each item were given. Perhaps the second volume is intended to establish standard abbreviations. However this seems unlikely since Wall presents more than one choice in some cases without indicating that one is preferred. Most libraries already have enough general and specialized dictionaries to find meanings of abbreviations.

James Rettig *is head reference librarian, University of Illinois at Chicago.*

Almanac of the Federal Judiciary, edited by Susan Alexander. Law Letters, Inc. (332 S. Michigan Ave., Suite 1460, Chicago, IL 60604), 1984. looseleaf $125. 0-914239-02-3 84-080461

The American Bench (Minneapolis: Reginald Bishop Foster & Associates), an apparently defunct annual published during the late 1970s, served as a who's who to 15,000 federal and state judges. *Almanac of the Federal Judiciary* fills a part of the void left by the *American Bench*'s collapse; it covers 550 active judges serving in United States district courts. In addition to the usual who's who biographical information about birth date, family, education, work history, memberships, honors, awards, and address, each entry lists publications and information of special value to lawyers who appear before the judges. A table lists statistics on the judge's case load and speed in dealing with criminal and civil cases. Noteworthy decisions of recent years are summarized, as is the tenor of the judge's coverage in the popular and the professional press. Most significant for lawyers, however, are their colleagues' comments about each judge's prejudices and talents. These comments follow a set pattern supplemented by brief direct quotes. The profiles, arranged by court districts, are indexed by name. Law school libraries will want this on principle. Lawyers will turn to their office copies whenever one of their cases is assigned to a judge they do not know.

Biographical Dictionary of Psychology, by Leonard Zusne. Westport, CT: Greenwood, 1984. 563p. $49.95. 0-313-24027-2 83-18326

Zusne has revised his *Names in the History of Psychology* (New York: Wiley, 1975) by adding biographies of 101 contributors to psychology. Eleven of these are recently deceased; most of the other additions died before 1600. As in its predecessor, most of the subjects were selected by a panel of nine judges whose rankings of 1,040 psychologists from between 1600 and 1967 were published in a paper in the *Journal of the History of the Behavioral Sciences* in 1968. That survey produced a list of 526 leaders and Zusne enriched the list by adding earlier psychologists. The brief biographies, now more sensibly arranged by the subjects' names rather than by their birth dates, offer birthplace and date, death date and place, highest degree, honors, and career before discussing the subject's psychological theories, major publications, discoveries, new methodologies, and influence on others. A bibliography of additional sources concludes each biography. A majority of the subjects receive similar treatment in Corsini's *Encyclopedia of Psychology* (reviewed in *WLB*, November 1984), but without the useful bibliographies. A library can get by without the *Biographical Dictionary* if it owns Corsini, but having the bibliographies and the biographies for which there are no counterparts in Corsini is an undeniable plus.

Contemporary Theatre, Film & Television, Vol. 1, edited by Monica M. O'Donnell. Detroit: Gale, 1984. 545p. $85. 0-8103-2064-9 ISSN 0749-064X

The verso of the title page notes that "special acknowledgement is due to the *Contemporary Authors* staff members who assisted in preparation of this volume" which is identified as "a continuation of *Who's Who in the Theatre*" (17th ed., Detroit: Gale, 1981). In other words, no new editions of *Who's Who in the Theatre* will be forthcoming from Gale; instead libraries will have to buy its successor, a serial modeled after *Contemporary Authors*. In compensation for the increased cost, buyers will receive a crisper format and a broader scope encompassing numerous actors, writers, producers, and directors from the worlds of television and film. The "purists" who were assured that the seventeenth edition of *Who's Who in the Theatre* remained "true to its original editor's intentions" may wince to see the likes of Bill Murray now sharing pages with Laurence Olivier. Others will welcome the more popular approach to entertainment and the occasional inclusion of first-person comments along with the traditional lists of credits and biographical facts. The old book's pages look dull and dowdy when compared to the new work's portrait-sprinkled pages. In Gale's house style, there is a cumulative index incorporating the last edition of *Who's Who in the Theatre*. This will have wider appeal, especially in public libraries, than *Who's Who* had before the curtain was lowered on it.

The Country Music Book of Lists, by Fred Dellar and Richard Wootton. New York: Times Books, 1984. 175p. pa $9.95. 0-8129-6339-3 84-40110

Few people have neutral feelings about country and western music; they either love it or loathe it. The former group's enthusiasm will extend to this compendium of trivia. In sixty lists, each given the title of a hit country song, it identifies crossover hits, horses of singing cowboys, members of the Country Music Hall of Fame, stars' personal favorite songs, rare country singles, origins of stage names, the people stars would choose for company on a desert island (Janie Fricke would want President Reagan along because "he reminds me of my daddy") and more. A selection of publicity color shots complements the profusion of black-and-white photographs. One section places "yesterday" and "today" pictures of the stars side-by-side. The only index is a concluding alphabetical list of all the song titles used as headings, included to identify the performers of the songs. Public libraries in communities whose clientele are apt to put a "Nashville or Bust" sign on their cars at the start of a vacation will want this, but not necessarily in the reference collection.

A Dictionary of Sexist Quotations, by Simon James. Totowa, NJ: Barnes & Noble, 1984. 206p. $23.95. 0-389-20501-X 84-11108

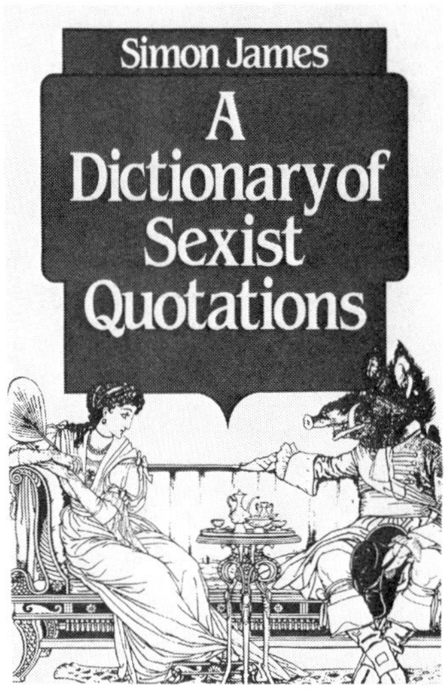

One can easily understand the reason for Simon James's *Dictionary of Economic Quotations* (reviewed in *WLB*, November 1981) and other subject-specific quotations dictionaries. However one cannot imagine why, or for what audience, James compiled this one. His only explanation is that an editor suggested the idea. One still asks, "Why?" Under 105 alphabetical headings from, appropriately, Adam and Eve to Work, James arranges quotations, most of them from British writers of the past five centuries. Not all of the quotations can be called sexist, but those that merit the label are equally divided between misogyny and misandry. Sources of the quotations are well documented. The keyword index, a more sophisticated retrieval device than specialized quotation dictionaries generally feature, overcomes the limitation resulting from assigning each quote to just one of the 105 headings. It is all ably done, but also unnecessary. It may appeal to some patrons, not as a reference work, but as a bedside book to be dipped into briefly before dozing off.

Encyclopedia of Community Planning and Environmental Management, by Marilyn S. Schultz and Vivian L. Kasen. New York: Facts On File, 1984 475p. $45. 0-87196-447-3 82-7366

The field of community planning has developed at the intersection of a number of disciplines including law, economics, sociology, transportation, civil engineering, real estate, medicine, and ecological studies. In clear articles, Schultz and Kasen define and explain the significance of more than

2,000 relevant terms and concepts from these and allied fields. The definitions are as important as the explanations because many of the terms (e.g., corridor study, parking ratio, sector analysis) exemplify the social sciences' penchant for impenetrable jargon. Occasional photographs and diagrams enchance the text. Many articles conclude with copious *see* reference that function as *see also* references. The index groups article titles by major subjects such as architecture, buses, insurance, and storm sewers. Planning professionals will find this a convenient desk reference and newcomers and lay persons will appreciate its clear explanations of unfamiliar ideas. It can serve this latter group especially well in public and academic libraries.

The Encyclopedia of Mammals, edited by David Macdonald. New York: Facts On File, 1984. 895p. $45. 0–87196–871–1 84–1631

Approximately 180 scholars at universities from throughout the English-speaking world contributed the signed articles in *The Encyclopedia of Mammals,* a breathtakingly beautiful book planned and produced in Britain. The seven hundred entries are arranged into broad headings (e.g., carnivores, sea mammals, primates, small herbivores). Related species are group together. Popular names are used in both headings and text, but the index includes scientific names for additional access. Articles describe the animals' physical characteristics, differences among species, habitat, behavior, diet, social organization, range, and information specific to each group of animals. Fact boxes summarize some of this information. The long articles enable a reader to get to know the animals well. Sidebar articles touch on matters such as why elephants are so large and how hyenas communicate. The text alone is an impressive achievement. When coupled with the 1,000 color illustrations, most of them photographs, the whole defies adequate description. If the text acquaints the reader with the animals, the pictures place him in their presence. Submarine hippos, feeding vampire bats, zebras in combat, fetal possums, and much, much more enliven the pages. Informative captions give the pictures inestimable value. All in all, a real treat!

The Free Software Catalog and Directory, by Robert A. Froehlich. New York: Crown, 1984. 475p. pa $9.95. 0–517–55448–8 84–12107

Microcomputer users who employ the CP/M operating system can go to local user group meetings or log on to electronic bulletin boards to obtain free public domain software. Or, they can consult this directory of free software available from two major user groups, CPMUG (CP/M Users Group) of New York City and SIG/M (Special Interest Group for Microcomputers) of Clifton, New Jersey. The complete libraries of both groups are listed separately, each entry listing the program's number, name, size, author's name, language, and keywords. A series of cumulative indexes to both lists indexes them by keyword, language, author, and file name. The book concludes with directories of bulletin boards and user groups. Introductory chapters explain how to use electronic bulletin boards and other means of receiving free software. Sensibly, the book has been printed on pulp paper. Its life will be brief but its utility great.

A Guide to American Screenwriters, by Larry Langman. New York: Garland, 1984. 2v. $88. 0–8240–8927–8 84–48018 (Garland reference library of the humanities, v. 501)

The computer-produced typeface makes one speculate that this work, the product of much indexing, would not have been produced in the pre-computer era. The first volume lists more than 5,000 American screenwriters and the feature films, full-length documentaries, and animated films each wrote during the sound era from 1929 through 1982. The year of each film is given and the name of the writer's collaborator appears after the title, unless there was more than one collaborator. In these cases, an asterisk follows the title. The second volume indexes the first by title, listing year and writers(s) of each of the 20,000 films. Many reference sources tell who wrote particular screenplays, but none is as effective as *American Screenwriters* in listing the works of each screenwriter. It will help fill out comprehensive film collections.

The Hardcore Bodybuilder's Source Book, by Robert Kennedy and Vivian Mason. New York: Sterling, 1984. 256p. $19.95, pa $12.95. 0–8069–4186–3; 0–8069–7894–5 84–8821

Interspersed amidst endless pictures of make and female bodybuilders sporting bikinis and grotesque poses, lurks a multifaceted reference work. Bodybuilding, formerly confined to ads placed in the back pages of comic books to appeal to the proverbial ninety-eight pound weakling, is unaccountably growing in popularity. The *Source Book* illustrates the way a field's reference literature develops as it grows. Between the *Source Book*'s covers are several separate reference works: a directory of equipment suppliers, lists of award-winning bodybuilders, directories of organizations and competitions, the exercise routines of twenty-two famous bodybuilders, a glossary, and a bibliography of books and magazines. One cannot help but notice that the only part of their bodies these latter-day Charles Atlases have not enlarged is the cranium. That aside, true enthusiasts of the art of distorting flesh on command will firmly embrace the field's fledgling reference work.

Historical Dictionary of Egypt, by Joan W. King. Metuchen, NJ: Scarecrow, 1984. 719p. $47.50. 0-8108-1670-9 83-20247 (African historical dictionaries, no. 36)

Even though it excludes ancient history, this volume is the most substantial of the African Historical Dictionary series, both in size and in content. Beginning with the seventh-century ascendancy of Muslims, the selective introductory chronology concludes with the assassination of Anwar Sadat in 1981. The extensive dictionary observes the same time span, identifying rulers, soldiers, events, political groups, organizations, wars, laws, agreements, and other relevant items from Egypt's past. The theme of conquest by foreigners (Arab, French, and British) and the counterthemes of Egyptian nationalism weave together six hundred disparate items. Entries do not stint on detail or analysis; some are several pages long. The sixty-seven page topical bibliography includes a significant number of Arabic titles. The dictionary clarifies the significance of persons and events in more than a millenium of Egyptian history. It will serve anyone who is curious about that past.

An Ibsen Companion, by George B. Bryan. Westport, CT: Greenwood, 1984. 437p. $49.95. 0-313-23506-6 83-18551.

From the inauspicious beginnings of his *Catiline,* published in 1850 in a press run of 250 copies, 200 of which were eventually sold as scrap paper, Henrik Ibsen, "an unknown author writing in Norwegian at a time when there was no Norwegian theatre and no professional actors," came eventually to be recognized as a genius of drama. In dictionary form, the *Companion* digests and organizes many of the raw materials for a critical biography. Production histories and lengthy, very detailed act-by-act summaries and structural analyses of Ibsen's plays are the *Companion*'s centerpiece. Shorter entries explain how family members, other writers, actors, directors, critics, characters, translators, and books relate to Ibsen's life and works. Many articles include bibliographic references. A chronology of Ibsen's life, a list of translators of his plays into English and other languages, and a selected bibliography are also provided. The twelve-page index is worthy of inclusion in a full-length biography of Ibsen. Bryan pays obeisance to Michael Meyer's *Ibsen: A Biography* (Garden City, NY: Doubleday, 1971). Even while acknowledging Meyer's accomplishment, the *Companion* is done well—done so well one wonders why Bryan did not instead work it into another full biography.

International Center of Photography Encyclopedia of Photography, edited by Cornell Capa. New York: Crown, 1984. 607p. $50. 0-517-55271-X 84-1856

The *Focal Encyclopedia of Photography* (New York: Hastings House), often reprinted, was last revised in 1969. Even though *Focal* remains competitive as a source of technical information, professionals and librarians may now turn instead to the *ICP Encyclopedia* for all types of photographic information because it is more current and far more attractive. *Focal*'s densely printed, cramped, sparingly illustrated, gray pages may be a fit medium, considering its emphasis on technical matters, but the format is off-putting. *ICP*'s bright, bold layout, including sixty-four pages of color plates and two hundred duotone photographs, sets the standard for a one-volume photography encyclopedia. It includes 250 biographies of photographers and innovators in the field who were born before 1940. Other entries cover types of photography, equipment, processes, and aesthetic concerns from the time photographic media came into being to the present. The articles explain technical details for the professional, but also dispense some how-to advice for amateurs. The 400,000-word text if far stronger than *Focal* on biographical information, an emphasis reinforced by an appendix briefly identifying the nationality, dates, and photographic interests of an additional 2,000 persons. A directory of professional societies and bibliography of 3,000 books arranged under one hundred subject headings round out the volume. Current, comprehensive, and brimming with eye appeal, *ICP* has become the new focal point of photography reference collections.

International Directory of Special Events and Festivals, edited by Lesa Ukman. Special Events Report (213 W. Institute Pl., Chicago, IL 60610), 1984. pa $65. 84-90118 ISSN 0743-4170

Guide to Fairs and Festivals in the United States, by Frances Shemanski. Wesport, CT: Greenwood, 1984. 339p. $35. 0-313-21437-9 82-21080

Depending upon one's purpose, there are now three major guides to festivals. *Festivals Sourcebook* (2nd ed., Detroit: Gale, 1984) tells would-be tourists where and when festivals of all sorts are held in the United States, briefly describing them and listing a contact person, address, and phone number for additional information. Its geographic, chronological, and subject indexes are helpful in travel planning.

The *International Directory,* while it includes much the same information plus a twenty-page international section, appeals to a different audience. It tells events' attendance, budget, and prior corporate sponsors in addition to the standard directory data. Organized by type of event and indexed by place, by subject, and by month, it is aimed at advertising agencies and corporations looking for events they can sponsor, at which they can plaster their name on posters, painters' hats, tickets, food booths, T-shirts, etc. Therefore this directory includes an index of events considered to be sponsorship opportunities and an "Industry Yellow Pages" directory of promoters and marketers. While this undeniably serves the marketing world well, some of the business information may get in the way of the personal travel planner simply looking for entertainment. The directory's purpose—to aid profit-seekers—explains why a supplement will be issued in March and why it will become an annual in 1986.

A Guide to Fairs and Festivals, the most selective of the trio, would best suit the armchair festival-goer since it does not include addresses or phone numbers for additional information. Instead, it surveys festivals state-by-state, describing their origins, their history, their activities, and their parent organizations. If they depended less on hype borrowed from civic boosters' brochures, the descriptions could be reprinted as innocuous features in Sunday newspapers' travel sections. Selection criteria are vague. For example, the *Guide* includes the defunct Chicagofest, but not the thriving Dayton Air Fair, largest air show in North America. A calendar of festivals lists them by state, then by month. They are also indexed by type, by subject, and by name. Only the *Guide* tells the origins of festivals. Yet in nearly every case, the other two books will be more useful.

Jay Robert Nash's Crime Chronology, by Jay R. Nash. New York: Facts On File, 1984. 224p. $19.95. 0–87196–663–8 83–14046

To his numerous criminal whodunit reference books, Nash adds a "when they dunit." His chronology opens in London on January 9, 1900 with the hanging of Louise Masset for the murder of her three-year-old bastard son and concludes October 16, 1983 with the conviction of Kakuei Tanaka, former prime minister of Japan, for accepting bribes from the Lockheed company. It is surely the largest, most cosmopolitan, and most sensational police blotter ever compiled. Within the annual listings, murder, robbery, white-collar crime, organized crime, and miscellaneous crime news have separate chronologies. The one-paragraph entries tell who did what to whom, when, and what retribution the law exacted for their misdeeds. Black-and-white photographs show that despite their notoriety, most criminals look normal, even nondescript. The personal name index of criminals and victims unfortunately excludes nicknames. So, unless one knows that "Son of Sam" is David Berkowitz, one must first consult another source such as Carl Sifakis's *Dictionary of Historic Nicknames* (reviewed in *WLB,* May 1984) to pinpoint the date of a crime. If the index included dates as well as page numbers, fact retrieval would be faster. This simply shows that the perfect reference work is as difficult to pull off as the perfect crime. The indexing deficiencies will not diminish the book's popularity.

The London Stage, 1920–1929, by J. P. Wearing. Metuchen, NJ; Scarecrow, 1984. 3v. $89.50. 0–8108–1715–2 84–10665

This is the fourth in a series of calendars detailing the public offerings of the London stage beginning with 1890. Year-by-year it chronicles 3,980 productions at fifty-one theaters, listing each play's title, genre, theater, length of run, cast, production staff, bibliography of contemporary reviews, and comments about the production. The third volume indexes the other two by title and by personal name as well as by theater name. This installment covers a very fertile decade of the theater, a time that saw productions of plays by Maugham, Yeats, Shaw, and Pirandello and performances by Olivier, Gielgud, and Richardson. Wearing's series is an essential tool for scholarly study of British theater.

The New Unger's Bible Handbook, by Merrill F. Unger. Chicago: Moody Press, 1984. 720p. $24.95. 0–8024–9049–2 84–1032

A revision of *Unger's Bible Handbook* (1966), *New Unger's* in many ways resembles *Eerdman's Handbook to the Bible* (Grand Rapids: Eerdman's, 1973). Both are heavily illustrated with maps, charts, and color and black-and-white photographs; both are written from a Christian evangelical point of view; and both lead the reader through the Bible, book-by-book and chapter-by-chapter. Both also use effective sidebar articles to evoke the life and places of biblical

times. Commentary on specific verses is brief, usually for the purpose of making moral messages explicit. Unger takes as its text the New International Version of the Bible. Cross-references between passages are plentiful. Appendixes tell the Bible's history, outline Christianity's history, and describe the early church, the medieval church, and the modern church. The index is very brief, but adequate for a book whose modus operandi is the structure of the Bible. Libraries can choose either handbook as a source of brief, nonscholarly explanations of Bible passages as interpreted from an evangelical Protestant point of view.

The Oxford Companion to American Theatre, by Gerald Bordman. New York: Oxford, 1984. 734p. $49.95. 0–19–503443–0 83–26812

The accompanying publicity blurb hopes readers will "spend some happy hours with *The Oxford Companion to American Theatre.*" Those with a passion for the theater could easily while away many happy hours in this storehouse of thespian lore and history. The three thousand entries discuss playwrights, individual plays, actors, producers, directors, lyricists, composers, theaters, theater companies, and movements. From the European settlement of North America to the present, the *Companion* identifies both the well-known and the obscure, an example of the latter being the Ravel family, a family of French rope dancers who debuted in New York in 1832 and whose careers seem to have unraveled some thirty years later. Even though the *Companion* has escaped the New York chauvinism that afflicts so many discussions of American theater, its coverage of contemporary regional troups is less than comprehensive. Effective cross-references abound. The highly readable articles draw on social history to place the theater in context. The *Companion* is the source of choice for brief, factual information about American theater.

Reference Service, Supplement 1976–1982, by Marjorie E. Murfin and Lubomyr R. Wynar. Littleton, CO: Libraries Unlimited, 1984. 353p. $35. 0–87287–402–8 84–16388

Bibliographies rarely stir excitement. However, this bibliography and its predecessor (1977) covering the first century of reference service, should excite reference librarians. Indexed by author, title, and subject, and arranged in fourteen topical chapters, the 1,688-item supplement surveys the voluminous and diverse literature of the field. The compilers exercised selectivity about online services but strove for comprehensiveness in other areas. They have come remarkably close. Annual surveys of the state of reference service that appear in the *ALA Yearbook* have been overlooked, but no other omissions could be identified. Books, articles, conference papers, dissertations, and ERIC documents are included and nearly all have been annotated. It is impossible to say whether the compilers or the copy editors are to blame for several errors in the index. It hardly matters; the errors are so minor they do not interfere with retrieval. This bibliography and its predecessor are essential tools of the trade for any reflective reference librarian.

Science Fiction, by Phil Hardy. New York: Morrow; 1984. 400p. $24.95. 0–688–00842–9 84–60579

This year-by-year survey of science fiction films produced throughout the world from 1895 through 1983 charts the development of the genre through text and film stills. Both show that science fiction's concerns recur in every decade, offering moviegoers extraterrestrial aliens, resurrections of the dead, hybrid humans, superheroes, laboratory accidents, giant insects, and interplanetary travel. The photos, however, tell an additional story. They show that the special effects that enable science fiction audiences to willingly suspend their disbelief have progressed. From basement workshop tin-can robots, filmmakers have advanced to computer-generated graphics and laser light. The concise summaries-cum-credits of some 1,300 films judge their quality and discuss their contribution to or use of the science fiction genre and its conventions. Comprehensive and critical, *Science Fiction* belongs in every serious film reference collection.

The World Atlas of Architecture. Boston: G. K. Hall, 1984. 408p. $75. 0–8161–8716–9 84–6576

Born as *Great Architecture of the World* (London: Mitchell Beazley, 1975) and then transformed into *Le Grand atlas de l'architecture mondiale* (Paris: Encyclopaedia Universalis, 1982), *The World Atlas* is a translation, rewrite, and expansion of the French work. Rather than leaving a jerry-built appearance, the remodelings become it. Text and numerous illustrations, many in color, bear the load equally. By period and country, chapters explain and illustrate the features of architectural styles throughout history, concentrating on the mainstream of western culture. The text relates each style to its society's needs and the building materials and techniques of the times. A rather selective glossary has been integrated into the index, heavy with place names. Because it is a popular treatment and heavily illustrated, the *World Atlas* can be used most profitably when teamed with other architecture reference books.

Library World

News of announcements, new posts, retirements, and deaths should be sent to "Library World," WLB, 950 University Ave., Bronx, NY 10452.

ANNOUNCEMENTS

Joseph Becker, president of Becker and Hayes, Santa Monica, Calif. has received the ASIS Award of Merit. Currently chairman of Section T of the American Association for the Advancement of Science, he was an NCLIS commissioner from 1971 to 1979.

Norman Horrocks has been named chairman of Canada's Advisory Board on Scientific and Technological Information (ABSTI). He is SLS director and dean of the faculty of management studies at Dalhousie Univ., Halifax, Novia Scotia.

Martha Williams has received the ASIS Award of Merit for achievements in electronic information storage and retrieval systems. She is a professor of information science and directs the Information Retrieval Research Laboratory at the Univ. of Illinois, Champaign.

NEW POSTS

Rita Altomora

Rita Altomara, formerly assistant library director at the Fort Lee (N.J.) PL, is now library director.

Barbara Baker has been appointed branch librarian of the Centennial and Maring branch libraries of the Muncie (Ind.) PL. She was previously children's librarian in the Indianapolis Marion County (Ind.) PL.

David Bryant

David Bryant is the new deputy assistant state superintendent for educational media and technology services with the North Carolina Department of Public Instruction. He was formerly senior project manager of the student information management system for the North Carolina Department of Public Education.

Beverly Bury is now assistant director for branch services with the Charlotte and Mecklenburg County (N.C.) PL. She was previously director of the Campbell County (Ky.) PL

Henry Dutcher, formerly reference librarian at Springfield (Mass.) College, is now public services librarian at Asnuntuck Community College, Enfield, Conn.

Joseph Green has been appointed director of the Nassau (N.Y.) Library System. He replaces **Andrew Geddes,** who retired.

Carolyn Greufe, formerly head of reference and young adult services at the Southeast Branch of the Moline (Ill.) PL, has been named head of the adult circulation department at the St. Joseph (Mo.) PL.

Patricia Hannon, formerly director of public libraries in Wanaque and Woodridge N.J., has been appointed director of the Oakland (N.J.) PL.

Sandi Kaplan, formerly senior librarian at Simi Valley Library, Calif. is now supervising librarian at Camarillo Library, Calif.

Richard Maynard has been appointed supervising librarian at the E.P. Foster Library in Ventura, Calif. He was formerly acquisitions librarian for the Ventura County library services agency.

Dilys Morris has been promoted to assistant director for technical services at the Iowa State Univ. Library. She was formerly head of the monographs department at Iowa State.

Judith Muck, formerly director of the Pottawatomie-Wabunsee Regional Library, St. Marys, Kansas has been named director of the Northwest Missouri Library Network, St. Joseph.

Elizabeth Titus has been appointed assistant director for public services at Northern Illinois Univ., Dekalb. She was formerly associate professor at the Oakland Univ. Library, Rochester, Mich.

John Ulmschneider, formerly systems librarian at the National Library of Medicine, Bethesda, Md. is now library automation systems manager at the Earl Gregg Swem Library of the College of William and Mary, Williamsburg, Va.

Carroll Varner has been named assistant director for technical services at Northern Illinois Univ., Dekalb. He was previously chairperson of the technical services department at the Univ. of Nebraska at Omaha.

Announcements

☐ Deltiologists of America, an international society of postcard collectors, is developing a list of picture postcard collections in public and academic libraries. Cooperating libraries will receive a free copy of *Over 900 Things to Know About Postcard Collecting* by George Wolstenholme. The listing of libraries with picture postcard holdings will appear in *Deltiology,* the society's bimonthly publication. A copy of the listing form can be requested from Deltiologists of America, 10 Felton Ave., Ridley Park, PA 19078.

☐ With the pound still slipping against the dollar, even librarians can afford a trip to the United Kingdom. And those who can't stay away from libraries even on vacation can arrange a visit to libraries in London and southeast England through the London and Home Counties Branch of the Library Association. Supply detailed information on your areas of interest at least one month before your trip and a program of visits tailored for you (or your group) will be arranged. There is no charge for the service, but an informal report on your experience would be welcome. For more information write Eric Winter, 19 Cricketers Dr., Meopham, Kent DA13 0AX, England.

☐ There's no need to go overseas to see the "Raleigh and Roanoke" exhibit, originally mounted at the British Library in April 1984 and traveling to the United States this year. The exhibit, celebrating the 400th anniversary of Sir Walter Raleigh's Roanoke voyages (1584–1587), features 157 documents and artifacts, many of which are displayed in this country for the first time. Fittingly, the exhibit will first appear in Raleigh, North Carolina at the North Carolina Museum of History from March 8–June 6. Lectures will be given March 11–14. After June 6, the exhibit will travel to the New York PL.

☐ ALA has several versions of a three-by-five-foot blue nylon flag with the library symbol in white. A flag with the symbol silk-screened costs $20, a flag with the symbol appliqued costs $30, and the appliqued flag with a library's name costs $30 plus $1 per letter. Order from Public Information Office, ALA, 50 E. Huron St., Chicago, IL 60611.

Children's Specials

☐ The Ontario Library Service—Escarpment Area (formerly South Central Regional Library System) has developed a summer reading program in conjunction with the 100th anniversary of Parks Canada. Materials produced for the program include 17-by-24-inch color posters ($1.10 each, fifty for $50, plus shipping), buttons ($.50 each, 100 for $46, plus shipping), and a reproduction kit ($9.50 each, plus shipping, for a coloring sheet, four bookmark designs, a certificate, and recommended book titles). All materials are available in French and English; specify when ordering. Order from Carol Smith, Ontario Library Service—Escarpment Area, 220 Dundurn St. S., Hamilton, Ont. L8P 4K7, Canada, 416/525-2610.

☐ The Combined Book Exhibit at seventeen library, academic, and book trade meetings in the first half of 1985 will feature Reading Rainbow displays within the regular CBE exhibits. The displays will enable visitors to examine books that have been or will be covered on the PBS television series, as well as a poster, the *Reading Rainbow Gazette,* and the *Reading Rainbow Teachers Guide.* Free bookmarks are also available. For a list of the meetings or additional information contact Combined Book Exhibit, 100 Providence Highway, Westwood, MA 02090, 617/329-7493.

☐ In the twenty-eight-minute videotape "Grandmas Can Live Longer If They Eat," produced by Alice Naylor for the Association for Library Service to Children, twenty-five children from kindergarten through eighth grade express their opinions of ALSC Notable Books. A brochure accompanying the tape provides discussion questions for teachers, parents, and librarians. The videocassette is available in ½- and 3/4-inch for $50 (inquire about rental) from Alice Naylor, Department of Library Studies, Applachian State University, Boone, NC 28608, 704/262-2243.

☐ The New York PL's annual roundup of the year's best in children's books, "Children's Books 1984," has just been published. The list divides its 100 titles into eight categories: picture books, folk and fairy tales, nonfiction, poetry, stories for younger readers, stories, new editions, and recordings and computer software, with brief annotations of each title. The poster-size folded sheet can be ordered for $2 from the Office of the Branch Libraries, 455 Fifth Ave., New York, NY 10016.

Continuing Education

☐ The theme of the seventh Library History Seminar, to be held March 6–8 at the University of North Carolina at Chapel Hill, is "Libraries, Books and Culture." The conference will explore the historical role and significance of graphic records in society, particularly the preservation of records in collections. Four speakers will address plenary sessions, and twenty-four papers will be given. There will also be tours, book exhibits, and social gatherings. The sessions are free, but there is a $30 fee for the two luncheons offered. For more information write Donald Davis, Jr., Graduate School of Library and Information Science, University of Texas at Austin, Education Building 564, Austin, TX 78712.

☐ A conference on "Library Preservation: Implementing Programs" will be held March 8–9 in Alexandria, Virginia. Sponsored by the Resources and Technical Services Division of ALA and first offered in April 1984 in St. Louis, the conference provides information on establishing a local perservation program. The registration fee of $205–255 includes some instructional materials and one meal. For further information write RTSD, ALA, 50 E. Huron St., Chicago, IL 60611.

☐ How children recreate experience from reading and the interaction between the author and the young reader will be examined at "The Reader Becomes the Book," a conference to be held March 22–23 in Madison, Wisconsin. To obtain a brochure, contact Barbara Arnold, University of Wisconsin Extension Library and Information Science, 610 Langdon St., Room 220, Madison, WI 53703, 608/262–6398.

Film and Video

☐ The San Francisco PL has produced a video series on deaf culture in the United States. The four films in "American Culture: The Deaf Perspective" are *Deaf Heritage, Deaf Folklore, Deaf Literature,* and *Deaf Minorities.* All are close-captioned, available in all video formats, and run thirty minutes. Purchase price is $400 for the set, $125 for each film, rental is $25 for each film, and a twelve-minute preview reel is free. The library has also produced *What Is a Bank?,* an eleven-minute program in American Sign Language with voice narration. It explains basic banking services (3/4-inch and Beta II, $75). For more information write Friends of SFPL: Video Acct, c/o Special Media Services, San Francisco PL, Civic Center, San Francisco, CA 94102.

☐ Karol Media has published a new catalog of National Geographic Society 16mm films. Among the titles listed are over fifty of the society's hour-long television specials, and shorter films for use in science, social studies, and literature. For a copy of the catalog write Karol Media, 22 Riverview Dr., Wayne, NJ 07470.

☐ "Revising Romance: New Feminist Video" is a traveling exhibition whose eleven films (ten by women) examine popular ideals of romantic love in entertainment aimed at women: soap operas, juvenile literature for girls, "women's pictures," and romance novels. Organized by the American Federation of Arts in cooperation with the Institute of Contemporary Art, Boston, the exhibit will travel to Houston, Rochester, New York, Columbus, Ohio, Philadelphia, and Portland, Oregon. For more information contact the American Federation of Arts, 41 E. 65th St., New York, NY 10021, 212/988–7700.

Finding Aids

☐ A set of three bibliographies on health information has been prepared by the New York Metropolitan Reference and Research Library Agency. Included are a selected list of indexes and reference sources of medical materials for the nonmedical librarian, a selective resources list of patient health information, and a list of sources of free or inexpensive health education materials. METRO member libraries can obtain one set free and additional sets at $15 each; other libraries can order sets for $20 (invoiced orders add $5). Order "Health Information Update '84: Reference Sources for the Non-medical Librarian" from METRO, 57 Willoughby St., Brooklyn, NY 11201.

☐ *Minority Women's Organizations and Programs: A Partial Annotated List,* published by the Project on the Status and Education of Women, describes organizations that serve the educational and career needs of minority women. Over seventy groups are listed with a brief description of goals, activities, and publications. The directory is available for $2 from PSEW, Association of American Colleges, 1818 R St., NW, Washington, DC 20009.

☐ Peace Issues Bibliography Service will provide an annotated bibliography on peace resources for children geared to specified grade, format, and subject for $2. Write for a brochure from Center for International Cooperation, National College of Education, 2840 Sheridan Rd., Evanston, IL 60601 or call 312/256–5150.

☐ Wisconsin Women Library Workers has published *The Music of Women; A Selection Guide, 1984,* an 18p. pamphlet compiled by Nancy Vedder-Shults. With sections on concert music, jazz, blues and gospel, folk, and contemporary women's music, the guide provides a brief bibliographic essay on each subject and an annotated list of recordings that are basic or representative in the field. Funded by a grant from the Wisconsin Humanities Committee, the guide was distributed free to public libraries in Wisconsin, and can be purchased by others for $3 from Wisconsin Women Library Workers, Box 1425, Madison, WI 53701.

Idea Exchange

☐ The latest library PR fad seems to be calendars. While some are literary, some historical, and some just promotional, the Prince George's County (Maryland) Memorial LS 1985 calendar is strictly commercial. The calendar costs $2.50 ($3 mailorder), but it contains coupons good for over $9 worth of library services (film, video, and art print rental fees), items from the book sale, and even a free PGCMLS pen or note pad. For more information contact the Office of Information Services, Prince George's County Memorial LS, 6532 Adelphi Rd., Hyattsville, MD 20782.

☐ Many libraries have instituted job information centers, but these do not fully serve patrons who first need further training and education. The Boston PL has opened a Higher Education Information Center to offer high school students, out-of-school youths, and older adults information and counseling on education, financial aid, and career opportunities. Library staff are assisted by counselors on loan from local institutions, graduate student interns, and trained volunteers. For more information contact the center at the Boston PL, 666 Boylston St., Boston, MA 02117, 617/536-0200.

☐ An event that can raise money on the West Coast, but probably not in Maine, was staged last fall by the Atascadero (California) Friends of the Library. For the Lobster Fly-In the group sold tickets for live Maine lobsters for $10 each, Blue Point oysters for $5.50 a dozen, and cherrystone clams for $3 a pound. Buyers encouraged to plan a BYOL (bring your own lobster) party. All proceeds went to the Atascadero Library building fund.

Media Center World

☐ The National Library of Canada and the National Film Board have produce a sound filmstrip to introduce young students to library facilities. *All About Bicycles—And Libraries, Too!* shows a group of elementary school students who use library resources to collect information for a class project. A sound commentary is provided by a sixteen-minute cassette, which can be used in machines with or without automatic cueing. Kits can be obtained for a fifteen-day examination. The English-language version (cat. no. 123801A4) is available for $39 from McIntyre Educational Media Ltd., 30 Kelfield St., Rexdale, Ont., M9W 5A2, Canada, and the French-language version (cat. no. 215 C 023 010) for $36 from Multi Media Audiovisual Inc., 5225, rue Berri, Montreal, Quebec, H2J 9S9, Canada.

☐ The third annual National Council of Teachers of English Teachers' Choices list of outstanding books for children includes twenty-nine titles of fiction, nonfiction, and poetry from 1984 in three categories: preschool to grade 3, grades 4–6, and grade 7 and up. The annotated list was published in the January 1985 issue of *Language Arts,* journal of the Elementary Section of NCTE, but a copy of the unannotated list can be obtained by sending a SASE to Teachers' Choice List (LSH), NCTE, 1111 Kenyon Rd., Urbana, IL 61802.

☐ The AASL/Follett Library Book Company Microcomputer Award will be given annually beginning this year to recognize the creative use of microcomputers in school library media centers. Awards of $1,000 each will go to two individuals for innovative use of the microcomputer in library management and integration into the curriculum, and the schools represented by the winners will receive $500. Applicants must be personal members of AASL and school library media specialists. Send for an application form from AASL, ALA, 50 E. Huron St., Chicago, IL 60611.

☐ Appropriate for Women's History Week (the second week in March), but usable all year are the eleven-by-seventeen-inch TABS posters on women. Single posters are $2.50, the entire forty-seven-poster set is $88.50, the twenty-four-poster Women of Achievement set is $48, the twenty-eight-poster Women's History Week set is $56, the eight-poster career set is $16, and the ten-poster introductory set is $20, all plus shipping and handling. Other quantity discounts are available. For a brochure and order form write to Organization for Equal Education of the Sexes, Dept. 85, 744 Carroll St., Brooklyn, NY 11215.

Products and Services

☐ Libraries that circulate filmstrips, cassettes, and computer software may be struggling with display systems, especially if there is accompanying material such as booklets. A solution from Monaco is their clear plastic envelopes that can be hung on racks, peg boards, and even bookshelves. Catalog pockets and label holders are also available, and the envelopes can be custom printed. Prices range from 25¢ to 40¢ per envelope. For a brochure write to Monaco, Box 765, Wilton, CT 06897 or call collect 203/834-0855.

☐ The OPIX-DS Dual System Projector from Constantin Systems combines the functions of an opaque and a transparency projector in one portable unit. The projector weighs twenty-nine pounds and measures 7-by-14-by-20½ inches; the projection platform is 12-by-12 inches. Detailed literature is available from Constantin Systems, Inc., 645 N. Michigan Ave., Suite 620, Chicago, IL 60611.

☐ The ideal place for the new Sharp SF-815CN is not a quiet study area—this coin-operated copier talks to the user. The purpose of the built-in voice synthesizer is to reduce operator error by giving audible instructions. Other features of the copier are a dual cassette paper system, setting for two vend rates, automatic change function, bypass service key, two-key security system, and three meters, one for each paper feed and one for total copies. For information contact Copier Products Division, Sharp Electronics Corp., 10 Sharp Plaza, Paramus, NJ 07652, 201/265-5600.

Sharp SF-815CN copier

☐ A new brochure describing 3M products useful in schools and libraries is now available. Included are artist's, drafting, and book tape, labelers, custom-printed Post-it notes, mounting and matting products for art and photography, and films, pens, and kits for making overhead transparencies. There is also a full-page chart showing which 3M diskettes are compatible with major brands of personal computers and word processors. For a copy of the brochure write 3M, Dept. CS-99, Box 33600, St. Paul, MN 55133.

Professional Reading

☐ Maygene Daniels and Timothy Walch, directors of the Modern Archives Institute, the archival education program sponsored by the National Archives, have compiled *A Modern Archives Reader*. The collection includes classic essays that outline the basic theories of archival administration as well as recent articles that demonstrate the practical application of archival principles. The 365p. book costs $14 in hardcover and $12 in paper. Make checks payable to National Archives Trust Fund Board and send to National Archives, Dept. 501, Box 37066, Washington, DC 20013.

☐ Funds were granted in 1981 to the Nioga LS and the Onondaga County PL for two pilot projects in New York State to improve health information service. Results of the projects are published in *Health Information from the Public Library: A Report on Two Pilot Projects*. The programs described and evaluated and materials created by the libraries, such as bibliographies, brochures, and training matrials, are reproduced. Copies of the 204p. paperback are available for $5. Make checks payable to the New York State Library and send to Henry Ilnicki, Gift and Exchange, New York State Library, Cultural Education Center, Albany, NY 12230.

☐ The Wisconsin Association of Academic Librarians has published *Minimum Library Use Skills*, which presents minimum competency standards, a test of minimum library use skills, and a brief bibliography on evaluating library competency. The 25p. publication is $3 from the Wisconsin Library Association, 1922 University Ave., Madison, WI 53705.

Software

☐ Formation from Software Concepts enables the IBM PC, TRS-80 Models II, III, 4 and 12, and several dedicated word processors to fill out pre-printed forms. On-screen questions are answered by the operator and the program formats the answers for each form. The same information can be shared between forms and used to create data files for other uses. The software costs $299. For more information contact Software Concepts, Inc., 1116 Summer St., Stamford, CT 06905, 203/357-0522.

☐ Approximately 3,000 software titles are listed in *Swift's 1984-1985 Educational Software Directory, Apple II Edition* and approximately 1,500 in *Swift's Directory of Educational Software for the IBM PC and PC jr, 1984-85*. Both are organized by subject and publisher with a title index. The Apple II edition is $24.95 and the IBM edition is $19.95. For more information or to order contact Sterling Swift Publishing Co., 7901 South IH-35, Austin, TX 78744, 512/282-6840.

☐ Learning Well has two new language arts programs for grade 2 and up. Vocabulary Challenge contains four games which reinforce word association, definitions, and understanding of analogies. Over 3,000 words are used, with the ability to add words and choose difficulty levels. Question-and-answer sequences are followed by explanations. Poetry Express provides samples, explanations, and line-by-line guidance in creating and printing poetry. Both are available for $39.95 from Learning Well, 200 S. Service Rd., Roslyn Heights, NY 11577, 800/645-6564.

Write for These

☐ Four new ERIC digests (formerly known as fact sheets) are now available from the ERIC Clearinghouse on Information Resources. Each of the two-page digests provides a brief overview of the topic and selected references. The titles are "Computer Literacy for Teachers," "Electronic Networks," "A Review of Reviews of Research on Computer-Assisted Instruction," and "Teleconferencing in Education." There are also two new two-page bibliographies: "Interactive Video" and "Online at the Reference Desk." Request by title and send an SASE to ERIC Clearinghouse on Information Resources, Syracuse University, School of Education, Syracuse, NY 13210.

☐ A directory of federal and state technical assistance centers which offer help to small businesses has been published by NTIS. The eighty federal centers are arranged by subject such as agriculture, building technology, energy, and ocean sciences, and the 100 state centers are arranged by state. Address, phone number, and name of contact person are given. Copies of the 8p. brochure are free. Request booklet PR-767 from NTIS, Springfield, VA 22161.

☐ Businesses listed in the 1985-1987 edition of the *Source Directory* of the Indian Arts and Crafts Board are cooperatives, tribal arts and crafts enterprises, and businesses and galleries owned by Indians and Eskimos. Also included are several nonprofit organizations. Single copies of the 46p. booklet are free from the U.S. Dept. of the Interior, Indian Arts and Crafts Board, Washington, DC 20240.

Preservation *(cont'd from page 388)*

accidents can happen, even with professional exterminators. Librarians have become increasingly aware of the necessity of taking steps to preserve library materials. Now they need to learn in addition how to protect the health of patrons and staff.

Footnotes

1. Frank J. Duffy and James L. Burchfiel, "Long Term Effects of the Organophosphate Sarin on EEGs in Monkeys and Humans," *Neurotoxicology*, 1 (1980), 667–89.

2. Illes Desi and others, "Neurotoxocologic Studies of Two Carbamate Pesticides in Subacute Animal Experiments," *Toxicology and Applied Pharmacology*, 27 (1974), 65.

3. *Clean Your Room: A Compendium Describing a Wide Variety of Indoor Pollutants and Their Health Effects* (Sacramento, California, Department of Consumer Affairs, 1982), pp. III.I. 18 and III.I.21.

4. Mary-Lou Florian, remarks during "Fumigation: Effects on Objects and People," American Institute for Conservation of Historic and Artistic Works Annual Meeting, Baltimore, Maryland, May 1983, taped by Cassette Recording, Inc., Dayton, Ohio.

5. Arthur J. Slater and others, "An Integrated Approach to Cockroach Control," *Lab Animal*, January/Feruary 1981, pp. 44–45.

6. *Environmental Protection of Books and Related Materials,* Preservation Leaflets, No. 2 (Washington, DC: Library of Congress, 1975), n.p.

Portrait *(cont'd from page 402)*

commission's bidding to improve education or organize themselves for other national crises? "I don't think you will find many libraries saying that they can do it. They will say, 'We can help if you will help us to do it.' But we can't afford to say, 'We will help only if you help us.' The funders might say, 'If we have to pay, we can go elsewhere'—to the computer and information industry, for example."

Eileen Cooke has spent twenty years in the ALA Washington Office, the last twelve as director. A Minnesotan, she began her library career as a bookmobile librarian in Minneapolis and held other positions in the city's library system until 1963. In 1964, she went to ALA's Washington Office as assistant director. She established strong working relationships with members of Congress and leaders in education and related fields. She is a veteran of innumerable battles and campaigns to restore or increase appropriations for libraries and can "write the book" on strategic planning—one doesn't want to apply the word lobbying to her efforts on behalf of reading and learning.

Her well-known persistence and refusal to take no—or zero—for an answer were important in extending library funding laws and in obtaining supplemental money for the White House Conference on Libraries and Information Service. She has served as consultant to the Commission on Federal Relations of the American Council on Education and is a member of the President's Committee on Employment of the Handicapped and may other government and private organizations.

I asked Senator Claiborne Pell to comment on her service and contributions over the years. "She and her staff have been indispensable to my work on behalf of libraries and to many others on the Hill," he said through a spokesman.

Library to Library *(cont'd from page 403)*

sharing, serves as an impediment, particularly for document access and delivery beyond the local or regional level. Despite the good intentions of the ALA code, libraries with large collections, accessible via national databases, feel compelled to protect themselves from the burden of excessive lending by instituting high loan fees. The absence of nationally coordinated interlibrary loan protocols fuels the brushfire of spiraling loan fees. Access is restricted if not denied.

Continuing to encourage the distribution of the interlirary loan traffic through local and state resource-sharing programs is essential. So is research on borrowing and lending patterns and the economics of document delivery. As former director of the National Library of Medicine Martin Cummings recently remarked in a speech, "There is a need for a constructive federal information policy that recognizes that information collected and organized by our nation's libraries should be disseminated as a public good, not solely as an economic commodity." Certainly there is a clear and present need for an aggressive approach to planning on a national level and coordination of document delivery. We need an improved networking structure that makes better use of the abundance of information resouces residing in the nation's libraries.

Recently such network "ecology" issues as telecommunications, database copyright, and network contracts have dominated the resource sharing dialogue. These are all vital issues, but shouldn't we identify the bait before building a better mouse trap?

Our Profession *(cont'd from page 417)*

without undue explanation, of what Congress, the Executive Branch, and the Library of Congress can do in this noble cause. Boorstin has issued a ringing call to action that we should all read and that we would all do well to heed.

Credits:
p. 375—Scott McKiernan and Anne Day; 377—Univ. of Texas/El Paso; 378—Los Angeles County Public Library; 396—Leo Cullum; 404—E.P. Dutton, Houghton Mifflin; 406—Bradbury Press, Viking Krestrel; 407—Lippincott, Viking Penguin; 409—St. Martin's Press; 410—Columbia Records, Geffen Records, O.D.N. Production; 416—American Eagle Software; 417—Peterson's Guides; 419—Barnes & Noble; 420—Facts on File; 422—Facts on File, Moody Press; 423—Oxford Univ. Press

WLB Classifieds

Classified Advertising is accepted six weeks preceding date of issue. Charges are: minimun 3 lines—$10; each additional line—$2.50. If voucher forms are required, please send them when submitting copy. All advertisements for positions must exclude reference to race, creed, color, age, and sex as conditions for employment. The publisher reserves the right to reject any advertising considered unacceptable as to wording or appearance or for any other reason. Submit classifieds to: Brian Bavolar, Wilson Library Bulletin, 950 University Ave., Bronx, NY 10452.

Announcements

EARN UNIVERSITY CREDIT for your personal travels/vacation anywhere in the world. Write Univ. of Calif. Travel/Study, Box 16501, Irvine, CA 92714.

THE FOOTLOOSE LIBRARIAN newsletter & network. Money-saving travel news + U.S. & overseas librarians offering Bed & Breakfast, housing exchange, more. "Good, practical information" M.S., IN; "An excellent publication" S.R., Tunisia. Free brochure. TFL, Box 972, Minneapolis, MN 55440.

MILITARY BOOKS for identification of shoulder patches, medals, insignia . . . U.S. and foreign. Military history, etc. Send for free catalog, M.C.N. Press, Box 52033 WLB, Tulsa, OK 74152.

NEWSLETTER FOR YOUR SUMMER, SPRING, CHRISTMAS COURSES in London, Paris, Mexico, Hawaii, etc.! Visit libraries, theatre productions, galleries. Exciting study/vacation options for librarians, plus work in foreign libraries. Subscription: $25/yr. NEWSLETTER, Box 5513, Santa Monica, CA 90405.

NOW FREE LIBRARY shelving servicing for Eastern Half U.S. Call 10–4 EST 615-588-6114 for free Kanecrest Systems Packet Guide, Solid Oak Sample, and free, no obligation counseling/estimating your needs!

THE ONE-PERSON LIBRARY: A NEWSLETTER FOR LIBRARIANS AND MANAGEMENT. Professional isolation is one of the major problems of working alone. We want to change that. This new newsletter is informal, informative, and, above all, quick and to the point. Charter subscriptions (one year, 12 issues) for $35, a savings of over 20%. Pre-paid orders to OPL RESOURCES, LTD., Box 948, Murray Hill Station, New York, NY 10156.

For Sale

BRUCE TEGNER'S self-defense/judo/karate/aikido/martial arts books in hardcover and trade paper editions from your jobber or the publisher. Current list from Thor Pub. Co., Box 1782, Ventura, CA 93002.

CAN-DO CARDS: RESEARCH REPORTING—A proven method for teaching students in grades 4-8 how to write research reports. $6.95. The Curriculum Exchange, 71 Longview Dr., Marblehead, MA 01945.

". . . get ideas from every issue."
M.S. High School Media Center, NY
Subscribe (and send *your* nitty gritty ideas) to The U*N*A*B*A*S*H*E*D Librarian™, the "how I run my library good"℠ letter, Box 2631, New York, NY 10116. Four issues $20 US funds (add $5 Canadian and foreign postage).

THE "GRAND CANYON" VIDEO, helicopter exploration. Breathtaking music. Details FREE. Beerger Productions, 3217 Arville, Las Vegas, NV 89102, (702) 876-2328.

HOBBY BOOKWATCH: Military, gun and hobby book review. Approximately 600 new titles each year. Small and large publishers. One year, $2; two years, $3.50; three years, $5. Published six times a year. For free sample write: HB, Box 52033, Tulsa, OK 74152.

Librarians Love TFL!
"Everyone on our staff is interested in the Travel Exchange, either as a traveller or a host" M.H., San Diego. Free brochure on THE FOOTLOOSE LIBRARIAN newsletter & travel network. TFL, Box 972, Minneapolis, MN 55440.

LIBRARY NEWSLETTERS. Let a librarian prepare camera-ready copy for your newsletter. $1 for samples. Library Newsletter Service, Box 637, Belleville, NJ 07109.

The MILITARY BOOKMAN—Military, Naval, and Aviation History. Out-of-print and rare books, 3 catalogs per year. 29 East 93rd St., New York, NY 10128 or call (212) 348-1280, Tues.-Sat. 10:30-5:30.

PUT SEARS TO WORK. 1,200 "see" and "see also" cards plus Manual/List of Headings with DEWEY numbers. From *Sears* 12th ed., $49.95. Woods Library Publishing Co., 9159 Clifton, Evergreen Park, IL 60642.

SOLID OAK SHELVING

YES, there is still time to get your Direct Institutional Purchase Order to us for April/May delivery of your demountable-remountable solid oak Kanecrest Furniture Shelving. Act now by calling 615-588-6113 between 10 and 4 EST for your FREE "Packet Parcel" to make your selections from hundreds of combinations of beautiful hardwood shelving. Give name, position, institution, and UPS delivery address for prepaid shipment of Packet Guide, Actual Sample, and Prices Delivered from our Kanecrest Solid Oak Furniture Facility in Tennessee. Also see our WLB Classifieds in each issue since September. The Kane Company, Box 10505, Knoxville, TN 37939-0505.

"WOW!" "Do not pass go without collecting this PR gem . . ." LJ
GO, PEP AND POP! 250 TESTED IDEAS FOR LIVELY LIBRARIES by Baeckler and Larson. Order from: The U*N*A*B*A*S*H*E*D Librarian™, the "how I run my library good"℠ letter. Dept. GPP/WLB, Box 2631, New York, NY 10116. Send $4.50 check and mailing label with order. Libraries add $1 for billing. Canadian and foreign add $1 in US funds. 6 to 8 weeks delivery. LC 75-20328 CIP.

Wilson Library Bulletin
March 1985

OCLC UPDATE

OCLC MicroSystems

We Have the Answers

For 18 years, OCLC has been meeting libraries' automation needs. The strength of that commitment is evident from our Online Systems, with a variety of efficient and cost-effective services, and more recently, with the introduction of the LS/2000 system, OCLC's powerful local option.

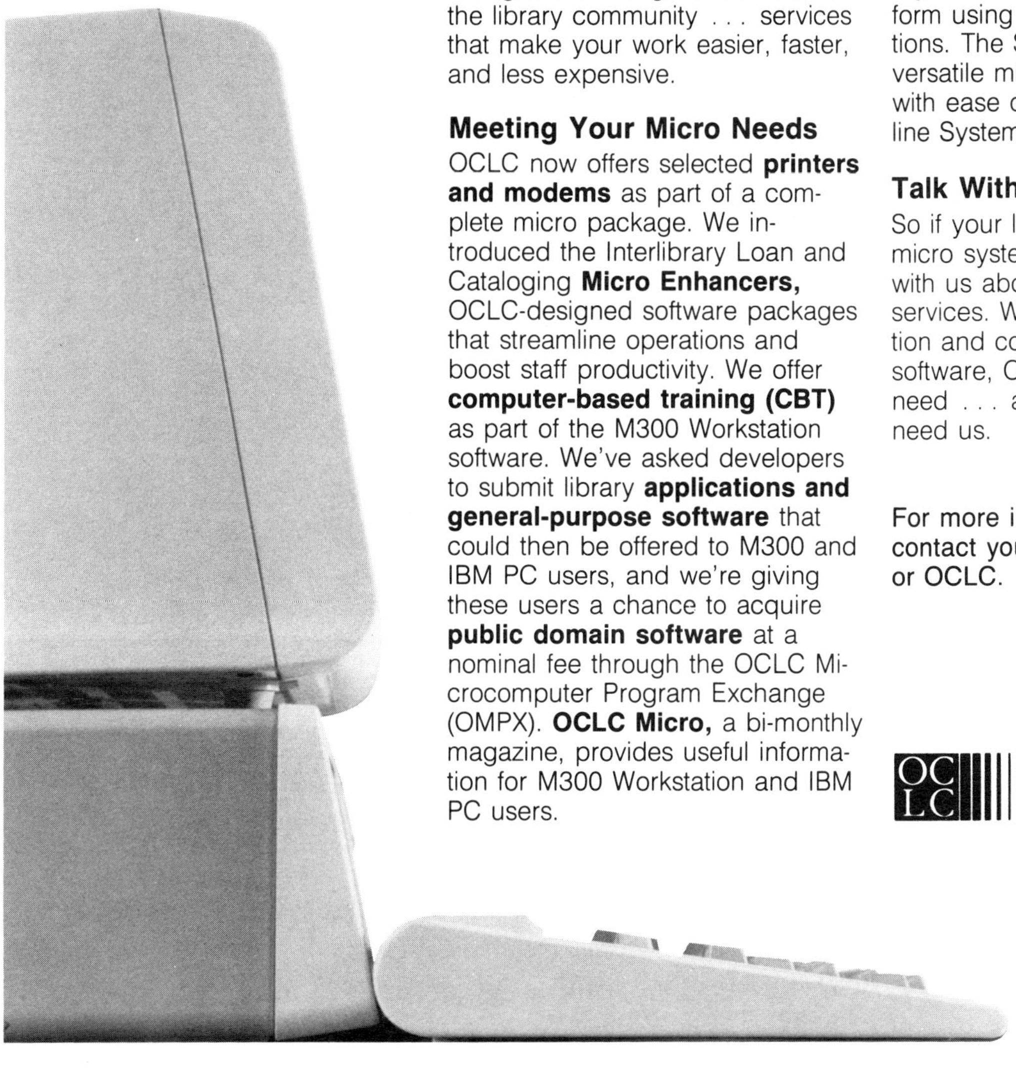

The M300 Workstation

When libraries asked for micro-based systems, we responded with the **M300 Workstation,** a modified IBM® Personal Computer designed with OCLC users in mind. The first M300 Workstation was installed in March, 1984. Just one year later, more than 1,500 M300s are providing a wide range of services to the library community . . . services that make your work easier, faster, and less expensive.

Meeting Your Micro Needs

OCLC now offers selected **printers and modems** as part of a complete micro package. We introduced the Interlibrary Loan and Cataloging **Micro Enhancers,** OCLC-designed software packages that streamline operations and boost staff productivity. We offer **computer-based training (CBT)** as part of the M300 Workstation software. We've asked developers to submit library **applications and general-purpose software** that could then be offered to M300 and IBM PC users, and we're giving these users a chance to acquire **public domain software** at a nominal fee through the OCLC Microcomputer Program Exchange (OMPX). **OCLC Micro,** a bi-monthly magazine, provides useful information for M300 Workstation and IBM PC users.

MICROCON and SC350

The past few months also saw the introduction of two new M300 Workstation-based services: **MICROCON** and **Serials Control 350 (SC350).** Our MICROCON service is an economical batch retrospective conversion option that enables libraries to convert cataloging records to machine-readable form using rent-free M300 Workstations. The SC350 system combines versatile micro-based serials control with ease of access to OCLC Online Systems.

Talk With Us

So if your library is considering a micro system, we invite you to talk with us about OCLC MicroSystems services. With the M300 Workstation and compatible hardware and software, OCLC has what you need . . . and we're here when you need us.

For more information, contact your network office or OCLC.

OCLC MicroSystems
6565 Frantz Road
Dublin, Ohio 43017-0702

(800) 848-5878
(800) 848-8286 (Ohio)

IBM is a registered trademark of the International Business Machines Corporation

Wilson Library Bulletin

March 1985, Volume 59, Number 7 ISSN 0043-5651

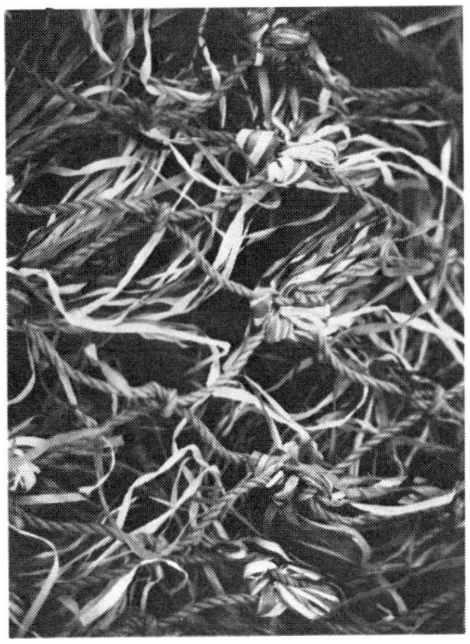

Streamers, our cover for March, represents fishing nets bound together by colored ribbon to attract a catch. The image was taken by **Gary San Pietro,** a Philadelphia photographer and frequent contributor to *WLB*.

Departments

Letter from New York/Editorial 436
Correspondence 438
Upfront/News—*Zero budget for libraries; SLA considering move to Washington, D.C.; Vermont creates statewide information system; LC to build deacidification facility; WLN introduces Micro-Recon; National Archives to use RLIN; Minneapolis Public signs with Geac; Rare book sales benefits Dartmouth; late news.* 440
Calendar 446
Library World 505
Marketplace 506
WLB Classifieds 512

Articles

The Computer Backlash: Why I Hate IBM *James LaRue* 447
High Tech Breakthrough: Interactive Videodisc *Rebecca Sturm* 450
Hispanex: Serving Libraries Serving Hispanics *Brian Aveney and Vivian Pisano* 453
The First of Four More Years: ALA in Washington *The Editors* 456

Features

Dateline—Washington *Dale Nelson* 467
Eye on Publishing *Anne McGrath* 469
Facing the Public *Will Manley* 471
School Library Technology *Patricia Berglund* 473
Future Libraries *Tom Surprenant* 475
Online Update *Martin Kesselman* 477
Portrait: James O'Neill *Joseph Deitch* 479

Reviews

Picture Books for Children *Donnarae MacCann/Olga Richard* 482
The Young Adult Perplex *Patty Campbell* 484
Murder in Print *Kathleen Maio* 486
Front Row Center *Judith Trojan* 488
On Record: Popular Music *Bruce Pollock* 490
Magazines *Gail Pool* 492
Our Profession *Norman Stevens* 494
Software for Libraries *Patrick Dewey* 496
Current Reference Books *James Rettig* 499

The *Wilson Library Bulletin* is published monthly except in July and August by The H. W. Wilson Company, 950 University Avenue, Bronx, N.Y. 10452. Second-class postage paid at Bronx, N.Y. and additional mailing offices. The *Wilson Library Bulletin* is indexed in *Education Index, Library Literature,* and *Popular Periodical Index* and abstracted in *Library & Information Science Abstracts, Historical Abstracts,* and *America: History and Life*. Book reviews are indexed in *Book Review Index*. Subscription $30 a year, U.S. and Canada; $35, foreign. Single copies $4, U.S. and Canada; $4.50, foreign (remittance with order, please). Address all correspondence about subscriptions to the publisher. No subscriptions through agents. Telephone: (212) 588-8400

Letter from New York

Editorial

An awkward silence in Chicago

Amanda Rudd, commissioner of the Chicago Public Library, resigned her position on February 26 (see *Upfront/News*) to assume a position as fulltime consultant to the library system until 1986, when her contract expires. The action was taken after several months of speculation that Rudd and the library board of trustees were having difficulty agreeing on policy and six months after James Lowry, board president, created performance measures to evaluate how the library system was being managed. A member of the board who asked not to be identified, told a reporter for the *Chicago Tribune* that Rudd had been asked to resign.

Rudd's letter of resignation was read to the library board by Lowry. After the statement was read, Rudd refused comment. Nor did she respond to reporter's questions afterwards.

The search for a new library commissioner is to begin immediately. According to Lowry, the board is interested in "someone who can take this library, with all its problems, and really get things going in terms of fund-raising."

Rudd had replaced Donald Sager, who resigned in 1981 under similar circumstances. In both cases the commissioners were largely silent, the board of trustees unwilling to be perfectly open, the mayor's office without a known position. And, in each case, the board president found public praise for the departing librarian. Lowry declared that "We have been very consistent in saying that Amanda Rudd has been a tremendous resource. She brings over twenty years of library history, knowledge, and experience with the Chicago Public Library. To lose that, we would be losing a valuable resource." Even so, the board was not reluctant to endure the loss.

The reasons behind Rudd's decision to resign are based on hearsay. Board members have said that Rudd and Lowry had a clash of management styles, that there were leadership problems, personality difficulties, and that fund-raising was not proceeding as planned.

It's not easy to manage the Chicago Public Library. The library has vacillated for several years over a site for the new central library, only recently having decided, once again, on the Goldblatt Bros. department store building located in the south loop at State and Van Buren streets. The board was not unanimous in approving the action, some members believing the location too remote from the Cultural Center, the former home of the central library which is used for special exhibits and programs.

The library has experienced legendary difficulties with installation of a local automated system by Data-Phase, the negotiations, claims, and counterclaims continuing for several years. The Chicago Public Library hasn't made automation look easy.

The library board has historically been accused of being politically motivated, tolerating appointments, reassignments, and terminations based on political ties of board members and displaying susceptibility to pressures from the mayor's office.

Rudd herself has attracted criticism by suspending a deputy commissioner in a controversy involving the theft of library property, a move reversed by a U.S. district judge. And an alderman found fault with Rudd when it was discovered that the commissioner had approved trips for seventy librarians to attend the 1983 annual conference of the American Library Association in Los Angeles, an amount he termed "most distressing."

With no central building, no permanent home for its collection, no operational automated system, no freedom from outside influences, no absence of political maneuvering, and no concord among the board of trustees, it is difficult to imagine what formula for success the next commissioner will find useful.

It is not hard to imagine a large urban library system plagued with problems, but it is less easy to accept a situation where there is so little candor, such disbelief in the healing virtues of forthrightness.

All parties involved in the latest incident at the Chicago Public Library are depending on the amenity of silence, withdrawing with a smile like a courtier backing out of an audience with a sovereign. An ancient custom for dealing with an immediate predicament, the strategy doesn't contribute much to a lasting resolution of difficulties.

But that's life, that's Chicago, that's politics, and that's that.

—*Milo Nelson*

Correspondence

Acting in advance of change

Perhaps the reason that many people have such difficulty with planning (Editorial, *WLB,* December 1984) and its process is the inexact nature of planning. The majority of organizations tend to be reactive and therefore are acting on known changes. The danger in this is, of course, that your destiny is always in the hands of others.

The American Medical Association is rapidly losing members, revenue and public trust. They know this and are now reacting to changes in public values and perceptions about the AMA but they are coming from behind and reacting. With fewer than half of physicians belonging to the AMA the time is ripe for an assault on doctors. Who will protect them?

With library schools closing, private providers of information and entertainment popping up right and left, new technology, a middle-aged population growing older, women becoming mainstreamed into better paying jobs, fewer children, changing lifestyles, and a host of other dramatic changes in our population's expectations it is commendable that ALA is planning.

Planning should consist of creating various scenarios and visualizing the approaches the organization should take if one or a combination of several should occur. Once this is done the signs of change become more obvious and the organization can act in advance of the change rather than react after it has passed.

At one time it was thought that doctors existed because people needed them. Today with thousands of unneeded operations and a revolt on the part of the public it would appear that doctors need people and will have to change the whole nature of health care. Do people need libraries or do libraries need people?

TONY LEISNER
Quality Books, Inc.
Northbrook, Illinois

Concise and diverse

First of all, a couple of compliments are in order. *WLB* is far and away the best of the periodicals aimed at librarians. I find it to be concise, diverse, controversial, and never burdened with gossip. And, speaking of controversial, Bruce Pollack's column is my favorite. His knowledge of the field and his propensity for speaking his mind would keep me subscribing to *WLB* even if I was no longer a librarian.

Your covers are always superb.

KAREN GERDETZ
Kingston, New York

New federal audit law

The Single Audit Act of 1984 (Public Law 98–502) was signed by President Reagan on October 19, 1984. The new federal audit law establishes statutory policy concerning audit of many federal assistance programs. Libraries receiving direct grants from the federal government or pass-through grants as a subrecipient, such as grants to local libraries under the Library Services and Construction Act, will be affected by this new legislation. The new law applies to all fiscal years of recipients that begin after December 31, 1984.

The Single Audit Act addresses a number of the criticisms voiced against Office of Management and Budget (OMB) Circular A–102, Attachment P. (The A–102, Attachment P audit was reviewed in *Wilson Library Bulletin* in February 1984.) The new legislation outlines a uniform approach by the federal government for the audit of all federal assistance programs, including general revenue sharing, and should improve the coordination and coverage of required audits. It is expected that almost ninety percent of federal funds paid to state and local governments will be covered under these audits.

State and local governmental entities that get less than $25,000 per year in federal financial assistance will not be required to have audits performed under the Single Audit Act. Retention of accounting records will be expected to document grant and program compliance, or for use if audits are necessary.

Recipients of $25,000 to $100,000 per year will have the option of conducting an audit annually or complying with audit requirements of the federal program under which they receive the funds.

For those receiving over $100,000 per year in federal financial assistance, an annual financial and compliance audit will be required. If they are already required under state or local law to perform such audits on a biennial basis, they may continue that schedule. Those doing biennial audits because of a non-statutory policy will be required to move to the annual audit cycle within three years.

Federal funds may be used to pay for a proportional share of required audits. The recipient may be allowed to use federal funds for more than the proportional amount if appropriate documentation is provided to OMB.

The single audit will contain three sections and must be performed using generally accepted government auditing standards as prescribed in "Standards for Audit of Governmental Organizations, Programs, Functions, and Activities" (also known as the General Accounting Office Yellow Book).

First, the audit must have the auditor's opinion on the financial statements and operations as they relate to generally accepted accounting principles along with the auditor's opinion on the supplemental statement of selected grant activity.

Second, it must have the auditor's statement whether the internal control system provides reasonable assurance that federal funds are managed properly. The auditor must report any material weaknesses found in the system.

Third, the audit requires an auditor's statement about compliance with grant requirements, with enough information to allow federal reviewers to determine if the programs are being administered in compliance with applicable laws and regulations. This statement, or a summary statement, must include a complete description of all instances of noncompliance or questioned costs disclosed in the audit. The single audit report must be sent to the appropriate federal officials and be available for public inspection within thirty days after it is completed.

The Office of Management and Budget will have the responsibility of drafting the rules and regulations to implement the audit bill. The General Accounting Office has been instructed, in the Act, to review all future legislation concerning audits to assure consistency with the Single Audit Act of 1984.

RICHARD WILSON
Idaho State Library
Boise, Idaho

Lessons of patience and compassion

While working as a reporter for *Cognotes* at the ALA Midwinter meeting I heard librarians discussing the article in *WLB* about the demise of the children's librarian. "It's true," they said, "I can't fill my openings because nobody wants to begin their career as a children's librarian." "Why is that?" I wanted to know, for I had begun professional life as a children's librarian. They responded in unison, "Just read Will Manley's September column in the *Wilson Library Bulletin.*" So, upon returning to Dallas I made a special effort to find the article that had generated such heated discussion.

Manley's points are well made and certainly ring true, especially in the points made about some of the hassles that children's librarians encounter on a daily basis. However, I find it hard to believe that a new graduate would seriously accept a low paying position simply because of an interesting title and the beginnings of "the road to riches." I would like to offer another point of view from personal experience—that youth work is both personally and professionally enriching as well as a legitimate way to begin one's career as a librarian.

First of all, where else is youth and general inexperience considered an asset to employment? I had never done a puppet show, run a reading club, or organized a craft program. I had enjoyed my one course in children's literature and was interested and willing to take on the job.

In the beginning, the job was lots of fun. I really enjoyed throwing outlandish parties, having ambitious craft programs, and my boss loved the constant growth in statistics. Juvenile literature was also a nice change from AACR II. There were times when I could hardly believe that I was being paid to have such a good time.

There were many new faces and lots to learn about the system. At the Dallas Public Library there were rules for everything and an organizational handbook that took me three days to read. As a children's librarian I had the time to learn procedures gradually and thoroughly as well as opportunity to work closely with many key people in the system who were kind and patient with the latest recruit.

As most librarians know, a great percentage of branch activities are generated by the children's department. In the summer, the statistics alone are staggering and the monthly reports usually reflect this truth in the following blurb: "Youth circulation increased twenty-one percent for the month of June and program attendance hit an all time high of 1,987 children attending eighteen programs. Ruthie the clown was especially popular. . . . "

I quickly learned to keep a calm exterior when faced with a large crowd, limited supplies and other "crisis" situations. Other children's librarians can relate to the "behind-the-scenes" activities that include a projector that refuses to focus, the loyal volunteer who has left for camp, and the handicapped child that requires special attention. One does learn to "rise to every occasion."

I soon became a walking advertisement for the library and met young patrons at almost every social gathering. Local recognition increased with appearances on the short-lived cable "Storytime" and the locally popular "Mr. Peppermint" program.

All of these activities helped to build confidence as well as provide solid experience in time management, program planning, collection development, cable TV certification, as well as the usual amounts of adult reference and experience with online computer searching. When the time came to explore new areas, I had developed a solid record and many new skills. Therefore, I highly encourage the new professional to at least consider youth work as a solid career move as well as a golden opportunity to learn lessons of patience, understanding and compassion, lessons that you will apply on a daily basis with adult patrons.

ELENA CARVAJAL
Dallas Public Library
Dallas, Texas

Reaching but not selling

How does Will Manley explain his interest in reaching out to his colleagues (thus not too incidentally advertising both himself and his institution) in a regular column entitled (of all things) "Facing the Public" when he would have us believe that "Public libraries should not be selling" (*WLB,* January).

He is and we are and good for us both.

SUZANNE SUTTON
Bloomfield Township Public Library
Bloomfield, Hills, Michigan

UPFRONT NEWS

West Virginia Secretary of State A. James Manchin *(right) presents* **State Library Commission Director Frederic Glazer** *with the first official notary public commissions for librarians throughout the state. Manchin called the commissioning of almost 200 librarians throughout West Virginia as notaries public a "benchmark" and said it would bring such services closer to the citizens who require them. "Until now," Manchin said, "there were areas in West Virginia that were literally without the necessary services of a notary public. If a person needed to have a document notarized, he would often be forced to travel to the county courthouse in search of a notary public." In addition to providing notarial service, the action will also establish many West Virginia libraries as voter's registration offices. Utilizing the postcard voter's registration form which allows individuals to register to vote by mail, librarians can now act as voter registrars. "What we have done," Manchin observed, "is to make it much simpler and much easier for people to take advantage of their right to suffrage. We have brought government to the people it is designed to serve."*

Amanda Rudd resigns from Chicago Public Library

After a closed meeting of the Chicago Public Library board of trustees on February 26, board president James Lowry announced the resignation of Amanda Rudd as library commissioner. Lowry read a letter to the press prepared by Rudd in which she stated her wish to step down from the position. Rudd offered no comment after the letter was read. The resignation was effective upon the announcement.

Rudd will serve as acting commissioner until April 15 at which time she will begin serving as a fulltime paid consultant at a minimum salary of $50,000 and a maximum set at her current salary of $63,000. Her consulting contract will expire in November 1986.

Lowry stressed that Rudd had been a valuable library director and refused comment when questioned by reporters about the existence of frictions between Rudd and the board and speculation that the commissioner would have been asked to resign had she not done so voluntarily.

Rudd was described by an observer present at the press conference as "very positive and upbeat."

SLA considering move to Washington, D.C.

The Special Libraries Association, presently located on Park Avenue South in New York City, is considering moving its headquarters to the District of Columbia. The four-floor property in Washington is located at 16th and R Streets, in proximity to Dupont Circle. David Bender, SLA executive director, is currently negotiating a final contract for the new facility, pending an engineer's report.

SLA's lease on its present site expires in 1987 and the organization has been engaged in both a search for a new location and a fund-raising campaign to purchase a suitable headquarters. SLA's New York City offices are no longer capable of accommodating its staff of twenty-seven employees.

If the contract for the building in Washington is successfully completed, SLA plans to move sometime this year.

LC to build deacidification facility

The Library of Congress plans to begin construction in early 1986 on a book deacidification facility to be located at the U.S. Army's Ft. Detrick in Frederick, Maryland. Congress has approved an $11.5 million appropriation for construction of the facility.

The preservation unit will have the capability of treating from 500,000 to one million books per year, converting paper in the books from an acidic to a mildly alkaline condition. The facility will have two processing chambers each of which will hold a maximum of 9,000 volumes.

The deacidification facility will be operated twenty-four hours a day, seven days a week and involve three shifts. The staff operating the facility will be employed by a technical services firm under contract to the library. It is estimated that 7,500 books will be processed per chamber using a five-day operational cycle.

Operational costs for the facility will run approximately $2.5 million per year which will yield a unit cost of $2.00 to $3.50 per volume. The library is interested in licensing the process to institutions and corporations who wish to make use of the service directly or market it to potential customers. Only Library of Congress materials will be processed at the Ft. Detrick facility. The thirteen million items in the library's general collections and the new incoming material (over 300,000 items per year) will require the full capacity of the Ft. Detrick plant for the next twenty years.

All books processed through the facility will be stamped upon their return to the library on the back of the copyright page. The symbol will show the letters dez for the diethyl zinc treatment and the year that the book was treated.

It is expected that the deacidification facility will be operational in late 1987.

Vermont creates statewide information system

The University of Vermont Library, the Vermont Department of Libraries, and Middlebury College Library, the three major research collections within Vermont, have entered into a collaborative project to develop a statewide information system. The Vermont Automated Libraries System (VALS) will result in geographically distributed access to library and national information databases from any library, office, or home within the state which has access to an appropriately equipped computer terminal. The statewide information network is expected to be a prototype for other libraries and academic institutions that require a distributed network. Two vendors who have the resources to implement the information network for the state of Vermont are now in the final stages of undergoing consideration.

In 1985 three separate, hardware-compatible computer systems will be installed in Middlebury, Montpelier, and Burlington. Author, title, and subject databases for the cooperating libraries will be loaded into three separate computer systems. The systems will then be linked by dedicated telephone lines and hardware and software tested so that the three systems are accessible to anyone on the network as if they were one system. The library network will then be linked to the University of Vermont's IBM/ROHM digital PBX to make the information network accessible to all faculty and students from their own microcomputers or terminals. The system will also provide gateways into national telecommunications networks so that off-campus users can obtain access to other databases across the nation via the library network.

When these additional network linkages are in place, attention will focus on adding local databases, on evaluation of microcomputer software that can simplify direct user online searching, and on teaching students, faculty, librarians, and the general public to search and download data onto local microcomputers for personal use. By 1988 every student at the University of Vermont is expected to own a personal microcomputer.

According to Nancy Eaton, director, University of Vermont Library, the AT&T divestiture and the ensuing struggle of large organizations to plan for their new communications links made it even more necessary for smaller systems to create their own telecommunications networks. VALS, Eaton noted, will have "design potential for larger states."

Berkeley Public votes to unionize

The Berkeley (California) Public Library has recently voted to unionize, eighty-three percent of the staff voting to affiliate with a union and seventeen percent voting against the move. For the past year the library staff has been embroiled in pay equity and comparable worth disputes. Staff members participating in the decision included professional librarians, paraprofessionals, and clerks.

As a result of the action, library staff members have joined the Service Employees International Union Local 535, an AFL-CIO affiliate, which currently represents Berkeley city health care workers and miscellaneous administrative employees.

Harvard Library receives $1 million gift

John Blodgett, Jr., an alumnus of Harvard University, has donated $2 million to the institution, $1 million of which is designated as an unrestricted gift to Harvard University Library.

Sidney Verba, director of the library, said "I learned from my predecessors of Jack Blodgett's ongoing involvement with the university library and the many ways he has expressed his support. One primarily associates the name Blodgett with athletics and with Harvard's splendid swimming pool. This gift will remind everyone of Jack Blodgett's strong personal interest in history, in books, and in the Harvard Library."

In the past Blodgett provided funds for the acquisition of books for the Widener, Hilles, and Lamont libraries and underwrote the library's acquisition of Leon Trotsky's papers. Installation of a Halon fire-protection system in the Pusey Library was also underwritten by Blodgett.

National Archives to use RLIN

The National Archives and Records Service recently announced that it will conduct an archival automation project using the Research Libraries Information Network as its computer system. The project will test the suitability of RLIN's implementation of the USMARC Archival and Manuscripts Control format for controlling federal records throughout their life cycle and for improving access to the records.

Barbara Brown, associate director of Program Coordination for RLG, welcomed the NARS decision as "an important step in the development of a national database of archival and manuscript records."

Created in 1949, the National Archives and Records Service is the agency responsible for the publication, management, distribution, and preservation of federal records. Among its divisions are the Office of the National Archives, the Office of Presidential Libraries, and the Office of the Federal Register. On April 1, NARS, which has been under the General Services Administration, will become an independent federal agency.

California to create "talking" terminal

The California State Library has awarded $52,000 to the University of California Division of Library Automation to develop a "talking" terminal for the visually impaired. The terminal will interface with the university's MELVYL online catalog. The catalog combines library holdings of all nine University of California campuses into one source, accessible to patrons by computer terminals located in the libraries.

Marion Bourke, principal librarian of the California State Library's Braille and Talking Book Library, has been designated primary consultant for the project.

Nevada installs online data network

The Nevada State Library has installed the first phase of its online data communication network designed to provide information sharing between different library computer systems in the state. Using equipment from Doelz Networks, Inc., three library computers used in the state will be connected, providing all libraries on the network, regardless of size, with access to the same information. The network, which requires fewer phone lines for terminal connection than traditional networking systems, will transfer information over phone lines and via the state-owned microwave link.

Four Doelz Elite One high-speed concentrator switches will provide four libraries with access to two of the library system's databases from any terminal in the network. Elite One switches were installed in Carson City at the Nevada State Library and Ormsby Public Library, in the Douglas County Library, and in the Clark County Library District in Las Vegas.

The Doelz equipment will connect different library computer systems regardless of any difference in transmission media, processor speed, attached devices, or protocols.

Mark Scully appointed to USGPO post

Mark Scully has been named Director of Library Programs Service at the U.S. Government Printing Office. Scully will be responsible for administering the Federal Depository Library Program and for directing the agency's staff of 130 employees. Under the Depository Program, U.S. government publications are centrally acquired, cataloged, and made available to the American public through 1,388 depository libraries nationwide.

A GPO employee since 1981, Scully holds an MLS degree from the University of Maryland and received a master's degree in public administration from American University.

OCLC introduces microcomputer magazine

This month OCLC plans to premier *OCLC Micro,* a magazine for users of its M300 Workstation and the IBM PC. The publication will incorporate articles, advice from OCLC and network staff, user comments, solutions to problems, hardware and software reviews, and article abstracts. Some issues will include diskettes with programs that users can take advantage of immediately.

Ginni Voedisch, of OCLC's Documentation Department, will edit the magazine. *OCLC Micro* will be issued every other month, with monthly issues during November and December. The subscription cost is thirty dollars per year.

IFLA to meet in Chicago

The International Federation of Library Associations and Institutions will meet in Chicago, August 18–24 at the Palmer House. The conference theme is "Libraries and the Universal Availability of Information." Major components of the theme to be discussed during the week include access to information, publishing, formats of information, and issues of bibliographic control, resource sharing, and networking. Conference papers may be obtained by delegates free of charge before each meeting in the room assigned to that session.

Simultaneous translation services will be available in the four official languages of IFLA (English, French, German, and Russian) and in Spanish. This service is available for the Council meetings, opening and clos-

From its opening in 1983, more than sixty companies have made use of the Federal Government Procurement Center located in the Business Department of the **Toledo-Lucas County (Ohio) Public Library**. *Of the more than thirty bids submitted on federal contracts, fourteen were accepted by the government and as a result $4,066,753 was added to the area's economy in the past eighteen months.*

The Procurement Center is a joint venture of the library, the Toledo Area Chamber of Commerce, the Private Industry Council, the Toledo Area Small Business Association, and the Lucas County Improvement Corporation. The center serves as a clearinghouse for information services designed to help local firms identify government bidding opportunities and compete successfully for contracts.

The library was selected to serve as the provider of information relating to the procurement process because of its central location and its ability to maintain the voluminous listing of current government specifications which a company must take into consideration when it prepares a bid.

The center subscribes to Commerce Business Daily, *a government publication which lists bidding opportunities for civilian and military agencies, and has commodity lists from more than 100 federal purchasing centers in the U.S. which indicate what products and services each unit is interested in buying. The library also provides local businesses with assistance in complying with bidding protocol. The library holds copies of the* Federal Acquisition Regulations *and other materials on submitting contract bids.*

In the photo above **Galen Avery,** *Business Department librarian for the Toledo-Lucas County Public Library, explains some of the materials housed in the Procurement Center to Toledo Mayor Donna Owens (left) and Congresswoman Marcia Kaptur.*

ing sessions, plenary sessions, and the open forums.

Approximately 100 commercial and educational exhibits have been organized for the conference. Exhibits will feature vendors of online data services, software, library equipment, and high technology applications. A model information center will be exhibited by NCLIS.

A reception for all delegates will be hosted on the evening of August 19 by the State of Illinois and a reception will be held two nights later at the Chicago Public Library Cultural Center. A block party will take place on August 22 on East Huron Street in front of the ALA headquarters building.

Registration fees are $175 per person. The fee provides for admittance to all meetings, receptions, exhibits, and tours, as well as copies of all papers presented. Registration forms are available from IFLA '85 Coordinator, 50 East Huron Street, Chicago, Illinois 60611.

Zero budget for libraries

For the fourth consecutive year, President Reagan has proposed elimination of library programs. The fiscal year 1986 budget transmitted to Congress on February 4 requests no funds at all for LSCA or HEA II. Revenue sharing, postal subsidies, and NCLIS are also proposed for elimination.

Rare book sale benefits Dartmouth

Proceeds from an auction of the Doris Benz collection of rare books and manuscripts surpassed estimates of what the Dartmouth College Library, Hanover, New Hampshire, will receive from the trust held in her name. The library expects to realize over $1 million when all sales are concluded.

Last November the auction firm of Christie's sold over 400 lots which yielded $885,675, substantially more than pre-sale estimates. A 1928 Cresset Press edition of Bunyan's *Pilgrim's Progress* sold for $22,000 rather than the anticipated figure of $5,000 and a first edition of *Seven*

Pillars of Wisdom by T. E. Lawrence went for $13,000, up from an expected $5,000.

The terms of Benz's will specified that money from the sale of her collection of books and manuscripts was to be placed in an endowed fund for the acquisition of rare books thought important to the Dartmouth College Library.

Ruraline now in operation

The Center for the Study of Rural Librarianship at Clarion University of Pennsylvania has established an electronic mail service, Ruraline, for rapid transmission of messages via microcomputers. Ruraline is part of TYMNET's OnTyme-II network with more than 500 member libraries. The OnTyme-II message system allows libraries to communicate simultaneously to any number of users across the country. Ruraline will also allow local libraries to refer reference questions to regional centers or to the Center for the Study of Rural Librarianship in Clarion, Pennsylvania.

ITT Dialcom expands services

ITT Corporation's electronic mail unit, ITT Dialcom, is now providing subscribers with access to Dow Jones News/Retrieval. The News/Retrieval comprises business, financial, and general news sources, including the *Wall Street Journal*, *Barron's*, and the Dow Jones News Service. Late-breaking news is available to ITT Dialcom subscribers within ninety seconds of its movement on the main Dow Jones news wire. At 6 a.m. each morning, ITT Dialcom subscribers have access to the full text of that day's edition of the *Wall Street Journal*.

Dow Jones News/Retrieval contains thirty databases, including current and historical stock market quotes, profiles of major U.S. companies, a stock symbol directory, a weekly economic survey, and electronic transcripts of the "Wall $treet Week" television program.

Other news services available from ITT Dialcom include the Associated Press, United Press International, Deutsche Press Agentur, and the White House News Service. Users may access ITT Dialcom through any communicating terminal, including personal computers, word processors, and data communications terminals.

The New Mexico Military Institute Library, *now under construction (above), will be fully automated when it opens in August of this year. The Institute, located in Roswell, New Mexico, selected the LIBS 100 System 73, manufactured by C L Systems, Inc. The library will use the computer system for a public access catalog, circulation control, reserve book room operations, and interlibrary loan.*

Founded in 1891, the New Mexico Military Institute is a four-year high school and two-year junior college.

Reagan to nominate new NCLIS commissioner

President Reagan has announced his intention to nominate Daniel Carter to be a member of the National Commission on Libraries and Information Science for a term expiring in 1989. Carter is vice-president for strategic business services at Walter Ulrich Consulting, a management and technology consulting firm in Houston, Texas. Prior to this assignment Carter was associated with Texas Instruments.

Rochester receives $500,000 grant

The University of Rochester, Rochester, New York, has received a grant of $500,000 from the Pew Charitable Trust of Philadelphia toward the development of a fully automated information system for the university's libraries. The grant will support the installation of an online public catalog and an automated circulation system. The library also plans to automate systems for managing serials and acquisitions.

Negative reaction to software numbers

At a recent meeting held in New York City by the Association of American Publishers, a negative reaction to a proposed draft of a Standard Computer Software Number (SCSN) was demonstrated by major software publishers, software distributors, and software outlets. The proposed standard, composed of thirteen digits and developed by a subcommittee of the National Information Standards Organization (NISO), differs significantly from the ISBN and ISSN which are employed by similar groups as international standards.

Several publishers noted that they have applied the ISBN to software products for a number of years and found it an effective identifier. Representatives from Prentice-Hall and Addison-Wesley voiced strong objections to the adoption of a new number since they have based warehouse and inventory systems on the ISBN.

Representatives of software outlets and distributors indicated displeasure for a number that would not be internationally accepted and is too long to be effectively bar-coded (the ISBN requires ten digits, the ISSN only eight digits).

NISO seeks input from all interested parties. Copies of the proposed standard may be obtained by writing to NISO (Z39), SCSN Comment, National Bureau of Standards, Administration 101, Library E106, Gaithersburg, MD 20899. All negative comments will receive an individual response.

WLN introduces Micro-Recon

The Washington Library Network has introduced Micro-Recon, a software program for Apple and IBM PC microcomputers that will assist member libraries in converting holdings to machine-readable form. Micro-Recon will allow libraries to create search keys which can be matched against the WLN bibliographic database. This new method of retrospective conversion provides a formatted screen and prompts the terminal operator for each type of data to be keyed in. Diskettes containing search keys are mailed to WLN where they are periodically matched against the database. When a match occurs, the library's holdings are added. The holdings then become available to WLN users online and may be included in COM catalogs and the WLN resource directory.

Micro-Recon was developed by the Washington Library Network with the help of a development grant from the Alaska State Library. The software is available only to WLN member libraries.

Minneapolis Public signs with Geac

The Minneapolis Public Library has signed a contract with Geac Computers International for a $604,785 automated circulation control system. The circulation system, which will use a Geac 8000 computer and fifty-six terminals, includes online catalog software. The system has a capacity for 100 terminals.

The first of fourteen Minneapolis community libraries is expected to be online this summer, with the remaining branches and the central library in full operation within two years.

RLG receives funding for conversion program

The William and Flora Hewlett Foundation has awarded $1,050,000 to the Research Libraries Group to support the RLG cooperative retrospective conversion program. This grant completes funding for the first phase of the project, which has also received a $750,000 grant from the Andrew Mellon Foundation and a $350,000 contract with the J. Paul Getty Trust.

Roger Heyns, president of the Hewlett Foundation, said "Converting libraries' card records to computer form is an important step toward creating a national bibliographic system. For many libraries, RLG's cooperative retrospective conversion program will reduce the costs of this work."

Thirteen retrospective conversion projects have been approved at the following member institutions: the American Antiquarian Society, the University of California at Berkeley, Brown, Columbia, Cornell, Iowa, Johns Hopkins, Michigan, Minnesota, New York University, Stanford, Temple, and Yale.

Vendors to use OCLC's direct transmission service

Blackwell North America, Coutts Library Service, Midwest Library Service, Research Micropublishers Service, and the Yankee Book Peddler are the first vendors to make use of OCLC's Direct Transmission (DX) service. The DX service enables OCLC Acquisitions Subsystem users to place orders electronically rather than through the mail. Orders are generated at the library using the subsystem and then forwarded electronically to OCLC where participating vendors retrieve their orders by dialing into OCLC's computer.

The DX service accommodates a wide range of data processing capabilities, enabling vendors with different automation levels to benefit from electronic order transmission. Any vendor with a "dumb" terminal and a telephone can use DX. A vendor communicating in BISAC (Book Industry Systems Advisory Committee) format may completely eliminate manual processing of incoming orders.

OCLC's DX service is available ninety-two hours per week, the same hours during which the OCLC Online System is available. Orders can be transmitted in a print image format or in the BISAC fixed-length format. Should a vendor fail to "pick-up" orders during the seventy-two hour waiting period, the DX service automatically prints and mails them.

New York approves construction grants

New York Commissioner of Education Gordon Amback has announced that 160 public library construction grants totaling $2.9 million have been approved. The state grants will be matched with more than $16.3 million in local funds to support construction projects totalling $19.2 million.

Legislation enacted in 1984 authorized a $3 million state aid program for public library construction, renovation, and rehabilitation. Funds are allocated by public library systems and grants made by the Education Department upon recommendation of public library system boards. The grants range from $425 for energy conservation in a small library to $150,365 for major renovations to a branch of the New York Public Library. About thirty percent of the new funds will expand library service to the handicapped, including construction of exterior and interior ramps, installation of elevators, and widening of aisles and doorways.

Calendar

Announcements should be sent at least 60 days in advance to "Calendar," WLB, *950 University Ave., Bronx, NY 10452.*

MAR. 27–29—*North Carolina Community College Learning Resources Association,* annual conference. Greensboro Sheraton, Greensboro, N.C. Theme: "The Past a Foundation; the Future a Challenge." Inf.: Lynette Finch, Nash Technical College, Box 7488, Rocky Mount, NC 27804.

MAR. 27–30—*Kansas LA, Kansas ASL, Kansas Association for Education, Communications and Technology,* annual tri-conference. Broadview Hotel, Wichita, Kansas. Inf.: Kay Mounkes, Hillcrest Jr. High School, 9300 Nieman, Shawnee Mission, KS 66214.

MAR. 29—*Archives and the Law: Keeping It Straight,* seminar. Education Bldg., Room 468, Univ. of Texas at Austin. Inf.: Mel Boggins, GSLIS, EDB, 564, Univ. of Texas at Austin, Austin, TX 78712–1276.

MAR. 29–30—*Subject Analysis,* symposium. North Carolina Central Univ., Durham. Inf.: D. McAllister-Harper, North Carolina Central Univ. SLS, Durham, NC 27707.

MAR. 31–APR. 3—*Softcon,* international software conference. Georgia World Congress Center, Atlanta. Inf.: Softcon, c/o Northeast Expositions, 822 Boylston St., Chestnut Hill, MA 02167.

APR. 1–2—*Coordinating Cooperative Collection Development: A National Perspective,* conference. Allerton Hotel, Chicago. Inf.: Office of the Dean, Library Services, Eastern Illinois Univ., Charleston, IL 61920.

APR. 8–11—*Catholic LA,* annual convention. Marriott Pavilion Hotel, St. Louis. Theme: "The Library: Gateway To Global Understanding." Inf.: John T. Corrigan, CLA, 461 W. Lancaster Ave., Haverford, PA 19041.

APR. 11–13—*Pennsylvania School LA,* annual conference. Americana Host Farm, Lancaster, PA. Theme: "Kaleidoscope: Changing Images." Inf.: Rebecca Frost, 2422 Riverview Ave., Bloomsburg, PA 17815.

APR. 12—*Syracuse Univ. SIS,* spring conference. Sheraton Hotel Conference Center, Syracuse, N.Y. Theme: "The Young Adult: A 'Totally Awesome' Phenomenon." Inf.: Spring Media Conference Coordinator, Syracuse Univ. SIS, 200 Huntington Hall, Syracuse, NY 13210.

APR. 14–16—*Library Applications of Data Processing,* annual clinic. Illini Union, Univ. of Illinois at Urbana-Champaign. Theme: "Human Aspects of Library Automation: Helping Staff and Patrons Cope." Inf.: Robin Caton, Univ. of Illinois at Urbana-Champaign GSLIS, 1407 West Gregory Drive, Urbana, IL 61801.

APR. 14–16—*Missouri Association of School Librarians,* spring conference. Lodge of the Four Seasons, Lake Ozark, Mo. Theme: "Spring Alive in '85." Inf.: Barbara Simonie, 10407 Walrond, Kansas City, MO 64137.

APR. 14–17—*Basic Library Management Skills,* institute. Centre Hotel, Philadelphia. Sponsor: Office of Management Studies of ARL. Inf.: OMS/ARL, 1527 New Hampshire Ave., N.W., Washington, DC 20036.

APR. 16—*Betty Burrows Memorial Seminar.* Ramada Inn Akron-Fairlawn, Akron, Ohio. Theme: "Getting Your Own Sweet Way: How to Make Your Library Visible in a Corporate Setting." Sponsor: Cleveland chapter of SLA. Inf.: Ellen M. Smith, Plain Dealer Library, 1801 Superior Ave., Cleveland, OH 44114.

APR. 16–17—*Connecticut LA,* conference. Park Plaza Hotel, New Haven. Theme: "The Real World." Inf.: Mary Balmer, Homer Babbidge Library, Univ. of Connecticut, Storrs, CT 06268.

APR. 17–19—*New Mexico LA,* conference. Sweeney Convention Center, Santa Fe, N.M. Theme: "Blazing New Trails: Library Issues in '85 and Beyond." Inf.: William C. Foege Jr., Publicity Committee, New Mexico LA , 2844 Calle Princesa Juana, Santa Fe, NM 87505.

APR. 18—*Records Management,* seminar. Driskill Hotel, Austin, Texas. Theme: "Exploring the Dynamics of Records and Information Management." Inf.: Steve Broberg, Austin Chapter of ARMA, Box 12455, Austin, TX 78711.

APR. 18–20—*Tennessee LA,* annual conference. Opryland Hotel, Nashville, Tenn. Inf.: Betty Nance, Tennessee LA, Box 120085, Nashville, TN 37212.

APR. 22–23—*Records Management: Enhancing the Profession,* seminar. Downtown Hilton, Dallas. Inf.: (see Mar. 29 for address.)

APR. 25—*Marian McFadden Memorial Lecture.* Indianapolis-Marion County PL. Sponsor: The Indianapolis-Marion County PL Foundation Inc. Inf.: Judith Miller, Indianapolis-Marion County PL, Children's Services, Box 211, Indianapolis, IN 46206.

APR. 26—*Improving Management Skills,* meeting. State Univ. of N.Y. at Geneseo. Sponsor: Western New York/Ontario Chapter of ACRL. Inf.: Ray Metz, Univ. of Rochester, Rush Rhees Library, Rochester, NY 14627.

APR. 26—*Western New York/Ontario Chapter of ACRL,* meeting. State Univ. of N.Y. at Geneseo. Theme: "Improving Management Skills For New Or Prospective Managers." Inf.: Ray Metz, Rush Rhees Library, Univ. of Rochester, Rochester, NY 14627.

The Computer Backlash: Why I Hate IBM

James LaRue

Mark my works, a computer backlash is a-comin', spearheaded by people and libraries that bought Apples, TRS-80's, or any of the many CP/M computers.

Item: "You Don't Necessarily Need a Big One" by Paul Kittle (*Small Computers in Libraries,* September 1984)—"Within five years many 'experts' agree that the 32-bit systems will be well established. So why jump on the 16-bit bandwagon when a 8-bit will do the job?"

Item: "The Trailing Edge" by Edgar Coudal (*Infoworld,* December 17, 1984)—"So here I am, back on the trailing edge of microcomputer technology but doing everything I want to do with speed and efficiency."

Item: The entire issue of the January 1985 *The Whole Earth Review,* titled "Computers as Poison." Stewart Brand, editor of the *Whole Earth Catalog,* the man who made every small press publisher in America dream big, takes us all to task for just jumping on board this whole computerized train bound for ...? ("Biting the Hand That Feeds: Ungrateful Wretches Criticize Munificent Benefactor.") Brand suggests that our entire society has accepted the "computer revolution" far too easily. "All the usually reliable liberal critics," he writes, "have Kaypros and Wordstar and pride in their new computer skills, and they're hushed."

This article is being written with Wordstar (not my usual word processor). I am writing it at home, on my Kaypro. Consider it an act of karmic penance.

James LaRue *is assistant director, Lincoln Library, Springfield, Illinois.*

My story

In 1983, I bought a "portable" personal computer. It was called a Kaypro II, and it was the biggest financial commitment of my life. I took out a loan.

In 1984, just five days before my final payment, I read a review of the new Kaypro 2. This newer model had a central processing unit that ran twice as fast as the one I'd bought. It had "primitive" graphics (mine didn't have any). Its disk drives took up half the space mine did, and were faster, quieter, and more reliable. The two came bundled with a complement of software that many feel is superior to the batch I got with mine. The whole package was $500 less than what I'd paid.

Truly, none of that bothered me. Even back in the dim computer antiquity in 1983, I knew that increasing performance and dropping prices were trends. Besides, I had more than earned the difference between the prices of the models during the nearly two years since I had put my life in hock, and the Kaypro had had a lot to do with that.

But the reviewer said the Kaypro 2 was a bad buy. Why? *It was obsolete.* According to him, an 8-bit CP/M machine just wasn't a good offering on today's market. All the new software was being developed for 16-bit, MS-DOS machines. Software that had been developed for the old 8-bit was not being updated. Why bother? People were buying IBM PCs or compatibles.

The reviewer also said that the Kaypro was ugly. That was unnecessary. Baby Kay (OK, I call my computer Baby Kay) is not ugly. Nor, as some have averred, is she merely "utilitarian." Compact, rather. Sleek. My Aunt Hazel was right: "Journalists are not gentlemen."

But gentleman or no, the reviewer was essentially correct. I know of only one new and innovative program produced exclusively for 8-bit machines: an outline processor called KAMAS. By all accounts it is excellent, and I will certainly buy it. But I can't help but feel it's a sop thrown to us Neanderthals. We *have* to buy it.

What happened was, I got the computer blues. I read hacker magazines until dawn. It was the same pattern I'd followed two years earlier: the eagerness to buy, the restless, almost frantic combing of computer stores, the same questions asked over and over, the balancing and rebalancing of my checkbook. Previously, I had had nothing but disdain for Compaqs, the stunted IBM PC (you call that a keyboard?) and the host of pale imitations. And the Macintosh? For all its promise, in its 128K incarnation it was little more than a glorified Etch-a-Sketch. Now I lusted for them all.

I imagine this cycle is common among most fanatics. First, you go through a period of obsession. Then there is the need to proselytize. Then comes the disillusionment—then, the fervent reconviction to the cause.

Finally, I decided the ACT Apricot was the machine of choice. A clean break with the past. An alliance with the future. An elegance and beauty even a journalist could recognize.

But just before I signed my life over for a few more years, the cool breath of reason calmed my fevered brow. Why did I have to buy another computer? I drive a 1973 Maverick, why can't I use a 1983 computer? What's the real difference between my humble Z-80 (8-bit) computer, and the 8088 or 8086 (16-bit)?

I got to nosing around, and I found out some things I hadn't realized before.

Battle of the bits

If you want a computer to work primarily with numbers, a 16-bit machine makes sense, as numbers like to be shuffled around a computer in 16-bit chunks. Calculation works out to be at least twice as fast. That comes in handy for the more powerful programs. Of course, something like the best-selling Lotus 1-2-3 is expensive thrice: once to buy the program, once to buy the extra computer memory you'll need, and once to learn how to use it all. But if you need it, you need it, and a compatible is the only game in town. (Actually, if it's speed you're after, you probably want an AT, which is still something of an incompatible. But that's another story.)

If, however, your fundamental use of a computer is word processing, you're as well off with an 8-bit computer. Each individual character you type, no matter what kind of computer you use, is made up of one byte. That's 8-bits. So the basic unit of the word exactly matches the basic (central processing) unit of the many inexpensive Z-80 computers.

Byte magazine routinely measures the performance of each new word processor—almost all of them designed to run on one compatible or another—against the venerable Wordstar. Now up to Version 3.3, Wordstar is a program originally designed for 8-bit machines, then modified to run on the compatibles. By and large, Wordstar does pretty well in these comparisons. (See issues of *Byte* for an explanation of their word processing "benchmarks.")

Depending on the machine, Wordstar itself runs at different speeds. Surprisingly, it runs faster on a Kaypro than it does on the IBM. Again, this mostly results from the nature of word processing itself, and the original design of Wordstar.

Even for number-crunching, 16-bits is overkill for most sorts of library calculation. An 8-bit will do the work, and still leave you whistling at its speed.

If performance is the issue, where's the IBM advantage?

Now compare prices. The Kaypro 2 costs $1,295. For this, you get the following hardware: computer, detachable keyboard, monitor, and two disk drives. Also included in the $1,295 is Wordstar, a spelling checker, a spreadsheet, a database program, a couple of programming languages, CP/M, and a few odds and ends. An IBM PC runs about $2,500. The monitor will cost you extra. Oh, and you'll need a card to drive the monitor. Add $60 for the operating system, MS-DOS, without which nothing can be done with the computer at all.

I love it. Imagine buying a car: the salesman names a price, it sounds good, and you sign. Then he mentions that you'll probably want tires, an "option." As you take the key, and start walking out to the car, he smacks his forehead and wonders, "Oh, gee—did you want a *steering wheel*?"

If this is a good buy, goodbye.

Always of interest to libraries on tight budgets is cheap software. There are volumes of public domain software for CP/M. Ditto for Apple. There's nowhere near as much free software available for the IBM—although some of it, such as PC-Write, and PC-File, is quite good.

So for most library applications, an 8-bit, CP/M machine is as good as a 16-bit. Yet virtually every new library application for microcomputers is built around MS-DOS, and depends upon machines that must be considered expensive alternatives to computing power. Why?

What's happened to us? Behind all the razzamatazz of "windows" and "gateways" and "integrated packages" and "workstations"—what's really going on with librarians and computers?

Putting it in perspective

I'm not selling Kaypros. But I am in favor of the concepts it embodies: good value, reliable performance. There are several other computers that offer the same price-for-performance ratio, such as the Morrow computers, and Osborne's latest, the Vixen. Even in the 16-bit world, the Seequa Chameleon, and even a Compaq, offer more computing bang for the buck than an IBM.

If your library is about to make use of OCLC for the first time, fine, buy an IBM. It has more general utility than a dedicated OCLC terminal, and even if you get locked into the every-three-years IBM upgrade pattern, you're still saving money.

If you've already bought an "old"

8-bit computer, don't feel you need to rush right out and buy an IBM. Unless you require a program that runs only on MS-DOS, you'll probably do all right with what you have.

If you must have a 16-bit computer, why buy an IBM PC? There are other computers that not only work faster, come bundled with software, and even have more storage, but they are still cheaper than the PC. In particular, I would recommend the Tandy 1000 or 2000, and NEC's latest APC. And let's not forget the stunning Apricot ACT (but check to make sure you can get local service on the ACT —it's manufactured in the United Kingdom).

There is something ludicrous about us librarians, most of whom are certainly not qualified in any field of hard science, yet who embrace the new technology, utterly without reservation, as if it were the answer to all of our problems.

I'm not saying we should junk all our microcomputers. They have proven their utility to us. Microcomputers are good for lots of things, including but not limited to: statistics, budgeting (depending on how much of a budget you've got), word processing across the board, circulation control for the smaller libraries (and most of them are), such database management applications as mailing lists, and various telecommunicating tasks. Microcomputers can and have saved months of staff time each year.

Going with a brand name

I question not the value of the microcomputer but the price tag. We need to shop around a little more. I think many librarians do not feel competent to make judgments about just what they're being offered. To mask their ignorance and insecurity, they go with a brand name.

In some respects, this is prudent. The library that ran out and bought Franklin's Ace—the Apple II clone that was not only cheaper than its template, but in most respects superior—must now face Franklin's bankruptcy and liquidation. Reliable service and company longevity are valid organizational concerns.

IBM seems safe. They are the proven, the not-likely-to-fail (excluding the PCjr). They will be here in the future. Admittedly, there are some compatibility problems between their various models. The 8-bit internal bus limits the 16-bit PC. The XT is fast, but the PC is faster with a Tallgrass hard disk attached. The AT only claims ninety percent compatibility with the PC. But nobody expects technology to hold still. Past a certain point, asking for "compatibility" is like asking a Volkswagon engine, without modification, to power a Cadillac. That's clearly unreasonable.

For all its faults, IBM never forgets a customer, right? There's always someone to hold your hand—if you like men in blue suits. But does buying an IBM PC really insure good service? Most of us buy our micros from local dealers. Thus, dealer reputation is far more important to us than whether a particular computer company is truly monolithic, or merely well-established. Unless we give all our business to IBM, there are several other companies that may also be expected to survive.

Most libraries simply cannot afford the equipment, software, peripherals, and staff necessary to develop high-powered automated solutions to daily problems. Nor is it always wise to attempt this. For many routine library operations, a manual system is more than sufficient—it may well be superior to most computerized procedures.

The crux of the matter is this: if we must buy computer solutions, do we have to spend so much money shoring up people only marginally interested in our real aims? As Hamlet said, sort of, What are we to IBM or IBM to us?

I don't *hate* IBM, not really. But I don't trust them either, any more than I trust R. R. Bowker publishing *Small Press*. Bowker is hardly a small press, and has chiefly ignored those people published in the small press—unless these same people make it big. The little guys make the world safe for democracy; the corporations clean up.

IBM is an easy target, I know that. If I really wanted to find a computer company to pick on, I'd choose Digital, who came along with 8-bit, 16-bit coprocessing, which seemed like a sure bet. Then I discovered that they had made it impossible to format your own disks. You had to buy them direct from the company, at a high markup. Although that particular problem has been rectified, it soured me on Digital, and the Rainbow still tends to be more expensive than the IBM PC. This kind of difficulty is illustrative of the mainframe and minicomputer mindset, and may be a sign of things to come. If I were to evaluate the IBM PC and (to be evenhandedly malicious) the DEC Rainbow as if they were reference books, I would conclude that these exorbitantly priced works provide little that is unique. The field is better covered by the Kaypro on the low end, and the NEC APC on the other. Not recommended for smaller libraries.

Call it paranoia, but I think IBM and their ilk may well sweep the library market—and it will not work out to our advantage. OCLC has settled on the IBM PC; CLSI has begun pushing a Rainbow "work station." I fear that microcomputer applications will become more and more narrowly defined. Libraries will have to buy dedicated machines, running software that only works with IBM or Digital equipment, and then we'll have to dish out the same kind of "upgrade" money we currently spend on our minicomputers. These "information appliances" will diminish the chief power of the micro—flexibility—and restrict our ability to develop our own responses to the unique needs of our communities.

Perhaps we should all band together and agree to buy cheap, small-scale computer solutions. That way maybe we'll have some money left for books. Our job is to be not state-of-the-art, but Good Enough. As any software test-site will tell you, he who lives on the cutting edge—is usually down. ▣

High Tech Breakthrough: Interactive Videodisc

Rebecca Sturm

"Videodiscs and computers offer too much learning and storage capabilities for libraries to ignore."

During the last year, I have been following the development of the interactive videodisc (IVD) via my interest in computer-assisted instruction (CAI) for academic libraries. Recently, I was awarded a small grant from General Electric in Cincinnati to explore the implications of the IVD for higher education. The project's goal was to gain this information by attending the Fifth Annual Nebraska Video Disc Symposium (in Lincoln on August 27–30, 1984) and share this experience with our faculty and staff. The Nebraska Videodisc Design/Production Group is internationally known in this field; the over three hundred symposium participants included individuals from Great Britain, Australia, France, Italy, Japan, Belgium, Canada and the Netherlands. These people were a mix of hardware and software representatives and developers in the areas of the military, business, industry and entertainment.

During the course of multiple conversations with other participants, surprise mixed with curiosity at my presence would change to understanding and agreement when I expressed *library* interest in this technology. Throughout the symposium, I heard about the millions spent on research and development for the videodisc—millions that will be directed elsewhere unless libraries throughout the U.S. begin to express interest in the IVD and its variety of applications.

The IVD combines the videodisc (videotape in disc format), with its various visual and audio information, and the computer, either as part of the disc player or as an external interface. Because the reflective optical videodisc is "played" by a laser beam without physical contact, these discs are considered to be quite a durable and stable format. One thirty-minute disc can hold 54,000 individual frames, obviously valuable to any library for archival purposes. Because of the rapid access, a videodisc can be programmed for very sophisticated

Rebecca Sturm *is head of public services, Northern Kentucky University Library, Highland Heights, Kentucky.*

CAI; a number of programs can be written for the same videodisc; programs can offer the user a choice of languages; and computer graphics can be superimposed on other images or even as material presented on a second screen. Combining this technology with that of a touch screen, light pens and barcoding, the IVD offers instruction that can be truly "user friendly" yet also highly individualized and interactive. It offers us the best of the videotape and the computer. The major drawback at this point is cost. For production, a disc must be created from a high quality 1´´ or 3/4´´ videotape plus the costs of any computer programming. Whether you elect to produce or purchase discs, you still have the initial cost of playback equipment, at least $1600 for a player plus computer interfaces, and monitors.

Here are just a few examples of programs in a variety of applications. Probably the most familiar to us as librarians is the Library of Congress's recent videodisc project that involved putting thousands of prints, photographs, and posters (all of various sizes) onto a few videodiscs. One disc is currently being used at LC by library patrons, the others are pending distribution due to copyright conflicts. (The IVD does offer some challenges to current copyright laws.)

It is admirable that LC is setting an example for other libraries to follow—the completion of a videodisc project and its ultimate distribution to other libraries. A similar project has also been completed by the National Gallery of Art. One side of their disc has over 1,000 oil paintings, along with identifying information, with access to any painting available within a second or two. The other side is a tour of the museum itself. This videodisc is available from Videodisc Publishing for $95. The military and private industry have both been quick to recognize the potential uses of the IVD for training, especially in the simulation of expensive and dangerous pieces of equipment. By utilizing headsets and voice-activated equipment, videodiscs can be used at time of need to lead the user through exacting, yet infrequent repair procedures.

Another industrial/educational use involves the ActionCode (ICS-Intext) which employs a touch screen or light pen (to avoid use of a keyboard) and a workbook for the learner to use, refer to away from the videodisc setup, and ultimately to keep. In addition to being highly interactive (the learner can "touch" actual dials/controls on the monitor and experience the response), the workbook has barcodes throughout. When the user wants to review or go to any portion of a training lesson, touching pen to barcode immediately accomplishes this.

An industrial use that is both archival and interactive is an inventory project designed for Westinghouse by Digital Video Corporation. Based on diagrams of their steam turbines and built on a hierarchical approach, a plant manager can use a touch screen to successively move from the turbine itself down to any individual part, review the ordering information on a second screen and then actually place the order. By having one screen act as the other's "slave," a plant and the warehouse can view the same material to decide on the correct part to order and send. While discs are available to teach various physics, chemistry and biology theories (GPN, Nebraska Videodisc Design) that are unwieldy or impossible to stage in the classroom (a bridge collapse, for example), two simulation examples I saw at the symposium were particularly exciting and illustrate the immense capabilities of the medium.

One videodisc was designed by a physician (Intelligent Images, Inc.) for emergency room physicians to aid them in developing decision-making skills without risk to patients. Through the combination of live action, real time and a teenager with a simulated gunshot wound, the audience experienced all the stress of the

An Easy Introduction to IVD

Gindele, John and Joseph Gindele. "Interactive Videodisc Technology and Its Implications for Education," *T.H.E. Journal* (August 1984): 93–97.

Levin, Will. "Interactive Video: The State-of-the-Art Teaching Machine," *The Computing Teacher* (September 1983): 11–17.

The Library of Congress Optical Disk Pilot Program. Booklet available from the Information Office, Library of Congress, Washington, DC 20540.

Melin, Nancy. "Library of Congress Pilots Optical Disks, *Information Today* (September 1984): 23+.

Melin, Nancy. "Optical Disks in Libraries," *Information Today* (October 1984): 7+

Price, Joseph. "The Optical Disk Pilot Program at the Library of Congress," *Videodisc and Optical Disk* (November–December 1984): 424–432.

actual situation. A second screen allowed "the learner" to order tests and make judgements and the subsequent action was based on these decisions. The program also kept track of lab costs, comparing them to "ideal" care and when the user did not react quickly enough or appropriately, the nurse in the simulation would offer verbal prompts to the doctor in the video.

A final example is not as dramatic, but is perhaps more impressive because it was produced at the University of Iowa using modest resources—not by an independent producer with a large budget. Their program is designed to educate junior medical students in the identification of a number of muscular syndromes in infants. Filmed at the University of Iowa Hospitals and Clinics, it alleviates the problem of a few weeks on a given medical service providing the unlikely chance of seeing all of these syndromes in actual patients. To program a series of lessons that may take four to six hours to move through but are contained on one videodisc and one computer diskette, stills were used unless movement of the children was necessary and sound was kept at a minimum. Again, using two screens, the user moves between the two, viewing children, questions, printed material, and graphics, and making responses as needed. The University of Iowa projects (they have others on dance and film editing) are proof that quality programs can be designed without exceptional cost.

If either the educational or the archival aspects of IVD sound appealing, I believe you must be prepared to act now—hardware and software producers are looking for some interest from the educational sector to encourage further development. Here are some things to try:

• Read and become more familiar with this marvelous technology—a few sources are included at the end of this article.

• Contact hardware and software producers; find out what they have and let them know what you want to see.

• Ask for demonstrations from producers or even from industries in your area that may be using IVD for their own training (DEC or NCR, for example). See if your local high school has "College USA" (Info-Disc Corp.)—videodiscs containing information about colleges, often in a choice of languages.

• Purchase existing programs—this is a sure sign to producers that the interest in this technology exists. The $95 art disc mentioned earlier may be a reasonable beginning. You may wish to cooperatively purchase the playback equipment with other libraries, rent it, or try to get such equipment in return for serving as a demonstration site.

• Finally, I think we need to begin to cooperatively produce interactive videodisc programs that are generic enough to share, yet specific enough to be useful. A natural beginning is to make an existing videotape interactive by writing a computer program for it. Grant money is also another way to get started in this area. These programs can then be marketed to help recover costs and to "spread the word."

Videodiscs and computers offer too much learning and storage capabilities for libraries to ignore. Here is a chance for librarians to join forces with others—programmers, instructional designers, video experts and other subject specialists—to create the demand for a technology that can reshape the world of learning and information retrieval for society. Let's not ignore the lead that business, industry, the military, travel, entertainment, retail sales, and most of all the Library of Congress, have forged for us. ▣

Further Reading

Daynes, Rod and Beverly Butler. *The Videodisc Book 1984.* New York: Wiley, 1984.

Journal of Computer-Based Instruction. Association for the Development of Computer-Based Instructional Systems, Western Washington University, Bellingham, WA 98225.

News. Nebraska Videodisc Design/Production Group, Box 83111, Lincoln, NE 58501 (Free)

T.H.E. Journal (Technological Horizons in Education). Information Synergy, Inc., Box 17239, Irvine, CA 92713 (Free)

Videocomputing. Videosoft, 109 South Miramar, Indialantic, FL 32903

Videodisc Market Survey and Report 1984. Meckler Publishing, One Ferry Lane West, Westport, CT 06880

The Videodisc Monitor. Future Systems, Inc., Box 26, Falls Church, VA 22046

Videodisc and Optical Disc and *Videodisc and Optical Disc Update* (a bimonthly journal and biweekly newsletter). Meckler Publishing, One Ferry Lane West, Westport, CT 06880

Hispanex: Serving Libraries Serving Hispanics

Brian Aveney and Vivian Pisano

Roberto Cabello-Argandona and **Vivian Pisano**—Meeting the growing needs of Hispanics

The Hispanic Information Exchange (Hispanex) is a non-profit organization established to support libraries in their attempts to meet the information and cultural needs of the nation's growing Hispanic population. Its programs include current and retrospective bilingual cataloging services, publication of a review journal to support library selection activities, cooperative acquisitions services for Spanish and Latin American materials, and publication of materials relevant to the Spanish-speaking population.

Automation has been an important component of the Hispanex program since its beginning. National and international standards have been carefully adhered to so that Hispanex records can be easily merged into other bibliographic databases. Wherever possible, Hispanex projects have built upon systems and procedures already developed.

In the beginning

In the mid-1970s, a number of California public libraries submitted LSCA proposals designed to enhance the use of libraries by the state's five million Hispanics. Statistics showed that while ninety percent of this population could read Spanish, only twenty-one percent reported that they could read English well. A number of proposals to address this problem were consolidated under the wing of the Ethnic Services Task Force, directed by Yolanda Cuesta of the State Library, and the Spanish Catalog Project was organized in 1977.

The original focus of the project was on the provision of catalog access. Spanish-language titles often ended up in cataloging backlogs, not because of any intentional neglect on the part of libraries, but simply because centralized cataloging was not available for many of these titles. Additionally, Spanish-language subject headings were needed to make these materials truly accessible to patrons who did not read English. Working with a variety of national and international groups, the Spanish Catalog Project initially concentrated on defining MARC fields to support bilingual cataloging, and on development of a Spanish-language subject heading list.

These efforts built towards the development of a state-wide Spanish-language union catalog. In early 1980, an initial book catalog (*Catálogo Español*) listing over 7,000 titles with bilingual subject headings, representing titles in the Oakland, Alameda County, Alameda City and Contra Costa County public libraries, was produced with technical support from CLASS, BALLOTS (now RLIN) and Auto-Graphics.

In 1980, emphasis shifted from the creation of a union catalog to the development of a bibliographic database which could support a variety of applications including acquisitions, cataloging, and processing. Roberto Cabello-Argandoña was appointed Executive Director, and the name of the project was changed to the California Spanish Language Data Base (CSLDB) in 1981.

The programs have continued to grow in both size and number. In addition to holdings of other public libraries such as Los Angeles Public and Los Angeles County, cataloging for titles in UCLA's Chicano Studies Research Library and rare Hispanic materials from the Sutro Library of the California State Library have been added. In 1984, the first step towards a more national role was taken with the input of 11,000 retrospective Spanish-language titles from the Chicago Public Library's collections.

Brian Aveney *is president of Information Works, El Granada, California.* **Vivian Pisano** *is program manager for the Hispanic Information Exchange, Oakland, California.*

Hispanex today

In recognition of the extension of services beyond the simple creation of a database, and to emphasize the organization's emerging national role, the board of directors approved a change of the name of the organization to Hispanic Information Exchange (Hispanex) in December 1984. Hispanex is a non-profit association governed by a board of directors composed of both librarians and non-librarians. John Bareño, a San Diego lawyer, is chairman of the board, which also includes Elizabeth Martinez Smith of the Orange County Public Library and Gary Strong, California State Librarian.

SPANCAT: Cataloging Support

The automated cataloging activities were the reason Hispanex was originally conceived, and remain today the most active services. Both current and retrospective cataloging support are offered. The MARC II format records include full AACR2 cataloging, Library of Congress subject headings and Spanish equivalents, and Dewey and LC classification numbers. Both catalog cards and machine-readable records are made available.

The union bibliographic database has now grown to over 58,000 titles representing the holdings of about thirty California and Illinois libraries. In addition to monographs, records for journal citations and government reports on the Chicano urban experience, U.S.-Mexican relations, Hispanic women, folklore, labor and immigration are now being added to the database.

In addition to being used for Hispanex's own current and retrospective cataloging services, the database is made available on both RLIN and AGILE II to encourage libraries to take advantage of this unique resource. A portion of the database is being made available on UCLA's ORION online information system, as well. This spring, Hispanex anticipates beginning to use the Adlib integrated library system for its cataloging activities. Use of a local system will both lower costs and provide more control over system operation. The bibliographic database and both name and subject authority files will be mounted on the local system.

Bilindex: Bilingual subject headings

Bilingual subject access was one of the project's initial objectives. Hispanex's bilingual subject heading thesaurus, *Bilindex,* contains Spanish equivalents for over 15,000 current Library of Congress subject headings. It expands and updates the Organization of American States' (OAS) 1967 *Lista de Encabezamientos de Materia para Bibliotecas,* compiled and edited by Carmen Rovira, and its supplements, and Gloria Escamilla Gonzalez's *Lista de Encabezamientos de Materia* published by the Universidad Nacional Autónoma de México (UNAM).

The thesaurus contains the Spanish headings and Library of Congress equivalents, appropriate cross-references, and explanatory and source notes. Regional variants are included so that headings can be retrieved using Southwestern, Cuban, Mexican, Mexican-American, Puerto Rican and other Spanish forms. An especially useful feature is inclusion of Spanish equivalents for many technical and scientific terms. The Spanish headings are established with approval of a resource group of librarians who serve Hispanic communities.

Bilindex is available online on the Auto-Graphics AGILE II system. Users may use either English or Spanish terms to retrieve the records stored in the MARC II format for authority data. The availability of the authority records online in AGILE II is especially useful to California public libraries who produce their COM catalogs through Auto-Graphics. It is important to note that there are only two online thesauri in the Americas, the French-English Canadian thesaurus and the Spanish-English *Bilindex.*

The thesaurus is also available in print form. The preliminary edition, *Catálogo Español. Lista Bilingüe de Encabezamientos de Materia* (1980), included 6,000 headings. The most recent printed edition of *Bilindex* (1984) contains 13,000 headings. The printed thesaurus includes a brief explanatory preface, Spanish equivalents to LC standard subdivisions and LC subject headings for children's literature, a guide to establishing Spanish personal names, a list of Spanish-language geographic names, and an English to Spanish index to provide access to the main Spanish-language sequence. A supplement of 3,000 additional headings and subdivisions is in preparation.

Lector: Reviewing Current Publications

To aid libraries in selecting currently available Spanish-language and bilingual materials, Hispanex launched *Lector* in 1982. Now in its third year, *Lector* is a bimonthly review journal containing in-depth evaluative reviews of books, records and films suitable for library purchase. Reviews are contributed by a nation-wide body of 350 reviewers from the library and academic community. About 100–150 titles are reviewed in each issue. In addition, citations for another fifty titles not reviewed are provided in the "Briefly Noted" section. *Lector* is designed to meet the need of public libraries for current Spanish and bilingual material, Hispanic literature, Latin American studies, and ethnic studies.

Reviews in *Lector,* organized into two dozen broad subject areas, provide full bibliographic information including imprint, collation and price, and signed evaluations of one to a half dozen paragraphs. Codes below each review indicate recommended reading levels and audiences for each title, as well as type of binding. At the end of the review section, full addresses are provided for publishers and distributors who supplied materials reviewed in the issue.

Columns, news items, a calendar of events, and articles of interest to book selectors and public service librarians are also included. Bibliographies on special topics are a frequent feature. A recent three-part series, by Sylvia

Flores Johnson of the Los Angeles Public Library, provided an extensive annotated subject list of readily available titles suitable for a core collection of popular materials. Another article reviewed eleven major U.S., Spanish-language newspapers and provided brief listings for another sixteen.

An editorial advisory board of librarians and scholars guides the journal's development. Free sample issues are available by writing to Hispanex on library or institutional letterhead.

COPAS: Cooperative Acquisitions

Libraries in the U.S. have often encountered difficulty in obtaining materials suitable for their Hispanic patrons. Further, materials purchased often languish in cataloging backlogs because of the unavailability of adequate cataloging copy. Hispanex's Cooperative Acquisitions System (COPAS) was initiated in 1983 to assist libraries in purchasing materials reviewed or listed in *Lector.*

COPAS acts as a cooperative ordering agent for current books, records, audio cassettes, videocassettes, films, and other library materials from publishers in Spain, Latin America and the U.S. By consolidating orders and simplifying time-consuming ordering and acquisitions procedures for Spanish-language and bilingual materials, COPAS cuts costs and indirectly improves library service to the Hispanic community. Full AACR2 cataloging with bilingual subject headings is available for all titles ordered though the system. Overprinted catalog card sets are provided with books upon request.

Libraries looking to develop or strengthen their Spanish-language collections will find the LIBROS database maintained by Hispanex a unique source for selecting current titles. The LIBROS database provides brief bibliographic information and prices for approximately 2,000 selected in-print titles organized under broad subject categories. Citations to reviews in *Lector* are included when available. All prices are converted to U.S. dollars for convenience in ordering.

Floricanto Press

The original focus of Hispanex was publication of a printed union catalog. Over the years, additional publications were produced from various projects. Floricanto Press was created to draw together the existing publications such as *Bilindex,* to develop further Hispanic-related reference materials aimed at the U.S. Hispanic population, and to initiate a new line of quality bilingual children's books.

Developed in cooperation with the UCLA Chicano Studies Research Center, *Statistical Sources on the California Hispanic Population 1984: A Preliminary Survey,* compiled by Eudora Loh and Roberta Medford, identifies, describes and evaluates selected data sources from the maze of materials published by the state and federal governments. Topics covered include population and vital statistics, housing, employment and economics, education, health and social services, crime and law enforcement, agricultural workers, and consumer patterns and leisure. A substantial annotated selected bibliography is included.

The Chicano Public Catalog, compiled by Roberto Trujillo, is an annotated bibliography of about 700 recommended popular titles for a Chicano collection. Currently in press, this volume is intended to be used as a selection aid, a source of cataloging data, and a reference tool.

Manuscripts directed at children ages 5–9 (grades K–3) and suitable for bilingual publication are currently being sought. Titles must be non-stereotypical, non-sexist, and present a multi-ethnic environment that is positive, educational, and entertaining. Manuscripts, correspondence, inquiries, and orders may be addressed to Claire Splan of the Floricanto Press at the Hispanex address.

Can Hispanex help your library?

According to Director Cabello, Hispanex sees its mission as developing a pragmatic infrastructure from which to develop basic high quality services and products to assist all types of libraries who serve Hispanics wherever they are. This includes both public and academic libraries, as well as school, corporate, and institutional libraries. Hispanex is engaged in an expanding role in online infomation and reference retrieval service through a newly created program enitled Hispanic Online Access (HOLA). This new development is aimed at creating an online database of 200,000 bibliographic citations on U.S. Hispanics and other related subjects. The first organizational meeting was conducted at Stanford University on February 1, 1985. With a record of successful support for library services to Hispanics in California, and more recently in Illinois, Hispanex today is ready to work with libraries across the country to make effective use of its unique resources.

Hispanic Information Exchange Publications:

Bilindex; A Bilingual Spanish-English Subject Heading List; Spanish Equivalents to Library of Congress Subject Headings. 1984. 533p. $65 plus $2 shipping and handling. 0-915745-00-3 83-25285; Supplement. Forthcoming. approx. 250p. 0-915745-02-X

Chicano Public Catalog, compiled by Roberto Trujillo. Forthcoming. approx. 275p. 0-915745-03-8

Lector. The review journal for Spanish language and bilingual materials suitable for purchase by public, school, college, university, and special libraries in the United States. Bimonthly. $20 per year. 0732-8001

Statistical Sources on the California Hispanic Population 1984: A Preliminary Survey, compiled by Eudora Loh and Roberta Medford. 1984. 210p. $19.80 plus $2 shipping and handling. 0-915745-01-1 84-5897

The First of Four More Years: ALA in Washington

Members of the American Library Association who assembled in Washington, D.C. for the midwinter meeting of the organization held January 5–10 met only weeks before the swearing-in of President Reagan. The largely hospitable weather that prevailed then was to change so completely by the end of the month as to make an outside inaugural ceremony impossible. While zero temperatures were not foreseen, the likelihood of zero budgeting for federal library programs was already projected, less of a trauma now than a predictable annual event for which it is necessary to draft letters, dial numbers, arrange meetings, twist arms, squeeze hands, and generally lobby for our cause.

For the fourth year in succession President Reagan has proposed elimination of library programs. The fiscal year 1986 budget transmitted to Congress on February 4 requests no funds at all for LSCA or HEA II. Postal subsidies, revenue sharing, and NCLIS are also proposed for elimination. The ECIA Ch. 2 school block grant would be level-funded. The first year of Reagan's second administration promised to pose as many challenges for librarians as the year just passed.

In 1984 Congress gave library programs a forty-four percent increase in funding and passed a five-year extension of LSCA. The Library of Congress received funding for construction of a mass deacidification facility, proposed increases in library telecommunications rates were postponed, and Senator Claiborne Pell (D–R.I.) promised to introduce legislation calling for a second White House Conference on Library and Information Services in 1989. President Reagan vetoed the Health Research Extension Amendments which included an extension of the Medical Library Assistance Act, the National Archives was separated from the General Services Administration, and the U.S. withdrew from UNESCO. OPM Director Donald Devine suspended all standards projects and placed the proposed librarian standards on hold pending an internal review by the Office of Personnel Management. Senator Larry Pressler (R–S.D.), concerned about telecommunications developments affecting libraries, asked the FCC to consider a library private line service. Said Pressler, "Our libraries are our good friends. We cannot allow the divestiture of AT&T to prevent them from performing their historic role of providing universal access to information."

Also in 1984 the FCC pronounced AT&T's proposed interstate private line service tariff to be unlawful. Major increases proposed in the tariff would have had an impact on libraries connecting through networks to bibliographic databases. Finally, the Department of Education published *Alliance for Excellence,* calling for an alliance of school, family, and library, and the Library of Congress released *Books in Our Future,* a report calling for initiatives to end illiteracy and new means to promote books and reading.

If it was not a perfectly good year for the cause of libraries and librarianship, it was not terribly bad either. What was clear at this midwinter meeting is that libraries would once again have to lobby for their cause, not taking any support for granted, realizing that the value, place, and significance of libraries is not universally accepted. That this was nothing new, and that we are now accustomed to raising our voice in Reagan's Washington, provided some measure of collective self-confidence.

Executive Board: Four more days

The ALA Executive Board, meeting on four occasions during the week, heard a report on January 5 from Regina Minudri, chair of a board subcommittee that examined AASL's Future Structure Report, a study critical of AASL's role within the parent organization. Of seven major issues brought forward by AASL, it was the subcommittee's opinion that some of these matters could be dealt with by present policy, some would have to be studied by other units of ALA because of wider implications inherent in them, and some were simply not issues of contention. The Executive Board decided "there was no compelling reason to recommend changes in the Constitution and Bylaws as a result of the inquiry into AASL's Future Structure Report." Noted the subcommittee, "It is clear that AASL is now and will always be an essential unit of the ALA. Just as the ALA bears responsibilities for and to its divisions, so do ALA divisions bear responsibilities to the association as a whole." The board voted to accept the report from Minudri and discharged the subcommittee.

At its meeting on Sunday the board undertook a discussion on the proper use of ALA's imprimatur in issuing reports, endorsing causes, and boycotting products. "I think," said Arthur Curley, "there is confusion in the use of ALA's name." William Summers agreed: "Much of our policy is written to protect our right of deniability." At discussion's end it was agreed to ask the Committee on Organization to prepare a position paper on the use of the ALA name.

The ALA Strategic Long-range Planning report, a three-phase program "to provide the association with a structured and identifiable mechanism for determining future trends and needs," was introduced by Brooke Sheldon. Although some board members felt Council would need a full review of the background and purposes of the rather undefined study, Executive Director Robert Wedgeworth disagreed: "Do we need to go through a full goal-setting hearing when we have done this in the recent past?" Beverly Lynch was not convinced: "It is exceedingly hard to budget in the absence of any specific plan." The board, nevertheless, recommended adoption of the long-range study.

Other action on this day consisted of debate on a bylaws change presented by Ernest DiMattia, chair of the Constitution and Bylaws Committee, that would allow ALA members to attend Council and membership meetings without registering at the particular conference during which they were held. While proponents of the change argued that the present arrangement disenfranchises members not wishing to pay conference registrations Curley sharply disagreed: "I for one think this is a terrible idea." He suggested that "we refer it somewhere where it will die a slow and deserved death." The board voted to refer the recommendation to the Membership Committee.

Ceilings and deficits

At the third meeting of the board on January 8, the group went over an audit report from Gary Longman and Mark Arvin of Peat, Marwick, Mitchell. ALA received an unqualified audit report, no longer qualified because of the challenge to its tax exempt status by the Illinois Department of Revenue. The report noted that a major use of funds in 1984 was for equipment acqusitions ($585,000) which caused an increase in bank borrowings of $350,000 and pointed out that ALA has a great deal of unused borrowing capacity represented by its new headquarters building. All operating funds had excess revenues over expenses of $96,000; the plant fund deficit was $310,000; the endowment fund deficit amounted to $76,000; and the prior year adjustment of deferred subscription revenue was $220,000. The 1983–84 year ended with a total fund balance deficit of $510,000.

The group approved January 14 as an official holiday for ALA staff honoring Martin Luther King and accepted a report from the Awards Committee recommending against a proposed Exemplary Service Recognition Award. The committee, chaired by Linda Pierce, held that "the proposed award would lessen the prestige of existing awards."

The 1985–86 Executive Board met on Thursday morning. Those in attendance included President E.J. Josey, President-elect Beverly Lynch, past-President Brooke Sheldon, Treasurer Patricia Schuman, Executive Director Robert Wedgeworth, and board members Margaret Chisholm, Arthur Curley, Judith Farley, Elizabeth Futas, Regina Minudri, David Snider, William Summers, and Lucille Thomas.

Barbara Markuson, chair of the Committee on Program Evaluation and Support, presented a report calling for a general fund budgetary ceiling of $9,566,532 and a division fund budgetary ceiling of $952,166. The written report also embodied an opinion on the feasibility of a graduated dues structure. Refraining from endorsement of such an innovation, the committee noted that a graduated structure might decrease divisional membership, would be complex to administer, and difficult to monitor for accuracy in reporting. COPES also observed that "benefits of membership in a professional society do not accrue on a salary basis."

"One of the amenities . . . "

A briefing on the present status of the Business Support for Libraries Council was offered by Carol Nemeyer and John Hoving. Nemeyer acknowledged that the council is "still a concept and not in action," and suggested that it might be a logical activity for the Public Library Association to assume. The board approved a motion to refer the proposal to the PLA board of directors, asking for a progress report by January 1986. Hoving stated that there has been a shift of business interests from the 1960s and 70s, moving away from a national viewpoint to a local, more parochial one. "Libraries," said Hoving, "are one of the amenities of a modern, technological society."

The president of Independent Sector, Brian O'Connor, appeared before the board to make an appeal for ALA affiliation in his organization, an agency that grew out of the former National Council on Philanthropy. O'Connor explained that "there has been an erosion in giving over the last twenty-five years" as well as increasing tax laws and government regulations pertaining to philanthropy. O'Connor characterized independent giving as "the third way by which the nation deals with its problems." The base of giving, said O'Connor, is moving downwards, most of it coming from families earning less than $25,000 annually. The board authorized Wedgeworth to undertake procedures resulting in affiliation with Independent Sector. The membership fee was estimated at approximately $6,000.

WLB conference analysis

Organization: American Library Association, 1985 Midwinter Meeting
Dates: January 5–10, 1985
Place: Washington, D.C.
Membership: 39,400 (August, 1984)
Attendance: 5,607 (including 1,527 exhibitors)

In final action Judith Krug, Office for Intellectual Freedom, presented an overview of the case of *American Booksellers Association, et. al.* v. *William Hudnut, et. al*, which challenges the constitutionality of Indianapolis's recent ordinance proscribing pornography as sex discrimination. The U.S District Court in Indianapolis subsequently held that the ordinance violated the First and Fourteenth

Amendments. In December 1984 the City of Indianapolis filed a notice of appeal with the U.S. Court of Appeals for the Seventh Circuit in Chicago. Krug related that the Freedom to Read Foundation has joined the American Booksellers Association as a plaintiff in the case and stated that the FTR board of directors voted to invite ALA to participate in an *amicus* brief on the appeal. The board voted to authorize the Executive Director to begin the process of filing an *amicus* brief with the Court of Appeals.

An historic year

At Council I, President E.J. Josey termed 1984 an historic year both for the nation and for ALA. It was the year, said Josey, in which we underwent a national election, survived the predictions of George Orwell, and celebrated the thirtieth anniversary of *Brown* v. *Board of Education* in which the U. S. Supreme Court ruled that the equal protection clause of the Fourteenth Amendment prohibits racial segregation in public schools. The Court opinion said Josey, also constituted "the elimination of racial barriers to library service."

Taking note of accomplishments in his presidency, Josey reported that the Process Planning Committee submitted a long-range plan for ALA, a Task Force on Bibliographic Databases had been formed, the Committee on Accreditation received a grant to study how other information organizations can become involved in the ALA accreditation process, and ALA and the Association of American Publishers are going to look into what they can do to export books abroad as a result of discussions at the IFLA conference held in Nairobi.

Referring to the Executive Director's decision not to renew his contract, Josey said "While we regret Mr. Wedgeworth's decision, we are well aware of the fact that as an imaginative administrator he has a right to pursue other career interests."

Declaring that "the membership is ALA's greatest asset," Josey emphasized that "it is essential and vital that we work together." Concluded Josey, "Libraries are faced with increasingly sophisticated demands by the American people."

The Freedom to Read report, prepared by FTR President Ella Yates, was read in her absence by Dorothy Broderick. The document listed a number of cases in which ALA has an interest, including *American Library Association* v. *Faurer* in which the National Security Agency placed some 300 library items on restriction, and *Marian English et al.* v. *Evergreen School District, el al.* in which thirty-three books had been removed from a junior high school library in the state of Washington. "We remind the Council," read the report, "that the foundation represents your insurance against censorship attack and coercion. With the wave of conservatism sweeping the country, it could be any of you, your libraries, or your library collections being challenged tomorrow."

Tremendous assets

"We have tremendous assets, financial and otherwise," remarked Patricia Schuman, opening Council II with the treasurer's report. Stating that "ALA is an asset-rich, rapidly growing association," Schuman led Council through a twenty-two page financial statement and fourteen exhibits in as clear, candid, and forthright a fiscal presentation as the body had ever experienced.

In light of the $76,000 deficit in the ALA endowment fund caused by portfolio neglect when funds were transferred from the First National Bank of Chicago to the Northern Trust Company, councilor Daniel Casey suggested a lawsuit against the responsible bank might be an appropriate action. Wedgeworth, however, stated that "we had a difficult time in assigning responsiblity for the loss."

In presenting his annual report, Wedgeworth observed that federal funding of library programs will continue to be an important issue. "We must broaden our agenda for ALA in Washington," asserted Wedgeworth, and "we must reestablish what we want money for in terms of the American people."

Wedgeworth asked Council to support the ALA long-range plan, stating that "the longer we delay, the more it will cost." Wedgeworth said that "at the moment planning is only done in conjunction with the budget" and stressed the need for "an effective mechanism to pursue planning."

Taking account of the diminishing time left to him as Executive Director, Wedgeworth confessed that "this position has brought me more attention than I ever imagined." But, he added, "the honors were not for me, they were for ALA."

Our best thinking

Council III was gavelled to order on Wednesday morning with memorial tributes to Bradford Chambers, who died in September 1984, and to Clara Lacey Jones, who passed away in December.

Brooke Sheldon and Roger Parent, ALA Deputy Executive Director, presented the Strategic Long-range Planning report to Council. Sheldon endorsed the need for "a full-scale,

Total Assets—$8,217,053

Current Assets	1984	1983	Change 1983-84
Cash	$ 142,000	$ 49,000	$ 93,000
Receivables	863,000	693,000	170,000
Inventory	873,000	828,000	45,000
Prepayments	316,000	239,000	77,000
Total	$2,194,000	$1,809,000	$385,000
Property and Equipment	$4,319,000	$4,093,000	$226,000
Non-Current Assets			
Restricted Cash	$ 102,000	$ 85,000	$ 17,000
Investments (Endowment)	1,602,000	1,603,000	(1,000)
Total	$1,704,000	$1,688,000	$ 16,000

long-range planning program," observing that "COPES frequently receives requests for funding with no supporting documentation to point out the merits, to fit in the request with larger ALA objectives." Parent said the long-range plan represented "the best thinking of some of our most experienced members and staff" and characterized the scheme as "a more sophisticated and rational approach to planning than anything we have ever tried before." A motion to approve the plan was passed with few dissenting votes.

In matters brought to Council by Eric Moon, chair of the Intellectual Freedom Committee, the body voted to take a position against deregulation of the broadcast media and repeal of the Fairness Doctrine, agreed to rescind a statement on Freedom of Expression of Foreign Nationals, and endorsed a resolution directing the ALA Commission on Freedom and Equality of Access to Information to hold open hearings on its findings at the 1985 ALA conference in Chicago.

Ching-chih Chen, chair of the Committee on Legislation, won Council approval of seven resolutions: that Congress fund federally legislated programs in support of public and academic libraries; that Congress fund all Higher Education Act Title II programs at the authorized levels; that Congress and the Department of State facilitate reforms that will permit the U.S. to rejoin UNESCO; that ALA encourage implementation of programs outlined in *Books in Our Future*; that the Office of Management and Budget remove "Library operations" from the list of commercial activities included in its Circular A–76; that the U.S. Department of Labor exclude librarians from the *Register of Wage Determinations Under the Service Contract Act*; and that ALA form a coalition of organizations to study the dissemination of vital government information.

In other action Council expressed concern over the intention of the Italian Ministry of Cultural Affairs to suspend publication of the *Bibliografia Nazionale Italiana*; agreed to have the endowment trustees make regular reports to Council; and expressed support for International Youth Year, 1985.

Arthur Curley and **Mary Futrell**—The Library doors must swing open

Lengthy debate ensued over a proposal to allow personal members of ALA to attend membership and Council meetings without registering for the conference. James Matarazzo objected, stating that the effect of the resolution would be to make registration an option: "I honestly think this is irresponsible." The resolution won narrow approval, sixty-eight for, fifty-nine against.

Council concluded its agenda with consideration of a resolution calling for formulation of a minimum annual salary for entry-level librarians possessing the MLS degree. Councilors argued that a minimum salary guideline would work against graduates seeking higher salaries and that organizations now offering high entry-level wages might readjust them downward. Several members of the body found fault with the figure of $17,500, finding it inappropriately low. As the hour for adjournment approached it was agreed to forward the resolution to the Office for Library Personnel Resources, soliciting their opinion and response.

The Public Good

The President's Program, held at the Sheraton Washington on Monday afternoon, was devoted to "Forging Coalitions for the Public Good."

Arthur Curley, Deputy Director, New York Public Library, stated that the public good represents "a vagueness that has been somewhat of a danger to us," but added, "It is encumbent upon us to do something dangerous—to have faith in the public good." Curley praised E.J. Josey, calling him "a pioneer in broadening the objectives of this association to social issues." He emphasized that "there are larger purposes of our libraries for which the term information is not sufficient."

"I have alway had a great deal of difficulty," said Mary Futrell, president, National Education Association, "in wondering how we could advocate excellence without advocating libraries." Futrell told the audience in the Washington Ballroom that "we must make sure that our library doors swing open to all Americans" and "we must be prepared to reach to all our population the best education possible." Said Futrell, "We have a cultural heritage to preserve that cannot be measured in dollars." She told an enthusiastic audience that "libraries are fundamental to our economic wellbeing."

A bracing look

During the Legislative Workshop, sponsored by the ALA Legislation Committee and the Legislation Assembly, several hundred invited participants devoted over five hours to a program designed to strengthen ALA chapter and state school library media association legislative networks. Speakers on the first part of the program included Joseph Shubert, chair of the ALA Task Force on Excellence in Education, Bill Doswell, lobbyist for the Virginia LA, and Roger Fry, director of the Division of Library Programs, Department of Education.

After the participants studied and discussed various PR leaflets and fact sheets designed to be used in local lobbying efforts, a panel discussion was held to provide guidance on coalition building. The panelists all represented agencies that are National Partners with ALA in National Library Week.

Marlene Blum, a PTA member active in Virginia, spoke of her frustration at the low profile school librarians keep in the community and her difficulty in getting them involved in parent-faculty committees. Hope Dougherty, National Director of 4-H, pointed out that libraries and 4-H have a similar image problem with the public, which is often ignorant of the full range of activities of both. Dougherty also cautioned against the dangers of turf-protection, which can prevent coalitions useful to everyone. Bella Jacobs of the National Council on the Aging outlined three NCOA programs librarians should be aware of, including a literacy program just getting underway that will train older adults as tutors (she noted that there are nine million functional illiterates in the U.S. over the age of sixty). Other speakers were James Rutherford, of the American Association for the Advancement of Science, and Dennis Labuda, of the Institute of Lifelong Learning of the American Association of Retired Persons. The panelists' remarks were frank and sometimes unflattering, providing the audience with a bracing look at how others see their efforts.

The session ended on a more upbeat note with an encouraging luncheon talk by Representative Major Owens (D-N.Y.), a member of the House Education and Labor Committee.

An uproar over copyright

The Task Force on Bibliographic Databases, created last June in response to membership concern on the copyright of databases, held an open hearing at which six persons had requested to speak. Rowland Brown, president of OCLC, was not able to get through all of his statement in the five minutes alotted to each speaker, but ended up spending more than twice that time in later responding to questions.

Brown was placed on the defensive because the task force's mandate to analyze the state of copyright for bibliographic records in fact referred to OCLC, since OCLC's registration of copyright is the only test case in existence. (It was noted that the UTLAS database is copyrighted in the U.S., but this is because of the international copyright convention that gives U.S. copyright protection to material copyrighted in Canada.)

The first speaker, Louella Weatherbee of AMIGOS, stated their vehement opposition to the OCLC copyright registration. A joint meeting of AMIGOS and SOLINET in October 1984 reaffirmed this, with a suggestion that protection against database misuse be provided by a cooperatively developed code of conduct for bibliographic utilities and their members. Charles Lowry, vice-chair of SOLINET, in agreement with Weatherbee that database copyright threatens the concept of library cooperation, made another suggestion that received an appreciative response from the audience: as an act of good faith, OCLC should re-register the copyright with all 4,000-some members as co-authors. James Schmidt, vice-

Conference quotes: "We need a greater commitment to research in the profession."—Donald Sager; "ALA makes haste slowly."—Regina Minudri; "Divisions have to take their own reponsibility and not blame central."—Al Trezza; "Libraries are faced with increasingly sophisticated demands by the American people."—E.J. Josey; "A threat to the flow of information is a threat to the library community and to society."—Arthur Curley; "Most of the books being censored are written by or about minorities."—Mary Futrell; "We have tremendous assets, financial and otherwise."—Patricia Schuman; "ALA may not ever count the majority of librarians working in the U.S. as its members."—Robert Wedgeworth; "Strategic long-range planning is more necessary for an association even than a corporation."—Brooke Sheldon; "We cannot be in the business of establishing minimum salary standards."—James Matarazzo; "The unfettered use of bibliographic data will depend on networks and libraries."—James Schmidt; "OCLC membership is not an inherent right."—Rowland Brown; "The extent of OCLC's ownership of its database, if any, is still to be decided."—Charles Lowry

president of RGL, while affirming RLIN's intentions not to copyright its database, felt that the copyright of a bibliographic utility's entire database would not interfere with a member's use of its own database.

Richard Boss, speaking as a consultant with who has been in contact with over 100 libraries in the past year, conveyed the anxiety many librarians have now about the legality of such arrangements as shared local systems in which not all libraries are OCLC members. While acknowledging that many of these fears are groundless, he painted a picture of poor communications between OCLC and its members on this issue.

Elaine Rast, of Northern Illinois University, a member of the Illinois OCLC Users Group, made explicit what Boss's remarks had implied: the uproar caused by OCLC's copyright move was a result of poor PR; OCLC did not "respond in a clear, straightforward manner." She concluded by saying, "We all need OCLC, and I hope we have all learned something from this episode."

Significant Board/Council actions: Approved adoption of a strategic long-range plan; Voted against an Exemplary Service Recognition Award; Agreed to affiliate with Independent Sector; Resolved to file an *amicus* brief in the case of *American Booksellers Association* v *William Hudnut*; Voted to take a position against deregulation of the broadcast media and repeal of the Fairness Doctrine; Urged Congress to facilitate reforms that would permit the U.S. to rejoin UNESCO; Urged Congress to fund HEA Title II programs at the authorized levels; Referred a resolution calling for a minimum annual salary for entry-level librarians; Endorsed a measure directing the ALA Commission on Freedom and Equality of Access to Information to hold open hearings.

Rowland Brown downplayed the importance of the copyright issue; the real issue, he contended, is how to make the database available to all libraries (including nonmembers) on a cost-effective basis. The copyrighting of the database is an attempt to regulate third party use, and will not be invoked against members. (Member usage is regulated by the contracts between OCLC and each of its members.) The damages he cited in unauthorized third party use are loss of revenue and loss of data that third party users do not contribute to the database.

In fact, there seemed to be a general acceptance of the copyright as a fait accompli, leaving only legal and technical questions about what constitutes misuse of the database and how to prevent it. Brown conceded that the problem of misuse is not black-and-white, but with many grey areas, since the possible situations are so complex.

One final area of concern seemed to be the contract language OCLC would be using to forestall member misuse of the database. Brown reported that this would be determined by the OCLC Board of Trustees, who in February will be receiving reports from OCLC management, the Users Council, and two special committees, the Committee on Copyright Alternatives and a Select Committee on Third Party Use.

The task force, which at the time of the hearing was still undecided about what recommendations to make, will offer its final report at the annual conference in July.

Little disagreement

There was little disagreement over basic issues among the candidates for ALA president during a presidential forum held by the Social Responsibilities Round Table, with the main differences appearing to be in style and emphasis. Particular points were brought out by each candidate during the prepared remarks. Regina Minudri stated her commitment to pay equity, calling it "the issue of the eighties." Alphonse Trezza stressed his knowledge of ALA structure and politics, stating that if elected he would pick one important topic to make the focus of his year in office. Donald Sager wished to make ALA's leadership role its most important goal.

Questions from the audience covered predictable social responsibilities ground: the status of women in libraries, library service to minorities, whether the association should take stands on social issues, whether fees should be charged for some services.

It came as no surprise that the candidates were all for women and minorities, and against user fees, at least in principle.

New definitions

The Accreditation Committee held an open meeting to provide an update on the Accreditation Project. The project, funded by the Department of Education, is seeking to determine whether other professional societies should become involved in the accreditation of library schools. Chair Robert Hayes outlined the structure of the project, which consists of a steering committee, comprised of representatives of the participating professional societies, and various working groups. Draft working documents will be studied and discussed at the annual conference this summer, and a draft report will be prepared in the fall, to be considered at Midwinter 1986. The final report will be delivered March 1986.

The participating societies are the Association of American Law Libraries, American Society for Information Science, Association of Library and Information Science Education, Association of Reseach Libraries, Canadian Library Association, Medical Library Association, Special Library Association, Association for Records Managers and Administrators, National Federation of Abstracting and Information Services, and the Society of American Archivists. Other organizations may join at a later date, Hayes noted.

Beth Miller of the Canadian LA spoke of her organization's enthusiastic reception of the idea of cosponsorship of accreditation (ALA currently accredits library schools in Canada). SLA president Vivian Arterbury, who also spoke briefly, felt that as one of the by-products of the process, "we will have a new definition of the information profession."

Several audience members questioned how a new accreditation program would be structured. Hayes, while mentioning possible solutions, refused to speculate on the project's final recommendations.

Grassroots action, personal contact

The Legislation Committee held an update session to report on recent action and on what to expect in the 99th Congress. Eileen Cooke, director of the ALA Washington office, feels the the make-up of the new Congress is only slightly different from the old. A key appointment is Senator Paul Simon (D–Ill.), a friend to libraries from his House days, who will probably chair the Senate Labor and Education Committee, which will be reviewing the Higher Education Act. Cooke predicted a zero budget for libraries (LSCA and HEA both zeroed out) in the 1986 budget, just as in the past three, and strongly urged the necessity for grassroots action and personal contact with legislators, stating that the existence of the Washington office does not take the responsibility off individual librarians for lobbying their representatives.

Nancy Kranich, chair of the ACRL Legislation Committee, spoke in more detail on HEA, which is up for reauthorization. ACRL will be focusing on HEA Title II–A (college libraries), which has not been funded for two years. A new funding bill will probably require a needs criteria from college libraries to receive aid. An ACRL committee was working at the conference on defining such criteria.

Walter Bolter, director of the Bethesda Research Institute, spoke on telecommunications. An upcoming issue of importance to libraries is in the private-line area. For instance, the FCC seems intent on de-averaging rates, so that telecommunication rates in outlying areas could become very expensive.

Adelaide del Frate, chair of the Federal Librarians Round Table A–76 Task Force, reported on the trends and implications of the government contracting out library services. ALA feels this puts government information and library services at risk. Through what appears to be a clerical mistake, the Department of Labor has for the first time included librarians on the list of nonprofessional employees, assigning them the minimum wage of $9.62 an hour. FLRT also objects to the job description which accompanies the wage classification. FLRT has written to the Office of Management and Budget to recommend removal of librarians from this list.

Some unresolved questions

The Copyright Subcommittee of the Legislative Committee asked two representatives of the Copyright Office to provide background on two issues of current interest. Dorothy Schrader, Associate Register of Copyright for Legal Affairs, outlined the Copyright

Office's actions in the registering of copyright by OCLC. The Copyright Office first determined that databases of bibliographic records are copyrightable as are any other compilations resulting from the original selection and arrangement of material. Some legal objections were made to the Copyright Office in attempts to prevent the registering of OCLC's copyright, and Schrader explained why they were found to be insufficient. She emphasized that the Copyright Office does not rule on the validity of a copyright claim—it only registers claims. The only determination the Copyright Office made in the OCLC case was whether the nature and scope of the claim were sufficiently defined—which OCLC had done to their satisfaction.

The office has already registered some libraries' contributions to online databases, and ten to twelve applications are pending of libraries who claim to be joint authors with OCLC of the database. Schrader brought up some interesting unresolved questions on exactly what entity a copyright claim should be made for, and how often, when registering a database that is continously being added to. There is as yet no legal determination of this question, and copyright claimers can use any approach they wish (OCLC is registering its database once a month).

Lewis Flacks, also of the Copyright Office, spoke on international copyright. He reminded the committee that UNESCO administers the Universal Copyright Convention—which the U.S. was instrumental in establishing—and it is our only copyright agreement with seventy-five countries. The Universal Copyright Convention is important to the U.S. because we do not subscribe to the Berne Convention, but renewed efforts are underway to bring this about. Private and government working groups have already been formed on this issue, and Flacks urged librarians to study Berne and its implications (it contains regulations that provide certain exceptions for schools and libraries) and provide input in as early a stage as possible in these discussions.

He briefly outlined the difference between Berne and the Universal Copyright Convention. The Universal, and the other individual copyright treaties we have, result in authors in one country becoming subject to the laws in another. Berne is an international agreement that creates rights all countries recognize. Berne is also much more detailed and theoretical. Flacks concluded by noting that plans are being made to have a program on Berne at the ALA conference in Chicago this summer.

E. J. Josey, presiding—"This has been an historic year."

Networking for equity

The Commission on Pay Equity met immediately after the President's Program, dovetailing nicely with the presentation of the final speaker, Winn Newman, a lawyer active in wage discrimination cases. Cynthia Johanson, co-chair of the commission, noted that Newman had donated his honorarium to the legal fund of the Fairfax County (Virginia) librarians who have filed a sex discrimination complaint with the EEOC over salary inequities.

Present to informally share information were representatives from the AFL–CIO Department of Professional Employees, the American Association of University Women, Federally Employed Women, the National Education Association, the National Organization for Women, the National Committee on Pay Equity, the Newspaper Guild, the Service Employees International Union, the Virginia Commission on the Status of Women, and the Women's Legal Defense Fund.

After each representative outlined her group's present activities, there was discussion on job evaluation studies used to document systematic pay inequities, and which can be time-consuming, expensive, and even result in "proving" that no inequity exists. Some participants felt that after enough studies had been done, the existence of pay inequity would be established and would not have to be proved again for every case. Other methods mentioned that would not require evaluation studies were approaching pay equity as a collective bargaining issue (for union staff) or as a management-personnel issue.

At an earlier meeting the commission discussed a proposal to hold a preconference training session to prepare library staff to select the most effective methods to establish pay equity. Participants would then set up similar training programs in their home states. It is hoped this would establish a national network to further the progress of pay equity. Funding has been applied for through the World Book–ALA Goal Award.

Covering the Floor: ALA Midwinter Exhibits

Bibliofile

The display of new laser and microcomputer-based technology at the Midwinter Meeting made the library exposition one of the most provocative ever. The following sampler highlights some of the most exciting new technology demonstrated at the conference. Further information about these products and services may be obtained directly from the individual vendors.

Bibliofile

The Library Corporation exhibit was wall-papered with hundreds of complimentary compact laser discs containing the complete Library of Congress MARC English language cataloging database that forms the backbone of its Catalog Production System. With the aid of an industry standard disc drive plugged into the IBM PC or OCLC's new M300 Workstation, special access software, and application programs created by TLC, librarians may use the keyboard's ten function keys to perform current cataloging or retrospective conversion work.

The Catalog Production System retrieves a MARC record via LCCN, ISBN, ISSN, author or title key, and title. It accepts "qualifiers"—publication year or year range, for example—to identify the specific work. The system offers a full-screen editor for record modification; accepts original cataloging input; displays a catalog card image of the record; orders a MARC or REMARC record from other vendors; and validates and saves the record to diskette for later use or conversion to MARC tape. In addition, the program prints sets of headed catalog cards as well as spine and pocket labels.

The Library Corporation touts several advantages to the Catalog Production System over traditional long distancc mainframe access including the elimination of telecommunications costs and mainframe downtime. And while the MARC database on the compact laser disc is recompiled, reindexed, and replaced only quarterly at this time, TLC plans weekly replacements by mid-1985. (Contact The Library Corporation at Box 40035, Washington, DC, 20016 or call 800/624–0559.)

InfoTrac

Information Access's videodisc storage system is designed to solve the document delivery problem. Speed of access to indexed information along with guaranteed availability of the full text is the basis of InfoTrac. Referred to as an "automated periodical literature reference system," InfoTrac makes it possible for up to four users to simultaneously search by computer fully-indexed references recorded on a videodisc and then to print these citations and later the full text on the spot.

The first disc to be produced contains nearly half a million citations indexed from over 1,000 business, technical, legal and general interest periodicals which reflect the collections of major libraries. This disc, along with one laser disc player, one laser disc interface, one silent printer and four microcomputers (for four separate users) is the basic configuration of the system. Citations may be located with specific words or phrases, with "see" or "see also" headings, or through a "browse" function.

A printed copy of the search results may be made immediately and, if an Information Access Company accession code is included with a citation, the searcher may also obtain the full text of the article either from IAC's Magazine Collection or Business Collection. Subscribers will be provided with a new videodisc each month containing the full updated and cumulated InfoTrac database which includes several years of retrospective material. (Contact Information Access Company at 11 Davis Dr., Belmont, CA 94002 or call 800/227–8431 or 414/591–2333.)

Eastwind Micro Circulation

Although microcomputers were hardly common in most libraries one year ago, their recent introduction by the bibliographic utilities (Washington Library Network, UTLAS, and OCLC) for use as cataloging workstations has opened up a brand new marketing opportunity for the more ambitious vendors. Many are relying on the power and speed of IBM products including hard disk support for the PC and XT and the new AT.

DataPhase's Eastwind Micro Circulation Software is a full function standalone system running on the PC/XT (DataPhase also announced an auxiliary system for the PC, XT or Apple IIe and IIc for users of their ALIS II and III system). It is as sophisticated as their larger systems and, because it is built on a MARC compatible database, smaller libraries may combine conversion to a online circulation system with conversion of these same files to MARC. Furthermore, this database may later be used in networking with other MARC libraries or for migrating with comparative ease to a larger system.

Eastwind, utilizing a ten-megabyte hard disk, offers charge, discharge, renewal, fines, recall, blocks, holds and notices functions. Parameters supports include library system name, loan period matrix, default loan periods, processing fees, call number breakdown, fine codes and manual block maintenance messages. The system, without the micro, is offered at an introductory rate of $1500. (Contact DataPhase at Box 797, Shawnee Mission, KS 66201 or call 913/262-5100.)

PAC/II and Series 3000

Not to be outdone, rival circulation vendor CLSI demonstrated its "Next Generation Online Catalog," PAC/II, which runs on mini- and microcomputer configurations. Using CLSI's new Series 300 workstation with terminal emulation software one may access the local LIBS 100 system and operate it in an online mode for data entry and revision. The workstation may also be employed as a standalone word processor or database manager for library administrative work; or, finally, it may be employed as an interface to several bibliographic utilities including RLIN, WLN, UTLAS, OCLC, or Autographics.

The Series 3000 includes the 3100, a floppy based system, the 3110, which can allow the addition of a Winchester hard disk, and the 3110W, which has a built-in disk. At this time Lex II software is available for word processing, and Super Comp Twenty for database management. CLSI will shortly offer a report generator, the CLSI/Datawriter which will allow the Series 3000 Workstation to download from the LIBS 100 and produce reports locally without interfering with the work of other LIBS 100 terminals. (Contact CLSI at 1220 Washington St., West Newton, MA 02165 or call 617/965-6310.)

SC-350 and MICROCON

OCLC's announcements of a new micro-based serials system and a floppy disk batch process retrospective conversion service were the highlight of a special press conference at which it unveiled these two new software programs designed to run on their own M300 Workstation.

The first, Serials Control 350 (SC 350) allows users local serials control as well as access to the OCLC Online Union Catalog of over 600,000 records. It supports a full range of technical services needs including bibliographic record selection and transfer, automatic check-in and claiming, routing, binding, financial control, and report generation, as well as a public searching capability. This combination of local control along with the possibilities of participation in nationally maintained online union lists sets it apart from many of the new serials systems on the market. The software was developed by MetaMicro Library Systems of San Antonio, Texas and requires a hard disk storage device. OCLC plans to convert all users of its online serials systems to SC350 over the next few years.

MICROCON, the new batch conversion service, allows libraries to use their own staff to enter search keys and local data onto diskettes using rent-free M300 Workstations provided by OCLC. When the diskettes are full they are returned to OCLC where the data are transferred to tape and compared with the Online Union Catalog for matching records. When a hit—an exact match—is made, the contracting library's holding symbol and local data are then added to those records. Libraries are charged only for those search keys that result in a single hit. (Contact OCLC at 6565 Frantz Rd., Dublin, OH 43017 or call 614/764-6000.)

Microcon—OCLC's new conversion service

MICROLINX

Faxon's new MICROLINX, not yet commercially available, was a surprise announcement at Midwinter. Working right up to the official exhibits opening hour, Faxon staff were able to demonstrate a standalone IBM PC-based (hard disk required for collections of more than 600 serials) serial control system including telecommunications software with which users may connect with Faxon's mainframe serials database for use of their highly successful LINX network system. No documentation of the system is yet available for review. (Contact Faxon, 15 Southwest Park, Westwood, MA 02090 or call 800/225-6055.)

Dale Nelson:

Dateline Washington

Loyalty and libraries

While he was a student at the University of the District of Columbia, Harry Kenneth Clark worked part-time reshelving books at the Library of Congress. He also attended some meetings of the Young Socialist Alliance.

The two may seem unrelated, but the library's personnel office ordered a full field investigation of Clark by the FBI. When it was over, the library concluded that the young reshelver was "suitable for retention" in his job.

After Clark was graduated from college he sought to get a full-time job at the library. Although he applied for forty low-level jobs—none of which were much, if any, more sensitive than reshelving books—he failed to get any of them.

As a result, Clark has won a case in the U.S. Court of Appeals in Washington on the question of how far a government agency can go in investigating lawful political activities of its employees.

"It is unquestionable that investigations such as the one at issue here are justifiable under certain circumstances, especially in cases of persons in sensitive positions," Judge Edmund L. Palmieri wrote for a three-member panel of the appeals court.

"However, to hold that the full field investigation of Clark was justified on the basis of the record here would be to sanction intrusive and injurious investigations initiated on the basis of minimal information regarding an employee's association with a lawful political group, no matter how menial or inconsequential the position of the employee might be."

Clark worked full-time at the library and went to college part-time

from 1973 through 1976, when he switched to part-time work and full-time college. He attended several meetings of the YSA, an affiliate of the Socialist Workers Party, and his name was put on the group's mailing list. Informers told the FBI, the FBI told the Civil Service Commission, and the commission told the Personnel Security Office of the library.

In June, 1976, the library asked the FBI to investigate Clark's activities, including "(1) his motivation for joining the YSA, (2) the nature, extent and objective of his involvement in YSA activities, (3) any comments or conduct on his part which indicates he is aware of and/or supports the philosophy and objectives of the Socialist Workers Party/Young Socialist Alliance, (4) whether or not he has indicated or expressed advocacy of overthrowing the U.S. Government by force, violence or other unlawful means, and (5) whether or not any other information exists which might give rise to a reasonable doubt as to subject's loyalty to the United States or otherwise reflect adversely on his suitability for continued federal employment."

According to the court record, the FBI interviewed Clark's co-workers, former teachers, former neighbors in New York, and neighbors of his family in Washington. The agents asked, among other things, about his activities while on vacation, his involvement with religious groups, and whether he was a homosexual.

Joseph Love, one of the library personnel security officers responsible for Clark's case, testified that the library's concern about Clark was not

---

Dale Nelson *is a journalist who covers the Washington scene for WLB.*

related to national security, but solely to his loyalty.

According to a 1974 Supreme Court ruling, incidentally, the Socialist Workers Party "does not advocate the use of violence. It seeks instead to achieve social change through the political process, and its members regularly run for public office."

The library conceded during the trial that Clark was qualified for at least seventeen of the positions for which he applied over a two-year period before quitting in discouragement in 1979.

Clark filed suit in U.S. District Court, claiming that the investigation violated his First Amendment rights and led to rumors and gossip that prevented him from getting a promotion so he could pursue his ambition of a career at the library.

Clark sought $100,000 damages, "reinstatement" to one of the positions he sought, and an injunction against further investigations of him.

The trial judge ruled against Clark, holding that the government had a right to make at least "some enquiry into the employee's suitability" and that in any event the FBI, not the library, was at fault if the investigation was too intrusive.

He was overruled unanimously by the appeals court panel made up of Chief Judge Spottswood W. Robinson III, Judge Patricia Wald and Palmieri, a senior district judge from New York sitting as a member of the District of Columbia court.

They held that the government's sovereign immunity barred Clark from collecting money damages and that his request for an injunction was premature because it was too early to tell what damage future investigations might do.

But they ruled that the library had "failed to demonstrate the existence of any legitimate, much less compelling justification for the full field investigation of Clark." They sent the case back to the district court for consideration of Clark's requests for reinstatement and for correction of his record.

At that time the library will have another chance to show that its action was justified. But, the court said, it must prove that the full field investigation "was necessary to serve a vital governmental interest and . . . was the available means least restrictive of Clark's first amendment rights."

Ban on sleeping and smelling

While agreeing that the invasion of the street people may be a nuisance, most librarians do not seem to be following the lead of the Ann Arbor, Michigan library system in banning people who sleep or smell bad.

"We don't feel that it's necessary," said Mark Merrifield, reference librarian at the Alexandria, Virginia public library.

And Betsy Pinover, manager of public relations for New York's eighty-six-library system, said, "We refrain from any policies which exclude or deny access. Making the library accessible to the public is our first and foremost responsibility."

Pinover added, however, that the increase in the number of homeless people is a problem and library officials are considering how to deal with it.

The Ann Arbor library dealt with it by adopting a rule against "the disturbance of other library patrons and interference with other library patrons' use of the facility through extremely poor personal hygiene." In addition, while permitting patrons to nod briefly over their books, the rule prohibits sleeping in the library for more than ten minutes.

The Washtenaw County ACLU Lawyers Committee has expressed concern that the rules will be enforced unequally, discriminating against the homeless.

Our friend in the Senate

Illinois's new senator, Democrat Paul Simon, is expected to follow up in the Senate on the reputation he earned in ten years in the House as a strong supporter of education and libraries.

Simon, who was chairman of the higher education subcommittee of the House Education and Labor Committee, applied for a seat on the corresponding Labor and Human Resources Committee in the Senate.

Committee assignments for members of the Senate minority are up to the Democratic leadership, but with his credentials Simon was expected to get his choice.

Simon was the author of last year's rewrite of the Library Services and Construction Act, including a $5-million-per-year program to provide start-up grants of up to $25,000 to encourage neighborhood libraries to double as tutoring centers for illiterate adults. ▣

Stanford approves site for Reagan library

The trustees of Stanford University have approved a proposed site for the Reagan Presidential Library on a twenty-acre plot in a visually screened part of the foothills adjoining the central campus. Edwin Meese III, counselor to the president, said "The president would be favorable to a building design that blended into the Stanford hillsides and complemented the natural setting." Meese also noted that "President Reagan strongly prefers the kind of architecture that predominates on the Stanford campus, including red tile roofs."

It is estimated that it will be at least two years before groundbreaking. Interim steps include formation of an independent foundation to raise funds for the library, selection of an architect, agreement on a contract between the university, the foundation, and the National Archives and Records Service, which will operate the library, and local hearings and governmental approvals.

The trustee resolution approving the site stipulated that interior space allocated to exhibits should not exceed fifteen percent of the gross square feet of the facility. The trustees also stated that the library should contain conference areas and meeting rooms "of such an extent and character as to maximize its usefulness to undergraduate and graduate students and faculty." Meese noted that President Reagan was especially concerned that the library be "readily accessible" to students.

Anne McGrath:

Eye on Publishing

1985: Another good year for book publishers

Publishers who have been waiting with bated breath for evidence that the economy's expansion will continue to mean prosperity for their industry in 1985 now have some concrete figures to give them hope. According to *The Industrial Outlook,* a report recently released by the U.S. Department of Commerce, revenues will indeed continue to grow in 1985, albeit at a slower pace. The report assumes that the gross national product will increase 4.3 percent this year and that the rate of inflation will remain constant at 4.5 percent.

The Commerce Department recognizes increased library and school funding as one factor in sustained growth, additional sales outlets as another, and greater pools of discretionary income as a third. Book shipments in 1985 should exceed those of 1984 by 4.5 percent, the report predicts, taking inflation into account. Furthermore, shipments should continue to grow for another five years at an annual rate in constant dollars of 3.5 percent. In 1985 an additional 200 publishing jobs are likely to be created, which would bring total employment to 67,500.

Book sales in the United States rose an inflation-adjusted 5.1 percent in 1984 over the 1983 figure, to a total of nearly $9.4 billion.

A recent study by New York investment banker Veronis, Suhler & Associates found the book publishing industry's performance from 1979 to 1983 in comparison to its competitors in other segments of the communications industry to have been less than "stellar." The latest *Communications Industry Report,* issued annually, surveyed some thirty publishers and ranked them according to such measures as revenue growth, operating income, and return on assets. The highest that publishing ranked in any of the categories was sixth among ten segments of the communications industry that include radio and television, cable and pay television, newspaper publishing, advertising, and recorded music.

Anne McGrath, *a freelance writer based in New York City, covers the publishing world for WLB.*

But can publishing survive illiteracy?

A study issued early last December by the Library of Congress identifies illiteracy and aliteracy as two true threats to the future of the book in America and calls on publishers, booksellers, librarians, and government to help stamp them out by the end of the decade. Technology, so often considered to be the culprit behind any decline in reading ability, is let off the book by the LC report. "Technology is not the problem," the report states. "It is our opportunity. Illiteracy and aliteracy were not created by technology, but technology can help us abolish them."

At the same time, the study warns, the excitement and challenge offered by new technologies should not be allowed to overshadow for students the possibilities for discovery presented by books. Those in the business of publishing and providing books to the public can do more to make their books accessible and attractive to intransigent nonreaders, the report concludes.

Publishers and booksellers are encouraged to find new and "unexpected" outlets for their books, for example, and to campaign for new readers with innovations like Great Britain's redeemable book certificate program. To ensure that efforts to promote and facilitate reading are as effective as possible over the next few years, the report suggests that sound research on the book trade and the American public's reading habits be undertaken. Even though economics may militate against it, the study beseeches publishers to join librarians in the struggle to lengthen book life by turning to acid-free paper and stronger bindings. The Library of America series, the report points out, is an example of a successful effort to combine quality subject matter with conscientious design and manufacture.

Government has its own work to do. One suggestion calls for federal, state, and local government to assess the impact on literacy that various pieces of legislation might have. Such assessments, the report proposes, should address specifically the serious issues of how "new legislative actions will directly or indirectly affect the world of reading and learning." When Congress is drafting legislation affecting day-care centers or services to the elderly, opportunities for minority groups, those in vocational training, or those in prison, it should whenever possible consider how to provide access to reading material to those the legislation affects.

More money, of course, is a key requirement if members of the book community are going to successfully eradicate illiteracy and thus assure the book a future. Libraries, the report points out, can't buy books unless they're properly funded.

How Vintage aims to promote reading

The new Vintage Contemporaries series of paperback fiction, which made its debut last fall, is one good example of a publisher's determination to lead readers to critically fine reprint fiction that—perhaps because of its lack of tremendous commercial promise—has

not enjoyed wide distribution before; and to introduce deserving original work by young new writers that might otherwise never see the light of day. Seven titles appeared on the fall list, and five are scheduled to come out this spring. You can tell them by their distinctive, colorful design—and if you haven't already picked one up, they are definitely worth a look.

Like Vintage's Aventura series—which in 1983 began giving Americans a taste of modern foreign fiction in translation—the Contemporaries are intended to call the best of today's writing to the attention of readers hungry for thoughtful literature and to put the books within their financial reach. Fall titles (ranging in price from $4.95 to $6.95) included one humorous original novel, *Bright Lights, Big City,* by Jay McInerney, about a young man's not-very-well-managed personal life and career in New York, and six reprints: Raymond Carver's collection of short stories *Cathedral,* James Crumley's novel *Dancing Bear,* Janet Hobhouse's *Dancing in the Dark,* Paule Marshall's *Chosen Place, Timeless People,* Peter Mathiessen's *Far Tortuga,* and Thomas McGuane's *The Bushwhacked Piano.*

Among the books to follow are *The Debut,* by Anita Brookner, *A Fan's Notes,* by Frederick Exley, *A Piece of My Heart,* by Richard Ford, and *Taking Care,* a book of short stories by Joy Williams.

E.P. Dutton to be part of New American Library

Independent publisher E.P. Dutton, founded more than 150 years ago, has agreed to be acquired by paperback publisher New American Library. The move is expected to benefit each house because it teams a leading paperback operation with a respected hardcover house and should enable the new entity to acquire both hardcover and paperback rights to a book.

Dutton's list of authors boasts such notables as Joyce Carol Oates, Jayne Ann Phillips, Jorge Luis Borges, and Benjamin Spock. The firm publishes some 120 titles a year for adults and approximately 130 juvenile titles. The New American Library, started in 1948, ventured into hardcover publishing several years ago—and in fact is responsible for the currently popular *Weight Watchers Quick Start Program Cookbook*—but in Dutton it gains a truly solid and diverse hardcover program.

***Time*'s best books**

Time magazine recently surveyed the field of books published last year and came up with its own list of the best ten—five fiction and five nonfiction. Which titles does *Time* recommend? Fiction choices: Padgett Powell's novel *Edisto,* about a boy's adolescence on a South Carolina island, Saul Bellow's collection of short fiction, *Him with His Foot in His Mouth and Other Stories,* Norman Mailer's unusual murder mystery, *Tough Guys Don't Dance, The Unbearable Lightness of Being,* a look at life under a totalitarian regime by Czechoslovakia's Milan Kundera, and John Updike's fantasy of satanism in modern New England, *The Witches of Eastwick.*

The nonfiction recommendations include Wallace Terry's collection of interviews with twenty veterans, *Blood: An Oral History of the Vietnam War by Black Veterans, Churchill & Roosevelt: The Complete Correspondence,* edited by Warren F. Kimball, Joseph Frank's *Dostoevsky: The Years of Ordeal, 1850–1859,* the second volume in his five-volume study, Susan Cheever's painstakingly honest portrait of her father, John Cheever, *Home Before Dark,* and Evan S. Connell's version of the Little Big Horn disaster, *Son of the Morning Star: Custer and the Little Bighorn.* ▣

Will Manley:

Facing the Public

"Sorry! For tax questions you'll have to ask your local librarian."

It's probably apt testimony to my inabilities as a reference librarian that for the life of me I can't locate an article which I seem to remember reading a year or two ago. It concerned an obscure functionary in the Internal Revenue Service who was awarded either a medal of honor or a citation of commendation by some other federal functionary for saving the government millions (or was it billions?) of dollars.

Even if you didn't see this article, you are, I am quite confident, well acquainted with the way all that money was saved. If you are a reference librarian in a public library you have probably already guessed. That's right, that proudly decorated I.R.S. bureaucrat is the one who decided that public libraries should be the main dumping ground for tax forms and should serve as a community's central distribution point for same.

I suppose we should all be flattered. At least that's what I thought several years ago when the feds began sending us box upon box of form 1040s, Schedule C's, and instruction booklet E's. Along with those massive looseleaf notebooks containing a myriad of laminated reproducible forms that the I.R.S. had so thoughtfully designed specifically for public library use, I figured we'd really be in an excellent position to a) pull in new patrons and b) increase photocopy revenues.

It didn't occur to me at the time that distributing federal tax forms to the taxpayers is not the same thing as distributing federal financial aid applications to high school students. I was too myopic to realize that on the one hand you're helping the government take money out of people's pockets while on the other hand you're helping them put it in their pockets. Rather I figured that going whole hog into distributing tax forms would be a good way to be patriotic without putting on a uniform and shooting at someone. Everybody's always talking about how terrible the federal deficit is and nobody ever does anything about it. Here, it seemed to me, was a perfect opportunity to help our nation out by doing our part in the patriotic process of assisting people to pay their taxes.

Also, for those of us who have been making pretentions about the library being more than just a repository for James Michener, Rosemary Rogers, Janet Dailey, and Louis L'Amour, the income tax thing presented endless possibilities for us to prove our worth as an "Information Center" with professionally trained reference librarians more than eager to turn their attention from simply checking in microfiche copies of the *Wall Street Journal* to attacking difficult financial questions that require a sophisticated knowledge of complex informational resources.

The best aspect of the income tax service, however, was that it seemed utterly utilitarian and so obviously essential. That's where we've always been weak in our defense of the public library. You know how the old song goes at budget time. Cut the police department and you're inviting rape, murder, and anarchy. Cut the street department and you'll need a Sherman tank to get around in the winter. Cut the sanitation department and we're talking widespread cholera. Cut the public library and people will have to go to a bookstore for their daily dose of Janet Dailey. But now the real prospect looms that if you decide to cut the public library our whole tax structure, not to mention the entire federal government, will collapse.

What I didn't figure was that tax forms (any kind of tax forms) from a public relations standpoint are not good to be associated with. For some strange reason the phrase "tax forms" has a connotation of taxes for most people, and if you want to know how people feel about taxes just ask Fritz Mondale. He can give you about fifty-five million reasons why you might not want to be associated with them.

Other than trying to help our reference staff figure out a place to store all the boxes of tax forms, my only connection over the years with our li-

Will Manley *is director of the Tempe (Arizona) Public Library.*

brary's tax reference/distribution service had been, along with thousands of other procrastinators, limited to late night April 15 cramming. Like the typical uninvolved, uninformed, and office-isolated library director I thought that tax form distribution was the best thing to happen to reference services since Constance Winchell descended from the mountaintop with her stone tablets.

If wasn't until I ended up filling in for our reference staff, who had migrated en masse to the Holidome in Peoria (AZ) to be lectured to by Nora Rawlinson, that I clearly understood what income tax distribution/reference service was all about. I naively assumed that it was Nora's wit, wisdom, and flair for the dramatic that had motivated our entire reference staff to go conferencing and leave me holding the bag.

In all due respect, however, to Nora's eloquence it didn't take me long to figure out that their main motivation was to flee (at least for a day) the horrors of our income tax services. To put the situation in its proper perspective, let me add that this occurred during the second week of April on a Friday. Since Friday is normally a very slow day, I was confident that the rustiness of my reference skills brought on by administrative inactivity would not be fatal.

And the first few questions were harmless enough. One older gent had forgotten his spectacles and couldn't seem to locate the card catalog. Another person wanted to know who the Bhagwan Shree Rajneesh was. I quickly found out that he's the Indian mystical leader in Oregon who's taken a vow of silence but not poverty (he owns a fleet of Rolls Royces).

Everything was going unexpectedly well until, like a surprise military attack, the income tax barrage began: "The people at the post office sent me here. Where is form 6251, Schedule G, and the Tax Tables for Form 1040A/EZ?"

"We don't have the actual forms, but we do have a master form that you can photocopy. It's only a dime."

"Photocopy! A dime! You mean I have to pay to get my bleeping tax forms! I have to pay to have the privilege of paying my bleeping income tax. That's adding bleeping insult to injury. That's like being told to print up your own death notice. You I.R.S. people have nerve!"

"I'm sorry, sir. I'm not with the I.R.S. I'm with the Tempe Public Library."

"It's the same thing. You're both bleeping government," and with that impeccable piece of logic he stormed off toward the bleeping photocopier.

Another patron: "I need form 5498. At the bank they told me that you have *all* the tax forms."

"Yeah, I think that's right," I said as I picked up that two-ton binder of a thousand and one tax forms that the I.R.S. sends to librarians. "Let's see, you want form 5498. We've got forms 5329, 5695, and 5884 but no form 5498. You must have the wrong number."

"No, I don't. It says so right here." He showed me a citation from an I.R.S. tax document that said that form 5498 is for "individual retirement arrangement."

"Oh, wait a minute, look at this," I said pointing to a footnote that read: "The following forms are not contained in this kit of reproducible forms because they are specially printed. They may be obtained by sending a self-addressed, stamped envelope to the I.R.S."

"A self-addressed stamped envelope! Do you realize it's April 10 already? I'll never get it back in time. This is horrendous—you people should be sued!"

But my problems didn't end there. Since our reference desk has the word "Information" on it, a surprising number of people assumed I could give them some kind of definitive, authoritative answer on figuring their tax.

For example, a man approached me with the following problem: "Under the terms of our divorce, my wife was allowed to stay in our house for five years and I had to move out. The time is up and I've agreed to let her buy my half. I'm fifty-nine and would normally qualify for the one-time $125,000 capital-gains exclusion on the sale—if I'd also lived in the house for three of the past five years. Can I still claim this exclusion on my income tax return?"

When I said, "Let me show you how to use Prentice-Hall, CCH, or Lasser's so that you will have access to all the information that you'll need to make a logical decision," he got annoyed, angry, and finally outraged. He apparently thought my role was to serve as a government-appointed tax adviser whose instantly made decisions would carry the imprimatur of the I.R.S. and save him the expense of going to H & R Block. "Why do you make tax instructions we can't understand if you're not willing to help us with them?" was his final complaint.

The underlying assumption by the people who came in solely for tax forms throughout this entire painful period was that I was a lackey for the federal government and that the library was tied up in some vague sort of bureaucratic way with the Internal Revenue Service. People tend not to make a distinction between local, state, and federal government. It's all the same free-spending and tax-robbing bureaucratic mess to them.

Personally, I think it's time to tell the feds to get lost. Sure we're saving our country some money, but for all the time and trouble of pandering tax forms how much of the federal budget do we get? We don't even get peanuts; we get the shells. If there's a $250 billion federal deficit it's not because anybody in Washington is throwing money at libraries.

If there's a deficit it's because of the military's overkill complex. If the I.R.S. doesn't want to distribute its own tax forms, then I suggest they delegate that responsibility not to libraries, but to the Army, Navy, Air Force, and Marines. They're the ones who are getting the benefit. If the public doesn't like it, all we have to do is mimic Ronald Reagan of the 1984 presidential campaign by saying: "What tax increase? What deficit?"

Patricia Berglund:

School Library Technology

While some media specialists are yearning for erasable optical disks, the rest of us aspire to having a record player that works. In many districts, this gap between what technology offers and what we use is distressingly large.

California surely must be an exception, you say. The state that's home to Silicon Valley, the birthplace of Hewlett-Packard and Apple Computer—surely the schools there must utilize the latest in electronic learning aids to ensure that the students of today turn into the technologically capable employees of tomorrow. Wrong.

Every California school does have at least one computer, courtesy of Apple, but other equipment is conspicuously lacking. An informal survey of my colleagues in and around San Francisco reveals what I've long suspected: very few schools have videocassette recorders or even color televisions. It's not unusual to find school media centers that don't even have carousel slide projectors.

The lack of VCRs in the schools is particularly noteworthy given the amount of publicity surrounding this communication medium. At ALA's 1984 Midwinter Meeting, Arch Lustberg of the U. S. Chamber of Commerce declared, "Video tape is the greatest teaching tool since the printing press. In fact, it may be an even better tool." Last Christmas, *Time*'s cover story was "VCR . . . the magic box that is creating a video revolution." An article in the September/October 1984 issue of *Instructional Innovator* actually complained that there were too many stories in other journals that described the educational uses of video (particularly interactive video) or concentrated on the functions and capabilities of the hardware. Those subjects are old hat, argued the author, an assistant professor at Ohio State University.

Patricia Berglund *is a librarian in the San Francisco Unified School District.*

Dr. Vladimir Sakovich *in the instructional TV control room*

Old hat it may be on the university level, but the video revolution has yet to penetrate the public schools around here. Many teachers and librarians are still unsure what VCRs are good for in the school setting. Seeking to clarify these issues, I contacted Dr. Vladimir Sakovich, coordinator of instructional television services at San Francisco State University.

Sakovich discussed three main styles of educational VCR use. The easiest and cheapest use is showing instructionally valuable films. It is less expensive to purchase a film on videocassette than on 16mm reels, and it's also easier to store and maintain videocassettes. Additionally, schools may tape programs directly from television for reshowing to their students, as long as they obey copyright laws. These laws are complicated, but Sakovich says they allow a taped program to be played back for students within ten days, viewed thirty-five days after that and then erased. In many cases, educational institutions can, for a fee, obtain licenses to reshow the films indefinitely.

If schools invest in a camera and other peripheral equipment, they can make their own videotapes. Besides the value of having a custom-made product for instruction, public relations, or evaluation, such on-site work provides children with experiences in research and scriptwriting and practice cooperating with a crew. Students also learn standard television techniques.

With a special interface card, a VCR can be married to a computer. This arrangement, known as interactive video, allows the computer to stop the videotape and ask questions to evaluate how well students are learning the material. If the set-up is sophisticated enough, the program will branch to different lessons or repeat unlearned material depending on the student's progress. Potential interactive video users should note, however, that the best systems are now using videodiscs instead of videotapes.

Why are there so many schools without VCRs? Dr. Sakovich has given a lot of thought to this question. "The first people who get new equipment are in the Department of Defense," Sakovich says. "They are the ones who will experiment, and they have the money. Then the military passes it down to business, and last of all it filters down to education."

In the case of instructional video, it has filtered down to colleges and some well-off high schools, but there has been a noticeable lack of support for including it in the educational program of the average public school. Sakovich says that both teachers and parents have resisted its introduction.

Sakovich, the father of a sixteen-year-old son, notices that parents are very upset about the keen competition their children face for jobs and for places in the best schools. "They think the educational answer is to have the child sit in the classroom and do something with a pencil, even if it's a twenty-year-old ditto from McGraw-Hill," he says. "I hear parents saying, 'what these kids need is reading, writing and arithmetic. They shouldn't be watching TV or fooling around with all this equipment.'"

Sakovich admits that there is no clear-cut evidence that instructional video is superior to other methods of instruction. "Out of 500 studies, 250 will say it's better; and 250 will say it's worse. You have to decide what your goal is and what's the best way to achieve it. There are certain things that TV is best for: taking you places, showing you visuals, giving constant stimulation to the easily distracted learner. Computers are better for other things—for math or for things that are routine or tedious."

One point Sakovich is adamant about: machines will never replace teachers. "Some people worry that you will bring in a lot of equipment and replace teachers," he says, "but nothing will take the place of a personal relationship between students and their instructors. You never want to send the student to the learning center and say, 'Watch this tape and then do this assignment' without personal interaction. But as a supplement or complement to your live presentation of the subject matter, it's fantastic to have an outstanding videotape at your disposal."

Other factors work against the use of VCRs in the schools. People teach the way they were taught to teach, Sakovich notes, and older teachers have had no training in video technology. And since few people went into teaching or school librarianship in the seventies and early eighties, there aren't many schools that have staff members with up-to-date audiovisual training.

Too often, public school personnel are overworked and underpaid and don't want to cope with anything additional. "If you are a teacher, you have enough just dealing with those students. It's going to be difficult for you to start learning about the new technology—you're going to be drained. If we come in and say, 'Hey, we're going to get you some TV equipment,' you'll say, 'Oh no, you're not!'" The solution, Sakovich says, is a media specialist outside the classroom to bring expertise and assistance to those who need it.

His insistence on the importance of a non-classroom teacher to help with equipment use is seconded by Joanne Troutner, a pioneer in the use of interactive video and the author of the recent book, *The Media Specialist, the Microcomputer and the Curriculum* (Libraries Unlimited, 1983). Troutner, currently a junior high school librarian in the Tippecanoe School Corporation in Indiana, began developing a series of interactive video programs when she worked for the neighboring Lafayette School Corporation in 1981. Working out of the district's central office, she organized teams from several different schools that included at least one teacher and the school librarian.

Since producing interactive video programs was her only job, she could take the time to learn procedures thoroughly and facilitate the use of the programs by others. Recalling those days, she said, "I knew a little bit about BASIC; but we did not know, any of us, that much about computers. I had a very good team and an excellent consultant from Purdue University to work with; and I had the time during the day to work on things."

Some tasks took more time than others, according to Troutner. "The programming is fairly simple," she says. "When you buy the interface card, they send all the subroutines you need, so all you do is figure what number you need to plug in where, but somebody has to have the time to write the units. Teachers are not going to do it."

Producing her own videotapes was difficult because the pace and editing have to be precise for an interactive program. "I can still remember sitting and looking at this one program for a whole week trying to get it to stop right where I needed it to," recalls Troutner. "I was so sick of that thing." Using commercial tapes produced especially for interactive video saves a lot of time.

Funded by Title IV-C money, Troutner worked on the project for two years and produced a number of units on different grade levels. "I would take the programs and the equipment to the school, and then the teacher would use it; but I transported it, hooked it up, all that. The biggest stumbling block I see in interactive video right now is the fact that, by the time you connect all those wires and everything, the setting up of the equipment looks so threatening to a teacher. Teachers are not going to take the time to do it."

Troutner knows whereof she speaks. The interactive videotapes she worked two years to produce are no longer being used. "They are locked up somewhere," she says. "When there's no one to transport the equipment and hook it up, that's what happens."

Will the promise of VCR teaching technology go unfulfilled for lack of equipment, time, and personnel? California hopes not. The State Department of Education recently decided to spend one million dollars on videocassette recorders for California schools. They also purchased tapes of outstanding public television programs. Jim Fryer, Director of Educational Technology Services, Alameda County Office of Education, is providing copies of these programs to any school, district or county office in the state. Recipients pay only for the cost of the blank tape and a small copying charge.

Sakovich is hopeful about money and personnel: "I'm optimistic about the future because people are talking about education. They recognize the fact that teachers are underpaid, and the support staff is underpaid. They are trying to do something about it. I really look for an upswing. People are going back into educational careers. We'll teach them here at the university about educational video and educational television. They'll take these skills and, if they can be enthusiastic and keep pushing, they'll find a way to get them into schools."

Tom Surprenant:

Future Libraries

"It's the Johnsons brought to you via satellite."

Predictions abound concerning the information millenium, with speculation ranging from the strictly fanciful to a cautious extension and projection of present trends into the future. Trying to predict where the culture is headed at any point in our history has been chancy at best. But, despite all of the problems inherent in attempting to predict the future we continue to try to gain a perspective on where we are now and where we are going. Southern New England Telephone Company sponsored a study by Louis Harris and Associates entitled "The Road After 1984—The Impact of Technology on Society." A total of 1,256 randomly selected adults were interviewed along with 100 members of Congress, 100 science editors, and 100 superintendents of schools. These groups were asked over 150 questions on topics in four categories: information abuse in the computer age, the computer revolution, assessing the consequences of the new technology, and leaders vs. the public. This survey has provided us with current information on how our society assesses the impact of new technologies and their effect on cultural values and norms. The tendency to be optimistic about new technological developments has long been a significant American trait, and the survey showed that this optimism is shared by even the most disadvantaged groups in American society. And this is but one of many insights provided by the survey.

The abuse of information was a major concern of all of those surveyed. There was support from all groups for the enactment of effective federal legislation to deal with the problem. A definite fear was expressed that the government would be able to intimidate citizens in a variety of ways because of the availability of increasingly sophisticated technologies. The monitoring of individual and group activities as well as the erosion of personal liberties were high on the list of feared abuses. Belief in the ease of creating a master file on individuals was prevalent and this was seen as a potential invasion of privacy. There was also concern that some of these files of unknown purpose already exist. Harris provided evidence that those suspicious of these files have grown over the past decade from 44 percent in 1974 to 67 percent in 1983. Specifically, four threats to privacy and freedom were identified as both possible and likely: disclosure of

Tom Surprenant *is director, Graduate School of Library & Information Studies, Queens College, City University of New York.*

damaging facts about individuals, use of confidential information to intimidate enemies of the government, use of closed circuit TV by government to document compromising activities of citizens, and the use of confidential information to take away privacy and liberty. The Orwellian specter of 1984 was raised by the researchers with mixed responses. A majority of the public viewed it as possible, although not likely, that the combination of computerized information and electronic surveillance could control the population under a totalitarian state. The computer was seen as playing a critical role in any information abuses that do, or will, occur.

The results of the survey indicate that the computer revolution is advancing even more rapidly than many have predicted. Of the general public, 45 percent stated that they knew how to use a computer. In some of the leadership groups surveyed the figure went as high as 90 percent. In the overall population 36 percent of the employed used a computer at work, with 60 percent for office workers. When the educational system was examined it was evident that the move towards computer implementation has been considerable. Nearly 40 percent of the households with school age children reported that computers were used in their education. The survey also revealed that, within the next five years, ownership of home computers would reach as high as 50 percent of the general public and 75 percent of some of the leadership groups.

The possibility of the establishment of technological elites was confirmed in the demographic analysis of the survey that showed startling variations by societal subgroups. College graduates were more likely to know how to use the computer than high school grads. The disparities increased when income and profession were examined, with higher income (over $35,000) individuals 44 percent more likely to know how to use a computer than those in the lowest income brackets. Professionals were 38 percent more likely than unskilled laborers to know how to use computers. These same factors were highly related to present and planned future ownership of a home computer. Those on the lower end of the spectrum, in terms of social and economic status, were not as likely to own a computer. It was not surprising that the one key factor related to familiarity with the computer was age. Those in the 18–29 age group were more likely to know how to use a computer than any other age category.

The survey confirmed the general optimism of our society regarding technology. Increased efficiency and productivity were seen as positive results of technological innovation. Those surveyed expressed strong support and approval of technology when it was viewed as enhancing human capabilities. But some serious doubts were revealed. Fear about displacement of human functions was a major concern. If a specific technological development was viewed as a threat to human capabilities it created far less enthusiasm. Most of the polarization in attitude occurred between the use of computers in the factory and in the office. In the latter setting, the introduction of new technologies was viewed in a much more positive way. However, the majority of those surveyed still saw more good than harm coming from science and technology in future years. One important manifestation of this attitude was general support of basic research. Thus, the report concluded that Americans hope for the best from new technologies while, at the same time, seeking remedies from potentially harmful consequences.

It is gratifying to note that the leadership group surveyed seemed to have an accurate perception of public opinion on science and technology, information abuse and privacy. At the same time the leadership group differed from the general public on certain critical issues. Because they know a bit more about science and technology and computers, the leadership group tended to be more optimistic about many of the future developments than the general public. They tended to be less fearful about threats to privacy and freedom. But it is also a relief to note that differences disappeared among all groups when it came to the need for legislative remedies for scientific and technological abuses.

While this survey did not reveal any startling new trends it can still serve to remind librarians of some of the issues that have to be confronted as a result of current technological innovations. Prime among them are the real, and potential, abuses of information by institutions in the society. Since librarians are a key component of the information industry this is a subject of critical importance. The profession must address the fear of information abuse clearly and directly in order to maintain a high level of public confidence. Active participation in the evolution into the silicon culture must also continue. The survey also showed that the computer is going to become an integral part of everyday life for an ever increasing group of people. It is obvious that a new class of clientele is being established which will make many new demands on libraries because of their increased technological sophistication. And the potential for a class of information poor will present similar challenges. To ignore either group is to place the entire profession in peril. Careful attention must also be paid to implementing technology in such a way as as to preserve and enhance the humanistic values of the culture. Librarians can make a major contribution by designing new or improved information systems that serve as models of the proper use of technology. Creative as well as effective leadership is necessary if the library is to survive these times of change. It has to occur at all levels of librarianship and needs to reflect a dynamic, flexible, and concerned approach to the information problems of the society. Hopefully, when another survey is conducted ten years from now significant progress will have been made by both the culture and the library in the improvement of the quality of life in the information society. ▣

Martin Kesselman:

Online Update

"Can you recommend a computer book that's entertaining, exciting, humorous, easy to read, and short?"

Microcomputers have dropped in price and have become widely available so that they are now a common purchase for many. In addition, microcomputer users have taken advantage of low-cost modems and after-hours online services such BRS After Dark and Dialog's Knowledge Index and are taking an interest in doing their own online searching.

To help meet the need for current information on online services and databases, several popular books have appeared on the market during the past year aimed directly at the home end-user market (although librarians will find them useful too). The list that follows is intended as a guide for librarians in making purchase decisions or in suggesting appropriate sources to interested end-users.

• Cane, Mike. *The Computer Phone Book.* New American Library, 1983. pa $14.95. ISBN 0-452-25446-9

Introductory sections explain how to make a computer communicate and provide an overview of online systems, explaining how to use several of them, including Delphi, CompuServe, and Knowledge Index. Most of this book, however, consists of directories of online services with information on hours, costs, access, and available databases for each, and of U.S., Canadian, and overseas bulletin board systems.

• Gilreath, Charles. *Computer Literature Searching: Research Strategies and Databases.* Westview, 1984. $22. ISBN 0-86531-526-4

Whereas the other titles listed are popular in their approach, this is a book geared for the "wired scholar" such as a scientist, graduate student or other serious researcher. The basics of computer literature search systems and how they're indexed and organized as well as the role of the search analyst as a partner to the researcher are discussed. The rest of the chapters deal with searching and databases in agriculture and life sciences, social sciences and education, physical sciences and engineering, business, humanities, arts and architecture, and legal research. A glossary is also included.

• Glossbrenner, Alfred. *The Complete Handbook of Personal Computer Communications.* St Martin's Press, 1983. pa $14.95. ISBN 0-312-15718-5

Glossbrenner's book begins by telling how to get started in telecomputing by choosing modems and communications software. Subsequent chapters cover online services such as the Source, CompuServe, Dow Jones, Dialog, BRS, Orbit, and Newsnet, accessing free computer bulletin boards, shopping and banking online, teleconferencing, and telecommuting. In addition there is a chapter that deals with the technical side of data communications. The appendix discusses troubleshooting, using the Telenet and Tymnet telecommunications networks, and electronic mail. A glossary is also included.

• Hansen, Carol. *A Microcomputer User's Guide to Information Online.* Hayden, 1984. pa $14.95

While not giving much detail on particular databases, this book does provide a good introduction to how online systems work, information available online, and the search process. Information utilities such as the Source and online vendors such as Dialog are treated in some depth with descriptions, and information on subscribing, training, and system protocols. These sections also include some case studies, providing examples of each system's usefulness. Other chapters deal with equipment and communications software, transferring files (uploading and downloading), and software for use with offline files. Also included are a glossary, bibliographies, and lists of database produc-

Martin Kesselman *is life sciences librarian at Bobst Library, New York University.*

ers and manufacturers.

• Howitt, Doren and Weinberger, Marvin. *Inc. Magazine's Databasics.* Garland, 1984. $19.95. ISBN 0-8240-7287-1

Databasics includes a wealth of online information, with a slant toward business-related sources. Part I, "All About the Information Industry," explains the concepts of databases, indexing, database producers, and online systems. It also discusses costs, tips on database searching, and electronic mail. Part II, "A Guide to Selected Business Databases," reviews broad-coverage business databases, general news databases, and databases in other areas such as advertising and marketing, science and technology, and energy and the environment. Part III discusses the database vendors in detail. Part IV reviews the nuts and bolts of using microcomputers for online searching, communications software, and modems. Part V, on online information in the future, includes a look at networking and gateway services, speech synthesis, storage, and knowledge bases. An appendix includes a bibliography, directory of information brokers, and a "smorgasboard" of terminals, communications software, and modems. Coupons for discounts on many online services and products are included as a bonus.

• Lesko, Matthew. *The Computer Data and Data Base Source Book.* Avon, 1984. pa $14.95. ISBN 0-380-86942-X

Lesko's book serves as a comprehensive "road map" to commercial and government databases and public data sources. The first section provides several examples and uses of online databases in fulfilling information needs. Following this brief section, most of the text is a directory of databases arranged alphabetically, divided into sections on commercial and government databases. Each entry includes information on subject, source, contents, inclusive dates, the database producer, the online system(s) on which the file is available, and approximate costs. The Public Data Sources section includes data in both printed publications and computer tapes. Subjects covered in this section include education, energy, economics, health statistics, industry, and population and vital statistics. Lesko also provides advice on requesting and obtaining needed information and data from government agencies.

• McMullen, Barbara and McMullen, John. *Microcomputer Communications: A Window on the World.* Wiley, 1983. pa $14.95. ISBN 0-471-87335-7

Most of the information presented in this book is easily available elsewhere. The volume consists largely of brief listings of public access bulletin boards, access phone numbers for Telenet, Tymnet and Uninet, the CompuServe subject index, and the Dialog blue sheets. An introductory section reviews equipment and communications software, but many of the other titles reviewed here do it much better.

• Newlin, Barbara. *Answers Online: Your Guide to Informational Databases.* Osborne McGraw-Hill, 1985. pa $16.95. ISBN 0-88134-136-3

Newlin concentrates on databases and the information one can expect to get from them. Chapters are devoted to business databases, scientific databases, and news, general information, and social science databases. Each entry includes database contents as well as a sample online record. Newlin also reviews electronic mail, the afterhours service via BRS After Dark and Knowledge Index, full-text services and databases, numeric databases and services, basic and advanced online search techniques, and document delivery. A very nice feature is the chapter on evaluating services and databases.

• Stone, M. David. *Getting On-Line.* Prentice-Hall, 1984. $14.95.

Most of Stone's book deals with preparing to go online, reviewing decisions concerning terminals, modems, and communications software, and putting them all together as well as developing effective search strategies. The rest of the book is a catalog of information utilities and online systems including access, price structure, description, and detailed listings of available databases. Stone's book also includes information on bulletin board services, an overview of videotex, and advice on staying current in the field. ▣

Other titles that may also be appropriate for end-users but were not examined first-hand are:

Edelhart, Mike. *Omni Online Database Directory 1985.* Collier Books, 1985. pa $12.95. ISBN 0-02-079920-9

Haas, Lou. *Going On-Line With Your Micro.* TAB Books, 1984. $17.95, pa $11.95. ISBN 0-8306-0746-3; 0-8306-1746-9

Shafritz, Jay and Alexander, Louise. *The Reston Directory of On-Line Databases: Your Computer Phone Book.* Reston, 1984. $24.95, pa $17.95. ISBN 0-8359-6668-2; 0-8359-6666-6

Stoner, Donald. *Personal Telecomputing.* Compute! Publications, 1984. $12.95. ISBN 0-942386-47-7

Also during the past year, some new periodicals have appeared on the market dealing with online searching for end-users:

Dial-Out. Monthly. $25/yr. Mike Cane, 175 Fifth Ave., Suite 3371, New York, NY 10010.

Link-Up. Monthly. $23.95/yr. On Line Communications, 3938 Meadowbrook Rd., Minneapolis, MN 55426.

Micro Communications. Monthly. $22/yr. Miller Freeman Publications, 500 Howard St., San Francisco, CA 94105.

Modem Notes. Monthly. $24/yr. Katherine Ackerman, Box 408472, Chicago, IL 60640.

Joseph Deitch:

Portrait: James O'Neill

Nothing surprises Dr. James O'Neill about gifts received by presidents. The Assistant Archivist of the United States for Presidential Libraries of the National Archives and Records Service knows that expressions of esteem can range from diamonds and wool socks knitted by solicitous ladies in northern states to portraits of presidents made on typewriters and embroidered flour sacks sent to President Hoover by grateful Europeans for his relief work in their countries after World War I. President Reagan was engulfed by an avalanche of jellybeans early in his first term.

But Dr. O'Neill, whose scholarly discipline is 20th-century American presidents, seemed vastly amused when I noted that President Ford had got a gift of the Declaration of Independence printed in alphabet-soup letters. The typesetter, possibly a chef in a busy diner, did not say how many cans of soup—or pounds of dry letters—it took to do the job, nor could the Campbell Soup Company come up with an estimate. But it did say it was pleased that one of its soups might be on display in the President Ford Library and Museum.

The 198,000 gifts to presidents since Franklin Roosevelt's first term far outnumber books in the seven presidential libraries built for Hoover, Roosevelt, Truman, Eisenhower, Kennedy, Johnson and Ford. A library for President Carter will open next year. Papers of the Nixon administration are in the custody of O'Neill's agency, awaiting the outcome of pre-library litigation. "The fact is," O'Neill said in an interview, "books are not a major component of presidential libraries." They house the "large and complex bodies of historical evidence" known as presidential papers, from casual reflections dictated or jotted down at day's end by Presidents Nixon and Carter, to documents that changed the course of history.

Joseph Deitch *writes for* The New York Times *and other publications.*

The first presidential library, repository for the fifteen million or so papers from the FDR administrations, was opened in 1941 at Hyde Park, New York. O'Neill, who was its director from 1969 to 1971, said that this storehouse alone has provided material for 500 books, the largest book yield of any of these libraries. Some have been bestsellers.

O'Neill with President Ford

O'Neill said that the FDR Library has helped make Roosevelt the most written-about president. Within five years of his death, the vast bulk of his papers was open for research. At that time, in 1950, the papers of John Adams and John Quincy Adams were still closed. And the main part of the Abraham Lincoln papers, in the Library of Congress, had been open only about two years. "There was also no access to the historical material of the principal early 20th-century presidents," O'Neill said. "So the presidential library system has had a tremendous impact on opening documents related to presidents and their administrations. That is why there is so much writing on FDR."

O'Neill said that modern presidential papers tend to be opened within five to seven years after the end of an administration. "That may not sound fast to a journalist, but believe me, to historians, it is very fast."

With 500 books on Roosevelt and his administrations, is there anything left to be told about the man and his years in the White House? "Each generation of historians and other writers looks at a segment of the past with somewhat different perspectives and they may pose new questions or pose old ones in a new way," O'Neill asserted. "I think it unlikely that there will be explosive new facts suddenly appearing about FDR. But there will be new looks at Roosevelt in the New Deal, his diplomacy preceding the war, his decisions as Commander-in-Chief, his place in history. In recent months, there has been a spate of news stories on his role at the Yalta Conference. I thought that was a dead issue. But people want to reexamine it, and rightly so, in the light of a new generation's questions. That will happen to all these presidents."

Are historians using computers and other time-saving systems or are they still combing card catalogs? "It depends on whether the data they look for is in computer form. Quantitative historians have been using computers for some time. They analyze voting patterns in Congress and make similar studies. Then they put data into computers, manipulate it and see what comes out. But for traditional forms of political history, not quite yet. It will happen, however."

Dr. O'Neill does not think the early presidents will get their own libraries. Are their papers too scattered? "No, most of their papers are in the manuscript division of the Library of Congress. The library holds the principal body of papers of the twenty-three presidents who preceded Herbert Hoover, from Washington to Coolidge. Some presidents' papers are not in the Library of Congress, and there is a large variation in the completeness of the documentary record for them."

The early presidencies did not generate the enormous volume of material that has come out of recent administrations, beginning with Franklin Roosevelt. There is a correlation between the activism of a president and the government's role and the quantity of paper produced in his administration. O'Neill sees no indication of separate buildings for 19th-century and pre-FDR presidencies. But there is a presidential library outside of the National Archives, much like the ones that he administers. This is the Rutherford Hayes Library in Ohio. It contains the personal and family papers and the White House files of this one-term president in America's Gilded Age. Hayes was not one of the most active and voluminous chief executives in the archival sense, though major scholarly projects on him make a visit to the library a necessity, especially on civil service reform.

In June, 1984, the House of Representatives approved legislation requiring private interests to share the cost of operating presidential libraries, an expense that has soared more than twelve times beyond original estimates. Currently, private organizers must raise the money to build libraries not donated to the federal government. The Senate has not passed this or related bills. But O'Neill said that presidential libraries may come up again and perhaps pass both houses this year.

Besides seven presidential libraries, O'Neill's agency supervises the Nixon and Carter presidential materials projects, the first in Alexandria, Virginia, the second in Atlanta. The papers of the two former presidents are awaiting the move to library buildings. Access to the first of the Nixon papers, set for 1983, was delayed by a lawsuit by some of the president's former White House aides, which they partly won. This led to further delays and to new public-access regulations issued by O'Neill's office, as required by special legislation on the disposition of the Nixon materials. The government, with authorization by Congress, had seized the Nixon papers—documents, files, and tapes. The presidential libraries system has custody of them and government archivists are processing them.

O'Neill expects new access regulations to be issued in the next few months, depending on what happens if his agency is taken to court again. But he hopes the first block of Nixon material can be opened this year. There is no access to the Nixon White House files as such, although photographs and other non-textual material may be seen.

The materials in the Carter pre-library project includes his files, audiovisual holdings and, for the first time, a significant quantity of machine-readable documents. It will be the first of the libraries in which researchers will use computers to access certain materials. The library will be completed next February and dedicated in the spring.

Asked about new approaches to cataloging in the presidential libraries, O'Neill said there is one innovation in use. Traditionally, presidential archivists depend on "finding aids," also called inventories and registers. They do not lead researchers to individual documents because, unlike a book library, presidential libraries store "staggering quantities" of documents. Finding aids are descriptive and lead to groups of documents in folders. "Think of a file of folders with subject labels on them that have to be looked through for the items you need," O'Neill explained. "We cannot catalog hundreds of millions of individual documents. Archivists have never had the personnel to go beyond the folder level."

A major new development in presidential libraries is the use of computers to prepare and organize finding aids. The first phase of a two-year study has resulted in the installation in all these libraries of "fairly powerful" microcomputers. They are used for word-processing, administrative functions, and to develop finding aids—all leading to easier access to materials.

"Our intent, in the long run," O'Neill said, "is to create an online database made up of all finding aids in all our libraries. It will be accessible from any of the libraries and to other national archives needing information on someone, for example, who served under two or three presidents, like W. Averell Harriman. Other institutions may want to link up with presidential libraries. A researcher using the Ford Library at the University of Michigan would go to a terminal that links up with presidential libraries that have files on Harriman's service to presidents, including oral history interviews. Before the researcher embarks on travel to do that kind of detailed study, he will have the road map well laid out for him."

Local public and university libraries do not have access to presidential libraries "at this stage," O'Neill said. "Not until the computer system to store finding aids is completed. Once it is done, and assuming the researcher or librarians have access to a terminal, they can learn what material is in our libraries and we could make photocopies for them." But presidential libraries rarely deal with local libraries. Their users are historians and researchers for books and articles. "Sometimes they work through university or public libraries, but they usually come to our libraries in person, having written in advance to make sure we have enough material to warrant the trip."

If a researcher only wants two presidential letters, "we can make copies and send them to him." Scholars and book and magazine writers may spend weeks and months in residence in a community close to a presidential library if they are working on major projects. For the first volume of his biography of Herbert Hoover, George Nash lived in West Branch, Iowa, home of the Hoover Library. A Ph.D. student working on a topic in diplomatic history may want to use several federal depositories—the National Archives, the Library of Congress and a presidential library.

"By listing his needs in advance, wc can have material ready for him. He may spend two or three days at our library. If he has a small research fund, he can tell us what he wants and we can mail him the copies after he leaves," O'Neill said.

Many writers work that way, particularly in the recently opened Johnson, Kennedy and Ford libraries. Random browsing for articles isn't feasible in presidential libraries or in an archive as one would in a book collection, because presidential material is stored in boxes, which are brought to the writer. The researcher may then browse through them for article ideas.

Each presidential library lists its holdings. They cover titles and references to individuals, institutions and organizations that have a body of material in a library, including oral history transcripts. Relevant lists are available. The staffs of the libraries usually hold graduate degrees in fields like American history and government. Those with degrees from library schools "do not, by any means, comprise the largest number of our personnel," O'Neill said. The National Archives system operates its own internal training and internship programs. Instruction includes courses and such rotational assignments as work in preservation, processing, and reference duty. At the end of the first year, trainees are promoted to GS 9 and to GS 11—journeyman's level at about $20,000—at the end of the two-year program.

Researchers work with the original documents in presidential libraries. Some files get such intensive use that they wear out. When signs of wear show up, the originals are "retired" and copies are substituted. It is rarely essential that researchers must use the originals. Papers in the FDR, Truman and Johnson libraries have had to be duplicated.

On security, O'Neill said that some documents are valuable "from the monetary point of view." Others are "secured" because they have been pulled from the files and are vulnerable. For a time, depending on the terms of the deed of gift from a former president, documents may be removed from public use to prevent "a real invasion of personal privacy." Use of papers with a national security classification is prohibited.

All of a president's papers go into his library. None may be withheld. They are safeguarded by special security. With a few exceptions, his entire presidential record will be open to public scrutiny.

The libraries have not fully moved into the computer age. The archival field is not as advanced as the library profession in the use of technology, O'Neill said. But it is advancing, and the presidential libraries are among the more progressive in the archival field, he added. The database as master storage for all holdings is progressing. For manuscripts, the libraries are using the MARC format of the Library of Congress. The presidential library system will also become, "in one way or another, part of RLIN, the Research Library Information Network."

At the end of the Reagan administration, Dr. O'Neill's agency will bodily take over the whole of the White House files. No special preparation of the files is needed while Reagan is serving. There is a White House filing manual, a central filing station, and various offices have their own files. No individual is collecting or preparing the files for a presidential library takeover. "We don't operate that way," O'Neill said. "We take over the whole filing operation—there is nothing selective about it."

"The president sees a very small percentage of the paper generated in the White House. A lot of it never gets to his level." If anyone saves papers at the doodle level, it is a staff member close to him. Perhaps the most famous doodling in American history was that done by President Kennedy during debates on the Bay of Pigs. Doodled pages from his yellow pad were saved by his secretary, Evelyn Lincoln, and may be seen in the Kennedy Library. Papers misfiled in the White House—it happens elsewhere all the time—are correctly refiled for posterity by O'Neill staff.

Some presidential papers remain closed, in whole or in part, on grounds of family privacy, especially those on financial matters, and for national security reasons. Unil four years ago, the Roosevelt Library was the most heavily used presidential library. Now it is neck-and-neck between the Kennedy and Johnson Libraries, with the Roosevelt third. This indicates a rush to make use of the libraries to get into print fast with new disclosures.

Gifts received by presidents from foreign officials in their position as head of state automatically, by Constitutional decree, become the property of the United States government. They are logged in at the White House and are earmarked for the relevant presidential library-museum. O'Neill's agency takes custody of them early in a president's administration. It already has possession of a large number of gifts to President Reagan.

Gifts from private citizens belong to the president. He may keep a few as mementos, O'Neill said, but ordinarily they are deeded to the government for display in his library-museum. "We end up with both categories of gifts, but the route to us is slightly different," he said.

The Nixon Library will contain some forty-five million documents—three times the number generated in FDR's three terms. That amount of paper was produced by the copying machine and its ruthless ability to proliferate material, not necessarily by the president but by federal agencies in his administration. It is also an outcome of the sheer growth of government. "If, in Roosevelt's day, you wanted to make a duplicate of a letter or memo, you had to use carbon paper or sit a secretary down and have her type it out all over again," O'Neill said. "The electronic copier has had a powerful impact on the content of presidential libraries." ▣

Donnarae MacCann/Olga Richard:

Picture Books for Children

Excellence and unusual productivity are the norm for a small group of author-illustrators. In the case of Ivan Gantschev and Tony Ross, their output is so consistently creative and multifarious that it is hard to give their work adequate coverage. They are poles apart in terms of goals, but their books highlight the fact that artists can have different motivations, but similar degrees of commitment.

In the Gantschev picture books, technique, subject emphasis, and emotion create a distinctive imagery—a style that makes a Gantschev illustration immediately identifiable as the work of this Bulgarian artist. Three titles published in 1984–*RumpRump, Noah & the Ark & the Animals* (text by Andrew Elborn), and *The Christmas Train*—exemplify his wet-on-wet and free-form technique, with objects from nature in each book an important subject focus. These preferences in method and content are a means to an end, a way to convey warmth, serenity, grandeur, and a deep humanism. Such qualities in his work are as much a part of his trademark as the less subjective features.

Working with such a clear-cut technique and intention, Gantschev gives himself, in one sense, a greater burden than that faced by a more eclectic artist. That is, his visual imagination must not lapse, despite the pressure of producing page after page of scenic beauty, and despite the fact that he is not altering his basic approach. The three books from 1984 illustrate how he performs this feat.

The eponymous hero of **RumpRump** is a friendly bear who is something of a bungler when it comes to finding breakfast. When searching out honey, he disturbs a nest of hor-

From *RumpRump*

nets. When fishing, he "grabbed and clawed and slapped and jumped" to no avail. Eventually he meets someone who shares her garden with rabbits and is hospitable to bears as well. Camaraderie is the simple theme, but how intensified it becomes through Gantschev's tenderness in depicting the visible world.

This illustrator has a remarkable talent for producing nuances in color variations and in the massing of shapes. The soft edges from the wet-on-wet device are delicate, while lines drawn on a drier surface balance this effect with sharper definitions. And by building in and out of the edges when he is using the entire picture space, he suggests an enormous vista. The overall result is a large, strange, magical realm—a place the reader can extend with his or her own visual fantasies.

The free-form shapes that are a hallmark of Gantschev's style are visible in the illustration printed here from **Noah & the Ark & the Animals**. The presence of God in this familiar legend is suggested by two images: the shimmering gray and white ovals with radiating circles in the sky above Noah, and the unexpected bluish shape that is among the sculptural-looking rocks. Noah seems small in this universe of sky and mountains, but he is firmly placed and solidly formed. He can hold his own in this larger environment because Gantschev softens the vindictive element in this tale with the non-threating aura of his technique. And the author of the text, Andrew Elborn, softens this biblical object lesson by adding a frame narrative about a mare and her colt on a rainy day.

The explanatory ("pourquoi") formula is emphasized in this version as the colt learns about rainbows. First he cries: "I think it's going to rain for weeks and weeks, and we'll all be washed away!" This is not an irrational conclusion in the child mind, and after the mare tells the Noah legend, she explains that the rainbow means God is keeping his promise. Then the colt returns to childlike restlessness: "Well, I want to go out now."

The animal portraiture is not entirely successful on Gantschev's part, perhaps because so many diverse kinds of beasts must be brought into the ark. Some he hardly bothers with, some are given a too precious treatment. They blend into his designs in a general way, but they can't be compared with the superb delineation of Noah as he farms, receives God's message, builds the ark, and rides out the storm.

From *Noah & the Ark & the Animals*

The best qualities in the Noah book are present in **The Christmas Train.** Again the environment is depicted as powerful and awesome, and yet there is an impression of security and peace that is in keeping with the

Olga Richard *and* **Donnarae MacCann** *are the authors of* The Child's First Books.

plot, but is also characteristic of Gantschev's whole attitude. The narrative is based on an incident in the life of the author's aunt when she was a child. Her father's job was to protect trains in a mountainous region by watching for landslides. At the conclusion of the story, he gives his daughter a lamb for Christmas, but the essence of this Christmas theme has already been illustrated through action. The lamb is simply an apt symbol for the child's subordination of her own interests and safety. During her father's absence, she has burned her Christmas tree on the tracks to save an oncoming train.

Rounded forms, soft edges, indistinct shapes, and subdued color—these convey the tender "lamb" qualities and a feeling that things will work out. But the lamb as a Christian symbol also connotes strength—the capacity to sacrifice for others—and this dimension is captured not only through the contrast between a small child figure and a "huge, hissing train," but through a careful modulation in the illustrator's style. When the train appears, he designs with more geometric precision. A splendid arrangement of triangles, rectangles, squares, and circles delineates the engine, and the human figures are defined with a similar array of shapes and colors. These geometric improvisations are a creative shift, and yet the engine is a free-form machine and never out of key with Gantschev's mysterious, impressionistic landscape.

As a storyteller, Gantschev is drawing from a range of sources (family lore, natural history, the folk tradition, and so on). As an illustrator, he is drawing upon his training as a masterful graphic technician, and more important, he is invariably making his art responsive to his basic aesthetic.

The British cartoonist Tony Ross illustrates with the same identifiable authority as Gantschev, but in a different mode and for different purposes. He has a comic imagination and a superb sense of theater. The latest Ross book, **I'm Coming to Get You!**, plays the "monster" game of

From *I'm Coming to Get You!*

mock fear and leads into it gradually with lively endpapers and an intriguing jacket. A monster appears to be breaking through the paper cover, and the endpaper design suggests an extraterrestrial theme. The reader is prepared for a spoof about a ghoulish creature who gobbles up a planet inhabited by banana-people, and then heads for earth. As he circles in his spaceship looking for Tommy Brown as his next snack, Tommy Brown is listening to a bedtime story about scary monsters. The suspense for a six- or seven-year-old is almost unnerving as he or she wonders how Tommy can escape the fate of an anthropomorphized banana. But in the last scene it is the monster who trembles. He is scarcely taller than the thick soles of Tommy's sneakers—the brunt of Ross's joke about illusive fears.

Ross works with strong contrasts of light and dark and big and little. He uses many diagonals and varied approaches to perspective. The effect is a sly, ebullient humor. The toy-littered bedroom of Tommy is a satirical comment on suburbia, but the child will find it an amusing place to explore. The partially-eaten banana planet looks like an apple core in the midst of a whole galaxy of monster-nibbled planets. Such images are saturated with energy, and seldom lacking in the sense of control that sustains tension.

Ross's version of **The Three Pigs** offers a huge cast of carefully selected players. And although these players have only supporting roles, we see fascinating and novel types, rather than the same folks in a costume change. A goat plays the bank president with a "securipig" on hand to guard the safe. Assorted birds are hod carriers for the last pig, and numerous streetwise dudes from the animal kingdom are his neighbors. A brief frame narrative was added to the tale to accommodate this array of personalities—that is, Pig and his two friends, Pig and Pig, first live in an apartment and decide to move to the country; in the end the city has sprawled its way into Pig's pastoral haven.

Characters are posed with such spontaneity that the book has the quality of a choreographed performance, rather than a sequence of stills. And despite the longevity of the original Three Little Pigs story, in Ross's version, it is the kaleidoscope of changing environments and city slickers that capture one's interest. Everything is in flux except the last of the three wacky pigs. Change does not seem inherent in his character.

It is hard to think of many cartoonists in recent years who have developed as rapidly as Ross with both a comic touch and a serious design interest. And with respect to pure inventiveness, he is now in the company of such comedic compatriots as Quentin Blake, Graham Oakley, and John Burningham. ▣

Elborn, Andrew. *Noah & the Ark & the Animals.* Illus. by Ivan Gantschev. Picture Book Studio USA, 1984. (A Neugebauer Press imprint; dist. by Alphabet Press, 60 N. Main St., Natick, MA 01760). $10.95. ISBN 0-907234-58-5

Gantschev, Ivan. *The Christmas Train.* Little, Brown, 1984. $12.95

Gantschev, Ivan. *RumpRump.* Picture Book Studio USA, 1984. (A Neugebauer Press imprint; dist. by Alphabet Press) $11.95. ISBN 0-907234-53-4

Ross, Tony. *I'm Coming to Get You!* Dial Books, 1984. $10.95

Ross, Tony. *The Three Pigs.* Pantheon, 1983. $10.95. ISBN 0-394-86143-4 LC 83-2356

Patty Campbell:

The Young Adult Perplex

"The minute you get near a girl you lose your brains. Sometimes I think you boys have your brains in your pants," complains Mrs. Belco bluntly to her son Danny in Harry Mazer's new novel, *Hey, Kid! Does She Love Me?*

"In case you're wondering why I decided to write a book, all I can tell you is that I'm seventeen years old and for the last three years I've probably spent an average of 47% of each day thinking about sex," writes Scott Tauscher in Todd Strasser's *A Very Touchy Subject.*

"It's hard enough to find someone who'll do it with you, let alone someone you can love," moans Mike Petrino in Peter Filichia's *A Matter of Finding the Right Girl.*

Clearly, young males have a different perspective than young females on the search for love and romance. And a different set of goals and standards. These three recent books have set out to explore the hard life of being young, male, and horny—distinctly a minority point of view in a literary field that is dominated by feminine perceptions of romance. The twittering heroines of the paperback series might be roundly shocked to discover the thoughts that lie behind the warm blue eyes and cute smiles of their broad-shouldered objects of adoration.

In the past, teachers and librarians—a predominantly female group—have also had negative reactions to YA novels that attempted to be realistic about the thoughts of sex-starved adolescent boys. The tendency to perceive girls as collections of interesting body parts, while attributable to high hormone levels, is not easily understood or forgiven by women. It is also a tricky stylistic problem for the writer to give the impression of genital preoccupation without resorting to a parade of overwhelmingly graphic images. All of this has had a chilling effect on novels of teenage male sexuality, but with these three perceptive and funny books that chill seems to have melted.

Patty Campbell *teaches young adult literature at UCLA and is a library consultant and freelance writer. She is currently at work on a book about YA novelist Robert Cormier.*

Each of the protagonists is seventeen going on eighteen, which makes for a very different situation than, say, a thirteen- or fourteen-year-old with sex on his mind. Each feels that everyone else is Doing It, and that he is the last male virgin left in the western world. Each feels driven by his hormones and is embarrassed and guilty at his compulsion to sneak peeks and cop feels. In a post-feminist age, sensitive young men know better, but they still feel like it. Each has a sexually experienced best friend who eggs him on in his quest for a willing female body and disparages his search for a congenial female person. None of the three has anyone he can really talk it over with. As Scott says, "If you're a guy and you talk to other guys about sex, they either don't know the answers or they just BS you to death. And forget about parents and teachers. This may make a lot of adults mad, but frankly I think you'd have to be an absolute nerd to sit down and discuss the intimate aspects of your life with your biology teacher or someone." So they muddle through, groping in an obscuring fog of lust toward a glimmering of understanding of love and relationships.

The dynamics of this universal masculine problem are most clearly laid out in **A Matter of Finding the Right Girl.** Mike and his best friend Wally three years before made a Vow—a solemn promise that by the time each was eighteen "he would get it or would die trying." Now Wally has already achieved the objective, but for Mike, two weeks before his birthday, it is T minus 335 hours and counting. He has set his calculator watch for the countdown, and as the minutes and hours tick by his search for the right girl grows more desperate. He really likes red-headed Leslie, who works beside him at Zella's Superette. They have fun together and are good friends, and besides, he can't help noticing her nice breasts. But Leslie is going with someone else, so Mike dates Corinne (who on their third date tells him she has decided to become a nun) and then little Rochelle Twombley (whose reputation for easiness turns out to be based on one pathetic incident). At last with only three hours, twenty-nine minutes, and thirty-five seconds left to go he "gets it" in the back seat of his car with Susan, an angry girl who is bent on getting back at her parents for uprooting her from her beloved Wyoming. It isn't as great as he'd expected. In fact, it's pretty mechanical, and Mike, in a neat switch on the usual way of the world, has the distinct impression he's been used. For a while he worries that he might even be gay, until his Uncle David, who *is* gay, reassures him: "My guess is that you're going to feel a lot better about making love when you make love with someone you love." It looks like this is going to turn out to be gloriously true when Leslie breaks up with her boyfriend and she and Mike discover that their friendship has laid the basis for some very satisfactory passionate caring.

Filichia treats this story with refreshing humor and honesty. He treads delicately in the areas of graphic sex and sexual language: there is very little here explicit enough to offend cautious librarians. Minor faults are the occasional awkwardness that comes from his use of the present tense and one or two clumsy shifts of voice. More careful editing would have been appropriate. Although Fawcett Juniper is to be commended for an original title of such quality, it is a pity that a book this good will not have the longer shelf life of a hardcover printing.

A Very Touchy Subject by Todd Strasser is a bit slicker, but the conflict is the same. "Sex alone isn't a good enough reason to be interested in someone," says Scott Tauscher, sounding like a sex ed manual. "You should enjoy being with her, you should like and admire and respect her, you should feel some kind of emotional caring that's different from your desire to jump in bed with her." Scott is sophisticated enough to know the right attitudes, but it's hard for him to remember them when his longtime girlfriend, wealthy Alix, continually refuses to have sex, for no special reason (it seems to him) except that she wants to exercise the right to refuse. In the vacuum he finds himself reluctantly attracted to his fifteen-year-old neighbor Paula, mostly because he knows she has a lover and therefore (by male teenage logic) is available for sex. But Paula is a waif,

and Scott finds himself unwillingly drawn into helping her deal with her alcoholic mother and abusive boyfriend. When his romance with Alix dies of malnutrition he finds that he has become Paula's friend and has grown past his desire to exploit her for sex (although he makes her promise never to tell his buddies that he has passed up the Golden Opportunity).

Hey, Kid! Does She Love Me? is more sentimental—a touching story of a young man's unrequited grand passion for an older (but not much older) woman. Jeff Orloff more than anything wants to become a film director. Two years ago, when he was a sophomore and she was a senior, he was smitten with Mary Silver's acting talent but never got up the nerve to speak to her. Now she is back in town—with a baby—and living at the boardinghouse run by his best friend's mother. Jeff plots and schemes to get near her, and eventually does break through her prickly defensiveness to win her trust and that of her adorable baby Hannah. But all his romantic daydreams come to nothing against Mary's cool determination to stay just friends. Distressed at her abandonment of her acting career, he persuades her to try for a scholarship to a weekend acting workshop. Mary wins, and Jeff offers to care for Hannah, privately planning to hand the baby over to his mother. But his parents have arranged to be out of town that weekend, and Jeff finds himself singlehandedly (in one of the funniest passages in all of realistic YA fiction) taking care of a squalling, diaper-filling, utterly charming baby girl for four endless days. Fantasies sustain him of Mary falling into his arms (and bed) with gratitude. Eventually he gets pretty good at the job of baby-tending and begins to feel a new emotion of tenderness for the bossy little creature in his care. And he begins to understand the life-changing demands that women accept when they decide to bear a child. "Maybe it's a good thing men don't get pregnant. We're too selfish to have babies. I am, anyway," he muses, in a striking monolog. "Now, in a just world, pregnant women—pardon me, pregnant persons—would have time off for good behavior, check out of the scene when it got to be too much." Finally Mary returns, aglow with new plans and opportunities, and although she is grateful, she makes it plain that they are still no more than friends. Jeff's fantasies die hard. For a while, even after she has left town to live with a young theater troupe, he clings to hope. Only after he has punctuated the end of the romance by getting drunk, wrecking his friend's truck, and spending a night in jail is he able to get on with his life and let his passion for Mary be transformed into the same tenderness he feels for Hannah. Mazer, with his usual mastery, has written an amusing and sensitive novel anatomizing the varieties of love. ▣

Filichia, Peter. *A Matter of Finding the Right Girl.* Fawcett Juniper, 1985. 199 p. $2.25. ISBN 0-449-70107-7 LC 84-90923
Mazer, Harry. *Hey, Kid! Does She Love Me?* Crowell, 1985. 224 p. $12.50; lib. ed. $11.89. ISBN 0-690-04275-2; 0-690-04276-0 LC 83-45054
Strasser, Todd. *A Very Touchy Subject.* Delacorte, 1985. 183 p. $14.95 ISBN 0-385-29378-X LC 84-16963

Kathleen Maio:

Murder in Print

About a year ago I reviewed the first Benny Cooperman novel by Howard Engel and suggested that he and Ted Wood represented new hope for the Canadian mystery. A Canadian reader later chastised me for not mentioning Eric Wright. Mea culpa, that *was* a grave oversight. As the most pleasant bit of penance possible, let me draw attention to Eric Wright's **Smoke Detector** (Scribner's, 1984, $12.95). This is the second appearance of Wright's police sleuth, Charlie Salter of the Toronto police, and a further indication that Wright is one of the most exciting voices in the police procedural field today.

Charlie's career is still stalled when he is given the chance to temporarily help out the overextended homicide squad and tackle an arson and murder case involving a fire at an "antiques" shop. The shady owner died in the fire, and Salter must sift through the rubble and a score of the owner's customers, lovers, and associates to crack the case.

Wright has written a tightly plotted and fairly clued mystery. Like Charlie, we wonder how an elusive old Japanese, interned during World War II, fits into the puzzle. We are likely to follow the same red herrings, too. Wright handles a suspense storyline with the best of them, but that is not his greatest gift.

Wright focuses on the man, Salter, and his relationship with his family and society. When Charlie worries about his health, or wonders how to deal with his son's discovery of skin magazines, we too want to hear the urologist's verdict and Charlie's awkward fatherly counsel. We know how the hassle of a simple household repair can complicate our lives for days, and become involved with his search for a screen door part almost as much as his search for a killer.

Is all this extraneous? I think not. Like the much missed team of Sjöwall and Wahlöö, Wright is interested in more than whodunit. He cares about the life of a good if buttoned-down guy living in Toronto today who happens to be a cop, and makes us care too.

Not every mystery writter seeks to study modern society. **Death in a Deck Chair** by K. K. Beck (Walker, 1984, $12.95) is an unabashed throwback. Set in 1927, this shipboard puzzle features young and lovely Iris Cooper as heroine and sleuth.

The trouble with nostalgic mysteries is that they are so hard to pull off. The characters and dialogue here are stilted and unnatural. Ladies "twitter"; they wave to and greet one another "gaily." And just in case we've forgotten what era we're in, a matron will examine "her blue marcelled coiffure critically."

The fact that the plot revolves around the lost prince of a miniscule European country and dastardly schemes against him by a group called the "Comrades of the New Dawn" doesn't help. I found *Death in a Deck Chair* neither believable nor entertainingly campy. Cozy fans who wish a wholesome night's reading may feel differently. But I'd suggest re-reading Christie's *The Secret Adversary* for real period enjoyment.

If I found Beck's first mystery a trifle dull, I found another more than a little offensive. **Embrace the Wolf** by Benjamin M. Schutz (Bluejay Books, 1985, $13.95) introduces us to a hardboiled detective named Leo Haggerty. Leo is hired by a woman to find her husband, who has disappeared on a manhunt for the psychopath who abducted their twin daughters five years earlier. Haggerty eventually tracks hunter and prey to North Carolina where the plot climaxes in a dramatic, ludicrous scene of deep-sea violence.

In fact, violence seems to be the only thing Schutz can write about. He creates a world where women and children are tortured, battered victims and men are either weak or intensely vicious. In Schutz's story we do not meet one psychopath or sicko: we meet at least a half dozen. When Haggerty stops in a Carolina bar to use the rest room there is, of course, a gang-bang in progress. This complication provides a chance for a sub-

Kathleen Maio *is a freelance writer based in Somerville, Massachusetts. She has contributed to* Twentieth Century Crime and Mystery Writers, Murderess Ink, *and numerous magazines.*

plot with more episodic violence perpetrated by examples of that classic stock character, the Southern redneck neanderthal.

I worry about a hero who, when interviewing a vice king, flashes back on a nun from school days, concluding his thoughts with "You heartless cunt." I worry too about an author (a clinical psychologist we are told) who displays some talent but buries it under a mountain of excessive violence and human degradation.

One does not have to live in the gutter to be a tough guy. Loren D. Estleman proves that in **Sugartown** (Houghton Mifflin, 1984, $13.95). Amos Walker's new adventure opens with an ironic twist on the classic scene of the beautiful dame entering our hero's office. Martha Evancek is a beauty, of sorts—a very old, physically disabled, yet fiercely proud Polish immigrant—who wants to find her grandson, the sole survivor of a domestic murder/suicide tragedy some nineteen years earlier.

Walker eventually finds himself searching for a missing jewel-studded crucifix as well as the long-lost grandson. The search forces him to untangle old crimes as he stumbles over fresh corpses. There are bizzare elements to the plot (e.g., Walker held a drugged captive by a mad collector and his malodorous goon), but these cannot blemish the basic credibility of Estleman's story. Estleman writes so well of the threadworn respectability of working people stranded on the edge of an urban wasteland. His vivid and merciless descriptions of the revitalized Detroit root his complex story in reality.

Walker is all a tough guy p.i. should be with his superhuman talent for the cheap comeback line and his sex appeal that works well, but not in lasting relationships. Estleman's Amos Walker series remains one of the best the hard-boiled field has to offer.

Someone equally good in a completely different mystery format is June Thomson. Her tenth mystery, **Sound Evidence** (Doubleday/Crime Club, 1985, $11.95), while not her strongest, shows her talent for the hybrid formula mixing police procedure with psychological suspense and a touch of the golden age puzzle. Detective Chief Inspector Rudd becomes especially eager to find the murderer of a young hood when he discovers that his victim's gang is implicated in a cop killing. The hoodlums are gay, as is a sympathetic bureaucrat involved in the plot by his young lover.

Meanwhile Rudd has developed a crush on the new woman pathologist, bringing to mind Jonathan Ross's similar alliance. The inspector may be an awkward beau, but he remains a highly effective sleuth. And Thomson's observations of the Essex and Suffolk countryside enrich her story of human folly and dishonor among thieves.

Also in the police procedural line is Mark Hebden's **Pel and the Bombers** (Walker, 1985, $12.95). Although Hebden has written several novels about his Burgundian police inspector, this is the first I've read.

There is certainly enough going on in this novel. Pel and his squad are faced with the murder of a young boy, the shooting of a farm wife, and the massacre of several policemen by a group of radicals who may be planning to blow up the French president. Despite all that, I often found myself losing interest.

Hebden never gave me a feel for his Burgundy locale except perhaps in the xenophobia expressed in his pages. The police decentralized hero has worked well for writers like Ed McBain, but is less successful with Pel and his numerous sergeants. *Pel and the Bombers* is a competent police procedural, but one with little beyond an active story line to recommend it.

A well-realized milieu is a requisite for a good mystery, but it can also create problems. Take the case of Laura Munder's maiden mystery, **Therapy for Murder** (St. Martin's, 1984, $13.95).

Sara Marks is a recently qualified Ph.D. and family therapist who enjoys her new career and life until one of her young female clients falls from a bridge to her death. The police say suicide. Sara isn't so sure, especially since the girl has died soon after breaking up with one of the center's disturbed (and sometimes violent) male patients.

The mystery focuses on the two families involved and on the mental health professionals working to heal them and solve what turns into a multiple murder plot. The problem is that, as with therapy, nothing happens quickly in Munder's novel. The first death doesn't occur until the tenth chapter and the entire action takes a full year. Moreover the jargon-hurling and psychologizing will alienate many readers. But for those who are willing to accept that one of the greatest mysteries is how the family organism with its delicate system of love, hate, dependence, and misery survives, *Therapy for Murder* should prove very satisfying.

On the comeback trail is a new edition of Dilys Winn's **Murder Ink** (Workman, 1984, $9.95 paper). Although I could do without some of the cutesy new touches, like a scratch 'n' smell tea spill inside the front cover which ties in to a mystery "book within a book," I welcome many of the new essays. These include Martha Grimes on the British mystery, Eric Wright on the Canadian mystery, Joseph Hansen on homosexuals in mystery fiction, and John Leonard on William F. Buckley's Blackford Oakes thrillers.

The many new contributions and the easier to handle (and shelve) trade paper format makes the new *Murder Ink* a worthwhile purchase.

Judith Trojan:

Front Row Center

Before Jane Fonda mounted her fitness crusade against fat thighs, she denounced the exploitation of pink-collar workers in **Nine to Five.** As naive divorcée Judy Bernly, Fonda and her co-stars, Dolly Parton (sexy Doralee Rhodes) and Lily Tomlin (efficient Violet Newstead), literally hogtie their boss, Franklin Hart, Jr., played by Dabney Coleman. In a riotous role reversal, the women stand in as Hart's surrogates and initiate widespread improvements in their office. They manage to increase morale and productivity tenfold by eliminating sex discrimination and harassment. Although their alcoholic rehabilitation program, daycare facilities, flextime and job sharing for working mothers, and new salary policies bring Hart unprecedented kudos, the three protagonists are indirectly rewarded when he is ordered to implement "his" modern ideas at a new plant in Brazil. In true Hollywood fashion, Hart is kidnapped by some "headhunters," and never heard from again.

By fulfilling the fantasies of every exploited secretary who's ever dreamed of strangling her chauvinist boss, *Nine to Five* provides a giddy catharsis. Unfortunately, this celluloid fantasy has little in common with real life. Thousands of women slave away in pink-collar "ghettos," with no hope of positive change—women like Violet, who devote many years to a firm in order to win a promotion, only to be passed up by the young men they helped train; or Doralee, whose well-endowed figure makes her the object of sexual harassment and innuendo.

Judith Trojan *is editor-in-chief of* Sightlines *magazine, editorial coordinator at the Educational Film Library Association, and a staff member of the American Film Festival.*

While *Nine to Five* awards some measure of comeuppance, in reality women continue to be second-class citizens in the workplace, and pink-collar jobs remain bastions of inequity, sexism, and servility. Several current documentaries address these issues seriously, noting the frustrations as well as some channels for change.

On first look, Laura Sky's half-hour film, **Good Monday Morning,** portends to be a whining, self-serving catalog of feminist, workaday woe. Not so. The film spotlights some articulate, young Canadian women who have such valid complaints as wage discrimination, mindless drudge work, hazardous working conditions, oppressive management, and little or no chance for advancement. Even the promise of new technologies has soured.

From *Good Monday Morning*

A hoped-for avenue for advancement, computers have ironically pushed these women further back into the Dark Ages. Bookkeepers and high-level secretaries are being relegated to the basement to sort old files and records for keying into new computer systems. As these women are caught in an endless chain of sorting, collating, stapling, and keying, men are being trained for the advanced computer jobs. This mind-dulling phenomenon is called "de-skilling."

VDTs are a more insidious threat to women of child-bearing age. Emitting low levels of radiation, VDTs pose a real danger to fetuses. In a shocking sequence, one new mother laments the hours she spent working on a VDT while pregnant. Her child was subsequently born with blind eye (microopthalmaya). A relatively high number of birth defects were found in her co-workers' children as well.

Another young mother shows off her healthy baby, and recalls how she fought management for a job off VDTs during her pregnancy. Initially given a pay cut, the woman took her case to final arbitration and was awarded her original salary. These two mothers agree that during future pregnancies, if not given transfers off VDTs they will quit their jobs rather than risk hurting their unborn children.

Motherhood also suffers indirectly from the emotional drain of monotonous, exploitative jobs. A single mother describes her growing activism in the workplace. She justifies her fight for equal rights and better pay as a legacy for her young daughter. One woman resents bitterly the damage her boring job has on her relationships with her child, husband, and close friends. Her self-esteem can't rise above the degrading sameness of her job.

A final sequence profiles several female aeronautics workers who staged a strike against an unsatisfactory government pay raise. Since many of these women were originally anti-union and apolitical, their newfound pride is an inspiration, reminding one of the travails beautifully documented in **The Willmar 8,** Lee Grant's award-winning film profile of eight women who staged a historic strike against a Minnesota bank for its discriminatory practices.

Female exploitation is ironically addressed in **Yes, Ma'am,** Gary Goldman's documentary about black housemaids in the enclaves of upper class New Orleans. In this hothouse environment, the patronage system is still a viable but dusty reminder of Old South plantation life. Longtime, live-in black retainers cook, clean, and raise generations of rich kids (their "blue-eyed children") for a secondhand share of the good life. Elderly maids, who have served generations of one family in the "mammy" tradition for forty or fifty years, recollect the many kindnesses bestowed upon them as a result of their devoted service. Their employers reply in kind, pampering their servants like royalty especially for the camera. But it soon becomes evident that this mutual admiration society has its limits. With few exceptions, the "blue-eyed children," now young adults, talk about their maids in patronizing tones. "Even a child knows how to love a maid," cracks one young woman. Another belle shamelessly professes her love for "genuine" mammies, but recalls her disbelief when her maids wouldn't join the civil rights movement to better themselves. Intercut with these often crass remarks are the sincere and loving reflections of the elderly maids who coddled and amused these pampered darlings into adulthood.

Goldman contrasts these fading servants with a new generation of black maids who unionized in 1973 and now call themselves "household technicians." These women perform household chores and child care duties for various employers, from whom they are careful to maintain their personal distance. It is clear from interviews with these workers that no young black woman will ever again work solely for the joys of service to a "fine" family. Insistence on market value wages, health and retirement benefits, and professional respect are the keys to their new savvy.

Although *Yes, Ma'am* appears somewhat jumbled and lacks clear identification of its cast of characters, it makes some fascinating comparisons between the attitudes held by the old and new breed of household workers. As such, the film gives unique perspective to woman's eternal role as servant—on the job, at home.

Before Congress passed the Pregnancy Discrimination Act in 1978, pregnant women faced stiff job discrimination. Women with children who worked outside the home were often considered to be temporary workers. Badgered into taking early maternity leave with no disability benefits or job security after giving birth, many quit their jobs early in their pregnancies rather than suffer the stress of fighting for their jobs and benefits. The Pregnancy Discrimination Act went into effect in April 1979, making it illegal for employers to discriminate against pregnant workers in hiring, firing, seniority, or benefits.

Judith Pomer's **Pregnant But Equal: The Fight for Maternity Benefits** outlines women's rights under the law, and takes a brief look at specific cases won and lost by women in a union shop in Cincinnati. The videotape also catalogs the pre- and post-history of the act (it was made possible by the passing of the Civil Rights Act in 1964), and the hidden agendas that many firms still use to stifle it. In the Cincinnati factory, for example, the act was poorly promoted in benefit packages to female workers, hence many women didn't know they had any rights when they became pregnant. And since doctors are often averse to handling the excessive paperwork involved in substantiating requests for early maternity leave with disability or requests to take on less strenuous jobs, they may refuse to acknowledge a woman's claim. The Cincinnati women recall a twenty-four-year-old co-worker, subject to fainting and with a history of high blood pressure, whose doctor would not back up her request for early maternity leave with disability. Instead of changing doctors, she worked at her demanding factory job through her eighth month of pregnancy. She died after giving birth.

An information-packed tape, *Pregnant But Equal* will be useful as an educational tool at union meetings and for women's groups in business and industry to apprise female workers of their rights under the law. This, like the other films reviewed above, will encourage women to know their rights and to fight for them in the proper channels. All the films and tapes are suitable for senior high, college, and adult audiences of working women and their employers. Labor studies classes in schools and universities and general audience programs dealing with work-related issues will also find these films informative. ▣

This month's films:

Good Monday Morning. 16mm & video. color/b&w. 30 min. 1982. Director: Laura Sky. Dist: Fanlight Production, 47 Halifax St., Boston, MA 02130. 16mm—$500 (rental $50). Video—$435 (rental $50).

Nine to Five. 16mm. color. 110 min. 1980. Director: Colin Higgins. Screenplay: Colin Higgins and Patricia Resnick. Cast: Jane Fonda, Lily Tomlin, Dolly Parton, Dabney Coleman, and Elizabeth Wilson. Released by 20th Century–Fox. MPAA rating: PG. Dist: Films Inc., Inc., 1144 Wilmette Ave., Wilmette, IL 60091. Rental: $100.

Pregnant But Equal. video & 16mm. color. 24 min. 1982. Director: Judith Pomer. Dist: Icarus Films, 200 Park Ave. S., Suite 1319, New York, NY 10003. Video—$240 (rental $45). 16mm—$415 (rental $45).

The Willmar 8. 16mm & video. color. 49 min. 1980. Director: Lee Grant. Producers: Mary Beth Yarrow and Julie Thompson. Dist: California Newsreel, 630 Natoma St., San Francisco, CA 94103. 16mm—$700 (rental $75). Video—$600 (rental $75).

Yes, Ma'am. 16mm & video. color. 48 min. 1981. Director: Gary Goldman. Dist: Filmakers Library, Inc., 133 E. 58th St., Suite 703A, New York, NY 10022. 16mm—$700 (rental $65). Video—$600.

Bruce Pollock:

On Record: Popular Music

In the fractionalized world of rock radio East is East and West is West and never the twain shall meet except on MTV, or CHR, which is the new name for good old Top 40. To translate, where once, in the heyday of the Beatles, rock was a generic term for everything from Leonard Cohen dirges to the bubblegum of the Monkees, now the word hardly explains anything at all. On the airwaves rock is dead. It has been replaced by New Music (which used to be New Wave and Punk), Urban Contemporary (which used to be Disco, which used to be R'n'B), Heavy Metal, AOR, Lite, Power Pop and Golden Oldies. If you want to hear a certain sound you switch to the station in your area carrying that sound and only that sound—and two or three spins ought to be enough to tell you what sound a station is featuring on the current rating sweep. MTV and CHR are a little different—they will play the hits, no matter what race, creed or musical labels they carry. Of course, for those with even a pinch of taste, the hit single is a musical label itself—sometimes more limiting than any of the others mentioned above.

Other forms of music do exist in the eighties—contrary to popular belief—among them punk/folk, hip-hop, rap, pop/metal, pop 'n' roll, funkabilly, Outlaw Country, EOR, and Dance. And there are stations that sample each, but you have to manage to catch these specialized, once-a-week shows.

But the point for a true music fan is that there's no radio that simply samples the best of the month's new releases, regardless of the package, and that plays songs as songs regardless of the format of the music or the track record of the group. The only way that such music could be played with regularity is to create a format large enough to encompass all these wonderful sounds, and yet narrow enough for potential advertisers to feel they were getting their money's worth.

As difficult and idealistic as such a proposition may sound, I believe I have come up with this format. I call it Middle of the Dirt Road.

Far from being a replay of the excesses of the sixties, where Ravi Shankar's sitar nestled down with the likes of Ginger Baker for a thirty-seven-minute drone session, Middle of the Dirt Road would be consistently clean and classy. No one could accuse it of catering merely to the sixties intelligentsia, although, of course, those musical veterans would be among the first to pick up on and then flock to its signal.

Here's why: of all the musical generations since the inception of rock, those who came of age during the reign of the Beatles (circa 1964–1973)

John Fogerty at bat

Bruce Pollock *is the editor of* Guitar *magazine and the author of* Popular Music: An Annotated Index of American Popular Songs, Volumes 7 and 8.

were the most diverse in their taste, the most musically well-read; they understood rock at its farthest extremes, could listen as well as dance—and dance as well as listen. They dug the Velvet Underground and Creedence Clearwater Revival, The Fugs and the Beach Boys and Otis Redding, the Mothers of Invention, Rufus Thomas and Buffy Sainte-Marie. Not to belabor the obvious (and not to get too painfully nostalgic), but it was that diversity which formed a generation's taste—upon a foundation of soul and Top 40, folk/rock and psychedelia. Which is not to say that any of the above forms of music ever died. In fact, they are all quite healthy, with new practitioners redefining their genres even as Tom Rush pushes his records via ads in *The New Yorker* and New York deejay Pete Fornatale recreates his progressive playlist from 1968.

No, the answer is not an updated oldies format. Middle of the Dirt Road would have a library of artifacts, to be sure: Richie Havens, Ritchie Blackmore, Buffalo Springfield, Janis Joplin, Janis Ian. But, for the most part, MODR would focus on brand new stuff. In the mold of the old, maybe, but if so only because that mold is too good to be broken. Are you going to throw away the Roche Sisters just because they sport folkie harmonies and beatnik slouches? Lou Reed is singing and writing better than ever, many people feel. Bob Dylan has returned to at least a shadow and a half of his former self. But you've got to include Big Country in all of this, and in the same breath U2, Talking Heads, Los Lobos, Joe Ely, Steve Morse, and Triumph. There's a smattering—more than a smattering, actually—of every format on the boards today that could qualify for Middle of the Dirt Road. These are the songs with just a little more depth, more soul, a touch of class, with hooks a bit more irresistible than the rest. This is music with a past, like the country song "Good Old Boys Like Me," sung by Don Williams, which contains the line: "Those Williams boys sure meant a lot to me/Hank and Tennessee." This would be a format for music fans who are familiar with those two Williamses—and the Elvis Sun sessions, Buddy Holly, Sonny Boy Williamson, Muddy Waters, the early Stones, vintage Kinks, the late great Marvin Gaye, the Shirelles, the Dovells and the Bonnies, Raitt and Koloc. Living in the present, this format would not discriminate against the guitar or the synthesizer, Cyndi Lauper or Huey Lewis (Duran Duran might be another story). It is, at last, a format for the rock connoisseur, who is surely doomed in a marketplace that favors trash over taste, the paperback romance, the TV Movie of the Week. And yet in a society as diverse as ours there's always the odd "Hill Street Blues" that breaks through.

Finally, as the generation that discovered the Beatles and was in turn discovered by the Beatles gets older, and as musicians influenced by the Beatles and all the music that followed for about a decade continue to ply their trade, the generation and the music will constitute an inevitable marketplace. Middle of the Dirt Road: it's only a matter of time.

An MODR candidate

John Fogerty. *Centerfield* (Warner Brothers 25203-1)

In the meantime, we'll have to be content to catch the occasional cut from albums like this, wherever and whenever they pop up on commercial radio. Fogerty, erstwhile leader of the late great Creedence Clearwater Revival, has come up with a package, after a decade off to test the waters, of medium-rock, medium-backwoods, medium-tempo tunes, designed to fit some formats, if not to show off the artist at the top of his game.

Using Fogerty's own metaphor of himself as a ballplayer on the comeback trail, as delightfuly espoused in the title ditty, Bayou John has only lost a step or two since the glory days. "I Saw It on TV" and "Vanz Kant Danz" (the latter about a pocket-picking pig, the former a rock equivalent of the Peter Sellers film *Being There*) are nearly as good as anything from his heyday—and that's pretty damn good. On "Searchlight," especially, the old gritty swamp-soul voice is back in force; on "Mr. Greed," the ear for injustice that gave us "Fortunate Son" and "Bad Moon Rising" is tuned in once again. Yet overall there is a tone of acquiescence (befitting his advanced years perhaps) that's years removed from the fierce and pungent essence of Fogerty's Creedence days. Perhaps to fit in with the sound of today, he's had to mellow out, explain himself a bit too much. The album is very nice, as far as it goes. On the new MODR format, guys like Fogerty would be allowed to really cut it loose. ▣

Gail Pool:

Magazines

These are challenging times for those ill at ease with technology. Even if we hadn't been told a thousand times that we're in the midst of a technological revolution, the message could hardly have escaped us. Whether we're struggling to master the new equipment at the office or trying to assess the feasibility of the president's "star wars" concept of defense, we have become increasingly aware that technological developments, despite the term's abstract sound, have down-to-earth implications which we had all better understand.

For those not drawn to technology for its own sake but concerned about its implications for human affairs, I recommend a magazine called **Technology Review.** *Technology Review* is not "technology made simple." Nor is it a guide to "how things work." Rather, it is a "thought magazine," more akin to *The Atlantic* than to *Byte,* which examines technological issues for the intelligent reader, placing them within the context of social, political, and economic affairs.

Technology Review, for example, does not merely describe how cable television works; rather, its series of articles explored the implications of cable. It doesn't rave about the capabilities of the latest computer or the hottest new software. But it has discussed the impact of computers on labor relations—how they are being used by management and labor—and the potential impact of computers on urban life. Recent articles such as a series on "Women in Technology," "The Ultimate Head Waiter: How the Brain Controls Diet," "The Other Industrial Revolution: Lessons for Business from the Home," and "The Fallacy of Laser Defense" indicate the magazine's lively range.

As a genre, technology magazines have proved surprisingly problematic in the publishing world. The science niche is well established, with such excellent publications as *Scientific American, Science,* and *Science News.* Computer magazines are flourishing. But technology magazines have not fared well. *Technology Illustrated,* a

Gail Pool *holds an M.L.S. degree from Simmons College and presently works as a freelance writer based in Cambridge, Massachusetts.*

"how things work" guide for laymen, folded last year. *Technology* failed after three issues. The highly technical *High Technology,* to judge from both its circulation figures and its editorial content, continues to search for an audience.

Technology Review seems to know just whom it is written for, and its strong identity is all the more impressive in view of its dual role as a national magazine and as MIT's alumni magazine.

Technology Review was founded in 1899 by MIT's Alumni Association, an organization independent of the university, which remains responsible for the publication. Initially, like other alumni publications, *Technology Review* was intended to extend an understanding of the institution among alumni and the general public.

In 1965, however, John Mattill was hired as editor with a specific mandate to broaden *Technology Review*'s scope. By then MIT itself had widened the range of its offerings to include such non-technical departments as political science and humanities. The feeling was that a broader magazine would better reflect the university and better serve alumni by keeping them informed and equipped to act upon issues.

But as the magazine developed its current thrust, focusing on the relation of technology to a broad range of social and political issues, the Alumni Association and editors realized that their magazine's content was not well represented in the magazine world and that there might be a public for it. By the late sixties they had decided to market the magazine nationally, developing a two-edition system: one, a national edition for a general audience, and the second, comprised of the national edition plus some forty-eight pages of MIT-related material, for alumni.

MIT's *Technology Review,* though it is the most ambitious alumni publication and the only one, I believe, to be actively seeking a national audience, is part of a trend toward more sophisticated alumni magazines. A number of universities and smaller colleges have begun turning out colorful, professional magazines in recent years—perhaps because academic institutions, like many companies, have come to recognize how effective a magazine can be for image and public relations.

Harvard Magazine is a notable example of an alumni publication that has developed into a lively general interest magazine. Founded in 1898 as the *Harvard Bulletin, Harvard Magazine* during the sixties broadened its editorial scope. Editor John Bethell says they took the *Smithsonian* as a model for a magazine that served its constituency well with educational journalism, colorful layout, clear writing, and an adventurous range of articles.

By the seventies, Harvard found it had a good cultural magazine on its hands and, like MIT, decided to market it nationally to non-alumni. But, says Bethell, it proved an expensive business. Perhaps they underestimated the competitiveness of the magazine marketplace. And culture magazines, even good ones, are historically big money losers in America. Ultimately, Harvard decided it wasn't worth the effort. *Harvard Magazine* today has retained its editorial range (Boy George was on a recent cover), but while the magazine will hardly turn away outside subscriptions, it isn't seeking them out.

Technology Review, because of its more specialized content, is likely to meet with more success in a national marketing program. The magazine today reaches 35,000 nonaffiliated readers in addition to 35,000 alumni—not an enormous circulation but a respectable one.

Just how viable a product *Technology Review* is became clear last year when the British-based *Economist* made an offer to acquire the publication. The Alumni Association considered the offer, but in the end rejected it—partly, says Mattill, because they were concerned that MIT's name might be attached to a publication that no longer had any MIT connection, and partly because they saw benefits to keeping the magazine as it was. Interestingly, several months after the rejection, *The New York Times* reported that the *Economist* had announced its own new technology magazine, a bimonthly called *Innovate*—which has not yet, as far as I know, appeared.

Technology Review is an ambitious magazine, editorially and commercially, and it faces an unusual set of publishing problems. As an alumni magazine that also serves a general audience, as a technology magazine that is also a "thought" publication, and as an eight-times-a-year frequency magazine, it may be something of a puzzle to advertisers and even to readers. As yet advertising has not been voluminous and MIT continues to pick up the publication's deficit.

Does *Technology Review*'s value to MIT outweigh its cost? "Well, obviously some see it as having great value, but others see it as an extravagance," says Mattill. "If you think an alumni magazine should simply carry the alumni message, it could be done a lot less expensively than *Technology Review.*"

But *Technology Review,* of course—to those of us who subscribe to it, or buy it at the newsstand, or read it in the library—is not an alumni magazine. It's a magazine that happens to be edited at MIT. Most universities subsidize an assortment of magazines but many of these titles, scholarly or esoteric, serve the academic community alone. *Technology Review* is one of the few that is meant for the rest of us. By focusing on a subject of importance to us all, by elucidating material that is often both controversial and obscure, and by uncovering the general interest in topics that seem at a glance to be merely technical, *Technology Review* reflects the university at its best: generously making its resources available to those outside the ivory tower. ▣

Technology Review. 8/yr. $24/yr. Subscriptions: Room 10-140, MIT, Cambridge, MA 02139.

Norman Stevens:

Our Profession

There is so little library humor published that almost any venture into such an odd subject is worth mention. Andy Gibbons's and Jeanne Nelson's cartoons in **"Shhh" Is a Four Letter Word** offer the views of librarians, not professional cartoonists, on the lighter side of librarianship. Almost all of their cartoons, as you might suspect, are based on the image of the librarian and draw on the usual foibles and stereotypes. Some of their humor is good but much of it, to my mind, is not. None of their work elicited more than a chuckle. Still, library humor is such a personal matter that others may well find much greater enjoyment in this view of libraries and librarianship than I did.

Most of our work, of course, is all too serious. Certainly retrospective conversion has little to amuse us. The challenge of finding effective ways of converting the millions of catalog records that American librarians have produced in the past hundred years into a machine-readable form is substantial. Only for libraries with new or small collections is retrospective conversion not one of the critical issues of the day. Jutta Reed-Scott's study, **Issues in Retrospective Conversion**, conducted for the Bibliographic Service Development Program of the Council on Library Resources, is the best available summary of these important issues. It should be read, along with Dick Boss's article "Retrospective Conversion: Investing in the Future" in *WLB,* November 1984, by those facing this challenge either in their own library or in a cooperative setting. To date retrospective conversion largely has been dealt with as a task for the individual library with some assistance from national and multi-state network services both in the techniques of conversion and in access to already converted records.

The thrust of Reed-Scott's study is to suggest new initiatives in the form of a national strategy for retrospective conversion. She offers these five alternatives: (1) establishment of a central agency to coordinate the process; (2) establishment of a central data resource file for pre-LC MARC records; (3) expansion of the University of Chicago/Library of Congress retrospective conversion project; (4) record sharing among national network services; and (5) a planned, coordinated program by the major research libraries and the Library of Congress. Each option is described briefly and evaluated. She then concludes with six recommendations based largely on her last option, in addition to access to records through the national network services. The scope and the cost of what she recommends is enormous but it is, perhaps, something that all libraries could support as they increasingly need such records to operate the automated systems that are becoming a way of library life. Retrospective conversion is, indeed, a sound investment in making the records of the past available in the future.

Given the magnitude of the retrospective conversion work that faces American libraries, even if a coordinated national approach is developed, the more widespread organized use of volunteers to assist in that effort would seem to be a natural solution. To date, however, academic and public libraries have made less effective use of volunteers than school libraries. Linda Bennett's **Volunteers in the School Media Center** reflects that unfortunate fact. It is the only major monograph available on the use of volunteers in libraries and serves an important need. Bennett does an excellent job of summarizing each of the issues that a library faces in using volunteers, including the impact of a volunteer program, apprehensions, preplanning, the role of the volunteer coodinator, attracting volunteers, screening and placement, training and implementation, predicting and alleviating problems, recognition, and the evaluation and modification of programs. Some of the details of such matters as appropriate tasks and programs that volunteers can assist with and the practical examples are oriented to the school media center and may not seem relevant to those in other kinds of libraries. In general, however, Bennett's coverage of the issues involved, such as the potential objections to the use of volunteer help, is broad enough to be of value to all librarians. Throughout her advice is sound and well thought out. She dem-

Norman Stevens *is university librarian at the University of Connecticut and the author of* Communication Throughout Libraries.

onstrates that a volunteer program is something much more than a few mothers offering to come in and tend an elementary school library a few mornings each week. In particular larger libraries of other kinds that have not considered the use of volunteers may find what she has to offer stimulating.

While designed, and most useful, as a library school textbook, A. Robert Rogers and Kathryn McChesney's **The Library and Society** has other potential uses. It might well, for example, be read by library volunteers, or new non-professional staff, who want some background in the concept and role of libraries. The standard library school course in The Library and Society is traditionally considered one of the least challenging and interesting components of a library school education, perhaps because of its catch-all nature. As we all know from experience, such a course can be downright boring. One textbook cannot change the situation but this one, if wisely used in conjunction with a range of other material, may help improve matters. It offers a reasonable approach to, and some useful introductory material on, the following broad areas: the social, philosophical, and historical background of librarianship; major types of libraries; libraries and librarianship in other countries; and professional concerns. Some critical issues, such as library literature, are given inadequate treatment and others, such as professional ethics, are almost entirely omitted but, on the whole, Rogers and McChesney manage to touch on most issues of importance accurately and in reasonable detail. The chapter, by Rogers and McChesney, on "Professional Issues in Industrial and Post-industrial Societies" covers, for example, in twenty-five pages: the shift to a "service" economy, productivity, libraries in the political process, public relations, computers in libraries, national information policy, copyright, multi-type library cooperation, censorship, racism and sexism, service to special groups, education of information professionals, and library research. For each of those topics a short summary of the issues and the important literature is followed by a few well thought out questions designed to stimulate thinking and discussion. The practicing librarian may learn little from such an approach but for students and other beginners the summary and questions offer a good starting point for a first introduction to the issues. The coverage of librarianship outside the United States is both welcome and useful. Ezekiel Kaungamno's essay, "Books and Libraries in the Third World: Problems and Prospects," provides an especially good introduction to those issues although his omission of any reference to such essential material as the work of Anthony Smith and the McBride Commission is unfortunate.

American librarianship too often tends to be isolated from what is happening elsewhere and what has happened in the past. The treatment that Rogers and McChesney give to foreign librarianship in a basic text is, for example, unusual. One of the neglected classics of librarianship is Wilhelm Munthe's **American Librarianship from a European Angle** which was first published in 1939 and was reprinted in 1964. Although, unfortunately, now out-of-print and somewhat outdated, it remains worth reading especially for its sharp critical insights on our approach to librarianship. The reviews by such luminaries as Bishop, Hoole, and Metcalf when this book was first published commented on the extent to which it "set American librarians to thinking about fundamental problems which they face" (Metcalf). Powell called attention to Munthe's work in a 1962 essay which led to its reprinting and in reviewing the reprint he cited it as "an example of what can be done when vision and imagination illuminate knowledge and experience."

In 1936 Frederick Keppel, president of the Carnegie Corporation, asked Munthe, a prominent Norwegian librarian, to visit libraries in the United States and to report on what he found. Munthe's incisive report covers major topics including books and reading, college and university libraries, public libraries, education for librarianship, librarianship as a feminine vocation, staffing, and library buildings. Along the way Munthe also touches on a host of minor topics such as open shelves, fines, smoking, genealogy, pay collections, the master's thesis, and celibacy. Often critical, but always stimulating, Munthe's views helped a generation of American librarians, who set the stage for the libraries of today, to think about what they were doing. His report was undoubtedly one of the most influential books of its time. It deserves to be rediscovered again. It also is a model of the kind of critical examination of contemporary librarianship that is once again badly needed. Some imaginative organization needs to commission another Munthe to do a report on the present state of American librarianship from a foreign angle. ▣

This month's books:

Bennett, Linda Leveque. *Volunteers in the School Media Center.* Libraries Unlimited, 1984. 236p. $23.50. ISBN 0–87287–351–X

Gibbons, Andy and Jeanne Nelson. *"Shhh" Is a Four Letter Word.* R&E Publishers (Box 2008, Saratoga, CA 95070), 1984. 120p. pa $11.45. ISBN 0–88247–702–1 LC 83–62296

Munthe, Wilhelm. *American Librarianship from a European Angle.* American Library Association, 1939; Shoe String, 1964. 191p. o.p. ISBN 0–208–00120–4

Reed-Scott, Jutta. *Issues in Retrospective Conversion.* Council on Library Resources (1785 Massachusetts Ave., NW, Washington, DC 20036), 1984. 57p. $3 (prepaid)

Rogers, A. Robert and Kathryn McChesney. *The Library in Society.* Libraries Unlimited, 1984. 285p. $28.50, pa $19.50. ISBN 0–87827–379–X; 0–87827–398–6

Patrick Dewey:

Software for Libraries

A wonderful, lively interactive introduction to the alphabet for kids aged three to six is provided by the five games in **Easy as ABC** (Springboard Software, Inc., 1984). To play the games—*Match Letters, Leapfrog, Lunar Letters, Honey Hunt,* and *Dot to Dot*—children, using either a joystick or keyboard, select and move large, friendly letters about on the screen to form words or patterns of animals, or to plot a course to another planet. In *Honey Hunt,* for example, guiding the honey bee to flowers with only upper and lower case letters is rewarded with a ration of honey. By connecting all of the letters in alphabetical order, *Dot to Dot* players finish with an outline of an animal which is finally transformed into a delightful picture. In fact, all of the graphics in this educational package are superior, though there are no color-dependent aspects to the games. The booklet that serves as documentation for this package contains not only instructions for use, but a number of additional activities for improving learning as well. Each game is described in detail to help adult companions see the purpose behind each, with hints for making the games more enjoyable. For use with Apple II+, IIe, IIc, Commodore 64, IBM PC, PCjr. Cost: $39.95.

Logical practice

What's My Logic by Michael O. Baker and Tracy Valleau (Midwest Publications, 1984) is a delightful, challenging logic game, designed for use with third and fourth graders and up. Simple in design, the program is reminiscent of an IQ test, but it is similar enough to traditional puzzles to attract many adults and children. The game is played on a checkerboard grid

with each square containing a different object varying in shape, color, and size. Players attempt to move an oversized cursor, step by step, from the bottom left of the grid to the top right. To do so, however, it is necessary to follow the rules, which change with each game. For example, one rule might be that it is only possible to move from one shape to an object of a different shape, or, more difficult, from an object to an object that is "same size or same shape," but not "same size and same shape." Rules of logic covered are: negation, conjunction, inclusive or, exclusive or. The package contains twenty puzzles, each progressively more difficult. An answer sheet is included. For use with: Apple II+ (48K), IIe, IIc (important: there is a separate version for color computers and one for black and white), Commodore 64; TRS-80 version due out soon. Cost: $39.95.

Sights and sound for Commodore

Commodore 64 Graphics and Sounds (Sams, 1984) is a software package with a success story behind it. The author, Timothy Orr Knight, is just seventeen years old, and has now written three books. He began working with micros at age thirteen and has even established his own company. This new software package, well worth its modest price, is a concise guide to Commodore 64 sound effects, low and high resolution graphics, three dimensional graphics, multiple graphics combinations, and three-voice music. The program disk contains forty-seven programs, some serving as simple illustrations of a particular solution to a basic programming problem, though all may be listed out for study and manipulation. The source code for each program is also listed in the manual. Some of the programs are interactive in nature, allowing users to experiment with musical notes and graphics. Many programs are quite simple which makes the package good for use with young people. (In fact, I watched some kids at our branch library who loved it; they not only made it work, but took great delight in being able to demonstrate various programs to me.)

For use with: Commodore 64. Cost: $19.95.

Patrick Dewey *is administrative librarian, Maywood (Illinois) Public Library and author of* Public Access Microcomputers: A Handbook for Librarians.

Electronic nursery rhymes

Mother Goose (Sunstar Systems, 1984) is a software package for preschool through early grade school which displays the text of eighteen nursery rhymes with accompanying tunes, and a graphic of some kind; e.g., for "Hickory, Dickory, Dock," there is a grandfather clock with a little mouse climbing up it (though most of the rhymes have nothing as spectacular as climbing mice). Other rhymes include: "Pat-A-Cake," "Humpty-Dumpty," "Twinkle, Twinkle," "Mary, Mary, Quite Contrary," "Rain Rain, Go Away," and "Ride a Cock-Horse to Banbury Cross." The colors are quite good, and so are the drawings. Unfortunately, the program itself provides little in the way of interaction, and for the most part just turns pages. Scrolling both forward and backward is permitted. The program does allow the user to make a backup, but the process of preparing the disk for use can be confusing (it is necessary to copy IBM DOS onto the program disk; I had to try four different IBMs at two locations and get the assistance of an IBM salesperson who also found it confusing), but once the disk has been prepared this chore need not be repeated. The musical tunes are all about the same: dull. And while I don't want to sound down on Mother Goose, it's unfortunate that the idea wasn't carried just a bit further to provide more interaction as do many of the other fine preschool and early grade materials currently available. For use with: IBM PC/XT, PCjr, 64K RAM, one disk drive only required, and color monitor. PC DOS 2.0 or higher. Cost: $34.95.

Fractions hold librarian hostage

Fractions, Decimals, & Percent (Society for Visual Education, 1983) is a well-crafted package of six diskettes. The programs are extremely easy to use, and though a "Management System" for classroom use is included, users may easily bypass this feature by typing "Student" when asked for their last name. All material is presented in the context of a game, such as *Free the Librarian* (correct answers will set the librarian, tied up in a chair, free—some game!) and *Become a Star-Agent.* The manual is not essential to the program's use, but it does contain a great deal of material that is especially useful for both a classroom setting and individual study. Included in the manual are a student progress chart, operating instructions, disk summaries (objectives, menu, summary), "Quick Reference Sheet for Easy Lesson Preview," skill sheets for each lesson, and other worksheets for students. Permission is granted in the documentation to reproduce all of the worksheets. Sound may be turned off, a bonus for libraries with the micro in a reading room. The program makes good use of graphics and color. Good interaction is produced by giving hints to users when a wrong answer is made. Lessons cover quite a large territory, including dividing decimals by decimals, using equivalent fractions to find percent, finding base amount given rate and percent, decimal word problems, reading a graph, finding percent, and many others. For use with: Apple II+, IIe. Cost: $239 without backups; $299 with backups.

Simulations and a fish story

Simulation Collection (Educational Computing Network) states that over sixty "simulations" are included in this package. While there are over sixty programs, no more than a dozen are simulations. There are a few good ones, such as *Dairy Farm,* a simple grade school simulation of buying and selling cows to produce milk, and *African Cocoa,* a simulation that will teach the basics of supply and demand. A good version of *Oregon Trail* with graphics is also included. Many of the other programs contained in the package (six diskette sides, three diskettes formatted on both sides) are just fine, but few have anything to do with simulations as most people would normally define them. One entire disk side is taken up with the Bible story *Jonah.* It's quite good, but has nothing to do with simulations; instead, it contains three different versions of this story: adult, easy, and all pictures. As with any other public domain collection being offered as a bargain, some of the programs do not work, there is no documentation, and many programs (or their equivalent) are available through other, less expensive sources, including the local computer club. For use with most Apple IIs (most of the programs are in Applesoft). Cost: $75.

Publisher addresses for this month's software:

Educational Computing Network, Box 8236, Riverside, CA 92515.

Howard W. Sams & Co., Inc., 4300 West 62nd St., Indianapolis, IN 46268.

Midwest Publications, Box 448, Pacific Grove, CA 93950.

Society for Visual Education, 1345 Diversey Parkway, Chicago, IL 60614.

Springboard Software, Inc., 7807 Creekridge Circle, Minneapolis, MN 55435.

Sunstar Systems, Route #4, Box 368, Ogdensburg, NY 13669.

James Rettig:

Current Reference Books

Correspondence and review copies for this column should be directed to James Rettig, University Library, Box 8198, University of Illinois at Chicago, Chicago, IL 60680.

The American Historical Supply Catalog, by Alan Wellikoff. New York: Schocken, 1984. 240p. pa $16.95. 0-8052-0775-9 84-5579

Last fall an intrepid band of four Minnesota men set out on horseback across the northern plains. They used authentic clothing and supplies, right down to the one-lens-suits-all-eyes spectacles, of the 1870s. It was not an enjoyable experience, especially after an early snow increased their hardship and discomfort. They tried to live the nostalgic dream others express by incorporating artifacts of the past into contemporary lifestyles. For the latter group, the *Historical Supply Catalogue* tells where to order some 500 reproductions of nineteenth-century American furniture, housewares, clothing, sporting goods, toys, musical instruments, food, stoves, carriages, farm implements, and more. Illustrations of 350 of the items accompany their descriptions, histories, and the address and phone number of the supplier. Not all descriptions include prices, as these are subject to change. The index is helpful, even though the items are grouped in a logical order. Most of the articles are useful as well as decorative. House restorers and others who dote on the past century will revel in the *Catalog*.

Biographical Directory of American Territorial Governors, by Thomas A. McMullin and David Walker. Westport, CT: Meckler, 1984. 353p. $75. 0-930466-11-X 84-9095

Meckler has published historical biographical dictionaries covering American colonial and revolutionary governors and governors of the states through 1978. This volume covers the remaining gubernatorial territory in thirty chapters, one for each of the incorporated territories that existed during the period opened by the enactment of the Northwest Ordinance in 1787 and concluded by conferral of statehood on Hawaii in 1959. The introduction explains the legal distinction between an incorporated and an unincorporated territory; suffice it to say that the limitation excludes territories such as Samoa and Puerto Rico. The biographies, arranged chronologically by the governors' terms, emphasize the governors' political careers and analyze their administrative efforts. All conclude with a brief bibliography. An introductory overview of each territory's history would have been convenient, although readers can construct their own by reading all of a territory's governors' biographies. In the case of Alaska, this would mean reading twenty-four pages covering the fifteen governors during Alaska's seventy-four years as a territory. The *Biographical Directory* is a helpful source for anyone studying the political antecedents of twenty-eight of the thirty-three states admitted to the union since Ohio entered in 1803.

Bowker's 1985 Complete Sourcebook of Personal Computing. New York: Bowker, 1984. 1,050p. pa $19.95. 0-8352-1931-3 84-20460

Now in its second year, much has changed in this annual, expanded by more than 400 pages, since it was reviewed here last March. The brief descriptions of 750 PCs, an increase of 150 percent, have been reorganized to group machines by manufacturer. In recognition of the way IBM has shaped the PC marketplace, a separate section lists 127 IBM-compatible microcomputers. Another section identifies lap-sized portables. To help users through the thicket of competing machines and software, new sections cite more than 3,000 reviews of programs and hardware in popular computing magazines. Directories of user groups and magazines and the list of books have grown dramatically in the past year, in some cases by more than double. Each of the book's nineteen sections has been organized to be user-friendly. This annual has rapidly become a convenient and, as far as possible, comprehensive guide to the booming PC field. Standing orders are in order.

Catalogue of Vocal Solos and Duets Arranged in Biblical Order, by James H. Laster. Metuchen, NJ: Scarecrow, 1984. 204p. $15. 0-8108-1748-9 84-14187

A companion to the compiler's *Catalogue of Choral Music Arranged in Biblical Order* (Metuchen, NJ: Scarecrow, 1983), *Vocal Solos and Duets* will be every bit as useful a reference and planning tool for church choir directors, enabling them to select vocal pieces to coordinate with a service's Scripture readings. Entries list biblical reference, citation of other Scriptures incorporated into the piece, composer's name, language if other than English, accompaniment, vocal

James Rettig *is head reference librarian, University of Illinois at Chicago.*

range, publisher, and date of publication. Laster identified solos and duets through bibliographies and by querying music publishers. The works are indexed by both composer and title. Many of the entries cite anthologies as the song's sources, yet the book lacks a bibliography of these anthologies, a slight hindrance to retrieval. This does not diminish the book's usefulness as a guide; it merely burdens a desirable book and its users with unnecessary inconvenience.

The Consumer Protection Manual, by Andrew Eiler. New York: Facts On File, 1984. 658p. $29.95. 0-87196-310-8 82-1464

Sooner or later everyone has the unpleasant experience of a dispute with a mechanic, a mail–order house, a repair shop, a contractor, or a bank,but not everyone knows how to negotiate

a satisfactory settlement. Some demand and some plead, but others succeed. Eiler offers the know-how for success when trying to cancel an order placed with a door-to-door sales person or get a refund for a credit. Drawing on his experience as director of legislation and research at the Michigan Consumers Council, Eiler explains the consumer's rights in a variety of common situations, cites FTC regulations and provisions of the Uniform Commercial Code, and outlines an effective negotiating strategy consumers can use in a dispute. Eiler displays equal parts of knowledge and common sense in explaining what can go wrong in each type of transaction, how to prevent problems, and how to solve them. Consumers locked in battle with sellers will eagerly adapt sample letters to their cases. The subject index allows quick reference to discussion of those cases. It would be ideal if people use this before they buy, but libraries can expect demand to come when a patron's checks have unaccountably turned to rubber or a repair shop is spinning excuses about why the spin cycle on the washing machine is not covered by the warranty.

Dictionary of American Catholic Biography, by John J. Delaney. Garden City, NY: Doubleday, 1984. 621p. $24.95. 0-385-17878-6 83-25524

Because all 1,500 subjects profiled in this dictionary are deceased, author Delaney had the opportunity to assess their contributions to American society and the Catholic Church in America. He passed it up, choosing instead to stick to the facts. And so, the biographies read like who's who entries or newspaper obituaries, telling the tale of parentage, birth, education, employment, accomplishments, and finally death. Clerics and laymen from all walks of life from the time of the Spanish explorers to the recently deceased are included. Delaney has his facts straight, but exaggerates one. Jacques Marquette's remains, except for a few bone chips, are buried at St. Ignace, Michigan, not at Marquette University in Milwaukee as Delaney states. The university has only the few fragments. Several brief appendixes list Catholics who have held national political office. The book would more clearly illustrate the diversity of backgrounds of American Catholics had Delaney indexed it by occupation, schools, and birthplace in the fashion of the *Dictionary of American Biography*. This workmanlike biographical dictionary will answer factual questions about the lives of individuals, but it could have answered others as well.

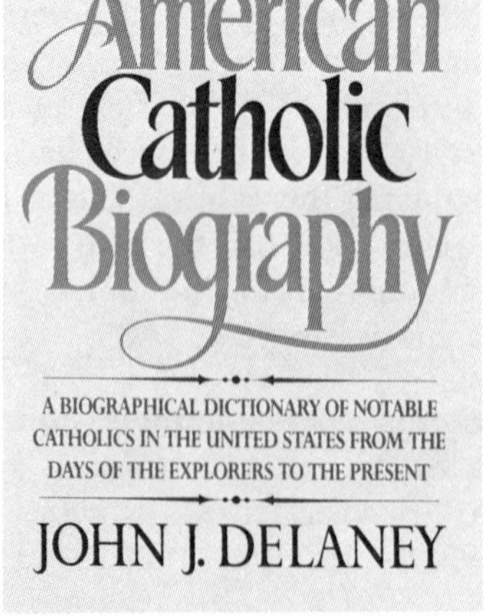

Directory of Nursing Homes, edited by Sam Mongeau. 2nd ed. Phoenix: Oryx, 1984. 1,301p. pa$125. 0-89774-145-5 84-18994

It is not the nearly 900 new entries that make the second edition vastly superior to the first edition (1982) of this directory. The biggest improvement is the tremendous expansion of those entries. Instead of just name, address, phone number, name of administrator, type of licensure, number of beds, level(s) of care, type of ownership, and certification, most of the 16,139 entries also describe admission requirements, religious or organizational affiliation, size of staff, types of specialists on staff, facilities, recreational activities, and special features. The convenient state-by-state format and the index by facility name have been carried over from the first edition. The added information, gathered mostly by questionnaire, makes this attractive to public libraries and broadens its usefulness in medical and nursing collections. It can be helpful to concerned health care consumers who must place a relative in a nursing home and by health care professionals seeking employment in these facilities.

Emily Brontë Criticism, 1900-1982, by Janet M. Barclay. Westport, CT: Meckler, 1984. 162p. $40. 0-930466-63-2 83-17433

Since a first edition of this annotated bibliography was published in 1974 as *Emily Brontë Criticism 1900-1968* (New York Public Library), the Brontë bibliographic landscape has become more crowded. First, Anne Passel's annotated *Charlotte and Emily Brontë* (New York: Garland, 1979) appeared. As a consequence of its more ambitious scope, its coverage of twentieth-century criticism is not as thorough as Barclay's. Second, R. W. Crump's *Charlotte and Emily Bronte, 1846-1915* (Boston: G.K. Hall, 1982) came upon the scene, claiming supremacy in nineteenth-century coverage. These developments have not dislodged Barclay's book which retains its place by virtue of its comprehensiveness for the twentieth century. Barclay organizes the criticism by type of publication (books, articles, introductions, etc.). This will suit the patient scholar, but the hurried term paper author will prefer Passel's approach, in which she gathers criticism of *Wuthering Heights* in one section and puts general criticism, criticism of Emily Brontë's poetry, and criticism of Charlotte Brontë poetry in discrete sections. Furthermore, only Passel supplies a subject index, albeit an inadequate one. The landscape, though getting crowded, is not yet cluttered. Barclay's book will be most useful in research collections.

Encyclopedia of American Political History, edited by Jack P. Greene. New York: Scribner, 1984. 3v. $180. 0-684-17003-5 84-1355

In the tradition of Alexander DeConde's *Encyclopedia of American Foreign Policy* (New York: Scribner, 1978) and Glenn Porter's *Encyclopedia of American Economic History* (New York: Scribner, 1980), *Political History* consists of ninety lengthy articles by a variety of scholars. A sort of *Dictionary of the History of Ideas* with a distinctly American twist, *Political History* explores the development of American political ideas, institutions, and movements. The authors were encouraged "to take a strong personal line of interpretation," sometimes giving the set the feel of an extremely well–planned anthology rather than that of an encyclopedia. A short list of its topics demonstrates the set's encyclopedic scope: American Revolution, authority, cabinet, Congress, crime and punishment, egalitarianism, feminism, land policies, machine politics, New Deal, populism, separation of powers, suffrage, tariff policies, and voluntary associations. The extensive index complements the broad sweep of the articles. The approach also complements the narower articles in the *Dictionary of American History* (rev. ed., New York: Scribner, 1976). The encyclopedia's articles and their bulging bibliographies offer term paper writers or the merely curious an excellent starting point.

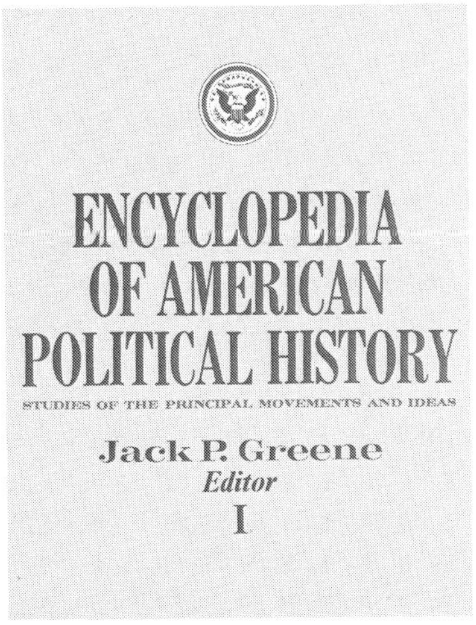

The End of the Beatles? by Harry Castleman and Walter J. Podrazik. Ann Arbor: Pierian Press, 1985. 553p. $39.50. 0-87650-162-5 84-60639 (Rock & roll reference series, no. 10)

There may have been an end to the Beatles more than a decade ago, but the end of books on the Beatles has not yet arrived. The newest continues the authors' *All Together Now* (Ann Arbor: Pierian, 1976) and *The Beatles Again* (1977). Its first section carries through 1983 the earlier books' year-by-year discography of albums and singles by the Beatles singly or as a group. Other sections provide background on records connected to the Beatles cult or by members of the Beatles' circle. Still others describe bootlegged records, including the group's 1962 Decca audition and BBC broadcasts. Thirteen of the fifteen indexes to songs, song writers, and individual Beatles cover all three volumes. This authoritative trilogy more than likely will grow into a quaternion for, as its concluding words declare, to baby boomers like the authors, "there will never really be an 'end' to the Beatles."

The Essential Jazz Records, Vol. 1, by Max Harrison, Charles Fox, and Eric Thacker. Westport, CT: Greenwood, 1984. 595p. $39.95. 0-313-24674-2 84-7926 ISSN 0192-334X (Discographies, no. 12)

Not content merely to enumerate and describe jazz recordings, the compilers of this 250-item discography hope it will provoke students of jazz to view in new ways the development of this distinctly American art. They especially take issue with accepted evaluations of the jazz of the 1930s. This volume covers jazz from its origins through ragtime to swing; a second volume will continue the story. Most of the topical chapters fit into a chronological structure. The detailed entries list the disc's title and label numbers and describe each track in detail, giving its title, musicians, their instruments, vocalists, and place and date recorded. A lengthy critical commentary accompanying each description places the recordings in context, frequently by comparing or contrasting a recording to others treated in the book. The compilers write for a jazz-savvy audience conversant with a technical vocabulary. Most of the recordings are 78 rpm LPs, so those who use this as a collection building guide can expect countless frustrations but hope for ample rewards should they succeed.

Future War Novels, by John Newman and Michael Unsworth. Phoenix: Oryx, 1984. 101p. $25. 0-89774-103-X 83-43245

Last year "The Day After" grabbed

headlines and generated considerable discussion about the possibility of nuclear war and its grim aftermath. Consistently but more quietly novelists since World War II have created visions of future conventional and nuclear wars, some of those visions more horrific than "The Day After." The lengthy annotations in this bibliography of 191 English-language novels published between 1946 and 1983 summarize the novels' plots and assess their literary merit. Newman, compiler of *Vietnam War Literature* (reviewed in *WLB,* September 1982), wrote the annotations, arranged chronologically by the novels' date of publication. This permits users to place them in the context of their times or to search for patterns or progressions. Author and title indexes conclude the volume. The uses of this bibliography by literary scholars and students are self-evident. It can also be used to advantage by political scientists, sociologists, and students of popular culture.

Hollywood and American History, compiled by Michael R. Pitts. Jefferson, NC: McFarland, 1984. 332p. $24.95. 0-89950-132-X 84-42733

Hollywood and American History lists credits, complete cast, studio, date, and running time of 245 films depicting people and events from American history. Even a brief perusal would convince the most casual browser that the phrase "based on" means a variety of things. Many Hollywood features "based on" the nation's past rely on historical verisimilitude, not necessarily historical fact. The most frequent liberty with history is the introduction of romances which may not have—indeed, almost surely did not—take place. In addition to listing the facts about the films, entries summarize the plot and evaluate the films, both as aesthetic works and as accurate tellings of history. Pitts pulls no punches, praising the praiseworthy and panning the poor. Since the majority of the films sensationalize the past, this is not suitable for use as a guide to curriculum materials. Instead it is another specialized tool for film studies collections.

The Hollywood Novel and Other Novels About Film, 1912-1918, by Nancy Brooker-Bowers. New York: Garland, 1985. 293p. $30. 0-8240-9007-1 83-49307

Within the field of film studies, the study of adaptations of novels and short stories has become a speciality. It is just, then, that novels about Hollywood and films should be organized for comparison and study by literature specialists. Indexed by author and title, *The Hollywood Novel* treats its 694 entries chronologically. The novels were selected because their characters are involved in the film industry. Annotations describe plots and characters and note relations between sequels and among novels in series. They also show that the Hollywood novel intersects with every other genre: the western, romance, mystery, detective, *roman à clef, Kunstlerroman,* even the epistolary novel in Albert Martin's self-published *Dog Gone Hollywood* (1947), letters written by a star's dog describing other stars' dogs. A number of the novels verge on the pornographic and many of the plots and situations are as fantastic as any Hollywood has produced on celluloid. Works by unknowns surround novels by F. Scott Fitzgerald, Aldous Huxley, Gore Vidal, and Evelyn Waugh. Even without a thematic index, the bibliography opens the door to a collection of Americana that would otherwise be difficult to identify.

Kentucky Place Names, by Robert M. Rennick. Lexington: University Press of Kentucky, 1984. 375p. $30. 0-8131-1503-5 84-7441

At the beginning of a two-year exile in western Kentucky, this native Yankee was baffled by locals who said they were from "Kaydeeze," for no such place appeared on the region's map. Finally it became clear. They were from nearby Cadiz. Unexpected pronunciations of place names are as common in Kentucky as tobacco farms or coal trucks. It is a blessing, therefore, that this thorough, carefully researched dictionary of Kentucky county and town names includes their local pronunciation. In addition to pronunciation, each entry describes the place's location, its history, and the derivation of its name. Entries conclude with numbers referring to the 1,461-item bibliography of books, pamphlets, journal articles, newspaper articles, manuscripts, letters to the author, and personal interviews conducted over the past fifteen years. Most of the 2,000 places, only a fourth of the names in the files of the Kentucky Place Name Survey, still exist. Carpetbaggers ought to pack this to avoid embarrassing mispronunciations in Versailles or Cadiz. But more importantly libraries in Kentucky and libraries with large geography collections will add it to their collections because it is authoritative, a model of its kind.

Marquis Who's Who Directory of Online Professionals. Chicago: Marquis, 1984. 829p. $85. 0-8379-6001-0

During December some stores offered a coveted Cabbage Patch doll to anyone who bought a Coleco video game; some people bought the game to get the doll. Some libraries may buy this biographical directory to get the eleven coupons that come with it. These entitle buyers to discounts on books, subscriptions, a search software package, and an information broker's service as well as free time on the Marquis PRO-files database, the online counterpart of this international directory. It identifies users of online search systems in libraries, government, industry, and academe. The fact-packed biographies focus on online expertise and experience, listing name, position, online role, systems used, access equipment, time spent searching each month, databases frequently searched, career history, selected publications, professional memberships, address, and phone number. The online function index indicates that librarian/intermediaries make up the directory's largest single group. Other indexes identify biographees by database subject expertise and geographic location. One person profiled identified five errors of fact in her listing, even though she had sent the publisher corrections on the galley submitted to her for verification. Several others, however, could find no fault with their listings, all of which measured up to the Marquis reputation for accuracy. The coupons will have a good deal of appeal to online professionals, but so will the book.

National Directory of Newsletters and Reporting Services, Parts 1-8, edited by Robert C. Thomas and Brigitte T. Darnay. Detroit: Gale, 1978-1984. 1,873p. in eight issues. pa$240. 77-99180 ISSN 0547-6232

When the fourth issue of this second edition of *The National Directory of Newsletters* was published in 1981, it carried the note: "This part completes the second edition." Yet four more issues followed because new newsletters continued to be created at a rapid rate and because additional existing newsletters continued to come to the editors' attention. Even after excluding house organs and newsletters of strictly local appeal, the eight-issue second edition describes 6,271 newsletters, reporting services, association bulletins, and financial services published in the United States. Publications such as *Frontiers in Immunoassay, Ghost Trackers Newsletter,* and *The Canal Zone Philatelist* and subject headings such as Skye terrier dogs, pet cemeteries, and infanticide demonstrate that no matter how esoteric, a topic will probably spawn a newsletter. The entries, indexed by title, publisher, and subject in the final issue, list title, address, phone number, editor, date of first publication, frequency, circulation, trim size, length, advertising policy, and types of illustrations. Each entry also describes the newsletter's purpose and scope. The improved bibliographic access to newsletters this directory gives libraries will highlight their chronic shortcomings in providing physical access to these publications.

The National Prison Directory, edited by Mary L. Bundy and Alice Bell. 3rd ed. Urban Information Interpreters (Box AH, College Park, MD 20740), 1984. 205p. $39.95.

Despite the seemingly straightforward title, the subtitle, "A Prison Reform Organizational and Resource Directory," clarifies this directory's scope and purpose. The directory retains the organization of the second edition (1979), the first section being a topical index to the second section, state-by-state descriptions of 367 organizations. Descriptions include a statement of objectives, a list of "change activities," and the history of the organization. The directory of national organizations has been retained. The bibliography of materials on the criminal justice system has been condensed and updated and the text of proposals for reforms of that system has been dropped in favor of a second state-by-state directory. It lists and describes the services 143 public libraries provide to inmates in 242 adult and juvenile correctional facilities. This directory is an obvious choice for academic criminal justice collections, and its new feature will make it attractive to library science collections and public libraries engaged in service to inmates.

Rolling Stone Rock Almanac, by the editors of *Rolling Stone*. New York: Macmillan, 1983. 371p. pa$10.95. 0-02-081320-1 83-16178

A scan of the holdings on OCLC shows that many libraries either missed or chose to ignore the publication of the *Rolling Stone Rock Almanac* in hardcover in 1983. Now it has been reissued in economical paperback. Given the perennial popularity of the topic, it deserves wider distribution, particularly in public libraries. Covering from the advent of rock in 1954 through 1982, the *Almanac* uses short paragraphs to describe in chronological order each year's events in the rock world. In addition to these news notes on performances, record releases, marriages, divorces, drug overdoses, and other fixities of the rock world, the chronology lists each week's chart-topping pop LP and pop, R&B, and British pop singles. Small black-and-white photos work well in the four-column, newspaper-like format. However, lacking captions, they will have significance only to real rock buffs. If the names index referred to dates rather than to page numbers, specific fact retrieval would be faster. There are thousands upon thousands of facts here. As a chronology of rock, this greatly outdistances Herb Hendler's pretentiously titled *Year by Year in the Rock Era* (reviewed in *WLB,* May 1984). Now that the *Almanac* is in paperback, it is an especially good value.

Scholars' Guide to Northwest European Studies, by Louis A. Pitschmann. Washington: Smithsonian Institution Press, 1984. 436p. $29.95, pa$15. 0-87474-754-6; 0-87474-753-8 84-600036 (Scholars' guide to Washington, D.C., no. 10)

Several other volumes in this carefully edited series spice their descriptions of scholarly resources in and around Washington with mention of the locations of cafeterias and advice on short-term living accommodations and getting around in the metroplex. Little of that is in *Northwest European Studies,* a guide to resources on the region which more than any other embodies the Protestant work ethic. In detail scholars will appreciate, the guide describes the resources of libraries, government agencies, and private organizations relating to northwest Europe. These countries, from Belgium north to Scandinavia and including Ireland, Great Britain, Iceland, and Greenland, have deep ties to North America through colonization, immigration, trade, and military alliance. Thus it is not surprising that a number of public libraries rate inclusion along with the expected entries for the Library of Congress and its neighbor, the Folger Shakespeare Library. Several indexes offer access to collections by name, size, and subject strengths. Not only will the guide help area studies scholars judge the value of a trip to Washington, it will also allow them to plan for a productive one.

The Social Security Book, by Jack E. Gaumnitz and Erwin A. Gaumnitz. New York: Arco, 1984. 161p. $12.95, pa$6.95 0-668-05958-3; 0-668-05960-5 84-9172

Librarians should not make the mistake of assuming that *The Social Security Book* is a private-sector reprint of the public-domain *Social Security Handbook* (8th ed., Washington: GPO, 1984, SuDocs He3.6/2:So1/3/984). Rather than a reprint of the turgid bureaucratic prose of federal regulations, it is a fresh and lucid explanation of how the Social Security system operates, the problems it faces, and eligibility for benefits. Numerous examples illustrate how a worker earns eligibility for benefits and exactly how much should be paid per month. The book embraces all of the programs loosely known as Social Security: retirement pensions, disability payments, survivor's benefits, Medicare, and Supplemental Security Income, each covered by a separate chapter. The book reflects the law as of 1984. Unless the promises of the president and other November winners are to be believed, benefits will change as budgets are cut and taxes raised. Nonetheless, the book will remain a useful guide to the system's fundamental principles.

State Maps on File. New York: Facts On File, 1984. looseleaf. $55/binder 84-675108. **Mountain and Prairie**. 0-8160-0121-9. **Southwest**. 0-8160-0122-7. **West**. 0-8160-0123-5

In 1983 Facts On File announced its Librarian's Award for Reference Publishing Ideas. The first idea to be awarded and published is *State Maps on File,* an idea submitted by Susan Jamison, librarian at the Corbit-Calloway Memorial Library in Odessa, Delaware. In the style of *Maps on File* (reviewed in *WLB,* January 1982), *State Maps* is a compilation of black-and-white maps intended to be photocopied. The clear maps lend themselves to overhead projection as well as to shading and labeling for inclusion in a report. Each state's section consists of a series of approximately twenty maps showing the state's location on the continent, its position among neighboring states, routes of exploration and settlement, major cities and highways, legislative districts, counties, landforms, climate characteristics, mineral deposits, agricultural products, Indian settlements past and present, and other information lending itself to cartographic display. Four additional volumes will cover the states from Missouri, Iowa, and Minnesota east to the Atlantic. These maps can be used in imaginative ways in schools. Any library that has been pleased with *Maps on File* will also be pleased with *State Maps on File.* Susan Jamison deserves her award.

U.S. Employment Opportunities, edited by Joseph Ryan. Washington Research Associates (2103 N. Lincoln St., Arlington, VA 22207), 1983— . Annual. looseleaf $184/yr.

Career guidance reference sources usually suffer from one of two polar limitations, either too much generality or too much specificity. Some, especially imitators of the U.S. Labor Department's *Occupational Outlook Handbook,* give good overviews of a field, but are too general to help a job hunter. Others are little more than corporate directories giving loads of specific information but none of it connected well enough to help a job hunter plan a strategy. *U.S. Employment Opportunities* hits the happy medium in its two-part annual reports on eighteen broad fields (e.g., health care, real estate, computers, banking, broadcasting, federal government). The first part of each original report offers an overview of the field and a thoughtful analysis of present and future employment opportunities in specific occupations. Part I generally concludes with a list of industry associations and major trade journals. Part II tells where the best job opportunities are, naming companies and describing them and the sort of people they hire. Specific job vacancies are also listed in Part II. The second part of every report is updated quarterly and the publisher hopes to increase the frequency of updates. Reports can be purchased separately in a minimum order of five. The reports take a little time to read, but job hunters who take that time will have a better understanding of the market when they hit the streets.

The World's Whales, by Stanley M. Minasian, Kenneth C. Balcomb III, and Larry Foster. New York: Norton, 1984. 224p. $27.50. 0-89599-014-8 84-14142

Because both are organized by the eleven families of whales and dolphins and both cover the seventy-six species in those families, *World's Whales* demands comparison to Lyall Watson's *Sea Guide to Whales of the World* (reviewed in *WLB,* February 1982). Both describe each species' size, color, markings, feeding habits, breathing and diving behavior, herding, and global distribution. Watson offers more thorough natural history information as well as local names and an explanation of the rationale for each species' classification. An almost tabular presentation of each of these items in *World's Whales* makes for quick reference, but is not as cohesive as Watson's more discursive approach. *World's Whales* sports impressive color photographs, but these sometimes depict only part of the whale, often partially obscured by the water. Watson's color drawings of each species, while clearer, lack photographic drama. Interestingly, the index to *World's Whales* uses *see* references from scientific names to popular names, just the opposite of Watson's practice. Because the strengths of these fine guides to cetaceans complement one another, these books can be recommended equally.

Library World

News of announcements, new posts, retirements, and deaths should be sent to "Library World," WLB, *950 University Ave., Bronx, NY 10452.*

ANNOUNCEMENTS

Charles Benton, past chairman of NCLIS, has been presented with a special award by the White House Conference on Library and Information Services Taskforce (WHCLIST). He was recognized for his commitment to and special support for the improvement of libraries and library services in the U.S.

John Frantz, city librarian for San Francisco, has received that city's 1984 Department Head of the Year Award. He was previously director of the Green Bay (Wisc.) PL.

NEW POSTS

Linda Barb, formerly regional services librarian at Fairbanks North-Star Library, Alaska, has been appointed regional reference librarian for the North Central Regional Library System, Wenatchee, Washington.

J. Edward Briggs has been named head of reference at Handley Library, Winchester, Va. He was formerly fine arts reference librarian at the State Univ. of N.Y. library, Binghamton.

Eloise Fasold has been appointed director of the Arapahoe Regional Library District, Littleton, Colo. Formerly assistant director, she replaces **Ann Kelver,** who retired.

Karen George, formerly assistant director, has been promoted to director of the Atlantic County library, Mays Landing, N.J.

Eloise Fasold

Marsha Grove, formerly Bordeaux Branch librarian with the Cumberland County PL system, Fayetteville, N.C., is now head of extension services for the system.

Ann Hutton is the new regional librarian for the Southeastern Libraries Cooperating/Regional library system, Rochester, Minn. She was previously library development consultant for the Illinois Valley library system, Pekin, Ill.

Ann Joslin, formerly automation consultant at the Idaho State Library, has been promoted to associate director.

Vicki Kreimeyer, formerly assistant director for public services at Lewis and Clark College library, Portland, Ore., has been appointed associate director at the Idaho State Library.

Ian MacPhail is now research fellow and curator of rare books at the Morton Arboretum, Lisle, Ill.

Anna Martinez, formerly supervising librarian in the extension division, has been promoted to deputy library director for the extension division of the San Diego (Calif.) PL.

Rita Padden has been appointed coordinator of public services for the North Central Regional library system, Wenatchee, Wash. She was previously head of children's services at the Sno-Isle regional library, Marysville, Wash.

Karen George

Shirley Payne, formerly coordinator of reader's services, has been promoted to director of the North Kingstown Free Library, North Kingstown, R.I.

Julie Quain has been named manager of library and medical school programs at BRS/Saunders. She was previously online training coordinator for the Greater Northeastern Regional Medical Library Program.

Martita Schwarz, formerly head of information services at Yonkers (N.Y.) PL, has been named head of the art/music/films department of the Minneapolis PL.

Elliott Shore has been appointed director of the historical studies/social science library at the Institute for Advanced Study.

Gail Terwilliger has been promoted to assistant head of extension services with the Cumberland Country PL system, Fayetteville, N.C. She was formerly coordinator of children's services for the library system.

Kristine Thurman, formerly director of the learning resources center at Western International Univ., Phoenix, Ariz., is now acquisitions librarian for the Ventura County Library Services Agency, Ventura, Calif.

Antoinette Walder, formerly with OHIONET, has been appointed head of the Xenia branch of the Greene County (Ohio) district library.

PLACE • MARKETPLACE • MARKETPLACE • MARK
MARKETPLACE • **MARKETPLACE** • MARKETPLACE
PLACE • MARKETPLACE • MARKETPLACE • MARK

Announcements

☐ The Minneapolis PL celebrates its centennial this year with events in March, April, and May. On March 2, the anniversary of the legislation creating the Library Board, libraries throughout the city held birthday parties. Other events include appearances by ALA President E. J. Josey, March 20, and Librarian of Congress Daniel Boorstin, April 25, at a gala banquet, lectures in May by David Godine, Frances Butler, Lowell Martin, and Eileen Cooke, and a variety of special exhibits. For more information contact Ruth Humleker, Minneapolis PL, 300 Nicollet Mall, Minneapolis, MN 55401, 612/372-6613.

☐ The 1985 Zena Sutherland Lectureship is held by Katherine Paterson, who received the Newbery Medal twice and the National Book Award for Children's Literature twice. She will give the lecture May 3 at the Chicago Cultural Center. Tickets to the lecture and reception are $10. Contact Sutherland Lectureship, Graduate Library School, University of Chicago, 1100 E. 57th St., Chicago, IL 60637.

☐ "Project Bookshare" is a new American Chemical Society program which collects chemistry textbooks and back issues of journals from donors and makes them available to libraries at small U.S. colleges, and to college and university libraries in developing countries. Donors should list their available books by title, with author, publisher, and date, and journals by title with dates. Books, except for classics, should be no more than ten years old, and materials should be in good condition. Send lists and inquiries to Gordon Bixler, Department of International Affairs, ACS, 1155 16th St., NW, Washington, DC 20036, 202/872-4449.

☐ Beginning in 1985, the Chinese-American Librarians Association will annually grant two $500 scholarships to full-time students in an ALA-accredited library school. CALA will also award an annual grant of $2000 to support research projects. Application deadline is May 1. Application forms and information are available from Eunice Ting, 2537 Cordelia Rd., Los Angeles, CA 90049, 213/825-5801.

☐ Two libraries have recently commissioned striking posters from graphic artist Lance Hidy. LC's Center for the Book poster promotes reading aloud with its depiction of a man seated outdoors reading to two children. The lettering is by calligrapher Julian Waters. The signed and numbered poster is available for $50 plus $5 for postage and handling; make checks payable to LC. A poster honoring New England bookbinder Arno Werner was commissioned by the Homer Babbidge Library at the University of Connecticut. Copies of the six-color signed and numbered serigraph are $75 plus $5 for postage and handling. Proceeds will go to the library. Order the reading aloud poster from the Information Office, Box A, LC, Washington, DC 20540, and the Arno Werner poster from Diane Castillo, Homer Babbidge Library, Business Services Office, U-5, University of Connecticut, Storrs, CT 06268.

Children's Specials

☐ Public libraries which have or are planning services and projects (other than traditional story hours) for children up to age five, and their parents or caregivers, are being asked to supply information on these projects to the Association for Library Service to Children/Public Library Association Task Force on the Development of a Preschool Project. To participate, send materials used in the program, publicity items, and a one-page description of objectives, size and age of target audience, funding, cooperating agencies, methods of service, and evaluation. Libraries with ideas for such projects are also encouraged to submit a description. Information should be submitted by April 15 to Craighton Hippenhammer, Cuyahoga County PL, 4510 Memphis Ave., Cleveland, OH 44144, 216/398-1800.

☐ One of the events in LC's celebration of Children's Book Week last year was a lecture given by Newbery Award-winner Madeleine L'Engle on the reading and writing of children's books, sponsored by the Center for the Book and the Children's Literature Center. The lecture, *Dare to Be Creative!*, has been published, along with a description of the activities of the Children's Literature Center by Sybille Jagush, the center's chief. Single copies of the 30p. booklet are available free from LC, Central Services Division, Washington, DC 20540.

☐ A new book from ALA for children looking for a good read uses subject headings that are meaningful to young readers. Thus the descriptive, but hardly catchy title: *Exciting, Funny, Scary, Short, Different, and Sad Books Kids Like about Animals, Science, Sports, Families, Songs, and Other Things.* Edited by Frances Laverne Carroll and Mary Meacham, *Exciting,* etc. lists approximately 1,000 books for children in grades 2–5 under 100 categories. More than fifty children's librarians contributed the brief annotations, composed to appeal to and be understood by children. Order the 168p. paperback for $10 from Publishing Services, ALA, 50 E. Huron St., Chicago, IL 60611.

Continuing Education

☐ Preservation of modern manuscripts on paper is the focus of the fourth annual seminar on the conservation of archival materials sponsored by the Harry Ransom Humanities Research Center at the University of Texas at Austin, to be held April 10–12. Contemporary conservation processes will be presented through lectures, demonstrations, and hands-on workshops. Registration is $235. For more information call Patricia Palmer at 512/471-9117 or write HRHRC Conservation Department, Drawer 7219, Austin, TX 78713.

☐ "Management of the Online Catalog," a two-day institute, will be presented April 8–9 at the University of Arizona Graduate Library School in Tucson. The program, cosponsored by the Library Administration and Management Association and the GLS, will be led by Joseph Matthews and Charles Hildreth and will feature demonstrations of existing online catalogs, with discussion of components, implementation, and the future of the online catalog. For more information, contact Roger Parent, ALA, 50 E. Huron St., Chicago, IL 60611, 312/944-6780.

☐ An intensive two-week program for library administrators, held at the University of Maryland, is now in its nineteenth year. The Library Administrators Development Program sessions, May 5–17, will cover such topics as leadership, decision making, financial planning, motivation, legal issues, marketing, and the impact of technology. Application deadline is April 1. For an application form or more information write Library Administrators Development Program, College of Library and Information Services, Hornbake Library, Room 4120G, University of Maryland, College Park, MD 20742.

☐ An audit or credit workshop for children's librarians and teachers, "The Illustrator as Storyteller," will be offered June 20–22 by the University of Iowa School of Library and Information Science. The children's picture book will be considered as a form of communication, a social, cultural, and historical document, and a prelude to literature, with a survey of types of picture books, evaluation, children's responses, and ways of sharing picture books with children. The fee is $63, and those taking the course for credit will be required to submit a written project. For more information contact Ethel Bloesch, SLIS, University of Iowa, 3087 Library, Iowa City, IA 52242, 319/353-3644.

☐ Children's librarians interested in a CE locale a bit more exotic than Iowa can enroll in "Children's Literature in China," a travel seminar offered June 14–30. The group will visit schools, libraries, and other educational settings in Beijing, Shanghai, Xian, Giulin, Hangzhou, and Hong Kong. Cost is $2990. For more information write CE-xchange International Planners, Inc., 132 Madison Ave., New York, NY 10016.

Film and Video

☐ Librarians visiting Chicago this summer who don't want to embarrass themselves by mistaking the John Hancock Building for the Sears Tower will be interested in two new releases from International Film Bureau. *Pioneers of Modern Architecture in Chicago* covers the work of Richardson, Sullivan, and Wright, and *Chicago's Modern Architecture* discusses the development of the skyscraper in Chicago, and works by Mies van der Rohe, Yamasaki, and Tigerman. Video sale price for each film is $350, for both, $625; 16mm sale price is $425 for each, $750 for both; 16mm rental is $35 for each film. Contact International Film Bureau Inc., 332 S. Michigan Ave., Chicago, IL 60604, 312/427-4545.

☐ Computer literacy is the goal of "Understanding Personal Computers," a series of videotapes from Metrics Research Corporation. Topics covered on the tapes include hardware, software, printers, word processing, and "starting out right." The tapes are twenty-five to thirty minutes long, and are available in VHS, Beta, and U-Matic for $129 each plus $4 shipping ($159 plus shipping for U-Matic). For more information write Metrics Research Corp., 130 W. Wieuca Rd., Suite 200, Atlanta, GA 30342.

☐ Every year the Academy of Motion Picture Arts and Sciences lends a film of the Student Film Achievement Award winners without charge to educational institutions so that it can be viewed by student filmmakers. This year's film, running approximately ninety minutes, includes films from New York University, the University of Illinois, Stanford, and the State University of New York. To request a viewing date contact Elaine Richard, Program Coordinator—Student Films, AMPAS, 8949 Wilshire Blvd., Beverly Hills, CA 90211.

Finding Aids

☐ Bill and Linda Sternberg Katz, who have guided librarians through the perils of magazine selection for many years, have now turned their attention to equally daunting fields, self-help and how-to books. *Self-Help: 1400 Best Books on Personal Growth* covers such subjects as health, education, etiquette, financial matters, job-hunting, and genealogy. *How-To: 1400 Best Books on Doing Almost Everything* lists books in such areas as how to perform sports, create crafts and art, and carry out DIY projects. Both books provide evaluative annotations, and include titles published between 1980 and 1984. They are available for $29.95 each or $53.95 for both from R. R. Bowker, Box 1807, Ann Arbor, MI 48106.

☐ A new newsletter on books by women on women's issues, *Women's Words,* provides annotations of about twenty-five books per issue, including fiction, nonfiction, and poetry. Published ten times a year, *Women's Words* is available for $12 for individuals and $18 for institutions from Kathy McLaughlin, 8 Fort Point St., #12, East Norwalk, CT 06855.

☐ The American Bar Association has published a directory of over 725 organizations, agencies, projects, and individuals that provide advocacy services to persons with mental and developmental disabilities. The 29p. publication, *Legal Resources for the Mentally Disabled: A Directory of Lawyers and Other Specialists* is available for $5 from the ABA, Commission on the Mentally Disabled, 1800 M St., NW, Washington, DC 20036.

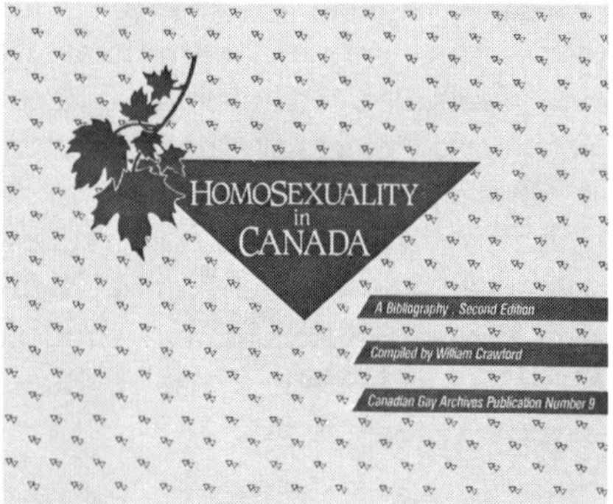

☐ *Homosexuality in Canada,* 2nd edition, compiled by William Crawford, is greatly expanded from the first edition, published in 1979. Entries are arranged by subject or format and include, in addition to books and articles, films, videotapes, government publications, and archival materials from the Canadian Gay Archives. The 378p. spiralbound book is available for $20 plus $3 postage and handling from the Canadian Gay Archives, Box 639, Station A, Toronto, Ont. M5W 1G2, Canada.

☐ A complement to *Legal Looseleafs in Print,* which lists legal reporters that require interfiling, *Legal Newsletters in Print 1985* lists newsletters and reporting services that do not require interfiling. The approximately 1,000 entries are arranged by title with address, frequency, price, where indexed, and a brief description of contents. There are publisher and subject indexes. The 228p. paperback is available for $50 from Infosources Publishing, 118 W. 79th St., New York, NY 10024.

From the GPO Presses

The following titles are a sample of recent publications available from the Government Printing Office. Specify stock number, price, and quantity when ordering. You may pay by check payable to the Superintendent of Documents or by Visa or Mastercard (give card number and expiration date). Send to Superintendent of Documents, United States GPO, Washington, DC 20402. Or call the order desk at 202/783-3238.

☐ In anticipation of a meteor shower of questions on Halley's Comet, libraries would do well to have on hand *Halley's Comet, a Bibliography,* by Ruth Freitag of LC's Science and Technology Division. It lists 3,289 references to the popular as well as scientific literature on the subject and includes a table of computed perihelion dates (when the comet was visible) beginning in 1404 BC. The 585p. volume, stock number 030-000-00158-3, is priced at $26.

☐ *Perspectives on Child Maltreatment in the Mid '80s* from the Department of Health and Human Services Office of Human Development Services contains papers on various aspects of child abuse. Topics include combatting child abuse and neglect, community involvement, overview of child neglect, sexual abuse, and emotional abuse. The 70p. publication, stock number 017-090-00076-3, is available for $2.75.

☐ Published on the occasion of an exhibition held last year, *Exposed and Developed: Photography Sponsored by the National Endowment for the Arts* is a catalog of the best photographs in the National Museum of American Art. Both color and black-and-white photographs are included. The 144p. publication, stock number 047-000-00396-2, is available for $11.

☐ *Age Pages* gives practical advice on health for the elderly, their families, and those who work with them. It includes articles on accidents, crime, arthritis, nutrition, high blood pressure, flu, and other concerns. The 52p. publication, stock number 017-062-00132-4, is available for $2.

Idea Exchange

☐ The Plainedge (New York) PL has added another title to its already long list of newsletters. The new bimonthly, *Tot Talks,* provides parents of toddlers and preschoolers with information on encouraging reading readiness and suggestions on other home activities. It is mailed to parents of children in that age group who attend library programs. The other newsletters produced by the library are *News for the Consumer, Community Courier* (community news), *Discovery* (for senior citizens), *Sunburst/ Expand* (for parents of gifted children), *Pierre the Pelican* (for expectant and new parents), and *Business Information from Your Library.* Sample copies of any of the newsletters can be obtained by sending a SASE to Joseph Eisner, Plainedge PL, 1060 Hicksville Rd., Massapequa, NY 11758.

☐ A special Sight Saving Room equipped to help those with limited vision has been opened at the Daniel Boone Branch of the St. Louis County (Missouri) Library. Those with low vision can use the room to read, draw, sew, study or listen to talking tapes. Equipment available includes five magnifier lamps, a reader which projects enlarged type on a video screen, the Talking World Book (the *World Book* encyclopedia on cassettes), and a collection of large print

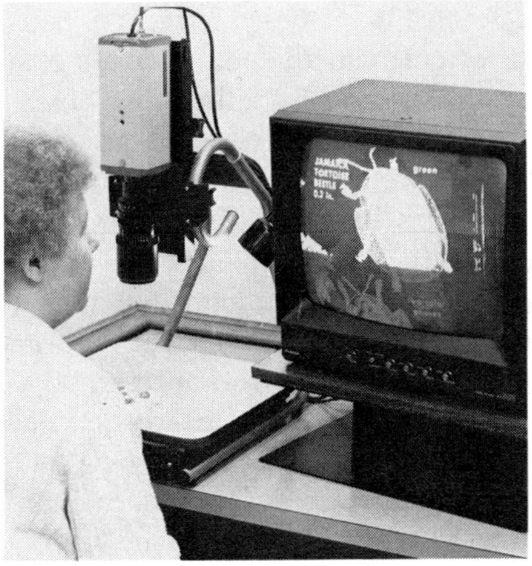

Equipment in use at the St. Louis County Library Daniel Boone Branch

books. The Ellisville Lions Club assisted in equipping the room.

☐ Young theatergoers in Birmingham, Michigan can attend a semi-monthly dinner theater at the Baldwin PL. Children from kindergarten age up bring a sack lunch (punch is supplied by the library) to the library's auditorium, where they dine at tables set with a seasonal theme. Post-dinner shows have included performances by a drama troupe, a puppeteer, and a mime. The program was inspired by a similar one at the Los Angeles PL.

☐ In a program that might work equally well with school boards or city commissions, the Connecticut LA Legislative Committee is assigning a librarian to each state legislator as a source of information on library issues. A training session for the Library Links was held, with advice from a lobbyist and a former state representative.

Magazine Notes

☐ A new semi-annual, *France Today,* caters to Americans with a business or a cultural interest in France. There are regular features on business, economics, technology, and law, as well as culture, food and wine, and travel. Subscriptions are $7 for two issues and $12 for four issues from *France Today,* Box 2510, Santa Ana, CA 92707.

☐ If Francophiles deserve their own magazine, so surely do the estimated 2.5 million Americans living abroad. *The International American* (formerly *Living Abroad*) provides legal, tax, financial, health, and travel information for both overseas Americans and frequent business travelers. In addition to practical matters, problems and tensions which expatriate Americans face are also addressed. Subscriptions to the monthly newsletter are $22 per year in the U.S., $26 overseas. Order from *The International American,* 201 E. 36th St., New York, NY 10016.

Media Center World

☐ Ruth Toor and Hilda Weisburg, the editors of the monthly *The School Librarian's Workshop,* have compiled thirty-three activities from that publication and thirty-three new ones in *66 Media Skills Puzzlers.* Providing exercises for students at all levels up to grade ten, the puzzlers teach and reinforce media use skills. Priced at $17, the book is available from Library Learning Resources, Inc., 61 Greenbriar Dr., Box 87, Berkeley Heights, NJ 07922.

☐ University Microfilms International has created two new microfiche sets for students from material published in the *New York Times. Great Personalities V* will support research with news, feature articles, and editorials on forty-one world figures. *The New York Times File: A Nation of Immigrants* contains over 2,000 articles spanning the years 1776–1984. Both sets are accompanied by a research guide which includes an index, discussion questions, and suggested research topics. *Great Personalities V* costs $105, with catalog cards for $10; *A Nation of Immigrants* costs $145, including catalog cards. For more information write Judy Carlson, Curriculum Products, UMI, 300 N. Zeeb Rd., Ann Arbor, MI 48106.

☐ To celebrate the centennial of the Statue of Liberty, the Photoduplication Service of the Library of Congress is making available prints of twelve views of the statue from the collections of the Prints and Photographs Division. "Selected Views of the Statue of Liberty," a flyer depicting the prints, and an order form/price list can be obtained by writing the Photoduplication Service, LC, Washington, DC 20540.

☐ Alarion Press has three new sound filmstrip series on the art of the Italian Renaissance. *Italian Renaissance Architecture and Sculpture* and *Italian Renaissance Painting* are for high school students. Each set consists of two cassettes, two filmstrips, a teaching manual, and a poster and is priced at $85. Both sets are available for $149. *History Through Art and Architecture* Ren 603 is for grades 4–9. It contains two cassettes, two filmstrips, a teaching manual, and a poster, and costs $85. For more information write Alarion Press, Box 1882, Boulder, CO 80306.

Products and Services

☐ The Worden Media Transport System is designed to cope with the

Worden Media Transport System

processing, sorting, and transporting of media in all shapes and sizes. The system consists of large coated wire baskets that attach to wall brackets or to a cart. The frame of the cart, which can revolve 360° in a standard thirty-six-inch aisle, is coated to act as a bumper. For more information contact Worden, 199 E. 17th St., Box 915C, Holland, MI 49423, 616/392-1848.

☐ Fiesta Publishing Corporation, a long-time distributor of Spanish-language books, is now publishing a catalog specifically for the library market. Mysteries, science fiction, classics, bestsellers, and children's books are listed, with package prices available for many combinations of titles. Fiesta is also actively seeking suggestions of types of books to distribute. For the catalog write Fiesta Publishing Corp., 6360 NE 4th Court, Miami, FL 33138.

New England Security Secure-A-Pen

☐ The annoyance factor may be worse than the budgetary impact, but pens disappearing from the public service desk is a recurring library plague. Pen-nappers can be stopped in their tracks by Secure-A-Pen, which attaches permanently to desk or counter tops with double stick tape. The pens use standard Parker refills. For more information write New England Security, 804 Broadway, Box 248, Raynham, MA 02767.

☐ Chief Manufacturing's Selectra-Set projector stand permits the use of up to three slide projectors at once. The projectors sit on cantilevered bases which can be adjusted in all directions. The Kodak EK-III, EK-II and S-AV, the Elmo, and the Telex/Singer slide projectors can be accommodated. The entire stand breaks

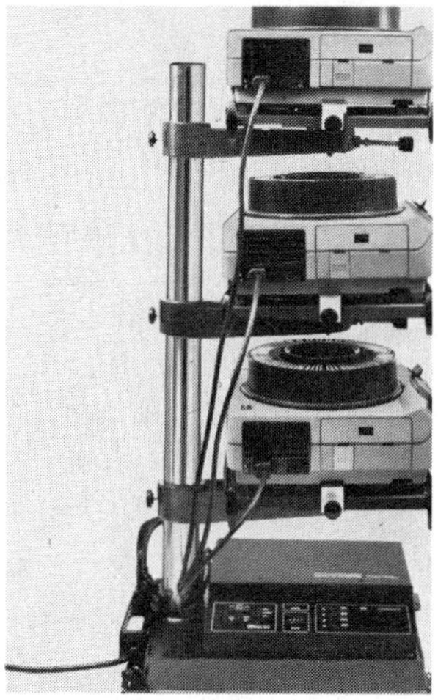

Chief Manufacturing Selectra-Set projector stand

apart for storage or transport. A one-tier unit costs $165, a two-tier unit, $249, and a three-tier unit, $339. For more information write Chief Manufacturing, Inc., 14310 Ewing Ave., S, Burnsville, MN 55337.

Professional Reading

☐ *Sheet Music Cataloging and Processing: A Manual,* by Sarah Shaw and Lauralee Shiere, has been published as MLA Technical Report No. 15. Steps in authority searching, cataloging, and processing, using AACR2 rules, LC subject headings, and the MARC Scores Format are detailed. A bibliography of reference sources useful in authority work is included. The 51p. manual is available for $11.74 ($9.40 to members) from the Music Library Association, Box 487, Canton, MA 02021.

☐ The National Information Standards Organization has published American National Standard Z39.48–1984, *Permanence of Paper for Printed Library Materials,* to establish criteria for uncoated paper. Paper which conforms to this standard's requirements for pH, alkaline reserve, and freedom from groundwood is anticipated to last several hundred years. The standard is available for $5 from ANSI, Sales Department, 1430 Broadway, New York, NY 10018.

☐ A new journal beginning this year is devoted to fee-based services in both the commercial and not-for-profit sectors. *Infomediary,* edited by Susan Klement, will address both practical and theoretical aspects of entrepreneurship within the information field. In addition to articles there will be reviews of interdisciplinary literature and reports on technological innovations and other relevant events. A subscription to the quarterly journal costs $92.50 plus $8 for postage and handling from Elsevier Science Publishers, Journal Information Center, 52 Vanderbilt Ave., New York, NY 10017.

☐ *dBASE II and dBASE III: An Introduction for Information Services,* 2nd edition, by Roger Palmer is designed for users of the database management program dBASE II in a library setting. Written for the novice, the chapters provide an introduction to file and database management, a crash course

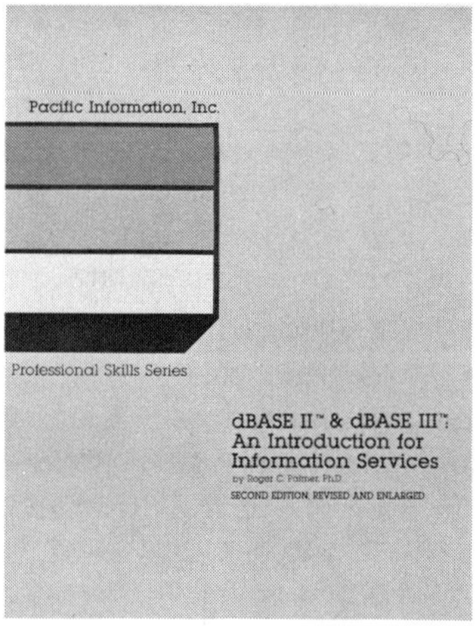

in dBASE II, instructions on file design, and directions for using dBASE III. Specific library functions addressed are sorting by library filing rules, subject headings, and creating a catalog. The paperback costs $25 from Pacific Information Inc., 11684 Ventura Blvd., Suite 295, Studio City, CA 91604.

Software

☐ A new program from Combase can teach index use skills to middle-school through adult patrons. *Using an Index to Periodicals* provides individualized, self-paced instruction, using the

Readers' Guide as an example. There are two levels of the program, one for novices and one for those with some familiarity with indexes. Each costs $50, including a back-up disk, from Combase, Inc., Suite 890, 333 Sibley St., St. Paul, MN 55101, 800/328-6795, ext. 264.

☐ Increasing reading speed and improving the ability to scan material for key points is the goal of *Excel-A-Read* from American Educational Computer. Intended for use by adolescents through adults, the software tests comprehension after each scanning or reading exercise, and advances successful learners to a higher level of instruction. The three-disk set costs $69.95 and can be used with IBM PC, PCjr, Atari, Apple, and Commodore computers. For more information write American Educational Computer, Inc., 2450 Embarcadero Way, Palo Alto, CA 94303.

☐ Palantir has announced price reductions on its word processor ($250, formerly $395) and filer ($145, formerly $195) programs. There is also a speller, priced at $145. All can be used with IBM PC, PCjr, XT and compatible systems, Apple II and III, DEC Rainbow, and CP/M-80 systems. For more information contact Palantir Software, 12777 Jones Rd., Suite 100, Houston, TX 77070, 713/955-8880.

Write for These

☐ *American Indians: A Select Catalog of National Archives Microfilm Publications,* compiled by Cynthia Fox and edited by Constance Potter describes microfilmed federal records that relate to American Indians, the formation of federal Indian policy, and the personnel involved. The 103p. catalog is available for $2 to the general public, but there is no charge for libraries requesting copies for public use. Order on official letterhead from National Archives Catalog, Box 2580, Potomac Station, Alexandria, VA 22301.

☐ The International Communication Industries Association report, *Computer Assisted Instruction (CAI): The Bottom Line,* prepared by Education Turnkey Systems, summarizes recent studies on the effectiveness of CAI and highlights the characteristics of quality courseware. The report was designed to be used as a selling tool by the educational software industry, but educators can use it to promote their needs to adminstrators. *CAI: The Bottom Line* is available for $2 (inquire about quantity prices) from ICIA Training Department, 3150 Spring St., Fairfax, VA 22031, 703/273-7200.

☐ The Ohio Regional Association of Law Libraries' *Guidelines for Legal Reference Service* can assist librarians in developing policy and strategy for handling legal reference questions from the public. To obtain a copy, send a SASE to Anita Shew, Butler County Law Library, 141 Court St., Hamilton, OH 45011.

INDEX TO ADVERTISERS

Gale Research Company .... 4th cover
Gaylord Bros., Inc. .... 2nd cover
OCLC 433
Unlisted Marketplace 437
H. W. Wilson Company .... 434, 498, 3rd cover

Credits:
p. 467—Kathy Walker; 471—David Jacobson; 473—Patricia Berglund; 475—Artemas Cole; 477—Joseph Farris; 482—Picture Book Studio USA; 483—Dial Books; 484—Crowell; 485—Fawcett Juniper; 486—Scribners; 488—Fanlight Productions; 490—Victoria Pearson; 500—Doubleday, Facts on File; 501—Scribners; 509—St. Louis County Library.

WLB Classifieds

Classified Advertising is accepted six weeks preceding date of issue. Charges are: minimum 3 lines—$10; each additional line—$2.50. If voucher forms are required, please send them when submitting copy. All advertisements for positions must exclude reference to race, creed, color, age, and sex as conditions for employment.

Positions Open

Announcements

For Sale

Wilson Library Bulletin

April 1985

Wilson Library Bulletin

April 1985, Volume 59, Number 8 *ISSN 0043-5651*

Our cover for April was taken by freelance photographer **Nino Mascardi**.

Departments

Letter from New York/Editorial 516
Correspondence 517
Upfront/News—*Five libraries to receive ALA awards; U.S. Court of Appeals finds against Merwine; Memphis-Shelby Library considering action against Data-Phase; Illinois and Wyoming to build new state libraries; Cooke objects to elimination of postal subsidies; Curley appointed director of Boston Public Library; Nemeyer resigns from Library of Congress; late news.* 518
Library World 567
Marketplace 568
WLB Classifieds 575

Articles

Video Technology: Conveying Information Visually *D'Ellen Bardes* 524
Computerized Braille: The Boulder Story *Fran Hooker* 527
Children's Librarianship: Doing a Better Job *Linda Braun* 531

Features

Dateline—Washington *Dale Nelson* 534
Eye on Publishing *Anne McGrath* 536
Facing the Public *Will Manley* 538
Online Update *Martin Kesselman* 540

Reviews

Picture Books for Children *Donnarae MacCann/Olga Richard* 542
The Young Adult Perplex *Patty Campbell* 544
Murder in Print *Kathleen Maio* 546
Front Row Center *Judith Trojan* 548
On Record: Popular Music *Bruce Pollock* 550
Our Profession *Norman Stevens* 552
Software for Libraries *Patrick Dewey* 554
Current Reference Books *James Rettig* 556
Editor's Choice *Gail Pool* 562

The *Wilson Library Bulletin* is published monthly except in July and August by The H. W. Wilson Company, 950 University Avenue, Bronx, N.Y. 10452. Second-class postage paid at Bronx, N.Y. and additional mailing offices.

The *Wilson Library Bulletin* is indexed in *Education Index, Library Literature,* and *Popular Periodical Index* and abstracted in *Library & Information Science Abstracts, Historical Abstracts,* and *America: History and Life.* Book reviews are indexed in *Book Review Index.* Subscription $30 a year, U.S. and Canada; $35, foreign. Single copies $4, U.S. and Canada; $4.50, foreign (remittance with order, please). Address all correspondence about subscriptions to the publisher. No subscriptions through agents. Telephone: (212) 588-8400

Letter from New York

Editorial

Food, gas, lodging, and library

The national library symbol promoted by the American Library Association for the past three years has finally been accepted by the Federal Highway Administration for inclusion in thir *Manual on Uniform Traffic Control Devices*. Although the agency had not initially shown much enthusiasm for the symbol, finding it "ambivalent," its acceptance statement conceded that the device has received widespread use and support. Like Niagara Falls, it seems to be working.

To insure that the public understands the meaning of the symbol, all new signs errected over the next four years must be accompanied by the designation "library." The sign, for highway use, will be white on green.

"This is," said Bob Garen, chair of the ALA Committee on Library Symbol Implementation, "a hallelujah day." Perhaps he is right.

We were certainly not an early advocate of the library symbol. Designed by Ralph Devore for use in the Western Maryland public library system, the emblem seemed almost too abstract, passive, bookish. We had little idea as to what might constitute an improvement. It would only provoke confusion to portray a library ladder, a book truck, a date-due card, or a Bruning electric eraser. But couldn't the sign achieve at least some low-grade level of excitement? Did it have to be a faceless, round-shouldered robot hunched over a titleless book? Must it be blue and white?

As librarians we have a rich tradition of searching for our identity, fashioning a proper image, reaching out for status, and attempting to establish some small degree of public insight into the work we practice. If it has been difficult to understand who we are, it has been equally troublesome to maneuver our public into comprehending what we do. For many librarians it has not only been the work of a career to establish their professional identity, but the labor of a lifetime to induce library patrons to appreciate the significance of libraries as an institution.

The prosaic library tour and current proposals for an International Year of the Library are only the unfortunate extremes of our effort to educate users. We provide handouts explaining ourselves by the millions, hold open houses, receptions, and grand openings, provide lectures, mount exhibits, and support National Library Week. In the last several years American libraries have done a commendable job of explaining themselves, of inviting use, of beckoning generously.

Much of what has been done was merely in the cause of keeping our users aware of our historic purposes—offering information, providing reference assistance, loaning books. Advances in communications technology, however, have thrown us into the future, placing us miles down the road from where we once stood and where, in most cases, our users still are.

Our ability to identity and locate books and other library material has largely been solved in our time, making it more obviously purposeful to share our resouces on both a local and national level. We are dealing with clients, however, who largely see us as operating in the manner characteristic of us in the early part of the century. We are viewed as keepers and archivists, as a quaint and enduring profession of people with backroom expertise in cataloging, classification, order and procedure, pattern and ritual. Libraries are still viewed as an adjunct to one's education, not at the heart of it, and certainly not at the cutting edge. The truth, however, is rapidly becoming otherwise.

Librarians have also changed. Slipping out of the Victorian garments of our earlier life, we have become as diversified as any other professional group in this country. Librarians are information specialists, media experts, database searchers, budget planners, lobbying activists, fund-raisers, writers, speakers, and consultants. Modern librarians are familiar with computer applications, telecommunications, preservation techniques, and copyright law. What we were is not what we are.

Our new, elaborate, and complex persona notwithstanding, we are now the owners of an officially sanctioned highway marker to advertise and make known our presence.

To motorists out on the freeway we will take our chances on recognition and patronage along with the neighboring Mobil station, McDonalds' restaurant, and Holiday Inn. We can't offer assistance to a motorist who has driven for the last twenty miles with his fuel gauge on empty, or the small comfort of an envelope of french fried potatoes, or the general salvation of a cocktail and soft bed. No gas, food, or lodging.

We can only offer what we have always offered—some lasting directions. If our final stand for recognition is to be at the exit ramp on Interstate 480, so be it. Maybe we should have been there years ago.

—Milo Nelson

Correspondence

WLB welcomes letters from its readers. Correspondence should be sent to Wilson Library Bulletin, 950 University Avenue, Bronx, N.Y. 10452.

Rising up in protest

With reference to "Ladies of the Club: An Arkansas Story" (*WLB,* January).

"But the story of the library in Helena is really about southern ladies, not coy belles cooing over their beaux, but resourceful and determined women who moved here from the North and East after the Civil War and replanted the culture of literacy they brought with them."

Well, sho' 'nuff, the po' lil southern ladies be too hep-less and mushmouf to have any literacy. What an asinine statement! All Southerners, past and present, should rise up in protest of such a remark. Shame on *WLB* for an editor not catching it.

SHARON BODKIN
Jefferson County Library
Chimacum, Washington

Luck and allergies

Thank you very much for Mary Davis' article in the February *WLB* ("Preservation Using Pesticides: Some Words of Caution").

In addition to being the only clear article on the pesticide deal, I now have a beaut of an excuse for why my poor, old brain has gone bye-bye.

I had noticed some problems with No-Pest strips several years back and discontinued their use. Now I see why. The annual black widow spider thing and after-effects is now clearer. We still have the interesting problem of which one is going to kill a patron first . . . or the staff. Depends on their luck and allergies, I guess.

A very valuable article.

HELEN PRESCOTT
Imperial Public Library
Imperial, California

Living under a new name

Thank you for reviewing my book, *A Guide to Fairs and Festivals in the United States* ("Current Reference Books," *WLB,* February).

However, I would like to point out that the "defunct Chicagofest" is still well and alive and living under a new name. This change came months after my book was published.

As for the Dayton Air Fair (real name: Dayton International Airshow and Trade Exposition, Vandalia, Ohio), they asked not to be included in my books. They felt that they were more trade oriented.

FRANCES SHEMANSKI
Bronx, New York

Working on their behalf

Thank you for publishing the article on Eileen Cooke in your February issue. It is helpful to have handy for all the people who keep asking me why they should pay dues in ALA, even as they benefit from Cooke's work on their behalf.

MARY CHELTON
Department of Public Libraries
Virginia Beach, Virginia

Further reading

Ellen Fecher's article, "Consumer Health Information: a Prognosis" (*WLB,* February 1985), overlooks the health information and health education materials collected and announced by federal health information clearinghouses. Although the extent to which these clearinghouses collect consumer-oriented material varies, many of them produce bibliographies of patient education materials—with complete bibliographic citations and availability information—that will assist the public librarian in collection development.

Three of these clearinghouses made their bibliographic files available in the Combined Health Information Database (CHID), which is searchable via BRS. The original participants in CHID were the Arthritis Information Clearinghouse (AIC), the National Diabetes Information Clearinghouse (NDIC), and the Center for Health Promotion and Education CHPE). The National Digestive Diseases Education and Information Clearinghouse and the High Blood Pressure Information Center have recently joined CHID as well.

Librarians may also find CHPE's monthly abstracting publication. *Current Awareness in Health Education,* to be a valuable source of health education materials. It is available from the Government Printing Office by subscription for $34 per year.

A listing of federal health information clearinghouses and other public and private resources to which library patrons may be referred is maintained by the National Health Information Clearinghouse (NHIC), whose reference file is also searchable on BRS. Its directory, *Health Information Resources in the Federal Government,* is available on request from the National Health Information Clearinghouse, Box 1133, Washington, D.C. 20013.

NANCY WRIGHT
Herner and Company Library
Arlington, Virginia

UPFRONT NEWS

University of Michigan Law Library

Folger Shakespeare Library

Vail Public Library

NYU Graduate School of Business Library

San Francisco University High School Library

Five libraries to receive AIA awards

Five libraries have been selected to receive Awards of Excellence for Library Architecture in the eleventh library buildings award program jointly sponsored by the American Institute of Architects and the American Library Association. Recipients are the Folger Shakespeare Library, New York University Graduate School of Business Library, San Francisco University High School Library, University of Michigan Law Library, and the Vail (Colorado) Public Library.

The awards are given every other year by the AIA and ALA's Library Administration and Management Association to encourage excellence in the architectural design and planning of libraries.

The Folger Shakespeare Library addition was designed by Hartman-Cox Architects, Washington, D.C., to achieve "a remarkable incidence of alchemy" in blending "monumental Washington" with the Elizabethan interior of the library, according to the awards jury. The New York University Graduate School of Business Library, designed by Voorsanger & Mills Associates, New York City, was described by the jury as "a significant renovation" that transforms an existing library and loft space within a highrise office building into "an exciting place to study." The San Francisco University High School Library was designed by Robert Herman Associates, San Francisco, to create a human-scale orientation for students at a small private school. The jury observed that the architect's solution, built on top of an existing two-story steel and concrete auditorium, "admirably plays off design elements of the original school building and then deftly inserts a new level under the recreational surface on the roof." The University of Michigan Law Library, designed by Gunnar Birkerts & Associates, Birmingham, Michigan, is a three-story underground structure, featuring two light wells sheathed in a bronze curtain-wall with tinted insulating glass units. The jury called the below-grade expansion a "masterstroke of campus planning and design." The Vail Public Library, designed by Snowdon & Hopkins, Vail, Colorado, has "a strong sense of being indigenous to the regional architecture," according to the jury. "The architect," said the jury, "produced a library that evokes the duality of rustic informality and sophisticated library planning."

Court of Appeals finds against Merwine

On March 8 the U.S. Court of Appeals, Fifth Circuit, found against Glenda Merwine in the case of Merwine *v.* Board of Trustees for State Institutions of Higher Learning. Merwine had alleged intentional sex discrimination against Mississippi State University and members of its hiring committee under Title VII of the Civil Rights Act of 1964. She also alleged that the imposition of MSU's entry-level requirement for a librarian to hold the MLS degree from an ALA accredited library school had an adverse impact on women in violation of Title VII. Merwine's complaint arose from her unsuccessful application for a position as head librarian at a branch of MSU's School of Veterinary Medicine.

In the March 8 decision, Judge Robert Hill held that "Applicant who did not possess published mimimum educational requirement of a master's degree in library science was indisputably unqualified for position and could not recover from university or members of its hiring committee under civil rights statute." Hill also stated that the "record would not support a finding that degree requirement was pretextual" and held that the requirement that applicants hold a master's degree from a school accredited by the American Library Association "has a manifest relationship" to the position open for hiring.

The written opinion handed down by the appellate court states "While administrative convenience alone does not validate MSU's imposition of the degree requirement, we believe that MSU's preference for an objective degree requirement that is widely recognized by academic and professional employers and that is required by approximately eighty percent of college and university libraries is supported as a valid business necessity."

Cooke objects to elimination of postal subsidies

Eileen Cooke, director of the ALA Washington Office, told the House Postal Operations and Services Subcommittee that the Reagan administration's proposals to eliminate all postal subsides would have a devastating effect. Said Cooke, "The library community is shocked at the administration's proposal to zero out the revenue foregone appropriations for the library rate, the free mailing for the blind and physically handicapped, and the nonprofit mailers. And we're flabbergasted at the mischievous administration proposal to cross-subsidize free and reduced rate mail by having the other 'ratepayers' lift that burden from the 'taxpayers'—as if we were not all ratepayers as well as taxpayers. The administration is completely overlooking the statutory criteria for setting postal rates and fees which include special recognition of the 'educational, cultural, scientific, and informational value to the recipient of mail matter.'"

The Senate Budget Committee has approved elimination of all postal revenue foregone appropriations and adoption of the Office of Management and Budget proposal to retain some nonprofit subsidies by raising nonsubsized rates.

Memphis considering action against DataPhase

The Memphis-Shelby County Public Library, Memphis, Tennessee is considering legal action against DataPhase over a computer installation that still isn't working to capacity. The $438,800 DataPhase contract was signed in January 1981 with the provision that $21,000 be withheld until the computer system was tested and found acceptable. The money is still being withheld.

Robert Croneberger, library director when the computerized circulation system was put in place, said DataPhase provided an inadequate system out of "either ignorance or maliciousness." Croneberger is now the state archivist.

Although the branch libraries are connected to the system, the main library, comprising over 600,000 volumes, was not able to be accommodated because of limited memory and storage space.

To date the library has spent more than $720,000 on the DataPhase installation, including an upgrading of additional disk drives. In spite of the upgrading, the system is still not capable of handling the workload.

Sallie Johnson, acting library director, has asked the city attorney to explore the possibility of legal action against DataPhase.

Wyoming to build new state library

A $500,000 appropriation for architectural plans and specifications for a new state library building has been included in Wyoming Governor Ed Herschel's recommendations for capital outlay. The appropriation is included in the current state budget.

The Wyoming State Library is presently located in a building that also houses the Supreme Court and the state law library. The structure, completed in 1937, is no longer adequate in office and stack space.

The state library has been in existence since 1871 when it was established by the Second Territorial Assembly.

Illinois Governor proposes new state library

In his State of the State message in February, Governor James Thompson of Illinois endorsed the construction of a new state library facility. "I propose that we build a new state library in Springfield for all of Illinois—a library that works—not a warehouse that doesn't—and that we spend $25 million over the next two years to do it," said Thompson.

Governor Thompson also recommended that the legislature "help local libraries throughout the state educate our children and grandchildren, and that we spend $8 million over the next four years to do it."

Curley appointed director of Boston Public

Arthur Curley, deputy director, Research Libraries, New York Public Library, has been appointed director of the Boston Public Library. The board of trustees of the Boston Public Library thus ended the search for a new director that began almost two years ago with the retirement of former director Philip McNiff.

Curley was deputy director of the Detroit Public Library prior to assuming his post at New York Public and has directed libraries in Massachusetts, Illinois, New Jersey, and Ohio.

A Boston native, Curley holds an AB degree from Harvard University and received his MSLS from Simmons College. He presently serves on the Executive Board of the American Library Association.

Nemeyer to leave Library of Congress

Carol Nemeyer, associate librarian for national programs, Library of Congress, has resigned her position effective May 15, a post she has held since 1977. From 1971–77 she was employed by the Association of American Publishers and prior to this assignment worked as a librarian for McGraw-Hill, Inc. In 1982 Nemeyer served as president of the American Library Association.

Nemeyer and her husband plan to set sail around the world on their forty-four foot ketch, *Rainbow,* to "explore and discover." Nemeyer said she hopes to become the "first floating library emissary."

Michigan acquires Zenith microcomputers

The University of Michigan Library has acquired seventy Zenith 150 microcomputers from Zenith Data Systems for the use of library staff. The computers, which will be distributed to library units across the campus, have an internal modem, printer, and an integrated software package. In addition to the initial purchase of microcomputers, Zenith has donated fifty Zenith 150 machines to the undergraduate library's microcomputer center.

Richard Dougherty, library director, said "At a time of reduced and reconfigured library staffs, we see the library's microcomputer network as providing critical support for communication, for operations, and for innovation. Perhaps more importantly it will provide a vital link with faculty and researchers already involved in the emerging electronic environment on campus."

CRL receives grant for building renovation

The Center for Research Libraries, Chicago, has received a $150,000 grant from the Joseph Pew Charitable Trust for renovation of the consortium's original building at Cottage Grove. Constructed in 1950, the building housed most of the center's collections and staff up until the completion of the organization's new structure on Kenwood Avenue in 1982. The older building continues to hold nearly all of the center's monographs and is used as a headquarters for CRL's bibliographic retrospective conversion projects.

The grant will be used to renovate exterior and interior walls and to repair an elevator system serving seven floors of book stacks.

Philadelphia Mayor W. Wilson Goode *presents a $75,000 check to* **Keith Doms** *(left), director of the Free Library of Philadelphia, to purchase materials for the library's Reader Development Program, part of the city's literacy effort. The funds were donated to the city by the William Penn Foundation and the Glemede Trust Company. Marciene Mattleman, executive director, Mayor's Commission on Literacy, assists in the presentation.*

The funds will supplement the library's support of the Reader Development Program which, since 1967, has provided instructional materials for adult learners and agencies in Philadelphia that are teaching adults to read. In 1984 the program served ninety-nine such organizations, ranging from formal classes to small neighborhood tutoring programs.

Rutgers receives grants for training information specialists

The School of Communication, Information, and Library Studies at Rutgers, the State University of New Jersey, has received two grants to develop programs preparing information specialists for careers in a technological age. A three-year federal grant totalling $220,000 to develop graduate education focusing on the impact of electronic communication on training for information science and communication positions has been awarded by the Fund for the Improvement of Postsecondary Education. A three-year state grant to develop similar programs at the undergraduate level has been awarded by the Fund for the Improvement of Collegiate Education.

In the first phase of the grants investigators will use focus groups, interviews, and surveys to identify the needs and issues that people in education and business consider critical for the development of information specialists.

Illinois adds books at lower cost

A study sponsored by the Council on Library Resources reveals that the University of Illinois at Urbana-Champaign spends less money to put new acquisitions on its shelves than seven other libraries examined in the study. Paul Kantor, president of Tantalus, Inc., a Cleveland library management consultant firm that undertook the study for CLR, said, "Of the eight libraries in the study, Illinois had the best ranking for the cost of processing volumes." Illinois spends an average of $25.52 for the combined costs of all the processes a book can go through. The same total costs for each of the other libraries ranged from $26.76 to $66.42. "According to published statistics, Illinois also adds more volumes every year than any of the other seven libraries," Kantor said. "The correlation between low cost and adding a large number of volumes is one of the most important general findings of the study."

Michael Gorman, director of general services for the library, said, "The management policies largely responsible for keeping operating costs low are giving clerical workers as much work as possible, designing efficient work procedures, and using an online computer system for cataloging." Gorman noted that "you will probably find in the higher-cost libraries there are a number of professional librarians and faculty members doing clerical work. Also, high-cost libraries don't make much use of automation."

The other libraries in the study included those at the University of Georgia, Northwestern, Cornell, Emory, Vanderbilt, Johns Hopkins, and New York University.

Kentucky forms literacy commission

Kentucky Governor Martha Collins recently announced the formation of a statewide literacy commission to "confront head-on the problem of illiteracy among adults." The twenty-member group will work with the state's Department for Libraries and Archives and the Department of Education in an effort to coordinate ongoing literacy projects. The commission will also serve as an advocacy group to gain private, community, and legislative support for the statewide literacy initiative.

ALA Publishing Services to reorganize

The American Library Association Publishing Services Department is planning a reorganization to strengthen management of the association's $5 million publishing business and enhance services to ALA members and customers. Individual marketing units will be combined in a marketing services section that will develop services for all ALA divisions and offices. Order billing, customer service, subscription, and central production units will work together as the production and distribution services section, taking advantage of recent automation enhancements.

Reference Books Bulletin, published as a part of *Booklist* for nearly thirty years, will move administratively under the *Booklist* editor. Helen Wright, who has edited *Reference Books Bulletin* for twenty-six years, will leave that post for a new position in Publishing Services—assistant director for new product planning.

The reorganization of ALA Publishing Services will take effect in September.

Kentucky to study state library needs

The Kentucky Department for Libraries and Archives has signed a contract with Peat, Marwick, Mitchell and Company to do a major study of public library needs in Kentucky, with recommendations for services which the state might provide to meet those needs. The project is expected to be the most comprehensive effort yet made in Kentucky to identify local public library needs.

The consultant firm intends to draw on their special expertise for multi-disciplinary planning by utilizing investigative methodologies taken from such areas as urban planning, high technology, corporate strategy, and creative financing.

"Libraries, Books and Culture," an international library history seminar recently held at the University of North Carolina at Chapel Hill, was dedicated to **Haynes McMullen** *(shown above left, with Dean Edward Holley), professor of library science at the university. The seminar, seventh in a series of meetings held every five years, was sponsored by the UNC School of Library Science, the Graduate School of Library and Information Science at the University of Texas, and the Journal of Library History.*

A UNC faculty member since 1972, the seventy-year-old McMullen will retire in May. Holley called McMullen "one of the top two or three library historians in the country. He has made many contributions through scholarship and writing during his fifty-year career."

The project is funded through LSCA Title I from the Kentucky Department for Libraries and Archives under the general oversight of the Kentucky Advisory Council on Libraries. The project is targeted for completion in the summer of 1986.

RLG announces IBM PC version of RLIN terminal

The Research Libraries Group has announced its intention to distribute software that allows an IBM PC to operate like an RLIN-programmed terminal. The terminal emulation software is the first of three stages in RLG's development of additional character set capabilities for RLIN.

The RLIN terminal emulation software, available on diskette, will enable libraries to use an IBM PC as a standard RLIN input terminal. The software will support input and display of the full Roman alphabet, including the ALA extensions to the American Standard Code for Information Interchange.

The second stage of development will be completed later this year when RLG will offer support on the IBM PC for Cyrillic input, searching, and display in RLIN. Support for the Cyrillic alphabet will be based on the stage one RLIN terminal emulation software.

In the final stage, RLG will release software to support Hebrew input and display on the IBM PC/AT. In 1986, support for Arabic will be added to the software.

At the present time RLG supports the input and display of Chinese, Japanese, and Korean vernacular in RLIN using specially designed RLG CJK terminals.

The RLIN software can only be used on the RLIN synchronous telecommunications network. If a user is not replacing an existing RLIN terminal with an IBM PC, this may require installation of a leased telephone line and a modem.

Chicago Public transfers Hebrew materials

The Chicago Public Library recently transferred 5,000 volumes in Hebrew and Yiddish from its collection to the holdings of the University of Illinois at Urbana-Champaign. The library decided to transfer the material because the population of Yiddish and Hebrew readers in Chicago has declined and the books were seldom borrowed.

Video Technology: Conveying Information Visually

D'Ellen Bardes

Visual communications technologies—videotape, videodisc, and graphic-imaging boards—are changing the usage, sales/evaluation process, and design of institutional information management systems.

Video literacy, or a fundamental understanding of video technologies, needs to be attained by individuals responsible for the planning and control of data, soon to be data/image, management systems and software.

Video, taken directly from the Latin word meaning "I see," is increasingly changing inter- and intra-business communications. Videotapes and videodiscs are cost-effectively replacing person-to-person, printed, and electronic media. Videotape, magnetic tape with a sensitive surface of iron oxide particles, is easy to duplicate, edit, and transport. Videotape recorders are devices which rearrange the iron particles on magnetic tape so that video signals can be stored on tape to be played back later. A reflective laser optical disc, or videodisc, has the capability to store the equivalent of 3,500, 5 1/4-inch computer floppy disks, 108,000 individual frames (still-video pictures), an hour of moving video, or any combination of the three, as well as an hour of audio, on its two sound tracks.

Featuring consistency of message delivery, "time-swapping," and visually personalized electronic information, video is being used in addition to, and in place of, technical and marketing company and product brochures, users guides, salespersons, training manuals, annual reports, maintenance manuals, and live seminars.

DEC's Interactive Video Information System

Timely information, cost savings

Providing timely information and hard dollar cost savings, videotaped communications are beneficial to both purchasers and vendors within the public and private library vertical market segment. Minicomputer Systems, Inc., Boulder, Colorado, the custom software developer of The Irving Library Network, is planning an end-user training tape to augment their personalized support effort. Well-known for their sophisticated, real-time, customized communications software, MSI is tying together dissimilar central processing units within the association of Denver metropolitan libraries.

Carlyle Information Systems, Berkeley, California, reveals that they receive up to thirty requests per week for demonstrations of their online catalog system, which was recently purchased by the New York Public Library system. Yet, Stephen Salmon, chief executive officer, indicates that it is not feasible to send a representative with a Carlyle UP5 computer and TOMUS (The Online Multiple User System) software out to so many libraries and educational institutions around the country in an efficient or timely manner. Thus, Carlyle is planning their first videotape production.

The tape will introduce computerized, online, direct access to entire library systems' textual (bibliographic) database, display the actual computer screens with which the TOMUS user interfaces, and graphically symbolize Carlyle's distributed, networked, systems configuration. "A videotape is the next best thing to having the actual system there," Salmon explains. "A tape makes it a lot easier to tell if it is the kind of system they want and to grasp TOMUS technically."

New video users, such as MSI and Carlyle, have a lot of company. Annual nonbroadcast (excluding commercial network and cable television programming) video expenditures by private industry, organizations, and institutions is currently in excess of $2

D'Ellen Bardes *is president, AllTech Communications, Denver, Colorado.*

billion—and growing. More than 11,000 organizations have recognized the high level of viewer acceptance, and the cost-effectiveness of well planned, electronic visual communications.

Of equal, or perhaps greater significance, is the coming integration of image management and visual enhancement of existing application software with traditional information management systems. Today, technology is available which provides the capability to capture and display video images on a personal computer's CRT, to store and modify high-resolution image/ data/ graphics files on optical laser discs and digital laser discs, and to transmit high-resolution, exact "pictures" across regular telephone wires from your PC.

But, without a fundamental understanding of "video software," or video programming, it is difficult to judge and to control the quality of product received for either informational or educational purposes—let alone to plan to incorporate visuals into the organization's probably only partially integrated computer and communications system.

AllTech Communications, a Denver-based video integration and market research firm, conducted an independent survey of the use and application of video technologies at the fall meeting of COMDEX in Las Vegas, Nevada. As the computer and communications industries' major semi-annual trade show, The Computer Dealer Exposition, sponsored by The Interface Group, Needham, Massachusetts, included over 1,400 exhibitors vying for the attention of the dealers and distributors among the almost 100,000 attendees.

Exemplifying how video is changing the marketing, management and design of technical information products, tapes used at COMDEX fell into four distinct classifications:

- **MARKETING:** Thirty-second film or tape "broadcast-quality" commercials, or three- to five-minute videotapes designed to attract dealers' attention, deliver a sales pitch, visually describe a company's performance, or highlight product benefits.
- **INFORMATIONAL**: Nine- to twenty-minute videotaped demonstrations, customer installations, or product feature/benefit guides—often "bundled" with its respective product for "free" distribution to dealers and distributors.
- **END PRODUCT**: Thirty- to 150-minute step-by-step training manuals, both tape and disk, for popular software packages or microcomputers, and developed by third-party companies strictly for resale.
- **DEMONSTRATIONAL**: One second to sixty minutes of demonstrational material, either still, real-time images or individual frames of motion, which are stored on a videodisc and played on a player powered by a computer.

After reviewing several productions or products within each grouping, the extension of the information system to include visuals becomes evident. COMPAQ, Texas Instruments, and Dennison were most successful at maintaining a captive audience to view their products in their entirety.

Marketing

COMPAQ Computer built a huge COMPAQ Portable within which a comfortable living room with plush couches welcomed weary dealers to view "Going Places." Produced in-house by Ken Price, Director of Communications, in only six days, the fast-moving, four-minute picture essay used only music with no narrative. The tape depicted escalating revenue charts, efficient manufacturing facilities, Portable to DeskPro product-line succession and the people comprising the COMPAQ team. "Some attendees, new to the industry, are not familiar with who COMPAQ is. In light of the shake-out occurring among weaker competitors, we wanted to visually convey our track record," explained Kim Hercules, manager of exhibits and special events.

Come "See the Lite" was Texas Instruments' theme to attract attendees to a private room, off of the convention center's main floor. There, a hands-on demonstration of TI's new, 10 1/2-pound, Pro-Lite lap-size computer, a live presenter, and a three-minute application videotape awaited the audience. "Try the Lite," an upbeat, music-video tape, pictured the TI Pro-Lite managing the accounting functions on location at a woman's apparel shop. TI's Richard Doan, advertising/merchandising manager, Data Systems Group, indicated that it was originally shot on 16mm film, and then transferred to one-inch videotape for final editing and viewing.

Dennison Computer Supplies, the manufacturer of Elephant Memory Systems, positioned three eighteen-inch televisions across the back top of the booth. A four-minute tape featuring their Premium and Yellow floppy diskettes and microcomputer ribbons alternately played with a lively thirty-second network commercial spot. While the well known "Elephant Walk" tune played in the interlude, Paul Vizzini, director of marketing, kept his audience patiently waiting in strategically angled lines for free yellow T-shirts with a large Elephant logo. He explained, "Our staffing ensures that the average wait-in-line is ten minutes, so each prospect views our product message approximately twice."

Humorous "broadcast-quality" productions—such as those used by Orchid, Pick, and Versa Tec—seemed to most easily attract busy, strolling attendees.

Orchid Technologies, the manufacturer of a powerful IBM PC adapter board, called PCturbo, continuously packed the aisles with viewers caught up in a suspenseful drama. Awarded AllTech Communications' Most Effective Video Honor, for fall COMDEX 1984, "PC-Rescue" starred "Turboman." The practical, but colorfully caped hero, with Intel 80186 expansion-board in hand, saves an unsuspecting buyer from a salesman throwing his IBM PC into the garbage can (literally), and replacing it with an IBM AT. Product manager Ron Wiener scripted the lively four-minute tape in two weeks and production was jointly managed by Robert Davi, Orchid's director of marketing and Marijane Lynch, of Dudkowski-Lynch Associates.

Pick Systems, developer and marketer of the Pick operating system, featured an actor representing "Dick Pick" on a rear projection system. Now that Pick is available on IBM PC compatibles, rather than just larger systems, W.B. Donor, a Los Angeles ad agency, visualized the new product anouncement through "the son of Pick" who answered questions about "himself."

The manufacturer of CompuCart products, wood veneer mobile cabinets which hold video and computer components, Versa Tec answered customer questions through "The Lady and the PC." First-time user President Ted Fielland confessed that once he learned what could be added through animation and special effects production time actually quadrupled.

Existing tape footage was cost-effectively recycled by Data General, Apple and Hercules. DG boasted comedian Rich Little introducing the DG-One Portable, originally shown at the New York financial analysts' product introduction. Apple Computer aired Macintosh Test Drive commercials, many of which, according to spokesman Alfred Mandel, have never been shown on television. Hercules showed network spots on its graphics and color cards from little sets perched atop simulated Greek columns.

Informational programs

Both the production quality, content, and ability to hold viewers' attention varied significantly within this classification. Among the higher quality productions: MicroPro and Tallgrass unwittingly received attention; one had to make a definite commitment to watch NEC's and Sharp's tapes, while Zenith preferred to not have their audio track even audible; Stride Micro featured a computer-controlled flying camera.

MicroPro lined up chairs classroom style to encourage attendees to relax and view nine minutes of "Introducing Wordstar 2000" on a giant free-standing screen. Originally created on 35mm slides by Chris Haigh & Associates, San Francisco, the voluminous nine-projector slide show was transferred to one-inch videotape to facilitate its usage in an eight-city traveling tour. Wink Grelis, director of marketing communications, has distributed the training tape to MicroPro's twenty-one direct sales offices and to select dealers across the U.S., U.K., and France. The data-intensive tape, produced in two weeks, begins with a humourous animated caveman scenario prior to outlining Wordstar 2000's technical features.

Tallgrass Technologies, a manufacturer of 12MB to 70MB mass storage systems for the IBM PC/XT, created a wild African jungle in their booth, dressed representatives in authentic safari attire, and convincingly dramatized the purchase process in a dynamic, similarly themed eleven-minute videotape. Steve Volk, vice-president of marketing, even had a full crew videotaping the activity in their booth to be used as footage in subsequent tapes.

With dealers scattered around the world, NEC Information Systems has adopted videotape to strengthen the timeliness and consistency of marketing and technical information on the NEC Advanced Personal Computer. Director of marketing communications Peter Ferguson created two versions of their booth's tape: a twelve-minute tape which was sent to dealers in Australia and England and a condensed four-minute tape for internal marketing to NEC corporate brass.

Franklin Barbosa, general manager, computer systems, indicates that Sharp Electronics produces numerous videos in-house for their distribution channels. Their latest tape on the Sharp PC-5000, a portable ten-pound, 16-bit, MS/DOS computer, has already been distributed to over 300 dealers nationwide.

Zenith Data Systems projected its Z-SHOW videotapes from television sets recessed in the booth. Soundlessly, five different twenty-minute videotapes continuously played, produced by Zenith's training department, in conjunction with SkillTec, Inc. Skokie, Illinois. Over the past year, their dealers have been trained via these tapes on software packages from Lotus, Condor, and Microsoft, as well as on Zenith's Z-150 desktop IBM PC compatible computer and 3-COM Networking. According to Sharon Segall, field instructor, portions of the tapes are designed for sales people only which outline how to qualify a prospect, and offer sales tips and insights as to how to prepare a sales demonstration, while other sections present overviews of Zenith hardware and software for potential buyers.

A "flying camera" was the subject of a curious attendee-stopper. Featuring a unique customer installation, the video starred a Stride Micro computer and joystick controlling "Skycam," an aerial videocamera, while it was suspended via moving wires over a football stadium. Skycam was invented by Garrett Brown who developed "Steadicam" in 1978, a technique which smooths handheld camera motion.

End-product programs

Effective video-based computer training programs, both tape and disc, are proliferating.

Chase Scientific, Santa Monica, California, was running "Using Your Machine for the Apple IIe" on their television monitor. Cathy Buchanan, director of marketing, indicates that Chase's Compututor, The Plain Language Audio-Video Tutorial, consists of a series of 1½-to-2-hour videotapes which easily trains novices to understand popular software and hardware. Other microcomputer training videotapes available include Cine-Mac, an official upgrade manual on Apple's Macintosh, from Micro-Graphic Images, Chatsworth, California; "The Video Training Series for Educators on the IBM-PC," from IBM Corporation, Armonk, New York; and "The Video Learning Library" including "How to Use your . . . (Apple IIe; Apple III; IBM PC; IBM PCjr) from Kennen Publishing, Mill Valley, California.

Videodisc courseware was projected from seven stand-alone Learning Center devices at Digital Controls' (Norcross, Georgia) booth. Each Learning Center consists of a twelve-inch optical laser disc player, an intelligent "video" terminal (which ideally sits next to a personal computer running the actual software), a set of educational videodiscs, an EPROM cartridge (for reprogrammable control of content and learning sequences), and a printed workbook. Educational programs explaining Lotus's 1-2-3, MicroSoft's Multiplan, Multimate word processing, Ashton-Tate's dBase II, MicroPro's Wordstar, and introductions to the IBM PC and MS-DOS/PC-DOS operating systems were featured. Mike Macke, chairman of the board, indicates that courses vary in length from two to twelve hours of self-paced instruction.

Demonstrational programs

Although their videos were insignificant in terms of production value, the capabilities which Panasonic, DEC, AT&T, and Innovion demonstrated, and their implications, seemed almost futuristic.

Although "First into the Future," an elaborate automated three-screen, twelve-projector slide-show on their office automation products, was featured by Panasonic Industrial, one monitor quietly played a scenic ocean tape. But that tape was stored on Panasonics' state-of-the-art TQ-2023F Direct Read After Write Optical Disc Recorder. Marty Frange, product manager, computer products division, explained that this videodisc recorder/ player's capability to record high quality moving pictures in real time was revolutionary. This feature, which allows an institution to master discs in-house, expands the immediate application potential of discs for security, archival, information communications, and training applications.

Beneath a colored laser light-show projected in Digital Equipment Corporation's booth, a low key, in-house-produced tape on "VAX Services Offering" was playing. With a closer look it was apparent that text and graphics had been overlaid on the moving tape, which was really demonstrating IVIS courseware. DEC's Interactive Video Information System consists of a DEC Professional 350 computer, videodisc player, touch-screen monitor, and earphones.

IVIS studies have determined that students retain twenty-five percent of what they hear, forty-five percent of what they see and hear, and seventy percent of what they see, hear and practice. When a videodisc player is connected to a microprocessor-based computer, an "intelligent" digital-video information system is created which allows a user to interact with the data, text, graphics, or individual images displayed on the monitor. According to government reports: "Microprocessor controlled microprocessor/videodisc systems is a more efficient provider of Equipment Independent Maintenance Training Program in terms of practise time and is less expensive" (Wilkinson, 1982) and "Flight simulators, computer-based instruction and maintenance training simulators appear as effective as methods of training as they replace and can reduce the cost" (Orlansky and String, 1982).

By "capturing" a viewer's image via a videocamera attached to the ATT 6300 personal computer, and digitizing it, or translating the image into digital code, ATT Electronic Photogaphy and Imaging Center, Indianapolis, Indiana, demonstrated their Video Display Adapter and Image Capture Board. Joseph Haaf, sales and marketing manager, cropped, moved, and inverted the image while explaining how both graphics and text could be added before the final, realistic image is sent over ordinary phone lines at 1200 baud, in as little as fifteen seconds.

Lastly, a stand-alone electronic paint box, the Innovion Personal Graphics System, Innovion, Layton, Utah, displayed an enhanced picture taken from a video. With thirty-two different brushes, sixteen patterns, and a palette of 2.1 million colors, users may creatively touch up images before restoring them on videotape.

The proliferation of video-based information tools, as represented by video usage and products shown at COMDEX, is just beginning.

An exploding era

A twelve-year production veteran, Michael Theis, vice-president of Telemation Productions/Denver, Colorado, the largest full-service production company in the country, projects that video will increasingly solve an organization's need for consistent, professional information delivery. Theis recognizes five primary catalysts which are fueling organizations' adoption of video—high production values (price/quality); overwhelming cost justification; inexpensive tape and disc volume duplication; viewer acceptance; and established delivery systems.

Steady advances in optical and digital disc technologies will soon integrate laser discs as cost effective mass storage devices and interactive communicators into major information networks.

Additionally, video boards, or computer graphics expansion cards, portend an exploding era of inexpensive visual communications. Often providing both higher resolution and more simultaneously displayable colors, realistic video images may be displayed, digitized, modified, stored, retrieved, transmitted, overlaid, and enhanced.

As video-based corporate communications, optical/digital discs, and video graphics boards merge with imbedded information management systems, informative electronic pictures will become the standard communications medium.

Thus, a serious new threat is posed to the long-term viability of existing information and communications systems: the possible integration of inadequate, and inaccurate visuals, whether for education, marketing, archival, or internal/external visual communications purposes.

It is nothing that a little knowledge, careful planning, and adequate controls can't avert, and turn into an unforeseen opportunity. ◙

Computerized Braille: The Boulder Story

Fran Hooker

Braille Computer Center director Priscilla Simmons at the Thiel Embosser

Fran Hooker *is a freelance writer and a volunteer at the Boulder (Colorado) Public Library.*

Recently Judy Dixon, a Boulder, Colorado graduate student, wrote, edited, and printed a paper using her local library's computer equipment. There would be nothing unusual about this—many libraries now provide word processors—except for one thing. Dixon is blind, and the paper she produced was printed in Braille. For the first time she and the 4500 other visually impaired people in Colorado can fully participate in the computer age. The reason is the Boulder Public Library's new Braille Computer Center, which celebrated its grand opening in February. It's one of the first centers of its kind in the United States.

A printing revolution

The library's electronic equipment consists of an Apple IIe with an Echo II Voice synthesizer, an IBM PC, Braille software packages, and a Thiel Braille Embosser. This last machine, which was purchased with funds from an LSCA grant, is the cornerstone of the center. Used in conjunction with a computer, the Thiel Embosser (pronounced "teal") revolutionizes the printing of Braille. Transcribers no longer have to sit for hours punching out the characters by hand, wasting a page every time they make a single mistake. The system works like a word processor, allowing both sighted and visually impaired users to edit their work before printing. It produces a page in about ten seconds. This works out to about 130 characters per second. The Cranmer "Perky" embosser, by contrast, prints about ten characters in the same length of time.

"I can see it opening up all kinds of information the blind haven't been able to have before, because it took so long to produce materials," says Priscilla Simmons, head of the Braille Center project. "Braillists will be able to do a great many more pages than they've ever done in the past. And visually impaired people will be able to come in and use the equipment for themselves."

"I intend to use the system to write and edit my own materials," says Homer Page. Page, who is blind, is a member of Boulder's City Council; he also teaches at the University of Colorado and is director of that school's Office of Services to Disabled Students. Page will enter his work in standard English on the Apple. The voice synthesizer will read back what he has written. He will edit the manuscript, then a program called Braille-Edit will translate it into Braille. He'll then print a copy in Braille for his personal use, and perhaps standard copies for the use of his co-workers and students. "Before, I had to write it in Braille and dictate it to someone, dictate it directly, or type the material then sit down with a reader to go over it and do the editing. Now I can develop a finished copy myself."

Page says he is also excited for the visually impaired students in his program. "It opens up a whole lot of things that their peers are doing," he says. "You're told that if you can't use computers you can't participate in the twenty-first century." He says that computer literacy will make more careers available to the sight-handicapped.

Barbara Angevine is a volunteer braillist for the Red Cross. She is using the system to transcribe the popular *Colorado Cache Cookbook,* which was requested by a Boulder resident. Angevine enters the information on the IBM, using a program called MicroBraille. (She could also use an Apple and its similar program called Edit-Braille.) Each of these programs renders all but six of the letter keys inoperable, essentially transforming the keyboard into a Perkins Brailler. Barbara checks over her entry, making any additions, deletions, or changes required. When she is satisfied that her copy is error-free, she has it printed on the Thiel embosser.

She use to do this work by hand. When she made a mistake, even on line 24 of 25, she had to discard the entire page, because there is no way to correct an error. If more than one copy was needed they had to be produced by heating a sheet of plastic that was placed over the original, a procedure that took about a minute per page. With the new system, the information can be stored on the diskettes, and multiple copies may be printed as required. In addition, if a braillist owns or has access to an IBM or Apple, as Angevine does, she can do the transcribing at home, then mail or bring the diskette to the library to print.

Judy Dixon is the director of Boulder's Center for People with Disabilities and is studying for a master's degree. Her work requires that she read reams of memos, budgets, reports, and agendas. Since she's blind she used to rely on her secretary to read all such paperwork aloud. Now her secretary, who doesn't know Braille, can take a report to the library, enter it on the Apple, use the translation program, and have a Braille copy for Dixon's use in minutes.

At the forefront

The Boulder Library is the first public agency in the west to own a Thiel embosser, and is believed to be the only institution in the country making such equipment available to the public. Why is a library at the forefront of this new technology?

"A lot of sight-handicapped people are very independent, yet they are always dependent on somebody to translate material into a form they can use," says Library Director Marcelee Gralapp. "With this center they don't have to be dependent on somebody else. It's not that they aren't willing to have someone help them, but it's human nature to want to do it yourself. The sight-handicapped people ought to have that right."

Gralapp says she views the center as just another facet of library service. "I feel that the library is an information resource, and that we should provide all kinds of information to the citizens of this community. People should have access to material in all forms when they need it. Sometimes it's a film, sometimes it's a magazine, sometimes it's a copy of something in Braille. They just ought to have access to it. It's a more expensive kind of service to give, but we're supported by tax dollars and our job is to provide information to all our citizens. It's important to me. That's why I'm a librarian."

The center's director agrees, adding that the library is the logical place for such equipment. "We're open seven days a week and most evenings," Simmons says. "We're providing more hours than anyone else could possibly offer." (The library is open Monday through Thursday from 9 a.m. to 9 p.m.; Friday and Saturday from 9 a.m. to 6 p.m.; and Sunday from noon to 6 p.m.)

Also important is that by being in a public library the center is open to all citizens rather than a particular segment of the population, such as elementary children or college students. "This makes it much more acceptable for adults to use," says Page. "It's really the appropriate place. If I choose to go into the library and work on a paper, I can do that. If it's at the Red Cross or some other agency, it's much more difficult. This emphasizes the independence of the blind user. We become just regular library users."

Frustrating archaic methods

The Braille Computer Center is something that Gralapp had been thinking about for years, ever since she signed up for a course in Braille and became frustrated at the archaic methods being used. When Simmons joined the library staff two years ago as Coordinator for Homebound Services, she shared Gralapp's interest in providing the visually-impaired with the most up-to-date technology possible.

At that time the library's facilities for the sight-handicapped included large print books (which now number 1800), talking books (there are now about 500 in the collection), recorded bus schedules and grocery store ads, and a table staffed by volunteers who assisted patrons with reading problems. A Visual-Tek Reading Machine was donated by the Boulder Lions Club last year. This closed-circuit machine magnifies print up to thirty times.

About a year ago, Simmons decided to study Braille. Like Gralapp, she became dismayed at how archaic parts of the sytem for reproducing materials were. They knew that someone somewhere must be applying computer technology to the problem. "We did a lot of research," says Gralapp. "Priscilla looked up a lot of people who had jerry-rigged things, people who were trying to make home-grown things, and finally the Thiel printer came into our purview. We knew that it was what we wanted."

The printer, developed in West Germany, is distributed by only one firm in the United States—Maryland Computer Services in Forest Hill. It has a price tag of $17,000.

Simmons consulted a number of Boulder and Denver agencies that work with the blind. She compiled information on how many visually impaired people might benefit if such a machine were available. She researched the distribution of such embossers throughout the country, finding that while there are about thirty of the machines in use, most are owned by private agencies and aren't available for the public's use. The nearest centers accepting disks for embossing were in Rochester, New York and Chicago. After determining that the embosser would be an important addition to the Rocky Mountain region, Simmons wrote the grant. It was approved, and the library received $22,000 with which to purchase and set up the embosser.

Simmons feels that one reason the grant was approved was that the library wasn't asking for the whole system. "We already had the computers, and have had for several years," she says. "All we were asking for was the embosser." The Apple was donated by the Boulder Library Foundation, and the IBM was given by the Buckingham Trust, a Boulder philanthropic organization. The library paid for the software packages, incidentals such as Braille manuals and cable locking systems, and is also paying for the overhead.

Gralapp had few doubts that the grant would be approved. "When federal money is tight the money that is there is going to go for programs for those groups that are less likely to have materials and facilities," she says.

After receiving the grant approval, Simmons's next step was to set up an advisory committee comprised of experts from local agencies for the disabled. Participating groups include the Red Cross, the university's Office of Services to Disabled Students, the Colorado State Library for the Blind, the Boulder Valley School District, Colorado Instructional Materials Center, the Boulder Center for People with Disabilities, and the local chapter of the National Federation for the Blind.

"They've all been working with Braille and services for the blind a lot longer than we have," Simmons says. "We've used them to help determine how to handle this thing."

Setting up shop

The committee met once a month for the first six months, and will meet bimonthly until at least the end of the year. One of the first decisions was to compile a list of potential users and to notify them of the center's facilities. The group's main task was to determine how to organize and administer the center. They tackled such questions as how much training to provide, how much to charge for paper, where to store diskettes, and where to bind books.

The LSCA grant provided enough money to hire a one-quarter-time assistant for one year. Aside from the project director and the assistant, all staffers will be volunteers. Nancy Morgan, the library's Volunteer Coordinator, developed three job descriptions. Plans call for people to train patrons, people to assist with embossing, and record-keeping personnel.

Training proved to be more difficult than anticipated. "We're finding that it takes more time to learn to use the equipment than we thought it was going to," Simmons says. The committee paid for two sessions with computer experts and spent a great deal of time practicing with the equipment. When the center opened Simmons was the only person fully competent in using the system, but she expects to have at least one volunteer ready to train patrons by April. A major task was deciding just how much instruction to provide.

"With the regular computers we have, we just give a general orientation—how to turn the computer on and off, where the manuals are, what the programs look like—so a person can come in and be able to teach himself." Current plans are to offer similar training for the Braille center.

Homer Page agrees with the plans in general, but as a city council member he has some reservations. "Like any relatively complex system, it's going to require a good deal of practice on the part of people who are using it. You certainly can't punch a little hole in somebody's head and pour it in. It's really an experiential process. But it's not going to work if people aren't given adequate training. I'm going to want to watch carefully to determine just how much training is really needed and to make sure that enough is provided. I guess if we need to find more funding we'll just do that."

Available to all

The center's equipment, like the library's other computers, are available to anyone who has taken the orientation program. The only charge will be the five cents per sheet the center pays for the heavy, extralarge paper. The terminals are always available for walk-in use, but appointments are required for the use of the embosser. This was unexpected.

"We thought people would be able to use the Thiel just like the printer on a regular computer," Simmons says. "It turns out that it's more delicate. We've decided that someone involved with the project will have to be on the site when the embosser is running." She doesn't anticipate that this requirement will pose any significant problems. "We've printed 1000 pages so far. About 500 of those were done in one shot. It took fifteen minutes." Eventually enough volunteers will have been trained to staff the center full-time.

Volunteers will also process diskettes sent by mail for embossing. The center will accept disks from around the state, and perhaps from thc entire Rocky Mountain region. The committee has decided that Boulder and Denver residents will receive first priority, although, Gralapp says, "when we're funded with federal money coming into the state of Colorado, I find it hard to say I can't serve the state. The only place I would really consider cutting it would be outside Colorado." The LSCA grant was channeled through the Colorado State Library.

People requesting the transcription of entire books will still be required to go through the Red Cross, which oversees volunteer braillists in Colorado. When a visually impaired resident requests a book, the Red Cross checks to see if it has ever been brailled, obtains the necessary permissions from the publisher, and assigns a volunteer to the project. The committee has decided that the current system will remain unchanged, and has further determined that books will be returned to the Red Cross for binding.

All agencies involved agree that the ease and speed of transcribing books using computers will greatly increase the numbers of Braille books being printed. Storage, another major problem, will be simplified as well, since the information can be retained on a disk until it's needed. A brailled version of a pocket dictionary takes up seven of the extra-large volumes. The current process of brailling by hand and copying by heating sheets of plastic will not be obsolete for many years to come, however. Many volunteers don't have access to computers, and others wouldn't feel comfortable using them in any event.

The right decisions

Because the Boulder library is a pioneer in establishing an output center for Braille, they have had to tackle many problems with minimal information to guide them. "Even though we did a lot of planning we had to go back and redo many things because this had never been done before and we weren't able to make the right decisions," Simmons says. For example, it took volunteer coordinator Nancy Morgan months to determine the optimal paper weight for the embosser and to locate an inexpensive source for that paper. "One of our goals is to be an example," says Simmons. She has prepared a packet of information for anyone who is interested in learning more abut the center. (Write: Braille Computer Center, Boulder Public Library, Drawer H, Boulder, CO 80306.)

"It's a major project," Simmons says. "It took a lot of work and a lot of time to put it together. It's not something we just thought of and went after in a couple of weeks." She feels there are certain minimum requirements for anyone considering setting up such a center. "One of the more important things is that somebody have a knowledge of Braille. You can't run the printer otherwise, because all of the instructions on how to set up the configurations are in Braille." She also says that it's important to have staff members who are experienced with computers.

Another factor in the library's success with such projects is that the city's residents are extremely supportive of their library. One patron commented that Boulder is a place where you can really sense that the library is the nerve center of the community. "This library is really used," says Simmons. "It's always busy. Our community really appreciates the library and wants to do everything they can to make it better."

Far-reaching dreams

What's in store for the Braille Computer Center in the future? Simmons would like another computer, which would be used solely for printing. She would like to improve the voice quality of the Echo synthesizer, which drones, has an annoyingly repetitive rhythm, and pronounces sounds which should be silent (such as the "s" in "islands"). Volunteers are currently working to improve the English-to-Braille program, which occassionally produces copy that does not follow the grammatical conventions of Braille. Her dream list—things she would like to get someday—includes an Omni-Reader, a wand that scans, print, making it possible for blind users to read typewritten documents; and a VersaBraille, a portable brailler that stores information on cassette tapes.

Gralapp's dreams are even more far-reaching. She envisions a time when libraries are the central source of such equipment, making the machines available to everyone through a kind of inter-library network. "I can't say every library in the country ought to get a Braille embosser, because they're very expensive. But it is a service that could be offered through a central source. These printers might be regionally located." She feels that libraries are the ideal place for the new technology because everyone in a community knows where the library is and because there is no stigma attached to going to the library. "It's an information source, that's all it is," she says. But all that is in the future. For now she and the rest of the people involved with the Braille Computer Center are concentrating on making it as good as it can be. ▣

Children's Librarianship: Doing a Better Job

Linda Braun

"I had a student who had experience in the business field," says Margaret Bush, associate professor at Simmons College School of Library and Information Science. "At the graduation breakfast Dean Robert Steuart asked this student, 'What are you going to do now?' The student answered, 'I was going to work in the business field, since that's where my experience is, but I took Professor Bush's course and I've decided to work with children.'" Bush recounts this story laughingly and adds, "It was good for him to hear that."

Why was it good for Dean Steuart to hear? Because many library school administrators are beginning to believe that students only want an education which will prepare them for high-paying prestige jobs. This student verged from the supposed norm. She turned her back on what can be a big money, glamorous field and chose to pursue a career in what is considered to be a nowhere profession.

In the 1981 *Library Journal* annual report on placements and salaries Carol Learmont and Stephen Van-Houten wrote, "Many placement officers believe that children's work is perceived by students as a dead-end but see a shortage ahead in the field." As library administrators begin to agree with placement officers a new problem needs to bc faccd. Library schools must begin asking themselves some questions: How significantly do we change our curriculum to reflect the changing needs and desires of the student body? Do we get rid of courses, such as children's librarianship, which do not prepare students for big money careers?

Linda Braun *has been a children's librarian at the North Adams (Massachusetts) Public Library and the New York Public Library. She is presently a librarian at CBS News, New York City.*

Low wages, little reward

What worries children's librarians and specialists in the field is that some schools have started to answer these questions and are making changes in curricula. Children's librarianship courses have been dropped from some schools' programs. And, it is possible that those who are interested in becoming children's librarians are being discouraged by faculty and administrators. As Bush says, "I think library schools reinforce the mythology that children's work means low wages and little reward. You still find a lot of people who are humanists, where ideals are operative. Human needs and interests are still there. It depends on how much you nurture the student."

Before looking at what is happening at some library schools throughout the country (some that are nurturing their students and some that are not), it is important to look at the truth about salaries and career possibilities of the professional children's librarian.

Evelyn Daniel, dean of Syracuse University's School of Information Science, has found that librarians working in the private sector make between $5,000 and $10,000 more in starting salary than librarians starting out in public library work. She says this happens because our society tends to place more value on private business than it does on supplying tax supported goods.

There is little doubt that many special library people and information specialists make more money than a children's librarian working in a public library. But generalizations are hard to prove true in any field. Salaries for a children's librarian range from $9,000 in Indiana to close to $19,000 at the New York Public Library. "It's impossible for the New York Public Library to offer so little money [because] the cost of living is so high," said Barbara Rollick, head of children's services at the New York Public Library. In fact, $19,000 is more than the $15,000 entry level salary made by a librarian at CBS News, headquartered in New York City. CBS is a special library which many would believe has a high wage scale. Both the $19,000 and the $9,000 reflect the cost of living in the locations offering these wages.

A difficult career ladder

Job advancement for the children's librarian depends on the place where one is working. In a small town advancement often equals leaving children's services for a library administration job, whereas a large public library system offers opportunities to move up the career ladder and remain in children's work. For instance, many of the branch directors in the New York Public Library are also the branch children's librarian.

If assumptions about salary and career possibilities for children's librarians could be made, the question still arises: Can we justify dropping children's services programs at library schools? Judy Davie at the University of North Carolina at Greensboro asks, "If that [the training of children's librarians] is not considered important in a program then how in the world is anybody going to know that children need to be served?" And children do need to be served. Going to the library, whether it be school or public, and picking out a book with the help of a children's librarian, is as much a part of a child's education as sitting at a desk in a classroom.

The concern is that schools which have often acted as role models in the field of librarianship are shifting their priorities. As a result their commitment to the education of children's librarianship is changing. "Two things happen," remarked Bush. "School administrators perceive that no one is taking courses in children's services and that students want information science courses. Then there is a spiral downward as the school deemphasizes courses students no longer show an interest in."

Ten years ago Columbia University's School of Library Service school catalog listed four graduate level and two post-graduate level courses in children's library service. Jane Anne Hannigan, who used to teach some of these courses, says, "We probably had the richest range of courses of any school in the country." At that time there were three full-time faculty members at Columbia who specialized in children's services. Library services to children and young adults and school media service were listed in the catalog as programs of study that students could pursue. In the current school catalog little that has to do with children's or school librarianship remains the same. "Books for Young Adults" is the only related course that is listed in the catalog, and this course is taught only in the summer by an adjunct faculty member. The school media service program is still listed in the catalog but it requires this explanation: "The program in school media service is a joint program with Teachers College, Columbia University." Since no children's courses, except young adult literature, are given at Columbia library school, most school media students end up taking all their non-core courses at Teachers College.

Information technology winning out

"Columbia, I understand, has decided they would concentrate not on public library librarianship but on academic libraries, computers, and information science," remarked Rollick. Columbia had to decide at a time of financial restraint what programs would draw the most students. Information technology has possibly won out over children's and other public library services.

Kay Vandergrift taught some of the courses in children's librarianship at Columbia. She says, "I think there was no real attempt to recruit people. In the last two years I was there the school program was dropping. On the other hand, the children's literature courses had begun to grow again. The beginning enrollments [those newly interested in the field] were not high because recruitment was nil. In fact people were being discouraged."

The acting dean at Columbia's library school, Kathleen Molz, insists that statements alleging that Columbia is making a concerted effort to stay away from teaching courses in school and children's librarianship are "rumors." She believes students at the present time are not interested in public and school library work. Dean Molz said, "If students show an interest in public library, children's, or school library service, the courses will be reinstated."

It is questionable whether or not a student interested the children's work would even apply to Columbia's School of Library Service. Vandergrift has said that if today she were looking for a library school program in children's services she would eliminate Columbia after looking at their catalog. In fact, this year there are fewer students enrolled in the Teachers/Columbia school media service program than were enrolled in the program last year. The trend is likely to continue.

More openings than students

Graduates trained as children's librarians would find jobs available to them. The administration of the New York Public Library has come to Barbara Rollick and said that they can't find children's librarians. The New York Public Library has been hiring for the past two years, but as Rollick says, "We still have gaps." Kay Vandergrift has noticed that school media specialist positions are available throughout the country. "For the last three or four years there were a number of jobs that we just couldn't fill. We had a lot more job openings than we had students," she said.

In northern California there are also job openings for children's librarians. The University of California at Berkeley has a vacancy. At Berkeley there is no full time faculty member in the field of children's services. Robert Harlan, the school's acting dean, says, "There has always been an interest there." In fact, the Berkeley catalog lists several courses which are relevant to children's librarianship. At first glance the program looks to be stable and well rounded. But each of the children's courses is taught by an adjunct faculty member. Adjuncts have very little input in a school's curriculum development. Since they are not at faculty meetings one might wonder who is speaking up for children's services during these discussions. Selma Richardson, who teaches at the University of Illinois, says the Berkeley situation means to her that "children's services really aren't integrated into the rest of the program."

Under pressure from the California Library Association, Berkeley had undertaken more than one search to find a qualified children's specialist to fill the faculty opening. The second search came to fruition when a person was hired. Two months before the faculty member was to start Berkeley said they had changed their mind. The job still remains open.

In the late 1970s Californians passed Proposition 13. This tax law affected the funding of public institutions such as public libraries and public schools. In the mid seventies New York City went through a fiscal crisis which affected the same public institutions. During the past two years, at the Deans Roundtable of the New

York State Library Association annual meeting, children's librarians have brought their concern about library schools' changing curricula to the deans' attention. As Barbara Rollick recalls it, "The deans have said 'You told us not to hire children's people because you had no positions.' It was true," continued Rollick. "I remember a young librarian coming to me and she couldn't decide if she should go to Boston or stay in New York. I knew what the situation was at the time so she went to Boston."

The market for entry level children's librarians was tight at that time. Nonetheless, those who were already working in the field were interested in continuing education courses in order to secure the positions they already had. "We found a huge constituency. It was the people who wanted continuing education. At that point Columbia should have built continuing education programs," said Vandergrift. It is possible that by exploring continuing education possibilities Columbia and Berkeley would now be struggling less. Says Greensboro's Judy Davie, "That's the only way it's going to work. To me it just seems so obvious. It's recognizing what the market conditions are and then recognizing how we make adjustments so we can work together, because these people are needed out there." Greensboro has made adjustments like scheduling courses at night and on Saturdays (recommendations Vandergrift and Hannigan made that were turned down). Library directors are taking advantage of these adjustments and are targeting staff members who could advance in their careers by pursuing a library degree. Children's library courses, like other courses at Greensboro, are attended by professionals with MLS degrees, library clerical staff, and newcomers to the field. An open dialogue is preserved where the newcomer can learn from the practitioner. If the problem of how to handle a noisy child at storyhour comes up in class someone is there to provide first hand examples.

Greensboro's library program does attract newcomers to the field of librarianship as well as seasoned professionals. "Serving youth has always been a basic philosophy at UNCG," says Davie. "I talked with one of my students who has just entered the program and is interested in youth services. I asked Judy, 'Why are you here?' One of the things she said was, 'There was a real sense of interest that it was an important thing to do. That to serve this population was exciting. And that's what made the difference for me.'"

At Greensboro there has been an increased interest in the special library field over the past few years. The university's program started as a school library program and after several years public library service courses were added to the curriculum. More recently special library offerings have been added. This addition of a special library program has in no way caused a de-emphasis of children's services. And even though the entire university is going through program review there is no plan to change the children's program in any major way.

A few dynamic people

"There are pockets of dynamic people, at schools here and there, which are doing good things in children's librarianship," says Bush. Greensboro is one of these pockets as is the University of Illinois at Champaign. The good health of the program at Champaign can be seen in the fact that a second faculty member in the children's services field has recently been added to the staff.

What is noticeable at Champaign is the integration of the children's program into the rest of the curriculum. Champaign does have several courses listed in its catalog which are geared specifically to the person interested in children's services. But even the courses which don't sound specific, such as "Library Buldings," are open to the children's services student who can pursue a special project to suit special needs.

At Champaign there is no sign that students are losing interest in children's librarianship. The enrollment this term in the course which covers school and public library service to children and young adults is about twenty students. "So it's not dying," says Champaign's Selma Richardson. At a time when library schools are talking about dwindling enrollments Richardson is trying to figure out what is the best way to handle such a large class.

Simmons College School of Library and Information Science had thought students were losing interest in children's librarianship. When the children's faculty position opened up recently the school was not going to fill it. "The New England Library Association got political with the dean and encouraged him," said Bush. The result of the encouraging was the hiring of Margaret Bush.

Some signs of health

Hiring Margaret Bush is seen by many in the field of children's librarianship as a sign of good health at Simmons. Bush remarked, "I enjoy the support of the faculty and deans here. But the changing curricula in library schools, in terms of children's librarianship, is a problem. It's the reason I'm back at Simmons." Bush first taught at Simmons in the mid-seventies. At that time the classes in children's librarianship had enrollments of twenty to thirty students per class each semester. In the years after Bush left Simmons enrollment dwindled to as low as eight people in a class. "Now each course is given once a year and there are ten to fifteen pupils in a course. People are requesting the young adult course be given in summer school. It will be given because of the demand," Bush related. What is happening at Simmons is an example of what can happen when the faculty and administration of a school work towards showing students that children's library work is not a "dead end."

But what about elsewhere? Margaret Bush, speaking as president of ALA's Association for Library Service to Children, said, "We are finding it

(continued on page 575)

Dale Nelson:

Dateline Washington

Sharpening reading skills

A computer program developed by the Navy to sharpen recruits' reading skills is being tested in libraries in West Virginia and Maryland as a weapon against illiteracy.

At the Enoch Pratt Free Library in Baltimore, Jane Heiser, director of literacy resources, says the program is working well enough that the library is raising funds to buy the equipment it is now leasing.

The project is also being tested at the Weirton, West Virginia library, serving an economically distressed steel town of 27,000 people near the Ohio line.

So successful has it been that a consortium of the Carnegie Library in Pittsburgh, the Pennsylvania State Library, Pennsylvania Department of Education, University of Pittsburgh and Carnegie-Mellon University are proposing a more ambitious version in Pittsburgh.

A proposal received by the National Commission on Libraries and Information Science from the Carnegie Library calls for a research and development center plus three or four literacy tutoring satellites.

The project stems from a meeting in 1983 between NCLIS and a Department of the Army representative to discuss resolutions of the 1979 White House Conference on Libraries and Information Service concerning literacy.

A steering committee was formed to look into ways that federally developed technology could be used to increase literacy among adults and high school dropouts with basic reading skills between zero and fifth-grade level.

After looking at many possibilities, the committee chose a computer program of vocabulary building and comprehension that was developed by Drs. Robert Wisher and Thomas Duffy when they were employed by the Navy Personnel Research and Development Center in San Diego, California.

"The Navy discovered that many of its recruits could read well enough to pass a basic test, but when they wanted them to take technical training, they soon discovered their reading skills were not sufficient," Heiser said.

The Baltimore library was chosen to test the idea in an urban setting, and developed programs on consumer awareness, driver education, and taxes at its Pimlico branch.

"Probably the tax section is going to be the most used," Heiser said. "I may go and use it myself."

Weirton, chosen to try the program out in a non-metropolitan setting, developed a pilot dealing with money management.

The Enoch Pratt library runs the program on an Apple IIe computer on a six-month budget of $6,998, covering lease of the computers, disk drives and printers, plus the time spent by a supervisor.

"We are finding that someone to manage it is absolutely essential," Heiser said.

At first, she said, the unskilled Pimlico tutors and their students were "so fascinated by the idea and the equipment that it was hard to focus on the lessons that were supposed to be happening."

"It makes a far better program to have knowledgeable people to answer questions," she said. "The machine won't do it for you."

Heiser said fifteen people were expected to have completed the project when it wound up at the end of March.

She said the Navy used the program for retraining recruits who read at the seventh or eighth-grade level, but most of the people being trained at the Pimlico branch were at about the fourth-grade level.

"Basically what it does is to teach vocabulary in the context of reading comprehension," she said. "The student users are so interested that we think we can lower it to begin to reach the very lowest, the first or second-grade level or the brand new reader."

Not high priorities

Libraries are taking at least their share of cuts as President Reagan tries again to whack away at the federal deficit.

The budget submitted to Congress on February 4 eliminates the six programs supporting state, local and research library activity, as well as the National Commission for Libraries and Information Science.

The budget notes that federal grants to state and local governments for library purposes totaled $80 million in fiscal year 1984 and $118 million in the current fiscal year.

"These programs are not high priorities for federal funds, and most have met their objectives of stimulating other sources of funding," the budget says.

The total budget for the Library Services and Construction Act, for all purposes, would be cut from $125 million to zero under the administration proposal.

The newly independent National Archives and Records Administration would also be cut, going from a current appropriation of $100.6 million to $99.4 million.

The budget calls for reducing the National Library of Medicine from $55.5 million to $53.3 million, and the National Agricultural Library

Dale Nelson *is a journalist who covers the Washington scene for WLB.*

from $11.4 million to $11.1 million.

Only the Library of Congress, whose spending plans are not subject to the scalpel of White House budget cutters, would get an increase.

Total federal funds for LC would go from $324.7 million to $337.8 million. The Copyright Office would increase from $11.5 million to $12 million, based on an estimated 500,000 copyright registrations, the same as in 1985.

The Government Printing Office, reflecting economies instituted under the Reagan administration, would go from $122.9 million to $122.2 million.

Deacidification priorities

The Library of Congress says it does not expect to make its new book deacidification facility available to other libraries, at least for the next twenty years.

"Our expectation is that only LC collection items will be processed at Ft. Detrick primarily because the number of books to be treated in the Library's general collections (13 million) and in the new incoming material (over 300,000 per year) will take up the full capacity of the Ft. Detrick facility for the next twenty years," the library says in a fact sheet.

Construction of the facility at Ft. Detrick, Maryland is expected to start early in 1986. Processing of books is scheduled to begin late the following year.

Reagan nominates NCLIS commissioner

President Reagan plans to nominate Daniel Carter of Houston, Texas, to be a member of the National Commission on Libraries and Information Science. He would succeed Margaret Warden and his term would expire July 19, 1989.

Carter is vice president for strategic business services at Walter Ulrich Consulting, a management and technology consulting firm, in Houston. He was with Texas Instruments from 1966 until this year.

Bowing out gracefully

The Folger Shakespeare Library board announced in January it would close the Folger Theatre, saying continuing operating losses were too great a drain on resources needed for the library.

Negotiations between library director Werner Gundersheimer and theater staff heads have been continuing, however, to determine what, if any, role the library might play in a reconstituted theater company.

Meanwhile the company decided that if it was going to bow out, it would bow out fittingly with a Shakespearean production.

The Folger replaced the originally scheduled *Marriage of Figaro* with *A Midsummer Night's Dream*. The Shakespearean comedy will cost more to produce than *Figaro* would have, but the library agreed to make up the difference. ▣

Anne McGrath:

Eye on Publishing

"Here's a little off-beat novel. In the whole book, there isn't one mention of sex."

Push to close "book gap" overseas

In 1983, the late Curtis Benjamin reported in his unsettling *U.S. Books Abroad: Neglected Ambassadors,* published by the Center for the Book, that overseas sales of serious American books had declined steadily and dramatically during the previous fifteen or so years, putting the United States far behind the Soviet Union in the battle to spread ideas through literature. A year ago, National Security Council Director Robert MacFarlane acknowledged the gravity of the problem by calling upon the U.S. Information Agency to study possible solutions.

The outcome? An analysis prepared by the Helen Dwight Reid Educational Foundation in Washington that identifies eleven aspects of bookselling abroad in need of attention and the establishment of a task force to look into appropriate legislative action. Implementation of the recommendations based on the study's findings will require Congress to appropriate some $12 million annually.

Some of the report's most significant recommendations:

• *Copyright law and intellectual property protection.* The International Copyright Information Center should be given increased support, and the USIA should beef up its educational programs on the importance of copyright and the insidiousness of piracy. The government should weave copyright guarantees whenever possible into its economic and cultural agreements with foreign governments.

• *Better dissemination of information about the content of American books.* Subscriptions to review journals such as *Booklist* and *Library Journal* should be provided free of charge to members of Third World education and book communities, and journalists and scholars around the globe should receive the review sections of our major newspapers. A machine-readable bibliographic tool kit could be developed that would drastically streamline the selection and ordering of U.S. books by foreign booksellers and librarians.

• *Exposure at fairs.* American publishers and the U.S. government can do much more than they are currently doing in the way of physically showing their books to foreign markets. More extensive paticipation in local and theme book fairs and exhibits at professional conferences is encouraged, as is the establishment of permanent book display centers abroad for American works.

• *Information exchange.* Members of the foreign book trade should be brought here to gain understanding of American publishing; U.S. publishers and booksellers should participate in educational seminars abroad. International book fairs provide an outstand-

Anne McGrath, *a freelance writer based in New York, covers the publishing world for WLB.*

ing opportunity as well to bring bookmen of all nationalities together for an exchange of ideas.

• *Expansion of the USIA publishing program.* In 1965, USIA-supported translations numbered 10.2 million volumes; today, that figure is only 500,000. Over the past ten years, on the other hand, the Soviet Union's book exports have jumped two and a half times. The wherewithal must be provided to bring agency programs and libraries back up to the levels of two decades ago. Furthermore, the selection of content and titles for the USIA program should be carefully handled to provide understanding of American culture, values, and policies; to recognize local needs; and to emphasize children's books.

Oxford to bring out ex-slave's writings

Two recently discovered books by traveling Methodist preacher and one-time slave John Jea, printed in England in 1815 and 1816, are to be republished by Oxford University Press in a single volume. The two works, a collection of hymns and Jea's autobiography, are significant for the illumination they shed on black American culture of the early nineteenth century. According to Yale University professor Henry Louis Gates Jr., who identified both books, Jea is as far as can be determined the first black American to publish both a collection of verse and an autobiography. (Single poems by blacks and first-person writings by slaves began appearing during the mid-eighteenth century; a volume of poetry by Phyllis Wheatley was published in 1773.)

Gates's research during the past several years as director of the Yale Black Periodical Fiction Project led him to Jea. He first became aware of the autobiography, *Life, History and Unparalleled Sufferings of John Jea, the African Preacher,* when he saw it listed in a bookseller's catalog two years ago. (Brown University and Columbia University hold the two copies Gates has found.) Careful analysis of the people and events described in the book led Gates to believe that the work was indeed authentic—and that a book of hymns remained to be found. The 251-page *Collection of Hymns,* roughly half of which can probably be attributed to Jea, was discovered last year in Oxford University's Bodleian Library.

Both works, while they focus on religious themes, do provide snatches of the author's personal history and glimpses of contemporary life. Jea was born in 1773 in West Africa, the son of Hambleton Robert and Margaret Jea, and was captured and brought to America as a slave at age two. After a religous conversion at fifteen that he claimed also gave him his ability to read, Jea was freed. He worked as ship's cook on a number of trans-Atlantic crossings, and eventually preached to audiences in the Netherlands and Ireland as well as in New York and Boston, and in several English cities. Many of the hymns are easily identifiable as Jea's as they mention occurrences from his life and, although in the book's introduction he attributes many to other writers, he often took the liberty of embellishing an already existing hymn with his own touches.

Grove Press sold

An agreement between Barney Rosset, founder of the decidedly individualistic Grove Press, and Ann Getty and British publisher George Weidenfeld will allow the publishing house to continue bringing out the kinds of works that have made its reputation. A company headed by Getty (the wife of Gordon Getty, heir to the Getty oil fortune) and Lord Weidenfeld of Britain's Weidenfeld Ltd. reportedly paid $2 million for Grove, publisher of the first complete versions of D.H. Lawrence's *Lady Chatterly's Lover* and Henry Miller's *Tropic of Cancer* in this country.

Rosset founded his press in New York's Greenwich Village thirty-four years ago, and since then has introduced his readers to such luminaries as Bertolt Brecht, Samuel Beckett, and Jean Genet. Recently, the press gained attention as publisher of *The Freedom Fighter's Manual,* the Central Intelligence Agency manual for rebels in Nicaragua that caused such a storm of controversy when its existence became known. After Rosset published the Lawrence and Miller books, both of which had been banned in the United States, he went on to defend them against charges of obscenity in court. While Rosset has had offers from major publishing houses for the undercapitalized Grove before, he has refused to let his firm be absorbed by a huge organization. Under the current agreement, the press maintains its identity as a literary house and Rosset stays on as president and publisher for five years.

One of Grove's first projects under its new owners will be to bring out a six-volume series of Beckett's works: his correspondence and notes on his plays. A second is the revival of *Evergreen Review,* a literary magazine which published many of Grove's authors during the press's first two decades.

National Book Critics Circle awards

Winners of the tenth annual National Book Critics Circle awards, recently announced at the New York Historical Society, are: freelance reviewer Alida Becker, a critic whose work appears regularly in *The Philadelphia Inquirer* and the *St. Petersburg Times,* for excellence in reviewing; poet Sharon Olds, for her collection *The Dead and the Living* (Knopf); biographer Joseph Frank, for *Dostoevsky: The Years of Ordeal 1850–1859* (Princeton University Press); critic Robert Hass, author of *Twentieth Century Pleasures* (Ecco Press); poet and short story writer Louise Erdrich, for her novel based on the lives of the Chippewa Indians, *Love Medicine* (Holt, Rinehart & Winston); and Freeman Dyson, whose *Weapons and Hope* (Harper & Row) was recognized in the general nonfiction category. In addition, a special Ivan Sandrof/Board Award went to the Library of America for its "ongoing publication of American classics in compact permanent editions."

Will Manley:

Facing the Public

Back in October last year I got a letter from ALA Executive Director Bob Wedgeworth. It wasn't a "Dear Will" personal letter. Rather it was a "Dear ALA Member" form letter that, conservatively speaking, was probably received by at least 40,000 other people. So I wasn't real excited about getting the letter and I wasn't all that interested in reading it.

Yet for some reason I read it. I guess I decided that if what I was waiting for was a personal, handwritten letter from Mr. Wedgeworth, then I'd better expect to be around at the millennium. Figuring that that might require more patience than I now possess I decided to read the form letter instead. One of the things that I did appreciate was that it made no pretenses about knowing me. It was not addressed hypocritically to "Dear Friend," "Dear Ms. Manley," or "Dear Colleague," as so many other computer-generated form letters are.

As form letters goes this one had integrity. And predictably it was an unabashed plea for money. Bob wanted me to renew my membership in ALA even though dues were about to be raised for the first time in five years. Since one dues increase in five years is not at all a bad track record and since I was flattered that Bob thought that the continuation of my ALA membership (along with 40,000 others) would help make the ALA voice stronger than ever, I decided to read on and seriously weigh the benefits of ALA membership against the cost of its increasing fees.

I'm really glad I read the letter because I didn't know that ALA was doing so much for me. For instance, did you realize that ALA's amicus brief helped bring about a favorable ruling for libraries in the Sony Betamax case or that under ALA's aegis a new continuing education series was published in *American Libraries*? If that's not enough motivation for you to reach for your checkbook, just consider that according to Bob the ALA National Library Week Committee secured fifty million allies for libraries including Lions International and the AFL-CIO in the "National Library Week Partnership Program." As if that's not enough incentive to sign on the dotted line, Wedgeworth goes on to mention that ALA's office for research did some exciting work "analyzing problems in the field of library statistics."

At first glance to those of us who are busily trafficking in the real world of library services and who are actively involved in the difficult and challenging process of providing a diversity of front-line services to a multitude of people, these accomplishments may seem like nothing more than organizational nonsense. There is the greatest temptation for us to condescendingly sneer at "how much" a distant ALA is doing for its members when we're in the midst of telling stories to thirty noisy children or trying to juggle two phone calls and three walk-in patrons at the reference desk.

But the way I look at it is that somebody's got to do that organizational work and it's a nice secure feeling to know that while most of us are preoccupied with facing the public everyday the whole area of library statistics is being researched by ALA. Also the capability of ALA to produce a competent amicus brief is comforting and convenient. As a direct result of the Sony Betamax decision I can tape the "Smurf Show" on Saturday morning and show it to my kids all week. Who could ever get enough of the Smurfs? Therefore, there's a lot to be thankful for with regards to ALA.

My only quibble with our national organization has to do with that four letter acronym LSCA. In his letter, Wedgeworth mentions that another big benefit of ALA is the legislative effort by the Washington Office in "combating the current administration's recommendation to eliminate Education Department library grant programs" and in "securing reauthorization legislation for LSCA."

That's precisely the problem with ALA. As long as it's setting up harmless little conferences, doing useless statistical studies, writing insignificant legal briefs, publishing a little-read series of articles, or striking up alliances with fifty million Lions members (are they the ones with the funny hats?), it is doing its job in its own unsung and quietly effective way. But when it comes to lobbying for federal funds, specifically LSCA monies, ALA begins to get out of its league and show the limitations of its vision.

First of all, LSCA, despite all the help it has gotten from "the unified voice" of ALA, has never been what you would call a big success story. What started out as a small federal program designed to provide rudimentary library services in unserved areas has developed into a small federal program that has attempted to create rudimentary library bureaucracies on both the state and local levels. LSCA funds in 1984 totalled $118 million. The Pentagon spends that much for a coffee maker, doesn't it?

But that $118 million is not just $118 million. It's a matter of pride. Forget the thought that LSCA money has done a lot more for bureaucracy than it has for libraries. In the present day, unfortunately, a measurement of a thing's value is its relationship to the federal government. The federal government, rightly or wrongly, is seen as society's long-term stamp of approval, for to become "federalized" means to become "bureaucratized" which means to become "permanentized." As our present budgetary defi-

Will Manley *is director of the Tempe (Arizona) Public Library.*

cit woes would suggest, there is nothing more deathless than a federal program. That, I think, is why federal money is so important to us. It legitimizes what we do. LSCA is the official imprimatur of the federal government. Never mind that in all honesty it hasn't amounted to a hill of beans in terms of developing libraries in the seventies and eighties. Just getting funded by the federal government is the important thing.

I mean, just think, where would we be without LSCA? It's our rallying cry. It's what unifies us. It's what we can all get righteously indignant about. Even though a bond referendum in Glendale, Arizona is something that will have a drastic impact on the development of library services in that community, folks in Oregon can't get concerned about it and can't jump to get on the bandwagon. But LSCA is different. It affects us all. We all get our $1.99 from it. So legislative lobbying days are held, ivory tower library commentators write impassioned editorials, and library professionals get on their soapboxes and villify any president or congressman who might question the philosophy of the federal government giving token support to locally financed public libraries.

That's what bothers me about the LSCA phenomenon. It develops into such an adversarial situation. It's unfortunate that we use a weak federal program of such dubious potential value to engage in what Wedgeworth terms "combating the current administration." It's too bad we can't find some more appropriate national forum to exercise our need to eloquently orate the value of libraries.

If our objective in these days of the eroding federal government really is to pursue federal funding and get as much of it as we possibly can, why don't we get smart and try to cooperate with the administration, not "combat" it. If what we're after are some really big bucks rather than simply winning our usual few dollars that are of value only to the bureaucracies that administrate them, then we should make an alliance not with fifty million Lions members, but with the free-spending, pistol-packing Pentagon. What, after all, would do more for the esteem of public libraries in the eyes of President Reagan than taking a more militaristic posture?

Think of all the exciting public relations possibilities. Instead of continuing to propose that LSCA monies be used for such mundane and timeworn purposes as interlibrary cooperation, we could suggest that federal funding be used for such new and innovative adult programming as teaching anti-Sandanista Nicaraguan rebels how to overthrow unfriendly governments. Or libraries could be used as sites to house the MX missile. For more traditional librarians the possibility always exists of requesting collection development grants in the areas of military science and nuclear weapon systems.

Better yet, why don't public librarians just forget about LSCA completely. The program could be dropped tomorrow and I'm sure the negative impact would be minimal, especially when you consider that for most public libraries LSCA funds constitute less than 3 percent of their operating budgets.

Instead of fighting to keep the LSCA flame burning, imagine the impact if ALA were to make a statement that since public libraries are traditionally locally supported institutions, and since in order for the economy to function at optimum levels the federal deficit has to be brought under control, ALA has decided that it is in the best interests of the country for such wasteful and counterproductive federal programs as LSCA to be eliminated.

That would be news—a special interest group voluntarily surrendering its federal peanuts. What a public relations coup. Before you dismiss the idea out of hand remember one thing. Nothing helps public libraries more than a strong economy. Public libraries get the vast preponderance of their operating budgets from sales tax and property tax. A strong economy significantly bolsters both. If federal deficits threaten the economy, why are we so obsessed with obtaining federal funds? Maybe, with all due respect to Mr. Wedgeworth, Mr. Reagan, by penciling in "0" for LSCA, knows what in the long run will really help libraries. Why "combat" it? Under Reagan the local tax base of many libraries has never been better. ▣

Martin Kesselman:

Online Update

This past December, I attended the International Online Meeting in London, England to read a paper co-authored with Irene Iwan of Cooper Union on database indexes and end-users. (Database indexes and their importance in online searching by both experienced searchers and new end-users will be the subject of a future column.) Over 2,000 attendees, most from the United Kingdom and other European countries, but with several from other parts of the world, were present at this year's meeting so that it truly had an international flavor. The papers presented also reflected the international scope of this meeting and included such diverse topics as online public search services in Hungary, an overview of databases produced in Italy, an online information system in Japan, and legal databanks in France.

Martha Williams reviewed highlights of the database field during the past year, as she has done at the National Online Meetings held in New York. Her talk noted that within the past year the number of hours of online usage has increased dramatically from 1.4 million to 1.7 million. Also of interest was the fact that Mead Data Central and Dialog together account for 82 percent of all revenues from online services and 69 percent of the usage in the United States.

On the lighter side, following William's talk Elizabeth Ferrarini, a free-lance writer specializing in telecommunications and microcomputers, spoke about her book, *Confessions of an Informaniac.* Ferrarini related how she not only became a whiz at various online activities such as accessing information services, and shopping and booking airline tickets online, but how she also met men through various online bulletin board services, for which she has coined the term electronic "male."

A major focus of the meeting and of much current interest in the online industry was the subject of the user interface in online searching. Included are subtopics such as artificial intelligence, expert systems, and front-ends and gateways, each of which adds value for the experienced searcher and eases the search process for the new or inexperienced searcher.

Chris Armstrong of the College of Librarianship, Wales in his paper, "Command Languages and the Intelligence Factor," presented his opinion that end-users require a great deal of training as most of them search inefficiently. He noted that although online searching has been available for over ten years, few major advances have been made in retrieval languages up to now. Only recently have some simplified versions of retrieval languages become available for end-users such as BRS After Dark and Dialog's Knowledge Index; Dialog 2, although a greatly improved rewrite of the Dialog search software, provides enhanced search capabilities for intermediaries only. Armstrong expressed surprise that there has been little movement made by online services in the use of artificial intelligence, which is instead being developed by various front-end systems. Pat Ryan of the Massachusetts General Hospital Health Sciences Library spoke about one such front-end, *Paperchase,* a service available since June 1984. *Paperchase* accesses the Medline database since 1977 and provides for vocabulary matching, whereby any term typed in by the user is cross-referenced to applicable medical subject headings. Institutions can also input their own collection of journals into the system so that they are displayed first in retrieved items. Hopefully we can look forward to similar vocabulary matching techniques with subject headings in online catalogs.

Alan Burns and John Robinson of the University of Bradford (U.K.) stressed the need for the development of acceptable user interfaces that can communicate with users of different backgrounds and levels of experience. Whereas new users require a great deal of help facilities and occasional users may need a few examples to refresh their memory, experienced users want to use a system directly without having to wade through several redundant sets of instructions. This concept of variable interfaces has many implications for users of online catalogs as well.

A special session at the International Online Meeting was held to explore the developments and options for improving intelligent interfaces to online services, specifically to EURONET DIANE, the telecommunications network of the Commission of the European Communities, which co-sponsored the session. Kate Birins Noerr of Information Management and Engineering Limited (U.K.) developed a wish list, based on a survey of users, of features desirable in an intelligent interface including automated logon, cross-file searching across different online systems, options for menu or command-driven systems, multilingual systems, variable help capabilities, and electronic

Martin Kesselman *is life sciences librarian at Bobst Library, New York University.*

mail. Marino Saksidas of the European Space Agency Information Retrieval System (Italy) gave an overview of the use of gateways, whereby a user accesses one host computer which in turn switches to other hosts when appropriate. Dick Kollin of Telebase Inc. (U.S.A.) discussed his company's gateway, *Easynet,* which provides access to numerous online systems and databases without the need for a knowledge of online searching. With a credit card number as a password, the user inputs a search question and *Easynet* selects an appropriate database and host. It then automatically translates the search statement into the command language of the chosen vendor, runs the search, and downloads the results to the user via the *Easynet* gateway computer.

Rounding out this session, Ian Croall of the Atomic Energy Research Establishment (U.K.) discussed the promise of expert systems in facilitating online searching. Expert systems mimic a human expert in a narrow subject area and require a flexible user interface. In online searching, expert systems would help the user through the search by asking questions to determine specific needs. Expert systems are comprised of a knowledge base of facts and rules (i.e., for searching, the numbers and types of documents and how they are organized or indexed), an inference engine (the central processing unit or CPU), an interface with the user, and an explanation system.

Also dealing with expert systems, Phil Williams of Userlink (U.K.) discussed his model for automated information retrieval and software for unskilled end-users being developed under a grant from the British Library. End-users are assisted by a feature called EXPLORE which allows them to scan the index terms in a preliminary set of retrieved items and then to use some of these terms to improve the search. A similar capability for experienced searchers, known as the zoom command, is available on the European Space Agency Information Retrieval System. According to Williams, expert systems must take into account the precision and recall required by the user as well as the total number of references the user wants and expects to retrieve.

Besides artificial intelligence, other emerging trends discussed included new methods for document delivery and for training online searchers. Nancy Fjallbrant of Chalmers University of Technology (Sweden) discussed what the user wants in a document delivery service and how delivery by satellite may be the most efficient method. Such a satellite transmission system, the Apollo Project, which has been undertaken by the Commission of the European Communities, was described by Carlo Vernimb of the commission. The Apollo service is expected to commence in 1986. For training online searchers, Smith and Roach of University College Cardiff (U.K.) described an innovative videodisc program under development whose interactive capabilities can be used to simulate various online searching situations.

New online products and services were also highlighted at three special exhibits, which included a software rendezvous with displays of front-end, database management, and search software packages, a technology rendezvous of new hardware such as touch terminals, videodiscs, optical character readers and microcomputers, printers and modems, and an electronic mail rendezvous which included Dialog's new DialMail service.

In addition, there were, of course, the usual exhibitors and several product review sessions held throughout the meeting, although many of these were geared towards the largely European audience. A nice feature I would like to see duplicated at other online conferences was an enquiry/help desk, where representatives of the U.K. Online Users Group provided unbiased answers and advice on questions dealing with any aspect of online searching.

For a change of pace and to find out what's going on in other parts of the online world, you might consider attending next year's International Online Meeting. For me, it was truly exciting to be a part of this informative and friendly conference.

Donnarae MacCann/Olga Richard:

Picture Books for Children

Joey

Cat & Canary

Funny Bunnies

The Witch's Hat

Picture books perhaps make the most of their comic possibilities when narrative and visual components are both incongruous. A disproportionate or inverted world is depicted, and while such a world is accessible to the young as slapstick, it often has satirical nuances as well, as child characters get the better of the grown-ups. In such cases, the story-hour becomes a shared experience on several levels.

In four recent picture books, the images create an out-of-kilter environment, while the plots invert the roles of the powerful and powerless. In **Funny Bunnies** by Robert Quackenbush, a crowd of rabbits have jammed into a tiny hotel room. A child rabbit has been having a dip in the pool while the maids, plumber, plumber's assistant, janitor, window washer, and room service waiter all try to perform their duties simultaneously as Mother and Father Bunny unpack. The scene is reminiscent of the Marx Brothers and their numerous shipmates in an ocean liner cabin in *A Night at the Opera.*

In **Joey** by Jack Kent, an overprotective kangaroo confines her youngster in her pouch in order to keep track of him. But Joey is not outsmarted, even though Mother counters his complaints about wanting his playmates by saying, "Ask your friends to come HERE and play." Joey invites friends with a TV set, a hi-fi, and eventually a grand piano, tuba, and bass drum. All fit into Mother's marvelously capacious pouch, but the commotion is finally too much for her. She gains control over her insecure maternal tendencies (but just barely). "'May I go play?' asks Joey. 'Yes,' Mother said with a deep sigh. 'But don't get lost.'"

A witch and her supernatural pot are the main contenders in **The Witch's Hat** by Tony Johnson (illustrated by Margot Tomes). A "wise child" type is not represented as a character in this tale, but a young listener can enjoy a certain sense of triumph by witnessing a line of command turned on its head. The witch's cauldron has more authority than the befuddled maker of its magical brew, and turns hat to bat to rat

---

Olga Richard *and* **Donnarae MacCann** *are the authors of* The Child's First Books.

to cat. And just as the witch feels she is regaining her proper prerogative, her hat becomes a fat frog and she is none the wiser.

With similar intrigue; a man's pets turn him into the innocent one in Michael Foreman's **Cat & Canary.** The naive soul goes off to work each morning in the mistaken belief that his cat and pet bird will have a cozy, uneventful day. On the contrary, this enterprising pair ends up having a thrill-packed adventure on the roof of the apartment. A kite lifts Cat into the sky over Manhattan, and Canary's many feathered friends bring him safely home. Child readers share with the author the excitement of this adventure, while the fictional adult is entirely in the dark.

The pleasure children derive from such books may have several sources. It appears as if the "wise child" theme is a major attraction, but it may also be safe to say that the picture book genre has now been developed to the point where it fits a young readership rather precisely. That is, the brevity fits the child's attention span. Rhymes fit the child's sense of play (e.g., in *The Witch's Hat*, "It was a magic pot, in case you forgot"). Parallel phrasing fits the child's pleasure in rhythm and a sense of anticipation. For example, in *Funny Bunnies* most of the text is a suspense-building alteration between these two groups of lines: "Came another knock at the door. Papa Bunny went to see who was there," and "A janitor [plumber, maid, etc.] wanted in to fix the lights [pipes, beds, etc.]." In other words, even when the narrative seems a bit mechanical—as in the predictable shape-changing scenario in *The Witch's Hat*—the text can be tailored in a playful way.

Yet the "tailoring" will have limited appeal if an illustrator is not on hand who can bring visual life to the verbal conventions. Robert Quackenbush makes his own illustrations for *Funny Bunnies*: bold, brassy, contemporary cartoons. In their humor they are so easy to comprehend that they may seem ordinary at first, but a closer look leads to enjoyment of a unique style. His technique is a blend of strong line and strong pattern. In the often repeated scene in which Papa opens the door, Quackenbush uses vertical patterns on the wall paper, wheel-like patterns on the rug, and palm fronds in a manner that accents the flashiness of the hotel decor. In other scenes he builds a vivid sense of place with dotted, checked, and striped objects, and he organizes all this to avoid a sense of clutter. That is, until the next to the last scene, when "Out tumbled all the bunnies!" Here he lets a great visual confusion enrich the narrative climax: an avalanche of distraught rabbits.

The book's witty endpapers—sixty hotel doors and an occasional bunny-occupant peering through a crack—are more than an embellishment. They lead the viewer into the book's art, and they cap the whole experience with a delightfully expressive and fitting image.

Joey is the other book in this group by a cartoonist. Jack Kent has a comic touch with characterization, and he gives Joey and his mother a directional push that sustains a sense of energy. The variety of diagonal lines in tail, face, legs, and ears enhance the animation. Behind the figures is a flat, opaque blue and green area that fixes the setting for action, and is only altered when the parent is approaching a four-star crisis over Joey's rock band assembled in her pouch. The sudden switch to a glaring red and yellow background conveys her state of mind.

In *The Witch's Hat,* Margot Tomes is also interested in amusing distortions. The entire anatomy of the witch—the thrust of elbows, hands, feet—make one smile. Yet the overall mood is one of warmth and sympathy, as well as playfulness, and the style provides a subtle treatment of three-dimensional forms. Each vignette and full-page composition is elegantly drawn, and the artist's talent for creating effective design structures shows throughout. For example, she places two small sketches on the page where "the cat ran downstairs like an inky streak." The one at the top contains the figure of a cat within a triangle (part of the stairwell). The upper part of the stair includes a dark, inverted triangle of shaded lines and brown color. The lower sketch depicts witch, stairs, and shadows with another set of triangular constructions—all beautifully planned.

Michael Foreman's *Cat & Canary* is an unabashed celebration of Manhattan—a group of spacious, panoramic views of skyscrapers, as well as dramatic impressions of their enormous height. In one scene, as Cat sails above the rooftops with his precarious kite, the artist intensifies the vertical distances by including a horizontal band of citizens of all sizes, shapes, and colors at the bottom of the picture. The figures are blocked in a colorful design and the effect is a rich, mosaic-like panel.

Foreman uses color and perspective to create intense moods. The night scene with Brooklyn Bridge is one example; another is a scene where Cat glides down "through the snow toward the bright flashing lights of the city." In this snowscape, Foreman really outdid himself with the gem-like treatment of city lights and threads of traffic. Finally, the cat portrait reproduced on this page is actually a bigger-than-life rendering that surprises the reader in the same way a movie close-up is sometimes startling. But the image fits the bigger-than-life drama. Foreman's picture books are exciting and complex, without being slick and pretentious. He respects the difference.

This month's books

Foreman, Michael. *Cat & Canary*. Dial Books for Young Readers, 1984. $11.95.

Johnston, Tony. *The Witch's Hat*. Illus. by Margot Tomes. G.P. Putnam, 1984. $9.95 ISBN 0-399-21010-5.

Kent, Jack. *Joey*. Prentice-Hall, 1984. ISBN 0-13-510348-7

Quackenbush, Robert. *Funny Bunnies*. Clarion Books, 1984. $11.95. ISBN 0-89919-267-X

Patty Campbell:

The Young Adult Perplex

All twenty copies of *Breakdancing: Mr. Fresh and the Supreme Rockers Show You How to Do It!* have disappeared from the library shelves, never to return. The fifteen copies each of five other titles, all named (more or less) *Breakdance,* have still not arrived, even though they were ordered last January. The YA librarian, unfortunately, is not authorized to make a quick run to the paperback store. As another summer of street dancing comes on, how to cope with the clamor from the kids for something—anything—on the subject? A photocopy-and-clip job for the vertical file can tide the library over till the jobber comes, but it would be best to do it quickly before the kids hit *The Readers' Guide* and the magazine stacks with scissors in hand.

In the effort to sort it out, get it all categorized and sanitized, a wealth of journalistic talent has attempted to explain the cultural phenomenon of hip hop, of which breakdance is a part. Some surprising publications have anatomized for middle America the whence and whither of this new blast of aesthetic energy from the grass roots (asphalt roots?) of the ghetto: *Wall Street Journal, Christian Science Monitor,* even the scholarly *American Book Review.*

None of these articles will teach the kids how to do the windmill or the float. (Tell them that learning to breakdance from print without a live teacher is dangerous anyway.) But a judicious selection of some of the more knowledgeable pieces will provide descriptions of moves and styles, color photos of dancers in action, histories, glossaries, news and good words from famous breakers, rappers, and their crews. But they can provide more. By tracing the several civic controversies between street dancers and city fathers, young adults may find a new sense of immediacy in the concept of civil liberty. And in the best of these writings, they will glimpse the complexity of the shifting American social consciousness, whose essence is and always has been defined by a watered-down version of the latest music and dance from the ghetto.

Patty Campbell *is a freelance writer who teaches young adult literature at UCLA.*

Glossaries

Breakdance has generated a whole vocabulary of new expressions that name not only dance movements but also attitudes about their performance, other dancers, and life itself. The first linguistic confusion to clear up is that "breaking" refers technically only to the extremely athletic moves done down on the floor. Other forms of breakdance (or more correctly, "street dance") are "electric boogie," "uprock," and "freestyle." They are all part of hip hop, which includes the wild style of graffiti, music, "rapping," and dress that originated in the Bronx about ten years ago.

• Barol, Bill. "The New Language of Dance." *Newsweek,* July 2, 1984, p. 48.
A cautious list of dance moves and styles.

• "Break Dance Moves: How They're Done, What They're Called." *Glamour,* August 1984, p. 72.
A brief description of a half dozen moves, worth mentioning only because the feminine pronoun is used throughout.

• Goldstein, Patrick. "Street Dancing: A Glossary." *Los Angeles Times,* March 25, 1984, Section C, p. 6.
The West Coast version.

• Hoare, Rosanne. "A Breaking Glossary." *Dancemagazine,* April 1984, p. 72.
Rosy Hoare is a name to watch. Trained as a jazz dancer at Marymount Manhattan College, she is house choreographer at New York's Roxy, the leading breakdance club, and works with crews of breakdancers as manager, choreographer, and mother hen. This list of breakdance expressions reflects her expertise.

Exegesis

Street dancing may have originated in the Bronx, but it also has a bewildering variety of other sources: Fresno electric boogie, Los Angeles "popping," the Brazilian dance-battle copoeira, kung fu, television cartoons, Ukranian folk dance, mime, even Egyptian wall paintings. Everybody has a different version of its history, and they're probably all true. Most of the following articles also invoke some of the big names and try to put the whole thing in cultural perspective.

• Cocks, Jay. "Chilling Out on Rap Flash." *Time,* March 21, 1983, p. 72.
Concentrates on the anthropology of the clothes of hip hop.

• Foster, Catherine. "They're a Human Earthquake!" *Los Angeles Times,* October 28, 1983, p. 26.

• Kendall, Elizabeth. "Breaking." *Vogue,* June 1984, p. 263.
An appreciation from outside. Includes a color photo of young breaker Robert Taylor from *Beat Steet.*

• Koepp, Stephen. "Breaking Through to Big Profits." *Time,* October 1, 1984, p. 52.
Commercial spin-offs from boards to board games.

• McGuigan, Cathleen and others. "Breaking Out: America Goes Dancing." *Newsweek,* July 2, 1984, p. 46.

Long, well-researched article concentrating on breakdance and other popular dance styles in the ballroom. Lots of detail about crews and rappers. Many photographs.

• Pierpont, Margaret. "Breaking in the Studio." *Dancemagazine,* April 1984, p. 82.
Brief remarks on the status of teaching breakdance. "We have housewives flinging their arms and saying, 'We bad!'"

• Robertson, Deborah. "Breakdancing." *American Book Review,* November-December 1984, p. 7.
Thoughtful analysis by a professor of dance at Montclair State College, who also performs with a professional tap dance company.

• Rosenwald, Peter J. "Breaking Away 80's Style." *Dancemagazine,* April 1984, p. 70.
Detailed report on the state of the art by the dance critic of the *Wall Street Journal.* Many color pictures of breakers performing on the street and the stage; the cover features Funky Frank.

Controversy

A new form of dance is always controversial, and when it's done in the street and crowds collect to watch, merchants and city councils can get very tense. The most widely reported breakdance hassle took place in San Bernardino last spring when the city banned breakers from the mall and then discovered they had stuck their fingers in a hornet's nest. Accusations of racism and violation of First Amendment rights made them modify their ruling to allow dancing in the parking lot. First Amendment rights were also the issue in Chicago, when the "old-fashioned" street performers (mimes, musicians, etc.) saw their new, hard-won license law threatened by civic resentment over uncontrolled breakdance crowds. The city moved to forbid street dancing, but the ACLU filed a successful injunction claiming the right of free speech for street performance.

• Adler, Jerry and Barbara Burgower. "Beating the Devil." *Newsweek,* July 2, 1984, p. 52.
The Ministerial Alliance bans all dancing in Mesquite, Texas—as in the fictional town of Bomont in the movie *Footloose.*

• Brotman, Barbara. "Street Musicians Sing a Song: 'Down with Break Dancers.'" *Chicago Tribune,* August 7, 1984.

• "C'mon, Gimme a Break." *Newsweek,* May 14, 1984, p. 28.
Outcome of the San Bernardino controversy.

• "Give Break Dancing a Break." *Christian Science Monitor,* March 28, 1984, p. 19.
Plea for appreciation from an unlikely source.

• Greenhouse, Steven. "Chicago Trying to Restrict Street Performers." *New York Times,* September 10, 1984, p. A19.

• Grubb, Kevin. "Banning Break Dancing—Another Fahrenheit 451?" *Dancemagazine,* June 1984, p. 4.
Once-over-lightly of several trouble spots across the nation. "The American Way seeks to educate people to the danger of limiting freedom—whether it be by banning break dancing or by burning books."

• Hughes, Wesley G. "Ban on Break Dancing Up for Vote." *Los Angeles Times,* March 5, 1984, Section II, p. 1.
San Bernardino attempts to impose a dance freeze.

• McGarry, T. W. "Curtain Falls on Westwood Sidewalk." *Los Angeles Times,* January 16, 1984, Section II, p.1.
L.A. police arrest teenage performers and audience by the hundreds for curfew violation.

Personalities

The essence of breakdancing is aggressive expression of the self, and so it is not surprising that it has given rise to a host of new celebrities and would-be celebrities. Not only dancers and their crews, but rappers, DJs, and impresarios are interviewed and photographed in the following.

• Barol, Bill and Jennifer Smith. "A Street Spinner's Big Break." *Newsweek,* July 2, 1984, p. 50.
Shabba-Doo (a.k.a. Adolfo Quinones), the star of *Breakin',* has come up the hard way.

• Cox, Dan. "Brooklyn's Furious Rockers: Break Dance Roots in a Breakneck Neighborhood." *Dancemagazine,* April 1984, p. 79.
The crew who call themselves the Furious Rockers, from poverty to stardom in *That's Dancing* to a European stage tour. Includes color pictures of this group with their choreographer Rosy Hoare. Rock Steady and other young New York street dancers show their moves in photographs.

• Goldstein, Patrick. "Shrimp and Crew: Street-Wise Boogaloo." *Los Angeles Times,* March 25, 1984, Section C, p. 5.
Breaker Boogaloo Shrimp explains his ambitions.

• Grubb, Kevin. "Hip-hoppin' in the South Bronx; Lester Wilson's *Beat Street.*" *Dancemagazine,* April 1984, p. 76.
The choreographer of *Saturday Night Fever* talks about his work in *Beat Street,* the first big-budget breakdance film.

• Grubb, Kevin. "Shabba-Doo: Street Dance's First Matinee Idol." *Dancemagazine,* October 1984, p. 66.
Formerly a lead dancer on *Soul Train* and the youngest member of the L.A. Lockers, Shabba-Doo at twenty-nine is almost as famous as Afrika Bambaataa.

• Lindsey, Robert. "Dancing in the Streets with a Dream." *New York Times,* January 27, 1984, p. A10.

• Sandler, Ken. "Break Dancers Twist, Turn Way Uptown." *Los Angeles Times,* March 25, 1984, Section C, p. 4.
Two articles showing the poignance of young street unknowns who hope that breakdance will be their ticket to ride.

And a word of caution

• Hamilton, William G. "What Can Break While Breaking." *Dancemagazine,* July 1984, p. 76.
Presents minimal advice on avoiding injury from a specialist in dance medicine. ▣

Kathleen Maio:

Murder in Print

There will be little argument that the British are champions at the "cozy" mystery. The sophisticated dilettante and the comfy auntie who fits detection in between the garden club and tea time are both mystery figures long associated with British detection. England has also produced many a lovable rogue and good inspector of the CID. Sherlock Holmes aside, the British have not, however, dominated the private eye novel. The p.i., with his roots in the pulps, is very much an American hero created by American authors.

There are, of course, examples of the British private eye. Two of the finest recent examples, at least according to my selective memory, have come from women authors and feature women detectives.

P.D. James's Cordelia Gray is the first of these, and Liza Cody's Anna Lee is the second and more active. Lee was introduced in *Dupe* (1981), which won honors on both sides of the Atlantic. Her second case, *Bad Company* (1983), was a disappointment to some, but Liza Cody is clearly back on target with **Stalker** (Scribner's, 1985, $11.95).

Lee is not a loner detective. She continues to work for Brierly Security where she is the only woman operative, condescended to and ogled by male colleagues and harassed by the bitchy receptionist. Anna's current assignment is tracking a carpenter who absconded with an investor's money, an assignment that would seem to be predictable and tedious. Cody does show us the tedium of Lee's job, but it turns out to be anything but predictable, especially after a tip leads Lee to a deserted moor and the badly decomposed body of a man shot with a crossbow.

There are many complexities to Cody's story, and she wisely does not attempt to have Lee solve them all single-handedly. In a touch of realism too often avoided by p.i. writers, Lee is even forced to back off from the case when it clearly becomes a police matter. It is the realism and subtlety of *Stalker* that makes it such an unusual and successful detective story. We are shown our hero's frustrations and humiliations—which are frequent—and also the small lucky breaks, like a London stakeout with legal parking, or a chance to get the week's laundry done while doing a little surveillance from a launderette.

Anna is intelligent and tenacious, but no superwoman. She is vulnerable and is in need of the help of friends. She has much in common with her hard-boiled American counterparts, but she is more different than alike. Whether it is violence or lovemaking, we are made party less to the acts thereof than to their effects on the people involved. There is quiet humor here, and the kind of credibility few American detective writers can match.

By way of comparison, **The Rainy City** (Avon, 1985, $2.95) by Earl W. Emerson is a good example of that predictable American p.i. product. Emerson's novel, which introduces a Seattle private detective named Thomas Black, is intensely derivative but generally enjoyable and a promising series start.

Black is a likable fellow who left the Seattle police force after becoming gun-shy. On the same day that his dog is murdered, his attractive downstairs tenant asks him to find an old friend who disappeared, leaving a passive husband and a small daughter. Things heat up quickly when the

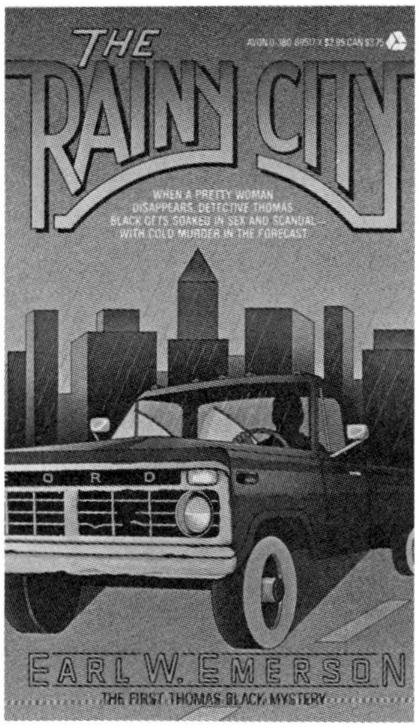

daughter is abducted by her grandfather and those who might provide clues in Melissa Nadisky's disappearance start dying.

Emerson provides violence, often graphic. There is human degradation to spare and enough foul language to satisfy the salty-minded. The plot of family skeletons and hatred goes exactly where we expect it to but travels well. I was especially struck by the figurative language in Black's first-person narrative. We may not be surprised to hear the sky described as being the "color of a bad bruise," but the frequent comparisons to cats ("She had the eyes of a three-week-old kitten being flushed down the toilet") demonstrate a singular prose style.

Kathleen Maio *is a freelance writer based in Somerville, Massachusetts. She has contributed to* Twentieth Century Crime and Mystery Writers, Murderess Ink, *and numerous magazines.*

Harder to categorize is William G. Tapply's **The Dutch Blue Error** (Scribner's, 1985, $12.95). Tapply was last year's winner of the Scribner Crime Novel Award, and his second mystery warrants equal attention. Lawyer to wealthy Yankees, Brady Coyne is again drawn into murderous doings. This time a wealthy, crippled client wants Coyne to negotiate the purchase of a rare stamp. The client, who believed he owned the only "Dutch Blue Error," must authenticate, and if it is genuine, buy a newly discovered duplicate stamp to protect his original investment.

When the prospective seller is murdered, the stamp vanishes, and Coyne must hunt for a murderer as well as the fragile bit of paper. I liked Brady's new assistant, a black law student named Xerxes Garrett, even though he could be viewed as yet another token minority sidekick. It is the suspicions by a racist cop of "Zerk" that really motivates Coyne's feverish detecting. Philately fans won't want to miss this one, but other readers are just as likely to take pleasure in Tapply's second novel.

A journeyman jack-of-many-formulas returns to mystery with **A Graveyard of My Own** (Walker, 1985, $13.95) by Ron Goulart who has written countless books under his own name and many a pseudonym. His first mystery for Walker follows a cartoonist turned commercial artist named Bert Kurrie. When Kurrie and his wife move into their new home in a prosperous Connecticut town, he starts discovering corpses, all of them former colleagues in the comic biz.

While Goulart provides a lot of interesting background on the cartooning field, it isn't enough. The banter among his characters sounds as phony as cartoon dialogue and the plot is equally forgettable. *A Graveyard of My Own* is a good-natured mystery best suited to those with fond memories of the garish comics of yore.

Another near miss is **Come Back, Alice Smythereene!** (St. Martin's, 1985, $12.95) by N. J. McIver. Arnold Simon is a poet and professor who supplements his income by pandering to pop. cult. tastes. When he can no longer sell his carefully crafted mystery series (!) he turns to writing bodice-ripper romances under the name Alice Smythereene. His wife leaves him, and the woman who plays Alice in public appearances and his agent both disappear. Soon Arnold is walking in on murders and having his property and person attacked.

Perhaps the moral of the story is that wealth and fame gained through the writing of romances can't make you happy. Certainly writing romance seems to have turned Arnold's mind to mush. He runs away from the scene of a murder. He repeatedly lies to the police. In short, he is the dim-witted damsel turned male, and the sight is not a pretty one.

McIver's eccentric literary characters are sometimes amusing but the mystery storyline is predictable and the boy-loses-girl plot between Arnold and his angry wife is worse, reminiscent of the "Three's Company" school of sexual sit-com.

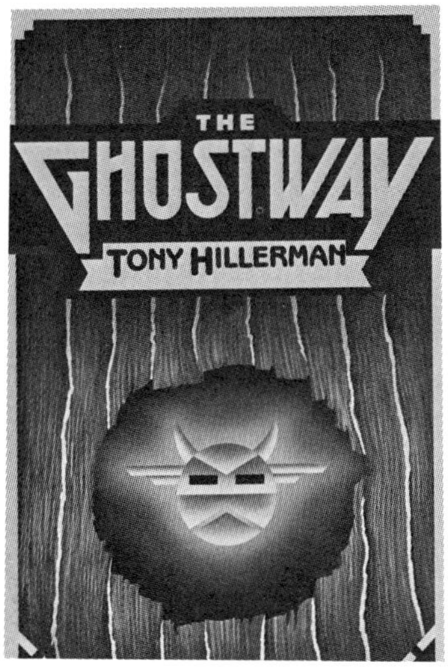

Tony Hillerman continues his series like nothing you'll ever see on TV with **The Ghostway** (Harper and Row, 1985, $13.95). Again Hillerman follows Jim Chee of the Navajo Tribal Police. The investigation of a shoot-out on the reservation leads to an old man's hogan which the lawmen find empty, abandoned to an evil "chindi" or ghost of the dead.

The case involes an FBI-"protected" witness, the survivalist enforcer out to find him, and the federal agents trying to keep him hidden. Jim Chee is caught in the middle, searching for the old man and his young granddaughter, innocent pawns in the war between law officials and organized crime. While the chase leads from Indian land to Los Angeles and back to the most isolated reaches of the reservation, the key to the mystery remains what happened in the hogan of Ashie Begay. Navajo practices regarding the dead and their survivors are more than local color, they are essential to the tale and its telling. This is another fine novel of Southwest suspense.

Last Judgment by Anna Clarke (Doubleday/Crime Club, 1985, $11.95) is certainly not for every taste. It is a novel of psychological suspense in which all the characters feel hatred and jealousy, resentment and ambition, in various configurations. They all plot away according to their own desires, but with the deep foreboding that Something Terrible Will Happen. Something does, but not until the end of the book.

Those who want a lot of action or a murder puzzle with plenty of suspects will abandon *Last Judgment* by chapter five. This is malice domestic with a literary bent. At issue are the papers of an ancient and disagreeable literary giant that provide motivation for various machinations, madness, possibly even murder. Such slow-building suspense is certainly not everyone's cuppa, but those with a taste for such a brew should sample *Last* Judgment. ▣

Judith Trojan:

Front Row Center

This months's column is a departure for me. In the past, I've tried to highlight films and videotapes of unquestionable merit: top-notch festival award winners, small, unheralded gems, classic treasures, or productions that make up in utilization potential what they lack in technical panache. This month, I have no easy answers, only questions. I feel obligated to raise some serious doubts about the numerous festival awards, strong word-of-mouth, and rave reviews piling up around Joel DeMott and Jeff Kreines's **Seventeen**, a disturbing cinema vérité portrait of working-class teenagers in Muncie, Indiana.

The film's original premise was a good one. Like the rest of the films in the much heralded "Middletown" series, created and produced for public television by Peter Davis, *Seventeen* was made-to-order in a sense. Six "Middletown" films were conceived by Davis to update the pioneering sociological studies, *Middletown* (1929) and *Middletown in Transition* (1937), conducted in Muncie by Robert and Helen Lynd. As Executive Producer, Davis wanted the films to reflect areas that concerned the Lynds fifty years before: local politics, leisure, religion, work, family life, and education. Davis personally directed one of the six films, *Second Time Around,* a tense look at the remarriage of two Muncie citizens. The five other programs were researched and filmed by noted independent documentarians from 1979 through 1981, with Davis acting as benevolent overseer. *The Campaign* chronicles a local mayoral race, *The Big Game* clocks a pivotal basketball game, *Community of Praise* profiles a family of Christian fundamentalists, *Family Business* details the ups and downs of a family's foundering pizza franchise, and *Seventeen* highlights the high jinks of a teenager, her family, and friends during their senior year at Muncie's Southside High.

It's interesting to note here that, although Peter Davis did not create *Seventeen,* he was its spiritual father. Having turned his sights from such anti-establishment, investigative documentaries as *The Selling of the Pentagon* (1971) and *Hearts and Minds* (1974), which sent conservatives Spiro Agnew and Bob Hope into a tailspin, Davis entered the eighties with a new focus—hometown America. He wrtoe *Hometown,* a nonfiction book published by Simon & Schuster in 1982, and he conceived the "Middletown" series, both to explore and celebrate life in representative American communities. Davis was quoted in *The New York Times* on March 14, 1982, saying, "If I were still reporting on people in power, I would again take an adversary stance, but . . . I have shifted. There's very little of the spirit of conventional journalism in "Middletown"—who wants an exposé of a small city in north central Indiana?" But, that's just what he got from Joel DeMott and Jeff Kreines, the filmmakers of *Seventeen.*

In the provocative tradition of Fred Wiseman's *High School* and Alan and Susan Raymond's *An American Family, Seventeen* was filmed in the cinema vérité manner, a seemingly freestyle technique—handheld camera and sound, no script and no narration—that evokes a sense of realism and objectivity. However, the technique also carries with it a history of heated debate over the ethics and validity of that very same "objectivity."

Alabama-based filmmakers DeMott and Kreines lived in Muncie for two-and-one-half years to research, film, and edit *Seventeen.* They claim to have "mixed easily with the kids because we each used a one-person rig—a camera/tape recorder combination that allows the filmmaker to work by himself, unhampered by sound people, lights, crew, or crates of paraphernalia." Because Joel (a woman) followed the girls and Jeff followed the boys, they were able to "film moments of high girlishness and boyishness that arose only out of earshot of the opposite sex."

Seventeen was the only "Middletown" film not to air on PBS in the spring of 1982. A hot potato from its two-and-one-half-minute preview reel, the film was attacked by one of its corporate sponsors (Xerox), by PBS, and by Muncie school board officials and parents for a variety of ills, chief among which were the kids' explicit sexual rap and profanity, and the film's focus on interracial dating. Xerox threatened to pull its promotional support from the series if *Seventeen* were aired, PBS demanded cuts in the language in an effort to placate Xerox. Threats of lawsuits filled the air as Muncie parents challenged the manner of permission granted by the filmed teenagers, and educators refuted its narrow view of Muncie's school system. Caught in this complicated web of bureaucratic maneuvering, the filmmakers at first conceded to a five-minute cut; but eventually they opted to withdraw the film.

Three years later, *Seventeen* is still not a pretty picture, but its filmmakers are trying again. They've released the film in theatrical and nontheatrical markets to great applause. Why? The film is as rough and controversial as it was in 1982. Its portrait of one teenager, her family, and her black and white friends is unrelentingly bleak and unflattering.

Seventeen's protagonist of sorts is Lynn Massie. With her sweet face

Judith Trojan *is editor-in-chief of* Sightlines *magazine, editorial coordinator at the Educational Film Library Association in New York City, and a staff member of the American Film Festival.*

and foul mouth, Lynn is the orbit around which the rest of "the cast" revolves. Lynn may have typical teenage fantasies and concerns—boys, dating and sex; best girlfriends; parties; smoking dope and drinking beer; loud music—but she also has no manners, no goals, and no observable set of values. Like all good film subjects, however, she has an easy rapport with the camera, which makes her an apt choice for its "star".

Day-to-day life inside Lynn's classes approximates the boredom, bedlam, and blatant disregard of authority that one might find in a minimum security facility for juvenile offenders. Lynn's cooking class, in particular, seems to be the perfect place for the kids to act up. The white girls and black boys who predominate in these scenes are so busy "playing" to the camera and sassing and mocking their teacher that cooking is the last thing on their minds. These kids make one fear that the prophecy of *A Clockwork Orange* (1971) is close at hand.

Lynn's behavior is understandable once we meet her parents. One tough lady, Shari Massie, at age thirty-four, acts more like Lynn's sister than her mother. Her father is a beer-guzzling macho-man who seems to have stepped right out of the wrong side of *Deliverance*. The Massies throw a beer party for Lynn's friends and neighbors. It turns into a drunken revel that wastes young and old alike, including Lynn's thirteen-year-old brother, Robbie. Police arrive to subdue the festivities.

An insidious sort of racism permeates Lynn's world. Southside High is integrated, and whites and blacks mix well at basketball games and in class. Lynn and her girlfriends date and pal around with black boys, which, the girls admit, makes them off-limits to white boys. Lynn is especially smitten with one black boy who is indifferent to her. A cross is burned on the Massie's lawn because Lynn dates black boys, and black girls harass her because she dates their boyfriends; so Lynn can't seem to win. Mrs. Massie tolerates Lynn's black male chums, but she's ready to whip out her gun and shoot the black girls if they come after her family.

Seventeen threatens to end on an uncharacteristically sweet note as the kids dress up in tuxes and gowns to attend their senior prom, where they are the picture of innocence. But the most offensive "neighborhood" sequences are yet to come. The adult men return home from a fishing trip with a live snapping turtle, which they proceed to torture unmercifully in the street. And a white boy stands in the middle of the same street bragging, in detail, about his sexual conquest of a local girl, while his neighbors—men, kids, girls, the cameraperson—all gather around and egg him on. This sequence sparked the film's initial controversy.

Although *Seventeen* appears to provide a realistic alternative to most of the white-washed TV teen sitcoms and the overly nostalgic teen comedy/dramas glutting the feature-film mar-

(continued on page 574)

Lynn Massie (left) and Wendy Gregory: A bleak and unflattering portrait

This month's films:

Seventeen. 16mm. color. 120 min. 1982. Directors: Joel DeMott and Jeff Kreines. Dist: DeMott-Kreines Films, 5330 Kennedy Ave., Millbrook, AL 36054. 205/285-6179. Apply for prices.

High School. 16mm & video. b&w. 75 min. 1969. Director: Frederick Wiseman. Dist: Zipporah Films, One Richdale Ave., Unit #4, Cambridge, MA 02140. 617/576-3603. 16mm lease—$1,200 (rental $150). Video lease—$900 (¾- and ½-inch).

Sixteen in Webster Groves. 16mm & video. b&w. 47 min. 1966. Producer: Arthur Barron for CBS-TV. Dist: Carousel Film & Video, 241 E. 34th St., Room 304, New York, NY 10016. 212/683-1660. 16mm—$550 (rental $55). Video—$400 (¾-inch); $300 (½-inch).

Webster Groves Revisited. 16mm & video. b&w. 53 min. 1966. Producer: CBS-TV. Dist: Carousel Film & Video. 16mm—$625 (rental $65). Video—$450 (¾-inch); $337.50 (½-inch).

Bruce Pollock:

On Record: Popular Music

Complete with competing world views, contrasting musical styles, parallel galaxies of superstars, the realms of country music and heavy metal could scarcely be further apart. And yet, on **19 Hot Country Requests** and **Metalmania**, two recent collections of supposedly classic reissues, as many cliches are broken as left standing. The standing cliches are by far the more interesting, however, serving to define issues much larger than the occasional heavy metal ballad, the all-too-frequent pop crossover hokum.

Dreaded by anyone over the age of consent (down from twenty to twelve this year), heavy metal is widely thought of as the music of the devil incarnate, played in fact by devil-worshipping bands of marauding, debauching musicians, to whom music is a mere means to venal ends—lust, blood, raw power, ready cash. While this is of course true for the most part, the Columbia heavy metal collection, limited by its catalog, delivers quite a few clunkers in the midst of genuine bloodcurdlers.

The same is true of the (less than) Epic country music collection, which cheats a bit on the typical country concoction of one part hiccup, two parts yodel. Dreaded by anyone under the age of retirement (down from sixty-five to forty-two, according to certain radio programmers), country music is fond of hoisting the verities in song: home, country, liquor. Replete with cheating men and fallen women, fallen men falling on cheating women, and whiskey-drinking preachers hopping southbound freights, the country world is easily as amok as that of heavy metal. In fact, a case could be made that the country cheater is merely the heavy metal egg-beater grown from dissolute youth into a kind of dilapidated prime. Certainly they both tend to favor the same brands of beer—and plenty of it.

None of this can explain, though, the unaccountable poignance of "Pancho and Lefty," by Willie and Waylon, from the country sphere, or the aching passion behind "Fool's Game," by the otherwise undistinguished Michael Bolton, on the metal collection. True music survives any genre, you might say, or thrives on its very limitations. Rare is the music fan, however, who might have the pleasure of experiencing both of those gems on any commercial radio station.

Running down the metal works, we find a generally uninspired mixture of outtakes by sometimes inspired artists. Mountain, represented by a live version of the seminal and murderous "Mississippi Queen," suffers from a poor recording. Fastway, considered in some circles the next best thing to Motorhead, won't gain any new converts with "Say What You Will." And Frank Marino, the underdog's guitar hero, has only the moderately affecting ballad "Strange Dreams" to carry his chalice to the unconverted. Closing side one, Joe Perry delivers the finest guitar moments in "Let the Music Do the Talking." Perry's music, away from his once and current band, Aerosmith, apparently was voiceless, leading him to rejoin his old cronies, who appear on side two with their chestnut, "Dream On." Those hungering to learn who Tommy Bolin was, and why millions of metal fanatics worship him, won't find out much from "Shake the Devil." But "(Don't Fear) the Reaper" by Blue Oyster Cult is the one very nearly pyrotechnic mo-

---

Bruce Pollock *is editor of* Guitar *magazine and the author of* Popular Music: An Annotated Index of American Popular Songs, Volumes 7 and 8.

ment on the LP.

Rather than heavy metal, this album seems to be merely rock and roll to me, and not particularly exotic at that, which leads me to believe that Columbia is at fault, at heart too conservative to really dig too deeply in the heavy metal mind. And neither is Epic, Columbia's sister label, in a position to offer us a wide enough selection of truly juicy country tidbits, although the nineteen tunes on this LP far outstrip Columbia's paltry eleven.

Aside from the absence of anything like a propulsive drumbeat, the thing you notice most about country music is the preponderance of great titles. In this random set alone you have some of the all-time best—"He's a Heartache (Looking for a Place to Happen)," "The Last Thing I Needed the First Thing This Morning" and "You're Going to Ruin My Bad Reputation." Once past the title, interest rapidly declines, except in a few cases. Through the gin-soaked whining and monotone groaning, Mickey Gilley's easy crooning is like hot chocolate on "Talk to Me." David Allan Coe's "The Ride" is properly mystical and moving. Willie Nelson on "The Last Thing I Needed . . . " is aching simplicity itself. Country women, while far from being feminists, are independent sorts nevertheless. Both Charly McClain ("Paradise Tonight") and Janie Fricke ("Tell Me a Lie") portray themselves as frankly out for passion, in a world that limits chances for same with every new release by B. J. Thomas, represented here by two of his more typical reactionary ditties: "Whatever Happened to Old Fashioned Love" and "New Looks from an Old Lover." Like I said, the titles say it all.

Either of the B. J. Thomas titles could be applied to the case of Richard and Linda Thompson, a saga so soapy it not only could have made a decent country song, but will probably soon turn up as a TV Movie of the Week. We'll have to settle for a pair of wonderfully expressive and revealing albums that make a mockery of those two lesser art forms.

Once married to each other, once dynamic and mystical musical partners, the pair broke up a while back and have now (coincidentally?) released simultaneous solo albums, each detailing the breakup, plunging to the heart of the relationship and its painful aftermath in song upon searing song of personal travail and discovery, life-imbued and folkishly melodic.

Richard's album, **Across a Crowded Room**, opens on a note of truth from which he does occasionally waver, but only because his emotions are the more firmly guarded of the combatants—announcing in "When the Spell Is Broken," the ending of a cherished dream, the echoed lines "Can't cry if you don't know how." He picks up on this lack in "I Ain't Gonna Drag My Feet No More," with a similar sentiment: "Where I come from feeling is a crime," he tells us. Though strongly told, the feelings come through loud and clear. Linda opens her album, **One Clear Moment**, with a more optimistic sentiment, in "Can't Stop the Girl," but proceeds through "One Clear Moment," "Telling Me Lies" and "In Love with the Flame" to detail a star-crossed romance that burned in its own passion's flames. The folk airs on both LPs are nothing short of sheer bliss for a fan of such things—existing midway between frothy country laments on the one hand and the more pungent sensations of rock on the other.

On side two Richard shows signs that his manly juices are beginning to flow. In "Fire in the Engine Room" and "Little Blue Number" he's clearly on the prowl. But he reaches an epic breakthrough in "She Twists the Knife Again," as agonizing a portrait of a miscast relationship as you're apt to find on record this side of Talking Heads. Linda, too, has had some experiences of life renewed, yet on the whole she's a good deal more reflective and forgiving than her former partner. Working with a new musical partner, Betsy Cook, "The Best of Friends" is a gesture of enormous magnanimity, considering to whom it's directed. It's just one of the reasons *One Clear Moment* is the more satisfying album to me, and one of the best I've heard all year.

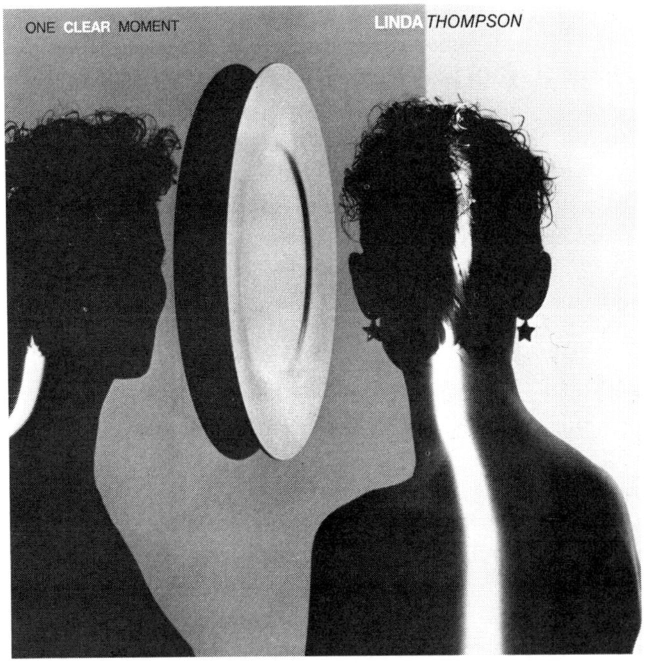

This month's albums

Metalmania. Columbia PC 39948

19 Hot Country Requests. Epic FE39597

Linda Thompson. *One Clear Moment.* Warner Brothers 25164-1

Richard Thompson. *Across a Crowded Room.* Polydor 422-825 421-1

Norman Stevens:

Our Profession

In an era when information, including library service, has a greater economic value than ever, and when technology is weaving information into the fabric of society, professional ethics take on an even greater importance for us. **Professional Ethics and Librarians,** which reflects that increased concern, serves as an excellent starting point for what I hope will be further treatment of such a critical issue. As the authors of the first monograph on the subject, Ann Prentice and Jonathan Lindsey give what may seem to be undue, but is necessary attention to the concept of professional ethics and the history of the way American librarians have dealt with it. After a brief discussion of the development of ethical concepts in various professions, Prentice and Lindsey present a lengthy historical treatment of the development of a code of ethics in the American Library Association, with details of codes from that first suggested by Mary W. Plummer in 1903 through that adopted by ALA in 1981 including the official statements of 1929, 1938, 1975, and 1981. Their documentary treatment provides no commentary on the approach or content, and makes no effort to trace influences or interrelationships. Still, Prentice and Lindsey have done us a substantial service by bringing together in one place all of those statements so that we now have a basis for further comparison and analysis. They also offer brief commentaries on the current ALA code by Page Ackerman, Caroline Arden, Lester Asheim, Jack Dalton, Brooke Sheldon, Robert Vosper, Robert Wedgeworth, William J. Welsh, and Virginia G. Young which are, for the most part, pious statements of little value. Only Arden, who suggests the possibility of an ethics tribunal and questions the appropriateness of professional gossip, and Sheldon, who raises the topic of truth in professional recommendations, make us think about the issues. The nature of those statements by professional leaders with roots in a more genteel era demonstrates the importance of ethics for our time. Commentaries by younger professionals, with, for example, roots in the activism of the 1960s, would offer, I suspect, more challenging and relevant observations. Before concluding with a detailed and useful bibliography, Prentice and Lindsey provide a short set of cases which summarizes some recent examples of ethical issues but this section lacks direction. *Professional Ethics and Librarians* is a much needed start towards the consideration of what is becoming a critical question for our profession. Perhaps because it is the first book on this subject, it offers too much information and too little opinion. If it is to serve us well, we must use it extensively as the basis for discussion and for the development of firm statements of opinion that can guide us through difficult ethical issues.

Conventional wisdom would have us believe that those of us, such as twelve-year-old Jason Hardman who established a library in his hometown of Elsinore, Utah (pop. 680), who provide library service in rural America have such a built-in sense of personal ethics that such issues are of lesser urgency. The report of the 1982 **Joint Congressional Hearing on the Changing Information Needs of Rural America** certainly raises no question, in any of its testimony, on such issues. It does raise the larger, and equally critical, ethical issue of equality in the distribution of, and access to, information so that citizens in rural areas are not put at an information disadvantage. The eleven individuals, including Jason Hardman, whose testimony is presented offer the usual assortment of descriptions of existing situations and programs to document the kind of support that is needed. As hearing testimony this report, like *Professional Ethics and Librarians,* offers too little in the way of guidance and direction, but serves as a good starting point for further discussion and work.

Ethical issues are only one of a number of complex matters which have received attention in a recent spate of publications on the organization and management of large urban public libraries. Snunith Shoham's **Organizational Adaptation by Public Libraries** is a summary of empirical research she conducted in 1983 in six California public libraries using general organizational theories and concepts. It is a theoretical work and, as such, not always easy to understand and to convert into action. Shoham examined such issues as adaptive behavior, the public library's response and adjustment to environmental demands, and the decision-making process involved in adapting to the environment. In particular her study focused on responses to changes in the

Norman D. Stevens, *University Librarian at the University of Connecticut, is the author of the forthcoming book* A Guide to Collecting Librariana.

population served and changes in resources. Her concluding chapter, "Retrospect and Implications," is a strong call for the public library to become more responsive to the community's needs and more involved in the political process, and for library schools to maintain their role in teaching the social value of libraries.

T.D. Webb's **Reorganization in the Public Library** examines that adaptive process in considerable detail. It grew out of a project to reorganize the Phoenix Public Library during which Webb found that, although public library reorganization was a widespread phenomenon, little information was available on organizational theory or strategies for reorganization. His work is an effort to provide a starting point for further discussion on aspects of reorganization. It is built around five themes: goals and organizational change, departmentation and organizational style, consolidation and cooperation, staff participation, and the use of consultants. In each case a short chapter on the general theme by Webb is followed by a case history from a major public library (Free Library of Philadelphia, Baltimore County Public Library, Phoenix Public Library, Montgomery County Department of Public Libraries, and Tucson Public Library) by people from those libraries. This somewhat unusual approach makes for an interesting blend of theory and practice which clarifies the interrelationship between the two. The case studies also demonstrate how some of the issues raised by Shoham have been dealt with in a more practical fashion. Webb suggests, for example, that one way to achieve greater political clout, and greater access to power and resources, is to provide the local government budget makers with services they need and to become an integral part of their organizational structure. Webb's comments are direct and to the point as he recognizes the strengths, as well as the weaknesses, of these various efforts to reorganize a public library.

The evaluation of the Dallas Public Library in its **Library Service Goals 1972–1982** is, as one might expect, less honest than those in Webb's book. This internal report, prepared by Librarian Gleniece A. Robinson examines the extent to which the library met the ten-year goals it set for itself in 1972. The goals, dealing with user-oriented service, materials collection and selection, organization of materials, staffing, and management and communications, were each a general statement of purpose accompanied by a brief set of specific goals that, unfortunately, in most cases were not directly measurable. Robinson has reviewed each general and specific goal and has sought objective information about the extent to which they were met. While the results may seem unduly optimistic, it is encouraging to have an example of a commitment to carry out a formal evaluation as a follow-up to the establishment of institutional goals. Too often, individually and collectively, we set goals but then neglect to evaluate our performance in meeting them. There are some useful lessons to be learned by looking at what the Dallas Public Library set out to accomplish and what it feels it has accomplished.

A more intriguing, and exciting, effort at evaluation is found in **Citizen Participation in Library Decision-Making,** a lengthy examination of reorganization, change, participation, community priorities, and the political process as experienced in the recent history of the Toronto Public Library. It is an analysis of the political process at work through a series of twenty-two essays by seventeen different individuals, largely private citizens, involved in one way or another with developments at the Toronto Public Library between 1974 and 1979. For the most part the essays present a positive view of how the library adapted to community needs by the direct and active involvement of citizens in its decision making processes. There are, particularly in an essay, "TPL Unionizes," by an anonymous insider and another, "The Struggle for Canadian Materials," by Marian Engle, some critical comments on the processes and the results. As personal testimony from citizens, not librarians, involved in the process to help improve library service in a large metropolitan public library, this work has much in common with the NCLIS/USDA report on rural public library service. The views of citizens on such issues are always refreshing and often a welcome change from our own jargon and self-congratulation.

Together five of the volumes reviewed in this month's column provide a fascinating assortment of views and information on the role of the public library today. Many of the issues that lie behind those views are examples of the kind of critical ethical issues that face us as we seek to make public library service available. ▣

This month's books

Joint Congressional Hearing on the Changing Information Needs of Rural America: The Role of Libraries and Information Technology. National Commission on Libraries and Information Science and U.S. Department of Agriculture, 1984. 83p. free

Library Service Goals 1972–1982 for the Dallas Public Library: An Evaluation Report. Dallas Public Library, 1983. 75p. $6.50

Marshall, John. *Citizen Participation in Library Decision-Making: The Toronto Experience.* Scarecrow Press, 1984. 392p. $25. ISBN 0-8108-1709-8 LC 84-10617

Prentice, Ann and Jonathan Lindsey. *Professional Ethics and Librarians.* Oryx Press, 1985. 184p. $32.50. ISBN 0-89774-133-1 LC 83-43244

Shoham, Snunith. *Organizational Adaptation by Public Libraries.* Greenwood Press, 1984. 163p. $29.95 ISBN 0-313-24406-5 LC 83-22738

Webb, T.D. *Reorganization in the Public Library.* Oryx Press, 1985. 120p. $35. ISBN 0-89774-074-2 LC 82-42917

Patrick Dewey:

Software for Libraries

The electronic bulletin board system (BBS) **People's Message System** (Bill Blue) can be used by libraries to turn an Apple Computer into an online database for communication with patrons or with other librarians: it provides an electronic window on the world. There are dozens of such software programs available for most of the major microcomputers. Typically, such a system is operated while the library is closed; in this way, a computer used for other things during the day may be used as a BBS at night, a sort of bonus. Users of the *PMS* have a variety of features available: electronic mail (approximately 100 messages may be left online by callers at any one time, with the oldest message deleted when a new message is added, eliminating the need for the housekeeping chore of a periodic manual purge); posting of articles, columns, or information modules; and downloading and uploading of software or other data. The volume of material that may be posted depends upon how much disk memory is available. The *PMS* also maintains a file of comments left by callers, and a logfile of who called and from where. A very special (and, as far as I can tell, unique to *PMS*) feature is the obscenity filter. This allows the library staff to create a file of forbidden words against which all messages left by callers are checked. If a message is found to contain any of the forbidden words, it is refused without comment. The best argument for the *PMS* over other BBS software, however, is that it has exceptional error-handling.

A word of caution: a BBS is not a project for beginners; it requires considerable familiarity with a microcomputer. A number of libraries are using a BBS, whether *PMS* or another system, some for internal use and some for public use. Those which have had success with the *PMS* have all had micro projects going for some time; these include the North-Pulaski (Chicago) Library and Liverpool (New York) Public Library. Typical material posted on a library BBS includes general information about the library, freelance columns, advice columns, puzzles for the kids, book and movie reviews, consumer information, calendar of events, municipal telephone numbers, book sale time and location, and bibliographies. In some rare cases, reference and interlibrary loan are provided. Librarians tend to think, however, that the greatest benefit is good public relations among the growing number of people with microcomputers and modems. The development of such a system is limited only by the external memory of the computer being used, and the creativity of the library staff. *PMS* documentation unfortunately leaves something to be desired; it is apparently a first draft that was never revised. For use with: Apple II+, IIe with two five-inch or eight-inch disk drives or a hard disk, and modem. To upload files, at least three five-inch drives are required. Cost: $300.

Patrick Dewey *is administrative librarian, Maywood (Illinois) Public Library and author of* Public Access Microcomputers: A Handbook for Librarians.

Electronic teacher

The DOS Teacher (AV Systems, Inc., 1984) is an inexpensively priced collection of programs on the operation and function of the Apple Disk Operating System (DOS), as well as many other programs, including utilities, that together make a good addition to a public access collection. Among these are programs which allow the copying of a whole disk or an individual file, a binary/text converter, a disk mapper and analysis program, a disk or file encryption system, a DOS command locator, a DOS command changer, a special catalog program, an illustrated high resolution graphics tutorial of what happens when a disk is initialized, and lots more. A few of the programs have notable and obvious deficiencies. For instance, a tutorial about mylar disk data storage is nothing more than several pages of text scrolled on the screen, and the sections on DOS language statements and disk trivia are merely automated glossaries. The authors have also introduced what they consider clarification by renaming Apple's "Housekeeping" routines "Operations." They may have a point, but the term "Housekeeping" is so well established that the change is confusing. But on the whole, there are more pluses than minuses. Special review copy sent on thirty-day approval. For use with: Apple II+, IIe, IIc. Cost: $29.95.

Dynamite math

Demolition Division (Developmental Learning Materials and Argue Communications, 1984) makes one wonder where education is headed. There is no better way to describe this program than the rather bizarre comment in the program documentation: "In *Demolition Division*, your child practices basic division facts in a warlike environment. He or she controls anti-tank guns and attempts to ward off advancing enemy tanks. Five tanks containing division problems approach and attack guns sheltered by walls. As the tank fire hits the walls, the walls begin to crumble. Your child must defend each gun before the walls collapse!" While playing this game, I kept thinking, "If I don't answer these problems correctly, I'll be

blown out of creation." It strikes one as infantile, though the game itself is fairly well designed; a typical youngster can have quite an exciting time. One answer at a time is displayed by the computer. Just "aim" the cursor (answer) to hit the corresponding tank (problem) using a joystick, paddle or keyboard, and "fire." If the answer is correct, the tank is pulverized. Players may choose the level of difficulty which governs the digits in use (easy to hard; from 0 to 3, 0 to 6, or 0 to 9), and play time may be adjusted from one to five minutes. Appropriate (according to the box) for use with ages six to fifteen. For use with: Apple II+, IIe, IBM PC, Commodore 64, Atari 400/800/1200. Cost: $34.

Discover America

Coast to Coast for ages eight to fourteen (CBS Software, 1984) is an excellent elementary tutorial which consists of five separate games, program guide, and keyboard overlays (in the case of the Apple II+ and IIe package—the version used for this review—two overlays are included). The high resolution graphics for the national map of the states is outstanding. The games include: "State Facts," "Quiz," "Mystery State," "Across the USA," and "State Shoot." They are all rather straightforward. Players, however, can get more out of the program than just state facts and geography; i.e., eye-hand coordination and the judgment of distance are needed to play "State Shoot," a non-violent game, the object of which is to hit the state outlined on the map with an arrow. "Across the USA" lets the player make an imaginary trip in the shortest distance by guessing which states border each other without the aid of state lines. Programs may be adjusted to easy, medium, or hard levels. The booklet not only helps to get the system up and running, but includes separate summaries of facts about all fifty states, Washington D.C., and commonwealths and territories. While I'm not too keen on keyboard overlays, they do work and provide a way of simplifying what would otherwise be a difficult procedure which can detract from learning. For use with: Apple II+, IIe, IBM PC, PCjr., and Commodore 64. Cost: $39.95.

Programs for the precocious

Hello Apple (AV Systems, 1984) is the perfect package for those whiz kids who come back day after day, exhausting the collection, since it consists of a large number of entertaining and educational programs. This well-organized collection contains dozens of games, utilities, statistics, and other useful software. The categories include Skills for Computing, Personal Programming, Business Programming, Entertainment, Graphics, Science, Applications, Mathematics, and Time Machine. Games range from an all-text Star Wars adventure, to "Marooned in Space," in which the player attempts to identify one of the planets or moons in the solar system based upon clues provided by the computer. For variety, there is a brief program on sound effects that produces noises ranging from "Zapper" to "The Crazy Moth." Other programs include math calculator (to perform basic math, check the area of a circle, or convert Fahrenheit to Celsius), an interactive graphics demo that explains rotation and other concepts, and a program that calculates eighteen business statistics (i.e., mortgage payments, interest, etc.). "Time Machine" is a single program which will produce a calendar for a month of any year. (I cannot say how accurate it is, but from experience with other calendar software, I believe that it's a good idea not to rely seriously upon such programs since authors often forget to calculate such things as extra days at the end of a century, or leap years.) A few of the programs appear to be in the public domain, since I have seen some of them elsewhere. I did uncover one (but only one) tiny bug in one program, at which point it bombed, but startup again is simple. It comes with a liberal backup or classroom use copy policy. Special review copy sent on thirty-day approval. For use with: Apple II+, IIe, IIc. Cost: $29.95.

Publisher addresses for this month's software:

AV Systems, Inc., Box 49210, Los Angeles, CA 90049.

Bill Blue, Marilla Corp., 1274 Del Monte Dr., El Cajon, CA 92020.

CBS Software, Inc., One Fawcett Place, Greenwich, CT 06386.

Developmental Learning Materials, One DLM Park, Allen, TX 75002.

James Rettig:

Current Reference Books

Correspondence and review copies for this column should be directed to James Rettig, University Library, Box 8198, University of Illinois at Chicago, Chicago, IL 60680.

Abstracts and Indexes in Science and Technology, by Dolores B. Owen. 2nd ed. Metuchen, NJ: Scarecrow, 1985. 235p. $17.50. 0-8108-1712-8 84-10902

Bigger and better are the words to describe this second edition. Enlarged in coverage from 125 to 223 titles, it now also indicates the online availability of the indexes and abstracts. The 223 indexes are arranged into eleven broad categories such as chemistry and physics, nuclcar science and space science, engineering and technology, agricultural sciences, health sciences, and a general section, with a title index. Entries describe the tools' arrangement, subject scope, types of materials indexed, most useful approach for use, nature of abstracts, type of internal indexing, availability of a list of the periodicals indexed, and online database availability. Each title is listed only once, even if its interdisciplinary nature would qualify it for inclusion in more than one of the broad categories. Like other guides to reference works, this can be used to identify indexes useful for solving particular information needs. The descriptive information also lends itself to use in bibliographic instruction with advanced students in academic libraries. It is a handy supplement to broader purpose guides such as Malinowsky and Richardson's *Science and Engineering Literature* (3rd ed., Littleton, CO: Libraries Unlimited, 1980).

James Rettig *is head reference librarian, University of Illinois at Chicago.*

Atlas of American History. 2nd rev. ed. New York: Scribner's, 1984. 306p. $50. 0-684-18411-7 84-675413
The Times Atlas of World History, edited by Geoffrey Barraclough. Rev. ed. Maplewood, NJ: Hammond, 1984. 360p. $75. 0-8437-1129-9 84-675088

With refreshing candor, the publicity release for the *Atlas of American History* notes that although this revision of the work originally published in 1943 and first revised in 1978 was "designed primarily for new . . . customers, we hope owners of older editions will also consider" it. Owners of the original should do more than consider it; they should definitely buy it. Owners of the 1978 edition can get by without it, although the 1984 incarnation offers new and revised maps. A map on universal male suffrage in the nineteenth century has been added and Norse voyages of discovery and national forests have been added to appropriate maps, but most revisions center on the past fifteen years, incorporating data from the 1980 census to display recent social and economic developments. Completely new maps deal with nuclear power plants, hazardous waste sites, and intercontinental ballistic missile bases. The black-and-white maps and their succinct captions convey considerable information. Ideally American libraries of all types will buy the 1984 revision; at the very least they should have the 1978 edition.

Revisions to the *Times Atlas of World History* are similar to those made in *American History.* First published in 1978, revised slightly the next year, and reprinted annually since, *World History*'s revisions reflect both recent scholarship about the past and recent political developments, with a distinct emphasis on revisions necessitated by the latter. Scholarship has driven changes in the text more than in the color maps, resulting in revisions to maps depicting things such as the spread of prehistoric man, the boundaries of the Roman Empire, and the travels of the Vikings. Updating in response to political events has resulted in considerable new text and some revision of maps of the Middle East, Central America, southern and southeastern Asia, and thematic maps such as the wealth of nations in the 1980s. The chronology of world history has also been brought forward. Advice on purchasing is also similar to *American History*; ideally libraries will be able to buy the 1984 revision but that is not essential if they have the earlier edition.

British Literary Magazines, 1837–1913, edited by Alvin Sullivan. Westport, CT: Greenwood, 1984. 560p. $75. 0-313-24335-2 82-21136 (Historical guides to the world's periodicals and newspapers)

A sequel to *British Literary Magazines, 1698–1788* and *British Literary Magazines, 1789–1836* (reviewed in *WLB,* April 1984), this is the third of four volumes which will recount the histories of the most significant British literary journals from the genre's inception to the present. It is also, surely, the most exuberant of the four by virtue of the period it covers. Increasing literacy and improvements in printing processes contributed to an explosion of periodical publishing in Victorian England, with perhaps as many as 50,000 titles appearing. From these, the team under Sullivan's capable editorial direction has selected and profiled approximately 100 addressing literary matters. These magazines have enriched the English-speaking world's culture. *The Cornhill Magazine* published essays by Matthew Arnold and Henry James's *Daisy Miller; Hard Times* appeared serially in Dickens's own *Household Words*; and since 1841 *Punch* has been poking fun at British society. This is an invaluable sourcebook for the study of these periodicals, for in addition to the profiles, it provides bibliographies, notes published indexes, lists reprint editions in hard copy and microform, identifies library holdings of complete or substantial runs on both sides of the Atlantic, and charts publication history, including a chronology of editors. The index enhances all these useful features. A model of its kind, *British Literary Magazines* deserves a place even in those academic libraries which have few of the magazines themselves.

Crittenden Directory: Real Estate Financing. Crittenden Publishing (Box 1150, Novato, CA 94948), 1983. 486p. looseleaf $237. **Buyers Directory.** Crittenden, 1984. 212p. looseleaf $287. **Dealmakers Handbook.** Crittenden, 1984. 75p. looseleaf $287. **Residential Lenders Directory.** Crittenden, 1984. 80p. looseleaf $287. **Syndicator Directory.** Crittenden, 1984. 119p. looseleaf $287.

For the first time, Crittenden is making available to libraries these five directories of major players in the commercial and residential real estate industry. The *Crittenden Directory* lists by regions of the country the 392 top mortgage lenders, describes their lending activity and interest in various types of projects, and states their minimum and maximum loans. An index for each region tells which companies make loans for various purposes, for example, business condos, farms, hotels, and retail shopping centers. The *Buyers Directory* lists 635 companies heavily involved in acquiring investment properties, listing for each the types of purchases it makes, maximum and minimum purchase amounts, territory, and contact person. The other three directories offer a single entry per page. *Dealmakers* tells what companies make loans and investments in all types of income property developments. *Residential Lenders* does the same for residential properties. The *Syndicator Directory* claims to be the only directory listing firms specializing in syndicating real estate investments. Some companies appear in more than one directory, but generally the name of the contact person changes to reflect the directory's special purpose. All five are updated quarterly. The lack of prefatory matter in the directories shows that these are intended for the knowledgeable professional, not the student or layperson. It is laudable in principle that these are now available to libraries; in practice, however, their cost and highly specialized nature are reasons for all libraries but those in the wealthiest graduate business schools not to buy them.

The Crown Guide to the World's Great Plays, by Joseph T. Shipley. Rev. ed. New York: Crown, 1984. 866p. $24.95. 0-5127-5392-9 83-27211

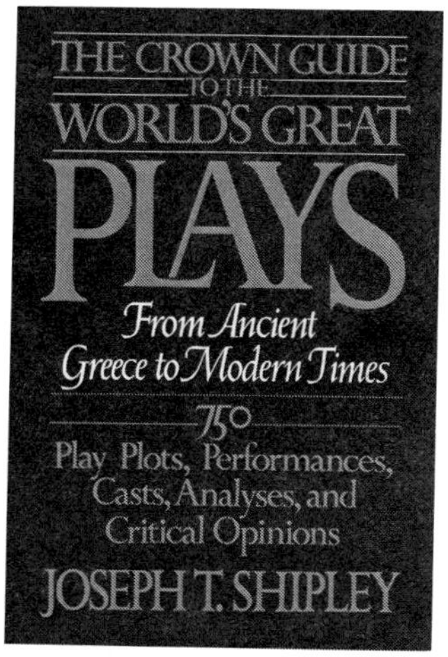

Nearly thirty years of new plays and new productions of old plays as well as changing critical judgments have necessitated a revised and updated edition of Shipley's *Guide to Great Plays* (Washington: Public Affairs Press, 1956). He has added coverage of approximately 100 plays, most written since the first edition was published. Some included in the first edition have been dropped because they have fallen out of public or critical favor, most notably ancient Greek and Roman dramas whose principal claim to fame rests on "the accident of survival." Librarians who banish plot summaries from their collections for ethical reasons have little to fear from Shipley's 750 entries arranged by the playwrights' names. Shipley epitomizes rather than summarizes each play, emphasizing its critical reception, its Anglo-American production history, and its place in its author's corpus rather than its sequence of dramatic events. Entries carried over from the first edition evidence revision mostly in the brief production histories. Shipley, an observer of the New York theater since 1918, writes with grace, wit, and verve. The title index cites not only the main entries, but also secondary references to the plays. *Great Plays* has been a standard in reference collections since 1956; the revision deserves an equally long run.

Dictionary of American Military Biography, edited by Roger J. Spiller and Joseph G. Dawson III. Westport, CT: Greenwood, 1984. 3 v. $145. 0-313-21433-6 83-12674

Unlike most historical biographical dictionaries published by Greenwood, not all of the biographees in *American Military Biography* are deceased. A few living military leaders, such as Elmo Zumwalt and William Westmoreland, who gained fame during the Vietnam war are included along with those from conflicts as far back as the French and Indian War. Although the majority of the 400 subjects served in the American military, especially the army, the editors have taken an expansive view of the subject, including entries on civilians who influenced American military history. Thus there are biographies of George Bancroft, Clara Barton, James Forrestal, Abraham Lincoln, Robert McNamara, Miles Standish, and Edwin Stanton, as well as biographies of seventeen famous Indian warriors including Crazy Horse, Geronimo, Chief Joseph, and Sitting Bull. After relating the birth-to-death biography of the subject, each two-part entry assesses his or her contribution to American military history and cites additional sources. With few exceptions the 200 contributors write with scholarly objectivity. Useful appendixes include a chronology of American military developments, the American military ranks in all branches during the past two centuries, definitions of various military units, and indexes of the entries by birthplace, by war, and by branch of service. Because most of these individuals can claim fame only through their military careers, biographical information in other sources can prove elusive. These brief biographies with bibliographies will thus be helpful to historians and others.

A Dictionary of Nicknames, by L. G. Pine. Boston: Routledge & Kegan Paul, 1984. 207p. $18.95. 0-7100-9582-1 84-3263

Pine's engaging dictionary is a cross between a historical dictionary of nicknames and a dictionary of generic nicknames. Of the first sort he includes "Divine Madman" for Michelangelo and "Non-jurors" for the dissidents who left the Church of England in 1689 after William III became king. Of the second sort are the very vivid "fullalove," "for an enormous person" and "scattergood" for "a spendthrift." In this second category Pine also includes the etymologies of many less colorful terms such as daft, new, and slow. All types of nicknames are entered in one alphabet. Historical entries identify the person or group so nicknamed and explain the origins of the names. By referring to page numbers rather than to specific sobriquets, the personal name index creates minor inconvenience even while providing access. Overlap with Carl Safikis's *Dictionary of Historical Nicknames* (reviewed in *WLB,* May 1984) is insignificant since Safikis treats only individuals and since Pine has a slight British emphasis.

Directory of United States Traditional and Alternative Colleges and Universities, 1984–1986, by Jean-Maximillien de La Croix de Lafayette. National Association of State Approved Colleges and Universities, Publications Division (4525 Lincoln Ave., Box 602, Beltsville, MD 20705), 1984. 476p. pa$38.
National Register of Social Prestige and Academic Ratings of American Colleges and Universities, by Jean-Maximillien de La Croix de Lafayette. National Association of State Approved Colleges and Universities, Publications Division (4525 Lincoln Ave., Box 602, Beltsville, MD 20705), 1984. 132p. $28.

These two books were sponsored not only by the National Association of State Approved Colleges and Universities, but also by the American Council for University Planning and Academic Excellence, non-profit organizations founded in 1981 and, according to the *Encyclopedia of Associations,* sharing not only the same Washington address, but also the same president, Jean-Maximillien de La Croix de Lafayette, editor of the books. A search of the indexes to *The Chronicle of Higher Education* for the past four years and a search of standard biographical sources failed to turn up a single additional reference to either organization or their president. Nor are their periodicals listed in *Ulrich's.* In short, something seems amiss.

The *Directory* lists colleges and universities which are legally empowered to grant degrees and identifies schools with non-traditional programs (e.g., weekend degree programs, independent study, study abroad programs, etc.). It also lists and warns against diploma mills. One curious chapter, "Colleges and Universities with Optional Class Attendance," runs only one page, indicating that such a list of more than 324 schools will appear in the next edition. It also notes that "Our survey indicated that 99% of students prefer not to attend classes if attendance is not required." In some chapters programs are described briefly; in others they are simply enumerated. John Bear's *Bear's Guide to Non-traditional College Degrees* (Berkeley: Ten Speed Press, 1983) has established itself as the authoritative guide to this field and is the only one libraries need.

The *National Register* immediately brings to mind the various "Gourman reports," a series of misleading rankings of colleges and universities. Librarians who have naively relied upon the Gourman reports should read David Webster's "Who Is Jack Gourman and Why Is He Saying All Those Things About My College?" *Change,* (November/December 1984, pp. 14–19+). All of the deficiences of the Gourman reports are present in the *National Register.* Schools and programs are ranked in various categories but the criteria for judging them are not stated. Students and parents persistently ask for rankings of schools. Jack Gourman and Jean-Maximillien de La Croix de Lafayette give them rankings. But that does not mean that libraries should, especially when the rankings are derived in an unknown manner. Caveat emptor!

Frew's Daily Archive, compiled by Andrew W. Frew. Jefferson, NC: McFarland, 1984. 374p. $24.95. 0-89950-127-3 84-42612

Librarians in school, public, and academic libraries have all faced crowds of students sent to the library, usually early in a new term, to find out what noteworthy events or other births have occurred on their birthdays. The purpose of his exercise as conceived in the student teacher's or the tenured professor's mind is to teach their students how to use and appreciate the library. What the students learn is that librarians have a remarkable ability to find obscure facts. *Frew's* will allow librarians to reinforce that lesson. For every day of the year, from 3,887,492,104 BC when allegedly "the first blue-green algae produced seventeen oxygen molecules" (February 29), to 1983 when American soldiers invaded Grenada (October 25), Frew identifies events, births, and commemorative days. He notes a surprising number of record-setting fish caught during recent years, possibly the reflection of a personal avocation. Birth lists emphasize entertainers and sports figures. They would be more useful, especially to students not yet conversant with the history of Western culture, if the persons' occupations followed their names. Johnny Carson (October 23,

1925) will be familiar enough to them, but one wonders how many, even among the college students, can state the significance of John Calvin (July 10, 1509). Linda Millgate's *The Almanac of Dates* (New York: Harcourt, Brace, 1977) offers more events, many of them obscure and even less accessible to today's students than the publication of *Pilgrim's Progress* (September 28, 1678). Of course the precise dating of prehistoric events is meant to be humorous, but it also makes one uneasy about the book's reliability. The more selective *Chase's Annual Events* (Chicago: Contemporary Books), with its lively, enlightening annotations, will remain librarians' first choice in this genre. However, so long as teachers believe the library can be understood after looking up a single date, few libraries can do without *Frew's* and a few others of its kind.

Global Guide to International Education, edited by David S. Hoopes. New York: Facts On File, 1984. 704p. $75. 0-87196-437-6 82-1545

In its effort to provide information "on international education organizations, academic programs, and printed and other resources" related to area studies programs for Americans, the *Global Guide* is perhaps too global in its listings of general resources. For example, it appropriately lists the Foundation for Ethnic Dance, but superflously includes *Dance Research Journal*. Such excesses are largely confined to the preliminary sections listing general publications and organizations in the field. Later sections on area studies, the study of particular countries, or international approaches to traditional disciplines list only organizations and publications directly related to their subjects. Brief annotations describe the purposes of organizations and the scope of publications. The guide keeps itself lean by excluding foreign language study programs, undergraduate international relations programs emphasizing political science, and study abroad programs. To students interested in studying an area of the world, the *Global Guide* offers useful lists of sources from which they can obtain additional information. Most of these sources can be identified by other means, but not with the one-volume convenience of this sourcebook. In academic libraries it will be a useful stepping stone to books with a narrower focus within the international education field.

Great Foreign Language Writers, edited by James Vinson and Daniel Kirkpatrick. New York: St. Martin's, 1984. 714p. $39.95. 0-312-34585-2 83-40552

Contemporary Foreign Language Writers, edited by James Vinson and Daniel Kirkpatrick. New York: St. Martin's, 1984. 439p. $25. 0-312-16663-X 83-40550

Who's Who-style biographies, bibliographies of primary works organized by genre, selective bibliographies of secondary works, and brief critical essays—the hallmarks of the *Great Writers of the English Language Series* of bio-bibliographies of poets, novelists, dramatists, and critics—characterize these two volumes created by the same editors directing new teams of specialists. The ambiguous criteria for inclusion, "the recommendations of the advisors," admitted a few to both volumes, some contemporaries (e.g., Jorge Luis Borges, Jean Genet, and Alexander Solzhenitsyn) having apparently already established their lasting value. Eclectically international in scope, these encompass writers from Hesiod and Homer to Mikhail Sholokov and Mario Soldati. The historical volume has far broader appeal since more of the writers it covers appear on high school and college reading lists and thus become objects of curiosity or topics for student papers. Like the volumes in the English language series, these provide solid foundations for investigations into a writer's life, works, and critical legacy. Essential purchases for academic libraries, they surely offer much to high school and public libraries as well.

How-To: 1400 Best Books on Doing Almost Everything, by Bill Katz and Linda S. Katz. New York: Bowker, 1985. 377p. $29.95. 0-8352-1927-5 84-24167

Self-Help: 1400 Best Books on Personal Growth, by Bill Katz and Linda S. Katz. New York: Bowker, 1985. 379p. $29.95. 0-8352-1939-9 84-24163

Because the fine line separating how-to books from self-help books inevitably blurs, these companion bibliographies carry the identical cumulative author, title, and subject indexes in addition to their individual tables of contents. The CIP information indicates this might create a small problem in some libraries; the recommended Dewey numbers use the same stem, but the LC numbers separate the two volumes. The tables of contents consist of subject headings and a plethora of *see* references to the headings. Most of the books have been published since 1980. *How-To* covers both expected (e.g., automobiles, computers, gardening, home repair, woodworking) and unexpected how-to topics (e.g., astronomy, cheerleading, gambling, juggling, tea). Some of the books explain the ins and outs of collecting various objects such as dolls or stamps. Despite a generally clear table of contents and a comparable subject index, a few things are elusive. For example, *How-To* includes books which might have saved this reviewer many blown fuses when fiddling with household electric wiring, but theses are listed under the heading "Appliances." Literate annotations not only describe and evaluate the books, they also convey their flavor, often comparing similar ones.

Self-Help gives similar treatment to books that can "help an individual improve, modify, or otherwise understand his or her physical or personal characteristics," excluding religious titles. Under more than 160 headings it annotates books on aging, beauty care, career changes, English usage, hair, management, personal finance, public speaking, sex, term papers, weddings, and numerous other topics.

The annotations evaluate the books within their class, rightly leaving to the reader the task of judging the value of astrology, exercise, yoga, etc.

The selection of 1400 rather than 1000 or 1500 or any other "magic" number of books for each bibliography is not explained. That hardly matters, as the two offer more than enough help to any and all no matter how much they want to do for themselves or improve themselves. These bibliographies will be particularly useful in reader's advisory service.

Knowing Where to Look, by Lois Horowitz. Cincinnati: Writer's Digest, 1984. 436p. $16.95. 0-89879-159-6 84-20876

Reference librarians will find little to argue with in this guide written by a reference librarian for nonlibrarians who need to do library research. Horowitz explains the benefits of independent library use and warns of its difficulties, even the difficulty of finding parking near many libraries. She lifts the veil of mystery from the research process by discussing the nature and use of various types of reference sources and research materials (e.g., dictionaries, encyclopedias, indexes, newspapers, microforms), citing and annotating examples of each type. She also discusses sources and techniques for finding types of information such as addresses, statistics, quotations, and legal information. The sample search strategies in the final chapter are too sketchy to integrate the type-of-source and the topical approaches. Nevertheless a careful reader of her guide can learn a great deal, at the very least when a library is likely to have resources relevant to a particular problem. Those who are not put off by the caveats early in the book may be overwhelmed by the number of resources discussed. Such readers may decide to ignore one of Horowitz's "myths about research," that "the best way to do research is to call your librarian." She says the librarian cannot give each individual more than a few moments. But most nonlibrarians would prefer to settle for those few moments than attempt to absorb everything in this book. It is well executed and reference librarians will enjoy the many excerpts from her regular San Diego newspaper column in which she answers tough questions; however, this book's audience is surely a small one.

The Oxter English Dictionary, by George S. Saussy III. New York: Facts on File, 1984. 277p. $14.95. 0-87196-962-9 84-13789

In his introduction Saussy quotes Anthony Burgess on the need for precision and clarity in language, advice he heeds by opening with the statement that "*The Oxter English Dictionary* is a collection of unusual words defined and used in context from the works of best-selling and less-selling writers published since 1945." Hence entries, sans pronunciation and etymology, for the likes of deipnosophist, frugivorous, ludibund, pinguid, and vespertine, each illustrated by a brief quotation from a post-war writer. These five esoteric terms and most of the others in *Oxter* are defined more thoroughly and illustrated by earlier quotations in the venerable *Oxford English Dictionary,* the reference work Saussy purports to honor in the title of his book. He points out that the *OED* cannot be carried about easily, whereas his book "can be tucked under the arm: hence the title," for "oxter," a British slang term used by Burgess in *Enderby,* means armpit. Odd homage to the *OED* indeed! *Oxter,* unlike the body part of the same name, has considerable appeal, although it can do little to improve one's vocabulary since these words call undue attention to themselves except when used in the proper context and by masters of the language. Although enjoyable for browsing, this is a luxury item for most reference collections.

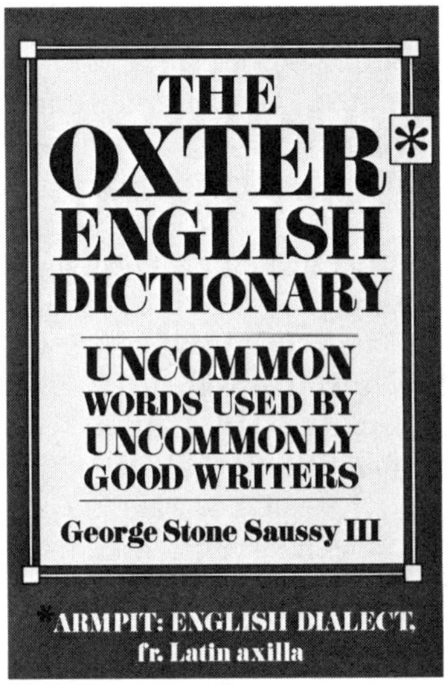

Psychware, compiled and edited by Samuel E. Krug. Kansas City: Test Corporation of America (dist. by Gale), 1984. 801p. $65. 0-9611286-5-8 84-16461

Creators of psychological tests have used the computer as a scoring tool for more than two decades. More recently, they have begun to use newer computers' more sophisticated capabilities to interpret scores. *Psychware* describes nearly 200 software products designed to help interpret tests in the areas of behavioral medicine, clinical assessment/diagnosis, educational evaluation/planning, personal/marriage/family counseling, personnel selection/evaluation, training/development, and vocational guidance. Arranged alphabetically by product name, entries list supplier, up to five applications from the list of seven above, sale restrictions (e.g., APA members), cost, type of service (i.e., mail-in, teleprocessing to a central computer, or local processing), and product description. Most entries also include facsimiles of the interpretive reports created by the products. Descriptions of products suitable for local processing specify the type(s) of compatible hardware. Indexes order the products by name, five broad categories, the seven narrower applications areas, supplier name, and type of service. *Psychware* holds greatest value, of course, to professionals in testing and counseling and will require periodic updating and revision. Graduate students in education and psychology will also find it useful in selecting not only testing instruments, but ways of using those instruments effectively.

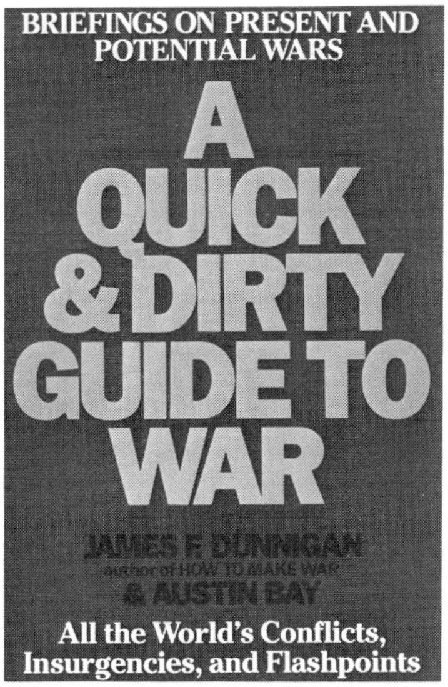

A Quick and Dirty Guide to War, by James F. Dunnigan and Austin Bay. New York: Morrow, 1985. 415p. $17.95. 0-688-04199-X 84-22797

Whereas *Border and Territorial Disputes* (reviewed in *WLB,* February 1983) explains the background and describes the status of all of the world's unresolved international border disputes, *Quick and Dirty* surveys the major trouble spots, including those which, though presently at "peace," are likely to develop into armed conflict. Thus it discusses the uneasy situations in South Africa and the Philippines as well as the political-military quagmires in Lebanon and Central America. Each conflict's history, its principal characters, the local geography, local political considerations, participants' strategies and goals, the superpowers' interest, and human and monetary cost to date fill a chapter. In a bit of daring, the authors have projected probable outcomes, assigning to them percentage values. By drawing on the facts of each case rather than their personal political biases, the authors offer a firm foundation to anyone—student or interested citizen—who wants to understand the Byzantine complexities of Lebanon or the nationalist yearnings of many of Spain's Catalans. They should, of course, build on this foundation by reading recent periodical and newspaper articles. Some significant conflicts have been ignored completely (e.g., the Quebec separatist movement and the IRA activities in Northern Ireland). Others rate only brief mention in the concluding summary chapters, one a series of one-paragraph surveys of wars and wars in the making throughout the world, the other an assessment of every nation's ability to wage war. *Quick and Dirty,* while testifying to nations' preference for swords to plowshares, offers convenient, current information behind the headlines of today and, one fears, tomorrow.

The Quotable Woman from Eve to 1799, compiled and edited by Elaine Partnow. New York: Facts On File, 1985. 533p. $29.95. 0-87196-307-8 82-15511

This companion to *The Quotable Woman: 1800–1981* (Facts On File, 1982) extends selection of noteworthy quotations from women back to the beginning of time. Like Bartlett's famous book, Partnow's is organized chronologically by the birthdates of the speakers. The header for each woman's section lists only her name and dates. A biographical index, in addition to providing alphabetical access, identifies each of the 804 women's nationality, occupation, and family ties to other women in the book. The collection would be richer if the biographical information had been included in the headers rather than relegated to the index. Partnow wisely opted for a thorough subject index rather than a first word/key word index, for only a fraction of the 6,000 quotations are known well enough to merit the latter treatment. Through their chronological order the quotations tell the history of women both mighty and humble in Western society. They address nearly every conceivable subject. A personal favorite comes from Lucy Hay (1599–1660), identified in the index as an English wit: "Spell well, if you can." Most reference collections, already well supplied with quotation dictionaries organized or indexed for a subject approach, will be still better supplied by the addition of *The Quotable Woman.*

The Record Producers File, by Bert Muirhead. Poole, England: Blanford (dist. by Sterling), 1984. 288p. $17.95, pa$9.95. 0-7137-1429-8; 0-7137-1430-1

Thankfully, this book's purpose—to list the rock albums produced by various record producers between 1962 and 1984—is virtually self-evident. This spares users from having to read the brief introduction. Its concluding sentence fragment unconnected to all else calls into question the entire introduction's credibility. What one can learn from the introduction is that the book's alphabetical listing of producers includes only those who produced albums which appeared on the charts in either England or the United States. Muirhead, editor of *Hot Wacks* magazine in Edinburgh, has the proper credentials to compile such a book and examined more than 75,000 album sleeves to gather his information. Each producer's entry, a list of his albums alphabetized by their artists' names, includes album title, label, and year of release. Collaborations with coproducers are noted. Although many producers have a personal and distinctive "sound," they do not enjoy the visibility of rock stars. Only true rock aficionados will fully appreciate Muirhead's contribution to rock music reference literature.

Gail Pool:

Editor's Choice

The Seven Mountains of Thomas Merton, by Michael Mott. Boston: Houghton Mifflin, 1984. 691 p. $24.95. 0–395–31324–4
Merton by Those Who Knew Him Best, edited by Paul Wilkes. San Francisco: Harper, 1984. 171 p. $12.95. 0–06–069416–5 84–47824

It is difficult to write about Thomas Merton without using the word *paradox,* and Michael Mott gets only to the bottom of page one before doing so. Merton was an unbelieving, rather wild young man who became a Catholic, then a monk in a religious order of legendary strictness; a Trappist who chose silence and solitude, then wrote a bestseller and had countless correspondents all over the world and a stream of visitors even in his "hermitage" apart from the monastic community; a monk who vowed fidelity to an abbey in Kentucky and died at a conference on Buddhism in Bangkok.

The publication of an authorized biography presents two more paradoxes: that of a man who had sought anonymity being analyzed down to the most private thought at a length of nearly 600 pages; and that of a man whose significance lies in his commitment to a contemplative religious ideal still holding the public interest today.

Though *The Seven Mountains of Thomas Merton* has an elaborate structure (hinted at in the title) and over two thousand footnotes, it is readable and fascinating. In the current style of biography, it is exhaustive rather than selective, and it is quite possible that we do not need to know every one of the details Mott records of visitors, letters, minor disagreements. But unlike many of these other huge biographies, it has an elegance of style and a wealth of perception. Mott quotes extensively from Merton's published writings, letters and unpublished journals, and from the letters and recollections of his friends. His account of the tensions and difficulties Merton experienced within the Trappist order does not overshadow the positive aspects of Merton's call to the contemplative life. In general he conveys the all-important spiritual dimension of Merton's long journey very well.

Some readers may find a few episodes disillusioning or the psychohistorical strand a virtual invasion of privacy, but given his subject, the author had to delve deeply. Mere recitation of the outward events of his life would have little meaning: it is the "why" of Thomas Merton that we are so eager to understand.

Merton by Those Who Knew Him Best is like a distillation of all the masses of information in *Seven Mountains.* Twenty friends, representing different periods and aspects of Merton's life, spoke in interviews of the Merton each one knew. The tone ranges from a fellow monk's "He had very profound insights that for him were more real than stones in a wall. They were concrete, God was concrete for him," to Joan Baez's "He was a living doll." The one constant in the book, as in Merton's life, is his gift for friendship; and although we learn few new facts in these pages, the vitality of the man comes through perhaps even more strongly than in Mott's book.

—Stephanie Martin

The Kindness of Strangers: The Life of Tennessee Williams, by Donald Spoto. Boston: Little, Brown, 1985. 416p. $19.95. 0–316–80781–8

Although Tennessee Williams has long been a favorite subject of writers—academicians and journalists published some 2,500 articles about him during his lifetime—there has been no comprehensive biography of this most inspired and complex of America's playwrights until this year, now two years since his death and forty years after the first production of *The Glass Menagerie.*

Based on hundreds of interviews with those who knew him and on other previously unpublished material, Donald Spoto in *The Kindness of Strangers* presents a portrait of Tennessee Williams which is both respectful and sensitive. Using a straightforward chronological format,

Gail Pool *holds an M.L.S. degree from Simmons College and presently works as a freelance writer based in Cambridge, Massachusetts.*

Spoto describes the early years in detail, sometimes even correcting Williams's own reminiscences from *Memoirs* (1975), which are noteworthy more for frank sexual confidences than for accuracy on crucial points in his life.

An indifferent student, a failure in ROTC and a failure as a shoe salesman—both undertaken to please his emotionally distant father—Williams embarked after graduation on a decade of odd jobs to support himself while he wrote. And, if anything is clear from this book, it is that Williams wrote constantly. Spoto observes, "He gave new meaning to the word prolific."

Between 1945 and 1961, Williams saw no fewer than ten of his plays acclaimed on Broadway; thereafter, success became more elusive as the pressures in his personal life increased. The death of his lover, Frank Merlo, in 1963 (perhaps no more supportive consort has ever been portrayed by a biographer) ushered in what Williams himself named his "stoned age." For the final twenty years of his life, dominated by alcohol and pill addiction, mental instability, hypersexuality and a restlessness which drove him from place to place when he could barely function, Williams was indeed—as Spoto shows—"dependent on the kindness of strangers."

—Marilyn Souders

Best of the Realist: The 60s' Most Outrageously Irreverent Magazine, edited by Paul Krassner. Philadelphia: Running Press, 1984. 256p. $19.80, pa $8.95. 0–89471–287–X;0–89471–289–6

Many magazines aspire to irreverence, but few are willing to be sufficiently offensive to achieve it. *The Realist* was willing. Between 1958 and 1974, Paul Krassner's sometimes witty, sometimes tasteless satirical magazine took on anything from chic liberalism to the Catholic Church and anyone from J. Edgar Hoover to Mahatma Gandhi. In such pieces as "Sex Education for the Modern Catholic Child," "The Parts Left Out of the Kennedy Book," "Too Late for the Sexual Revolution," *The Realist* proved time and again it was the magazine which was not edited for Middle America.

Because magazines are so ephemeral, this book is especially welcome as a more permanent representation of the magazine, which has all but disappeared. But the collection also reads well in itself. Particularly good are the series of "Impolite Interviews"—with Woody Allen, Dick Gregory, Jules Feiffer—and many of the cartoons. Surprisingly (worrisomely!) the material does not seem dated. Indeed, some of it seems uncannily timely: " . . . and dear God, let all those who are against school prayers be struck dead in their tracks . . . " prays the little old lady in the *Realist* cartoon.

Not all the pieces in this collection hit their mark. And some seem sadly misaimed. Satire only works if its object deserves—from some point of view—to be satirized. From what point of view do the handicapped deserve to be mocked? Such items as "Humor of the Handicapped" and "Bad Taste Coloring Books" are both gratuitously nasty and poor satire. Perhaps they represent one aspect of *The Realist,* but it seems to me they should not have found a place in a collection of its "best."

Since many readers of this collection will be unfamiliar with the original *Realist,* it is unfortunate that Krassner did not include a detailed profile of the magazine. The impact of a book is very different from that of a magazine. As it stands, *Best of the Realist* conveys the *Realist*'s vitality. But had it provided some knowledge of the publication's founding and struggles, of who read it, what it looked like, and why it died, it would have conveyed a keen sense of the *Realist*'s reality as well.

—G.P.

The Editors' Choice: New American Stories, Volume 1, compiled by George E. Murphy, Jr. New York: Bantam Windstone. 331p. pa $6.95. 0–553–34176–6 84–24157

The title of this new annual collection of short stories aptly points to what distinguishes it from existing annual collections. As George Murphy notes in his introduction to *The Editors' Choice,* the established and well-respected *O. Henry Awards* and *Best American Short Stories* are both limited to stories which reflect the tastes and sensibilities of only one editor. *The Editors' Choice,* on the other hand, includes stories "chosen as the best contemporary short fiction for 1984 by America's top magazine editors." This eclectic approach does reflect the range of fiction currently being published in periodicals, but the contributing magazines (*Playboy, Ms., Cosmopolitan,* and *Paris Review,* among others) have widely varying audiences. Thus one finds stories side-by-side which do little for each other by comparison, and whose sometimes startling differences in style and appeal confound the reader's expectations.

Some interesting trends are apparent in this collection. Women writers appear to be more active (or more successful) in the short story genre, comprising eleven of the eighteen authors. The four writers representing the Iowa Writers Workshop, published with one exception in literary magazines, are more ambitious in both their emotional and stylistic reach than those currently enjoying success in the glossies. Undoubtedly one of the benefits of such a collection is to give these writers increased exposure. Among the new writers, Charlie Smith, Amy Hempel, and Mary Hood stand out as having a unique and authentic voice and an easy way with storytelling. Readers will also find stories by established writers who deliver no surprises.

Murphy suggests in his introduction that aspiring writers would benefit from close study of this collection in their attempts to assess the market. This disturbing emphasis on editorial rather than authorial sensibilities, prevalent throughout Murphy's comments, may accurately reflect today's competitive market but it does not bode well for the future of the American short story. If these stories seem lacking in courage or vision, as most of them do, a remedy is certainly not to be found in encouraging writers to conform to editorial tastes, however important the role of those who "have painstakingly searched for great writing and pored over 'slush piles' for worthy new talent."

—*Candyce Dostert*

The Simple Life: Plain Living and High Thinking in American Culture, by David E. Shi. New York: Oxford University Press, 1985. 332p. $19.95. 0–19–503475–9

"Simplicity, simplicity, simplicity," preached Henry David Thoreau. "A man is rich in proportion to the number of things he can do without."

Thoreau remains the most conspicuous American proponent of the simple life, observes historian David Shi; but from colonial times to the present, numerous individuals and groups have embraced plain living as a higher way of life. For the Puritans, it was a religious precept; for the early republicans, a political precept; for the hippies in the 1960s, a social precept.

The Simple Life is the history of an ideal, a chronicle of its transformations, an examination of its place in American culture. As Shi makes clear, voluntary simplicity has always conflicted head-on with other American ideals: not only such worldly endeavors as the quest for wealth but the spirit of enterprise or of inventiveness, not ignoble in themselves, have worked against the realization of plain living. Efforts on the part of groups to actually live the simple life have invariably been defeated—sometimes by their own success. The Protestant ethic, for example, became a work ethic and led to the accumulation of wealth. The back-to-the-land movement was exploited and home gardening became an aspect of affluent cosmopolitan life. "But though a failure as a societal ethic," says Shi, the simple life has retained its power as myth, dream, challenge, ideal.

Shi never altogether convinces me that "the simple life" is an umbrella without holes. Plain living, moderation (the golden mean), and self-denial seem to me to differ more than they resemble each other. Some weakness in Shi's conclusions may derive from a weakness in the category of plain living itself. Yet in many ways the rubric serves well, and both the simple life and *The Simple Life* afford an interesting viewpoint on American culture and history.

—*G.P.*

Sisterhood Is Global: The International Women's Movement Anthology, edited by Robin Morgan. New York: Anchor Press/Doubleday, 1984. 815p. $24.95, pa $12.95. 0–385–17796–8;0–385–17797–6 82–45332

In *Sisterhood Is Global: The International Women's Movement Anthology,* edited and compiled by Robin Morgan, there are essays by women from seventy countries, from Afghanistan to Zimbabwe, telling stories of risk and imprisonment, poverty and invisibility, and of heroines and goddesses. The issues they describe are as diverse as the cultures themselves, from sati, purdah, or genital mutilation in the Third World countries to reproductive freedom and job discrimination in the West. Each contributor presents her own particular vision, which makes for some unevenness in the writing, but also for a fascinating miscellany: in India, there is a women's temperance movement called the Night Patrollers; in Thailand, a long tradition of economically independent women; in Kenya, more than 6,000 local women's groups; and in China, an alarming rise in female infanticide. In one of the best-written essays, Ama Ata Aidoo describes the solitary battle of an independent woman in Ghana. In another, Margaret Papandreou, wife of the Greek prime minister, tells of organizing village women in what sounds like the Greek version of consciousness raising.

Each article is preceded by a preface which includes statistics (population, the economy, education, literacy, health, marriage, divorce, rape, abortion, contraception, and other categories), laws—both in policy and in practice, and sections on Herstory and Mythography. Finally, there are chapter bibliographies, a forty-page general bibliography, and a glossary. Reference librarians, especially, should have respect for the massive research effort which went into the gathering of international statistics.

Whatever their apparent diversity, in the end, *Sisterhood Is Global* presents the unified voice of women who, as Morgan says, "passionately share a feminist vision of transforming the world." Taken all together, this 815-page document is truly an encyclopedia of women in the eighties.

—*Marilyn Souders*

The Selected letters of E.M. Forster, Volume Two, 1921–1970, edited by Mary Lago and P.N. Furbank. Cambridge, MA: The Belknap Press of Harvard University Press, 1985. 316p. $20 0–674–79827–9

The second volume of E.M. Forster's *Selected Letters* offers what might be called a portrait of the artist as an established, successful, and likeable man. The first few letters deal with Forster's second trip to India, and with the writing and publishing (in 1924) of his masterpiece, *A Passage to India.* This finest of his novels was also to be his last; the bulk of the letters included in this volume therefore document his transition from fiction writer to man of letters.

Given the current interest in India (in part due to the recent film adaptation of *A Passage to India*), readers might be particularly interested in Forster's comments on his Indian experiences. Although India does not occupy a major part of this volume (a lengthy selection of letters recording Forster's first reactions to India can be found in volume 1), Forster's attitude toward empire does emerge. He sees the importance of bridging the gaps between cultures and also the profound differences that prevent reconciliation. In a letter to British journalist Edmund Chandler, Forster writes:

> We both amuse ourselves by trying to be fair, but there our resemblance ends, for you are in the Club trying to be fair to the poor Indians, and I am with the Indians trying to be fair to the poor Club. . . . I have almost always felt miserable in a Club, and almost always felt happy among Indians, and I want to go back among them. They won't like my book, I know, because they don't like fairness, dislike it fundamentally, and here something in my own heart goes out to them again. God preserve us from cricket in Heaven!

The strength of this edition of Forster's letters lies in Mary Lago and P.N. Furbank's judicious selection. Represented are a varied sampling of Forster's relationships, activities, writing styles. Letters range from short housekeeping notes to his policeman-lover in London to lengthy literary critiques to fellow authors (Thomas Hardy, T.E. Lawrence, Christopher Isherwood, various members of the Bloomsbury group). One weakness of this edition is in the notes, which are sometimes overlong and repetitive, at other times skimpy or nonexistent.

While Forster was not one of the great letter writers, he is invariably interesting, often eloquent, and passionate. Evident throughout this volume is his commitment to literature, expressed in his generous support of other authors, his battles against censorship (even when disguised as part of a "war effort"), and his wrestling with issues in criticism and writing. The final impression of these letters is of a man "trying to be fair" indeed, and succeeding with intelligence and humanity.

—*Jeanne Anderegg*

Advertising, the Uneasy Persuasion: Its Dubious Impact on American Society, by Michael Schudson. New York: Basic Books, 1984. 288p. $17.95. 0–465–00078–9 84–45076

Vance Packard's "hidden persuaders" have long been out of the closet, and now Michael Schudson has diagnosed them, and the entire institution of advertising, as "uneasy." In *Advertising, the Uneasy Persuasion,* Schudson finds uncertainty in every corner of the institutional psyche. Yet amid all this uncertainty, he is sure of one thing: advertising does have an impact on our attitudes and beliefs, on our "behavioral environment," on our way of life.

Most of this well-researched, well-documented study is devoted to demonstrating the indefinite connection between advertising and consumer behavior. Schudson convincingly explains that all parties involved in the dynamics of advertising—advertiser, agency, consumer—operate within a complex environment within which many factors influence the development of a marketing strategy, the shape and placement of an ad, the behavior of the consumer; and many of these factors are not entirely understood or predictable at the time.

Schudson also goes to some length to show that advertising is not to blame for the materialistic values of our consumer culture. It is a result, not a cause, of that culture, he argues; historically, advertising has *followed* the acceptance of a product by consumers.

Much of this book will not surprise the reader who had thought critically about advertising's role in the marketplace, but Schudson's research is comprehensive and he provides a welcome and strong rebuttal to those critics and proponents of advertising who would place it at the very heart of the American consumer economy. It is simply not that powerful.

It is in Schudson's efforts to define the impact that advertising does have on our culture that his book is disappointing. He acknowledges that most people do not believe what they read and see in advertisements, but argues that since we, therefore, do not regard advertising as important, we do not pay critical attention to it; with our "perceptual defenses" down, we are then more vulnerable to the "larger" messages of advertising. These messages reinforce the values of a consumer society. The problem is that Schudson does not explain how this works in concrete terms; he does not identity the particular values as they are conveyed in particular ads. He omits concrete content analysis that would explain this phenomenon more convincingly.

Schudson's book ends on an optimistic note: he hopes that the "special cultural power" of advertising can be used for good causes. But he has already described advertising as an "art form of bad faith," one that "features messages that both its creator and audience know to be false and . . . honors values they know to be empty." It is difficult to share Schudson's optimism in the face of all the uneasiness he has stirred up.

—Steven Bloom

Station Island, by Seamus Heaney. New York: Farrar, Straus and Giroux, 1984. 123p. $11.95. 0–374–26978–5

In Seamus Heaney's new book of poetry, *Station Island,* Heaney addresses the felt conflict between his responsibilities as a Catholic from Northern Ireland, or more broadly, a person living in history, and as a writer, whose freedom seems at times too easy, whose role seems too insignificant. As Heaney put it in "Chekhov on Sakhalin," a writer's freedom is "his freedom/To try for the right tone—not tract, not thesis—/And walk away from the floggings." Like Chekhov in this poem, Heaney is haunted by those who cannot walk away.

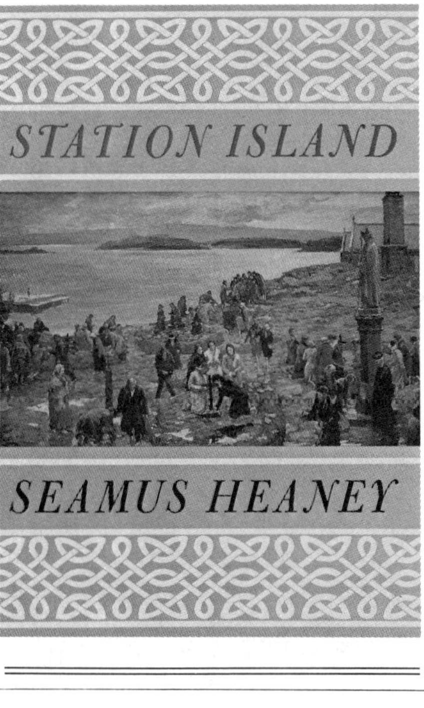

In "Station Island," the twelve-part middle section, Heaney gives voice to the dead, some of whom have died violently in Northern Ireland. They judge and advise him as they tell their stories. In his notes, Heaney calls this section "a sequence of dream encounters with familiar ghosts." Dante is the obvious and explicit examplar, and Heaney proves worthy of his model. In its range and depth, its unsparing honesty and closeness to felt life, this section is extraordinary. Interweaving meditation, description, stories, conversation, and revelation, Heaney's encounters are chilling and moving.

After repeatedly upbraiding himself in his own voice, and the various voices of the dead, for not being honest enough, bold enough, involved enough, Heaney gives Joyce's ghost the last word. "You've listened long enough. Now strike your note," Joyce tells him. And "You lose more of yourself than you redeem/doing the decent thing."

As always reading Heaney, the poems offer deep poetic satisfactions. The music is immediately recognizable as his own in its density and resonance. His metrics are varied and complicated, his ear flawless and bold. This is a book of immense conscience and mastery, extending Heaney's already formidable achievements.

—Carol Moldaw

Observations: Essays on Documentary Photography, edited by David Featherstone. Carmel, CA: The Friends of Photography, 1984. 118p. pa $12. 0–933286–39–2 84–80869

Beaumont Newhall begins his essay, the first in this volume of nine essays on documentary photography, with the statement: "*Documentary photography* is a term that has defied definition ever since it was first introduced in the 1930s."

While Newhall and the other contributors (critics and historians Maria Morris Hambourg, Bill Jay, William S. Johnson, Mark Johnstone, Estelle Jussim, Max Kozloff, Alan Trachtenberg, and Anne Wilkes Tucker) do not attempt to provide a rigid definition of the term, they do, by presenting different perspectives on the medium and raising thought-provoking questions, create "a complex exchange of ideas," which according to editor David Featherstone is the purpose of the book.

For example, in Trachtenberg's essay the reader is asked to consider whether Walker Evans's book *American Photographs* is an "inventory or transcription of a presumed reality" or rather "the making of a fictive world, an America of the imagination: a documentary invention," Hambourg discusses Eugene Atget as "the precursor of modern documentary photography," Kozloff writes about Helen Levitt's *A Way of Seeing* and explores why she is "a quintessential modern street photographer," Jussim addresses the question of "how documentary photography succeeds in persuading, how the photographs manage to influence public opinion."

This is not a book of photographs but a book of words about photography, and as such it contains only a few illustrations, which are reproduced in very reduced size. If the reader is not already familiar with the works of the photographers discussed in the text, then it will be necessary for him or her to have access to examples of these works. But the absence of photographs in no way diminishes the value of this collection's contribution to the on-going discussion of the nature of documentary photography.

—Lorna Condon

Library World

ANNOUNCEMENTS

Thomas Childers has been named the recipient of the Drexel Univ. (Penn.) Achievement Award. He has been a member of the Drexel Univ. faculty since 1970, and is currently professor in its college of information studies.

Jessie Carney Smith, university librarian at Fisk Univ., Nashville, Tenn., has been awarded the ACRL Academic or Research Librarian of the Year Award for 1985.

NEW POSTS

Gwenyth Arnold, formerly children's librarian at the Portsmouth (Ohio) PL, is now children's services consultant for the Ohio Valley Area Libraries (OVAL) in Wellston, Ohio.

John Berry has been appointed executive director of the Library Administration and Management Association (LAMA) of ALA. He was formerly head of the systems development dept. at the Northern Illinois Univ. libraries, and before that he served as public services coordinator at Elmira College, Elmira, N.Y.

Beverly Bower, formerly circulation librarian at the Milton campus of Pensacola (Fla.) Junior College, has been promoted to services coordinator for the college's learning resources center.

Arthur Curley has been appointed director and librarian of the Boston PL. He was previously deputy director of the research libraries of the New York PL.

Joseph Gabriel, formerly serials cataloger at the Harvard College library, Harvard Univ., has been appointed serials/periodicals librarian at the Univ. of Lowell libraries, Lowell, Mass.

John Berry

Michael Hill has been named president of the Fédération Internationale de Documentation (FID). He is the director of the science reference library at the British Library, London, and was previously vice-president of FID from 1981 to 1984.

Donald Napoli has been named executive director of the Cuyahoga County (Ohio) PL. He had been director of the South Bend (Ind.) PL since 1977.

Janet Pinkowitz has been appointed reference librarian in charge of subscription services at the Columbia Univ. law library, New York City.

Kate Purcell has assumed the position of special projects librarian for the Anne Arundel County PL, Annapolis, Md. She was formerly branch manager of the system's Broadneck branch.

Linda Resnik has been appointed executive director of ASIS. She was formerly with the Public Broadcasting Service (PBS), Washington, D.C., and before that was director of marketing for The Learning Channel, Washington, D.C.

Debra Rhodes, formerly extension services librarian at the John McIntire PL, Zanesville, Ohio, is now branch manager at the Churchland branch of the Portsmouth (Va.) PL.

Clarice Ruder, formerly assistant head of the special collections department at the Tampa-Hillsborough County (Fla.) PL system, has been promoted to head of the system's Riverview branch library.

Kate Purcell

Donna Serafin is now preservation officer for the State Univ. of N.Y. at Buffalo libraries. She was previously senior assistant librarian.

Nancy Smith has been appointed manager of branches and community services for the St. Louis PL. She was formerly director of the Lonoke County (Ark.) library.

Trudi Sommerfield has been named young adult librarian for the Prince William Library, Manassas, Va. She was formerly librarian/media specialist at Hackett HS, Kalamazoo, Mich.

John Sondheim has been appointed central library chief for the Enoch Pratt Free Library, Baltimore. He was previously assistant county librarian at the Johnson County library, Shawnee Mission, Kansas.

Eric Stocker, previously research associate for the Harry Ransom Humanities Research Center at the Univ. of Texas at Austin, is now rare books librarian for the St. Louis PL.

Gretchen Wronka, formerly children's librarian for the Hennepin County (Minn.) LS, has been promoted to senior children's librarian for the system.

MARKETPLACE

Announcements

☐ If necessity has mothered the invention of computer furniture in your library, the Library Administration and Management Association Building and Equipment Section Equipment Committee wants to know about it. The committee is sponsoring a contest of adaptations and original designs of furniture to accommodate computer and associated equipment such as an OPAC or a staff workstation. Submit a photograph or drawing and the dimensions of the furniture, along with a brief statement of its uses and features, by June 1 to Kazuko M. Dailey, Shields Library, University of California, Davis, CA 95616.

☐ The Continuing and Independent Learning Committee of the Adult Education Programs Section of the Public Library Association is seeking submission of papers, for possible presentation at the PLA conference, April 1986, on effective and innovative programs, plans, materials or concepts used for instructing patrons in the use of public library materials and services. A one-page typed summary and samples of materials should be submitted by June 1 for judging at the ALA conference in Chicago. Send to Marilyn Genther, Indianapolis-Marion County PL, Box 211, Indianapolis, IN 46206.

☐ The American Library Trustee Association has established an affiliate program designed as a networking opportunity for library trustee boards for which individual memberships may not be feasible but whose members do want access to helpful information. For the $50 annual fee per board, affiliates receive a "New Trustee Packet" of orientation materials and *Trustee Digest,* a quarterly newsletter. Personal membership ($45 annual dues) includes membership in ALA and subscriptions to the *ALTA Newsletter* and *American Libraries.* For more information contact Sharon Jordan, ALA/ALTA, 50 E. Huron St., Chicago, IL 60611, 312/944-6780.

☐ In an effort to more widely distribute locally produced recorded magazines for the blind, the National Library Service for the Blind and Physically Handicapped has established a quality assurance program to help local groups produce material of national caliber and to distribute them. Fifteen magazines have been accepted so far. Administered by one of NLS's four multistate centers, the Multistate Center for the Midlands, the program will eventually be extended to Braille material. Groups who wish to submit their magazines should contact Jacquelyn Hickey, Multistate Center for the Midlands, LC, 685 Redna Terrace, Cincinnati, OH 45215, 513/771-1125.

Children's Specials

☐ East Carolina University has established the National Clearinghouse for Information on Storytelling to be jointly administered by the Department of Library and Information Studies and Joyner Library. The clearinghouse welcomes published and unpublished materials on storytelling, the names and addresses of individuals and organizations to contact, and information of the use of storytelling in nontraditional fields. Those interested in being notified of information services as they become available should contact Constance Mellon, National Clearinghouse for Information on Storytelling, Department of Library and Information Studies, East Carolina University, Greenville, NC 27834.

☐ "Poetry for Children," a bibliography of recent poetry collections of high quality and popular appeal, first published in the June 15, 1984 *Booklist,* is now available as a reprint. A single copy is free for a self-addressed #10 envelope with 39¢ postage; multiple copies are 25¢ each. Request from Poetry for Children, *Booklist,* ALA, 50 E. Huron St., Chicago, IL 60611.

☐ Another booklist recently made available is *1983 U.S.A. Children's Books of International Interest,* prepared by members of the International Relations Committee of ALSC. The annotated list of eighty titles in the areas of picture books, fiction, folklore, poetry, biography, and nonfiction is designed to encourage international understanding through children's literature. Single copies are available for 75¢ and a stamped, self-addressed #10 envelope from ALSC/ALA, 50 E. Huron St., Chicago, IL 60611.

☐ *Bilingual Books in Spanish and English for Children,* by Doris Cruger Dale, annotates and evaluates 254 bilingual books for preschool through elementary school children. The entries are arranged by publishing date, with author, title, subject, and subject in Spanish indexes. The 173p. book is $23.50 from Libraries Unlimited, Box 263, Littleton, CO 80160.

Continuing Education

☐ Those willing to pass up hot dogs and parades can spend July 4 and 5 at "Successful Hiring Practices: Finding the Right Person for the Right Job," a preconference institute in Chicago sponsored by the ALA Office for Library Personnel Resources. Analyzing the job, the role of the job description, preparing for the interview, conducting the interview, and making the decision will be covered. Registration fee is $110 for ALA members and $125 for nonmembers; the deadline is June 13. For more information contact Sandra Raeside, ALA/OLPR, 50 E. Huron St., Chicago, IL 60611, 312/944-6780.

☐ Wright State University is offering "Southern Style: Children's and Adolescent Storytour of the Southeastern United States" June 15–19. The tour will feature speakers as well as visits to literary sites and collections. For more information write Mary Lou White, College of Education and Human Services, Wright State University, Dayton, OH 45435.

☐ A pre-festival conference, "New Developments in Children's Media," will open the American Film Festival May 27 in New York City. The all-day session will feature discussions and film showings by four children's filmmakers, a luncheon address by Twyla Liggett, executive producer of Reading Rainbow, talks by children's media researchers, and a panel discussion on the use of half-inch video. The fee is $100 before May 13 and $125 thereafter. For more information contact the American Film Festival, 45 John St., New York, NY 10038, 212/227-5599.

☐ The first international gathering on library continuing education will be held August 13–16 at Moraine Valley Community College, Palos Hills, Illinois, prior to the IFLA conference in Chicago. Lectures, meetings, poster sessions, and a consulting service will be featured. There is no registration fee but attendance is limited to 150 and preference will be given to those attending IFLA. For more information on the World Conference on Continuing Education for the Library and Information Science Professions contact Elizabeth Stone, SLIS, Catholic University, Washington, DC 20064, 202/635-5085.

☐ In addition to its two summer credit sessions (June 3–July 12, July 15–August 23), the University of Maryland College of Library and Information Services is holding five non-credit workshops. There are three workshops on online searching: DIALOG (May 18, 20, $135), ORBIT (May 30, June 1, $135), and BRS (July 13, 15, $150), one on archival automation (Tuesdays and Thursdays, June 4–July 11, $325), and one on information retrieval and database design for microcomputers (Mondays, Wednesdays and Fridays, June 3–21, $475). For more information write Jean Diepenbrock, Director of Admissions, CLIS, University of Maryland, College Park, MD 20742.

Film and Video

☐ If there are faculty in your college or university who always return library books late, perhaps they could profit from *Time Management: A Second Chance.* The twenty-two-minute color film summarizes principles of time management effective for faculty and staff in higher education, and suggests coping strategies. Included in the purchase price ($325 16mm, $150 U-Matic, VHS or Beta; $25 16mm rental) is a workshop facilitator's manual. The film can be previewed if return postage is paid. For more information contact Indiana University Audio-Visual Center, Bloomington, IN 47405, 812/335-8087.

☐ "Your Heart and Circulation," a series of twelve video programs from Medcom, Inc., covers how the heart works, how to avoid heart disease, how heart attacks are treated, types of heart surgery, and recovery from a heart attack. Medcom also has a new CPR training film, *CPR: A Second Chance for Life*, available in 16mm and all video formats. For more information write Medcom, Inc., Box 116, Garden Grove, CA 92642, 800/854-2485.

☐ An audio cassette and printed materials from a one-day seminar on video copyright for educators held recently by Ken Winslow and Jerome Miller are available from Copyright Information Services. Included in the materials from the Video/Copyright Seminar are a directory of low-cost videocassette distributors and an institutional copyright policy outline. The price is $39 plus $1.50 shipping and handling from Copyright Information Services, 440 Tucker Ave., Suite D, Friday Harbor, WA 98250.

☐ An explanation of the retirement, disability, and survivor benefits of Social Security and of the Medicare system is presented in *What You Should Know About Social Security Now,* a twenty-minute color film available in 16mm and all video formats. For more information or to arrange a preview, write 50 Plus, 850 Third Ave., New York, 10022, Attn: B.J. Dais.

☐ You can begin your collection of Shakespeare on video with *Macbeth, Richard II, The Tempest,* and *Antony and Cleopatra,* the first four films in Encyclopedia Britannica's "The Complete Plays of William Shakespeare," a series that will take five years to complete. The plays are filmed on a replica of the Globe Theatre stage, using American actors, with a running time of two to three hours. Each play costs $175 in VHS or Beta II. For more information contact Encyclopedia Britannica Educational Corporation, 425 N. Michigan Ave., Chicago, IL 60611, 800/558-6968.

Finding Aids

☐ EIC/Intelligence has started three new abstract services: *Acid Rain Abstracts, Artificial Intelligence Abstracts,* and *CAD/CAM Abstracts.* All have subject, source and author indexes, and selected documents listed are available on fiche from EIC/Intelligence. Subscriptions to the monthly *AI* and *CAD/CAM Abstracts* and to the bimonthly *Acid Rain Abstracts* are $295, including an annual cumulative index. Contact EIC/Intelligence, 48 W. 38th St., New York, NY 10018, 800/223-6275.

☐ For a number of years now LC has not provided an index to its *Information Bulletin.* To remedy this (and to raise money for its scholarship fund) the LC Professional Association has produced *LCPA's Index to Library of Congress Information Bulletin 1984.* The main index is by subject and title, and there is a separate index of personnel changes. The 30p. paperback can be ordered for $10 prepaid from LCPA, Library of Congress, Washington, DC 20540.

☐ Project: LEARN publishes *Books for Adult New Readers* to aid libraries in developing collections for adults who read at an elementary school level. The 1984 edition has 436 annotated entries, 60 percent of which are at a fifth grade reading level or below. Order for $6 from Project: LEARN, 2238 Euclid Ave., Cleveland, OH 44115.

☐ Useful for locating speakers or instructors for a genealogy program, *A Directory of Archivist and Librarian Genealogical Instructors,* by J. Carlyle Parker, lists professionals who give presentations on genealogical research, with index by subject. Almost half the instructors lecture for expenses only, and nearly all will provide free program planning consultation. The 24p. booklet is available for $5.95 from Marietta Publishing Co., 2115 N. Denair Ave., Turlock, CA 95380.

☐ The *Chicano Organizations Directory,* by Cesar Caballero, lists over 370 professional, political, social, cultural, educational, social service, and special interest Chicano organizations. A special section lists Chicano studies departments and programs in universities. There are indexes by subject, name, acronym, and geographic area. The 221p. book is available for $19.95 from Neal-Schuman Publishers, 23 Cornelia St., New York, NY 10014.

Idea Exchange

☐ Concerned that some of her small patrons could identify a picture of Mr. T but not one of farm animals, Rosalind NaPier, children's librarian of the Beauchamp Branch of the Onondaga County (New York) PL, began a weekly program on farm animals. After stories, songs, and films about the week's animal, the group of forty to eighty three-to-six-year-olds repaired to the lawn for a visit with the real thing. Guests included rabbits, pigs, ducks and geese, a calf, and a lamb. The lamb's owner demonstrated carding and spinning wool. As well as drawing a large turnout, the program also presented photo opportunities no newspaper could pass up.

☐ Many libraries provide brochures on community services to special groups, such as senior citizens, but the Mesa (Arizona) PL decided that young adults have needs special enough to justify their own publication as well. *Helplines,* prepared by the YA staff, lists eighteen agencies, many of them with twenty-four-hour hotlines, in the areas of health, mental health, education, and job assistance.

☐ The Annual Lincolnwood (Illinois) Library Literary Festival is an ambitious weekend-long event to which the library brings three nationally renowned writers. Authors read from their works and participate in a forum. Receptions and a buffet dinner provide opportunities for the public to meet the authors. A donation of $20 is required for participation and other costs of the festival are met by advertising sold in the festival program, and a local hotel and travel agency which underwrite travel expenses. This year's festival, to be held May 18–19, will feature Bette Bao Lord, John Toland, and C. D. B. Bryan.

Magazine Notes

☐ The fall 1984 *Mark Twain Journal* is a special issue: "Black Writers on *Adventures of Huckleberry Finn,* One Hundred Years Later." The writers, all black academics, discuss such topics as Twain's racial ambiguity, *Huck Finn*'s influence on Afro-American literature, and morality in the novel. Subscriptions to the semi-annual journal are $8 and single issues are $4, postpaid. Orders of ten or more copies of this special issue are $2 per copy. Order from Thomas Tenney, *Mark Twain Journal,* Department of English, College of Charleston, Charleston, SC 29424.

☐ Haworth Press's new quarterly journal *Computers in the Schools* provides practical articles on such subjects as guidelines for math problem solving software, computer use in the teaching of composition, and educational uses of LOGO. There are also book reviews and overviews of new hardware and software. Subscriptions are $24 for individuals, $30 for institutions, and $40 for libraries. For a free sample copy write on library letterhead to Haworth Press, Inc., 28 E. 22nd St., New York, NY 10010.

☐ Another, more narrowly directed computer journal, *Computers in Mathematics and Science Teaching,* has recently expanded its format. Aimed at teachers at all levels, the journal in addition to feature articles

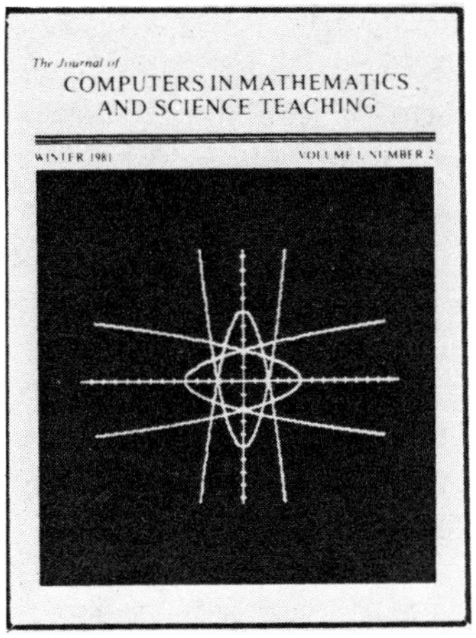

now presents software reviews, and to its previous columns on LOGO and BASIC now adds columns on educational communications and computer instrumentation in the school lab. Subscriptions to the quarterly publication are $18 for individuals and $36 for libraries from *The Journal of Computers in Mathematics and Science Teaching,* Box 4455, Austin, TX 78765.

☐ The National Geographic Society supports much scholarly research which does not get into the pages of *National Geographic.* Previously published in the annual *Research Reports* and other scholarly journals, this research now has a new home in *National Geographic Research,* a handsome quarterly publication combining the appeal of *Scientific American* and *National Geographic.*

Subjects covered are geology, archeology, anthropology, and the natural sciences. Subscriptions are $40 from *National Geographic Research,* National Geographic Society, Department 1675, Washington, DC 20036.

Media Center World

☐ Bullfrog Films is distributing two new Canadian nature films. *Cricket, Tiglet & Friends,* produced by OWL *Magazine* and the Young Naturalist Foundation, shows the dangers of "rescuing" nestling owls through a look at the work of an owl rehabilitation center. The nine-minute film for grades three and up is available for sale in 16mm for $200, in video for $95, and for rent for $25. *The Temperate Rain Forest* is a sixteen-minute color production from the National Film Board of Canada on the ecology of the northwest coastal rain forest. It is available for sale in 16mm for $290, in video for $95, and for rent for $35. Both films can be previewed. For more information contact Bullfrog Films, Inc., Oley, PA 19547, 215/799-8226.

☐ *Computer Use in Education* is a 116p. manual recently published by the Department of Library and Information Studies at East Carolina University. Author Veronica Pantelidis covers computer-assisted instruction, computer-managed instruction, interactive video, artificial intelligence, funding sources, electronic networks, word processors, database management systems, and spreadsheets. There is a selected bibliography for each topic. Order for $6 plus $1 for postage and handling from the author, 106 Lakeview Dr., Greenville, NC 27834.

☐ The National Center for Career Education will close August 31. In an effort to dispose of its inventory of career education materials, it has cut the price of lesson plan packets from $250 to $75 plus $5 shipping and handling. Available in four levels (K–3, 4–6, 7–9, 10–12)) each packet has about 2,600 non-copyrighted pages that tie career education into the math, science, social studies, language arts, and guidance curriculum. Orders must be processed before August 31. For more information contact Judy Wright, NCCE, 2400 West Central, Missoula, MT 59801, 406/721-7902.

☐ The unique challenge of collection development in high school media centers is addressed in *The Collection Program in High Schools: Concepts, Practices, and Information Sources,* by Phyllis Van Orden. It examines the relation of the media collection to the school, discusses general principles and practical considerations of collection development, and highlights the operations involved in developing and managing a collection to ensure its responsiveness. Appendixes list associations, agencies, selection tools, and related literature. Priced at $23.50, the 397p. book is available from Libraries Unlimited, Box 263, Littleton, CO 80160.

Products and Services

☐ Two markers for use on computer software have been developed by Sanford Corporation. The Diskribe marker can be used directly on software disk sleeves; its permanent ink, available in silver and gold, does not affect information on the disk. The Label Pen marker can write on slick-finish and other hard-to-mark labels on disks, diskettes, and videocassettes;

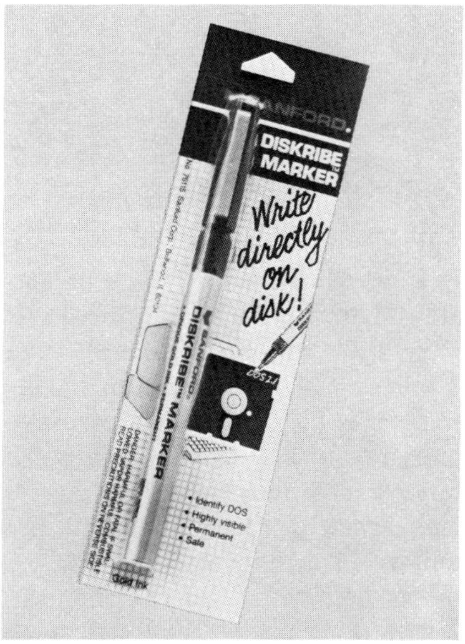

Research Technology International TapeChek 320

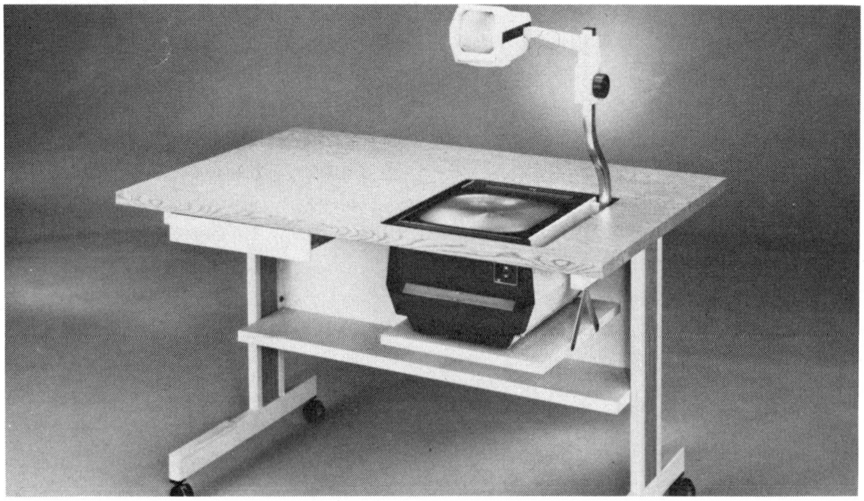

Bretford WSOH29 overhead projector workstation

Panasonic FP-1520 copier

it comes in black, red, and blue.

☐ Research Technology International has introduced a budget priced VHS videotape inspector/cleaner, the TapeChek 320, that can clean and inspect a T-120 tape in less than two minutes. An LED display reports the number of defects (wrinkles, creases and damaged edges) detected. The unit is 14 3/4 inches wide, 18 3/4 inches deep, 5 1/2 inches high and weighs thirty pounds. For more information contact Research Technology International, 4700 Chase Ave., Lincolnwood, IL 60646, 800/323-7520.

☐ The Panasonic FP-1520 copier, designed for varied and moderate copying needs, has three ratios of reduction and two of enlargement and can handle documents as large as eleven-by-seventeen inches. Priced at $2,495, the FP-1520 can produce fifteen copies a minute. For more information contact Panasonic, One Panasonic Way, Secaucus, NJ 07094.

☐ A new overhead projector workstation from Bretford Manufacturing, the WSOH29, provides ten square feet of work surface (48-by-30 inches) for organizing papers and transparencies. An overhead projector can be inserted into a 15 1/2-by-16 3/4-inch well in the table, and raised and lowered on an adjustable platform so that the projector's writing surface can be even with the table's work surface. For more information contact Bretford Manufacturing, Inc., 9715 Soreng Ave., Schiller Park, IL 60176, 312/678-2545.

Professional Reading

☐ Prior even to site selection, planning for a new library should be underway to avoid future problems. The guidelines in *Conservation, Safety, Security, and Disaster Considerations in Designing New or Renovated Library Facilities at Cornell University Libraries* can be useful to other libraries in the early planning stages. The 10p. booklet is available for $10 from Publications Committee, 015 Olin Library, Cornell University, Ithaca, NY 14853.

☐ Originating from workshops on private files sponsored annually by the Information Technology Division of SLA, *Private File Creation/Database Construction: A Proceeding with Five Case Studies* by Marjorie Hlava provides five case histories of libraries who successfully automated a file. An introductory chapter gives background on the design, creation, and maintenance of online bibliographic databases. The 108p. paperback is available for $15 from SLA, 235 Park Ave. S., New York, NY 10003.

☐ Dalhousie University School of Library Science Occasional Paper No. 34, *Urban Public Library Service for the Aging in Canada*, by Lois Bewley and Sylvia Crooks, is a study of the characteristics of the aging population in Canada, their implications for libraries, and current library services, with recommendations for better meeting the needs of the aging. The 123p. paperback is available for $11.50 from Norman Horrocks, School of Library Service, Dalhousie University, Halifax, N.S. B3H 4H8, Canada.

☐ There may be just enough time to catch your breath between adjusting to computers and the advent of the Next Big Thing in technology, video. Prepare yourself with *Video-Based Information Systems: A Guide to Educational, Business, Library, and Home Use,* by William Saffady, a non-technical introduction to video recording, digital television, video disks for entertainment and education, cable TV, low-power TV, videotext, microfacsimile systems, and optical disks. The 240p. paperback is $30 from Publishing Services, ALA, 50 E. Huron St., Chicago, IL 60611.

☐ The *Apple Library Users Group Newsletter,* containing questions and answers, articles, and reviews contributed by members of the group, is free of charge to individuals using Apple computers in a library setting. Request from Monica Ertel, Apple Computer, Corporate Documentation 26B, 20650 Valley Green Dr., Cupertino, CA 95014, 408/973-2552.

Software

☐ The recommendations of sixteen software evaluation services, many of them operated by state and local school boards, are consolidated in *Only the Best: The Discriminating Software Guide for Preschool–Grade 12,* prepared by the editors of *SchoolTechNews.* The 113 programs that received high ratings from three or more services are listed, arranged by subject, with producer's address, grade level, price, system requirements, description, and a summary of the evaluations. An additional 189 programs that ranked just below the top are briefly listed. The evaluation services consulted are also described. The 139p. paperback is $15.95 from Education News Service, Box 1789, Carmichael, CA 95609, 916/488-4623.

☐ Micro Learn has added four new programs to its tutorial series. *English SAT II* helps students prepare for the Scholastic Aptitude Test, with emphasis on word skills. The stories in *Myths, Magic, and Monsters* help improve reading skills for grades 4–8. *More Powers to You* teaches exponents and scientific notation through multiple-choice questions, help screens, and branching. *American History: Becoming a World Power, 1865–1912,* for grades seven up, covers Reconstruction, industrial growth, the frontier, the farm, urban growth, immigration, and foreign policy. All programs cost $35 and run on Apple IIs, IBM PC/PCjr, Commodore 64, and Corvus. Contact MicroLab, 2699 Skokie Valley Rd., Highland Park, IL 60035, 312/433-7550.

☐ An annotated list of forty-five astronomy programs prepared by the Astronomical Society of the Pacific includes graphic displays of the solar system and constellations, tutorials, simulations of space flight, and programs for astronomical calculations. There is also a brief reading list on astronomy software. This four-page reprint from *Mercury* magazine is $1 from Astronomical Society of the Pacific, Computer List, 1290 24th Ave., San Francisco, CA 94122.

Write for These

☐ The Kingfisher Independent Studies series has been developed by the Halifax City Regional Library for self-directed study on various topics. The 18p. pamphlets annotate recommended books on a high school to undergraduate level. Current titles are *China* and *The Middle East,* and titles in preparation will cover math, science, Latin America, and Russia. Copies are available for $1.50 from Administration Office, Halifax City Regional Library, 5381 Spring Garden Rd., Halifax, N.S. B3J 1E9, Canada.

☐ Every year students in entomology at the University of Florida compile the *Annual Entomology Booklist.* The 1984 list covers twenty-seven categories, with no more than five references in each category. Copies are available free from Annual Booklist, Department of Entomology and Nematology, University of Florida, Gainesville, FL 32611.

☐ A flexible-disc recording with information about the Department of Education's student financial aid programs is available to libraries, students, and organizations. The 33 1/3 rpm disc presents a dialogue between an information specialist and a handicapped student. Copies can be obtained from Flexi-Disc, DOE, Office of Student Financial Assistance, 400 Maryland Ave., SW, Room 4661, ROB-3, Washington, DC 20202.

☐ Each issue of the BOSC (Books on Special Children) catalog annotates new books for parents and teachers on dealing with handicapped and learning disabled children. Approximately thirty-five books listed in previous catalogs and still available are also included. For the catalog write BOSC, Box 305, Congers, NY 10920.

Front Row Center *(cont'd from p 549)*

ket today, it's questionable whether the film has any credibility beyond its very limited view of a small group of boorish people. Is this really what the Lynds had in mind when they recorded the status quo in working-class, middle America? I think not. With their cinema vérité mandate in hand, the filmmakers decided what to shoot, what not to shoot, and what footage to discard as they edited the film. They were also, no doubt, catalysts to some of the outrageous acts and posturing by the teens and adults who were unused to having a camera follow them around for a year. So, on a certain level, *Seventeen* is a performance film. When the filmmakers chose Lynn and her friends and family as subjects, and chose to include such controversial sequences as the sex tales, the soul kiss, the interracial dating, the dope scenes, they were consciously choosing to make a titillating statement.

Two basic questions remain: Would hard-working, goal-oriented teenagers make for hot film subjects? And secondly, does *Seventeen* fit in with the original goals of the "Middletown" series, or is it, in fact, an exploitative anomaly?

Despite and because of *Seventeen*'s provocative focus, it is suitable for selective programming, especially if juxtaposed with one or more classic films that cover similar terrain and now seem tame in comparison. For a real contrastive view, screen it with *Sixteen in Webster Groves.* In the mid-1960s, newsman Charles Kuralt and a CBS-TV news team examined what it was like to be a sixteen-year-old in Webster Groves, Missouri, a predominantly affluent, white Protestant suburb, where the values of the children turned out, in most cases, to be those of their parents—materialistic, success-oriented, and seemingly insulated from worldwide political, social, and economic realities. Utilizing CBS-TV's own brand of investigative journalism, Kuralt and his camera crew invaded the schoolrooms, streets, and homes of Webster Groves to hear what the kids, their parents, and teachers had to say about life. This excellent telecast should be piggybacked with *Webster Groves Revisited,* which documents the suburb's positive and negative reactions to the original program during and after its network showing.

And, of course, there's *High School,* Fred Wiseman's non-narrated look inside the walls of Philadelphia's Northeast High School. The film exposes the creaky philosophy of this typical, late sixties urban high school, including cinema vérité clips of academic and gym classes, guidance and disciplinary sessions, and forays into the corridors.

Seventeen should be programmed with caution, to mature senior high school, college, and adult audiences who are prepared for the profanity and sexual situations depicted.

Children's Librarianship
(cont'd from p 533)

[library school curricula] more of a problem than we wish it was. At ALA we're getting reports from different areas that library schools are dropping courses." Judy Davie is certain that these reports can't be ignored. "I think there should be concern anytime there is a reduction or a diminishing of attention to some aspect of librarianship." Concern is being generated throughout the children's service community. But what is the solution?

An integration of ideas

For people like Jane Anne Hannigan and Kay Vandergrift the answer may lie in the concept of specialization. "I think one of the things that will have to happen is what Hannigan recommended, we will have to identify certain schools and specialize," says Vandergrift. Specialization means that a few schools will each have several faculty members in children's librarianship. Any student who wants to work with children would have to go to one of these schools.

Specialization may insure that children's librarians will be trained but what would happen to the integration of fields that is so important and has worked so well at Champaign? The "Library Buildings" class would only cover buildings which pertain to children's librarians. All in all we might become a very segmented field. Davie says, "The world is not specialized and I think we need an integration of ideas. You can have things which are your particular strong suit but it has to be within a total framework to work on."

For Bush the solution comes with the politicization of children's librarians. "I'm convinced political strategies will work. It needs to be a kind of consciousness raising effort." Political action has worked at Simmons but it has as yet to work at Berkeley. Deans and other library school personnel need to recognize the worth of children's programs in library education. If this happens perhaps students' perceptions will change.

As Judy Davie says, "I think we need to educate everyone, and I'm talking about administrators, boards of trustees, and the citizens, to what children's services are all about. We need to do a better job in our education of librarians to the integration of the various elements of the library field. We need to show that children are patrons too and they have needs and interests. And, we need to show that children's services are important in the delivery of librarianship."

For Sale

INDEX TO ADVERTISERS

Ebsco 513
Gale Research Company
.... 4th cover
Gaylord Bros., Inc.
.... 2nd cover
Holt, Rinehart & Winston
.... 535, 539
H. W. Wilson Company
.... 514, 3rd cover

Credits:
p. 526—Fran Hooker, Ben Grzenda; 536—Joseph Farris; 547—Avon, Scribners; 548—Harper & Row, Crime Club; 558—Crown; 561—Writer's Digest Books, Facts on File; 562—Morrow; 563—Harper & Row; 565—Oxford University Press, Anchor/Doubleday; 566—Basic Books; 567—Farrar, Straus, Giroux.

Wilson Library Bulletin

May 1985

Wilson Library Bulletin

May 1985, Volume 59, Number 9 ISSN 0043-5651

May Colors, this month's cover, is a tempera on paper by **Jennifer Nelson,** a student at Julian Curtiss School, Greenwich Connecticut.

Departments

Letter from New York/Editorial 580
Correspondence 582
Upfront/News—*Pikes Peak Library District to create Maggie III; SLA to move to Washington, D.C.; Chicago Public looking for new commissioner; Library security legislation introduced in Massachusetts; AMIGOS claims co-ownership of OCLC database; Mathias reintroduces bill to study public lending right; late news.* 583
Library World 633
Marketplace 634
WLB Classifieds 640

Articles

The Electronic Book of the Very Near Future *Charles Goodrum and Helen Dalrymple* 587
The Once and Future Book: Preservation Strategies *Jay Ward Brown* 591
Information Around the Clock: Atlanta's Channel 16 *Ron Chepesiuk* 596

Features

Dateline—Washington *Dale Nelson* 600
Eye on Publishing *Anne McGrath* 602
Facing the Public *Will Manley* 604
School Library Technology *Patricia Berglund* 606

Reviews

Picture Books for Children *Donnarae MacCann/Olga Richard* 608
The Young Adult Perplex *Patty Campbell* 610
Murder in Print *Kathleen Maio* 612
Front Row Center *Judith Trojan* 614
On Record: Popular Music *Bruce Pollock* 616
Our Profession *Norman Stevens* 618
Software for Libraries *Patrick Dewey* 620
Current Reference Books *James Rettig* 622
Editor's Choice *Gail Pool* 629

The *Wilson Library Bulletin* is published monthly except in July and August by The H. W. Wilson Company, 950 University Avenue, Bronx, N.Y. 10452. Second-class postage paid at Bronx, N.Y. and additional mailing offices. The *Wilson Library Bulletin* is indexed in *Education Index, Library Literature,* and *Popular Periodical Index* and abstracted in *Library & Information Science Abstracts, Historical Abstracts,* and *America: History and Life*. Book reviews are indexed in *Book Review Index*. Subscription $30 a year, U.S. and Canada; $35, foreign. Single copies $4, U.S. and Canada; $4.50, foreign (remittance with order, please). Address all correspondence about subscriptions to the publisher. No subscriptions through agents. Telephone: (212) 588-8400

Letter from New York

Editorial

Proletarians of the World, Unite!

Communist Party of the Soviet Union

PRAVDA

Organ of the Central Committee of the CPSU

Established the 5th of May 1912 by V. I. LENIN

Price 4 Kopeks

DIARY OF COMPETITION

RAISING THE MILITANCY OF THE KOMSOMOL

NEWS

Atomic Energy

A Giant in the Making

THE USUAL ROAD TO THE FARM

The Horizons of Russia

SOCIALIST COMMITMENTS

of the workers of the Russian Federation for 1985

Nothing lost in translation

There are a lot of things we are afraid of without quite knowing why—that might be the motto of the twentieth century. In America our burden of dread is not light. For years we have been concerned about the San Andreas fault, the Mafia, dark alleys, the Bermuda Triangle, people who talk in theaters, slow-moving traffic, extra-terrestrial life, sardine cans with no keys, the Reverend Moon, computers that are down, high-speed elevators, barking dogs, burnt toast, nuclear warfare, and the personal happiness of Elizabeth Taylor. But our number-one anxiety, at the top of the chart for the past forty years—ahead of cancer, lunacy, and even death—has remained constant: Russia. For sheer dread, unrelenting apprehension, and chronic fear, nothing surpasses our awe of the U.S.S.R. or, in the strangely vague usage of Secretary of State Shultz, the "other side."

It is certainly true that much of what we associate with the Soviet Union has a daunting effect: Siberia, vodka, borscht, the KGB, sub-zero weather, endless chess games, Stalin, *Crime and Punishment,* hammer and sickle, bread and salt. The Rooskies weigh too much, wear too much, like to stand in rows, bury their leaders in walls, work on state farms, devise five-year plans every five years, and hold a May Day parade without one single clown or fire engine.

Were it not for the fact that the U.S.S.R. possesses nuclear weapons of all descriptions we would probably have little to do with them. As it is, there is no great pleasure in talking to them and U.S. presidents plan outings to thc Kremlin with all the joy of a long-deferred trip to the dentist.

In spite of all our traipsing back and forth to summits, state visits, embassy parties, and the installation of hot lines and priority telephones, our relations with the Union of Soviet Socialist Republics are in about the state they have been in since 1950—tenuous, fragile, and easily disconnected.

Recently a small but significant attempt to increase our common, lay level of awareness of Russian life and outlook was undertaken by Charles Cox of St. Paul, Minnesota. Organizing a small firm known as Associated Publishers, Cox has begun translating *Pravda,* the official organ of the CPSU, into English. To call it required reading is understatement.

Making use of graduate students, scholars, and Russian specialists in the Minneapolis area, Cox is able to produce a verbatim translation of *Pravda.* The newspaper is published seven days a week and usually runs to six pages. The translation of text and reproduction of graphics is complete and includes news, articles, party information, cartoons, television schedules, chess scores, and weather. Each article is gone over twice by Russian-speaking editors. The complete translation of *Pravda* into English is, according to Cox, "a world first."

The subscription price for 365 issues a year mailed second class from Minneapolis is $630. Reasonable excerpts may be reprinted without special permission and bulk copies for classroom use are available at no additional cost.

As librarians and members of ALA we have taken positions on a number of social issues, including the Equal Rights Amendment, the U.S. withdrawal from UNESCO, and the practice of apartheid in South Africa. We guaranteed maximum information to the public about the activities of the Ku Klux Klan, expressed concern over limited public access to data gathered by the U.S. Census Bureau, objected to President Reagan's executive order on Safeguarding National Security Information, and supported legislative action to ensure affordable access to telecommunications. In 1983 we urged libraries to make information available about the ongoing debate on proliferation of nuclear weapons and last year joined Citizens Against Nuclear War as a member organization.

In a world of large causes it is not easy for a single professional group to exert influence. Even though we like to talk about the value of the "free flow of information" and "transborder data flow," these are largely terms without meaning.

Here, however, with an English translation of an important Soviet publication, is a cause that is easy to embrace and that invites individual action. Providing American library users with an insight into contemporary Russian life (even though official) would be an act of immeasurable worth.

In the short run this constitutes an expensive decision. Not taking advantage of such opportunities will also have a price.

—Milo Nelson

Correspondence

A library like a bakery

Will Manley's column ("Facing the Public") in the March issue certainly struck a responsive chord in me. In Yonkers, the library is not only handing out the tax forms, but also running a volunteer service which helps patrons fill out their returns. If Manley thinks handing out the forms is a headache, I've got news for him. Managing the Vita (Volunteers Income Tax Assistance) Program is far worse.

New York State collects taxes, but offers no help at all. The IRS, which has an office about a block from the library, will look over the returns but for real help they send everyone to us. Response has been so great we had to set up a numbering system, not unlike what one would find in a bakery.

Naturally, with help being offered, every library employee is now considered to be a tax accountant. Some patrons are irate, to say the least, when we cannot help them. We have enough volunteers to schedule twenty-two hours a week, and they are trained only for the simple forms, a fact which does not endear us to the patrons with Capital Gains forms who are hoping to save accountant fees. Add these problems to the difficulties of working with volunteers—no-show volunteers with the cancellation of assistance five minutes before we are due to start and twenty people waiting—and you can get an idea of the horror this program entails.

This is a great service to the public, there is no denying that, but I am beginning to wonder where the library's responsibility ends. Perhaps, in these days of staff shortages, we are spreading ourselves too thin. Especially since I see in this very same issue of *WLB* that Reagan has again proposed a zero budget for libraries. I say, let the government do their own dirty work from now on.

ELEANOR WOLVEN
Yonkers Public Library
Yonkers, New York

A cruel oxymoron

We read with rueful amusement Will Manley's account of distributing IRS forms and propaganda to testy taxpayers ("Facing the Public," March).

In our library, the IRS forms occupy a freebie shelf for four months, from whence they leer at us over a sign that reads Free Literature. To label these forms "free literature" seems a cruel oxymoron closely related to "military intelligence."

GEORGE CARLSON
State Library of Iowa
Des Moines

Back in print

Although the review of the *Almanac of the Federal Judiciary* in the February issue of the *Wilson Library Bulletin* ("Current Reference Books") indicates uncertainty as to the status of *The American Bench,* I want to assure you that it is not "defunct."

The 1985/86 edition of *The American Bench* is currently being completed and will be available in August, 1985. It will continue to be published *biennially.* We appreciate your making reference to the "void" created by *The American Bench* not being in print since 1979.

As you know, *The American Bench* is a biographical reference guide to the more than 17,000 judges at all court levels within the American judiciary. *The American Bench* also includes descriptions of every court in the United States.

JAY LONG
Reginald Bishop Forster & Associates
Sacramento, California

Clarifying Mother Goose

In reference to the review of Mother Goose ("Software for Libraries," *WLB,* March) there are several points that I would like to clarify.

It is Sunstar Systems contention that when we think of computers for very young children we *can* think of something other than games. We feel that young children can profit greatly from the experience of viewing children's literature on a computer in the same way that they view literature in a library setting. The same skills and benefits obtained from reading a book can be obtained through this new medium adding animated graphics and music.

In reference to Dewey's difficulty in preparing the disk for use, it is not stated in the directions for the user to copy DOS onto the Mother Goose diskette. The procedure is only to copy IBM's BASICA onto the disk to make the program easier to use.

Finally, while the review of our Mother Goose program states that there are eighteen nursery rhyme screens, there are in actuality twenty-four screens with text of nursery rhymes and original color graphics.

ANITA LENES
Sunstar Systems
Ogdensburg, New York

UPFRONT NEWS

The seventy-fifth anniversary edition of the **Thomas Register of American Manufacturers** *has recently been issued by the Thomas Publishing Company. The new edition, the largest yet published, has grown to nineteen volumes and sells for $190. In the photo above the new edition of the directory is displayed before a painting of the company's founder, Henry Mark Thomas.* **Carl Holst-Knudsen,** *president of Thomas Publishing, holds a copy of the first one-volume edition published in 1905.*

Pikes Peak Library District to create Maggie III

The Pikes Peak Library District, Colorado Springs, Colorado, has signed a contract with Eyring Research Institute, Provo, Utah, to build a new generation of Maggie's Place, a library resource management system widely acclaimed for its computerized community resource files and home user dial-up service.

The $1.3 million contract with Eyring calls for computer installation, customization of software, training, documentation, maintenance, and four megabyte processors that have the power to grow 100 times more powerful than the current Maggie.

The new Maggie will use the Colorado Alliance of Resource Libraries (CARL) online catalog and circulation system, making the library district part of a statewide network. The network includes the libraries at the University of Denver, University of Colorado at Boulder, Colorado School of Mines, Denver Public Library, and the University of Northern Colorado at Greeley.

The CARL software and Eyring's conversion and upgrade of Maggie will run on Tandem Computers "non-stop" processors, promised to run 99.9 percent of the time. The Tandem processors total sixteen megabytes, will support 300 terminals, and will increase Maggie's disc storage three times over.

Currently, Maggie's Place handles book circulation, purchasing and cataloging, budgets, payroll, word processing, and electronic mail.

Maggie III will be expanded to handle an additional 200 computer terminals. The CARL resource management system will charge out and check in books, create overdue notices, and handle patron registration. The card catalog will be replaced by an online one. Eyring also plans to develop a radio-frequency data-link between bookmobiles and Maggie for uploading patron charge-out information.

Maggie's name was derived from a librarian who retired from the Pikes Peak Library District in 1976—Margaret O'Rourke. The computer (Maggie) was installed in the area once occupied by O'Rourke's desk.

Chicago looking for "radical recommendations"

James Lowry, president of the Chicago Public Library board of trustees and interim library commissioner since the resignation of Amanda Rudd on April 15, has said, "We will give free rein to a new commissioner to make radical recommendations on staff changes." Lowry observed that "there are some people who should not have been appointed. Where we can't get them out we'll have to train them and motivate them."

Lowry made his remarks on a WBBM radio program, "At Issue," broadcast April 14. He defended the award of a $50,000 consulting contract to Rudd: "Amanda Rudd is a highly professional person in the library field. She can serve as a skilled professional. She has a lot of experience and knowledge of the Chicago library system. That does not mean to say she is a skilled management person."

Lowry observed that the board of trustees will place emphasis on management skills in their selection of a new library commissioner. "People have been wedded to the idea that a librarian must head up a library. We want the best and the brightest. We will look for a skilled librarian," said Lowry, "and if we can't find one we will opt for a skilled manager."

The board intends to assume day-to-day control of the library until a new commissioner is hired. Board members will work under Lowry in two-person committees to oversee finances, fundraising, and administration.

Lowry, who heads a private consulting firm, will receive no salary as acting commissioner.

Mathias reintroduces bill to study public lending right

Senator Charles Mathias, Jr. (R-MD) has reintroduced legislation in the U.S. Senate to establish a commission to study whether authors should be compensated when their books are borrowed from public libraries. Stating that "this question clearly deserves serious study," Mathias said the purpose of to he commission would be "to give the Congress the expert guidance it needs to evaluate the public lending right in the American context." He noted that at least ten nations, including Great Britain and West Germany, have adopted public lending right regulations.

The commission would consist of eleven members appointed by the President representing authors, publishers, librarians, and the public. The group would submit a report to the President and the Congress two years after it has been established.

Mathias said the report "would include recommendations and proposals regarding the appropriate procedures to carry out such financial compensation, if the idea seemed workable."

The proposal has been referred to the Senate Judiciary Subcommittee on Patents, Copyrights, and Trademarks, a body chaired by Mathias.

SLA to move to Washington, D.C.

The Special Libraries Association, presently located at 235 Park Avenue South in New York City, has completed negotiations for the purchase of a new headquarters building at 1700 18th Street N.W., Washington, D. C. The final closing is scheduled for May with the staff completing the move from New York to Washington by the end of August. The decision to relocate in the nation's capital was made after a four-year unsuccessful effort to locate suitable housing in the New York metropolitan area.

The $1.4 million purchase price includes the cost of remodeling and refurbishing the site, to be completed prior to the move.

The new headquarters, a four-story neo-Georgian townhouse, is situated near Dupont Circle. Constructed in 1909 as a private residence, the building was later used as the headquarters for the American Psychiatric Association.

SLA Executive Director David Bender called the relocation a "wonderful opportunity" and said, "By purchasing its own building, SLA will create a sound financial base for the association and will protect itself from the inflationary pressures of the rental market."

AMIGOS claims co-ownership of OCLC database

The AMIGOS Bibliographic Council, Dallas, Texas, has voted to file a copyright claim for co-ownership of the OCLC Online Union Catalog on behalf of AMIGOS and its member libraries. Edward Johnson, chair of the AMIGOS board of trustees, said, "This decision emphasizes our consistent desire to insure parity in the relationships among OCLC, the network, and member libraries. In addition, filing for co-ownership confirms AMIGOS's desire to continue and to protect the cooperative and joint development of the database in which we have been involved for the last decade."

It has been the position of the board of trustees that if the OCLC copyright claim were registered, "AMIGOS as an organization and each of its members must be co-owners of the database." In a survey of AMIGOS members last year, ninety percent of the respondents stated their agreement with the board's position.

RLG continues work on eighteenth century database

The Research Libraries Group and the British Library plan to activate a dedicated telephone line between Palo Alto and London to facilitate work on the Eighteenth Century Short Title Catalog (ESTC). The project was begun by the British Library in 1977, with RLG participating since 1981. There are now more than 165,000 entries in the ESTC database at RLG.

According to John Haeger, vice-president for programs and planning at RLG, "It is probably the largest bibliographic project ever undertaken. It is a multi-million dollar, multinational project to catalog or recatalog literally everything that was printed in the English language anyplace in the world between 1701 and 1800, or in any language in the United Kingdom or any of its dependencies."

The North American editorial office, the largest outside of London, is at Louisiana State University in Baton Rouge. RLG was chosen as the master file because the RLIN software, based on Stanford's SPIRES database program, offers better editorial capabilities than the system presently available in London.

The final database is expected to list about 350,000 unique items.

Washington receives grant for collection management

The Graduate School of Library and Information Science, University of Washington, has been awarded a $165,338 grant by the Fred Meyer Charitable Trust to train Pacific Northwest librarians to manage their collections more effectively. This training is part of a larger library program begun by the Meyer Charitable Trust in 1984 to improve access to information resources in the northwest. More than 300 librarians from Alaska, Idaho, Montana, Oregon, and Washington will be trained to profile library collections and assisted in creating a database of management information about single collections and regional holdings. The project will involve 220 libraries and will be overseen by Margaret Chisholm, director of the University of Washington Graduate School of Library and Information Science.

DIALOG to put McGraw-Hill publications online

DIALOG Information Services has announced that it has signed an agreement with McGraw-Hill, Inc. to make thirteen McGraw-Hill periodicals available online through the DIALOG system. The magazines will include, among others, *Business Week, Byte, Electronics Week, Aviation Week and Space Technology, Popular Computing,* and *Data Communications.*

Library security legislation introduced in Massachusetts

An act designed to deter library larceny has been introduced in the Massachusetts House of Representatives. House Bill 4819, now before the Justice Committee, provides that whoever "willfully conceals a book or other library property, while still on the premises of such a library, or willfully or without authority removes any book or other property from any library or library collections shall be deemed guilty of larceny thereof, and upon conviction shall be punished as provided by law."

A second measure, House Bill 4875, now before the House Judiciary Committee, would protect the library staff from civil liability. The bill states "A library or agent or employee of the library causing the arrest of any person suspected of the crime of larceny shall not be held civilly liable for unlawful detention, slander, malicious prosecution, false imprisonment, false arrest, or assault and battery of the so arrested," assuming there was "probable cause to believe that the person committed willful concealment of books or other library property."

The tenth annual Curtis Benjamin Award for creative achievement in publishing was presented to **Frederick Ruffner, Jr.** *(above, left), president of the Gale Research Company. The award presentation was made by Carol Nemeyer, associate librarian for national programs, Library of Congress. Also pictured above is Townsend Hoopes, president of the Association of American Publishers.*

The plaque given to Ruffner cited him as an individual "Whose vision, imagination, and entrepreneurial spirit have generated publications which set new standards for information publishing."

Cost of academic books up by 2.8 percent

The average list price for an academic book published in 1984 rose 2.8 percent to $26.71, according to Baker & Taylor's annual analysis of academic book prices. The annual study is based on pricing and subject information extracted from the company's approval program. Statistics also reveal that the number of titles published last year rose five percent, to 34,206.

LC and CBS announce new television venture

The Library of Congress and CBS News have announced a joint venture to produce a series of 100 different informational broadcasts for young viewers for the CBS Television Network's 1985-86 season.

The series of one-minute spots, entitled "American Treasury," will focus on interesting and unusual facts about people, places, and events. Each segment will be based on materials and information found in the collections of the Library of Congress. Daniel Boorstin, Librarian of Congress, said, "We look forward to this collaboration, which will use the power and excitement of televison to extend the reach of America's Library to all the people to whom it belongs."

The narrators of "American Treasury" will be popular personalities familiar to a young audience. They will include Olympic boxing champion Mark Breland, Olympic champion skater Scott Hamilton, actresses Stephanie Mills and Ann Reinking, and model Cheryl Tiegs.

Chicago Public votes to pay DataPhase

The Chicago Public Library board of directors has authorized a $500,000 payment for their automated circulation system, leaving only $82,000 unpaid in their $2.1 million contract with DataPhase Systems of Shawnee Mission, Kansas. Completion of the installation has been delayed for over three years. The board also agreed to delay releasing DataPhase from a $596,000 performance bond that guarantees the system will perform to library specifications.

Although problems with the system persist, the remaining difficulties are scheduled to be resolved with rewritten computer software DataPhase has promised to deliver in May. The library has the option of seeking up to $200 a day in penalty charges from DataPhase if the software proves inadequate. Richard Friedman, an attorney who has advised the board on the contract with DataPhase, has cautioned that there are "considerable risks" in suing the vendor. Friedman noted that if they are challenged in court, DataPhase may accuse the library of failing in its obligation to provide sufficient technical personnel to monitor the installation of the system.

Fennessy appointed president of CCC

The board of directors of the Copyright Clearance Center, Salem, Massachusetts, has appointed Eamon Fennessy president of the organization. Before joining, CCC Fennessy had management responsibility for monitoring federal, state, and local legislation that affected the British Oxygen Company, a world-wide manufacturer of industrial gases and health care equipment for hospitals.

The CCC was established in 1977 by photocopy users, authors, and publishers in response to the wish of Congress that a service be created to facilitate implementation of the new U.S. copyright law which took effect January 1, 1978. The CCC operates a centralized photocopy authorizations and payment system serving both users and copyright owners.

USC receives major Latin American collection

A 60,000-volume collection of Latin American materials has been given to the University of Southern California Library by San Fernando business and civic leader Herbert Boeckmann II. The H.F. Boeckmann II Latin American Collection, valued at $1.7 million, contains materials published in Latin America from the seventeenth to twentieth centuries, primarily in Mexico, Brazil, Central American, and the West Indies. More than 50,000 of the volumes are nonfiction works.

The collection will be available for use by students and faculty and will be housed in the new Boeckmann Research Center in Latin America and Iberian Civilization at USC's Doheny Memorial Library.

The library intends to catalog 20,000 volumes representing that portion of the collection least likely to be found in existing databases. The cataloging will then be input into RLIN, making the material available nationally.

Honeywell introduces videotex system

Honeywell Information Systems has announced the availability of the InfoNow Videotex System, a computerized information retrieval system that works through a central system. Based on a dedicated Honeywell DPS 6 minicomputer, the InfoNow system is designed for major corporations, manufacturers, distributors, and federal, state, and local governments who wish to dial into a central computer for instant retrieval of textual and graphic information.

The InfoNow system is based on the French Antiope protocol, but otherwise is protocol independent. Information is stored on "pages" in a central database. Users access the information base from portable Minitel terminals, manufactured by the French firm Telic-Alcatel. The terminals contain a fold-down keyboard, a nine-inch diagonal, 40-line-by-24-character monochromatic display screen, and a built-in modem for communication with the central system. A VT-Link adapter board and emulation software are available to allow a Honeywell microSystem PC, IBM PC, or IBM PC/XT to function as a user terminal. Guided by menus that work like a book's table of contents, users can locate the category of information they want without knowing anything about how the database is structured. The number of end user terminals on any InfoNow system can be approximately ten times the number of actual communications lines.

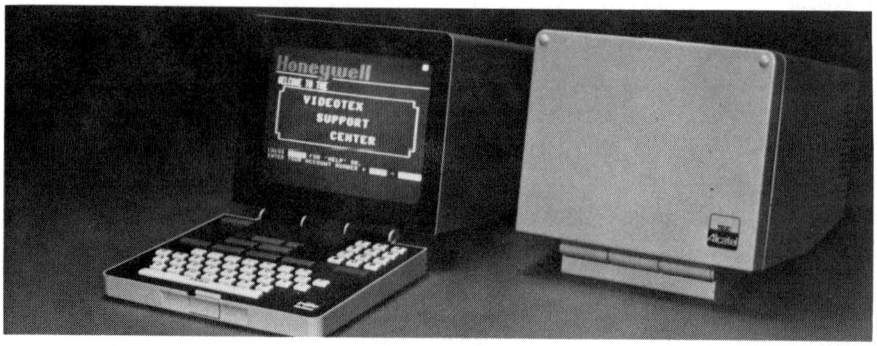

InfoNow: Honewell's new videotex system

The Electronic Book of the Very Near Future

Charles Goodrum and Helen Dalrymple

Obviously the reason we all are interested in what is going to happen to the book in the future is so we can know how to deal with it today. Whether we are librarians, teachers, bookstore owners, or simply household consumers, we would like to know what we should be doing now so we will not wish we had played it a different way when we get to then. Thus, we need to have some reasonably valid images of what the world of the book will be like tomorrow, and in this case tomorrow is defined in the way the staff with whom we spoke at United Technologies defined it: "Very little of this will have come to pass in the next five years, but all of it will be here by the end of fifteen."

The first point to be dealt with is: Just what devices are we talking about? What will they look like? What will they do? Barbara Tuchman used the traditional phrase, "You can't take a computer to bed or to the beach" meaning it literally. Of course, you *can* take a computer both places. The book the specialists are talking about can either be one of the briefcase-sized computer screens that are increasingly seen on people's laps in airplanes, or the flat screens seen on designers' work benches. The latter are the size of a *Life* magazine, about three-fourths of an inch thick, with a color screen, and definition so sharp you can read the serifs on ten-point type. But their chief charm is that they can carry a 600-page book in their memories, the book pages are white with black letters, and you can dial whatever size type you want. The young people use ten or twelve point, the middle-aged use twelve or fourteen and the vision-impaired can take the text up to a single word filling the entire screen. Knowing what the coming machines will be like makes considerable difference to our ability to guess with accuracy what will be done with them. Let's describe a few that were either shown or described to us as we pursued the 100 interviews.

Printed by permission from the Center for the Book and the Library of Congress. From the forthcoming Books in Our Future: A Resource Volume, *the second work in a study of the book authorized by the U.S. Congress.* **Charles Goodrum** *and* **Helen Dalrymple** *were consultants for this project.*

Liquid crystal type

We can start with the TV screens that will be coming on the market very soon. We all know that a present day nineteen-inch color television set is sharper than the same one was only five years ago. We also know that a nine-inch TV is even sharper than the nineteen-inch, but you have to sit closer to get the benefit. The same is true of monitors. The original Apples and Commodores were legible, but the letters were blockish and you certainly couldn't sweep-read them as you would a book page. Last year's monitors like the IBM or the Amdeks are much sharper. The letters look like typewriter characters with serifs, high resolution, and crisp appearance, but very soon the screens will be as sharp as a good magazine page.

A home television set has 525 lines of resolution; the new Sony screens (and their fellow companies) are 1100 lines, and the improvement is far more than doubled. Color pictures look like magazine pictures, and print looks like type. The Sony handles ten-point type as sharply as a newspaper page.

The CrystalVision screens are barely an inch thick and their type appears in liquid crystal in a form that is a modern day extension of the early technique used in digital watches. Nowadays you can have your "page" either as white letters on black, black on white, or the "page" in dark green or soothing amber.

Where will the letters come from? We saw models using all sorts of storage devices. You can get a complete novel on a piece of plastic the size of a credit card which is slipped into the side of the frame of the digital page. This "Drexon Card" is laser formed, with the digital record either in pits drilled into the plastic or bubbles raised on the surface; it holds 160,000 words. Or the words can go into a silicon chip that can be screwed into the back of the flat screen, or if you can tolerate the briefcase thickness, it can simply be on a small, floppy disk the size of a Mason-jar lid slipped in a slot in the front (here the words are magnetic charges on plastic).

Note the immediate effect of the change of the monitor screen and the computer. The Book of the Month Club can send its volumes around in envelopes instead of the complicated cardboard packages it now uses; disks or chips or plastic cards all offer cheaper postage, less damage in transit. If the television screen is so sharp that it can show book print, the cable companies can offer the bestseller of the week via a simple pager tied to the selector dial. They can also offer how-to books, probably sent in response to a telephone call to the local TV station.

Just to confuse things, the new Sony Mavica snapshot camera paints pictures not with dyes or silver salts like a traditional photograph, but with digital charges like the magnetic records on a tape cassette. It was invented as a photographic device (you point the camera at the Washington Monument, it records it digitally, and when you get home you show it on your television set). But the specialists are intrigued with the thought that you can take similar pictures of a book page, put these on the plastic card and when you get home you can either read them off of your television set or off a special table-top screen. Obviously we are again back to the digital page, this time by way of your home snapshot camera rather than via the home computer. In all of the above instances, the present book page ends up on a screen.

Printers and paper

The screen is probably acceptable when we are dealing with facts and information; it is probably not acceptable for recreational reading or for material on which we wish to reflect or with text we wish to change. This will take print on paper. When we try to think about what the book will be like tomorrow, we must force ourselves to realize that printing on paper, at home, on-demand will be much faster and cheaper than anything we have known to date.

We first had to adjust to the fact that IBM's spinning ball typed much faster than individual keys hitting a platen when the Selectric displaced the trusty Woodstock. Next came the dot matrix printers the Japanese tied to our home computers. While the Selectric could comfortably produce 325 characters a minute, the Epson dot matrix gave us 4,800 characters a minute on a machine that cost barely half as much. The next generation of home printers will produce 120,000 characters a minute on an even cheaper machine. That is a page a second, sixty pages a minute, a 360-page novel in six minutes. These machines are already in existence, and, depending on which patents the parent companies own, will arrive at their product either by chisel head printers or laser ink jets. The common dot matrix printer now creates a letter by hitting the ribbon with eight tiny chisels; the next step is a single head that runs completely across the page and 640 chisels slam out the complete line. The ink jets are even faster since they don't have to wait for the head to move in and out, but paint the characters from flying pin points in a tube.

Strangely enough, these incredibly fast machines are not very expensive. Most futurists think they will be cheap enough that the book clubs and videotext newspapers can afford to give one free with each subscription in return for savings on distribution via mail or newspaper carriers.

We heard applications of these inexpensive, high speed printers coming from a variety of sources:

Robert Badger, editor at John Wiley: "The future of the book is largely entwined with laser print technology and its ability to supply quality reproductions of the printed word and graphics. People will not want to only read from screens, so the printed word will still be with us." He believes that within ten to fifteen years most journals will be on-demand, printed out in the home or office only.

Elie Shneour, director of the Bio Systems Research Institute, pictures a cable or telephone system in which blank books are supplied to every subscriber and placed in a "black box" on top of the television set. By punching a code into a keypad, the user can request any available book which is then printed via laser printer on to the blank book which slides out of its slot "after a few minutes . . . now filled with beautifully typographed text and illustrations, some in color."

New ways of delivering words

Fred Croxton of the Library of Congress, Ithiel de Sola Pool of M.I.T., and Tom Surprenant of Queens College, City University of New York expressed concern about the effect of the on-demand book on libraries. All three expressed the belief that this innovation will come in the working lifetime of present library administrators and should be anticipated by present supervisors. Kenneth Dowlin of the Pikes Peak Library System thinks that home, on-demand printing holds the greatest threat/challenge to American booksellers and American libraries of all the electronic points of impact. Harry Gray of United Technologies believes that digital transmission and storage will explode into our ways of keeping and delivering words, but warns that the resulting on-demand printing will "double . . . treble the amount of paper that we now produce." He thinks that we will continue to read the important words on paper—but we will throw the paper away when we've finished that day's use of it, knowing we can always get it back quickly from the computer when we need it. Filing cabinets and shelves and libraries as we know them will be a thing of the past. Pool refers to this form of printing as "editions of one" and Jacques Barzun reminds us that computer printouts "are a reversion to the scroll." It should be explained, however, that Shneour's blank books are single sheets printed on both sides and held in hardback binders. The inside of the spine comes with adhesive into which the sheets are dropped.

When the American Heritage and Random House dictionaries were first offered as floppy disks, they were add-ons, separate mini-programs for slipping into the home computer. In just three years' time, however, they have become a part of word processing programs and now are appearing resident in the computer's permanent memory when the units are purchased; they are being used as spelling checkers. As the user types into the computer, the memory automatically checks each word against the dictionary and if the dictionary does not find a spelling that matches, it flashes the word on the screen until the writer either corrects it, or passes the signal that that is the way he wants it and to forget it. Originally intended as a device to help the author with spelling problems, they have become a device for proofreading. The programs can scan a thousand words in a matter of seconds, and pick up miskeys and transpositions as the text develops. Over 100,000 of these spelling checkers were sold in 1982 and by 1985 the figure is expected to have exceeded half a million.

Similar computerization of basic reference books has already started: thesauri, almanacs, one-volume encyclopedias all included as part of the computer's built-in programs so the reference works can be consulted without leaving the keyboard as the writer needs the information. Increasingly these reference books are being included free with the purchase of the computer as an attempt to get ahead of the competition in a field where most of the machines do about the same thing at the same price. Andrew Rosenheim believes that "by 1990, if not sooner, sales of electronic dictionaries will exceed sales of printed ones." As soon as the built-in memory goes one step higher in its steady annual increase, one need not be a visionary to foresee a complete reference shelf of the basic information volumes as the standard inclusion on all computers capable of word processing.

Books turning to dust

Most of what we have discussed thus far relates to the creation and distribution of the word. The preservation of the word beyond its immediate use is another area of potentially great change. The printed word on rag paper (up to the 1860s) is holding up reasonably well. But print on wood pulp paper (since 1860) is in terrible shape. Major libraries are at the point of near despair with the way their collections are turning, literally, to dust on their shelves. Between four and five million volumes in the Library of Congress collections have already reached a state of severe deterioration.

About fifty years ago, the libraries decided that the answer to the preservation problem was microform: microfilm, microcards, or microfiche—miniaturization on chemically stable plastic film. Since that time most newspapers and magazines have been so preserved, and many documents and archival materials. The idea has been a great success until, to the horror of the librarians and archivists, they discovered that after thirty to forty years, the microfilm began to deteriorate. Now the libraries' reels of microform are crystallizing, the emulsion is separating from the base, and the impressions are being lost. Once this was discovered, the preservationists began re-microfilming—new pictures of the old microfilms on new emulsion and new film. This has proved to be quite unsatisfactory. It has been discovered that when the first microfilms were made, the photographic process degraded the image of the letters by about twenty percent. Re-filming them degrades it another twenty percent—to the extent of closing up e's, a's, and o's, filling in serifs, making manuscripts almost illegible, and in general defeating the purpose of the project. From the preservationist's point of view, the problem is the failure of support material, not the print itself. Paper rots away, now film is splitting and falling apart.

The preservationists are trying two paths. The first is to deacidify paper so it does not deteriorate. They are now able to do this by fumigating books in huge vaults filled with diethyl zinc gas. The problem is that even when done in quantities of thousands of books at a time, the process costs between four and five dollars per volume. You also must then house the books in air-conditioned space forever.

The other way is the digital solution. This involves either going back up the printing chain and capturing the digital text that drove the photocomposition machines, or taking a picture of the complete printed page (or map or manuscript or photograph) and capturing the digital data which would traditionally be used to produce wirephotos, television pictures, or *USA Today.* Once the preservationists get the words or pictures in digital form they then must solve how to save these little off-or-on signals. Putting them on floppy disks or mainframe tapes or disks is not the answer, since these develop reading errors over the years as the magnetic charges fade. But putting them on optical discs appears to be the exact solution to all kinds of ills. An optical disc can be a sheet of non-corrosive metal or it can be glass or ceramic. The bits and bytes can be preserved by drilling pits into these materials by laser beam, or creating blisters by heat. Preservationists are pleased by the thought that even if they are wrong again and glass or gold or silver alloy does change in a hundred years, they can hastily recapture the digital pattern on new materials without the degradation they suffer when they do the same thing with photographic processes.

The effects on the book, however, are a result of all the effort of preserving it: 1) it is incredibly compressed. A single optical disc holding digital type can hold 15,000 pages of print. The same disc holding five-color pictures of paintings, or reels of Technicolor motion picture images can hold only one-fifth of this amount of information, yet a hundred-disc carousel can hold the color image of every painting in every museum in the U.S.

From this great compression (with no deterioration) comes the next advantage: 2) when used in a library, dozens of people can be reading the same book simultaneously, no book is ever lost, stolen, or off the shelf, and all further library construction can cease. The old cliché that the whole Library of Congress collection can be put in a closet comes to pass.

How will people read from optical discs? Either at CRT monitors, or if they want printed text, from printouts produced on a "Xerox machine"-like copier where the sheets come out by the page or on a traditional digital personal printer where they are produced by the line. Where will they read this text? Anywhere you can run a telephone wire. So far as the videodisc-to-screen link is conerned, you can put the discs in the basement and the monitors in the reading room overhead—or you can put the discs in the basement and the monitors on the other side of the continent.

How close is this to reality? It is already here. The Library of Congress has discs filled with 50,000 rare photographs that are being searched and viewed today, and it is putting on the text of seventy current magazines so they can be viewed on computer screens.

At the present time 100 discs are housed in a device that both looks and operates like an old-time jukebox. One of these jukeboxes can hold more than a trillion digital bits, which is the equivalent of ten thousand pictures or over one hundred thousand books if the text is taken from a word processor or character scanned. Ithiel de Sola Pool notes that at the present time it costs about forty cents per book to get a full-sized, printed volume on to the optical disc, but near-term projections expect the cost to get down to between a nickel and a penny per volume within a decade.

Creating our own characters

Lane Jennings, World Future Society, thinks that in another generation people will use paper mainly for preserving data with the emphasis on convenience, and they will use the computer for creative activities—speculation and emotional involvement. He thinks that when we grope for "how will things be different in the future world of the computer?" we should use the phenomena we can observe in the video arcade as the analogy and guide. Here we see young people of high energy—both physical and mental—captured by the sense of personal involvement. The very complex adventure games (different levels, different screens) let the reader create characters and manipulate them and relate to them. Essentially what they are doing is what their parents did in books—building characters and scenes in their own minds, "surrogate memory experience." But in many cases when these young people grow older, they are turned off by books because a book has become passive: the reader can't do anything different with the characters.

Some speculators think that is one way the computer may direct the energy now invested in fiction. Books were descriptive and philosophical until the invention of the novel in the mid-eighteenth century. At that point, made-up characters like Tom Jones and Pamela *did* things, had things happen to them in places and times that the reader could imagine. Using the arcade analogy from above, instead of playing dungeons and dragons in mystical kingdoms, it is possible that future videodisc novels will provide scenes of historic crisis, or fantasy castles and chateaux, or exotic modern locales which the readers will people (both visually and imaginatively) with characters of their own choosing.

Several people with whom we spoke believe that the present preoccupation with laser painting and electronic music may be a hint of the way art and music will go. Walt Disney's early mixture of graphic images tied to music in *Fantasia* have not only spoken to audiences and stood the test of time, but now seem to be appearing in the video music pieces that again are attempting to project sound and rhythm visually. What does a Chopin prelude "look" like? How about a Beethoven quartet? Can the electronically produced visual image of a computer give us a new way of expanding our appreciation of the creative genius of the sound of music? Jennings sees these examples less of the way the next creative step will go, than indicative of the fact that the computer is going to bring something new to our experience. Fred Kilgour of OCLC expressed the same thought when he told us, "The computer is not going to do old things in new ways; it is going to do entirely new things in new ways and we should be ready to recognize them when they come and go with them when they appear."

The word at the threshold

How we get from here to there is intriguing writers and artists across the literary spectrum. At one extreme we find Arthur Clarke and Byron Preiss making "electronic books" out of their *Rendezvous with Rama* and *Dragonworld* novels. Joanne Davis of *Publishers Weekly* describes the technique: "the reader (who is transmogrified into Amsel, the hero of *Dragonworld*) is presented with one or two pictures at the top of the screen and a body of text at the bottom describing the situation. He or she then types in commands to travel through the network of screens that comprise the simulated Dragonworld, encountering various adventures and characters (who can be spoken to and asked questions) in the process."

At the other extreme we have children's book illustrator and writer Mercer Mayer of the "Little Critters" and "Little Monster" series, who is creating digital children's books called TinkTonks. "These colorful, robot-like characters live deep inside your computer on little disks that float above the CrissCross Sea." Again, each time the child turns on the computer the characters are in their home at the start of a new day and the reader determines which way they go and whom they meet at "crossroads" in the story. The story then follows a new path each time. The endlessly changing stories are reputed to be totally engrossing to children four to eight. Mayer is internationally known for his Little Golden books, and describes his present explorations in the same metaphor we heard so often: "The appeal is that it is the next quantum leap from a communications standpoint. What the printing press was back in the 1400s is what the computer is today. It's going to radically change everybody's way of communicating."

Of the one hundred people we interviewed, the overwhelming majority looked at the future of the book with eager, optimistic anticipation. The world of the word was perceived to be at the threshold of its most triumphant period. ▣

The Once and Future Book: The Preservation Crisis

Jay Ward Brown

A book is somehow sacred. A dictator can kill and maim people, can sink to any level of tyranny, and only be hated. But if books are burned, the ultimate in tyranny has happened.

—**John Steinbeck**

The ultimate in tyranny is happening right here in America, though not quite in the way Steinbeck characterized it. Our books are burning—while they sit on our library shelves. Carlton Rochell, dean of libraries at New York University, describes it this way: "There are no flames. No smoke. But the paper is burning, nonetheless. It turns yellow, then brown. It becomes crisp and eventually crumbles to dust."

"When you go into the stacks and look at the books all neatly lined up row after row, they really don't look so bad," explains John Baker, the New York Public Library's chief of conservation. "It's when you take a book off the shelf and open the book and discover its covers are falling apart and you can't turn the pages without cracking them, and after using the book for half an hour, there's all this book dandruff around on the floor—that's when you know how rapidly our books are approaching the end of their lives. That happens many times a day in our reading rooms."

On the brink of disintegration

"The knowledge of our country is crumbling just sitting there," says Madeline Davis, chief conservator at the Buffalo Public Library.

As we sit in front of the fire with Shakespeare, or curl up in bed with a novel, most of us find such statements hard to believe. The truth is, our books are disintegrating as we hold them in our hands: The New York Public Library estimates that half of its five million volumes are falling apart. The University of Minnesota reports that one million of its four million books shouldn't be circulating. The Library of Congress, founded on the philosophy that every book is invaluable, reports that one-fourth of its twenty-five million volumes are on the brink of disintegration. A nationwide study of public libraries, conducted in the late 1970s by the William Barrow Laboratories, concluded that ninety-seven percent of the non-fiction books published in the first half of this century won't last until the beginning of the next.

The irony of the problem is that its cause lies between the covers of our books: the acidic paper on which we print them. Although acid-free papers were developed decades ago, inertia in the paper and publishing industries has prevented a switch to permanent papers. Librarians have had to develop their own means of preserving our rapidly evaporating heritage. With time, money and luck, their innovations may save our burning books.

The writings found on "primitive" cave paintings and clay tablets have endured for as long as 35,000 years. Scraps of the first paper, produced 2,000 years ago, exist in fine condition. Numerous copies of the Gutenberg Bible, circa 1456, sit firmly on their shelves, their pages white and supple, their bindings sound. Understandably, twentieth century readers expect that the comparatively modern book should be just as durable.

But the pages in a 1912 edition of Henrik Ibsen's works are so brittle that merely closing its cover sends up a puff of paper dust. The pages in more recent books, such as Steinbeck's *The Grapes of Wrath,* are yellowed and stiff and beginning to crack. With all our modern technology, a book published today will have a useful life of no more than fifty years, and probably closer to thirty.

The explanation is easy: older books were printed on better paper. Before the nineteenth century, most paper was made by boiling cotton and linen rags. The resulting cellulose fibers were mixed with animal or vegetable gelatin and dried into sheets. The paper was strong. And because of the natural materials, it was highly alkaline, or acid-free.

But during the 1800s, several changes took place. The explosion in literacy gave rise first to the penny press newspapers and then to a huge new audience for books. The paper industry began to run out of rags.

Seeds of disaster

As early as 1600, manufacturers had discovered that wood chips could be used instead of rags. By 1900, wood was the major source of cellulose fiber. But wood chips had to be boiled with caustic chemicals and bleached with chlorine in order to produce useful cellulose. Papermakers found that alum/rosin sizing, rather than vegetable gelatin, was better for use with wood cellulose.

Therein lay the seeds of disaster. Alum/rosin breaks down into sulphuric acid. That acid is now rapidly consuming our written heritage.

It wan't long before nineteenth

Jay Ward Brown *is a freelance writer who lives in New York City.*

century librarians noticed the deterioration of their books, but it wasn't until 1929 that Edwin Sutermeister, a paper chemist, correctly identified alum/rosin as the culprit. By 1959, researchers were able to produce paper using calcium carbonate and synthetic alkaline sizing in place of the alum/rosin.

Today, experts say alkaline paper has a life expectancy of over 1,000 years for the best types and 500 years for average grades. Alkaline paper cannot be distinguished from acidic paper on the basis of quality and, in general, it is no more expensive to make than acidic paper. That is partly because alkaline manufacturing makes it easier to meet environmental safety requirements, since the process doesn't involve the disposal of caustic chemicals. Another boon to manufacturers is that alkaline paper is easier on plant equipment: acid from traditional methods corrodes the papermaking machinery.

But today, fewer than fifteen manufacturers regularly produce alkaline paper in the United States. Together, they make only twenty-five percent of the nearly one million tons of paper used in books each year.

With all of the advantages of alkaline paper, it is hard for some booklovers to understand why so few manufacturers have switched. The cost of converting mill equipment is the main reason, according to papermakers. New papermaking machines, often the size of a city block, cost as much as $100 million. But in 1980, the last year for which figures are available, manufacturers spent over $6 billion refitting their plants. At the time, industry association president Louis Laun called the expenditures a massive effort at increasing productivity. Little of the $6 billion was spent on conversion to acid-free paper.

Finch Pruyn & Company of Glens Falls, New York, is one of the few companies that did convert when it refitted its plant. Elaine Ryder, the company's customer service coordinator, said that Finch Pruyn needed to replace its aging equipment. Because most of their regular customers, which include both major publishers and specialty houses, were asking them for acid-free paper, Ryder said, Finch Pruyn made the switch to alkaline manufacturing. She also noted that Finch Pruyn didn't change its prices by a penny after the switch.

Most manufacturers deny there is a demand from publishers for alkaline paper. Olin Corporation fell into alkaline manufacturing more by accident than by design. Headquartered in North Carolina, Olin originally produced cigarette paper, which has to be alkaline—acidic paper produces an unpleasant taste when smoked. The company discovered that it could also sell the light-weight paper to pharmaceutical companies to use for the instructions included with medications. The thin paper was also suitable for Bible publishers. As it expanded its operations, Olin found a market for alkaline book papers.

Other manufacturers tell similar stories. S. D. Warren converted half of its mills to alkaline manufacturing during the 1950s because it wanted to produce a stronger paper and alkaline manufacturing is an economical way to do so. As was the case at Olin, according to Marketing Manager Lewis Brown, S. D. Warren's switch had "absolutely nothing" to do with demand for longer-lasting paper.

Paper-producing behemoths

One thing all of these smaller companies have in common is that book papers are now their main product. Thus, they are particularly sensitive to quality concerns in the book market. But the vast majority of book paper—seventy-five percent of it, according to industry estimates—is manufactured by huge companies with diversified interests. Less than five percent of industry giant International Paper's 1984 production was for the publishing industry. These behemoths produce most of the paper used in publishing each year, but that production is only a small fraction of their total sales. There isn't enough demand for acid-free to encourage International, or giants like it, to make the switch, according to International's Product Development Manager Bruce Stone.

In addition, demand for book paper has been heavy and is expected to increase about fifteen percent each year, at least through 1986. An industry report indicates that manufacturers won't be able to increase productivity fast enough to keep up with the new demand. This means that publishers, even if they want to use acid-free, will have to buy what paper they can find without being choosy.

"There is simply a resistance within the industry to changing technology," says Paul Royster, production manager for the Library of America, a specialty publishing house. Royster has a keen appreciation for the ravages of acidic paper—he studied nineteenth century literature as a college student. The books from that period are among the hardest hit by acid deterioration.

Anthony Liberatore, production manager at P. H. Glatfelter Company, an alkaline manufacturer, agrees with Royster. "The conversion process is very, very slow because there are a lot of manufacturers like International Paper that don't have a product mix that requires it."

Many manufacturers blame publishers for failing to demand acid-free. Liberatore says that most publishers just aren't interested in making longer-lasting books. S. D. Warren's Lewis Brown agrees: "Selling books is a money-making institution and until someone sees a way of increasing their profits by using acid-free paper, the idea won't get much play from publishers."

"That's not true," says Howard Goldstein with more than a little anger in his voice. Goldstein is production director for Simon & Schuster, a major publishing house. He has been active nationally as an advocate of acid-free paper.

"If acid-free were available, we would give the consumer the best possible product," he said. He points out that acid-free paper isn't available from most manufacturers. "If I'm using Mill A and Mill A makes nonacidic, then I'm a hero because I can say all my books are on acid-free. If, on the other hand, I am using Mill B, and Mill B makes acidic paper, then I'm no good."

Goldstein admits that Simon & Schuster hasn't gone out of its way to look for acid-free mills. But he argues it would be nearly impossible for his company to change from one mill to another. Because transportation is a major factor in the cost of paper, publishers need to buy from the mills closest to their printing plants. And Goldstein says that for Simon & Schuster, there aren't enough acid-free mills nearby.

Accusatory fingers

Both sides have a point. After jabbing the accusatory finger at each other, most publishers and paper manufacturers end up blaming the reading public for the failure to print books on acid-free paper. If consumers were to insist on it, both sides say, industrial hesitation would evaporate and the switch would take place almost overnight. Everyone involved admits that is unlikely to happen any time soon.

"The libraries of the world would love to have everything on acid-free paper," Brown said. "The problem is that they don't have the marketplace muscle to demand it from the publishers." And he doesn't think commercial booksellers, who do have the muscle, have much interest in the subject at all.

Brian Baxter, a buyer for B. Dalton's, one of the nation's largest commercial booksellers, confirms Brown's assertion. According to Baxter, paper quality is not a primary concern. He said it wouldn't have any effect on his decision to carry a book because his customers aren't interested in it. As another buyer put it, "The average consumer doesn't have the slightest idea what's going on, and doesn't care. They read a book and put it away. They don't think about who will have it when they're gone."

Librarians agree. Peter Sparks, director of preservation at the Library of Congress, points out that most consumers think in terms of their own lifetime, if even that long. Librarians, he says, think in terms of centuries.

In the absence of public concern, librarians have been trying to foster an official one. With intense lobbying, the Council on Library Resources persuaded the American National Standards Institute to adopt guidelines for book paper quality. The standard, which took effect in January, 1985, specifies the type of alkaline paper that should be used in publishing. It also recommends that publishers include a message on the flyleaf of a book, advertising the fact that it is printed on permanent-durable paper.

Almost no one thinks the voluntary standard will have much effect on either publishers or consumers. Alan Calmes, preservation officer at the National Archives says, "No manufacturer will come near to following those standards."

Howard Goldstein, who sat on the committee that drafted them, said, "I doubt very seriously whether Simon & Schuster would be in a position to adopt all the standards when weighed against the economic considerations of publisher-paper manufacturer relationships."

B. Dalton's Baxter says of the message printed on the flyleaf of books: "It's like a cigarette package warning. Only these will be ignored more because you can't say acidic books are dangerous to your health."

Sparks is not surpised by those responses. He compares book preservation to the status of the environmental movement twenty years ago. "We're at the starting point. The average person is just beginning to show concern about preserving our cultural heritage for their children and the publicity accompanying developments like the standard will foster that concern."

But as Sparks points out while standing amidst the bustle of activity in the LC preservation workroom, with collections turning to dust on their shelves and millions of acidic books being printed every day, librarians cannot wait years for public pressure to affect the book industry.

Massive deacidification

If there is no hope in the near future of getting more publishers and paper manufacturers to make books that last longer, then librarians will have to do it themselves. That is exactly what they are doing. Preservation activity is currently concentrated in three areas: deacidification, microfilming, and computerization. No one method is yet a perfect solution to the problem of our burning books, but librarians say recent developments have taken them much closer to their preservation goals.

Deacidification is not new—book conservators have been hand-treating rare volumes for many years. After removing the book's binding, a conservator coats each page with alkaline chemicals to neutralize the acid, and the book is then rebound by hand. This process extends a book's life by 300 to 400 years. It can cost as much as $1,000 for a single volume and takes a week or more to treat each book. Hand-treatment is hardly practical for general collections. Indeed, even if the money could be found, the vast majority of books would disintegrate long before they could be treated.

Researchers in the United States have been striving for an effective way to deacidify books on a massive scale. The most advanced process was first patented in 1976 by the Library of Congress and is just now moving into practical application.

In the LC method, books are loaded into a vacuum chamber and then dried for three days to remove all water vapor. (During a recent test on 5,000 books, over 600 pounds of water were removed.) Then diethyl zinc (DEZ) gas is introduced into the chamber. A molecule of DEZ measures about ten angstroms—it would take nearly two million DEZ molecules to fill the eye of a needle—so the chemical easily permeates stacked books. As it reacts with chemicals in the paper, DEZ neutralizes the acid. DEZ also leaves an alkaline buffer of zinc oxycarbonate in the paper. This protects the book from future acid attacks, including human ones. Pens, pencils, and highlighter pens all contain acid which eats into the paper. Even turning the pages leaves acidic fingerprints behind. Sparks said the DEZ process extends the life of a book by five to six centuries and the treatment can be repeated if necessary.

Vacuum chambers are required because DEZ ignites when exposed to oxygen and explodes when it comes in contact with water. Researchers George Kelley, Jr. and John Williams began their experiments with DEZ in an ordinary pressure cooker and concluded them in the gigantic vacuum chambers at NASA's Goddard Space Center. As one librarian explained, "The equipment that helped us get to the moon helps preserve the books that tell us how we got there."

Congress provided $11.5 million this year to build a full-scale DEZ treatment facility at Fort Detrick, Maryland. Sparks said that he had no trouble getting the appropriation once librarians made Congress aware of the seriousness of the problem.

Site preparation began last spring and will be completed in 1986. The 40,000-square-foot facility will house two vacuum chambers each capable of holding 7,500 books. The treatment center is scheduled to operate twenty-four hours a day. At the estimated cost of $3 to $5 per volume, mass-deacidification would be the cheapest and most effective means of prolonging the shelf-life of a book. Depending on how fast they can be trucked in and out of the facility, Sparks hopes to be able to process one million volumes each year.

Even at that rate, Sparks points out, it will be at least twenty years before LC will be able to treat even the most important books sitting on its 532 miles of shelves. Sparks added that half the facility's capacity will be reserved for new acquisitions since it is important to treat books before they start to deteriorate. "In twenty or thirty years we will have stemmed the tide of acid material in the collection," he said.

Although he praises the new technology, NYPL's John Baker is quick to note that if the Fort Detrick facility is ever available for use by other libraries, it won't be until well into the twenty-first century. That will be too late for most of his collection.

According to Sparks, LC will license the technology to other responsible organizations. He said there have been a number of inquiries, including requests from the University of Wisconsin, an Arizona library and the Japanese government. Sparks thinks the National Technical Information Service, the agency that controls government patents, may be ready to license the technology within a few months.

University of Chicago Professor Richard Smith says that libraries don't have to wait for LC because his own method of mass-deacidification is already available. The process is called Wei T'o, named for the Chinese god responsible for protecting books. It uses different chemicals than LC and administers the gas under pressure instead of in a vacuum chamber. Although Smith disagrees with Sparks about the relative merits of the two systems (he claims his is less expensive), the effect is the same.

Aggressive microfilming

Mass-deacidification may be an effective stabilizer, but it does not restore strength to the paper. A book will eventually wear out from regular use, even if acid is no longer burning the paper. In that case, another form of technology is necessary to preserve the information contained in books.

Since its development in the 1930s, microfilming has been the most widely used means of reducing the bulk of printed material for storage. However, early films deteriorated even faster than books. Over the past decade, new films have been developed. Bohdan Yasinsky, preservation microfilming officer at LC, says that when stored in an acid-free box under constant temperature and humidity, silver halide film will last as long as 1,000 years. He adds that libraries now rely exclusively on the halide film.

The Library of Congress has the most aggressive microfilming program in the world, according to Yasinsky. Since 1968, LC has filmed some 60,000 titles comprising over 100 million pages. Its goal this year is to commit another nine million pages to film. Eight thousand volumes are currently being processed, but Yasinsky says that over four million books need to be filmed before they fall apart. Another 77,000 are added to that list each year. "We have made only footsteps on the moon," Yasinsky says.

At a cost of about $45 per volume and four months to process each book or document, no library can afford to microfilm all of its endangered books. In fact, most public libraries can't afford to film any. The New York Public Library is one exception. It is second only to LC in the amount of filming done. This year its preservationists will process close to 10,000 volumes. For smaller libraries in Buffalo or Minneapolis or San Antonio, budgets won't allow it. About all most can do is rely on commercial microfilmers that mass-produce films of newspapers, magazines and other materials. By buying the film instead of the original, libraries save time, money and storage space. At LC, which currently subscribes to 75,000 magazines and 1,459 newspapers, microfilming is a necessity.

Bohdan Yasinsky explains that during filming at LC, a master negative and duplicate are created. The master negative is stored in specially adapted caves in Pennsylvania from which it can be retrieved should something happen to the duplicate negative at the library. The working copies to be used by patrons are made from the duplicate, which is stored in an acid-free box in a climate-controlled, fire-proof vault at LC. As the working copies wear out from use, new ones can be made from the duplicate negative at a cost of about $15.

Because the master negative is never used, there is no chance of damaging it. In seven or eight hundred years, before the master starts to deteriorate, more duplicates can be made, extending the life of the material indefinitely, Yasinsky said. Among the volumes currently awaiting filming in the NYPL workroom are the paperback science fiction books of Issac Asimov, books and papers from the gay press and a collection of Jewish monographs from the late nineteenth century that may be the only copies of the works in existence. That highlights one of the biggest advantages of microfilm: inexpensive copies can be distributed to libraries around the world, making rare books easily accessible to all. The National Register of Microfilm Masters provides a yearly index of titles available on film.

Deterioration plagues the books even as they wait to give over their contents to microfilm. During a tour of the NYPL facility, Baker picked up a volume of World War I battle plans. A cloud of yellow dust settled to the preservation office floor as Baker turned its pages. He carefully placed the book back on the shelf, shaking his head as he moved on.

Despite being a permanent means of preservation, there are some drawbacks to microfilm, in addition to its cost. Patrons have been less than enthusiastic about the bulky viewing machines and the necessity of working in darkened rooms. Librarians admit it is impossible to tuck a microfilm reader under one's arm and head for the park. The University of Minnesota's director of preservation, Donald Kelsey, says "Microfilm is a long way from an acceptable medium for users," particularly because it does not provide random access to a book's contents. The user must crank back and forth through the roll of film to the desired pages, wasting time, and with manual machines, expending considerable effort.

In addition, microfilming usually necessitates the destruction of original books. In order to get quality images, it is necessary to split the spine of the book and cut apart the pages. To some, this is a heinous crime for a librarian to commit.

"Some call us butchers when we have to destroy a book to save its content. But I think preserving the intellectual content is what is most important," Bohdan Yasinsky says. "And until now," he adds, "that has meant microfilming."

Yasinsky is alluding to a new computer technology the Library of Congress began using in December 1984. Tests completed earlier indicated that optical disc technology may replace microfilm as the most important and effective means of preservation.

Digitizing information

The heart of the prototyope system, the "jukebox," as it has been dubbed, sits in Room G51 of LC's Madison Building. If it had flashing lights and a slot for a quarter, you would expect it to play Elvis Presley songs.

But this jukebox costs $2.5 million. It contains 100 optical discs, each the size of a phonograph record. And each of these glass-covered twelve-inch discs contains more than 15,000 images, the equivalent of 100 books.

In a process akin to photocopying, the page of a book or a photograph is scanned by a computer that records the information in digital electronic form. That digitized information—essentially a series of numbers that tells the computer what the original page looks like—is engraved by laser on the metal surface of the disc. When the disc is plucked from its rack and "played" by the jukebox, another laser beam reads the tiny ridges on the surface of the disc. The computer translates the digital information back into an image, and the page of the book is displayed on a high-resolution television screen at a computer terminal.

For the just-completed test program, some 30,000 photographs, prints, and posters have been digitized and placed on a disc. The access terminal sits in the middle of a third floor reading room. With a hand-held remote control device, the user turns on the TV. The disc's table of contents is displayed. The user can go through the collection one page at a time, or, by entering the appropriate page number, the user can "flip" to a specific page. Those who tire of cranking through rolls of microfilm will appreciate the fact that it takes the optical disc scanner a mere five seconds to skip over 39,500 pages to find the one requested by the user. Unlike microfilm, the optical disc image is a full color duplicate of the original.

Last December, LC began digitizing print materials, concentrating at first on popular and scientific journals, law materials, and manuscripts. These documents will form a database on public policy issues intended for use by the Congressional Research Service and available to the public on eight terminals to be installed in various reading rooms.

It will take some time to fill up the first jukebox. Audrey Fischer, operations coordinator for the program, says she hopes by then the cost of each unit will have decreased so that LC can add jukeboxes as necessary.

"The immediate emphasis of the program is service to readers," Fischer said. Currently, readers must run back and forth between LC's three buildings as they do their research. Sometimes it takes up to two hours for librarians to retrieve periodicals or books from the stacks, assuming that the materials are shelved where they are supposed to be. The optical disc system eliminates all those problems, she said.

From a single terminal, a reader will be able to access every book, magazine, and photograph available on disc. After typing in the item's call number, the reader's computer will search the system to find out which jukebox contains the item. Once it is located, the jukebox will play the disc, feeding the information into the reader's computer terminal. The whole process will take a matter of seconds. The reader can then manipulate the information, flipping back and forth between pages of books on the disc. A printer attached to each reader station will produce high-quality copies of the page. Color printers will be available for reproducing photographs. As Bohdan Yasinsky points out, each copy made from the disc will be a "spitting image" of the original.

One of the big advantages of the jukebox is that more than one person will be able to look at the same book at the same time. Once the jukebox has relayed the contents of a disc to the reader's terminal, the disc is available for use by other readers. "The book is always on the shelf," Fischer said, and because of the jukebox's mechanical accuracy, it is always returned to its proper place. Yasinsky said that LC might even transfer its microfilm holdings to disc, for ease of use.

The glamour of the technology makes it easy to forget the optical disc's more mundane preservation capabilities. Each minute, LC adds ten more items to its collection of eighty million. Miniaturized storage is essential, because LC is already running out of shelves. One page of a standard book occupies 54,000 square millimeters. The same page on optical disc occupies four square millimeters, or about 1/13,000 the amount of space.

First generation copying

Each optical disc has a life expectancy of about twenty years. Now, that would seem to make them a poor means of preservation. Not so, says Fischer. By inserting a quality control code on the disc, it is possible to monitor the oxidation of the metallic alloy. Before any of the material on the disc has a chance to deteriorate, the computer will automatically copy the entire disc onto a new one. Because the computer is transferring digitized codes and not the actual image, the copied disc will be absolutely identical to the original. "You are always dealing with a first generation copy," Yasinsky says, "and you can keep making first generation copies indefinitely."

Copies of the discs can also someday be distributed to other libraries, in the same way that microfilms are. And, like any computerized information, optical discs can eventually be used to transfer the contents of entire books over the telephone lines.

Walking through the stacks at the University of Minnesota, Donald Kelsey said he doesn't think that such technology will ever completely replace the book. Most people agree with him. "But then," Kelsey added, "the clay tablet people didn't think they'd be replaced either." In fact, in one sense, optical discs are a return to clay tablets: they are carvings, made by laser instead of sharpened sticks.

Librarians argue that, given enough money, deacidification, microfilming, and computerization could save all of our written knowledge. LC has every intention of saving everything in its collection, according to Peter Sparks.

LC may have the money to carry out its ambitious goal, but almost every other librarian, in libraries large and small, agrees with Marsha Moss of the 200,000-volume Concord, Massachusetts, Public Library: "We just don't have the money."

Bound by their budgets, librarians must pick and choose what to save. Therein lies the potential for social censorship. "As librarians, we don't want to act as censors of the present generation for the future," NYPL's John Baker said. "On the other hand, preservation deferred is preservation denied. Deciding what to preserve is very difficult, but the decision has to be made."

Toward that end, librarians have been trying to establish preservation priorities. Types of books frequently cited by librarians as low priorities include: workbooks, anthologies, vanity publications, athletic and political hagiography, novelizations of films, formula novels and most paperbacks.

Librarians are understandably uncomfortable at having to impose such restrictions on themselves. They emphasize that everything, including science fiction and romance novels, tells a great deal about our culture. It is, in the words of one, "the height of arrogance for us to choose what future generations will know about us." It seems clear that decisions about what to save should include the input of librarians, archivists, scholars, government, and the public.

"In the end," says Carlton Rochell, sitting in his book-lined office on the eleventh floor of the NYU library, "I guess it does become a selective form of censorship."

"Nobody's God," adds Baker. "All we can do is try to arrive at the best judgment."

A moral victory only

Excited as they are by the preservation potential of deacidification, microfilming, and computerization, librarians also sense the irony of it. Preservation budgets in major libraries run into the millions every year. Smaller libraries devote hundreds of thousands of dollars. Often, they spend as much on preservation as on acquisition. Said one librarian: "Just think of all the different books we could buy, if we didn't have to spend that money to save the books we already have."

With the adoption of the new paper standard in January, librarians have achieved a moral victory in their battle to get publishers and paper manufacturers to switch to acid-free paper. But the "standard" is just that, it is not a requirement. Without pressure from the majority of consumers, the book industry isn't likely to complete the switch.

Unfortunately, most people don't consider the crisis until a book falls apart in their hands. That is happening more and more frequently. One person described his experience to Carlton Rochell this way: "The front part of the book I took from the shelf was in my left hand, the back was in my right hand, and in between was this yellow snow drifting to the floor." That yellow snow is an idea that has been destroyed.

As classics scholar Gilbert Highet once asserted, "These are not books, lumps of lifeless paper, but minds alive on the shelves. From each of them goes out its own voice and just as the touch of a buttton on our set will fill the room with music, so by taking down one of these volumes and opening it, one can call into range the voice of a man far distant in time and space, and hear him speaking to us, mind to mind, heart to heart."

Unless that voice falls fractured to the library floor in a flurry of yellow snow. ▣

The Channel 16 crew

Information Around the Clock: Atlanta's Channel 16

Ron Chepesiuk

The listings in the television guide read "Realms of the Unknown"—an exploration of paranormal and strange phenomena and "Life in the Universe"—a discussion of the possibility of intelligent life on planets other than earth.

These listings may look like the usual programming guide information about the local educational television station, or perhaps even the commercial station, but they're not. They actually describe programs appearing on the Atlanta-Fulton Public Library's Channel 16 (Cable 5), the country's only library television station to produce programming twenty-four hours a day, seven days a week.

Bob Miller, who oversees the library channel, describes it as "Atlanta's information station, dedicated to providing people with the kinds of information that are readily available in the public library." Channel 16 is also Atlanta's innovative channel, one that obviously is not afraid of experimentation. It is the only library in the country to regularly broadcast its monthly board of trustees meetings.

Located in the APL's central library, the library channel is under the administration of the video department. The spacious new central library stands in the city's downtown business district amidst towering office buildings and hotels next to the Peachtree Center MARTA Station. It has been called "the busiest downtown library in the United States," circulating over 700,000 items and serving more than two million patrons a year.

But in the words of its own administration, it is a "starving library system," one that, when compared to other library systems of similar size throughout the United States, "ends up at the bottom of the heap." Why then a television channel? Considering the basic functions of a library, isn't a round-the-clock television channel a luxury?

An extension of the book

On a recent visit to Atlanta, I posed these questions to the central library's administration. Brenda Knight, the APL's public relations director, says that Channel 16 is definitely not a luxury but serves a unique role. She says, "Like many other agencies, the library believes in using the television screen to help provide information in a way that this generation can relate to. Television broadcasting is just another way of disseminating information to the public. The only difference is that we are bringing it to the patron's house rather than having them come to the library."

Casper Jordan, deputy director of the APL, describes the library as being on the cutting-edge of the new frontiers of librarianship. "Cable television," he explains, "is really an extension of the book, another way of

Ron Chepesiuk *is head of special collections, Dacus Library, Winthrop College, Rock Hill, South Carolina.*

providing information to our users who, in this case, are our viewers." Jordan adds that the station has great utility for the library. "The system is allowing the library to experiment for the future when it expects to increase its electronic capabilities significantly."

Other library staff members believe that cable television is helping the APL deal with a rapidly changing library world. Greg Heid of the film department summed up what many said: "The Atlanta-Fulton Library has to adapt to cable inter-link technologies to facilitate information transfer. Otherwise, we will merely become a warehouse of books and magazines. The public won't think of the library as a place to find current information."

Although the development of the APL's broadcasting capability began over a decade ago, it has only been since 1981 that the library started broadcasting to the public. When the central library was completed that year, it included a small television studio.

Bob Miller, who joined the APL in 1981, talked about Channel 16's beginning. "The library got involved with cable television because of Channel 2001, which had a franchise in Atlanta. The library was approached by city officials who asked if it could make use of the channel. The library administration quickly said yes because it realized that there was potential for the home delivery of information via an existing new method—the television set."

The APL's start in public broadcasting began in September, 1981, when it developed a general program that presented the different types of information to be found in the library. The weekly program is still on the air. Explains Miller, "We may talk about a particular reference tool or have a very practical feature; for instance, a home economist may talk about how to prepare the Thanksgiving dinner."

During that first year, the library's programming was limited to the daytime. In 1982, however, the station

Bob Miller

decided to try to reach a larger audience and began broadcasting during the evening hours. It has had round-the-clock programming ever since.

Miller describes the library's twenty-four-hour programming as the most "amazing thing the video department has done. We really have nothing for staff." There are only two full-time employees: one is in charge of day-to-day programming, while the other is an electronic technician responsible for repairing equipment. In addition, three part-time "library associates" each work thirty hours a week, and a "library aid" works fifteen hours per week.

Miller says that, although staff members do many jobs, each has a specialty. For example, one is involved with editing, another writes, while a third is adept at handling a camera. Miller is the only member of the video department with a library background.

Because of the small staff, other APL departments have tried to help out. APL staff members are allowed to volunteer up to two hours of their time per week to work in the studio. Compensatory time is left to the discretion of the volunteer's supervisor. The channel has also hired what it calls "field contributors"—various specialists who assist in producing programs. Video artists are also brought in to help with production. Occasionally, college and university students are allowed to work at the studio and gain valuable experience. Course credit is given at the discretion of the student's institution.

Each department at the central library has appointed a liaison to the video department. That person is responsible for providing the library channel with information about a particular department, including the programs and services provided, the collections housed, and other pertinent information that may potentially have broadcast value.

The channel's budget is as small as its staff. Miller says that the video department's budget, including salaries, totals $250,000. About $200,000 of this amount is used to run the library's inhouse broadcasting system and television channel.

In 1983 a budget crunch chopped fifty percent of the equipment money. Explains Miller, "Until recently, when the APL was transferred to the county's control, my department was in real bad shape. We were still using the equipment that we started out with in 1976. That's really bad news because video is like the computer industry. It's constantly changing. Each day, there is new and better equipment on the market. Under county control, the department had received its first substantial funding. It has taken some maneuvering to convince people that we needed the equipment to do the job."

Much of the library channel's success can be attributed to Bob Miller's leadership and hard work. He has brought a wealth of video experience to the APL. Miller's video background goes back almost twelve years when he started as a paraprofessional in the New York Public Library.

Miller recalls, "The young adult department of the NYPL got a grant to have a teenage video workshop. I got my first portapack, although I didn't know what it was. I had to learn from scratch."

This experience stimulated Miller's interest in media, so he enrolled in the community media program at Columbia University. The program required that he study almost a full year at New York University's film school. Upon completing the program, Miller moved to Chicago where he taught media courses and, along with two others from the National College of Education in Illinois, built his first studio. Miller began working at the APL in 1981.

Miller's style and personality is stamped on all aspects of production. Most importantly, he has the final say in programming. Although using several methods to decide what to air, Miller says the most important is demand—what the public wants to see.

He gives an example to explain the decision-making process. "We have a program called 'Healthy, Wealthy, and Wise.' One of our staff members is interested in paranormal psychology. He did a segment on the program about tarot cards. People kept calling in and asking for that particular segment. We then did a survey and found it was very difficult to find this type of information in the books on the shelves. We had a winner. That is how 'Realms of the Unknown' started. The response has been tremendous."

Miller has different ways to measure viewer response. One of his favorite ways is the "big brain quiz." He says, "We ask a question. If a person phones in and gets the right answer, he receives a prize. To encourage phone calls, we mention the winner's name over the air, praising him as a big brain."

The printing of the televison guide provides another good measurement method. Viewers get a free television guide if they write or call the station. "In addition, we mail them a form," says Miller, "that asks a series of questions. How did you learn about the free guide? How much do you watch Channel 16? And so on. These names also allow us to compile a mailing list that has proved quite useful."

Interactive information

Despite limited resources, Channel 16 has managed to bring a very creative touch to broadcasting, especially in producing live television programs. "On Line" is what Miller calls "an interactive information program designed to connect people to the experts by using cable as a funnel." He sees this process of information exchange as similar to what a librarian at a reference desk might do. "If a patron comes into the library and asks a reference question," he explains, "the librarian will give him a book that might help. Instead of books, we provide people that help."

Televising the library's board of trustees meetings can't be considered a creative project, but Miller believes it has been effective nevertheless. "A board meeting may look rather dull on television," he says, "but when an issue affects people and their communities, you can bet your boots that they will be watching."

In 1982 the library board was divided evenly about whether to televise board meetings. The chairman broke the tie, and the channel began broadcasting them. After a six-month trial period, the board meetings became a regular part of the programming schedule. The monthly meetings are aired live and then video-taped for rebroadcast during the week. Miller believes that the telecastings have helped take the mystery out of the board meetings. Trustees have frequently been stopped by people in the street who watch the televised board meetings.

The library channel also plays an important role in the central library's efforts to reach out to the community, providing yearly support for various library-sponsored events. The Black History Essay contest, the Friends Author Christmas Show, and Opera Week are examples.

The library channel has even found the time for some self-promotion. Last year it sponsored a logo contest to choose the station's official design. The contest was open to the general public with the exception of Fulton County employees and their families. All of the winning designs are now used as library channel identifiers, on promotional pieces and as equipment decals.

Despite its initial success, the video department continues searching for ways to improve its programming and to increase its financial support. An APL programming study indicates ninety-seven percent of all programs shown on the library channel are repeats. According to a recent department report, plans are in the works to seek grant money and other funding sources for the additional staff needed to increase the production volume as well as improve quality control. The money will also be used to purchase special equipment.

The same report states that "funding and continued support is more easily attracted by an organization with a proven track record." One major departmental goal for 1985 is to win a prestigious award. To do this, the department plans to enter projects in several contests during the year.

Do what you do best

As for the future of Channel 16, Miller says that it is inextricably linked with the cable industry. "American cable television is in a survival mode right now," explains Miller. "The industry has been operating in a deficit for the past four or five years. I see major bankruptcies coming. If the industry is going to make it, it will be in the next five years."

Miller says that the cable television industry has tried to be too much like commercial television. He believes that it must stop thinking in terms of entertainment. If it does, he then foresees libraries playing a big role in the industry's future.

To any library interested in developing a cable television station, Miller advises, "Don't try to do what commercial television does. Do what you do best. Give the public hard information. Look for ways to use cable television as a means of providing people with information that you are already providing. The ideas are out there. But you have to think imaginatively to pull them in." ▣

Dale Nelson:

Dateline Washington

Government overprinting

When the Reagan administration came into office in 1981, government files indicated federal agencies had 234 printing plants scattered around the world. By the time the new team at the Office of Management and Budget had finished checking, it turned out that there were in fact about 1,000.

"No systems existed to identify unnecessary publications and to curb wasteful spending," OMB says in a new report on government management mandated by Congress. The report outlines savings made during President Reagan's first term and details future plans including greater OMB control over agency publication programs. It says the government was spending more than $165 million per year to publish and distribute approximately 16,000 publications at the time the "Reagan revolution" began.

Since then, it boasts, 3,848 publications have been eliminated or consolidated—amounting to 150 million individual documents or about 25 percent of the total federal inventory. The report says costs of an additional 3,100 publications have been reduced and further savings of approximately $71 million are expected this year.

In addition, OMB is revising its rules to set up an annual approval process for periodicals and require continued monitoring of publications programs. The new rules are due out in late spring.

The report says the first inventory of federal printing and duplicating facilities, made in 1983, showed that in some cases there was more than one plant in the same geographic area, in the same city, and even in the same federal building. It noted, "Many of the presses were underutilized, overstaffed, and operated at more than three times the cost of private printers."

Agreements were negotiated with agencies to eliminate or downgrade 111 printing plants, cutting 564 full time equivalent positions and saving $11 million in fiscal year 1985. Savings by 1988 are estimated at $38 million.

Most of these investigations have been in civilian agencies, but the Defense Department is conducting onsite regional studies of a cross-section of its nationwide printing and duplicating facilities. A report and recommendations are expected by the end of the year.

Speaking of printing and publications, if you want more information about this, you can order government document S/N 041-001-00287-1, "Management of the United States Government; Fiscal Year 1986" from the Superintendent of Documents, Government Printing Office, for $3.75.

OCLC scoreboard

Henry Kissinger far outdistances William Shakespeare in popularity on the nation's library shelves, but neither of them can hold a candle to the authors of *Anglo-American Cataloguing Rules*.

At least that's the conclusion of OCLC in Dublin, Ohio, which compiled a list of the top forty books from its records of volumes held by about 4,000 libraries.

OCLC didn't say what its list was supposed to prove. What it may prove is that a computer can't tell you much about what actually goes on in a library.

According to the study, *Anglo-American Cataloguing Rules* is the fourth most commonly shelved book. But that is because it is a standard book on cataloging that most libraries would need for their own purposes.

On the other hand, almost any library has volume after volume of the works of Shakespeare. But he doesn't show up in the top forty at all, because the computer counts each edition of a work as a separate book.

Phil Scheiber, the center's manager of public relations, told a reporter that there are almost 12,000 entries

Dale Nelson *is a journalist who covers the Washington scene for WLB.*

on the computerized list for various editions of Shakespeare's plays and poems. For the same reason the list misses the Bible, the book most commonly cited as the best seller of all time. Kissinger's *White House Years* ranks thirtieth on the list of forty. At the top of the list is *Megatrends* by John Naisbitt, a best selling analysis of changes in contemporary life.

Presidents and preservation up

President Reagan's proposed budget for presidential libraries may raise eyebrows on Capitol Hill, where some lawmakers have been fretting over the rising costs associated with former presidents.

For the first time this year, it will cost more than $1 million to keep just one of the libraries going. The Lyndon B. Johnson Presidential Library in Austin, Texas, is slated for a shade over a million in the Reagan budget.

The budget also includes $4.7 million to build an annex building and a boat dock for the John F. Kennedy Presidential Library in Boston. Members of Congress who have questioned the value of the museum functions of the libraries are likely to take a long look at that boat dock.

Elsewhere in the $100 million budget for the National Archives and Records Administration, Reagan is proposing for the fourth straight year to eliminate the grants program operated by the National Historical Publications and Records Commission. The commission provides about $5 million in grants each year to help state and local governments compile and preserve records. So far, Congress has kept the program alive.

The biggest increase in the Archives budget is for preservation, which would be allotted about $3 million as the first step in a twenty-year plan to improve preservation of the three billion pages of records the agency is responsible for. The agency would expand its staff by seventy-six persons to do the added preservation work.

La Follettes memorialized

The late Wisconsin senators Robert M. La Follette and Robert M. La Follette, Jr. are best remembered as supporters of such progressive causes as direct primary elections, conservation of forests, and the rights of labor. But they were also pioneers in the use of libraries as a legislative tool, and they are being remembered for that role by the Library of Congress.

On March 4, the library dedicated the reading room of the Congressional Research Service as the La Follette Congressional Reading Room.

La Follette, Sr. established a legislative reference service for Wisconsin when he was governor and later, as senator, sponsored an amendment that created the Legislative Reference Service within LC in 1914. La Follette, Jr. played a key role in passage of the 1946 Legislative Reorganization Act, which greatly expanded the role of the reference service.

Anne McGrath:

Eye on Publishing

Soviet novel, bestseller in France, to be published here

A scathingly critical account of life under the Soviet Union's Stalinist system, published by Julliard in France as part of its dissident literature series under the title *Vie et Destin,* will be brought out in the United States this fall by Harper & Row, a quarter of a century after the manuscript was completed. *Life and Destiny* is the long-suppressed novel by Vassili Grossman, a novelist whose work was pro-Soviet—and even merited a Stalin Prize—before he learned the horrible extent of the Holocaust and saw his own motherland enforce anti-Semitic policies after the war. Grossman died in the Soviet Union in 1964, several years after his attempt to publish the novel at home led to its confiscation by the KGB, along with all his notes and drafts.

According to a companion volume also published by Julliard, *Le Cas Grossman* by Simon Markish, Grossman served as a war correspondent during the Battle of Stalingrad and the fall of Berlin. His discovery of the existence of concentration camps led him to co-write a book critical of the Holocaust in 1943 that was no sooner written than destroyed. The post-war publication of his account of a Jewish family and the siege of Stalingrad put him in immediate disrepute with the state; that experience cemented his resolve to expose the injustices of the Soviet system. *Life and Destiny,* which builds on the experiences of his fictional Jewish family and depicts the siege and Battle of Stalingrad, the Holocaust, the bitter famines of the Ukraine, and the horrors of the Soviet prisons, was completed in 1960. The manuscript was brought to light years later, reports *Le Cas Grossman,* by a Soviet dissident who managed to get it out of the country in 1980.

Anne McGrath, *a freelance writer based in New York City, covers the publishing world for WLB.*

Encyclopaedia Britannica further revamped.

In 1974, the 200-plus-year-old *Encyclopaedia Britannica,* the oldest reference work of its kind in the English language, took a revolutionary approach with its fifteenth edition. Rather than arranging entries alphabetically in one sequence, the fifteenth edition presented information in three ways. A new ten-volume Micropaedia provided succinct 750-word summaries on its multitude of topics; a nineteen-volume Macropaedia presented long and thoughtful discussions by experts of broader, significant subjects; and a Propaedia, in one volume, set forth ten categories of knowledge. In March a further revamped *Britannica* was published, a revised fifteenth edition, in a $24 million effort on the part of the Chicago company to improve upon its 1974 concept.

The revised edition consists of thirty-two volumes, two of which provide a new and much-needed index. The Micropaedia now has twelve volumes and contains some 86,000 entries, including most of the encyclopedia's biographies. The Macropaedia, which previously offered more than 4,200 articles by such scholars as Linus Pauling, Milton Friedman, and Arthur Koestler, now presents its discussions under only 681 headings; most of these are now book-length. The World Data Annual, another innovation, reviews events of the preceding year and surveys statistical information about some 200 countries. All told, the revised edition boasts signed contributions by approximately 4,000 specialists, one-third of which were originally written in more than fifty foreign languages and translated.

Publishing shuffle at Gulf & Western

The world's largest publishing company (sales for 1985 are expected to top $800 million) has announced a reorganization that puts six broad categories of publishing operations under one umbrella. Richard Snyder, who has headed Simon & Schuster since Gulf & Western acquired it in 1975 and has been its chairman since 1981, will preside over the new G & W Publishing and Information Resources Group. Six group presidents, each directing the activity of one of the new units, will report to him. Prentice-Hall, the educational publisher added to the Gulf & Western publishing stable last December, becomes part of the new Education Group.

Simon & Schuster, the backbone of the Publishing and Information Resources Group, takes its place under Jack Romanos as the mainstay of the Trade Publishing Group. Romanos, whose career has taken him from Fawcett through the ranks at Bantam to the position of publisher there, will also oversee trade paperbacks, Pocket Books, juvenile books, and audio and visual publishing.

The General Reference Group will handle publication of the Webster's dictionaries and the Prentice-Hall trade books. Travel guides, J. K. Lasser books, Brady computer books, and all software publishing for personal computers will also be part of this group, under the direction of Frank Schwartz, who has headed electronic publishing at Simon & Schuster since 1983.

John Davis, who has worked in a number of capacities for Prentice-Hall during his thirty-year career there, most recently as president of the College Division, will take charge of the new Education Group. (Donald Schaefer, formerly president of P-H, intends to work with the company as a consultant.) Elementary and secondary school textbooks, college texts, and vocational materials under the P-H, Allyn & Bacon, Globe, Reston, and Cambridge Book Co. imprints, among others, will be published by this group.

The Business Information and Training Group merges the business book publishing operations of Prentice-Hall with information services of the Executive Reports Corporation and the Bureau of Business Practice. Resource Systems International, the New York Institute for Finance, and Deltak join the group as well. Robert Martin, whose responsibilities with Prentice-Hall's Business and Professional Books Division have been extensive, heads the new group. Edward Hutton of Prentice-Hall takes charge of the Professional Information Services Group, which is to handle medical books, Appleton-Century-Crofts journals, the P-H tax services, and Brentwood's trade magazines.

Finally, an International Group has been formed that will join Simon & Schuster's International Division with Esquire and P-H's foreign operations.

1984: A great year for bestsellers

The *Publishers Weekly* roundup of last year's bestsellers (in the March 15 issue) pointed out some interesting facts. For one thing, 1984 saw an amazing feat by the hottest seller ever, *Iacocca.* The autobiography by Chrysler's head sold more than a million copies inside of two months. So many copies of so many bestsellers were bought last year that *PW* stretched its runners-up lists from ten to fifteen—and still left several books that hit the 100,000 unit sales mark off the fiction and non-fiction lists. For the first time since 1977, nary a first novelist showed up among the top fiction sellers—and only three of the top fifteen novels this year were by first-timers on the list! The number-one novel, *The Talisman,* enjoyed the largest-ever (600,000 copies) first printing for a hardcover novel. Below, last year's most popular books:

Fiction: *The Talisman* by Stephen King and Peter Straub (Viking); *The Aquitaine Progression* by Robert Ludlum (Random House); *The Sicilian* by Mario Puzo (Linden Press/Simon & Schuster); *Love and War* by John Jakes (Harcourt Brace Jovanovich); *The Butter Battle Book* by Dr. Seuss (Random House); *. . . And Ladies of the Club* by Helen Hooven Santmyer (Putnam); *The Fourth Protocol* by Frederick Forsyth (Viking); *Full Circle* by Danielle Steele (Delacorte); *The Life and Hard Times of Heidi Abromowitz* by Joan Rivers (Delacorte); *Lincoln: A Novel* by Gore Vidal (Random House); *The Walking Drum* by Louis L'Amour (Bantam); *The Haj* by Leon Uris (Doubleday); *Strong Medicine* by Arthur Hailey (Doubleday); *First Among Equals* by Jeffrey Archer (Linden Press/Simon & Schuster); and *The Dune Storybook* adapted by Joan D. Vinge (Putnam).

Nonfiction: *Iacocca: An Autobiography* by Lee Iacocca with William Novak (Bantam Books); *Loving Each Other* by Leo Buscaglia (Slack/Holt, Rinehart & Winston); *Eat to Win: The Sports Nutrition Bible* by Robert Haas, M.D. (Rawson Associates); *Pieces of My Mind* by Andrew A. Rooney (Atheneum); *Weight Watchers Fast and Fabulous Cookbook* by Weight Watchers International (NAL Books); *What They Don't Teach You at Harvard Business School: Notes from a Street-Smart Executive* by Mark H. McCormack (Bantam Books); *Women Coming of Age* by Jane Fonda with Mignon McCarthy (Simon & Schuster); *Moses the Kitten* by James Herriot (St. Martin's Press); *The One Minute Salesperson* by Spencer Johnson, M.D. and Larry Wilson (Morrow); *Weight Watchers Quick Start Program Cookbook* by Jean Nidetch (NAL Books); *Chef Paul Prudhomme's Louisiana Kitchen* by Paul Prudhomme (Morrow); *Putting the One Minute Manager to Work* by Kenneth Blanchard and Robert Lorber (Morrow); *Tough Times Never Last, but Tough People Do!* by Robert H. Schuller (Thomas Nelson); *The Bridge Across Forever* by Richard Bach (Morrow); and *Dr. Burns' Prescription for Happiness* by George Burns (Putnam).

Will Manley:

Facing the Public

"It says here you were loitering, gambling, and carrying a concealed weapon. Sounds like you've been at the public library again."

During spring break one year I was in college I had some research to do for an Irish history class. The term paper I was working on had to do with the origins of leprechaun mythology. Since my university library was closed, I went to the local branch of the county library.

This turned out to be a mistake because this place had been turned into a kind of circus by a new librarian named Mr. Procter. Frankly I thought the guy was more qualified to be a motorcycle mechanic because the day I was there he was giving a program on how to repair motorcycles. His audience consisted of what appeared to be a ring of pre-adolescent Hells Angels in training. He had an old Harley-Davidson strewn around in pieces throughout the main reading room on oily newspapers. To find the book you wanted you had to step over a carburetor, fender, and headlight. Feeling some frustration, I went up to Procter and asked him if the library had any books on leprechauns. He looked at me quizzically and said, "What's that, some new kind of mini-bike?"

So I decided to get on the train with my roommate and visit the Chicago Public Library. Actually it wasn't much better. It seemed like everytime I turned around I bumped into an elderly gentleman with a scraggly beard and a runny nose who kept trying to tell me that the Cubs were going to win the pennant. Or else there was some old shopping bag lady sitting next to me breathing real loud as though she'd just jogged through two miles miles of smog. But the most unique incident of the day occurred when two bums (Joe and Lubie) started hassling over the newspaper.

What happened was that Joe had fallen asleep on top of the early morning edition of the *Chicago Sun-Times.* This made Lubie mad because he had been waiting a half-hour to read it. So he tried grabbing it away from Joe who suddenly awoke when he felt the sports section slipping away from under his face. Then Joe got mad and poked Lubie in the face with the wooden rod that the paper was attached to. Not to be outdone, Lubie reached back into the newspaper rack and pulled out the Sunday edition of the *New York Times* and began using its rod as a sword.

What I thought was unfortunate was the fact that my roommate and I were the only ones who seemed to be paying attention to them. He had his money on Joe and I favored Lubie. Everyone else was either buried in a book or just staring at the floor. Apparently this was just another day at the library.

Pretty soon you'd have thought they were holding the Olympic fencing championship right there in the reading room as Joe and Lubie went at it like a couple of real swashbucklers. Finally a security guard, who was insanely waving a gun around, came and took them away, though not before Lubie had smashed Joe twice on the head with the *Times.*

Just when I was finishing taking some notes a guy wearing an African jungle helmet and an orange shirt decorated with swaying palm trees came up and asked me, "What is time?" I glanced at my watch and said "5:05."

"No, what *is* time?" he asked again.

"Well, time is, well, it's time," I answered exasperated.

He looked at me very seriously and said, "You are a wise man." Then he walked away quickly.

My roommate, who had been reading some back issues of the *National Geographic,* glanced up at me and

---

Will Manley *is director of the Tempe (Arizona) Public Library.*

shook his head with a smile. "Better check your wallet," he joked. "Nobody calls you a wise man in Chicago unless they're after your money."

Even though he was trying to be funny I instinctively felt against my back pocket. My God. No wallet. I rushed over to the security officer who appeared to be a really young guy, maybe nineteen or twenty. He had one of those really thick beards that comes right up to the eyes. I got the funny feeling I was talking to a Muppet.

"I got ripped off!" I yelled at him as if it were his fault.

"Hey, man, slow down. Now, what happened?"

"I got pickpocketed."

"Do you know who did it?"

"Yeah, that guy in the jungle helmet who wanted to know what time is."

"Oh no, you don't mean Willie, the Cubs fanatic, do you?"

"Who's he? The guy with gross whiskers and a runny nose?" I asked.

"Yeah, that's Willie," he answered with a nod of the head.

"Then, no, it wasn't Willie. It was the guy with the jungle helmet."

Suddenly he remembered. "Oh, that guy. I've seen him around before," he said. Then he drew out his pistol and began looking around the library—under chairs, behind bookshelves, and even in the back of a huge lighted globe by the newspaper rack. You'd think he was trying to hunt down a rabbit for heaven's sake.

"I guess he's not here anymore," the guard finally said.

"What should I do now?" I asked.

"Get a new wallet," he answered.

On my way back to the train station my roommate and I bumped into one of Chicago's finest. I told him about my misadventure at the library. "What are two nice boys like you doing in a place like that?" he asked as if we had been in the corner tavern.

"Don't kid yourself," said the officer, "I know some pool halls I'd feel safer in. The library is full of sharpies. The guy you have to especially watch out for is the one with the real thick beard who wears a security guard suit and packs a pistol. The suit is from the Salvation Army and the pistol is a water gun. He's already spent half his life at the Mental Research Center. Now, look, I feel sorry for you guys getting pickpocketed, but stay away from that library."

Anyone who has habitually frequented public libraries either as an employee or as a user has met with a wide variety of people including the types I met in Chicago a number of years ago. That, of course, is the public library's uniqueness as a quasi-cultural educational institution. Young people rub shoulders with old people as they grovel for the latest bestsellers. Rich kids make as much noise in story hour as poor kids. The well educated are as apt to attend a great books discussion group as the poorly educated. And, of course, overdue book delinquencies are totally non-discriminatory. They cut across all barriers of religon, sex, or age. All studies indicate that that copy of "The Snows of Kilimanjaro" which has been overdue for eight weeks is as likely to be held by a young Caucasian male as it is by an elderly Oriental female.

The public library is then the common ground for all kinds of cultural, informational, educational, and recreational interests of a widely diverse clientele. We can complain all we want about understaffing, poor pay, long evening hours, weekend schedules, and inadequate working conditions, but the fact remains that the vast majority of us remain in the field of public library work because, unlike most occupations, our daily, workaday world is a quickly changing, always varied set of challenges calling for us to use all our formal training, and all our informal street smarts. The irony always amuses me when I'm on an airplane and the man in the three-piece suit sitting next to me asks, "What do you do?" You know from his Brooks Brothers suit, his manicured nails, his Gucci shoes, and his Pierre Cardin tie that he's something boring like an attorney, a business executive, or a computer systems salesman. But when you tell him that you're a librarian he shakes his head and says something patronizing like "nice quiet work, but I imagine it's secure." If only the world knew what we know.

We could all regale many an unsuspecting fellow airplane traveler with stories about the time the Olympic fencing championship was held on the second floor of the library, the time two young boys brought in a fifteen-foot live snake to identify, or the day you discovered that the "good old boy" reference room regular, who wears the spectacles held together by Band-Aids, the necktie speckled with chili sauce from a taco eaten in the 1950s, and the double pin-striped pants propped up by suspenders like worn our rubber bands, is actually a millionaire who uses *Standard and Poor's* not as a pillow, but as an investment guide.

Unfortunately, however, out strong commitment to providing services, our unflagging energy in solving problems, our admirable openness in helping others, irrespective of who they are and what they look like, has sometimes been abused. Because we, more than most municipal workers, take seriously the term "public servant" we are at times taken advantage of and treated as "public slaves."

Public libraries everywhere are to an increasing degree becoming refuges for the homeless, the mentally disturbed, the violently insane, and the sexually perverted. Because of this unfortunate fact of life the off-beat situations that front-line librarians have always been confronted with in their daily duty of facing the public are shifting from the realm of tragicomedy to just plain tragedy. Correspondingly the lives of these librarians are becoming more stressful and less satisfying. The very aspect of our lives that we previously found fulfilling—the opportunity to bring a diversity of books together with a diversity of people—is now becoming alarmingly fraught with tension and fear. The anti-social behavior of a minority of users is souring the process of serving the ma-

(continued on page 639)

Patricia Berglund:

School Library Technology

A chapter in the new edition of the classic *Children and Books* argues that computers can replace books for the teaching and enjoying of reading. "You can sit and hold a child and read a story from the computer just as well as from a book," writes Dr. Philip Turner, of the University of Alabama Graduate School of Library Science. "You can tell a story to a group of kindergartners from a terminal. I don't think there's anything in a book per se that will appeal to children more than a color computer terminal. We must discard our prejudices against reading on the computer."

I consider myself modern, liberal, a computer proponent—but what a reactionary I turn out to be when I hear such a proposal.

Turner is especially in favor of interactive computer fiction such as the Twistaplot stories on Scholastic's Microzine disks. In this type of software, the child reads a portion of the plot on the computer screen and then types in the answer to the question, "What do you want to do?" The computer program branches to different segments of the plot depending on the child's answer. The child, rather than the author, thus controls the development of the story.

The computer also has the ability to personalize a story. The child may type in his or her name and the name of a friend, and the ensuing story will weave those names into the plot.

Children may well enjoy what they do on the computer with Dr. Turner's type of program, but the activity they are engaged in is not what I mean by *reading.*

In *The Second Self,* Sherry Turkle points out that many young children think computers are alive. When children read books, they are interacting with their own thoughts and feelings, developing their imaginations, responding to the various shapes, sizes, and textures of the physical book. Children reading from computer screens will be denied this private voyage of discovery. They will be attached to a machine, one to which they may attribute living powers. Every story will be delivered to them on the same screen while they sit in the same relative position. They may be performing the physical act of decoding, but I will cry "No, no, no," until my dying day to the proposition that this stultifying activity is as good as, or better than, reading a book.

Author Irving Stone writes, "Books change lives. They enrich lives. They push back horizons. They bring understanding along with joy." John Milton knew that books were something beyond a means of communicating information: "Books . . . contain a potency of life in them. . . . [They are] the precious lifeblood of a master spirit," he wrote. "Reading a good novel is a one-on-one experience that a movie can never quite duplicate," columnist Bob Greene says. I have a feeling that if asked he would include computers with movies.

If you didn't develop a love for books in your younger years, no quotations from famous people or words of mine will convince you that they are special. If you don't know it now, you probably will never know how the words of an inspired writer, the feel and smell of a book and the security of a favorite reading corner combine to make life more worthwhile. However, I have an abiding belief in the power of books and libraries to make life better; and I want today's children to have the opportunity to adopt that same philosophy.

In my own childhood and early adult years, it was not socially suspect to love books. The reading child was well thought of, and adults who read were likewise admired. I didn't really notice that trouble was brewing until the explosion of media libraries in the early seventies. I was given an indication when I read a media center director's claim that reading was elitist in the April/May, 1974 issue of *K-Eight.* Teacher Irene Zabawski declared that reading was an obsolete style of learning. "Pushing reading as the way to get information is foolish and useless," she said as she argued for self-education through television and films. Happily for me, Zabawski and her supporters did not prevail. Children did watch more and more television, but, officially at least, reading books remained a linchpin of education.

What happened to change the way children read was not TV, but the appearance of The Test as the almighty judge of reading. The Test was whatever standardized test the school district used to measure the degree of skills mastery in your city against that of neighboring cities. If your students failed silent e's while the next district's kids excelled in medial i's, you were in trouble. Administrators lived and died by test scores, and they turned to an impressive array of reading machines, workbooks, and flashcards to produce the treasured headline, "Reading scores go up."

A few perceptive individuals began to see what that headline really meant: "We produce good little decoders in this area." Some people penetrated the sham further with questions such as: "Our children have good reading scores, but do they actually like to read? Do they feel comfortable and competent about finding information that they need to live pro-

Patricia Berglund *is a librarian in the San Francisco Unified School District.*

ductive lives?"

I thought we were on the brink of using the solution that had seemed so obvious to me all along: make classes smaller and increase children's contact with teachers and librarians who know how to foster a love of reading and learning.

Alas, the microcomputer then entered the field of reading education. How much easier this machine will make the automated delivery of separate decoding skills. How much faster it will be to keep those lengthy record sheets of individual skill mastery. Administrators will feel oh-so-au courant when they report to parents that their children are in a computerized reading program. Teachers will be relieved that they don't have to spend so much time filling in dots on the student checklists.

If you seek to oppose such a program, you embark on a very risky venture. There is nothing in the education field today that begins to compare with the clout of the computer. A high school librarian told me that kids who used to argue until they were blue in the face about overdues meekly accept their fate now that circulation is computerized. If the computer says it's so, it must be so, they believe. If the printout of the skills checklist says the kid is a reader, can I convince anyone that he isn't really?

I do have some allies who will help me try. Susan Ohanian is a former reading teacher and currently is contributing editor of *Classroom Computer Learning*. Working for a computer magazine, she of course supports computers in the schools. Yet her perceptive article, "How Today's Reading Software Can Zap Kids' Desire to Read" (November/December 1984) offers hope to those of us who think reading books is what reading is all about.

"When all is said and done," she writes, "the computer is not going to stimulate much reading. Reading a screen filled with type is neither amusing nor inspiring. . . . Certainly it is not something we should inflict on children we are trying to encourage as readers."

She continues, "I don't see reading as a steady progression along carefully sequenced rungs of skill development. The skill-and-drill fix is about as helpful to children's intellectual development as sucking on jujubes."

According to Ohanian, children need teachers who are passionately and personally involved with books. "Disk-drive partisans justify their use of computers by bragging about the bonanza of immediate feedback. . . . If a child is to become a reader he must be willing to take risks. Do we want to be too quick to label such risks as error?. . . . And then there is impersonal feedback. Now there's a notion to make a granite wall weep. I want my students to become personally involved with books—to puzzle over them, laugh over them and, when necessary, to get angry with them. . . . I did not become a teacher to replace enthusiasm with anomie."

Ohanian understands how powerful a force computers are in education. She notes that bureaucrats can find thousand of dollars for computerized reading programs at the same time they are laying off librarians for lack of money. Such electronic programs may be convenient, but "we must demand more of our reading paraphernalia. We must insist that it be good for our kids," she says. "Software reviewers . . . seldom measure the electronic hugger-mugger against, say, *Charlotte's Web* or *King Arthur* or *Never Cry Wolf*. . . . One good book is worth 1,000 floppy disks."

Library conferences now routinely feature computer workshops. Any state, regional or national library conference will include the obligatory sessions on comparisons of library management software, tips on computer maintenance or programming, curriculum guides, demonstrations of educational programs, and reports on circulation or cataloging software. There are certainly many people still seeking answers to questions in these areas, and I do not suggest that we abandon such courses.

We must, however, guard against a certain smug self-satisfaction. We cannot suppose that with symposia of this kind we have sufficiently covered the computer field. We cannot believe that the only computer topics with which we must concern ourselves are ever increasing technical expertise and software awareness.

Publishers Weekly reports a boom in the production of computerized fiction for young people. Turner's *Children and Books* chapter encourages the substitution of CRTs for books. Something radical is happening in our world. If we do not pay professional attention to it now, traditional reading by children may be swept away before the computer juggernaut in our lifetime. ▣

Donnarae MacCann/Olga Richard:

Picture Books for Children

Greedy Zebra

A beast fable with a picture book format is a considerable improvement over an unadorned version. Animal antics have often been converted into object lessons, with the instructive purpose overshadowing the cast of characters. However, the beasts in a well-designed picture book parable are important in their own right. They are presented to the reader in their formal beauty and they are often surrounded by a rich environment. Adrienne Kennaway shows what can be done in **Greedy Zebra** (text by Mwenye Hadithi). Her designs match the ingenuity of Hadithi's cautionary myth about how the animals of the world came to be variously patterned.

It all happened in a far-off time when creatures were uniformly and monotonously gray. Zebra was too greedy to stop eating, and he arrived late at the gathering where animals decked themselves out in new, flashy garments. Only a few pieces of black cloth remained when Zebra finally decided to pause a moment in his dining. They made a fine suit, but Zebra's appetite for leafy bushes made all the seams pop open; thus the illusory stripes. We are really seeing a creature in an undersized suit with split seams.

Kennaway's stylized treatment of Zebra is in tune with her many rhythmic clusters of plants, animals, hills, and valleys. In order to highlight vibrant patterns, she uses an abstract style with a great sense of abandon. Distortions in shape suit the compositional needs, as when tree limbs are extended to take care of what would have been a bland corner, or when animal sizes are scaled to the aesthetic needs of the space.

The illustrator uses a palette of many hues, but some of the most successful color ideas are found on pages where her color range is more restricted. For example, on the page where the zebra's "tubby tummy squeezed through the seams," the artist is underscoring strong value contrasts, rather than the exotic range of color that defines the jungle environment in other parts of the book. In general, Kennaway's design sense is consistent, and her pages are exciting in their abundance of flowing, vigorous, visual ideas.

At the opposite pole from the cautionary element of this beast fable is the extravagant farce of an alphabet book such as Jane Bayer's **A My Name Is Alice** (illustrated by Steven Kellogg). It is a superlative blend of visual and textual nonsense because the visual surprises keep the repetitive pattern in the text from becoming tedious. The verbal parts gradually expand in their ludicrousness, in their cataloging of zany characters and occupations. The first page reveals the sequence that is repeated throughout:

> A my name is Alice and my husband's name is Alex.
> We come from Alaska and we sell ants.
> Alice is an APE. Alex is an ANTEATER.

Such bland assertions have no special charm until they begin to mount up. There is Doris and Dave who sell dust, Gertrude and George who sell giggles, Rosie and Richard who sell rubbish, and so on. The silliness becomes contagious.

The pair reproduced here—two Xigertlings who sell Xofersizers—are the only purely fanciful extensions to the known world. This page is one of Kellogg's best because it is not as agonizingly detailed as the others. Kellogg's technique is looser and fresher in this illustration—more rhythmically and delicately detailed in both line and color. It is sketchier, and not burdened with "rendering" techniques. It would be interesting to see an entire book in this style, a lighter, more original, and somehow more contemporary mood. Portraits of the Xigertlings and the small mouse in the lower corner of the page suggest a century-long culture gap in illustration styles. The contrast is seen again where Hannah and Henry are riding a surf board. Kellogg gives us some gorgeous, frothy water as this hippo and hamster hawk their harps.

The "pure Kellogg" cast in the rest of the book amuse us with incredibly detailed costumes, absurd posturings, and the slapstick dilemmas that arise from selling noodles by the running inch or emu eggs in boxes of exactly eight. All the scenes are expertly drawn and comically intricate, but it may be time for Kellogg to explore some of the aesthetic directions sug-

Olga Richard *and* **Donnarae MacCann** *are the authors of* The Child's First Books.

gested in the "X" page—to let children see some of the marvelous drawing that gets smothered in many Kellogg designs, but turns up in the Xigertling's feet!

Tony Auth's cartooning in **Mean Murgatroyd and the Ten Cats** (text by Nathan Zimelman) is an example of how humor and stylistic originality can blend. Auth's art is spontaneous, fresh, bold. He combines color and line in a unique manner, using line to contour some objects, but a combination of line and color in other images. For example, in the illustration reproduced here, the line on the heroine's leg stops, then color is used for some of the form, then line continues again. At times the objects are drawn completely, but more often the specifics are left to the viewer to fill in. This technique—a studied incompleteness—brings tremendous action and energy to the illustration. There is a visual tempo that is in keeping with the narrative line: the proverbial chase when dogs gang up on cats.

Mean Murgatroyd and the Ten Cats

The cats in this case belong to Arabella, who decides that a lion companion would be the best way to deal with the lawless canine leader, Murgatroyd. Since the zoo keeper and pet dealer are fresh out of lions, Arabella makes do with a lion suit from the local costume shop. The overbearing bulldog doesn't know the difference, and child readers have the pleasure of seeing the child protagonist as problem-solver; as protector of her large, amiable cat family.

Zimelman's minimal text is as speedy as Auth's rendition of Arabella and her pets. However this author/illustrator compatibility is not repeated in the illustrator/book designer teamwork. The beauty of a page depends upon a pleasing synthesis of typeface and illustration. In Arabella's story, the type intrudes upon the illustration, and the typeface style is too heavy and large to be well-suited to Auth's graphic style. Auth's work has the liveliness and improvisational quality that demands some breathing space. The tinted pages work fairly well since the background color subdues the type, enabling the illustration and type to blend to a degree. This kind of accommodation should have been made throughout the book. The publisher's inattentiveness to book design is surprising in this case because Auth is a Pulitzer Prize-winning cartoonist. It is glaringly apparent that his work for children warranted a felicitous showcase. ▣

A My Name Is Alice

This month's books

Hadithi, Mwenye. *Greedy Zebra.* Illus. by Adrienne Kennaway. Little, Brown and Co., 1984. $10.95. ISBN 0–316–33721–8

Bayer, Jane. *A My Name Is Alice.* Illus. by Steven Kellogg. Dial Books for Young Readers, 1984. $10.95. ISBN 0–8037–0124–1 LC 84–7059

Zimelman, Nathan. *Mean Murgatroyd and the Ten Cats.* Illus. by Tony Auth. E.P. Dutton, 1984. $9.95. ISBN 0–525–44116–6 LC 84–1635

Patty Campbell:

The Young Adult Perplex

"Black and White, Unwed All Over" punned *Time* in the title of a 1981 article that laid out the dimensions of the teen pregnancy epidemic. Today's facts are too appalling for humor. An international study released in March by the Guttmacher Institute laid the statistics directly on our national doorstep. The United States has the highest rate of unwed teenage pregnancy in the Western world—ninety-six per thousand girls aged between fifteen and nineteen. Among the thirty-six other developed countries studied, those with the lowest teen pregnancy rates were also those with the most liberal attitudes toward sex education and contraception. Conservatives who blame the epidemic on the teaching of family planning are having a hard time refuting this clear evidence. Guttmacher Institute president Jeanie Rosoff claims that in industrial societies worldwide, sexual activity begins at an earlier age because young people are healthier and mature earlier. When confronted with the ideal of abstinence until marriage by an opponent on the "MacNeil-Lehrer Report," she responded realistically. "Well, that seems to me perfectly fine, but when the behavior of other human beings does not conform to the ideal, what do you do?"—an urgent question for conservatives and liberals alike.

One thing we can do as youth advocates—besides keeping our sex ed collections up-to-date and highly visible—is to be aware of the sexual attitudes and expectations that are being taught to young adults in books that are not usually defined as sex education. There are many romances, for example, in which sexual feelings are euphemized as "tingles," and in which, after one passionate (but never French) kiss, the boy pulls away and suggests nobly that maybe it's time to go home now. A girl who in real life floats dreamily off on a date with such a script in mind is likely to come home pregnant, if not this Saturday night, then next week, or the week after. Virginity should be armored with values and knowledge, not sweet dreams. This knowledge has been kept in a compartment labeled "sex education" and the romantic feelings in another, and too many girls are not making the connection. God forbid that anybody in a romance novel should ever carry a condom. It would spoil the mood. But then, so does an unplanned pregnancy.

Perhaps we can make a small beginning in the library to spark that connection. What if we should throw the classification scheme to the winds and shelve multiple copies of *Under 18 and Pregnant, A Woman's Guide to Safe Abortion, What Are You Using?*, and *Facts About STD* in among the multiple copies of Sweet Dreams, Wildfire, and Heart to Heart? Imagine the shock. Imagine the association of ideas from the association of volumes.

Here are some good ones to include in that outrageous display, some titles that have not previously been reviewed in this column.

Mom, I'm Pregnant; A Personal Guide for Teenagers by Reni L. Witt and Jeannine Masterson Michael is a real gem: complete, authoritative, readable. It lays out the choices clearly and gives calm step-by-step guidance for the girl whose pregnancy has thrown her into a terrified muddle. "The decision you make about the outcome of your pregnancy may be the most difficult one you have ever had to face," the authors level. "Yet the problem of what to do can be broken down into small pieces." In five basic steps they show how to weigh alternatives and accept the consequences of choice. Co-author Jeannine Masterson Michael counsels pregnant teens at Eastern Women's Center, a gynecological health care facility in New York City, and her years of experience show as she leads the reader skillfully past the first stages of denial to seek help and take action. Michael knows all the myths and excuses and secret reasons. She gives careful unflinching explanations of the pregnancy test, the pelvic exam, the difficult task of telling boyfriend and parents, and the primary decision of whether to continue or end the pregnancy. Chapters on abortion, marriage, adoption, and foster care are detailed and realistic, presenting facts but also helping the girl deal with feelings about each choice. A final section outlines prenatal care and birth and works through the negative feelings many young women have about contraception. An invaluable feature of the book is the exhaustive (sixty-seven-page) list of hotlines and agencies in the United States and Canada. The excellent bibliography includes both articles and books (unfortunately books addressed to teens are not listed separately). The tone throughout is friendly but tough, and many brief quotations from girls add anecdotal interest. The underlying theme, as the authors explain in "A Special Word for Parents," is "Achieving self-knowledge and independence, as well as accepting responsibility"—a vision of hope for the young women who can gain self-respect and strength from these hard decisions well made.

Handbook for Pregnant Teenagers by Linda Roggow and Carolyn Owens is a much slighter work, but is appropriate for girls whose religious convictions preclude abortion as an option. In an opening scene a young girl agonizes about her decision to abort and finally cancels

Patty Campbell *teaches young adult literature at UCLA and is a library consultant and freelance writer. She is currently at work on a book about YA novelist Robert Cormier.*

her appointment because "abortion means taking a human life." From there the book goes on to thoughtfully consider the alternatives of marriage, adoption, or raising the baby alone. The orientation is middle-class, and many of the factors for decision-making are financial. With the exception of a final chapter titled "Faith Helps" there is very little specific religiosity. The authors often make points in the form of reasonably believable anecdotes or quotations. Although there are a few general remarks about the advisability of good prenatal care, there is no description of birth, the pelvic exam, attitudes or feelings about past or future sex, or any other physical matters. The only form of contraception mentioned is repentance and prayer. An appendix lists "Crisis Pregnancy Centers" that offer counselling for those who do not wish to consider abortion. A page of "Suggestions for Further Reading" lists other relevant books from fundamentalist publishers—a type of bibliography that is often hard for librarians to find. In general this is a sound book for the readership for which it is intended, although it certainly should not be the only book on the subject in the library collection.

"Mom . . . I'm Pregnant" by Bev O'Brien is written by a mother, ostensibly for other mothers, but some girls with a born-again Christian orientation may find this story of a close mother-daughter relationship inspirational. (Care should be taken not to confuse this book with the Witt and Michael volume of the same title reviewed above.) When nineteen-year-old Sandy turned up pregnant her mother Bev was numb with shock that her good Christian daughter could ever do anything that would lead to such a result. She needed to work through her own anger and grief before she could help her daughter. During the pregnancy Bev and Sandy come to terms with the shame and guilt and make the decision to allow the baby to be adopted, although this causes them both great pain. A highly emotional book, this has little factual information to offer and what there is centers on legal matters—the rules of adoption, the laws on discrimination against pregnant women, the statutes concerning paternity (a rather distasteful chapter describes their attempt to punish the young non-Christian father by taking him to court). In the last two chapters Bev ponders whether she, or any mother, should give her daughter detailed birth control information. She dismisses this idea on the grounds that no contraceptive method is foolproof, and "she may construe this to mean that we expect her to experiment with sex." Sexual values, if not clinical facts, should be taught in the home, she maintains, difficult as it may be for parents to speak of such things. Unfortunately her short unselective bibliography gives little help. In general, this book has mostly scare value. It should be balanced by more objective and factual titles, and is useful only for libraries serving a large fundamentalist population.

Facts About STD by Sol Gordon is a new edition of *Facts About VD for Today's Youth* (1973, 1979). This short, easy-to-read guide is a dependable resource that gets straight to the latest data on sexually transmitted diseases. It minces no words, and even reluctant readers will find it easily understandable. The new edition, besides adjusting the title to current usage, adds significant information about herpes, chlamydia, PID, AIDS, and other recently recognized horrors. Good news, too, appears in the form of new research on prevention and cure. It makes sense for libraries to replace the older title with several copies of this new one, and to shelve them, preferably open to the diagram of how to use a condom, right next to Janet Quinn-Harkin's latest. ▣

This month's books:

Gordon, Sol. *Facts About STD.* Ed-U Press (Box 583, Fayetteville, NY 13066), 1983. 49 p. $5.95 ISBN 0-934978-04-2

O'Brien, Bev. *"Mom . . . I'm Pregnant."* Tyndale House, 1982. 127 p. $3.95. ISBN 0-8423-4495-0 LC 82-50437

Roggow, Linda and Carolyn Owens. *Handbook for Pregnant Teenagers.* Zondervan, 1984. 142 p. $5.95. ISBN 0-310-45821-8 LC 84-15317

Witt, Reni L. and Jeannine Masterson Michael. *Mom, I'm Pregnant; A Personal Guide for Teenagers.* Stein and Day, 1982. 239 p. $10.95; pa $6.95. ISBN 0-8128-2874-7; 0-8128-6173-6 LC 82-40009

Kathleen Maio:

Murder in Print

Against all odds, the city of Seattle seems to be on its way to becoming a mystery capital. Although there have been mysteries set in Seattle before, they were few and far between. Yet I have read three Seattle mysteries in the past four months: the radical first mystery, *Murder in the Collective,* a private eye debut in the paperback original *The Rainy City* (the second in that series, *Poverty Bay,* has also been released), and this month, the latest John Denson mystery, **Fish Story** (Viking, 1985, $13.95) by Richard Hoyt.

Hoyt is a veteran of five years of prolific mystery and thriller publishing and he furthers his reputation as a major new voice in mystery fiction with *Fish Story.* For John Denson, life is complicated enough when the fates conspire to close down his favorite dive and transform it into a chichi restaurant for North Pacific yuppies. But the question of where to play darts with his friends Willie Prettybird, "Rodent Clone," "Scabby," et al., soon becomes the least of his worries.

Willie asks his help because a man keeps breaking into his sister's apartment and beating up her boyfriends. Threats are delivered by the masked assailant. Melinda and Willie suspect that it is her Anglo ex-husband. Another possibility is that the terrorism is related to a suit the Prettybirds have filed to regain salmon fishing rights for their tribe, the Cowlitz. If this is so, the list of suspects grows considerably to include both professional and sports fishermen.

As Halloween approaches, the case becomes more and more macabre as chunks of human flesh start turning up in Pioneer Place, a park where Native American winos gather in the evening to "powwow" and pass the bottle. It is feared that the frozen chops and steaks are part of the missing federal judge assigned to the Cowlitz fishing rights case. When police technology fails to trace the meat delivery, Denson and his distinctly mismatched crew of volunteers take to Seattle's underground to track the butcher.

This is an underground city in the literal sense. Below the streets and ground floor storefronts of old Seattle is another set of streets, alleys, and rooms. Inhabited by rats and the haunted cries of an unseen dog or coyote, the underground is as eerie a locale as you could find for a horrific climax to a mystery—and Denson plays it for everything he's worth.

The recent paperback release of two of the earlier Denson mysteries, *Decoys* and *30 for a Harry,* will be the perfect supplement for those collections that don't yet have the entire Denson series. I quarrel with the cover notes on those editions, however. Denson is described as a "soft-boiled" sleuth. He is not. He may not pack a gun (except for the figurative variety—I refer the reader to the sex scene midway through *Fish Story*) but there is a harshness and profanity to Hoyt's fiction that true soft-boiled fans will likely find distressing.

Hoyt is undoubtably a major talent and *Fish Story* lives up to its name. It is an outrageous piece of storytelling that most mystery fans will swallow hook, line, and sinker.

Another unusual mystery locale is effectively used in a December 1984 release I've just gotten around to reading. It is **Prophet Motive** (St. Martin's, 1984, $12.95) by Cleo Jones. The locale is a suburb of Salt Lake City, Utah, and the mystery focuses on the Mormon community.

Jones is an ex-Mormon and her attitude toward the Church of Jesus Christ of Latter-Day Saints is far from benevolent. The plot starts off on a snowy night with the stabbing murder of the "Iron Rod Saint," Bishop Manion. Harsh though he was, everyone claims, Manion was a good man who had no enemies outside of an evil hussy named Naomi Green, who had the audacity to open a Planned Parenthood office in this Mormon stronghold. The fact that the Bishop dies not far from Green's door, with footprints leading from the scene of the crime to that door and no where else, helps the community decide that it's an open and shut case.

Chief Christopher Danville of the Magpie Police, himself a fallen Saint, is not so quick to pass judgment, especially when he finds himself drawn to the forbidden "evil" of his primary

Kathleen Maio *is a freelance writer based in Somerville, Massachusetts. She has contributed to* Twentieth Century Crime and Mystery Writers, Murderess Ink, *and numerous magazines.*

suspect. Danville is an unhappy, believable fellow, and a dogged sleuth as he chases a murderer, a missing husband, and the thief of a collection of "death tapes."

While there is no doubt that practicing Mormons would be horrified by Jones's novel, others will find it fascinating. The author tells us much of the history and present practices of a religion with which few of us are conversant. The sum total of this information could be labelled an exposé, and at times Jones's/Danville's angry indictments threaten to swamp the narration. Luckily, Jones manages to skirt this danger, and the mystery's surprising conclusion, directly linked to the religion and the character of its practitioners, justifies any excesses. *Prophet Motive* is a fascinating first mystery.

Actress and busybody detective Tessa Crichton returns in Anne Morice's **Getting Away with Murder?** (St. Martin's, 1985, $11.95). There is no sex and no violent action in the Crichton series. Everyone is well-bred and civilized at all times. Even a ménage à trois is handled in the most wholesome and homey manner.

Tessa and her policeman hubby, Robin Price, are off for a holiday at a reputable country inn. They talk themselves into making it a busman's holiday as they re-examine an unsolved murder case. The couple lures Tessa's cousin Toby into joining them, and the three spend much of their time debating over the dining table, sifting through evidence, and deflating one another's theories.

The plot, which touches on the horsey set and the landed gentry, is the kind of thing Morice handles so well. There are new murders and robberies to complicate matters, and everything works out nicely in the end. For those who have not yet sampled Morice's work, *Getting Away with Murder?* is representative and a good measure of whether the author's easy, classical style is to taste.

Ray Harrison brings us the second in his historical series starring Detective-Sergeant Bragg and his aristocratic subordinate, Constable Morton,

in **Death of an Honourable Member** (Scribner's, 1985, $11.95). When an anonymous note forces the coroner and police into a highly sensitive investigation of the seemingly accidental death of a member of Parliament, Bragg and Morton are given the difficult assignment. Harrison writes a well constructed story that is faithful to his turn of the century period yet modern in style with short dialogue-intensive scenes. On the debit side, the frequent discussions of the victim's financial dealings and political maneuverings have a stagnating effect on the story. The fanatical murderer makes matters worse. *Death of an Honourable Member* does not live up to the talents of the author but leaves hope for a more satisfying

book next time.

Velda Johnston is the prolific author of passable romantic suspense. Her latest is **Shadow Behind the Curtain** (Dodd, Mead, 1985, $13.95). Beautiful Deborah Channing had led the pampered life of a well-to-do New Yorker until the death of her step-father inadvertently leads to the discovery that her real father is a convicted child murderer serving a life sentence in a New Mexico prison. After the death of her mother, and a separation from her society fiancé, Deborah goes to New Mexico to explore her roots and, if possible, vindicate her father.

Perhaps if the theme had not been employed already with more skill by P. D. James and others, Johnston's story might come off better. There is very little detecting into either the crime or the human heart in this account. When a sufficient number of pages have been filled, the schizophrenic murderer merely exposes his identity to Deborah and attempts to murder her. A happy ending is assured, but the overall effect is quite flat.

Murder on the Hudson (Walker, 1985, $13.95) by Don Flynn is his second mystery to feature Ed Fitzgerald of the New York *Daily Press*. Like Johnston, Flynn suffers in comparison with other authors, this time with those who have set their mysteries within the fourth estate. I kept wishing that Flynn would do more (like Richard Hoyt, for example, in his second Denson mystery) with his newsroom characters and situations.

Fitzgerald covers a story involving the murder of a messenger on a Hudson cruise ship. Soon, he is involved with the victim's daughter and is running from thugs who claim the young woman owes them big bucks. Flynn's plot is nice and twisty but his characters, including city desk editor Ironhead Matthews, are stereotypes straight out of *The Front Page*. The euphemistic swearing ("grumper," "patoot," "butt") in his dialogue completes the old-fashioned picture. George Harmon Coxe fans may well enjoy *Murder on the Hudson*.

Judith Trojan:

Front Row Center

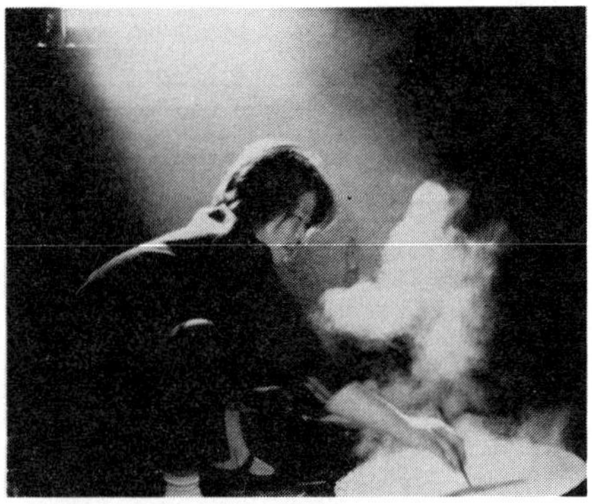

A Taste of China

Films about food fall into three main categories. There are the "food as product" films that promote foods produced and packaged by the film's sponsor, Nabisco or General Foods, for example. Such films often distance viewers through their use of authoritative, voice-over narration and minimal on-location dialogue. They also make little effort to hide their commercial intent. Usually available for free loan, these films are easily accessible to large, non-specialized audiences.

"Food as art" films, in contrast, make the most of close-up photography and natural sound to enhance the intrinsic beauty of food—its texture, color, and shape. The art and craft of food processing and preparation are also common themes in "food as art" films—bread-baking and chocolate-making are two favorite subjects. Most films in this genre reflect the personal visions of their makers rather than commercial points of view.

Finally, there are the "food as culture" films that study food as it reflects the living environment, customs, and traditions of a country, region, or a particular group or class of people. Basically anthropological or geographical in focus, these films educate audiences about gastronomical lifestyles.

Sue Yung Li's **A Taste of China** series of four, half-hour films combine the best elements of all three genres. Ostensibly an exploration of food as a mirror of Chinese culture, the series, in fact, works successfully on several levels. Blending the art and craft of Chinese cuisine with a strong cultural and philosophical bent, the films make a positive pitch for various Chinese foods and demystify agrarian and urban Chinese lifestyles. Connections are made between food and the earth, food and spiritual well-being, and food and physical health. Born in Shanghai, producer Sue Yung Li is a product of Chinese culture; but she is now an American and in a perfect position to translate the edible landscape of her ancestors into terms that will tempt Westerners.

Exquisite cinematography captures the visual poetry of growing, harvesting, preparing, and eating various Chinese delicacies and everyday foods. The use of natural sound is also top-notch—whether in the farm fields, over the stove, or at the table, every crackle, chop, swish, and slurp is heard to full effect. The tranquil voice-over narration replaces subtitles, which are not missed except during a lengthy sequence featuring an itinerant entertainer.

The first film in the series, *Masters of the Wok,* serves as a perfect appetizer to native Chinese cuisine. Both peasant and banquet fare are highlighted; and the wok, a trendy piece of cooking gear in many American kitchens, is very much in evidence throughout this film. In the northern plains region of Shandong, we watch young chefs prepare a twenty-eight course banquet for a government conference, under the critical eyes of master class chefs. The training is gruelling. The master chefs perform great feats of wokmanship—flipping and sloshing the sizzling ingredients over the open flames. In the pastry kitchen, breads, noodles, cakes, and such delicate one-of-a-kind items as orange jelly "goldfish" and thin "dragon whisker" noodles are hand-fashioned.

Chinese cooking is elevated to an art in this film. Entertaining images of the chopping, cutting, and slicing of vegetables and meats, and the "pulling" of noodles are highpoints. Great things are done with slow-motion cinematography, close-ups, dissolves, and electronic music to project the texture, color, and even the aroma and taste of the foods handled by these highly skilled chefs.

During a visit to nearby Qufu, the birthplace of Confucius, three generations of rural women prepare a noon-

Judith Trojan *is editor-in-chief of* Sightlines *magazine, editorial coordinator at the Educational Film Library Association, and a staff member of the American Film Festival.*

day meal, which is the largest of the day. In the north, wheat, millet, and corn are staples, so breads, pastries, and "longevity noodles" are very much in evidence. To assure good luck, these five-foot noodles must be eaten in one continuous piece.

In Sichuan Province in central China, spices and hot peppers are a delicacy. Here, we witness the consumption of various stages of a twenty-five course chrysanthemum banquet. Toasts are made in between each course of contrasting foods—sweet and salty, smooth and crunchy—and as the feast draws to a close, the seventy-eight-year-old master chef takes his bow to applause and one last toast. There's no doubt he deserves it!

Food for Body and Spirit opens with an arduous journey up Blue City Mountain in Sichuan Province to the Taoist Temple of the Celestial Master. The aim of this second film in the series is to examine religious influences on Chinese cuisine, with focus on the forces of yin and yang and their incarnation in Chinese attitudes toward food.

Rare herbs are collected at this site. They are an important ingredient in the preparation of healthy meals as well as the medicines sold in herbal shops. These highly respected institutions dispense time-honored herbal medicines to sophisticated customers who come with prescriptions in hand. Since it is believed that ill health arises from an imbalance of yin and yang, blends of herbs and other natural substances are used, instead of chemicals, to correct that bodily imbalance.

Behind the herbal shop profiled in this film sits a restaurant that invites patrons to "eat their way to health." The restaurant serves herbal medicine food. A third-generation herbalist—a cross between our Western pharmacists and nutritionists—recommends dishes to restore or maintain the health of patrons. Senior citizens, young athletes, pregnant women, and impotent men are just a few of the clients who frequent this place to partake of individually prescribed foods made from ancient, secret recipes. Garnishes include such delicacies as tiny seahorses or winter caterpillars; the latter are recommended for virility.

The origins of vegetarianism in China are traced to Buddhism. The many skilled culinary transformations of high protein soybeans and other vegetables into unique edibles that mock meat, fish, poultry, and milk are demonstrated. A visit to a Buddhist vegetarian restaurant is also on the itinerary.

Taoism and Buddhism are shown to be so well integrated into the daily life of the Chinese people that they've ceased to regard them solely as religious pursuits. The most fascinating film in the *Taste of China* series, *Food for Body and Spirit* can easily stand on its own as a portrait of an ancient, yet still revolutionary way to "eat healthy."

The Family Table contrasts the culinary tastes and talents of two quite different Chinese families. The Za family, a four-generation farm family living in a Sichuan village, work side-by-side to grow, harvest, and prepare mouth-watering food fare for their large family table. Rice, vegetables, and spices are staples in Sichuan households. Most of the villagers are related by marriage, and their lifestyle centers around the agrarian seasonal cycles. During rare slack periods, families gather for outdoor entertainment and games like Chinese chess and Chinese jumprope.

In urban Hangzhou, the three-member Xu family lives in cramped but stylish quarters. (Only 15 percent of China's population live in urban areas.) Although the Xus wear contemporary clothing, have only one child and many modern conveniences—a black and white TV, a stereo cassette player, an electric fan, potted plants, and goldfish—they share a small kitchen with their neighbors and have no refrigeration.

While the rural Za women prepare an elaborate Sunday lunch of homegrown foods for the extended family, Mr. Xu must shop for and cook dinner for himself, his wife, and son because his wife works the nightshift at the local silk factory. Perishable foods must be purchased on the day of use to avoid spoilage, and convenience foods fit the Xus' hectic lifestyle.

The Family Table closes during the annual Moon Festival, which signals the completion of harvest and the eighth full moon. As villagers gather in lakeside gazebos and in brightly lit floating barges to gaze at the full moon, they enjoy the fruits of harvest, munch on moon cake, and regale the youngsters with moon legends. In this spectacularly photographed sequence, the moonglow and shimmering boat lights cast a mysterious spell over the water, perfectly capturing the fantasy of this shared ancient ritual.

The last film in the series, *Water Farmers,* similarly transforms a rather mundane landscape into one of lyrical beauty. Natives glide effortlessly and quietly in boats through the Yangzi River Delta south of Shanghai. Miles of these "liquid highways" criss-cross the region, linking towns and villages. Farmers cultivate and harvest "water" crops of lotus, bamboo, fish, and river clams for pearls. Funeral boats pass by, as do wedding barges laden with dowry.

One of the staples of any Chinese social gathering is warm rice wine, and wine taverns are the mecca for many Chinese seeking rest and relax-

(continued on page 639)

This month's films:

A Taste of China is a series of four films produced by Sue Yung Li and directed by Michael Lerner. Individual titles are: *Masters of the Wok, Food for Body and Spirit, The Family Table,* and *Water Farmers.* 16mm & video. color. 29 min. each. 1983. Dist: University of California Extension Media Center, 2223 Fulton St., Berkeley, CA 94720. 415/642-0460. 16mm—$1,750 series; $500 each (rental $45). ½/¾-inch Video—$1,350 series; $375 each (rental $35).

Bruce Pollock:

On Record: Popular Music

Sade

In the fifties it was the big beat, rock and roll; in the sixties, the college educated, Beatle-influenced sound of folk/rock; in the seventies, no contest, disco. Each decade, usually around the mid-point, has found a defining sound that captures the essence of its music and its music fans. The ducktailed delinquents of *Blackboard Jungle,* the long-haired hippies of Golden Gate Park, the oily-locked scions of John Travolta's Infinity Disco in Brooklyn—these were the images rock drummed into the heads of its dancing denizens as the beat repeated through the years. In the eighties, though MTV reigns supreme, proliferating images at the speed of light, separated only by commercials, we have yet to come upon the all-consuming sound, the all-encompassing single image uniting a generation not only in the hand-in-hand sense, but to all its rock and roll predecessors. With 1985 upon us, the fateful time is nigh. If such a sound is to emerge, and such a crew of nightlife revelers to cheer it on, the records bearing that sound could well be in our midst even now, in our very collections still in shrink wrappers, waiting to reveal the secrets of the contemporary age—carrying on the traditions of antiquity.

Bruce Pollock *is the editor of* Guitar *magazine and the author of* Popular Music: An Annotated Index of American Popular Songs, Volumes 7 and 8.

Bronski Beat. *The Age of Consent* (MCA 5538)

The first place we look, creatures of old bad habit that we are, is to the college campus, long a spawning ground of future trends, where music is an intellectual as well as physical passion. One of the top-sellers on campus this year, Bronski Beat is an unusual looking band, but that is not the half of it. "Openly gay," they deliver an emotional message that extends far beyond whatever stereotypes that label may imply, creating an album that is lifted and purified by the pain of self-discovery and self-realization, brought on by the epiphanies of Jimmy Somerville's aching lyrics and piercing falsetto. In "Why," "Screaming" and "Smalltown Boy," there is confessional poetry that nearly amounts to gospel music. Their surprising and scintillating remake of "It Ain't Necessarily So" is eerie, sultry, Near Eastern and totally magical. There's the anti-war song that you'd expect to be big on college campuses; the questioning-the-future song. There's the explicit "Need a Man Blues," that carries the refrain: "The sweetest thing of all is men loving men." Above it, through it, and beyond it is the sound, the all-encompassing, rapturous ambience of the music, obliterating much of the lyrics, becoming a message in itself.

Sade. *Diamond Life* (Portrait BFR 39581)

At the after-hours, invitation-only, ultra chic nightclub, replete with intimidating hatcheck girls and bare-chested male bartenders, we come upon Sade, an ex-fashion designer, currently the rage of Europe, bewitching South African lady of many talents. Buried in the dense tropics of this album, with its lush atmosphere of steamy encounters and heated exchanges, are several songs that go beyond the requirements of dance music (admittedly a bit more stringent than the meager components of disco music). In "Frankie's First Affair," "Cherry Pie" and "Sally," Sade (pronounced Sha-day) becomes, for those fifteen minutes or so, the updated equivalent of Nico, the smoky chanteuse who sang of decadence in the dungeons of New York's Lower East Side in the late sixties (and who is apparently still singing somewhere of seedy sex). Stepping outside herself on those songs, Sade becomes a spokesperson for the nightlife volunteers of the eighties, those plucky well-dressed urbanites who dance from midnight to dawn and still put in forty hours behind a desk. Even the other songs on this debut album (already a worldwide smash) are a cut or two above the norm, not as moving or pointed as the standouts, but connected by the album's superior sound, the cascading, relentless push of eager bodies seeking solace under a beat.

John Hiatt. *Warming Up to the Ice Age* (Geffen GHS 24055)

In another neighborhood entirely, our tour bus gets a flat outside of a neon bar and grill, where the headline act tonight is a wiry rocker by the name of John Hiatt. Not by nature a sentimental man, he nevertheless is the central figure in a soap operatic album of no small dimension. Hiatt sings about the plight of the common man, not with the mythical urgency and bombast of a Springsteen, or the pop syrup schmaltz with lemon of a Billy Joel, but merely with bedrock lust and soul in his socks. Hiatt is the little guy who's been kicked by the eighties once too often. He can't comprehend modern relationships with demanding and designing women. Even when such a relationship is in danger of approaching, on the brink of becoming real, both he and the lady co-protagonist are apt to run away. He consoles himself at the bar and grill, with raunchy jokes about lewd women (and vice versa), cold beer, and hot rock and roll. As served up by Hiatt, this concoction offers about as satisfying and visceral an album as any man has produced this year. (Don't let him near the Bronski Beat; they're likely to beat him up.) Especially on the title tune, "The Usual," "Zero House," "She Said the Same Things to Me" and the exceptional "Living a Little, Laughing a Little," a duet with Elvis Costello, the sound here is infectious blue-eyed soul of the highest order, with a side of crackling guitar and wit. "When We Ran" is something else again, a lament so searing and believable it must be heard.

John Martyn. *Sapphire* (Island 90248-1)

Filling a spiritual need for the eternal questing visionary on a reef, John Martyn assumes his stance high on a windy cliff, taking up where Van Morrison left off, with his tales of inner torment. Evoking other hopeful voices of our time, from Garland Jeffreys to (especially) Tim Buckley, the Martyn sound is spacey but sincere, imbued with jazz leanings and folk longings, blues inflections and rock influences. In keeping with the era's return to tradition, Martyn gives us a moving remake of "Over the Rainbow." Aside from "Sapphire" and "Fisherman's Dream," no other individual tunes emerge, but instead what lingers, as on the other records, is the overall sound, utterly convincing, captivating.

We are in an abundant time. There are some musical visions being formed and magical sounds around us. If no one central theme has surfaced, let's count our blessings. ▣

Norman Stevens:

Our Profession

Recent years have seen the publication of an increasing number of reference books specifically designed to assist us professionally. We have been surprisingly imaginative in developing new kinds of reference tools. This month's books include two such titles that take an approach that is slightly different from previously available ones. Mary Ann Bowman's **Library and Information Science Journals and Serials**, the first in a new series of such guides for various subjects, is described as an analytical guide. It is an annotated alphabetical listing of 311 current library science journals and serials in English published throughout the world. For each title Bowman provides basic information on as many as twenty-one points including title, date founded, frequency, price, publisher, circulation, manuscript selection process, book reviews, target audience, and the like. There is the usual assortment of preliminary information and indexes to help use the book and locate titles. All of that information is, for the most part, straightforward and not much different from what is readily available in other more general sources, but it does help to have a reasonably comprehensive list of library science titles available in one source. Bowman's brief annotations, in general, are entertaining and do a good job of succinctly characterizing the content and nature of each of the journals. Although some of the information is dated, this is a useful guide for the selection of titles by libraries, the identification of potential sources for publication of articles by would-be authors, and even for the determination by the individual librarian of titles to subscribe to, or read, on a regular basis.

Norman Stevens *is university librarian at the University of Connecticut and the author of* Communication Throughout Libraries.

David Kohl's **Administration, Personnel, Buildings and Equipment** is also the first volume of a series but the subsequent five volumes will cover circulation, reference, library education, professional issues and other subject areas within librarianship. Kohl provides a unique approach by summarizing the content of articles published in major American journals between 1960 and 1983 that report on quantitative research in librarianship. Quantitative information selected from these articles is summarized and arranged in a series of topical headings under the three main topics. Each citation is accompanied by a reference to a comprehensive standard bibliography of the articles cited in all six volumes in the series. Under the heading user fees in the administration section, for example, there are five sets of facts summarized from one article and two from two other articles. This kind of text does not make for inspiring reading; the summary of the facts cannot adequately substitute for the articles themselves; and Kohl does not evaluate the accuracy of the techniques or the findings. As a starting point for administrators, managers, staff, and students examining a particular issue, Kohl's guide provides an approach that is somewhat more useful than the standard indexing found in *Library Literature* because it is more selective and the facts, not the citations, are emphasized. These two books are important for demonstrating that new reference tools of potential value to librarianship can still be developed and that there may even be a market for them.

The cantankerous Sanford Berman might well object to the vanilla approach to the literature of librarianship presented by Bowman and Kohl both in terms of the content of their work and the subject analysis of that content. His tireless crusade for what he regards as significant improvements in cataloging and classification practices to bring them in line with contemporary needs and reality is continued in **Subject Cataloging**. Here his theme, and that of his colleagues, is that subject access potentially represents the most powerful means of access to library materials available but that we have not yet adequately developed that means. His purpose in this volume is to try to identify what is wrong with current subject cataloging techniques, to report on techniques being used that are more responsive to user needs, and to suggest constructive reforms.

The thirteen articles in this volume, five of which are by Berman himself, deal with topics ranging from subject headings for children's fiction, to PRECIS as an alternative approach, to the subject approach to health information, to multilingual access. Much of what is said here is not new and has been put forward elsewhere. Likins's listing of strange subject headings (e.g., one-legged resting position) from the Library of Congress and Berman's parody of such headings (e.g., see also one-eyed, one-horned flying purple people eater) are especially amusing even though those jests sometimes fail to recognize the reality of the literature being analyzed. Whether these radical views will ever be incorporated into the reality of our cataloging practices is open to question, but it seems likely that most of these suggestions will fall on deaf ears. The best we can hope for is that this kind of criticism may force those in the mainstream to be more receptive to criticism and more open to change. We badly need this kind of critical appraisal. Those involved in developing cataloging policies and procedures, including the development of techniques of online public access, should read and understand the points that Berman and his colleagues make here and elsewhere. As new systems of subject access are developed, we will be ill-served if they only incorporate all of our old practices and prejudices.

While subject access may be an important way of helping users locate information, strong reference service is unquestionably the most effective means that a library has of offering users the most comprehensive access to the contents of its collections. For too long we assumed that good reference service consisted simply of such things as an adequate number of staff, a good collection, and reasonable hours of service. In recent years we have realized that there is also a need to measure and evaluate the quality of reference service. A variety of methods and techniques for evaluating reference collections, departments, service, and staff have been developed. Bill Katz and Ruth Fraley helped put all of that work into perspective by assembling twenty-five articles, mainly written by the leaders in developing those methods and techniques, in the **Evaluation of Reference Services.** Included are contributions by Bundy, Bunge, Crowley, Emerson, Katz, Lancaster, McClure, Rothstein, and Weech that deal with topics such as the need for evaluation, referred reference questions, evaluating the reference librarian, performance standards, and output measures. Much of the emphasis is on quantitative techniques but, questions of quality are not overlooked. With the related information to be summarized by Kohl in a subsequent volume and a number of the classic works, such as those of Childers, Crowley, and Lancaster, this volume should serve as a basis for further work in this important area. Administrators and managers concerned with how effectively their department and staff function, as well as staff concerned with ways of evaluating and improving their own work, will find this among the more useful recent publications on reference services.

Neither reference books nor collections of essays make for stimulating reading. The polished writing of a single author on a well-defined topic, such as Kathleen Molz's **National Planning for Library Service 1935-1975,** is far more enjoyable. This adaptation of her dissertation is a fascinating study, approached from the framework of public policy analysis, that deals with the evolution of the concept of an acceptable national plan for library service in the United States. That concept grew, largely through the dedicated efforts of Carl Milam, Carleton B. Joeckel, and Louis Round Wilson, from an idea that was nonexistent in the early 1930s to one that led to the passage of the first federal library legislation in 1956. Molz uses as her boundary points the national plan developed by ALA in 1935 and the national program put forth by NCLIS in 1975. She has done an outstanding job of locating materials and of describing how over time financial support for public libraries was brought into focus as an issue of national concern through the concerted effort of a number of librarians. By concentrating on the concepts and not the facts, Molz has produced a work valuable in its own right as well as an example of how others should examine similar issues. All of that is done extremely well and in a readable fashion. Because of her emphasis on the concepts and the efforts behind national planning, Molz sheds considerable light on some of the questions that still face us as we deal with the issues of a national information policy and other aspects of library planning at the national level.

This month's books:

Berman, Sanford. *Subject Cataloging.* Haworth, 1984. 252p. $22.95. ISBN 0-86656-265-6 LC 84-10554 (also published as v. 2, #1/2, Fall/Winter 1984 of *Technical Services Quarterly*)

Bowman, Mary Ann. *Library and Information Science Journals and Serials.* Greenwood, 1985. 140p. $29.95. ISBN 0-313-23807-3 LC 84-157787

Katz, Bill and Ruth A. Fraley. *Evaluation of Reference Services.* Haworth, 1984. 334p. $29.95 ISBN 0-86656-377-6 (also published as #11, Fall/Winter 1984 of *The Reference Librarian*)

Kohl, David F. *Administration, Personnel, Buildings and Equipment.* ABC-Clio, 1985. 304p. $35. ISBN 0-87436-431-0.

Molz, R. Kathleen. *National Planning for Library Service 1935-1975.* American Library Association, 1984. $15. ISBN 0-8389-0422-X LC 84-18407

Patrick Dewey:

Software for Libraries

Based on the novel, **The Hitchhiker's Guide to the Galaxy** by Douglas Adams and Steven Meretzky (Infocom, 1984) is interactive fiction for those who like to take silliness seriously. This program comes complete with its own microscopic space fleet (in a small plastic bag), a piece of fluff (for inserting in your ear, pocket or navel), a pair of Joo Janta 200 Super-Chromatic Peril-Sensitive Sunglasses, and, of course, a red "Don't Panic" button (which is great to wear to board meetings or just around the library). Also, for those who don't like tea, no tea is included. Aside from all this intergalactic hitchhiker's paraphernalia, there is a diskette and an instruction manual to play one of the best "books" since *Zork* (also produced by Infocom). You awaken and it's pitch black. What do you do? As in all interactive fiction (and *Hitchhiker's Guide* is 100 percent text—no graphics), the decisions will lead you to unravel the story, or to a quick end (as someone bulldozes your house away). *Hitchhiker* also seems to be a step up from other games of this kind in that it allows you to use longer sentences to communicate with the computer. As a result, it's possible to carry on a more normal conversation, instead of being reduced to simple sentences such as "Open door." For example, "Put the banana peel in front of the beggar" will work (though it won't do much for the beggar). Typing N, S, NE, NW, etc. works conveniently for the compass points. The game also comes with two copies of a "House Destruct Order," one in English, the other in Vogon (fortunately, it's for Arthur Dent's house and not the library). It's good to see such a popular book made into a quality software package. For use with: Apple II series, Macintosh ($44.95); Atari ($39.95): IBM PC, PCjr, XT, AT ($44.95); Radio Shack I, II, 2000, Color Computer ($44.95); and others, including CP/M computers.

Patrick Dewey *is administrative librarian, Maywood (Illinois) Public Library and author of* Public Access Microcomputers: A Handbook for Librarians.

News in a flash

The Newsroom (Springboard Software, 1984) is a complete program for producing a newsletter or small newspaper. Aimed at junior and senior high school journalism students who are putting out a school paper, it could probably serve the needs of many struggling adults, too. As a teaching tool, it performs admirably, demonstrating all of the various components of a newsroom: photo lab work area, layout work area, copy work area, the printing press, the wire service, and the banner work area. As a utility, it has a lot of power, operating like a specialized but sophisticated word processing system. With it you can prepare blocks of text and banner headlines, or choose from among two disk sides of clip art that contain everything from aliens and dinosaurs to maps of the United States (all of which may be modified to meet custom needs). Once complete, these parts may be assembled (laid out) into the finished product. Most of the system is driven with icons, tiny pictures that represent various commands. In case of error, there is an "OOPS" icon that lets you undo the last action. There is also a telecommunications feature, making it possible to send or receive files over the phone. About fifty printers are listed as compatible, including the Epson, and the IDS 460 (with graphics). As with any package requiring a printout, the quality of the work depends upon the quality of the printer. Like other Springboard software, this comes in a durable plastic, book-size container for convenient storage. This is a great idea and is highly recommended. It comes with an excellent eighty-six-page manual that contains illustrations of the clip art, and sample completed pages. The sound may be turned off. For use with: Apple II series (64K required); available soon for the IBM PC, PCjr; Commodore 64; dot matrix printer required. Cost: $49.95.

Test yourself

Lots of people seem excited to take a test outside of the classroom if they think it will tell them something about themselves—such as an I.Q. test. **The Brain Game** by Rita Aero and Elliot Weiner, Ph.D. (Millennium, 1984) is just that: a battery of intelligence and aptitude tests. Included are: I.Q. Test, Art Judgment Test, Recall of Observations Test, Computer Science Aptitude Test, Opposites Test, Science Vocabul ary Test, Creative Associations Test, Repertory Test, Minnesota Vocabulary Test, Memory Recognition, and others; a total of thirteen. All of the tests are timed by the computer, and require thirty minutes or more to take. The package is well-designed; the tests are self-documenting, the menus are easy to follow, the graphics are well done, and the sound can be turned off. An individual record of progress can be created and stored on the disk. Several of the tests come with special cards (e.g., the Computer Science Aptitude Test has a paper "Calculator Simulator" that allows calculator kinds of questions). This is a professionally constructed package that should prove fun and interesting to many people. For use with: Apple II series. Cost: $39.95.

Automated oldie goldie

The Three Bears by Gladys J. Reich and Laura Boxer, and illustrated by A. Barbara Jurgensen (Millennium, 1984) is an automated, interactive picture book for ages three through seven. The text is simple (e.g., Here is Goldilocks, Watch Momma Bear cook, etc.), and the drawings excellent. Unlike a book, children can direct the course of the action, and usually decide who will eat porridge first, who will sit down in a chair first, etc. The bears can also be sent on a walk or take a nap while their porridge cools. In either case, Goldilocks rampages through the house, destroying furniture and devouring porridge. The ending is very special, because the user can decide on one of three conclusions: Goldilocks and the bears become friends, Goldilocks runs away, or Goldilocks apologizes. Several skills are improved during all of this drama, including learning some letters of the alphabet (press C to help Momma Bear cook, etc.), and size relationships. It comes complete with a set of black-and-white line drawings on sturdy cards, and is packaged in a convenient book-size case (as is the other Millennium software reviewed this month). For use with: Apple II series, 48K. Cost: $39.95.

Mental Workout

Concentration by Gladys J. Reich, Laura Boxer and Ronald S. Lizzi (Millenium, 1984) is a new version of computer games we have seen before, but this is the best yet. Designed for ages five through adult, players choose from six games. In *Morse Code Concentration,* there are sixty-four cards, each turned face down, with a letter hidden on the other side. Instead of revealing the letter during your turn, the game beeps the Morse code equivalent. Some games come in a beginner's level and an advanced level, the only difference being the number of cards or boxes. Other games include: *Flag Concentration,* which uses flags of different nations; *Box Concentration,* a game played matching "presents" in boxes; *Card Concentration,* the more traditional game; *Matrix Concentration,* a tutorial on matrix skills to help children with the other games; and *Balloon Concentration,* a game for young children matching different color balloons. For use with: Apple II series. Cost: $34.95.

Publisher addresses for this month's software

Infocom, Inc. 55 Wheeler St., Cambridge, MA 02138.

Millenium (Distributed by Facts on File), 24 E. 22nd St., New York, NY 10010.

Springboard Software, Inc., 7807 Creekridge Circle, Minneapolis, MN 55434.

James Rettig:

Current Reference Books

Correspondence and review copies for this column should be directed to James Rettig, University Library, Box 8198, University of Illinois at Chicago, Chicago, IL 60680.

The Baby Boom, by Greg Byerly and Richard E. Rubin. Lexington, MA: Lexington, 1985. 238p. $25. 0–669–08903–6 84–47904

They (or rather we) were *Time*'s "Man of the Year" in 1967; we have our own edition of the Trivial Pursuit game; and now we have our own annotated bibliography. The "baby boomers," the generation born in the United States between 1946 and 1965, has affected school enrollments and building programs in the 1950s, campus protest movements in the 1960s, the me-decade of the 1970s. In the 1980s and beyond the baby boomers will affect politics, consumption trends, and the liquidity of the Social Security system. Despite its importance, especially to marketing specialists, no standard subject headings have been established for this group. This selective bibliography identifies 702 otherwise hard-to-find books, journal articles, dissertations, ERIC documents and government publications. Books, dissertations, and government publications are grouped in one chapter. Articles have been placed in six topical chapters, dealing with demography, economics, marketing, management, and education. By far the largest number deals with marketing. A final chapter consists of citations to articles from popular magazines and newspapers. All are indexed by author and subject. The subject index, with entries for the children's shoe industry, housing prices, microcomputers, physical fitness, and Skippy peanut butter reveals the baby boom generation's broad impact on business and society. It is ironic that none of the subject headings in the CIP copy relates specifically to the baby boom generation. This bibliography will greatly simplify the search for information about that group, but first someone will have to dig it out of a library's catalog.

James Rettig *is head reference librarian, University of Illinois at Chicago.*

Baker's Biographical Dictionary of Musicians, edited by Nicolas Slonimsky. 7th ed. New York: Macmillan, 1984. 2,577p. $95. 0–02–870270–0 84–5595

Baker's provides basic biographical information on some 13,000 musicians living and dead. Entries run through the chronology of events in a subject's life and list his or her works; some include bibliographies of writings by and about the subject. Many would consider this enough to ask of a reference book, but *Baker's* does this and more, much more, with a gusto uncommon in reference works. Under the editorship of Nicolas Slonimsky since the fifth edition (1958), it has established its well deserved reputation for being authoritative. In the preface to the sixth edition (1978), prudently reprinted here, Slonimsky explains his methods for verifying dates, places, and events. His distrust of facts repeated in other reference works should admonish reference librarians to verify facts in more than one source. Readers' deep faith in the accuracy of his biographies rests on this painstaking research. In the preface to the seventh edition Slonimsky is too hard on himself; it is an extended public *mea culpa* for errors of fact and even for typographical errors in the sixth edition. Like the pessimist, he sees a bottle as half empty; he has every right to view his work like the optimist who sees the same bottle as half full.

From the prefaces (written in such an engaging manner that they are harder to put down than a good mystery), one can learn just how much labor goes into the compilation of a reference work, even a revision. But this edition is no more revision, for Slonimsky has revised 80 percent of the biographies and added new ones. Among the thousand new biographees are Michael Jackson and Loretta Lynn since Slonimsky chose "to include a number of rock-'n'-roll musicians, crooners, songstresses, [and] movie stars, who occasionally sang, in fact, everyone with an operative larynx short of singing whales." The entertainment and enlightenment the prefaces alone provide would be reason enough to acquire *Baker's,* but Slonimsky's wit and playfulness are all through the biographies, especially his autobiographical entry. Just as this edition is no mere revision, the biographies are no mere catalogs of facts; Slonimsky judges his subjects' contributions to music, sometimes caustically but deservedly. For example, of Elvis Presley he says, "He captivated multitudes of adolescents by the hallucinogenic monotone of his vocal delivery." Several more examples should whet the appetites of readers of this review to feast in the pages of the book itself. On J. S. Bach: "Supreme arbiter and lawgiver of music, a master comparable in greatness of stature with Aristotle in philosophy and Leonardo da Vinci in art." On Luciano Pavarotti: "Like most tenors, he likes himself immensely. Unlike most tenors, he does not get involved in scandal." On Handel: "Physically, he tended toward healthy corpulence; he enjoyed the company of friends, but had a choleric temperament, and could not brook adverse argument." Buy it; use it; but most of all, enjoy it.

Concerned Investors Guide, edited by Sharen D. Knight and Deborah Knight. Resource Publishing Group (1401 Wilson Blvd., Suite 101, Arlington, VA 22209), 1983. 356p. $167, $117 to libraries if ordered directly. 0-915619-00-8 ISSN 0741-1995

Although it was published in 1983 and has been displayed at ALA conferences in the Combined Book Exhibit, the *Concerned Investors Guide* has yet to be reviewed in the library press. The concerns addressed are not those appealled to by brokerage firm commercials when the tense, driven young broker leaves the enjoyment of a dinner with friends to call the office for the latest market developments. Unlike any other reference publication tracking the performance of publicly held companies, the *Guide* reports on their "social responsibilites" performance, to use the best term available, over a five-year period. Drawing most of its information from government regulatory agencies, the *Guide* profiles each company listed on the New York Stock Exchange in terms of environmental protection, fair labor practices, occupational health and safety, product safety, anti-trust cases, the civilian nuclear industry, nature of involvement in South Africa, and weapons contracts. In the areas of environment, labor, health and safety, product safety, and anti-trust, the reports list cases, their dates, sometimes brief notes on their nature, and their outcomes if known. Since many of the outcomes are not known, users of the directory might easily conclude guilt lies where none has been proved. The civilian nuclear industry reports list not only violations and penalties paid, but also sales of equipment for nuclear power plants. The weapons contracts reports simply list the company's dollar total for weapons contracts received in a year. If no information was found on a company in a category, this is noted. Some companies were not reported in any category; a note to this effect appears in its alphabetical listing and these companies are listed in a separate index. Another index lists the companies followed by the categories in which each has been reported while yet another index reverses this, listing each of the categories followed by the names of the companies which have been reported in it.

The data reported are hardly surprising. For example, the Mercantile Texas Corporation, a bank holding company, has no reports in any category whereas the next entry, Merck & Company, Inc., a pharmaceuticals company, has had several product recalls. Some businesses face greater risks than others. It is unlikely that many investors will pass up *Value Line* in favor of the *Guide,* but some may want to examine both sources. It is more likely that students and social activists interested in any of these categories will turn to this. Even then, they will have to go to the regulatory agencies for full reports on the incidents noted. In mid-1985 a second volume treating the companies traded on the American Stock Exchange will be published.

The Constitutional Law Dictionary, vol. 1, by Ralph C. Chandler, Richard A. Enslen, and Peter G. Renstrom. Santa Barbara: ABC-Clio, 1985. 507p. $47.50. 0-87436-031-5 84-12320 (Clio dictionaries in political science, no. 8)

Since the bicentennial of the Constitution's writing, ratification, and enactment (1987-89) lies in the offing, constitutional topics will certainly receive increased scholarly and popular attention. When questions about these topics come to the library, *The Constitutional Law Dictionary* will help answer them. The first volume treats individual rights; the second volume, to be published a year hence, will treat governmental powers. Within thematic chapters on constitutionalism; the first, fourth, fifth, sixth, and eighth amendments; and equal protection and privacy, the dictionary defines key concepts in terms of cases adjudicated by the United States Supreme Court. The index, an alphabetical list of cases entries, and a table of contents at the beginning of each chapter provide access to the discussions of particular ideas and cases. The clearly written, lengthy two-part entries define a concept or describe the facts of a case and then explain its significance and practical implications. A warning should be made about the use of legal language that may trip up lay readers. For example, in the description of a case that "involved a warrantless inventory search of an impounded automobile," "warrantless" means, not "without cause" in its popular sense, but "without a search warrant." The chapter on constitutionalism serves as a convenient overview of the development of the Constitution and its major provisions. The dictionary is not as basic as the Constitution, but it will be very helpful to people who want to understand that document.

Contemporary Designers, edited by Ann L. Morgan and Colin Naylor. Detroit: Gale, 1984. 658p. $95. 0-8103-2036-3 (Contemporary arts series)

The Facts On File Dictionary of Design and Designers, by Simon Jervis. New York: Facts On File, 1984. 533p. $24.95. 0-87196-891-6 83-25350

Through its scope, each of these biographical works attempts to give definition to the amorphous field known as design. *Contemporary Designers* profiles 600 designers from throughout the world, most still living; most of the deceased subjects lived into the 1960s or later. By its inclusion, it defines the design field as encompassing graphic, typographical, industrial, consumer product, book, fashion, textile, interior, costume, and theatrical set design. The detail-packed biographies list basic biographical and career facts, individual and group exhibitions, major design accomplishments, and books and articles by and about the designers. The lengthy entries also include signed critical essays evaluating the designers' work and in some cases comments by the designers on their own work. Black-and-white photographs of indifferent quality do not do justice to samples of their designs. Some of the subjects—for example, Laura Ashley, Bill Blass, and Halston—have become household names through their aggressive marketing programs. Others—for example, the late William Golden, designer of the CBS "eye" symbol—have labored without popular recognition despite the ubiquity of many of their designs.

In addition to biographical entries, the *Facts On File Dictionary* includes journals, selected institutions, and famous nineteenth-century exhibitions that have been important in the history of design. Through its scope, *Facts On File* defines design as a field including ceramics, furniture, glass, interior, metalwork, and textile design, with lesser emphasis on graphic and typographical design and design of durable consumer goods. It excludes industrial, theatrical, and fashion design. Limiting itself to Europe and North America, it reaches back to 1450. One-paragraph entries summarize the designers' lives and note their chief contributions. Numerous cross references embedded within the articles link members of schools and movements.

With interest in design on the upswing, these two books respond to a need in public, academic, and art museum libraries. No matter what definition of itself the field eventually settles on, these will retain their value as ready sources of biographical information on important designers.

Critical Survey of Long Fiction, Foreign Language Series, edited by Frank N. Magill. Englewood Cliffs, NJ: Salem Press, 1984. 5 v. $275. 0-89356-369-2 84-51791

A companion to *Critical Survey of Long Fiction, English Language Series* (reviewed in *WLB,* January 1984), this set covers 182 novelists from throughout the world who wrote in languages other than English, among them Heinrich Böll, Gustave Flaubert, Günter Grass, E. T. A. Hoffmann, Luigi Pirandello, Erich Maria Remarque, George Sand, Alexander Solzenitsyn, Miguel de Unamuno, Jules Verne, and Elie Wiesel. Although writers from the Orient and the third world are represented, most are Europeans of the nineteenth and twentieth centuries. Entries are unmistakably patterned after the companion set, consisting of a list of principal works of long fiction, brief mention of works in other genres, an explanation of the author's overall achievement, biography, analysis of novels, and a very selective bibliography of secondary works. The final volume includes an index and lengthy essays on the development of long fiction in various cultures or historical periods. These essays offer a context for the individual author treatments. While the "Analysis" sections on the authors tend to approach their works of long fiction chronologically and treat them individually, few of them would be confused with the plot summaries Magill has published for some of these works in *Masterplots.* Criticism of these authors is available in a variety of sources, but often those sources are inaccessible to students because of their language, their scarcity, or both. *Long Fiction* helps meet the demands created by such esoteric plenty.

Exciting, Funny, Scary, Short, Different, and Sad Books Kids Like About Animals, Science, Sports, Families, Songs, and Other Things, edited by Frances L. Carroll and Mary Meacham. Chicago: American Library Association, 1984. 192p. pa $10. 0-8389-0423-8 84-20469

The editors surveyed a number of children's librarians to determine two things. First they wanted to learn what subjects children request books about these days. Second, they wanted to learn what books the librarians recommend on these subjects. The result is *Books Kids Like,* an annotated guide to books on thirty-five broad topics such as those listed in the lengthy title as well as holidays, computers, war, dinosaurs, cars, and history. Genre books (historical fiction, mystery) are treated as well as popular series such as the "Little House" books and the Will Stanton series. Many of the broad subject sections are subdivided; for example, the section entitled "I Like to Read About Kids Like Me" breaks down into kids at school, being blind, black children, doing fun things, friends, in the city, super kids, kids who can't hear, and kids with handicaps. There is no particular order to the sections since "there is not any reason from a child's point of view to put Halloween books with Christmas books, for example, together in a division of holiday books." This may or may not be true; since the index lists authors and titles of the recommended books but not the subject sections, one must scan the table of contents carefully lest a desired topic be overlooked. The arrangement implies that children themselves should use the book as a selection guide and indeed the annotations of a sentence or two are written so that children can comprehend them. Perhaps this explains the absence of grade or age level indicators which children might find patronizing or offputting. When used carefully, in the hands of either a young reader or a children's librarian, *Books Kids Like* will be a helpful reader's advisory tool. Librarians may also want to comb it systematically as a collection development/evaluation guide.

The Harlem Renaissance, edited by Bruce Kellner. Westport, CT: Greenwood, 1984. 476p. $45. 0-313-23232-6 83-22687

Langston Hughes, premier poet of the Harlem Renaissance, wrote of the time "when Harlem was in vogue," the time between the anti-lynching Silent Protest Parade down New York's Fifth Avenue in 1917 and the first Harlem race riot in 1935. Although centered in Harlem, the artistic and intellectual ferment among blacks extended well beyond its confines. This historical dictionary describes the writers, musicians, songwriters, playwrights, actors, clergymen, educators, civil rights leaders, painters, entertainers, novels, plays, periodicals, theaters, films, organizations, and events that made up the Harlem Renaissance. And so it has entries on the Apollo Theater, the *Liberator,* the NAACP, Carl Van Vechten, James Weldon Johnson, Paul Robeson, and many more. The articles explain the subject's role in the period and cite sources for additional reading. Appendixes present a chronology, a bibliography of primary materials, plays and serials relating to the movement, a glossary of Harlem slang, and a bibliography of secondary works. The index differentiates between a term's main entry and other mentions of it. Because other sources tend to neglect the period, this will enrich both black studies collections and collections on American history and arts.

Macmillan Illustrated Animal Encyclopedia, edited by Philip Whitfield. New York: Macmillan, 1984. 600p. $35. 0-02-627680-1 84-3956

Monkeys and Apes, by Gotthart Berger. New York: Arco, 1985. 240p $24.95. 0-668-06204-5 84-2846

A veritable zoo between covers, the *Illustrated Animal Encyclopedia* describes the range, habitat, size, physical characteristics, habits, and mating behavior of members of every family of vertebrate animals. Thus it excludes worms, corals, insects, mollusks, and crustaceans. Grouping animals into the broad classes mammals, birds, reptiles, amphibians, and fishes, the table of contents lists the popular names of the families within these classes. This, along with the index listing animals by both popular and scientific names, makes for speedy access to the descriptions. Coverage of families is comprehensive except in the fishes class where, because the families are so numerous, representative ones have been described. Most entries consist of two paragraphs, the first giving the animal's characteristics and habits, the second describing gestation period, size of litter, and weaning period. The attractive format pairs these descriptions on the left side of each two-page spread with eye-catching color drawings of the animals on the right side. Were it not so large a book, it could serve as an identification guide in the field. The encyclopedia's brief entires provide quick reference to basic facts about thousands of animals. The descriptions will satisfy the curiosity of adults, and junior high students should be able to comprehend them without difficulty.

Monkeys and Apes puts only the zoo's primate house between its covers, but a full house it is. Family-by-family (except for the family Hominidae, i.e., humans) it describes the physical characteristics, range, habitat, social behavior, foods, and gestation period of each genus of monkeys and apes. Descriptions of the distinguishing characteristics of individual species follow. Berger, director of the Dresden Zoological Gardens in Germany, often notes zoos' success in housing and breeding various species and summarizes findings of zoologists' research studies. When his text was translated into English, metric weights and measures were retained. In this respect, in its references to the bibliography at the back of the book, and in its vocabulary level, *Monkeys and Apes* aims at a more sophisticated audience than the *Illustrated Animal Encyclopedia.* Although the book's organization lends itself to reference use, other features do not. The index does not include popular names and there are no direct links between the text and the color and black-and-white photographs. The classification chart of primates allows a user to translate scientific names into popular names and vice versa, a needlessly cumbersome process compared to using an index employing both forms of entry.

Online Database Search Services Directory, edited by John Schmittroth, Jr., and Doris M. Maxfield. Detroit: Gale, 1983-84. 1,184p. in two parts. pa $110. 0-8103-1698-6 ISSN 0741-0077

The information in *Online Database Search Services Directory* used to appear in the *Encyclopedia of Information Systems and Services* (6th ed., Detroit: Gale, 1984) until it became too voluminous as online search services became the norm rather than the exception. The first part of *Online* was issued in late 1983, the second part a year later. Together they describe the search services of 1,145 organizations, nearly all of them libraries. Entries include the name of the service's contact person, institution name, number of searchers, annual search activity level, systems accessed, subjects searched, frequently searched databases, clientele served, fee policy, search personnel, and search request procedure. Cumulative indexes in part two provide access to the services by organization name, systems accessed, databases frequently searched, subject areas searched, personal names, and geographic location. The organization name index confirms that the directory falls short of comprehensiveness, for neither of the institutions at which this reviewer has worked as a searcher is included although the libraries of the professional schools at both institutions are. Much of the directory's information, especially lists of personnel, is, of course, subject to frequent change. Even if it were not, one would have to question the practicality of the directory. Contacts made through local online user groups are likely to be as informative and more likely to be current if a searcher needs to refer a client to another nearby institution for a database not available at his or her own. However, searchers investigating distant potential employers will value its wealth of information about individual services.

The Population of the United States, by Donald J. Bogue. New York: Macmillan, 1985. 728p. $55. 0-02-904700-5 84-18688

The many tables in this volume have

appeared in a number of government publications, most emanating from the Census Bureau, and their sources are duly noted. More than simply a statistical abstract of recent population trends in the United States, this goes beyond the presentation of the numbers to their interpretation. Twenty chapters in five major sections give an overview of the population; chart the forces of population change; and describe its social, economic, and other characteristics such as housing and political and religious affiliations. The text accompanying the borrowed tables and the graphs and pie charts created for the book explains how the data in them were gathered, the meanings of technical terms employed, and the relationships between variables. The text also analyzes trends and projects them into the future. A bibliography at the end of each chapter lists additional statistical and interpretive sources. Subordinate index entries vastly outnumber principal entries, providing access to very specific types of demographic data. Tables and text generally reach back no more than forty-five years unless a topic (e.g., immigration) demands greater historical perspective. Librarians in public, special, and academic libraries will frequently find that they have cause to use this interpretive source in conjunction with the *Statistical Abstract* or *Historical Statistics of the United States.*

Songs of the Theater, by Richard Lewine and Alfred Simon. New York: H. W. Wilson, 1984. 897p. $70. 0–8242–0706–8 84–13068
American Song: The Complete Musical Theatre Companion, by Ken Bloom. New York: Facts On File, 1985. 2 v. $95. 0–87196–961–0 84–24728

When placed side by side by side, these two guides to the songs of American musicals are strikingly similar. *Songs of the Theater* covers more than 17,000 songs from 1,200 Broadway and off-Broadway shows produced between 1891 (the year of Reginald De Koven's *Robin Hood*) and the end of 1983. Its main section is an alphabetical listing of the songs, identifying composer, lyricist, show, and year of each. A second section lists the shows alphabetically, giving for each its opening date, number of performances, songs, and notes on the show, including the availability of a record album, piano vocal score, or vocal selections. The book concludes with a chronology of shows, an index of film and television productions of musicals, and an index of composers, lyricists, and authors. Entries in the index of film and TV productions list songs dropped from or added to these versions.

American Song places its alphabetical list of shows first. Although it covers the shorter time span of 1900 through 1984, *American Song* lists approximately 1,100 more productions and 25,000 more songs than *Songs of the Theater* since it also includes off-off-Broadway productions and shows which flopped on the road in tryouts and never opened in New York. *American Song*'s entries give much more information about each show, listing not only the composer, lyricist, and songs, but also the producer, director, librettist, choreographer, costume designer, other technical personnel, and cast. Symbols beside song titles tell which ones were added in film or TV productions, which ones were dropped from these productions, and which ones were added or dropped during the stage run. Bloom often adds notes explaining his source of information on a show, assessing its worth, or relating an interesting anecdote about a show. The second volume indexes the first by personal names and song titles. It also has a chronology of shows.

Songs of the Theater, although it covers fewer shows and songs, is more convenient when one wants to learn simply who wrote the lyrics or music for a particular song or the name of the show that gave it birth. *American Song* provides the same information, but only by going through one of its indexes. Both are ably done, yet if a library can afford only one of these and does mind losing coverage of the five shows produced during the 1890s, it should buy the more comprehensive *American Song.*

Subject Compilations of State Laws 1979–1983, by Cheryl Nyberg and Carol Boast. Westport, CT: Greenwood, 1984. 556p. $55. 0–313–23335–7 84–12813

Nyberg/Boast, as the authors refer to their compilation, updates and continues Foster/Boast, Lynn Foster and Carol Boast's *Subject Compilations of State Laws* (Westport, CT: Greenwood, 1981). The entry-numbering system of Nyberg/Boast, a bibliography of 1,466 "treatises, pamphlets, reference books, journal articles, legal newspapers, state and federal documents, looseleaf services, and cases that contain compilations of state laws," picks up where Foster/Boast leaves off. The bibliography is arranged in 327 subject headings, most carried over from Foster/Boast. Annotations tell what sort of information the items contain and how many states they cover; many include references to entries in Foster/Boast. An author index and a directory of publishers follows the bibliography. A fifty-page research guide, updated from Foster/Boast, opens the volume. This guide serves as a state-of-the-art survey of compilations of state administrative regulations and commercial looseleaf compilations of state statutes and regulations. It has its own index apart from the bibliography's author index. People often want to know what the laws on a particular matter are in the various states. Only in the largest law libraries can one compile for oneself such a list, and then only at the cost of considerable time. So, until Nyberg and Boast get their wish of being "put . . . out of business" by a continuously updated database produced by one of the legal resource publishers, the base volume and this supplement are invaluable aids to research in comparative state law. Meanwhile, Nyberg and Boast offer a monthly update on subscription.

Undying Passion, by Joseph R. Orgel. New York: Morrow, 1985. 379p.

$16.95. 0–688–02218–9 84–61797

Most public and academic library reference collections have heavy concentrations of literary biography. The staple of these books is the formula birth-to-death comprehensive overview sprinkled with criticism of major works. Such workmanlike biographies of even the most flamboyant figures (for example, Byron, who, since dogs were forbidden, kept a bear as a pet while at Cambridge) fail to bring their subjects to life. These collections are redeemed from pedestrian emphasis on fact by the presence (and the best reference librarians' hearty recommendations) of Donald Hall's *The Oxford Book of American Literary Anecdotes* (New York: Oxford, 1981) and its older British sibling, James Sutherland's *Oxford Book of Literary Anecdotes* (New York: Oxford, 1975). Orgel's *Undying Passion,* subtitled "A Book of Anecdotes About Men, Women, Love, Sex, and the Literary Life," is worthy to stand beside them. "And So to Wed," at a hundred pages the longest of the seventeen chapters, tells how famous writers from the United States, England, and the continent came to their decisions to marry. Thus can a reader learn of W. H. Davies's search for a whore fit to become his wife, of Yeats's persistent pursuit of Maud Gonne and her equally persistent resistance, and of Robert Frost's secret marriage to his wife preceding their public wedding. Other chapters discuss writers' trips to brothels, the loss of their virginity, affairs, homosexuality, adultery, cases of mistaken identity, refusals, and other experiences. Orgel cites his sources in notes clustered at the back of the book just ahead of the personal name index. The brief anecdotes, some a paragraph, others several pages, invariably amuse or offer insight into their protaganists' personalities. The format (as well as the subject matter) makes this the ideal bedside book for anyone interested in literary lives. Although by conventional definitions not a reference book, it will enliven the literature section of reference collections.

Ward's Directory of 49,000 Private U.S. Companies. Baldwin H. Ward Publications (929 Petaluma Blvd. N., Petaluma, CA 94952), 1984. 1,184p. pa $195. 0–913482–02–1 ISSN 0737–4445

What *Ward's Directory of 51,000 Largest U.S. Corporations* (reviewed in *WLB*, January 1985) does for those companies, this directory does for the nation's 49,000 privately owned companies with annual sales of between $2 million and $10 million. Even though most of the companies in *51,000 Largest U.S. Corporations* are private, no company is listed in both directories. Like other Ward directories, *49,000 Private U.S. Companies* ranks the companies by sales within three-digit SIC categories and lists them in state and zip code order as well as alphabetically. Entries in all three sections include name, address, name of chief executive officer, phone number, a four-digit SIC number, annual sales, number of employees, whether or not the company exports, and year of founding. This directory includes a master index to the 100,000 companies listed in the two directories. It also has special lists of the 1,000 private companies with sales of $10 million, and the 1,000 having between 200 and 500 employees. The publisher verified the information in the directory in mid-1984. No other business directories attempt to rank companies nor do any others list as many obscure companies as do the Ward directories. Because they are often the only source of any published information about companies that don't rate inclusion in the Moody's manuals or other corporate directories, these directories have become essential purchases for comprehensive business collections. It is unfortunate that libraries that buy this new directory will not be able to use it immediately upon its arrival. The perfect binding could not hold up during the mild treatment of the review process; if the book is to survive daily use, it will need to take a detour through the bindery before reaching its destination in the reference collection.

What's the Difference? by Jane B. Stump. New York: Morrow, 1985. 247p. $12.95. 0–688–04192–2 84–20569

The difference in the title is the difference between men and women. A few of the answers are that more women than men are churchgoers but that 95.8 percent of the clergy is male; that in 1980 more men than women earned doctorates in psychology but more women than men earned master's degrees in psychology that year; that men with type O blood usually outlive men with type B blood but that women with type B blood tend to outlive women with type O; and that 75 percent of men surveyed said their jobs were the most important things in their lives but the same proportion of women said their families were most important in their lives. Organized alphabetically by key word, hundreds of paradoxes and simple facts about how men and women compare tell "what's the difference." Many deal with emotional health, physical strength and stamina, longevity, sexual activity, occupations, and income. A small number of the "facts" are vague verging on meaninglessness, for example, "Thirty thousand older men and sixteen thousand older women wed each year," with "older" not defined. A brief citation to its source follows each comparison; full citations for the sources are given in the eclectic bibliography of approximately 350 items, most published since 1975. Sources cited include *World Almanac, Ms., Science Digest, Parade Magazine, Psychology Today, Sex Roles: A Journal of Research,* and an equally diverse collection of books, among them Joyce Brothers's *What Every Woman Should Know About Men* and Sylvia Farnham-Diggory's *Learning Disabilities* (Cambridge: Harvard University Press, 1978). In other words, this should be used as a sort of statistical abstract; the prudent user will go to the cited source of any comparison to verify its authority.

Who's New Wave in Music, compiled and edited by David Bianco. Ann Arbor: Pierian Press, 1985. 430p. $39.50. 0–87650–173–0 84–61228 (Rock & roll reference series, vol. 14)

A directory, a discography, a bibliography, a glossary, an index to performers, and an index to songs, *Who's New Wave in Music* is the all-purpose reference work for punk rock, new wave, and other rock styles between 1976 and 1982. Those other styles include "the ska and mod revivals, power pop, electro- and technopop, [and] rockabilly." Those who think that the Sex Pistols were the entire movement will be surprised that Bianco lists 854 groups, some with endearing names such as Parasites of the Western World and Throbbing Gristle. Each group's entry lists its name, home base, founding date, style of music, personnel (including dates of membership and instruments played), chronology, articles about the group, reviews of live performances, discography, and address. This comprehensive directory is indexed by personal name, record label, song and album titles, musical style, and geographic location. A second directory organized by record company lists the new wave, punk, etc., records each one released. Appendixes annotate books, new wave and mainstream rock magazines, new wave fanzines, and anthology albums illustrating the new wave style. The glossary defining the vocabulary of this part of the rock music world bristles with more *see* and *see also* references than a punk's spiked hairdo; synonyms abound in this field and seemingly identical terms possess subtle differences in meaning. One can understand the lack of biographies of the performers since most are still in their twenties or early thirties. The various parts of the book work well together, making this the complete reference source on the first wave of new wave.

Women in Particular, by Kali Herman. Phoenix: Oryx Press, 1984. 740p. $95. 0–89774–088–2 84–1019

The idea, an index to biographies in a number of biographical sources and general purpose reference works, has become commonplace in recent years. Nevertheless, Herman has given it a new twist in this index to biographies of more than 21,000 significant American women in an eclectic assembly of fifty-four reference works. Similarities between *Women in Particular* and Norma O. Ireland's *Index of Women of the World* (Westwood, MA: Faxon, 1970) are obvious. In a single alphabet, Ireland indexes biographies of women of all ages and nations in numerous works. Herman groups the women into categories such as civil rights, fashion and etiquette, labor welfare and reform, oratory, photography, sports, and the temperance movement. Within each category the entries, arranged chronologically by the subjects' birthdates, list name, dates, occupation or achievement, ethnic background or religious affiliation, and sources in which additional information can be found. One source which figures prominently is Ireland's book, itself an index to other books. Herman's innovations in the biographical index genre are the arrangement by occupational category and the inclusion of religious affiliation, ethnic/racial, and geographic indexes. Entries in these indexes conveniently include all of the information of the entries in the main occupational section. A cumulative name index indexes all of the other sections, permitting a user to locate entries of particular women. Herman's special indexes and the chronological arrangement of subjects in all sections facilitates historical approaches to the progress of American women in an occupation, area, or religious tradition. Because of these indexes, this work does more than supplement Ireland. Academic and public libraries in particular will want to acquire *Women in Particular.*

World Artists 1950–1980, by Claude Marks. New York: H.W. Wilson, 1984. 912p. $70. 0–8242–0707–6 84–13152

World Artists immediately invites comparison to *Contemporary Artists* (2nd ed., New York: St. Martin's, 1983). Rather than compete, they complement one another. Their selections of illustrations reveal their emphases: *Contemporary Artists* decorates its pages with black-and-white reproductions of art works; *World Artists* choses instead photographs or self-portraits of its subjects. If the artist's work and criticism of that work can be construed as two dimensions of an artist's biography, then *Contemporary Artists,* with its brief critical essays by scholarly contributors, can be taken as an exemplar of two-dimensional artistic biography. The succinctness of its biographical facts and the clarity of its layout of lists of individual and group exhibitions, collections, and writings about the artists serve as the setting for the jewel of its criticism. *World Artists* also concerns itself with the artists' works, but approaches them through the lives of their creators. Its 312 biographies, running between 1,500 and 6,000 words in length and rich in anecdotes and autobiographical quotations, exemplify three-dimensional artistic biography; they combine the works, criticism of the works, and consideration of the creators' personal lives. Events such as associations with other artists, marriages and divorces, and international moves to flee oppressive governments often help explain the development of an artist's work, especially those artists who came to prominence just before and since World War II. *World Artists* draws its strength from emphasizing this dimension of biography. The opening paragraph of every biography in *World Artists* concisely summarizes the artist's significance and identifies his or her membership in schools or movements. As in *Contemporary Artists,* entries in *World Artists* include lists of group and individual exhibitions, significant museum and private collections, and selected books and articles about the artists. Each of these fine books sets the value of the other in relief. ▣

Gail Pool:

Editor's Choice

White Noise, by Don DeLillo. New York: Elisabeth Sifton Books: Viking, 1985. 326p. $16.95. 0-670-80373-1 84-40375

White Noise deals with the most familiar material—strange new viruses, meaningless sex, chemical waste, physical and spiritual decay and death, the decline of the West. But DeLillo, with his streamlined, supple prose, matches everything up in astonishing combinations. From the opening description of possession-laden students arriving in their parents' station wagons for the fall term at a small college somewhere in the heartland's industrial desert, straight through to the finale set in an emergency room run by blasphemous nuns, the novel is gripping, with very few lulls along the way.

DeLillo is an original. His characters are cartoons, but he treats them with respect. Jack, the "most prominent figure in Hitler Studies in North America," fears that his colleagues will learn that he knows no German; his wife Babette teaches senior citizens how to sit and stand, and takes a pill designed to deaden those brain cells that activate the fear of death; their children (from previous marriages) are maddeningly smart about environmental toxins and their parents' hangups, and tirelessly castigate the adults while munching junk food and watching devastation footage on the tube. As the disasters multiply and the hilarity rises, DeLillo is able to flood the book with emotion so that the deadpan comic-strip creatures are glimpsed as tragic figures. *White Noise* isn't as densely poetic as *The Names* (1982), nor does it quite achieve that novel's mysterious power, but it's much more accessible and may open up a large audience for DeLillo's fiction.

—*John Alfred Avant*

Gail Pool *is former editor of* Boston Review *and has reviewed for* The Nation, Christian Science Monitor, *and the* Washington Post.

The Discovery of King Arthur, by Geoffrey Ashe. New York: Doubleday & Co., 1984. 192p. $16.95. 0-385-19032-8

At first, one might expect the "discovery" in the title of this book to refer to the discovery by the reading public of the quasi-historical, Dark Age warrior Arthur, as opposed to the legendary King Arthur of romance. After all, it was Geoffrey Ashe himself who was influential in popularizing this view of Arthur. In fact, the book is about Ashe's discovery of a documented Briton of the late fifth century who, Ashe now believes, was in [fact] "King Arthur."

The book has an engaging style and all the virtues of Ashe's other works: it is imaginative, well-informed, and communicates a lively enthusiasm for the time and place. It also displays his most notable failing, a too ready transition from "could have," "may well have been," and "plausibly" to "on the basis of Arthur's identity, there need never have been any mystery at all." Of course, the coulds and might haves are unavoidable in this context; that's why the Dark Ages are so called. But Ashe, despite protests to the contrary, gives in just a little to the temptation to seize on the best possibilities and call them facts.

Ashe prefaces his new theory with a clear summary of the known and knowable Arthurian background that provides a good, brief introduction to the period and the historical problems it entails. The author's useful bibliography suggests other books, notably John Morris's *The Age of Arthur* (New York: Scribner, 1973), that treat the history in greater depth. Ashe's later chapters trace the Arthurian idea from history into legend; this is well done, but the final pages on Arthur in modern literature are perfunctory. (An interesting recent book on that topic, *The Return of King Arthur,* by Beverly Taylor and Elisabeth Brewer, Barnes & Noble, 1983, was published too late for inclusion.)

This is not a definitive treatment of the "Arthur Question." But it makes delightful reading, the controversy is stimulating, and *The Discovery of King Arthur* should inspire in a whole new audience a lasting fascination with the subject.

—*Stephanie Martin*

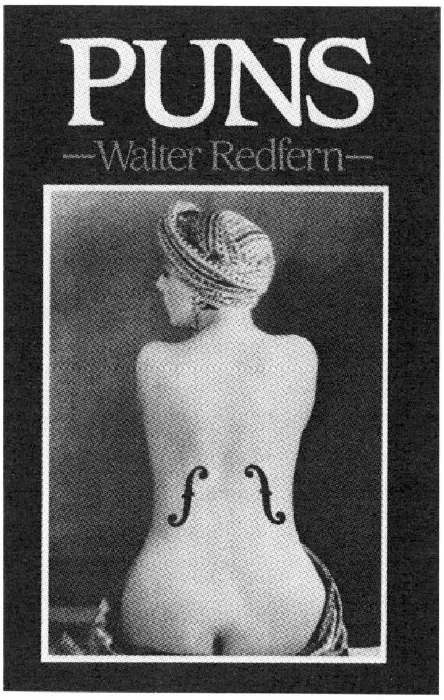

Puns, by Walter Redfern. Oxford and New York: Basil Blackwell, 1985. 256p. $14.95. 0-631-13793-9

"Puns," said Arthur Koestler, "represent the most primitive form of humor." Ambrose Bierce defined the pun as "a form of wit, to which wise men stoop and fools aspire."

The pun, one might say, has suffered from a poor image and bad press. Walter Redfern has sought to redress this situation in *Puns,* a full-scale defense of this much-maligned form of word play.

Redfern, a professor of French studies at the University of Reading and himself a punster, explores his subject from historical, psychological, cultural, and linguistic points of view. He shows how puns have been used in various literatures, from Sanskirt writings to Flaubert, and he examines theories of punning posited through the centuries. Redfern offers some good insight into the appeal of puns: their economy, their playfulness, the dimension they add to language. Of the numerous theories put forth to account for our negative reaction to puns, however, I think none convincingly explains why they make us "groan, squirm, flinch, grimace or wince."

"Part anthology, part gloss, part invention, part speculation," *Puns* brings together a large body of commentary on puns. One might not have suspected how many people, from Coleridge to McLuhan, have applied themselves to the subject. An appealing part of the book are the puns themselves, of which I should have liked many more: "It takes a lot of excises to keep Uncle Sam fiscally fit." "A critic is a man who pans for gold." Despite the injunction that "unlike children, puns should be heard not seen," one reacts strongly to the printed pun, even giving the requisite wince.

In many ways a rich book, *Puns* is stylistically frustrating. "My tone swivels between academic pedantry, journalese and the gutter; between the pedestrian and the jaywalker," says Redfern in his conclusion. But I think he is too easy on himself. His style is excessively convoluted, often obscuring where it should illuminate. If the book's intention is "to let in some bracing air on a cloistered topic," a less dense hedge of prose might have served the purpose better.

—*G.P.*

Habitations of the Word: Essays, by William H. Gass. New York: Simon & Schuster, 1985. 228p. $17.95. 0-671-52726-6

To read William Gass is to accompany an extraordinary mind on a quest for perfection, an invigorating voyage for the strong of heart. "There are truths," asserts this philosopher/fiction writer/literary critic, and while these truths cannot be named, they can be realized and encountered in language, for the word is the essence of consciousness, and "consciousness is all the holiness we have."

In this new collection of essays, written for different occasions over the past five years (symposia, commencement addresses, publication in journals), Gass returns to the same themes he explored in his last volume of essays, *The World Within the Word.* Again it is language that is celebrated, examined, and put to use in startling new ways. In this volume we are urged to seek out the "habitation of the word" in the great lines of literature, for there both reader and writer share a moment of immortality. Each of these essays resounds with a faith in the power of language well-used; their various subjects provide Gass with different materials and strategies for coming around to this one injunction: Read; Use language with care and joy; Live it so that you sing the word, dance it, taste it.

"When Ideas and things are separate, the word is torn in two," says Gass in his title essay. In keeping with this vision of the essential unity, in language, of Ideas (or Forms) and things, Gass undertakes this spiritual quest in the most physical terms. His imagery is earthy and sublime, his style one of luxurious excess, where things are called by all their names. His essay devoted to exploring the multiple meanings of the word "and" reveals that he is aware of his place in the tradition of expansive American writers which includes Gertrude Stein and Hemingway as well as Whitman and Melville.

It is a keen pleasure to accompany so erudite and energetic a reader over the terrain of great writers, Henry James, Rilke, Sir Thomas Browne, and Plato among many others. "It is the words of others which most often bring the essay into being," he notes in his introductory essay on Emerson, and here these words have sparked reflections on such subjects as the importance of talking and reading to oneself in exercising the gift of language and the writer's necessary struggle with the barriers of his unconscious in the quest for "the soul inside the sentence."

This volume is a call to join this celebrant of words in realizing the infinite possibilities of the human spirit. It is a challenge only the faint of heart would refuse.

—*Candyce Dostert*

Film Forum, by Ellen Oumano. New York: St. Martin's Press, 1985. 400p. $15.95. 0-312-28932-4

Buried within *Film Forum* is the nucleus of a good book. To create this "symposium" on filmmaking, Oumano interviewed thirty-five independent filmmakers, a category she defines as those directors and cinematographers who maintain significant control over the making of their films. Mainstream directors such as Sidney Lumet are included along with more maverick and less commercially successful directors like Chantal Akerman and Jean Rouch. Filmmakers, especially those as articulate and engaged with their art as many of Oumano's interviewees, are inherently interesting when they comment on the techniques and theories behind their works. Since printed information on most independent filmmakers is scarce, a publication dealing with this neglected aspect of cinema is all the more welcome.

The serious flaw in this book lies with its unfortunate organization. Oumano chose to chop up her interviews, and group related comments by various filmmakers under broad topical headings. In the aggregate, these comments supposedly shed light on the processes behind the films. Instead, we get snippets that tantalize more than they reveal, and the individual filmmaker's perspective and voice are lost. Since the volume is not indexed, it is impossible even to piece together the remnants of the original interviews. Moreover, Oumano's own profiles of the filmmakers border on the sophomoric in their totally uncritical appraisals of the personalities and careers involved. Perhaps a filmmaking student might find some value in having glimpses into the working methods of different directors brought together. For most of us, this book represents a missed opportuity.

—Jeanne Anderegg

Christine de Pizan: Her Life and Works: A Biography, by Charity Cannon Willard. New York: Persea Books, 1984. 266p. $19.95. 0–89255–084–8

In 1442, not long after Christine de Pizan died, Martin le Franc said, "Though death may draw the curtain around her today, her name shall endure."

His prophecy may finally be fulfilled—but not, it seems, without a struggle. Christine, often called "the first professional female writer," was the author of more than twenty works, successful and influential in her own time, and one of the few women of her era to enter into public intellectual debate. But her works were largely forgotten until the eighteenth century, and the process of rediscovery has been slow. Until recently, many of her writings were unavailable except in manuscript, and most still cannot be found in modern English. Without texts, readers and critics have necessarily been scarce.

The first modern-English translation of Christine's remarkable *Book of the City of Ladies* in 1982 was one major step toward recognition of this fourteenth century author, and Charity Cannon Willard's biography is another. Dr. Willard, a medieval scholar and a recent recipient of the French government's Order of the Academic Palms, has spent most of her life on the study of Christine de Pizan. This distillation of her studies is a fine elucidation of Christine's life and works.

Born in Venice in 1365, Christine was brought to France at the age of three to join her father, a municipal counselor to Charles V. Her childhood was comfortable, her young womanhood conventional. At twenty-five, she was left a widow with three children, a widowed mother, and a niece to support—and no inheritance.

That Christine turned to writing to earn a living is extraordinary; that she succeeded is still more so. Between 1390 and 1429, she won recognition with a diverse body of poetry and prose, including ballads, a commissioned biography of Charles V, a highly respected military essay ("The Book of Feats of Arms and Chivalry") and *The Book of the City of Ladies,* a history and defense of women that was both a personal and an intellectual response to the widespread misogyny of her era.

Willard chronicles Christine's life and examines her development as a writer, analyzing specific works in relation both to biographical data (which Christine used freely in her poetry and prose) and to the political and social milieu of medieval France. Balanced, scholarly, lucid, *Christine de Pizan* brings to light the life and work of a writer who has been invisible for far too long.

—G.P.

The Bicentennial of John James Audubon, by Alton A. Lindsey. With chapters by Mary Durant, Michael Harwood, Frank Levering, Robert Owen Petty, and Scott Russell Sanders. Illustrated by Robert A. Petty. Bloomington, IN: Indiana University Press, 1985. 175p. $17.50 0–253–10650–8 84–47791

This assemblage of well-crafted essays marking the bicentennial of John James Audubon's birth shows that the famous "bird man" was hard to classify. He was, of course, artist-naturalist extraordinaire, head of the family enterprise which gave us monumental masterpieces—*Birds of America, Ornithological Biography,* and *Quadrupeds of North America.* Till his mid-thirties he fitted bird watching and painting into the spare time his dry goods business allowed, but once he turned pro, he burned the candle at both ends, blazing new trails in the ornithological wilderness of limited equipment, scarce literature, and hundreds of as-yet-unidentified species. As Alton Lindsey remarks more than once, Audubon had the great good luck to work in a magnificient America that we will never know. In Europe Audubon made his mark as the quintessentially American (despite his thick French accent), rough-and-ready woodsman, selling subscriptions of his work to drawing room society. Back home, he was an ebullient teller of yarns and anecdotes, and a consummate player of practical jokes. But admirable as he was, "the father of American ornithology" had his flaws. He often lied about his illegitimate birth to a French seaman and his mistress on the island of Santo Domingo. He probably didn't study with the famous painter David as he sometimes claimed. His grounding in science was so poor that a Scottish zoologist had to give the middle-aged master a crash course in ornithology. Occasionally he misclassified species or painted birds with the wrong accompanying flora. Perhaps most disturbing to those who revere him as a patron saint of conservation, he indulged in wasteful shooting sprees, banging down scores of birds, then keeping only a handful for study specimens.

The book is occasionally repetitive, especially about Audubon the woodsman. And if the excellent chapter, "The Man Himself," had occurred early on rather than smack in the middle, it would have spared this reader some confusion. But there are moments of pure poetry here—stories of Audubon observing a flock of chimney swifts in a hollow tree, or nestling a mother hawk in his palm as he gently measured her beak and body, or finding the joy of birdsong even on his darkest days. And there's the moving tale of a fourteen-year-old boy's saving the oxidized plates for the magnificent *Birds of America* from meltdown into copper bars. Altogether this handsomely illustrated book with its multiple viewpoints on Audubon and his legacy gives a balanced assessment and is a worthy addition to our shelves of Audubonian a.

—*Peg Padnos*

Louise Bogan: A Portrait, by Elizabeth Frank. New York: Alfred Knopf, 1985. 460p. $24.95. 0-394-52484-5 83-48853

Louise Bogan, who died in 1971, and whose poems, collected in *The Blue Estuaries,* first appeared in the 1920s, wrote lyrics of extraordinary intensity and beauty. They are personal, but distant; as she observed, "the rough and vulgar facts are not there." Bogan's guarded reticence, which extended to public statements about herself, has a powerful effect upon one's imagination, and makes her an excellent subject for a biography. *Louise Bogan: A Portrait* is a thorough, cogent, and dispassionate account of Bogan's life, offering clues as to why she was so private and why it became increasingly difficult for her to write.

Until now, readers interested in Bogan's life had two sources: a volume of letters, *What the Woman Lived,* and an autobiographical "mosiac," *Journey Around My Room,* assembled by Ruth Limmer, Bogan's literary executor, who also edited the letters. From the letters, written to Edmund Wilson, Theodore Roethke, May Sarton, and many others, one could discern Bogan's wit, both caustic and playful, her pride, honesty, and dedication to self-knowledge. In her criticism, collected in *A Poet's Alphabet,* she was often ruthlessly judgmental (and perceptive) about her contemporaries, but in the letters one saw that she also applied her impossible standards to herself. They show her most often high-spirited; but her autobiography shows her depressed. The overall sense is of a supremely talented and engaging woman overcome by demons she fought, but could not master; a woman whose fighting spirit often masked inner inertia.

Frank's account fills in many gaps, but does not alter the basic portrait Bogan herself left, though her temper, paranoia, and jealousy are shown to be even greater than one had guessed. Most surprising is Frank's assertion that overcoming these traits, and finding emotional equilibrium, had a deadening effect upon Bogan's ability to write poems. She overcame her demons, and then, unable or unwilling to risk her peace, she was "becalmed," plagued only by her desire for poems.

A Portrait, like its subject, is discreet; even so, there is plenty of interesting, well-developed material here. Frank is particularly good in describing Bogan's childhood, and her problematic relationship with her mother; her independent stance amidst the politics of the 1930s; and the difficult break-up of her marriage to Raymond Holden.

Louise Bogan's best poems will last as long as people read lyric poetry, and *A Portrait* brings to life the enigmatic woman who wrote them.

—*Carol Moldaw*

This Place, by Andrea Freud Loewenstein. Boston: Pandora/Routledge & Kegan Paul, 1984. 440p. $14.95. 0-86358-039-4

"This Place" is the prison setting Loewenstein utilizes as background for her examination of women's relationships with each other as lovers, as therapists, as inmates, all dealing with power transactions. The novel covers four months of journal entries of four women: Ruth Foster, the traditional therapist who teaches inmates how to name their reality, yet can't define her own; Sonya Lehrman, the "expressive" therapist, an artist who self-consciously creates film footage of her life; Candy Peters, the white "'ho"; and Telecea Jones, a paranoid schizophrenic whose visionary rantings evoke a Greek chorus to the action of the novel.

The central relationship in the book, between Sonya and Ruth, is characterized by manipulation: the dominant artist and her victim, the woman she seeks to objectify and use. Sonya devises a sculpture of Ruth and herself: "Two female figures, balancing each other as they jockeyed for position." Ruth's attraction to Sonya leads to her unraveling and ultimate collapse. Marge Piercy's "Song of the Fucked Duck" applies here: "In using there are always two./The manipulator dances with a partner who cons herself./There are lies that glow so brightly we consent/To give a finger and then an arm/To let them burn. . . . " *This Place* offers grim evidence that love relationships between women may parallel the most destructive love relationships between men and women.

Loewenstein's setting is unique. The women's prison and its cottage, softball diamond, yard, and mental health corridor become familiar ground upon which the four major players present themselves. One is drawn into caring deeply about their intermeshed lives, becoming very much involved with Ruth Foster's struggle with her sexual and professional identities; and with Candy's similar tasks. There's nothing artificial in the complicated lives and feelings of Loewenstein's women. Their separate struggles to become new and the despair of backsliding, "losing it," speak vividly.

—*Clare Marie Ackroyd*

Library World

News of announcements, new posts, retirements, and deaths should be sent to "Library World," WLB, *950 University Ave., Bronx, NY 10452.*

ANNOUNCEMENTS

Paul Galdone, illustrator and author of children's books, has received the sixth annual award for outstanding contributions to children's literature given by the School Library Media Specialists of Southeastern New York (SLMSENY).

The Hawaii LA as elected officers for 1985. They are: **Arlene Tibayan,** pres.; **De Etta Wilson,** vice pres./pres. elect; **Amy Nogami,** secy.; and **Vernon Tam,** treas.

NEW POSTS

Michael Bilhorn, formerly reference librarian at the Univ. of Houston libraries, is now librarian for the Yorktown branch campus of the Mercy College libraries, Westchester County, N.Y.

Mary Ellen Bowman-Ritz has been promoted to librarian II/cable television coordinator at the Buena Park library district, Buena Park, Calif. She is executive producer of the Library Channel, which cablecasts library programming and educational shows.

Edith Branman has been named coordinator of outreach services at the Queens Borough PL, N.Y. She was formerly director of public relations for the library.

Barbara Brown has been appointed head librarian at Washington and Lee Univ., Lexington, Va. She was previously associate director of program coordination for Research Libraries Group, Inc., Stanford, Calif.

Linda Silver

John Corbett has joined the staff of the Finkelstein Memorial Library, Spring Valley, N.Y. as media librarian. He was formerly media librarian at the Passaic County (N.J.) College Library.

Robert Daw has been named head of the art and music dept. of the Omaha PL, Omaha, Neb. He was formerly head of the Topeka (Kansas) PL fine arts dept.

Suzanne Fedunok has been promoted to assistant director for resources at the Columbia Univ. libraries. She joined the staff as math/physics librarian in 1977, and became head of collection development/reference, science and engineering, in 1983.

Sue Fontaine, previously associate manager of public relations for the New York PL, has been appointed director of public relations for the Queens Borough PL.

Peter Graham has been promoted to assistant director for bibliographic control at the Columbia Univ. libraries. He joined the staff as head of book acquisitions in 1981.

Michael McCaslin has been appointed deputy executive director for the resources and technical services division (RTSD) of ALA. He was formerly collection development/technical services coordinator at the DuPage library system, Geneva, Ill.

Donna Skvarda

Marlene Ogg has joined the staff of the Oak Park (Ill.) PL as head of the technical services dept. She was previously head of technical services at the Crown Point (Ind.) Community Library.

Linda Silver, former public services director of the Cuyahoga County (Ohio) PL, has been promoted to deputy director of the library.

Donna Skvarla, formerly head of children's services for the Norman (Okla.) PL, is now the adult program consultant for the Oklahoma Dept. of Libraries.

Mona Stevenson has been promoted to assistant director of the Warren Trumbull County (Ohio) PL. She was formerly head of the main library.

Barbara Sullivan, formerly periodicals/circulation librarian at Gary Memorial Library, Vermont College, Montpelier, is now librarian of the Bronx Extension Center of the Mercy College libraries, Westchester County, N.Y.

Shirley Sykes has been named adult materials specialist for the Oklahoma City metropolitan library system, Okla. She was previously acquisitions librarian for Kilgore College, Kilgore, Texas.

MARKETPLACE

Announcements

☐ This year marks the fortieth anniversary of the United Nations and observances will culminate October 24, United Nations Day. The UN Publications Division will be cooperating with libraries that wish to set up special UN exhibits. Those interested should contact Nina Leneman, Deputy Chief, Sales Section, Publications Division, UN, New York, N Y 10017.

☐ The President's Committee on the Arts and Humanities in cooperation with the Exxon Corporation has established a pilot project to use the PBS series "Great Performances" in public library programming. Four public libraries have been chosen as test sites: those in Baton Rouge, New York City, Baltimore, and Shepherdstown, West Virginia. Each library will receive a set of videotapes, playback equipment, $3,000 for expenses, and the services of a programming consultant.

☐ Lilian Moore has been named winner of the 1985 National Council of Teachers of English Award for Excellence in Poetry for Children. The award is given every three years in recognition of a poet's work for children ages three to thirteen. Moore is the author of a number of poetry collections, the first of which, *I Feel the Same Way,* was published in 1967. The presentation of the award will take place November 23 at the Books for Children Luncheon at the NCTE annual convention in Philadelphia. For book jacket seals, imprinted with the award medallion, contact NCTE, 1111 Kenyon Rd., Urbana, IL 61801.

☐ Three annual awards for the best catalogs published by U.S. or Canadian institutions for exhibitions of books or manuscripts will be granted for the first time next year by the Rare Books and Manuscripts Section of the Association of College and Research Libraries. Catalogs published between January 1, 1983 and August 31, 1985 are eligible and must be submitted by September 30, 1985. Awards will be granted in three budget categories: expensive, moderately expensive, and inexpensive, based on the production costs. For entry forms write Sally Leach, Chair, RBMS Committee for Awards for Exhibition Catalogues, Harry Ransom Humanities Research Center, Drawer 7219, Austin, TX 78713.

Children's Specials

☐ The Children's Science Book Review Committee, sponsored by the science and mathematics program of Boston University's School of Education and the New England Roundtable of Children's Librarians publishes *Appraisal,* a quarterly review of children's science books. Each book is reviewed by both a children's librarian and a scientist. Subscriptions are $16 from Diane Holzheimer, Editor, *Appraisal,* 605 Commonwealth Ave., Boston, MA 02215.

☐ An anthology of criticism from the Children's Literature Association *Newsletter* and *Quarterly* (prior to the establishment of the present journal) has been edited by Patricia Dooley, former editor of both publications. The articles in *The First Steps: Best of the Early ChLA Quarterly* are arranged chronologically with a subject index. Topics include the canon of children's literature, children's science fiction, folklore, children's book awards, and illustration. The 150p. paperback is available for $17.50 from ChLA Publications, 210 Education, Purdue University, West Lafayette, IN 47907.

☐ Children often wish to have some kind of contact with a favorite author, and in response Canadian mystery writer Eric Wilson has set up the Eric Wilson Mystery Club. Membership is free and includes a semi-annual newsletter to which children may contribute reviews and stories, or ask Wilson questions. Write the Eric Wilson Mystery Club, Collins Publishers, 100 Lesmill Rd., Don Mills, Ont. M3B 2T5, Canada.

☐ Elaine Moss continues to proselytize for the use of picture books by older children in the second edition of *Picture Books for Young People 9–13.* The evaluations of recommended titles, arranged by broad subject, have been increased to 101. The 46p. paperback is available for $4.75 from the Thimble Press, Lockwood, Station Rd., South Woodchester, Stroud, Glos. GL5 5EQ, U.K.

☐ To steer children to book sequences (in which characters grow and develop) rather than sequels (in which changeless characters meet endless adventures), *Sequences: An Annotated Guide to Children's Fiction in Series,* by Susan Roman, lists selected fiction for children from grade three through young adult. Approximately 125 authors are represented, many of them with two or more sets of stories. There are indexes by main character, book title, and series title. The 116p. clothbound book is available for $17.50 from Publishing Services, ALA, 50 E. Huron St., Chicago, IL 60611.

Continuing Education

☐ Pearson '85, sponsored by the University of Victoria, is a week-long immersion program designed to provide experienced school librarians information on new trends, techniques and directions in learning materials management, program development, and instructional strategy. Two sessions will be held, July 28–August 2 and August 4–9. Tuition is $240 and meals and housing are $260. For more information write Donald Hamilton, Coordinator, Pearson '85, Education Extension, University of Victoria, Box 1700, Victoria, B.C. V8W 2Y2, Canada, 605/721-7899.

☐ Miami University is offering three programs this summer to improve the effectiveness of library administrators. The two five-day programs, Middle Management, July 21–26, and Advanced Management, July 21–26, cost $495 for tuition, materials, lodging, and most meals. Strengthening Your Communication Skills, July 17–19, primarily for those who are past participants in the management programs, costs $245. For further information contact Richard Vandegrift, Director, Center for Management Services, 103 Laws Hall, Miami University, Oxford, OH 45056, 513/529-2132.

☐ Scheduled for the summer quarter at the Graduate School of Library and Information Science at the University of Washington are five week-long three-credit courses: online reference services (July 8–12), information policy (July 22–26), microcomputer software (July 29–August 2), corporate libraries (August 5–9), and promoting mathematics and science through the school media center (August 12–16). Tuition is $135. For more information contact Summer Quarter, University of Washington, GH-26, Seattle, WA 98195, 206/543-2320.

☐ An ALA preconference for children's librarians to help increase their understanding of the needs of children with learning disabilities and foster broader use of the library by this group is being held by the Association for Library Service to Children July 5, 8:30–6:00. Group seminars and AV presentations will provide an overview of what learning disabilites are, highlight successful library programs, offer help in selecting materials, and describe strategies for working with other community agencies. Registration fees are $50 for ALSC members, $75 for ALA members, and $85 for nonmembers, and include materials and lunch. The deadline is June 14. For more information contact ALA/ALSC, 50 E. Huron St., Chicago, IL 60611.

Film and Video

☐ With the Little League season fast approaching, *Coaches World* offers advice for coaches and parents on developing a positive, healthful sports program for children. Produced by the Sports and Physical Fitness Committee of the American Academy of Pediatrics, Minnesota Chapter, the videotape covers coaching philosophy, developmental differences in children, and sports physiology, psychology, and injury. Examples used are from boys and girls basketball, swimming, gymnastics, hockey, and soccer. Formats are ½-inch Beta or VHS for $125, ¾-inch U-Matic for $150, and 16mm for $350, with a reproducible handout sheet included. A preview sampler is available. Order *Coaches World,* order number HS-19, from University of Minnesota Media Distribution, Box 734 Mayo Building, 420 Delaware St. SE, Minneapolis, MN 55455, 612/376-8340.

☐ Random House has just released its first videocassettes, based on children's books. The catalog includes some original videotapes, some adapted from filmstrips, and some transferred from film. With any order a free 17-by-22-inch poster will be sent. Request the 1985 elementary catalog

from Random House Video, Random House School Division, Dept. 9249, 400 Hahn Rd., Westminster, MD 21157, 800/638-6460.

☐ The prevalence of videocassette players in schools and libraries has led to growing requests to AV producers to provide video versions of their films. Weston Woods now has forty of their titles in video, ranging from the venerable *Mike Mulligan and His Steam Shovel* to *Really Rosie* and *Harold and the Purple Crayon*. Each is available for $50 on VHS or Beta. For an annotated catalog contact Weston Woods, Weston, CT 06883, 800/243-5020.

☐ Further good news for library budgets is that distributors that already have large video collections seem to be engaged in a price war. Learning Corporation of America has lowered the price on its Basic Concepts Series to $79 each from $175. The seven-to-twelve-minute films present elementary school students with such concepts as energy, elections, reading, taxes, and money. Titles in the twenty-six-part series Leaders of the 20th Century, for a high school through adult audience, running time twenty-four minutes each, are $89, reduced from $300. The prices are for all one-half-inch formats; ¾-inch U-Matic is slightly higher. For more information contact Learning Corporation of America, 108 Wilmot Rd., Deerfield, IL 60015, 800/323-6301.

☐ Not to be outdone, Films Incorporated has reduced the prices on all its videocassettes. Series available include *Heritage: Civilization and the Jews* and the Annenberg/CPB productions on the brain, the Constitution, Congress, and writing. Request the updated price list from Films Incorporated, 1213 Wilmette Ave., Wilmette, IL 60091, 800/323-4222.

Finding Aids

☐ Universal bibliographic control advances another step with the publication of *Irish Books in Print 1984*. It covers books published in Ireland (north and south), in English and Irish, and Irish-interest books published in English abroad. The 30,000 entries are by author, title, and subject. The 1,010p. book can be ordered for $79.50 from S&J Cleary Publishers, Keshcarrigan Bookshop, 90 W. Broadway, New York, NY 10007.

☐ Recognizing its usefulness to practitioners who may never have had a chance to take a similar course, Pratt Institute is making available the 65p. syllabus, consisting mostly of bibliographies, for a class in business, economics, and statistics sources. Prepared by Joan Canning of the Brooklyn PL Business Library, the sections cover statistics; advertising, marketing, and public relations; finance and investment; money and banking; and business databases. Order *Business, Economics and Statistical Sources* for $10 from Pratt Institute, GSLIS, Brooklyn, NY 11205.

☐ The new field of men's studies is old enough to have at least 600 books, as annotated in *Men's Studies: A Selected and Annotated Interdisciplinary Bibliography*, by Eugene August. The entries are arranged by subject and cover such topics as images of men, men's rights, minority men, men in families, and health. The 230p. book is $30 from Libraries Unlimited, Box 263, Littleton, CO 80160.

☐ *Subject Guide to Book Reviews*, a new monthly publication, provides citations to book reviews in *Booklist, Kirkus, Library Journal, New York Times Book Review,* and *Publishers Weekly*. Citations are arranged by LC subject headings, with the book's author but not title given. Subscriptions are $60 from Daniel Hill, Box 646, Salem, OR 97308.

From the GPO Presses

The following titles are a sample of recent publications available from the Government Printing Office. Specify the stock number, price and quantity when ordering. Payment is by check payable to Superintendent of Documents or by Visa or Mastercard (give and card number and expiration date). Send to Superintendent of Documents, United States GPO, Washington, DC 20402. Or call the order desk at 202/783-3238.

☐ An updated edition of the *Handbook for Small Business,* which consolidates information on government programs and services to assist small businesses, has been published. Compiled by the Senate Committee on Small Business, the handbook describes the assistance programs offered by twenty-five federal agencies and departments. The 228p. publication, stock number 052-071-00680-0, is available for $7. Send prepayment to Dept. 36-LM.

☐ A publication from the National Bureau of Standards discusses issues in personal computer security management, such as physical and environmental protection, system and data access control, integrity of software and data, backup and contingency planning, and communications protection. Appendixes include a list of references, a self-audit checklist, and a guide to security products for personal computers. The 68p. *Security of Personal Computer Systems: A Management Guide,* stock number 003-003-02627-1, is available for $3. Send prepayment to Dept. 36-LR.

☐ *The United States and Sub-Saharan Africa: Guide to U.S. Official Documents and Government-Sponsored Publications, 1976-1980,* compiled by Julian Witherell, chief of LC's African and Middle Eastern Division, covers over 5,000 publications that express American policy and provide background on such issues as the civil war in Angola, South African apartheid, and the Sahelian drought. The term "government-sponsored publications" includes studies issued under government contract by universities and other research centers, or reproduced or translated by the government. The 721p. book, stock number 030-000-00160-5, is available for $17.

☐ The National Agricultural Library's Food and Nutrition Information Center has published a new bibliography, *Promoting Nutrition Through Education: A Resource Guide to the Nutrition Education and Training Program.* This is number 31 in the Bibliographies and Literature of Agriculture series of the Department of Agriculture. The bibliography, stock number 001-000-04436-2, is available for $7.50.

Idea Exchange

☐ Joining forces with technology to keep alive the tradition of reading aloud to children, a Bloomington (Minnesota) project funded by the state department of education will videotape amateurs (who will receive coaching) reading children's stories. The tapes will be cablecast and will be available in all school and public libraries in Bloomington.

☐ In a similar use of the media, mini book reviews (one minute and forty-five seconds) are being taped by staff of the Framingham (Massachusetts) PL for weekly broadcast over a local radio station. The reviews take the form of interviews, with the director asking questions of the staff member who has prepared the review. Cassettes of the interviews will be placed in a listening corner of the library, with a cassette player, headphones, and copies of the books.

☐ The Body Shop, a health awareness fair, was held at the Arlington Heights (Illinois) Memorial Library in February. Sponsored by the Youth Services Department of the Library, and the local department of health services and the fire and police departments, the day-long program provided information on health services, blood pressure, hearing, and vision screenings, a paramedic van to examine in the parking lot, and healthy refreshments.

Media Center World

☐ Developed in cooperation with the Anne Frank Center in Amsterdam, *Anne Frank: A Legacy for Our Time* is a filmstrip program to help junior high students examine their attitudes about human rights, prejudice, morality, justice, and the responsibility of the individual in society. Priced at $81, the set includes two filmstrips, two cassettes, sixteen skill sheets, and a guide. For more information write the Society for Visual Education, Dept. 20324, 1345 Diversey Parkway, Chicago, IL 60614.

☐ The Women's Educational Equity Act Publishing Center has resources ranging from bibliographies and curriculum guides to career choice materials developed to help promote sex equity and educational excellence. The materials are designed for all grade levels and cover the math, history, science, career, women's studies, and language arts curricula. For a catalog contact the WEEA Publishing Center, 55 Chapel St., Newton, MA 02160, 800/225-3088.

☐ Now available from the publisher, the American Map Corporation, Colorprint-Schick anatomy charts come in several different formats. Thirty 8½-by-11-inch color charts with overlays in a spiral binding are $17.95. These charts are also available individually for $1.50 each, in English or Spanish. Thirteen 23-by-29-inch wall charts of major body systems are $7.95 in paper or $14.95 laminated. For more information contact the American Map Corp., 46-35 54th Rd., Maspeth, NY 11378, 718/784-0055.

☐ The Milwaukee Public Museum has a series of posters featuring the new earth science exhibit, "Continents, Oceans and Life in Motion . . . A New View of the Third Planet." On one poster Tyrannosaurus rex and Triceratops battle it out in the museum's largest diorama, depicting life in Montana sixty-five million years ago. The other poster, of a Silurian reef, shows the marine life that existed in a shallow inland sea that covered Wisconsin 410 million years ago. Posters measure 25-by-18 inches and are available for $3.50 each plus $2 shipping and handling from Publications, Milwaukee Public Museum, 800 W. Wells St., Milwaukee, WI 53233, 414/278-2787.

Products and Services

☐ The new self-instructional language catalog from Audio-Forum features audio and videotapes in forty-two languages. Many of the intensive tapes were developed by the Department of State, and there are also briefer courses for those who wish to acquire only a working vocabulary. Also listed are books on tape in foreign languages, including the Bible in nine languages, six different foreign language Scrabbles, and a Spanish Monopoly. For a copy of the 1985 catalog of language courses contact Audio-Forum, Dept. R, On the Green, Guilford, CT 06437, 203/453-9794.

☐ Alos Micrographics' Planetary Recorder 26 is a table-top camera for producing 16mm rollfilm from loose or bound documents. The camera operates simply with automatic film advance and changeable film units. For more information write Alos Micrographics Corp., Box 407, Walden, NY 12586.

☐ Geac's Gigadisc is an optical disc for data storage that can hold up to two billion bytes of data on a single disc. Now personal computers can have access to this storage medium through the use of Gig-Attach, a single circuit board and accompanying software that allow a microcomputer to read and write on Gigadisc under MS-DOS. With one of the $1,195 attachments an entire network can have access to Gigadisc storage. The first product available is compatible with the IBM PC/XT and versions are being developed for other microcomputers and the Unix operating system. For more information contact Geac, 350 Steelcase Rd. W, Markham, Ont. L3R 1B3, Canada, 416/475-0525.

☐ The Paddy Wagon, a designer of printed note pads, has developed a line of humorous notepads for librarians and book lovers. For a list of the available items, write to Librarians List, The Paddy Wagon, 2421 W. Pratt Ave., Suite 294V, Chicago, IL 60645.

Professional Reading

☐ The first volume of the new semiannual *International Journal of Reviews in Library and Information Science* has been published by the Rosary College Graduate School of Library and Information Science. Edited by Rosary library science professors, the journal will review books, periodicals, AV materials, and other resources. Surveys of bibliographic services in a particular subject or country will also appear. Submission of manuscripts is invited. For more information write managing editor Patrick Williams, GSLIS, Rosary College, 7900 W. Division St., River Forest, IL 60305.

☐ Art Libraries Society of North America has published two more of their Occasional Papers. *Current Issues in Fine Arts Collection Development,* 36p. $7.50, contains five papers on collection evaluation, collection development policy, allocation of book funds, automatic acquisitions plans, and starting an art library. *Reference Tools for Fine Arts Visual Resources Collections,* 56p., $12, annotates works in three sections: professional literature for visual resources, general art reference works, and art historical sources. Both are available from Art Libraries Society of North America, 3775 Bear Creek Circle, Tucson, AZ 85749.

☐ The Office for Library Personnel Resources' latest Topics in Personnel Kits are *Employee Selection and*

Minimum Qualifications for Librarians, with material on the MLS as an employment requirement, and *Writing Library Job Descriptions,* which includes sample job descriptions for public, school, and academic librarians. Each kit is $10 prepaid from OLPR/ALA, 50 E. Huron St., Chicago, IL 60611.

☐ The Rare Books and Manuscripts Section of ACRL will be publishing a new journal devoted to special collections librarianship. Each issue will carry three or four articles, book reviews, and news notes. The emphasis will be on the theory and practice of special collections librarianship. Articles are being solicited, and to be included in the first issue should be submitted by December 2, 1985 to Ann Gwyn, Editor, Milton S. Eisenhower Library, Johns Hopkins University, Baltimore, MD 21218. For information on subscriptions contact Sandy Whiteley, ACRL/ALA, 50 E. Huron St., Chicago, IL 60611.

Software

☐ Menlo Corporation has expanded the capabilities of its *In-Search* gateway software, for end users searching DIALOG, to create *Pro-Search,* for professional online searchers using DIALOG and BRS. *Pro-Search* has a cost accounting feature for creating invoices and monthly search summaries, and allows searches to be formulated before going online, and then executed with a keystroke. The program costs $495 and runs on the IBM PC, AT, and XT, IBM-compatibles, and the TI Professional. A trial size version is available that accesses a limited number of databases and operates for three connect hours. For more information contact Menlo Corp., 4633 Old Ironsides Dr., Suite 400, Santa Clara, CA 95054, 800/221-4237.

☐ There are already several services that index software reviews, but Facts on File's new *Software Reviews on File* provides extracts from reviews appearing in over 150 publications. Review summaries are arranged by subject with address of software pro-

ducer, price and system requirements. The monthly issues and cumulated index come with a three-ring binder. Subscriptions are $145 from Facts on File, 460 Park Ave. S, New York, NY 10016.

☐ An interest inventory for the field of home economics, *There's a Career for You in Home Economics* matches student interests against the characteristics of fifty-three occupations. The software runs on Apple computers and includes an 80p. career guide. For more information contact MCE Inc., 157 S. Kalamazoo Mall, Kalamazoo, MI 49007, 800/421-4157.

☐ The first two software packages in McGraw-Hill's FastStart Tutorial series teach the use of *Lotus 1-2-3* and DOS 2.0. The tutorials run simultaneously with the application so that users learn through performing typical tasks. They operate on IBM PC, XT or compatible computers with 128K of memory for DOS and 256K for *Lotus 1-2-3.* The *Lotus 1-2-3* tutorial, including two diskettes and a reference manual, costs $79.95, and the DOS tutorial, including one diskette and reference manual, costs $59.95. For more information contact McGraw-Hill Training Systems, Box 641, Del Mar, CA 92014.

☐ The Central Illinois Libraries Microcomputer Users Group has completed its first software union list, which includes a directory of the forty-seven participating libraries with address, contact person, and hardware owned. Entries are arranged by title of software with subject, age level, system requirements, and holding libraries. The group also publishes a quarterly newsletter. Order the union list for $4 from Randy Wilson or Lori Logsdon, Parlin-Ingersoll Library, 205 W. Chestnut, Canton, IL 61520.

Write for These

☐ The National Center for Missing and Exploited Children has recently published two free booklets. *Selected State Legislation,* 54p., describes state laws that address child abuse and kidnapping, with excerpts given from various state laws now in effect. *Parental Kidnapping,* 40p., is a workbook helping parents prevent or deal with kidnapping. Legal rights are outlined and addresses given of support groups. Write to National Center for Missing and Exploited Children, 1835 K St. NW, Suite 700, Washington, DC 20006.

☐ Helen Hooven Santmyer (. . . *And Ladies of the Club*) is only the most recent example of an active and productive octogenarian. The Manhasset (New York) PL has produced a booklist of works by and about her and thirty-four other ageless seniors. The *Octogenarian Booklist* is 60¢, a set of five other adult booklists is $3, and a set of three YA booklists is $1, all produced by library staff. Order from Manhasset PL, 30 Onderdonk Ave., Manhasset, NY 11030.

☐ The Center for Early Adolescence has published *Discipline and Young Adolescents, The Learning-Disabled Student,* and *Girls, Math, and Science* for teachers of ten-to-fifteen-year-olds. Each publication summarizes current research and suggests books, AV materials, and other resources. To order a summary, send a self-addressed envelope with 39¢ postage and the title of the summary in the lower left-hand corner to the Center for Early Adolescence, Suite 223, Carr Mill Mall, Carrboro, NC 27510.

Facing the Public *(cont'd from p. 605)*

jority of our patrons.

That is why the much publicized action of the Ann Arbor Public Library to get tough with problem patrons is so refreshing. According to a recent AP news story the library's governing board has voted to revoke the library privileges of individuals who violate guidelines regulating fighting, loitering, gambling, alcohol, drugs, weapons, sleeping, and disturbing others through poor personal hygiene. Predictably the American Civil Liberties Union was critical. Their spokespeople felt the new rules might discriminate against street people and that the board was attempting to outlaw poverty in Ann Arbor.

The word "poverty" is the key to the problem. As I understand it, the Ann Arbor Library is concerned not necessarily with people who are poor, or who live in the streets, but rather with people who are violent, antisocial and engaging in illegal activities. Just because some of the people who display anti-social and violent tendencies happen to be poor does not excuse their offense. Public libraries are not social service agencies charged with the responsibilities of solving serious societal and economic problems. Rather they are reading, informational, and research centers that can only function in a safe, sane, and secure environment in which librarians and patrons alike can be free from the fear of being raped, mugged, or molested. The public library community owes a debt of gratitude to the governing board of the Ann Arbor Public Library for showing courage and foresight in dealing with the problem head on. ▣

Front Row Center *(cont'd from p. 615)*

ation. Since the best rice wine is produced in this region from the pure water in Mirror Lake, the highlight of *Water Farmers* is its focus on the making and drinking of rice wine. One sidelight—people are warned not to look into Mirror Lake if they have something to hide because the lake will reflect one's true nature.

Often shot subjectively from water level, with strong emphasis on calming natural water sounds, *Water Farmers* does much to underscore the continuing interdependence of man and nature in China today. It will also calm jittery nerves in the audience.

The series is suitable for senior high through adult audiences. General social studies, geography, and anthropology classes will find it enlightening, as will general adult library programs featuring films on China, food, or Chinese cooking. An in-house demonstration would make a wonderfully aromatic finale to your screening of *A Taste of China*! ▣

WLB Classifieds

Classified Advertising *is accepted six weeks preceding date of issue. Charges are: minimum 3 lines—$10; each additional line—$2.50. If voucher forms are required, please send them when submitting copy. All advertisements for positions must exclude reference to race, creed, color, age, and sex as conditions for employment. The publisher reserves the right to reject any advertising considered unacceptable as to wording or appearance or for any other reason. Submit classifieds to: Brian Bavolar, Wilson Library Bulletin, 950 University Ave., Bronx, NY 10452.*

Positions Open

SCHOOL LIBRARIANS. Mesa County Valley School District #51, Grand Junction, Colorado has openings for three secondary school librarians. Requires M.A. degree in Library Science. Must hold or be eligible for Colorado Certification as school librarian. Salary commensurate with experience and education. Contact Mesa County Valley School District #51, Personnel Office, 2115 Grand Ave., Grand Junction, CO 81501. Phone: (303) 245-2422.

Announcements

EARN UNIVERSITY CREDIT for travel anywhere in the world. Write Univ. of Calif. Travel/Study, Santa Barbara Extension, Santa Barbara, CA 93106.

THE FOOTLOOSE LIBRARIAN newsletter & network. Money-saving travel news + U.S. & overseas librarians offering Bed & Breakfast, housing exchange, more. "Good, practical information" M.S., IN; "An excellent publication" S.R., Tunisia. Free brochure. TFL, Box 972, Minneapolis, MN 55440.

For Sale

INDEX TO ADVERTISERS

Advanced Binding Methods, Inc. 607
Baker & Taylor Company 577
CLASS 622
Gale Research Company . . . . 4th cover
Holt, Rinehart, and Winston 611
Krieger Enterprises 617
OCLC 578
Unlisted Market Guide 581
United Nations Publications 601
H.W. Wilson Company . . . . 2nd cover, 3rd cover

Credits:
p. 602 — Lo Linkhart; 604 — David Jacobson; 608 — Little, Brown; 609 — E.P. Dutton, Dial Books; 616 — Joe Bangoy; 629 — Blackwell; 634 — Persea Books

Any day is a holiday if you have a good book to read

Celebrations

Read-Aloud Holiday and Theme Book Programs

by Caroline Feller Bauer

301pp. 1985. ISBN 0-8242-0708-4. LC 85-714. $35 U.S. and Canada, $40 other countries.

From the Pied Piper of reading, here is a highly unusual collection of 16 children's book programs based on holidays, events, and other phenomena—some real, some make-believe. Sure-fire enticements to the practice and enjoyment of reading, the complete, ready-to-use programs in *Celebrations* combine prose and poetry selections, crafts, games, recipes, book lists, and displays that bring to life such readable floating holidays as National Nothing Day, Gone Fishin', and Pigmania, as well as traditional occasions like Christmas, Valentine's Day, and Halloween.

Sixteen Ready-to-Use Read-Aloud Book Programs

Each celebration features:

- **Prose selections**—stories, folk tales, and book excerpts suitable to be read aloud and listened to in a single sitting.
- **Poetry**— both light verse and more thoughtful poetry.
- **Bulletin board displays**—simple ideas to draw attention to the programs.
- **Treats**—recipes for easy-to-make, fun-to-eat snacks.
- **Activities**—ideas for simple crafts and souvenirs, drawings, puppets, mobiles, jokes, riddles, and games.
- **Creative writing**—related topics that can be used as writing exercises or for group discussions.
- **Book lists—**selective lists including classics as well as the newest titles available.
- **Bookmarks—**an illustration for each celebration can be reproduced directly from the book and handed out as a bookmark.

With just the right mix of fun and good literature, each of these book programs is complete and can be used at a moment's notice—just add your own enthusiasm.

Also by Caroline Feller Bauer:

This Way to Books

376pp. 1983. ISBN 0-8242-0678-9. LC 82-19985.
$35 U.S. and Canada, $40 other countries.

"Contains more suggestions than one person could use in a year of teaching."
—TOP OF THE NEWS

"The inviting format, enthusiastic writing, clear directions, and helpful index contribute to the usefulness of the handbook." —THE HORN BOOK

To order call toll-free 1-800-367-6770 (In New York State, 1-800-462-6060).

THE H.W. WILSON COMPANY

950 University Avenue, Bronx, NY 10452
212-588-8400

Wilson Library Bulletin
June 1985

Wilson Library Bulletin

June 1985, Volume 59, Number 10 *ISSN 0043-5651*

Our cover for June, **Chicago Marquee**, was taken by freelance photographer **Nick Nicolson**.

Departments

Letter from New York/Editorial 644
Correspondence 645
Upfront/News—*Thomas Galvin named ALA executive director; International Thomson acquires R.R. Bowker and Gale Research; DataPhase sells ALIS III software to UTLAS; TBG acquires CLSI; California to offer integrated online database; Stolen books returned to Crerar; Daniel named dean at North Carolina; late news.* 646
Library World 712
Marketplace 713
WLB Classifieds 719

Articles

Microcomputers in Libraries: The Quiet Revolution *Richard Boss* 653
Online Databases: Some Questions of Ownership *Sally Drew* 661
Pioneering New Services: Videocassettes *Don Julien* 664
Information for All: ALANET *Joel Lee* 668

Features

Dateline—Washington *Dale Nelson* 673
Eye on Publishing *Anne McGrath* 675
Facing the Public *Will Manley* 677
Online Update *Martin Kesselman* 679
Future Libraries *Tom Surprenant* 681
Portrait: Charles Scribner, Jr. *Joseph Deitch* 683

Reviews

Picture Books for Children *Donnarae MacCann/Olga Richard* 686
The Young Adult Perplex *Patty Campbell* 688
Murder in Print *Kathleen Maio* 690
Front Row Center *Judith Trojan* 692
On Record: Popular Music *Bruce Pollock* 694
Magazines *Gail Pool* 696
Our Profession *Norman Stevens* 698
Software for Libraries *Patrick Dewey* 700
Current Reference Books *James Rettig* 702
Editor's Choice *Gail Pool* 708

The *Wilson Library Bulletin* is published monthly except in July and August by The H. W. Wilson Company, 950 University Avenue, Bronx, N.Y. 10452. Second-class postage paid at Bronx, N.Y. and additional mailing offices. The *Wilson Library Bulletin* is indexed in *Education Index, Library Literature,* and *Popular Periodical Index* and abstracted in *Library & Information Science Abstracts, Historical Abstracts,* and *America: History and Life.* Book reviews are indexed in *Book Review Index.* Subscription $30 a year, U.S. and Canada; $35, foreign. Single copies $4, U.S. and Canada; $4.50, foreign (remittance with order, please). Address all correspondence about subscriptions to the publisher. No subscriptions through agents. Telephone: (212) 588-8400

Letter from New York

Editorial

The house that Bob built

We are familiar with the facts of his life. Robert Wedgeworth was born in 1937 in Ennis, Texas, retrospectively the most important library event that ever occurred in that small, north Texas community. He received an AB degree in 1959 from Wabash College, Crawfordsville, Indiana and his MSLS from the University of Illinois at Urbana-Champaign in 1961. He began his career as a cataloger at the Kansas City (Missouri) Public Library in 1962. He then served as assistant head librarian at Park College, Parkville, Missouri; as head librarian, Meramec Community College, Meramec, Missouri; as assistant chief order librarian, Brown University; and from 1971–72 as assistant professor of library service at Rutgers University. The event with which we chiefly associate him, however, was his appointment in 1972 as executive director of the American Library Association.

Wedgeworth officially revealed his intention not to renew his contract at the 1984 spring meeting of the ALA executive board in Chicago. In announcing his intention to resign, Wedgeworth took the opportunity to summarize what he considered his major achievements as executive director. He noted that personal memberships are at a record high, that "more varied and democratic decision-making procedures" are in effect at ALA headquarters, that the image of librarians is more prominent in the public consciousness than ever before, and that the ALA complex at Huron Plaza has become a model for similar association facilities.

When Wedgeworth arrived at ALA headquarters the organization, in his words, was in a state of "general malaise." The credibility of the association was at a low ebb and a number of staff had submitted resignations. Wedgeworth proceeded to turn this around. "I have been," he has said, "extremely successful in attracting first-choice candidates to create an outstanding senior staff."

Wedgeworth's definition of a successful executive director is one who is "able to exploit opportunities," to "move among the competing interest groups," and to decide "what will be done, not done, put on hold."

Wedgeworth takes satisfaction in the recent fiscal turnaround of ALA: "We rebounded and shocked many members of Council." He has called ALA an "asset-rich" association: "ALA doesn't have financial problems, it has management problems."

Viewing ALA as a "shared enterprise," Wedgeworth has characterized the relationship between divisions and the central association as one of "healthy tension." ALA, commented Wedgeworth, is "a spreading oak tree."

There is certainly tangible evidence of Wedgeworth's presence at ALA headquarters. A new association building, a young and talented staff, a reorganized salary structure, a revitalized publishing program, computerized fiscal services, a highly responsive administrative staff, and a showcase communications system. In handling information, Wedgeworth has said, "we are the cutting edge."

It is no surprise that Wedgeworth is much more proud of his less visible accomplishments, of representing ALA and American librarians all over the world, of traveling down the "back-roads of Idaho going to a meeting, perhaps being the first presence of a representative from ALA." Being executive director of ALA, said Wedgeworth, has been "the most exciting, productive, and educational experience of my career."

The executive director oversees a staff of 220 people and manages a budget of approximately $12 million. He plans and directs the daily operations of the association and serves as secretary to the executive board, Council, and membership. The job description for the position, drafted after Wedgeworth made his decision to step down, states that the official must "provide leadership, guidance, and direction for the association" and that he represent the body "in ways that will enhance the good will, credit, and reputation of the association and the position."

For thirteen years Robert Wedgeworth has held this position with distinction—it is a sequence of years that are particularly his, that he shaped and defined. It is a tribute to his extraordinary abilities and his enlargement of the position that the newly appointed executive director, Thomas Galvin, comes to the assignment with a background already rich in experience and responsibility.

Wedgeworth has been right not to allow Huron Plaza to be seen as a monument to his accomplishments. No one is lastingly influenced by a building, but by the force that caused it to be erected. Wedgeworth's achievement resides in the manner in which he represented the cause of American librarians and libraries—with dignity, diplomacy, intelligence, and forthrightness. He created his own memorial.

It is a pleasant irony that one's more invisible contributions outlast all others. "Memory is all," said Gertrude Stein, "and all the immortality there is."

From 1972 to 1985 Robert Wedgeworth kept house well. No one could have done it better. The proof is no one did.

We wish Bob good luck. Although of all the professional colleagues we know, he probably relies on it least.

—Milo Nelson

Correspondence

WLB welcomes letters from its readers. Correspondence should be sent to Wilson Library Bulletin, 950 University Avenue, Bronx, N.Y. 10452.

Playing big league ball

Your April issue was the appropriate one to carry the Will Manley column ("Facing the Public") slamming ALA's Washington operations—April Fool, indeed.

As one who for ten years was on the professional staff of the Senate subcommittee handling library legislation and then for another ten years served as AAP's director of Education and Library Affairs, I have had ample opportunity to observe ALA's Washington activities from both sides of the desk. My conclusion: They continue, as *Time* magazine once observed, as one of Washington's most effective lobby groups.

ALA's effectiveness is not only measured in what it has accomplished with respect to LSCA—even the Department of Education reports that LSCA is a successful program—but it has run up successes for college and research libraries, freedom of information, copyright, civil service classification of librarians, special libraries, rural and urban problems, and many other areas.

Manley writes that ALA's Washington operation is "out of its league." Wrong. ALA in Washington is playing big league ball—and at minor league salaries. If you don't believe me, ask your Congressman.

ROY MILLENSON
Government Relations Consultant
Washington, D.C.

Waiting for the new professionals

Encomiums to Linda Braun for her excellent, timely article on children's librarianship ("Children's Librarianship: Doing a Better Job," *WLB,* April). Temporarily, work with automation is "sexy" and higher-paying, but that situation is bound to change. The next generation of gadgetry will require far less technical expertise. What now seems new and exciting about high tech will become humdrum. Meanwhile, children will still be waiting for "live" story hours, book talks, and reading guidance from the new wave of human service professionals.

MARY SOMERVILLE
Louisville Free Public Library
Louisville, Kentucky

Brightening the landscape

Thank you for publishing Linda Braun's report on the state of childrens services ("Children's Librarianship: Doing a Better Job," *WLB,* April). Her article deserves thoughtful consideration by all who profess an interest in libraries and literacy in America. Despite Braun's gloomy picture of library school administrators and faculty voting to drop courses that prepare students for the "nowhere profession" of children's services, some library schools brighten the landscape.

Prospective students interested in working with children would do well to consider the two-year master's program in the School of Library Science at the University of North Carolina. Three members of a full-time faculty of fourteen teach a total of seven different graduate courses—two materials courses, history of children's literature, reading guidance, storytelling, administration of children's services in the public library, and a seminar in children's literature. In addition, the curriculum includes three other graduate courses dealing with school media centers. All ten of these courses are taught at least once (and several twice) every two years. In addition to these specialized courses, students interested in children's services can select from related offerings such as online databases, and seminars in popular materials, public services, and public library systems and management. Finally, each student does a field experience in a library or information center of choice.

Despite the bleakness of the national landscape, a person interested in working with children in public or school libraries will find that Chapel Hill really is "the southern part of Heaven."

MARY KINGSBURY
School of Library Science
University of North Carolina
Chapel Hill

Author query

For a study on how U.S. publishers, authors, and libraries have been adversely affected by IRS ruling 80-60, the tax rule based on the U.S. Supreme Court's *Thor Power Tool Company* decision, please send information (hard or soft) to the undersigned.

MARY LOE
150 E. 2nd Street
Oswego, New York 13126

UPFRONT NEWS

Galvin named ALA executive director

Thomas Galvin, dean of the School of Library and Information Science at the University of Pittsburgh since 1974, has been named executive director of the American Library Association effective December 2, 1985. He will be responsible for managing a staff of 244 and overseeing a budget of $13 million.

Galvin was president of ALA in 1979–80 and served three terms on ALA Council. A member of ALA's International Relations Committee, he also serves on the International Relations Committee of the American Society for Information Science. In 1980 Galvin was appointed to the United States National Commission for UNESCO.

Prior to his appointment at Pittsburgh, Galvin was associate director and professor in the School of Library Science at Simmons College in Boston. He has served as chief librarian at the Abbot Public Library, Marblehead, Massachusetts and as reference librarian at Boston University's College of General Education.

Galvin holds a BA degree in English from Columbia College, Columbia University, an MLS from Simmons College, and a Ph.D. in library science from Case Western Reserve University, Cleveland.

Galvin succeeds Robert Wedgeworth, ALA executive director since 1972. The appointment is the result of a nine-month nationwide search directed by a seven-member search committee.

There have been seventeen executive directors of ALA, known as "secretaries" up until 1958 when David Clift became the first executive director. Melvil Dewey served as the first secretary of the association.

"I have a wide familiarity with the profession"
—Tom Galvin

Chicago Bound: An Interview with Tom Galvin

by Carol Bleier

This interview took place in Dean Galvin's office at the School of Library and Information Science, University of Pittsburgh, on May 28. Carol Bleier is a graduate student in the school.

Bleier: Libraries and librarianship are in the throes of change. In fact, F.W. Lancaster wrote an article on the future of librarianship (*WLB* May 1983) stating that libraries as we know them seem likely to disappear. What do you see happening? What about print on paper?

Galvin: I think the importance of the library as a facility will diminish somewhat, not disappear but diminish. The importance of the services that libraries provide to their clientele will increase. Librarians will have to think of delivering information to people outside of the facility we call a library. It suggests a more active role for librarians in bringing information to where people live and work, using technology to do that. One of the things we have learned in studying how people use information is that if you look at any specialized population, such as university professors, the extent to which they do or do not use library materials, more than anything else, is determined by the physical proximity between where they work and where the library materials are kept. In the past the only way we could deal with this was by the very expensive method of duplicating collections. Now we have alternatives as we move information electronically from one location to another.

A major change that is significant for libraries is that library service is shifting from a focus on document delivery to a focus on information transfer. Technology makes it possible to enhance the quality of information service. As a consequence, it becomes necessary to redefine norms and standards of quality in library service.

Bleier: There seems to be a growing emphasis on information science. What is the future of library science?

Galvin: Certainly, there has been a dramatic decline nationally in library education programs. Schools have closed largely because job markets for librarians have diminished over the last ten to fifteen years. The distinction between library science and information science is becoming less sharply drawn and more schools are broadening education to include extensive information technology to prepare a wider range of information professionals.

Bleier: I realize your new position doesn't take effect until December 1, but I would like to know what you see as priority issues that ALA will be addressing over the next few years. Will you follow or have similar priorities as Robert Wedgeworth?

Galvin: I am a great admirer of Robert Wedgeworth. When he assumed the position thirteen years ago, his priorities included turning around a declining membership and establishing a stronger financial base, which he has done. I see a number of priority issues. A major task for ALA is to reach agreement on a few priority concerns and channel resources to support those priorities. Another issue is to deliver more service to where members live and work, for those who can't come to conferences or participate in committee work. ALA has recently established ALANET, an online information network, and has been experimenting with teleconferencing.

A third priority is forming coalitions with other state and national organizations so as to magnify the impact of what ALA can accomplish. ALA, for example, has taken the lead with other national organizations in forming a literacy coalition to support a national literacy program to aid the 27 million people in the U.S. who can't read well enough to read directions on a medicine bottle. As another example of coalition, ALA is currently in discussions with other national professional societies in the library and information field to focus attention on quality control in information science where there is no accreditation and I believe there needs to be.

Bleier: There has never been a woman as executive director. In an organization predominantly female, how do you respond to why a man was selected again to head ALA?

Galvin: This is a very important and sensitive issue. I believe the search committee and executive board made a strong and aggressive effort to assure that all qualified candidates had an equal opportunity to be considered. There are several who would have been well qualified this time in the candidate pool as well as among those who did not want to be considered. It's difficult for me to know what led to their decision. I know the association well because I have been active in a wide variety of offices. I have a wide familiarity with the profession, a broad international experience, a sensitivity and appreciation of the political process in a membership organization, and have developed strong contacts in Washington, D.C.

Bleier: You have mentioned in several articles your concern with the library user rather than documents or computers. Is this a trend in library and information science? Will you pursue this concern as executive director?

Galvin: Libraries primarily exist to respond to human information needs so the focus of the library must be on the client. The collection is a tool to meet information needs of the client. This is consistent with the direction of the information field. Computer and other technologies are important but not central. The executive director can exercise substantial influence on the direction the profession takes. This will be a continuing priority concern for me.

Bleier: After spending eleven years at the University of Pittsburgh's School of Library and Information Science, what do you see as major changes that have occurred?

Galvin: The major changes have been in the growth and size of the school, particularly the expanding of programs in information science. The enrollment has increased from 324 to 710 students over the past eleven years. There are eighteen degrees and certificates offered and there were six in 1974. Currently, the School is developing a new program offering a Master of Science in Telecommunications beginning this fall. Initially, the program will be part of the information science department but may develop into a separate department. The purpose of this program, which is the first of its kind in the country, will be to educate a new kind of information professional who can design, create and manage integtrated information systems that include data, voice and image. It will also be possible to have an undergraduate minor in telecommunications combined with a minor in information science, computer science, electrical engineering and communications.

Bleier: What has been personally re-

(continued on page 718)

R.R. Bowker sold to International Thomson

The Xerox corporation has sold R.R. Bowker to International Thomson Ltd. in a $500 million divestiture of all six of its publishing companies. Thomson also bought University Microfilms from Xerox.

In addition to the sale of R.R. Bowker, Ginn and Company was sold to Simon & Schuster, Xerox Educational Publications was sold to the Field Corporation, and Xerox Learning Systems was acquired by the Times Mirror Corporation.

International Thomson, a Canadian firm, also owns Carrollton Press, Research Publications, Inc., and UTLAS.

International Thomson acquires Gale Research

The International Thomson Organization Ltd. of Toronto has acquired the Gale Research Company for $66 million cash. Gale Research, based in Detroit, is the publisher of the *Ency-*

clopedia of Associations, Contemporary Authors, Contemporary Literary Criticism, and other reference works. Gale was founded in 1954 by Frederick Ruffner, Jr. who will continue to serve as chairman and chief executive officer. Gale will be a member of International Thomson Information Inc., a subsidiary organization.

"The International Thomson philosophy of commitment to an ever-increasing scope of high quality service to the library market makes them an ideal partner for Gale," said Ruffner. "We share their management philosophy and operating style and are looking forward to this new relationship."

Other International Thomson companies include Van Nostrand Reinhold and Jane's Publishing.

Library of Congress implements UNIMARC

The Library of Congress recently announced the availability of its machine-readable catalog records in UNIMARC, the international exchange format developed by the International Federation of Library Associations and Institutions (IFLA). All major Library of Congress MARC distribution services, including books, serials, music, maps, and visual materials will now be available in UNIMARC as well as in the standard USMARC format. Foreign libraries and bibliographical agencies are expected to be the chief users of the international format. UNIMARC will permit national bibliographic agencies that exchange records internationally to maintain only two format conversion programs—one from the national format into UNIMARC, and one from UNIMARC back into the national format.

DataPhase sells rights to ALIS III software

DataPhase Systems, Inc. of Shawnee Mission, Kansas has signed an agreement with UTLAS, Inc. giving the Canadian firm exclusive marketing rights to DataPhase's ALIS III software. ALIS III is a circulation and online catalogue system that utilizes Tandem computers. DataPhase is keeping its smaller ALIS II system which uses Data General computers.

At the Chicago Public Library, where installation of an ALIS III automated circulation system is now three years behind schedule, there is concern about the sale of DataPhase marketing rights and whether or not UTLAS will assume responsibility for liabilities. The library has invested $2.1 million in the DataPhase system, as yet inoperable, and has not yet released the company from a $596,000 performance bond required by the original contract.

James Lowery, acting commissioner of the Chicago Public Library, said the DataPhase action "may just lead us to end up throwing the whole system in the lake and starting over with another company." Although the library has still not received computer software that is intended to correct two basic flaws in the circulation system, Robert Levy, an attorney representing DataPhase, has said that the firm believes its contractual obligation to the library has been fulfilled.

California to offer integrated online database

California will soon have an online integrated statewide database available through OCLC that will represent the largest online public library union database in the nation. The California Library Services Act (CLSA) Statewide Database, consisting of over 650,000 bibliographic records and more than 3 million location listings, is currently being loaded into the OCLC Online Union Catalog. Access to the database, which comprises the post-1978 acquisitions of CLSA's public library participants, was previously possible through microfiche only.

"From Eureka to San Diego, we will have an online California Union Database of over 150 public libraries," said Gary Strong, California State Librarian. "This project furthers the intent of the California Library Services Act which seeks to make library resources acquired and maintained with public funds readily available to as many California taxpayers as possible."

Access to OCLC will be extended to all CLSA participant public libraries and they will also have access to OCLC subsystems for acquisitions, cataloging, interlibrary loan, and serials control.

"Besides online access to the CLSA Database, the program also brings to California taxpayers access to the library resources of nearly 6,000 libraries in the U.S. and nine other countries through the OCLC Online Union Catalog," said Strong. "In addition to an incredibly rich source of bibliographic information, libraries can also achieve real staff time savings using OCLC to determine the location of a needed book."

"This is a landmark project," said Rowland Brown, president of OCLC. "The California database demonstrates how OCLC can facilitate statewide sharing and at the same time pursue its objectives as a national membership organization."

"While this is a landmark in library resource sharing for California," remarked Strong, "I do not see in this arrangement a model for database development elsewhere. I doubt that any other state or region shares our history or eclectic approach to library database building. We are very pleased that OCLC was able to put together a program so well suited to our unique resource sharing needs."

Chicago Public begins search for commissioner

The Chicago Public Library has begun its search for a new library commissioner with the selection of Heidrick and Struggles, Inc. and ASI Personnel to work as consultants in the hiring. James Lowry, president of the board of directors, will serve as acting commissioner until an appointment is made. The search is expected to take four months to complete. Ten Chicago-based employment agencies were interviewed by the library board before the selection was made. "It was a difficult choice," said Lowry, "but we feel confident that we have chosen the best and most knowledgeable people. They are familiar with the problems of large metropolitan libraries and have a working knowledge of the best people in the fields of library science and management."

"Rebuilding the library system is the most important need in the life of the city right now," said Mrs. Astor. "I hope that this grant, the most sizable the foundation has ever made, will encourage the generosity of the library's 40,000 other donors and underscore how much all of our gifts matter."

Andrew Heiskell, chairman of the library board, said the award would "encourage the library's board, management, and staff to further the process of rebuilding the New York Public Library."

Massachusetts Governor Michael Dukakis *(above) signs a commemorative copy of a new depository law that formally recognizes the State Library's role in collecting, preserving, and distributing Massachusetts state agency publications. The State Library, founded in 1826, has the most complete collection of Massachusetts state documents in existence. Since 1975, the State Library has provided state documents to a network of depository libraries, including the Boston Public Library and the University of Massachusetts at Amherst.*

Pictured with Governor Dukakis are (from left) Secretary of State Michael Connolly, State Librarian Gasper Caso, State Archivist Albert Whitaker, and State Library trustees E. William Johnson, Frances Faletra, and Marie Parente.

New York Public receives record grant

The New York Public Library announced May 29 that a $10 million grant, the largest in the institution's history, has been pledged by the Vincent Astor Foundation. It is also the largest gift the Astor Foundation has ever bestowed. Of the amount, $7 million is designated for the library's unrestricted endowment and $3 million will be used to support the research library's annual operating costs from 1986 to 1988.

TBG acquires C L Systems

The Systems and Technologies Strategic Unit of TBG (formerly Thyssen-Bornemisza) has acquired C L Systems, Inc. (CLSI), a prominent library automation vendor. A worldwide corporation with 1984 sales in excess of $1.7 billion, TBG has its U.S. headquarters located in New York City.

CLSI's basic product is the LIBS 200, a turnkey mini- and micro-computer-based system used by libraries to manage circulation, acquisition, data retrieval, and public access catalogs. The company's systems are based on Digital Equipment Corporation computers. CLSI will continue to serve the library market, supplying turnkey automation products to public, special, and academic libraries.

CLSI president Richard Goldberg will remain as president and chief executive officer. William Marovitz, an executive of the Systems and Technologies Strategic Unit, will become chairman of CLSI's board of directors. Marovitz commented, "This acquisition represents a further strengthening of our position in the growing information industries. CLSI will provide us with a unique opportunity to bring a variety of information services directly to the users of the largest group of information centers in the world—libraries."

OCLC to offer micro-based acquisitions system

OCLC is developing a microcomputer-based acquisitions system, ACQ350, that is scheduled for release in early 1986. ACQ350 is designed for use with the OCLC M300 Workstation. Software written for the system will combine the advantages of microcomputing with access to the OCLC Online System. Acquisitions functions such as accounting, file maintenance, and offline reports will be part of ACQ350 software.

ACQ350 will maintain links to the Online System for bibliographic verification and name-address information. Users will be able to download bibliographic and address information and upload Direct Transmission (DX) information for electronic ordering. ACQ350 will interact with SC350, the OCLC micro-based serials control system, and with LS/2000, OCLC's local automated library system.

Other planned ACQ350 features include automatic claims and cancellations, an allowance for hierarchical funds, use of default records for permanent constant data, accommodation of all MARC formats, and multi-user, multi-tasking capabilities.

Combined Book Exhibit dissolved

The Combined Book Exhibit, the industry's oldest cooperative book display service, has announced that it is ceasing operations and will close its North American office June 30. The announcement was made by Richard Rowe, president of the Faxon Company, CBE's parent corporation. According to Rowe, Faxon has concluded that CBE, a service used primarily by book publishers, does not significantly contribute to Faxon's goal of servicing the periodical trade. Faxon has owned CBE for the past nine years.

The dissolution of CBE has resulted in the cancellation of all upcoming domestic exhibits.

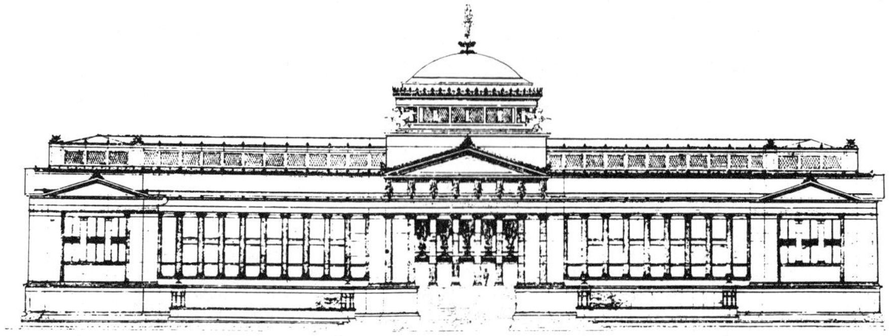

Treasures of the Milwaukee Public Library, *a recent exhibit held by the institution, featured a rendering of a library by Frank Lloyd Wright (above). Wright submitted the work in a design competition for a central library in Milwaukee in 1898. The architect, twenty-nine years old at the time, lost the competition to the architectural firm of Ferry & Clas. The Ferry & Clas design eventually achieved landmark status for the library. There is no known evidence that any library designed by Wright was actually constructed.*

Meese names panel to study pornography

Attorney General Edwin Meese has appointed an eleven-member panel to study the effects of sexually explicit material and to recommend new ways to control it. "Re-examination of the issue of pornography," said Meese, "is long overdue." The commission will be headed by Henry Hudson, chief prosecutor for Arlington County, a suburb of Washington, D.C. Meese stated that members of the panel had been selected to "carefully balance the need to control distribution of this material and the need to protect First Amendment freedoms." Barry Lynn, legislative counsel to the American Civil Liberties Union, said "I'm afraid there is a train marked 'censorship' which has just left the station."

New York consortium dissatisfied with DataPhase

Tri Li, an informal consortium made up of the Brooklyn Public, New York Public, and Queens Borough Public Libraries, recently announced that they have opened parallel negotiations with C L Systems, Inc. while continuing to negotiate with DataPhase over installation of an automated circulation system. According to a news release from the New York Public Library, "This decision follows some six months of negotiations with DataPhase during which time adequate progress was not made toward an agreement on a performance-oriented and remedy-insulated contract." The consortium noted that the action had been taken to ensure its interests and those of the City of New York.

Stolen books returned to Crerar Library

Over 400 rare books and manuscripts stolen from the John Crerar Library in Chicago have been returned in an out-of-court settlement. The books were removed from the library by Joseph Putna of Brookfield, Wisconsin who subsequently sold them to Warren Howell, a rare-book dealer in San Francisco who died in 1984. Attorneys for the library filed suit in U.S District Court asking nearly $1 million in damages from Putna, his wife, and the estate of Warren Howell. Precise terms of the settlement were not revealed.

Anton Valukas, an attorney for the Crerar Library, told the *Chicago Tribune* that "we are pleased with the settlement. The library has been made whole and the books we were most concerned about are being returned to the library."

Material stolen from the library included works by Copernicus, Galileo, William Harvey, and Leonardo da Vinci. At the time of the theft the library was located on the campus of the Illinois Institute of Technology.

Of the approximately 100 books still missing, only a handful are said to be of high value. Putna is serving a two-year sentence in federal prison.

Case Western closes library school

The board of trustees of Case Western Reserve University, Cleveland, have approved closing the Baxter School of Information and Library Science on June 30, 1986. The move was earlier recommended by the university faculty and admission to the school was frozen in 1984. Declining enrollment, which led to financial difficulties, was chief among the reasons for the decision.

The university has notified the Ohio Board of Regents and the American Library Association of the pending closing to assure them that every student's academic requirements will be met.

Illinois funds library literacy programs

Illinois Secretary of State and State Librarian Jim Edgar has announced $489,538 in grants to libraries throughout Illinois to provide for the development of local literacy programs for children and adults. The first major award of library funds for literacy in Illinois, the grants will fund seventeen literacy programs in which local libraries and library systems will work with other agencies to support a wide variety of reading programs.

"Libraries play an important role in this state's literacy effort by providing a pleasant environment for reading tutors and their students to work," said Edgar. "In addition, many of the libraries will be using grant funds to obtain special collections for adult new readers."

Los Angeles considering master plan

The Los Angeles board of library commissioners has been presented with a proposed master plan for the Los Angeles Public Library's branch libraries prepared by the library administration. Entitled "Libraries for the Future—the Los Angeles Public Library's Branch Facilities Master Plan," the 300-page report contains recommendations for each area of the city in terms of new, renovated, and expanded branch facilities.

The Los Angeles Public Library currently has sixty-two branches, including one under construction. Nearly one-third of the buildings were constructed prior to 1931, over half before 1961. The report concludes that most branch buildings are too small, are highly vulnerable to burglary, vandalism, and arson, and have inadequate parking. Forty percent are not air-conditioned; nearly one-third are not accessible to the handicapped.

"Most important of all in terms of usage, our branch libraries have, with only a few exceptions, poor locations," said Wyman Jones, city librarian. "Public libraries have learned they have everything in common with retail businesses when it comes to site selection. Relative to their potential, public libraries located in or at the very edge of heavily used retail business centers record high usage. Los Angeles' branch libraries are nearly all located in residential areas and parks, locations that public library consultants and planners warn against."

If the report is approved, it will replace the "Public Library's Plan of 1968," an element of the Master Plan of the City of Los Angeles.

Daniel named dean at North Carolina

Evelyn Daniel, dean of the School of Information Studies at Syracuse University, has been named dean of the School of Library Science at the University of North Carolina at Chapel Hill. Daniel succeeds Edward Holley, dean of the school since 1972. Holley will return to full-time teaching and research.

Daniel, dean at Syracuse since 1981, has taught at the universities of Rhode Island, Kentucky, and Maryland and held a variety of positions in school, public, special, and academic libraries. She earned her MLS and Ph.D. in library science at the University of Maryland. Her appointment at the University of North Carolina is effective July 1.

The Milwaukee Public Library *recently opened two Career and Job Information Centers in neighborhood libraries with special resources to assist patrons looking for employment. The centers, funded by an LSCA grant, include directories, videocassettes, out-of-town newspapers, special handouts, listings of classified ads, and electric typewriters for preparing resumes. The job centers are designed to allow individuals to use the resources on their own, although librarians will provide additional assistance on request.*

The Reynolds Corners Branch of the Toledo-Lucas County Public Library, *the newest and largest branch in the Toledo system, recently opened for service. The single-level building was designed by the Toledo architectural firm of Munger Munger & Associates and constructed at a cost of $1,298,699. The facility, which will accomodate 75,000 books, features a glass-enclosed courtyard.*

Members of the Oklahoma Historical Records Advisory Board recently presented **Governor George Nigh** *(above, center) with the results of a year-long assessment of the condition of the state's historical documents. The report, entitled* "Preserving Today's Records for Tomorrow's Use: A Mandate for Action," *was the result of a survey, public meetings, and on-site visits. Concludes the report, "The conditions under which the majority of Oklahoma's most valuable records are maintained and preserved are barely adequate at best, and often appalling." The study recommends improved storage facilities, more equitable management of records, training and assistance for records custodians, statewide microfilming, a field advisory service, conservation treatment facilities, and new legislation regarding maintenance and destruction of historical records.*

Pictured with Governor Nigh are (from left) Earle Metcalf, executive director, Oklahoma Historical Society; Lloyd Lentz, director, Logan County Historical Society; Robert Clark, director, Oklahoma Department of Libraries; and Louis Coleman, deputy director, Oklahoma Historical Society.

California State Library opens capitol branch

The California State Library has opened a Capitol Branch in a room of the State Capitol to serve legislators, their Sacramento and district office staffs, and executive departments located in the building.

The branch resources include online access to over 200 databases through information systems such as NEXIS and DIALOG; online access to the catalogs of major research libraries; the ability to produce computer printouts of citations to books, articles, and documents; and telefacsimile transmission of article-length texts to fill rush requests.

Spaulding elected SLA president

Frank Spaulding, a member of the Special Libraries Association board of directors, has been named president-elect of SLA. Spaulding, who will succeed H. Robert Malinowsky as president in June 1986, is manager of library services at the AT&T Bell Laboratories, Holmdel, New Jersey.

LC and National Library of Canada to coordinate standards

The Library of Congress and the National Library of Canada have begun work to coordinate the standards activities of the two institutions, particularly in the area of protocol development for data transmission. The National Library of Canada, through its Office for Network Development, is operating two types of application protocols in a pilot project. The first type represents computer-to-computer links transferring MARC records between the National Library and the computer systems of Carleton University, the Université du Québec, and the University of Waterloo libraries. The second type comprises message-oriented links between microcomputers for interlibrary loan messaging. Protocol specifications have also been completed for book order messaging and a prototype system for distributed databases is currently underway.

The Milwaukee Public Library's *new mascot (above) made its debut during National Library Week and Imagination Celebration, a week of city-wide art events for children held in late April. The lion-like creature, intended to convey a visual impression of the library, incorporates books and a model of the central library in its design. Creation of the mascot was funded by a grant from the Dayton Hudson Foundation on behalf of B. Dalton, Booksellers.*

Microcomputers in Libraries: The Quiet Revolution

Richard Boss

What is a micro? is probably one of the most difficult questions to answer in computing today. Micros range in capacity from one user performing one function to as many as sixteen users performing several functions concurrently. Some light can be shed on the question by separating micros into three categories, personal, desk-top and multi-user devices.

The personal micros, such as the Apples, the IBM PCs, and the DEC Rainbows, are the most visible. Approximately 160 different makes are now available. These micros consist of a keyboard, a central processing unit (usually behind the keyboard or the screen), a storage device (generally a floppy disk drive), and a screen that looks like a television monitor. While we normally call it a micro, it is in fact a micro-based system. Only the central processing unit—where the actual manipulation of data takes place—is the microcomputer.

Bigger and better

When the CPU is on a single board—*all* the wiring on a single board—the machine is generally what we have called a "micro." That was the initial definition of a micro. Now bigger and better micros have multiple boards.

When all the components—the keyboard, the central processing unit, the disk drives, the screen and the printer—are combined in a "package," costing $3,000 to $5,000, the designation is usually a personal micro, although the term "professional" micro is becoming increasingly popular for machines targeted to the office market. That doesn't mean that it is not possible to spend more than that, but that is the basic configuration. Personal computers are usually sold through computer stores, and constitute about ninety-three percent of all micros over $3,000 in value sold to date.

The next level of micro is the so-called desk-top micro. This is a somewhat more powerful and robust machine. It contains more memory, a somewhat faster processing speed, a better-quality screen, more storage even on floppy disk, and more commonly, a Winchester hard disk drive with much greater storage capacity. About one million characters, or one megabyte of data, can be stored on the largest floppy disk. This is enough to store about 125 pages of typewritten text. The equivalent of about 600 to 1,200 pages of typewritten text can be stored on the 5MB–10MB disk drive of a desk-top computer. There are now disks with even greater capacities associated with desk-top computers.

"Desk-tops" also tend to have more useful, more sophisticated operating systems, and the desk-top dealers tend to offer a greater level of post-sales support than do personal micro vendors. As a result, a desk-top microcomputer such as a Decmate II, a Wang or Philips single-user system is rarely priced much under $10,000. And they are normally sold through business centers rather than through the popular retail computer stores. Many of the single-user word processing systems are actually turnkey desk-top micro-based systems. A manufacturer bundles the hardware and software together and thus develops a word-processing device that is a special application desk-top micro. Desk-tops represent only about two percent of sales if dedicated word processing systems are excluded. If word processors were to be incorporated into the figures for desk-tops, the desk-top share of the market would turn out to be closer to five percent.

The third category of microcomputer is the multi-user, multi-tasking micro, or supermicro. Unlike the personal and desk-top, the multi-user, multi-tasking micro can support—on the single CPU—more than one keyboard, more than one screen, and if required, substantial hard disk storage. Normally, this system has shared

Richard Boss *is senior consultant, Information Systems Consultants, Inc., Bethesda, Maryland.*

storage. The most common installed multi-user, multi-tasking micros are Cromemco and Altos, but Data General and Digital Equipment Corporation, the leading makers of minicomputers, have now aggressively entered the market. They are sold in computer business centers and by vendors that combine hardware and software as "turnkey" systems for specific applications.

True microcomputers

The Cromemco and Altos are true microcomputers, built from the ground up on a single CPU that has been designed to provide increased computing power. Thus, they are distinguishable from machines such as DEC's PDP 11/23 used by CLSI and OCLC in some of their library systems. The 11/23 is a microcomputer in name only. It is actually a stripped down version of a minicomputer. Architectually, the design concept is that of a minicomputer that has been reduced in size and processing power in order to bring the price down to that level at which the machine can compete with micro-based, multi-user, multi-tasking systems. Typically, a buyer will spend $20,000 for minimally configured multi-user, multitasking micro system hardware. The key concept in multi-user, multitasking systems is that such machines allow several users to share the resources of the CPU, and each may use the system for totally different tasks or functions.

The multi-user, multi-tasking micro is beginning to threaten the lower end of the minicomputer line, because it can do almost all of the things that a minicomputer can do except that it is somewhat slower and somewhat less expandable. And, currently, there is a more limited range of software available for the micros.

The multi-user micros will probably affect sales of the desk-top units because the desk-tops do not have the prospect of developing into the true multi-user, multi-tasking systems that more and more people are demanding, and because the desk-tops are too expensive to be considered as workstations for larger computer systems. In this latter application, personal micros are becoming increasingly popular.

The emerging pattern in micro use is one of gravitation toward the personals and the multi-user systems. It might be that five years from now there will be basically two types of micros; one type functioning as an individual workstation, and another supporting several terminals whose users perform different functions at an activity level too low to require a more powerful minicomputer or mainframe.

Expanding memory

A very significant basis for differentiating among the various types of computers used to be primary memory capacity. A typical microcomputer would have about 64,000 characters, or 64 KB (kilobytes) of primary memory. The typical minicomputer had about 128 KB of memory, and the mainframe or full size computer—the kind that usually carried the label of IBM—had a million or more characters (one megabyte) of primary memory. The ratio of 64,000 to 128,000 to 1 million was an important sizing difference. Presently there are very few personal micros with fewer than 128,000 characters, and few minicomputers with fewer than 256,000 characters. A personal micro's memory begins at about 128 KB. It is now possible to expand that capacity up to 512 KB or even one million characters by adding boards.

The capacity of the primary memory of a mini now goes to two million or more characters. Mainframes (full-size computers) still begin at a million and can go up to more than fifteen million characters of primary memory. The more primary memory, the more the computer can be doing at any one time: more programs can be loaded, more data can be manipulated. It is no longer a question of getting the most primary memory available, but of getting enough primary memory for the application. To buy a micro with fewer than 128,000 characters, or 128 KB, would be foolish because a number of the programs that libraries want to use require more than 64 KB of primary memory. One of the reasons it had not been possible to build a database on a microcomputer until recently was because the smallest database management systems required more primary memory than the largest micro provided. Now database management systems require less space, and the power of micros has increased, with the result that they can accommodate these types of programs.

Floppy disks—slow but cheap

Storage of data is most often provided by floppy disks which now come in a variety of sizes. Floppies are economical, but they are also slow in terms of the speed with which information can be retrieved from them. More and more, micro buyers are purchasing systems that use a hard disk. The medium that is most commonly used is called a Winchester disk. The Winchester disk normally used with a personal micro has a capacity of five to ten megabytes. When planning micro-based applications and determining the amount of storage required, it is important not to overlook the fact that storage will be required in excess of that needed to accommodate the records to be created. If an application calls for the creation of 5,000 records, each with 500 characters, the system will need more than 5,000 x 500 characters of storage. This is so because the computer may transfer some programs to storage when they are not actually being used but must be available to be drawn on in a later stage of processing. In addition to the overhead storage requirements, indexes to records will also require storage.

In most recently installed mini-based, multi-function library systems, the average MARC record has a length of 704 characters, but its impact on a computer system in terms of secondary storage requirements is 3,000 characters. In other words, more than four times the amount of space required for the record is needed to accommodate that record, the associated indexes, and all of the overhead in the system. No one has done the same kind of calculation for micro-based systems because there is much greater variance among the various software packages in terms of overhead requirements. As a rule of thumb, one should allow a minimum of two to two-and-one-half times the projected size of the database for indexes and other types of overhead when calculating secondary storage requirements.

Floppy disk-based storage offers infinite expandability at a relatively low price. Provided that only the most recent disks need to be accessed frequently, indexing and control of the disks are not a problem. But if regular access to all data is required, control of a large number of disks can cause considerable frustration and time wasted in locating and loading the appropriate disk. Floppy disks are a very slow form of retrieval, though an economical form of storage. Winchester disks offer immediate access to much more information. If an active file of any significant size—more than one floppy disk—is being created, ideally hard disk storage would be used.

There are differences between disk-based storage for micros and similar storage on larger computer systems. The disk drives available for micros are smaller and slower, though they are beginning to creep up to 80 MB and more. Also, the Winchester disk drives associated with micros tend to be less reliable as they get larger. The 5 and 10 KB drives are quite good, as are most of the 20 KB drives. Inefficiencies increase at around 60 KB, and 100+ MB Winchester disk drives for micros are a still somewhat unreliable technology.

Fifteen seconds and counting

The speed of accessing and retrieving information from a Winchester hard disk can also present problems. The typical Winchester disk drive for a microcomputer has only one channel; the relatively slow microcomputer has to go through that single channel to access a fairly slow spinning disk drive to retrieve information. Every time a single record is accessed, the process actually involves making multiple accesses to the disk. The response time performance of such a system tends to be poor.

In a minicomputer environment, such as that used by turnkey vendors to support local patron access catalogs, circulation systems and the like, it is possible to specify that the system should provide average response time of two seconds, and get a contractual commitment for a maximum response time of five seconds. These kinds of response times cannot be achieved with micros. Fifteen seconds is generally the average that can be achieved with a personal micro, and it can take much longer to get a response to a particular search. After eight seconds a user's patience becomes strained. With regard to processing speed, a typical personal micro may have one-fourth the processing speed of a mini and one-sixteenth that of a mainframe. A multi-user, multi-tasking micro is usually two to three times faster than a personal micro.

One of the important considerations in buying a micro is expandability. It is important to avoid a situation in which, acting on advice that the required applications will need 128 KB, the purchaser chooses a micro which has an upper limit of 128 KB. Ideally, the machine will be expandable to about four times the initial projected maximum memory requirement. This is true irrespective of whether the unit is a micro, a mini, or a mainfame. An expansion path is essential to support more activity and more sophisticated programs that require more space.

This is particularly important in the case of micros because most micro users' applications requirements increase rapidly once they have purchased a machine. Contrary to a lot of the marketing pitches of micro vendors, it appears that the average personal computer buyer does not want to write computer programs. The buyer more often wants to use the computer as a tool, and wants to be able to start using it as quickly as possible. This means there is a demand for off-the-shelf programs that are user-friendly and can be dealt with on an English-language basis rather than on a computer-language basis. The more friendly the program, the more computer resources are required to support that friendliness. The new programs, therefore, require much more memory to operate than the older ones. An expansion path is essential.

Definite limitations

Consideration also needs to be given to the expandability of other parts of the system. What alternatives are available when more storage is required? Most small computers—all sizes of micros and even some small minicomputers—have definite limitations as to how much secondary storage can be added and how many printers and terminals can be supported. The buyer has to be aware of the upper limits in these areas.

It is easy enough to determine present requirements, but what of the growth in demand that can be expected over a five-year period? Might the need be three times that of current requirements, five times as much? If so, does the system have the capability of being expanded to that extent? How much would such expansion cost? Will the system need a second printer? Can it be supported? How much would it cost? Does that system have the capability of supporting x additional terminals, and how much would it cost to add them?

These kinds of questions about expandability: 1) is it feasible? and 2) what is the cost?, are even more important than that of the initial start-up cost. Very often the systems that will look most attractive from a cost standpoint initially are those that offer the least expansion in the longer term. Why? Because it usually costs extra to build expansion capabilities into the system. A rock-bottom priced system may be compromised in terms of that invisible quality of expandability.

Another consideration when purchasing a micro is the operating system. An operating system is the operating environment for which computer programs are written; the operating system provides the basis on which the application programs are designed. It acts as the organizer for the system, handling scheduling and other chores. A program will work only with the operating system for which it is designed. To run on another system, the program would have to be re-written. Different micros support different operating systems. Some micros will support multiple operating systems, but most support only one. Common operating systems in the personal micro environment include MS-DOS and CP/M. Desk-tops often use operating systems developed by the manufacturers. Multi-user, multi-tasking micros often use the same operating systems as minis.

De facto standards

A micro manufacturer has the choice of using an existing operating system, or developing a new operating system (there is no standard operating system, but for some time there have been two de facto standards for personal micros: CP/M and MS-DOS). The decision about the operating system is important because it determines whether or not the micro will be able to support specific existing programs, or whether currently available programs will have to be rewritten for the new operating system.

When IBM entered the micro marketplace it decided against using CP/M, then the de facto standard. Instead, it decided on a proprietary operating system—one designed specifically for IBM equipment, but a variant of MS-DOS. Because IBM is such a strong marketing force, it did not have to worry about the availability of programs compatible with its "non-standard" operating system; software producers would be so interested in capturing the IBM users' market that they would quickly re-write their programs to operate on the IBM micros using the PC-DOS operating system. Software producers with only limited resources to devote to their programming have shown a distinct inclination to concentrate their initial efforts on producing programs that will run on the IBM PCs.

On the other hand, a small micro manufacturer cannot really afford to adopt a proprietary operating system. Such producers lack the clout or market share to persuade software producers to create versions of their software for a small and limited market. Such manufacturers are increasingly choosing to adopt operating systems that are very similar to the IBM PC-DOS. These may not be clones, but they are sufficiently similar and can use software designed to work in the IBM PC environment with minor modification. Apple and Radio Shack each has its own operating system, and the Digital Equipment Corporation has been using not only MS-DOS, but also the CP/M operating system which has been adopted by 130 of the 160 micro manufacturers. However, all of these operating system choices were made before IBM entered the personal computer market. Many companies are now moving toward PC-DOS.

While the choice of an operating system has certain technical ramifications for the operation of a computer system, it is significant for the standpoint of a personal micro buyer that the operating system be one for which a lot of people are writing software. Of the available operating systems, those for the IBM PC, the Apple II and for DEC micros are those for which most software developers are choosing to develop software first. Only if the software product is incredibly successful do the producers tend to rework it to use on other operating systems.

Transferring downward

The problem in terms of library automation is that the operating systems which support the software developed for minicomputers are generally not available in versions for use on microcomputers. Thus, a vendor that has developed a minicomputer-based system cannot readily move it onto a variety of microcomputers. Only a few companies have that capability. Three companies—AdLib, Dynix, and Library Information Systems—use the PICK operating system in their minicomputer-based systems. PICK is one of two major operating systems that is available for microcomputers, minicomputers, and full size or mainframe computers. Although they initially wrote their programs for minicomputers, these companies can move upward into mainframes, or down onto micros relatively easily.

The other operating system which has this capability is UNIX. There is no commercially available library applications software which uses the UNIX operating system. UNIX is a product of Western Electric, and one of the consequences of deregulation is that Western Electric now has far greater freedom to aggressively market this product. There are predictions, which are probably valid, that UNIX will become the de facto operating system for the multi-user, multitasking micros—the so-called supermicros. Some vendors in the library automation market are considering rewriting their software into UNIX for greater flexibility. In the meantime, software written for the Data General line can run on the new S/120, and that for the Digital PDP/11 can run on the PDP 11/23, both minis scaled down to supermicros.

There is a large base of general software that has been developed for minis using UNIX. This could be easily transferred downward to micro-based systems. Most of the development work on the design of new computers done by companies like Digital Equipment Corporation and Data General is done using the UNIX operating system.

Intimately concerned with databases

When selecting a micro, one must also consider database management systems. Libraries are intimately concerned with databases: card catalogs are nothing more than databases that are not machine-readable. In the distant past, every card for a card catalog was typed separately, the main entry card was typed in full and the added entries were prepared as brief entries.

Then the idea of the unit card was developed. The same basic unit card was printed again and again, and the appropriate headings were added later on a typewriter. The concept of a database management system in an automated environment is very much the same. The information is recorded only once and multiple access points are provided. A database management system allows the creation of one bibliographic record and provides support for the development of the multiple access points: author, title, and call number, without the need to create duplicate records under each access point. Before the availability of database management systems, such access could only be provided by setting up duplicate files under the required entry/access points. The data redundancy was time consuming and used a lot of computer storage and other resources.

Database management systems not only support the development of multiple access points to a single unit record, they allow the user to determine what access points are required after the records have been input. Before database management systems were developed, the system user had to define all access points at the time the system was designed and the records input. A subsequent decision that another access point was required entailed considerable reformatting and manipulation of the data.

A database management system makes it possible to make changes in programs and the database independently of one another. Database management systems also protect the data, shielding it from operator error and tampering to a certain extent. While the database management systems available for most micros are not yet as sophisticated or powerful as those for minicomputers and mainframes, exciting developments are taking place.

A single supplier, legally obligated

Applications software are those computer programs that address a specific application or need. Checking books in and out, calculating a payroll, and maintaining a mailing list are all applications. While the operating system is normally provided by the company that manufactured the hardware and database management systems are normally obtained from large software companies, applications software is usually bought from a specialized software development company. These sell by mail, through magazines, and in computer stores. Libraries tend to buy personal micro applications software from traditional library supply houses like Gaylord and Highsmith because local computer stores do not consider the library market to be sufficient to warrant the investment in the cost of carrying such specific purpose applications packages. Libraries tend to obtain multi-user, multi-tasking micros and minicomputer applications packages from a turnkey vendor as part of a package that also includes the required hardware. This has the advantage of giving the library a single supplier who is legally obligated to ensure that the hardware and software actually work together. The other route is to purchase a software package from an organization such as Northwestern University (the NOTIS package) or Virginia Tech (the VTLS package).

Another consideration in purchasing a computer system is the transportability of the software. This is to provide protection in case the hardware proves unsatisfactory, or the manufacturer or hardware maintenance company goes out of business. If this happens, the hapless user could be left with software packages and a database and no machine on which to run them. Can these be transported to another computer system? Often the answer is no. Thus it is important that if there are two seemingly equal choices, the software alternative that will offer more than one hardware option should be given preference over the one that does not.

A major factor in the transportability of software and files from one computer to another is the operating system for which the software was developed. A CP/M operating system offers the possibility of transportability to other personal micros using CP/M. This is a tricky area, however. Many computers support CP/M and one might expect that all versions of CP/M would be the same. This is not necessarily the case. Frequently CP/M is rewritten in order to make a product run better on a particular line of computers. Thus, it should be expected that in terms of moving from one CP/ M system to another there will be some time and cost entailed in making the transfer. Normally the rewrite will be done by the vendor of the software package, rather than the purchaser.

The larger multi-user, multi-tasking micros, which will play a very major role in library automation, are lagging behind the personal micros. One of the reasons for this is that automated library system vendors are finding it difficult to get the costs of multi-user, multi-tasking micro systems low enough to make them viable alternatives to mini-based systems. If all a vendor does is replace the mini with a micro, the cost of the system changes by only fifteen percent and that is not enough to open up an entirely new market. If all of the other aspects of the system are also stripped down, including the amount of support given to customers, the price can be further reduced, but the vendor may no longer have an attractive product. The question of how to make an automated library system based on a multi-user, multi-tasking microcomputer attractive is a major issue in library automation today, and one that has yet to be fully resolved.

Painting oneself into a corner

Software has been developed to support a number of library applications on personal micros. There are several micro packages that will write purchase orders, support claiming, and handle funds accounting. These are available for a variety of machines, from the Apple II to the IBM PC. Both Gaylord and Highsmith sell software for these purposes. Expect, however, that by the time the software package and the required hardware are purchased, the total cost will be in the range of $6,000 to $9,000. And this results in only a single function system, which can support only a single user. For such expenditure to be justified, a library must be in a situation in which its current needs as well as five-year growth can be accommodated by the system. It should also be noted that the database created on the single function system may not be usable in any other way. Given these factors, it is difficult for a library to avoid painting itself into a corner. It could have an acquisitions only system, and no place to go in terms of adding more functions or users. With careful selection, the library might be able to provide enough expansion capability for growth with such a system.

There is a multi-user, multitasking micro-based system for acquisitions called Innovacq, developed by Innovative Interfaces of Berkeley, California. This system can cost from $30,000 to over $50,000, but it will handle the acquisitions of any library except for the very largest. However, it is relatively expensive on a per terminal basis, and while it will support multiple users it has, until the recent addition of serial control functions, supported only a single function—acquisitions. The company is developing patron access catalog application software.

A system developed to support acquisitions is not usually intended to handle the complex searching strategies with Boolean capabilities that are required for patron access catalog functions. Generally, the type and frequency of access required in an automated acquisitions system will be relatively straightforward and will not require the substantial computer resources needed in the most sophisticated patron access catalog applications.

Automated serials control support is also provided on a range of machines, from a personal micro to a multi-user system. Perhaps the most successful package in terms of sales is the Checkmate software developed by CLASS. Checkmate was initially designed for the Radio Shack TRS-80 on which it could handle up to 2,000 serials for check-in, claiming, and routing. CLASS later developed a hard-disk version that can handle up to 6,000 titles. The rights to distribute Checkmate have been assigned to the Capital Systems Group based in Kensington, Maryland and to Gaylord Brothers. Gaylord has rewritten the system to run on the IBM PC. But again, this is a limited function capability that can handle only a limited number of titles, and only one user at one time. A library may again find that it has painted itself into a corner. This might be a conscious decision based on the reasoning that the library's serials problems are so great that the potential benefit to be realized by the expenditure of $7,500 on hardware and software, for a limited period of four or five years, is worth the investment even though the system will not provide for a natural migration to a multi-function system.

Why do keyboarding?

Cataloging can also be done on a micro. That is, the micro can be used to create cataloging records, and even records of sufficient detail for the MARC format. The Library Software Company of Pleasant Hill, California has several products. However, the question is one of whether any library today would wish to create records de novo by doing all the keying. It costs at least $1.40 to key in a typical shelflist card, but for less than $1.40 a machine-readable retrospective conversion record can be obtained from OCLC or some other source. In this case, why do the keyboarding? After keyboarding, the record still has to be proofed and corrected. For these reasons, the extraction method of creating records—drawing machine-readable records from a resource data-base—is by far the more popular. But, if a library prefers to key in its own records and recognizes the diseconomies inherent in such an approach, a micro and an appropriate software package can be a perfectly good cataloging tool. The problem will not be the keying, but the maintenance of the database created by that cataloging activity. It is difficult to manipulate a database on a personal micro. Of course, a personal computer can be used as a workstation to access a remote resource database for cataloging.

Circulation control systems based on personal micros can be purchased from Highsmith, Gaylord and several other sources. Most of them run on the Apple II or on the IBM PC. Generally these systems can handle circulation volumes of up to 100,000 transactions. However, the circulation support offered on personal micros is fairly basic: check-out, check-in, and the preparation of overdue notices.

Libraries that installed automated circulation systems in the early-to-mid 1970s very quickly began trying to use these systems to support additional activities. Reference librarians started to use them to determine what the library held, and some libraries began to put terminals where they could be used by the public for database inquiry. Librarians soon realized that the real value of the systems was not to check books in or out, but to control the inventory and provide access not only to holdings information but also to current availability data in a single screen display.

There are so many other applications for circulation systems that they should really not be called circulation systems any more. For instance, a circulation control system can be a powerful inventory tool if the system has sufficient processing power. A portable terminal, or a Motorola radio broadcast terminal, can be taken to the shelves and each book tipped outward so that its bar coded label can be scanned. By comparing the results of this shelf inventory with the information in circulation, the system can identify which items are missing from the collection. If a long cable were attached to the portable terminal to give it two-way communications capability, the inventory operations could be extended so that the scanner would give an audible signal when the items on the shelves were out of order. There are all sorts of ways of exploiting what was formerly a mundane technology to handle charging and discharging of library materials.

Personal micro-based circulation control systems do not handle more than the basic circulation tasks. Micros, for the most part, will not speed the charging and discharging of library materials very much. In a typical library, the length of time that a circulation transaction takes is determined by the time required to scan a label or to put a transaction through a charging machine.

A Gaylord model C electromechanical charging device will accommodate the transaction load of a library with up to a quarter of a million circulations as effectively as any automated system, if all that is required is to check books out quickly. Automated circulation control systems really don't offer tremendously improved performance in this area. Automation will help, though, in the holds or reserves operation, and in getting overdue notices out. If a library has problems in this area, automation may be the answer.

A treacherous decision

The problem with the available micro-based circulation systems is that they utilize brief bibliographic records. This limits a library to using the system only for circulation control, and developing a database that will support only circulation control. The system itself will not physically support detailed database inquiries and, more importantly, the database developed on the system will not be satisfactory for use on more sophisticated systems later on. The database would have to be upgraded at considerable cost. For these reasons, using micros for circulation control can be rather treacherous.

Many libraries can successfully justify going into automated acquisitions or automated serials control as a short-term interim step on a limited function micro-based system. But circulation control as a short-term interim step has generally not worked out as well.

It is most unwise to mount an online catalog on a micro, especially a personal or desk-top sized micro. The emphasis given to this viewpoint in a brief article in the January 1984 issue of *Small Computers in Libraries* is particularly interesting, as the newsletter is published by a group that is particularly enthusiastic about using micros for library applications. The article points out that personal micros are not well suited for patron access catalogs or any kind of online file that is to be accessed regularly through relatively sophisticated multiple access points. A personal micro simply does not have the power to sort complex searches against large data files. Even if there were a reliable disk drive big enough to hold the files, the processor cannot support the required sorting, selection, and display procedures to provide a result in a reasonable time. Some companies do offer patron access catalog software for personal micros but if this application is to be automated, a larger machine should be used.

Dumb and intelligent terminals

The library application that represents the most successful use of a personal micro is that of using the micro as a workstation. A workstation is a personal micro that can function both as a terminal and as a separate processor. Information retrieved using the personal micro as a terminal can subsequently be manipulated using word processing or other packages running on the micro's CPU.

Many libraries accessing both local systems and remote databases use "dumb" or ASCII terminals that do not contain communications protocols. Because of the lack of communications protocols in the terminals, the only way a computer being accessed by such a terminal knows which terminal is calling is by identifying the port or channel of the computer through which the terminal is communicating. On the other hand, an "intelligent" terminal has communication protocols; it can identify itself to the computer. This is important because telecommunications efficiencies can be realized using terminals that have built-in protocols. However, these terminals are also more expensive. A personal micro can be made to emulate or pretend to be either a dumb or intelligent terminal just by loading suitable software.

With this flexible access device, users soon developed techniques that increased the efficiency of computer access. They soon found that, when accessing remote databases such as BRS, Dialog, and SDC, telecommunications costs could be reduced by preparing the initial search statement offline on the micro and going online to the remote system only for transmission. Similarly, as soon as a satisfactory search result was obtained, the data would be downloaded from the screen into the storage of the micro. After signing off from the remote sytem one could perform any further data manipulation to convert the results into a format suited to the end user. Such techniques have been found to cut online communications and system usage costs by more than half.

Recognizing that this approach to database searching is becoming common, database vendors are examining their pricing structures with a view to moving from the established system of charging on a connect-time basis to one based on the number of units of data being removed from the system, irrespective of whether that removal is by offline or online printing, or by downloading. Even if these pricing structures change to accommodate the new database access methods, the user will still realize savings in telecommunications costs because the online connection is of shorter duration. The added benefit is that the end result is more manipulable, and therefore more useful. The typical remote database service printout is not particularly well formatted for the needs of the end user. However, transferred to a micro and manipulated by a word processing software package, it becomes much more useful.

Downloading information

Three years ago, one out of ten Dialog users was using a workstation approach. It is now estimated that, of the heavy users who collectively account for eighty percent of all Dialog use, two-thirds are using personal computers and downloading information rather than using dumb terminals.

OCLC's decision to adopt the IBM PC as a workstation to its system will accelerate the trend, and Mead Data—the vendor of NEXIS and LEXIS—has abandoned its dedicated terminal approach (which required that these files could only be accessed using a terminal supplied by Mead Data) in favor of an IBM PC or any one of several other micros equipped with a special software package. Increasingly, database vendors of all types—Mead, OCLC, Dialog, ISI, etc.—are developing micro software packages to facilitate workstation access to their systems.

Turnkey automated library system vendors are also moving towards personal computers to provide data collection back-up for circulation, acquistions, and serials control when the host computer system is down. If the host goes down, staff can continue to enter data and record transactions on the memory of the personal computer being used as a workstation rather than in the memory of the main system. The same workstation can be used to perform other functions as well.

Every library is an office

Libraries often overlook the administrative applications potential of personal micros—word processing, accounting, and scheduling. In addition to being a library, every library is also an office. If a library can reduce its office workload by thirty-five percent or so, this is an impressive saving. And there is no question that this can be done. The applications packages available for the office environment are superior to those for the library environment because the office market is much larger and more competitive. A word-processing package may sell 200,000 copies and VisiCalc may sell 450,000 copies. Such levels of sales provide not only enough income to refine the product, but also a client expectation that the products should perform very well. Provided some care is taken in the selection process, it is possible to obtain very good display sheet, word processing, accounting, and other software packages for almost any available microcomputer system.

However, once an organization's interests extend beyond basic word processing and financial work, the choice is more limited. A library might wish to identify a software package to schedule student assistants, for instance. Software for this function is not as widely available as that for more common office applications, and the choice is more or less limited to packages designed for use on the IBM PC, DEC Rainbow, Apple II, and Radio Shack TRS-80. There just hasn't been the demand for those developing scheduling packages to offer them for sale to a larger user group; a larger group but one comprised of numerous small subgroups each using a different micro, all of which are less popular than the market leaders.

In selecting a personal micro for office applications, it is not necessary to define all possible applications and survey the availability of software for each. The trick is to choose hardware from one of the companies expected to survive in the marketplace. Services such as Datapro have undertaken numerous studies to identify the likely survivors in the microcomputer industry. Not surprisingly, these are companies such as IBM, Apple, and the Hewlett-Packard Corporation.

In selecting a micro for a library it is important to know why automation is being considered. Is the library trying to demonstrate that it is up to date? Is there a specific problem which must be solved immediately? Is the intent to contain or reduce costs? In relation to this last question, no documentation comes to mind that indicates that the automation of library applications, other than shared cataloging, reduces costs. Automation contains costs, yes; improves service, unquestionably; but reduces costs? No.

A library administration needs to acknowledge why automation is being considered so that the decisions made throughout the process of procurement and implementation are consistent with the objective. What function or functions are to be automated? The decision should not be based solely on what is currently available, but on what functions really should be automated. A few years ago everybody was saying that they wanted to automate circulation. Undoubtedly this was because the only systems in the marketplace that had a high visibility were circulation systems. Now everybody wants to implement patron access catalogs. Many librarians do not give a high priority to serials control automation because they believe that the vendors haven't yet addressed this function. While serials control remains the least developed area and implementation may have to be postponed, the function should be included in a library's planning.

The fifth year postion

It is critical to think in terms of the fifth year position. Where does the library want to be five years from now? Where will investment in this system leave the library after five years? Is it going to have a database that has been created for a circulation system that has brief records and that cannot possibly be used any other way, leaving the library to start all over again creating a new database? Is the library going to be using a system from a small hardware company that is unlikely to survive? If the worst happens and the company isn't around any more, what equipment will the software package run on?

It is extremely important that all automation planning—even with a micro, even with a proposed $5,000 investment—starts five years from now and works back to today. Such a planning approach gives five years in which to take those steps necessary to get one to where one wants to be. Even more importantly, such planning ensures that one doesn't take steps that will move the library in the wrong direction. ▣

Online Databases: Some Questions of Ownership

Sally Drew

"Barriers to basic information of critical importance to the mission of libraries threaten the services provided and the efficiency and cost effectiveness of providing them."

Libraries create, use, reuse, and purchase machine-readable bibliographic records, or access to them, for many purposes from a wide variety of sources. Arrangements for obtaining bibliographic records and the relationships between creator, owner, user, and data processing agent have become increasingly complicated. A library may play several roles as its service needs and working relationships with other libraries and vendors change.

Such complexities and complications are already causing and will continue to cause barriers to the access to information in general and bibliographic information in particular. Barriers to basic information of critical importance to the mission of libraries threaten the services provided and the efficiency and cost effectiveness of providing them.

Some articles have discussed the steps involved in and methods of converting card catalog information to machine-readable form for use in automated library systems. Others have discussed in great detail the process of contracting for the automated system itself. Few have given equal attention to the concepts that should be addressed in contracting for creation of machine-readable data. The value of the product to the library has rarely been analyzed except to simply calculate the actual costs of the initial creation of the database.

I wish to discuss the long-term value of bibliographic records to the library and the cost and service implications of that value. I will also describe potential relationships between creators, users, and providers of bibliographic data and offer some guidelines for contracting with providers.

Sally Drew *is director, Bureau for Interlibrary Loan and Resource Sharing, Wisconsin Department of Public Instruction, Madison, Wisconsin.*

Assigning value

The simplest way to assign value to any product is to calculate how much was paid for it. The creation of bibliographic records certainly has associated labor, supply, vendor fees, and other costs that can be calculated. The value to the library is enhanced, however, by factors other than initial cost. If machine-readable records are created according to Library of Congress MARC standards, in all likelihood it will be possible to use these records for purposes other than those originally planned. For example, MARC records created as a by-product of cataloging materials can be used in an automated circulation system, even though the services may be provided by different vendors and utilize different hardware and software, assuming each vendor adheres to use of MARC standards.

Future applications may involve the association of one library with other libraries, and an automated system originally planned for one library may be extended for use in another. All libraries associated with the project may use the same database. Sharing of the database may have an economic advantage to all parties because they can all contribute to it and eliminate duplicate effort.

The existence of the shared project can also enrich the services of all involved libraries in a variety of ways to which it is more difficult to assign costs, such as ease of identification of needed materials and their location and sharing of reference information and materials. The ability to share a bibliographic database can help build stronger relationships among libraries of all types. This can enhance the services of all parties and is a very important value in its own right. Certainly, taxpayers benefit when public agencies cooperate in this way.

Prior to purchasing bibliographic records, a library should carefully review its overall mission and the purpose for which records are being created. Most publicly funded libraries (public, school, academic) share a common goal of dissemination of information in as free and open a manner as possible. Libraries perform the task of creating and distributing information that is used to assist in the storage and retrieval of other information. Bibliographic information, whether included on catalog cards or in computer systems, falls into this category.

Publicly funded libraries generally create and use bibliographic information for a public purpose, and in many states and communities bibliographic records may be considered public. Public records, by their nature, are available to be shared. They are normally not copyrighted by the institution creating them, nor is exclusive license given to any party for their use.

Questions regarding the handling of copyrighted material can be confusing, especially when copyright is applied to bibliographic records. Library staff are comfortable working with copyrighted materials and are familiar with copyright issues and law. Most of the books, periodicals, and other materials purchased by libraries are created by others and are copyrighted. Library staff respect the owner's rights in circulating and using these materials.

However, most of the bibliographic records held in databases operated by bibliographic utilities and, in many cases, by vendors were created by library staff, and many were created with public funds. The data created by the library staff should not be confused with the data processing services needed for accessing or processing this data.

Public domain

For example, the Library of Congress MARC records are considered to be in the public domain. To obtain or use these records it may be necessary to contract or work with another library, a bibliographic utility, or a vendor. The fact that the information is processed by an organization does not necessarily remove it from the public domain. However, some organizations, by invoking copyright or contract provisions, may attempt to limit your library's use of this public domain material because you purchased it from them.

> ***"Questions regarding the handling of copyrighted material can be confusing, especially when copyright is applied to bibliographic records."***

If the mission of your library involves the creation of public records or consistently involves interaction and working relationships with other libraries, communities, and political jurisdictions (school districts, vocational-technical schools districts, counties, or towns), the value to your organization of the bibliographic records will be enhanced if it is possible to use them in a manner consistent with the use of public records. This may well involve sharing them with other libraries or organizations with which you routinely cooperate. Use of these records will be limited if restrictions are imposed or if complex royalty provisions are involved.

Most library services can be assisted and improved by some level of automation. Libraries have gained positive experience in automation of circulation, catalog record production, patron catalog access, acquisition of library materials, serials control, interlibrary loan, and reference services. Services can be used online with staff and patrons interacting directly with the computer, or the machine-readable database can be produced in the form of computer output microfiche or printed copy for other uses. In most cases the same database can be used for all these applications if care is taken in creating it and if compatible automated systems for these services are selected.

A library can gain access to or purchase machine-readable bibliographic records from a wide variety of sources. The records may include bibliographic information and library holdings. The following sources are most common:

- Bibliographic utilities: Examples include OCLC, RLIN, WLN, UTLAS.
- State and multistate networks offering the services of a bibliographic utility and additional independent services: Examples include AMIGOS, SOLINET.
- Commercial vendors: Examples include Autographics, Brodart, GRC, Computer Company, MARCIVE, Library Corporation, REMARC.
- Federal agencies: Examples include the Library of Congress, National Library of Medicine, Government Printing Office.
- Libraries and groups of libraries: Examples include local libraries of all types, public library systems, and associations of libraries.

Claiming ownership

The relationship between a library and any of the above sources of bibliographic records will vary depending on whether the library creates, uses, shares, or claims ownership. Depending on the terms of the agreement or contract between a library and the source of bibliographic records, ownership may be claimed by either party. A library may obtain ownership either by creating the records from scratch (in most cases copyright will apply) or purchasing ownership rights to a product.

In arranging or contracting for creation, use, or reuse of bibliographic records, library staff must be careful to fully describe the relationship to the vendor or agency providing the records as well as the rights and obligations of both parties. In addition, it is important to understand the future implications of this relationship and the agreement on rights. From a library's perspective, the following relationships are not uncommon:

- Library creates bibliographic data, claims ownership of that data, and contracts with a vendor, utility, or other agency to store, maintain, or produce various products from the data.
- Library purchases data or access to the data for a particular purpose but does not obtain ownership and has no rights of use for other purposes.
- Library purchases data for one or more purposes and obtains nonexclusive ownership and rights of reuse.
- Library retains rights to the data cooperatively with other libraries or agencies, and rights of use and reuse described in the cooperative contract.

Several bibliographic utilities, libraries, and vendors claim ownership rights through copyright or contract to the entire compilation of the database operated, created, or compiled. However, use of a subset of the database may not be covered by the copyright or contract, and it may not be clear which party has ownership rights to the subset.

Rights and ownership

The concepts of either ownership of data or unrestricted rights to use the data once purchased are important to the library. In order to protect their market, some vendors, bibliographic utilities, or libraries have placed restrictions on the use, reuse, or sharing of the data purchased. Some libraries have mistakenly assumed that purchase of data includes ownership only to find that only access to the record was actually purchased. The type of access may be limited and may not include all legal rights of ownership.

While libraries may assume that they are paying an agency to perform work for hire, the agency may attempt to claim ownership rights to the data on the basis of the computer processing entailed to produce the records or the database as a whole. The fact that the library actually created or edited a record may not establish ownership if rights are relinquished by contract. Records in the public domain may cease to be so if the vendor claims that value has been added and the library agrees in a contract to limited use. Restrictions commonly take the following form:

- Purchase, through the agency operating the computer equipment, of online access to records only.
- Restrictions on use of records in more than one automated application.
- Restrictions on the format of data that may be used or distributed.
- Restrictions on sharing records with other libraries.
- Requirement of royalty payment if records are used in more than one system or shared with other libraries.

For example, REMARC created the data in its database under contract with the Library of Congress, and even though LC MARC records are in the public domain, ownership of REMARC records has been assigned to REMARC. OCLC libraries have long shared records among themselves as members of a cooperatively based organization. Recently, OCLC copyrighted its database and has attempted to restrict, through contract, sharing of bibliographic records by asking the participating libraries and networks to restrict access to bibliographic records to any "third party," that is, a library which is not a member of OCLC. Whereas many libraries assumed they had the right to share records (derived from the archival tapes which they purchased) with other local libraries which may not be OCLC members, they now find they may not be able to do this without requesting permission from OCLC.

In some cases, a library may acquire rights to some but not all of the records in its database. This can occur if the library creates some records but purchases others without gaining nonexclusive ownership rights to those purchased. Some records may be in the public domain (Library of Congress records), while others are owned by the agency selling them (REMARC). If both types of records are combined into a single database in such a way that it is impossible to determine the original source of individual records, the library may have an impossible task in claiming ownership. In practical terms, the library may not be able to use any of the records for another purpose without violating the rights of other libraries, agencies, vendors, or utilities. Even if ownership of individual records can be determined, it may not be economically feasible to do so in order to extract records or reuse them.

Defining responsibilities

Libraries frequently take a great deal of care in defining the requirements of an automated circulation system or online catalog and in defining the responsibilities and obligations of the vendor or agency supplying it. Frequently, the same libraries do not take the same care in developing a contract with the agency that provides the source for bibliographic data to be used in the automated system. As is the case with other types of purchases, the lowest bidder may not be the best. Both short-term and long-term costs should be taken into consideration at the time of original purchase. In developing a contract, libraries should attempt to negotiate the following:

- Rights to nonexclusive ownership in the data purchased.
- Unlimited rights to reuse the data for a purpose different from the one for which the data was originally purchased.
- Unlimited rights to share the data with other libraries without payment of royalties or other fees.
- Unlimited rights to transfer data from one agency or vendor to another for any purpose specified by the library.
- Unlimited rights to use or share the data in any format, including machine-readable records.

Libraries should approach the contract with a bibliographic supplier with the same care as any other contract by establishing the product to be delivered, its quality, and the right to use the product or derivatives of it. ▣

Pioneering New Services: Videocassettes

Don Julien

The King County Library System, Seattle, Washington, has a long tradition of actively supporting a wide range of information formats: books, periodicals, 16mm films, and disk and cassette audio recordings. In 1980, the administration realized that home videocassette recorders in the library system's service area numbered in the thousands, that the video store business was in its infancy and few stores offered a wide selection of tapes at a low cost. The library system supports an extensive 16mm film collection comprised of entertainment, documentary and general interest short subjects, but the audience for videocassettes was a different clientele, seeking feature films, entertainment shorts (such as music), and how-tos, in a convenient format for casual home use. Here was a format growing in demand and appropriate for library service. In 1982, King County Library System introduced a series of videocassette projects leading to a current collection of over 5,600 tapes representing over 1,100 titles, available in all thirty-seven libraries. Videocassettes represent at least ten percent of a 1984 circulation of six million items and, in 1985, the library system budget includes $200,000, 8.9 percent of the total materials budget, to support this service.

Don Julien *is head librarian, Lake Hills Library, Bellevue, Washington. The library is an affiliate of the King County Library System.*

A videocassette audience awaiting

King County Library system serves approximately 770,000 people in the 2,012 square-mile suburban and small-town environs of Seattle, through thirty-seven libraries backed by an administrative center closed to the public. Traditionally, library collections and services have been dispersed throughout the libraries rather than centered in one major facility. Five of the libraries serve as area resource centers, carrying microfilm, 16mm films, business, reference, and foreign language collections. In recent years several of these special services have expanded to additional libraries as various communities and local demand have grown.

The population in the library system's service area is predominantly white (94 percent) with Asian the largest ethnic population (2.8 percent). The black and Spanish-origin populations are very small (1.2 percent and 1.8 percent). In age, the population is slightly higher than the national average in the 25–45 category (32.6 percent) and slightly lower than the national average in the 55 and over categories (15.5 percent). The population tends to be well educated, with 26.2 percent of the adults over 25 having four or more years of college; the median years of education is thirteen. Employment is heaviest in management, professional, technical, sales, and administrative support occupations (61.4 percent). Manufacturing is important, especially in electronics and aerospace. Special areas of growth are manufacturing and warehousing industries in the Kent valley, financial and professional services in Bellevue, and the electronics industry in the Redmond valley. The 1979 median income was $20,717, with a mean of $24,114. The local communities ranged from $19,215 to $34,477 in median income and from $21,012 to $41,800 in mean income. The population is very mobile—only 4.2 percent of the households have no vehicle, 39.4 percent have two vehicles, and 28.5 percent have three or more.

Local branch library collections range from 1,000 to 100,000 volumes. The collections have for the most part developed individually to provide full range service to each local community, with some attention paid to being part of a larger system. This type of collection development produces a great deal of duplication, but was necessary when travel was difficult between communities. A few branches have local, informal arrangements for special collections development. Only recently has the library system begun a central selection program to purchase timely, widely popular materials in larger quantities. The library system also recently improved interbranch delivery so that requested items could be retrieved from other branches or the administrative center in timely fashion. Each branch, however, still feels the local pressure to maintain full range, general interest collections. The area resource libraries make an attempt to meet the demand for depth, but are still limited by collection size and space. The facilities range from 600 to 18,500 square feet and cannot adequately house both general and special collections.

Book, film, and magazine selection has emphasized general interest, entertainment, and some support for local school curricula. The library system purchases very few textbooks and shies away from technical works such as industrial specifications, trade and professional journals, and extensive literary criticism. The generalized, dispersed approach to library service was carried over to the videocassette collection, with limited attention paid to growing special interests.

Exploring the marketplace

When the library system first approached videocassettes the administration reviewed the system's overall materials selection philosophies, analyzed the clientele, and explored the marketplace. By far, most video cassette recorders were being sold for entertainment purposes rather than for training or education. It was discovered that 85 percent of the machines sold in the service area were VHS format. The videotapes available commercially were predominantly entertainment, and the very few instructional or training tapes available were crudely produced and overpriced. Most business-oriented tapes were available only for rental. Since most available tapes were feature film releases, the media department also examined the local film theater market to find patterns or gaps that would be useful in selection. The Seattle area has a reputation for high theater attendance, indicating an interest in a wide range of feature film productions. The department found that most theaters in the system's service area were members of large multitheater chains, while most independent theaters, noted for special showings and art house titles, were in the city of Seattle. Foreign films, as well as occasional box-office blockbusters, tended to be shown in downtown locations inaccessible or inconvenient to our patrons. Many fine films played limited engagements and never moved out to suburban theaters.

The theatrical market suggested a similar high interest in blockbuster and general interest feature film cassettes and a latent demand for art house and limited engagement titles. In a deliberate, planned move, the administration decided to enter into video service in a highly visible and popular way, carrying the blockbuster feature films, popular art-house films, children's films, a limited number of classics, a few music concert tapes, and a very selective number of general interest instructional tapes. A highly visible and popular service would encourage public support for spending large sums on video. Once the service was well established, selection could move into more traditional library-type titles: cultural, educational, and informational. The system continues to give full budgetary support to its more traditional 16mm film collection which is still growing in patronage.

A specialist in the media department is responsible for keeping up on the mass-market film and videocassette industry, reading *Variety, Box Office, Billboard, Moviegoer, Films in Review, Video Review,* local newspaper reviews, and general circulation magazine reviews, such as *People, Us, Time* and *Newsweek.* Film reviews on "Entertainment Tonight" and "At the Movies" are also monitored. The specialist keeps up on the specialized film and video market, talking with distributors and representatives and scanning traditional library review media, although the system has not as yet purchased videos in specialized fields.

The media department is responsible for purchases. Titles that have been smash hits across the country, especially Academy Award nominees, titles that have been particularly big in the Seattle/King County area, and children's titles are purchased in quantities as high as thirty copies. Art house titles such as *Another Country, Eating Raoul,* and *Android,* a limited number of classics, and non-fiction titles that from past experience should be popular, such as *Warren Miller's Ski Time,* are purchased in quantities of five to twenty copies. The department purchases review copies of non-fiction and children's films that it has questions about and has not been able to preview on television, 16mm film, or in the theaters.

The library system purchases from Commtron, a local, regional outlet for a national wholesale distributor. Cost analysis indicated that volume business with a local jobber was more cost-efficient than dealing with traditional library jobbers. As one of its major accounts, the media department is kept up-to-date on new releases for pre-release purchasing. The local warehouse and offices enable the media department staff to deal with Commtron's staff personally, picking up rush orders and handling problems. As far as purchasing is concerned, the library system views itself as a customer entitled to the same service as a video store, and has convinced Commtron to share that view.

A role to play

Some concern has been expressed that the library system is providing a service that is readily and inexpensively provided by private industry—the video stores, supermarkets and others. However, the number of tapes and titles the library system has to serve 770,000 people comes nowhere close to the stock of two video stores serving a town of 20,000. If a patron wants a wide selection, or a particular title at a particular time, there is one choice—the video store. Video stores, like all commercial retail outlets, must be conscious of turnover. A title that turns over slowly takes up valuable space. Video store owners admit a difficulty generating any significant rental activity in children's and instructional videos, and are amazed at the quantities the library system purchases. Video stores also use turnover as a major criteria for deleting titles from the collection, while libraries traditionally hold titles much longer than the retail outlets. The library also has a role providing titles on which a patron might be willing to gamble time but not money. Patrons are also willing to watch a title for the third, fourth or fifteenth time if free, but are reluctant to pay a rental for it.

In many cases, the library has generated video store business; patrons have commented that they have purchased a videocassette recorder because the library had tapes, and they now use both the library and the store as sources of entertainment. Libraries have never been a threat to bookstores, even used bookstores, which more closely fit the profile of a rental video store. Libraries, even those with popular-oriented collections, will continue as always to identify and serve those segments of the market which cannot or will not be served by private industry.

The videocassettes are fully cataloged and entered in both the automated circulation system database and the COM catalog. The videocassettes are also entered in the WLN database using the WLN format. Ninety-five percent of the cataloging is original, since very few of the titles are on the MARC tapes or have been entered by other libraries. When the system originally decided to catalog and classify videocassettes, the cataloging department was instructed to classify a title in Dewey if a comparable book would be classified Dewey. This would identify informational and instructional tapes for later integration of collections. Most feature films were classified as fiction, but a few, such as *The Right Stuff, Never Cry Wolf* and *Prince of the City* ended up with Dewey numbers or as biography.

Packaging the product

Packaging was deemed important. The library system wanted to take advantage of the original, attractive packaging provided by the distributor. Although some library systems use uniform labels with the title typed in, the library felt the point-of-purchase appeal was important to the success of the project. After some experimentation, the media department found Mid-America Plastics' videocassette case with a clear plastic window completely covering the front, spine and back (the Warner Roundback). The original box is trimmed and slipped into the plastic window. The cassette boxes are prominently displayed, while the tapes themselves are housed at the checkout desk. Some of the libraries have chosen to forgo the point-of-purchase benefits and have set out 3x5 cards representing the tapes currently in-house.

Originally, when the libraries did not permit browsing of the videocassettes, twenty-to-forty word annotations were written for all titles. Annotated lists were then printed in quantity quarterly and distributed free to the public until gone. Now that the library system has moved to browsing collections with original packaging, new titles are not annotated. Each library provides reference sources such as Consumer Guide's *Rating the Movies, Halliwells Film Guide,* and *Filmgoers Companion* for patrons who need more information.

The branch libraries and the Youth Service Center (the county juvenile detention facility) are divided by size into four tiers for videocassette distribution. The tiers in April, 1984, were five libraries with 175 titles each, nine with 125 titles each, nine with 75 titles each, and fifteen with 30 titles each. Currently, they have 300, 220, 125, and 60 titles respectively. The multiple copies of new titles are distributed by formula to keep a relative balance among the tiers.

Putting a price on it

Few guidelines were available for setting circulation and fines policies. Video store rentals ranged from overnight to three days, at charges from $2 to $6 per tape. A committee arbitrarily chose something easy to remember: three tapes, three days, $3 fine. Further refinement followed: three titles per patron, three calendar days, $3 per title per day overdue. Later, the system changed the policy to two tapes, two days. Tapes must be returned to the library from which they were checked out, even though all other materials can be returned to any branch. Videocassettes are also not to be returned in the night book return. A label designed for recordings was affixed to the cassette boxes, claiming damage might be caused by return in the drop, but the real motive was to avoid the "claims returned" problems that seem to hover over the night drop, to get a faster turn-around on the cassettes, and to force the patron into the library.

A hoary problem for libraries and films is the question of ratings. At the outset, the system decided to use the ratings of such sources as *Seventeen, Consumer Reports, Consumer Guide,* and MPAA as evaluation resources but not as purchasing restrictions. The system felt it had a responsibility to select titles for adults, and not just for families, children, and young adults. The use of a film by an inappropriate audience does not fall within a selection policy but within a circulation policy, and an open access circulation policy could not be a restraint on purchasing. Open access and labeling policies were extended to videos—the system intended to put no restrictions by age upon their circulation, and processing neither affixes nor deletes any ratings or recommendations on the original packaging. The system does recognize a public obsession with various ratings systems and provides resources for identifying various recommendations. An early decision required all videocassette borrowers to fill out a media/equipment responsibility card. The one restriction that applied to age required that a parent or guardian sign a minor's responsibility card. The card contains a statement that the King County Library System carries a range of videocassettes, including R-rated material. Local library staff attempt to discuss with parents the range of materials available and offer suggestions on how they can keep informed about the films available. This required card has been extended to include viewing videocassettes in the library as well as for checkout. Although there is a public demand in the marketplace for erotic adult videos, the library decided they were inappropriate for our collection.

An improving turnaround

When the library system introduced the service, the libraries accepted requests on all titles. The response, however, was overwhelming. By April, 1984, 50,000 requests were waiting on 3,000 tapes. Additional copies were purchased as the budget allowed to hold the ratio of requests per tape down to twenty to one, but the usual wait for a title was still three to five months. After considering other options, the administration decided to discontinue taking requests on videocassettes, fill the existing requests, and move to strictly browsing collections in all facilities. The demand for tapes remains high, with very few tapes "on the shelf" when patrons walk in, but turnaround time has improved from once a week to three times a week and a short wait usually yields a returned tape a patron has not yet seen. Some problems have arisen with patrons hounding the circulation desk or waylaying incoming video patrons, but overall most patrons exercise restraint.

Videocassettes classified as nonfiction, however, tend to be more suitable for filling non-entertainment subject requests than for browsing entertainment. The library system is now taking requests on these titles, entering the requests into the automated circulation system. When a request is triggered, the tape is mailed to the patron for a two-week chargeout period.

After three years of heavy use, the lifespan of a videocassettte remains a mystery. Several tapes have survived 250 circulations without appreciable damage. Community libraries send 'damaged' tapes to the media department for checking or replacement. The department finds that half of the reported damage is really unfamiliarity with equipment. The patron may not know how to adjust the videocassette recorder with the tracking knob. One of every ten "damaged" tapes, reported as having no picture, has just not been rewound. Among the tapes that are actually damaged(ten to fourteen per month), the most damage has been caused by magnetic fields, either by staff placing the cassette in a security system or by a patron placing the cassette on a stereo speaker or a television set. Some tapes suffer from "flaking," caused by a misadjusted rewind mechanism. A few cassettes suffer from snapped or stretched tape or a leader plug coming loose from one of the reels. The only damage that can be fixed easily is the re-siting of the leader plug. All other damaged tapes are replaced by new copies, if still available. The media department estimates that approximately seven percent of the 1985 videocassette budget will be for repair and replacements.

Some damage is still mystifying. Cassettes have cracked or popped-out windows that suggest they have been dropped on an edge or poked. A number of cases are crushed in the upper-right-hand corner. The media department continues to experiment to find the causes. One question that arose is the library system's responsibility in the case of a library tape damaging a patron's equipment. Apparently, a spliced tape (whether by staff or by a helpful patron) can ooze adhesive and cause damage to a playback head. Since library staff conduct only a cursory inspection, if any at all, they most likely would miss such a "repair." The library system has, at this point, accepted no responsibility.

Continuing to experiment

The marketplace is changing. Business titles are no longer rentals only. Informational titles are better produced, although still pricey. Major classics are just beginning to be released in video. Our 1985 purchasing will look more closely at these markets. The media department is watching and purchasing kidvid—mass-marketed children's video such as Rainbow Bright, Care Bears, and He-Man, what might be termed the "Golden Books" of video. The library system continues to experiment: the system purchased for a year the rights to duplicate the American Short Story series, placing a full set in seven libraries; the media department negotiated the rights to transfer from film to video the *Horror of It All* and the Paddington Bear films, creating attractive packaging; and the system purchased several sets of a business series and is trying browsing, booking, and requests to see which service is appropriate. Approximately fifteen percent of the current videocassette budget will be devoted to picking up and experimenting with cultural and educational tapes.

As the local communities grow and change, the library system expects to keep the changing needs in mind. Some communities are seeing exploding business and educational development, as they develop into new urban centers. Others are growing with high-density multi-family housing in a new suburban sprawl. The somnolent rural towns are awakening to find themselves as commuter bedroom communities. The marketplace and public demand will continue to strongly influence what the library system buys. ▣

Information for All: ALANET

Joel Lee

```
              W E L C O M E   T O   A L A N E T  (R)

THE AMERICAN LIBRARY ASSOCIATION'S ELECTRONIC INFORMATION SERVICE

PLEASE REVIEW THE FOLLOWING MENU AND MAKE A SELECTION. . .


   CODE          DESCRIPTION

 * MAIL          Electronic Mail System
 * SYSTEM        Instructions for System Use
 * ALANEWS       ALA News Bulletin UPDATE 5/20/85
 * ALAPUBS       electroCitations: ALA Publications News UPDATE 5-3-85
 * DCNEWS        ALA Washington Newsline 4/15 and 4/30 issues online
 * OIFALERT      Intellectual Freedom Alert UPDATE 4-25-85
 * CONFER        Conference Program and Preconference Schedules--UPDATE 12/26/84
 * FORMS         Online Order, Registration, I.L.L. and other Forms
 * PRPOST        The ALANET Bulletin Board
 * SERVICE       The Library Supplier's Service Center
 * UNITS         ALA Unit Newsletters--LION for 3-25-85 now online!
 * GATEWAY       Database Services (BNA Advanceline, NEWS, ABI, UMI and more)
 * QUIT          System Level Prompt

Type "INFO MORE" for more instruction.
```

ALANET, the American Library Association's electronic information service, had its official start-of-service at the January, 1984 ALA Midwinter Meeting, following first announcements and promotional mailings the preceding fall. By mid-April, 1985, some 900 "electronic mailboxes" had been activated, representing every kind of library, state and federal agencies and national libraries, library suppliers and publishers, associations and networks, ALA units and many of their members, and even individual librarians throughout the U.S., Canada, and abroad. This rapid growth, along with press coverage, articles in the library literature, and word-of-mouth, have begun to make firm ALANET's position in the electronic communication marketplace and highlight its growing role as supporter and facilitator of a variety of networking activities and in providing information services for the library/information community.

Joel Lee *is ALA Headquarters Librarian and ALANET System Manager. ALANET is a registered trademark.*

Improving communications

The goal for the ALANET program was not simply to create an electronic mail system, but to develop a wide-ranging information service that would permit the association to improve communications between members and the staff in Chicago, Washington, D.C., and Middletown, Connecticut (where *Choice* magazine is headquartered), and at the same time improve access to the information resources of ALA—resources that are extraordinarily rich, but that are dispersed among many units, staff in Headquarters, and members in the field. While electronic mail is the most visible feature of the service, and the one most easily applied to existing programs, it is only a technological structure upon which a variety of information-related activities are built and through which a growing number of information services are provided—for communication channels are an absolute requirement for access to information.

Two converging paths of development can be identified in ALANET's origins. The first and most widely known is the test of electronic mail using Tymshare's Ontyme II system, beginning in 1981 with LITA and RTSD through CLASS in California and with the ALA Executive Board directly through Tymshare. The second was a major grant project developed in the Headquarters Library in 1981–82 that sought to improve ALA's information services through the Headquarters Library and through the development of databases and other electronically-based services derived from ALA's own resources. The electronic mail experiments represented recognition of the serious need to expand and improve ALA's means for communication. The database grant project represented recognition of the need for improved access through technology to the profession's own information resources; for me personally it was a culmination of much of my work as a library science librarian at ALA since late 1977. While the Executive Board gave its authorization to seek funding for the project, no funds were forthcoming from the granting agencies. The entire program was placed "on hold" until winter, 1982–83, when the time came to develop the Executive Board's embryonic network, dubbed ALANET by Executive Director Robert Wedgeworth (whose insights had also initiated the database project), and I was brought into the program as the search began for a vendor whose computer hardware, software, and telecommunication services would support it.

Three criteria guided the selection: the service had to be both powerful and easy to use, it had to be accessible through all the major telecommunication networks currently used in the field, and it had to enhance the provision of information services to ALA's members and to the library/information community. As various firms' offerings and proposals were reviewed it became clear that ITT Dialcom, Inc. of Silver Spring, Maryland was the vendor of choice. Dialcom offered a variety of powerful and responsive, but still "friendly," electronic communication facilities, with dial-access through Telenet, Tymnet, Uninet, and even a private telecommunication network, and, significantly, electronic publishing and database facilities that would enable ALA to begin fulfillment of the goals of the database grant project. With this technology the ALANET program could expand and improve ALA's communication and information services for libraries and librarians; it could also form a technological and programmatic base for beginning to further develop ALA's own Headquarters Library (which had, like other ALA units, suffered staff cutbacks in 1982).

Conceptual underpinnings

Perhaps the most important element of ALANET is its programmatic roots: the fact that it has as conceptual underpinnings the provision of information services to meet a primary ALA objective—access to information. The combination of a powerful technology and this programmatic orientation not only have begun to achieve the desired improvements, but also have led to the replication in local and regional settings of some of the same services ALA offers system-wide and to the growth of many networks within the larger ALANET network—with all participants throughout able to communicate with one another.

There are three components to the ALANET electronic information service, the first of which is the group of features that form the electronic communication system. The basic electronic mail system, with its capacity for instant transmission, group mailings and special options (*e.g.*, automatic acknowledgements, courtesy and blind copies, express priority, electronic filing, security passwords), is enhanced by such features as interactive forms, where the user is prompted by the system to "fill in the blanks" in purchase order, claim, registration, interlibrary loan and other forms; a system-wide bulletin board (in which special categories are available to subscriber networks); online conferencing systems; an interface with the Telex/Mailgram/Telegram network; and file transfer capabilities that maximize the time and cost savings of microcomputers and high speed transmission and that permit ALANET to be the transfer point between both compatible and incompatible hardware and software regardless of location. (This article was sent to the editor through ALANET; a document this length can be transmitted in about six minutes at a cost of about $1.80.)

The second component of ALANET is a group of external databases, including the Official Airlines Guide Electronic Edition, the ABI INFORM management database, an Electronic News service including AP, UPI and other wires, BNA ADVANCELINE, UMI ARTICLE CLEARINGHOUSE, and other information sources offered to all organizations using Dialcom's facilities (totalling about 90,000 mailboxes). These databases are in a way "frosting on the cake" in light of ALANET's primary goals, but in fact are an attractive part of the service because of their ease of access and modest cost, and because of the convenience of "one stop shopping" that the call to ALANET can provide in terms of information services for the library's clients in addition to the librarians. Moreover, this feature is in process of further expansion with "gateways" into additional services supported by Dialcom as well as to other host computers. ALANET is the first electronic service that a number of subscribers have ever used, and many others have had only limited experience with machine-readable information sources. The easy availability of these databases through ALANET provides an opportunity to explore or expand subscribers' use of online information services.

Professional information services form the third part of the ALANET service. The five electronic newsletters currently being produced with Dialcom's electronic publishing (epub) facility are the first to use the immediacy of the electronic medium to "short-circuit" the time lag of print publications. The most popular of these newsletters is the ALA WASHINGTON NEWSLINE, prepared at the ALA Washington Office and designed to present brief, action-oriented reports to the library/information community on legislative and policy issues of concern. (The Washington Office also uses the communication features extensively to maintain contact with state agencies and members in the field.) The ALA NEWS BULLETIN presents general ALA and library news and update information on ALANET services and participants. Other newsletters provide news about intellectual freedom and new ALA publications, and the LITA ONLINE NEWS (LION) is the first of what will be a number of newsletters by ALA units.

The epub facility is also used to publish preliminary schedules for ALA Annual Conferences well in advance of the printed conference materials; the schedules are input as newsletters, but keyword search capabilities—just expanded to include Boolean searching—permit profiled searching through the schedule by subject, unit acronym, day, or date. Fully tagged and retrievable databases can also be created on the system, and there have been plans for developing some databases on the system. The bulletin board is another means for the interchange of professional information, with participants posting free-form notices of their ideas and queries for others to review and answer.

These kinds of information services are more complex to develop and implement than some of the communication features because they involve content that must be gathered and prepared for presentation. ALANET's first newsletters have been those for which there was known interest and that would be simplest to produce editorially. This component of the service will grow as more ALA units develop their own newsletters and as more of ALA's and the profession's information resources are made available through ALANET. A staff planning committee involving staff from various ALA divisions and other units is developing these services and the ALANET program.

Some guinea pigs

The first communications networks established in ALANET were in ALA units, and I am frank to admit that ALA staff and participating members served as much-appreciated guinea pigs in the earliest months of the service. In addition to the Executive Board, whose members in spring 1983 were the first users to teach themselves to use the Dialcom system, the LITA and RASD boards at the 1984 Midwinter Meeting adopted ALANET for communications. Other busy communicators among some two dozen ALA units online include several ACRL staff and member groups, including *Choice* with daily communiques to Chicago and the Strategic Planning Task Force (which gave its distribution list the charming code name of "SPLAT"); ALA Publishing Services, with online order forms and frequent Telexes to its overseas agents; *American Libraries,* with a mailbox for news and a form for placing LEADS classified ads; the Federal Librarians' Round Table; the Washington Office; and, of course, the Headquarters Library.

ALANET's very first external subscriber was Quality Books of Northbrook, Illinois, the first of a number of library suppliers in ALANET whose roster lists subscription agents, book publishers and wholesalers, independent consultants, and others. The first ALA chapter to subscribe was the Illinois Library Association, whose legislative development committee has been online since October 1983, and whose members regularly communicate with project coordinator Deborah Miller (a trustee of the Schaumburg Township Public Library and active ALA member), who uses a home computer and ALANET to prepare and "upload" an electronic news bulletin.

A number of other associations and networks selected ALANET to support board, committee, and other business communications and to permit communication with ALANET ID holders outside their organizations. Among them are NELINET, INCOLSA, AMIGOS, the Academic Librarians Association of Ohio (ALAO), and the Association for Library and Information Science Education (ALISE). Other key nodes in the library/information community that can be reached through ALANET include NCLIS, ERIC/IR, ARL's Office of Management Studies, Special Libraries Association, and three national libraries: the Library of Congress, the National Library of Medicine, and the National Library of Canada.

Assisting interlibrary loan

As the number of mailboxes active on the system has grown steadily, so too has ALANET's prominence in supporting major networking activities in local and regional organizations to meet a variety of needs. Interlibrary loans were among the first transaction-oriented communication needs that subscribers addressed as ALANET applications; in many cases ALANET serves to supplement existing interlibrary loan channels. The North Suburban Library System, headquartered in Wheeling, Illinois, for example, has been conducting increasing numbers of loan transactions through the system since early 1984, with first statistics suggesting that while only 10–12 percent of loans were conducted through ALANET, these were loans that otherwise would have gone unfilled using their other available systems. ILLINET, the Illinois Library and Information Network, replaced a network of TWX machines in July, 1984, with use of ALANET and custom-designed forms to transmit interlibrary loan referrals among system headquarters throughout the state in an LSCA-funded project.

In spring 1985, three additional major networks were brought online. In mid-March ALINE, the Arkansas State Library Network, was inaugurated with a series of training workshops at the Arkansas State Library in Little Rock. ALINE offers its group of some thirty public, academic, special, and school libraries and agencies services similar to those offered to direct ALANET subscribers: a special menu of services for ALINE participants, an electronic newsletter called ALINE NEWS NOTES, an ALINE category within the bulletin board, and access by electronic mail to the entire network and to selected ALANET services including the Library Supplier's Service Center.

Later in March came a series of demonstration and training sessions for MEDLINK, the Massachusetts Medical Information Link, a program of the Massachusetts Medical Society, publishers of the *New England Journal of Medicine.* MEDLINK selected ALANET to support its interlibrary loan and communication network and uses the same technology to provide its participants with their own menu of services, an electronic newsletter, a bulletin board, and three interactive forms for interlibrary loan of books, AV materials, and photocopy requests; the forms are accepted by the National Library of Medicine. The Society offers grants to libraries in MaHSLiN, the Massachusetts Health Science Library Network, to support their activity for the first six months, with participants assuming costs thereafter; MEDLINK will offer additionally other information support services for its medical library constituents. The new program had already brought in over thirty libraries at this writing, less than a month after formal invitations were sent to MaHSLiN members.

The New York Library-Line (NYLINE) was introduced in late April through a series of workshops in Albany, Buffalo, and Syracuse. The LSCA-funded program brings together about sixty libraries, systems, and other agencies in the state for communication within the state and with the entire ALANET network. Among the services in its menu, NYLINE has four separate bulletin board categories, including a calendar of events, and the New York State Library is electronically publishing the NYLINE NEWS.

In addition to these networks' primary services, their participants are given access to a selection of other ALANET offerings and are encouraged to subscribe directly to ALANET for access to professional information services and external databases. In some other states, notably Connecticut and Wisconsin, systems within the state have been provided with full subscriptions to ALANET. Further regional networking is being developed through brokers of the ALANET service, including INCOLSA and AMIGOS, and through several projects scheduled to begin with the fiscal year start date of July 1. All the groups supported by ALANET have benefited the service in developing networks of experienced users and by improving training materials and documentation; an RASD committee is drafting a "quick reference" guide for the service, while other subscribers have helped review drafts of new manuals in preparation by ITT Dialcom.

The marketplace observed

The communications I have had with ALANET's users, potential users, and non-users (and there are some, of course), and the experience I've had "on the road" in training workshops, conference exhibits, and network planning sessions, have led to the formation of a certain picture of the electronic communication marketplace and of the way libraries operate and communicate with one another and their suppliers.

My experience suggests that the number of individuals actually using electronic mail services in particular, and other online information services in general, is overestimated. While the current literature demonstrates the unquestionable growth in volume of library automation activities, microcomputers, and use of databases, there are still many, many libraries that cannot afford, or choose not to afford, use of such services, and still more that make only very limited use of them. As for individual librarians and other staff members, there is still considerable resistance to or fear of using computer equipment; moreover many administrative structures are (quite naturally) such that the number of persons who actually use computers or terminals with any regularity is relatively small. (Of about 200 people who have attended training sessions I've conducted in spring 1985, perhaps 10 percent had never used a computer terminal, and at least half were making no use whatever of online information services.) In many cases, limited funds rather than computer resistance have kept libraries away from technology, despite the longer-term cost savings and service enhancements it provides. Those of us with microcomputers become easily and quickly spoiled; it's easy to forget how things were before we could acquire our micros, and even easier to forget that there are still libraries in the U.S. without telephones, or that have difficulty paying their electric bills.

While I may speak in glowing and altruistic terms about ALANET, it must still function within the library marketplace. There are other electronic mail systems available, some of them cheaper than ours, and several already in use for a number of years by librarians; there was indeed some criticism of ALA's selection of ITT Dialcom when there were other services already being used by some in the field. The selection was based, however, on a set of programmatic goals and criteria which the technology had to meet, and it is the combination of multiple access points, special features, and information services ALANET offers that makes ALANET unique in the marketplace. Within any realm of library and information services, where automation is a part, there are several different independent vendors from which to choose, just as there are many book and journal publishers in the field.

Still, people tend to do that which they are accustomed to doing. Those who regularly and effectively use one electronic system for communication (or anything else, for that matter) will be reluctant to learn and integrate operationally the use of another, until some application-oriented need arises, or until it is clear that the additional system will help expand upon existing activities or contacts.

A subscription to ALANET is no guarantee that the organization will use it; some individual or group within the organization must first recognize the need for such a service, and most important must take responsibility for applying and integrating its use into the regular daily operations of the organization. Use of electronic mail decreases as the distance between the user and a terminal increases, and it is not easy to incorporate this different pattern of working and communicating into an operation, especially for a vendor, who must integrate it not only into the workflow but also into the firm's marketing and service program. We do have, unfortunately, some moribund subscribers.

Our growth patterns demonstrate that simply promoting electronic mail is not enough to make people want to use it, particularly among those who have never been exposed to it before. The technology must be closely related to existing activities and, most significant, to existing communication needs before the real and significant, but rather intangible benefits of speed, efficiency, and cost effectiveness can be perceived and realized. ALA and its constituents are excellent candidates to be electronic mail users, with the many communications that take place among them; such transactions as interlibrary loans, conference registrations and purchase orders or claims are activities more readily translated into the electronic mode. But a common reaction to exhibit demonstrations of electronic mail has been, "It's terrific, but what would I do with it?" (By contrast, the report of AMIGOS's twenty-five-library study of electronic mail through ALANET from May to October, 1984, noted that a substantial number of communications that took place electronically would not have been made at all without e-mail.)

Moreover, ALANET has sought to create a well-rounded package of information services to meet a variety of interests and user needs. The combination of varied offerings that distinguishes ALANET provides a number of different elements to attract different kinds of users from throughout the library/information community; the diversity of ALANET's subscriber base proves the importance of this consideration.

We also attempt to back this up by taking what I regularly describe as a "Jewish Mother" approach to service, despite our small staff, occasional *faux pas,* and the need to improve documentation and training offerings in our service.

The technology offered must be both easy to use and powerful enough to support a variety of applications. Dialcom's system is sufficiently easy to learn (despite the weaknesses of current editions of their user's manuals) that even novices have been able to perform basics of the mail, newsletters, and some other services without formal training classes, using only materials prepared by Dialcom and ALA. The system can be either menu- or command-driven, thus accommodating different levels of expertise. A less powerful or less accessible system would not be as hospitable to the varied needs of ALA or ALANET subscribers, nor would it provide as many access nodes to our geographically dispersed ID holders.

The potential of the ALANET service is limited only by the creativity of its users. ALANET has offered its subscribers, among them in particular the various networks, not only ALA's own information services, but also the opportunity to replicate them in their own organizations. The many and varied applications we see among our users reflect their varied needs and their creativity in using this technology to meet them. ALA's strengths as a program-oriented organization, supported by its members in the field and a staff of specialists in its headquarters units, certainly come into play in its network support services, but the networkers within ALANET are really the ones who have created their networks.

Because the communication features and applications of ALANET are so prominent, its broader information service orientation and goals may not always be perceived as readily by our constituents. As I have stated, however, it is these goals that have guided ALANET's conceptual, technical and programmatic development and that give ALANET its unique character among electronic services in the field. Librarians and other information professionals have come to learn well (and often the hard way) the fundamental importance of communication mechanisms (including among them marketing) to providing library services. Without effective communication techniques, information service cannot be delivered. Communication with other professionals and access to professional information resources are critical to professional development and expansion of information services.

The Headquarters Library's goals as formulated in the 1982 grant require a program like ALANET for their support and implementation, and they will be achieved very gradually as the service grows, as ALA units expand their use, and as the technology helps ALA to bring more order and integration to its information resources.

Information for all

The communication that forms the basis for so much of the networking activity now going on within ALANET demonstrates the need for such a basis to the development of other information services. Those networks that are disseminating and exchanging information through electronic bulletin boards and newsletters, in addition to carrying on electronically their various transactions, recognize that they have a need to expand their information services; they recognize that the technology can help them perform many of their services differently, and in many cases more effectively, than the print-based modes they have traditionally relied upon. The availability of a powerful technology and hospitable organizational structure—as the ALANET service itself seeks to provide—fosters broader attention to the profession's information needs, because there is now a recognized means for addressing them.

While these networks focus first on immediate organizational needs, their development within the context of a larger ALANET network suggests the potential advantages to be secured by extending beyond local or regional or organizational boundaries.

The networking that has begun to flower in the ALANET information service is the natural product of the creative work of those individual users who have worked toward developing it. It is also consonant with the ALANET program's goals and objectives, those of the ALA Headquarters Library, and indeed of ALA itself—expansion and improvement of information services for the library/information profession and improved access to information for all. ◙

Dale Nelson:

Dateline Washington

Just another special interest group

While a committee named by President Reagan seeks to raise $100 million for his presidential library, his administration is balking at applying congressional cost-cutting measures to the institution once it is built.

The House, controlled by Democrats, voted last year to require the private organizations that build presidential libraries to set up an endowment, equal to 20 percent of their cost, to help pay for maintenance. At the request of the administration, however, the proposed Reagan library on the Stanford University campus in California was exempted. The Republican-controlled Senate took no action, allowing the bill to die.

This year, the bill's sponsor, Representative Glenn English (D–Okla.), introduced substantially the same measure again and wrote to the president urging him to withdraw administration objections to having the Reagan library covered.

"Library operating costs are ongoing in nature," English wrote. "Consequently, to exclude your library from the endowment requirement would mean the additional appropriation of at least $750,000 per year, in perpetuity.

"Mr. President, I think it would be unconscionable to ask future generations to be saddled with the cost of operating your library, when funds for an endowment could easily be raised as an adjunct to the general library fundraising effort."

Budget Director David Stockman, however, wrote back that the administration now wanted an exemption, not only from the endowment, but also from another provision of the bill giving the National Archives veto power over the design of a proposed presidential library.

The House Government Operations Committee refused to go along with the additional administration request, with both Democrats and Republicans insisting that the same architectural standards should apply to the Reagan library as to any other.

"The president's staff acts just like most special interest groups," said English. "They all seem to favor spending cuts, except when it comes to them."

The ranking Republican on the committee, Representative Thomas Kindness of Ohio, said he found Stockman's suggestion "surprising if not offensive."

The architectural standards provision would give the sanction of law to guidelines which Archives already supplies to groups planning presidential libraries. The committee also suggested that Archives consider making the standards more stringent. The present guidelines, for instance, do not require that the libraries be equipped with telephones, security systems, furnishings or archival equipment such as microfilm readers, storage racks and shelving.

"The committee recommends that the National Archives and Records Service consider adopting, in the guidelines which it formally promulgates, fixed rules as to responsibility for each of the costs," the committee said in a report sent to the House floor with the bill.

National Archives officials told the committee that the archival suitability of the seven existing presidential libraries varies widely. At the Hoover Library, 71 percent of the gross square footage is usable space; but the Kennedy Library, with its impressive but inefficient central atrium, has only 46 percent usable space.

The bill was expected to pass the House easily, but the Senate is more likely to heed the administration's objections.

Named to the committee to raise funds for the Reagan library were Attorney General Edwin Meese III; his predecessor, William French Smith; former Secretary of the Interior William P. Clark; and two former White House aides, Michael K. Deaver and Martin Anderson.

Endangered materials

The National Endowment for the Humanities says a fourth of the books in the nation's research libraries are at risk from the ravages of decay, and has set up an Office of Preservation to do something about it. Congress has been asked to appropriate $5 million for the office in fiscal 1986.

Harold Cannon, director of the office, told a news conference in March that 75 million of the estimated 305 million books in 263 American research libraries "cannot be handled without suffering further deterioration, literally crumbling to pieces." In the next twenty years, Cannon said, an additional 38 million books will join the total of endangered materials.

The new office will administer a program of grants to support preservation efforts. Initial grants, totaling more than $900,000, went to the Research Libraries Group, the Northeast Document Conservation Center, the University of Delaware, the Rochester Institute of Technology, the University of California, and the State Historical Society of Wisconsin.

Nixon tapes: another wait

If you have been waiting eagerly since 1974 to get at those bottled-up tapes

Dale Nelson *is a journalist who covers the Washington scene for WLB.*

and documents from the Nixon White House, be patient; you have a while longer to wait.

On March 29, the National Archives issued regulations providing for public access to records of historical significance among the materials, as provided by Congress eleven years ago. This is the sixth time such regulations have been issued, however, and so far only twelve-and-one-half hours of the tapes have been made public. All of the documents are still sealed.

"The intent of Congress to provide public access to the materials has been thwarted," Dr. John Brademas, who was the principal author of the law as a Democratic representative from Indiana and is now president of New York University, told the *New York Times*.

Three sets of regulations were vetoed in the 1970s by congressional Democrats who thought they did not go far enough. Others were delayed by lawsuits, one by former President Nixon and two by former Nixon aides.

Among the nineteen Watergate era veterans who blocked the last set of regulations was Patrick Buchanan, now President Reagan's White House communications chief.

The regulations provide sixty days for public comment, another sixty for congressional review, an additional thirty for objections by people involved, and another thirty for them to file suit if their objections are overruled.

All in all, it could take a while before we find out what Tweedledee said about Tweedledum in the confines of the Oval Office.

Tackling pornography again

Another federal commission is tackling pornography, in a climate much changed since 1970, when a federal report found little concern about the subject.

A Justice Department announcement in the *Federal Register* said the eleven-member commission will recommend "initiatives . . . government could pursue in controlling, consistent with constitutional guarantees, the production and distribution of pornography."

Barry Lynn, legislative counsel of the American Civil Liberties Union, expressed the traditional civil libertarian objection to such initiatives, saying the proposed study "poses great, great dangers to the First Amendment."

That view is likely to be challenged more sharply than it was fifteen years ago, as women's groups have become increasingly outspoken in opposing pornography on grounds that it dehumanizes women.

Show may go on at Folger

Things are looking up for the Folger Theater. Not only does the theater have a hit in its critically praised *Hamlet*, but it turns out *Hamlet* isn't going to be its last production after all.

The theater decided to mount the tragedy of the prince of Denmark, feeling it should go out on a Shakespearean note, after trustees of the Folger Shakespeare Library said they could no longer support a theater.

In March, however, the library's director, Dr. Werner Gundersheimer, rescinded the eviction notice he had presented to the fifteen-year-old theater organization in mid-January. Gundersheimer said he would commit $300,000 in cash over two years, plus $260,000 in maintenance money, while a way is being sought for the theater to become independent of the library.

Despite Gundersheimer's announcement, the House Administration Committee's task force on libraries and memorials went ahead with a planned hearing on the theater's future.

Gundersheimer testified that the theater "is a very dynamic organization, but a very expensive one" that took up 40 percent of the library's budget last year.

Anne McGrath:

Eye on Publishing

Mr. Chow critics cleared

A recent ruling by three judges for the federal court of appeals sets to rest concerns of critics—and in particular restaurant reviewers—whose vulnerability to libel lawsuits has of late appeared appreciably more pronounced. The decision in the Mr. Chow case, written by Judge Thomas Meskill, overturns a district court ruling made in 1983 to award New York restaurateur Chow $20,005 after a jury found that a negative review published in a French-language guide to New York City had indeed been libelous. The defendants in the case were Henri Gault and Christian Millau, authors of *Gault & Millau Guide New York.*

Journalists and publishers were angered by the district court's apparent unwillingness to distinguish criticism—expressions of opinion—from statements of fact. The Libel Defense Resource Center, the Association of American Publishers, the National Book Critics Circle, the Magazine Publishers Association, Consumers Union, and the New York Film Critics, among others, joined in articulating their support for the defendants in a "friends of the court" brief that staunchly defended the tradition of absolute privilege reviews have enjoyed under the First Amendment.

The Chow review, the brief pointed out, contained the "obviously figurative or hyperbolic statements" that characterize expressions of opinion, and that are "almost always literally false." The district court judge, they held, had been incorrect to instruct the jury to measure those statements against a standard of literal truth or falsity. Furthermore, it would be impossible to prove actual malice in the case of a review, an expression of "personal perception that cannot be proven 'false' in any meaningful sense. Nor can the reviewer's knowledge of their falsity be established."

Judge Meskill found statements made by the guide to be consistent with the "natural function of a review," the communication of the reviewer's opinion. "The author obviously believed that the service was bad, the pork was too doughy, the peppers were too cold, the rice was too oily and the pancakes were too thick. The average reader would understand the author's statements to be attempts to express his opinions through the use of metaphors and hyperbole."

Moreover, even one possible error of fact the appeals court recognized (having to do with the number of dishes containing Peking duck) could not be considered libelous because there was no proof it had been made with malice.

Avon and the Northern California Booksellers wrap up

The battle between Avon and the Northern California Booksellers Association—the determined group of independent booksellers that took the paperback publisher to court several months ago over a discount policy favoring chain bookstores—has ended, although no decision in the case is likely to be forthcoming before this summer. U.S. District Court Judge Thelton Henderson heard the final witnesses in the trial at the beginning of April.

The NCBA has contended that the 7.3 percent additional discount given over a number of years by Avon to

---

Anne McGrath, *a freelance writer based in New York, covers the publishing world for WLB.*

Dalton, Walden, and Crown Books has effectively subsidized the expansion of the chain bookstore business, improving cash flow and making it easier for the chains to qualify for bank loans, and has greatly reduced the independents' ability to compete. Such a pricing policy, the association argued, must be in violation of anti-trust law. The Hearst Corporation, Avon's parent, has justified its policy on the basis of a cost-of-selling study that shows how significantly more expensive it has been for the publisher to service its independent accounts than it has been to sell to the chains. Avon's study shows in fact that the publisher spends 16 percent less to do business with the chains than to put its books on the shelves of the independent booksellers.

A primary reason, and one that the plaintiffs have not accepted as legitimate, is Avon's practice of sending sales reps to handle the independents' accounts. Most of the booksellers object strenuously to being forced to pay for rep service, desired or not, when they—particularly those specialist booksellers with an expertise in their specialty or those who carry a large backlist inventory—could just as easily order from a catalog. They cite New American Library's strategy of giving all booksellers the same 46 percent discount and the same disincentive to return books as an example of a fair system.

By contrast, the booksellers have found Avon's prerequisites for the most favorable discounts—$1 million in net sales of Avon books, a centralized ordering location, and an inventory system the publisher approved of—to be discriminatory. The outcome of the trial, most expect, will have considerable impact on the future of the small, independent, specialist book trade.

New mystery book line

Warner Books has committed itself to the cultivation of mystery and detective fiction as one important aspect of its business by joining forces with a real pro in the field, The Mysterious Press. More than 200 titles are planned over the next several years under a joint Warner Book/Mysterious Press imprint; next year some fifty works, hardcover and paperback reprints, are scheduled to be published. The Mysterious Press's current distributor, Farrar, Straus & Giroux, will carry on with hardcover distribution. Warner, which will handle production of the new line as well as promotion and advertising, will also take responsibility for distribution of the paperback reprints. Editorial responsibilities will be shared by both houses.

The Mysterious Press, established by New York City's Mysterious Book Shop owner Otto Penzler in 1973, published some thirty-five titles last year. Among the hardcover originals and reprints it has brought out over its eleven-year history are works by Ross Macdonald, Mickey Spillane, Isaac Asimov, and James Cain. Warner has published suspense novels by Gregory McDonald, William Goldman, P.D. James, and Mignon Eberhart, among others. This fall, Warner will inaugurate a new series by Roman Catholic priest and bestselling novelist Andrew Greeley, featuring a mystery-solving priest.

Books to note for summer reads

Herewith, a number of recent prize-winners well worth adding to the shelves. First are those works receiving the five 1985 Pulitzers awarded for letters. Fiction: Alison Lurie's *Foreign Affairs* (Random House), general nonfiction: Studs Terkel's *The Good War: An Oral History of World War II* (Pantheon), history: Thomas McCraw's *The Prophets of Regulation* (Belknap Press/Harvard University Press), biography: Kenneth Silverman's *The Life and Times of Cotton Mather* (Harper & Row), and poetry: Carolyn Kizer's *Yin* (Boa Editions).

Next, the three books honored this year in the Robert F. Kennedy Memorial Book Awards Program. Raymond Bonner's *Weakness and Deceit: U.S. Policy and El Salvador,* published by Times Books, took first place. Bonner, who spent time in El Salvador as a reporter covering the war, received a $2,500 prize for his work. The two works that received honorable mention are David Haward Bain's *Sitting in Darkness: Americans in the Philippines* (Houghton Mifflin) and Joel Williamson's *The Crucible of Race* (Oxford University Press). The Kennedy Award has been given annually since 1980, from a fund established by historian Arthur Schlesinger, Jr.

The body of work produced by Milan Kundera, the Czech novelist who lives in exile as a French citizen, has just garnered him Israel's most coveted literary award, the Jerusalem Prize for Literature on the Freedom of Man in Society.(Other recipients of the prize have included such luminaries as Eugene Ionesco and Graham Greene.) Kundera's most recent works are *The Book of Laughter and Forgetting* and *The Unbearable Lightness of Being.*

Nine works on Jewish themes, in such categories as social and political analysis, religious thought, children's books, and art, have been recognized for their superiority in the Kenneth B. Smilen awards sponsored by New York City's Jewish Museum. Saul Bellow's *Him with His Foot in His Mouth and Other Stories* (Harper & Row) won the award for fiction. Primo Levi's *The Periodic Table* (Schocken Books) was singled out as the biography/autobiography winner.

Last, but not least, here are a few of the Mystery Writers of America selections for best late-night read: *Briarpatch* by Ross Thomas (best novel of the year; Simon & Schuster), *Strike Three, You're Dead* by R.D. Rosen (best first novel; Walker & Company), *Grandmaster* by Warren Murphy and Molly Cochran (best paperback original; Pinnacle Books), *Double Play: The San Francisco City Hall Killings* by Mike Weiss (best fact crime; Addison-Wesley), *Novel Verdicts: A Guide to Courtroom Fiction* by Jon L. Breen (best critical/biographical work; (Scarecrow Press), and *Night Cry* by Phyllis Reynolds Naylor (best juvenile novel; Atheneum).

Will Manley:

Facing the Public

"Yes, I went to graduate school to become a librarian. But no, not to learn how to make photocopies."

Lately I've been doing a lot of speaking at state and regional library conferences and I've learned that airplane travel has some real hazards. Predatory DC–10s, overworked air traffic controllers, Bermuda triangles, renegade pilots, turbulent weather, and clumsy flight attendants aside, your biggest threat in the airways today is usually the person sitting next to you. No matter what you're doing, whether it be donning a Walkman, burying your face in an unabridged edition of *Moby-Dick,* or clutching a string of rosary beads, the people sitting next to you always want to talk. And the problem is they never want to talk about anything interesting.

That's because the only people who travel regularly on airplanes are prosperous-looking businessmen, and they are categorically the most boring people in the world. All they want to talk about are new cures for crabgrass, the relative merits of Audis and BMWS, the validity of the Dow-Jones average as a stock market measurement, the unfairness of the graduated income tax, the price of real estate in California, the historical inevitability of the Chicago Cubs winning the World Series, the unfairness of the local property tax, the need for nuclear power plants, the capabilities of office computers, the parameters of government versus the parameters of private enterprise, and the unfairness of the sales tax.

No matter how much you clear your throat, blink, yawn, or adjust the volume on your Walkman, your neighborly businessman continues to prate on about Japanese import quotas and his house in the suburbs. But the minute you tell him you're a librarian, he'll say something condescending like, "Do you have to go to school for that?" and then drop suddenly and silently into the friendly confines of his *Wall Street Journal.*

I'm not sure our sociological status as librarians would be significantly elevated if the general public began to perceive that in order to become a librarian one has to successfully pass through the rigors of a formal library science training curriculum on the postgraduate level. One thing that is certain, however, is that most librarians who are clad with the MLS degree feel not only that they are professionals because of it, but that they should also be recognized by the world at large as professionals because of it. This of course puts those practitioners in the library field who do not have the MLS shield in a somewhat precarious and insecure position.

What results is the aeons' long debate concerning a) what a "professional" is, b) whether librarians qualify as professionals, c) whether the non-possession of an MLS is what makes other people who work in libraries non-professionals.

I first started working at a public library reference desk exactly one week after I got my MLS degree. After twelve months of studying the intricacies of the Dewey Decimal Classification, researching the complexities of *Poole's Index to Periodical Literature,* learning the murky idiosyncrasies of

---

Will Manley *is director of the Tempe (Arizona) Public Library.*

Ranganathan's Colon Classification scheme, reading about the secular riches of the Vatican Library, and expanding my vocabulary with such words as "Festschriften," I was ready to turn my newly acquired bibliographic skills loose on the world. I wanted to test my abilities to the limit and justify to myself that my MLS not only was worth the time, money, and trouble, but that it truly set me apart as a professional. With my MLS I was confident that if I got questions on the value of American currency in 1829, the reproductive cycle of a fruit fly, or the name of the monarch of the principality of Liechtenstein I would know right where to look. Also I knew that the degree would prove invaluable on that fateful day when my library director would ask me to write a book selection policy. I had learned enough jargon and had been sufficiently indoctrinated into ALA's Library Bill of Rights that I could have done as professional a job on it as any other MLS. But to my great disappointment nobody asked me to explain the reproductive cycle of a fruit fly or to write a book selection policy. I did, however, get a lot of questions like "Where's the photocopy machine?" "Do you have back issues of newspapers?" "Does this library have any books about dogs?" and "Can you recommend a good, wholesome book that doesn't have a lot of sex in it?"

For several months I took a very negative and condescending attitude toward those kinds of questions. "I spent four years of college and one year of graduate school for this?" I kept asking myself over and over again. What upset me even more was the fact that the public thought that everyone who worked in the library was a "librarian." Book shelvers, circulation clerks, the maid who watered the plants, the janitor who slept in the back of the periodicals room, and even the technician who came in periodically to service the photocopier were often referred to as "librarians" by the general public. I was so frustrated that I was almost ready to suggest to the library director that all staff should be required to wear a badge stating their name and correct job title. Without an MLS clerks and aides had no right to be thought of as librarians. It also occurred to me that signs should be posted in the library that read: "Questions should only be asked of librarians possessing MLS" until it dawned on me that most people associate MLS with the real estate term "multiple listing service."

The bottom line is that it was bugging the heck out of me that most of the library staff, irrespective of educational levels, IQs, or degrees, were quite capable of handling most of the questions I was being asked at the reference desk. What bugged me even more was that it appeared from time to time that many of the non-degreed staff could answer some of the questions better than I could. With their years of checking-in thousands upon thousands of titles it was quite obvious that many of the old line circulation staff knew the collection better than the reference librarians. After all, they were the only ones on the staff who could actually answer that frequent, but elusive question, "Could you help me find that tall, skinny, yellow book about cats?"

Perhaps most humiliating, however, was the phenomenon that I grudgingly began to notice of certain patrons going out of their way to avoid me in order to seek out someone at the circulation desk for help or guidance. Why did they do this? Perhaps it was my attitude. In those first few months of MLS fervor when I saw someone approach my desk I desperately wanted that person to ask me to convert the monetary currencies of twenty-seven obscure Middle Eastern countries into dollars. And when all he wanted was a good book on dogs, all I could do was wave him off into the direction of the 636s and mutter something about wouldn't he really prefer to know the exchange rate of the drachma.

Day after day, question after question, it finally dawned on me that in the public library setting the reference librarian is usually not called upon to exercise any sophisticated techniques in the discipline of information retrieval. The main skill required is the ability to communicate. Nine times out of ten the patron who wants to know if the library has any books on dogs wants something much more specific than a general book on dogs. He may want material on the breeding habits of Great Danes, instructions on housebreaking poodles, or information on entering dogs in blue ribbon competitions, but he does not simply want a "book about dogs." It's the job of the reference librarian to identify in a diplomatic and friendly manner exactly what the patron wants.

That's why the MLS is overrated as a criterion for working in the public library. Give me a personable, inquisitive, well read, and articulate person any day over a "professional" with an MLS whose idea of reading literature is perusing *Library Journal* and who is lost without a computer terminal. Obviously this is somewhat of a generalization bordering on a stereotype, but my point is that the public simply wants good service, and couldn't care less if it is delivered by someone with an MLS.

The purpose of all this is not to belittle library schools or even to suggest that their curricula be more practically oriented or more job related. I enjoyed library school and am grateful for the sense of historical perspective and future possibilities it gave me about libraries. Rather, my purpose is to suggest that it's time to recognize in our library literature, our library conferences, our library associations, our library hiring practices, and our eyeryday library working conditions that non-degreed library practictioners are just as valuable and sometimes even more capable than their library-schooled colleagues.

It's time to acknowledge that even as the clientele of the public library is varied and diverse our library staffs can also be multifaceted with individuals qualifying for jobs on the basis of a diversity of criteria not just oriented around library degrees or library experience, but also upon other forms of educational training and other forms of public service experience. ▣

Martin Kesselman:

Online Update

Aside from the databases offered and cost considerations, each online system has features that make that system particularly attractive to search on. It is certainly reason to sit up and take notice when one of these online services, Dialog, adds many new features and enhancements, some of which have been strengths of other online systems, and some of which are unique. Dialog had remained basically in the same format since it first became commercially available in 1972. However, in December 1984, Dialog began introducing a completely new rewrite of its search software, known as Dialog 2. Initially supported on Dialog 2 were Dialog's new REPORT feature, allowing searchers to print retrieved items from various business databases in a tabular format, to access the menu-driven Bureau of the Census database, CENDATA, and to use a gateway service, OAG, the Online Airline Guide. Most of Dialog 2's features are those that have been requested by customers over the years; others improve internal processing. The best thing about Dialog 2 is that it is backwardly compatible; most of Dialog's basic search commands and techniques remain the same. At present users have the option of searching Dialog or Dialog 2 (Dialog 2 requires a special logon procedure), but eventually Dialog 2 will replace Dialog completely. Because almost all of the familiar Dialog features are still available, I would strongly encourage searchers to use Dialog 2, explore its new features and not be wary of making mistakes.

Martin Kesselman *is life sciences librarian at Bobst Library, New York University.*

Among Dialog 2's capabilities: the number of sets in a search has been increased to 200 from 98, any SELECT command can now have up to 240 characters (up from 50), EXPAND displays can be up to fifty lines, up to fifty items can be combined with an OR command, the user's workspace has been doubled to two million records, truncating terms will now work for up to 2,000 index entries, up to 100 databases can be chosen for a search in DIALINDEX, and up to 5,000 records can be printed with each print command.

Many Dialog 2 attributes make it a more "forgiving" system. As examples, in many cases spacing is less crucial around the = sign in searching prefix fields and some commands have optional formats such as END/SAVE which may also be entered as just SAVE.

Other Dialog 2 features provide additional options for searchers to revise their search strategies easily and cost-effectively. The SELECT STEPS (SS) command now provides postings for each element in a search statement and will provide a set number and postings for each term, even when terms are combined by proximity operators. These set numbers can then be selected later by themselves or in conjunction with other terms in new proximity combinations. Sets can also be qualified "after the fact" with various suffix fields. For example, the set number for a term first searched free-text could be later post-qualified to the descriptor field.

Some of the new Dialog 2 features also provide short cuts for cross-file searching. As an example, in searching prefix fields, more than one prefix can be searched at once, such as when one database uses JN for journal name and another uses JO. Searching more than one suffix field is a feature of the original Dialog system that continues on Dialog 2.

Several new features for proximity searching have been added with Dialog 2. With the new NEAR (N) operator, terms on either side of the operator need to be next to or near each other within a specified number of words, but in any order, as compared with the (W) operator which specifies order. For example energy (1N) shortage will retrieve items with either "energy shortage" or "shortage of energy." Also added is the not proximity feature, e.g., (NOT W), for users who do not wish to retrieve citations in which a particular term is within a certain proximity (i.e., adjacent to, in the same subfield as, in the same descriptor, or in the same field) of another term. As with any NOT operation, caution should be used so as not to lose citations that might prove useful. Proximity operators can now be distributed among groups of search terms, a nice feature that has long been available on BRS. For example, selecting (eating or food) (W) (habits or patterns) will retrieve citations with eating habits, eating patterns, food habits, or food patterns.

On the original Dialog system, limiting a search statement requires a separate step. On Dialog 2, LIMIT functions can now be searched directly as suffix fields (e.g., /ENG or /PATS). LIMITALL features have also been expanded. LIMITALL allows the searcher to save a great deal of processing time and costs by restricting a search in advance, such as by language or to particular years. On Dialog 2, searchers can now also use LIMITALL to restrict a search in advance to any suffix field such as to the title or descriptor fields. Dates can also now be directly selected as suffixes instead of being selected with the PY-prefix.

Cost estimates on Dialog 2 are much clearer and include a total cost which is an estimated cost of the search session since logon. New options for printing include the possibility of having the offline search printed on vertical sheets of paper rather than the usual horizontal format, using ALL in a print statement to have all items in a set printed, adding comment lines (preceded by asterisks) to be included as part of the search strategy on the offline printout, and finally, the option of cancelling an offline print for up to two hours after logoff.

In the coming weeks and months Dialog will continue to add new search features and enhancements. Some of the new Dialog 2 features users can look forward to include: options for user-generated print formats, having offline prints mailed by express delivery, a mailing label service that allows searchers to request labels for records from directory files such as the Electronic Yellow Pages (late 1985), an electronic mail service, DIALMAIL, which became available on Knowledge Index in April and will be available on Dialog 2 later this year, access by many new cities to DIALNET, Dialog's telecommunications service which provides direct access to Dialog and places the user on the least loaded of Dialog's three computers, and the exciting possibility of multifile searching, searching a topic on several related files at once, a feature Roger Summit, Dialog's president, announced at the past year's Dialog Update and which is expected sometime in 1986.

Although their changes are more subtle than those of Dialog, BRS has also added some new features to their search system with the implementation of their BRS-Search software. These include: a new command, SET HIGHLIGHT=ON, which will highlight (place asterisks on either side of) search terms, an abbreviated print command, leaving out DOC= and just entering the document numbers to be printed, the capability for left-handed truncation on the current files of MESH (Medline) and CHEM (Chemical Abstracts) in order to search for terms that end with the same base, and inclusion of the search strategy on all offline prints automatically.

Searchers will need to keep up to date with these new features in order to be able to search cost-effectively. For more information on any of these new features and enhancements on Dialog and BRS, consult their newsletters and for Dialog, the series of Technical Memos they have developed. In a future column I will be providing an update on the special features and databases of another, much younger, online system, Wilsonline. ▣

Tom Surprenant:

Future Libraries

"Parading the horribles" is a phrase seldom used these days. It suggests a look at people, things or events that everyone would rather ignore because of their distasteful nature. Every culture has had its own set of horribles, and one could easily show that this century has spawned a larger number of them than most. However, one should be aware that despite the predictions of Armageddon that have been made throughout history we have managed to survive. Given that admonition, there can still be little argument that the menace posed by nuclear weapons truly threatens to extinguish mankind or, at best, to reduce cultures to Stone Age levels. In terms of overall impact the effects of this genre of warfare are well documented in both the popular and technical literature. Nevertheless, in spite of all that we know, the so-called limited nuclear war has come close to becoming an acceptable risk. This shift in attitude from the unthinkable to the thinkable is forcing every cultural institution to reassess its role in society. Should librarians seriously consider the ultimate survival of the library in a limited nuclear war and prepare for this eventuality? As keepers of information we have developed a series of myths concerning our central place in the civilization. Logically it would seem that we should do all that we can to insure that both information and the accumulated wisdom of our culture is preserved and passed on to future generations whatever their condition.

Electronic technology, in the guise of the microchip, is developing into

Tom Surprenant *is director, Graduate School of Library & Information Studies, Queens College, City University of New York.*

the driving force of our age of information. With it come many benefits for all, especially librarians. But it has an Achilles' heel that is just now becoming frightfully apparent. The entire technology in which we are becoming intertwined is fatally vulnerable to the effects of electromagnetic pulse (EMP). Simply put, EMP burns up electronic circuits by overloading them; the smaller the circuitry, the easier it is to destroy. It would take only one nuclear weapon, exploded in space over North America, to produce a large enough EMP to completely wipe out the entire electronic culture that we have so carefully nurtured. This attack would destroy no cities and would directly kill few people. Instead, it would render all microchip circuitry useless and effectively eliminate the functioning of anything in which it was embedded. Since librarians are becoming increasingly dependent upon electronic access to information, and many are eagerly awaiting the day when the entire base of information can be stored electronically, EMP is the ultimate threat because it would reduce the entire technology to useless junk. It seems that we should begin to think about the potential of EMP to create a sudden loss of access to library information before we become so totally dependent on the microchip that it is virtually impossible for most librarians to get information in any other way.

From what we can glean from the literature, the aftermath of this type of limited nuclear war would have catastrophic effects in terms of information and information access capabilities. There would be little possibility of maintaining the extensive telecommunications grid. Rebuilding it, essentially from scratch, would be an almost impossible task. Thus, reliance on local sources of information would become the norm. Dependence on these resources would be critical because of the strong likelihood that the country would split up into a number of distinct and autonomous regions. Survival in small and self-sufficient units would be the order of the day. Consequently, the role of the librarian would be to provide information to assist in the process of rebuilding some semblance of society and, hopefully, to act as the conservator of the past so that the thread of history would remain unbroken. The library would serve as both a cornerstone of survival and a direct link to the past. In order to act in this role some fundamental conditions would have to be met. Those librarians that survived would have to be able to afford easy access to available and necessary information, with some form of manual system in place to allow users access to the collection. The information necessary for survival would have

to be an easily identified part of the library collection. Long before the need there would have to be a systematic acquisition of those materials that would be essential to the rebuilding of a stable society. This assumes that some form of basic survival bibliography would be available that would serve as the basis for an active collection building policy. There would also have to be a disaster plan for providing an easy path to needed information as well as protecting the library collection from theft or destruction. To be effective such a plan would have to be coordinated with other governing institutions. Thus, the library and its collections would be forced to meet the ultimate test of value during times when the very existence of life would depend, in large measure, on what information was available. Even though we may not want to deal with the realities posed can we be sure of providing basic survival information from our local collections right now? If not, we should become concerned enough to do something about it.

This is not a plea for a return to the past, nor an attack on the age of electronic information. Rather, it is an attempt to take a more realistic view of the potential of the library in a hostile future. We cannot remain behind the march of technology because of the wants and needs of our society. The electronic technology is here to stay and our dependence upon it will increase dramatically. What we have to be careful of is not to put all of our reliance on a technology that may not be there to serve a future need for information. We must be aware that there may come a time when we will need to get at certain types of locally stored information in a quick and efficient manner for purposes of survival. What we have to do is to plan for the eventuality of a limited nuclear war while praying that it will never occur. This means that we must identify and collect information that will be of critical use in the event of such a disaster. A core "basic survival" collection must become a part of every library so that each locality will have a chance at survival. Access to it must be simple and cannot depend on electronic means. To do otherwise is to neglect our responsibilities as professionals and to be so pessimistic as to think that there could never be a recovery from a limited nuclear war.

Planning for the continued survival of the library is not outside the tradition of librarians throughout history. In every age, and in every culture, those responsible for the collected store of information have been ready to attempt to preserve the essence of their collections in the face of imminent disaster. The only difference is the scale of the job and the reluctance of most, if not all, of us to face the necessity to plan for such an eventuality. If we are really serious about our role in a future world that might be far different than anyone has visualized, then we must prepare for a number of alternative scenarios. The only way that we can achieve this goal is through ALA or some other nationally oriented professional organization that is interested in the survival of information. Now is the time to begin to parade the horribles. ▣

Joseph Deitch:

Portrait: Charles Scribner, Jr.

Charles Scribner, Jr.—A nose for talent and loyalties

"Can I fix you a drink?" Ernest Hemingway asked Charles Scribner, Jr., chairman of Charles Scribner's Sons and publisher of Hemingway's books. Scribner, who is of Quaker descent, declined the drink, he recalled in his office on lower Fifth Avenue in New York City. Perhaps because "he leaned over backward to be nice to people—he was a great friend of my father," Hemingway renewed his offer. "How about a little vermouth and ginger ale, then? There's practically nothing to that, but it lights a little fire." "No, but I'll settle for the ginger ale," the publisher compromised.

Hemingway was "sweet-tempered and very nice to me, and it was about this time that he gave me a small traveling bag and said to lock it up in my safe." Scribner said he would do so and locked it in a filing cabinet. "Don't lose it or anything in it," Hemingway instructed. He was sensitive about losing things. As a young man, his wife had lost a suitcase containing all of his unpublished manuscripts. "I'll kill myself if I lose it," Scribner said, to which Hemingway replied, "That wouldn't do me any good."

What was so valuable in the case? "Among other things, his will," Scribner said. A few days later Hemingway returned and asked to see the bag. The publisher removed it and Hemingway riffled through it on top of the cabinet. Scribner watched with bemusement. "I knew perfectly well that he had come back to see that I hadn't lost it. I got a hundred on that one." Then the author went into Scribner's private office and "absolutely discombobulated" him by sitting down at his desk. "For a businessman, that is about the most demasculating experience you can have. I stood there, not knowing what to do with myself," Scribner said. But Hemingway was only trying to put his publisher at ease. Scribner wondered if he would like a cup of coffee. "Sure." A secretary brought him a cup. "Cream?," inquired Scribner. "Just enough to change the color."

Did Hemingway—big-game hunter, marlin-catcher, survivor of airplane crashes, occasional bullfighter, and boxer who once slugged Max Eastman in a Scribner office—have a bone-crushing handshake? Scribner shook his head. "He was not well at that time and I had an impression of frailness. If he had a crushing grip I would have noticed it, because I have a strong handshake myself."

Charles Scribner, Jr. is a tall, erect, and white-haired executive with the ruddy complexion of a seaman who has just finished deck duty in a winter gale. He did, in fact, spend five years in the Navy, completing a Korean duty tour in 1952. He became president of his firm in that year. A classics major at Princeton, he was commencement salutatorian, in Latin, though the family motto is in French—*Il faut (d'abord) durer*: Above all, to continue.

Joseph Deitch *writes for* The New York Times *and other publications.*

The company's first book, issued in 1846, its founding year, was probably *The Puritans and Their Principles,* by Edwin Hall. *Napoleon and His Marshalls* by the Rev. J. T. Hadley, also an early Scribner book, was its first bestseller. It launched the firm, financially.

As the decades went by Scribner became a household word and a standard supplier of books for homes and libraries. In those earlier eras, a home library was as much an educational and entertainment necessity as the phonograph, movies, radio, and television were to become. In proportion to population, earlier Americans read more than they do today. Aside from arts, crafts, and conversation, what else was there to do at home but read?

This particularly applied to children. Their reading needs were gloriously met by Scribner which began to publish many of its classics for the family. In 1873, for instance, it began its famed *St. Nicholas* magazine under no less an editor than Mary Mapes Dodge, who wrote *Hans Brinker, or the Silver Skates.* The popular novelist, Frank Stockton, was assistant editor. Henry Steele Commager prepared two *St. Nicholas* anthologies.

Charles Scribner, Jr. is continuing his family interest in children's books, a key part of the Scribner list since the days of Robert Louis Stevenson. He has written several of them himself. Another big early seller was the *American Boy's Handy Book.* Its author was Dan Beard, a founder of the Boy Scouts of America. Scribner's son, Charles Scribner III, reported that Beard's immortality is sustained by the letters still addressed to him at the firm. Beard died in 1941.

Charles Scribner III also recalled that Henry van Dyke, an American clergyman, author, teacher, diplomat, and outdoorsman, "almost instantly put Scribner's out of business and himself (van Dyke) in an early grave" when a book of his, *Fisherman's Luck,* was printed with a prominent, single-letter misprint in the title. This momentary reversal was more than made up for with the publication, at about the same time, of three Scribner classics: Edward Eggleston's *The Hoosier Schoolmaster,* Howard Pyle's *The Merry Adventures of Robin Hood,* and Frances Hodgson Burnett's *Little Lord Fauntleroy.*

There followed, over the next half-century, a succession of titles by now-famed novelists, important reference works, biographies, histories, scientific and technical books, criticism, and drama. Among the fruits of vast research and planning was the *Dictionary of American Biography,* produced in cooperation with the American Council of Learned Societies. The entries, by top scholars, many of whom had written full-scale biographies of people they wrote about for the DAB, are models of accuracy, concision, and good, often elegant, writing.

Mention great book editors in twentieth century literature and the name apt to come up first is Maxwell Perkins of Scribner's. He made novels of Thomas Wolfe's truckloads of manuscripts. There was also Alice Dagleish. At Scribner's, during the 1930s, she built one of the most distinguished lists of children's books in American publishing. The first thing she did was to separate these books from general adult titles and form a children's department. Three days after she joined the firm, she was summoned by Scribner's father. He wanted to know how she was getting on. "Oh, just fine, Mr. Scribner, but there is one thing I'd like." "Of course," he said. "What is it?" "Do you think I might have a desk?" "I don't see why not. It never occurred to us you'd need one." Dagleish was not only the pioneer in her field for the house of Scribner, but she broke the office-equipment barrier for women at the firm. One wonders how Scribner's founding fathers would have reacted to the recent appointment of Mildred Marmu as president and publisher of Charles Scribner's Sons, the company's first woman president and only one of its three presidents not named Scribner.

A glance at personnel listings of other old American publishing houses shows virtually no descendents of the firms' founders, at least not by original names or among top executives. Scribner men, father to son, continue to run the firm or have key responsibilities. The full history, based on the archives at Princeton, the family university—Charles Scribner, Jr. was a trustee for ten years and a trustee of its press for over thirty years—is still to be written. The resultant book will document one of the most colorful segments in American publishing history.

A man with an infectious enthusiasm for his firm, Scribner Book Companies, and for his job, Charles Scribner, Jr. took this writer on a tour of the company. It covered seemingly acres of space on one floor for Scribner and its subsidiaries—Atheneum Publishers, Leisure Press, and Rawson Associates.

In June, 1984, Scribner took the most important step since its founding when it accepted an offer to merge with Macmillan and became part of its publishing family. "A better and more permanent home could not have been invented for our reference, juvenile, college, and trade departments and authors," Charles Scribner III, now director of special projects at Macmillan, said at the time. The link with Macmillan is not new. Just 125 years earlier, Charles Scribner introduced and distributed books of Macmillan of England in this country.

The most interesting sight on the tour was the name, Jacques Barzun, in gold letters, on an office door. The eminent historian, critic, man of letters, and retired Columbia professor and administrator is Scribner's literary adviser. Scribner considers him one of the firm's great assets.

Scribner also made a stop at the office of Karen Day, promotion manager for reference works. "She's the czar of this important department," he said. "Czarina," she gently corrected.

Scribner's sale of its famous Fifth Avenue bookstore to Rizzoli International Bookstores last December made major news of its kind. Rizzoli is owned by Italian and Swiss interests. The store has been a mellow landmark for New York City and suburban bookbuyers—and browsers—for seventy-four years. Nothing will be changed. The Scribner name, staff "and everything else," Scribner said, will stay the same at the store, designed by a family-related Beaux Arts architect.

Why was the store sold? "When we sold the building," Scribner related, "it was no longer practicable for us to maintain our offices in it and to keep the store. The sales were arranged by my son, the fifth Charles Scribner. If we were going to make corporate changes, the sale was the most benign way we could do it, since all would be virtually the same."

Scribner said he has no "self-reproach at all" for selling the bookstore. "Would that every change of that kind were as benign," he said, and drew these analogies: Einstein said that "one of the happiest fates that can befall a physical theory is to be an exceptional case in a more inclusive theory." "And one of the happiest fates that can befall a building is to be part of a larger entity, where it is appreciated. You can also say that about a publishing company—one of the happiest things that can befall a smaller publishing house is to be taken over by a larger one that shares the same goals and ideals."

Scribner is pleased, because he would be "lost without a place like the Scribner bookstore." It is there that he can buy books on the history of science, one of his personal interests. A paper of his, "Henry Poincare and the Principles of Relativity," has been published in the *American Journal of Physics*.

Publishing sentimentalists may wince at the trend toward mergers and acquisitions involving old American book firms but Scribner does not think this a dismaying development. "It is not a bad thing if it is done well," he commented. "As for the trend, I think it is over, because almost every major publishing firm has become affiliated with a larger one. In our case, it was Macmillan, which is about as old as Scribner's. So the coagulation process in the industry is virtually complete. What happens is that the acquiring company becomes aware of the individuality, the distinction, and if I may use the word, the genius of the acquired company and it usually respects and wants to retain these qualities. This can lead to a very happy and constructive merger. The acquired company is in a better position to fulfill its publishing program and the public is the winner because, economically, it is often hard for a smaller company to make a go of it today."

Scribner recalled that Hemingway said it best in *To Have and Have Not* when Harry Morgan, a big-game fisherman, observed, "No matter how, a man alone ain't got no bloody fucking luck." "That," Scribner added, "can be translated to companies. Worrying about finances all the time is a form of tyranny and is not conducive to good publishing. In the Aristotelian sense, you have two extremes. One is where the acquired company is wholly dominated, loses its soul, and goes out of business. The other is when there are no operational differences, after acquisition, but new strength for the absorbed company."

"Scribner will retain its identity—I am absolutely sure of it," Charles Scribner, Jr. said. "Macmillan wants us to do the publishing that we have done best." The chairman's personal interest is in reference works, primarily in the humanities. "We brought out the first major dictionary on the history of science—the *Dictionary of Scientific Biography*." Other Scribner publishing projects that Macmillan and Scribner "find congenial" cover the Middle Ages, the history of ideas, American and British writers, and American history and foreign policy. Scribner is one of the most avid readers of the works, especially in the sciences.

I noted that the quality of fiction in this and other countries seems to have declined over the past thirty years. Perhaps ninety percent of new novels are publishing ephemera. These books are printed, reviewed, and forgotten in a matter of months, casualties of low publishing standards and the lower standards of book review editors.

"I tend to agree that the quality of literature and writing is in something of a decline, though there are notable exceptions," Scribner responded. "I attribute the decline to two things: a completely laissez-faire attitude toward grammar and lexicography that has become fashionable. Many people in education, who ought to know better, say that the spoken language is *the* language and that whatever is, is right. I think that is wrong. Second, the humanities have been dehumanized by the introduction of scientific methods for the study of literature, and the challenge or use of literature is to make 'discoveries,' as in science. Teachers of literature are becoming technical specialists without the broad, humanist scope needed for the study of the subject and to write about it.

"Consequently, since people are not being taught to read, speak, or write well, it would be surprising if there were no decline in literature and in literary standards and values. It's a subtle phenomenon and I feel, particularly for fiction, that the decline has been global."

Scribner defended the commercial novel and the blockbusters among them as providers of the financial support for publishing genuine literary and artistic fiction that may not sell. He is interested in all branches of publishing, he said, including mysteries. Scribner cited P. D. James's books as examples of writing far better than that found in mainstream novels.

Giordano Bruno said, "Each individual is the result of innumerable individuals, each species is the starting point for the next." Charles Scribner, Jr. embodies almost a century-and-a-half of family experience in publishing. Each Scribner generation has learned from predecessors who have contributed to its leadership and distinction. What, I asked Scribner, were the main ingredients for the firm's longevity and success? Without thinking, Scribner said "A nose for talent—and loyalties." ▣

Donnarae MacCann/Olga Richard:

Picture Books for Children

Effective author-illustrator teamwork has been a characteristic of picture book publishing for much of this century. But in the field of controlled vocabulary books, there are relatively few teams that warrant special notice. Joan Robins, author, and Sue Truesdell, illustrator, are an exception. In **Addie Meets Max** (an "Early I Can Read" book) the interplay between text and pictures produces a remarkably authentic vision of childhood—a mirror of youthful feelings that is rare except in novel-length works.

Addie Meets Max

Joan Robins has only a few oversimplified lines of dialogue and description to use in this drama about new neighbors. But the skeletal prose of the "I Can Read" formula is not a serious problem because Robins has selected revealing episodes about how children move beyond shyness and anxiety. Sue Truesdell fleshes out the minimal text with humor, warmth, and an unusual blend of spontaneity and verisimilitude.

The plot's brief encounters are thoroughly plausible: colliding bicycles, the sharing of a pizza (arranged by Addie's no-nonsense mother), the examining of wounds incurred in the crash, the ritualistic burial of Max's tooth (prematurely jarred loose in the accident). Max's large, scruffy dog seals the new relationship on Addie's part, embodying at first her worst fears and then her highest pleasure. It is this combination of fascination and resistance in Addie that the book conveys so convincingly.

The illustrator's style makes for a warm, free, lumpy feeling that suits the story. Truesdell uses a traditional technique—wiggly lines around objects, scratchy, close-together lines to suggest mass and depth, and low-keyed color washes of compatible yellow, yellow-orange, and orange. Her drawing skills enabled her to use such elements spontaneously. Perspective awareness is always present and expertly handled, but not belabored. Details are suggestive, not burdensome. Compositions are casually designed—sketchy assemblages that suggest the ambience of the setting and the personalities of the youngsters and the dog.

Addie Meets Max evokes the positive side of a new relationship whereas Laura Joffe Numeroff's **If You Give a Mouse a Cookie** reveals a potentially negative side. With illustrator Felicia Bond, Numeroff profiles and satirizes a friendship that is exploitative, that presents a comically naive and willing victim. It *is* easy to be "put upon" in a relationship that is highly extraordinary—for example, when a boy and a mouse share a snack. The mouse in this case is like a spoiled child. The opening lines show how one thing leads to another until the boy (the parent symbol) is an exhausted wreck.

If You Give a Mouse a Cookie

If you give a mouse a cookie,
he's going to ask for a glass of milk.
When you give him the milk,
he'll probably ask you for a straw.
When he's finished, he'll ask for a napkin.
Then he'll want to look in a mirror
to make sure he doesn't have a milk mustache.
When he looks into the mirror,
he might notice his hair needs a trim.
So he'll probably ask for a pair of nail scissors.
When he's finished giving himself a trim,
he'll want a broom to sweep up.

At this point the mouse becomes a compulsive little helper. He sweeps and washes all the floors, and this leads to weariness and a box-bed, blanket, pillow, and bedtime story. The progression from one demand to another is both ingenious and natural. Numeroff keeps the telling terse while Bond reveals the bedlam and the increasing bewilderment of the

Olga Richard *and* **Donnarae MacCann** *are the authors of* The Child's First Books.

boy. As in the Robins/Truesdell book, author and illustrator are perfectly in tune.

Felicia Bond's graphic style is familiar (a superlative example is seen in her 1983 title, *The Halloween Performance*), and yet she puts something new into each effort. In the Numeroff book, she groups many tight, miniature patterns—seen in wallpaper, floor tiles, kerchief, etc.—and produces striking arrangements in space. She sometimes uses large objects linked together with many small shapes, as when a kitchen island builds into another object (the refrigerator) which in turn builds into the kitchen counter. Each object repeats lines of the other, but the verticals vary somewhat for they are all slightly skewed. Many smaller objects are arranged on the tops of the larger ones, making an interesting contrast of sizes throughout the design. The protagonist is integrated with the other shapes and treated in the same manner: with clean, precise contours. It is as if Bond were designing with "rest" spaces in mind, as in a dance where you glide for a while, then take some bouncy steps, then glide some more. As in the scene reproduced here, there is a pleasing array of household paraphernalia in the busy spaces.

Maria Theresa

Problems of being alone and being together are resolved more conclusively in the Felliniesque picture book, **Maria Theresa,** by Petra Mathers. A middle-aged woman, Signora Rinaldo, sings to her coop full of chickens on the roof of her New York apartment building, listens to the opera, and reads *The New York Times.* The author/illustrator doesn't say that this is a regimented and alienated lifestyle, but by the end of the story, the reader is glad the pattern has changed. And it is a pleasure throughout the tale to follow the adventures of a strange and incongruous character—a chicken, Maria Theresa—who expands the Signora's relationships as well as her own.

The book's theme, Italian references, urban and provincial settings, trappings of the circus—all bring to mind elements of a Fellini film. But the chief tie with this cinematic artist is seen in Mather's seductive, surreal imagery. While the story is set in New York, the real milieu is European.

When the coop is accidentally left open, Maria Theresa sallies forth and lands with a thud on East 77th Street. She moves with the crowd to the Lexington Avenue subway, stows away in a woman's shopping bag, rides on a bus, and ends up in the open countryside not far from a crowded circus tent. She joins the act of Miss Lola, a performer who juggles eggs from the back of a cow. Meanwhile, the Signora is so miserable she allows a Neapolitan tenor to court her, they visit the circus, the Signora and Maria Theresa are reunited, and they both accept new "destinies," agreeing to meet only once each year in Vermont. (It seems the chicken wants to learn to ski!)

If this sounds to you like a mishmash of kitsch and slapstick, it is because you are not taking account of the illustrations. Petra Mathers uses a flat, primitive style that produces a consistently engaging, other-worldly quality. She tells us in the text that Maria Theresa spread her wings and sailed down to 77th Street, but the bird looks like a mobile hanging on an invisible string—permanently suspended in one spot. This same sense of fixed objects in a fixed space is repeated in the circus scenes where both Miss Lola and Maria Theresa are spotlighted in a lasting time frame. The visuals underscore Maria Theresa's message to the Signora on a post card: "The stage is my destiny!" The dichotomy between frozen time and the dramatic changes in the lives of the protagonists adds to the surreal atmosphere, yet neither illustrations nor narrative are ambiguous. The images are the result of incredible planning on Mathers's part.

She defines all objects as stylized, simple, clean-edged shapes, all painted quite solidly and arranged in overlapping masses. The one exception to this illusion of flatness is in the chicken coop scene; here the forms are modeled and depth is achieved through gradations of brown from light to dark. On other pages, Mathers models objects primarily for the sake of varying the color. She produces a sense of perspective by modulating color, but it is not the same kind of depth probing that is noticeable in the interior of the chicken coop.

Mathers's colors are unusual. She uses many, but most are tints or subtle shades. When raw hues are incorporated into her complex designs of flat objects, the accents add to the enchantment of her surreal arrangement. ▣

This month's books

Mathers, Petra. *Maria Theresa.* Harper & Row, 1985. $13.95. ISBN 0-06-024109-8 LC 84-48346.

Numeroff, Laura Joffe. *If You Give a Mouse a Cookie.* illus. by Felicia Bond. Harper & Row, 1985. $9.95. ISBN 0-06-024586-7 LC 84-48343.

Robins, Joan. *Addie Meets Max.* illus. by Sue Truesdell. Harper & Row, 1985. $7.95. ISBN 0-06-025063-1 LC 84-48329.

Patty Campbell:

The Young Adult Perplex

The silk weavers' quarter in Kyoto in the first months of the American occupation of Japan—the Orthodox Jewish synagogues and households of New York in the last years of the Depression—what might two novels set in such different times and places have in common? Could two writers coming from such contrasting worlds struggle with the same problems and find reassuringly similar answers—and questions? A comparison of **Cranes at Dusk** by Hisako Matsubara and **Davita's Harp** by Chaim Potok shows an astonishing number of parallels of structure and character and theme, parallels that reinforce the message of each but also throw into sharp relief the separate uniqueness of these superb novels.

Both authors are critically acclaimed master storytellers, and both are ordained in the faith with which their protagonists struggle. Hisako Matsubara grew up in Kyoto as the daughter of a Shinto priest and is herself a priestess of that religion. Her three novels and five nonfiction books have won her international respect as the most distinguished Japanese woman writer of our time, although her reputation in the U.S. rests almost entirely on the novel *Samurai,* first published in English in 1979. Matsubara lives in Cologne and writes in German. (The excellent translation of *Cranes at Dusk* was done by Leila Vennewitz.) She is a new name to young adult literature. Chaim Potok, on the other hand, is an old friend; *The Chosen, The Promise, My Name Is Asher Lev* are YA classics. His novels of American Jewish life come from his own experience as an ordained rabbi.

Both *Cranes at Dusk* and *Davita's Harp* tell the story of a young girl in a time of political and social turmoil when old values are shifting and giving way, a young girl with daring and intelligence beyond what is allowed to women in her culture, who tests the old ways and samples the new to find her own meaning and direction for the future. Saya is the ten-year-old daughter of a Shinto priest, who is the Guji of a famous shrine high on a hill above the street of silk weavers in Kyoto. The time is September 1945. The Emperor has just announced that the war is over, and the American victors have arrived with their blue eyes and big feet and loud voices. Life is hard just now—there are food shortages and confusion over Japan's defeat and the new official attitudes toward the gods and the Emperor. But the people make do and try to understand the new ways of the Americans as they also celebrate the old religions—the earthy, life-loving household gods of Shinto, the children's festival for the beatific Jizo, the austerity of Zen Buddhism for times "when people think of death." The Christian church, too, has gained new prominence since it is now the religion of the victors. Saya sees all this through curious eyes, cheerfully sustained by her love for her wise, kind father and her beloved little brother, three-year-old Bo. She is contemptuous of her teacher's sudden hypocritical shift from fervent nationalism to empty praise of freedom. At home she is caught between her bitter mother's fierce devotion to ancient Samurai rituals and her father's bland disregard for formality. One day, drawn by the music and the strangeness, she wanders into the Christian church, where her lively curiosity is soon caught by trying to reconcile the words of Jesus and the deeds of his followers. Later when her precious Bo dies suddenly in the night, she seeks blindly for answers in all the old and new faiths and finds comfort only in the strong love of her father.

Ilana Davita, too, in *Davita's Harp,* searches for meaning in a confusion of old and new ways and at last finds strength only in the memory of her father's love. Davita is the child of Michael and Anne Chandal, young intellectuals who are ardent and active party members at a time when communism seemed the only way to fight against the approaching threatening Fascist shadow. "My mother was a nonbelieving Jew, my father a nonbelieving Christian," she remembers. In a series of cold and shabby "proletariat" apartments, she listens from her bedroom to the passionate discussions and singing at party meet-

Patty Campbell *is a freelance writer who teaches young adult literature at UCLA.*

ings. She hears her parents' talk of labor unions, bloody strikes and the Civil War in Spain, and soon grows into an understanding of world conditions too heavy for her years. Michael and Anne are a brilliant and beautiful couple, whose every action is consistent with their commitment to making a better world. They bring the same devotion to parenting as they do to politics, giving Davita unstinting love and answering her questions with scrupulous honesty, but being careful to leave room for self-determination. When Michael goes off with his wife's approval to be a journalist in Spain, Anne does not interfere when Davita is drawn to the warmth and security of the Orthodox synagogue, although she herself had long ago bitterly rejected the Jewish beliefs and rituals imposed on her by her hated father. At the same time Davita is also intrigued by Christianity, which she learns about from her father's sister Sarah, a homely missionary nurse of great spiritual beauty. When Michael is killed in Spain, Davita and her mother experience great suffering, which is greatly intensified for Anne when the Stalinist purges in Madrid destroy her trust in the infallibility of communism, and with it the purpose of her life. Gradually Davita becomes more and more immersed in the intellectual challenge of Talmudic study at a yeshiva, and Anne, too, very slowly and reluctantly, returns to her tradition and a new and happy marriage. But Davita's commitment to patriarchal Judaism is deeply shaken at her graduation when the Akiva award for which she has studied so hard is given to a boy to save the school the public shame of a girl as best student. Taking courage from her father's memory, she accepts her "sacred discontent" and knows that she cannot settle with life so soon.

To summarize both stories in so few words gives no sense of their richness of detail, the fascination of character, and above all, the veracity of time and place. The strange and exotic is made real in a wealth of colors, smells, and sounds. The idealistic underworld of American communism in the thirties leaps out in evocative details: Anne's beret, the melody of "Joe Hill," the receptions in houses where there are crystal chandeliers but no books, the voices heard from the next room arguing long into the night. The exquisitely groomed asters and pines of the Shinto shrine are as immediate as the drone of Kaddish recited behind a canvas divider in a warm and stuffy shul. The dancing children at the Jizo festival are figures on a silken scroll, but the sound of their laughter and stamping and the drifting smoke of sweet potato slices on a grill make the picture come sensually alive for the reader.

In addition to the obvious parallels in theme, other striking contrasts and echoes can be readily spotted. The central (but offstage) event that moves the lives of both sets of characters is World War II—as a looming future in *Davita's Harp* and as a fearful past in *Cranes at Dusk*. Each is symbolized by a horrifying description of Air Raid: Guernica and Hiroshima. Both mothers have been shaped by fanatical paternal figures: the Guji's wife by her stern Samurai grandfather and Anne by her scrupulously devout Talmudic scholar father. In both stories a death gives urgency to the search for meaning. Both young girls gain from their fathers the strength and permission to search for themselves. Both must swallow their hot resentment at injustice in the treatment of women. Each eagerly learns a new language—Hebrew, English—better to explore new mysteries. Each turns away from Christianity in puzzlement because "the Nazis were Christians, too, weren't they?" Both cultures find spiritual order in a ritualization of the homely details of daily life: Saya's mother, like a good kosher housewife, keeps many separate sets of dishes for different foods—but carries the principle on into vice in her obsession with correctness. Both books have titles which refer to a story told to a child in which the flight of birds is the central metaphor. And at the end of both novels, the young women have returned to an acceptance of tradition but must now not reject, but move beyond it. As Aunt Sarah tells Davita in a dream, "Be discontented with the world. But be respectful at the same time."

This month's books:

Matsubara, Hisako. *Cranes at Dusk*. Translated from the German by Leila Vennewitz. Dial Press, 1985. 253p. $14.95. ISBN 0-385-27858-6 LC 84-7031

Potok, Chaim. *Davita's Harp*. Alfred A. Knopf, 1985. 371 p. $16.95. ISBN 0-394-54290-8 LC 84-48526

Kathleen Maio:

Murder in Print

There have been several attempts at a comprehensive bibliography of mystery criticism in recent years. All have been gratefully received by scholars and fans. All have had their problems. *Crime, Detective, Espionage, Mystery and Thriller Fiction and Film* by David and Ann Skene Melvin (1980) was, as the title indicates, the most ambitious. It was also the most troubled. An attempt to cover the mystery, fiction and film, including Sherlockian studies, in a "comprehensive" manner, requires much more than 204 entry pages. A lack of annotations or contents analysis leaves the user without adequate guidance.

Crime Fiction Criticism by Timothy W. and Julia Johnson (1981) dropped film coverage and added annotations of a non-critical nature. But it too is difficult to use because of a lack of adequate indexing or cross-referencing of entries. Like the Skene Melvin volume, it largely ignores the great body of critical work in the mystery fanzines.

Now a third general bibliography of criticism has been produced: **Detective and Mystery Fiction: An International Bibliography of Secondary Sources** by Walter Albert (Brownstone Books, 1711 Clifty Dr., Madison, IN 47250, 1985, $60).

This massive volume of almost 800 pages finally approaches the definitive mystery bibliography. Albert wisely refrains from trying to cover Sherlockiana (which, as experience has shown, would require at least another 800 pages) or suspense film, except where it intersects with the discussion of mystery fiction. He has added coverage of pulp and juvenile sleuth series, and far-reaching coverage of the American mystery fanzines. Moreover, through the help of an international band of mystery scholars, Albert cites a treasure trove of critical work by mystery fans in France, Scandinavia, Japan, and other cultures rich in mystery authorship and fandom.

We might occasionally find a translated novel by a Maria Lang or a Seicho Matsumoto but before now we could not locate references to critical commentary. The downside to these discoveries is that Albert's intriguing annotations make us want to read sources that have never been translated, in journals almost impossible to track in the U.S. These foreign sources can cause confusion as well as frustration. For example, when an article title needed no translation (as with an author's name as title) it is not always clear in what language the source appears. More obvious notations for language and a descriptive key to foreign fanzines would have been extremely useful.

The bibliography is organized in four major sections. The last of these, "Authors," shows how useful this bibliography can be. Following a list of abbreviated citations to entries in other reference works, and another list of interviews with the author (which can include more than ten citations in the case of a major author), cross-references are provided to other applicable internal entries. Finally a mix of references from academic, news, and fan journals on several continents appears with sometimes terse, sometimes expansive and pithy annotations.

There are undoubtedly items that slipped through the cracks, and typos appear, but this cannot mar the monumental accomplishment of Albert's work. As one of the twenty-two mystery folk who assisted Walter Albert in gathering his more than five thousand entries, I am, perhaps, not an impartial judge. That admission over, it is my partial opinion that *Detective and Mystery Fiction: An International Bibliography of Secondary Sources* is an essential source for all libraries seeking to support the study of mystery fiction and authors.

One of the authors woefully neglected in mystery criticism and still generally unknown to U.S. readership is the late Gladys Mitchell. Her death, in 1983, at age eighty-two, cut us off from one of our last links to the Golden Age of mystery fiction. Her first mystery was published in 1929. The last, **The Crozier Pharaohs** (Michael Joseph/Merrimack Publishers' Circle, 1985, $12.95), has just been released.

As with the majority of Mitchell's work, *The Crozier Pharaohs* features Dame Beatrice Lestrange Bradley and her trusted secretary and "Watson," Laura Gavin. I wish I could say that this final volume is one of Mitchell's finest; it is not. The plot having to do with two sisters who raise Pharaoh hounds and are plagued by madmen and murderers is less a case of detection than luck and "surmise."

Those who have read and loved the series will not want to miss this chance to see Dame Beatrice's "reptilian smile" one last time. New Mitchell readers should instead read

the recent first American edition of *The Rising of the Moon* (St. Martin's, 1985, $11.95), a 1945 title that shows just how good she could be.

Another (self-proclaimed) "Classic

Kathleen Maio *is a freelance writer based in Somerville, Massachusetts. She has contributed to* Twentieth Century Crime and Mystery Writers, Murderess Ink, *and numerous magazines.*

Mystery" is Paul McGuire's **Enter Three Witches** (Harper Perennial, 1985, $3.50), first published in 1940.

After an odd encounter with a beautiful young woman and a ghost from the past on Rome's Spanish Steps, Tony Grant is invited to a deadly country houseparty. Set in 1939, after the failure of the Spanish Civil War, but before the darkest days of World War II, the novel's elegant writing and the air of weltschmerz about its hero will likely appeal to fans of the mannered school.

A very different kind of manners can be found in **Bare Acquaintances** by Karin Berne (Popular Library, 1985, $2.95). A proponent of the *Compromising Positions* school of mystery fiction, this paperback original is less a mystery puzzle than a social comedy concerning the sexual liberation of a thirty-eight-year old displaced homemaker.

A mystery puzzle there is, but whether by fluke, skill, or transparent plot, I was able to spot the murderer even before the crime occurred. The mystery exposed, I found it hard to concentrate on the sexual misunderstandings between the heroine, Ellie Gordon, and her wheelchair-bound lover and boss.

As a comedy of sexual politics, *Bare Acquaintances* definitely has its strong points. Enough so that I will look forward to more from the two women who are "Karin Berne." And, assuming she can learn to stop talking in extended metaphors, I would have no objection to meeting heroine Ellie Gordon again either.

The academic mystery is a favorite formula among "cozy" fanciers. The mild-mannered and absent-minded professor, that wise innocent who happens upon clues and corpses littering the halls of ivy, is a beloved stock character. **Doubting Thomas** by Robert Reeves (Crown, 1985, $12.95) is most certainly not *that* kind of college mystery. It is, nonetheless, one of the best academic mysteries of recent memory.

Thomas Theron is a professor of Am. Civ. coming up for tenure at a prestigious Massachusetts university suspiciously like the Harvard wherein author Reeves once toiled. He is a classic professor of sorts—the burnt-out, post-sixties sort. His self-destructive bent includes a regimen of beer, bourbon, Lucky Strikes, and blowing his wad playing the ponies at Suffolk Downs.

Operating on a tip from a urine-soaked drunk in the track's men's room, Theron puts a bundle on a long-shot filly called Jesus Saves and cleans up. The drunken tout is not so lucky. He is dead of a drug/alcohol overdose. Whereupon Theron's troubles really begin.

Against his will, the professor is drawn into the world of a pedantic mafioso who is also a literal-minded student of literature. Vincent Ciullo wishes life, specifically Theron's, to imitate art in the form of the masculinist classics.

A man's gotta do what a man's gotta do, but Theron would rather pass, thanks. Our reluctant hero isn't a particularly nice guy, but he is absolutely convincing as a fellow strong-armed by fate into living dangerously.

If horse racing doesn't provide enough color, Reeves throws a religious cult and various vice operations into his unusual first mystery. It all adds up to a winning debut with a good deal of wit and hard-boiled insight.

For those who prefer a homier brand of wit and absurdity, there is **The Grub-and-Stakers Quilt a Bee** (Doubleday/Crime Club, 1985, $11.95) by Alisa Craig. As many already know, Alisa Craig is the Canadian alias of Charlotte MacLeod, the current queen of the gentle, screwball mystery. This is her second book about the Grub-and-Stake Gardening and Roving Club of Lobelia Falls, Ontario. And there is more whimsy here than you could shake a stake at.

When the new director of the equally new Aralia Polyphema Architrave Museum takes a dive from its mansard roof, Dittany Henbit Monk, husband Osbert, and Sergeant MacVicar of the local constabulary investigate in a way that is sure to gain even more fans for Craig and MacLeod.

If anyone doubted that Sierra Club Books is new to the mystery biz, they need only read their press releases. "We give away little of the plot," they claim, "by mentioning that the villain is. . . . "

Such a spoiler blurb is forgivable from a nature publisher known for their celebrations of the wilderness.

The Turquoise Dragon by David Rains Wallace (Sierra Club, 1985, $12.95) is a departure for nature writer Wallace as well as for his publisher, but not as much of a departure as you might think.

Set in the Klamath Mountains of northern California, the plot concerns outrages of man against man and nature, but focuses on a lost breed of salamander called the Turquoise Dragon.

Wallace's hero is a forest ranger drop-out who became a private reforester via a short but lucrative career as a pot farmer. Through the character of George Kilgore, the novel expresses well the limbo quality of the lives of baby-boomers who couldn't manage (or rejected) lasting yuppiehood.

More to the point, Wallace tells a very entertaining suspense tale. Much of the action, including the extended confrontation with the baddies, takes place in the wilderness the author loves. Wallace is mercifully controlled with his environmentalist propaganda, however. There is nothing here that smacks of sermon, only a beautifully realized natural backdrop for a skillful first thriller.

Judith Trojan:

Front Row Center

Like it or not, abortion is a fact of life. With the recent rash of abortion clinic bombings, spurred on by President Reagan's anti-abortion campaign, the fiery debate between freedom-of-choice advocates and anti-abortionists continues, unabated.

Two fine, new programs explore the abortion issue—past and present—and its reverberations both here and abroad. Whether they're from the hills of Thailand or the suburbs of Pennsylvania, women are the focus in both documentaries. For it's women, ultimately, who must come to terms with the consequences of choosing abortion. Aside from the difficult moral, physiological, emotional, and economic dilemmas, the legal ramifications of abortion remain a real concern in most parts of the world today. In Peru, for example, women caught having abortions are imprisoned and must often wait as long as one year or more for a trial. If their children have no other caregiver, then they, too, must reside in prison alongside their mothers. "Babies-behind-bars" seems an ironic price to pay for aborting unwanted pregnancies.

Abortion: Stories from North and South, written and directed by Gail Singer for the National Film Board of Canada, provides a fascinating cross-cultural survey of current, indigenous abortion practices. After a brief, information-packed recap of abortion history, incorporating fascinating archival photos and drawings, the film singles out abortion in Ireland, Canada, Colombia, Thailand, Japan, and Peru for primary attention. The film's point-of-view is pro-choice and, as a result, it is often guilty of over-dramatizing that bias with ominous music and urgently read, voice-over narration.

In Ireland, where abortion is emphatically illegal, a sad-faced young woman is counseled on-camera about options for her unwanted pregnancy. Ashamed and fearful that her parents and employer will find out, she travels quietly to London for a legal abortion. This sequence, although touching, seems frankly staged. The young woman's fear of exposure is ludicrous given the fact that she consented to be filmed. Thankfully, the rest of the film lacks this phony docu-drama quality.

Although abortions are technically illegal in Thailand, women are not persecuted if they choose to have abortions. Pregnant women often utilize massage abortionists, one of whom is shown performing a daily, half-hour massage on her own unhappily pregnant daughter. After seven days, the girl's placenta fails to dislodge on schedule, so the girl must go to a clinic to have a vacuum abortion. A physician speaks about her own problematic position as a professional abortionist at this clinic in a society that theoretically frowns upon abortion.

Thai authorities do promote family planning efforts since they are paid for by international development dollars. Even in the remotest areas the villagers are familiar with modern forms of contraception and sterilization. In one sequence, a mixed audience of northern hill people giggle as a paramedic describes the use of condoms. The incentive system—pigs and chickens for using birth control pills or IUDs, a water tower for having a vasectomy—works wonders in rural regions to lower Thailand's birthrate and raise the gross national product.

In contrast to Thailand, where the people are "contraceptively" sophisticated but still lack exposure to modern technology, Japan, the technological giant, still can't come to terms with the sexual revolution. Japanese kids learn about sex from porno comics; and healthy, open dialogues about sex and birth control are stifled. Although abortion is permitted (originally as a form of birth control to monitor fertility, genetic defects, and family size), religious guilt is still ominously present. New Japanese feminists speak out about the double standard that continues to bind Japanese women.

While not illegal, abortions in Canada must be reviewed on a case-by-case basis by a three-person medical team. This bureaucratic shilly-shallying dangerously delays abortions, which makes Canada the country after India to engage in the most second trimester abortions. A thirty-five-year-old pregnant Canadian woman is filmed as she makes her initial phone call to locate a faster abortion, as well as during her abortion 400 miles away in Quebec, where free-standing abortion clinics are allowed.

Backstreet abortions and infanticide are the key forms of birth control in Colombia. Infectious hospital wards are filled with maimed victims of botched abortions. One lucky survivor of an abortion, self-induced with an onion, talks about her ordeal from her bedside in one such ward. In a horrifying sequence, the camera pans a city dump where murdered infants are discarded like yesterday's garbage.

With its highly dramatic soundtrack and visuals, *Abortion: Stories from North and South* underscores its plea for safe, legal abortions, liberal sex education, and family planning clinics. To its credit, the film boasts a large, mostly female crew.

The bias, for or against abortion, is less clear-cut in Mark Obenhaus's brilliant, hour-long documentary, **Abortion Clinic.** Originally aired in 1983 as a part of the PBS "Frontline"

Judith Trojan *is editor-in-chief of* Sightlines *magazine, editorial coordinator at the Educational Film Library Association in New York City, and a staff member of the American Film Festival.*

series, the videotape opens and closes with stage-setting remarks by series host Jessica Savitch. Savitch provides an uncharacteristically soft-spoken pitch for the unique graphic quality of the program and its admirable focus on how individual women choose to deal with unwanted pregnancies.

Because *Abortion Clinic* is apparently the first American TV program to show graphic abortion procedures on camera and due to its often heartbreaking personal intimacy, the video is, at times, harrowing to watch. It is certainly not for the squeamish.

Abortion Clinic profiles four young women—two of whom choose to have abortions and two who choose to carry their pregnancies to term. The Reproductive Health and Counseling Center in Chester, Pennsylvania, is a logical focus for the tape. Ironically, the Center is located in a building that once housed a seminary. A private facility, the Center performs more than 3,000 first trimester abortions annually; its major clients are young, white, and single. Outside the Center, "pro-lifers" picket and pray under the leadership of Right-to-Lifer Dr. George Isajiw; Isajiw, an internist, and his small band of followers attempt to divert women before they enter the Center. Sequences featuring the work of Dr. Isajiw as he counsels clients in his office and houses low income, pregnant women with his own family balance the tape.

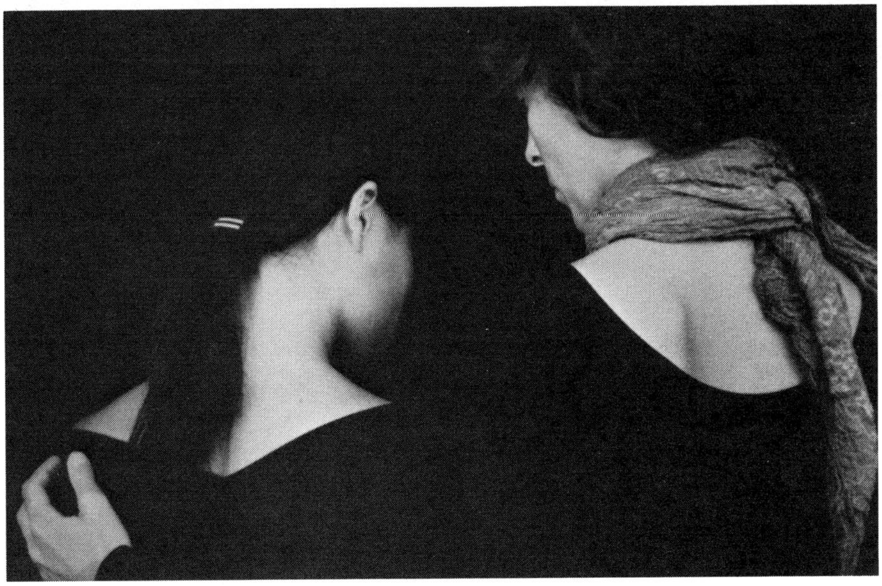

Abortion: Stories from North and South

At the Center, the most revealing moments come during counseling and admission sessions with individual women; and especially during the lengthy sequences featuring Helen and Barbara, both of whom are seventeen, single, and pregnant. Helen naively believed her boyfriend's lie about having a vasectomy. Helen's mother—young, abused, and abandoned by Helen's father—has four kids to raise; she sensitively discusses and supports Helen's decision to abort. This is Helen's second abortion; she manages to smile and remain calm during the abortion procedure, which is captured on-camera from a discreet angle. Views of the instrument insertion and rather cursory inspection of the embryonic or placental material are, however, somewhat hard to take. A wonderful female counselor gently hand-holds Helen during the abortion, a service she also provides for the much more fragile Barbara.

Barbara chose to have her first child, now two years old; but she painfully decides to abort her second for sound reasons. Abused regularly by her boyfriend, she is thin, undernourished, and simply worn out. She manages to feed her son as best she can on food stamps; she supports her own apartment, and has admirably returned to school to finish her high school education. Although she's obviously not a quitter, Barbara is wasted physically and emotionally by the abortion, which is viewed here from start to finish. Despite the presence of the sensitive female counselor and a female cameraperson—Nancy Schreiber shares "camera" credit with director Mark Obenhaus—the footage taken during Barbara's abortion seems much too intrusive, given her frailty. Barbara's sequence will do much to muddle the most stalwart pro-choice advocates in the audience.

Two other young women opt to carry their pregnancies to term after being counseled by Dr. Isajiw. Young and poor, both women, however, have supportive male partners. One of the women is a rape victim who glowingly commends the doctor for educating her about the horrors of a saline injection abortion. She eventually moves in with the doctor and his wife; the latter is also a Right-to-Lifer and a one-time rape victim.

Despite Dr. Isajiw's somewhat simplistic and insensitive counseling techniques—he uses plastic models and photos of developing embryos and fetuses and botched abortions—his case against abortion is clearly heard here to balance the work of the Reproductive Health and Counseling

(continued on page 719)

This month's programs:

Abortion Clinic. video. color. 52 min. 1983. Producer/Director: Mark Obenhaus. Dist: Fanlight Productions, 47 Halifax St., Boston, MA 02130. 617/524-0980. Video—$300 (rental—$75) ¾ and ½ inch.

Abortion: Stories from North and South. 16mm & video. color. 55 min. 1984. Writer/Director: Gail Singer. Producers: Signe Johansson & Gail Singer for the National Film Board of Canada. Dist: The Cinema Guild, 1697 Broadway, New York, NY 10019. 212/246-5522. 16mm—$895 (rental $100). Video—$595 (rental $100) ¾ and ½ inch.

Bruce Pollock:

On Record: Popular Music

Approaching its midpoint, the eighties is no longer a decade in search of a sound to call its own, some searing image or guitar lick around which to rally the troops and wave the banners. While in the decade's first four years we've seen a number of contentious noises vie for the honor of a generation's fondest remembrances, all of these assorted beats have fallen by the wayside like nervous twitches under mass sedation. Now that Heavy Metal has been effectively modified by MTV, the last bastion of corporate rock, previously the sound, if there ever was one, of not only the eighties, but of the past ten years, has been whittled to a sliver of its former glory. High-gloss, overly made-up, but researched to the nines, corporate rock was the essence of soulless perfection, the type of sound omnipresent in the corridors as you skulked through any major multinational cartel that housed a record company (soon to be heard inside its elevators as well). For females in spandex it might have been called Journey, Styx, REO Speedwagon. For males in heat you had Van Halen, Def Leppard, Scorpions. For purists of either gender there was Judas Priest, Iron Maiden, Rush. When Heavy Metal

made the charts, you called it Hard Rock. In any case, it was strictly choreographed, costumed, tailored for TV and nationwide radio. In fact, with MTV in the ballgame since 1981, the very notion of having to spend thirty to fifty grand per video to promote a band made virtually everything a captive of the corporate dollar—which was not about to be invested foolishly, on anything smacking too much of experimentation, protest, creativity or reality.

About a year ago, this new sound arose anyway, not exactly coming up from underground, but once planted through the good works of its natural champions, its roots exposed a veritable flower garden below the surface of public awareness. If we think of this sound as American Rock, and its champions as Bruce Springsteen and John Fogerty, then the works of such disparate entities as R.E.M., the Bangles, the Blasters, George Thorogood, even Huey Lewis and Cyndi Lauper begin to seem connected. It's just the next latest greatest thing since New Wave, which gave way to New Music (and which was basically British in derivation) and Disco, which gave way to Techno-Dance Rock (also basically European in derivation)—ephemeral musical notions destined to pale before the onslaught of American Rock throughout the remainder of the eighties. A whole new set of archetypes will be resurrected, the glory of rock and roll reborn.

Evolving country

Jason & The Scorchers. *Lost & Found* (EMI-America ST 17153)

Journeying back to rock's beginnings, here's a band of country slickers who segue from stone country twanging to punk/rock yowling before settling into a folkish groove that fits them best. Not sophisticated and cynical enough to pass for an updated Eagles, and not goofily mellow enough to pose any threat to Poco, these boys are merely singing what they feel, without limiting stereotypes. Based in Nashville, they offer us their rendition of "Lost Highway," and then update it poignantly in "Broken Whiskey Glass." They have a fondness for acoustic guitars, mandolins, and mournful singing, yet they open up the album on a rockish note. Is it pure American ingeniousness, this hick schtick, or a distinct, evolving blend? I vote the latter.

Just another pretty face

Janey Street. *Heroes, Angels & Friends* (Arista AL8 8219)

Not that we lack for female archetypes in this rock and roll Year of the Woman, but ever since the advent of Chrissie Hynde (originally from Akron) the image has added new substance. Street (now there's an evocative name) looks quite a bit like Hynde, and also reminds me of another rocker I once fell heavily for, named Carolyne Mas, a slick city chick songpoet with far-away eyes, a battered past and a definitely windblown presence. Not surprisingly, she sings like an East Coast Rickie Lee Jones, of street creatures and nightscenes, only her Sunset Boulevard is more like Queens Boulevard, a middle-class enclave of miniature upheavals and the occasional transit strike. No young Laura Nyro out of young Janis Ian (actually, was Janis Ian ever young?), Street adds little to the recorded annals of urban neurosis other than a pretty face and the usual punchlines.

Tex-Mex cuisine

Los Lobos. *How Will the Wolf Survive* (Slash/Warner Brothers 25177-1)

Another type not recently heard from is the lowdown, juke joint combo—five scruffy guys in zoot suits, horns and (of course) an accordian for the ethnic numbers from the 1940s. Welcome Los Lobos, a Tex-Mex band from East Los Angeles, who not only fill the bill and your dancecard, but wail like Haley. The album is a stew pot of rock Americana, with a carrot of fifties honking, a bubbling broth of New Orleans funk, that Mexicali beet/beat, etc. The title song is a masterpiece of a metaphor, equating the noble wolf to the individual's last cry of uniqueness in a world of researched romances and corporate caution. You even get to hear them play a polka. Let's see Van Halen try *that*.

Sensible songs

The Replacements. *Let It Be* (Twin Tone TTR 8441)

Virtually shut out of the corporate rock jungles for the past decade has been the truly American garage band sound so popular in the early seventies before video and hi-tech made it passé. The Replacements, a cross between the Clash (but not political) and the Ramones (but not instrumentally inept), revive that sound with a vengeance. Located far from the corporate centers, in Minneapolis (first stomping ground of Bob Dylan), they've managed to produce three LPs of raw, unrefined rock and roll, laboring on the nearly forgotten premise that the record can be its own reward, a creative release, an emotional statement. In an era when rock groups take to their roles like graduates of Wharton, where success is the bottom line and personal taste virtually an afterthought, the Replacements are doggedly anti-capitalistic in their disdain for the college of musical polish. The first few passes through *Let It Be* may not even reveal the sensibility that courses through this band like a Mississippi River of influences and tributaries, washing over the Beatles, the Kinks, the MC5 and others in its wake. In fact, only the energy and the urgency may reach you, but that ought to be enough to coax the few more spins necessary to reach the heart of the matter. And, as it was at the beginning, the heart of the Replacements resides in their songs. Listen to "Unsatisfied," "We're Coming Out," "I Will Dare" and "Sixteen Blue" and then ponder the fate of American rock in the eighties. ▣

Bruce Pollock *is editor of* Guitar *magazine and the author of* Popular Music: An Annotated Index of American Popular Songs, Volumes 7 and 8.

Gail Pool:

Magazines

Confronted with the **Utne Reader**, I realized I have always harbored some prejudice against digest magazines. Digests, after all, sin twice over: by reprinting material from other magazines and by condensing the material to boot. I suppose the purist in me has always believed that magazines should offer original material and that no work except Webster's should ever be abridged.

As it turns out, the *Utne* (rhymes with chutney) *Reader* is an interesting magazine, and it has led me to think more highly of the digest genre. For one thing, the *Utne Reader* has a distinct personality of its own; and it is clear that though the digest, like the cuckoo, may do some borrowing, what emerges in the end is an independent entity. For another, the digest, if it is well done, really can be useful. Consider how much is being published, how inaccessible much of it is, and how poorly written. Here is a digest promising to sift, select, and print a compressed readout of the best. It is an offer that is hard to refuse.

I suspect that for most of us, the term "digest" instantly calls to mind the *Reader's Digest,* one of the most influential, profitable, and ubiquitous magazines of all time. Actually the digest genre has a long and full history. According to historian Theodore Peterson, the first publication to call itself a magazine was a digest: the *Gentleman's Magazine,* founded in London in 1731, was comprised of items culled from other papers.

In America, Funk and Wagnall's *Literary Digest* and Albert Shaw's *Review of Reviews,* both founded at the end of the nineteenth century, grew to be respected publications. Through the years, a fanciful assortment of material has been "digested":

Gail Pool *holds an M.L.S. degree from Simmons College and presently works as a freelance writer based in Cambridge, Massachusetts.*

Cartoon Digest offered newspaper art, *Column* collected newspaper columns, *Listener's Digest* summarized the best radio programs, and one digest selected the best letters to the editors of newspapers.

The *Utne Reader,* a new variation on the digest theme, was started in February 1984 by Eric Utne. A co-founder of *New Age* magazine and clearly a sixties man, Utne seems to have initially aimed to create a digest of "the best of the alternative press," which is the magazine's subtitle. In its early form as a sixteen-page monthly newsletter, the *Utne Reader* was something of an alternative digest. Since he has transformed his publication into a 128-page bimonthly magazine, Utne is giving us something broader and better.

It is not that the *Utne Reader* ignores the alternative press: the 1,000 periodicals Utne and friends comb for material include such titles as *Rain,* the *Multinational Monitor,* and *Yellow Silk*; and the *Utne Reader* is an excellent source of information about little known magazines. But recent issues include numerous reprints from *The Nation,* the *Progressive,* the *Village Voice*—magazines I would call only borderline alternative; and many other from such titles as *Playboy,* the *New York Review of Books, Harper's,* and *Esquire*—magazines that are not alternative at all.

"Even mainstream magazines can offer enlightening thoughts, and we don't want you to miss them," writes Utne in justifying his inclusion of these magazines. But why, one wonders, does he need to justify? Perhaps his sixties conscience is nagging him. But the *Utne Reader*'s mix of mainstream and alternative is effective in its variety and contrast. I suggest he lay aside his guilt and his subtitle and continue in his current direction.

The *Utne Reader* falls into two sections. Its departments, all originally written, provide a guide to some of what's in print. "In Brief," for example, gives synopses of a selection of articles in magazines as diverse as *The Atlantic* and *Covert Action Information Bulletin.* Especially good are "Some of a Kind," an annotated bibliography of outstanding periodicals in a particular field—American Indian magazines, for example, or Canadian magazines; and "Recommended Reading," comprised of reviews of staff and adviser recommended periodicals, that tell what the magazines are about and how to get hold of them.

The rest of the *Utne Reader*—which is most of it—is made up of excerpted articles and interviews. Several articles in each issue focus around a theme: "Kids: Should You Have One?," for example, offered pros and cons by writers from the *Village Voice,* the Vanguard Press, and *Mothering Magazine,* as well as the hilarious "Babies and Other Hazards of Sex," excerpted from the book of that title. Other themes have included "Soviets and Americans: Searching for Common Ground" and "Vietnam: Can We Heal the Wounds?"

If some of the themes seem trendy, in a sense that cannot be helped. If a digest limits itself to material that has been published elsewhere, and if it is looking for several articles on a single subject, it is almost bound to follow trends. Within the trends, the *Utne Reader* has managed to find some unusual pieces. But it is easy to see why many digests, frustrated with the parameters of the genre, turn increasingly to original material.

In addition to the thematic pieces, each *Utne Reader* carries ten to twenty other pieces selected, as the editor has said, "idiosyncratically." They have included—to give some sense of the range—"Being Dead Is Bad for Business," from *Inc.*; "Advertising Is Capitalist Realism," from *Harper's*; "The Murder Epidemic," from *Science 84*; and two pieces on poet Gary Snyder, one from *California Living* and one from *Mother Earth News.*

In general, these articles are interesting and they blend well to form a magazine. Though they are condensed, they do not seem overly simplified. And they are well-edited to read smoothly. I doubt that a reader coming upon them for the first time would be aware they had been compressed.

And what of the basic question asked by *Reader's Digest* founder DeWitt Wallace: Are these articles "of enduring value and interest"? Do they deserve to be reprinted?

On the whole, I would say yes. Most of the *Utne Reader*'s articles take on subjects that matter; they are well written; they make points worth making. I do question the value of some of the selections. I couldn't help wondering, with all the corruption evident these days in the United States, whether Robert Coles had nothing better to criticize than nuclear-freeze advocate Dr. Helen Caldicott, and whether the *Utne Reader* (and also *Harper's*) had nothing better to do with their space than to reprint this criticism.

I also wondered whether the platitudes that make up most *Esquire* articles really deserve extended life. I was especially disappointed to see the sophomoric and simplistic "Why Men Love War" by William Broyles *again*—though I admit that the *Utne Reader* handled the piece well. Placed within a different context—alongside an opposing viewpoint—the article had a different impact, even a different message, than it had in its *Esquire* environment. Proof, should we need it, that the digest really isn't simply a replay but the creation of a new publication.

As periodical literature continues to mount, the times would seem to be propitious for a digest magazine. One simply hasn't time to read everything from *Processed World: The Magazine with a Bad Attitude—Created by and for Dissident Office Workers* to *The Economist.* Even a magazine junkie, as Eric Utne likes to call himself, is likely to discover articles he missed—and will be glad to find—in the wide-ranging and entertaining pages of the *Utne Reader.* ▣

This month's magazine:

Utne Reader. Bimonthly $24/yr. Subscriptions: Box 1974, Marion, OH 43305

Norman Stevens:

Our Profession

This month's books present a varied approach to librarianship. Two of them touch on basic routines; two deal with service to specialized groups; and the last is a highly personal testimony to the virtues of a particular, and one is tempted to say peculiar, school of librarianship. Each has something to offer.

It is no longer fashionable for library schools to teach such mundane practices as the use, production, and evaluation of bibliographies. An understanding of the basic principles of bibliography remains, however, an essential element of our professional skills and, with the current emphasis on bibliographic instruction, is perhaps more essential than in the past. In **Bibliographies: Their Aims and Methods**, Krummel has done a skillful job of presenting in a short space, but at a relatively high price, a fundamental manual on bibliography. His work should serve as a standard text for some component of library school programs and should, in particular, serve practicing librarians in good stead. Each chapter is short but succinct. The end result is a wealth of general information about the history and role of bibliographies as well as the more practical aspects of scope, citation style, annotation, organization, collecting entries, presentation, and evaluation. There is also an excellent bibliography, which itself serves as a model, of some 110 of the major writings on the compilation of bibliographies from 1883 to 1983. Krummel is a fluent writer with a witty approach to what is most often a dull subject that rivals the best of Paul Dunkin's work. He tells you all that you need to know about why and how certain things are done without embellishment. He obviously understands the nuances of such things as citation style without feeling compelled to write a treatise on that, or other topics, or to belabor any particular point. This book is apt to be overlooked because it is on a mundane subject and is not from a major publisher, but it is well worth reading and using on a regular basis. It may well turn out to be one of the best books of the year.

Budgeting, perhaps even more so than bibliography, is regarded as a routine library task that must be done but has little glamor to it. Spending money can be fun; planning for and controlling expenditures is hard work. Budgeting is also a subject whose practical aspects, like those of bibliography, are too often ignored in our education and training. It is something that we most typically learn by doing and do not always learn correctly or well. Fortunately there have been several excellent books in recent years to assist us in understanding more about this essential aspect of our work. Alley and Cargill's *Keeping Track of What You Spend* (1982), which was the first book on library budgeting, remains the best. Smith's *Accounting for Librarians* (1984) presents a somewhat more detailed and sophisticated approach but it is also extremely useful. Margo Trumpeter and Richard Rounds's **Basic Budgeting Practices for Librarians**, like Alley and Cargill's work, offers another very simple and straightforward approach to the subject. It requires little in the way of previous understanding of the complexities of large-scale budgeting operations or accounting techniques. The authors proceed, in a logical fashion, to describe various aspects of library budgeting, the projection of expenditures and revenues, the oral and written presentation of budgets, the budget cycle, and managing what you ultimately receive. They, like Krummel, have packed a sizeable amount of information into a short space. Their writing, while easy to follow, lacks his charm and style which are needed as much in thinking about budgets as in thinking about bibliographies. Nevertheless their text will be especially useful for students, others wanting to know more about the mysteries of library budgeting, and for librarians in smaller libraries of all types.

As many aspects of our work have become more specialized, and as the literature of librarianship has grown, we have moved away from a reliance

Norman D. Stevens, *University Librarian at the University of Connecticut, is the author of the forthcoming book* A Guide to Collecting Librariana.

on generic texts on, for example, the university library, or technical services, to ones that deal with a more specific component of library services. Ellis Mount's **University Science and Engineering Libraries**, while it is representative of that newer kind of text, is also unique. It is the only work that deals with specialized library units in an academic library setting. For many larger, and even some smaller, academic libraries one or more departmental or divisional libraries in the sciences or engineering are an important part of their structure and services. Such libraries have their own set of relationships and their own problems so it is especially useful to have a text that deals specifically with the issues that they face. This second edition improves on the previous edition by providing more specific treatment of sci-tech libraries in colleges, dealing more extensively with computer applications and networks, and, in general, covering the numerous changes that have taken place since the publication of the first edition in 1975. After a brief overview of the historical background and the general nature of these specialized units, Mount deals with the management of such libraries, their technical services requirements, their user services functions, their collections, and their facilities and equipment. He concludes with the results of a survey based on visits to sixteen academic institutions in 1983 which provided a setting and data for this volume. While he uses that information and includes some bibliographic references, the work is primarily an outstanding statement of Mount's own philosophy of library service in a specialized setting in a larger institutional and library structure. Mount writes in a concise, straightforward, and easy to understand style and, in doing so, offers a clear picture of virtually every aspect of the management and operation of these vital library units.

Phyllis Dalton's **Library Service to the Deaf and Hearing Impaired** is yet another example of the rapid specialization that continues to occur in our literature. The relatively recent publication of such works as the Thomas and Thomas's *Library Services for the Handicapped Adult* (1982) and Wright and Davie's *Library and Information Services for the Handicapped* (1983) marked an awareness of the increased need for substantial general texts on serving users with specialized needs. Now, only a few years later, we have a substantial text on serving one group of these users and others are certain to follow. Apart from creating an awareness of the needs of such users, and the fact that meeting those needs requires a range of specialized activities and not just some modest additions to library services, Dalton provides a wealth of specific information and ideas that will be of considerable use to library administrators, managers, and practitioners in libraries of all types. She places the issues into an excellent general perspective and provides some historical background before dealing in-depth with services and resources, the evaluation of such programs, and the potential for such services. Above all Dalton demonstrates the need to consider in detail the ways in which libraries can meet their responsibilities to this particular group of potential users who, for a variety of good reasons, have tended to ignore libraries as an institution interested in and able to meet their needs.

Scarecrow seems to have a knack for publishing unusual books and with **Library Literacy Means Lifelong Learning**, or *LLMLL,* as Carolyn Michaels consistently refers to it, they have certainly won the prize for the strangest book of the decade. *LLMLL,* which purports to be a revised version of the author's *School Libraries Worth Their Keep,* can best be described as a stream-of-consciousness, and thoroughly jumbled and intertwined, recounting of Michaels's personal and professional life and career and her philosophy of librarianship. The arrangement, the content, and the chapter headings make little sense and what much of the content has to do with librarianship is beyond me. Michaels's writing style is highly personal, primitive and unskilled, and full of strange turns of phrases (e.g., "librarians will have joined . . . the team to defuse America's illiteracy bomb"). Since Michaels asserts that she produced this work at the urging of Scarecrow, one must assume that there is a market for this "patchwork . . . philosophy distilled from experience into a working paper on professional problems . . . [and] a very real map of my feminine, marriage-directed professional odyssey." As peculiar and as unusual as *LLMLL* is, it nevertheless has a certain kind of naive charm lacking in some of our more formal and polished writings on school librarianship. I can hardly recommend Michaels's odd personal testimony to everyone but it is, at least, worth dipping into to obtain a very different perspective on librarianship and for amusement. Its intended audience, which may represent a more sizeable portion of our profession that I would like to think, will undoubtedly greet *LLMLL* with unbridled enthusiasm. ▣

This month's books:

Dalton, Phyllis I. *Library Service to the Deaf and Hearing Impaired.* Oryx Press, 1985. 371p. $39.50. ISBN 0–89774–135–8 LC 83–43242.

Krummel, D.W. *Bibliographies: Their Aims and Methods.* Mansell, 1984. 192p. $30. ISBN 0–7201–1687–2.

Michaels, Carolyn. *Library Literacy Means Lifelong Learning.* Scarecrow, 1985. 365p. $27.50. ISBN 0–8108–1719–5 LC 84–10705.

Mount, Ellis. *University Science and Engineering Libraries.* 2nd ed. Greenwood, 1985. 303p. $35. ISBN 0–313–23949–5 LC 84–6530.

Trumpeter, Margo C. and Richard S. Rounds. *Basic Budgeting Practices for Librarians.* American Library Association, 1985. 164p. $25. ISBN 0–8389–0399–1 LC 84–20503.

Patrick Dewey:

Software for Libraries

Computer illustrator Sally Tobin's **1 Hunter** (Millennium, 1984), adapted from a work by Pat Hutchins, is a set of five programs for children ages three through six. The main program, "Hunter's Story," has a "Hunter" taking a walk past nine groups of animals, beginning with a pair of elephants and ending with ten parrots. At each stop, the animals are hiding in various ways. The program then waits for the child to press the correct number on the keyboard. If correct, the animals come out of hiding. All of the animals within a group are the same. "Mixed-Up Animals" is essentially the same format, but one group consists of more than one type of animal. In "Pick and Count" the child picks the animal and then attempts to count out the number associated with that animal by pressing the space bar an equal number of times. "A Photo Opportunity" is simply a view of all of the animals together. Many of the games may be "frozen" or speeded up to increase the action. The colors and format are superb. The documentation consists of an instruction card and "a note to the grown-up," which is a list of suggestions to help get the most out of the program for your kids, including extra activities. All "hunting" is done with a camera; no guns are seen or mentioned. It comes complete with a wall poster of the animals and a set of five-by-eight-inch cards of line drawings of the animals and the "Hunter." Both disk and documentation are packaged in a durable, book-sized binder for convenient shelf storage. For use with: Apple II series. Cost: $34.95.

Patrick Dewey *is administrative librarian, Maywood (Illinois) Public Library and author of* Public Access Microcomputers: A Handbook for Librarians.

Computerized calendar

The Millennium Electronic Almanac: 1985 (Facts on File, 1984), edited by Anthony S. Kleckner and Belinda S. Tan, and programmed by William Ying, is a beautiful electronic version of a traditional type of reference volume combining excellent graphics with a highly interactive presentation of facts. The four diskettes (eight disk sides) are divided into Summer, Spring, Winter and Fall, and before they will work it is necessary to transfer DOS to at least one of them. It is completely menu driven, and as a bonus, the program will act as a personal calendar by allowing up to four lines of text to be entered for any date (the first day of winter, 1984 through December 31, 1985). When a date has been selected, a variety of information is displayed, including several events of significance which occurred in history on that date, famous birthdays, a daily word, a computer word for the week, and more. From a menu of two-letter commands, a brief quiz of additional trivia may be selected. There is also a daily tune which you attempt to guess. Fortunately, this element may be turned off if desired (it is also possible to play the tunes one after the other which might be troublesome in some libraries). The program is easy to use. An initial concern that it would go out of date before it could get on the shelves is true of some of the material presented. However, it is not true on the whole, as much, maybe 90 percent of the material, will remain relevant and interesting to younger users perennially. Presumably, this will be a continuation. What's next—Guinness on disk? For use with: Apple II Series; IBM PC or PCjr. with 128K color card, and DOS 2.0 or 2.1; Compaq and other compatibles. Cost: $49.95.

Barbaric adventure

Conan (Datasoft, 1984) by Eric Robinson and Eric Parker, and graphics by Eric Parker, Kelly Day, and Russ Wolvek, is described on the box in this fashion: "Trap doors are waiting to swallow you up; floating ledges may at times help you, or demolish you instantly. Poisonous scorpions and giant ants creep through the hallways. Hungry bats seek to devour you! . . . Intense battle action."

(This is actually more descriptive of several Chicago branch libraries at which I've worked than it is of this new game.) I usually find it difficult to recommend any sort of arcade game for libraries, believing that we can put our money to better use, but some libraries may not suffer from this aversion, nor a lack of cash, and others may even wish to circulate such games. Fortunately, *Conan* is more closely an adventure game than an arcade, possessing elements of both. As an arcade game, Conan jumps across crevasses, climbs ladders, and avoids killer ants and bats. Even here the game is only mildly arcade, and nearly always slow-paced. Conan is represented on the screen by an inch-size, muscle-bound speck, not at all the burly brute he was in the adventure books, hurling his sword at anything that flashes on the screen. The graphics, on the other hand, are excellent, and if a joystick is used, it is delightful (though keyboard is supported). As an adventure, Conan encounters more strange sights and villains than Indiana Jones. As Conan you get ten swords (to throw), and three lives. None of it, I am afraid, comes close to being as hair-raising as the cover description above would lead us to believe. Sound effects may be turned off. For use with: Apple II Series. Cost: $39.95.

Picture this

Stickers (Springboard, 1984) is an excellent multiple skill learning tool for ages four through twelve. Though this is not quite in the format of a traditional coloring book, kids have access to a large number of different sized and shaped stickers that can be pulled from the side of the screen and "stuck" wherever desired. Users

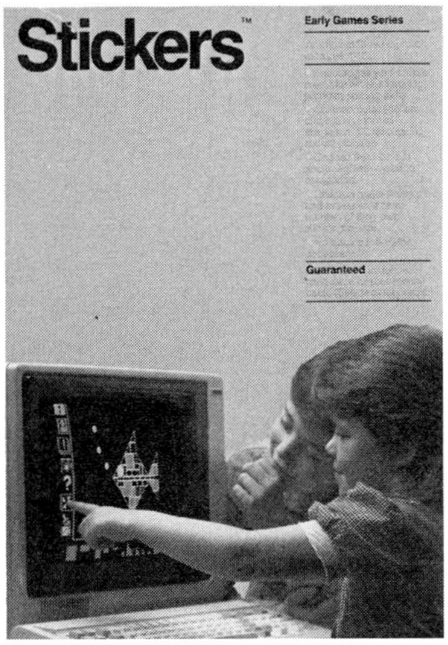

choose the color by changing the palette. This can be on a "blank" form as in coloring books, but composed of outlines of the sticker shapes (circles, squares, triangles and rectangles). In just a few minutes, kids can produce beautiful pictures. They may also produce their own original drawings using either the stickers which come with the set or by creating their own customized stickers of any shape. Prefabricated designs come in groups of monsters, vehicles, people, space ships, animals, dinosaurs, and other forms—about 100 pictures in all. For use with: Apple II Series; Commodore 64; IBM PC, PCjr. Cost: $34.95.

Database management simplified

Bookends: The Reference Management System (Sensible Software, 1984) by Jonathan D. Ashwell, is a specialized database for keeping track of references. It can be used in several ways, including maintaining a file of special materials (local history, plays, etc.), and as a replacement for a card file, if the necessary hardware is available and convenient (sometimes, it's just better to stick with a card file, so be careful when considering a change). It can also be used to maintain and print bibliographies of books or journal articles. Use of the program is rather straightforward, and you can be up and running in a couple of minutes. Each citation allows for author, title, journal, volume, page number, date, publisher, keywords, location, and an abstract. All fields, except classification, which is limited to one character, allow for a maximum of 720 characters. These may also be modified as required, to include other labels as desired. Printing out this material is fairly easy, too, and printer options include slot #, page dimensions, extra line feeds, etc. Clearly, there are better database programs around, including just about any of the well-known database systems (Data Factory, PFS-File & Report, dBase, etc.), but they nearly all cost more. Other databases allow for more fields, greater flexibility in the format process, etc., but these also require more time to configure and "set up" for a particular application (it may also take you some time to work out all of the bugs). For use with: Apple II series (64K required) with PRODOS operating system. If you don't have PRODOS or don't wish to use it, you may obtain a special DOS 3.3 version for no extra charge by writing the publisher after purchase of the PRODOS version. According to the package, *Bookends* translators are available to convert MEDLINE and DIALOG MEDLINE dial-up sessions into *Bookends* ($49.95). The excellent documentation is about 100 pages and indexed. For use with: Apple II series (64K). Cost: $124.95. ▣

Publisher addresses for this month's software:

Datasoft, Inc., 19808 Nordhoff Place, Chatsworth, CA 91311.
Millennium Group (Facts on File), 24 E. 22nd St., New York, NY 10010.
Sensible Software, 210 S. Woodward, Suite 229, Birmingham, MI 48011.
Springboard Software, Inc., 7807 Creekridge Circle, Minneapolis, MN 55435.

James Rettig:

Current Reference Books

Correspondence and review copies for this column should be directed to James Rettig, University Library, Box 8198, University of Illinois at Chicago, Chicago, IL 60680.

Almanac of the 50 States, edited by Alfred N. Garwood. 1985 ed. Information Publications (Box 1536, Burlington, VT 05402), 1985. 446p. $42.50, pa$35. 0-931845-03-3; 0-931845-02-5

Places Rated Almanac, by Richard Boyer and David Savageau. 2nd ed. Chicago: Rand McNally, 1985. 448p. $24.95, pa$14.95. 0-528-81091-X;0-528-88008-X 84-43149

One of these titles covers states as a whole, sticks to the facts, and lets those facts speak for themselves; the other covers metropolitan areas and unhesitatingly evaluates them in comparison to one another. The *Almanac of the 50 States* draws data from census reports and other sources to create statistical portraits of each state, the District of Columbia, and the nation as a whole. The eight-page profiles cover the states' geography, demographic characteristics, vital statistics, health, education, Social Security and welfare programs, election results, government finance, crime, labor, income, agriculture, business, and energy and transportation. A second section ranks each of the states in all of these areas. Unlike the subjective ratings in *Places Rated,* these are objective rankings. *Almanac of the 50 States,* a convenient statistical digest, will be useful in all types of libraries.

The first edition of *Places Rated Almanac* (reviewed in *WLB,* March 1982) rated the quality of life in 277 metropolitan areas in terms of their climate, terrain, housing, health care, environment, crime rate, transportation, education, recreation, cultural attractions, and economic conditions. The updated edition ranks 329 metropolitan areas in these same categories, each chapter providing information on the appropriate amenities or omissions of the metro areas. Each chapter also lists the areas from best to worst and indexes this list by city name. Subtle changes have made for a more useful book. For example, the recreation chapter now includes information on quality restaurants and college sports and the housing chapter now lists average rent and tells what percentage of dwellings are houses, mobile homes, and apartments. Sidebar articles have been revised extensively; some have been dropped and new ones have been added. Every chapter is filled with careful explanations of how its ratings have been derived and what they mean. Thus it is ironic that this very useful book's most publicized feature—its cumulative ranking of the 329 areas—is its only useless feature. Asheville, North Carolina, has displaced Atlanta in the top spot and the Lawrence, Massachusetts-Haverhill, New Hampshire SMSA (now in 154th place) has vacated the cellar to make room for Yuba City, California. As a high rating of twenty-first for dirty, overcrowded, expensive Chicago and an almost equal rating of twenty-sixth for dirtier, more crowded, more expensive New York demonstrate, these ratings are, of course, absurd. The authors sensibly counsel readers to weigh various factors to suit their tastes and desires. If readers heed that counsel, this is an almost inexhaustible treasure trove of data for comparing cities. In our mobile society it will be very useful to many.

British Novelists, 1890–1929, edited by Thomas F. Staley. Detroit: Gale, 1985. 387p. $85. 0-8103-1714-1 84-28613 (Dictionary of literary biography, v. 36)

Libraries that have bought volumes of the *Dictionary of Literary Biography* selectively will want to select this one since it profiles the lives and works of some of the most read and most studied modern English novelists. Among the twenty-nine novelists treated are Aldous Huxley, James Joyce, D.H. Lawrence, W. Somerset Maugham, and Virginia Woolf. For these and others (including Bram Stoker) specialists have written lengthy critical biographies and compiled bibliographies of primary and secondary works. The biographies, illustrated by photographs and facsimiles of manuscript pages and corrected proofs, go beyond the "irritable reaching after fact" of who's-who works to convey the character of the writers' lives and works. Eight essays from the early part of the century discussing the novel of the period have been reprinted as an appendix. Like its predecessors in the series, this volume carries a cumulative index of authors. These biographies will answer the needs of many patrons, especially high school students and undergraduates, better than lengthy monographic biographies.

Chicano Organizations Directory, compiled by Cesar Caballero. New York: Neal-Schuman, 1985. 221p. pa$19.95. 0-918212-65-0 83-8333

As the country's Chicano population has grown and the Chicano cultural heritage and social condition have come under scholarly scrutiny, Chicano orginizations have come into being. Some have been founded to carry out an agenda of social change, some to preserve a distinctive culture, and others to facilitate scholarly discourse. All Chicano organizations that com-

James Rettig *is head reference librarian, University of Illinois at Chicago.*

pleted the compiler's questionnaire have been included in this directory. It also includes nonprofit agencies whose principal mission is serving Mexican-Americans. Caballero hopes that publication of the first edition will attract the notice of organizations he has overlooked and that a second edition will have twice as many entries. The 378 entries list addresses, type of organization (i.e., national, regional, state, local), founding date, administrators' names, statement of purpose, publications, and, as appropriate, number of courses/type of degree(s) offered or frequency of meetings. Geographic, subject, and organization name indexes round out the volume. Even though the directory is organized alphabetically by name, this last index is justified since it permutes names susceptible to being garbled. This directory will obviously be useful at colleges with Chicano studies programs and in communities with concentrations of Mexican-Americans.

Collins Australian Encyclopedia, edited by John Shaw. Sydney: Collins (dist. by G. K. Hall), 1984. 848p. $49.95. 0-8161-8738-X

North American libraries that need a comprehensive encyclopedia of *res Australiana* have but one choice: the twelve-volume *Australian Encyclopedia* (4th ed., Sydney: Grolier Society of Australia, 1983). Both it and the *Collins* encyclopedia focus on the history, the people, the institutions, the flora, the geography, the fauna, and the culture of Australia. The major difference between the two is not scope but magnitude. Their respective treatments of Australia's railroads illustrate that difference. The *Australian Encyclopedia* devotes eight-and-one-half pages to the topic versus less than a page in *Collins.* The longer treatment surveys the history of rail development, its current state, and recent freight carrying statistics in each state and territory. The shorter treatment condenses this, discussing nationwide history and current conditions rather than more local situations. The only statistics given are of the number of miles of rails in service at several widely separated dates. Other differences are less pronounced and less significant. The *Australian Encyclopedia* provides more numerous bibliographic references at the ends of articles and treats minor geographical features, towns, plants, and animals in greater detail. *Collins* is stronger in its treatment of popular culture, especially of world class athletes. More than 1,000 black-and-white photographs and forty-eight pages of color plates illustrate the 3,000-plus articles. The subject index organizes entries into broad topics such as education, exploration, natural resources, and religion. The *Collins* work delivers essential factual information about Australia past and present while offering economy and one-volume convenience.

The Complete Guide to Cabins and Lodges in America's State and National Parks, by George Zimmermann. Boston: Little, Brown, 1985. $19.45, pa$12.95. 0-316-98808-1; 0-316-98837-5 84-25065

Because most of the nation's state and national parks will begin accepting reservations for the 1986 summer vacation season at some point between now and December of this year, this is the time for public libraries to order this useful addition to travel reference collections. When Joe and Jane Vacationer return from their summer sojourn disappointed because the Oceanbreeze Inn was a mile from the beach or because the Forestview Motel looked out over a row of gas stations, *Cabins and Lodges* will guide them to better digs next year. In it outdoors enthusiast Zimmermann describes the accommodations at all 300 state parks and 36 national parks that offer lodging. Grouping the states by region, each section shows the location of parks on a regional map. Entries always give addresses and phone numbers. By way of introduction to the accommodations, individual park profiles describe the park's overall environment, its history, outdoor activities, and noted flora and fauna. Descriptions of lodging include number of rooms or cabins, sleeping capacity, age, construction materials and style, cooking facilities, type of heating and cooling systems, rates, forms of payment accepted, dates of operation, minimum length-of-stay requirements, and earliest date reservations can be made for the next season. Booking park cabins and lodges for prime vacation periods is very competitive; people smart enough to go to libraries for information about them deserve the edge this book gives them.

Contemporary Stage Roles for Women, compiled by Sandra Heys. Westport, CT: Greenwood, 1985. 195p. $35. 0-313-24473-1 84-19218

In its effort to redress a traditional "lack of rewarding roles " for women in theater, *Contemporary Stage Roles* goes overboard by all but ignoring the male characters in plays. Its alphabetical guide to approximately 200 plays lists the playwright, the number of male and female characters, a one- or two-sentence plot synposis, and a description of each female character. The male characters are not even named, much less described. Ancillary sections classify the plays by age of female characters, by character types (e.g., heroic, comic, villainous, high brow), by unusual physical characteristics (e.g., overweight, wheelchair bound), and by minority group. An appendix analyzes the casts by size, but only in terms of the number of women required. Indexes of playwrights and characters close the book. It achieves what it sets out to do: identify plays in which actresses can perform meaningful roles. However it should have done this without ignoring the fact that half the human race is male, a fact reflected in many of the plays' mixed casts. In the principal list, male characters should have been named and described. Such a note of realism permitting better informed selection of roles for women would not have detracted from the value of the other sections of the book. The book serves its purpose, but not as effectively as it could have. It will be useful as a flawed adjunct to *Play Index* (New York: H.W. Wilson).

A Dictionary of British and American Women Writers 1660–1800, edited by Janet Todd. Totowa, NJ: Rowman and Allanheld, 1985. 344p. $45. 0-8476-7125-9 84-2123

Reference works usually form the last link in the bibliographic chain of articles, books, dissertations, and conference papers. The systematic study of British and American women authors has been stalled, however, by the difficulty scholars have had in identifying women writers of the period this

biographical dictionary covers. It provides the missing link and fulfills its dual purpose of illuminating "the forgotten writers" and of re-examining "the major accepted ones in light not only of new scholarship but of new consciousness." Given the state of study of the period's women writers, the great majority of the 500 belong to the ranks of the forgotten, now at long last remembered as the era's Ann Radcliffes and Mary Wollstonecrafts have always been remembered. Specialists in the period's literature have written bio-critical essays discussing each writer's achievement in the context of the art and society of her time and place. Understandably, most are British. The index consists mostly of proper names. A chronology of the writers by birthdate would have been a useful feature enabling students and scholars to make comparisons and to explore developments in styles or conventions. Even without this, the *Dictionary* will straighten the very crooked path that has made these writers generally inaccessible. As they are studied more, new reference works, particularly bibliographies, will add links to the chain and strengthen it.

Directory of Residential Treatment Facilities for Emotionally Disturbed Children, by Barbara S. Sherman. Phoenix: Oryx Press, 1985. 231p. $45. 0-89774-118-8 ISSN 8756-2170

Since the implementation of Public Law 94-142 in the late 1970s, the nation's eight million handicapped children have been guaranteed needed special educational services through their local school districts. The great majority of these children receive these in their own schools provided by a speech therapist, a learning disabilities teacher, or some other specialist. However some children are best served by being placed in residential facilities. This directory's descriptions of some 300 public and private residential treatment facilities in forty-six states and Puerto Rico are based on questionnaire responses and other information supplied by the homes. Each facility profile lists the facility's name, address, phone number, contact person, types of placements accepted, history of the home, age levels and types of handicaps served, tuition and other fees, social and rehabilitative services, educational and vocational programs, and referral and placement requirements. Indexes list facilities by type of placements accepted (e.g., educational, psychiatric, group, therapeutic), by age ranges served, by characteristics of the children served (e.g., autistic, emotionally disturbed, learning disabled, minimal brain dysfunctioned), and by types of funding available (e.g., private, state, insurance). Information on each facility is more detailed than that supplied in *The Directory for Exceptional Children* (10th ed., Boston: Porter Sargent, 1984); however this latter directory lists many more facilities, organizing them by type of services offered rather than by state. The compiler's introduction explains the rights of handicapped children under P.L. 94-142 and the ways parents and schools can meet these children's needs. The directory will be most useful to education professionals who assess children's special education needs, helping them to make proper referrals in the cases of children who can benefit from residential treatment.

The Hard-Boiled Explicator, by Robert E. Skinner. Metuchen, NJ: Scarecrow, 1985. 125p. $13.50. 0-8108-1749-7 84-20246

This bibliography of secondary works on the hard-boiled detective fiction of Dashiell Hammett, Raymond Chandler, and Ross Macdonald, the masters of the genre, contains a number of mysteries to be solved through hard-boiled bibliographic detective work. One of its chapters consists of eight items which the compiler could not retrieve because their citations in other sources contain errors. Skinner gives all the clues he can from the original citing sources, but these were not enough for him to locate the citations. Other chapters, hopefully free of error, list popular and scholarly periodical articles, books and dissertations, and major book reviews. Brief descriptive annotations accompany all 650 items. Annotations of reviews generally indicate only whether they were positive or negative. Only the reviews chapter is divided into three sections for each of the authors; the others are organized by the names of the authors of the items cited. The subject index subdivides major topics by the names of the three writers, but this would have been much easier to use if each chapter had been organized into separate author bibliographies with needed cross references. Nonetheless, scholarly interest in the detective genre has been on the rise in recent years and *The Hard-Boiled Explicator* leaves future investigators a clear trail of bibliographic footprints to follow.

The Macmillan Book of Business and Economic Quotations, edited by Michael Jackman. New York: Macmillan, 1984. 302p. $19.95. 0-02-558220-8 84-14415

Whether or not they own Simon James's *A Dictionary of Economic Quotations* (reviewed in *WLB,* November 1981), libraries will want to consider *Business and Economic Quotations.* Although like the newer work it includes witticisms by Oscar Wilde and ironic observations by Mark Twain, James's slim volume emphasizes the writings of economic theorists. Jackman is more catholic and more popular, freely quoting ancient philosophers as well as more recent dramatists, politicians, novelists, judges, poets, newspaper columnists, and even Lenny Bruce and Rod Stewart. Both books arrange quotations topically, Jackman under 62 headings and James under 133, many of these 133 derived from the technical vocabulary of economics as a social science. Due to the differences in the nature of the sources the books draw on, their two collections of quotations on the same subjects exhibit considerable differences and little overlap. James gives full citations to the quotations' sources; Jackman lists only the speaker's name and the quotation's year. Jackman's key word index refers to page numbers rather than to specific quotations, an economy one can understand but cannot condone. With its wide variety of 5,000 quotations compared to James's fairly specialized selection of 1,700, Jackman's collection is the best choice for public libraries; academic libraries will probably want both.

More Memorable Americans, 1750–1950, by Robert B. Downs, John T. Flanagan, and Harold W. Scott. Littleton, CO: Libraries Unlimited, 1985. 383p. $30. 0-87287-421-4 84-27780

A continuation of *Memorable Americans, 1750–1950* (reviewed in *WLB,* June 1983), *More* provides the same sort of brief, popular biographies of approximately 300 Americans who made significant contributions in literature, the arts, the military, politics, government, law, religion, science, journalism, medicine, historical studies, business, and other fields. It is an eclectic convocation of achievers, among them Charles Lindbergh, Abigail Adams, General George Patton, Douglas Fairbanks, Winslow Homer, William Rainey Harper, Crazy Horse, Carl Sandburg, Marshall Field I, Alfred Kinsey, Emily Post, Duke Ellington, and Charles Goodyear. Perhaps only in America would one find such diversity. The biographies, one to six pages in length, open with a general assessment of the subject's contribution and then shift into a birth-to-death survey of his or her life before concluding with a brief summation paragraph. Appendixes list the biographees by date of birth and by principal occupation. Although not essential, there is an eight-page subject index. Like those in the first volume, these compact, highly readable biographies are a pleasant alternative for those who do not need or feel intimidated by the amount of detail in the *Dictionary of American Biography.*

Newspeak, by Jonathan Green. Boston: Routledge & Kegan Paul, 1984. 263p. $19.95. 0-7100-9685-2

The first of a projected two-volume set, *Newspeak* identifies and briefly defines the obfuscatory euphemisms of democracy that are "designed to allay suspicions, modify facts and divert one's attention from difficulties." It draws its terms from British and American governments and their faceless bureaucracies, the news media, the military, economists, advertising, pop therapies, and numerous trades and professions that use specialized vocabularies both to communicate among practitioners and to confuse outsiders. The overwhelming majority of entries belongs to this last category (e.g., "chapel" meaning a printers' union local, *nolo contendere,*

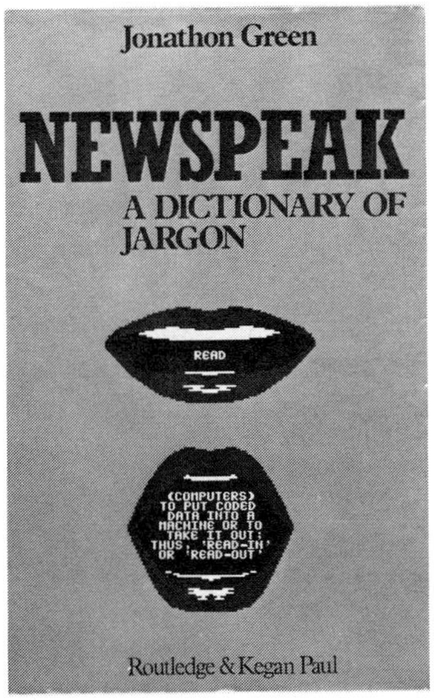

a plea in court). Although euphemisms are relatively few, those included are dandies such as "executive action" meaning assassination or "to organise," a term meaning to steal among British soldiers. Most of the terms are very matter-of-fact words in some specialized field; the field of origin is specified in each definition. As a work of lexicography *Newspeak* is not nearly as satisfying as *The Second Barnhart Dictionary of New English* (Bronxville, NY: Barnhart Books, 1980) and its predecessor. These give parts of speech, pronunciation, etymology, and illustrative quotations along with clear, succinct definitions. *Newspeak* includes many more terms than the Barnhart dictionaries and provides adequate information—their definitions—about them for most people. It is a serviceable supplement to standard English dictionaries.

Science Reference Series, edited by David Jollands. New York: Arco, 1984. 8 v., 64 p. $9.95. each. Vol. 1, **Exploring Space and Atoms.** 0-668-06175-8 83-26623. Vol. 2, **Language and Communication.** 0-668-06176-6 83-26651. Vol. 3, **Sight, Light, and Color.** 0-668-06177-4 83-26645. Vol. 4, **Energy, Forces, and Resources.** 0-668-06178-2 83-26619. Vol. 5, **Machines, Power, & Transportation.** 0-668-06179-0 84-6449. Vol. 6, **Measuring and Computing.** 0-668-06180-4 84-6307. Vol. 7, **Earth, Sea, and Sky.** 0-668-06181-2 84-6312. Vol. 8, **Patterns of Life on Earth.** 0-668-06182-0 84-6318

This attractively illustrated set introduces young adult readers to basic concepts of science and explains how these concepts function in the physical world. The structure of the whole as well as the organization within each thematic volume lends itself to extended browsing but not to a systematic survey of the world of science. For example, the final volume includes discussions of how animals fly, animal courtship rituals, animal ecology on islands, hibernation, conservation of species, and predators. The simple text in each two-page article is amplified by the plentiful color photographs and drawings with lengthy explanatory captions. Terms defined in the volume's glossary are printed in boldface. The explanations of fundamental concepts are clear and concise. However since each volume is indexed separately, it will be difficult to use the set for specific fact retrieval. Elementary and junior high students and teachers can use it for a basic introduction to the workings of the beam steam engine, electricity, volcanoes, or fiber optics. It is difficult to classify this work; it is not strictly a reference tool nor a textbook nor a survey. Whatever one calls it, it will be welcome in school and public libraries.

Software Reviews on File. New York: Facts On File, 1985. Monthly. Looseleaf. $145/yr. ISSN 8755-7169

When the scramble for a secure place in the market among microcomputing reference works ends, *Software Reviews on File* will have firm purchase on its place. In the course of each year it will publish hundred-word excerpts from some 3,000 reviews of more than 500 new programs for microcomputers. Each sixty-four-page issue covers approximately forty programs, introducing each in a factbox telling its name, author, producer, date, price, physical contents, and system hardware requirements. The producer's description precedes the review excerpts. The arrangement of the programs by type (i.e., business, communications, programming languages, education, games, personal) is laid out clearly on the front page along with the titles of the programs in each category. The cumulative monthly index includes entries for software producers, titles, hardware, and subjects. This will be especially useful in libraries that have not been able to keep up with the proliferation of microcomputing magazines; in the absence of the full reviews, software shoppers will be able to rely on the excerpts. Such libraries can compensate, at least in part, by subscribing to *Software Reviews on File.*

The Sourcebook of Franchise Opportunities, by Robert E. Bond. Homewood, IL: Dow Jones-Irwin, 1985. 509p. pa$19.95. 0-87094-475-4 84-71569

In his introduction Bond decries the existence of other guides to franchise opportunities which are simply reprints of the United States Commerce Department's *Franchise Opportunities Handbook* (1984 ed., SuDocs C61.31:984). Nevertheless it appears that Bond himself owes a debt to the *Handbook.* Both books are organized by a very similar list of businesses by type. The lists of franchisors within each type are also very similar; the differences show in the franchisor descriptions. Those of Bond's descriptions that list only the name, address, president's name, number of franchishees, and a brief statement of purpose seem to have been borrowed from longer profiles in the 1983 edition of the government-produced *Handbook.* In these cases the language of the descriptive statements is very similar and the number of franchisees is identical; in every case checked, this number had increased in the 1984 edition of the *Handbook*! However, the majority of Bond's profiles consists of the franchisors' responses to a questionnaire he sent them to learn their history, financial requirements for franchisees, and training and other services provided by the franchisors. The *Sourcebook* provides fuller information on some franchise opportunities and the *Handbook* provides fuller information on others. Libraries should be franchisees for both.

Stage Lives, compiled by George B. Bryan. Westport, CT: Greenwood, 1985. 368p. $49.95. 0-313-24577-0 84-19833 (Bibliographies and indexes in the performing arts, no. 2)

In compiling *Stage Lives,* Bryan has taken care to minimize overlap with the *Performing Arts Biography Master Index* (2nd ed., Detroit: Gale, 1979), *Theatre, Film and Television*

Biographies Master Index (Detroit: Gale, 1979), and several other similar although more specialized indexes to biographies of actors and actresses. Bryan, a professor of theater at the University of Vermont, annotates 154 collective biographical works and lists some 2,500 monographic biographies and dissertations on individuals. These sources, all in English, are indexed by the names of the persons they treat, a total of some 4,000 actors, critics, playwrights, managers, dancers, and producers. In addition to citations to the list of works indexed, index entries include the person's name, dates, nationality, and role in the theater. Citations to the collective works identify relevant page numbers. Because most of the citations refer to monographic biographies of individuals, this should be viewed as a supplement not only to the collective indexes listed above, but also to a library's subject catalog. As such its use can be expected to generate interlibrary loan requests. This will fulfill a need in comprehensive theater collections; elsewhere it will be a luxury item.

The Wisdom of the Novel, by David Powell. New York: Garland, 1985. 729p. $50. 0-8240-9017-9 83-490808

From Hugh Henry Brackenridge's *Modern Chivalry* compiler Powell quotes: "I read with great pleasure oftentimes a book which has not a single idea in it except the quotations." So it is with this book of quotations from several hundred British and American novelists from 1470 through 1900. One can readily read it with great pleasure; one cannot, however, so easily use it as a reference book. Powell has organized several thousand quotations under approximately 800 thematic headings, listed in the front matter. Some of the headings should have been combined (e.g., "peace" with "war and peace," "instruction" with "teaching"), others are archaic (e.g., "agitation," "coxcombry"). Some, actually *see* references in disguise, are unmasked only after a user turns to the appropriate page. The cross referencing used through the body of the book is inconsistent and unconventional. The choice of thematic headings sometimes appears to be the result of a key word in a quotation; other times it appears to be the result of a high level of abstraction. Only the latter can explain phenomena such as placing "Their tongues quivered like aspen leaves" under the heading "expression." Since each quotation's author is cited, the author index operates efficiently. However, the key word index, citing page numbers rather than specific quotations, is cumbersome. In some cases, a key word is followed by more than hundred page numbers. As a source to find quotations about a topic, *The Wisdom of the Novel* supplements the standard quotations dictionaries, especially those favoring more memorable verse quotations. Its best use, however, is to be read with great pleasure.

World Book Encyclopedia. Chicago: World Book, 1985. 22 v. library binding $403 to schools and libraries, other bindings and prices available 0-7166-0085-4 84-50815

Like many other general purpose multivolume English-language encyclopedias, the *World Book* is revised continuously, each annual edition incorporating changes made since the previous year's was issued. The 1985 edition continues to embody the qualities which have made *World Book* a perennial leader on the Chicago Public Library's list of its most used reference tools and have made it a selection of many of the librarians who have accepted the challenge from *Reference Services Review* to list ten reference works they consider the most essential. *World Book* has gained and maintains its respected position through currentness of contents, clear writing, careful editing, authoritative articles, useful special features, clear graphics, and a thorough index. It is effective both as a ready reference source and as a tool for learning. To carry out this latter role, topics have been selected to reflect the contents of the curricula of North American schools. So, although cosmopolitan in its coverage, *World Book* is strong on western history and culture and gives special treatment to United States and Canadian historical figures, politicians, cities, states, and provinces.

The 1985 edition includes results of the 1984 Olympics and the November presidential election as well as balanced articles on AIDS, the political situation in Nicaragua, and Geraldine Ferraro. Throughout the encyclopedia one finds careful attention to current fact and recent breakthroughs in scientific knowledge. Fully a third of the set was revised to some degree during the past year.

Even though the 19,000 articles have been written by more than 3,000 scholars and other specialists, the editors have controlled the reading difficulty of the set to keep its contents accessible to a wide audience ranging from grade schoolers to adults. The reading level escalates in articles on complex subjects, especially scientific and technical topics, so that a young reader can gain a basic knowledge from the early paragraphs and a more mature reader can gain more by reading further. Technical terms are defined within the articles, an effect no doubt wrought by careful editorial control rather than a consistent awareness of their audience among the authors. The list of contributors is impressive, among them Harold Bloom on Percy Bysshe Shelley, Tom Landry on football, Isaac Asimov on science fiction, and Daniel Levinson on middle age.

More than 1,400 of the articles include brief, up-to-date bibliographies of books, many of them divided into two difficulty levels. Major articles also include outlines of their contents, extensive cross references to other articles, and questions such as one might find in a grade school textbook. Some 200 articles on popular topics (e.g., the elements, Japan, Michelangelo, stars) also refer to Reading and

(continued on page 719)

Gail Pool:

Editor's Choice

Correspondence and review copies for this column should be directed to Gail Pool, 75 Summit Ave., Brookline, MA 02146.

Brett: From Bloomsbury to New Mexico, by Sean Hignett. New York: Franklin Watts, 1985. $22.95. 0-531-09775-7

The life of Lady Dorothy Brett began in Victorian England where her father was an adviser to the Queen and "Doll," as she was then called, attended dancing classes at Windsor Castle. Ninety-three years later her life ended in Taos, New Mexico where, known simply as Brett, she had become one of the living icons surrounding the memory of D. H. Lawrence. Sean Hignett, whose own background is similarly cross-cultural, has produced a well-documented biography in which some of the minor players are Aldous Huxley, Bertrand Russell, Virginia Woolf, Alfred Stieglitz, Georgia O'Keefe, and Leopold Stokowski.

Breaking free of her family at the relatively late age of twenty-seven, Brett became an art student in London where she began a succession of passionate—but mostly platonic—attachments, a habit which was to be a leitmotif throughout her life. A regular at the salons of Lady Ottoline Morrell, a friend to Katherine Mansfield and a lover of John Middleton Murry, Brett's life changed forever when she became the sole recruit to the utopian community "Rananim" in Taos, New Mexico then being promoted by D. H. Lawrence.

Life in Taos was hardly utopian. A contentious lot, there was constant strife among Frieda Lawrence, Mabel Dodge Luhan and Brett over Lawrence's attentions while he remained in America and over the proper disposition of his memory, and even his ashes, during the decades following his death. Despite an isolating deafness, constant money problems and a lack of critical attention to her work, she was to find, as had Lawrence, a liberation in the rugged southwest. In the end, she experienced moderate artistic success with her paintings of Indian ceremonies, but it is realistic to assess Brett's true fame as deriving from her brief association with D. H. Lawrence and surviving till 1977 to tell about it.

—*Marilyn Souders*

Collected Stories of John O'Hara, selected and with an introduction by Frank MacShane. New York: Random House, 1984. 414p. $19.95. 0-394-54083-2

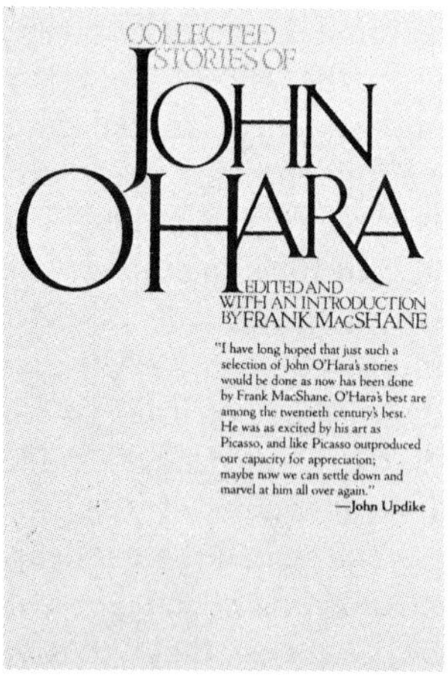

In only five pages, the 1934 story "Over the River and Through the Wood" sets the stage for a seemingly casual confrontation—a feeble old man opens a door on an almost naked girl who puts him down with a contemptuous "Get out of here, you dirty old man." Then, with a few crisp closing sentences, O'Hara opens up abysses, and one realizes that the man is psychically destroyed and by no means guiltless. In "The Doctor's Son," a longer story from the following year, Jimmy Malloy, an autobiographical character whom O'Hara used many times, recalls the 1918 influenza epidemic during which he, aged fifteen, closely observed many of his father's patients die and silently witnessed an adulterous affair which ended with the death through illness of the unsuspecting cuckold. The story doesn't dwell on connections between sex and death, they're just there, sensed by Jimmy, who can't quite express what he knows. This coming-of-age story is swift, funny, horrific, and humane. Lost innocence isn't mourned; as ever in O'Hara, the loss is inevitable and necessary. Adult life is hard and often inexplicable, but there are usually some good times. These two works are the strongest in this loosely chronological book's first part, a sampling from the thirties and forties. Most of the others from this period, including one *Pal Joey* episode, seem tailored for *The New Yorker*; although their bluntness and witty detail are recognizably O'Hara's, they tend toward the shapely vignette that focuses on a bit of character revelation. This is not to discount them as much as to contrast them with what follows. O'Hara wrote no stories during the fifties. He had quarreled with *The New Yorker* over its attack on his first blockbuster, *A Rage to Live,* and abandoned the short form along with the magazine. His return, "Imagine Kissing Pete" in 1960, clinically follows the sexual activities of the wife in a marriage that starts on a rebound, gets shakier and shakier, and, after thirty years of infidelity and sliding socially downhill, is

Gail Pool *holds an M.L.S. degree from Simmons College and presently works as a freelance writer based in Cambridge, Massachusetts.*

going to work. This fifty-page novella, with its compression and flow over long stretches of time, has the impact of a full-length novel. The narrator is Jimmy Malloy, who, in the stories O'Hara wrote in the sixties, mystery readers may connect with Archie Goodwin, Nero Wolfe's assistant and chronicler. Jimmy and Archie share a similar sexy tone of having been around; both are cool, knowledgeable, detached from the action they often precipitate, and laconically hard-boiled. This later O'Hara's techniques often seem derived from detective fiction. One reads these stories of O'Hara's final decade not for the craft of the young O'Hara but to be caught up in the older man's storytelling. He almost always leaves springs hidden for the reader to trip over; his stories can shock and move you in ways that are difficult to anticipate.

—*John Alfred Avant*

The Soong Dynasty, by Sterling Seagrave. New York: Harper & Row, 1985. 532p. $22.50. 0-06-015308-3 83-48802

The "dynasty" of the Soong family was short-lived, in Chinese terms, lasting only about fifty years. But as Sterling Seagrave demonstrates in this carefully researched and very readable book, the story of how this family came to play such a major role in the revolutionary transformation of Chinese society is as full of intrigue and drama as that of any true dynasty. While this tumultuous period in Chinese history (roughly the first half of the twentieth century) has been extensively covered, Seagrave is the first to do so from the perspective of this family, whose influence on China's destiny was profound, if hardly propitious.

As central figures in China's Nationalist movement, the Soongs were well known to Americans, but their dazzling public image kept their more nefarious deeds in the shadows. Making use of recently available studies, as well as the results of his own tenacious research, Seagrave reconstructs their story, and the portrait that emerges is not a flattering one. Seagrave believes that "such a biography did not exist earlier because the Soongs did not want it to." Indeed, part of his mission here is to reveal just how this grand deception was perpetrated, at the expense of both the Chinese people and the American taxpayers.

The first third of *The Soong Dynasty* covers the early stages of patriarch Charlie Soong's career, the education of his children in America, and the incipient Chinese revolution. A runaway to America, Charlie made the contacts here that would later translate into wealth and power in China. After an initial stint as a Methodist minister, a position for which he had been groomed by North Carolina Methodists, Charlie made his fortune in China publishing bibles. He then became chief fundraiser for Dr. Sun Yat-sen's revolutionary organization. Seagrave's interesting portrait of Sun Yat-sen reveals him to be an ineffectual visionary whose ability to inspire revolution far exceeded his ability to carry one out. There are no heroes in this book, but at this point the villains have yet to emerge.

In the last two-thirds of the book, Seagrave reveals in great detail how the Shanghai underworld, specifically one Big-Eared Tu of the notorious Green Gang, orchestrated the rise to power of Chiang Kai-shek. The story that unfolds is a vast web of corruption, greed, and brutality, which implicates every one of Charlie's offspring except daughter Ching-ling, the idealistic wife of Sun Yat-sen. Eldest daughter Ai-ling, wife of financier H. H. Kung, was a shrewd manipulator who financially bled China nearly dry; youngest daughter May-ling married Chiang Kai-shek and acted as his spokesperson to the West, her magnificent powers of deception earning billions for the corrupt regime. Harvard-educated T.V. Soong held many positions of power in the Kuomingtang goverment (KMT), but as financial adviser he made himself very rich by "controlling" the flow of American aid to China.

Though the grim dealings of the KMT have been well documented by others, Seagrave's book reveals for the first time the extent to which the KMT depended for its control of China on the Green Gang and its opium trade. Also new is the full story of the role of the Soong family in this perfidy. Seagrave writes forcefully and convincingly, with rich detail. *The Soong Dynasty* is an important book for any student of modern China, as well as anyone interested in the intricacies of American policy toward China.

—*Candyce Dostert*

Nero: The End of a Dynasty, by Miriam T. Griffin. New Haven: Yale University Press, 1985. 320p. $25. 0-300-03285-4 85-51761

The emperor Tiberius Claudius Nero Caesar has achieved fame as a ruler of unique wickedness. Unlike, for example, Richard III, he has had no partisans, no revisionist biographers. Miriam Griffin, summing up in her masterly work just about everything there is to know about Nero, cannot alter the traditional verdict. She finds in Nero some intelligence and ability, and a surprisingly serious artistic dimension, but no heart of gold.

Nero: The End of a Dynasty is not light reading—true, all your friends from *I, Claudius* are here and up to their lurid tricks, but this is a serious, scholarly book that gives equal attention to Nero's character and to his place in the Roman state. It demonstrates that his failure was also the failure of the government structure.

Oddly enough, the account of

Nero's life is the book's least successful aspect for the general reader. Because the author presumes a knowledge of first-century history, the narrative contains frequent references to events in the past and developments still to come. The reader, feeling inadequate, wishes guiltily for a cast of characters. However, the longer sections that treat various subjects in depth are absorbing and readily comprehensible, especially the extended treatment of Nero's artistic interests and talents. These discussions certainly reward the effort of following the narrative.

The book is handsomely produced with attractive, readable type (something not to be taken for granted these days). Unfortunately, the all-important family tree is reproduced in smaller, fainter letters.

—*Stephanie Martin*

Illiterate America, by Jonathan Kozol. New York: Anchor Press/ Doubleday, 1985. 270p. $15.95. 0-385-19536-2 84-20487.

"One out of every three adult Americans *cannot* read this book." This statement is splashed across the cover of *Illiterate America* by Jonathan Kozol, education activist and author of *Death at an Early Age*. In this latest book Kozol outlines the scope of a major national disaster in vivid terms. He tells of people who eat only in restaurants with illustrated menus, of parents who strive to hide from their children that they can't read the note the teacher sent home, and of tenants who sign leases they do not understand. The cost of this problem is staggering, both in direct payments by the government to those unable to find and hold jobs and in lost productivity. But the human costs, the denigration of self, the agony of blame, are the saddest, and out of them has grown Kozol's passionate commitment to a vision of change.

Kozol's vision is based on an uprising, a national overflowing of energy and determination to empower all segments of society. This will not occur easily, for the politics of oppression are deeply embedded. In Kozol's view certain groups in our society feel their best interests are not served by the education of the poorest class, that the existing power structure is most stable when large numbers of people do not have the skills to gain the information needed to make informed choices that might bring about change. The military, for example, is dependent on personnel who are literate enough to read and follow complex technical directions, but whose education does not encourage them to question orders or seek reasons.

The existing literacy programs, underfunded, understaffed and often poorly designed, barely scratch the surface of what is needed. Kozol envisions a national commitment, similar to the Civil Rights movement of the sixties or the WPA of the Roosevelt era, which would provide the money and the impetus for the development of grass roots programs.

This is a powerful book. Kozol is angry that our society allows this problem to exist and enthusiastic when he describes what could be done. In his boundless optimism he even suggests that the millions of books that are shredded annually by publishers should be distributed free to everyone, the piles of books in laundromats, daycare centers, and supermarkets a visible incentive to learn to read. It is a wonderful idea, and we know (and so does he) that in our profit-based society it won't be done.

This kind of broad, sweeping view occasionally weakens Kozol's argument. In his passion to make us comprehend the scope of the problem, he sometimes overstates his case. The decline in the sale of hardcover books, for example, probably has little to do with illiteracy, and much to do with economics. Similarly, the fact that the TV is on constantly in many households seems unrelated to the family members' inability to read the TV schedule.

Despite his unfortunately realistic assessment that very little will probably be done to combat illiteracy in the next decade, Kozol challenges us to take action. The well-being of our nation depends on it.

—*Barbara Scotto*

Plausible Prejudices: Essays on American Writing, by Joseph Epstein. New York: W. W. Norton & Co. 1985. $17.95. 0-393-01918-7

Of the two words that make up the title of this collection of essays, the second, "prejudices," is very apt. Chief among Joseph Epstein's many prejudices is a disdain for the literature of the past quarter century, a period he sees as producing no great works of art. To prove this point, he draws portraits of current novelists including Robert Stone, John Updike, and Cynthia Ozick. Their works fail, Epstein claims, linking their separate failures to several broad trends outlined in his introductory essays. Responsibility for the mediocrity of recent literature lies with universities that provide safe havens for too many writers; critics, particularly deconstructionists, who champion obscurity at the expense of straightforward literary judgment; book reviewers who regularly indulge in hyperbole; literary biographers who invade the private lives of their subjects in search of sexual or psychological revelations: in short, the present literary establishment which, Epstein believes, places politics above literature. To buttress this charge, Epstein turns to literary figures from the past such as Van Wyck Brooks and James Gould Cozzens whom he considers to be undervalued for political reasons.

As a self-described "sheriff," Epstein effectively calls a halt to unquestioned acclaim for leading contemporary writers. The weakness of the book, however, lies with the first word of the title, "plausible." Epstein generally doesn't truly argue or marshal evidence. Instead, in his attacks, Epstein commits many of the same sins he sees in others. One wonders, for example, whether Epstein himself does not place politics above literature in his criticism. In his dismissal of such authors as Robert Stone and Gabriel Garcia Marquez he seems to point his objections specifically to their leftist perspective, so that one senses he is objecting more to the particular political bias than to a political bias in general. Moreover, in rejecting various works, Epstein uses quotations unconvincingly and draws on the personalities and personal lives of authors for ammunition. His underlying critical principle, that literature must show a "love of Life" to be good, is insufficient, as are his simplistic explanations for the gloom and doom in much of contemporary literature. Provocative and often fun, *Plausible Prejudices* ultimately fails to persuasively argue its point of view.

—G.P.

Secret Gardens: A Study of the Golden Age of Children's Literature, by Humphrey Carpenter. Boston: Houghton Mifflin, 1985. 235p. pa $16.95. 0-395-35293-2

What prompted the wave of imaginative children's literature between 1860 and 1930? Humphrey Carpenter, author of acclaimed biographies of C.S. Lewis and J.R.R. Tolkien, as well as editor of *The Oxford Companion to Children's Literature,* now answers this question in an elegantly written survey that blends the best of literary criticism, biography, and social history.

As Carpenter sees it, a central factor for this flowering of children's literature lies in the home-bodied temper of the times. The late Victorians and the Edwardians lavished attention on their smaller families and sought enjoyment in children's books set in a safe enchanted place—Arcadia, to use the author's consistent metaphor.

For the most part, this image works in explaining how the new vision evolved in children's literature. In the 1860s Charles Kingsley's *The Water-Babies* and Lewis Carroll's "Alice" books unseated the sentimental evangelical novels popular the decade before. Ruralist Richard Jeffries laid the groundwork for an alternative world with *Wood Magic* and *Bevis.* Similarly, Frances Hodgson Burnett's *Little Lord Fauntleroy* advanced the notion of the beautiful child in an Arcadian setting. But the true mantle of leadership fell to Kenneth Grahame who expressed a safe, snug world in terms of the symbol popular with his own generation, the River Bank. An interesting contrast is Beatrix Potter, "the ironist in Arcadia," whose world is as alarming as Alice's. With his ingeniously-named "child-god" Peter Pan, J.M. Barrie "invoked something akin to religious feeling." To visit his Never Never Land, however, "requires an act of belief which the children cannot sustain as they grow up." The end of this "golden age" coincided with the post-World War I era. In Carpenter's view, A.A. Milne bade farewell to Arcadia: Winnie-the-Pooh's ideal world is "not a dream-come-true land at all" and Christopher Robin's beauty is really a camouflage for "ruthless egotism."

Insightful and persuasive as this analysis is, the most appealing sections of *Secret Gardens* are those that deal with the lives of the writers themselves. Carpenter's skillfully compressed biographies show that many were misfits: Kingsley relished cold baths and equated sexuality with penance; Carroll stammered and photographed little girls in the nude; Barrie impersonated his dead brother and was, like his creation, frozen in boyhood; Grahame yearned to escape married life. But the best of them kept their own childhoods close by; their frequent visitations of youthful experience were symbolic encounters with an Arcadia deep inside their memories. Depending on their taste for biography versus literary analysis, readers may decide whether the linkages between the authors lie more in the warped lives or in the deeper, spiritual levels of the works themselves.

—Peg Padnos

Pioneer Jews: A New Life in the Far West, by Harriet and Fred Rochlin. Boston: Houghton Mifflin, 1984. 243p. $17.95. 0-395-31832-7

Studies of the Hebrews in the Far West are few, but two recent books help fill the void: *Pioneer Jews* and Irving Howe's *We Lived There Too* (New York: St. Martin's Press, 1984). Both books are beautifully illustrated with photographs, etchings, advertisements, and portraits, and although both would well adorn a coffee table, Howe's work seems the more substantial.

These publications are the products of a renaissance of American Jewish culture, as witnessed by the number of academic programs, publications, and young scholars entering the field. American Jewish scholarship since the 1920s has produced such works as Solomon Schechter's *Studies in Judaism* (Philadelphia, 1924); A.J. Heschel's *Maimonides* (New York, 1983), which was first published in German in 1935; Joseph L. Baron's *Candles in the Night* (Philadelphia, 1940), stories of "righteous Gentiles," or Christians who have rendered aid and comfort to individuals and communities of an often persecuted people;

In *Pioneer Jews,* the Rochlins present a well illustrated history of the first Hebrew settlers in the southwestern United States, beginning in the 1500s, when the Hebrews "fled the fiery stake" of the Mexican Inquisition. The study ends with the year 1912, when the last two western territories were granted statehood. The area is the Far West, the Rockies to the Pacific, and Texas and South Dakota. Although by law a Hebrew must be born of a Jewish mother, the term "Jew" in this study includes people not technically Jewish, such as those born of a Jewish father and non-Jewish mother.

The text is written as an anecdotal account of these early pioneers—businessmen, farmers, financiers, an actress. Through their lives and the stories of their families, careers, and relationship to their religion, a panorama of the great glories of the western United States, its people and settlement is painted before us.

From a "bank of file cabinets" and an accumulation of two walls of books, journals, and monographs from western Jewish historical societies, museums and archives, the authors have extracted an attractive work on Hebrews in the American West.

—Karen Ami

Library World

Janet Husband

Ray Riddle

John Tooth

NEW POSTS

Rich Bowra has been named assistant director of the Dauphin County LS, Harrisburg, Pa. He was formerly director of the system's central library.

Susan Clarke has joined the reference dept. at the Lincoln Park campus of the DePaul Univ. libraries, Chicago, as reference librarian.

Lon Dickerson, formerly director of the Lake Agassiz Regional Library, Moorhead, Minn., is the new library director for the Timberland Regional Library, Olympia, Wash.

Marc Gluck has been named branch manager of the Broadneck branch of the Anne Arundel County PL, Annapolis, Md. He was previously general services librarian for the Annapolis branch of the library.

Michael Golrick, formerly head of the technology and business dept. at the Bridgeport (Conn.) PL, has been named director of the Wilton (Conn.) PL.

William Griffin has joined the staff of the Southwest Texas State Univ. library as acquisitions librarian.

Jan Hanson is now reference and young adult librarian at the Croton Free Library, Croton-on-Hudson, N.Y. She was formerly with the literature dept. of the Seattle PL.

Janet Husband, formerly acquisitions librarian at the Thomas Crane PL, Quincy, Mass., is now director of the Rockland Memorial Library, Rockland, Mass.

Gail Junion has been promoted from assistant head to head of the catalog dept. for the Univ. of Rochester libraries. She was previously head of the catalog dept. at Bowling Green Univ., Ohio.

Abolghasem Khosh-Khui has joined the staff of the Southwest Texas State Univ. library as serials cataloger.

Michael Richardson has been named assistant director for budget and personnel for the general libraries at the Univ. of Texas at Austin. He was formerly assistant director of the Frank Erwin Center at the university.

Ray Riddle, formerly director of the Cass County PL, Harrisonville, Mo., has assumed the post of director of libraries for the Kansas City PL, Kansas.

Richard Riley, previously director of library services at the Univ. of Texas of the Permian Basin, has been appointed chief administrative services librarian at the Southwest Texas State Univ. library.

Gail Schlachter is now president of Reference Service Press, Los Angeles. She was previously vice-pres./general manager of ABC-Clio Information Services, Santa Barbara, Calif.

Lois Stephens has been promoted from assistant head of reference to head of extension services at the Warren-Trumbull County PL, Warren, Ohio.

Sylvia Tiffany has been promoted from assistant director to director of the central library of the Dauphin County LS, Harrisburg, Pa. Previously, she was research associate at the Becton Dickinson Research Center, N.C., from 1977 to 1984.

John Tooth has been appointed editor of *School Libraries in Canada,* the official journal of the Canadian School LA. He is the chief librarian of the Manitoba Education Library.

C. Daniel Wilson has been named chief librarian of the New Orleans PL. He was formerly director of the Davenport (Iowa) PL.

Catherine Wilt has been appointed resource center manager in the college of information studies, Drexel Univ., Philadelphia, Pa. She was formerly director for public services for the Ursinus College library, Collegeville, Pa.

Beverly Wood is the new director of the Bayouland LS, Lafayette, La. She was previously cataloger and science reference librarian at the Louisiana State Univ. Eunice campus.

MARKETPLACE

Announcements

☐ The American Friends of the Hebrew University have formed a new group, Friends of the Jewish National and University Library. The library is Hebrew University's central library and the national library of Israel, with over three million volumes and, among other special collections, Albert Einstein's personal archives. First on the agenda for the Friends is supporting the periodicals collection, which has suffered recent cuts. For more information contact Peggy Rackett, American Friends of the Hebrew University, 11 E. 69th St., New York, NY 10021, 212/472-9800.

☐ Free speech/free press will be the theme of "Banned Books Week '85—Celebrating the Freedom to Read," September 7–14. The 250th anniversary of the libel trial of John Peter Zenger, a Colonial printer successfully defended by Alexander Hamilton, will also be celebrated that week. Promotional packets ($10) that include an annotated list of banned books, a selection of quotations on the First Amendment, three posters, and suggestions for media coverage are available from ALA and will be sold at the annual conference in Chicago in July.

☐ The recipients of the first Children's Book Council Everychild Honor Citations have been selected: author Beverly Cleary, for books, J. Larry Brown, founder of the Massachusetts Advocacy Center, for child advocacy, and Fred Rogers, of "Mister Rogers' Neighborhood," for communications. The citations will be presented at a luncheon on August 24 during the Everychild conference in New York City. The event will be open to the public; reservations are $37 from the Children's Book Council, 67 Irving Place, New York, NY 10003.

☐ *Openers,* the publicity newsletter libraries can offer their patrons, has jazzed up its look and added new features, including reference questions and answers, a TV tie-in alert, and record reviews and information. A two-year subscription to the quarterly is currently being offered at a $25 savings. For more information write Lukie Marriott, Circulation Manager, *Openers,* ALA, 50 E. Huron St., Chicago, IL 60611.

Children's Specials

☐ Children's Radio Theatre has twelve new audiocassettes of plays written by children aged ten to sixteen. One of the releases is *Children's Playhouse 15: The Sixth Annual Henny Penny Playwriting Contest,* an hour-long program of four plays recorded at the Kennedy Center by professional actors. Another program, *Galaxy Girl in the Case of the Disappearing Damsel,* was recorded at the Smithsonian Institution's Discovery Theatre. One to two cassettes cost $8 each, three to twelve, $7 each, and thirteen or more, $6 each. Contact Children's Radio Theatre, Box 53057, Washington, DC 20009, 202/234-4136.

☐ Since its inception in 1919, Children's Book Week has been held annually in November. It has been suggested that the date be changed to a time of year when teachers and school librarians have more time to devote to planning and events. Opinions should be sent to It's Time for Book Week, CBC, 67 Irving Place, New York, NY 10003.

☐ A fundraiser for the Warren-Newport (Illinois) PL can brighten up children's rooms in homes and libraries. The fourteen-by-sixteen-inch prints of a bear family at bathtime and bedtime have been created by local artist Virginia Bleck (who has also donated her drawings to the library's children's room). Unmatted prints are $12.75 each to Illinois residents, $12 to out-of-staters, and matted prints (with mats in several colors) are $16 and $15, respectively. Order from the Warren-Newport PL, 224 N. O'Plaine Rd., Gurnee, IL 60031, 312/244-5150.

Teddy bears' bathtime from Warren-Newport PL

☐ The Association for Childhood Education International has published a revised edition of *Bibliography of Books for Children,* with annotations of fiction, nonfiction, and reference books, and periodicals. Ordering information and age levels are given. The 112p. book is $6.55 prepaid from ACEI, 3615 Wisconsin Ave. NW, Washington, DC 20016.

Continuing Education

☐ Connections, an institute on young adults and reading, will be held July 24–25 in Durham, New Hampshire. Librarians, teachers, editors, and other speakers will cover trends in YA reading interests, adult books for YAs, science fiction and fantasy, boys and reading, booktalking, and other topics. The cost of $75 includes two lunches. Housing in campus dormitories is available. For more information write Susan Snider, New Hampshire State Library, 20 Park St., Concord, NH 03301.

☐ The 1985 Annual Conference of the National Genealogical Society is being held in Salt Lake City, August 6–9. There will be advance meetings for librarians and professional genealogists, and classes and lectures on the last three days. A banquet will feature the Archivist of the United States as speaker. The registration fee is $75. For more information write 1985 NGS Conference, Box 1053, Salt Lake City, UT 84110.

☐ The University of Southern Maine at Gorham is sponsoring "In Celebration of Children's Literature: 1985," July 17–19. Elizabeth George Speare, Ethel Heins, Charles Mikolaycak, Karla Kuskin, and Laura Simms will be among the participants. Recertification credit is available. Write Joyce Martin, University of Southern Maine, Gorham, ME 04038.

☐ Programs at the Out-of-Print and Antiquarian Book Market, a seminar/workshop for librarians and booksellers, August 11–16, at the University of Denver, will cover information systems for bibliographic description, pricing and appraisals, using bookseller catalogs, the auction market, care and preservation of antiquarian books, and other topics. The fee is $315, with a $100 deposit payable by July 1. University of Denver housing is extra. Three continuing education credits are available. For a registration form write the Graduate School of Librarianship and Information Management, University of Denver, Denver, CO 80208.

☐ A five-day workshop for personnel who are responsible for repair of nonrare library items but who have had no formal training is being offered August 26–30 at Stanford University by the Resource and Technical Services Division of ALA, with the cooperation of the LC National Preservation Program. The eleven workshops will teach skills that can be used in libraries without sophisticated repair shops and binderies. Housing and meals are $47.75 per day for a single and $42 per person per day for a double. Registration fees are $190 for RTSD members, $215 for ALA members, and $240 for non-ALA members. Registration will be accepted through July 22. For more information contact Ann Menendez, ALA/RTSD, 50 E. Huron St., Chicago, IL 60611, 312/944-6780, ext. 319.

☐ The Rosary College Graduate School of Library and Information Science is offering certification programs in law librarianship, library administration, and technical services beginning with the fall 1985 semester. The certificate of special studies requires either fifteen hours of study beyond the MLS or a forty-five-hour course of study that combines the MLS and special certification program. For more information write Rosary College GSLIS, 7900 W. Division St., River Forest, IL 60305.

Film and Video

☐ On a rainy day this summer golfers can stay inside and watch the play-by-play action in two golf tournament films being given away by the Kemper Group. The twenty-six-minute films cover the 1981 Kemper Open and the 1982 Women's Kemper Open. Because of limited quantities, the films will be given away on a first-come-first-served basis. Send requests, indicating which film is wanted, to Film Promotion, Advertising D-5, Kemper Group, Long Grove, IL 60049.

☐ "The Abilene Paradox" is a situation in which group members fall into a false consensus because they feel they have to go along with the group, and it is also the title of a new film from McGraw-Hill Training Systems on recognizing and overcoming this obstacle to decision making. The twenty-seven-minute color program in ½-inch VHS, ¾-inch U-Matic, and 16mm rents for $125 a week; free preview is available. For more information contact McGraw-Hill Training Systems, Box 641, Del Mar, CA 92014, 619/453-5000.

☐ The National AudioVisual Center has released a catalog of the seventy National Park Service Films it distributes, twenty-five of which are new. Among the new films are *Eleanor Roosevelt—First Lady of the*

World, Frederick Douglass: An American Life, Cape Cod by Henry David Thoreau, and several films on native Americans. Programs are available in 16mm and video, and nonprofit organizations can preview free. Request the catalog from National AudioVisual Center, Customer Services Section EB, 8700 Edgeworth Dr., Capitol Heights, MD 20743, 301/763-1896.

☐ Originally designed for employee safety programs at AT&T, *The Time Line: Managing the Moment for Safety* shows how mental preoccupation is often the hidden cause of accidents. The thirteen-minute program is available in all video formats for $250 purchase or $75 for a three-day rental. Order from Simon & Schuster Communications, 108 Wilmot Rd., Deerfield, IL 60015, 800/323-5343.

Finding Aids

☐ The Special Libraries Association has published the fourth edition of

Map Collections in the United States and Canada, last issued in 1978. The 804 collections are listed by state and province with name of collection head, address, telephone number, hours, size, area and subject specializations, and other information. The 192p. book, priced at $35, is available from the Special Libraries Association, 235 Park Ave. S., New York, NY 10003.

☐ *Consumer Drug Information on Disk* provides information on over 250 generic drugs representing more than 50,000 brand name drugs. The disk is searchable by generic name, brand name, and illness, and by all information categories for each entry, such as dosage, side effects, interactions, pregnancy cautions, and diet. The disk runs on IBM PC and compatible computers. For more information contact Dwight Tousignaut, CDID, American Society of Hospital Pharmacists, 4630 Montgomery Ave., Bethesda, MD 20814, 301/657-3000.

☐ Engineering Information, Inc. has added a second volume on robotics to its Technical Bulletin series. *Robotics,* vol. II contains over 1,000 abstracts dealing with the science and technology of design, operation, and application of industrial robots. Other Technical Bulletins cover remote sensing, ultrasonics, nuclear safety, and wastewater treatment. All are available for $49.50 each, and with an order of four, a fifth title is free. Write for an order form from Engineering Information, Inc., 345 E. 47th St., New York, NY 10017, 800/221-1044.

☐ Over 25,000 periodicals covered by 375 databases are listed in *Directory of Periodicals Online: Indexed, Abstracted & Full-Text.* Each title entry gives publisher, frequency, subject, and database availability, with length of coverage, and whether a citation, abstract, or full text. There is also a subject index. Volume one, covering over 6,000 titles in news, law, and business is available now; volumes on medicine and social science, and science and technology are forthcoming. Volume one, plus a six-month update, is $90 from Federal Document Retrieval, Inc., 514 C St. NE, Washington, DC 20002, 800/368-1009.

☐ Public schools now have many programs for the learning disabled, but these students may not get the support they need in college. *Lovejoy's College Guide for the Learning Disabled* by

Charles Straughn and Marvelle Colby identifies over 380 colleges that admit LD students and offer special services. After an introductory section covering whether an LD student should consider college and what to expect, the colleges are listed by state, with enrollment, tuition, special admission procedures for LD students, support services, and a summary of academic programs offered. The 118p. paperback is $9.95 from Simon & Schuster, 1230 Avenue of the Americas, New York, NY 10020.

From the GPO Presses

The following are a sample of recent publications available from the Government Printing Office. Specify stock number, price, and quantity when ordering. You may pay by check payable to the Superintendent of Documents or by Visa or Mastercard (give card number and expiration date). Send to Superintendent of Documents, United States GPO, Washington, DC 20402. Or call the order desk at 202/783-3238.

☐ The National Bureau of Standards has prepared *Introduction to Software Packages* to aid in choosing business software. It offers an overview of the kinds of business tasks for which software is currently produced, from budgets to inventory control to statistical analysis. To simplify journal selection a chart is provided which lists journals and magazines and describes the areas of software information each one covers. The report, stock number 003-003-02569-1, is available for $2.25 from Dept. 36-HM.

☐ Five new publications from the Department of Transportation discuss urban transportation planning. The titles are: *Urban Transportation Planning in the United States; An Historical Overview* (stock number 050-000-00485-6, $4.25), *Planning Services for Transportation-Handicapped People: Data Collection Manual* (stock number 050-000-00489-8, $7), *Special Paratransit Service for Elderly and Handicapped Persons: Operational Experience* (stock number 050-000-00216-1, $6.50), *Use of Volunteers in the Transportation of Elderly and Handicapped Persons* (stock number 050-000-00495-3, $5), and *A Case Book of Short-Range Actions to Improve Public Transportation* (stock number 050-000-00494-5, $7). All the reports are available from Dept. 36-LX.

☐ The report of the President's Commission on Industrial Competitiveness, *Global Competition, the New Reality,* examines evidence of American industry's competitive decline. It offers a policy framework to improve America's ability to compete, with specific remedial actions outlined for both the federal government and private industry. The report, stock number 003-009-00438-1, is available for $2.75 from Dept. 36-MF.

Idea Exchange

☐ A Big Balloon Launch was held to mark the beginning of a series of cooperative programs by the Oak Lawn (Illinois) PL and the Oak Lawn National Bank. Over 1,000 helium balloons were released with names attached. Prizes will be awarded to both the launchers and the finders for balloons returned from the three farthest distances. Balloon tracking

Oak Lawn Balloon Launch

charts will be on display at the bank and the library. The library is undergoing a major remodeling and the joint effort with the bank provides an opportunity to continue public service activities, such as displays in the bank lobby.

☐ Now in its second year, the adult spelling bee sponsored by the Nebraska Literary Heritage Association in cooperation with the Lincoln City Library Foundation is part of an effort to raise funds for a matching grant from the NEH for the Heritage Room of the Lincoln City Libraries. Contestants or their sponsoring organizations are charged a $25 registration fee and the public is charged $2 admission to the event, held at the Zoo Bar. The first place winner receives a dictionary donated by a local bookstore.

☐ The Public Library of Columbus and Franklin County (Ohio) has inaugurated two innovative services. A media production center is open to the public for producing a number of graphic materials. There is equipment for mounting, laminating, transparency and slide production, drafting, visual and audio production, and binding. Use of the equipment is free but users must provide their own materials. Training sessions are available. To aid program planners for local organizations, the library staff has prepared the *Directory of Resources for Program Planners,* listing 195 companies and associations that provide free or inexpensive programs, other resources, and meeting rooms available at area libraries. A program planners institute was also held during which nineteen local organizations presented samples of the programs they offer. The directory is being sold by the library's friends group for $3. Write to the Public Library of Columbus and Franklin County, 28 S. Hamilton Rd., Columbus, OH 43213.

☐ Approximately 200 parents and children attended a Demonstration of Preschool Skills held at the Kinchafoonee (Georgia) Regional Library last year, jointly sponsored with the Terrell County Board of Education Curriculum Department. Kindergarten teachers, aides, and children demonstrated skills children should know upon entering kindergarten. Handouts on the skills, a schedule of summer library activities, and an exhibit of books and AV materials were also available. School officials were on hand to meet with parents. For more information send a SASE to Sue Jones, Kinchafoonee Regional Library, 334 N. Main St., Dawson, GA 31742.

Media Center World

☐ Ranger Rick, the National Wildlife Federation raccoon-in-residence, has expanded his publishing empire. *Ranger Rick's NatureScope* is a new bimonthly (during the school year) whose goal is to help elementary school children understand and appreciate nature. Intended for teachers,

the magazine contains activities and crafts, graded by age (preschool through grade 7), with pages of games, puzzles, and quizzes to photocopy. Each issue concludes with an extensive list of other resources. Subscriptions are $18 from *NatureScope,* National Wildlife Federation, 1412 16th St. NW, Washington, DC 20036.

☐ All map projections are distorted, but some are more distorted than others. The traditional Mercator projection maps, originally intended for navigation, show Europe and North America as unduly large. The more representative Orthogonal or Peters projection, which shows relative sizes more accurately, is now available in a 35-by-50-inch color map, with a panel detailing the misconceptions fostered by traditional maps. The map can be ordered for $8.95 from the CIBC Resource Center for Educators, 1841 Broadway, New York, NY 10023.

☐ *Perspectives* is an Ohio-based journal that reviews books for elementary school children and offers suggestions for incorporating literature into the language arts, social studies, science, art, and music curricula. Reviews are written by teachers and librarians. Published three times a year, it is available free to teachers in Ohio and for $7.50 to teachers elsewhere. Write to Hughes Moir, Cooperative Services for Children's Literature, Snyder Building, University of Toledo, Toledo, OH 43606.

Products and Services

☐ Dukane Corporation's new Manual Direct Projection Microfilm Reader, the MDP, projects images downward onto an 18-by-20-inch screen angled fifteen degrees. The MDP is available with an 18X lens or a 13X to 23X zoom lens and features 360° image rotation and a 1,000-hour quartz halogen lamp. The manual film drive permits high speed advance and rewind as well as slow speed location of material. For more information on the MDP Model 27A88A

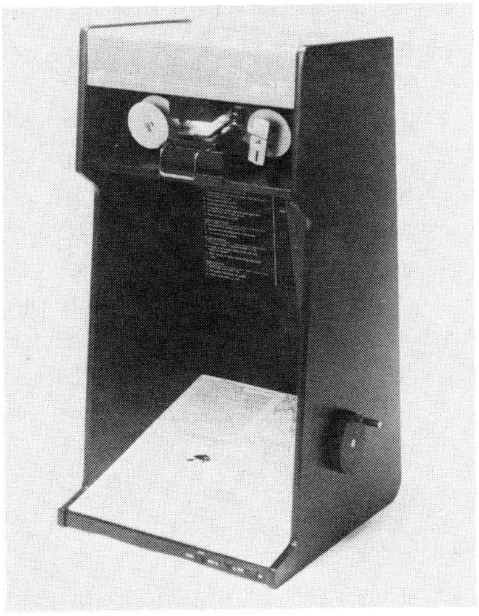

Dukane MDP 27A88A

contact the Dukane Corporation, Audio Visual Division, 2900 Dukane Dr., St. Charles, IL 60174, 312/584-2300.

☐ The Institute for Scientific Information is offering a new online database covering arts and humanities literature, to complement their existing databases Scisearch and Social Scisearch. The new file, available on BRS, will cover about 1,300 journals in the arts and humanities, as well as selected articles from 5,600 social science and science publications, and will be updated every two weeks. For more information on Arts & Humanities Search contact ISI, 3501 Market St., Philadelphia, PA 19104, 800/523-1850.

☐ A more specific area of the arts is covered by another new database, BASEline. It provides information on films, television shows, and stage shows, with dates, credits, distributors, and ratings; projects still in production; and literary properties available. The service fee of $90 a month includes one hour of connect time; time beyond that is charged at 75¢ a minute. For more information contact Baseline, Inc., 80 E. 11th St., New York, NY 10003, 212/254-8235.

Professional Reading

☐ Intended as a replacement for the *Unesco Journal of Information Science, Librarianship and Archives Administration,* which ceased in 1983, *Information Development* is a new quarterly journal that will cover current developments in information work internationally, with special emphasis on the developing countries. The first issue contains articles on UNESCO, information policy in India and China, information training in Pakistan, and the information workforce supply, as well as news items, book reviews, conference listings, and other brief items. Subscriptions are $58 for institutions and $29 for individuals from Carfax Publishing Co., Box 25, Abingdon, Oxfordshire OX14 3UE, U.K.

☐ The Computer and Information Technology Committee of the Missouri Library Association has published *Library Applications of Microcomputers: A Bibliography,* listing materials published between 1982 and 1984 in such categories as acquisitions, reference, public use, circulation, and serials. There are also citations to articles on specific pieces of hardware and on evaluating and circulating software. The 59p. bibliography is available for $5 ($3 for MLA members) plus $1 postage and handling from the Missouri Library Association, Parkade Plaza, Suite 9, Columbia, MO 65203.

☐ Two new sibling periodicals are *Database End-User,* a monthly newsletter, and *Database End-User Specialist,* a bimonthly journal, both edited by Barbara Quint. *Database End-User* will include tips and techniques, new product news, conferences, and other brief items. Each issue of *Database End-User Specialist* will cover one of six areas: law, health sciences, business management, science/engineering, new developments, and end-user support, with feature articles and regular columns, including reviews of online databases in subject areas. Subscriptions to the newsletter (premiering in July) are $37; the journal, beginning January 1986, is $75. For more information contact Meckler Publishing, 11 Ferry Lane West, Westport, CT 06880, 203/226-6967.

Software

☐ If shooting down aliens can make math fun, trivia questions should be able to take the boredom out of database management. The *Atari Trivia Data Base* teaches the fundamentals of database management with two programs. Using modules of Atari BASIC, users construct a database management system and load it with data in the form of trivia questions and answers. Other modules are used to build the second program, a game that uses the stored trivia data. Both programs can be used with data other than trivia. The program is available as a book for $8.95, or combined with a program disk for $19.95. For more information write Howard W. Sams & Co., 4300 W. 62nd St., Indianapolis, IN 46268.

☐ Libraries setting up an electronic bulletin board now have another software package to consider: BBS-PC, from Micro-Systems. It provides sixteen sections, four different file transfer protocols (for uploading and downloading), 256 possible security levels, and a "terminal mode" feature that supports a second modem, COM port, and phone line to permit answering one modem and dialing out on the other. The BBS-PC for IBM PC, XT, PCjr (with 256K), and compatible systems is $249. For more information contact Micro-Systems Software, Inc., 4301-18 Oak Circle, Boca Raton, FL 33431, 305/391-5077.

☐ Professional Software's new Serial Control System's main module provides automated check-in, renewal, and claiming for $900. Additional modules are holding lists, $400, bindery/microfilm management, $300, and routing, $700 (available in the fall). The system operates on the IBM PC and compatibles with 256K RAM, two disk drives, and a 132-column printer. A demo is available that includes a manual and all programs for $75, with a $65 credit toward purchase. For more information contact Professional Software, 21 Forest Ave., Glen Ridge, NJ 07028, 201/748-7658.

Write for These

☐ The Law Library of the Library of Congress has recently prepared *A Guide to Official Gazettes and Their Contents* to give legal researchers a brief summary of foreign official law gazettes, including such information as whether a gazette contains the text of treaties, court decisions, or an index. The 205p. publication is free (but supplies are limited) from LC, Law Library, Washington, DC 20540.

☐ To help parents of communicatively disabled children ensure an appropriate public education for their children, the National Association for Hearing and Speech Action has prepared *A Free Appropriate Public Education for Your Communicatively Impaired Child.* It describes Public Law 94-142 (Education for All Handicapped Children Act) as it relates to the communicatively disabled, explains what the education program should include, and provides a resource list of organizations. For a free copy write NAHSA, Box L, 10801 Rockville Pike, Rockville, MD 20852, 800/638-8255.

☐ *A Guide to Selecting Canadian Materials* lists sixty information centers and 190 publications that can aid in materials selection, arranged by subject. The 18p. guide is free from the Canadian Book Information Centre, 70 The Esplanade, Toronto, Ont. M5E 1A6, Canada, 416/362-6555.

☐ An annual Braille anthology of current children's literature published by the Braille Institute, *Expectations,* is available free to any blind child in grades three through six. The 36th edition includes five complete books as well as chapters from four books and several poems. Organizations serving blind children should request *Expectations* on official letterhead from Jody Avery, Braille Institute, 741 N. Vermont Ave., Los Angeles, CA 90029. ▣

Upfront/News

(cont'd from p. 647)

warding for you in the profession?

Galvin: I have spent so much time in education for librarianship that I had the opportunity to know and work with people in all the specialized areas of librarianship. That is a major attraction to the position at ALA, to continue to work with people in all specialized fields, to know the profession broadly. My own vision of librarianship as a field has expanded as I have had contact with those in various specializations.

Bleier: With your international background, will you find it difficult to relate to, let's say, school librarians?

Galvin: There are many active international library programs and organizations in the field of service to children and youth. These include the International Association of School Librarians affiliated with the International Federation of Library Associations, and an active U.S. chapter of the International Board on Books for Youth. The children's field could be a model for other specializations that want to develop an international orientation. The children's field is very well organized internationally. Many other specializations are not.

Bleier: There is a conference in August of IFLA and you have been on the organizing committee. What are some of the current issues and concerns on the international scene relating to librarians and will we see a world library system?

Galvin: No, we will not see a world library system. What we will see is more information moving more readily across national boundaries. There is a concern to make sure national borders don't become barriers to the free flow of information. IFLA is concerned with copyright, tariff barriers to the free flow of information, and equality of access to information so that people in undeveloped countries enjoy access to information comparable to those in developed countries.

Bleier: There has been recent publicity in the state of Pennsylvania about having a state access card. Small libraries are concerned that people would not continue to use their libraries. What is your view?

Galvin: I think it's a fine proposal and I support it enthusiastically. Whatever enhances access to information to people is good. Details would have to be worked out so the existence of the small libraries is protected. ALA is thinking about a universal borrowers card which would work like a network bankcard. A mobile society should not be limited to a single access point for information. ▣

Front Row Center *(cont'd from p. 693)*

Center. Although the Center appears to be a clean, safe clinic with a highly skilled, caring staff, the experience of actually viewing abortions—if only from a safe and distant angle—is jolting and will force audiences to face the reality of the procedure head-on.

In the end, viewers may find themselves changing sides or at least reconsidering their past biases. *Abortion Clinic* is fair because it uncompromisingly shows women in the difficult position of weighing their options, making a choice, and living with the consequences, for better or worse. This engrossing program shows that there are no easy or right answers.

Both *Abortion Clinic* and *Abortion: Stories from North and South* are suitable for senior high (with reservations) through college and adult audiences.

Current Reference Books

(cont'd from p. 707)

Study Guides in the index volume. These suggest topics for study, list additional books with annotations, and recommend other reference tools including specific headings in the *Readers' Guide.* How-to explanations (e.g., how to carve meat) and science projects which can be performed at home also encourage further pursuit of topics such as heredity or how detergents interact with water. Sidebar articles explain how rockets work, the parts of AC and DC generators, and how clouds form.

In *World Book* graphics team up with text to convey information clearly. Nearly half of the 29,000 illustrations are in color. The drawings illustrating the heart and a plaque-clogged coronary artery are exceeded in vividness only by the photograph of a heart undergoing surgery. More than 2,300 maps of various types have been created specifically for *World Book.* Cut-away drawings are used extensively to explain the how of things. Other illustrations also carry out the set's educational purpose by concentrating on the relationships among things and their how and why. Whenever possible, *World Book* consistently emphasizes *how* over *what.*

In its 150,000-entry index volume *World Book* gives *what* its due. Entries include brief glosses clarifying just what a thing is (for example, "Jackson's Mill [farm, Weston]" for General "Stonewall" Jackson's boyhood home in West Virginia). Fact boxes, chronologies, and tables of specialized terms also aid in specific fact retrieval.

The 1985 *World Book,* as intelligent as it is intelligible, is a solid selection for home or library. It will meet the general information needs of children and young adults and satisfy many of their parents as well. Its special features serve the didactic purpose of *World Book* well, suiting it to heavy use in elementary schools and high schools by students and teachers alike. Some have claimed that very soon online access will make printed general purpose encyclopedias as extinct as dinosaurs. *World Book* will prove them wrong since it is the sort of information tool a student can use without special instruction and since its pictures, which cannot (at least not yet) be distributed via online systems, form an integral part of it. Furthermore, it is not just a reference tool that can be picked at in the black box of an online search system; it is also an educational instrument to be used in the systematic manner suggested by the Reading and Study Guides. The hard copy codex, not the scroll printed from a terminal, is ideal for this purpose. Clear, current, authoritative, the *World Book Encyclopedia* continues to earn respect.

WLB Classifieds

Classified Advertising *is accepted six weeks preceding date of issue. Charges are: minimum 3 lines—$10; each additional line—$2.50. If voucher forms are required, please send them when submitting copy. All advertisements for positions must exclude reference to race, creed, color, age, and sex as conditions for employment. The publisher reserves the right to reject any advertising considered unacceptable as to wording or appearance or for any other reason. Submit classifieds to: Brian Bavolar, Wilson Library Bulletin, 950 University Ave., Bronx, NY 10452.*

Positions Open

LIBRARIAN. Responsibilities: Coordinating activities of main library and eight branches. Guiding transition to an automated system including an online catalog. Working with technical services. Requirements: MLS from an ALA-accredited school; three to five year's library experience—managerial experience preferred. Salary and benefits competitive. Send application letter, resume, transcript, references to: Theda F. Gibson, Director, Lonesome Pine Regional Library, Box 1739, Wise, VA 24293.

LIBRARY DIRECTOR, City of Troy, Mich. Admin. of med.-size class 6 Pub. Lib. (43,000 sq. ft., 161,000-vol. collection), incl. 3 non-full-serv. mini-branches and outreach prog. Incl. supv. of staff and vol. Req. MLS; 7 yrs. prog. resp. lib. work exper., last 4 yrs. as Dir. of class 6 Pub. Lib. with 40,000+ popn. and 100,000+ vol. collection; exper. with outreach prog. and automated circ. sys. Salary open. Write for appl. to City of Troy, Personnel Dept., 500 W. Big Beaver Rd., Troy, MI 48084. Deadline: July 1, 1985. EOE.

Announcements

THE FOOTLOOSE LIBRARIAN newsletter & network. Money-saving travel news + U.S. & overseas librarians offering Bed & Breakfast, housing exchange, more. "Good, practical information" M.S., IN; "An excellent publication" S.R., Tunisia. Free brochure. TFL, Box 972, Minneapolis, MN 55440.

HELPING YOU INFORM YOUR PATRONS is our business. Write for our free catalog of: Signs, Floor Plan Directories, Displays, etc. The Library

For Sale

INDEX TO ADVERTISERS

Advanced Binding Methods, Inc. 609
C L Systems, Inc. . 3rd cover
Gale Research Company .... 4th cover
Krieger Publishing Company 674
Psychological Abstracts ... 641
Standard Change-Makers 680
H. W. Wilson Company .... 2nd cover, 642

Credits:
p. 664—Paramount Home Video; 675—Joseph Farris; 677—David Jacobson; 681—Ronald Chironna; 686, 687—Harper Junior Books; 688—Alfred A. Knopf; 690—Merrimack Publisher's Circle; 691—Sierra Club Books; 693—The Cinema Guild; 703—G.K. Hall; 704—Rowman & Allanheld; 705—Macmillan; Routledge, Kegan Paul; 708—Random House; 709—Harper & Row; 716—Oak Lawn Public Library.

Decision Maker

6

Vincent Richards
Director
Edmonton Public Library
Edmonton, Alberta,
Canada

Edmonton Public Library staff catalogue new volumes by terminal connection to UTLAS.

How to increase your budget for collection development by 396% and save money at the same time.

"Find the Best Library Automation Company"

"Late in 1976 we decided to automate. We knew we had to have the best, biggest, fastest and most dependable automation system. We chose CLSI. They were the only people with a track record that proved they knew how to install really large systems and make them work.

Since then circulation has increased 158%; doubling in the past 4 years. Over half of our 565,000 population are registered users. Last year we moved 2.1 million items a year between branches, as a result of CLSI's easy, automated place-a-hold and change-agency features. That comes to 17.6 tons of books a week. CLSI's LIBS 100 Circulation Control Module handles our 7.5 million annual circulation, and tells us the location and status of every single item."

"Go First-Class With Your Catalogue"

"When we selected CLSI we decided to go first class with our bibliographic control: we chose UTLAS, the Toronto-based bibliographic utility, to produce a system-wide catalogue of all our holdings. We worked with CLSI and UTLAS to the point that their respective automation services complement each other perfectly, both built on the full MARC record.

With UTLAS, we maintain our own private database and yet have continuous, all-day-long access to UTLAS's 23 million records."

"Build A Cultural Juggernaut"

"Using the two best automation systems gives you very powerful tools. Users at any service point know what you have, using the full system-wide catalogue. The free place-a-hold service and detailed circulation statistics give you vital information for proper user-oriented book selection and collection management. A good electronic security system, in all service points, stops material being stolen. The efficient and cost effective computerized production of overdue notices by the LIBS 100 gets books back quickly. Fines get collected and revenues go up. Readers' frustrations are greatly reduced—they can get what they need quickly and far more easily than in non-automated libraries. Use soars!

Properly implemented automation translates into real cost savings, better and faster service, improved public relations, and enthusiastic public support. Cost savings can be re-allocated to where it counts: improving book and audio-visual collections. The attendant public enthusiasm influences funding authorities and keeps the book budget booming—ours increased 396% in 7 years and helped make us Canada's busiest library.

When your library can do these things it will enhance its visibility, strengthen its popular support, and be in a much stronger position to secure the support it needs to do more of the same."

"Best of Both Worlds"

"In Britain, librarians say they pride themselves on the substance and quality of their collections above all else. Circulation of 12–13 books per capita, like Edmonton, is normal. Americans, they sometimes say, tend to point to their spacious new buildings and shiny new technology. Here in Edmonton, I am certain we have the best of both worlds. With CLSI and UTLAS you can too."

CLSI

CL Systems, Inc.
1220 Washington Street
West Newton, MA 02165
617.965.6310

Amsterdam
Boston
London
Melbourne
Milano
Toronto